Effective Practices
in Early Childhood Education

Fourth Edition

Effective Practices
in Early Childhood Education
Building a Foundation

Sue Bredekamp
Early Childhood Education Specialist and
Independent Consultant

 Pearson

Director and Publisher: Kevin Davis
Executive Portfolio Manager: Aileen Pogran
Managing Content Producer: Megan Moffo
Portfolio Management Assistants: Maria Feliberty
Development Editor: Krista McMurray
Executive Product Marketing Manager: Christopher Barry
Executive Field Marketing Manager: Krista Clark
Manufacturing Buyer: Deidra Headlee
Cover Design: Carie Keller, SPi Global, Inc.
Cover Art:
Media Producer: Daniel Dwyer or Allison Longley
Editorial Production and Composition Services: SPi Global, Inc.
Full-Service Project Manager: Heather Winter, SPi Global Inc.
Text Font: Times LT Pro

Credits and acknowledgments for materials borrowed from other sources and reproduced, with permission, in this textbook appear on the appropriate page within the text.

Every effort has been made to provide accurate and current Internet information in this book. However, the Internet and information posted on it are constantly changing, so it is inevitable that some of the Internet addresses listed in this textbook will change.

Library of Congress Cataloging-in-Publication Data

Names: Bredekamp, Sue, author.
Title: Effective practices in early childhood education : building a
    foundation / Sue Bredekamp, Early Childhood Education Specialist and
    Independent Consultant.
Description: Fourth edition. | New York : Pearson, [2020}.
Identifiers: LCCN 2018050832 | ISBN 9780135177372
Subjects: LCSH: Early childhood education—United States. | Child
    development—United States.
Classification: LCC LB1140.23 .B72 2020 | DDC 372.21—dc23
LC record available at https://lccn.loc.gov/2018050832

38 2023

ISBN-10:   0-13-517737-5
ISBN-13: 978-0-13-517737-2

Dedication

To Joe Bredekamp, for a lifetime of love, friendship, wonderful memories, and tolerance of craziness.

About the Author

Dr. Sue Bredekamp is an Early Childhood Education Specialist from Washington, DC. She serves as a consultant on curriculum, pedagogy, developmentally appropriate practice, and professional development for organizations such as the National Association for the Education of Young Children, Head Start, the Council for Professional Recognition, state departments of education, and universities. Her seminal work on NAEYC's best-selling publications on *Developmentally Appropriate Practice in Early Childhood Programs* has had a major impact on the education of young children and teacher preparation for more than 30 years. As NAEYC's Director of Accreditation and Professional Development, she developed and administered their national accreditation system for early childhood centers and schools, and wrote standards for curriculum and assessment, and teacher education.

Dr. Bredekamp is a frequent keynote speaker and author of numerous books and articles on professional practice. She has been a visiting lecturer at Macquarie University in Sydney, Australia; Monash University in Melbourne; New Zealand Tertiary College; University of Alaska; and University of Hawaii. Dr. Bredekamp holds a Ph.D. in Curriculum and Instruction and an M.A. in Early Childhood Education from the University of Maryland. In 2014, the McCormick Center for Early Childhood Leadership at National Louis University recognized Dr. Bredekamp with its Visionary Leadership Award.

Dr. Bredekamp serves as Chair-Emerita of the Board of HighScope Educational Research Foundation. She served on the National Research Council's (NRC) Committee on Early Childhood Mathematics which produced a landmark report, *Mathematics in Early Childhood: Paths toward Excellence and Equity*. She co-authored *Learning to Read and Write: Developmentally Appropriate Practices for Young Children* and was the content developer and on-air faculty for *HeadsUp! Reading*, a live satellite television course on early literacy disseminated to more than 10,000 early educators. For more than 45 years, Dr. Bredekamp has worked for and with young children toward the goal of improving the quality and effectiveness of early childhood education programs.

About the Contributors

Dr. Kathleen (Kate) Gallagher is the Director of Research and Evaluation at the Buffett Early Childhood Institute at the University of Nebraska. Dr. Gallagher is an educational psychologist and early childhood professional, with more than 30 years of experience teaching, home visiting, and leading early childhood programs, including early intervention and inclusive preschool programs. Her research, evaluation, and teaching focus on practices, programs, and policies that support the development and well-being of young children 0–8 years and their families, particularly in the contexts of poverty, disability, and cultural diversity. Her recent work is focused on how organizations can implement policies and practices to support the well-being of early childhood professionals. Kate holds a doctorate in educational psychology from the University of Wisconsin-Madison, a master's in education from Marquette University, and a bachelor's degree in early childhood education and special education from Cardinal Stritch University. Kate has presented two TED talks on the transformative power of early childhood education, and has published extensively on children's early language and literacy, social-emotional development, and early intervention.

Dr. Gail Joseph is an associate professor of Educational Psychology and Early Childhood and Family Studies at the University of Washington. She teaches courses, advises students, provides service, and conducts research on early learning and equity, child care quality, teacher preparation, early childhood mental health, and school readiness. She is the Founding Executive Director of Cultivate Learning at the University of Washington and was the Director of the Head Start Center for Inclusion and Co-Director of the National Center for Quality Teaching and Learning funded by the Office of Head Start. At Cultivate Learning she oversees the quality ratings system for all licensed child care and pre-K programs in the state, and is the creator of numerous professional learning resources such as *Circle Time Magazine* and the *Meaningful Makeover* series. Additionally, she is the Founding Director of the EarlyEdU Alliance. The EarlyEdU Alliance is improving the quality of programs for more than 30,000 children nationwide by making relevant, affordable bachelor's degrees accessible to the early childhood workforce. Using the latest research on optimizing child outcomes and adult learning, the technology-powered pedagogy of EarlyEdU creates degrees that make a significant contribution to individuals and the field. To serve as an innovation lab, Dr. Joseph led the development of the University of Washington's first online B.A. completion degree in early childhood education which was just ranked #1 in the nation. Dr. Joseph is the 2018 recipient of the the David R. Thorud Leadership Award at the University of Washington.

Megan Schumaker-Murphy has worked in early childhood education for 15 years as a special education teacher, early interventionist, and teacher educator. At last count, Ms. Schumaker-Murphy worked directly with more than 300 families and more than 150 teachers and early interventionists serving more than 1,000 young children across those settings. She is a doctoral candidate and instructor at DePaul University in Chicago where she lives with her family and two adorably naughty cats.

My motivations for writing the prior editions of this book were both personal and professional. I began my career in early childhood education more than 45 years ago as an unqualified child care teacher. During the intervening years, I've often wished that I had known even a fraction of what I know now about child development, and effective teaching and learning so I could have been a better teacher. I initially wrote this text to help ensure that new teachers get off to a better start than I did and that the children do, too.

My professional motivations emanate from the current explosion in research that should be informing our practice to a much greater extent than it is today. Neuroscience and research on child development, teaching, and curriculum provide considerable guidance about effective practices and what children truly need to be physically and mentally healthy and successful in school and life. In addition, I continue to feel the responsibility to clarify and explain what *developmentally appropriate practice* really means—that it is not ages and stages but rather a complex decision-making process on the part of teachers that is embedded in social and cultural contexts.

As I wrote this fourth edition, I reflected a great deal on my entire career. I had the privilege of spending time and videotaping at the Center for Young Children (CYC) at the University of Maryland, my alma mater. I'm proud of the fact that the CYC is NAEYC-accredited because I developed and directed the accreditation system. When I visit the program and many others like it in our country, I see what we early childhood professionals continue to envision for every child—a caring community of enthusiastic learners, effective teaching, engaging and challenging curriculum, and developmentally appropriate practice implemented as it is intended. My mentor, Dr. Carol Seefeldt was one of the visionaries whose work influenced the design and curriculum at the CYC. I feel her presence there and in my work every day.

Many parents, policy makers, economists, business leaders, and researchers now consider early education essential for long-term success in life. Our profession has a deep responsibility to meet these lofty expectations. But the power of early education depends on the quality of teacher-child interactions and the effectiveness of instructional practices. To achieve their potential, children need and deserve highly competent, well-educated, well-compensated teachers. But most of all, we have a responsibility to ensure that young children have safe, secure, and joyful childhoods. Only then can we fulfill the promise that lies within every child.

New to This Edition

- A new cross-cutting theme of the entire book is the importance of developing children's executive function, self-regulation, and positive approaches to learning. Every chapter and many established features, such as *Becoming an Intentional Teacher and Promoting Play*, present examples of effective curriculum and teaching to promote these goals for children.
- New *What Works* features in 10 chapters discuss executive function, self-regulation, approaches to learning, or brain development.
- The revised Chapter 13 is a STEM chapter with discussion and examples of engineering and increased emphasis on science standards and teaching practices in addition to mathematics and technology.
- Chapter 1 is updated with discussion of new policies, changing demographics, and new research on child development and effective early education. The chapter addresses both trends in the field and challenging issues such as adverse childhood experiences, stress in children's and families' lives, the opioid crisis, threats to children's play, bullying, and social media.
- Chapter 3 is updated with a discussion of new research and ongoing issues such as the importance of situating decisions in cultural context, scripted curriculum, and academic rigor and developmentally appropriate practice. The reorganized chapter includes learning materials with environments.
- Updated research and new strategies for dealing with toxic stress and challenging behavior appear in Chapter 8 and Chapter 14.
- The updated Chapter 2 includes the history of Reggio Emilia and discusses Loris Malaguzzi as a major historical figure.
- New *Promoting Play* features in six chapters emphasize protecting children's right to play, especially in kindergarten.
- Chapter 1 and Chapter 16 provide a discussion of NAEYC's *Power to the Profession*.
- Updated culture and language lenses are provided on culturally responsive curriculum, teaching, and learning, as well as discussions on professional ethics in challenging times.
- New examples of developmentally appropriate digital media for children, teachers, and families appear throughout the text.
- New artifacts of children's work appear throughout.

Book Organization Continues to Reflect *Guidelines for Developmentally Appropriate Practice*

This book is designed to teach the concept of *developmentally appropriate practice* for students, because an understanding of its principles is the foundation on which to build early childhood programs and schools for children from birth through age 8. Chapters are organized according to NAEYC's guidelines for developmentally appropriate practice, which I have coauthored for more than 30 years.

Part 1, "Foundations of Early Childhood Education," describes the current profession and the issues and trends affecting it today (Chapter 1), the rich history from which developmentally appropriate practices evolved (Chapter 2), and an overview of its principles and guidelines, which are described in depth in later chapters (Chapter 3).

Part 2, "Dimensions of Developmentally Appropriate Practice," includes chapters describing the key factors teachers must consider as they make professional decisions. Chapter 4 presents an overview of current knowledge about how all children develop and learn. Chapter 5 addresses the unique, individual differences among children, including children with diverse abilities. Chapter 6 discusses the critical role of social, cultural, and linguistic contexts on all children's development and learning and how teachers must embrace a diverse society to help every child succeed in school and life. Though addressed in different chapters, these three dimensions are integrally connected.

Part 3, "Intentional Teaching: How to Teach," describes the role of the teacher in implementing developmentally appropriate practices. Each of the interconnected aspects of the teacher's role is addressed in separate chapters: building effective partnerships with families (Chapter 7), creating a caring community of learners and guiding young children (Chapter 8); teaching to enhance learning and development (Chapter 9); planning effective curriculum (Chapter 10); and assessing children's learning and development (Chapter 11).

Part 4, "Implementing an Effective Curriculum: What to Teach," describes both *how* and *what to teach* children from birth through age 8 in language, literacy, the arts, STEM, social-emotional development, social studies, physical development, and health. Each chapter demonstrates how the continuum of children's development influences decisions about curriculum content and intentional, effective teaching strategies for children of different ages.

Early childhood educators join this profession and stay in it because they believe their work can make a difference in the lives of children and their families. But to make a lasting difference, our practices must be effective—they must contribute to children's learning and development. This book reflects this core goal by building on the basic framework of developmentally appropriate practice while going beyond to emphasize intentional teaching, challenging and interesting curriculum, and evidence-based, effective practices for a new generation of early childhood educators. Each of these key themes is discussed on the following pages.

Intentional Teaching of Young Children

This text builds on the framework of developmentally appropriate practice emphasizing that effective teachers are intentional, thoughtful, and purposeful in everything they do.

Intentional teachers know not only what to do with children but also why they are doing it and can explain the rationale for the decisions they make to other teachers, administrators, and families. To help students understand this concept, **Becoming an Intentional Teacher** features reveal what teachers are thinking in classroom situations, *how* and *why* they select the strategies they do, and challenge students to reflect further on these scenarios.

Current Research on Effective Practices

In an era of expanding research on child development and learning, Common Core State Standards, Early Learning standards, accountability, and rapid change in the field, the text makes research understandable and meaningful for students and illustrates the connections between child development, curriculum content, assessment, and intentional teaching.

What Works features present research-based practices in action, including descriptions of demonstrated effective practices such as strategies to develop executive function and using relaxation techniques to prevent challenging behaviors.

Lens features present insights on culture, language, and including all children. These features discuss practice through diverse *lenses*, expanding the sources of information teachers use to make decisions and helping them look at questions or problems from broader perspectives. Widening the lens with which teachers view their practice is a strategy to move beyond the persistent educational tendency to dichotomize difficult or controversial issues into "either/or" choices, and move toward "both/and" thinking.

Connections between Curriculum and Child Development

Unlike many early childhood texts that focus on child development only, this text shows how child development and curriculum content knowledge are connected.

In the **Developmental Continuum** feature, the text provides an overview of the continuum of learning in the areas of language, literacy, mathematics, and cognitive, social, emotional, and physical development and describes how child development is linked to curriculum planning for children from birth through age 8.

- Chapters 12 to 15 help early childhood teachers understand right from the start that there is content in the curriculum for young children. They describe the goals for young children's learning and development that predict success in school and life. Each of these chapters includes examples of effective strategies such as teaching children of diverse abilities in inclusive classrooms or ways to promote dual language learning.

The **Promoting Play feature** presents current research on the important role of play in development and effective strategies to help children learn through play or protect their right to play. These features address play across the full age range, from birth through age 8. Discussions of play are also integrated in each chapter throughout this book as an effective means to support all domains of development and promote learning in all curriculum areas. Today, many people are concerned about how the standards movement is negatively impacting play. We often hear statements such as "We can't let children play because we have to teach literacy," or "We don't have time for outdoor play in primary grades because we have to get children ready for standardized tests." Play should not be treated as a separate part of an early childhood program or day that can be cut if someone deems it unimportant. Therefore, you will find a discussion of play in every chapter of this book.

- The emphasis on effective curriculum reflects current trends such as the goal of aligning prekindergarten and primary education, NAEYC accreditation and CAPE professional preparation standards, and enhanced expectations for teacher qualifications as described in the 2015 report, *Transforming the Workforce for Children Birth through Age 9: A Unifying Foundation* by the Institute of Medicine and the National Research Council, the 2018 report of the National Academies of Sciences, Engineering, and Medicine (NASEM), *Transforming the financing of early care and education*, and NAEYC's Power to the Profession initiative.

Revel™

This fourth edition of *Effective Practices in Early Childhood Education* is available in Revel.™

- Provide an all-in-one solution
  - Fully digital and highly engaging, Revel gives students everything they need for the course—all in one continuous, integrated learning experience. Highlighting, note taking, and a glossary let students read and study however they like. Educators can add notes for students, too, including reminders or study tips.
- Engage students at they read
  - Revel was designed to help every student come to class ready to learn. To keep students engaged as they read through each chapter, Revel integrates videos, interactives, and assessments directly into the author-created narrative. Thanks to this media-rich presentation of content, students are more likely to complete their assigned reading and retain what they've read. So they'll show up to class better prepared to participate and learn.
- Encourage practice and review
  - Embedded *Check Your Understanding* concept checks afford students opportunities to check their understanding at regular intervals before moving on. Assessments in Revel let instructors gauge student comprehension frequently, provide timely feedback, and address learning gaps along the way.
- Foster critical thinking through writing
  - The writing functionality in Revel enables educators to integrate writing—among the best ways to foster and assess critical thinking—into the course without significantly impacting their grading burden. Assignable *Shared Writing* activities direct students to share written responses with classmates, fostering peer discussion.

Over more than four decades in early childhood education, I have had the privilege of working with and learning from countless friends, colleagues, teachers, and children. This book would not have been possible without the help and encouragement of the following people:

Deep appreciation goes to my three contributors without whom I would not have been able to complete this text. Dr. Kathleen Cranley Gallagher revised Chapter 4, Chapter 5, and Chapter 7. Kate's expertise on early intervention, social-emotional development, and mental health greatly inform this edition.

I am thrilled that Dr. Gail E. Joseph was able to revise Chapter 8 and 14. Gail wrote several chapters and the Including All Children features for the first edition. Her innovative work on early intervention, improving Head Start and child care, and cutting-edge professional development of teachers has made a significant contribution to the field and been a personal inspiration to me.

Appreciation goes to Megan Schumaker-Murphy for updating Chapter 11 on assessment. Her expertise and practical experience with assessment of children with and without disabilities provided practical examples that greatly enhance the chapter. Thanks to long-time colleague Dr. Gayle Mindes for connecting us.

Deepest gratitude goes to Carol Copple with whom I have collaborated on *Developmentally Appropriate Practice in Early Childhood Programs* for several decades and who will always be my best thinking and conceptualizing partner. Warm thanks to Laura Colker for her unequaled generosity, sharing of ideas, and gracious support.

I want to thank Carol Brunson Day for teaching me so much about diversity, anti-bias education, and cultural influences on development; and Linda Espinosa and Luis Hernandez for research and practical examples of teaching dual-language learners.

Closest colleagues whose wisdom and encouragement have educated and sustained me for decades include Marilyn Smith, Barbara Willer, and Barbara Bowman. The debt is never paid to the late Carol Seefeldt, who taught the first early childhood course I ever took and mentored me through my dissertation. I hope that my work continues to reflect her vision.

A sincere thank you goes to the administrators, teachers, children, and families at the Center for Young Children (CYC) at the University of Maryland for welcoming me to observe and videotape there. I especially want to thank Mona Leigh Guha, Director; Anne Daniel, Assistant Director; Leslie Oppenheimer, Curriculum Specialist; and Bernadette Daly, special educator. I'm particularly grateful to these outstanding teachers: Kristin Bowman, Kelsey Blorstad, Amy Laakso, Danielle Miller, and Cici Fowler. Thanks to the children and their parents who allowed us to use the artwork and artifacts found in this book.

I am grateful to the many schools, teachers, and administrators who welcomed me as an observer, shared examples, and contributed artifacts, including: K. W. Barrett Elementary, Arlington Public Schools (APS) in Arlington, Virginia; Hoaliku Drake Preschool, Kamehameha Schools Community-Based Early Childhood Education; The Shoenbaum Family Center in Columbus, Ohio, including Anneliese Johnson; Wickliffe Progressive Community School and the Jentgen family; Linden, New Jersey, Public Schools; Far Hills Country Day School in Far Hills, New Jersey; the HighScope Demonstration Preschool in Ypsilanti, Michigan; and Easter Seals Blake Children's Achievement Center in Tucson, Arizona.

I am grateful to my new editor at Pearson, Aileen Pogran, for stepping in and quickly becoming a true supporter, sharing her vast knowledge of educational content and publishing. I continue to be indebted to Julie Peters, my editor on the previous three editions, for her unwavering support of my work.

My life and work continue to be inspired by Patty Smith Hill, founder of NANE, whose vision for early childhood education laid the foundation for NAEYC's commitment to developmentally appropriate practice.

I would also like to thank the many reviewers who contributed to the development of this book. They are:

- **Tracey Bennett Carter, Vance-Granville Community College**
- **Dede Dunst, Mitchell Community College**
- **Hannah Mills Mechler, University of Texas at Dallas; Texas Woman's University; Tarrant County Community College**
- **Lucia Obregon, Miami Dade College**

Brief Contents

Table of Contents

Special Features

Developmental Continuum/Learning Trajectory

Including All Children

Culture Lens

Language Lens

1 Continuity and Change in Early Childhood Education

Learning Outcomes

After studying this chapter, you should be able to:

1.1 Describe early childhood education.

1.2 Explain the reasons for becoming an early childhood educator.

1.3 Explain high-quality early childhood education and how it is measured.

1.4 Report research about the positive effects of early childhood education.

1.5 Analyze the current trends and issues affecting children, families, and teachers.

© Kali9/E+/Getty Images

Case Study

At Cresthaven Primary School, teachers, children, and family members of all generations are viewing children's work and sharing memories during the year-end celebration. Cresthaven is located in a community that has adopted a birth-to-age 8 approach to education and child development. The public school serves children from pre-kindergarten to grade 3, and works in partnership with the local Head Start and Early Head Start programs. A nearby child-care program, the Reed Center, serves infants to 5-year-olds and provides before- and after-school care. The school principal, program directors, and teachers are committed to ensuring seamless transitions and aligned learning experiences for children. All are invited to the celebration.

Children who will attend Cresthaven next year get to see the building and meet teachers. The preschoolers are in awe of the "big school." Parents see children's work displayed in the hallway. "Look, Mommy! Here's my painting of the yellow fish," cries 4-year-old Amber as she tugs on her mother's hand. "See where I wrote my name. And here's Brenda's picture. She's my new best friend." Amber's mother smiles and tries to read what her daughter wrote: "I lk fsh." The teacher, Ms. Engels, comes up and says, "Amber knows a lot about writing and letters. She can write her name, and she is starting to write the consonants she hears in words." Mario, who attends Head Start, reminds his mother that he can write too.

For several years, Cresthaven School has been involved with its neighbors and the other early childhood education programs in a community garden project. In each class, the teachers connect the larger curriculum—especially science and social studies goals—to aspects of the garden project. Six-year-old Sergio and his grandmother walk down the hall to find the list of all the meals the kindergartners prepared with the vegetables they harvested. A Spanish-speaking teacher, Mrs. Zapeda, greets Sergio's grandmother and makes her welcome. Sergio explains, "And tonight, we get to eat strawberries!" Meanwhile, first-grader Mathias quietly explains to some parents, "Me and my friends made this graph. It shows the vegetables the kids liked most." Third-grader Carola describes her class project to her father. "You'll like this, Dad. For social studies, we're figuring out where food comes from and why it costs so much."

The second-grade teacher, Ms. George, gets everyone's attention. "Our class is going to present their video of the garden project in 15 minutes." Seven-year-old Kelsey takes 75-year-old Mrs. Carrero by the hand and invites her to see the show. The children share most of the food raised in the garden with elderly neighbors such as Mrs. Carrero. "I'll read you the story I wrote about the garden too," says Kelsey.

© AndrewLilley/E+/Getty Images

3

Four-year-old Cooper, who has autism, has been in Ms. Watson's Head Start class for two years. His mother comes up and quietly whispers to Ms. Watson, "I wanted you to know that Cooper got invited to Martie's birthday party. I never thought that would happen, but he's made more progress than I ever imagined."

As she's leaving, Nicky's mom stops to thank Isela and Evan, who are finishing their first year of teaching 2-year-olds at Reed Center. They remember their struggles with Nicky's tantrums as he hugs his mom's leg and playfully peeks around at Evan. She says, "I know he is growing up and has to move to preschool, but we are really going to miss you two." ■

Listening to these children, parents, and teachers, some new to the field and others with many years of experience, reveals the most exciting—as well as challenging—dimensions of early childhood education. Teaching young children is hard work. It takes energy, physical stamina, patience, a sense of humor, and a wide range of knowledge and skill. But early childhood professionals soon discover the rewards of their efforts. Nothing is quite as exciting as making a baby smile and giggle, seeing a toddler's grin as he climbs the stairs on his own, or observing a preschooler's serious look as she comes to the rescue as a pretend firefighter. And what can compete with a first grader's feeling of utter accomplishment that accompanies learning to read?

Early childhood education is a rewarding profession for many reasons. We describe the diverse field of early childhood education and discuss its rewards in this chapter. We also discuss why high-quality early education is now widely recognized as critically important for our country. We examine current trends and issues in the field and larger society that present both opportunities and challenges. We also describe how, in a period of rapid change, the early childhood profession continues to be shaped by its enduring values. Above all, early childhood educators enter and stay in the field primarily for one reason—they know that their work makes a difference in the lives of children and families. ■

What Is Early Childhood Education?

early childhood education Education and child care services provided for children from birth through age 8.

professionals Members of an occupational group that make decisions based on a specialized body of knowledge, continue to learn throughout their careers, and are committed to meeting the needs of others.

Early childhood education is a highly diverse field that serves children from birth through age 8. During these years, children participate in many different kinds of care and education settings. Regardless of where they work or what their specific job titles are, however, early childhood teachers are **professionals**. This means that they make decisions based on a specialized body of knowledge, continue to learn throughout their careers, and are committed to providing the best care and education possible for every child. The opportunity to make a difference in this exciting field has never been greater.

How Early Childhood Education Is Valued

In recent years, early childhood education has achieved increasing public recognition, respect, and funding. In a time of political polarization, a national bipartisan poll found that 79% of voters—equal proportions of Republicans and Democrats—believe that the federal government should improve the quality of child care and preschool, and make it more affordable for parents (First Five Years Fund, 2017). The same poll found that 85% of voters oppose cutting funding to programs, 74% believe that early education prepares children for school, and 69% agree that it leads to a more skilled workforce. Regardless of party affiliation, voters agree that the federal government should provide funds to states to improve access to high-quality programs for both low- and middle-income families, increase tax credits to help all families pay for child care, and increase Head Start funding.

Forty-three states—as diverse as Oklahoma, Georgia, New Mexico, New York, Illinois, Massachusetts, Tennessee, and Florida—provide funding for prekindergarten programs (Barnett et al., 2017). Continued funding even in challenging economic times reflects growing public recognition of the benefits of early education, especially for children at risk of later school failure, but also for middle-class children. A great many policymakers, parents, and researchers now consider early childhood programs essential for fostering school readiness and long-term success in life (Garcia, Heckman, Leaf, & Prados, 2016; Pre-kindergarten Task Force, 2017).

A national, bipartisan nonprofit organization, Council for a Strong America, is a coalition that includes law enforcement leaders, retired admirals and generals, business executives, pastors, coaches, and athletes who strongly support the value of high-quality early education, especially for children from low-income families. They believe it prevents crime, builds stronger families, and is necessary to prepare a qualified workforce for the military and economic prosperity (Council for a Strong America, 2017). A prestigious group of America's police officers and prosecutors call themselves "the guy you pay later" because America's failure to pay for quality services for children increases the costs of the criminal justice system (Fight Crime: Invest in Kids, 2017).

Nobel Prize–winning economist James Heckman is a powerful advocate for early education. His research demonstrates that investing in early education is a cost-effective strategy that will improve education and health outcomes, strengthen the economy, help solve America's social problems, and produce a more capable, productive workforce (Garcia et al., 2016).

Several factors have contributed to the rise in status of early childhood education. These include an impressive body of research on the positive effects of early childhood programs and concerns about the persistent achievement gap in our schools. Next, we examine the overall landscape of the field, including the types of settings where children are served.

The Landscape of Early Childhood Education

Although early childhood terminology is not uniform across diverse settings, throughout this text we will use vocabulary that is consistent with that used by the **National Association for the Education of Young Children (NAEYC)** and that we believe best represents the present and future of the field. NAEYC, headquartered in Washington, D.C., is the world's largest professional organization of early childhood educators. Founded in 1926, NAEYC's mission is to promote high-quality early learning for children birth through age 8 by connecting practice, policy, and research; to advance a diverse, dynamic early childhood profession; and to support all who care for, educate, and work on behalf of young children.

One way the association achieves its mission is by establishing standards for teacher preparation at the associate, baccalaureate, and graduate-degree levels (NAEYC, 2011). NAEYC's standards have considerable influence in the field; it is likely that the course you are now taking is designed to meet the association's professional preparation standards. NAEYC (2017) also administers an accreditation system for high-quality early learning programs for children and provides resources such as publications and conferences to support teachers' continuing professional development.

Given NAEYC's definition of the field—birth through age 8—early childhood teachers work with various groups:

1. *Infants and toddlers:* birth to 36 months
2. *Preschoolers:* 3- and 4-year-olds
3. *Kindergartners:* 5- and 6-year-olds
4. *Primary grades 1, 2, and 3:* 6-, 7-, and 8-year-olds.

Because early childhood is defined so broadly, the field encompasses child-care centers and homes, preschools, kindergartens, and primary grade schools. Figure 1.1 provides an illustration of the various settings where young children are educated and receive care. Young children are always learning, and they always need loving care. Therefore, it is important *not* to distinguish child care from early education, but rather to ensure that all children have access to programs that are both caring and educational, regardless of the length of day or who provides the service.

Child Care The term *child care* typically refers to care and education provided for young children during the hours that their parents are employed. To accommodate work schedules, child care is usually available for extended hours, such as from 7:00 a.m. to

National Association for the Education of Young Children (NAEYC) The world's largest organization of early childhood educators whose mission is to promote high-quality early learning for children ages birth through 8 by connecting practice, policy, and research; to advance a diverse, dynamic early childhood profession; and to support all who care for, educate, and work on behalf of young children.

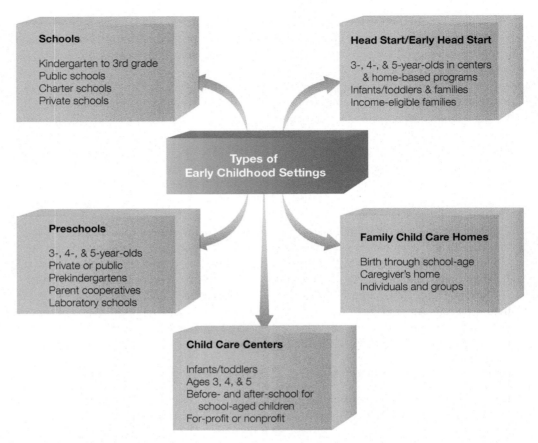

FIGURE 1.1 Types of Early Childhood Settings Early childhood education is a diverse field because young children's care and education occurs in a variety of settings, as depicted here.

Child care center Group program that provides care and education for young children during the hours that their parents are employed.

family child care home Child care in which caregivers provide care in their own homes for a small group of children, often multi-age groups.

preschool Educational programs serving 3- and 4-year-olds delivered under various sponsorships.

parent cooperative Preschool program owned, operated, and partially staffed by parents.

laboratory school School operated by colleges and universities that usually serves children of students and faculty and also acts as a model of excellent education for student teachers.

6:00 p.m. In some settings, such as hospital-affiliated child care centers, care is offered for longer hours to accommodate evening, weekend, or even night-shift employment.

Child care is typically provided in two types of group programs: child care centers and family child care homes. In either setting, children's care may be privately funded by parent tuition or publicly subsidized for low-income families. Child care centers usually enroll children from infancy through preschool-age children, and many also offer before- and after-school care for primary grade children. In family child care homes, caregivers provide care in their own homes for a small group of children, often of varying ages. Family child care is the setting of choice for many parents of infants and toddlers because of its home-like atmosphere.

Preschool   As their name implies, preschool programs serve 3- and 4-year-olds prior to their entrance into kindergarten. As of 2016, 42% of 3-year-olds and 70% of 4-year-olds attended preschool (Friedman-Krauss, Barnett, & Nores, 2016). These programs may be operated by community organizations or by churches, temples, or other faith-based organizations and also by parent cooperatives, which are run and partially staffed by groups of parents. Preschools often operate half-day, although extended hours—the school day— are becoming more common. Some colleges and universities operate laboratory schools, which usually serve children of students and faculty and also act as models for student teachers.

Preschools are called by various names, including *nursery schools* and *prekindergartens*. To further complicate matters, child-care centers are also called preschools. Preschool programs are both privately and publicly funded. Those that are funded by parent tuition primarily serve middle- or upper-income families. Two particular types of preschools are designed primarily for children from low-income families: public prekindergarten and Head Start.

Public Prekindergarten The term **prekindergarten (pre-K)** usually refers to preschools that are funded by state and local departments of education. Public prekindergarten is in the news media regularly and is the fastest-growing sector of the field, with enrollment increasing enormously in recent years. In 1980, 96,000 preschoolers were served in public elementary schools; in 2017, enrollment had increased to 1.5 million children across 43 states (Barnett et al., 2017).

The primary purpose of prekindergarten is to improve **school readiness**; that is, to prepare children for kindergarten. Although some state officials narrowly define readiness as literacy and math skills, the early childhood profession uses a broad definition of school readiness that describes the whole child (Head Start, 2017):

- Approaches to learning
- Social and emotional development
- Language and literacy
- Cognition, including mathematics and scientific reasoning
- Physical development and health

This multi-faceted definition of readiness was first promulgated by the National Education Goals Panel (Kagan, Moore, & Bredekamp, 1995). At that time, approaches to learning was a loosely defined construct. However, current research demonstrates that *how* children learn, their **approaches to learning**—enthusiasm, interest, motivation, curiosity, initiative, and engagement—affect all other areas and strongly predict their success in school and later life.

The majority of public prekindergarten programs are designed for children from low-income families or those who are considered at risk for school failure due to conditions such as low levels of maternal education or speaking a language other than English in the home. However, a growing number of people are calling for funding of **universal voluntary prekindergarten**, the goal of which is to make these programs available to families of all income levels that choose to use them. Publicly funded prekindergarten has contributed to the field's growth; today, the number of 4-year-olds in state prekindergarten programs exceeds the number enrolled in Head Start (Barnett et al., 2017).

Head Start **Head Start** is a federally funded, national program that promotes school readiness by enhancing the social and cognitive development of children ages 3, 4, and 5.

prekindergarten (pre-K) Educational program serving 3- and 4-year-olds, usually in public schools.

school readiness Children's competencies related to success in kindergarten, including physical development, health, and well-being; social-emotional development and learning; cognitive development and general knowledge such as mathematics and science; positive approaches to learning such as curiosity and motivation; and language development and early literacy skills.

approaches to learning Behaviors or typical patterns that children use in learning situations that include both how they feel about learning—their level of enthusiasm, interest, and motivation—and how they engage with learning—their curiosity, initiative, and creativity.

universal voluntary prekindergarten Publicly funded preschool, usually for 4-year-olds but sometimes 3-year-olds; available to any family that chooses to use it.

Head Start Federally funded national program that promotes school readiness by enhancing the social and cognitive development of children ages 3, 4, and 5 through providing educational, health, nutritional, social, and other services to the nation's poorest children and families.

© Jules Selmes/Pearson Education

Early childhood education includes child care centers, preschools, prekindergartens, family child care homes, and schools. But every high-quality program provides both loving care and education for young children and support for their families.

Early Head Start Federally funded program serving low-income pregnant mothers, infants, and toddlers that promotes healthy family functioning.

early childhood special education Services for children with disabilities or special needs who meet eligibility guidelines that are determined on a state-by-state basis according to the Individuals with Disabilities Education Act.

Individuals with Disabilities Education Act (IDEA) Federal law governing provision of services for children with disabilities and special needs.

early intervention Services for infants and toddlers who are at risk of developmental delay and their families.

inclusion Participation and services for children with disabilities and special needs in programs and settings where their typically developing peers are served.

kindergarten Typically considered the first year of formal schooling; serves 5- and 6-year-olds.

primary grades First, second, and third grade; sometimes includes kindergarten.

Video Example 1.1:

Inclusion

All early childhood educators are likely to work with children with disabilities at some point in their careers. This inevitability broadens what teachers need to know right from the start. In this video, consider these questions: how does inclusion require that early childhood teachers collaborate with special educators? What are the benefits of inclusion for all children?

Head Start provides educational, health, nutritional, social, and other services to the nation's poorest children and to families whose incomes fall below the official poverty level (Head Start, 2017). Head Start's goal is to improve school readiness by supporting all areas of children's development and learning needed for later success. In addition to these comprehensive services, parent involvement is a special focus of the program. Parents volunteer in the classroom and serve in governance roles with the goal of empowering families to move out of poverty. In fact, 23% of Head Start staff members are parents of current or former Head Start children (Head Start, 2017). Children with disabilities make up about 12% of Head Start's enrollment (Head Start, 2017).

Head Start programs are quite diverse. Most Head Start children are served in classroom-based preschool programs, although in rural or remote areas, a home-based option is available. One of the smallest serves 30 children on the Havasupai reservation in the Grand Canyon, accessible only by helicopter or donkey, while the largest programs serve over 22,000 children in 400 centers across Los Angeles (Head Start, 2008).

The families represent all the racial and cultural groups in the United States (Head Start, 2017). About 44% of the children are White, 37% are Latino, and 29% are African American. A sizable number of families—10%—report that their children are biracial or multiracial. In addition, the program has a special focus on serving American Indians, Alaska Natives, and migrant and seasonal workers. About 30% of the children speak a language other than English at home. Of these, 85% speak Spanish, but 140 other languages are spoken.

In response to brain research and concerns that age 4 or even age 3 is too late for services to be effective, the government launched **Early Head Start** in 1995. Early Head Start serves low-income pregnant mothers, infants, and toddlers, and promotes healthy family functioning in all 50 states, the District of Columbia, and Puerto Rico (Head Start, 2017). Research on Early Head Start (Vogel, Yange, Moiduddun, Kisker, & Carlson, 2010) demonstrates that it achieves its promise of lasting positive effects on children and families.

Early Intervention and Early Childhood Special Education **Early childhood special education** serves children with disabilities or special needs who meet eligibility guidelines that are determined on a state-by-state basis, according to the **Individuals with Disabilities Education Act (IDEA)**. In addition to serving children with identified disabilities, some states provide **early intervention** services for infants and toddlers who are at risk of developmental delay and their families.

Federal legislation enacted during the past three decades has fundamentally changed the way early childhood services are organized and delivered to children with disabilities and special needs (Division for Early Childhood & NAEYC, 2009). These children, including children who are at risk for disabilities or who exhibit challenging behaviors, are far more likely to participate in a typical early childhood program than in the past. This trend, called **inclusion**, is defined and described in the feature *Including All Children: What Does Inclusion Mean?*

Kindergarten and Primary Grades Most 5- through 8-year-old children attend public schools, although many attend secular or faith-based private schools funded by parent tuition. Typically considered the first year of formal schooling, **kindergarten** has traditionally been designed for 5-year-olds. States establish varying dates for the legal entrance age to kindergarten, but 44 states require that children who are entering kindergarten must have their fifth birthday before the end of September or earlier (Workman, 2014). This means that today's kindergartens enroll many 6-year-olds. By contrast, in 1975, only nine states required that children be age 5 by September (Colasanti, 2007)

First, second, and third grades are the **primary grade** years of school (6 through 8 years of age). These grades are especially important because

Including All Children
What Does Inclusion Mean?

Mark and Monique Berger operate a family child care program in their home. Their state permits group homes such as theirs to serve up to 12 children. The licensing agent informs them that they are required by law to serve children with disabilities and special needs. One mother, whose son Barry has cerebral palsy, has inquired about enrolling him in the Bergers' program. Mark wants to be sure that they abide by the law, but Monique is a little unsure about what it means to include a child with a disability in her child care home.

Although full inclusion of children with disabilities in early childhood programs has been the law of the land for many years, Mark and Monique are not alone in being unsure about what it means. To guide them and other professionals like them, the DEC & NAEYC (2009) jointly developed a statement defining early childhood inclusion:

> Early childhood inclusion embodies the values, policies, and practices that support the right of every infant and young child and his or her family, regardless of ability, to participate in a broad range of activities and contexts as full members of families, communities, and society. The desired results of inclusive experiences for children with and without disabilities and their families include a sense of belonging and membership, positive social relationships and friendships, and development and learning to reach their full potential.

The statement describes the key features of high-quality inclusive programs, which are (1) access, (2) participation, and (3) supports.

A defining feature of high-quality early childhood inclusion is *access*, which means providing children with a wide range of learning opportunities, activities, and environments. In inclusive settings, adults also promote belonging, *participation*, and engagement of children with disabilities and their typically developing peers in a variety of intentional or purposeful ways.

Finally, an infrastructure of inclusion *supports* must be in place to ensure a foundation for the efforts of individuals and organizations that provide inclusive services to children and families. For example, Mark and Monique will need access to ongoing professional development and support to acquire the knowledge, skills, and dispositions required to effectively meet Barry's needs and contribute to his development. In addition, specialized services and therapies for Barry will need to be coordinated and integrated with the other activities they offer the children.

Source: Division for Early Childhood and National Association for the Education of Young Children, 2009 *Early childhood inclusion: A joint position statement of the Division for Early Childhood (DEC) and the National Association for the Education of Young Children (NAEYC).* Retrieved November 4, 2017, from www.dec-sped.org/position-statements

during these grades, children are expected to acquire the fundamental abilities of reading and mathematics, along with the foundations of other academic disciplines including social studies, science, the creative arts, technology, and physical education. In first to third grade, children are learning to read; after that, they are expected to read to learn (Hernandez, (2011)). Therefore, if a good foundation is not laid during the primary years, children are likely to struggle in later years.

Forty states and the District of Columbia permit funding of public **charter schools.** Charter schools are independently operated, publicly-funded schools that have greater flexibility than regular schools in meeting regulations and achieving goals, but they must also meet accountability standards. They are operated under a contract with the state or district. In school districts in which charter schools are an option, parents have a choice of where to send their children. However, competition for spaces often means that families do not have meaningful choice. More than 3 million children attend charter schools, and the percentage is increasing (National Alliance for Public Charter Schools, 2017).

charter schools Independently operated, publicly funded schools that have greater flexibility than regular schools in meeting regulations and achieving goals.

How Early Childhood Education Is Expanding

Participation in early childhood programs has increased steadily for many decades as more children participate in group programs at younger ages. In 1965, only 60% of 5-year-olds went to kindergarten, whereas today about 95% do (National Center for Education Statistics, 2017). A similar but steeper growth trend is apparent for younger children. In 1960, only 10% of 3- and 4-year-olds were enrolled in any type of early childhood program. By 2015, 38% of 3-year-olds, 67% of 4-year-olds, and 87% of 5-year-olds attended a program prior to kindergarten (National Center for Education Statistics, 2017).

Growth in Early Childhood Program Attendance
All types of early childhood programs have seen growth over the years, including private preschools and child-care centers, state-funded prekindergarten, preschool special education, and Head Start (NCES, 2017; Head Start, 2017).

A fundamental change in preschool participation was apparent in the findings of the landmark *Early Childhood Longitudinal Study, Birth Cohort* (Jacobson Chernoff, Flanagan, McPhee, & Park, 2007). That study revealed that preschool, rather than kindergarten, is now seen as the first year of school for children. The percentage of children who attend center-based preschools is approximately the same whether or not their mothers are employed. This finding indicates that the growth in preschool enrollment is related to increased demand for early education as much as increased need for child care.

Child Care for Employed Families
Expansion of the early childhood field is directly related to the demand for child care for employed families. Two-thirds of children under age 6 have parents or their single parent in the labor force (Bishop-Josef, 2017). Infant and toddler care is a particular need, because 58% of mothers of children under age 1 are in the workforce. The likelihood of children being cared for by a non-family member increases with age: 21% of infants are cared for by non-relatives compared to 65% of 4-year-olds (Bishop-Josef, 2017). Almost 80% of school-agers need care for some hours of the day.

Recognizing how important good child care is to maintaining a productive workforce, some employers sponsor on-site child-care centers or subsidize child-care expenses as an employee benefit. Employers find that support for child care can reduce absenteeism and turnover.

In addition, the federal government provides child-care assistance through **Temporary Assistance for Needy Families (TANF)**. The TANF program provides temporary financial aid but requires recipients to move into the labor force or schooling, further increasing the demand for child care. The **Child Care and Development Block Grants (CCDBG)** program allocates funds to states for low-income working families to purchase their own child care. In 2014, Congress reauthorized the CCDBG for the first time since 1996, with significant bipartisan support. The new law significantly improved provisions designed to protect children's health and safety, and to improve the quality of care.

Access to High-Quality Early Education

Despite the overall increase in the number of children attending preschool, access varies considerably depending on family income and other factors. In fact, the children who are most likely to benefit from high-quality programs are the least likely to participate in them.

Consider the following statistics (NCES, 2017; Friedman-Krauss et al., 2016):

- Young children who live in poverty are less likely to attend high-quality preschool than children from higher-income families.
- African American and Hispanic children have less access to high-quality programs than White children.
- Head Start and state-funded prekindergarten programs increase the participation rates for low-income families, but insufficient slots are available to serve all the eligible children.

Temporary Assistance for Needy Families (TANF) Federally funded program, more commonly known as Welfare to Work, that provides temporary financial aid but requires recipients to move into the labor force or schooling.

Child Care and Development Block Grants (CCDBG) Federal funds allocated to states for low-income working families to purchase child care.

- Families with moderate incomes face the greatest hurdle because they are not eligible for subsidized programs and cannot afford private ones.
- Preschool participation varies considerably depending on the mother's education. Children of college-educated parents attend preschool at higher rates than children whose parents are high school dropouts. Again, the children who need preschool the most—those whose mothers are less likely to provide educational experiences at home—are the least likely to get it.

How Early Childhood Education Is Changing

Recently, several major transformations in the United States have had significant impacts on early childhood education—changing demographics, economics, and families. The nation is becoming increasingly diverse. At the same time, economic hardship and poverty—including homelessness—are affecting increasing numbers of families.

Changing Demographics In the last few decades, the population of young children in the United States has become dramatically more diverse, as depicted in Figure 1.2. From 1990 to 2017, the white population of children declined from 69% to 50%, while the percentage of Latino children increased from 16% to 26% (Annie E. Casey Foundation, 2017a). Relatively soon, the majority of young children will be children of color—members of groups currently identified as minorities. In many school districts, this is already the case. For example, 52% of young children in California are Latino (Annie E. Casey Foundation, 2017a).

Many of these children are **dual language learners** because they are learning to speak two languages at the same time—their home language and English. These demographic

dual language learners
Children who simultaneously learn two languages: the home or first language as well as English or another second language.

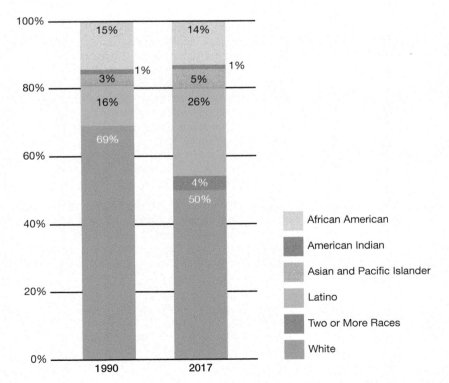

FIGURE 1.2 Child Population by Race and Ethnicity In the last two decades, the population of young children in the United States has become more ethnically and racially diverse.

Source: Based on Annie E. Casey Foundation, (2017). *2017 Kids Count data book: State trends in child well-being.* Baltimore: Author. Retrieved November 9, 2017, from www.aecf.org/2017

shifts have important implications for early childhood educators, as discussed in the feature *Language Lens: Preparing to Teach Dual Language Learners*.

Economic Challenges Despite an economic recovery since the 2008 recession, poverty is widespread. Of the 23 million children under age 6, 23% live in families with incomes below the federal poverty level, which is about $24,000 for a family of four with two children (Jiang, Granja, & Koball, 2017). Considering that families actually need twice that income to cover basic expenses, an additional 23% of all young children live in low-income or *near-poor* families. About 70% of these children have at least one full-time employed family member.

Poverty disproportionately affects children of color. Nearly one-third of African American and America Indian children and one-fourth of Hispanic children are poor, compared to one in nine White children (Children's Defense Fund, 2017). Most alarming, 6 million children live in extreme poverty—half the federal poverty level. Nearly 1 in 30 children experience homelessness, which occurs in every city and state in the nation (National Center on Family Homelessness at American Institutes for Research, 2015).

Language Lens
Preparing to Teach Dual Language Learners

Eight different languages are spoken among the children in Natalia's kindergarten class. Natalia and two of the children are the only ones whose first language is English. Natalia works hard to create a caring community where all the children comfortably experiment with learning English while also developing their home languages. She strives to communicate with the parents by using translators. Last year, Natalia's class also included eight languages—but some of them were different from those spoken this year.

The number of languages represented in Natalia's classroom may seem extreme, but linguistic and cultural diversity is now the norm in our nation's schools. In the next 20 years, the biggest single child-related demographic change is predicted to be an increase in dual language learners. Most of these children speak Spanish as a home language, but many others speak Asian, Middle Eastern, and African languages. California, Florida, and Texas continue to have the largest percentages of Spanish-speaking families, but the Hispanic population grew in many regions of the country. In fact, Georgia's Hispanic population more than doubled in two decades.

In the past, most teachers could safely assume that they would never encounter a language other than English in their entire careers. Today, Natalia's experience, or something like it, is not so very rare. New teachers may find it beneficial to learn another language themselves, but learning eight languages is not a reasonable expectation. What can new and experienced teachers such as Natalia do? They can start by remembering some important principles about dual language learners:

- People who speak the same language, whether Spanish or another language, are not all alike—they come from a variety of countries and cultures.
- Learning two or more languages does not confuse children as some people think, but rather enhances brain development.
- Dual language learners can better focus attention because alternating languages requires intense concentration.
- Supporting home language development is essential because children can learn many skills in their home language and apply those skills as they learn English.
- Teachers need to intentionally teach English vocabulary and provide lots of opportunities for children to play together and practice their developing language skills.
- Communicating with families is essential regardless of the effort required.

The children of today must be prepared to function as citizens of a global society. Speaking two or more languages is an important skill for the 21st century. When children enter early childhood programs speaking a language other than English, the foundation is already there on which to build.

Sources: Flores, 2017. *How the U.S. Hispanic population is changing.* Washington, DC: Pew Research Center; National Academies of Science, Engineering, and Medicine, 2017. *Promoting the educational success of children and youth learning English.* Washington, DC: The National Academies Press; Bialystok & Werker, 2016. The systematic effects of bilingualism on children's development. *Developmental Science, 20*(1).

These statistics are alarming given that the youngest children have the highest poverty rates. Growing up in extreme poverty can have potentially devastating impacts on health, brain development, and learning. These children are most in need of high-quality early childhood programs and good teachers. And yet, too many families do not have access to subsidized programs and cannot find affordable child care (Flores, 2017).

The effects of the economic downturn on children and families are real. However, increased political support for child care and early education at this difficult time in the nation's history is solid evidence of its broad support and the recognition of its value.

Diverse Families Young children's families today are a rich tapestry. Not only are they ethnically, racially, culturally, and linguistically diverse, the composition of families varies widely. More children are growing up with single mothers or fathers. Same-sex couples can now legally marry, creating loving families for their children. And grandparents are increasingly the custodial parents of their grandchildren. Many children live with large extended families that include aunts, uncles, and/or cousins as well as siblings. There is no such thing as the "typical" American family.

Choosing to teach young children, like every career decision, involves weighing many factors. Prospective teachers need to be familiar with what the work entails and the possible career options. Most important, they need to determine whether the demands and rewards of their chosen profession are a good match with their own strengths, dispositions, and personal goals (Colker, 2008).

The Joys of Teaching Young Children

Working with children demands patience and the willingness to care for and about other people's children, even or especially the least lovable of those children. Teaching young children is truly rewarding work, even when it is most challenging (Colker, 2008). Each day brings new discoveries, accomplishments, and joys for children and teachers.

Picture a 4-year-old child. What are the first thoughts that come to mind? Is he or she curious? Eager to learn? Excellent early childhood teachers take advantage of young children's deep desire to actively engage with and make sense of the world around them. Recall the sense of satisfaction you felt when you mastered a difficult task such as learning to read or ride a bike. Children gain great pleasure from the sense of mastery that comes from learning something new or overcoming an obstacle.

Another word that comes to mind when thinking of children is *fun*. Yes, early childhood programs prepare children for success in school, but they also provide them with joyful learning experiences every day of their young lives. Children should have fun in child care centers and homes, preschools, and schools. They love to joke, tease, and be silly; to sing, move, and dance; to play by themselves and with friends; to know that adults care

© David Kostelnik/Pearson Education

Intentional teachers are purposeful, but they are also playful. How can teachers keep the fun in childhood while helping children achieve important learning goals?

for them; to wonder about and explore the natural world; and to generally enjoy living. When teachers create a safe and supportive place for children to experience the unique joys of childhood, children will thrive—and their teachers will also.

Dimensions of Effective Intentional Teaching

One overarching theme of this book is that effective early childhood practice requires teachers to be intentional in everything they do. Intentional teachers have a purpose for the decisions they make and can explain that purpose to others (Copple & Bredekamp, 2009; Epstein, 2014). However, we believe that intentional teaching involves much more. Intentional teaching is a multifaceted, multidimensional concept that conveys many of the personal and professional qualities of an early childhood educator. Consider how well your own aspirations and dispositions fit with our description of the dimensions of intentional teaching that appears in Figure 1.3.

For an example of intentional teaching, read the feature Becoming an Intentional Teacher: Modeling Positive Approaches to Learning.

intentional teachers Teachers who have a purpose for the decisions they make and can explain that purpose to others.

Career Options for Early Childhood Educators

Now that we have described both the dedication and the delight that teaching young children entails, we turn to an overview of the job opportunities in the field. As the field of early education grows, so do the potential career options and opportunities for early childhood professionals. At the same time, however, the field is experiencing a shortage of qualified teachers (IOM & NRC, 2015). Even as a large percentage of the current teaching staff is nearing retirement, teacher qualification requirements are being raised in many sectors of the field.

Because the early childhood field is so diverse and covers such a broad age range, early childhood educators have many possible career choices. Careers tend to fall into two categories:

- Working *with* children involves daily interaction and direct responsibility for children's care and education, and includes positions such as classroom teacher or family child care provider.
- Working *for* children involves work that supports children's development and education, whether in proximity to the children, such as being a child-care center director, or at a further distance, such as being a teacher-education professor.

Over the course of their careers, many early childhood professionals move back and forth between these types of jobs. However, we believe that success in working *for* children is greater if an individual has actually worked *with* children. No one in the early childhood community can do his or her job well without knowing what life is like in an early childhood setting (Colker, 2008). This experience informs decisions at every level.

Working *with* Children   Early childhood teachers are usually the first to admit that they aren't in this profession for the money. It is the satisfaction they get from working with children that is deeply rewarding. For many of them, the fact that they make an impact

- **Caring and committed.** They recognize that developing a personal, positive, warm relationship with each child is the foundation for everything they do. Their commitment to children means putting children's needs before their own and recognizing that teaching young children is less a job than a calling.

- **Enthusiastic and engaged.** They genuinely enjoy being with young children however messy or challenging they may be, and share in the excitement of their discoveries. They become energetically and intensely involved in children's activity, whether it means getting down on the floor to play and talk with a baby or thinking through the solution to a problem with a kindergartner.

- **Curious and creative.** They are eager to learn, just as children are. Young children want to learn all sorts of things that teachers themselves may not know—what's inside a bug, why the sky is blue, how an airplane flies. Intentional teachers model an inquisitive attitude. They want to find out along with children, and they approach questions or problems in new, imaginative ways.

- **Respectful and responsive.** They value and treat children, families, and colleagues with dignity and esteem. They respond thoughtfully to diversity in all of its forms: language, culture, race/ethnicity, ability/disability, age, gender, and sexual orientation. They are open and accepting of perspectives that are different from their own.

- **Passionate and patient.** They bring into their work their own emotions and deep interests, such as a passion for music, painting, or poetry; a preference for belly laughs or quiet smiles. At the same time, they recognize that children have their own intense feelings that can spill over into anger, frustration, or fits of tears. Intentional teachers respond calmly and thoughtfully, without becoming upset or annoyed themselves.

- **Purposeful and playful.** They have important goals for children—to help them make friends, regulate their emotions, control their bodies, learn to read and write—and they plan carefully to help children achieve their goals. But along the way, they joke and laugh with children, accept silliness, encourage and support play, and make learning itself playful. A sense of humor is a necessity.

- **Focused and flexible.** They are like cameras that can scan the entire classroom and then narrow their attention to meet one child's need or respond to her question or idea. They can be teaching a reading lesson with a specific goal in mind and switch gears when a child starts talking about his brother's illness.

- **Aware and accountable.** They are self-aware, they reflect on and evaluate their own performance, and they strive to improve. But their judgments are not made in isolation; they compare their performance to a standard of excellence. Intentional teachers are willing to be accountable; they accept responsibility for their actions.

- **Informed and effective.** They know how children develop and learn; they know how to teach and what to teach. They use research-based teaching practices that lead to positive outcomes for children and help children make sense of the world around them. Intentional teachers also regularly check to see if what they are doing is actually working. Are children making progress toward developmentally appropriate goals?

- **Listening and learning.** They realize that the more they learn about children, the more they need to know. They understand that choosing to teach is choosing to be a lifelong learner. Intentional teachers learn from children every day; they listen to children, and they pay close attention to all of children's cues. They stay up to date about new knowledge and continue to grow as professionals.

FIGURE 1.3 Characteristics of Professional Intentional Early Childhood Teachers Intentional teaching involves a wide range of personal and professional qualities, such as those listed here.

on the life of every child they encounter is a powerful incentive and the reason that, once they enter the field, they are there to stay (Colker, 2008).

Early childhood teachers work with different age groups from infancy through primary grades in a wide range of settings. The qualifications and required certifications for specific jobs will vary, but a broad-based education in the field is necessary preparation.

Becoming an Intentional Teacher

Modeling Positive Approaches to Learning

Here's What Happened One wintry morning in my Head Start class, I brought in my guitar and started playing and singing happily as the children arrived. This was a surprise for them because I usually greet them at the door and help them with their coats. Instead, they managed on their own, began to gather round me, and asked lots of questions. "I've been learning to play guitar, and I just love it," I said. "It takes lots of hard work and I make mistakes, but as long as I keep trying, my songs sound better." Nico enthusiastically danced along to the music. Wide-eyed Elena concentrated very hard on my fingers as I changed chords. "Can I try?" she asked hopefully. "Later, I will let each of you have a turn, but first I'm going to play a song I made up, and I want you to make up some new words for it," I replied. The children laughed at the challenge and agreed that would be fun.

Here's What I Was Thinking As a Head Start teacher, I have a responsibility to help children make progress on important early learning outcomes, including a strong emphasis on approaches to learning. I used my personal passion for playing guitar and writing songs to intentionally model my enthusiasm, interest, and creativity. I also talked about hard work to demonstrate my motivation, initiative, persistence, and engagement. Young children often want to be like their teachers, so I think their curiosity about the guitar and writing songs will promote positive approaches to learning but also their language as they attempt to compose songs and their fine motor development as they pluck the strings.

Reflection Reread the Characteristics of Professional Intentional Early Childhood Teachers in Figure 1.3. Which ones are the same positive approaches to learning that children need to develop? What other ways could this teacher intentionally support children's enthusiasm and engagement?

Following are some of the options and opportunities available for interesting and rewarding work:

- *Head Start* teachers can alter the life trajectory of young children and their families who are most in need. They help ensure that children from low-income families receive an excellent education and comprehensive health, nutrition, and other services.
- *Early Head Start* teachers intervene early with mothers and their babies to help set them on a course of healthy development.
- *Child-care center* teachers provide loving care and education to children for extended periods of time each day, and help employed parents feel secure about their children's care so they can do their jobs. Careers in child care offer the option of teaching various age groups: infants and toddlers, preschoolers, and school-age children before and/or after school. Although teaching in child care pays less than does teaching in other settings, many teachers relish its flexible and creative environment. Conditions also vary by administrative agency; for example, an employer-sponsored child-care center may offer more benefits and higher compensation than a community-based one.
- Teachers in *family child care homes* literally open their doors to small groups of children from infancy through school age, providing a home-like atmosphere of care and education. Family child care means being your own boss, but requires administering a small business as well as caring for children.
- *Preschools* vary a great deal—public, private, faith-based, and so on—each with its own benefits that will appeal to different teachers' interests and match their goals. A public prekindergarten, for example, may provide better salaries, whereas a private one may be more flexible about curriculum and expectations for children.
- A teacher in a *parent cooperative preschool* has the opportunity to develop particularly close relationships with families but also needs the ability to work with parents as co-teachers, an acquired skill.

- Teachers in *public schools* have the option of teaching different age groups from kindergarten through primary grades. Schools are bureaucracies with regulations and an established curriculum and tests, but as professionals, teachers make hundreds of classroom decisions every day. Salaries and benefits in the public schools are the most secure of any sector in early childhood.
- *Early childhood special educators* and *early intervention specialists* are qualified individuals who work with children with special needs in various settings such as in school systems, Head Start, or child care. Inclusion of children with special needs means that early childhood special educators work closely with regular classroom teachers. In fact, in some states, the same teacher education program prepares teachers for certification in both fields simultaneously.
- *Mentor teacher* is an evolving career option for more experienced, outstanding professionals. It is helpful for new teachers to work with a mentor teacher to improve their skills or to get help for children with particular learning challenges. Mentor teachers are becoming more common in elementary schools, preschools, and child care programs.
- The need for *bilingual or multilingual teachers* and those who are qualified to teach dual language learners is growing. As the population becomes ever more diverse, these qualifications will be useful in any early childhood setting.

Given the variety of careers available, early childhood teachers have many options. Even when an entire career is spent teaching the same age group in the same workplace, teachers will always encounter new challenges and new experiences. I once asked a former teacher who had taught for 40 years, "Didn't you ever get tired of teaching first grade?" She looked stunned and replied, "Never, because every group was different." Having been a child in her class at one time, I clearly understood what she meant—that every child is different and unique, and that being a teacher never loses its fascination.

Working *for* Children At some point in their careers, all early childhood professionals should work with children in order to understand firsthand how educators help shape our young children. However, there are many opportunities for early childhood educators to pursue positions working *for* children. With additional education, specialized training, and experience, a background in early childhood can lead to positions such as these:

- *Director* of a child care center or preschool, or school principal (with additional course work in administration)
- *Curriculum developer* for an individual school, network of schools, or publisher
- *Home visitor* or *family services worker* in Head Start, Early Head Start, or another community agency
- *Policy staff* at local/state/federal agencies, associations, and organizations
- *College faculty* teaching teachers and/or conducting research
- *Writer/producer of resources for children* such as children's book author, technology developer, children's museum staff, or media performer

In previous sections, we discussed what it means to be a professional intentional early childhood teacher. These definitions reflect the profession's core values and beliefs, a topic to which we turn next.

© Pearson Education

Video Example 1.2:

Career Options in Early Childhood Education

In this video, Sue Bredekamp interviews a director of an NAEYC-accredited program about the qualifications she looks for in hiring teachers and the career options available in the field. Consider what you've done or could do in the future to begin your journey as an early childhood educator.

The Culture of Early Childhood Education

A key theme of this book is the important role that culture plays in development and learning. Broadly defined, **culture** comprises the rules and expectations for behavior of members of a group that are passed on from one generation to the next. These rules determine to a large extent what group members regard as important and what values shape their actions and judgments.

culture The explicit and implicit values, beliefs, rules, and expectations for behavior of members of a group that are passed on from one generation to the next. These rules determine to a large extent what group members regard as important and what values shape their actions and judgments.

Like other professional groups, the early childhood profession has its own culture. This culture is transmitted both explicitly and implicitly from more experienced, competent members to new initiates in three ways: through formal education, through on-the-job experiences, and through mentoring in either setting. New teachers may become confused or flustered when the cultural rules transmitted in one setting, such as their college classrooms, do not seem to match the expectations for behavior in another, such as their first teaching assignments.

Cultural groups define themselves in many ways, including through the language they use, how they identify themselves, the values they share, and their fundamental beliefs. We discuss these topics in the following sections.

Shared Vocabulary

One aspect of early childhood culture is a shared vocabulary. Shared language facilitates communication and minimizes misunderstandings within groups. The profession gives particular meaning to terms such as *developmentally appropriate*, *play*, *relationships*, *comprehensive services*, or *inclusion* (all of which are defined in this book). Their definitions are tailored to our profession, and may not mirror how these words are used in other professions or everyday life.

An essential part of joining a profession is learning its language. For example, although the larger society uses the term *day care*, within the profession, the accepted term is *child care*. We believe that saying *child care* is more respectful of children and a more accurate description of the setting and the job.

Shared Identity

Most professionals feel a sense of belonging to their group. They identify themselves as members of the profession, whether it is as a doctor, a lawyer, or an accountant. In early childhood education, it is often harder to "name" ourselves. The profession itself has been called by many names—*early care and education*, *child care*, *early education*, and *early development and learning*. In this book, we refer to the field as *early childhood education*. We prefer this term because it contains the word *child*, which is an ever-present reminder of the primary focus of our work. We also believe that the term encompasses the key elements of caring, development, and learning.

Another challenge to establishing a clear identity is what to call the role itself. Infant/toddler teachers and teachers in center-based care are often called *caregivers*. In family child care, adults are called *providers*. But we embrace the term *teacher* because it is the broadest term, it captures most of the job responsibilities, it commands society's respect and potentially increased compensation, and it is, after all, what children usually call the adults who care for and educate them no matter what the setting.

Shared Values

The early childhood profession is committed to a core set of values that is deeply rooted in the history of the field. NAEYC (2011) articulates these core values in its code of ethical conduct:

We have made a commitment to:

- Appreciate childhood as a unique and valuable stage of the human life cycle
- Base our work on knowledge of how children develop and learn
- Respect diversity in children, families, and colleagues
- Recognize that children and adults achieve their full potential in the context of relationships that are based on trust and respect
- Appreciate and support the bond between the child and family
- Recognize that children are best understood and supported in the context of family, culture (including ethnicity), community, and society
- Respect the dignity, worth, and uniqueness of each individual (child, family member, and colleague)

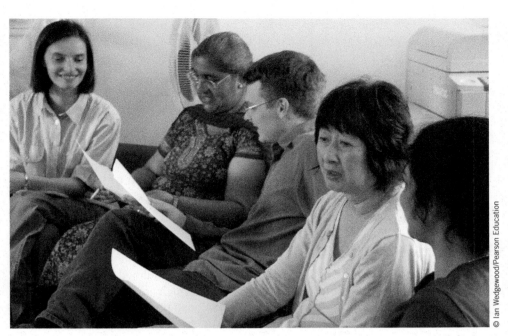

Early childhood educators are members of a profession that shares knowledge, values, and beliefs about children and their work. Meeting with more experienced teachers is one way of becoming a professional. Can you think of others?

I often take informal polls of teachers during speeches at education conferences. A question I always ask is: "What are your values as an early childhood educator?" Most of the core values just listed are mentioned. Yet there is one that is always stated emphatically and is usually first—"play!" Early childhood professionals strongly value play as essential for children's development and learning. Because play is so important in early childhood, we will revisit the topic throughout this book. Political and economic forces threaten these values at times, but they nevertheless endure.

Shared Beliefs   Although early childhood culture shares many beliefs, a few dominate:

- The strong belief in the potential of all children, regardless of their life circumstances and individual abilities or disabilities.
- The belief in the power of **developmentally appropriate practice (DAP)** to produce positive results for children. Developmentally appropriate practice is teaching that engages children's interests and adapts for their age, experience, and ability to help them meet challenging and achievable goals.
- The belief that early childhood teachers are professionals who make informed decisions about what is developmentally appropriate for each child in each situation.
- The fundamental belief in the potential of our work to make a real and lasting difference in the world.

developmentally appropriate practice (DAP) Ways of teaching that engage children's interests and adapt for their age, experience, and ability to help them meet challenging and achievable learning goals.

This is the final justification for joining the profession: the opportunity to make a contribution to children's lives. Many professions exist primarily to solve problems. Doctors and nurses treat illnesses. Firefighters put out fires and rescue people. Insurance agents help people recover from losses or catastrophes. The work of early childhood professionals, on the other hand, is to prevent problems from occurring. Our job is to set children on a positive course from the beginning. The proven effectiveness of early intervention when young children face difficulties creates room for optimism and hope.

✔ Check Your Understanding 1.2

🏠 Early Childhood Program Quality and Measuring Effectiveness

Growing attention to early education primarily results from impressive research demonstrating its effectiveness in improving outcomes for children. All of the research that has influenced policy, however, finds that the key ingredient in the effectiveness of early childhood education is the quality of the program for children. But what is quality?

Setting Standards for Quality

Earlier in this chapter, we described different types of early childhood programs. Various kinds of programs must meet different sets of standards, which are intended to determine the program's quality. Early childhood educators have been instrumental in setting standards for quality that, in addition to research, reflect the profession's core values and beliefs.

Child Care Licensing Standards   Child care centers and, in some states, family child care homes, are regulated by each state's **child care licensing standards**. These set minimum requirements for a program to operate legally. Such standards usually establish a minimum number of teachers required per child (teacher/child ratios), teacher qualifications, and health and safety requirements.

> **Child care licensing standards** Minimum requirements legally established by each state for a child care program to operate.

Quality Rating and Improvement Systems   These standards, designed to ensure children's protection, vary considerably from state to state. For example, one state requires 1 teacher for every 4 infants, whereas another permits a ratio of 1 to 6. Child Care Aware of America (Dobbins, 2017) evaluates state licensing standards and monitoring of centers' compliance. They find that many states' standards fall short of minimum protection for children's health and safety, and support for their development.

Because licensing standards vary and represent minimums, the quality of child care also varies considerably. Some licensed programs exceed the required standards, whereas others barely meet them (Child Care Aware of America, 2017). To address this issue and help parents make informed decisions, many states now operate **quality rating and improvement systems (QRIS)**. These tiered systems rate program quality according to achievement of benchmarks beyond those required for minimal licensing, such as having more highly qualified teachers or better ratios (BUILD Initiative, 2017). The state recognizes centers that meet higher standards with more stars and pays higher reimbursement rates for children served. In some states, achieving accreditation is the highest level. QRIS also helps families make informed decisions about choosing child care.

> **quality rating and improvement systems (QRIS)** State-operated tiered systems that evaluate and rate the quality of child care programs according to achievement of benchmarks beyond those required for minimal licensing, such as having more highly qualified teachers or better ratios.

Accreditation Standards   The early childhood profession under the leadership of NAEYC (2016) is committed to raising the overall quality of early education for all children. Toward this end, the association sets high-quality standards and administers a voluntary **accreditation system** for all types of early childhood centers and schools serving children from birth through kindergarten. The standards that programs must achieve to obtain accreditation are listed in Table 1.1. These standards apply to any early learning program regardless of length of day or sponsorship. NAEYC accreditation standards are designed to answer the question: "What is high quality?"

> **accreditation system** NAEYC's voluntary system for identifying high-quality early childhood centers and schools serving children from birth through kindergarten.

TABLE 1.1 NAEYC Early Learning Program Standards

NAEYC's accreditation standards describe all the key elements of a high-quality early childhood program.

Standard	Standard Description
1. Relationships	The program promotes positive relationships among all children and adults to encourage each child's sense of individual worth and belonging as a part of a community and to foster each child's ability to contribute as a responsible community member.
2. Curriculum	The program implements a curriculum that is consistent with its goals for children, and promotes learning and development in each of the following areas: social, emotional, physical, language, and cognitive.
3. Teaching	The program uses developmentally, culturally, and linguistically appropriate and effective teaching approaches that enhance each child's learning and development in the context of the program's curriculum goals.
4. Assessment of children's progress	The program is informed by ongoing systematic, formal, and informal assessment approaches to provide information on children's learning and development. These assessments occur within the context of reciprocal communications with families and with sensitivity to the cultural contexts in which children develop. Assessment results are used to benefit children by informing sound decisions about children, teaching, and program improvement.
5. Health	The program promotes the nutrition and health of children, and protects children and staff from illness and injury.
6. Teachers	The program employs and supports a teaching staff that has the educational qualifications, knowledge, and professional commitment necessary to promote children's learning and development, and to support families' diverse needs and interests.
7. Families	The program establishes and maintains collaborative relationships with each child's family to foster children's development in all settings. These relationships are sensitive to family composition, language, and culture.
8. Community relationships	The program establishes relationships with and uses the resources of the children's communities to support the achievement of program goals.
9. Physical environment	The program has a safe and healthful environment that provides appropriate and well-maintained indoor and outdoor physical environments. The environment includes facilities, equipment, and materials to facilitate child and staff learning and development.
10. Leadership and management	The program effectively implements policies, procedures, and systems that support stable staff and strong personnel, fiscal, and program management so all children, families, and staff have high-quality experiences.

Source: National Association for the Education of Young Children, 2016. *Overview of the NAEYC Early Childhood Program Standards.* 2016, by National Association for the Education of Young Children, Washington, DC, retrieved from http://www.naeyc.org/academy/files/academy/OverviewStandards.pdf

To understand what we mean by *quality*, it is important to see the relationships among the standards rather than see them as a discrete list. In the accreditation system, the primary focus is on *children*, as described in the first five standards: relationships, curriculum, teaching, assessment of children's progress, and health. The other five standards address teachers, partnerships with families and communities, and administration, including the physical environment, leadership, and management. Meeting these standards establishes a supportive context that makes it possible to achieve and maintain the quality of life for children described in the first five standards.

Head Start Program Standards
Quality is also a critically important issue in Head Start, particularly because it serves the nation's most vulnerable children. Head Start programs are regularly monitored for compliance

© Pearson Education

Video Example 1.3:

The Value of Accreditation

In this video, a program director describes the value of NAEYC accreditation for her school. Can you think of any additional ways accreditation benefits children, families, or teachers?

Head Start Program Performance Standards
National standards that establish the level of quality of services provided by every Head Start program.

with the national Head Start Program Performance Standards, which were significantly revised recently (Head Start, 2016). The new standards take a birth through 5 year old approach to reflect the process of children's development, and reflect the continuum of services from Early Head Start through preschool programs. These standards are similar to accreditation standards, but they also address the comprehensive services that are part of Head Start's mandate.

Military Child Care Act

The largest employer-sponsored child care system in the world is the U.S. military. Its voluntary workforce of men and women depends on the provision of high-quality child care. In 1989, Congress passed the Military Child Care Act to ensure consistently high standards of quality in these programs. The act required that centers seek NAEYC accreditation, and also included provisions for teacher training and a career ladder tying compensation to increased professional development. The Military Child Care Act resulted in significantly improved quality and learning outcomes for children that have been maintained for decades (Whitebook, Phillips, & Howes, 2014). In addition, the military child care system is now seen as a model for providing a universal child care system in the United States (Covert, 2017).

Measuring Quality in Early Childhood Programs

The early childhood field defines quality as having two dimensions: structural and process (Minervino, 2013). Structural quality includes features such as maximum group sizes, teacher/child ratios, and teacher qualifications, which are relatively easy to quantify and measure. Process quality, on the other hand, refers to the quality of the relationships and interactions among teachers and children, and the appropriateness of the materials, learning experiences, and teaching strategies. These features are more difficult to evaluate, and yet are the key aspects of the quality of children's experiences. They describe what life should be like for children in a program, how they should be treated, and how their learning and development should be promoted.

Structural quality and process quality are interconnected. For example, well-qualified teachers are needed to plan and implement an engaging curriculum and teach effectively. Similarly, positive relationships between teachers and children are more likely to be established when the size of the group and ratio of adults to children is relatively small. An age-appropriate, well-equipped, and organized environment is needed to protect children's health and safety, and to promote active learning.

The most difficult challenge is determining how to measure compliance with quality standards. To see if a program is meeting requirements, it is relatively easy to examine transcripts of teachers or count the number of children in a group. But it is much harder—especially for an outside evaluator—to decide if teachers have positive relationships with each child and family or if they are using effective teaching strategies. These standards can be assessed only by directly observing what goes on in classrooms.

To provide consistent ways of measuring quality, researchers have developed observation tools. The most widely used observational measure is the Classroom Assessment Scoring System (CLASS), with versions for infants, toddlers, preschoolers, and primary grades (Hamre, La Paro, Pianta, & Locasale-Crouch, 2014; La Paro, Hamre, & Pianta, 2012; Pianta, La Paro, & Hamre, 2008). The CLASS assesses the quality of teachers' relationships with children, the instructional strategies they use to support children's learning, and how well the classroom is organized. More than 150 studies demonstrate that how well classrooms and teachers score on these measures predicts how well children score on measures of language, literacy, mathematics, social-emotional, cognitive abilities, and engagement in learning (Teachstone, 2017). The CLASS is required as a tool for monitoring quality in Head Start, as well as some state prekindergarten programs and QRIS.

Another widely used program quality assessment is the Early Childhood Environment Rating Scale (ECERS-3) (Harms, Clifford, & Cryer, 2014) with versions for preschool, infant/toddler, family child care, and school-age programs. ECERS is used by many state QRIS systems.

structural quality Features of an early childhood program, such as maximum group sizes, teacher/child ratios, and teacher qualifications, that are relatively easy to quantify and measure.

process quality The quality of the relationships and interactions among teachers and children and the appropriateness of the materials, learning experiences, and teaching strategies occurring in an early childhood program.

Classroom Assessment Scoring System (CLASS) Preschool and elementary classroom observational instrument that assesses the quality of teachers' relationships and interactions with children and the instructional strategies used to support children's learning.

Early Childhood Environment Rating Scale (ECERS-3) Observational instrument used to rate program quality on a seven-point scale from inadequate to excellent.

The overall conclusion of all the research on the effectiveness of early education is that what teachers actually do with children is the most important determinant of the quality of children's experiences and their learning outcomes. After decades of research on quality in early childhood programs, one thing we know for certain is that teachers matter. If children are to reach their full potentials, professionals must also reach theirs.

Measuring Effectiveness

As we have seen, program quality is usually defined and measured in terms of "inputs"—the environments children experience and their interactions with teachers. However, program effectiveness is usually defined in terms of "outcomes"—the effects of these experiences on children's development and learning. As a result, effectiveness is measured against specific, usually age- or grade-related goals.

Children from Birth Through Age 5 The most common source of outcome goals for the youngest children are state **early learning standards** or guidelines, which describe what children should know and be able to do before entering kindergarten. All 50 states have comprehensive learning guidelines for preschool children, and virtually all have guidelines for infants and toddlers (National Center on Early Childhood Quality Assurance, 2017).

> **early learning standards**
> Guidelines that describe what children should know and be able to do before entering kindergarten.

Head Start Head Start has established its own set of comprehensive goals for children—the Head Start Early Learning Outcomes Framework (ELOF). Head Start programs are required by law to periodically assess children's progress toward the framework's goals. The ELOF includes approaches to learning; social and emotional development; language and literacy; cognition; and perceptual, motor, and physical development (Head Start, 2017).

Public Schools State departments of education establish outcome standards for children from prekindergarten through primary grades. Children's progress toward these goals is often measured by statewide standardized testing programs, usually beginning at third grade. Each state sets its own content standards for learning, which leads to great variability. To address this issue, in 2010, the Council of Chief State School Officers (CCSSO) and the National Governor's Association (NGA) released the **Common Core State Standards (CCSS)**, which are rigorous national standards in English language arts and mathematics for kindergarten through 12th grade.

> **Common Core State Standards**
> Rigorous national standards in English language arts and mathematics for kindergarten through grade 12 developed by the Council of Chief State School Officers (CCSSO) and the National Governor's Association (NGA).

The Common Core began as a bipartisan effort but became politically controversial. Some view it as a federal intrusion on state control of education. Others criticize the standards for being unachievable, narrowing the curriculum to two areas, and leading to overreliance on standardized tests for which students and teachers are not prepared (Carlson-Paige, McLaughlin, & Almon, 2015). Although the standards do not apply to preschool, like many elementary school initiatives, they have a "push-down" impact on younger children. Despite these concerns, the Common Core is used in 35 states and the District of Columbia. In other states, even though Common Core is technically not used, their standards are very similar.

 Check Your Understanding 1.3

The Positive Effects of Early Childhood Education

We began this chapter by citing ways that early childhood education is a field on the rise. The positive attention and support that the field has garnered is to a large extent the result of an impressive body of research on the importance of the early years and the lasting benefits of early childhood programs.

Brain research demonstrates the importance of early childhood education, especially for infants and toddlers.

© Carla Mestas/Pearson Education

Brain Research

Among the most exciting achievements in neuroscience in the past century were new insights into how the brain grows and functions during the earliest years of life. Brain research, which had previously been confined to laboratories, is now reported regularly in popular newspapers and magazines. Technologies such as positron emission tomography (PET) scans and functional magnetic resonance imagery (fMRI) reveal the inner workings of babies' brains to policy makers, educators, and the public.

Major conclusions from brain research have significantly lifted the profile of early childhood education—especially the importance of experiences in the first three years of life (Center on the Developing Child at Harvard University, n.d.):

1. Early life experiences build the architecture of the brain.
2. Positive experiences in the early years—especially warm, responsive, caring, and conversational relationships—literally grow babies' brains and lay the foundation for later learning.
3. Negative experiences such as prolonged stress, neglect, physical or sexual abuse, or exposure to violence can have dire and long-lasting effects on brain capabilities.
4. Early intervention, including intensive early education and comprehensive support services for families—the earlier and more intensive, the better—can ameliorate negative effects.

Dramatic evidence, along with powerful visual images of brain scans, has raised awareness of the vital importance of early experiences. For example, brain scans of maltreated children provide striking evidence of smaller brain volumes than those of children who have not suffered maltreatment, with more negative effects the earlier the abuse began and the longer it lasted (Center on the Developing Child, n.d.). Findings such as these demonstrate the critical importance of early intervention.

Brain research has also elevated the importance of children's approaches to learning, particularly their self-regulation and executive function abilities. These terms are often used interchangeably, which can be confusing. Generally, **self-regulation** is defined as the ability to adapt or control behavior, emotions, and thinking according to the demands of the situation, control impulses, and delay gratification—aspects of social-emotional development. On the other hand, **executive function**, sometimes called cognitive self-regulation, refers to mental abilities that enable children to remember, think flexibility, focus attention, plan, and think ahead. Although less easily measured than specific academic skills, self-regulation and executive function are very important indicators of a program's effectiveness because they enable children to learn in all areas. Read the feature *What Works: High-Quality Programs Promote Executive Function* to learn more about the connection between quality and effectiveness.

Video Example 1.4:

Brain Research

http://www.youtube.com/watch?v=tLiP4b-TPCA

In this video, Dr. Jack Shonkoff, founder of the Center for the Developing Child at Harvard University, presents the importance of positive early childhood experiences based on what scientists have learned by studying the brain. What should teachers of infants and toddlers do to "build" babies' brains? How can preschool teachers support children who experience extreme stress in their daily lives?

© Google and the google logo are registered trademarks of Google Inc., used with permission

self-regulation The ability to adapt or control behavior, emotions, and thinking according to the demands of the situation, control impulses, and delay gratification (sometimes called executive function).

executive function Mental abilities including working memory, mental flexibility, and inhibitory control that enable children to remember, think flexibly, focus attention, control impulses, plan, and think ahead (sometimes called self-regulation).

Lasting Benefits of Early Childhood Education

A large body of research demonstrates that high-quality early childhood programs can have long-lasting positive consequences for children, especially children from economically disadvantaged backgrounds, and can be cost-effective (Pre-kindergarten Task Force, 2017). Three well-designed longitudinal studies—the Perry Preschool Project, the Abecedarian Early Childhood Intervention Project, and the Chicago Child-Parent Centers—followed children from early childhood into adulthood. The findings of these studies are largely responsible for increased investments in early education.

What Works

High Quality Programs Promote Executive Function

The most frequently used observational measure of preschool quality is the Classroom Assessment Scoring System (CLASS). This tool assesses three aspects of program quality: the emotional climate, classroom organization, and instructional climate. Research shows that children in classrooms with higher scores on each dimension have positive outcomes in academic subjects such as literacy and mathematics, but notably in executive function, which facilitates learning across all areas. Teachers' positive, responsive relationships with children predict working memory, impulse control, and mental flexibility—that is, their executive functioning. The more emotional support teachers provide children, the better they are able to focus their attention, control their behavior, and engage in learning.

In addition, well-organized classroom routines promote executive functioning and positive approaches to learning. In such classrooms, children are more eager to learn, behave appropriately, pay attention, and persist at tasks. CLASS scores on instructional climate measure how well teachers support children's higher-order thinking, problem-solving, and language development. These teaching strategies have been found to help children behave more positively because they control negative impulses and use language and reasoning to solve problems rather than quarreling or fighting. Research in early elementary classrooms has similar results. For example, scores on classroom organization in kindergarten positively affect children's self-control, work habits, and engagement in learning.

Most standards for both program quality and child outcomes—NAEYC, Head Start, and state early learning guidelines—address these key elements of quality for a reason. They *work* in children's best interests.

Sources: Center on the Developing Child at Harvard University, 2017. *Executive function and self-regulation.* Retrieved November 5, 2017, from https://developingchild.harvard.edu; Teachstone, 2017. *Effective teacher-child interactions and child outcomes: A summary of research on the Classroom Assessment Scoring System (CLASS) Pre-K–3rd Grade.* Charlottesville, VA.

The Perry Preschool Project The Perry Preschool Project, which began in the early 1960s in Ypsilanti, Michigan, was one of the first studies to demonstrate the lasting effects of a high-quality preschool program on educational and economic outcomes. (Perry Preschool later became the HighScope Educational Research Foundation.) Researchers found that Perry Preschool graduates were less likely to be assigned to special education or retained in grade, and had better achievement test scores than children who did not attend preschool (Berrueta-Clement, Schweinhart, Barnett, Epstein, & Weikart, 1984). Preschool participation was also related to less involvement in delinquency and crime and to a higher rate of high school graduation (Schweinhart, Barnes, & Weikart, 1993). At age 40, program participants were significantly more likely to have higher levels of education, be employed, earn higher wages, and own their own homes; they were less likely to be welfare dependent and had fewer arrests (Schweinhart et al., 2005).

These outcomes benefited not only the participants but the larger society as well. Economists estimated that for every dollar spent on the program, as much as $10 was returned on the original investment (Heckman, 2008). This means that Americans saved money in terms of the decreased costs of crime, special education, grade retention, and welfare payments, as well as increased taxes paid by those who achieve in school and later earn higher incomes.

The Abecedarian Project The University of North Carolina's Abecedarian Early Childhood Intervention Project demonstrated that intensive early intervention—five years of full-day, high-quality child care with parent involvement—greatly enhances the development of children whose mothers have low income and education levels (Garcia, Heckman, Leaf, & Prados, 2016). The Abecedarian program produced positive effects on achievement in reading and mathematics throughout elementary and high school. Children who participated were significantly less likely to be retained in grade or placed in special

Video Example 1.5:

Benefits of Chicago Child-Parent Centers

http://www.youtube.com/watch?v=ToCbcbpEfDw

This video describes the Chicago Child–Parent programs and cites the results of the studies conducted on the success of the program. Why has participating in this program resulted in lasting benefits for children and families?

education, and were more likely to attend four-year colleges and have skilled jobs. Access to free child care improved the mothers' long-term employment opportunities and earnings. The researchers concluded that high-quality birth-to-5 programs for disadvantaged children can deliver a 13% per year return on investment.

The program was especially beneficial for boys (Garcia, Heckman, & Ziff, 2017). Later in life, they had lower drug use and blood pressure, and more education and income. By contrast, boys who attended low-quality childcare centers had the most negative consequences. The researchers emphasized that a program must be of high quality to result in positive outcomes.

Chicago Child–Parent Centers Perry Preschool and Abecedarian were relatively small-scale demonstration programs. A third longitudinal study of the Title I federally funded Chicago Child–Parent Centers reached similar positive conclusions with a large-scale, public school program involving more than 1,500 children (Reynolds, Temple, Robertson, White, & Ou, 2011). Since 1985, the Chicago Child–Parent Centers (CPC) have provided preschool and kindergarten for children from low-income families and family support services with continued intervention in early elementary school.

Children who participated in CPC demonstrated higher school achievement, better social adjustment, less frequent grade retention, lower dropout rates, and lower rates of juvenile arrest. A follow-up study conducted 25 years later found strong positive effects into adulthood (Reynolds et al., 2011). Children who attended the program at age 3 attained better levels of education, income, job skills, and health insurance coverage, and lower rates of substance abuse, arrest, and imprisonment.

The Positive Effects of Prekindergarten, Head Start, and Child Care

As publicly funded prekindergarten programs have expanded, a great deal of research evaluating their effectiveness has become available. More research is available on prekindergarten and Head Start effectiveness than on child care. However, all the research has one thing in common—programs must be of high quality to benefit children.

Prekindergarten Numerous states across the country have found positive effects of funded prekindergarten on children's readiness for school (Pre-kindergarten Task Force, 2017). For example, a longitudinal study of Michigan's program found that it decreased grade repetition and increased the number of children who passed the state's reading and mathematics tests and graduated from high school on time. The study also found that these differences were greatest for children of color (Schweinhart, Xiang, Daniel-Echols, Browning, & Wakabayashi, 2012). An evaluation of Virginia's state-funded prekindergarten involving more than 60,000 children found that it resulted in improved literacy and less kindergarten retention. Results were most positive for Hispanic and African American students and for children with disabilities, and persisted through first grade.

Most research demonstrates the value of preschool for children from low-income families, but research provides evidence of the positive effects of early education for *all* children. Oklahoma's state-funded prekindergarten is universal, based in the school system, and reaches a higher percentage of 4-year-olds than any other state pre-K program. Classes are located in public schools, Head Start, and child care programs that all meet the same standards for quality.

The Oklahoma program has the highest quality standards in the country. Lead teachers must have a bachelor's of arts degree and be certified in early childhood education. Notably, prekindergarten teachers earn the same wages and benefits as other public school teachers. Student–teacher ratios are 10 to 1 and class sizes are limited to 20. An evaluation of the program involving more than 3,000 children found strong positive effects for children from all income groups (Gormley, 2008). All children's language and cognitive test scores improved, regardless of their economic status or ethnicity. The largest gains were for poor children of color, with Hispanic children making the most learning progress, followed by African Americans. But even though gains were somewhat higher for low-income children, gains for children in the higher income group were almost as large.

Head Start   Perhaps no other federally funded project has been as thoroughly studied as Head Start over the nearly 50 years of its existence. An overall conclusion that can be drawn is that Head Start has positive effects on children's overall development, health and dental care, and preparation for school, including improved literacy skills and social-emotional development (Barnett & Friedman-Krauss, 2016). Although there is evidence that Head Start needs to be improved and participation does not close the achievement gap between poor and middle-class children, it does narrow the gap. The effects are most positive for children who enter at age 3 and participate in full-day programs that include regular home visiting (Walters, 2014; Yoshikawa et al., 2013).

Child Care   Research consistently finds that children who participate in high-quality programs demonstrate better short- and long-term outcomes, including better language and mathematics ability and health, and fewer behavior problems than children in poor-quality care (Garcia, Heckman, Leaf, & Prados, 2016; Vandell, Belsky, Burchinal, et al., 2010). Positive effects are evident for all groups of children but are greater for children from lower-income families.

A recent well-designed study of more than 200 children found that high-quality, full-day child care positively affected 2-year-olds' language development (Yazejian et al., 2017). Children had more positive parent-child relationships and fewer behavior problems than those in lower quality centers. High-quality, dependable child care is good for children, families, and employers who obtain a more productive workforce. Unfortunately, only 10% of child care programs are considered high-quality; most are mediocre or poor (Bishop-Josef, 2017). Parents struggle to find good child care programs and can't afford it when they do; costs may be greater than college tuition. And yet, the National Center for Education Statistics (NCES, 2016) finds that children who attend a center-based program the year before kindergarten score higher on reading, mathematics, and cognitive flexibility measures than children whose primary care arrangement is with their parents or a relative.

We could cite many other studies from states as diverse as New Jersey, Louisiana, Maryland, New Mexico, Massachusetts, and South Carolina that prove that high-quality early childhood programs can have positive short- and long-term consequences for young children. Research is also powerfully connected to another reason high-quality early education is essential—the country's need to close the achievement gap, as addressed in the next section.

Social Justice and Closing the Achievement Gap

One of our nation's greatest challenges is addressing the persistent gap that exists between the school achievement of African American and Latino children and their white peers (Friedman-Krauss, Barnett, & Nores, 2016). Scholars tend to agree that these differences result primarily from the fact that race and ethnicity are strongly associated with socioeconomic status (SES) in the United States (CDF, 2017). For example, 36% of African American children and 27% of Latino children under the age of 5 are in the lowest socioeconomic level of U.S. citizens compared with 11% of white non-Hispanic children (CDF, 2017). And children of color are much more likely to live in conditions of extreme poverty (CDF, 2017). Achievement differences between racial and ethnic groups narrow among children when they are from similar socioeconomic backgrounds (U.S. Department of Health and Human Services, 2014).

As we have seen, the number of young children growing up poor in our country is increasing, with the largest growth in poverty among children under age 5 and children of color, which could further widen the achievement gap in the future. The achievement

socioeconomic status (SES)
Family income level.

gap has profound consequences for our nation's future and its ability to compete in a global, highly technological society. Moreover, the potentially devastating effects on the life trajectories of individuals cannot be ignored.

Where the Gap Begins

Differences in children's cognitive abilities are substantial at a very early age and widen over time (Friedman-Krauss, Barnett, & Nores, 2016). By 18 months of age, SES differences in language development are evident, and by 24 months, economically disadvantaged children are as much as six months behind their more advantaged peers (Fernald, Marchman, & Weislader, 2013). At age 4, children who live below the poverty line may be 18 months below what is considered normal for their age group. Although socioeconomic status is a complex set of factors, inequity in opportunity is the most important predictor of children's cognitive skills (Duncan & Magnuson, 2012).

To describe this discrepancy, a more accurate term than achievement gap is really *knowledge gap* or *opportunity gap*. The differences in achievement are likely the result of differences in children's opportunities to gain knowledge from a variety of learning experiences. As we know, children from higher-income families are much more likely to attend high-quality preschool. Given these disparities, it is not surprising that 80% of U.S. public school superintendents think states should invest more on early childhood education programs (Calderon & Jones, 2017). Only 16% of them say most children are prepared when they start kindergarten. Urban school leaders are more likely to report that quality early education is unavailable.

Schools' Contributions to the Gap

Children from low-income families not only enter kindergarten with fewer cognitive skills than their more affluent peers, but also are more likely to encounter poorer-quality elementary schools (Neuman, 2008). These schools are likely to have fewer resources and qualified teachers, more negative teacher attitudes, and poorer neighborhood or school conditions. As a result, the inequalities in cognitive abilities that are present even before kindergarten entry are not eliminated, and often are magnified by their elementary school experience (Parkinson & Rowan, 2008).

One of the frequent criticisms of Head Start and prekindergarten is that the gains children make "fade-out" by later grades. These criticisms focus on standardized test scores rather than lasting social-emotional and meaningful life outcomes, and they fail to take into account the quality of children's education in primary school (Garcia, Heckman, Lead, and Prados, 2016). A more accurate term than *fade-out* is *convergence* (Yoshikawa et al., 2013). Children's achievement scores converge in the early grades because their school experiences do not build on preschool gains.

Children who begin school behind tend to stay behind. Although achievement has improved on average in the last few years, problems remain. By fourth grade, only 32% of public school students are proficient in reading (Annie E. Casey Foundation, 2017b). Reading achievement at the end of first grade predicts reading skill at the end of fourth grade (Hernandez, 2011), which subsequently predicts high school graduation. Moreover, deep-seated inequities in communities and schools tend to increase rather than diminish these early achievement gaps over time. As one child advocacy group states, "Our children are not failing to learn. Our schools are failing to teach them effectively" (Foundation for Child Development, 2008, p. 4).

Early Education and Social Justice

As we saw from research cited previously, these initial inequalities can be reduced. Children from low-income families who attend high-quality early childhood programs begin kindergarten with higher achievement, thus providing the potential to narrow the gap at the outset. This research, as well as studies on the effectiveness of services for children with special needs, proves that early intervention is less costly, more effective, and more humane than later remediation.

Improving quality and increasing access to early childhood education programs are important strategies for enhancing social justice in America and improving learning outcomes for all children. These goals can be addressed, however, only in the context of current trends in the field and the nation, which we discuss next.

✓ Check Your Understanding 1.4

 Current Trends and Issues in Early Childhood Education

Early childhood education is literally a field in transition, experiencing rapid growth and widespread attention. In the sections that follow, we describe both trends and issues. Trends are general directions in which the field is changing, while issues are problems confronting the field. A number of trends are worth discussing, but there are also challenging issues that pose threats to children and serious challenges to teachers. Even a cursory look at these trends and issues reveals that they are interconnected.

Trends Impacting Early Education

Current trends affecting the field include new policy initiatives at the federal and state level, rapidly changing technologies, more focus on scientific knowledge with calls for increased continuity in services for children from birth through age 8, and greater emphasis on professionalization.

Federal and State Policy Initiatives The first two decades of the 21st century saw enormous growth in public support and funding for early education to achieve high-quality early learning from birth to age 5 and to meet the following goals (Office of Early Learning, 2014):

- Provide access to high-quality infant and toddler care through Early Head Start-child care partnerships;
- Expand voluntary evidence-based home visiting to support our country's most vulnerable families; and
- Develop partnerships with states to provide voluntary, high-quality, full-day preschool for *all* 4-year-olds from families at or below 200 percent of the federal poverty line.

In response, a bipartisan group in Congress introduced the Strong Start for America's Children Act in 2014. The U.S. Department of Education distributed $1 billion in Early Learning Challenge Grants for statewide systems to improve the quality of early childhood programs and increase access for children who need them. Early Learning Challenge Grants supported state efforts to build high-quality, accountable systems of early education and provided grants for states to use the same learning standards across all programs, measure children's learning outcomes, and improve professional development and compensation for teachers. As a result, the grants led states to develop or adopt kindergarten entry assessments (KEAs) to help teachers adapt instruction to individual children's needs. Preschool Development and Expansion Grants were also distributed to states to move the country forward in achieving universal prekindergarten.

Expanding prekindergarten led to greater involvement of public schools in preschool education. In the past, young children rarely encountered a public school before kindergarten, but now the public education system is a major player in the early childhood landscape. As a result, laws that govern public schools as well as issues that dominate

accountability The process of holding teachers, schools, or programs responsible for meeting a required level of performance.

Elementary and Secondary Education Act (ESEA) Law governing how the federal government distributes education funds to states and holds public schools accountable for the use of funding.

Every Student Succeeds Act (ESSA) Reauthorization and revision of the Elementary and Secondary Education Act (effective 2016), provides for more local and state control of schools, new accountability systems, and more support for early learning.

K–12 education now affect programs for younger children, such as more focus on standards and accountability—holding teachers, schools, or programs responsible for meeting a required level of performance.

The federal government provides support to states through the Elementary and Secondary Education Act (ESEA). Now called the Every Student Succeeds Act (ESSA), the law took effect in 2016 and focuses on state and local control of public education. The law offers new opportunities for states to be creative in expanding educational services to young children. It also provides accountability systems other than test scores and the opportunity to focus support on the particular needs of local schools and communities. The law provides funds to states for Preschool Development Grants to expand early learning opportunities, support literacy instruction, and offer after-school programs.

One of the most exciting developments in recent history is the Bipartisan Policy Center's new initiative, *A Bipartisan Case for Early Childhood Development* (Bipartisan Policy Center, 2017). The initiative is chaired by former U.S. Democratic Rep. George Miller and former U.S. Republican Sen. Rick Santorum, whose political perspectives on most other issues are diametrically opposed. The report strongly emphasizes the vital importance of early childhood development to the future of our country and its power to unite lawmakers of both parties. The recommendations include ways to support families such as making child care more affordable by increasing CCDBG funds and the federal Child Care Tax Credit, a major discussion point in the 2017 tax reform debate. Among other goals, they propose increased funding to improve access to high-quality programs as well as tuition assistance and professional development for early childhood teachers.

Technology In no aspect of life is the speed of change as rapid as in the area of technology. In education, technology has a tremendous impact on how teachers teach and function in their work, but also on children's experiences at home and in school. The use of interactive media in all aspects of early education is a major trend. Given the demand for highly qualified teachers, online teacher preparation and professional development options are increasing rapidly.

As digital media such as handheld mobile devices and video games proliferate, so has the development of educational apps, the majority of which are targeted to preschoolers (Vaala, Ly, & Levine, 2015). In their position statement on technology, NAEYC and the Fred Rogers Center for Early Learning and Children's Media (2012) acknowledge legitimate concerns about potential inappropriate uses of technology but also promote the almost unlimited creative ways that interactive media can support learning and development. The question is no longer whether young children should be exposed to digital media, but rather what is the quality of technological tools provided for them.

New research is forthcoming almost daily about positive, effective uses of digital media with children and families as well as the risks. Teaching media literacy to children has become very important (TEC Center at Erikson Institute & NAMLE, 2017). The topic applies to all areas of effective teaching and learning, and therefore is discussed throughout this book.

Continuity from Birth Through Age 8 A highly influential report, *Transforming the workforce for children birth through age 9: A unifying foundation* from the prestigious Institute of Medicine & National Research Council (IOM & NRC, 2015), contains a review of the current scientific knowledge about child development and learning as well as effective educational practices. The research greatly strengthens our understanding of the full developmental and learning continuum from birth to age 8.

Alignment or Continuity— Coordination of the curriculum and experiences from one level of education to the next in order to build on what children have already learned and to ease transitions for students between schools and school levels.

Based on this research, the report calls for better continuity across the full age span from birth through age 8. Continuity, also called alignment, is coordination of the curriculum, experiences, and services from one level of education to the next in order to build on what children have already learned and to ease transitions for students between schools and school levels. Traditionally, preschool and K–3 have been two separate worlds with very little communication between them.

Many early childhood educators are concerned that the push for alignment will narrow the curriculum to literacy and mathematics, apply learning standards intended for older children, and lead to inappropriate testing of young children (Carlson-Paige, McLaughlin, & Almon, 2015). They are especially concerned that schools will eliminate valuable experiences such as play, the arts, and support for social-emotional development.

On the other hand, advocates for birth to third grade continuity support better connected education for preschool and elementary children. They stress that aligning curriculum does not mean that preschool children should learn primary grade skills at an earlier age (IOM & NRC, 2015). Rather, the curriculum should reflect what children can and should learn at each age, and teachers should know how to help children make continuous progress.

Application Exercise 1.1
Promoting Continuity for Young Children

Power to the Profession In addition to compiling the current knowledge base, the IOM report called for unifying and professionalizing the field by raising preschool teacher qualifications, with an emphasis on college degrees in early education or child development and improving teacher compensation (IOM & NRC, 2015). Several research reviews have concluded that having bachelor's degree–level teachers with specialized preparation in early education leads to better outcomes for young children. Although some research has not found clear benefits of degrees (Walters, 2014), studies tend to support the fact that the more specialized education teachers have, the better it is for the children they teach.

In 2016, NAEYC, as part of a coalition of 15 national organizations, launched *Power to the Profession*. The goal of this initiative is to address the fragmented nature of the workforce. A 4-year-old is a 4-year-old whether she is in Head Start, prekindergarten, or a child care center, and yet teacher qualifications and compensation vary considerably across these settings. Raising teacher qualifications has the potential to improve quality for children and also compensation and status for teachers. The biggest challenge is providing adequate funding to provide compensation commensurate with teacher qualifications, which is far from the case (Whitebook & McLean, 2017).

An additional concern is the need to maintain a diverse workforce that reflects the population of children served. State prekindergarten programs have a larger percentage of teachers with bachelor's degrees than do Head Start or center-based programs. However, Head Start teachers are much more likely to reflect the cultural and linguistic diversity of the community. For example, 30% of Head Start staff are proficient in a language other than English (Head Start, 2017).

Head Start's teacher qualifications have incrementally been raised over the years. The Head Start Act of 2009 required that 50% of teachers hold a bachelor's degree with early childhood specialization. The program has far exceeded that goal, with 73% of its preschool teachers holding a bachelor's degree or higher (Head Start, 2017). An additional 23% have an associate's degree.

Similarly, at least 50% of Head Start teacher assistants are required to have at least a CDA credential or be enrolled in a degree program. In addition, the CDA credential is the required qualification for teachers in Early Head Start. The **Child Development Associate (CDA) credential** is a competency-based credential that requires 120 clock hours of training (which may or may not be credit bearing) and 480 hours of experience with children, plus passing a written test and being observed working effectively with young children. The CDA Credential is recognized by state licensing as a qualification for child care teachers.

Child Development Associate (CDA) credential National competency-based credential for entry-level early childhood educators.

Current Issues Confronting Children, Families, and Teachers

Among the most problematic issues confronting early childhood education today are increased and almost unrelenting stress in the lives of children, the opioid crisis, threats to children's play, and the ubiquitous presence and impact of social media and technology. In addition, the divisive political climate cannot be ignored. Distressing stories of threats to immigrant families, Muslims, and increasing racism appear in the news daily. Teachers are not immune to these problems and sometimes suffer the effects themselves.

Stress in Children's Lives New findings from neuroscience have raised awareness about the negative impact of toxic stress that results from what are now called **adverse childhood experiences (ACEs)**. These include drug or alcohol abuse by parents; physical, emotional or sexual abuse; and chronic neglect; all of which endanger children's long-term mental and physical health (Center on the Developing Child, n.d.). The greatest risk is for children who experience multiple ACEs.

Factors such as poverty and violence are major sources, but stress affects the lives of all children to some extent. We live in a world where the daily news constantly reminds us of the threat of terrorism, mass shootings, and natural disasters such as hurricanes or wildfires. Every child care center and school must now be prepared for and practice "active shooter" drills that traumatize many children. Teachers and their families experience these same stressors, yet they can play a major role in helping build children's resilience. A specific source of toxic stress affecting almost every community is the opioid crisis.

Opioid Crisis The opioid epidemic in the United States has created trauma for children, families, and teachers. Every 25 minutes, a baby is born who has been prenatally exposed to opioids (Bipartisan Policy Center, 2017). They experience symptoms such as seizures, vomiting, crying, and fever as they go through withdrawal. Prenatal exposure can also cause developmental delays and behavioral and learning problems throughout life. Increasingly, addicted parents often abandon or neglect their children, a major source of injury to brain development. New research finds that drugs appear to impair parents' natural instincts to care for and bond with their children (De La Cruz, 2016).

As the epidemic explodes, families are disrupted. Child-welfare agencies are overwhelmed. Thirty thousand more children entered foster care from 2014 to 2015 (Annie E. Casey Foundation, 2017c). More than a third of these children are age 5 or younger, while an additional 23% are between ages 6 and 10. About 2.6 million children are being raised by grandparents or relatives, which is a far better alternative than foster care but places a serious emotional and financial strain on older adults (Generations United, 2017).

Threats to Children's Play Teachers and parents are concerned about protecting children, while at the same time they feel pressured to prepare them for the academic rigors of school. These conditions conspire to threaten one of the most important and beneficial activities of childhood—play. Teachers report that more children are aggressive and disruptive as a result of stressful events. Increasing numbers of children, especially boys, are inaccurately diagnosed as hyperactive and needlessly medicated. Childhood obesity is also endemic.

Research demonstrates that exercise and child-initiated play are effective stress relievers. Ironically, however, a survey of child care, preschool, and Head Start teachers found that they tend to limit children's opportunities for active play, especially outdoors, due to safety concerns and the need to prepare children academically for school (Copeland et al., 2012). Children living in poverty are most likely to suffer because they have less access to safe outdoor play areas, and programs feel extra pressure to focus on academics to close the school readiness gap.

adverse childhood experiences (ACEs) Parents' substance abuse, physical emotional or sexual abuse, or neglect that creates toxic stress.

Part of the solution is that teachers, parents, and administrators need to understand that play and school readiness is not an *either/or* choice. The American Academy of Pediatrics emphasizes that play is essential for children's physical health, emotional and mental well-being, social relationships, and brain development and cognition (American Academy of Pediatrics, 2013). Vigorous play develops large motor skills and can reduce obesity, yet one study found children in child care were engaged in active play only 12% of the day (Tandon, Saelens, & Christakis, 2015).

In an attempt to get children ready for school and protect them from injury, early childhood programs may actually be contributing to children's stress by minimizing their large muscle activity and child-initiated play time. Because children spend so much time in programs and school, it may be their only opportunity to have physical activity or outdoor play. Educators need to draw on the support of physicians and other experts to help educate parents and policymakers about the importance of play in children's lives and its essential role in helping children cope with stress and improve school success. They also need to advocate for funding to provide safe playgrounds and adequate spaces indoors and outdoors for active engagement. Play spaces and opportunities must be designed to protect children from injury, but protecting them from stress is equally important.

A growing concern of both early educators and parents is the loss of play in kindergarten. Read the feature *Promoting Play: Protecting Play in Kindergarten* to learn more about this issue.

Promoting Play

Protecting Play in Kindergarten

Early educators often say, "Play is a child's work." But play and work are really two different things, as most kindergartners will tell you. With increased emphasis on academic standards and testing, play has disappeared from kindergarten, which has become much more like first grade. Kindergartners are often in for a shock. Rather than having child-choice or center time, they are expected to pay attention during long periods of whole group literacy and math instruction, then sit at desks doing worksheets. One mother reported that her son did 70 worksheets during the first 15 days of school. Little time is devoted to the arts that children love. Even in full-day programs, there is less physical activity or outdoor play. After school, play is also threatened because 5- and 6-year-olds now have homework.

Teachers feel pressured to teach formal reading and prepare children for standardized tests. Parents lament that their 5-year-olds who loved preschool have tummy aches or are reluctant to go school. Many hold their children back a year so they will be older and better able to handle the demands.

So what's to be done? Resist the debate about play *vs.* academics. It is not an *either/or* choice. There is abundant research about developmentally appropriate, meaningful ways to promote literacy, language, and mathematics learning without lengthy didactic instruction or worksheets. At the same time, play opportunities in kindergarten should not be a free-for-all. Playful social interaction is necessary for language and social-emotional development. Neuroscience demonstrates the importance of self-regulation and executive function. These capacities are developed during teacher-supported play and may be impaired in stressful kindergartens. Children's approaches to learning—their enthusiasm, motivation, engagement, curiosity, and creativity—are strengthened when various kinds of learning-full play are both protected and provided.

Sources: Bassok, Latham, & Rorem, 2016. Is kindergarten the new first grade? *AERA Open*, *1*(4), 1–31; Abbott, 2017. Keeping the "kinder" in kindergarten: Developmentally appropriate practice in New York. *Preschool Matters Today.* Retrieved from NIEER.org; Brown, 2017. *All work and no play needs to change for kindergarteners. Here's why.* World Economic Forum blog.

Social Media and Technology

Although technology can promote children's learning and development in many positive ways as discussed throughout this book, there are also negatives. In every setting—homes, restaurants, playgrounds, museums—parents can be seen studying their phones rather than talking to or playing with their children, even their babies. Researchers have only just begun to analyze the impact on brain development and learning, but it is predictable. When parental relationships are impaired, children's language, cognitive and social development are also.

While social media has many positive uses, it has become a source of tension as well. Online bullying, false information, and cruel discourse are rampant. Children are growing up in a rapidly changing cultural context, the effects of which are a cause for concern. All the more reason every child needs a loving, well-qualified teacher and high-quality early childhood program.

Continuity and Change

One overarching trend always affecting education is continuity and change. As the field expands and changes occur in response to new cultural, political, and economic realities, many longtime early childhood professionals are concerned that the fundamental values of the field will be lost. Development, including development of professions, is characterized by both continuity and change. In this book, we describe how the fundamental values of early childhood education can be retained and enhanced (thus maintaining continuity with the important tenets of the past), while also presenting what is known from new research about effective teaching practices for *all* children. Some ways of thinking and practicing should be cherished and held onto, whereas others may need to be updated or abandoned.

Resolving Contradictions between Enduring Values and Current Trends

We propose that the way to resolve potential contradictions that arise over difficult or controversial issues is to "widen the lens." Widening the lens is a metaphor for expanding the sources of information professionals use to make decisions, gaining insights from diverse perspectives including through the lenses of culture, language, and ability/disability, and looking at questions or problems from broader perspectives. Widening the lens is a strategy to move beyond the tendency to oversimplify complex educational issues into "either/or" choices and to move toward "both/and" thinking.

Embracing *Both/And* Thinking

Widening the lens to consider diverse points of view—*both/and* thinking—is a constructive response to addressing both continuity and change in the field. Figure 1.4 illustrates how this process applies to the field today. The left side of the arrow describes traditional practices that have held sway in the past; the right side of the arrow illustrates how current views encompass these earlier approaches and extend beyond them, thus reflecting *both/and* thinking as well as continuity and change.

Throughout this text, we will revisit these issues as well as the profession's core values and demonstrate how new research can help teachers effectively put these values into practice. Chapters are devoted to each of the core values: child development and learning, relationships, families, communities, individuality, and cultural diversity. We discuss the overarching value of play in the context of all the key topics in this book.

We began by pointing out that early childhood education is highly valued in American society. The profession is expanding, growing in status, and gaining support from policymakers and the general public. A huge body of research supports the importance of the work. It is indeed an exciting time to be an early childhood educator.

Traditional Practices	Current Practices
• Processes of child development and learning	• **Both** how children learn **and** what they learn
• Inputs – standards such as licensing or accreditation that mandate what programs should do	• **Both** program standards **and** outcomes (early learning standards)
• Quality	• **Both** quality **and** accountability
• Activities	• **Both** coherent curriculum plans **and** links to learning goals
• Free play	• **Both** child-initiated, developmentally valuable play **and** playful learning
• Developmental appropriateness	• **Both** effectiveness **and** developmental appropriateness (Are children making progress from the experiences we deem appropriate?
• Observation of children	• **Both** observation **and** formal assessment of child outcomes
• Facilitating learning	• **Both** intentional teaching **and** positive, supportive relationships
• Development, not academics (viewing early childhood education as separate from primary grades)	• **Both** viewing learning and development as a continuum from birth to age 8 **and** alignment from pre-K to grade 3
• Typical, normative development	• **Both** adapting for individual variation of every child **and** intervention and adaption for children with disabilities and special needs, as well as children who are advanced

FIGURE 1.4 Continuity and Change in Early Childhood Education Early childhood education today builds on the enduring values of its past but also changes as we acquire new knowledge about children, families, and the contexts in which they live.

 Check Your Understanding 1.5

Revisiting the Case Study

Cresthaven Child Development Center

This chapter began by peeking in and eavesdropping on the end-of-the-year event for Cresthaven Primary School and its community Head Start and child care partners. Now that we have seen the broader picture of the early childhood landscape, the teachers' thoughts and emotions become more meaningful. At this event, we saw the wide range of age groups that early childhood encompasses as well as some of the diverse settings. In addition, these teachers exemplify the fundamentals of intentional teaching.

We've seen the value of promoting continuity from birth to age 8 in early education. The collaborative partnership between the school, Head Start, and child care program eases transitions for children and families, and supports alignment of curriculum from infancy through third grade. The garden project is one example of how these teachers connect the curriculum to the larger community and provide children with meaningful, hands-on learning opportunities. Children, families, and teachers not only celebrated the good times they'd had, but children also demonstrated how much they'd learned through the displays of their work and through technology.

Across the classrooms, we saw the value of communication and responsive relationships among teachers and families. New teachers Isela and Evan have learned that early childhood education is hard work but have also begun to experience the rewards. Their patience and focus on intentional teaching is paying off for Nicky. Cooper's experience demonstrates the power of inclusion and how it benefits children with disabilities and their peers. At the end of the day, these teachers go home feeling good about what they've accomplished while knowing that there is more to learn and new adventures awaiting them tomorrow. ■

1 Chapter Summary

- Early childhood education is a diverse field that covers the broad age range of birth through age 8. Teachers work in child care centers and homes, preschools, kindergartens, and primary grade schools.

- Becoming a professional intentional early childhood teacher is a challenging and rewarding opportunity. Early childhood education is expanding and is a field on the rise, benefiting from growing public recognition and support. Many career options are available to work with children or work for children.

- Early childhood professionals are part of a cultural group that shares a vocabulary, an identity, values, and beliefs. These include emphasis on the uniqueness of early childhood, the value of play, the importance of relationships and a sense of community, valuing and teaching each child as an individual, respecting linguistic and cultural diversity, and relationships with families.

- The early childhood profession sets high-quality standards for programs. The most important determinants of the quality of children's experiences and strongest predictors of positive outcomes are the social and instructional interactions that occur between teachers and children.

- Brain research demonstrates the importance of early experience to later development. A large body of evidence exists supporting the positive long-term and short-term consequences of high-quality early childhood programs.

- High-quality early education has an important role to play in improving children's school readiness and addressing social justice concerns about closing the achievement gap in our schools.

- Current trends affecting the field include new federal and state policies, more focus on current scientific knowledge and calls for more continuity in services for children from birth through age 8, and increased emphasis on professionalization. Challenging issues include stress in the lives of children, the opioid crisis, threats to children's play, and the impact of social media and technology.

- Early childhood education is a rewarding profession for many reasons, but above all, early childhood educators enter and stay in the field because they know their work makes a difference in the lives of children and families.

Key Terms

- Early childhood education
- professionals
- National Association for the Education of Young Children (NAEYC)
- child care centers
- family child care homes
- preschool
- parent cooperatives
- laboratory schools
- prekindergarten (pre-K)
- school readiness
- approaches to learning
- universal voluntary prekindergarten
- Head Start
- Early Head Start
- Early childhood special education
- Individuals with Disabilities Education Act (IDEA)
- early intervention
- inclusion
- kindergarten
- primary grade
- charter schools
- Temporary Assistance for Needy Families (TANF)
- Child Care and Development Block Grants (CCDBG)
- dual language learners
- intentional teachers
- culture
- developmentally appropriate practice (DAP)
- child care licensing standards

- quality rating and improvement systems (QRIS)
- accreditation system
- Head Start Program Performance Standards
- structural quality
- process quality

- Classroom Assessment Scoring System (CLASS)
- Early Childhood Environment Rating Scale (ECERS-3)
- early learning standards
- Common Core State Standards (CCSS)

- self-regulation
- executive function
- socioeconomic status (SES)
- accountability
- Elementary and Secondary Education Act (ESEA)

- Every Student Succeeds Act (ESSA)
- continuity
- alignment
- Child Development Associate (CDA) credential
- adverse childhood experiences (ACEs)

 Flash Cards 1.1

Readings and Websites

Chenfield, M. B. (2014). *Still teaching in the key of life: Joyful stories from early childhood settings.* Washington, DC: National Association for the Education of Young Children.

Colker, L., & Koralek, D. (2017). *High-quality early childhood programs: The what, why, and how.* St. Paul, MN: Redleaf Press.

Institute of Medicine (IOM) and National Research Council (NRC). (2015). *Transforming the workforce for children birth through age 8: A unifying foundation.* Washington, DC: The National Academies Press (available free online).

National Association for the Education of Young Children (NAEYC)

NAEYC's website has a wealth of resources on every aspect of early childhood education, including its publications, accreditation system, position statements on controversial topics, and public policy.

National Institute for Early Education Research (NIEER)

On this website, you will find summaries of research conducted by NIEER and other resources to learn about and advocate for high-quality, effective early childhood education for all young children.

National Center for Early Childhood Quality Assurance

The child-care licensing regulations for every state are maintained in a database on this website.

Head Start's Early Childhood Learning and Knowledge Center (ECLKC)

This website provides many valuable resources for all aspects of Head Start programming that are also useful for any early childhood program, including an interactive app for implementing the Early Learning Outcomes Framework and the newly revised Head Start Program Performance Standards.

 Shared Writing 1.1

Explain the Benefits of High Quality Early Childhood Education

2 Building on a Tradition of Excellence

Learning Outcomes

After studying this chapter, you should be able to:

2.1 Explain why it is important to learn from the past.

2.2 Describe how European educators influenced early education practices.

2.3 Describe the leaders and events that propelled the kindergarten, preschool, and child care movements in the United States.

2.4 Explain a wider view of early childhood history—the contributions of African Americans, Hispanic Americans, and Native Americans.

2.5 Discuss how early childhood history influenced the launch of the national Head Start program and early education today.

Related NAEYC Professional Preparation Standard

The NAEYC Professional Preparation Standard that applies to this chapter:

Standard 6: Becoming a Professional (NAEYC, 2011).
Key element:
   6a: Identifying and involving oneself with the early childhood field

Case Study

Grant, Melinda, and Reece are enrolled in an introductory course in early childhood education. Their first assignment is to observe a preschool classroom. The professor says, "I want you to pretend that you are from another planet or from such a remote part of the Earth that you have never seen a preschool classroom before. Observe for one hour and write down exactly what you see. Don't try to guess what I want you to observe or second-guess yourself, just write what you see."

After completing their observations, Grant, Melinda, and Reece compare notes. Their lists are different in some respects but the following items appear on all three lists: child-sized furniture, 1-inch cube blocks, and wooden parquetry blocks in various colors and shapes. They see groups of children building roads and towers with wooden blocks. Each classroom has a library area with picture books, alphabet books, and stories (each room even has a copy of *Goodnight Moon* on the bookrack). One class has sandpaper letters. There are also woodworking benches, sand tables, a posted recipe for cooking a snack, and dress-up clothes and props. In all three classes, children are actively playing or working with teachers in small groups. One group had visited the fire station, as evidenced by a chart on the wall recording children's remembrances, and there are firefighter hats and hoses to play with. Several classes have displays that clearly demonstrate projects they are working on—photos, children's drawings and writings, clay sculptures, and other visible evidence of what they are learning. At snack time in one room, the children sing "Happy Birthday" to their friend.

During class, the professor asks each student to share one thing on his or her list and then for a show of hands to see who else had seen the same thing. There is remarkable uniformity among the observations. The professor explains, "What you observed are traces of the history of early childhood education. Your unfiltered observations are like the first steps archaeologists take in uncovering what has gone before. You may be surprised to find that all these things you observed can be traced back to specific people or events in the history of the field. They were put there, and they remain there for a reason. First, we'll find out how they got there, and the rest of this course will help you understand why they are still there or how practices have changed in the intervening years." ■

© Andrew Lilley/E+/Getty Images

Early childhood educators tend to like stories. We love sharing stories about the enchanting things young children say and do. We listen to parents' stories about their children. And we exchange stories about our teaching—sometimes when we have a bad day, and almost always when we have a very good day. Those good days usually involve seeing an exciting example of a child's developmental progress.

Stories—that is what *history* is. The goal of this chapter, then, is to tell the story of early childhood education. We begin by describing how studying history is relevant. Next, we describe how the concept of childhood has changed over the course of history. Finally, we tell several stories about major historical movements and how they influence early childhood education practice today. Parts of these stories occurred simultaneously and overlap.

 Learning from the Past

Early childhood education is a field with a long and rich history going back to ancient times. Its history differs from that of education for older children, which has been considered a public responsibility for more than a century. By contrast, young children's care and education are so closely tied to families that private and public support for early childhood care and education is a very recent phenomenon. In addition, early childhood education is a more interdisciplinary field than is elementary education, with historical influences coming from not only child development and education but also from medicine, psychology, sociology, and other areas. As a result, many historical paths have converged to lead the field to where it is today.

Why History Is Relevant

The history of early childhood education, especially during the past 150 years, reveals that the past and the present are inexorably linked. Most of the current issues and controversies have been visited in some form in the past. For example, even all those years ago, teachers grappled with questions such as these: What environments and materials should be provided? What are the goals for children's learning and development? How should children be taught? What is the role of the teacher? How should parents be involved? Who is qualified to be a teacher? All of these issues have dominated debates about early education since its inception, and continue to do so.

Rather than assuming that these issues are being encountered for the first time, understanding how they have been resolved in the past can inform current discussions. One reason this is so important is that "the solution to every problem contains the seeds of a new problem" (Bredekamp & Glowacki, 1996). For example, early in the 20th century, advocates fought for kindergarten to be part of public schools. Succeeding in doing so eventually meant that kindergarten teachers were able to earn public school salaries and services became available for all children. But this solution created a new problem—kindergartens became, and still are, more like first grades in curriculum expectations and teaching methods. Today's advocates for public prekindergarten need to be aware of this history as they pursue their goals.

Consider how this phenomenon may be evident in your own life. A problem that many college students face is the high cost of tuition. Students solve this problem in

Traces of the history of the field of early childhood education can be found in any preschool classroom today. What in this classroom environment might have been present in a preschool 80 years ago? Why do you think it is still being used?

different ways—taking out loans, working full-time or part-time while going to school, or choosing less expensive schools. But each of these solutions can lead to new challenges. The loans need to be repaid; a full-time job delays graduation; the accessible schools may not meet the students' needs. In turn, each of these "problems" leads to a subsequent solution, and the process begins anew.

The idea that solving problems creates new challenges can be discouraging; however, it need not be. As long as we are working on solving new problems or challenges, we are making progress. History is composed of such progress in spurts as well as in setbacks. As you reflect on early childhood history, you will encounter many examples of solutions creating new challenges.

Avoid Getting Stuck in the Past Just as it is true that we continue to confront questions and challenges similar to those faced by our forebears, it is equally true that responses to these issues need to reflect current knowledge. As we will see, many of the principles and values that guide the field today are remarkably consistent with earlier views (Elkind, 2015). There are also essential differences based on newer research, theories, and realities. Getting stuck in the past can lead to defending past practices simply because we have always done it that way. Knowing why it was "done that way," however, can lead to changing it for the better.

Aspire to Make a Difference for Children History is not just the story of events, but the stories of people. The history of early childhood education is replete with inspiring stories of women and men who devoted themselves to improving the lives of children and families. Many "dauntless women" (Snyder, 1972) contributed in countless ways to early childhood education at a time when women's opportunities for higher education and careers were severely restricted. Similarly, men have been at the forefront of building the profession even though children were considered the purview of women.

The stories of these pioneers of early childhood education, who were forward-looking in both their thinking and their deeds, serve as inspiration and motivation for current and future professionals. Learning about their lives, the obstacles they faced in their work, and the brilliance of their minds sets a high standard for the rest of us.

Advocate for Change Understanding the paths history has taken is important if early childhood educators are to be successful in improving services in the future. Even a brief summary of historical underpinnings reveals that change is a constant. For example, at times services for children have been a priority while at other times (regularly, in fact), the services have been threatened. The Head Start program is a case in point. In the mid-1960s, Head Start was launched to great fanfare as a means to end poverty in this country, an impossibly unrealistic goal. But over the years, the program frequently has fallen prey to changing public attitudes and funding priorities.

Throughout these years, some advocates have set idealistic goals, which can be inspiring; yet history has taught us that unrealistic goals doom a program to failure. In the intervening years, advocates have made it plain that Head Start plays a key role in empowering low-income families to improve their lives and in preparing their children for success in school. However, Head Start is not a cure for the ills of poverty, nor is it an inoculation against poor school experiences that might follow. To be most effective, advocates for improving Head Start and other early childhood programs and services should apply lessons from the past to current issues.

Examining the history of childhood education reveals that there have been significant changes—transformations, actually—in how children are viewed. In the sections that follow, we examine the changing view of childhood and its effect on children's lives.

The Changing View of Children

Different periods of history have had differing perspectives on children and the idea of childhood itself (Aries, 1962). These perspectives matter because they have direct

Centuries ago, children were viewed as "miniature adults." Children today are once again dressing like adults, playing adult-type games, and being exposed to adult images through the media at younger and younger ages.

implications for how children are treated and what kinds of education they are provided. Different eras in history have tended to view children as miniature adults, born in sin, blank slates, innocent, economic valuables, competent, and as citizens with rights. At different times, one or the other of these perspectives has tended to prevail. To some extent, all these views of children persist to this day. In the sections that follow, each of the perspectives of childhood just mentioned is described, along with the potential positive and negative consequences for children's lives.

Children as Miniature Adults

From the Middle Ages to about the 17th century in Western Europe, children were basically seen as adults on a smaller scale (Aries, 1962). Children dressed like adults, did adult-like work, and even played the same games. In fact, it wasn't until the 15th and 16th centuries that children appeared in paintings wearing specialized children's clothing.

In the 18th century, discovery of smallpox inoculation and better conditions in general reduced the death rate among children, which likely contributed to changes in the idea of childhood (Aries, 1962). Previously, the extremely high infant mortality rate motivated families to produce a large number of children to ensure the survival of a few. Families depended on their children to provide labor to support the family. As children's survival became less precarious, so too did their value as individuals and the image attached to them.

Today, the image of children as miniature adults is apparent once again in the clothes children wear and the images to which they are exposed through the media. Primary-grade girls dress like teenagers or young adults. Concern exists that they are too sexy too soon (Levin & Kilbourne, 2008). Preschoolers engage in team sports previously reserved for older children. Children's toys have been replaced by adult-like video games and digital devices.

Children in Need of Redemption

The image of the child during the 1300s to 1800s was shaped by the religious belief that children were born in sin and needed redemption. Misbehavior of any kind was considered sinful and punished harshly.

Schools in Europe and America in the 18th and 19th centuries were based on this image of children. Children learned to read from the Bible, recited memorized passages, and were often beaten or ridiculed for errors. Many people today continue to believe that severe punishment is necessary to shape children's moral character.

Children as Blank Slates

English philosopher John Locke (1632–1704) countered the religious argument that children are born with a predetermined sinful nature. Instead, he believed that children are born as *tabula rasa*, blank slates. What gets written on the slates is determined by their experiences in the environment. Locke's view was a step forward because it rejected the notion of inherent sinfulness and strongly emphasized the importance and value of education.

Locke was accurate in assuming that environmental experiences play a major role in children's learning; however, he did not see individual differences in children or how they actively shape their own experiences. Nevertheless, Locke's image of children as blank slates persists. Many schools today still operate on the notion that children are empty vessels that need to be filled rather than active participants in the process of education.

Children as Innocents

In contrast to Locke's theory as well as the notion of children as sinners in need of redemption, French philosopher Jean-Jacques Rousseau (1712–1778) introduced the Romantic image of the child as innocent. Rousseau's book

Emile promoted the idea that children are born good rather than evil, and that they have inherent abilities upon which to build (Elkind, 2015). He thought education should build on children's natural goodness.

Rousseau believed it is important to observe children. He was among the first to propose the concept of stages of development. He believed that children should not be rushed through stages, nor that one stage was simply preparation for another, a concept that continues to influence practice more than 250 years later.

Rousseau's image of childhood was a radical departure from the views of his day. Although he did not put these ideas into practice, they influenced many thinkers who followed, and continue to have an influence today. Early childhood education has a strong tradition of focusing on the positive in children to develop individual potential.

Children's Economic Value At various points in history, children's value has been calculated in response to a number of factors. Even today, some consider children to be their parents' property. They were, and still are in some communities, economically necessary to contribute work to the sustenance and care of the family; this includes taking care of other children and parents in old age. In the 19th and early 20th centuries, however, child labor laws limited children's potential economic contributions to family well-being. As children's economic contributions diminished, they began to take on more intrinsic emotional value in the family. For example, insurance companies compensated parents for a child's death or injury not only because of the costs involved and the potential income lost, but also as an attempt to compensate for the emotional loss (Zellizer, 1981).

The Competent Child Scientific study of children beginning in the 20th century led to an alternative view of childhood—the **competent child**, the idea that children are active players in their own development and learning. The more researchers learned about children's competencies beginning at birth, the less plausible it became to see them as blank slates. Brain research in recent decades has further reinforced this image of children's innate competence.

competent child The image of children as active players in their own development and learning.

The image of the competent child has had a major impact on early childhood practices and the larger culture. But negative consequences can emanate as well. Producers of television programs and apps claim they can teach a baby to read or produce a future Einstein. In addition, the image of the competent child has contributed to the trend to hurry young children through childhood toward expectations or experiences more appropriate for older children or adults (Elkind, 2007; Levin & Kilbourne, 2008).

The Child as a Citizen with Rights The image of the child throughout history has come almost full circle in its relation to adults. But rather than seeing children as small-scale adults, a present-day development is to view children as citizens who have rights just as adults do (Hall & Rudkin, 2011). In a democratic society, rights are implemented as laws, such as those that protect children from abuse or prosecution as adults. Similarly, toys and products used by children must meet safety regulations.

Internationally, the image of a child with rights has gained widespread attention due in large part to the influence of the Reggio Emilia approach to early education (Reggio Children, 1995). In 1989, the United Nations Convention on the Rights of the Child went into effect. It has been ratified by every developed country in the world except Somalia and the United States. The declaration calls for protection of all children from physical, mental, and sexual abuse. One provision states that, although parents have primary responsibility for children's upbringing, states should provide appropriate assistance and support for child care programs. This is one of several provisions that have been politically controversial in this country. Although the United States has not endorsed the UN Convention, its existence promotes an image of the child with rights.

Images of Childhood Today Elements of all these images of childhood are present in children's lives today and influence how they are treated. Although our country tends to see children as innocents in need of protection by parents and the government, we also propel them into adult experiences at young ages. Our schools swing back and forth between taking an approach that children are empty vessels and viewing them as competent contributors to their own learning. On the one hand, children are highly valued, and on the other hand, they are abused and neglected. As we have seen throughout history, the prevailing image of children impacts their lives in many ways. One example is the role of play, which is described in the feature *Promoting Play: The Image of the Child and the Role of Play.*

As we explore the evolution of early childhood practice in the sections that follow, it will become apparent which of these images has had the greater influence on the field. We can only present highlights of the rich history of the field here.

Promoting Play

The Image of the Child and the Role of Play

Children always play. However, many factors influence how they play and the materials they play with. To some extent, children's play reflects the prevailing image of the child. For example, when children were considered miniature adults, there was little difference between their play pastimes and those of their elders. Adults and children played with hoops and danced the same dances. When children were thought to be born in sin, Puritanical adults frowned on play as idleness and thought children's time should be spent in Bible study or productive work.

The view that children are innocents who are inherently good meant greater freedom for children to play in less restricted, more creative ways. The late 19th and early 20th centuries saw changes in children's play as living conditions improved. When child labor laws went into effect, children enjoyed more time for free play unsupervised by adults. Children created their "toys" from real objects, such as bats out of sticks. Boys and girls played make-believe, often outdoors. Boys tended to engage in informal ball games and girls enacted housekeeping scenarios with dolls and pretend, rather than manufactured, props.

As scientific study of child development expanded in the later 20th century, the image of the "competent child" had a significant impact on children's play. Whereas previously toys such as balls, dolls, blocks, and cards were relatively open-ended and primarily designed for fun, "educational toys" began to flood the market. Middle-class parents purchased toys to teach rather than entertain their children. And

children's free time became much more structured with formal dance or music lessons and participation on sports teams at younger ages.

The recent image of children as citizens with rights is a noteworthy development relevant to play. Article 31 of the United Nations Convention on the Rights of the Child affirms that governments recognize the right to "engage in play and recreational activities appropriate to the age of the child."

Although play is influenced by adults' image of the child, children always exercise a certain amount of control over play, or the activity isn't play at all. And their play is often based on their image of adults. As a result, children prefer toys and play themes that are connected to the adult world. For instance, when horses were the primary mode of transportation, children played with hobby horses or stick horses. Subsequently, these were replaced by cars, then airplanes, and eventually spaceships.

The U.S. culture now seems to have come full circle. In many respects, children are once again seen as miniature adults. They dress like adults, play with adult-like toys (Barbies instead of baby dolls), and desire the same exact "toys" as adults—video games, cell phones, and iPads.

Sources: P. Aries, 1962. *Centuries of Childhood: A Social History of Family Life.* New York, NY: Vintage Books; J. L. Frost, S. C. Wortham, and S. Reifel, 2012. *Play and Child Development* (4th ed.) Upper Saddle River, NJ: Pearson; United Nations Convention on the Rights of the Child, 1989, retrieved from www.ohchr.org/en/professionalinterest/pages/crc.aspx.

Check Your Understanding 2.1

European Influences on American Early Childhood Education

Like much of American history, early education was strongly influenced by Western European ideas. Although European ideas were not the only, nor necessarily the best, educational concepts in the world, current practices in the United States strongly reflect these early influences. Later in this chapter, we consider early childhood history through a wider lens.

Rousseau's belief in the inherent goodness and potential of children had a strong impact on the educational ideas and practices that followed. Two other thinkers who shared similar views were Comenius and Pestalozzi. Unlike Rousseau, both created schools that implemented their visions.

John Amos Comenius

John Amos Comenius (Jan Komensky in his native Czech) (1592–1670) was a minister who wrote about educational reform and directed a school where he could put his ideas into practice. He believed in three key ideas (Elkind, 2015): (1) Teaching methods needed to be radically changed from punitive approaches to make learning easier, deeper, and more pleasant; (2) teachers should engage children with nature and follow their lead; and (3) children should learn in their own language, rather than in Latin.

To accomplish his last goal, Comenius wrote a new kind of book, *Orbis Pictus*, or "the world in pictures." Popular for the next 200 years, this was the first children's picture book or illustrated textbook ever published. It was organized around topics of interest such as birds and plants, and included pictures with labels attached. Comenius also wrote the first illustrated alphabet book to teach children to read in their own languages.

Some of the educational ideas that Comenius practiced in his school were radical for his time but sound familiar today. For example, he thought the early years were an extremely important foundation for later learning. He believed that children learn through their senses and need to be active, and he felt that children's interests and firsthand experiences promote learning and memory. Comenius believed that children are born in the image of God, and was vehemently opposed to physical punishment (Elkind, 2015). He was one of the first to identify developmental stages.

Comenius's ideas have endured for centuries. For example, in the 1990s, Eastern European countries that had been under Communist dictatorship moved toward democracy. One strategy was to reform previously rigid educational systems. With the help of American philanthropy, the International Step by Step Association was founded to develop Head Start-like preschool programs. There was some concern that these "American" ideas—such as child-centered education—would be culturally inappropriate. However, these concerns underestimated the lasting reverence for native son Komensky (Comenius)—who is, after all, the forerunner of much of American early childhood education.

Johann Pestalozzi

Johann Pestalozzi (1746–1827) was a Swiss educator who, like Comenius, founded his own school and trained the teachers. He believed that all children—including children who lived in poverty—could benefit from education (Nourot, 2005). The field's current views of best practice are remarkably consistent with many of Pestalozzi's ideas about teaching and learning.

Learning and Teaching in Pestalozzi's School Pestalozzi described his philosophy in a book titled *How Gertrude Teaches Her Children* (1894/2012). He believed that teachers must study child development. He thought that learning proceeds through stages, with children needing to master skills and knowledge before moving on to the next stage (Elkind, 2015). Pestalozzi promoted what came to be called the "whole child" point of view—that children's physical, emotional, social, moral, and intellectual development are integrated. He called these "the hand, heart, and head."

Other important ideas of Pestalozzi included the notion that children need to discover ideas for themselves through their own activity—a precursor of Piaget's theory of **constructivism**. He rejected punishment and threats, and felt that children are motivated to learn by their interests. Like many early theorists, Pestalozzi viewed development as a natural unfolding or blossoming from within, with teachers acting as gardeners who nurture the process rather than direct it. Although this view is simpler than our understanding of development today, it persisted well into the 20th century.

Impact of Pestalozzi's Work Pestalozzi's ideas directly influenced schools for young children in the 19th century. Particularly influential was his notion of object lessons—learning from direct observation and sensory experience in the natural world—that begin with the here and now and move beyond (Wolfe, 2000).

A well-known school influenced by Pestalozzi was founded by Robert Owen (1771–1858) as part of his idealized community in Scotland, New Lanark. Owen spread his ideas to America by founding a similar model community in New Harmony, Indiana. Although his experiment did not survive long, the school provided care and education for hundreds of children, from infancy to age 10, whose parents worked in the mills—one of the earliest examples of a child care center.

> **constructivism** Learning theory derived from the work of Jean Piaget, which assumes that children actively build their knowledge from firsthand experiences in stimulating environments.

Friedrich Froebel

Friedrich Froebel (1782–1852) built on Pestalozzi's ideas but extended them to develop educational materials. His view of development as a process of natural unfolding is evident in the name of his school, a "garden for children." Froebel is well known as the "father of the kindergarten."

Froebel believed in the innate goodness and capacities of children, and saw God's image in them. Like Pestalozzi, he believed that education should be based on children's interests and their active involvement, and that teachers need to understand children's development by directly observing their actions (Giardiello, 2014).

Froebel described stages of development that are similar to those Piaget articulated in the 20th century. He saw infancy (birth to 3 years) as focused on the family and the infant's relationship with the mother. He wrote *Mother Play and Nursery Songs* to assist mothers in their interactions with very young children—something most mothers today take for granted. Froebel's second stage (ages 3 to 7), for which he developed his kindergarten materials, was the focus of most of his work. The third stage (ages 7 to 10) focused on more formal school instruction.

Froebel's Kindergarten Froebel's metaphor of the children's garden was more than poetry. He strongly believed that children's learning is a process of unfolding from within. He also believed that learning would occur on the child's own timetable and not until the child was ready. Froebel's kindergarten emphasized children's free play, singing, and movement (Nourot, 2005). The materials he developed, which were called **Froebel's occupations and gifts**, were used to guide and structure children's play. As a result, Froebel's view of "free" play was not as free as some interpret today.

> **Froebel's occupations and gifts** Invented by Friedrich Froebel for kindergartners. Occupations were planned experiences designed to train children's eye-hand coordination and mental activity; gifts were concrete materials, many of which influenced later toy development.

Froebel's Occupations and Gifts Invented by Froebel for kindergartners, occupations were planned experiences designed to train children's eye-hand coordination and mental activity, and gifts were concrete materials, many of which influenced later toy development.

The role of the teacher in Froebel's kindergarten was to be like a gardener. Teachers were to observe, nurture, and help but not interfere with the natural growth of the child. They needed to be aware of children's development, however, so they could provide new challenges as children engaged with the gifts and occupations.

Another gift was a cube that could be divided into eight smaller cubes and put back together to form a whole. Children could play many games with this gift, but it also promoted basic math concepts related to number and geometry. Froebel also invented parquetry blocks—a set of flat, colored, wooden shapes that could be put together to form various designs. Other gifts included sticks and rings made of wire and natural materials such as seeds and pebbles. The same or similar materials are prevalent in early childhood classrooms today, where children use them in creative ways and to learn mathematics and science.

In contrast to the gifts, occupations were planned experiences designed to train children's eye–hand coordination and mental activity (Elkind, 2015). The occupations included activities such as drawing on grid paper, lacing paper strips, weaving mats, folding and cutting paper into designs, constructing with sticks, or making models from cardboard.

Froebel believed that the use of the gifts and occupations engaged children in symbolically representing objects and events in the real world—such as creating a model or drawing a picture of a building. The importance of representation, which Froebel presaged, is now supported by research.

Impact of Froebel's Work Froebel's work had a major impact on education in the United States, leading directly to a large-scale kindergarten movement here. Several teachers and teacher educators who studied Froebel's methods in Europe—"kindergartners" as they were called—transplanted his ideas to this country.

Kindergartens today increasingly bear little resemblance to Froebel's "children's garden"; today they are more like formal first grades (Bassok, Latham, Rorem, 2016). However, many of his basic ideas are still evident in preschool and child care programs, and continue to inspire early educators (Moore & Campos, et al., 2010). His gifts and occupations were clearly the prototypes for many of the toys and materials, such as 1-inch cube and parquetry blocks, that are pervasive in preschool classrooms. Common activities—constructing models or using natural materials in art and projects—also mirror some of his occupations.

Froebel's work had a significant impact on the development of American kindergartens, which we will return to later in this chapter. First, we will visit another European educator who lived a century later than Froebel but whose work also stands out for its contributions to the field—Maria Montessori.

Maria Montessori

Maria Montessori (1870–1952) was a major figure in the history of early childhood education (Giardiello, 2014). A brilliant woman, she was Italy's first female physician. She was nominated for the Nobel Peace Prize, and her face graced the 1,000 lira note until Italy abandoned the lira for the euro. Montessori was, and probably always will be, the only early childhood educator whose face adorned a currency.

History of the Montessori Method Montessori's contributions grew out of her work with poor children in the slums of Rome. The prevailing opinion was that these children were mentally deficient. However, Montessori believed that what appeared to be mental retardation was not biologically based but rather caused by the lack of stimulation in their environments.

Montessori classrooms are specially designed environments in which children learn by interacting with materials. What skills might children acquire by working with the Montessori materials depicted here?

In 1907, she started a program for children ages 4 through 7 called *Casa dei Bambini* (Children's House) and developed a highly successful approach to teaching the children, which revealed that they were not mentally disabled at all. Montessori demonstrated that educating needy children is a less costly and more effective strategy than waiting until they create problems for society. This is the same justification used to launch Head Start, and it is still the core rationale for much of the current investment in early education.

Key Elements of the Montessori Method

The Montessori method includes several basic elements. In the sections that follow, we briefly describe Montessori's views about children and learning, the environment, and the teacher's role.

Image of Children: The Absorbent Mind

absorbent mind Maria Montessori's image of the child as actively learning from sensory experiences.

Like other key figures in early childhood history, Montessori (1909/1964) believed that children develop naturally in an organized environment. Her image of the child is the absorbent mind—actively learning from sensory experiences. She also believed that children from 4 to 7 years old are internally motivated to interact with the world and do not need external encouragement or rewards.

Where Montessori deviated greatly from others in the field was in her opinion of play. Montessori dismissed play as a waste of children's time (Wolfe, 2000). She also minimized the value of social interaction for children's learning. As evidence, children each had an individual small mat on which to work and not be disturbed by others.

A Prepared Learning Environment

Montessori believed that poor children deserve high-quality experiences. She thought that children need an orderly environment that supports their ability to work on and complete tasks independently. Accordingly, she designed classroom environments and materials that demonstrate respect for children. Montessori innovations included child-sized tables and other furnishings as well as materials arranged on open shelves for easy access by children.

To facilitate learning and prevent wasted time, she developed educational materials for children to use in prescribed ways. Montessori designed self-correcting learning materials for children, many of which are still commonly used. For example, she created puzzles with little knobs attached to each piece for very young children to practice the pincer grasp used for writing; to practice fine motor skills, she invented a cloth board with buttons and buttonholes. Montessori emphasized that there was one right way to use each of her materials. She did not consider her materials to be toys; instead, she viewed them as educational tools. Children were also taught practical life skills such as washing a table and sweeping a floor.

Montessori's belief in sensory learning extended to academic areas as well, specifically writing, reading, and mathematics (Montessori, 1912/1964). For example, she created sandpaper alphabets so children could feel the shapes of the letters as a first step toward writing. She thought children should learn to write as a strategy to teach reading.

This was an innovative concept for its time (when promoting reading at an early age was not accepted by her peers in early education), and also presaged later understandings of the strong connection between writing and reading in becoming literate.

The Teacher's Role Montessori's view of the teacher's role is to prepare the environment, observe children, and demonstrate materials, but not to interfere with their natural exploration. Although teachers' interactions with children are very intentional in the Montessori Method, much of the learning is assumed to occur as children interact with materials. The teacher presents brief individual or small-group lessons, but during most of the day, children choose their activities. Their choices have limits, however, because the adults arrange those choices.

Impact of Montessori's Work From 1910 to 1920, interest in Montessori's approach gained popularity in the United States; several elements of her approach remain widely accepted. However, overall interest in her methods faded here, primarily due to her unwillingness to adapt to new knowledge and her rejection of key elements of American philosophy, such as the importance of play. Maria Montessori's lasting contribution to the field was her development of Montessori materials and her impact on the organization of environments.

Not until the 1950s was interest in Montessori revived in the United States. In contrast to Montessori's original intent to serve poor children, Montessori schools in the United States tended to be private, serving a more affluent population. In recent years, however, the approach has been embraced by some magnet and charter public schools. A study of a public Montessori school in Milwaukee found that the approach contributed positively to 5-year-olds' literacy, math, and social skills (Lillard, 2005) and to creativity and social skills at age 12 (Lillard & Else-Quest, 2006). With its emphasis on individualized instruction, the Montessori approach also has been found to be effective in improving the school readiness of Latino prekindergartners (Ansari & Winsler, 2014). Interestingly, the founders of Google, Larry Page and Sergey Brin, attribute their success to the self-motivation they gained from attending Montessori preschool, and Amazon founder Jeff Bezos is a Montessori graduate (Gaylord, 2012). To learn more about the positive effects of Montessori's educational approach, read the feature *What Works: Developing Self-regulation with the Montessori Method.*

Video Example 2.1:

The Montessori Classroom

This video gives an overview of the arrangement and materials found in a typical Montessori classroom. Which key elements of the Montessori Method do you notice? How do the materials themselves promote learning? What is the role of the teacher in a Montessori classroom?

Loris Malaguzzi

One of the most internationally influential educational leaders of the 20th century was Loris Malaguzzi (1920–1993), the founder of the Reggio Emilia approach. The exemplary municipally-run preschools and infant-toddler centers in the city of Reggio Emilia, Italy, had a significant impact on both theory and teaching practices throughout the world. The programs serving children from birth through age 6 originated as a movement among parents following World War II. Decades of Fascist dictatorship followed by a devastating war left much of the country in ruins. A small group of parents decided that the best way to rebuild their community and secure a better future was to build a school for young children based on democratic principles. Mothers and fathers literally built the first school "brick by brick" from the remains of bombed-out buildings and by selling a few horses, a truck, and a tank abandoned by German invaders (Barazzoni, 2000). As a young elementary school teacher, Loris Malaguzzi was inspired by these parents and committed himself to the continued evolution of the schools until his death in 1994. The schools struggled with little funding in the early years, and often relied on volunteer help until the city of Reggio Emilia took over administration in the 1970s.

What Works

Developing Self-regulation with the Montessori Method

Current research reveals that children's capacity to self-regulate affects all areas of their development and learning. Although neither Montessori nor any of her contemporaries used the term *self-regulation*, the goals of her method closely align with today's definition. Self-regulation is the ability to appropriately control emotions and behavior, focus attention, persist at tasks, and solve problems with competence and confidence. Self-regulation is one of the most important predictors of children's success in school and life.

To test the assumption that Montessori schools promote this critical ability, a three-year study compared the self-regulation and academic outcomes of 256 kindergarten, first- and second-grade children who attended Montessori school with children who were enrolled in regular public school classrooms in South Carolina. Teachers and parents were surveyed about children's work habits, emotional control, and social skills. Adults were also asked how accurately children judge their own capacities.

The results showed that the children who attended Montessori school were more likely to solve their own conflicts, engage in problem-solving, ask questions, and seek information if they didn't understand something. The Montessori children also developed their own internal standards for performance rather than relying on adults for external motivation or reinforcement, were more capable of evaluating their own performances and strengths, and performed better on reading and mathematics tests than their peers in non-Montessori classrooms. They were enthusiastic and curious learners, but they expected school to be challenging.

The researchers attributed these results to the fact that Montessori classrooms stress independent work habits and focused attention. Children have a lot of control and take initiative in a planned learning environment with specially designed materials. Undoubtedly, Maria Montessori would be pleased with these results but not surprised.

Source: B. Ervin, P. D. Wash, & M. E. Mecca, 2010. A 3-year study of self-regulation in Montessori and non-Montessori classrooms. *Montessori Life, 2,* 22–31.

Loris Malaguzzi's pedagogical and philosophical leadership in collaboration with parents, teachers, and children led to the evolution of the Reggio Emilia approach to early education, which has had enormous impact on the knowledge base (Cagliari, Castagneti, Giudici, Rinadi, Vecchi, & Moss, 2016). The principles of the approach are described in more detail in Chapter 12, but it includes several key elements: 1) the image of the child as rich, strong, and powerful imbued with rights; 2) the metaphor of "the hundred languages of children" referring to both how children display their learning through various media and how their understanding is transformed by working with diverse media such as clay, paint, drawing, video, and many others; 3) the role of documentation of both the process and products of children's learning; and 4) the co-construction of knowledge— children and teachers learning together.

In 1979, the practices began to be widely distributed throughout the world. An exhibit of children's work that demonstrated the processes of learning and teaching in Reggio, *The Eye Jumped Over the Wall*, was put on view in Scandinavia and other countries. An updated version of the exhibit, *The Hundred Languages of Children*, was exhibited in the U.S. beginning in 1990, and fresh exhibits continue to be displayed everywhere accompanied by educational seminars on the approach. In 1991, the cover of *Newsweek* magazine proclaimed one of the Reggio preschools, Diana School, the best early childhood program in the world.

Before his untimely death, Loris Malaguzzi received the prestigious LEGO award and was honored by the Kohl Foundation in Chicago. In 1994, Reggio Children—The International Center for the Defense and Promotion of the Rights and Potentials of All Children was launched with the mission of promoting the theory and practice of the Reggio approach through study tours to the schools, seminars, and publications.

Check Your Understanding 2.2

Leaders and Events in the Early Childhood Movement in the United States

The following sections present three interwoven stories of early childhood education in America—the kindergarten movement, progressive education, and the nursery school movement. These stories are described separately, but in reality, they happened simultaneously and were inextricably connected. A parallel story—the child care movement—was also occurring, but it played out differently, as you will read later in this section.

The Kindergarten Movement

The United States provided fertile ground for the growth of Froebel's "children's gardens." In the sections that follow, we describe how the movement began and spread widely, as well as its lasting impact.

Early Days of the Kindergarten Movement The earliest leaders in the kindergarten movement transplanted Froebel's ideas directly. The first kindergarten in the United States was founded by Margarethe Schurz (1833–1876) in Wisconsin in 1856 (Snyder, 1972). Schurz had studied with Froebel and, upon immigrating to the United States, started a German-speaking school to teach her own and neighbors' children. Later, Schurz met Elizabeth Palmer Peabody (1804–1894), and their encounter was the impetus for the American kindergarten movement.

Elizabeth Peabody was part of a well-known family of social reformers. Her sister, Mary, was married to Horace Mann, who is considered to be the father of public education in the United States. In Boston, Elizabeth Peabody organized the first English-speaking kindergarten in 1860, and soon after wrote the first American kindergarten textbook for teachers (Cantor, 2013). She understood that teachers needed to be trained in Froebel's philosophy to ensure the quality and integrity of the expanding kindergarten movement. She also traveled widely and became an outspoken advocate for the cause, inspiring new generations of leaders, the most influential of whom was Susan Blow.

Susan Blow's Leadership Susan Blow (1843–1916) was the major voice in expanding the kindergarten movement and in fighting to keep it true to Froebel's original vision. Inspired by Elizabeth Peabody's promotion of kindergarten, Blow visited Froebelian kindergartens in the United States and Germany, and became the leading interpreter of the approach at home.

Founding Public Kindergarten With the support of William Harris, a reform-minded school superintendent in St. Louis, in 1873 Blow founded the first public school kindergarten (Snyder, 1972) in response to Harris's concern that schooling did not begin until age 7. Blow was ambivalent about connecting kindergarten to public school, fearing that "the formality of the grades would seize kindergarten in its grip" (Snyder, 1972, p. 66). Nevertheless, she worked with Harris and launched more than 50 kindergarten classrooms. Teacher training was an essential part of her strategy, with teachers working with children in the mornings and attending lectures in the afternoons on topics such as the correct use of Froebel's gifts and occupations—a combination of theory and practicum that continues to this day in teacher education.

Upon Harris's departure from his post, a new school administration was less supportive of Blow's cause and threatened her ideal vision of kindergarten. Subsequently, Blow turned her energy from developing and spreading Froebelian kindergarten ideals to defending them (Snyder, 1972). Blow promoted a rigid application of Froebel's methods (such as using the gifts in narrowly prescribed ways), which was actually antithetical to his vision of kindergarten.

Founding the International Kindergarten Union   In 1892, Blow convened a group of ardent kindergartners from throughout the country and formed the International Kindergarten Union (IKU). (Much later, the IKU became the Association for Childhood Education International.) The original mission of the IKU was not just to disseminate information but also to protect the integrity of Froebelian kindergartens. Within two decades, this mission was to come into direct conflict with winds of change that were occurring in the wider educational world, emanating from the progressive education movement described in the next section.

Progressive Education

progressive education movement Major effort to reform schooling in the early 20th century to make it more democratic and responsive to children's needs. This movement was highly influential on early childhood education and later ideas about developmentally appropriate practice.

The progressive education movement was a major effort to reform schooling at all levels to make it more democratic. Its tenets were in direct contrast to the prevailing practices in schools of the time, which emphasized rote memorization, strict conformity, and harsh discipline. The traditional curriculum was limited to the "3 Rs": reading, writing, and arithmetic.

The story of the progressive education movement in the United States is integrally connected to the story of the nursery school movement (or preschool, as we now call it). Many principles of developmentally appropriate practice are derived directly from the work of early progressive leaders. Although differences exist between the earlier ideas and current views, the commonalities between the two visions—progressive education and developmentally appropriate practice—are striking. The following sections present the contributions of John Dewey.

John Dewey   John Dewey (1859–1952) was a professor of philosophy first at the University of Chicago and then for 47 years at Teachers College, Columbia University, in New York City. While in Chicago, John and his wife, Alice Chapman Dewey (d. 1927), founded the University of Chicago Laboratory School to implement their philosophy of a humane approach to education. Alice taught at the school, prepared the curriculum, and served as principal. The school, which they ran from 1893 to 1903, became a laboratory for developing and trying out their approach.

Principles of Progressive Education   Dewey (1916) believed that the purpose of education is to ensure the effective functioning of a democratic society. He believed the traditional approach to schooling could not produce citizen decision makers, and was concerned that in a democratic society, it is "impossible to foretell definitely what civilization will be twenty years from now" (Dewey, 1929, p. 6). Therefore, it is important to teach children to take initiative and use judgment. Dewey (1929) articulated his philosophy in *My Pedagogic Creed*. Let's take a look at some of the principles of progressive education as described by Dewey in that document.

What Education Is   "Education is the process of living and not preparation for future living" (Dewey, 1929, p. 7). This famous quote of Dewey summarizes his definition of education, and continues to influence early childhood education.

Dewey was a prolific writer whose words still inspire. The titles of his books alone convey his basic ideas about education: *Democracy and Education, Education and Experience, The School and Society, Freedom and Culture,* and *The Child and the Curriculum.* In Dewey's mind, schooling could not be separated from the larger needs of democratic society, and children rather than subject matter needed to be at the center of the curriculum.

What the School Is Dewey (1900) believed that the school should function as a community. The teacher's role is to be a member of the community. Teachers should not directly impose discipline but rather influence and assist children as they work together.

According to Dewey, teachers and parents should learn from each other—an accepted idea today, but radical for his time. In his school, parents and teachers met regularly to discuss topics such as why children should or should not learn to read at an early age—again, an issue that many educators and parents debate today (Wolfe, 2000).

integrated curriculum Learning plan that addresses goals across multiple areas of the curriculum at the same time.

What the Curriculum Is Dewey believed that subject matter—reading, writing, geography, history, science—should be introduced to children in ways that they can understand and that involve them in social interaction. He introduced the idea of integrated curriculum, now a staple of early childhood education, which addresses learning goals across multiple subjects at the same time. For example, children might learn economics, history, geography, and other subjects by studying the workers in their neighborhood. A tenet of Dewey's philosophy is that teachers should find ways to integrate traditional curriculum into topics of interest to children, such as building a model of the neighborhood. Dewey also brought expressive and constructive activities into the classroom such as cooking, sewing, and woodworking. He felt academic skills should grow out of these activities.

Video Example 2.2:

The Kindness Quilt Project

In this video, kindergarten children present their long-term project about making a kindness quilt. The project is an example of how integrated curriculum can be used effectively. Which key elements of John Dewey's educational approach are demonstrated? What are the children learning from this experience?

What Teaching Should Be Dewey (1929) believed that the traditional emphasis on children as passive learners was a "waste of time." He strongly emphasized the importance of teachers observing children and building on their interests. In progressive schools, the role of teachers is to guide or facilitate learning based on what they know about children and to choose the right problems and questions to further children's learning. For example, teachers don't simply teach geography as adults know it; rather, they teach the geography concepts and topics that the child is interested in and capable of learning. This approach, called the child-centered curriculum, has been falsely interpreted over the years to mean that children determine the curriculum (Bredekamp & Copple, 1997). Although teachers build curriculum from children's experiences and interests, Dewey felt strongly that teachers needed to know *both* what children are interested in *and* the content that children needed to learn. This *both/and* thinking principle in progressive education has often been lost in translation.

child-centered curriculum John Dewey's idea that curriculum should reflect the concepts and topics that the child is interested in and capable of learning.

The Impact of Progressive Education on Schooling Although progressive education has often been misinterpreted and periodically comes under attack by proponents of more traditional practices, its contributions to American education are profound. Lois Meek Stolz (1977), the first president of NAEYC and a contemporary of Dewey, eloquently captured the impact:

> I think it is very difficult for people of this generation to realize, or even picture, what the public schools were like in the early 1900s. Children were in their seats all day long. When they rose, they rose to count, "1, 2, 3," they then turned, marched, and went to the cloakroom. Then they did the same thing when they marched out of the school and when they marched in. Everybody read out of the same book at the same time. There was very little consideration for individual differences. (p. 103)

Earlier in this chapter, we talked about how solutions to problems contain the seeds of new problems. Progressive education was a case in point. Giving children more freedom meant that some people interpreted this as chaos, creating a backlash or a new problem.

And yet, as Stoltz points out, the efforts overall led to real change in schools—and that change is progress.

Although he was a philosophy professor, Dewey was strongly influenced by the trend in his day toward more scientific approaches in education. This trend, called the *child study movement*, is described in the next section.

The Child Study Movement

As far back as Pestalozzi, educators understood that teaching should be based on direct study of children. Beginning in the late 19th century, G. Stanley Hall (1844–1924) launched the child study movement. Hall was interested in understanding individual differences in children through direct observation.

Hall's students went on to develop systematic scientific approaches to studying child development. Arnold Gesell (1880–1961) is famed for launching a child study laboratory at Yale University called the Gesell Institute. There, he observed large samples of children and derived age-related norms for children's growth and development, such as by what age children should take their first steps or speak their first words. These norms were considered "universal" and have been widely influential. However, in the late 20th century, Gesell's age-related norms were criticized for understating individual differences and not using diverse samples of children.

Hall was a strong critic of Froebelian kindergarten. He thought its rigid methodology lacked a scientific basis. Thus, the child study movement played an important role in bringing about changes in the kindergarten movement, and also contributed in large measure to the growing nursery school movement. We tell this story in the section that follows.

The Nursery School Movement

Dewey's laboratory school and his emphasis on child observation reflected his understanding of the need to base education on the study of children. Similarly, other universities launched lab schools to train teachers and study children. Many of these schools served children younger than kindergarten age, and were called nursery schools based on their philosophy of nurturing development. Laboratory schools were established for the purposes of research and demonstration of teaching methods rather than to serve parents or neglected children (Hewes & NAEYC Organizational History and Archives Committee, 2001). As a result, many of these programs served middle- and upper-class children of faculty or community members.

The nursery school movement eventually launched the wider field of early childhood education. It grew out of the kindergarten and child study movements through the leadership of two women whose contributions to early childhood education are unparalleled: Patty Smith Hill, founder of NAEYC, and Lucy Sprague Mitchell, founder of Bank Street College. Every early childhood educator should know the stories of these women and their contemporaries, who played seminal roles in laying the foundation of early childhood education as we know it today. We who follow are their direct descendents.

Patty Smith Hill

Patty Smith Hill's life story parallels the early history of early childhood education, with each phase of her life connected to important developments in the field. She was a joyful child, teacher of young children, creator of resources for children, teacher educator, and national leader.

Hill's Early Life Experiences Patty Smith Hill (1868–1946) had an idyllic childhood. Her father believed that girls should be educated, a radical idea at the time. Her mother was a progressive thinker who secretly (and illegally) taught enslaved people to read, write, and calculate (Wolfe, 2000). Furthermore, Hill's mother believed that play was essential to childhood.

Work as a Kindergarten Teacher By the 1880s, the kindergarten movement was underway, and Anna Bryan launched a teacher training program in Louisville, Kentucky, where Patty Hill became one of the first students (Snyder, 1972). Hill started her own

child study movement Early 20th-century effort to scientifically observe and systematically document children's individual development under the leadership of G. Stanley Hall and Arnold Gesell.

nursery schools Schools serving children younger than kindergarten age; out-of-date term for preschool or prekindergarten.

kindergarten, where she encouraged creative uses for Froebel's gifts as toys and constructive materials such as blocks and clay. Her kindergarten evidenced her belief in the value of children's play as a way to learn.

In 1896, Hill and Bryan were among a group of influential kindergarten educators who attended one of G. Stanley Hall's lectures on new knowledge and insights gained from the systematic study of children's development. Hall's severe criticism of the Froebelian approach as unscientific outraged the attendees, all of whom stormed out of the meeting—with the exception of Hill and Bryan (Hewes, 1976). They stayed and continued to study with Hall, and developed a new curriculum for teaching young children.

In 1903, Louisville's kindergartens became part of the public schools. Hill was excited about the potential benefits, but feared that key kindergarten practices, including parent education, would be lost (Snyder, 1972). Hill's vision for kindergarten included three purposes: (1) to meet the needs of 4- to 6-year-olds, (2) to lay the foundation for the first-grade curriculum while ensuring the right of kindergarten children to develop at their own level, and (3) to connect the child's experiences at home and school, building on what children learn there (Hill, 1926/1987). This vision of kindergarten, especially the role of parents, was not just ahead of Hill's time, but one to aspire to today.

Early leaders of the nursery school movement in the United States, such as Patty Smith Hill, saw the value of pretend play for children's development. What might these children be learning as they play hospital?

Creator of Resources for Children Hill developed resources for children, including a set of lumberlike wooden blocks from which children could build structures large enough to play in. She and her musician sister, Mildred, wrote songs for children, using music as a teaching tool. Their most famous song is "Happy Birthday," although few people know its composers.

Hill also wrote many poems about children's interests as well as books to help children learn to read. Much like her mother, Hill was concerned about racial inequality. In the early 1940s, she worked for months on a set of readers showing African American children, but despaired when no publisher would consider them (Hewes, 1976). She believed that respectful images would help resolve racial prejudices.

Hill's Work as a Teacher Educator In 1905, Hill joined the faculty of Teachers College in New York, where she stayed for 30 years and was considered a master teacher (Snyder, 1972). She focused her work in the community school, which served poor children, as opposed to the campus lab school, which served well-off children of faculty.

The Dean of Teachers College, James Earl Russell, was famous for bringing together divergent points of view (Snyder, 1972). One of his provocative ideas was to bring Susan Blow to co-teach a course on kindergarten methods with Hill. Among the topics they debated were opposing views of work and play. Although students loved their lively debates, eventually it became clear that Hill's point of view was carrying the day (Snyder, 1972).

Hill's Contributions as a National Leader Hill was active in the IKU and served as its president. However, her more liberal ideas about kindergarten methods, including her promotion of play and creativity, came into conflict with others' more rigid interpretations of Froebel's ideas.

In 1904, the IKU formed the Committee of Nineteen, a group with varying perspectives on kindergarten practice, to resolve disputes on topics such as the role of play and the curriculum (Wolfe, 2000). Each year, the committee issued a report, and disagreements became more apparent over time. By 1909, differences could not be resolved and three reports were produced: one by Blow, another by Hill, and a compromise report by Lucy Wheelock (Snyder, 1972). Hill's report was to become the vision for early childhood practice as we know it today. Nevertheless, the process of debating conflicting points of view, which she embraced, continues to be an essential part of the work of early childhood educators (Bredekamp, 2001).

Founder of NAEYC As nursery schools began to proliferate in the 1920s, Hill was concerned about the lack of standards and curriculum, and about the threat of unqualified people taking leadership positions (Hewes, 1976). In 1926, she formed the National Committee on Nursery Schools, which became the National Association for Nursery Education (NANE). The committee included Lois Meek Stolz, Arnold Gesell, and Abigail Eliot. Stolz became the first president.

In the 1960s, NANE changed its name to NAEYC, the National Association for the Education of Young Children. Hill was its first member, and her views dominated the work of the nursery school movement during its early years. NANE's first publication in 1929 was *Minimum Essentials for Nursery School Education.* In this tradition, NAEYC has been involved in setting standards ever since (Bredekamp, 2001).

We have chosen to tell the story of Patty Smith Hill in such detail because she lived so many of the historical events that helped define present-day early childhood education. In the next section, we share the story of one of her close colleagues in progressive education, Caroline Pratt.

Caroline Pratt Caroline Pratt (1867–1954) attended the kindergarten education program at Teachers College. Like Hill, Pratt rejected the Froebelian approach. She believed it was far too structured and did not allow children to play freely or experiment with materials.

Pratt's Educational Philosophy Pratt focused her energies on studying children directly. Her motto, as well as the title of the book for which she is best known, was "I learn from children" (Pratt, 1948). She became intrigued by the potential of engaging children with open-ended play equipment and materials.

Like others in the progressive education movement, Pratt looked to education to transform society and worked in settlement houses with poor children. She set up classrooms with her own hand-made blocks and toys, crayons, and paper, and observed children's play. Based on her observations, Pratt realized the benefits for children of firsthand experiences, self-directed plans, field trips, and pretend play; letting children find answers to their own questions; the relationship of play and intelligence; and the need to nurture children's play (Wolfe, 2000). Pratt also saw an active role for teachers in supporting children's play. These conclusions have all been supported by empirical research in the intervening years.

Inventor of Unit Blocks Pratt's most lasting contribution is undoubtedly her design of wooden unit blocks. She admired Hill's blocks but found them difficult for younger children to manipulate. She wanted blocks that would allow children to openly express their ideas about the world. Her blocks are made of natural hardwood in various three-dimensional shapes, and are mathematically precise because each block is a fraction or multiple of the standard unit. For example, the standard unit block is one-half the next size block, one-quarter the size after that, and so forth. Research has proven what Pratt intuitively believed about the value of these tools for children's learning. Caroline Pratt's invention of wooden unit blocks was a major contribution that countless children have enjoyed and benefited from ever since. Research continues to uncover new and lasting learning benefits of block play to learning mathematics, engineering, language, social skills, creativity, and many other areas.

Pratt created wooden people representing families and community workers to add a pretend element to the block play. She also designed large hollow wooden blocks to encourage large muscle play and for outdoor use. For more than a century, millions of children have enjoyed and learned from these wonderful, creative materials. However, because she did not patent them, Pratt never benefited financially.

One of Pratt's closest colleagues was Lucy Sprague Mitchell. Mitchell's enormous contributions to the field are described in the next section.

✓ ## Application Exercise 2.1
Children's Block Play

 Lucy Sprague Mitchell Lucy Sprague Mitchell (1878–1967) has been identified as a major link between Dewey's progressive education movement of the early 20th century and NAEYC's current concept of high-quality, developmentally appropriate education (Field & Baumi, 2014; Greenberg, 1987). Indeed, her life spanned the period from the beginning of John Dewey's work to the birth of Head Start in 1965. In the sections that follow, we describe her early life, her educational experiments and ideas about curriculum, and the important role of Bank Street College, which she founded.

Mitchell's Early Years Lucy Sprague Mitchell was a brilliant woman who studied at Teachers College with John Dewey and Edward Thorndike, the father of educational measurement and statistical research. Her life's work drew on both of these influences—a progressive philosophy combined with research-based practice.

The Bureau of Educational Experiments Using inherited funds, Mitchell launched the Bureau of Educational Experiments (BEE) in 1916 to teach teachers and conduct research. The goals of the Bureau of Educational Experiments (Wolfe, 2000) were to:

- Focus on child development rather than learning specific curriculum
- Take a whole-child approach to learning and development
- Observe how children's development is stimulated by experiences and activities
- Focus on scientific measurement of stages of development and establishing norms (representing the influence of Arnold Gesell as well as Thorndike).

Bank Street College When the bureau moved to 69 Bank St. in New York City, its name was changed to Bank Street College of Education. A graduate program in teacher education, Bank Street College played essential roles in the history of early childhood education, and continues to do so. We can only mention a few here.

Most notably, Mitchell's educational philosophy emphasized children's firsthand experiences and play. Her ideas came to be called the **Bank Street approach**, later called the Developmental–Interaction approach to more accurately describe its tenets. In this model, children's experiences in the "here and now" provide the launching pad for their learning (Mitchell & David, 1992). These experiences, such as the field trips or projects described earlier, gradually widen children's horizons beyond the here and now. The concept is that curriculum should be based on individual children's development, and that learning occurs through interaction with the environment and other people (Biber, 1977; Shapiro & Nager, 1999). The Bank Street approach has been widely influential in early childhood curriculum development, especially in teaching social studies.

One element of the Bank Street approach that has sometimes been underemphasized is the role of the teacher. In Mitchell's words, "We were looking at children learning, and *intentionally* facilitating the process every day" (Greenberg, 1987, p. 75). Read the feature *Becoming an Intentional Teacher: Expanding Children's Experience* for an example of the teacher's role in the Bank Street approach.

The Writer's Workshops for Children's Authors Mitchell was a prolific writer and authored a series of children's books. She created a writer's workshop in 1937 for authors of children's books at Bank Street, which offered scholarships to ensure racial and socioeconomic diversity. The writer's laboratory was established to help authors better

Bank Street approach
Originating with Lucy Sprague Mitchell at Bank Street College and later called the Developmental–Interaction approach, a curriculum framework based on individual children's development, emphasizing that learning begins in children's experiences in the immediate environment (here and now).

Becoming an Intentional Teacher

Expanding Children's Experience

Here's What Happened   The preschool I work in is located in a rural community. Our curriculum is based on the Bank Street approach. At the beginning of the year, the children were very excited about riding the bus to school for the first time. They had so many questions that I decided we should pursue the topic. The children interviewed the bus driver, who is one of the children's mother. They drew pictures of the bus, sang "Wheels on the Bus," and played school bus. Based on the children's keen interest, I decided to introduce the idea of drawing maps of their bus routes. Some children have lengthy rides from the country while others live closer by.

Here's What I Was Thinking   The basic premise of the Bank Street approach is to begin the curriculum study in the "here and now" and expand children's experiences and learning from there. The school bus study began easily enough with the initial enthusiasm of riding to school. But I anticipated that these rides would soon become boring. Distracted preschoolers might create unsafe conditions on the bus. I decided to enhance the learning experience with the challenge of mapping their routes. This required keen observation and focused attention on the children's part. It also introduced them to geography and mapping skills.

Reflection   Many schools today are given a curriculum that prescribes certain topics of study such as *seasons* or *animals* that may not reflect the lives and experiences of the children. If you were a teacher in such a situation, how could you apply the principles of the Bank Street approach to make the experiences more meaningful?

understand children's development and interests, and to promote their use of the rhythms and rhymes of language that are so important and enjoyable for children (Wolfe, 2000). Among the best-known writers who participated in the workshop were Margaret Wise Brown and Ruth Krauss. Brown's books *Goodnight Moon* and *The Runaway Bunny* remain classics, as does *The Carrot Seed* by Krauss.

Near the end of her life, Mitchell was instrumental in numerous national efforts to expand early childhood education beyond laboratory schools and use it for true social reform (Field & Baumi, 2014). She lived to see the Bank Street approach used as the model for the Head Start program. Head Start is also known for its emphasis on parent involvement, which was another part of the nursery school movement described in the next section.

Parent Cooperative Preschools   As early as 1916, parents organized to start their own nursery schools. In these programs, which are called *parent cooperatives* or *co-ops*, the parents "own" and administer the program. They hire a teacher and take turns volunteering in the classroom as a second staff member. Most parent co-ops throughout the 20th century used a play-based, progressive education-influenced approach.

The number of parent cooperative nursery schools grew rapidly in the 1950s and 1960s, and through the leadership of Katherine Whiteside Taylor (1982), an association was formed, Parent Cooperative Preschools International. In recent years, the number of parent cooperative preschools has declined due to the increase in families with two employed parents. Nevertheless, the movement reinforced the integral role of parents in early education.

In the previous sections, we discussed the interconnected stories of the kindergarten, progressive education, and nursery school movements. Many more outstanding leaders contributed to these efforts than we can describe briefly. Next, we turn to the history of child care in the United States, which followed a different path from that of kindergarten and preschool.

The Child Care Movement

Kindergartens and preschools grew out of child study, were focused on middle-class children, and were associated with education and development. By contrast, child care grew out of social welfare efforts for poor families and focused on the need to support working parents. Consequently, child care became associated with physical care rather than education.

In the later part of the 20th century and into the 21st century, these differences became less distinct. However, these histories still play out in public policy and attitudes. For example, federal child care funding is part of public assistance for needy families, whereas prekindergarten support comes from state education agencies. In the sections that follow, we describe some of the key events and people involved in the history of the child care movement.

McMillan Sisters Margaret McMillan (1860–1931) and Rachel McMillan (1859–1917) worked to improve the lives of young children in London and North America during the early 20th century. The purpose of their work was to offer children a temporary alternative to the dreadful living conditions in the London slums, which severely damaged the health of most poor children. Accordingly, they set up a health clinic, a nursery school (they coined the phrase) for children under age 5, and teacher training.

The McMillan sisters developed a model open-air nursery that was unique in emphasizing outdoor play, nutritious food, cleanliness, and rest to promote healthy development. The program was also educational. These centers for working families were called **day nurseries**—the forerunner of present-day child care centers.

The McMillan sisters' work was influential in the United States. Several Americans studied with them in England, including Abigail Eliot (1892–1992), who subsequently imported many of their ideas and founded one of the first nursery schools in the United States in 1922 (Liebovich, 2016).

As always happens, events in the larger context had a major impact on early childhood education, particularly on the history of child care. These included the Great Depression and World War II.

day nurseries Programs designed to serve working families in the late 19th and early 20th centuries; the forerunner of present-day child care centers.

Works Progress Administration Nurseries During the Great Depression of the 1930s, the Works Progress Administration (WPA) was established to address the high unemployment rate (25%) and to build needed public works throughout the country. One of the WPA programs established in 1933 was the Federal Emergency Relief Nursery Schools. The purpose of the **WPA nurseries**, which were open from 9 A.M. to 5 P.M., was to support the economy by providing jobs for those who worked on the site and child care to families seeking work (Nourot, 2005). Like the day nurseries of the McMillan sisters, WPA centers focused on promoting physical care and healthy living habits (Nourot, 2005). But in contrast to the McMillan sisters' vision, most WPA centers did not emphasize education.

The WPA nurseries had both positive and negative effects on early childhood education. Because day nurseries served children from poor families, the idea of expanding nursery education to all children was born (Nourot, 2005). However, the rapid expansion of WPA nursery schools meant that teachers were hired with minimal training. This cycle of expanding services without attention to ensuring qualified staff has plagued the child care field throughout its existence. As the Depression ended, so too did the WPA nursery schools. But a major national crisis—World War II—followed shortly, leading to another important chapter in the history of child care.

WPA nurseries Federal emergency relief nursery schools funded by the Works Progress Administration (WPA) during the Great Depression. Designed to support the economy by providing jobs for those who worked on the site and child care services to families seeking work.

The Lanham Act World War II necessitated full deployment of not only men into the armed services but also women into the workplace to replace the men and support industry. This massive workforce shift required immediate child care assistance, which the federal government provided in the form of the **Lanham Act** (MacKenzie, 2011). This legislation funded emergency work-site child care centers, which operated for 10 to 12 hours per day.

One of the most famous centers was located at the Kaiser Shipbuilding company in Oregon (MacKenzie, 2011). Kaiser was the largest of the Lanham Act centers, operating 24 hours a day all year long. Lois Meek Stolz was the director, and the manager was Jimmy Hymes, who later became a professor and president of NAEYC (Anderson, 2013).

Lanham Act Federal legislation to provide emergency child care and other services for families employed in the war effort during World War II.

Still considered a model, the program provided health services and nutritious meals for children and mothers, parent education, teacher training, and a play-based educational experience for children.

As happened with the WPA nurseries, the Lanham Act centers ended along with the war. Child care was no longer supported because mothers left the workforce as fathers reentered it. These high-quality centers remain an ideal for working families; yet it wasn't until the 1980s that employer-sponsored child care again became a major sector of the early childhood field.

The stories related thus far of the kindergarten, nursery school, and child care movements were lived and recorded by members of the majority group—white, European Americans. However, various groups of Americans were also part of these stories and made significant contributions to the history of early childhood education, which we discuss in the next section.

✓ Check Your Understanding 2.3

A Wider View of Early Childhood History—Contributions of African Americans, Hispanic Americans, and Native Americans

History is written by those who gain the largest amount of power. It is important to note that the previous discussion is dominated by white European Americans because they were the individuals with the most power in the society, and their work is most often included in the "official" written history of the field. At the same time, however, parallel stories were occurring among the many groups that populated the United States. That history is less well known primarily because historical sources are scarce, but also because there is a strong oral rather than written tradition in these communities (Simpson & McConnell-Farmer, 2013).

These stories deserve our attention and respect because they also have made the field of early childhood education what is it today. Here, we briefly describe historical events and contributions from the perspective of African Americans, Native Americans, and Hispanic Americans. It is essential to point out that there is huge diversity within these population groups. In fact, they are hardly groups at all except as designated by the United States Census Bureau. To further understand history from an even wider view, read the accompanying feature, *Culture Lens: Early Childhood Education through the Lens of Non-Western Culture*.

African Americans in Early Childhood History

Throughout U.S. history, African Americans have been denied power. Before slavery was abolished, it was illegal to teach enslaved people to read and write, much less attend school. Once schooling became available, it was legally segregated by race until the 1954 Supreme Court's *Brown v. Board of Education* decision banned the practice. But even after desegregation became the law of the land, equal rights and equal educational opportunity for all racial groups were still denied.

During the centuries of enslavement, a few formal, mostly religious schools provided education for African American children (Cunningham & Osborn, 1979). By the 1830s, however, such schools were prohibited. Educating enslaved people was a clandestine and

Culture Lens

Early Childhood Education through the Lens of Non-Western Culture

Ideas from non-Western, alternative histories have much to offer early childhood education practices. One contemporary scholar who has written about diverse cultural approaches to educating children is Timothy Reagan (2005). He studies views from Africa, the Aztecs, North American Indians, the Rom, Chinese Confucians, Indian Hindus and Buddhists, and Islamic traditions.

Consider the African culture in which child-rearing practices and education are based on African people's view of the relationship between the physical and spiritual reality (Mbiti, 1992). They believe that understanding children requires understanding their spiritual purpose. Before a child is born, the child is a complete spirit—in some traditions, the child is an ancestor returning. At birth, children are celebrated, and the community is expected to make room for this child's purpose in the community. Because the spirit has come home to a community, not just to a biological set of parents, it becomes a community responsibility to take care of this child (Bunseki Fu-Kiai & Lukondo-Wamba, 1988; Some, 1999).

According to Dr. Itihari Toure (C. B. Day, personal communication, December 2008):

> The view of the spirit returning for the sake of the community also informs the responsibilities for the child. Child rearing is a collective process and children in different traditions not only have specific family responsibilities but partake in various community traditions as they must retain and transmit the values of the specific community. Biological parents

and community members take care of all children. Exposure to various crafts and skills needed for the community to thrive, songs and dances that represent various stages of life, and the countless stories that recall the history of the people are part of the child-rearing experience.... When children engage in formal schooling, the motivation is not based on personal achievement alone; there is a desire to bring pride and regard to the community through the personal achievement. This perception of purpose and success comes from a consistent socialization about the value of one's family and community interdependent with the value of oneself. It is often referred to as *Ubunutu* (I am because we are; we are because I am).

Understanding how other cultures rear children brings to light a very important consideration for all educators: Every child is a product of his or her own history. Knowing that other cultures rear their children according to non-Western beliefs deepens and broadens the possibilities for educating children to their full potential in ways that may resonate with their own historical and cultural realities.

Sources: K. K. Bunseki Fu-Kiai & A. M. Lukondo-Wamba, 1988. *Kindezi: The Kongo Art of Babysitting.* New York, NY: Vantage Press; T. Reagan, 2005. *Non-Western Educational Traditions: Indigenous Approaches to Education Thought and Practice* (3rd ed.). Mahwah, NJ: Lawrence Erlbaum Associates; S. Some, 1999. *Welcoming Spirit Home: Ancient African Teachings to Celebrate Children and Community.* Novato, CA: New World Library.

dangerous operation that required courage on the part of teachers as well as students. We saw earlier how Patty Smith Hill's mother was one of those who took that risk, and what its effects were on her daughter's life choices thereafter.

African American Kindergartens and Teacher Training

After the Civil War, education became the vehicle for advancement of African Americans, propelled by national leaders such as Mary McLeod Bethune (1875–1955), who founded Bethune-Cookman College in 1904 and became an effective voice for civil rights and equal educational opportunity. Between 1865 and 1890, prominent African American institutions of higher education were founded, such as Howard University (1867), Hampton University (1868), Tuskegee University (1881), and Spelman College (1881). These and other Historically Black Colleges and Universities (HBCUs) made important contributions to the study of child development, which was then usually housed in Home Economics departments (Cunningham & Osborn, 1979).

Historically Black Colleges and Universities have played important roles in the study of child development and the education of future generations of teachers. Although not well-known, the contributions of African American early childhood educators have been significant in the field's history.

Early childhood education was seen as an important foundation for future advancement. Many HBCUs operated teacher education programs and laboratory schools (Osborn, 1991). These programs reflected the prevailing philosophies of Pestalozzi, Froebel, and later Dewey and G. Stanley Hall. By 1873, Hampton Institute (now University) in Virginia had a kindergarten teacher-training program and a children's school that was influenced by Montessori's ideas about children learning practical skills (Cunningham & Osborn, 1979). Tuskegee in Alabama offered training for parents in child-rearing methods. In the early 1900s, Howard University in Washington, D.C., awarded degrees in kindergarten education, and Atlanta University operated a Froebelian kindergarten and an elementary and high school for African American students (J. E. Hale, personal communication, February 2009).

The National Association of Colored Women (NACW) was founded in 1896. Its first president, Mary Church Terrell (1863–1954), was the daughter of enslaved parents and one of the first African American women to earn a college degree and later a master's. She was a strong supporter of early education. Under her leadership, the NACW helped establish kindergartens for African American children throughout the country (Cunningham & Osborn, 1979).

African Americans and the Nursery School Movement In 1927, five years after Abigail Eliot started the first nursery school in the United States, Dorothy Howard founded the "first Black nursery school" in Washington, D.C., to serve professional families. She operated the school for more than 50 years (Simpson, n.d., p. 262). Spelman College in Atlanta opened the first laboratory school in an African American college in 1930 under the direction of Pearlie Reed (Cunningham & Osborn, 1979). This school used the "whole-child" philosophy of the larger nursery school movement. Still in operation, the school is named for Marian Wright Edelman, founder and president of the Children's Defense Fund, the nation's premier children's advocacy organization.

From 1929 to 1969, Oneida Cockrell (1900–1970) directed the Rosenwald-Garden Apartment Nursery School and Kindergarten in Chicago (Simpson, 2012). This program became a model for children's centers in urban apartment dwellings, and also served children with disabilities early on. Cockrell participated in the White House Conference on Children and Youth in 1950, and also taught at the University of Chicago laboratory school. She was a mentor to Barbara Bowman, founder of Erikson Institute and first director of the Office of Early Learning at the U.S. Department of Education, and to other African Americans who became national leaders.

Spelman College produced many future early childhood luminaries. Its first graduate student, Ida Jones Curry, became head of teacher training at Hampton Institute in 1932 (Cunningham & Osborn, 1979). Curry worked with the McMillan sisters for a time in London, and was a leader in NANE.

Among Curry's students at Hampton was Evangeline Ward (1920–1985), who made significant contributions to the field (Simpson & McConnell-Farmer, 2013). Ward was president of NAEYC from 1970 to 1974, and was not only the first African American president of the organization but also the only president to serve two terms. In the mid-1970s, Ward was the first to take on the challenge of developing a code of ethics for the profession. She was also the first executive director of the Child Development Associate (CDA) national credentialing program.

Many other African American early childhood leaders played major roles in the field's history. Space does not permit citing all their accomplishments. At a time when their educational opportunity was severely limited, these professionals overcame huge obstacles to earn doctoral degrees at major national and international universities, to educate and mentor future generations of teachers, and to voluntarily serve in professional organizations. Their work was essential as the field expanded tremendously, and the harvest of that work is still being reaped.

Native American Early Childhood History

The native population of this country is highly diverse within and among various tribes—each with its own cultural traditions, identity, and languages—and encompassing American Indians, Alaskan Natives, Native Hawaiians, and Pacific Islanders. Today, almost half of Native Americans live in urban areas rather than on reservations. However, the history of oppression, broken treaties, and removal from native lands has had a uniformly devastating impact on our indigenous population.

Schooling for Indian Children Historically, education was part of the government's strategy of oppression and control. For example, in the 19th century, children were often removed from the reservation to attend boarding schools in which they were not allowed to wear native dress, speak their language, or practice their cultural traditions (Wortham, 2002). Schools were also established on reservations but controlled by the Bureau of Indian Affairs with the goal of assimilating native peoples into the larger society and thus suppressing their cultural identity (Wortham, 2002). Surprisingly, one exception was William N. Hailmann, superintendent of Indian Schools both on and off reservations from 1894 to 1898, who tried to implement Froebel's ideas and methods and introduced kindergarten teacher training (Lascarides & Hinitz, 2000).

In 1928, a government investigation resulted in the Meriam Report, which concluded that previous policies toward Indians had been detrimental to their health, social, and economic well-being. The report led to a shift in Indian education toward more progressive practices—connecting education to family and the values of the community, and to relevant skills and knowledge (Lascarides & Hinitz, 2000). However, schooling continued to be mostly segregated and inferior.

Federal legislation between 1965 and 1978 brought about significant change in the education of Indian children. Funds became available to public schools to better meet their needs and to provide bilingual education, enabling transmission of the culture and preservation of the languages, many of which were becoming extinct. In 1972, the Office of Indian Education of the U.S. Department of Education was established. Regulations began to require that parents and tribal leaders be involved in setting policies.

American Indian/Alaska Native Head Start Head Start had a major impact on Native communities, bringing more emphasis on early education and comprehensive services. For example, Head Start played a significant role in ensuring that Indian children with disabilities receive intervention (T. Dobrec, personal communication, August 2, 2011). Dr. James Wilson, an Oglala Sioux, worked with tribal leaders to get them to accept programs on reservations (T. Dobrec, personal communication, August 2, 2011).

Today, American Indian/Alaska Native Head Start programs are located in 26 states (Head Start, 2016). Promoting home language and cultural identity are key goals of families and tribal leaders. Some, such as the Cherokee nation, are committed to tribal language preservation, and many Pueblos have teachers who are fluent in the tribal language. But generally, language preservation is a challenge because in many situations, only a few tribal elders still speak the language, and there is no written form. Head Start and foundations such as Kellogg have been instrumental in expanding teacher preparation by providing grants to tribal colleges.

Native American Early Childhood Leaders The early education field and Native American children and families have benefited from the contributions of many key leaders. One who was particularly important in higher education was Alice Paul (1930–2005). A lifelong educator in Tucson, she was the first Tohono O'odham woman to receive a Ph.D. from the University of Arizona. She served on the faculty of the University of Arizona from 1986 through 1999 and became head of Teaching and Teacher Education. Paul helped create the Tohono O'odham Community College and served on the board of NAEYC in the 1990s.

Winona Sample (1917–2008), another important role model and national leader, was involved with Head Start from its beginning. Born on the Red Lake Chippewa reservation in Minnesota, like many Indian children, Sample had to go away to school. She became director of a large Head Start program and eventually head of Indian Health Services for the state of California. She, too, served on the NAEYC Board. In her own words, "The highlight of my life was being selected as the vice chair of the International Year of the Child (1979–1980)" (Neugebauer, 1995, p. 57).

Helen Scheirbeck (1935–2010) has been described as one of the 20th century's most significant American Indian leaders. She was an untiring advocate for American Indian civil rights, Indian children and families, Indian control of their own education, and the sovereignty of her Lumbee Tribe of North Carolina. She served as director of the Office of Indian Education, where she led efforts to pass the Indian Education Act of 1975. She was the head of the Indian Head Start Program beginning in 1991. Notably, Scheirbeck was a member of the first Board of Trustees of the Smithsonian's National Museum of the American Indian in Washington, D.C., for which she planned museum exhibitions, cultural arts programs, and educational materials.

Hispanic/Latino Early Childhood History

As with African Americans and Native Americans, the history of early education among Latinos has involved social injustices and shifting political winds. We use the term *Latino* to describe a highly diverse population with countries of origin, including Mexico, Puerto Rico, Cuba, and various Latin and South American nations. Despite recent controversies surrounding immigration, most Latinos in the United States are American citizens and were born here.

In this brief overview of history from a Latino perspective, we address the two most significant influences: bilingual education in the K–12 sector and the history of dual language programming in preschool and Head Start. Of course, the topic of bilingual education is relevant to hundreds of language groups in this country, but we discuss it here because the Spanish-speaking population of children is by far the largest group. Only Mexico has a larger population of Spanish speakers than the United States (Rumbaut, 2006). Also, the issue of bilingual education is central to the history of early education from a Latino perspective.

American schools have always served large numbers of children who speak a language other than English at home. What do you think every early childhood teacher needs to know to teach dual language learners?

K–12 Bilingual Education Perhaps because the United States has always been a nation of immigrants, bilingual education has always been an issue. As far back as the colonial era, German, French, and Scandinavian immigrants provided bilingual schools (Cerda & Hernandez, 2006). In the 1870s, William Harris, the superintendent of schools in St. Louis who helped Susan Blow found the first public kindergarten, also founded the first kindergarten taught in German to help immigrant children get a "head start" on their education (Cerda & Hernandez, 2006). By the 1920s, however, most bilingual schools were abolished and children were expected to learn only English.

Modern bilingual programs began in the 1960s. The first two-way immersion program (taught in both Spanish and English) was established in Miami in 1963. Several important court cases in the 1970s, such as the *Lau vs. Nichols* decision in California and *Aspira vs. the City of New York* on behalf of Puerto Rican children, established that meeting linguistic and cultural needs, including providing bilingual education, was essential for children to have equal educational opportunity.

The federal government has played an important albeit changing policy-setting role in this history. Consider how names have changed in the U.S. Department of Education over time. In 1973, the Office of Bilingual Education was established to implement the first national Bilingual Education Act. From 1980 to 1995, the agency was called Office of Bilingual Education and Minority Languages Affairs (OBEMLA). Eugene Garcia, a highly respected scholar and advocate for early childhood education, was a director of the agency. Another important early childhood leader, Delia Pompa, also led the agency and was an executive at National Council of La Raza, recently renamed *Unidos USA*. OBEMLA's mission included helping school districts serve "limited English proficient" children (sadly called LEPs) and administering provisions in the Elementary and Secondary Education Act that included serving preschool children.

In the 1990s, bilingual programs came under attack as being ineffective, and voters succeeded in banning them in California, Massachusetts, and Arizona. Emblematic of this political shift, OBEMLA was renamed the Office of English Language Acquisition. These laws did not apply to preschool programs but certainly had an effect on how and by whom children were taught. Despite research in support of dual language programs, strong public sentiment against them prevails. In the words of Antonia Lopez, early childhood director at the National Council of La Raza: "The history of Latinos in early childhood education is tied into the history of not being seen as fully fledged Americans" (A. Lopez, personal communication, March 30, 2012).

Preschool Level   A slightly brighter picture of Latino history has prevailed at the preschool level, with Head Start leading the way from its earliest days in support of children and families who speak languages other than English. In 1972, *The Head Start Program Performance Standards* required that programs help each child build cultural identity, and that staff speak the primary language of the children and are knowledgeable about their culture. As part of the *Strategy for Spanish-Speaking Children* in the 1970s, Head Start funded development and dissemination of four Bilingual and Bicultural Curriculum Models. These models provided an important foundation on which subsequent curricula and professional development have been built.

In 1982, the Child Development Associate (CDA) Credential Bilingual Specialization was established for candidates who have a working knowledge of two languages and to provide more well-prepared staff to work with dual language learners. In 1991, *Multicultural Principles for Head Start Programs* were developed by a cadre of professionals such as Yolanda Garcia, who provided training on the four multicultural curricula. In 1996, they were incorporated into the revision of the *Head Start Program Performance Standards*. For decades, Head Start has served migrant and seasonal workers, most of whom now are Spanish-speaking, which has stimulated much of the bureau's work on linguistically and culturally responsive resources.

Despite these positive contributions to the field, Latino children were historically underrepresented in Head Start. The prevailing view was that Latino families have a cultural preference for in-home care rather than formal programs for their children. This view, which is not supported by research, masked the reality that Latino families did not have adequate access to programs in their communities, nor were all programs culturally and linguistically responsive (M. Lopez, personal communication, January 26, 2012). However, the expansion of Head Start and increase in Early Head Start programs led to its population now being 37% Hispanic. In 2009, Yvette Sanchez Fuentes became the first Latina director of the Office of Head Start.

Latina Early Childhood Leadership   As we have seen throughout this chapter, history is primarily the story of how people impact organizations. The efforts of a small but committed group of leaders brought about real change within the early childhood establishment. Leaders such as Antonia Lopez, Amie Beckett, Mary Margarita Contie, Lily Wong Fillmore, Lourdes Diaz Soto, and Marlene Zepeda launched the Early Childhood Interest Group of the National Association of Bilingual Education. A handful of people attended its first meeting, but before long, more than 400 people flocked to their sessions (A. Lopez, personal communication, March 30, 2012). These advocates were joined by many others, including NAEYC Governing Board member Rebeca Barrera. As a result, in 1995, NAEYC adopted a position statement, *Responding to Linguistic and Cultural Diversity*, and significantly revised its position statement on developmentally appropriate practice to reflect their input. Both of these statements are being revised once again.

This chapter demonstrates that many key individuals have had a significant impact on the history of early childhood education. Table 2.1 provides a brief synopsis of the major contributions of each historical figure.

In widening the lens on the history of early childhood education to include the perspective of African Americans, Native Americans, and Latino Americans, it is apparent that Head Start has played a key role in providing services for these populations of children and families. We conclude by describing how Head Start wound all the various strands of early childhood history together.

✔ **Check Your Understanding 2.4**

How History Influenced Head Start and Early Education Today

The separate stories described previously continue to influence early education today. For example, we struggle with the large gap between preschool practices and what follows in kindergarten and primary grades. Similarly, child care and preschool continue to be divided in terms of standards, funding, and populations they serve. But over time, the

Individuals	Contribution to Early Education
John Amos Comenius	Created the first picture books to teach children in their own language
Johann Pestalozzi	Promoted object lessons—learning from direct observation and sensory experience in the natural world
Friedrich Froebel	Founder of the first Kindergarten based on the idea that children's learning is a process of unfolding from within
Maria Montessori	The image of the child as the **"absorbent mind"**—actively learning from sensory experiences in a prepared learning environment with specialized materials
Susan Blow	Founder of first public kindergartens in the U.S. and the International Kindergarten Union, follower of Froebel
John Dewey	Developed the philosophy of progressive education, child-centered integrated curriculum, connected education and democracy
Patty Smith Hill	Leader of the nursery school movement with emphasis on play and learning, founder of NAEYC, wrote *Happy Birthday*
Lucy Sprague Mitchell	Founder of Bank Street College, developed the Bank Street curriculum approach moving from the "Here and Now"
Oneida Cockrell	Established Rosenwald-Garden Apartment Nursery School and Kindergarten in Chicago, a model for children's centers in urban apartment dwellings that also served children with disabilities early on
Evangeline Ward	Only NAEYC President to serve two terms, first Director of CDA National Credential Programming, wrote first Code of Ethics for the field

stories began to converge, most notably in the national Head Start program and, more recently, in the prekindergarten movement.

Application Exercise 2.2

Table 2.1: Historical Figures and their Contributions to Early Education

The Story of Head Start

The harvest of diverse leaders' past work is still being reaped, but the work was essential as the field expanded exponentially with the launch of Head Start in the mid-1960s, which brought together the strands of early childhood history (Hinitz, 2014). The Civil Rights movement of the 1960s brought about real change in virtually every aspect of society. Early childhood education was no exception. In response to the call for equal opportunity in this country, President Lyndon Johnson launched the War on Poverty. One of the cornerstones of this effort was the Head Start program. Head Start represents a coming together of the nursery school movement, which had previously served middle-class families, and the child care movement, which originated to serve the indigent and working poor. The following sections describe how the key elements of Head Start reflect the lessons learned from early childhood history.

Video Example 2.3:

Head Start Program Components

This video illustrates the key components of a quality Head Start program. How does Head Start today reflect the lessons learned from early childhood history?

A Comprehensive Program Just like Patty Smith Hill, Maria Montessori, the McMillan sisters, and so many others, the framers of Head Start believed in serving the whole child. Early childhood education has long been a multidisciplinary field. Head Start reflects this history as a comprehensive program providing health, mental health, social services, and parent involvement in addition to education.

Head Start was also a pioneer in fully including children with disabilities, who must constitute 10% of the population served. This mandate harkens back to the lessons learned from Montessori about the benefits of early intervention. Early education for all children with disabilities is a relatively recent phenomenon. For an overview of its history, see the lens on *Including All Children: Early Childhood Special Education in Historical Perspective*.

An Educational Program The educational model for the Head Start program is the nursery school, specifically the Bank Street model (Shapiro & Nager, 1999). Over the years, Head Start's educational program has changed as new knowledge has emerged. But its core is developmentally appropriate practice, with its foundation going as far back as Comenius and Pestalozzi.

Because it was based on the laboratory nursery school model, many Head Start programs were and still are half-day. This is changing as more families need full-day child care, but Head Start has yet to completely merge the child care and nursery school threads of the field.

The rapid launch and expansion of Head Start meant that, like the WPA and Lanham Act centers, a large workforce was needed on short notice. As a result, minimal training was required for teachers. In recent years, the program has raised qualifications significantly to require bachelor's degrees, but compensation remains a challenge.

A Parent Involvement Program A core component of Head Start's mission is parent involvement. Here, we see the influence of Lucy Sprague Mitchell and Jimmy Hymes, and of the parent cooperative movement. In Head Start, however, parents are not just involved in the classroom; they are also part of the governance of the program, acting in major decision-making roles.

As part of the War on Poverty, Head Start's mandate included hiring parents as teachers and in other positions. Currently, 23% of the staff are or have been parents in the program (Head Start, 2016). As in the case of WPA nurseries, however, hiring parents has presented the challenges of ensuring that the teachers are professionally qualified, and has created the need for a professional development system.

Including All Children
Early Childhood Special Education in Historical Perspective

When I first met my neighbor Clark—a large, friendly man about my age—I was struck by his delightful sense of humor and learned of his love of fishing and television. Even a brief encounter with Clark revealed that he had an intellectual disability, but spending time with him was always great fun. One day, while reading a book on my porch, I spied Clark watching me. When I asked him to join me, he replied, "I'd like to read a book." An older neighbor who'd known Clark since he was a child later explained, "Clark started school like all the other kids, back in the mid-1950s, but after a few days, they sent him home. They said, 'It didn't work out.'" Clark never returned to school.

If Clark had been born today, he would probably be diagnosed as having mild intellectual disability. His life experience would have been quite different due to major changes in special education services. In the latter part of the 20th century, parents of children with disabilities who were unable to obtain services formed organizations such as the Association for Retarded Children (ARC) and United Cerebral Palsy, and also started preschools for the children. With the advocacy of parents, special educators, and other professionals, public laws began to change. In 1972, the government mandated that 10% of Head Start's student population be children with special needs.

By far the most important event in the history of special education was the passage of Public Law 94-142, the Education for All Handicapped Children Act of 1975, which in 1990 was renamed the Individuals with Disabilities Education Act (IDEA). This law established standards for how public schools must serve people with disabilities from ages 3 to 21. A few years later, Public Law 99-457 extended services to children from birth to 3 years of age with emphasis on the role of families in early intervention. IDEA was reauthorized in 2004 with new provisions, and new revisions to the law were proposed in 2016. In addition, the Americans with Disabilities Act (ADA) of 1990 requires that programs be accessible for persons with disabilities and prohibits child care centers from discriminating on the basis of disability.

Early childhood special education today is the result of an amalgamation of traditional K–12 special education, regular early childhood education, and compensatory education including federal programs such as Head Start that were originally designed to "compensate" for areas of need in children's lives. The history of special education goes back to well before Maria Montessori demonstrated the power of early intervention to change children's lives. It is the story of many people such as Oneida Cockrell working together to make a difference on behalf of children like Clark.

The National Laboratory An important part of Head Start's mission is to act as the national laboratory for the field. In this role, Head Start has funded seminal research and contributed to the development of curriculum and teacher training models. Head Start programs also partner with universities on research projects. In this capacity, Head Start has supplanted the child study laboratory schools of the early 20th century.

Head Start programs are locally administered and controlled. But Head Start has maintained its integrity and consistency despite its national scope because every grantee must meet the Head Start Program Performance Standards. These standards address, at least for Head Start, the recurring questions that confront the early childhood field.

The Prekindergarten Story

Leaders such as Susan Blow and Patty Smith Hill were deeply concerned about the potential negative consequences of public school involvement in kindergarten and nursery school. Some of their deepest fears have come to pass. With kindergarten an integral part of the public school system, much of the child development focus they espoused has been lost. Similarly, with the movement toward universal, voluntary preschool and more states providing funding for pre-K programs, the rigid dividing line between preschool and public education no longer exists.

On the other hand, bringing the nursery/kindergarten movements together with public education has resulted in many more children having access to early education, particularly children whose families cannot afford preschool. The movement toward state education funding of prekindergarten has also led to improved standards for teacher qualifications, compensation, and curriculum. The National Institute for Early Education Research (NIEER) at Rutgers University annually evaluates and prepares a report on the status of prekindergarten. Since the first report in 2002, significant progress has been made on the number of states providing publicly funded prekindergarten, the number of children served, and the number of standards for program quality being met (Barnett et al., 2017).

Compared to the kindergarten and child care stories, the prekindergarten story is relatively new and rapidly changing. However, if Pre-K–3rd grade curricula were aligned based on child development knowledge and comprehensive services offered for all children from birth through age 8, all the stories could be brought together in the best possible way.

Building on a Tradition of Excellence

The fundamental questions that have faced the field since its inception continue to dominate the conversation: How is quality defined in programs for children? What should be the qualifications for teachers, and how should they be prepared? What are the goals for children's learning and development? What should be the content of the curriculum, and how should it be taught?

Looking back through history, we find that many ideas are revisited: stages of development, active learning, children's interests, sensory learning, positive guidance, image of the child, the teachers' role, and the role of materials and environments. But differences emerge as well. Today, we view the teacher's role as more intentional than our predecessors did, and we no longer see children's development as a natural unfolding. Instead, we better understand the interaction of environment and biology. In addition, developmental stages are not rigid as previously assumed. Standards and approaches need to be flexible and changing—based on new knowledge—unlike Maria Montessori and Susan Blow, who refused to change their views.

The most basic history lessons that early childhood teachers should never forget include these:

- We all need to learn from children, as did all the historical figures discussed in this chapter and as Caroline Pratt wisely put it.
- We need to draw on science and the wisdom of experience, as Patty Smith Hill and Lucy Sprague Mitchell modeled for us.
- As Patty Smith Hill believed, it is always valuable to listen to opposing points of view and to learn from them.

Check Your Understanding 2.5

Revisiting the Case Study

... the Preschool Classroom

Take a moment to revisit the classroom observations of the college students in the opening vignette of this chapter. The traces of early childhood history should now be apparent. The students saw John Amos Comenius's picture books and alphabet books, evidence of Friedrich Froebel's gifts in the wooden cube and parquetry blocks, and the legacy of Maria Montessori in the child-sized furniture and sandpaper letters. They also observed children's active play with Caroline Pratt's unit blocks and Patty Smith Hill's beloved dramatic play. Their fire station field trips are reminiscent of John Dewey's call for active learning and integrated curriculum as well as Lucy Sprague Mitchell's Bank Street approach. The woodworking tables and cooking are more evidence of Dewey's influence. The evidence of children's project work reflects the inspiration of Loris Malaguzzi and Reggio Emilia's concept of the "hundred languages of children." Finally, the students saw the lasting contribution of Lucy Sprague Mitchell's writer's workshops in Margaret Wise Brown's *Goodnight Moon* and the enduring joy of singing Patty Smith Hill's "Happy Birthday" on one child's most special day. ■

2 Chapter Summary

- Studying history is valuable because it helps people understand current issues, avoid getting stuck in the past, aspire to make a difference for children, and advocate for change.

- Different periods of history have had different perspectives on children and childhood, which have implications for how children are treated and what kinds of education they are provided.

- Early education in the United States was strongly influenced by Western European ideas and leaders, such as Comenius, Pestalozzi, Froebel, Montessori, and Malaguzzi. Although European ideas are not the only educational concepts in the world, current practices strongly reflect these influences.

- The kindergarten movement in the United States was based directly on the work of Friedrich Froebel and led by Elizabeth Peabody, Susan Blow, and others who spread his ideas widely through teacher training and founding the International Kindergarten Union.

- The progressive education movement led by John Dewey had a profound impact on education in the United States, especially early childhood education,

whose principles of developmentally appropriate practice are congruent with progressive ideas.

- The nursery school movement, which grew out of the child study movement, eventually launched the wider field of early childhood education through the leadership of Patty Smith Hill and Lucy Sprague Mitchell, among many others.

- The child care movement grew out of social welfare efforts for low-income families, which focused on the need to support working parents and became associated with physical care rather than education, although this division is changing.

- African Americans, Native Americans, and Latino Americans played significant roles in the history of early childhood education, although their contributions are not well documented.

- The launch of Head Start in the mid-1960s brought together the various strands of early childhood history, which are reflected in its comprehensive services, developmentally appropriate educational program, parent involvement, and role as a national laboratory.

Key Terms

- absorbent mind
- Bank Street approach
- child-centered curriculum
- child study movement
- competent child
- constructivism
- day nurseries
- Froebel's occupations and gifts
- integrated curriculum
- Lanham Act
- nursery schools
- progressive education movement
- WPA nurseries

Flash Cards 2.1

Readings and Websites

Elkind, D. (2015). *Giants in the nursery: A biographical history of developmentally appropriate practice*. St. Paul, MN: Redleaf Press.

Giardiello, P. (2014). *Pioneers in early childhood education: The roots and legacies of Rachel and Margaret McMillan, Maria Montessori and Susan Isaacs*. New York, NY: Routledge.

Hinitz, B. F. (Ed.) (2013). *The hidden history of early childhood education*. New York, NY: Routledge.

American Montessori Society

Check this website for information about the history of Montessori and its present-day practices, professional development opportunities, and other resources.

Association for Childhood Education International (ACEI)

Originally the IKU and now a global community of advocates for children, ACEI celebrated its 125th anniversary in 2017. Visit its website to view an excellent video on the history and current reality of kindergarten.

International Froebel Society

This organization's website provides an international forum and resources to learn about the child-centered educational theory of Friedrich Froebel, founder of the kindergarten.

Shared Writing 2.1

Past is Prologue

3

Understanding and Applying Developmentally Appropriate Practice

Learning Outcomes

After studying this chapter, you should be able to:

3.1 Define developmentally appropriate practice.

3.2 Identify the behaviors of intentional teachers.

3.3 Describe how teachers make decisions about developmentally appropriate practices.

3.4 Identify the complex roles of early childhood teachers.

3.5 Apply principles of developmentally appropriate practice in planning learning environments.

3.6 Discuss research about developmentally appropriate practices.

Related NAEYC Professional Preparation Standards

The NAEYC Professional Preparation Standards (NAEYC, 2011) that apply to this chapter:

1: Promoting Child Development and Learning
    1a. Knowing and understanding young children's characteristics and needs
    1b. Knowing and understanding the multiple influences on development and learning
    1c. Using developmental knowledge to create healthy, respectful, supportive, and challenging learning environments
4: Using Developmentally Effective Approaches to Connect with Children and Families
    4a. Understanding positive relationships and supportive interactions as the foundation of their work with children
    4b. Knowing and understanding effective strategies and tools for early education
    4c. Using a broad repertoire of developmentally appropriate teaching/learning approaches
    4d. Reflecting on their own practice to promote positive outcomes for each child

Case Study

Ms. Hakuta teaches kindergarten in a college town with people from all over the world. Each year, her group is very diverse. Some children start school speaking only their home languages, while others are multilingual. Some children don't know the alphabet, while others are reading at second-grade level. This diversity of abilities and individuality is one thing she loves about her job. It is never boring.

After the children arrive, eat breakfast and clean up, Ms. Hakuta's class gathers for Morning Meeting. They sing a greeting song and discuss the plans for the day. The children take turns describing what they will do and with whom they will play. Ms. Hakuta assures that no children are left out and pairs a few for specific tasks. She asks Noah, who is a native English speaker, to feed the fish with Leah, a dual-language learner. The class has been working on a long-term project about health and the human body. This project started after Ms. Hakuta was in a car accident and broke her arm and ribs. The children became very concerned. Their teacher helped turn their concern about her into a learning experience. At the end of their meeting, Ms. Hakuta chooses Domenica to lead the deep-breathing exercises they use to calm themselves when they are feeling stressed or over-excited. After Ms. Hakuta explained that her ribs hurt when she breathes, the children wanted to learn more. During these exercises, they feel their own ribs, their beating hearts, and their breathing. They also study anatomy picture books and photos of parts of the body, and continue to examine the skeleton that the local doctor loaned the class.

After Morning Meeting, they work and play in centers individually and in small groups for 45 minutes. One group is thinking of questions to ask a nurse when he visits the class tomorrow. Another is looking carefully at the X-ray of Ms. Hakuta's broken arm. As the children work in groups, Ms. Hakuta circulates, asking probing questions to expand their thinking and introducing new vocabulary words such as *circulation* and *blood vessel*. Everett and Daria are intrigued by the use of the word "vessel" to describe veins and arteries. They make a list of all the *vessels* they can think of. Felicia, Mona, and Finn are building a hospital in the block corner. The structure is quite sophisticated, and they post a sign requesting that it be preserved. Three children are in the pretend hospital providing emergency relief to dolls and to each other. Ms. Hakuta makes notes and takes photos of the children's work products to share with their families via email and on the class website. She also puts copies into digital portfolios to track their progress.

After clean-up and snack, center time is followed by a block of time devoted to literacy. Ms. Hakuta starts the session with a 15-minute whole group lesson to teach comprehension. She reads a short book and models, asking the questions who, what, when, where, and why. During the next 45 minutes, children read or look at books individually or in small groups guided by the teacher. Ms. Hakuta also works one-on-one with children who need individual help, and a few use skills apps on the iPad.

After literacy block, there is whole group music and movement time followed by lunch and outdoor play. Because they are studying health, while outdoors the children think of different kinds of exercise to work their muscles, bones, and respiratory systems. Following lunch, they have a quiet rest time, then a 30- to 45-minute mathematics and science time, during which they once again work in centers or small groups on games, word problems, and other learning experiences. Today, they are measuring and comparing their arms, legs, feet, hands, height, and weight. The day ends with a quiet group time of reflection on what they've learned and preparation for tomorrow. They will happily return to school, because their teacher uses developmentally appropriate practices. ■

T hroughout this book and throughout your studies and work as an early childhood educator, you will hear the term *developmentally appropriate practice*. In this chapter, we discuss the evolution of this concept and examine how it is used in the classroom. We also discuss the concept of becoming an intentional teacher. Next, we address the question of how to decide what is developmentally appropriate and the multifaceted role of the early childhood teacher. We apply this decision-making process to how teachers plan appropriate learning environments and daily schedules for children. Finally, we briefly describe the research base for developmentally appropriate practice.

The concepts addressed in this chapter are part of the foundational knowledge of early childhood education. These topics provide a basic framework for organizing much of your beginning knowledge. A large body of literature exists about the science of child development and its application to early childhood practice (IOM & NRC, 2015). This chapter considers some of this literature, as well as the definition, principles, and guidelines for developmentally appropriate practice as described by the National Association for the Education of Young Children (NAEYC, 2009).

🔺 What Is Developmentally Appropriate Practice?

Over time, the phrase *developmentally appropriate practice* (often abbreviated as D.A.P.) has been defined and used in different ways. Its definition has evolved as new research and knowledge have become available.

Developmentally appropriate practice is teaching that is attuned to children's ages, experience, abilities, and interests, and that helps them attain challenging and achievable goals. The foundations of developmentally appropriate practice as it is defined today lie in the history of early childhood education. Most fundamental is the premise that teaching young children should be based on what is known about how they develop and learn optimally.

developmentally appropriate practice (D.A.P.) Ways of teaching that engage children's interests and adapt for their age, experience, and ability to help them meet challenging and achievable learning goals.

Within the field of developmental psychology, the concept of *developmentally appropriate* has been widely used for more than a century, and refers to age-related and individual and cultural human variation. Early childhood educators have long used the phrase *developmentally appropriate* to describe high-quality environments, materials, learning experiences, or expectations for children of varying ages.

NAEYC'S Position Statement on Developmentally Appropriate Practice

The concept of developmentally appropriate practice gained widespread recognition and influence in the mid-1980s when NAEYC published position statements on developmentally appropriate practice (Bredekamp, 1987). A **position statement** is a document that articulates a research-based stance that an organization is taking in response to an issue or a problem. Based on new research, emerging controversies, and the changing contexts in which early childhood education occurs, NAEYC revised its statement on developmentally appropriate practice in the mid-1990s (Bredekamp & Copple, 1997) and again in 2009 (NAEYC, 2009). Because the knowledge base continues to grow and new issues emerge, NAEYC revisited its position in 2018–2019. The current statement and related resources are available on its website. At the same time, NAEYC developed an important companion position statement on advancing equity and valuing diversity.

> **position statement** A document that articulates a stance, usually research-based, that an organization is taking in response to an issue or a problem.

NAEYC's position statement describes principles and guidelines for teaching young children from birth through age 8. NAEYC also presents recommended practices for different age groups: infants and toddlers, preschoolers, kindergartners, and children in the primary grades (Copple, Bredekamp, Korelek, & Charner, 2013a, 2013b, 2014a, 2014b). The position statement is widely used as a summary of the field's best thinking, a defense of its valued practices, and an advocacy tool for improving programs for young children.

The position statement serves several purposes. Originally, NAEYC sought to clarify the term to help professionals consistently interpret its standards for early childhood program accreditation. A second purpose that continues to be an issue was to address the issue of appropriateness of expectations for children, as well as curriculum and teaching practices. In addition, the 1997 revision brought more attention to the critical role of culture and language in development, the inclusion of children with disabilities, and the teacher's role as intentional decision maker (Bredekamp, 1997a, 1997b). The 2009 statement continued these emphases and responded to issues such as addressing the achievement gap and alignment from pre-K to grade 3.

Current Issues in Developmentally Appropriate Practice

The early childhood profession continues to raise concerns about what is developmentally appropriate as new issues arise in the lives of children. Current issues addressed in NAEYC's 2018 update include the need to address the full birth to 8 age span—especially highlighting the importance of birth to 3 years and also ensuring that the statement "speaks" to the early elementary world in order to "push up" key developmentally appropriate concepts and practices. In this context, it is especially important to emphasize that although teachers are intentional decision-makers, they do not work in isolation. They need administrators and principals who understand child development and support working collaboratively with other teachers and families.

The revised statement also emphasizes every child's strengths rather than focusing on a deficit-based perspective, which is difficult to avoid when attempting to tackle the achievement gap which is actually an educational opportunity gap. The new NAEYC statement on equity and diversity is available on its website. It stresses the negative effects of inequity and income inequality on children's long-term development and school success. In addition, the association explicitly addresses the negative impact of racism and all forms of bias. One alarming example is the research finding that children in preschool and child care centers are expelled and suspended from school at higher rates than elementary or high school children (Gilliam, 2016). Obviously, expulsion and suspension are strongly related to negative educational and life outcomes. But most troubling is the fact that stark racial and gender disparities occur. Young African American boys and girls are suspended and expelled much more frequently than other children, an indicator of implicit bias among educators (Gilliam, 2016). The threat is so great that the U.S. Department of Health and Human Services issued a policy statement to eliminate expulsion and suspension from early childhood programs.

Other issues that continue to be seriously debated include push-down curriculum and appropriate practice in the digital age.

Push-down Curriculum Perhaps the most important motivation for defining developmentally appropriate practice over the years has been to counter the trend toward **push-down curriculum**, in which content that was previously taught in first grade is being taught in kindergarten or even preschool. This was one of the original motivations for writing developmentally appropriate practice. However, the problem is even more urgent today because the trend toward increased academic focus in kindergarten has accelerated (Bassok, Latham, & Rorem, 2016). For example, in 1998, about one-third of kindergarten teachers believed that most children should learn to read in kindergarten. By 2005, 65% of teachers held this expectation (Bassok, Latham, & Rorem, 2016).

Not surprisingly, these increased academic expectations led to changes in the curriculum. Time devoted to literacy in kindergarten has increased by 25%, and social studies, science, music, art, and physical education have decreased (Bassok et al., 2016). Increased academic demands have resulted in many teachers using practices such as worksheets and

push-down curriculum Content previously taught in a higher grade that's being expected to be learned in an earlier grade.

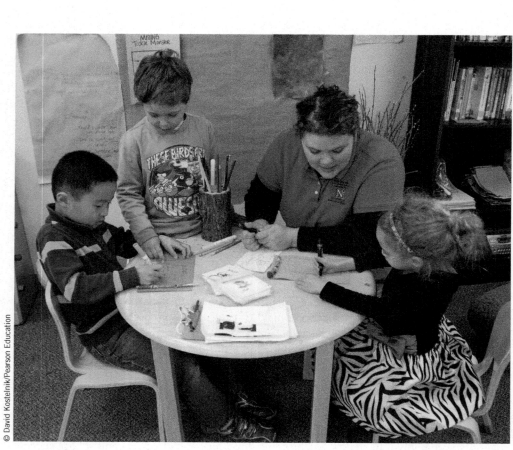

© David Kostelnik/Pearson Education

In developmentally appropriate classrooms, teachers get to know each child as an individual and build a positive relationship. What is this teacher doing to "meet children where they are" as individuals?

whole-group, didactic instruction that are not developmentally appropriate. A related trend is that young children no longer are given time or materials to play in school (Squires, 2014). As a result, increasing numbers of children are experiencing stress, being judged not ready for kindergarten, or struggling and failing in their earliest school experiences.

Push-down curriculum has been a trend for decades and is often attributed to the accountability movement, whereby teachers are held responsible if children fail to achieve certain standards. A particularly troublesome trend is the requirement in many states that children read by the end of third grade or be held back. This requirement puts additional pressure on teachers in the earlier grades, thus pushing down curriculum even more.

State Learning Standards and Testing

Another controversial issue is the impact on curriculum and teaching, especially on children, of both state learning standards and standardized testing. The *Common Core State Standards* (CCSS) have been the subject of much criticism (Common Core State Standards Initiative, 2011a, 2011b). The Common Core established national standards in English language arts and mathematics in kindergarten through grade 12 that were subsequently adopted in some form by most state departments of education. Some early childhood educators have expressed deep concern that the Common Core standards themselves are not achievable for most children in K–3, that they will lead to developmentally inappropriate teaching practices, and that they will narrow the curriculum further to the two subject areas (Carlson-Paige, McLaughlin, & Almon, 2015).

On the other hand, many of the standards call for the kind of higher-order thinking and problem solving that developmentally appropriate practices promote, and they should not automatically lead to bad teaching. The fact is that Common Core establishes standards for what children should know and be able to do, but does not address how teachers should teach. These words appear in the English language arts standards: "The use of play with young children is not specified in the Standards, but it is welcome as a valuable activity in its own right and as a way to help students meet the expectations in this document" (Common Core State Standards Initiative, 2011a, p. 6).

Nevertheless, some of the standards will be unattainable by many children in kindergarten through grade 3, especially those who have not had enriching prior experiences. Therefore, it is important that early childhood educators remain vigilant as the Common Core and any set of state learning standards are implemented and children's learning is assessed. Standards themselves are periodically reviewed, and if they are found to be unachievable for the majority of children (that is, are developmentally inappropriate), they should be revised.

Appropriate Practice in the Digital Age

One of the most frequently discussed topics in the context of developmentally appropriate practice is technology and interactive media. Some early educators are troubled by the fact that children spend too much time engaged with "screens," which takes away time from important activities such as play, outdoor time, conversations with other children and adults, and other joyful childhood experiences (Campaign for Commercial-Free Childhood, 2017).

On the other hand, technology and interactive media permeate children's lives and have demonstrated great potential to support young children's learning (Donohue & Schomburg, 2017; Donohue, 2015). Rather than simply "protecting" children from technology by limiting screen time, educators have a responsibility to promote the effective integration of high-quality, developmentally appropriate media (Donohue, 2015). Lisa Guernsey (2014), a national expert on children's media, advises that the most important considerations are the quality and appropriateness of the content on the screen, the context within which it is used (how long, under what supervision), and the age and characteristics of individual children. A major shift has been away from focusing solely on the amount of time a child spends with screens to emphasizing the quality and interactivity of the child's experience, including the engagement of parents, teachers, and other children.

The joint position statement on technology in early childhood programs by NAEYC and the Fred Rogers Center for Early Learning and Children's Media (2012) is an excellent guide for decision making in the digital age. More recently, the Fred Rogers Center and the TEC Center at Erikson Institute (2017) issued a new statement focusing on the whole child approach to using technology. The fundamental principle is that "Technology and interactive media are tools that can promote effective learning and development, within the framework of developmentally appropriate practice" (p. 5).

In short, interactive media require many professional decisions on the part of early childhood teachers and media developers to ensure they are of the highest quality and are used appropriately and effectively. In addition, we now must teach "media literacy" to help children and families become discerning and even critical consumers of apps and other interactive tools (Gee, Takeuchi, & Wartella, 2017).

Undoubtedly, other issues will arise as they have in the past. Over the years, the position statement has generated controversies, including questions about whether the recommended practices apply equally well to diverse groups of children (Dahlberg, Moss, & Pence, 2007; Graue & Delaney, 2011). In turn, new research and critiques will continue to stimulate productive discussions among early childhood educators about what is best for young children.

Developmentally Appropriate Practice in the Classroom

Developmentally appropriate practice begins with early childhood educators' knowledge of how children learn and develop. Its ultimate goal is to promote the development and enhance the learning of each child served. "Developmentally appropriate practice" is used by some as a shorthand term for the value of play or letting children be children, not pushing them to grow up too soon. Play is an integral component of developmentally appropriate practice; however, it is only one facet. To better understand how play relates to developmentally appropriate practice, read the feature *Promoting Play: Does Developmentally Appropriate Practice = Play?*

The term *developmentally appropriate practice* is used within the early childhood profession to describe the complex work of the early childhood teacher. Knowing how children learn and develop is essential for teachers of young children. The more they know about and are sensitive to the way children think and learn, the more effective their teaching and the more satisfying their work. To successfully engage in developmentally appropriate practice (Copple, Bredekamp, Koralek, & Charner, 2013b), teachers need to:

- Meet children where they are, as individuals and as a group.
- Use a variety of intentional strategies to help each child attain challenging and achievable goals that contribute to his or her ongoing development and learning.

Meet Children Where They Are Knowing what children within a given age range are generally capable of and how they learn provides teachers with a starting point for planning and organizing a program. But such a broad picture is not enough. Teachers must go beyond what is "typical"; they must recognize that they will have little success if they try to teach everyone the same way. They must also recognize that if their expectations are too high, children will become frustrated; if their expectations are too low, their students will become bored. In either case—teaching only what is "typical" or having unrealistic expectations—children will fail to make learning progress.

Good teachers continually observe children's engagement with materials, activities, and people in order to learn about each child's abilities, interests, and needs. Based on this information, they plan curriculum and adapt their teaching strategies to help children make continued progress. Meeting children where they are might look something like this:

Nathan knows only a few letters, he does not sit still during story time, and he is significantly behind on many of the kindergarten literacy goals. His teacher knows,

Promoting Play

Does Developmentally Appropriate Practice = Play?

For many early childhood educators, *play* is synonymous with *developmentally appropriate practice*. There are many reasons this is true. The primary reason is that a vast amount of research demonstrates that play is critical to healthy development and learning in the early years. To be developmentally appropriate, teaching practices *must* reflect what is known about how children develop and learn most effectively. Therefore, play *must* be an integral component of a developmentally appropriate program for young children.

But play is complex. There are many types of play that have different benefits for children, and children play differently depending on their age, level of development, and experiences. Observe how babies play, and you will notice that they tend to play with objects and explore the world using their senses—especially touch and taste. As toddlers gain mobility, their play involves their whole bodies, with running and climbing among their favorite activities. They begin to play more with toys, and occasionally with or near one other child. The preschool years are prime time for play, with children engaging in virtually every type of play both alone and with friends, such as block building, table toys, pretend, or rough-and-tumble play. Primary-grade children continue to need lots of play, including active outdoor free play, games with rules, and dramatization.

Children's play also varies with their individual interests and prior experiences. Girls and boys often gravitate toward different types of play despite the efforts of teachers and parents to discourage gender stereotyping. Some children prefer solitary play, while others take the lead in organizing a small group to build a fort or set up an airport.

Finally, children play the culture in which they live. Although children from diverse cultural groups play, the ways they play vary with the experiences and expectations of their groups. Play is a natural context for children to practice adult roles, and they mimic the activities, behaviors, and language of the adults and older children in their cultural groups. For example, in a highly technological society such as ours, children play with digital tools as well as the typical tools of daily life such as cars or microwaves.

Like all other aspects of development and learning, play varies in predictable ways by children's ages, individual characteristics, and the social and cultural contexts in which they live. To fully benefit children, teachers must intentionally promote children's play and use it to help children reach challenging and achievable goals. Developmentally appropriate practice is more than play, but play is developmentally appropriate.

however, that all kinds of transportation vehicles fascinate him. On a class visit to the library, she helps Nathan locate several information books on transportation to read with him and have him take home. He especially likes one book about all kinds of trucks. To interest Nathan in learning letters and words, his teacher prints the names of the different trucks on cards for him to match with the pictures. Soon, Nathan is drawing pictures of the trucks and trying to write the words himself.

Four-year-old Jamal speaks Arabic at home and is learning English at school. His teacher often reads to him in a small group that includes other children whose home language is not English, using books with limited vocabulary and clear correspondence between the pictures and words. She also uses other cues to aid his understanding. For instance, she uses real objects as props when she introduces new words, such as the kinds of food that the *Very Hungry Caterpillar* (Carle, 1969) is eating. She stays in close contact with his parents, communicating through a translator to learn about the competencies he demonstrates at home, and encourages the family to talk and read with him in their own language.

These examples demonstrate how teachers meet children where they are by assessing what they already know as well as learning about their interests. At the same time, teachers keep in mind the teaching goals.

Video Example 3.1:

Supporting Individual Children's Development

In this video, identify the challenging goals that the teacher has for the children. How does she intentionally use play to help them achieve those goals?

Help Children Reach Challenging and Achievable Goals

Meeting learners where they are is important, but it is just the beginning. As illustrated in the preceding examples, learning is most effective when materials or experiences not only build on what children already know and on what they can do, but also require them to stretch toward new skills and understandings.

Developmentally appropriate goals for a given group of children need to be realistic and attainable for most children within the age range of the group. However, developmentally appropriate practice does not mean making things easier for children. Instead, goals must be challenging but not so difficult that children are unable to achieve them. Further, children need to have plenty of opportunities to practice their newly acquired skills to the point of mastery. Young children often initiate such practice on their own, such as when they repeatedly count the steps they climb or try time and again to balance on one foot.

Once new skills have been mastered, children need new challenges to continue to learn. These new challenges should provide children with a reasonable stretch that is "just achievable." For example, consider a group of kindergartners learning to play catch. If the teacher consistently throws the ball way over children's heads, they will soon give up in frustration. But if she makes the task too easy—rolling the ball on the ground—most 5-year-olds will quickly grow bored and call it "baby stuff." Instead, a teacher who is taking into account what is developmentally appropriate will provide just the right amount of challenge. One child will need the ball thrown right into her extended arms, while another who has had more practice will joyfully leap to catch it over her head.

Teaching in a developmentally appropriate way brings together meeting the learner where he or she is and helping children achieve goals. Teachers keep the curriculum's learning goals in mind as they determine where children are and what the next steps forward should be. What is challenging and achievable varies from one child to the next, depending on each child's level of development; prior experiences, knowledge, and skills; and the context within which the learning takes place.

To be developmentally appropriate, teaching practices must be effective—they must *contribute* to children's ongoing development and learning. That is, if children are not learning and progressing toward important outcomes, then the practices and experiences in the program are not developmentally appropriate. To ensure their practices are in fact effective and developmentally appropriate, teachers need to be intentional in everything they do.

 Check Your Understanding 3.1

 What is Intentional Teaching?

To be effective in their work, teachers cannot leave important aspects of children's development and learning to chance. In everything early childhood teachers do—from organizing the environment and planning the curriculum to choosing specific teaching strategies or adapting their plans for individual children—effective teachers are intentional teachers. **Intentional teachers** have a purpose for their actions; they make decisions for a reason. The intentional teacher plans carefully in advance, but also has enough knowledge to make thoughtful decisions throughout the day, even during the unplanned, spontaneous "teachable moments" that inevitably arise.

intentional teachers Teachers who have a purpose for the decisions they make and can explain that purpose to others.

Developmentally appropriate teaching practices must be effective. Intentional teachers don't simply assume that play is developmentally appropriate. They support children's play so that it benefits children's development as much as possible.

Purposeful Planning

Intentional teaching and developmentally appropriate practice go hand in hand. Sometimes in early childhood classrooms where children spend significant periods of time in exploration, play, and activities that they choose and pursue independently, uninformed observers may think that the situation is "anything goes." However, if the child is in a program that truly is developmentally appropriate, teachers' intentionality undergirds the entire program and all of the experiences provided. The teacher carefully organizes the environment and selects and arranges the materials to promote children's active engagement, both mental and physical.

Video Example 3.2:

Helping Children Achieve Learning Goals

Observe how the teachers in this video engage the children in playful activities that are thoughtfully planned. What learning goals are the teachers intentionally helping the children achieve?

In planning the learning experiences, the intentional teacher thinks carefully about what will foster children's enthusiasm for learning and enable them to reach important goals in all areas of their development and learning. She regularly observes and assesses children, then uses the information gleaned to gauge her interactions with the children, both individually and in small groups, to promote ongoing learning and enable them to master new challenges.

Understand and Explain Practices

Intentional teachers are able to explain the rationale for their practices to administrators, other teachers, and family members. Intentional teachers are also alert to the need to modify plans, recognizing that there will be times when what they planned won't work out. Perhaps the children master a skill sooner than expected and lose interest in the activity; conversely, a task may be beyond the children's current abilities and they become confused or discouraged. In either case, an intentional teacher will have planned for such possibilities and be prepared to modify the learning experience or shift to another strategy that will be more effective in achieving the goal. Consider the following examples of practices, which are generally thought to be developmentally appropriate, and in light of the additional criteria of intentionality and effectiveness:

Tiana Carstairs teaches 4-year-olds. Each day, she reads a different Big Book (an oversized picture book with limited text per page) to the class. The children enjoy the readings and respond readily to Tiana's questions about the letters in print or sounds they hear. She also points out concepts of print by tracking the words on the page left to right and noting how to turn the pages. An observer in Tiana's class would probably view her practice as developmentally appropriate. What the casual observer would miss, however, is that 14 of the 16 children have mastered the print concepts that Tiana continues to teach. In addition, four children already know all the letters.

Rather than use this same teaching strategy every day without reflection, Tiana should regularly assess children's learning so that she continually adds challenges as children achieve new goals. Although the children enjoy the Big Book readings, the limited vocabulary contained in the books is not helping them learn new words. Tiana needs to be more intentional about building vocabulary in this group of children, who are already significantly behind in language development. She needs to employ effective practices, such as reading more complex stories and information books in small groups and engaging children in conversations about the readings.

Luis Gonzalez teaches in a full-day kindergarten. He believes strongly in the value of play for children's learning and development, and has been able to preserve time and materials for play in his classroom. In the early days of Luis's career, when parents or principals questioned him, he defended play by simply stating it was developmentally appropriate. But as pressures increased for literacy instruction in kindergarten, Luis found himself thinking more critically about his practice. He observed that during choice time, children's play had become repetitive. Boys built the same roads and towers in the block area. Few children engaged in dramatic play, and those who did pretended to be characters they had seen on TV or in video games. Other children wandered from one activity to another without engagement or sustained interest.

Luis realized that he didn't know enough about play; he couldn't explain clearly why it was valuable for children and didn't know how to enhance children's involvement. After attending workshops and reading professional journals, Luis became aware that there were many missed opportunities for learning in his classroom. He learned ways to help children engage in mature, sustained, sociodramatic play that builds social and emotional skills and language. He introduced board games to help children learn mathematics while cooperating and having fun.

Luis began to see that choice time provided many opportunities for him to engage in one-on-one, extended conversations with children or to build writing, reading, and math into their play. In short, Luis became intentional in his interactions with children during play and in the kind of play experiences he provided. As a result, play became a more effective teaching and learning experience for the children in his kindergarten.

Becoming an Intentional Teacher

© Monkey Business Images/Shutterstock

Easing Transitions through Developmentally Appropriate Practice

Here's What Happened In August before preschool began, I made postcards with my photo in the classroom and mailed them to the children in advance. When Olivia arrives on the first day of school, she hesitantly enters the building clutching the postcard. Her older brothers have been teasing her about how hard school is, and she is a little fearful as well as excited. Aware that several of the newly enrolled children and their families speak Spanish at home, I arranged for a translator to be present this morning. I also learned a few key phrases in Spanish, including how to introduce myself and say, "I'm sorry, I don't speak Spanish, but Ms. Lopez is here to help."

When Olivia's grandmother arrives with her, I greet her in Spanish and pull the translator into the conversation. Olivia's brothers and mother speak English, but her grandmother speaks only Spanish. Then I stoop down to Olivia's eye level, greet her warmly with a smile, and say, "I'm so happy that you are here, Olivia. We're going to have lots of fun playing, listening to stories, and making friends." Olivia takes my hand, and I escort her to a cubby with her name on it where she can store her belongings. "Would it be okay if I took a picture of you? We will print it and put it next to your name. Later, we can display a photo of your whole family on the wall with the other children's families." She shyly smiles for the camera and then asks to see herself.

"Now we're going to have some quiet play time while the children are arriving, and then we'll eat breakfast together. Your grandmother says that you like to do puzzles and read books, so I'll show you where we keep them." Olivia's eyes sparkle as she spies all the materials in the room, alighting on the iPad that two children are using to listen to a song in Spanish. She is especially delighted by the dress-up clothes, the painting easel, and the sand table. She seems to like the chairs and tables that are just her size.

Here's What I Was Thinking During the five years I've been teaching prekindergarten, I've found that the first month is usually a difficult adjustment period for many children. To smooth the transition, I decided to apply my knowledge of child development, connect with each child individually, and learn about and be responsive to their cultural background. I decided to use postcards because children today rarely receive snail mail (nor do adults, for that matter), which makes the communication more personal and meaningful. I used my photo and a picture of the classroom so they would feel more comfortable on arrival. I learned about Olivia's and the other families in advance and brought in a translator to ease communication. I wanted Olivia to know that I respect her grandmother and her family. She'll also see that when the photos are displayed. The classroom materials are at the right level for beginning preschoolers, such as the puzzles that Olivia can put together by herself.

Reflection Developmentally appropriate practices helped this teacher ensure that Olivia and the other children are already feeling comfortable on their first day of school. In what other ways did this teacher use developmentally appropriate, effective practices? What else could the teacher have done?

As we can see in the previous scenarios, intentional teachers continually reflect on their own decisions and gather evidence of how well children are doing. They may discuss their practices with colleagues and children's families. They modify their practices when they are not benefiting children. Read the feature *Becoming an Intentional Teacher: Easing Transitions through Developmentally Appropriate Practice* for an example of a teacher's actions and the thinking behind them.

Intentional teaching requires constant decision making. Next, we describe what teachers need to consider when making good decisions.

✔ **Check Your Understanding 3.2**

Developmentally Appropriate Decision Making

Teachers of young children make hundreds of decisions every day: which book to read to what size group, which questions to ask when, how to intervene with a child who is struggling to enter a play situation, and so forth. They must be able to negotiate difficult situations, such as what to do when a child shares a confidential family secret, how much support to give two boys who are trying to fairly divide blocks, and what intervention to try with a first-grader who is significantly behind in reading. The list goes on and on. Day after day and hour after hour, teachers are called on to determine what is developmentally appropriate.

In many cases, decisions are the result of careful advance consideration and planning. For example, teachers must consider what kinds of learning experiences will help the group achieve important learning goals. These decisions include planning curriculum so that the learning goals established for the group are achievable and challenging for the children. For instance, although the school district prekindergarten curriculum calls for teaching the alphabet, Ms. Jonas determines which children in her class have not yet achieved this goal and which have already mastered the alphabet. The curriculum plan as written may be appropriate for many children in the former group, but the latter group can connect letters and sounds, and use recognizable letters in their own writing.

Other decisions include setting up the physical environment, which materials to place where, how to schedule the day, or how to group children for various learning experiences. Ms. Jonas ensures that the alphabet is displayed at children's eye level as a model for children's writing, and that magnetic letters and alphabet puzzles are available for children to manipulate in their work and play. She organizes the daily schedule to ensure that children have ample time to write on their own, and during the day, she works in small groups with children who need extra help.

Some situations require teachers to make immediate decisions. For instance, suppose a dump truck pulls up outside the preschool window. The teacher may decide to interrupt his prior plans and follow the children's interest by taking them outside to observe the truck unloading the gravel for a new driveway. Or he may see that most of the children are engrossed in learning centers and decide not to interrupt. Likewise, if the story that a teacher is reading to a group doesn't hold the children's interest, she can readily switch gears and select another book or engage the children in an active song.

Primary-grade teachers must make numerous short- and long-term decisions as they support children's learning, particularly each child's reading progress. Some teaching decisions have lasting consequences for individual children. For example, identifying a child for special education services or determining a plan to work with a child who is extremely aggressive and disruptive has far-reaching consequences. When making such a decision, the teacher needs to take into consideration many sources of information, observations over time, and the diverse perspectives of family members and other professionals, such as special educators or social workers.

Make Informed Decisions

Large or small, all decisions teachers make should be informed decisions. NAEYC (2009) identifies three fundamental considerations that guide teachers in making decisions about what is developmentally appropriate for children:

1. *Consider what is known about development and learning of children within a given age range.* Having knowledge of age-related human characteristics allows teachers to make general predictions within an age range about what materials, interactions, and experiences will be safe, interesting, challenging, and within reach for children, and thus likely to best promote their learning and development. This dimension is sometimes called age appropriate.

2. *Consider what is known about each child as an individual.* Gathering information about the strengths, interests, and needs of each child in the group enables teachers to adapt and be responsive to that individual variation.

3. *Consider what is known about the social and cultural contexts in which children live.* Learning about the values, expectations, and behavioral and linguistic conventions that shape children's lives at home and in their communities allows teachers to create learning environments and experiences that are meaningful, relevant, and respectful of all children and their families.

Considering all this information is important, because it reflects what we know about how children develop. At each age, they share characteristics with other people within that age range but also develop as individuals and as members of cultural groups whose values and beliefs shape how their development occurs. Figure 3.1 depicts this model of child development.

In each of these three areas, the knowledge to be considered is substantial and changes over time. Intentional teachers make sure to stay informed both through ongoing professional development, which includes gaining information from new research, and through those avenues that will provide necessary information about the children they teach, their families, and their communities. Let's examine each of these areas more closely and see what each contributes to the decisions teachers make.

Consider What Is Known about Child Development and Learning

During early childhood, it is possible to make relatively accurate predictions about children's capabilities based on age ranges. Babies need constant care and careful supervision

> **age appropriate** Age-related human characteristics that allow teachers to make general predictions within an age range about what materials, interactions, and experiences will be safe, interesting, challenging, and within reach for children, and thus likely to best promote their learning and development.

✓ **Application Exercise 3.1**

Figure 3.1: Model of Child Development

- Unique
  - Individual abilities, strengths, needs
  - Personality, interests
- Predictable
  - Similar to children of same age
  - Predictable expectations
- Context
  - Values of cultural group
  - Community influence

© Monkey Business Images/Shutterstock

FIGURE 3.1 Model of Child Development This model illustrates the three core considerations of developmentally appropriate practice—child development in general, individual variation, and social and cultural contexts.

because they put everything in their mouths. Two-year-olds who have mastered walking waste no time in running head-long into furniture and walls. Preschoolers are fairly good communicators but need help expanding their vocabulary. Primary-grade children are reasonably independent learners when motivated by the topic or activity.

Adults—especially parents, family members, and teachers—consider what is developmentally appropriate every day without necessarily recognizing it. For instance, when selecting a toy for 2-year-old Hudson, his aunt chooses a schoolhouse with a handle for carrying. The toy has a label that indicates there are no small parts that can be swallowed. She determines that the toy is manageable for most toddlers whose fine motor skills are limited, so they are unlikely to become frustrated. Because the toy is age appropriate, it should hold Hudson's interest. Like most 2-year-olds, Hudson is beginning to engage in pretend play and also loves to carry his toys around with him. At other times, adults fail to recognize what is inappropriate, as when competitive soccer leagues for 4-year-olds are organized.

Some characteristics that young children typically demonstrate are common knowledge. For example, when a young panda cub makes his media debut, reporters observe that he behaves "like a toddler." Readers immediately get the picture even without the description—"He squirmed in the arms of his keepers, climbed and tumbled over a rock pile, and walked through a small stream. He also showed a penchant for putting things in his mouth" (Barker, 2005).

Knowing age-related characteristics helps guide teachers' expectations of children's behavior and abilities, the organization of the environment, and the materials provided. They also guide teachers' planning and affect their interactions with children. One example of age-appropriate interaction is how parents, teachers, grandparents, friends, older children, and even strangers talk to babies differently from how they do to each other. All over the world, people speak to babies in a high-pitched, repetitive voice called *motherese* or *parentese,* which infants consistently prefer hearing (Matychuk, 2005). Hearing the exaggerated sounds of *parentese* apparently makes it easier for babies to learn the sounds of their own language, and is emotionally engaging.

Consider What Is Individually Appropriate

One of the most basic principles of child development is that there are individual differences. In fact, children demonstrate a wide range of variability across every area of development—physical, cognitive, social, and emotional—while remaining within the range of "typical" development.

The development of some children falls beyond the range of what's predictable in one aspect or another. For example, in some respects, children with disabilities or developmental delays and children who are gifted add further diversity to the range of individual differences. A developmentally appropriate program accommodates individual variation. The feature *Including All Children: Developmentally Appropriate Practice and Children with Disabilities* illustrates this point.

Because children's needs, interests, and abilities differ as they grow and change, a developmentally appropriate environment for babies and toddlers looks very different from one for preschoolers or primary-grade children.

 Application Exercise 3.2
Age-Appropriate Environments

Including All Children
Developmentally Appropriate Practice and Children with Disabilities

People sometimes wonder if developmentally appropriate practices are effective for children with disabilities. The fact is that the basic elements of developmentally appropriate practice are necessary for inclusion to succeed. Consider the following example:

Isaac is 4 years old and has a diagnosis of autism. He is sitting on a brightly colored carpet square between two of his preschool peers at circle time. His teacher is reading a book the class made called *Friends, Friends, Who Do You See?* It is adapted from *Brown Bear, Brown Bear* (Martin, 1996), but features pictures of the children in the class paired with their names. Isaac loves the book, and reads along with the teacher. As the teacher reads each child's name in the story, he or she stands up and moves. After the story, it is time for singing. Isaac knows this because circle time happens in a similar routine each day.

The teacher pulls out a "song chart" featuring the pictures and titles of eight songs. One song is about a train. Isaac loves trains, and seems eager to hear the new song. He points to the "Trains on the track." The teacher helps Isaac remove the song card. Isaac holds the card while the children sing. Then Isaac makes the sign for "play" with his hands. The teacher says, "Yes, Isaac, it is time for centers." She lets Isaac choose a center first, because she knows it is hard for him to wait. Isaac brings the teacher the song card and points to the picture of the water table. His teacher models, "I want to play at the...." Isaac says, "Water table." His teacher, proud of Isaac's increasing verbal skills, gives him a hug and says, "Off you go to the water table." When Isaac's mother picks him up from school, his teacher describes how often he used his words and which friends he played with during center time.

By contrast, when children with disabilities are included in programs that are *not* developmentally appropriate, it becomes difficult for the child with special needs—indeed, for all the children—to make meaningful progress. Compare this child's experience to Isaac's:

Tara, also a 4-year-old with autism, is sitting next to her teacher at circle time. The teacher is reading from a small-sized book, and many of the children cannot see the pictures very well, including Tara. Circle time has been in progress for over 20 minutes,

and many of the children are getting restless. Tara begins rocking back and forth and looking at the door. Without warning, the teacher stops reading the book and tells the children to stand up for a finger play. Tara bolts from the circle and runs to the water table. She begins splashing and yelling. The teacher stops and asks Tara to return to the circle. When Tara does not return on her own volition, the assistant teacher physically moves her back to the circle, and a 10-minute struggle ensues. When Tara's father comes to pick her up, the teacher describes "her bad day" and asks him to talk to Tara about listening at school.

A child with a disability acts like a magnifying glass on the developmental appropriateness of an early childhood program. As is clear from Isaac's case and by contrast Tara's experience, developmentally appropriate practice provides the necessary foundation for his successful inclusion in the program. But individually appropriate adaptations are also essential for children with disabilities and other special needs.

The term individually appropriate refers to teachers using what they know about the personality, strengths, interests, and abilities of each individual child in the group to adapt for and be responsive to individual variation. Consider, for instance, two tricycle riders: The fearless rider may need more careful supervision to prevent injury, while the warier child may need extra encouragement and support to develop his large motor skills. Similarly, some children will need enriched experiences to accelerate their language development, while a few may need individual support to continue to build on their precocious reading ability. A withdrawn, timid child may need a great deal of emotional support to cope with life's challenges, while another may need help controlling aggression to make friends.

With the individual differences that exist, teachers clearly cannot expect all children in a group to learn the same thing in the same way at the same time. Even when the teacher introduces a concept or reads a book to a whole group, each child will take away something different from the learning experience. Therefore, to help children progress, teachers must continually keep track of what children know and are able to do, what they are struggling with, and what is engaging their interest and meets their needs.

Consider Children's Social and Cultural Contexts All learning and development occur in and are influenced by social and cultural contexts (Bronfenbrenner, 2004). In fact, *appropriate behavior* is always culturally defined. The cultural contexts in which a child grows up begin with the family and extend to include the cultural group or groups with which the family identifies. Culture refers to the behaviors, values, and beliefs that a group shares and passes on from one generation to the next. Because children share their cultural context with members of their group, cultural differences are differences between groups rather than individuals. Therefore, cultural variation needs to be considered as well as individual variation in deciding what is developmentally appropriate.

Children learn the values, beliefs, expectations, and habitual patterns of behavior of the social and cultural contexts in their lives. Cultural groups, for example, have characteristic ways of showing respect; there may be different rules for how to properly greet an older or younger person, a friend, or a stranger. Attitudes about time and personal space vary among cultures, as do the ways to take care of a baby and dress for different occasions. In fact, most of our experiences are filtered through the lenses of our cultural group. We typically learn cultural rules very early and very deeply, so they are not part of our conscious thought.

Social contexts of young children's lives differ in ways such as these: Is the child growing up in a large family, or in a family of one or two children? In a single-parent family, a two-parent family, with same-sex parents, or in a household that includes extended family members? In an urban, suburban, or rural setting? Has the child been in group care from a young age, or is this the first time in a group program? What social and economic resources are available to the family? All of these situations frame the social context and impact children's lives in unique ways.

For young children, what makes sense and how they respond to new experiences are fundamentally shaped by the social and cultural contexts to which they have become accustomed. To ensure that learning experiences are meaningful, relevant, and respectful to children and their families—that is, for those experiences to be **culturally appropriate** or *culturally responsive*—teachers must have some knowledge of the social and cultural contexts in which children live. Such knowledge helps teachers build on children's prior experiences and learning so that they can help children progress.

All young children must adjust when they move from the security and familiarity of their homes into schools or early childhood programs. The challenge is greatest, however, for children whose cultural experiences at home differ sharply from those predominating at the school or program. For these children, the transition can be confusing and frightening. Consider a Native American child, whose culture expects children to quietly listen and observe adults, entering a classroom where the teacher expects everyone to speak up. Think of how you feel, at least for a moment, when people around you are speaking a language you don't understand. Even as adults with all our coping mechanisms intact, we tend to feel uncertain, ignorant, and uncomfortable in environments different from those to which we are accustomed. (Are they talking about us?)

For teachers, being responsive to all social and cultural variation can be challenging. Our own cultural experience is so integral to us that we are rarely aware of it. If we are in the position of power as a teacher, we must be especially careful to be aware of and respectful toward those whose cultural backgrounds and accepted rules for behavior may be different from ours. Most important, we must be careful not to assume that our own cultural perspective is superior and make negative judgments based on our cultural variations. An example illustrates the potentially damaging result of such judgments:

> A European American teacher is employed in a school serving a predominantly African American community. One of her principal teaching strategies is questioning. But she finds that her questions are often met with blank stares or disdain from the children, and she assumes they don't know the answers. She doesn't realize that within their cultural community, people rarely ask questions to which they already know the answers.

individually appropriate Information about the strengths, interests, abilities, and needs of each individual child in a group that enables teachers to adapt to and be responsive to individual variation.

culturally appropriate Applying knowledge of the social and cultural contexts in which children live, which helps teachers build on children's prior knowledge and make experiences meaningful and responsive.

Culture Lens
The Role of Culture in Development

Take a moment to think about what you understand about culture. Do you tend to think about culture only as characteristic of children and families who are "culturally different"? Does the concept of culture apply only to some children? Actually, it is important to remember that *every* child is socialized in a cultural group, and that the most important elements influencing children's development are really aspects of their cultural experiences, which are often the hardest to observe.

What people sometimes think of as "cultural" are the products that culture produces, such as dress or holiday celebrations. These are the surface features of culture. But culture produces more indiscernible behaviors and attitudes that emerge from the same set of rules as the surface features of culture. These deep structural aspects of culture act as much more powerful influences on children's development than the surface features do. For example, if the cultural group believes that women should not be seen by men except for those in the immediate family, a woman's mode of dress will reflect this value. At the same time, this cultural belief will have much farther-reaching effects on her behavior and life choices than simply how she dresses. Consider an example in an early childhood classroom:

It is circle time in kindergarten, and the children are supposed to bring an object from home that has writing on it. Most of the children eagerly seek their turn, waving their hands widely, and showing off how well they can read the words. Jai has brought something, but is not eager to share. The teacher assumes he can't read the words, so she doesn't call on him.

As in all developmental domains, culture influences the expression of emotions. Although emotions such as fear, anger, and happiness are part of human interaction in all cultural groups, variations emerge in the way they are expressed. Jai, who is from India, is from a cultural group that avoids drawing too much attention to individuals or expressing emotions too openly. Children from other, more individualistic cultures such as the United States' are generally encouraged to express their feelings openly. These cultural differences account for Jai's behavior and that of the other children in his class more than their reading abilities do.

Cultural differences do not mean one way is right and the others wrong. They simply demonstrate that there is a wide variety of developmental patterns that can be explained best by understanding the cultural context in which development occurs.

To better accommodate the realities of cultural and linguistic diversity in schools and early childhood programs, teachers today need to work at being especially sensitive and responsive to the perspectives of children and their families that may be different from their own. To broaden your own perspective, read the feature *Culture Lens: The Role of Culture in Development*.

Consider All You Know When Making Decisions

The three considerations that teachers must take into account when making decisions—knowledge about children's learning and development, information about individual children, and information about the social and cultural contexts of children's lives—should not be viewed in isolation. All three considerations, in fact, interact with and influence each other; they are always intertwined in shaping children's development and behavior.

For example, children all over the world follow a similar developmental pattern when learning language. They progress from cooing, to babbling, to one-word utterances, to telegraphic speech ("Daddy up"), to short sentences, and finally to more complex sentences. However, a wide range of individual variation exists in language acquisition of children who are roughly the same age because of differences in language experience as well as developmental variation. At age 3, Joey speaks in three-word utterances, whereas his same-age cousin, Michael, expounds in paragraphs. Finally, each child speaks the language, including the dialect, of his or her own cultural group. Six-year-old Amelia speaks

English to her mother and Spanish to her father. All of these factors influence children's language development and how teachers think about supporting it optimally for all children.

Now let's look at how the meshing of the three considerations plays out in the decisions of one primary grade teacher:

> Frida Salzman has 22 children in her first-grade class. Her first challenge each year is to get to know the children well. She meets with their families, engages in one-on-one conversations with children, observes their behavior and skills throughout the day, and sets up specific tasks to evaluate their skills, such as literacy tasks or solving math problems with counters.
>
> As she gets to know her students, she regularly assesses their abilities and interests in relation to what she knows from her study of child development, the curriculum goals, and her experiences teaching other 6- and 7-year-olds. She finds that a few children exceed her expectations in reading or social skills, whereas others are significantly behind their peers in some areas. Each child has a unique personality and profile of abilities, and Frida becomes more aware of these.
>
> Neela has Down syndrome, and Frida has already met with her parents and the team of special education professionals who create and implement an individualized educational plan for her. After a few weeks, Frida becomes concerned that another child, Almonzo, might have an undiagnosed language delay. In the case of the six children whose home languages are not ones Frida knows, she recognizes that she must take extra steps to find out about them. Using community volunteers and, in one case, a paid translator, Frida connects with the families of her students to build relationships and learn what capabilities the children exhibit in their homes and communities.

We see that in meeting the children, Frida seamlessly draws on her knowledge of child development and learning, as well as her knowledge of them as individuals and members of cultural groups. Precisely because children are so different and their abilities vary so greatly, Frida will need to draw from a wide repertoire of teaching strategies to help them achieve developmentally appropriate goals.

So far, we have described the areas of knowledge that teachers consider in making decisions about developmentally appropriate practice—what teachers need to know and think about. Now we turn to the work of the teachers—what do early childhood teachers do? What are the dimensions of practice that describe the teacher's role?

© Pearson Education

Video Example 3.3:

Identifying Developmentally Appropriate Practice

In this video, Sue Bredekamp explains how to identify developmentally appropriate practices keeping the three considerations in mind. What other teaching practices generally appropriate for an age group might need to be modified considering individual and cultural variation of children?

✔ Check Your Understanding 3.3

🔺 The Complex Role of the Teacher

According to the NAEYC's (2009) guidelines for developmentally appropriate practice, the complex job of an early childhood teacher has five interrelated dimensions: (1) creating a caring community of learners, (2) teaching to enhance learning and development, (3) planning curriculum to achieve important goals, (4) assessing children's learning and development, and (5) establishing reciprocal relationships with families. One way to remember these dimensions is to visualize the five points of a star, as depicted in Figure 3.2. Each of the five points is necessary for the star to be complete, and they are all interrelated—take one away, and the figure is no longer a star.

It may be helpful, in fact, to think of it as a "mariner's star." Seafaring people use the stars to guide their way, but without considerable knowledge of the stars' positioning and

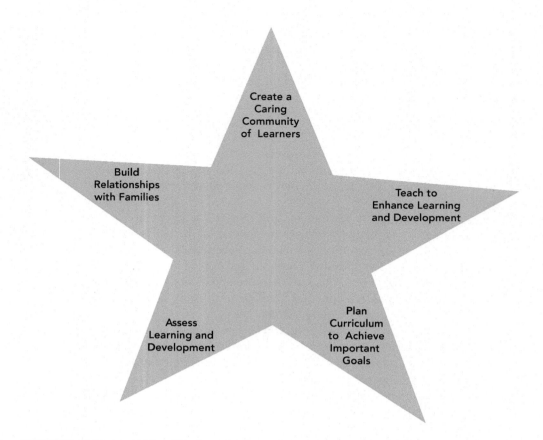

FIGURE 3.2 Mariner's Star: The Complex Role of the Teacher The image of the mariner's star illustrates how the teacher's many roles are integrally connected.

Source: Adapted from C. Copple & S. Bredekamp, 2006. *Basics of Developmentally Appropriate Practice: An Introduction for Teachers of Children 3 to 6*, p. 24. Washington, DC: NAEYC. Reprinted with permission from the National Association for the Education of Young Children.

their relation to navigation, mindlessly following a star won't lead to a destination. So it is with the mariner's star of early childhood teaching. Each of the star's points links to a set of guidelines that represent a large body of knowledge about early childhood education. Just as the stars guide seafaring people, the mariner's star helps guide teachers' professional behavior, but without that strong foundation of knowledge, the guidelines themselves have little meaning.

In the following sections, we introduce each aspect of the teacher's role in accordance with NAEYC's guidelines for developmentally appropriate practice. Each of these aspects of the teacher's role is described in later chapters.

Create a Caring Community of Learners

caring community of
learners A group or classroom
in which children and adults
engage in warm, positive
relationships, treat each other
with respect, and learn from and
with each other.

An early childhood setting—whether it serves infants and toddlers, preschoolers, kindergartners, or second-graders—needs to be a caring community of learners. The term caring community of learners incorporates several key ideas that characterize early childhood education: (1) Children's care and education are equally important; (2) children learn through positive relationships with adults and other children; and (3) the learning context matters—the indoor and outdoor environments, how the environments are organized, and the materials and equipment that they contain.

Children learn when they feel safe and cared for. They thrive in an environment in which they see positive images that reflect their own identities, such as photos of themselves and their families; where they see their own contributions to the community; and when they see their own work displayed. They also see examples throughout the community that reinforce their cultural identities. The messages are clear to each child: You belong here. We care about and support each other. You have important things to contribute to this group. You will thrive here.

The foundation of young children's learning is in positive relationships with other people who are responsive to them. At the same time, the early childhood setting is a learning community in which adults and children learn with and from each other. Each child's thinking can build on or challenge that of another. When Josué tells Willa she can't be the doctor because she's a girl, Willa promptly informs him, "I go to Dr. Ashai, and she's a lady, so there." Josué has to adjust his concept of *doctor* to include women as well as men.

In a caring community, children acquire the ability to regulate their own emotions and behavior and to make friends. Teachers actively teach children social and emotional skills and engage in individualized interventions for children who persistently demonstrate challenging behaviors, such as aggression.

© Pearson Education

Video Example 3.4:

Creating a Caring Community of Learners

In this video of an infant-toddler teacher, how does she foster warm and caring relationships among the infants and toddlers? How is she creating a caring community of learners for these very young children?

Teach to Enhance Learning and Development

Teaching seems the most obvious aspect of the teacher's role, but it isn't simple at all. Early childhood teachers typically do not conform to the images that come to mind for many adults when they think of "teaching"—the teacher standing in front of a blackboard or at a podium lecturing. Teaching simply looks different in the early childhood setting, and it takes many forms.

Effective early childhood teachers know the children in their groups very well. They thoughtfully plan the learning experiences and environment with these children in mind while also keeping in mind the learning goals. They use a variety of teaching strategies to help each child develop and learn. And they guide young children to become socially responsible, self-regulating, contributing members of the community.

© FatCamera/Vetta/Getty Images

Intentional teachers use every possible opportunity to promote children's learning, including preplanned small group lessons and conversations throughout the day.

Teachers also use various learning contexts such as teacher-guided group work, including large-group and small-group preplanned experiences, and periods of play and engagement in which children primarily guide their own activity with the support of teachers (IOM & NRC, 2015; Epstein, 2014). Teachers use various ways of grouping children for learning; they may gather a reading group of similar ability level or organize a group of children with different language abilities to work together on a project. Teachers' behaviors need to vary with the setting as well. In addition, routines such as eating meals and transitioning from one place or activity to another are all potentially valuable learning contexts if teachers use these activities as opportunities for one-on-one conversations with children or to reinforce a learning goal through singing a song or reciting a poem.

Plan Curriculum to Achieve Important Goals

curriculum A written plan that describes the goals for children's learning and development, and the learning experiences, materials, and teaching strategies that are used to help children achieve those goals.

If developmentally appropriate practice tends to focus on the *how* of teaching, then curriculum is the *what*—the content that children are expected to learn. A curriculum is a written plan that describes the knowledge and skills to be taught in the educational program and the learning experiences through which teaching takes place (Copple & Bredekamp, 2006, p. 61).

Currently, there is increased demand for evidence-based curriculum based on research about important learning goals that predict later achievement, the sequences in which concepts and skills build on each other, and the teaching strategies that have proven effective. Whatever the process through which a curriculum is selected, developed, or planned, to be effective, it must be implemented with attention to individual differences and cultural variation among children.

evidence-based curriculum Derives from research evidence about what kinds of learning outcomes relate to later achievement, and what types of teaching and learning experiences help children acquire those outcomes.

Good curriculum, whether published resources used in school districts or teacher-developed, offers teachers flexibility and ways of adapting, often providing many more suggested activities or materials than teachers could possibly use. Thus, they have many more decisions to make. Teachers need to be very familiar with the curriculum plan, especially the key learning and development outcomes for children—that is, what children should know and be able to do as a result of their participation in this program.

Assess Children's Development and Learning

assessment The ongoing process of gathering evidence of children's learning and development, then organizing and interpreting the information to make informed decisions about instructional practice.

In the current era of educational accountability, assessment is often a controversial topic. However, it is an integral component of developmentally appropriate practice. Assessment is the process of observing and documenting the work children do and how they do it as the basis for a variety of educational decisions. Assessment is important because teachers must draw on assessment information about individual children in an ongoing, systematic process to understand children's learning and development.

Children, especially very young children, are moving targets. What they can't do today, they can do tomorrow. What they didn't know or understand yesterday may gradually become clear, or they may have an "Aha!" moment of recognition. Their development may follow a predictable though somewhat slower trajectory in one area, or they may be in need of intervention for a serious developmental delay. To address any of these situations, teachers must use appropriate, accurate tools to assess children.

Each decision that teachers make about children has consequences. The more important and lasting the consequence, the more vital it is that the decision is based on multiple sources of information, including information from parents.

Build Collaborative Partnerships with Families and Communities

reciprocal relationship A two-way relationship in which information and power are shared evenly.

Young children do not come with résumés; they come with families. In effective programs, teachers and families work collaboratively as partners in children's care and education. NAEYC (2009) guidelines emphasize the importance of teachers and administrators developing reciprocal relationships with children's families. *Reciprocal* refers to a two-way relationship in which information and power are shared evenly. Such a relationship is based on mutual respect, trust, cooperation, and shared responsibility. A reciprocal relationship requires regular open communication and a willingness to negotiate differences toward shared goals.

We've already seen that to teach young children effectively, teachers must get to know each child well. The younger the child, the more teachers must rely on family members as key informants about the child's competencies, interests, needs, and cultural experiences. Young children's competencies are not always apparent, especially if they have been acquired in a cultural context different from that of the teacher. For example, a child may know colors and basic shapes and be able to count up to 20 in Russian, yet demonstrate none of this knowledge in English at school. Through a relationship with the parents, however, his teacher can ascertain that she needs to help the child learn the English words for concepts he already knows rather than teach these concepts. This allows both the teacher and child the opportunity to use what he already knows and move on to other important concepts more efficiently.

The Teacher's Role in Context

In each aspect of their work—whether creating a caring community, teaching, planning curriculum, assessing, or working with families—teachers must draw on a broad base of information to make useful decisions. The following example illustrates how the five dimensions of the teacher's role come together during a memorable experience for a beginning teacher:

> Scotty's teacher, Gina, believes he is the "bad boy" in his preschool class. Gina feels she is constantly correcting what he has done wrong. One day, a fight breaks out in the block corner and a chorus of voices arises, shouting, "Scotty did it!" Gina sighs, not surprised by these events, until she remembers that Scotty isn't there that day. She realizes that her focus on Scotty's misdeeds has made him the "bad boy" in everyone's eyes.
>
> Her realization forces Gina to reflect on her own and Scotty's behavior. She realizes that she doesn't really know Scotty, and spends time systematically observing him. Soon she discovers strengths on which she can help him build, such as his exceptional fine motor skills, and comes to see that there is much Scotty can do well. She gives him opportunities to use these skills (she allows him to cut up the oranges for snack under her supervision), and finally catches him doing something right for a change. Gina also meets with Scotty's mother so that together they can begin to focus on his positive behavior rather than his missteps. Gradually, Gina notices that Scotty's behavior improves. As a result, both Gina and Scotty's mother begin to enjoy him more. With more support and a sense of accomplishment, he makes friends with several other children.

Scotty's teacher wasn't named Gina. I was actually his teacher, and I learned a lot about developmentally appropriate practice from this firsthand experience. In making professional decisions, teachers should always consider strategies to broaden their own perspective, as illustrated by Scotty's situation. They need to take into consideration as many points of view as possible—to "widen the lens" with which they see children, their families, and the educational process.

Widening the Lens: Moving from *Either/Or* to *Both/ And* Thinking

Questions of educational practices in the United States are often dichotomized as either/or choices. Is phonics *or* vocabulary more important in learning to read? Should preschool stress social-emotional development *or* cognitive development? Should early childhood programs provide child-initiated *or* teacher-directed experiences? These either/or choices oversimplify the complex processes of becoming literate or developing the whole child. Either/or thinking assumes there is one right answer to a complex question. Instead, children would be better served and educators more effective if the questions were addressed with *both/and* thinking. Both/and thinking rejects simplistic answers to complex questions, and requires diverse perspectives and several possible answers to be considered.

To avoid either/or thinking, it is useful to use the analogy of *widening the lens*. Think of yourself as holding a camera and altering the view by adjusting the lens. Depending on how you adjust the lens, your view, and therefore your perspective, changes. You might zoom in on one child's expression, or you might zoom out to see the whole room arrangement. If you use a video camera, you could gain more information about the context over time, perhaps including the child's friends, extended family, or community. In fact, to engage in developmentally appropriate decision making, teachers must indeed widen their views. Just as the camera lens adjusts to display different views, teachers allow their minds to expand and accommodate several ideas at once.

As we have discussed, children of similar ages are *both* alike *and* different. Likewise, children of the same cultural group share some characteristics but not all. When you widen the lens, you will find that your view broadens and you can incorporate more information. As a result, you are less likely to get stuck in either/or thinking. When you widen the lens through which you look at children, the curriculum, teaching practices, assessment, and families—all aspects of your work—you begin to recognize the complexity and interrelationships among the principles that guide early childhood practice.

When teachers are willing to look beyond the views they have held, they enhance their effectiveness in their work with children and families. Consider the following example that demonstrates the power of widening the lens:

> Ms. Grantham is the director of a Head Start program. Several parents complain to her that they aren't seeing worksheets or similar products that show their children's learning coming home in backpacks or displayed in the classroom. Her program doesn't use worksheets because their philosophy of developmentally appropriate practice is based on children's active engagement. Ms. Grantham believes worksheets are just busy work for children and don't really teach them anything.
>
> At first, she thinks the parents are just uninformed about good early childhood education. But she asks a few more questions to better understand their perspective. Ms. Grantham comes to see that both she and the parents want the children to succeed—in the wider view, they are in agreement. And what the families are asking for is evidence that the children are in fact learning and on track to succeed in school.
>
> Reflecting on the parents' legitimate desire, Mrs. Grantham realizes that she could do a much better job of sharing with the families concrete samples of the children's work that show what they are learning and how they are thinking. She explains that worksheets are not effective because instead of active learning, they simply call for right answers ("circle the 4") and busy work, such as coloring. Worksheets are more like testing than learning. She begins to collect portfolios of children's drawings and writing, transcripts of their language, and photos of their project work, and meets with families regularly. She displays the children's work, describes what they have learned and will be learning next, and what she and the teachers are doing to help build the children's skills and knowledge. Along with the children, Mrs. Grantham develops a class website through which they communicate to families about their work in progress.

Now it's your turn. What do you see when you widen your lens? Try to think of several examples where widening the lens would help you be a better teacher or improve your relationships with family members, college professors, or work colleagues. For an example of the effectiveness of *both/and* thinking, read the feature *What Works: Rigorous Developmentally Appropriate Practice*.

What Works

Rigorous Developmentally Appropriate Practice

One issue that is often presented as an *either/or* choice is developmentally appropriate practice *vs.* academics. As with other false dichotomies, a *both/and* perspective is much more useful and accurate. In fact, several early childhood educators have begun to use the term "*rigorous developmentally appropriate practice*" to emphasize that good teaching based on child development also promotes children's achievement of important academic goals.

For example, when preschoolers "play" with various materials in the water table, they learn scientific concepts about the properties of water and ways to conduct experiments. With a teacher's support and language interaction, they learn vocabulary that provides background knowledge to achieve science standards in primary grades. The children develop social skills as they discuss their observations. Self-regulation is required to ensure that water is contained and that toys are shared. The teacher and the children may write down their observations, thus developing literacy skills. These and many other academic standards can be met by this favorite activity of young children.

Similarly, in kindergarten and the primary grades, where academic expectations for literacy and mathematics become more rigorous, developmentally appropriate teaching is more effective than long periods of whole-group instruction or worksheets. *Rigor* in this sense doesn't mean harsh or harder. Instead, in rigorous developmentally appropriate classrooms, children engage in interesting projects, work on teams, take initiative, learn from trial and error, solve problems, think critically, and persist at tasks. These important executive functions and social-emotional abilities are developed as they learn challenging content. And these 21st-century skills are essential for success in the future.

Sources: C. P. Brown, B. S. Feger, & B. Mowry, 2015. Helping others understand academic rigor in teachers' developmentally appropriate practices. *Young Children*, *70*(4), 62–69; V. Costanza, K. Northey, & S. Riley-Ayers, 2017. Academic rigor and DAP: Implementing high-quality teaching practices in K–3. Paper presented at annual conference of the National Association for the Education of Young Children, Atlanta, GA.

Now that we have defined developmentally appropriate practice and described the teacher's role, we turn to a discussion of how the environment impacts children's learning and development.

✓ Check Your Understanding 3.4

Developmentally Appropriate Learning Environments

How the learning environment and children's daily schedules are organized are the most obvious indicators of whether a program is developmentally appropriate. The environment should be rich in equipment and materials that are safe, healthy, interesting, and engaging for the age group of children for which it is designed. Because children's needs and abilities predictably vary by age, to be developmentally appropriate, environments should look different for infants, toddlers, preschoolers, and school-age children.

Organize the Physical Space

Environments send messages, often subtle or even subconscious, about how to behave or which behaviors are acceptable. Libraries convey the message that

Video Example 3.5:

Developmentally Appropriate Practice in Kindergarten

In this video, two kindergarten teachers describe their intentional teaching. How does a developmentally appropriate kindergarten differ from preschool? How do these teachers create lessons and experiences that are both developmentally appropriate and help children meet challenging and achievable learning standards?

soft voices and quiet reading are expected. Open spaces and playgrounds invite children to run and chase one another around. With the knowledge that environments send messages, teachers need to consciously think about the messages they want their classroom environments to send to children.

The classroom needs to be accessible to all children, including children with disabilities, and organized so that children can interact positively, function as independently as possible, and learn decision-making skills. For example, teachers should make sure there is enough space for active play that is protected from traffic. They should also make sure to provide enough age-appropriate materials and duplicates of popular toys so that children do not always have to share, which can lead to frustration and ultimately conflict.

learning centers Defined areas of the classroom that have a particular purpose and contain relevant furnishings and materials.

A developmentally appropriate preschool or kindergarten environment should be organized into separate **learning centers**, which are defined areas of the classroom that have a particular purpose and contain relevant furnishings and materials. Learning centers in a preschool typically include a library area; blocks; dramatic play, writing, and art centers; manipulative toys near tables; and a group meeting area. Learning centers enable children to focus their attention, promote small-group interaction, and require children to make choices and experience the consequences of those choices. Figure 3.3 depicts a room

FIGURE 3.3 Preschool/Kindergarten Classroom Arrangement A developmentally appropriate environment for preschoolers or kindergarteners is organized into learning centers that support child-guided and teacher-guided experiences.

arrangement for a preschool or kindergarten classroom organized with these guidelines in mind:

- Allow children to independently choose their own activities for part of each day.
- Establish clear boundaries between learning centers by using furniture, floor coverings (carpet, tile), or shelves that help limit the number of children who work or play in each area at one time.
- Locate quiet areas, such as the book, art, writing, and computer centers, next to each other and separate from noisier and more active centers such as blocks, dramatic play, or woodworking.
- Provide easily supervised places for children to be alone or with a friend.
- Locate messy activities, such as sand and water play and art projects, near a source of water for easy access and cleanup.
- Provide a comfortable meeting space for the whole group to engage in music, movement, book reading, and other large-group activities. Designate seating arrangements so that children are not crowded or distracted by toys within reach.
- Eliminate unnecessary clutter, which can distract and agitate some children.
- Avoid large open spaces or corridors that invite children to run.

An environment for babies and toddlers, on the other hand, should be more individualized, with large areas for active play and separate spaces for sleeping, feeding, and diapering. There should be carpeting for crawlers and soft furniture for children to snuggle with a teacher while looking at a book or to use to pull themselves up.

A classroom for primary-grade children would have tables or desks arranged in clusters so that children can face each other and work collaboratively. Primary-grade children should take an active role in designing the environment. Learning centers in a primary-grade school are more closely linked to curriculum areas such as a reading corner or a science observation area. Spaces for individual or small group work are also needed as well as a whole class meeting area.

Provide Developmentally Appropriate Learning Materials

Appropriate learning environments for children will vary depending on the age of the children, the time of the year, and the topic of study. Child-centered environments are organized so that many materials are accessible to children. In preschools, children have access to blocks, dramatic play props, puzzles and other manipulative toys, art materials, and books. In primary-grade classrooms, children might have books to read, science tools to explore and investigate, math games, computer centers, and other learning materials. Table 3.1 lists the types of centers available in a challenging and engaging early learning environment, as well as materials that they might include.

 Application Exercise 3.3

Developmentally Appropriate Learning Environments

Organize the Day

Another way for teachers to ensure developmentally appropriate learning experiences for children is to carefully plan how time is used. If the schedule is not carefully planned with children's developmental needs in mind, learning opportunities will be missed or children's valuable time will be wasted. Many of the difficulties that children exhibit in school are related to how the day is organized. Teachers can alleviate these difficulties by providing a consistent, predictable routine on which children can rely. At the same time, teachers need to be flexible so they can easily change plans in response to children's interests or to unanticipated events.

TABLE 3.1 Learning Centers and Suggested Materials

Developmentally appropriate learning environments include a wide variety of materials organized in centers to promote child-chosen experiences as well as small- and large-group instruction.

Learning Center	Examples of Materials
Library area	Culturally and linguistically appropriate books and literacy materials of all kinds (storybooks, information, poetry, wordless, leveled readers), listening center with earphones and CDs, puppets and puppet theater, flannel board
Writing center	All types of paper, envelopes, blank notebooks and journals, variety of writing materials (pencils, pens, markers), word walls, letter stamps, alphabet cards, computers with writing software and internet, mobile digital devices
Mathematics	Variety of objects to count, sort, and order (buttons, bottle caps); manipulatives (peg boards, Legos); tangrams; pattern blocks; number cards; interlocking cubes; attribute games; cuisinare rods; graphing mats; dice; card and board games; puzzles; gaming apps
Science	Plants, pets, fish tank, natural objects (shells, rocks, leaves, soil), tools for investigating and recording (magnifying glasses, stethoscope, magnets, funnels, lenses, balance scales, journals, clipboards)
Music and movement	Musical recordings from diverse cultural groups for listening and dancing, rhythm instruments, picture songbooks, props for movement (scarves, flags, streamers), CD player and headsets
Art	Many different kinds of paper; large variety and many colors of crayons, markers, pencils, chalks, and paint; easel; clay, Play-Doh, and tools for sculpting; scissors, paste, glue, and collage materials; construction materials (foam pieces, wood scraps, wire, pipe cleaners, recyclable materials); water and sand table; art and photograph books from diverse cultural groups; posters; light table; overhead or LCD projector
Dramatic play	Dress-up clothes; mirrors; home-like materials reflecting children's cultures; child-sized furniture; phone; empty food containers; cookbooks; junk mail; calendars; culturally sensitive dolls and accessories; props for pretending various occupations or settings such as store, restaurant or doctor's office; cash registers; measuring cups and spoons; store coupons; magazines; books; paper; open-ended materials (large pieces of fabric, cardboard boxes)
Blocks	Unit blocks, large hollow blocks, props (people and animal figures, transportation vehicles, dress-up clothes), open-ended materials (cardboard boxes, plastic tubing), literacy materials (writing tools and paper, signs, books about transportation and architecture)
Technology	Laptop computers, digital media (iPad, tablets, smartphone), printers, webcam, digital camera, scanners, digital microscope, whiteboard, apps

Sources: Based C. Heroman & C. Copple, 2006. Teaching in the kindergarten year. In D. F. Gullo *(Ed.), K Today: Teaching and Learning in the Kindergarten Year.* Washington, DC: NAEYC; M. B. Bronson, 1995. *The Right Stuff for Children Birth through Age 8: Selecting Play Materials to Support Development.* Washington, DC: NAEYC.

Young children are often thought to have short attention spans; however, the amount of time they engage in small-group activities that they have chosen is often considerably longer than adults would expect. Children's attention during activities that involve the whole group, such as story reading or morning meetings, is usually more limited and difficult to maintain because there are so many distractions. So, time should be planned accordingly. Figure 3.4 provides an example of a daily schedule loosely applicable to a preschool or kindergarten classroom.

A kindergarten schedule will be similar but with some important differences due to the curriculum goals. Morning center time will typically be followed by a block of time devoted to literacy learning that includes writing, reading, and small group activities to build skills and comprehension. There is also likely to be a 45-minute period devoted to individual, small group, and large group math and science experiences.

In an effective classroom, the schedule for the day is posted so that children can predict what will happen throughout the day. At times, the schedule will change for planned or spontaneous events, such as a celebration or finding a bird's nest on the playground. But for the most part, a regular schedule allows children to thrive in predictable environments.

Approximate Times (vary by program or school schedule)	Activity
15 to 30 minutes 8:00–8:30	**Arrival:** Teachers greet children and families. Children store belongings, wash hands, find a quiet activity such as looking at books or drawing, or eat breakfast.
15 to 20 minutes 8:30–8:50	**Morning meeting:** Teachers and children gather in whole group to plan for the day and encourage a sense of community and belonging in the group. They share music and movement.
60 to 75 minutes 9:00–10:15	**Center time and small groups:** Children play and work in learning centers that the teacher has prepared. Teachers observe and interact one on one with children and also work with small groups on projects, book reading, and playing a math game. Children clean up and wash hands.
15 minutes 10:15–10:30	**Morning snack time:** Teachers sit with children, engage in conversation, and model mealtime behavior. Children serve themselves.
15-20 minutes 10:30–10:45	**Group time:** Children share/revisit experiences of the morning. Teachers lead music, movement, and read and discuss a book.
30 to 45 minutes 10:45–11:30	**Outdoor play:** Teachers supervise children at play and as they make nature discoveries; they interact with them one on one or in small groups.
10 to 15 minutes 11:30–11:45	**Half-day program, group meeting:** Teacher and children reflect on the day and plan for tomorrow. **Full-day program, group meeting:** Do a calming activity, prepare for lunch.
30 to 45 minutes 11:45–12:30	**Lunch:** Teachers sit with children, engage in conversation, and model mealtime behavior. Children serve themselves.
60 to 90 minutes (varies with age and needs of children) 12:30–2:00	**Full-day program, group meeting, nap, or rest time:** Teachers help children relax. They also supervise and provide quiet activities for those who do not sleep.
15 to 30 minutes 2:00–2:30	**Afternoon snack and activities:** Children have an afternoon snack and engage in quiet activities such as putting puzzles together, book reading, drawing, or writing.
45 to 60 minutes 2:30–3:30	**Full-day program:** Children engage in outdoor play or large muscle experiences indoors. **Children continue projects from morning and/or make different choices or play outdoors:** Continue projects from morning and/or make different choices, or outdoor play.
10 to 15 minutes 3:15–3:30	**Group time:** Reflect on the day and plan for tomorrow.
60 to 90 minutes 3:30–4:30/5:30	**Full-day program center time:** Children play, continue projects from morning, and/or make different choices.

FIGURE 3.4 Sample Daily Schedule Young children need a predictable daily schedule designed to meet their developmental needs, but they also need flexibility.

Source: Based on The Creative Curriculum for Preschool, 5thed., by D.T. Dodge, L.J. Colker, and C. Heroman, 2010 Washington, DC:Teaching Strategies.

If the schedule has to be changed, teachers need to inform the children in advance. The daily schedule should be based on the following guidelines:

- Plan for a balance of learning experiences: large group, small group, and individualized; child initiated and teacher initiated; active and quiet; indoor and outdoor.

- Allow 60 to 75 minutes for learning-center time so children can become deeply engaged in play and projects. In a full-day program, allow at least 1 hour in the morning and another in the afternoon.
- Limit whole-group meeting times to 15 to 20 minutes (allowing more time as children get older) and give opportunities for children to be actively engaged during these experiences.

✓ Check Your Understanding 3.5

Research on Developmentally Appropriate Practice

The basic research question regarding any educational practice is this: Does it work? Is this educational practice effective in helping children achieve important learning outcomes? Because developmentally appropriate practice involves many different teaching behaviors and aspects of classroom organization, research on the broad construct of developmentally appropriate practice is difficult to conduct. However, subsequent chapters present the research base for each dimension of the teacher's role and area of the curriculum.

Research Reviews

Well-grounded research about learning and development is the foundation for NAEYC's work on developmentally appropriate practice, and provides solid guidance for early childhood educators. This knowledge is summarized in major scientific reports, such as *Transforming the Workforce for Children Birth through Age 8: A Unifying Foundation* (IOM & NRC, 2015), *Handbook of Early Childhood Education* (Pianta, Barnett, Justice, & Sheridan, 2012), *Handbook of Child Development and Early Education* (Barbarin & Wasik, 2009), *Eager to Learn: Educating Our Preschoolers* (Bowman, Donovan, & Burns, 2001), and *From Neurons to Neighborhoods: The Science of Early Childhood Development* (Shonkoff & Phillips, 2000).

A vast amount of evidence demonstrates the lasting positive effects of high-quality early childhood programs (see Cannon et al., 2017; Diamond, Justice, Siegler, & Snyder, 2013; Garcia, Heckman, Leaf, & Prados, 2016; McCoy et al., 2017; Pre-kindergarten Task Force, 2017; Teachstone, 2017; Weiland & Yoshikawa, 2013; Weiland, Ulvestad, Sachs, & Yoshikawa, 2013). Although the studies reviewed were not designed to evaluate developmentally appropriate practice per se, the practices employed in effective programs are consistent with NAEYC's guidelines.

One large-scale review identified the key components of effective early childhood education as "stimulating and supportive interactions between teachers and children that support learning *and* are emotionally supportive, and effective use of curricula" (Yoshikawa et al., 2013, p. 10). One review of research identifies the key components of effective early childhood education as a blend of "explicit instruction, sensitive and warm interactions, responsive feedback, and verbal engagement or stimulation intentionally directed to ensure children's learning while embedding these interactions in a classroom environment that is not overly structured or regimented" (Pianta, Barnett, Burchinal, & Thornburg, 2009, p. 50. They point out that this type of teaching is also related to children's achievement in K–12.

Evaluations of the impact of high-quality early education programs abound. For example, Oklahoma's universal prekindergarten program, which is the largest state-funded voluntary pre-K program in the country, found substantial improvements in school readiness for children from all racial and ethnic groups. The largest gains, however, were for Hispanic children and boys. When the children were followed through third grade, the most lasting benefits were found in mathematics (Hill, Gormley, Adelstein, & Willemin, 2012).

Similarly, a large-scale effort to address inequity in the quality of education in the Abbott School District in New Jersey focused on providing excellent prekindergarten programs for low-income children. The children who participated made strong gains in language, literacy, and math at kindergarten entry that persisted into second grade. Researchers followed the children through fifth grade and found that the program helped close the achievement gap and that fewer children were assigned to special education or retained in grade (Barnett, Jung, Youn, & Frede, 2013).

Research on Elements of Developmentally Appropriate Practice

Some studies have examined the effects of developmentally appropriate practice in preschool or kindergarten compared to "inappropriate" practices. These studies typically have defined appropriate classrooms as those characterized by child-initiated activity, active learning, problem solving, and positive, warm relationships between teachers and children. On the other hand, inappropriate classrooms are characterized by didactic lessons, heavy reliance on whole-group instruction, and emphasis on seatwork and rote learning. Much of the feedback in such classrooms tends to be teachers' correcting of children rather than expanding on their thinking and understanding (Ritchie & Gutmann, 2014).

Several studies compare the effects of such practices on children's social or emotional outcomes. For example, studies relating teaching practice to stress behaviors in children found significantly fewer stress-related behaviors in preschool and kindergarten children in more developmentally appropriate classrooms compared to children in less appropriate classrooms (Honig, 2010; Shanker, 2012). Children in less appropriate classrooms have also been found to score lower on measures of motivation (Stipek, 2011).

Over the years, a number of observational measures have been used to evaluate the quality of early childhood classrooms and the effects on children's outcomes. These tools, such as the CLASS and ECERS-R, are based on the same principles of child development and learning as developmentally appropriate practice. Children enrolled in classrooms that score higher on these measures are more likely to demonstrate positive outcomes, including language, early literacy, mathematics, social skills, self-regulation, and executive function (Hamre, Hatfield, Pianta, & Jamil, 2014; Teachstone, 2017).

Effects of Positive Teacher–Child Interactions

A large body of research supports the efficacy of one of the key aspects of developmentally appropriate practice— warm, responsive relationships between teachers and children (Teachstone, 2017). In observing numerous preschool and kindergarten classrooms, Stipek (2011) found that positive affect among teachers and children seemed to go along with developmentally appropriate practice, whereas negative affect was more likely to be found in classrooms using more inappropriate practices.

Observational research in preschool and primary classrooms has also found that positive, warm relationships with teachers that are developmentally appropriate promote academic success, social competence, and fewer behavior problems (Hamre & Pianta, 2005, 2007, 2010; Mashburn et al., 2008).

Effects of Teaching Practices

In recent years, more research has become available on the effectiveness of developmentally appropriate teaching strategies. About 150 studies using the CLASS have found that teachers' scores on instructional climate (which measures the quality of their language modeling, concept development, and feedback that engages children's higher-order thinking) predict children's language, literacy, and mathematics abilities and their on-task behavior (Teachstone, 2017).

Boston public schools are engaged in a highly successful early childhood initiative to close the achievement gap by instituting high-quality prekindergarten programs that are NAEYC accredited and use the same developmentally appropriate mathematics and literacy curricula with professional development for teachers. A rigorous evaluation found

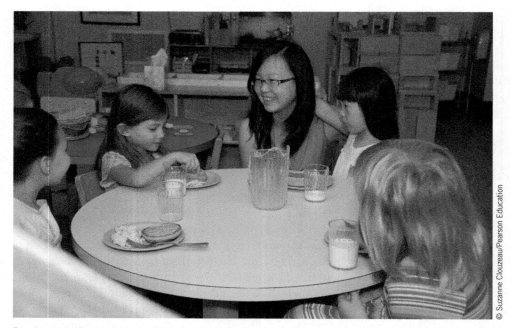

Developmentally appropriate classrooms function as caring communities of learners where each child is valued and families are welcomed.

substantial gains in language, literacy, mathematics, and executive function for all groups of children, but the largest gains were for Hispanic children (Weiland & Yoshikawa, 2013).

A classic longitudinal study compared the effects of the HighScope curriculum, or child-centered nursery school experience, with a highly scripted, teacher-directed curriculum called Direct Instruction (Schweinhart, Weikart, & Larner, 1986). The HighScope curriculum is a blended approach incorporating child-centered, active learning and intentional teaching. A longitudinal follow-up study (Schweinhart & Weikart, 1997) found that at age 23, the Direct Instruction group had three times as many felony arrests per person, especially those involving property crimes, and that 47% of the Direct Instruction group exhibited emotional problems during their schooling, as compared to only 6% in the other groups. Researchers attributed these results to the emphasis on planning, social reasoning, and other social objectives in the developmentally appropriate HighScope curricula, but not in the other curriculum.

More recent research demonstrates the effectiveness of building on a developmentally appropriate framework with evidence-based teaching strategies that focus on a content area such as literacy, mathematics, or social-emotional development (Jenkins & Duncan, 2017)—many of which we describe in this book. One effective Head Start intervention program (Bierman et al., 2008) involved brief lessons on literacy and social skills, hands-on activities, and specific teaching strategies designed to promote children's social-emotional competencies, language development, and emergent literacy skills. Materials were also provided to parents to enhance children's development at home. The program significantly improved children's vocabulary, emergent literacy, emotional understanding, social problem solving, social behavior, and learning engagement.

The Future of Developmentally Appropriate Practice

One of the most important functions of NAEYC's work on developmentally appropriate practice has been to further discussion and debate in the field about teaching practices. Given the history of the field, it is likely that this topic will continue to be debated. What aspects are most likely to continue to provoke thought? Undoubtedly, the realities of diversity and changing cultural contexts in our country will continue to raise questions about what is culturally responsive as well as developmentally appropriate. Increased demands for accountability, the challenge to close the achievement gap, and inequity of educational opportunities raise the stakes over which practices can be successfully defended. Likewise, debates about curriculum have been a constant and will continue in the future, but are likely to be driven more by research than in the past.

The word *appropriate* is a culturally laden term and thus will continue to provoke controversy. Similarly, it is difficult to counteract the tendency of teachers and other professionals to emphasize "typical development" over individual differences and cultural variations. After all, the first can be learned by reading books and journals, whereas the latter two require ongoing assessment of children, building relationships with families, and reflecting on how our own cultural perspectives influence our judgments and behavior.

To be developmentally appropriate, practices must contribute to children's learning and development. Therefore, this book focuses on recommended teaching practices, which must be responsive to children's individual development and cultural variation to be deemed appropriate. At the same time, we also focus on whether those practices help children achieve important learning goals. By definition, developmentally appropriate practices should be effective practices. To be effective, teachers must know children, they must know *how* to teach, and they must know *what* to teach. Each of these areas of knowledge must be informed by research. The following equation describes these components of effective, research-based practice:

Effective Practice = Knowing Children + Knowing How to Teach + Knowing What to Teach

Ultimately, the truest measure of developmentally appropriate practice is seeing children joyfully, physically, and intellectually engaged in meaningful learning about their world and everyone and everything in it (Copple & Bredekamp, 2009).

✓ Check Your Understanding 3.6

Revisiting the Case Study

... Ms. Hakuta's Classroom

At the beginning of this chapter, we visited Ms. Hakuta's kindergarten. Having explored the basic premises of developmentally appropriate practice, we can now view the kindergarten experience with a more informed eye. Her classroom, with its *age-appropriate* materials, furnishings, and environment, not only made the children feel comfortable but also encouraged their positive approaches to learning—initiative, engagement, enthusiasm, and interest. Furthermore, Ms. Hakuta drew on her knowledge of how children develop and learn by working to establish a warm, positive relationship with each child. She began each day with the Morning Meeting, which created a caring community of learners and ensured that no child was excluded.

At the same time, Ms. Hakuta demonstrated the importance of paying attention to what is *individually appropriate*. She provided individualized learning experiences that built on what the children were already able to do, and adapted her teaching to individuals and small groups.

Finally, Ms. Hakuta was *culturally appropriate*—responsive to the cultures and languages of the children. She provided opportunities for children to read, hear, and speak their own languages as well as English. In so doing, she demonstrated that she values and respects their families and cultural backgrounds.

Ms. Hakuta displayed all dimensions of intentional teaching—creating a caring community; teaching individuals, small groups, and the whole group effectively; partnering and communicating with families; assessing children's learning; and providing an engaging, challenging curriculum, as evidenced in their study of health and the human body. Taken together, the actions in that brief scenario demonstrate the teacher's broad base of knowledge, and bode well for her kindergartner's success in school. ■

3 Chapter Summary

- Developmentally appropriate practice is teaching that is attuned to children's ages, experience, abilities, and interests, and that helps them attain challenging and achievable goals.

- Intentional teachers have a purpose for everything that they do, are thoughtful and prepared, and can explain their decisions and actions to other teachers, administrators, or parents.

- Decisions about developmentally appropriate practice are based on knowledge of child development and learning (what is age appropriate), knowledge about children as individuals, and knowledge of the social and cultural contexts in which children live (what is culturally appropriate).

- The role of the early childhood teacher has five interrelated dimensions: (1) creating a caring community of learners, (2) teaching to enhance learning and

development, (3) planning curriculum to meet important goals, (4) assessing children's learning and development, and (5) establishing reciprocal relationships with families.

- "Widening the lens" is a metaphor to help teachers remember to consider diverse perspectives and move beyond *either/or* thinking to *both/and* thinking when solving problems or making decisions about practice.

- How the learning environment and children's daily schedules are organized are the most obvious indicators of whether a program is developmentally appropriate; therefore, they should look different for infants, toddlers, preschoolers, and school-age children, because abilities and needs predictably vary by children's ages.

- Well-grounded research about learning and development is the basis for NAEYC's position statements on developmentally appropriate practice and provides solid guidance for early childhood educators.

Key Terms

- age appropriate
- assessment
- caring community of learners

- culturally appropriate
- curriculum
- developmentally appropriate practice (D.A.P.)

- evidence-based curriculum
- individually appropriate
- intentional teachers

- learning centers
- position statement
- push-down curriculum
- reciprocal relationship

Flash Cards 3.1

Readings and Websites

Copple, C., & Bredekamp, S. (Eds.). (2009). *Developmentally appropriate practice in early childhood programs serving children from birth through age 8* (3rd ed.). Washington, DC: National Association for the Education of Young Children.

Greenman, J., & Lindstrom, M. (Ed.). (2017). *Caring spaces, learning places: Children's environments that work!* (3d ed.). Lincoln, NE: Exchange Press.

Kostelnik, M. J., Soderman, A. K., Whiren, A. P., & Rupiper, L. (2015). *Developmentally appropriate curriculum: Best practices in early childhood education* (7th ed.). Upper Saddle River, NJ: Pearson.

ASCD Whole Child Initiative

This website provides resources promoting elementary education that supports all areas of children's development and learning.

National Association for the Education of Young Children

NAEYC's website has a special section and the latest resources on developmentally appropriate practice and play, plus copies of all its position statements. Early childhood educators and students join this professional organization to stay up to date on effective practices.

ZERO to THREE—National Center for Infants, Toddlers, and Families

This website provides resources and practical tips for working with infants, toddlers, and their families.

Shared Writing 3.1

Explain Developmentally Appropriate Practice

4 Applying What We Know about Children's Learning and Development

Learning Outcomes

After studying this chapter, you should be able to

4.1 Describe development and learning, and how they are related.

4.2 Discuss how knowledge of brain development in early childhood informs teaching practice.

4.3 Identify key components of developmental theories (Erikson, Maslow, Piaget, Vygotsky, and Bronfenbrenner) and apply them to early childhood practice.

4.4 Identify key components of learning theories (Behaviorism and Social Cognitive theories) and apply them to early childhood practice.

4.5 Explain how play supports children's development and learning, and describe ways teachers can support play in early childhood settings.

4.6 Apply theories of development and learning to early childhood practice.

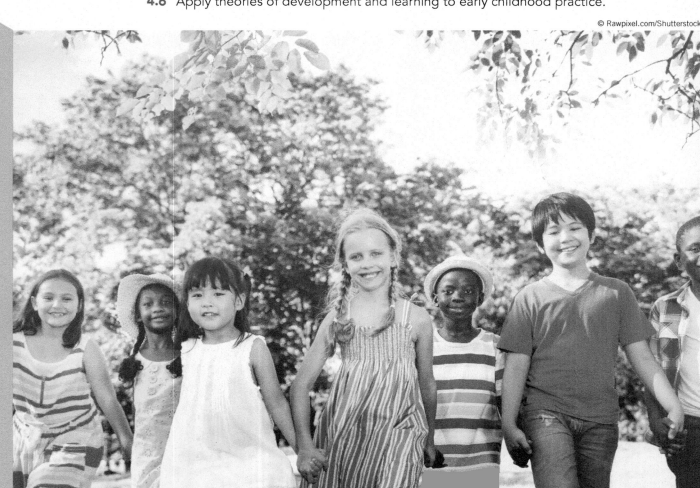

Case Study

Yvonne Donati is a prekindergarten teacher in an inclusive public school. One of her goals is to create a caring community in which her energetic youngsters learn how to get along and work together. Yvonne's approach to guiding children's behavior is to engage the children in lively discussions of the classroom rules and how to solve conflicts that arise with their classmates.

In planning curriculum, Yvonne draws on the children's interests to integrate literacy instruction with science study of plants or animals, and children often work on small-group projects, such as making a terrarium. She and the children have large-group meetings and she sometimes reads to the whole group, but she keeps these periods brief. She tries to find ways to make sure the children are physically active, such as doing motions to songs or fingerplays. She also actively engages children's minds, as when she gives clues for the children to guess what object is hidden in a paper bag or has them take turns figuring out what a new word means in a story.

When children encounter challenges in their play, Yvonne helps them come up with their own solutions rather than solve the problem for them. She asks probing questions: "Why do you think your tomato plant didn't grow tall?" "Let's compare your plant and Juana's—why is hers taller?"

Because some children in Yvonne's class have identified disabilities, she regularly meets with the special education team and cooperates in implementing the children's individualized education programs (IEPs). Maya has severe behavior problems, and the team works together to plan and implement a positive behavior support program to reinforce her desirable behaviors. After a few weeks of systematically working with Maya, Yvonne observes that the new strategy is working and that Maya is less aggressive.

After a month of school, Yvonne observes that every day, the block area is dominated by boys while girls prefer the dramatic play center. She isn't sure if this is just reflecting typical gender differences or if there is another reason. Yvonne knows from studying the importance of play that children benefit from both block building and pretend play, and that the benefits differ. She contemplates assigning children to areas but then designs an experiment. One week, she closes the dramatic play center; the next week, she closes the block center, observing and recording children's behavior each week. Yvonne finds that without the availability of the dramatic play center, girls freely enter the block area; some boys play with them while others go elsewhere. On the other hand, when the block center is closed, the girls continue to play in the dramatic center but the boys seem at loose ends and do not choose pretend play. Based on the results of her experiment, Yvonne institutes a play planning session each morning to make sure that girls have block-building opportunities. She also adds themes and props, such as creating a car wash, to interest more boys in pretend play. ■

his brief visit to Yvonne's classroom reveals several things about her approach to teaching. Although Yvonne may not be fully aware of it, the decisions she makes, like those of every teacher, actually reflect various theories of how children learn and develop. The purpose of this chapter is to help you understand and apply the prevailing theories of child development and learning. At times, beginning as well as experienced teachers wonder why theories matter or what relevance theories have to their work.

We begin by describing how theories of child development and learning are most useful in informing and influencing practice. Next, we describe research on brain development and its implications. Then we discuss all the major theories and how they apply to early childhood practice. Next, we explain the critically important role of children's play, which is supported by the key developmental theories. We conclude the chapter with a summary of the main principles of child development and learning derived from research and theory that guide early childhood practice.

Understanding Development and Learning

Intentional, effective teaching requires that teachers understand how children think and learn, and how best to support their healthy development at various ages in all areas—physical, social, emotional, and cognitive. Both development and learning are complicated processes requiring that teachers not only study research and theory but also study children themselves.

What Is Development?

development Age-related change that results from an interaction between biological maturation and physical and/or social experience; development occurs as children grow, adapt, and change in response to various experiences.

If you spend any time with early childhood educators, you are likely to hear that it is important for teachers to understand child development. This is true. But what do they need to know about development and why is it important? To answer these questions, we must first define terms. **Development** refers to age-related change resulting from an interaction between biological maturation and physical and/or social experience.

Development occurs as children grow, adapt, and change in response to various experiences. Consider how language develops. Biology plays a role, with babies all over the world producing similar sounds at about the same age. But language development requires more than maturation. Babies need social interaction with adults and older children who talk to them. As they grow physically and are able to get around on their own, infants and toddlers encounter more examples of language interaction, and their speech starts to take off around age 2 (just as their legs do).

Domains of Development Different areas of human functioning, including physical, cognitive, social, and emotional, are often described as **domains of development**. **Physical development** refers to biological growth and acquisition of fine motor skills, such as drawing, and gross motor skills, such as running. **Cognitive development** is a broad term encompassing thinking, intelligence, and language abilities. **Social development** refers to interpersonal relationships, such as the ability to make friends, cooperate, and resolve conflicts. **Emotional development** is the ability to regulate and appropriately express feelings.

Discussions of child development inevitably address these domains as if they were separate. In reality, of course, human development does not occur in different categories. Aspects of development are inextricably linked, which is one reason we often talk about social-emotional development as though it were a single construct. Domains of development are an artifact of how researchers study development, rather than how development actually occurs. The integrated nature of development requires that teachers maintain their awareness of the *whole child* at all times.

Recently, researchers and educators have begun to focus less on skills related to specific domains and more on abilities that cut across traditionally defined developmental domains, such as executive function and self-regulation (Jones & Bailey, 2014), which we discuss later in this chapter. Bolstered by new findings from brain research, we now know that such broad **domain-general processes** strongly predict children's success in school and life. For example, Galinsky (2010) identifies seven essential life skills that every child needs: focus and self-control, perspective taking, communicating, making connections, critical thinking, taking on challenges, and self-directed, engaged learning. A similar list is promoted by the Partnership for 21st Century Learning (2017): critical thinking, communication, collaboration, and creativity. Another way of describing these skills is children's approaches to learning—motivation, interest, persistence, curiosity, engagement, and enthusiasm (Bustamente, White & Greenfield, 2017). These lists of goals are overlapping and consistent, and they demonstrate the connection between development and learning, which we define in the next section.

What Is Learning?

Learning is a change in knowledge or skill that results from experience or instruction. Learning and development are not the same things, although they affect each other. Learning is a similar, though not identical, process whether a person is 3 years old or 33. For example, for a first-grader, learning to read isn't completely different from the way it is for an older person.

Because experience plays a role in both development and learning, there is a close connection between these processes, especially in the early years of life when children are growing and changing so rapidly. Sometimes development leads to learning (Piaget, 1952). For example, when a baby develops the ability to grasp objects and begins to put them in her mouth, she learns a lot about the objects in her world. Some are hard, others soft; some taste good while others don't. In this case, her development fosters her learning. Children's developmental level can also put limitations on what they are capable of learning. For example, preschoolers can do some abstract thinking but won't fully understand complex, abstract concepts, such as chronological time, until they are older.

© DaydreamsGirl/E+/Getty Images

During early childhood, children's development and learning are closely connected. Right from the start, babies put things in their mouths, which teaches them about objects in the world—how they feel and what they do.

domains of development
Areas of human development and functioning that include cognitive, social, emotional, and physical.

physical development
Biological growth and acquisition of fine-motor and gross-motor skills.

cognitive development
Thinking, intelligence, and language abilities.

social development The ability to establish positive relationships with adults and peers, make friends, cooperate, and resolve conflicts.

emotional development
Acquisition of important emotional skills, such as identifying feelings and learning to regulate emotions and express them appropriately.

domain-general processes
Broad abilities that cut across traditionally defined developmental domains.

learning A change in knowledge or skill that results from experience or instruction.

Learning also drives development. As children participate in the activities of their cultural groups and come to understand more complex concepts, their cognitive development is affected (Rogoff, 2012; Vygotsky, 1978). What children learn at home and in their cultural community powerfully affects their development. Consider the developmental differences between a 5-year-old child in America, whose primary "job" is to attend kindergarten, and a 5-year-old in rural Africa, whose primary responsibility is to transport water for the family.

The Role of Theory

Centuries ago, human beings thought the world was flat. No one wanted to venture too far out to sea for fear of falling off the edge. Slowly, more people traveled farther from shore, and others observed that the tops of arriving ships appeared first and then gradually the rest. If the Earth was flat, the entire ship would appear at once. These observations and experiences led to the conclusion that the Earth is not flat, but is actually a sphere.

theory An explanation of how information and observations are organized and relate to one another.

This simple example illustrates the power of theories. A theory is an explanation of how information and observations are organized and relate to one another. As we can see, theories are important because they affect how people think and behave. In education, theories of learning and development affect how people treat children, how they structure environments, and how they teach.

The Relationship Between Theory, Research, and Practice

Where do theories come from? Theories usually evolve from research, which can take the form of systematic observations over time or scientifically controlled experiments. In fact, a theory derives from a hypothesis, which is a tentative explanation for a phenomenon. The more research is available to support the "truth" of a theory, the more useful the theory becomes in guiding practice. Yvonne had a theory about why girls and boys play differently. She tested and then revised her theory by conducting an informal research study.

hypothesis An assumption about or tentative explanation of a phenomenon.

When research findings contradict earlier conclusions, theories evolve, are discarded, or are replaced with new ones. In the early part of the 20th century, the prevailing theory of child development was maturationist. According to this theory, derived from research by Arnold Gesell (1940; Ames & Ilg, 1979), the sequence of changes in abilities and behavior is largely predetermined by children's biological growth processes rather than by their experiences or learning.

maturationist Theory of development that assumes that the sequence of changes in abilities and behavior is largely predetermined by children's biological growth processes rather than by their experiences or learning.

Maturation theory led to the notion that teachers needed to wait until children were ready for experiences to be effective. Because it was assumed that children were not ready to read until first grade, few literacy experiences were provided in preschool or kindergarten. Research in the intervening years demonstrated that differences in children's abilities are heavily influenced by their experiences (Sameroff, 2009; Tierney & Nelson, 2009). As a result, maturationist theory has been displaced by other theories. Nevertheless, maturationist theory continues to influence some practices, such as kindergarten "redshirting"—holding children out of kindergarten until they are a year older and presumably readier to learn.

Theories can also drive the way research is conducted and findings are interpreted. For example, if a theory is assumed to be universally true for all children, then research that supports the theory is assumed to apply to all children. Even if the research has been conducted only with white, middle-class children, the findings are applied to children of color or children of different socioeconomic, linguistic, or cultural backgrounds. Understanding the role of culture in development and learning requires that theory and research be more cautiously interpreted through these lenses. Therefore, despite the frequent claim that theories are "universal" and apply equally well to all children, they need to be evaluated from a broader perspective, as described in the feature *Culture Lens: The Effect of Culture on Research and Theory*.

Culture Lens
The Effect of Culture on Research and Theory

An especially important consideration in evaluating theories is the cultural background of the children and families who participated in the research. For decades, one theory of how parental child-rearing affects preschool children's development has been assumed to apply to all children and families (Baumrind, 1971). The theory identifies three parenting styles:

- **Authoritative.** Loving, nurturing, involved, and sensitive parents who explain their reasons for discipline have children who are motivated to learn and are well adjusted socially and emotionally.

- **Authoritarian.** Restrictive, punishing, rejecting, and controlling parents have children who lack initiative and are inhibited.

- **Permissive.** Parents who are warm and accepting of children but minimally involved and laissez-faire about discipline have children with the lowest levels of motivation and achievement.

Authoritative parenting is found to be the most effective style of child rearing. Most research on the theory, however, has been conducted with Caucasian middle-class families. More recent research with Head Start families (McWayne, Owsianik, Green, & Fantuzzo, 2008) using culturally familiar language and behaviors identified similar, but not identical, types of parenting:

- **Active–responsive** (e.g., tell child "I'm proud" when he tries to be good).

- **Active–restrictive** (e.g., spank child when she is disobedient).

- **Passive–permissive** (e.g., tell child "I'll punish," but don't).

Research with low-income, urban, African American families found no relationships between these different parenting styles and preschool children's social-emotional skills. What might account for these contradictory findings between diverse cultural groups? When children grow up in poverty-stricken, dangerous communities and face possible discrimination and prejudice, parents' priorities reflect these conditions. They may express their love by focusing on survival skills and making sure their children behave maturely and competently in situations where people are biased against them. With these goals in mind, the effectiveness of restrictive parenting makes more sense.

In addition, compared to Caucasian middle-class families, African American child-rearing tends to be spread among a number of people in the extended family and community. The mother may be relatively passive and permissive, for example, whereas others in the child's circle, such as a grandmother or aunt, may be more restrictive or actively responsive.

What can we conclude from revisiting a widely-accepted child development theory like Baumrind's parenting framework? Research that leads to a new theory needs to be conducted with diverse populations of children and families. Otherwise, the theory simply can't be said to apply to them. In addition, research needs to be interpreted through a wide lens that considers the social and cultural contexts in which children live—in this case, the realities of life for low-income, urban, African American families.

Sources: D. Baumrind, 1971. Current patterns of parental authority. *Developmental Psychology, 4,* 1–103; C. M. McWayne, M. Owsianik, L. E. Green, & J. W. Fantuzzo, 2008. Parenting behaviors and preschool children's social and emotional skills: A question of the consequential validity of traditional parenting constructs for low-income African Americans. *Early Childhood Research Quarterly, 23,* 173–192.

Why Study Child Development and Learning?

Understanding theories of learning and development is particularly important for early childhood teachers for several reasons. During the first eight years of life, children grow and change more rapidly than at any other period of the life span. As a result, development and learning are more closely connected in early childhood, making the developmental accomplishments and learning that take place at this point critically important foundations for what follows.

Understanding child development and learning helps teachers in many ways, including:

- Setting and evaluating goals that are achievable for most children within a given age range and that also challenge children to go on learning
- Accurately interpreting children's behavior as predictable for their age or in need of intervention

- Knowing predictable sequences of development and learning to plan curriculum and adapt teaching to accommodate where individual children are in the sequence
- Predicting the kinds of topics and experiences that will be interesting and meaningful to children of different ages
- Understanding how children's social and cultural contexts affect their learning and development
- Using information about typical and atypical development to identify and diagnose potential disabilities or developmental delays in children, as well as to determine if children's development is advanced

In previous sections, we defined and described the relationships between development and learning, and between theory, research, and practice. Teachers have much to learn about these topics, but we begin with the most current area of new knowledge, brain development.

✔ Check Your Understanding 4.1

Brain Development and Implications for Practice

Some of the most exciting discoveries about human development have occurred in the past 40 years, as advanced technologies have enabled scientists to directly study how the brain grows and changes. Tools such as positron emission tomography (PET) scans and functional magnetic resonance imagery (fMRI) open windows into how the brain functions when people perform different tasks and how the brains of children and adults compare (Fusaro & Nelson, 2009). An explosion of brain research has captured the imagination of the general public and policy makers in addition to educators and parents.

A major conclusion of this research is that brain development results from an interaction between children's genetic make-up *and* their experiences in the world (Center on the Developing Child at Harvard University, 2016a). In other words, experiences both positive and negative affect brain development, and brain growth and change affect learning.

How the Brain Promotes Learning

The brain is the most complex of human organisms and the most important to overall functioning, yet we know the least about it. But we are rapidly learning more.

The Physical Brain The brain is composed of a massive number of nerve cells, or **neurons**, that receive information through the senses or from other neurons and then communicate information back to other parts of the body (Fusaro & Nelson, 2009). One connection might alert the baby to look at a human face; another might signal a smile in response to mommy's face. These connections that carry information between neurons are called **synapses**.

In utero, the baby's brain undergoes astonishing growth. Neurons are produced at a rapid rate, and they migrate (or move) to the places in the brain where they will develop and be used. They also begin the process of differentiation—specialization for particular functions. The processes of neuron production, migration, and differentiation are mostly

neurons Nerve cells in the brain that receive information through the senses or from other neurons, and then communicate information back to other parts of the body.

synapses Connections in the brain that carry information between neurons.

directed by genes. However, they are also affected by maternal health, nutrition, and environmental risks, such as alcohol or drug use.

The adult brain has about 100 billion neurons, about the same number that babies have at birth. The major difference between the newborn brain and adult brain, however, is the intricate network of connections (synapses) between the neurons, the brain's wiring system (Fusaro & Nelson, 2009). During the first two to three years of life, babies' brains overproduce synapses, going from about 2,500 at birth to 15,000—many more than adults have. After that, the brain starts **pruning** unnecessary or unused synapses. Throughout life, new synapses are formed and others are pruned away.

Pruning is important because it contributes to efficient brain operation, aids learning and memory, and increases the brain's flexibility—actions that neuroscientists term *plasticity*. **Plasticity** is the brain's ability to flexibly develop and change in response to experiences. After pruning, fewer and stronger connections among brain cells strengthen those that remain. This process is similar to pruning a bush that has grown too large; cutting off unneeded branches strengthens those that remain and may mean more blossoms in the future.

pruning The process whereby the brain eliminates unnecessary or unused synapses, which contributes to efficient brain operation, aids learning and memory, and increases the brain's flexibility.

plasticity The brain's ability to develop and change in response to experiences.

executive function The ability to control emotions, focus attention, plan and think ahead, and monitor cognitive processes.

Executive Functions of the Brain The activities of the prefrontal cortex region of the brain allow us to self-regulate—to manage our emotions, focus and shift attention, and regulate behavior to meet our goals—are known as **executive functions** (EF) (Jones & Bailey, 2014). They are some of the most important skills for learning and development (Gilpin, Boxmeyer, DeCaro, & Lochman, 2014). During preschool and the primary grades, considerable growth and change take place in the frontal lobes of the brain (Center on the Developing Child at Harvard University, 2016a). Given supportive experiences, the following skills improve considerably during these years: attention, impulse control, planning, reasoning, problem solving, and memory.

Now read the feature *What Works: Supporting Development of Executive Function in Young Children* to learn how teachers and parents can help develop these vital competencies.

Video Example 4.1:

Executive Function

https://youtu.be/efCq_vHUMqs

This video describes executive function and how it develops. Why is executive function so important? How can adults support its development in early childhood?

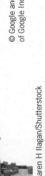
© Google and the google logo are registered trademarks of Google Inc., used with permission

What Works

Supporting Development of Executive Function in Young Children

© Karen H Ilagan/Shutterstock

Children are not born with the ability to focus their attention, remember directions, and plan their activities. They do not naturally control their impulses and emotional reactions; rather, they develop these abilities, known as executive function, over the course of early childhood with the help of caring adults. While infants are biologically prepared to learn to regulate their emotions and thinking, they rely on the serve and return interactions with adults to develop the skills they need for learning to learn.

Executive function is sometimes thought of as the brain's "air traffic control system" for its role in regulating our behaviors, thinking and emotions. Executive function abilities include working memory, inhibitory control and cognitive flexibility, and are essential for early learning. Children with well-developed executive functions are typically successful in early reading and math development. They achieve more in school, and have an easier time making friends and following school and activity routines. On the other hand, research suggests that children who do not develop strong executive

functions in early childhood experience poorer long-term health, lower achievement in school, and less job success as adults.

Families and early childhood teachers can support the development of executive function in young children by focusing on their social relationships, their daily experiences, and the settings in which they develop.

- Adults can help young children develop relationships by engaging in warm, language-rich serve and return, which helps children feel safe in addition to learning language. Consistent, reliable responding to children's needs (for example, crying when uncomfortable) helps young children know that adults can be relied upon for care.
- Most importantly, adults need to protect children from chaos, violence, and extreme stress. By helping children develop relationships upon which they can depend, adults prepare the child's developing brain for using reasoning rather than impulses when solving difficult problems later on.

- Adults, families and teachers help executive function develop when they engage children in experiences in problem-solving and complex interactions. They can "practice" emotions with children by playfully practicing and labeling expression of feelings, and by talking about when we might feel certain ways.
- Adults can scaffold interactions among children by providing a lot of support when children are learning how to play with others and gradually reducing support as children become more competent.
- Providing plentiful experiences for physical exercise reduces children's stress levels and provides a healthy way to deal with stress through the life span.

- Finally, children need to live and play in environments that are safe. When environments provide safe spaces and opportunities to play and explore, children develop better executive function. When adults are able to provide safe, economically stable environments that offer basic needs, children's brains are able to develop the "air traffic control" system to manage their behavior, thoughts, and feelings to match the demands of the home, school or play context.

Source: Center on the Developing Child at Harvard University, 2011. Building the brain's "air traffic control" system: How early experiences shape the development of executive function: Working Paper no. 11. www.developingchild.harvard.edu.

The Role of Experience in Brain Development During early childhood—a period of rapid brain growth—the brain is most receptive and responsive to experience. Experiences impact the child's developing brain architecture and interact with genes to influence development (Center on the Developing Child at Harvard University, 2016a; IOM & NRC, 2015). Children's relationships with the family and community impact brain development and influence how well the neurological system works. Both positive and negative experiences modify the brain architecture, with the most emotionally intense and most meaningful experiences having the greatest effects. For these reasons, highly stressful experiences during early childhood can have lasting negative consequences (IOM & NRC, 2015).

Although too little stimulation can lead to poor outcomes, exposing young children to overstimulating environments is not supported by brain research (Thompson, 2008). Babies and toddlers in particular become stressed when they are overstimulated. They either tune out (usually by going to sleep) or act out (usually by crying). Either way, they aren't learning.

serve and return the back-and-forth interaction between a caregiving adult and a child in which each response is contingent upon the response of the "partner."

A key concept in thinking about how brain architecture develops is called **serve and return**. Serve and return refers to the back-and-forth interaction between a caregiving adult and a child in which each response is contingent upon the response of the "partner." A baby may kick and coo, trying to get the adult's attention. The adult may respond by smiling and saying, "Are you ready to play?" The baby may kick harder, coo and smile, and so on. Through this type of interaction, the baby is learning about language, social interaction, and how to be in a relationship.

windows of opportunity Periods of time during which human brains are particularly susceptible and responsive to certain types of experience.

Brain research indicates that the early childhood years are a prime time for learning. The term **window of opportunity** is used to suggest that there are times in life when the brain is most open to certain types of experiences. For example, during the first three years of life, the brain is especially susceptible to learning language, and the amount and quality of language to which young children are exposed greatly influence which language(s) they acquire and their developing language ability (Kuhl et al., 2014). Young children's brains are much more active, connected, and flexible than are adults' (Thompson, 2008). However, this does not mean, as some people have concluded, that the first few years of life are such a critical period that after age 3 or 5, the window for learning closes. On the contrary, brains remain flexible throughout life, as demonstrated when an 80-year-old learns to knit or a 58-year-old learns Italian.

Implications for Children

As previously discussed, fostering optimal early brain development is essential for positive outcomes for children. Brain research (Center on the Developing Child at Harvard University, 2016a) concludes that:

- The brain's most significant development occurs before birth, placing great importance on prenatal care.

- Early experiences change and organize the physical structure of the brain.
- Severe negative experiences, such as neglect, abuse, and stress, pose serious threats to healthy brain development. Prevention and early intervention become even more important in light of the potentially lasting negative consequences for brain development.
- Brains develop best when children experience loving relationships; rich language interactions; play and opportunities to explore their worlds; interesting and engaging things to learn about; and healthy, safe environments.
- Brain development is integrated. Cognitive, emotional, social, and physical aspects of the brain are interconnected, and as children get older, the areas within the brain become better coordinated.

Implications for Practice

Brain research has electrified public interest in early childhood education. Nevertheless, neuroscience provides clearer guidance about the kinds of experiences that harm development, such as prolonged stress, rather than those that enrich it (Center on the Developing Child at Harvard University, 2010). Learning to handle the typical stresses of childhood is a normal part of growing up, such as when children go to the doctor or start a new school. At other times, children may experience more long-lasting stressful experiences, such as an injury or death in the family, which are difficult but tolerable as long as a caring adult is there for support. The biggest threat to children's developing brains is **toxic stress**, which occurs when children experience intense, frequent, and/or prolonged anxiety, such as abuse, neglect, violence, or economic deprivation, without adult support to help them cope (Shonkoff, Garner, & Committee on Psychological Aspects of Child and Family Health, 2012). Such prolonged stress can impair brain growth and have lasting negative consequences for physical and mental health.

> **toxic stress** Children's experience of intense, frequent, and/or prolonged anxiety such as abuse, neglect, violence, or economic deprivation without adult support to help them cope.

Threats to brain development reinforce the need to prevent child abuse and neglect, and to eliminate risk factors, such as poor nutrition and exposure to toxic substances (Center on the Developing Child at Harvard University, 2016a). Likewise, evidence from brain research supports the need for Head Start–like comprehensive family services to minimize stress and trauma in children's lives and to improve the mental and physical health of caregivers.

Many years of brain research have provided knowledge and guidance about specific ways to optimize young children's development and learning (Center on the Developing Child at Harvard University, 2016a). Warm, positive, language-rich interactions are essential components for healthy brain development and high-quality practice. Positive relationships build brain architecture and protect the brain from negative effects of stress (Lally & Mangione, 2017). Because the areas of the brain that contribute to social-emotional and cognitive development are connected, early childhood programs should focus on both.

However, we have much less knowledge of specific curricula or products that enhance brain development; therefore, teachers should be wary of products that claim to be based on brain research (Center on the Developing Child at Harvard University, 2010). Neuroscience is most useful when coupled with the larger body of knowledge about theories of development and learning, which we describe in the sections that follow.

 Check Your Understanding 4.2

 Child Development Theories

In this section, we present the theories of child development that are influential in early childhood education today. One of the most debated aspects of human development has been whether biology or experience (nature or nurture) plays the bigger role in explaining individual differences. Some theories place greater emphasis on inborn, biologically driven changes, whereas others consider the environment to be the primary influence. Most of the prominent theories, however, reflect the prevailing view that human development is a product of *both* biology/heredity *and* environment/experiences.

Multiple theories exist because of the various dimensions of development, such as social, emotional, and cognitive. The work of Erik Erikson and Abraham Maslow, which we describe in the sections that follow, has been influential in guiding practice in social and emotional development and motivation to learn. We follow with a description of two developmental theories that explain how children develop cognitive skills, Piaget's Cognitive Developmental Theory and Vygotsky's Sociocultural Theory. The section closes with Bronfenbrenner's Bio-Ecological Systems theory, a comprehensive theory of human development that explains how characteristics of the individual child and the settings interact.

Erikson's Psychosocial Theory of Human Development

Psychologist Erik Erikson (1902–1994) was influenced by cultural anthropologists and came to see the importance of culture and social experience in shaping development. Based on extensive investigations conducted with his wife, Joan, Erikson published his seminal book, *Childhood and Society* (1950/1963).

He proposed an eight-stage theory of personal and social development in which at each stage of life, an individual confronts a major challenge or "crisis." Successful negotiation of the crisis requires achieving a balance between two possible extremes. If crises are not resolved positively at particular points in the life span, Erikson postulated that later problems will ensue. Table 4.1 provides an overview of Erikson's eight stages, the typical crisis, and successful resolution.

TABLE 4.1 Erikson's Stages of Personal and Social Development

Approximate Age	Stage	Lessons Learned from Life's Challenges
Infants birth to 1 year	Trust vs. mistrust	Gaining feelings of security and positive attachment; learning to trust other people to meet needs as well as exert some control over environment
Toddlers 1 to 3 years	Autonomy vs. doubt	Becoming aware of increasing competence, strong will to practice new skills without restriction, and growing sense of self as individual
Preschoolers 3 to 5 years	Initiative vs. guilt	Becoming more purposeful in initiating play with other children and toys, increasing power and ability to act without taking too many risks
Elementary school-age 6 to 12 years	Industry vs. inferiority	Becoming confident in school work, mastering challenging tasks, and acting responsibly
Adolescence 10 to 20 years	Identity vs. role confusion	Finding sense of self and building relationships with peers
Young adulthood	Intimacy vs. isolation	Building close relationships with sexual partners, friends, and colleagues; beginning career
Middle adulthood	Generativity vs. self-absorption	Gaining satisfaction from life's work and contributing to larger society; nurturing next generations and caring for others
Late adulthood	Integrity vs. despair	Reflecting on life with contentment; engaging in rewarding activities; coping with loss and end-of-life challenges

Source: Based on T. M. McDevitt and J. E. Ormrod, 2018. *Child development and education* (6th ed.). Upper Saddle River, NJ: Pearson.

Application Exercise 4.1

Table 4.1: Erikson's Stages of Personal and Social Development

Stages of Personal and Social Development in Early Childhood

Erikson hypothesized the following four stages of psychological and social development in the lives of children. He assumed that mothers and other family members are the principal actors in children's lives during the first three stages. However, children today participate in out-of-home child care from birth. Therefore, teachers also play significant roles in helping young children negotiate these critical life events. Following are examples of how features of Erikson's stages can be seen in young children's behaviors and relationships.

Stage 1: Trust versus mistrust (birth to 18 months). Eight-month-old Martin is standing up in his crib sobbing and bouncing on his chubby legs. His family child care provider, Joanne, comes in and soothingly says, "I can tell you are wet and hungry. Let's change your diaper now." Martin sighs as she picks him up lovingly. Joanne knows Martin well enough to interpret his cries and respond accordingly; in turn, Martin is comforted by the fact that when he cries, Joanne is there for him.

The major task of infants and their caregivers is to develop a sense of trust in the world, a feeling that their needs for food and love will be met. Babies' trust develops through responsive relationships with caregivers. If adults are inconsistent or rejecting, the baby learns that the world is an untrustworthy place and that he has little power to influence what happens to him.

Stage 2: Autonomy versus doubt (18 months to 3 years). Belinda is 22 months old. She has been in the same child care center with the same primary caregiver, Sandy, since she was 5 months old. She and Sandy have a warm, loving relationship. But lately, Belinda has begun to resist just about everything Sandy wants her to do. As soon as Sandy finishes dressing her, Belinda starts pulling off her shoes or shirt. She yells, "I want red shirt." Sandy calmly says, "Okay, you can choose. Do you want your red shirt or your yellow one (the one she is already wearing)?" Belinda pumps up her chest and says, "Yellow one."

Belinda's behavior may seem like a step backward toward infancy, but actually it is evidence of her advancing development. By 18 months, most babies are mobile and soon able to communicate their wants and needs in words. They begin to separate from primary caregivers, try to do things for themselves, and assert their autonomy with statements like "Me do it!" or "Mine." This desire to break away from caregivers is sometimes called the "terrible twos" because it can lead to power struggles. One minute, the child wants to hold onto the adult, and the next minute, she wants to push away. But becoming a more autonomous human being is a major task of growing up. If adults are too harsh or restrictive with children at this age, children can feel powerless and doubt their own competence. One effective strategy is giving a toddler a manageable amount of power, such as Sandy did by offering a choice of two shirts.

Stage 3: Initiative versus guilt (3 to 6 years). Donald teaches 4-year-olds. He loves this age group because he finds that most 4-year-olds can do many things on their own while at the same time expressing their unbridled joy at every new accomplishment. He sets up his classroom and daily schedule to allow for as much choice as possible while also being available to assist children during these periods of child-initiated activity. Dorcas especially needs his help because her parents have been somewhat overprotective, and she is hesitant to try new experiences.

The preschool and kindergarten years are marked for most children by an increasing sense of their own abilities, especially improved motor skills and exploding language capacity. This sense of confidence, at times unwarranted, leads children to initiate their own activities. When children's initiatives are regularly punished or thwarted, they may begin to feel guilty and withdraw. The resolution for negotiating this stage is making sure that encouraging children's initiative and risk-taking is balanced by ensuring their safety.

Stage 4: Industry versus inferiority (6 to 12 years). Melodie's second-grade class is working in small groups on subtraction problems. One group works feverishly, arguing over the correct answers and giving each other high fives when they figure them out. Another group of children is quieter, appearing frustrated and unsure. Looking over at the others, Max says, "We're the dumb group. We'll never do good in math."

During the elementary school years, children's spheres expand, and the opinions of teachers and peers become more important and parents' less so. School work becomes a major part of children's lives, and they begin to find satisfaction in achievement and in mastering new skills. They also begin to compare themselves to others and are more capable of judging their own performances. When children's accomplishments are not up to their standards, they may develop a sense of inferiority.

Erikson emphasized that development does not end during childhood but continues throughout the life span. Adults—students, teachers, and parents—will see themselves in the later stages (see Table 4.1). Understanding the struggles of the later stages—identity versus role confusion, intimacy versus isolation, generativity versus self-absorption, and integrity versus despair—can provide teachers with insight into the behavior of adolescents (who may be parents) and other adults, including parents and colleagues. However, the first four stages are most relevant to the work of early childhood educators.

Implications for Teaching Erikson's theory has important implications for the social-emotional climates of early childhood programs, as we can see from visiting the Love and Learn Child Care Center. In this center, babies and toddlers have primary caregivers who stay with them for two or three years so teachers get to know them well and can provide consistent, responsive care. The preschool and kindergarten classes are structured with extended periods of time for children to initiate their own activities within the options that the teacher provides. Teachers encourage children to voice their opinions and ideas. The after-school program provides time, space, and materials for primary-grade children to pursue and master hobbies and interests, such as photography, computers, painting, sports, and writing stories.

In this book, we advocate a *both/and* approach to many questions regarding early childhood practice. Erikson's theory is an example of this approach, because each of the crises that children must negotiate is resolved by achieving a balance between the two poles. Trust is essential, for example, but children also need to develop a healthy sense of caution when interacting with strangers. Similarly, preschool children's initiative should be encouraged, but they also need to learn limits.

Erikson's theory emphasizes the role of the sociocultural context on children's personal and social development, but parts of his theory assume particular cultural perspectives. For example, his emphasis on the singular role of the mother during the first three stages doesn't reflect the value that some cultural groups place on multiple caregivers (see the *Culture Lens* feature on page 111).

Maslow's Self-Actualization Theory

self-actualization theory Maslow's view that behavior and learning are motivated by a hierarchy of needs.

Abraham Maslow (1908–1970) was part of a group of psychologists called humanists who studied healthy personality development rather than mental illness, as psychologists had done previously. Maslow (1954) developed self-actualization theory, which identifies a hierarchy of needs, as depicted in Figure 4.1, that motivate people's behavior and goals that are necessary for healthy personality development.

Hierarchy of Human Needs Maslow's hierarchy can be represented by a pyramid depicting the relationship between needs and goals. The bottom two layers represent the basic physical needs required to sustain life, such as food, water, and shelter, and the fundamental psychological needs for safety and security. Maslow postulated that unless these needs are met, humans cannot move up the hierarchy to achieve the next goals: love and a sense of belonging, and then self-esteem. The top of the pyramid represents self-actualization, which is achievement of life's goals in many individual forms. Goals that contribute to self-actualization are things that make life meaningful and satisfying. Maslow speculated that self-actualization is not achieved by everyone, although most people strive for it.

Implications for Practice Maslow's theory is useful as a framework for understanding how people are motivated. If children are hungry, it follows that they cannot focus their attention on anything else. Similarly, if children are frightened or emotionally insecure, they cannot learn effectively. Meeting children's basic physical needs as well as their need for psychological safety and emotional security is at the heart of good early childhood practice. Consider free school lunch programs and state licensing standards that set requirements for operating a child care center—these mandates are designed to protect children's health, safety, and security.

Effective early childhood programs go beyond meeting children's basic needs, however. Their goals include establishing positive, affectionate relationships among children and adults (the need for love and belonging) and building children's competence in all areas and therefore their self-esteem. Meeting children's needs and helping them achieve these goals contribute to life satisfaction and successful learning. Although children will not reach the pinnacle of Maslow's hierarchy—self-actualization—the foundations are laid during those early years. Adults might want to consider that a career teaching young children can be a self-actualizing experience, especially for those who find this work meaningful, playful, rewarding, and contributing to a better world.

The theories of both Erikson and Maslow apply primarily to social and personality development and the motivation to learn. Next, we turn to two theorists—Piaget and Vygotsky—whose work applies primarily to cognitive development. Because all domains of development are so integrally connected, however, these theories also have implications for social-emotional development.

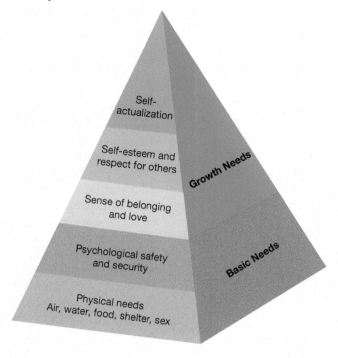

FIGURE 4.1 Maslow's Hierarchy of Needs Maslow's Hierarchy of Human Needs graphically depicts how successful relationships, positive self-esteem, and learning depend on a strong foundation of physical safety and security.

Source: A Maslow, © 2013. *Motivation and personality*. Reprinted and electronically reproduced by permission of Pearson Education, Inc., Upper Saddle River, NJ.

Piaget and Cognitive Developmental Theory

The cognitive developmental theory of Jean Piaget (1896–1980) has had enormous impact on early childhood education. Although parts of his theory—particularly the stages of cognitive development—have been criticized, he remains a towering and influential figure decades after his death.

Swiss-born, Piaget spent the greater part of his life observing and listening to children of various ages, beginning with detailed observations of his own children as infants. Piaget's wife, Valentine, did most of the minute-by-minute, day-by-day observing and recording of the children's behavior beginning at birth using the only tools available at the time, pen and paper (Gopnik, Meltzoff, & Kuhl, 1999).

Several aspects of Piaget's theory readily apply to education. The following sections present key concepts for teachers: constructivism, the process of learning (adaptation), types of knowledge, and the general idea of stages of cognitive development.

Constructivist Learning Theory Piaget's relatively complex theory can be summed up in a simple sentence: *Children think differently from adults.* Einstein called this discovery by Piaget "so simple that only a genius could have thought of it" (Papert, 1999). Piaget believed that children's minds are not empty vessels to be filled with knowledge by adults; instead, children actively make sense of their experiences by building or constructing their own knowledge. Piaget's theory of how children learn is called **constructivism**.

From his own perspective as a scientist, Piaget viewed children as little scientists who hypothesize about how the world works and continually test and refine their own theories (Piaget, 1952). The following example illustrates how Piaget (1930) did his work and how a young child thinks:

constructivism Learning theory derived from the work of Jean Piaget, which assumes that children actively build their knowledge from firsthand experiences in stimulating environments.

> *Piaget:* Where does the wind come from?
>> *Ost (age 4):* From outside.
>> *Piaget:* How is it made outside?
>> *Ost:* By the motor cars.
>> *Piaget:* What else can make the wind?
>> *Ost:* Bicycles, trams, carts, dust.
>> *Piaget:* What else?
>> *Ost:* When you blow, when you sweep. (p. 35)

This dialogue demonstrates Piaget's idea that children develop their own theories of how the world works. With their experiences, children test their theories and eventually either strengthen, change, or discard them.

How Development Occurs: The Process of Adaptation   One way we can tell that children construct their own knowledge is that they come up with their own ideas about or explanations for events. This is one reason young children can be so enchanting. Five-year-old Pearson arrives at kindergarten one morning and proudly announces to his teacher, "I know what A + A is—B!" Pearson hasn't discovered algebra, but he does apply what he has learned about how numbers work (1 + 1 = 2) to the alphabet. However mistaken Pearson is at this point, he is clearly thinking and trying to connect what he is learning to what he already knows.

Piaget believed that all children, like Pearson, have an inborn ability to organize and make sense of their experiences. Piaget coined the term scheme or schema for the organizing structures people use to think or guide behavior. Schemes develop and change with experience. Toddler Veronica has a big German Shepherd dog named Darby. When Veronica meets the Labrador next door, she calls him Darby, too. Her mom responds, "He's a doggie, but his name isn't Darby. It's Milo." Then Veronica sees a pony at the petting zoo and exclaims with glee, "Doggie!" But when she goes to pet the pony, she realizes he is much taller than either Darby or Milo. Again, her mother clarifies: "No, he has four legs like Darby and Milo, but he's a pony, not a doggie."

After many such experiences, Veronica changes her scheme for dogs (including the fact that dogs are not all the same) and another scheme for ponies. This process of changing schemes in response to experiences is called adaptation, and occurs in two ways:

scheme or schema
The organization of mental structures people use to think or guide behavior; the structures develop and change with experience.

adaptation   The mental process of altering concepts (schemes) in response to experience, which occurs in two ways: through assimilation and accommodation.

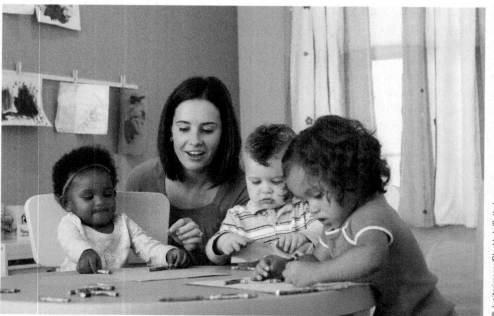

As young children play and interact with objects and other people, they construct their own understanding about the world, such as what a crayon can do and how paper is used.

through assimilation and accommodation. **Assimilation** occurs when new information or experience is understood in connection with an existing scheme. Veronica assimilated her experience with Milo into her scheme for dogs.

By contrast, if the new information doesn't fit within an existing scheme, the child must modify that scheme or construct a new one, a process called **accommodation**. In Veronica's case, the pony couldn't be assimilated into her doggie scheme, so a new scheme for pony had to be created. As Veronica gets older and has many more experiences, she will create different schemes to organize this basic information. Pony will be connected with the general scheme of animals, as well as the narrower scheme of animals you can ride.

When Veronica touched the pony and her mother gave her new information, she experienced **disequilibrium**, which is an imbalance in thinking that occurs when new information or physical experience cannot be understood in terms of what is already known (i.e., cannot be assimilated). Piaget believed that human beings seek equilibrium—we want the world to make sense, so we try to restore balance by creating new schemes or adapting existing ones, the process of **equilibration**.

Piaget theorized that learning depends on this process of adapting schemes through assimilation and accommodation in order to achieve equilibrium. He also believed that to change schemes, or accommodate, children need hands-on physical experience (they need to act on objects) and social interaction with peers and adults who help clarify their thinking. In the case of Veronica, her pony scheme was constructed through her real-life encounter at the zoo as well as her conversations with her mother.

Types of Knowledge   Another important point of Piaget's theory is that there are different kinds of knowledge. Piaget believed that children's minds develop as the result of interactions between experience and biology. But the process is not identical for every type of learning. In fact, Piaget (1952) identified three types of knowledge—physical, logico-mathematical, and social-conventional—each acquired in different ways.

- **Physical knowledge** is understanding how objects move and function in space—how the physical world works. Two-year-old Evan loves to watch the rubber ball roll down the ramp, and repeats the action over and over. Then he tries using a rubber block. Even though the block is soft like the ball, it doesn't cooperate. Evan's hands-on experience with the ball and block adds to his knowledge of how different objects function in the physical world.
- **Logico-mathematical knowledge** is the relationships that are constructed in our minds between objects or concepts. Unlike physical knowledge, logico-mathematical knowledge is not directly observable. While playing with his ramp, Evan sees that Delia has two small balls and he has one big one. He decides that he wants a second ball. The idea that two balls are more than one ball is an example of logico-mathematical knowledge. Evan created the relationship between the objects in his mind; it does not exist otherwise. He could just as easily have focused on the relationship of size instead of quantity and decided to keep the big ball.
- **Social-conventional knowledge** is the culturally agreed-on names and symbols that need to be transmitted to the learner directly. For example, the letters of the alphabet, number names, and the meaning of the colors on the stoplight are all arbitrary. This kind of knowledge can't be reinvented by every learner. Usually, children learn these symbols by repeated exposure (hearing and seeing them frequently) or being directly taught.

A challenge for teachers is that different types of knowledge require different types of teaching and learning. Just because social-conventional knowledge is most efficiently learned through instruction does not mean that other types of knowledge can be easily acquired this way. Complex concepts, such as counting, which is logico-mathematical knowledge, require much deeper understanding than simply reciting the number names. At the same time, children can't learn to count if they don't know the number sequence, just as they can't learn to read if they don't know the alphabet. Therefore, in constructing their understanding of concepts, children often draw on all three kinds of knowledge.

assimilation When new information or experience is understood in connection with existing knowledge (schemes).

accommodation When new information or experience doesn't fit within an existing concept (scheme), the child must modify it or construct a new scheme.

disequilibrium An imbalance in thinking that occurs when new information or physical experience cannot be understood in terms of what is already known (cannot be assimilated).

equilibration The process whereby humans try to make sense of new experiences by creating new concepts (schemes) or adapting existing ones.

physical knowledge Understanding how objects move and function in space and how the physical world works.

logico-mathematical knowledge The relationships that are constructed in our minds between objects or concepts.

social-conventional knowledge The culturally agreed-on names and symbols that need to be transmitted to the learner directly.

TABLE 4.2 Piaget's Stages of Cognitive Development

Stage	Approximate Age	Characteristics
Sensorimotor	Birth to 2 years	Learns through senses and physical movement, gradually moving from reflexes to conscious activity
Preoperational	2 to 7 years	Develops ability to learn through symbols—language and mental representations of thoughts; thinking is controlled more by perceptions than logic
Concrete operational	7 to 11 years	Able to think and solve problems more logically through concrete experience; abstract thinking is limited
Formal operational	11 years to adulthood	Can think and solve problems abstractly using symbolic thought and systematic experimentation

Source: Based on R. Slavin, 2015. *Educational psychology: Theory and practice* (11th ed.). Upper Saddle River, NJ: Pearson.

Cognition and Biology: Stages of Cognitive Development Piaget believed that biology plays a key role in cognitive development, with specific cognitive abilities changing in significant ways as children get older. His theory identifies four stages of cognition, as listed in Table 4.2. Piaget theorized that although the ages were approximate, the order of the stages is fixed and every child goes through each stage.

Sensorimotor Stage (Birth to Age 2) During the years from birth to about age 2, children learn about the world through a combination of their sensory abilities—sight, hearing, taste, touch, smell—and their motor skills. Newborn and young infants rely on reflexes, such as sucking and grasping to build schemes. When baby Sonia grasps her rattle and brings it to her mouth, she finds out lots of things about the rattle—it makes a noise she likes, and it feels hard and cold. Another characteristic of the sensorimotor period is that babies lack **object permanence**, which means that when an object is no longer in their sight, it ceases to exist for them. For example, if Mommy hides the favorite rattle under a blanket, Sonia won't look for it. When the blanket is removed, Sonia will inevitably be surprised to find the rattle there.

object permanence
A concept that babies lack early in the period of sensorimotor development so that when an object is no longer in their sight, it ceases to exist for them.

As children get older and are able to move on their own, crawling and toddling, they use more conscious movements to find out how things work. But their learning occurs through their actions; they don't yet think or plan in advance. Consider 18-month-old Ronde, who stacks his blocks in front of the cabinet door. When he opens the door, the blocks fall over, much to his surprise and dismay. Nevertheless, Ronde keeps stacking and knocking over the blocks, not realizing that if he moved the toys before opening the door, they wouldn't fall down.

egocentrism The process whereby very young children tend to see everything from their own intellectual and emotional points of view.

Very young children also tend to see everything from their own points of view, what Piaget called **egocentrism**. Their experiences, such as shaking the rattle or making milk flow by sucking, convince them that they are the center of their worlds and can cause events to happen.

By about age 2, young children begin to be able to use symbols, such as words, instead of relying on actions and objects to learn about the world, and they move into Piaget's second stage of cognitive development—preoperational.

Preoperational Stage (Ages 2 to 7) Several major cognitive developments occur during this stage. First, children's language development explodes, which provides symbols that enable children to think (that is, hold a mental representation) of an object or event. Ronde can now picture the door knocking down his blocks and therefore thinks ahead to building in a safer place. As a result of this new thinking ability, children are less dependent on sensorimotor learning, although active learning is still most effective.

Piaget did many classic experiments with preoperational children, trying to gauge their ability to solve various prearranged tasks. What he concluded from these studies is that preoperational children rely on their perceptions or intuitions about solutions rather than on logic.

For example, at snack time, 4-year-olds Isela and Ruth each have one graham cracker. Isela breaks hers into four pieces and tells Ruth, "Look! I have more crackers than you do!" Nothing her teacher says will convince Ruth that they have the same amount. Ruth is not content until the teacher resignedly breaks her cracker into four pieces as well.

From his observations, Piaget concluded that there are several specific limitations to the thinking of preoperational children. Ruth and Isela's situation demonstrates that they were unable to conserve quantity. Conservation is the concept that the quantity of objects or liquids does not change just because their physical appearance is transformed. If Ruth had a tall glass of milk and her teacher poured the milk into a short fat one, no doubt she would think that she had less milk and feel cheated once more. Ruth is unable to reverse the operation of pouring the milk in her mind and figure out that the amount has not changed. The same phenomenon—judging by appearances rather than logic—is observed when preschool children are presented with two equal rows of checkers. After one row is spread out and appears longer, even though no checkers have been added or removed, preoperational children will assume that the spread-out row has more checkers.

Preoperational children also continue to be egocentric—interpreting the world from their own points of view, though less so over time. During a visit to the Gettysburg battlefield, 3-year-old Ryan declares to his Nana, "I was too little to fight in the battle. I had to stay in the van."

conservation The understanding that the quantity of objects stays the same regardless of changes in appearance.

Concrete Operational Stage (Ages 7 to 11)
During the elementary school years, children's thinking becomes more logical, and they are able to solve problems mentally and reverse operations. They are no longer fooled by a conservation problem. Children are capable of carrying out mental actions. Piaget used the word *concrete* to refer to this stage of cognition because this age group is not yet capable of thinking about and fully comprehending complex, abstract concepts, such as historical time or death. Instead, they are most successful at solving problems they can directly experience. Piaget believed that abstract reasoning is not possible until the stage of formal observations in adolescence and adulthood, and that some people never reach this stage of cognitive development.

Criticisms of Piaget's Theory
Piaget's theory was first widely disseminated in the United States in the 1970s and had a major impact on views of how children learn and of appropriate ways to teach. Parents, toy manufacturers, and publishers were also influenced by Piaget's ideas about the competence of children, leading to an explosion in educational products for babies.

Piaget's stage theory emphasized the limitations of children's thinking at each stage, leading some educators to focus more on what children were *not* able to do rather than on their developing competencies. Preschool classrooms provided an interesting environment for children to "discover," with little interaction with adults to support expanding children's thinking. And most educators assumed that mathematics and literacy, which are based on understanding symbols, were too abstract for preoperational children and therefore not taught until children were older.

In recent decades, researchers and educators have challenged some of the fundamental tenets of Piagetian theory. Researchers have found that Piaget overestimated the role of biologically based stages and discovery in children's development, and underestimated the role of the environment and teaching. For example, researchers have found that Piaget underestimated children's abilities to think in more complex ways (Case & Okamoto, 1996; Eason & Levine, 2017; Gelman, 2000). Using carefully designed experiments, researchers have found that infants have object permanence much younger than Piaget theorized. With support, children can begin to understand the perspectives of other people at a much younger age than Piaget assumed. In addition, the inability to conserve quantity does not interfere with some preschool children's learning basic mathematics concepts, as Piaget assumed (Clements & Sarama, 2009).

Researchers today agree that a major, though gradual, transformation occurs in children's cognitive abilities around kindergarten age, known as the **5- to 7-year shift** (Berk, 2006; Sameroff & McDonough, 1994). Children don't pass through sharply drawn stages; rather,

5- to 7-year shift Major transition in cognitive abilities that gradually occurs between 5 and 7 years of age, resulting in increased ability to think logically, self-regulate, and solve problems.

their brain development and experiences contribute to their expanded memory and more logical reasoning (Center on the Developing Child, 2016; IOM & NRC, 2015).

Contributions of Piagetian Theory to Practice Despite the well-founded criticisms of Piagetian theory, the contributions of his work are enormous. Visit any good-quality early childhood program, and you will see evidence of these contributions. Children are actively engaged in learning—not sitting still and listening to a teacher talk most of the time. There are concrete learning materials, and children have time to use them on their own. The environment itself is designed to promote learning. While Piaget underestimated infant and toddler understanding, he was the first to suggest—correctly—that infants have an active intellectual life. Knowledge of the sensorimotor state of development literally launched the industry of toys and equipment for babies—mobiles over cribs, noise-making toys that babies control, and board books.

Piaget changed the way we view young children and how they learn. He believed that children developed understanding by interacting with objects and people in the environment. He relied on observing and interviewing to understand what children thought. However, Piaget overestimated the role of exploration and discovery in children's cognitive development, and underestimated the important role of the teacher. He also thought cognitive development was essentially the same across cultures. Lev Vygotsky, a Russian psychologist, studied Piaget's theory and expanded our understanding of children's development in important ways.

Application Exercise 4.2

Constructivism in Action

Vygotsky and Sociocultural Theory

Lev Vygotsky (1896–1934) was born in Russia the same year as Piaget. Although he died young, he was a prolific writer, and after his death, his theories were further developed and disseminated by his students. Because his work was not translated into English until 1962, it was unknown in the West until long after his death. The Stalinist regime also suppressed his work in his native country.

sociocultural theory Vygotsky's theory that children learn from social interaction within a cultural context.

Vygotsky's sociocultural theory is based on his belief that children learn from social interaction within a cultural context. He emphasized that *what* children learn is determined by the culture in which they grow up, such as an urban child learning to negotiate dangerous street crossings or a rural child learning to milk a cow. In recent years, Vygotsky's views on learning and teaching have become more influential than Piaget's, although the theories are actually complementary (Copple & Bredekamp, 2009).

Vygotsky's Theory of How Development Occurs Among developmental theorists, Vygotsky provided the greatest amount of guidance for educators (Stetsenko & Vianna, 2009). He viewed development as a continuous process driven by learning. At particular ages, the primary learning task differs. Babies learn through their senses and by manipulating objects (similar to Piaget's view). Relationships with adults, who talk and play with babies and often use objects when doing so, drive learning during the first two years of life.

From ages 2 to 5, children's development is dominated by their perceptions and reactions. They pay attention to what is interesting and meaningful to them, rather than to what adults prefer. They act and react without prior thinking or reflecting on past actions. For example, when Ms. Broyles says, "It's time to go outside, so put away your toys and get your coats," most 3- and 4-year-olds will run to the door. Much to Ms. Broyles's dismay, they still have this reaction after weeks of school. Vygotsky believed that a major goal of preschool is to help children move from such reactive thinking to the ability to think *before* they act (Bodrova & Leong, 2012b).

During the preschool years, children need to acquire cognitive and social-emotional competencies that shape their minds for all further learning—language, memory, focused attention, and self-regulation (Bodrova & Leong, 2012b). If these important foundations are in place, in the primary grades children acquire the ability to "learn on demand," as Vygotsky called it. They are more likely to cooperate with the school's agenda—learning to read, calculate, and follow group rules—even when they would rather be doing something else.

According to Vygotsky, cognitive development involves the zone of proximal development, scaffolding, social construction of knowledge, language and other symbol systems, self-regulation, and play. These concepts, discussed in the sections that follow, have important implications for practice.

Zone of Proximal Development

Twenty-month-old Ave is trying desperately to get on the pony riding toy. Her teacher, Khari, observes that she is about to cry in frustration. He could pick her up and put her on it, but instead he gently lifts her leg so that she gets over the last hurdle herself. Ave gives him a big smile as she pushes off with her feet and makes a circle around the room.

By giving Ave "a leg up," Khari helped her accomplish a goal that she couldn't do on her own, but could achieve with his assistance. Vygotsky (1978) identified this as the zone of proximal development (ZPD)—the distance between the actual developmental level an individual has achieved (their independent level of problem solving) and the level of potential development they could achieve with adult guidance or through collaboration with other children. The assistance, guidance, and direction teachers provide children in their ZPD is called scaffolding.

Scaffolding children's learning is a key instructional tool for children at all levels. It incorporates "serve and return," assessing a child's level of development and intervening with instruction matched to the child's level of ability and engagement to help them make progress.

Language and Thought

Because Vygotsky (1962) believed that learning depends on interaction with other people, he also believed that speech is the most important tool for learning. Babies begin by communicating through gestures, as when they learn that holding up their arms means "pick me up." Then they connect sounds and words with their meanings; saying "Da Da" gets a different result from saying "Ma Ma." Language growth during the preschool years enables children to learn through conversation. Speech gradually becomes internalized and used for thinking.

Think of a situation, such as learning a psychology concept or solving a mathematics problem, which you didn't really understand until you talked about it with someone else or at least stated your ideas out loud. According to Vygotsky, articulating an idea is necessary for real understanding. He described the relationship between language and thought as moving from interpersonal (between people) to intrapersonal (inside the child). Learning begins in conversation between people and then becomes part of an individual's thinking.

Interpersonal understanding or socially constructed knowledge is turned into intrapersonal knowledge through private speech (Vygotsky, 1962). For preschool children, private speech can look like thinking out loud. As 3½-year-old Ivor stands in front of the easel contemplating the next color to use, thick paint starts running down the paper. Ivor says, "Whoa, don't do that. I'm gonna get you with my brush," and proceeds to do so. By age 6 or 7, private speech becomes silent and is used for thinking and problem solving.

To summarize, children first use language for conversation. Then, through the vehicle of private speech, they literally use language to talk to themselves and to control their own behavior—that is, for self-regulation (Bailey & Brookes, 2012).

zone of proximal development (ZPD) The distance between the actual developmental level an individual has achieved (her independent level of problem solving) and the level of potential development she could achieve with adult guidance or through collaboration with other children.

scaffolding The assistance, guidance, and direction teachers provide children to help them accomplish a task or learn a skill (within their ZPD) that they could not achieve on their own.

© Pearson Education

Video Example 4.2:

Scaffolding Children's Learning

In this video, the teacher scaffolds Cooper's writing and story development. How does the teacher provide just the right amount of help at the right time? What do you think her goals are for Cooper in this activity? Does he meet these goals?

private speech The process whereby interpersonal understanding or socially constructed knowledge is turned into intrapersonal knowledge (thinking aloud becomes thinking to oneself).

Self-Regulation Vygotsky considered the development of self-regulation the primary task of the years before formal school entry. As we have seen, self-regulation is the ability to adapt or intentionally control behavior, emotions, and thinking according to the demands of the situation (Bodrova & Leong, 2012b). Preschool children's self-regulation ability is strongly related to their academic success in the early grades. When children have problems with self-control, they are more likely to experience health, economic, and social problems in school and in later life (Moffat, Arseneault, Belsky & Harrington, 2011). Teachers or parents may understand self-regulation as "the capacity to control one's impulses both to stop doing something that is unnecessary (even if one wants to continue doing it), and to start doing something that is needed (even if one does not want to do it)" (Boyd, Barnett, Bodrova, Leong, & Gomby, 2005, p. 4). This is why self-regulation is so strongly related to success. Every day, preschool teachers require children to stop playing (which they usually want to continue) and start cleaning up (which they don't want to do). Similarly, children in primary grades must attend to the reading lesson when they would rather go outside for recess.

Children who have Attention Deficit Hyperactivity Disorder (ADHD) often have developmental delays in their executive functions (IOM & NRC, 2015). They are often impulsive and have trouble paying attention. They also may have difficulty with working memory, the brain ability that allows us to remember information in the short term and use the information to understand and solve problems. While some children are identified with ADHD in preschool, children are typically diagnosed in early elementary school, when the demands of formal schooling require more focused attention and regulation.

Teachers can support EF in development of children with ADHD in several ways (Murphy, 2014). To help children focus better, teachers can break instructions and tasks into structured pieces, give individualized instructions, and check for understanding of instructions. Teachers can help children regulate their own behavior by providing positive reinforcement for positive behavior and by avoiding negative feedback, which can lead to poor self-image in children with ADHD. Many children with ADHD take medication to help them attend and regulate in the school setting; however, research suggests that the supports families and teachers can provide may help as much as medication in helping children experience school success.

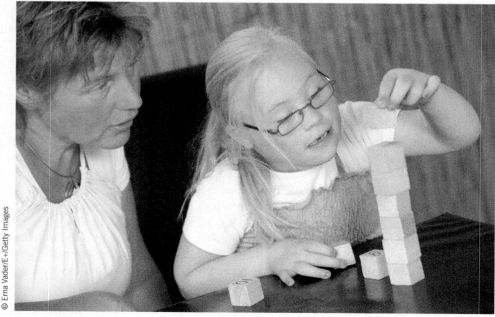

© Erna Vader/E+/Getty Images

Effective teachers draw on all the relevant theories to support children's learning progress. What strategies do you think this teacher is using to help this young girl accomplish a new skill?

Children with ADHD also benefit from an environment that allows for play and exercise. Recent research has examined the role of physical activity in children's attention and EF. Physical exercise enhances sustained attention in preschoolers (Palmer, Miller, & Robinson, 2013) and EF in elementary school children with ADHD (Gapin & Etnier, 2010).

Play and Vygotsky's Theory   According to Vygotsky (1978), make-believe play is the *leading activity* in children's development from about ages 2 through 5. Play creates a zone of proximal development in which a child behaves "as though he were a head taller than himself" (Vygotsky, 1978, p. 102). When children pretend to be adults—parents, teachers, or workers, as they often do—they use more sophisticated language than usual and model grown-up behavior.

Pretend play in small groups is especially valuable for promoting self-regulation because it is the one activity that requires children to regulate their own behavior, be regulated by others, and regulate others all within the same context (Leong & Bodrova, 2012). Picture 5-year-olds playing restaurant. Each child, whether playing customer, waiter, or cook, has an assigned role and must stick to the script. The customer can't say, "Can I take your order?" That's the waiter's role. If the customer begins serving the food, the play breaks down. The waiter says, "You can't do that. You have to sit down, look at the menu, and eat." The rules have to be renegotiated. The customer may say, "Okay, but I get to be the waiter next." So we see that the customer has to regulate herself (stay in her role and follow the rules), be regulated by others (the waiter), and regulate others (place her order so the waiter can do his job).

Sociodramatic play promotes children's ability to take another person's perspective (Vygotsky, 1977). Assuming a pretend role—being another person for a while—helps children move to another perspective and then back to their own. This ability to take another's perspective—to go beyond egocentrism—is necessary in school, where children need to see the perspectives of teachers and other children.

Elena Bodrova, who studied with Vygotsky's students, and her colleague, Deborah Leong, developed a Vygotskian curriculum model, *Tools of the Mind* (Bodrova & Leong, 2007, 2012b). The model focuses on teachers' building self-regulation in children through mature sociodramatic play.

Implications for Practice   Vygotsky's sociocultural theory has many implications for early childhood practice. Teaching in the zone of proximal development requires that children experience a challenging curriculum—not content that is meant for older children, but content that moves them ahead in thinking and problem solving.

Similarly, the role of the teacher becomes more important than ever, not as controller of the classroom, but as a collaborator with children. Teachers need to scaffold children's learning and set up situations where groups of children work together to solve problems and have the freedom to think out loud. During preschool and kindergarten, teachers need to intentionally support mature sociodramatic play to promote self-regulation, a topic we will return to later in this chapter.

Major contributions of Vygotsky's theory are his emphasis on (1) the role of adults in children's development, and (2) the transmission of cultural understandings as a part of children's development. We'll next consider a model that expands theory to a systems level, in which children develop in the context of many environments and interactions over time.

Bronfenbrenner's Ecological Systems Theory of Development

One of the most useful theories for understanding the interactive influence of social and cultural contexts on human development is the ecological systems model proposed by psychologist Urie Bronfenbrenner (1917–2005). Figure 4.2 illustrates Bronfenbrenner's

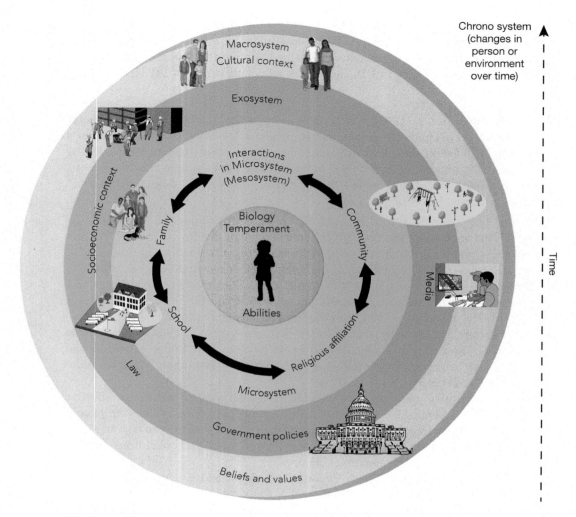

FIGURE 4.2 Model of Bronfenbrenner's Ecological Systems Theory

Source: T. M. McDevitt & J. E. Ormrod, © 2018. *Child development and education* (6th ed.). Reprinted and electronically reproduced by permission of Pearson Education, Inc., Upper Saddle River, NJ.

 Application Exercise 4.3

Figure 4.2: Model of Bronfenbrenner's Ecological Systems Theory

ecological systems theory Bronfenbrenner's theory that describes the diverse, interactive contexts that influence children's development over time.

microsystem System in which the child directly participates on a regular basis and includes the family, child care, school and faith-based settings.

proximal processes Interactions in the context of daily living that have the most impact on a child's development due to their frequent, ongoing nature, often over extended periods of time.

ecological systems theory (Bronfenbrenner, 1979, 2004), which describes the diverse, interactive contexts that influence children's development over time.

At the center of the model is the individual, whose development is influenced by his or her own biological factors, social interaction, and experiences in a variety of contexts. The environments, or systems, surrounding an individual from birth and beyond play significant interactive roles in a child's development. The systems in which the child directly participates on a regular basis are known as **microsystems** and include the family, child care, school, and faith-based settings. The child's daily interactions, which Bronfenbrenner called **proximal processes** (Bronfenbrenner & Morris, 2006), have the most impact on a child's development due to their frequent, ongoing nature, often over extended periods of time. Thought of as "drivers" of development, proximal processes include the physical care children receive, daily conversations with parents and teachers, and playground interactions with peers.

The next level of system that impacts a child's life is the **mesosystem**, which refers to the interaction of different microsystems in a child's life. Parent-teacher interactions, including conferences, phone calls, home visits, and back-to-school nights, are examples of a mesosystem—where the child's microsystems of home and school come together—and interact and influence each other. Bronfenbrenner believed that the strength of these mesosystems—the degree to which the systems work together—is important for supporting the child's positive development.

The exosystem consists of systems that affect the child's microsystems, but in which the child doesn't directly participate. This includes parents' employment, child care regulations, religious traditions, and school board decisions. When a teacher experiences stress in her home life, she may carry that stress into the classroom, impacting the quality of her relationships with students and the impact of her teaching. On the other hand, a teacher whose school board institutes policies that support good working conditions may be more likely to interact positively with children and provide effective instruction. An exosystem can include economic, media, education, health, legal, and political entities that directly effect a person or circumstance in the child's microsystem.

The outermost level of Bronfenbrenner's model is the macrosystem, which refers to the overarching cultural context of the values, beliefs, laws, and policies of a society. American society, for example, is strongly influenced not only by values of freedom and individual rights and responsibilities, but also by the value of collective responsibility for its neediest members. As a result, our institutions and social policies reflect these values, such as laws regarding provision of public assistance for families living in poverty. While it may not seem that macrosystems effect a child's daily life, they can exert a powerful influence over time. Bronfenbrenner uses the term chronosystem to refer to effects of circumstances over time. According to Bronfenbrenner, children who experience homelessness for a short period of time will likely suffer fewer negative outcomes than a child who is homeless for his or her entire childhood.

Bronfenbrenner's theory has helped educators and child development researchers realize the importance of considering the multiple, complex systems that impact children's development. Bronfenbrenner believed that society needs to attend carefully to supporting children by supporting all of the systems needed for a child to develop. Especially committed to supporting children and families who live in poverty, Bronfenbrenner was one of the key conceptual founders of the Head Start program. The comprehensive services (education, health, and family engagement) that are the hallmark of Head Start can be attributed in part to the influence of Bronfenbrenner's thinking.

In the previous sections, we described the developmental theories of Erikson, Maslow, Piaget, Vygotsky and Bronfenbrenner. Erikson's work, as well as that of Maslow, provides insights into children's social and personality development, and into their motivation. The theories of Piaget and Vygotsky cast considerable light on the processes of cognitive development and have much to teach teachers. Bronfenbrenner's ecological systems theory connects children's social and cognitive development with the many influential systems that surround them. In the next section, we turn to descriptions of the most influential theories of learning.

mesosystem Interaction of different microsystems in a child's life.

exosystem Systems that affect the child's microsystems but that the child doesn't directly participate in, including economic, media, education, health, legal, and political entities that directly effect a person or circumstance in the child's microsystem.

macrosystem System that includes the overarching cultural context of the values, beliefs, laws, and policies of a society.

chronosystem System that refers to effects of circumstances over time.

✔ Check Your Understanding 4.3

🔼 Learning Theories

In contrast to developmental theories, which are linked to age-related changes in children, learning theories are assumed to apply in the same way regardless of the age of the learner. In the following sections, we describe the work of two major learning theorists: B. F. Skinner and Albert Bandura. Another learning theory is Howard Gardner's multiple intelligences theory, which we discuss in the chapter on individual differences.

B. F. Skinner and Behaviorism

One of the most influential learning theories of the last half century is behaviorism or behavioral learning. According to this theory, learning is reflected in changes in behavior

behaviorism or behavioral learning Theory that learning is a change in behavior that is controlled by the consequences, either positive or negative, that follow the behavior.

operant conditioning The process of using pleasant or unpleasant consequences to control behavior.

that are controlled by the consequences, either positive or negative, that follow the behavior. Using pleasant or unpleasant consequences to control behavior is called operant conditioning.

Psychologist B. F. Skinner (1904–1980) developed the theory of operant conditioning through systematic experiments. Skinner discovered that he could train rats to press a lever by rewarding them with food. From experiments with animals and people, Skinner developed the core principles of operant conditioning, an example of which follows:

> During center time in her prekindergarten, teacher Nessa Stokes observes as Jemma struggles to print her name next to her artwork. As Jemma tires and looks as though she will give up, Nessa says, "You've almost got it, Jemma, J-E-M—two more letters and you will have written your name!" Jemma smiles proudly and continues her task. Nessa is reassured that her encouraging praise will keep Jemma working on a task that is difficult.
>
> Nessa also understands how technology can provide reinforcement to keep children motivated on difficult learning tasks. In the Tech Center, three children gather around a math game on the computer that has the boys distinguishing "more" and "less" in groups of dinosaurs. "More!" shouts Jessica, and Brian presses the button that indicates there are more dinosaurs in the new array than the previous. With the correct answer button pressed, the dinosaurs break out into a dance on the screen, leaving the children laughing. "Let's try the next one—a harder one," says Azim. "They get even funnier with harder ones." Nessa smiles, as in this activity she witnesses children cooperating, learning important math concepts, and getting positively reinforced for practicing skills while doing progressively more difficult math problems.

Although Nessa's actions in this brief scenario may seem relatively simple, she is in fact implementing several key principles of operant conditioning.

consequences Principle of operant conditioning that behavior changes as a result of what occurs immediately afterward.

Operant Conditioning
The most important principle of operant conditioning is that behavior changes as a result of its immediate consequences. Positive consequences strengthen the frequency of specific behaviors; unpleasant consequences decrease the frequency. Reinforcers are consequences that increase or strengthen behaviors. There are two kinds of reinforcers: positive and negative.

reinforcer Consequence—either positive or negative—that increases or strengthens a behavior.

Positive reinforcement is a reward or pleasant consequence that follows a behavior, causing that behavior to be repeated. In the previous example, Nessa reinforced or rewarded Jemma's writing efforts with a smile and positive words of encouragement. As a result, Jemma kept working at a difficult task. While Jessica, Brian, and Azim were sufficiently reinforced by the dancing dinosaur math game, Nessa knows to monitor their engagement in the activity to keep the learning and interactions positive and productive.

positive reinforcement A reward or pleasant consequence that follows a behavior, causing that behavior to be repeated.

Negative reinforcement also increases the frequency of a desired behavior, but in a different way. A negative reinforcer is an unpleasant consequence that is *avoided* if the person performs a behavior more frequently. For example, an annoying bell or buzzer—a negative reinforcer—signals when the seat belt is still unfastened after a car is started. To avoid the sound, most people fasten the seat belt as soon as they can. If Nessa had observed the children arguing over the computer game, she may have pointed out that they would lose computer time if they did not find a way to cooperate. Azim may have responded, "Let's take turns pressing the button, Brian." In this circumstance, negative reinforcement would have changed the children's behavior in positive ways.

negative reinforcement An unpleasant consequence that is avoided if the person performs a desired behavior more frequently.

punishment An unpleasant consequence that stops or decreases the frequency of a behavior.

Negative reinforcement is sometimes confused with, but is not the same thing as, punishment. Punishment is an unpleasant consequence that stops or *decreases* the frequency of a behavior. Many people, teachers as well as parents, think punishments are effective in changing behavior, and use them often. However, the problem with punishment is that it may temporarily stop an undesirable behavior, but it does not teach the child what to do instead. As a result, repeated punishment soon becomes ineffective in changing behavior. For example, when children misbehave in Tiffany's first-grade classroom, they get a red card and their name goes on the board, while those who behave well get a green card. But

When teachers use positive reinforcement, such as smiling or commenting on what a child is doing well, children are more likely to continue to stay engaged in learning.

day after day, the same children get the red card. Receiving the card—a punishment—does not improve their behavior.

Teachers need to understand that punishment only decreases an undesirable behavior temporarily. To increase a desired behavior, reinforcement is needed. In fact, in some cases, punishment actually serves as a negative reinforcer and increases the behavior. Consider the situation where a first-grade teacher decides to punish a disruptive child by making him miss recess. If the child wants to avoid recess because he doesn't get chosen for a team or is bullied, then removing him from recess is not a punishment but a reward, and thus will have the opposite effect from the one the teacher intended. When reinforcers are removed, the conditioned behavior diminishes and eventually disappears, a process called **extinction**.

extinction The process whereby a conditioned behavior diminishes and eventually disappears when reinforcers are removed.

What to Reinforce: Shaping Behavior Most human behavior is complex, much more so than that of the hungry rats Skinner studied. Children learn to take turns, follow classroom rules, or ride a bike over time and after many tries, some successful and others not. It would be impossible to wait to reinforce a highly complex behavior until a child performed it well. What if a kindergarten teacher only reinforced a child's writing when the letters were formed perfectly on the line? Many children would give up. Instead, an effective teacher recognizes the child's attempts, each step on the way to mastering writing the letters correctly. Teaching a new skill or behavior by rewarding each step toward the goal is called **shaping**.

shaping Teaching a new skill or behavior by rewarding each step or successive approximation toward the goal.

Shaping requires the teacher to carefully observe the **successive approximations**—not the actual desired behaviors, but each approximate behavior that is closer to the goal. For example, when 3-year-old Lola's scribbles begin to look like (approximate) a circle or straight line, her family child care provider Titia says, "Oh, look, Lola, you made an O like in your name." Lola didn't intend to draw an O, but it is likely that Titia's praise will result in Lola producing pages of Os to get more of Titia's positive attention.

successive approximations Behaviors that are reinforced (shaped) that are not the actual desired behaviors, but each approximate behavior that is closer to the goal.

Implications of Behaviorism for Practice Research supports the effectiveness of principles of behaviorism, especially for children with special needs (Division for Early Childhood, 2014). Some disabilities, such as cerebral palsy or Down syndrome, affect children's ability to perform functional behaviors (e.g., eating or dressing) that typically developing children learn relatively easily through imitation and repetition. Children with autism benefit from behavioral techniques to support learning social communication skills (Wong et al., 2014). In these situations, using behavioral learning techniques can be effective, as Yvonne learned in the opening vignette of this chapter. In the feature *Including All Children: Teaching Social Skills to Children with Disabilities*, note how a child's teacher and parents work together to support his developing social skills and friendships.

Behaviorism is a learning theory, not a theory of development. Therefore, the principles apply regardless of the age of the learner. However, as the name implies, the effectiveness of behaviorism is *limited* to teaching or changing observable behaviors. Even with this limitation, the important thing to remember is that behaviorism can be highly effective. At times, the wrong behaviors get reinforced, such as when an aggressive child gets what he or she wants by bullying.

Including All Children
Teaching Social Skills to Children with Disabilities

Children with disabilities may have difficulty making friends and being accepted by other children in the group. Peer rejection is harmful for every child, but especially painful for children with disabilities, who face multiple developmental challenges. And many parents of children with disabilities want most of all for their children to have friends and be treated like their typically developing peers. To achieve these goals, children with special needs often need adults—teachers and parents—to intervene, as the following example illustrates.

Tommy is a 5-year-old child with Down syndrome. He has attended preschool for the past two years and is now in kindergarten. Tommy's social relationships with the other children have been generally positive, especially with several children from his preschool. Recently, however, both Tommy's parents and teacher have noticed that other classmates have begun to avoid him, and former playmates are less interested in including him in their play. Children complain that Tommy "hugs too much," and in fact, Tommy hugs children and adults all day as a way of expressing joy and friendship. However, recently Tommy's hugs have gotten a bit too hard, and have even knocked a few children down. Children are seeing Tommy's hugs as aggressive.

Tommy's teacher, Ms. Wasky, has an early childhood degree but has little experience or knowledge of special education. She strives to provide interesting learning experiences that keep children engaged. She believes strongly in activating children's intrinsic motivation to learn rather than using external reinforcements, such as stickers or happy faces. She talks with the children and encourages them to include Tommy. Under Ms. Wasky's supervision, a few children grudgingly let Tommy join them, but then they ignore him. She is concerned that Tommy's social development is regressing.

Ms. Wasky and Tommy's parents discuss ways to help him become more accepted by his peers. The parents and teacher believe that Tommy can learn other strategies to express friendship and warmth with his peers. However, they want to give Tommy tools to interact independently, without adult participation all the time, and without disconnected external reinforcement.

Ms. Wasky and Tommy's parents decide to try a three-pronged approach. First, because Tommy uses little spoken language, they provide and teach him to use some social cue cards. When Tommy feels excited, he can share a friendship card with a peer. The card may show a picture of a child waving (saying "hello)" or showing playing children to indicate that Tommy would like to play. Next, Tommy uses a class picture to point to children he played with during the day, to share his friendship experiences with his parents. His parents ask questions to which Tommy can answer "yes" or "no" or point to a friend. Tommy circles the pictures of friends he wants to play with the next day, and puts a foil star by the pictures of children he has played with. He also has pictures of each of the classroom centers, so he can describe where he played. Finally, Ms. Wasky and Tommy's occupational therapist spend time several times a week playing popular games with Tommy and a few classmates. The presence of the teacher or therapist supports Tommy's appropriate interactions and increases the likelihood that classmates will feel safe playing with Tommy.

As a result of this intervention, Tommy experiences more success in his interactions with peers. When his needs for a hug are sensory-seeking, he can bring a "hug" card to his teacher, therapist, or family member, and they provide a good, strong hug. As a result of this explicit teaching strategy, Tommy not only experiences the fewer conflicted interactions with peers, but he begins to have enjoyable play times at school and better inhibits his impulses. Over time, Tommy may no longer need the picture supports, but while using them, he is better able to participate fully in the joys of classroom life.

Behaviorism, as epitomized by Skinner's work, is often pitted against developmental theories and teaching approaches. This is usually because behaviorism is connected to specific instructional practices, such as when teachers tell children facts and reward their correct answers. Another strong criticism of behaviorism is that overreliance on external rewards undermines children's internal motivation (Kohn, 2014). For example, paying children to read books may make them less motivated to read on their own when the payment isn't available.

But effective teaching is not an *either/or* choice between constructivism and behaviorism. These theories each apply best to different phenomena. Behaviorism may work to change observable behaviors, but it does not explain, nor is it effective in influencing, the less visible but essential processes of thinking, concept development, and problem solving. To explain this kind of learning, we must look to the theories of Piaget or Vygotsky, as described earlier. Building on the work of behaviorists and bridging the gap between behaviorism and cognitive theory is the work of Albert Bandura, described in the next section.

Albert Bandura and Social Cognitive Theory

Developed by psychologist Albert Bandura (born in 1925), social cognitive theory (also called *social learning theory*) is both a behavioral and cognitive theory, and therefore serves as a bridge between those two views of learning. Whereas Skinner's work emphasized that a person's behavior needs to be directly reinforced to change, Bandura demonstrated that people can learn more efficiently from observing the consequences of another person's behavior. This theory has important implications for classroom teaching.

social cognitive theory Bandura's theory that people can learn efficiently from observing the consequences of another person's behavior.

Bandura theorized that observational learning depends on learners having an image in their mind of the behavior they observed and its consequences—a memory of an event captured in pictures and/or words. This theory explains an important way that children learn—they observe and then model the behaviors they observe. Bandura's emphasis on the importance of a mental image adds a cognitive dimension to the learning theory and separates it from Skinnerian behaviorism.

To test his hypothesis that children would model observed behaviors, Bandura (1973) conducted hundreds of studies. In now famous research, he filmed situations in which an adult or another child were complimented or rewarded for beating up a plastic inflated clown named Bobo. Then, given the opportunity, kindergarten children who watched the demonstration not only beat up Bobo but also used the exact motions and expression, "Sockeroo!"

According to Bandura, children learn from watching what other children do and the consequences that follow. What do you think the teacher should do if one of the children is hurting other people?

modeling Teacher showing children a skill or desirable way of behaving or speaking; also children imitating the behavior of others.

vicarious learning Learning by observing the effects of other people's behavior, rather than experiencing rewards or punishments directly.

Modeling and Observational Learning

The basic principles of social cognitive theory are (1) children learn by **modeling**—that is, imitating the behavior of others—and (2) they can learn vicariously. **Vicarious learning** is based on observing the effects of other people's behavior rather than experiencing the rewards or punishments directly. Consider the following example of modeling:

> Mr. Evans's group of 3-year-olds is getting louder and louder as they boisterously encourage each other to jump up and down and scream at the top of their lungs. Wanting to scream himself, Mr. Evans chooses instead to tiptoe around the group, take Bettina by the hand, and whisper softly to follow him. One by one, the children stop their jumping and begin imitating Mr. Evans's toe walking. Gradually, their voices quiet in hopes of getting a turn to be the teacher's partner.

The children in Mr. Evans's group observed his behavior and saw that Bettina gained his favor by following his lead. According to Bandura (1986), observational learning has four phases:

1. *Attention.* The first step in observational learning is paying attention. Children pay attention to role models who are interesting, novel, or seemingly powerful. This is why action figures on television garner a lot of children's attention. Teachers use many fun and interesting ways to get and hold children's attention, such as talking through a puppet, having them guess what is hidden in a bag, or simply being excited themselves. Mr. Evans surprised the children with the novel behavior of walking on his tiptoes.
2. *Retention.* During this phase of the process, the teacher models the behavior and gives children a chance to practice it. Mr. Evans's goal was to get the children to lower their voices, so he modeled whispering and got the children talking softly.
3. *Reproduction.* The next step is for children to try to reproduce the behavior on their own. Mr. Evans and Bettina step aside from the group and observe as the other children take their turns whispering and tiptoeing.
4. *Motivation.* Observational learning works because children find that they will be rewarded in some way for imitating the desired behaviors. Such motivation can be based on something that happened in the past or is promised in the future. Or, as in Mr. Evans's class, the potential reward can be vicarious. Seeing Bettina rewarded with the teacher's positive attention encouraged the others to follow her lead.

Video Example 4.3:

Bandura's Theory of Learning

In this video, four preschool children are playing "helping hand," which is how their teacher identifies the class helpers each morning during meeting time. How is their behavior an example of Bandura's theory of learning? What are the children learning during the meeting time and also from this playful experience?

self-regulated learning Bandura's theory that people not only learn by modeling the behavior of others, but by observing and evaluating their own.

Self-Regulated Learning

Bandura's theory goes even further as a cognitive theory in his concept of **self-regulated learning**. Bandura (1997) postulated that people learn not only by modeling the behavior of others, but by observing and evaluating their own. Self-regulated learning requires that individuals have internalized standards and that they have the ability to reflect on their own performances and to reward or punish themselves. Bandura's emphasis on self-regulation is similar to Vygotsky's. Both theories view self-regulation as essential for cognitive and social-emotional development.

These high-level cognitive abilities are developing in preschoolers but are further along in most primary-grade children. Teachers can promote self-regulated learning by engaging children in setting goals, evaluating their own performances, and celebrating their successes. For example, Ms. Ross's first-graders do a lot of writing. Periodically, she sits down with one child to discuss various pieces of work. The child chooses a few to scan into the computer and preserve in a portfolio. When parents come for a conference, the children talk about why they chose this special piece of work.

Children in the primary grades become capable of setting standards for their own behavior and comparing their performance to that of others. Eight-year-old Melissa is unhappy with herself because she watched TV last night instead of studying, and today she got a failing grade in science.

We have now described the major theories that explain how children develop and learn. Table 4.3 summarizes the theories and their implications for effective teaching. In the following section, we discuss how play contributes to all areas of children's lives.

TABLE 4.3 Comparing Theories of Child Development

Theorist and Theory	Summation of Theory	Implications for Practice
Erik Erikson: Stages of Personal and Social Development	Through a hypothesis of four stages of psychological and social development in the lives of children, Erikson identifies how children might typically negotiate personal challenges and resolve them dependent on their age and stage of development.	Erikson's theory emphasizes the role of the sociocultural context on children's personal and social lives. Erikson provides useful observations of developmental patterns so teachers can anticipate and respond to children's needs appropriately.
Abraham Maslow: Self-Actualization Theory	Maslow identified a hierarchy of needs that motivate people's behavior and their ability to reach a hierarchy of personal goals. Maslow pointed out that if basic needs are not met, it is not possible for people to actualize personal satisfaction and succeed at a higher level of growth and learning.	The foundations for self-actualization of goals are laid early in life. Teachers may need to ensure that basic needs—food, water, shelter, safety, and security—are met to assist in helping children to develop a sense of community and belonging, self-esteem, and respect for others.
Jean Piaget: Cognitive Theory	According to Piaget, children learn by constructing their own understanding based on their direct experiences with people and objects. Piaget identified four age-related stages of cognitive development that describe how cognitive abilities change as children get older.	From birth, children are viewed as competent actors in constructing their own understanding. Teachers need to provide an enriching environment and hands-on materials for children to explore and investigate. Teachers facilitate children's engagement in projects.
Lev Vygotsky: Sociocultural Theory	Vygotsky described learning as the result of social interaction within a cultural context. He identified the zone of proximal development (ZPD)—the distance between the actual developmental level a child has achieved (their independent level of problem solving) and the level of potential development they could achieve with adult guidance or through collaboration with other children. The support that teachers provide children is called scaffolding.	What children learn is determined by the needs of the culture in which they live. Children learn by solving problems collaboratively with the teacher's support or by working with peers, which is called co-construction or social construction of knowledge. Teachers use many strategies to scaffold learning—gradually providing less assistance as children become more capable of performing on their own. Play is essential for children's development of self-regulation.
Urie Bronfenbrenner: Ecological Systems Model	Bronfenbrenner proposed that the child develops in interaction with many environmental systems—some in which the child doesn't even participate. Family life, parents' employment, state laws, and national culture all influence how each child develops. The most important influences on development, though, are the proximal processes, or daily routines, that children experience in their microsystems of family, school, and community.	Children do best when connections in the mesosystem are strong—when family, child care, and school communicate and work collaboratively to support children's development. The quality of children's daily experiences, though, is most important for development. Teachers emphasize building strong relationships with children and family members—strengthening the child's daily experiences in child care and school, as well as collaborating with the family to help the child develop and learn.

(Continued)

Theorist and Theory	Summation of Theory	Implications for Practice
B. F. Skinner: Behaviorism	Skinner developed the theory of operant conditioning that defines learning as a change in behavior that is controlled by the consequences that follow the behavior. Positive consequences strengthen the frequency of specific behaviors; unpleasant consequences decrease the frequency. Punishment temporarily stops a behavior but does not teach a new one.	Teachers use reinforcement to increase children's positive behavior and decrease their challenging behavior. They use shaping to teach a new, complex skill or behavior by rewarding each step—successive approximation—toward the desired goal.
Albert Bandura: Social Cognitive Theory	Bridging behaviorism and cognitive theory, Bandura demonstrated that people can learn more efficiently from observing the consequences of another person's behavior rather than having to directly experience them. Children learn by modeling the behavior of others. They also learn vicariously, whether the behavior of other people is rewarded or punished.	Teachers model and demonstrate the kinds of behaviors they want children to perform. They draw children's attention to other children's behavior and its positive consequences. Children are motivated to perform behavior that they see rewarded in other people.

© Pearson Education

Video Example 4.4:

Applying Development and Learning Theories in a Primary Grade Classroom

In this video, a teacher applies several theories of learning and development during a science lesson in a primary grade classroom. How does the teacher support children as they construct their own knowledge? How does he scaffold their scientific understanding? Does he apply behaviorist theory?

 Check Your Understanding 4.4

The Role of Play in Development and Learning

Psychologists and educators have studied children's play for a very long time. Despite the large body of research supporting its benefits, however, child-initiated play is becoming less valued, and is disappearing from children's lives today (Alliance for Childhood, 2010; Hirsh-Pasek, Golinkoff, Berk, & Singer, 2009). Many factors conspire against play: television and digital media, lack of safe playgrounds, overemphasis on direct teaching of literacy and mathematics, and highly structured activities or lessons, such as sports or ballet (Elkind, 2008).

Early childhood educators deeply value play. But to use play effectively in teaching children and to advocate for its value, it is important to be clear about what types of play matter and why it is worth defending. In the sections that follow, we describe what play is, how it develops, and how it benefits children.

Types of Play

Play is complex and difficult to define because there are different kinds of play: play with toys, movement play, rough-and-tumble play, make-believe play, and play with games and computers. Most often, *play* is defined as activity that is freely chosen, initiated and controlled by children, and enjoyable. Despite the lack of definitional clarity, most people would say, "You know it when you see it." And more important, children know when they are playing.

Different types of play have different benefits for children. Definitions for different types of play follow:

- *Functional play.* Children play with and manipulate objects, such as when a baby shakes a rattle or a toddler bangs a drum.
- *Constructive play.* Children use toys or objects to create something new, such as making a puppet from a sock, a design on a computer screen, or a castle out of Legos.
- *Symbolic play.* Children use one thing to represent or stand for another. Pretend play is a form of symbolic play. A stick becomes a magic wand. A piece of cloth becomes a veil or a cape.
- *Games with rules.* Children follow prescribed rules for playing together toward a common goal. Games include simple ones, such as *Candyland* or *Chutes and Ladders*, as well as complex ones, such as chess or baseball.

Piaget related types of play to stages of development (Johnson, Christie, & Wardle, 2005). He theorized that functional play dominates the sensorimotor stage (birth to 2 years) and that the preoperational stage (2 to 7 years) is characterized by symbolic and constructive play. Children in the concrete operational stage (7 to 11 years) tend to play games with rules. Children's pretend play becomes more complex over time, especially if people play with them and provide props. The following sections describe this sequence.

Functional Play
Babies and toddlers engage in functional play, focusing on objects and then on the people who use the objects with them. Toddlers enjoy repetition and practice as they play—for example, when they bang a toy hammer over and over.

If parents or teachers pretend with young children during functional play, toddlers will begin to pretend, too. Ms. Morgan sits next to 2-year-old Hester, picks up a cup, and pretends to drink. "This is delicious tea," she says. Soon Hester takes a cup and says, "Yum." This type of pretense is the foundation for later symbolic play.

Constructive Play
Constructive play begins as functional play and becomes more symbolic as children use objects to create new ones. For example, children act out pretend roles during block building. Constructive play aids logico-mathematical learning and can be as basic as a 2-year-old stacking three blocks or as complex as a second-grader building a model airplane.

Symbolic Play
Play helps build **symbolic representation**—using one thing to mean something else—such as when letters are used to represent sounds or number symbols represent quantities. At first, toddlers use real objects or toys in their pretend play, such as picking up the cup and pretending to drink. If adults encourage this type of play, children use other objects in their play. They might pretend that a block is a cup. Finally, children who have lots of experience with pretend play no longer need an object to pretend, using their hands to represent drinking from a cup or stomping their feet and saying, "I'm an elephant." This type of play helps children move from thought that is linked to physical actions to the ability to use words and other symbols to represent concepts (Piaget, 1962; Vygotsky, 1962).

symbolic representation The process of mentally using one thing to stand for something else.

By the time most children turn 4 years old, they begin to develop more complex play with roles and symbolic uses of props. Many preschool- and even kindergarten-age children, however, still play at the toddler level. Bodrova and Leong (2012b) define this kind of repetitive, unimaginative play as "immature play" to distinguish it from the "mature play" that is expected of 4- and 5-year-olds. Mature play promotes self-regulation, executive function, and other skills (Diamond & Lee, 2011).

Games with Rules

As children move into primary grades, they spend less time in pretend play and more time playing games with rules (e.g., sports and board or computer games). Games, including well-designed digital games, can build turn-taking skill, delay of gratification, problem solving, strategizing, and motivation to learn (Lieberman, 2006; Siegler & Ramani, 2008).

Games require children to follow the established rules; they rarely get a chance to discuss, negotiate, or change the rules—which would contribute to the development of social competence and self-regulation (Bodrova & Leong, 2012a). When pretend play is replaced by sports or other organized activities during the preschool years, these important foundational skills might not develop fully (Bodrova & Leong, 2012a).

Guided Play

Children can learn a lot by engaging in independent free play; however, guided play can enhance and extend learning. In guided play, an adult observes a child's play interests and joins the child's play, setting learning goals and gently scaffolding the child's achievement of the learning goals. The child is still the leader of the play experience, while the adult can assess and support child learning. Guided play can be used to enhance children's language and mathematics learning (Hassinger-Das, Hirsh-Pasek & Golinkoff, 2017). Read the *Promoting Play: Pet Project* feature to learn how pre-K teacher Aliana incorporates guided play into her interactions with children in ways that powerfully support children's relationships and executive function.

Promoting Play

Pet Project

Aliana had been observing her 4-year-old students in the dramatic play area for a few weeks. She noticed that the children's play was getting more complex: The story lines were more fantastical, and children were carrying their roles and play stories across days and weeks. They were designing new props every day and creating rules for play. Aliana knew from her child development classes that children learn to take turns and to take others' perspectives in the context of pretend play. She also learned that research has shown that children who spend more time in spontaneous pretend play demonstrate greater self-regulation and/or executive function and better memory skills.

Alexi and Marcus were also joining in the play, but they were struggling to keep up with the complex play,

and the other children were complaining and trying to exclude them. Aliana suspected that their difficulties were due to behaviors associated with their diagnoses of ADHD. Alexi was distractible; he struggled to remember the storylines and how to use the props. She made up characters that did not align with the children's storylines. Marcus wandered through the play area, creating his own stories and making up his own roles. He ignored the rules, and got frustrated and destructive when his peers protested his play choices.

Aliana began documenting the products the children were creating and listening to their conversations. She wanted to show the children's parents and her principal how much the children were learning in the context of play. Aliana also wanted to enhance Alexi and Marcus's experiences with their peers, so she started experimenting with using guided play.

Aliana's guided play looked like this: The children were pretending to have a pet grooming shop. Some children were playing the roles of groomers, receptionists, customers and pets. One child stood by as veterinarian for pets who might be sick when they arrive. With a variety of materials and by moving furniture around, the children had created and decorated a lovely world of pet care. Aliana noticed Alexi and Marcus watching, trying to figure out how to join. Marcus began calling directions from the sidelines, pointing out that people were waiting to get service. Aliana wondered aloud if it might help to have another receptionist to meet customers. Charlotte, the lone receptionist, nodded her approval, and Aliana suggested that Marcus hop in the play. She helped him gather his pencil and paper, and gave him a small table space at the shared reception desk. Whispering to Alexi, Aliana asked, "Would you like to be the pet or the owner, Alexi?" Instantly on all fours, Alexi started speaking in soft barks, her tail wagging. Aliana continued in the play, asking questions, offering suggestions, soliciting a bath for her dog (Alexi), and negotiating terms of service with Marcus and his partner receptionist. Aliana's presence and gentle verbal guidance provided the support Marcus and Alexi needed to successfully join in the play. She gently withdrew her support when she observed that her presence was not needed, ready to join again when new learning challenges emerged.

The Benefits of Play

Research demonstrates that play contributes to language development, self-regulation, attention, creativity, problem solving, and social and emotional skills (Bodrova & Leong, 2012b; Diamond & Lee, 2011). Play has been found to help prepare children for school (Frost, Wortham, & Reifel, 2012). Research also links play to children's literacy and mathematics skills (IOM & NRC, 2015).

Children's play can be enhanced through adult intervention, as in the *Tools of the Mind* curriculum described previously. Sara Smilansky (1968), an Israeli psychologist, conducted seminal studies of play among children living in poverty. She found that they did not engage in the same kind of mature sociodramatic play favored by their middle-class peers, and were behind in other areas as well. Smilansky trained children to play in more complex ways—using modeling and other techniques—which significantly improved their language and social and cognitive development, findings that have been replicated with other populations (Smilansky & Shefatya, 1990).

Karin Lifter and colleagues have studied the importance of play for all children, especially those with developmental delays (Lifter et al., 2011). They point out that play is not just an activity that feeds development and learning by providing a context for playful learning. Contending that play is in itself a domain of development, Lifter explains that it can be used to observe, assess, and set goals for children's learning.

© Pearson Education

Video Example 4.5:

Learning Through Play

This video provides two examples of play in a preschool classroom. What types of play do you observe? What are some things you notice about the children's play? How might the different theorists view the learning and development supported in the context of these children's dramatic and block play?

Play and Motivation

Although it is very important for children's development, play is not the only way that children learn, as we have seen from examining several theories. If so, why is it so important for teachers to defend and use play as a major context for teaching and learning? One reason is that preschool children themselves are intrinsically motivated to play. Play is so enjoyable for children that teachers don't need to coerce or cajole them to participate (Bredekamp, 2004).

In one study (Wiltz & Klein, 2001), preschoolers were asked what they like to do at school. Ninety-eight percent of the children said play was their favorite activity. When asked what they did not like about school, nearly a third of the children said meanness by teachers or peers, and others did not like naptime and time-out. But many also disliked circle time, especially in poorer-quality programs where it lasted 30 to 40 minutes and involved repetition of calendar, letters, and numbers. Even in high-quality classrooms where circle time was more interesting and engaging, many children reported disliking it primarily because it takes too long. As one little boy, Don, said, "Well, I don't really like … you know, like sit in circle and listen … I don't like that part [because] I think it's too long for me. I'd rather be playing" (Wiltz & Klein, 2001, p. 225)

 Check Your Understanding 4.5

 Connecting Theory and Practice

Too often, teachers think that theories of child development and learning have little relevance to their daily work with children, but the opposite is true. Theory and practice are, or should be, integrally connected. We conclude the chapter with an overview of the research-based and theory-derived principles that are the basis for developmentally appropriate practice.

Looking across theories and research, teachers can become confused. As we have seen, theories explain different aspects of children's learning or development, and at times they may seem contradictory. How can teachers make sense of diverse theories? To address these questions, we provide a framework for thinking holistically about development and learning.

NAEYC (2009) summarizes the research and theory undergirding developmentally appropriate practice in a list of principles. Although these principles do not cover everything teachers need to know about development and learning, they highlight some of the key concepts that have implications for practice. In Table 4.4, the principles are listed and illustrated with a few examples.

TABLE 4.4 Principles of Development and Learning to Guide Practice

Principle of Development and Learning	Implications for Practice	Example
Principle 1: Domains of children's development—physical, social, emotional, and cognitive—are closely related. Development in one domain influences, and is influenced by, development in other domains.	Curriculum should be comprehensive, addressing development and learning of the whole child.	During a project on animals, 4-year-olds learn science concepts about animals' natural environments, use language and literacy to tell and illustrate stories about their favorite animals, and act out those animals' movements.
Principle 2: Many aspects of children's learning and development follow well-documented sequences, with later abilities, skills, and knowledge building on those already acquired.	Teachers need to know the predictable, but not rigid, sequences of development and learning so they can assess children accurately and plan for children's continued progress.	Ms. Rodriguez is familiar with the scope and sequence in the first-grade reading curriculum, so she adjusts her expectations and works with children individually and in small groups at their various levels of reading ability.

Principle of Development and Learning	Implications for Practice	Example
Principle 3: Development and learning proceed at varying rates from child to child, as well as at uneven rates across different areas of a child's individual functioning.	Teachers need to get to know each child well, regularly observing and assessing each child's abilities, skills, knowledge, and dispositions.	Josh is 3 years old and very verbal, while Jon, also 3, seldom speaks. Jon has excellent fine motor skills that Josh lacks. Their teacher pairs them to play with interlocking blocks, with which they practice and improve their language and motor skills.
Principle 4: Development and learning result from a dynamic and continuous interaction of biological maturation and experience.	Teachers recognize that although there are inborn individual differences and limits on children's learning based on maturation, experience plays a large role in children's development. Teachers know the benefits of early intervention for preventing later problems.	Kindergarten teachers explain to parents that the "gift of time"—holding children out of school until they are older—is not a good policy, because children will benefit more from the experience of attending school rather than simply waiting to mature.
Principle 5: Early experiences have both cumulative and delayed effects on individual children's development. Optimal periods exist for certain types of development and learning.	Teachers need to know research on the short- and long-term effects of early experience.	In her family child care home, Mrs. Pickett rarely uses TV, because too much exposure can harm children's long-term attention spans and doesn't build language the way real conversation does.
Principle 6: Development proceeds toward greater complexity, self-regulation, and symbolic or representational capacities.	Teachers add greater complexity to learning experiences over time. Teachers engage children in conversations about thinking and problem solving.	Because young children often "think out loud," preschool teachers don't expect silent classrooms. They organize activities for children that encourage conversation.
Principle 7: Children develop best when they have secure, consistent relationships with responsive adults and opportunities for positive relationships with peers.	Teachers develop a warm, positive, trusting relationship with each child. Teachers protect the physical health and safety of each child.	At the beginning of the school year, Ms. Vargas conducts a home visit or meets with parents to get to know each child and family. She takes time to talk with each child every day.
Principle 8: Development and learning occur in, and are influenced by, social and cultural contexts.	Teachers recognize that children's competence acquired in their home culture may not be apparent in the school culture, and know that what is meaningful to children varies depending on their culture and language.	Concerned about Marta's language development, Ms. Kamp works with a Spanish bilingual teacher, Ms. Gonzales, to obtain an accurate assessment of Marta's vocabulary and grammar in her home language.
Principle 9: Always mentally active in seeking to understand the world around them, children learn in a variety of ways; a wide range of teaching strategies and interactions are effective in supporting all these kinds of learning.	Teachers use a variety of teaching strategies—both teacher-guided and child-guided—to meet the needs of individual children. Teachers use a variety of learning contexts—large group, small group, and individual—carefully considering each child's unique learning needs.	Ms. Hayes demonstrates and instructs the children in how to move the images on the computer screen for a new math program. The children take turns experimenting with the program, with Ms. Hayes close by to provide assistance as needed.

(Continued)

Principle of Development and Learning	Implications for Practice	Example
Principle 10: Play is an important vehicle for developing self-regulation as well as promoting language, cognition, and social competence.	Teachers purposefully plan time and materials for children's educationally valuable play. Teachers observe children at play and interact constructively with them.	Ms. Phillips models customer behavior in the grocery store center in her kindergarten, while children engage in counting money, reading labels, making lists, and using vocabulary as they play.
Principle 11: Development and learning advance when children are challenged to achieve at a level just beyond their current mastery, and also when they have many opportunities to practice newly acquired skills.	Teachers provide children with experiences at which they can be successful as well as providing them with some experiences that are at the "just achievable" level of challenge to stretch their learning and development.	Mr. Durkin observes that many children are interested in writing only their own names. He suggests that friends write each other's names, and provides name cards as models.
Principle 12: Children's experiences shape their motivation and approaches to learning, such as persistence, initiative, and flexibility; in turn, these dispositions and behaviors affect their learning and development.	Teachers draw on and cultivate children's interests to get their attention and keep them engaged in learning. Teachers encourage positive approaches to learning, such as curiosity and creativity.	Ms. Elias's kindergartners show little interest in the required reading workbooks. She encourages the children to act out the stories, make up songs, and write their own stories—experiences that encourage engagement with the literature.

Source: Based on C. Copple & S. Bredekamp (Eds.), 2009. *Developmentally appropriate practice in early childhood programs serving children from birth through age 8* (revised ed.). Washington, DC: National Association for the Education of Young Children.

In promulgating this list of principles, NAEYC (Copple & Bredekamp, 2009, pp. 10–11) offers several caveats. First, while the list is comprehensive, it is not exhaustive; other principles could be added. In addition, just as all domains of development and learning are interconnected, so too are the principles. For instance, cultural and individual variations are addressed in separate principles, and yet they play a role in all the other principles. In other words, decisions about applying any given principle should consider children as individuals and as members of cultural groups. Despite these limitations, the principles reflect a solid base of research to guide teachers' decision making.

Connecting theory and practice is a key component for becoming an early childhood teacher. Educating young children well necessitates having a sound knowledge base, well-developed skills, a commitment to children, and a reflective stance that allows the teacher to always be learning. In the feature *Becoming an Intentional Teacher: Mastering Serve and Return Interactions in Kindergarten*, read about the journey of a kindergarten teacher who believed she was doing everything needed to help children succeed, only to discover they—and she—were struggling. Observe how her openness to learning changed her practice—and progress for her children.

Becoming an Intentional Teacher

Mastering Serve and Return Interactions in Kindergarten

Here's what Happened I learned to observe children in my teacher education classes and to allow for plenty of play interactions. My kindergarten classroom is arranged beautifully, with interesting learning centers surrounding a large group area. I use a daily routine and engaging learning activities to support children's literacy, math, science, social, and artistic development. The children have opportunities to be active during outside play. But despite providing a rich and stimulating environment and experiences, my kindergarteners were not making the progress I—and the school district— expected. Their academic and social skills lagged behind the district averages. They displayed poor attention spans and frequent disruptive behavior. Many of children had gone to preschool, and almost all were living in homes and neighborhoods that lacked basic resources.

In response, I studied brain development and how interactions and relationships—not just curricula and enriched environments—dominate children's learning in the early years. I did some research about "serve and return" interactions, in which adults and children have conversational interchanges to understand children's needs and abilities, scaffold learning exchanges, and support children's developing executive function. I decided to try "serve and return" with children individually and in small groups.

Over the course of the week, I observed each child during play and in small and large group lessons. I noted who children played with well or poorly, what materials and interests each child pursued, and how they worked well independently or needed assistance. Then, for the next week, I planned conversation starters for each of the children, knowing that I would need to be flexible based on how they responded. I kept questions and comments open-ended, encouraging children to explain what they were learning and ask questions. I modified group lessons to be more about discussion and questions than telling the children information. Not only was I able to assess children's skills better, but they asked more curious questions. They solved problems together in groups and individually, using questions and wondering about different options to try. The first things that changed were children's vocabulary increased and their disruptive behaviors decreased.

Here's What I Was Thinking When learning about brain development in teacher education classes, I thought that "serve and return" was about interacting with babies. I just didn't realize that for children to be engaged and learning, they needed to be in exploring conversations— and they needed me to support this. I plan to attend professional development to learn how to use "serve and return" conversations more and better. In the meantime, my mantra is, "Listen. Ask open questions. Wonder aloud. Try things."

Reflection What led this teacher to explore new strategies to support her kindergarteners' learning? What are some other ways she could incorporate "serve and return" into her classroom interactions?

 Check Your Understanding 4.6

Revisiting the Case Study

... Ms. Donati's Classroom

We began this chapter by visiting Yvonne Donati's classroom. Having examined various theories of learning and their applications, we can see her practices in a clearer light. Yvonne operates from a constructivist perspective. She sees children as active learners, and structures her classroom and plans curriculum accordingly. Yvonne also implements sociocultural theory as she scaffolds children's learning in the zone of proximal development through appropriately timed prompts, questions, and assistance. She applies brain research, building positive relationships, and research on play.

Although Yvonne's teaching practices primarily reflect cognitive theories, she also applies principles of operant conditioning—reinforcements to increase positive behaviors. Yvonne discovers that behavioral principles can be particularly effective under certain circumstances, such as when she applies them for a limited period of time in working with Maya's special need.

Finally, Yvonne does some theory building of her own by testing her hypotheses about children's play with an informal research study. Theories are born, grow, or die from research that often begins in informal observations of children, such as Yvonne's. ■

4 Chapter Summary

- Development is age-related change that occurs as the result of an interaction between biological maturation and physical and/or social experience. Learning is a change in knowledge or skill that results from experience or instruction.

- A theory is an explanation of how information and observations are organized and relate to one another. Theories are important because they affect how people think and behave. In education, theories of learning and development affect how teachers treat children, how they structure environments, and how they teach.

- Early experiences change and organize the physical structure of the brain. Neglect, abuse, and stress pose serious threats to healthy brain development. High-quality, developmentally appropriate early childhood education can contribute to healthy brain development.

- The most influential theories of social-emotional development are Erikson's psychosocial theory and

  Maslow's hierarchy of needs. The most prominent theories of cognitive development are Piaget's theory of constructivism and Vygotsky's sociocultural theory. A theory for understanding the interactive influence of social and cultural contexts on human development is Bronfenbrenner's ecological systems model.

- The most prominent learning theories are B. F. Skinner's theory of behaviorism and Albert Bandura's social cognitive theory.

- Research demonstrates that play contributes to language development, self-regulation, attention, creativity, problem solving, social and emotional skills, and literacy and mathematics skills.

- Effective early childhood education is based on knowledge of child development and learning. NAEYC summarizes the key concepts of that knowledge base in 12 principles that can be used to guide practice.

Key Terms

- 5- to 7-year shift
- accommodation
- adaptation
- assimilation
- behaviorism or behavioral learning
- chronosystem
- cognitive development
- consequences
- conservation
- constructivism
- development
- disequilibrium
- domain-general processes
- domains of development
- ecological systems theory

- egocentrism
- emotional development
- equilibration
- executive function
- exosystem
- extinction
- hypothesis
- learning
- logico-mathematical knowledge
- macrosystem
- maturationist
- mesosystem
- microsystem
- modeling
- negative reinforcement
- neurons

- object permanence
- operant conditioning
- physical development
- physical knowledge
- plasticity
- positive reinforcement
- proximal processes
- pruning
- private speech
- punishment
- reinforcer
- scaffolding
- scheme or schema
- self-actualization theory
- self-regulated learning
- self-regulation
- serve and return

- shaping
- social cognitive theory
- social-conventional knowledge
- social development
- sociocultural theory
- successive approximations
- symbolic representation
- synapses
- theory
- toxic stress
- vicarious learning
- windows of opportunity
- zone of proximal development (ZPD)

Flash Cards 4.1

Readings and Websites

Bohart, H., Charner, K., & Koralek, D. (Eds.). (2015). *Spotlight on young children: Exploring play*. Washington, DC: NAEYC.

Copple, C. (Ed.). (2012). Growing minds: Building strong cognitive foundations in early childhood. Washington, DC: NAEYC.

Mooney, C. G. (2013). *Theories of childhood: An introduction to Dewey, Montessori, Erikson, Piaget, and Vygotsky* (2nd ed.). St. Paul, MN: Redleaf Press.

Mind in the Making website

Ellen Galinsky's book *Mind in the making: The seven essential life skills every child needs* and website of the same name provide very useful information for families and teachers on how to help children develop abilities that are essential for success in school and life, including executive function and self-regulation.

Center on the Developing Child at Harvard University

This website has rich resources about brain development and explains how early relationships and experiences shape the brain and behavior of the child. There are several videos and PowerPoints to use for teaching adults about the importance of healthy brain development, as well as activities to use with children and families.

ZERO to THREE

Explore this website for information on the development of infants and toddlers. You'll also find information for supporting brain development and young children's mental health, and resources for teachers and families.

National Association for the Education of Young Children (NAEYC)

The NAEYC website has a section dedicated to *Play and Learning,* including research, books, and teaching resources. Information on gender in play, how to choose toys, and how to support play at different ages is included.

Shared Writing 4.1
Explain Your Understanding of Child Development

5 Adapting for Individual Differences

Learning Outcomes

After studying this chapter, you should be able to

5.1 Describe the importance of understanding individual differences among children.

5.2 Describe what is known about individual differences among children.

5.3 Restate Gardner's Theory of Multiple Intelligences and discuss its implications for individualizing teaching practices.

5.4 Compare ways of providing responsive education for all learners.

5.5 Explain individual differences in ability, including legal requirements for serving children with disabilities and special needs.

5.6 Apply your knowledge of effective practices for teaching children with special needs to teaching all children.

© Kali9/E+/Getty Images

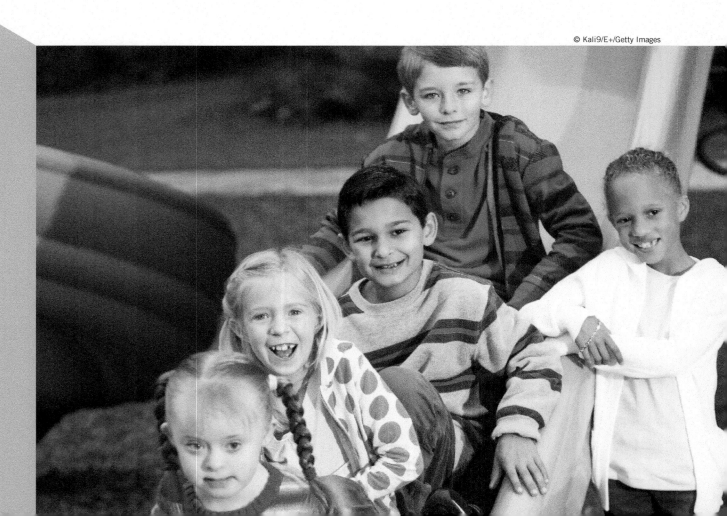

Related NAEYC Professional Preparation Standards

The NAEYC Professional Preparation Standards (NAEYC, 2011) that apply to this chapter:

1: Promoting Child Development and Learning
Key elements:
  1a. Knowing and understanding young children's characteristics and needs
  1b. Knowing and understanding the multiple influences on development and learning
  1c. Using developmental knowledge to create healthy, respectful, supportive, and challenging learning environments
2: Building Family and Community Relationships
Key elements:
  2b. Supporting and engaging families and communities through respectful, reciprocal relationships
  2c. Involving families and communities in their children's development and learning
3: Observing, Documenting, and Assessing to Support Young Children and Families
Key elements:
  3c. Understanding and practicing responsible assessment to promote positive outcomes for each child
  3d. Knowing about assessment partnerships with families and with professional colleagues
4: Using Developmentally Effective Approaches to Connect with Children and Families
Key elements:
  4a. Understanding positive relationships and supportive interactions as the foundation of their work with children
  4b. Knowing and understanding effective strategies and tools for early education
  4c. Using a broad repertoire of developmentally appropriate teaching/learning approaches

Case Study

Lindsay Creighton is ready for open house night. When Shira arrives with her mom in tow, she greets Lindsay with an exuberant hug, and turns to see Rohan coming down the hall. "Rohan! It's the open house!" Rohan clings to his father's leg. He is painfully shy, and seems unnerved by Shira's enthusiastic greeting. His father says, "Go play with Shira." But Rohan retreats and shakes his head "no."

The next to arrive are Cal and his grandmother. "Cal!" screams Shira, and the two embrace. Cal runs by his grandmother on his way to play, and she speaks sternly to him in Chinese. He stops running. Slowly, he moves to the block corner with Shira. When she hands him a pink car, Cal sighs, "This is for girls. I need a boy car."

Carter and his parents arrive. Shira says hello to Carter, but then speaks to his parents, "Carter can play if he wants." Carter flaps his arms and repeats a favorite phrase from a children's movie. He moves closer to Shira and grabs her cheeks. His parents intervene and say, "Too close, Carter." Behind Carter and his parents are the twins, Alice and Alexandra. Shira's mom, Beth, greets them by saying, "Hello, Alice. Hello, Alex." Alice rolls her eyes and says, "You got us mixed up again!" Beth apologizes, but the twins' mom says, "Even I get them mixed up sometimes, until they are in a place like this. Just watch. Alice will try to take over, and Alex will stay in a quiet corner until the open house is over." Ruby is the last to arrive. Her father immediately asks Lindsay if any of the food contains nuts. When Lindsay says, "No, I made sure," he still asks to see the ingredient labels due to Ruby's severe allergy.

Later, Lindsay reflects on the evening. Although the children are all about the same age, they are so different. She marvels at the fact that even the identical twins have such different personalities. She wonders if Rohan's shyness is influenced by his father's emphasis on participation. And what about Shira—how did she get to be such a social butterfly? Is it in her genes, or did her parents cultivate that?

Lindsay's thoughts turn to Carter, who has autism. She considers how well his parents coordinate with his teacher and other specialists to reinforce what he's learning in school. Lindsay also thinks of 5-year-old Cal, who is living with his grandmother after his mother's parental rights were revoked as a result of neglect. How is it that he is such a positive and vivacious boy given all he has had to deal with in his young life? Lindsay smiles when she thinks about Cal wanting a "boy car." How and when do these gender stereotypes crystallize?

Finally, her thoughts turn to the challenges she faces. How will she work with families to meet the needs of these children? How will she provide experiences that challenge Shira and Cal but don't overwhelm Carter? How will she make Rohan and Alex feel at ease in social situations? And how will she create a strong sense of belonging and friendship among these children? ■

I ndividual differences abound in every group of young children. As is evident from the open house vignette, even children of the same chronological age differ from one another in many ways. The purpose of this chapter is to examine what is known about the range of individual differences among children and how teachers can effectively adapt the curriculum and teaching strategies to help all children participate, develop, and learn to their fullest potential. Understanding individual differences is a critical dimension of developmentally appropriate practice.

We begin with a discussion of the range of individual variation that exists among all children and some of the origins of these differences. Next, we describe Howard Gardner's theory of multiple intelligences, which is a useful framework for thinking about individual children's strengths, needs, interests, and abilities. Then we discuss differentiating instruction and present a framework for responding to the diverse learning needs of all children. We conclude with a discussion of effective practices for teaching children with disabilities and special needs.

Understanding Individual Differences

Anyone who has been a parent or teacher is aware of the fact that every child is unique. Even people who do not have parenting or teaching experience have been children themselves and know that we are all different. Try to remember your earliest school experience and picture the children in your class. Were all the boys or girls alike? Did everyone enjoy and excel at the same activities? Did all of your classmates learn at the same pace and in the same way? Was anyone exactly like you? Of course, the answer to all of these questions is "no."

Acknowledging the uniqueness of each child is only the beginning. Effective early childhood teachers understand typical and atypical child development; they also understand the importance of knowing each child as an individual. They use this knowledge to plan and adapt curriculum, and to help each child meet important learning goals.

Why Pay Attention to Individual Differences?

One of the most well-known facts about child development is that there is a wide range of individual variation (IOM & NRC, 2015). But what does "wide range" mean, and what are the implications for teachers? The concept of a range of variation is based on an average; for example, we might say that on average, men are 5 feet, 10 inches tall. This average was calculated based on the heights of a huge number of men. When we consider their heights individually, however, they may range from 4 feet, 8 inches to 7 feet, 1 inch. Now consider a range of variation in relation to children's development. On virtually every characteristic we could measure—saying first words, balancing on one foot, knowing the alphabet—the pace and timing of children's performance vary. The average age at which most children master a skill, for example, doesn't tell us much without knowing the range, which gives us a far clearer picture of reality.

In general, teachers need to be cautious about focusing too much on averages. Many aspects of schooling, including the graded structure and power of standardized tests, tend to reflect the assumption that all children will achieve certain skills and knowledge at the same time. As a result, the tendency is for schools to ignore the range of variation and try to teach all children the same way.

But if we want every child to achieve the same goals, we must treat and teach them as individuals. Acknowledging that individual differences exist does not mean lowering expectations for some children. In fact, high expectations for children's learning are necessary if they are to succeed. In the sections that follow, we describe some important aspects of variation among children. But first we discuss theories about the origin of individual differences—the question of nature versus nurture.

Where Do Individual Differences Come From?

One of the most enduring debates in psychology is the degree to which development is the product of biology (nature) or environment (nurture). The question is often framed as whether nature or nurture is more influential in determining who we become as individuals. Although we know that physical characteristics are inherited, the genetic markers are less clear when it comes to an individual's behavior, intelligence, and personality. Consider the twins in Lindsay Creighton's classroom at the beginning of this chapter. Is Alice more outgoing and Alex more cautious because these personality traits are not part of the genetic pattern they share? Or does this difference result because their parents encouraged the girls in different ways?

The Influence of Biology on Development In the past, some psychologists (Jensen, 1980) proposed that people behave as they do because of inborn characteristics. This belief emphasizes the influence of **nature**, the hereditary or genetic contributions to human development. Whether we are male or female, have freckles, have black hair, or have a certain type of personality can be influenced by genetic factors.

nature The hereditary or genetic contributions to human development.

Nature also refers to the biological and neurological drivers of development. For example, physical growth and advances in motor skills for most humans develop in a predictable sequence. Newborn reflexes soon give rise to voluntary movements and the development of abilities such as rolling over, crawling, walking, and running. Similarly, language development has a biological component. The fact that most infants, regardless of culture, begin to coo and babble at approximately the same ages provides strong evidence that nature indeed affects development.

Whereas some aspects of nature influence a similar course of development for most children, genetics also affects individual differences. For example, most children take their first

Every class of young children is made up of unique individuals. Intentional teachers must find ways to meet the needs of every child while also challenging each one to make continued learning progress.

nurture Environmental factors and experiences that influence human development and behavior.

transactional theory of development Theory that development is the result of both biology and experience and how they influence each other.

steps by about 1 year of age, but there is a wide range of variation among individuals. David took his first steps at 7 months; his brother Jeffrey wasn't mobile until 18 months.

The Role of the Environment   Although biology influences individual differences, some scientists (Skinner, 1953, 1968) believe that people behave in certain ways more as a result of their experiences in the environment or because they are taught to do so. This belief stresses the influence of **nurture** on human behavior.

Heredity may play a role in influencing personality traits, but according to the nurture perspective, environmental factors ultimately determine who we become. Parents' discipline methods, for example, might have more influence on their children's behavior than the parents' genetic contributions. Other dimensions of the environment also influence children's development, such as the family's economic resources, the quality of their child care setting, the number of siblings in the home, and the safety of the community.

The Transactional Relationship Between Nature and Nurture   Although the nature versus nurture debate continues, the current thinking is that "nature and nurture are partners in how developing people interact with the surrounding environment" (Shonkoff & Phillips, 2000, p. 39). The **transactional theory of development** (Sameroff, 2010) explains that development is the result of *both* biology *and* experience and the ways in which they influence each other.

To illustrate how nature and nurture interact, consider the following examples. Myra, a highly verbal and inquisitive 6-year-old, seems to inspire her teacher to engage her in intellectually stimulating projects, such as finding out what causes earthquakes, which in turn further Myra's already accelerated development and learning. By contrast, Alyssa, who is deaf, is withdrawn and rarely joins in activities even though her teacher uses sign language. Alyssa's lack of responsiveness may provoke her teacher to initiate communication with her less often.

Both biology and experience play critical, interrelated roles in children's development. Therefore, the kinds of experiences children have become vitally important. As the Center on the Developing Child at Harvard University (2010) reports, "Experiences children have early in life—and the environments in which they have them—shape their developing brain architecture and strongly affect whether they grow up to be healthy, productive members of society" (p. 1).

How Experience Affects Outcomes for Children: Risk or Resilience

According to the transactional theory of development, children's experiences impact their overall development. Accumulation of certain kinds of experiences can place children at risk for negative outcomes. Similarly, if children have repeated positive experiences, their development is likely to be enhanced.

risk factors Inherited or experiential conditions that potentially contribute to poor developmental outcomes for children, such as peer rejection, academic failure, juvenile delinquency, and school expulsion.

Understanding Risk Factors   **Risk factors** are inherited or experiential conditions that potentially contribute to negative outcomes for children (Center on the Developing Child, n.d.). Among the most frequently identified risk factors are living in poverty, living with a single parent, low education level of parents, lack of nutrition, disability, and child abuse (Ali, 2013). The concept of risk factors has led to the use of the term *children at risk* of school failure.

When risk factors multiply in children's lives, they produce a growing number of poor developmental outcomes (Burchinal & Willoughby, 2013). That is, the more risk factors children have, the more likely they are to experience developmental delays and social or health problems. These conditions in turn can lead to a host of poor outcomes such as peer rejection, academic failure, dropping out of school, mental health disorders, or criminal behavior.

Promoting Resilience   Research on children with multiple risk factors demonstrates that exposure to risk and adversity does not necessarily result in negative outcomes for some children (Center on the Developing Child, n.d.). Positive, supportive experiences can mediate risk and help children become resilient (Masten, 2014). **Resilience** refers to a child's ability to overcome, adapt to, or minimize the damaging effects of adversity (Center on the Developing Child, n.d.).

Mechanisms—called **protective factors**—exist that may minimize the potentially negative effects for children living in identified high-risk situations. Like risk factors, protective factors are both inherited (nature) and experiential (nurture). A continuous, positive parent-child relationship has been found to be one of the most important contributors to the development of resilience (Masten & Cicchetti, 2016). Other protective factors include a variety of external social supports such as extended family, membership in a church or spiritual group, and close friends and neighbors.

Children's inherent characteristics also contribute to resilience. For example, resilient children often possess temperaments in infancy that elicit positive responses from their caregivers (Center on the Developing Child, n.d.). For example, Stefano is a happy, easily soothed baby who draws positive attention from everyone. Timothy, on the other hand, cries all night and doesn't nurse readily. His mother begins to feel inadequate and has difficulty attaching to him.

In short, risk and resilience are not the result of either biology or environment alone. Rather, the interactions between children's biological makeup and their experiences contribute to the wide variation among children and families. Teachers must remember that a child's genetic inheritance or environmental circumstances should never limit their expectations of children. In fact, one of the most important sources of resilience in children is positive relationships with teachers (Hamre & Pianta, 2010; Howes & Ritchie, 2002; Sabol & Pianta, 2013).

resilience A child's ability to overcome, adapt to, or minimize the damaging effects of adversity.

protective factors Mechanisms, both inherited and experiential, that may minimize the potentially negative effects for children living in identified high-risk situations.

 Check Your Understanding 5.1

What We Know About Individual Differences

Children whose development is well within the typical range differ from one another in many ways. Gender is a key area where biology and environment interact to influence development, as described in the next section.

Gender Differences

"Is it a boy or a girl?" seems to be the first question asked about a new baby. From the first moments of life, and even prenatally, powerful assumptions are made about children on the basis of their sex. These assumptions are soon influenced by experience. When 3-year-old Lucienne receives a soccer ball and a goal, she insists that she cannot play with them because "It's for boys." Her belief was reinforced by the fact that the packaging showed two boys playing soccer. Indeed, stereotypes about girls and boys are durable and pervasive, which raises questions about what the actual differences are, if any, in the development and characteristics of boys and girls.

Physical Development

There is little evidence of gender differences in most domains of development and learning. In some domains, however, the characteristics of females and males have been found to differ. Physically, for example, females are typically more mature at birth, and males are more likely to be miscarried, die in infancy, or develop hereditary diseases (Parke & Gauvain, 2008). On average, females also reach developmental milestones, such as talking a few months earlier, than do males (Özçalskan & Goldin-Meadow, 2010. Current research is beginning to reveal some sex differences in brain structure, but much remains to be learned before definite conclusions can be drawn (Woolfolk & Perry, 2015).

Cognitive Skills

Although there are no significant gender-based differences in overall intelligence, tests of cognitive abilities find some specific differences between girls and boys. Notably, boys demonstrate a slight but consistent advantage in the domain of visual-spatial rotation (Woolfolk & Perry, 2015), the ability to visualize and mentally transform or rotate figures or objects. While this ability is related to success in other mathematics areas, evidence suggests that early experience and attitudes toward mathematics may play a more important role in mathematical learning (Krinzinger, Wood, & Willmes, 2012).

Some evidence suggests, however, that gender differences in visual-spatial ability are to some extent a product of children's experience (Clements & Sarama, 2011). For example, during the preschool years, boys tend to spend more time than girls in the kinds of activities that build visual-spatial skills: building with blocks, playing with Legos, and putting puzzles together. When girls engage in such play and teachers make the experience meaningful, such as talking with them about what they are doing or reading a story about shapes, girls perform as well as boys on these visual-spatial tasks (Casey, Erkut, Ceder, & Young, 2008).

Social Behavior

Popular culture suggests that vast differences exist in social behavior between females and males; however, scientific research suggests that few broad gender differences exist in the area of social behaviors (Eliot, 2009). There are, however, subtle differences. Girls tend to engage in more imaginary play than boys do, while boys tend to play in slightly larger groups, and their play generally takes up more space (Woolfolk & Perry, 2015). Even as early as 2 years of age, girls talk more about emotion than boys do; however, these differences are not necessarily stable over time (Barbu, Cabanes & Le Maner-Idrissi, 2011).

Perhaps the most notable gender difference is that boys are more overtly aggressive than girls beginning in the preschool years. Possibly as a result of male hormones, boys are also more physically active and more likely to engage in rough-and-tumble play (Woolfolk & Perry, 2015). They display more physical aggression, try to dominate peers, and subsequently display more antisocial behaviors than females (Woolfolk & Perry, 2015).

Although it is tempting to think these gender differences are innate, the reality is more complicated. Current thinking is that sex differences in social behaviors are heavily influenced by the situation (Martin et al., 2013). Because boys and girls are often observed playing with their same-sex peers, differences between the sexes can appear to be greater than they really are and similarities less obvious. For example, preschooler Leo gets into frequent fights with his peers and appears to be more aggressive than Johanna. But this difference might have more to do with Leo's rough-and-tumble play than any innate tendency to aggressive behavior.

In addition, gender differences in aggression are largely a function of where the behavior occurs and how aggression is defined. The largest gender differences are found in less structured, natural environments such as on the playground. However, when aggression consists of attempts to hurt another person through manipulation, gossip, or exclusion from a social group, it is called *relational aggression*. When we consider relational aggression, girls are more aggressive than boys starting in the preschool years (Shahaeian, 2017). If Johanna were to be picked on as often as Leo, she might be perceived as being aggressive, too. There is also the possibility that Johanna would react differently from Leo. Rather than using physical aggression, she would probably resort to relational aggression, such as name-calling or saying, "I won't be your friend."

Gender-Related Expectations Although gender is a biological trait, much gender-related behavior is learned. From very early ages, children receive messages about what is expected of girls and boys that influence their behavior (Quinlan, 2016). By preschool age, children are beginning to firmly establish their gender identities, although they may still think that changing their clothes or activities can affect it. Sex-role stereotyping can play a powerful role in the classroom.

Among the individual differences that have the greatest significance for teachers are variations in cognitive development and abilities, social and emotional development (including temperament), approaches to learning, physical development, and interests. These topics are discussed briefly in the sections that follow.

Cognitive Development and Abilities

A major contributor to individual differences is variation in language development. Consider the fact that although on average babies say their first word at 11 months, the range is from 8 to 14 months (Hart & Risley, 1999). In addition, although the average age at which half of what children say is understandable is 19 months, the range is from 15 to 30 months (Hart & Risley, 1999), making teaching toddlers a challenging task indeed.

As children get older, variation only increases. Observations of 2-year-olds demonstrate that, on average, children produce 134 different words per hour, but the range is from 18 to 286 words (Hart & Risley, 1999). Such wide variation makes it challenging for teachers and parents to determine whether a child's development is just at the slow end of the range or is actually delayed.

By the time children reach kindergarten, their language, literacy, and mathematics abilities vary widely, and the achievement gap is already apparent (IOM & NRC, 2015). However, it is important to remember our earlier caution about averages when thinking about a large group of individuals such as children from low-income families. A wide range of variation exists within this group as well; although many children will be far behind, others will not. A large national study found that although Head Start children on average score below national norms, especially in vocabulary, the top one-quarter of the children scored at national averages on letter recognition and writing skills (Tarullo, Aikens, Moiduddin, & West, 2010).

© Pearson Education

Video Example 5.1:

Using Technology to Individualize Instruction

In this video, first graders are using tablets. What do you notice about their engagement and learning? How does using this technology effectively individualize instruction? And why does the teacher use technology this way?

Emotional and Social Development

Social skills and emotional self-regulation are among the most important skills for success in school and life. Positive social skills include the ability to make friends, join in play, and comfort other children in distress (Hemmeter, Fox, & Snyder, 2013). Children who have poor social skills are more likely to be angry and to argue and fight or withdraw from others.

Individual differences in social and emotional development are often related to temperament, and can often be observed when children are infants and toddlers. **Temperament** refers to individual differences in reactivity and self-regulation, as shown in children's emotions, activity level, and attention (Rothbart, 2011). One important aspect of temperament is how children react to new situations and people. Recall the twins, Alexandra and Alice, in the chapter-opening vignette. Alice confidently joins in

temperament The pattern of arousal and emotionality that is characteristic of an individual.

and becomes the life of the party, whereas Alex is fearful and inhibited in the new situation. While temperament has genetic and biological roots, research has shown that warm relationships with family members and teachers help all children develop positive social skills, regardless of their temperament type (Bates, 2012; Stright, Gallagher, & Kelley, 2008).

Some studies have shown that children with certain temperament characteristics struggle in school (Gartstein, Putnam, & Rothbart, 2012); however, warm and responsive relationships with caregivers help children be successful in academics and social relationships (Bates, 2012; Rudasill, Gallagher & White, 2010). Teachers who learn about and understand their children's different temperaments will learn how to adapt the learning setting to meet children's individual needs (Bates, 2012). Instead of assuming that a shy child has poor social skills or that an outgoing, energetic child is too aggressive or out of control, teachers should adapt to each child's needs. Alex's teacher will need to help her feel comfortable in new surroundings and teach her skills for making new friends (Gallagher, 2013). Alice's teacher may need to provide gentle guidance for following structured routines, redirecting her energy, and paying attention when needed. Temperament is one dimension of a larger topic, approaches to learning, which is discussed next.

Approaches to Learning

Early childhood educators are becoming increasingly aware that children's *approaches to learning* are critically important determinants of their success in school (McClelland, et al., 2013). As we have discussed, approaches to learning are "behaviors, tendencies or typical patterns that children use in learning situations" (Hyson, 2008, p. 10). These include both how children feel about learning—their level of enthusiasm, interest, and motivation—and how children engage with learning. Do they pay attention? Do they persist when tasks are challenging or frustrating? If one solution doesn't work out, are they flexible and creative in trying something new?

As with all other aspects of learning and development, there are individual differences in children's approaches to learning, which vary depending on the situation. For example, 7-year-old Wes enjoys taking things apart and putting them together; he will persist for hours working on his simple machines project for science. But during reading class, Wes loses interest and his attention wanders; his reading progress suffers. In response, his teacher brings in several books on machines, and Wes's enthusiasm for reading improves.

Even a brief visit to a classroom during choice time reveals the diversity of children's approaches to learning. Dontrelle can play with Legos for an hour. Ivy loves music, especially songs with movements, but wanders from one area to another, never alighting on one activity. Becca prefers painting but is perfectly happy if it is not available. The challenge for teachers is to foster children's positive approaches to learning and build on their strengths to help them acquire new abilities.

There are individual differences in children's approaches to learning. One child may be hesitants to join in play, while others may be enthusiastic and engaged right from the start.

Physical Development

Children of the same chronological age vary considerably in height and weight. Teachers sometimes inaccurately judge children's maturity based on their physical characteristics. For example, boys who are small for their age may be thought to be less mature than taller boys and inaccurately judged as not ready for kindergarten. At the same time, taller children, girls as well as boys, are often assumed to be older and more capable than they are.

Physical development is largely determined by biology; however, experience also plays a role in how physical skills and abilities develop, as when childhood malnutrition or chronic illness stunts growth.

On average, girls develop fine motor skills earlier than boys do, but cultural expectations for girls' behavior may contribute to these differences (Woolfolk & Perry, 2015). Girls, for instance, may be given dolls to dress with miniature clothes and shoes that require fine motor skills, and they may be encouraged by teachers or parents to play in a more restricted way than boys. Similarly, because boys may be less adept with pencils or unable to sit still for group time, teachers might think they are less competent. Just as teachers must understand each child's temperament, they must also come to understand each child's physical skills and capabilities in order to provide a wide range of learning opportunities to find the best match.

Seeing Each Child as an Individual

There is a scene in the movie *Mary Poppins* when Ms. Poppins meets her charges, Jane and Michael, for the first time. The star nanny pulls out her "magical measuring tape." The special tape measurer allows her to instantaneously surmise important and unique information about the children that helps her plan how she will best care for them. While this type of measuring tape does not exist in reality, it illustrates a necessary first step in working with children: getting to know them.

For teachers to build positive relationships and teach effectively, they need to understand children's preferences, interests, background, and culture. For children, this information is most often accessed by carefully and purposefully observing what they do, and by speaking with parents and other caregivers. The task of knowing children involves observing and assessing on a regular basis.

Some teachers find it helpful for parents to complete surveys about their child. Items on these surveys include family members; pets; fears; favorite foods, toys, or activities; how to tell when their child is upset; or what other special needs a child may have. With this information, teachers can help ensure that children are motivated to get involved, that the content of conversations and level of instruction are relevant, and that they communicate respect for children's families and cultural background.

As we have seen in previous sections, individual differences result from both heredity and experience. A key determinant of children's experience is their culture. For example, cultural groups differ in their views about appropriate behavior for males and females. Cultural differences and individual differences are not the same thing, but they are connected. The *Culture Lens* feature will help you understand the relationship between individual and cultural differences, and respond effectively.

All About Me

Name Molly

When I grow up, I want to be a vet

A food I really don't like is peas

A food I love is watermelen

My favorite animal is a dog and a lion

My favorite sport is soccer

When nobody is around I like to have a playdate

My favorite place to be is home and the beach

The things I like to make are freind ship brackets

The thing I like best about school is monkey bars freinds and studying animals

This All About Me interview helps the teacher get to know each child in her class.

© Rawpixel.com/Shutterstock

Culture Lens
Responding to Cultural and Individual Differences

Early childhood teachers must respond to both individual differences in children and to cultural differences. Why both? When teachers respond to the individual child, aren't they also responding to the cultural child? The answer is yes and no.

Every child is unique and develops an individual personality as a result of her or his personal history. At the same time, everyone develops some behaviors that are shared with members of his or her cultural group. Because culture is a group characteristic, the rules of a culture are shared by group members and are not unique to individuals. When teachers think of children only as individuals, they risk missing important information about what children have learned about group expectations. Consider this example:

> Edwin comes in from outdoor play crying; he is soaked and covered with sand and mud. His teacher, Ms. Amos, starts to undress him to help him get cleaned up, and he cries harder. When she tries to help him remove his shoes, he forcefully pulls away. Ms. Amos knows him to be stubborn. She tries to coax him into letting her help and consoles him while attempting to undress him, but to no avail. What his teacher doesn't know is that in Edwin's cultural group, you don't get your school clothes dirty, boys don't cry, and boys dress and undress themselves in private.

Had this teacher known more about Edwin's cultural group, she could have responded in a more appropriate way. She might have offered him a change of clothes and let him go to a private place to change himself. On the other hand, what teachers know about group differences when blindly applied to all individuals in a cultural group may be equally inappropriate because individuals within groups differ from one another.

After the incident with Edwin, Ms. Amos decides to learn more about his background. She talks to colleagues and becomes a more careful observer of Edwin and his family, as well as of other children from his cultural group. One day, Edwin's cousin Sammy comes in soaked and covered with mud. Ms. Amos decides not to help him clean up, but offers him a change of clothes. When he takes the clean clothes, returns to the playground, and throws them in the sandbox, his teacher is stunned, because she expected him to go in the bathroom and change. Sammy, however, was not at all upset by the wet clothes, and enjoyed acting contrary to expectations.

So why did the two boys—both from the same cultural group—behave so differently? Because culture is learned; it can be well learned by some people in the group and less well learned by others. Some families are tradition oriented, others less so. Further, even though families and individuals learn the cultural rules, some people conform to what they have learned, while others don't.

Thus, members of a cultural group will behave differently depending on how deeply embedded they are within the core of a culture. Thinking about differences in behavior in this way helps teachers understand why, for instance, all Japanese people don't always "act Japanese." And it helps teachers avoid stereotyping groups and applying untested assumptions about individuals.

An important thing to remember is that knowing who children are as members of cultural groups provides more information than simply knowing them as individuals. But the most important point is that children are both individuals and cultural beings at the same time and in the same place.

The connection between interests and abilities is the foundation of an important theory relevant to individual differences in human beings. This theory of multiple intelligences is described in the section that follows.

✓ **Check Your Understanding 5.2**

Gardner's Theory of Multiple Intelligences: Implications for Practice

A useful framework for thinking about individual differences among children is the **theory of multiple intelligences** developed by Howard Gardner (2004). Rather than thinking about intelligence as one score that can be measured by an intelligence test, Gardner

TABLE 5.1 Gardner's Theory of Multiple Intelligences

Intelligence	Definition	Child's Possible Interests in School and Later life
Logical/mathematical	Ability to reason, analyze, and solve logical problems	Earth, space, and physical sciences; mathematics; computers
Linguistic	Ability to communicate; sensitivity to words and functions of language	Reading, writing, teaching, public speaking
Musical	Ability to produce and appreciate music	Singing, playing instruments, composing, listening to music
Naturalist	Sensitivity to the natural world, plants, and animals	Outdoor play, nature, biology, environmental science, gardening
Spatial	Ability to perceive the visual-spatial world	Visual arts, photography, architecture, graphic design
Bodily/kinesthetic	Ability to control body movements and objects	Dancing, physical education, sports, movement exploration
Interpersonal	Sensitivity to the feelings and desires of others	Making friends, collaborative learning, social studies
Intrapersonal	Awareness of own feelings and strengths	Keeping a diary, reading, writing poetry, meditation

Sources: Based on Gardner (2004, 2006).

identified eight different intelligences, which are listed and described in Table 5.1. Gardner believes that people have different profiles of strengths and weaknesses among these intelligences. His theory challenges teachers to think of the many different ways children are intelligent and can demonstrate their competence.

Gardner (2004) points out that traditional schooling typically focuses on only two of the intelligences: logical/mathematical and linguistic. Consider the fact that college entrance exams result in scores for math and verbal ability. When educators test only children's verbal and math abilities, as is often the case, they miss children's strengths in other important areas such as sociability or psychomotor skills. Gardner also believes that attention to the full range of children's capabilities could help more children succeed in school, thus narrowing the achievement gap for children from low-income families and children of color, a conclusion that is supported by other scholars (Sullivan, 2016)

What are the implications of Gardner's theory for teachers? Consider the following example of teaching with multiple intelligences in mind. Hanita Blume teaches a mixed-age group of 4- and 5-year-olds. One of the primary goals of the math curriculum is to develop children's concept of number, which includes counting and beginning operations such as adding and subtracting. The range of ages and experiences among children within her group affects their levels of math ability. She takes these differences into account as well as the fact that each of these children has different capabilities and interests.

Hanita does not try to evaluate individual children's "intelligences." Instead, she plans a variety of learning opportunities to draw on children's strengths and interests to help them all achieve the math goals. Following are some of the learning experiences she provides relevant to each of the multiple intelligences:

- *Logical/mathematical.* Hanita engages children in solving real-world problems with numbers, such as "We have nine children and only five chairs. How many more chairs do we need?"
- *Linguistic.* Hanita reads a counting book in small groups and engages children in counting the objects on each page.
- *Musical.* In large and small groups, Hanita sings counting songs and does fingerplays such as *Five Little Monkeys* to engage children in counting forward and backward.
- *Naturalist.* During outdoor play time, Hanita works with children to make collections of natural objects such as leaves or stones. Children place the objects in categories (large or small, according to color), count the number in each category, and determine which has more or fewer.
- *Spatial.* Hanita provides many different kinds of blocks and small manipulative toys for children to count and categorize, and talks with them, supplying the counting words for those who need the help.

theory of multiple intelligences Theory developed by Howard Gardner that identifies eight different intelligences as opposed to a single score on an intelligence test; this theory is useful for thinking about variation among children and teaching to their strengths.

- *Bodily/kinesthetic.* Hanita engages children in using their bodies to learn the counting sequence and concept of number. Children stomp their feet or clap their hands three times, four times, and so on.
- *Interpersonal.* Hanita organizes small cooperative groups of children to work on math games such as *Chutes and Ladders*; children roll the die, read the number of dots, and count the number of spaces. There is no competition.
- *Intrapersonal.* Hanita works one-on-one with some children in tasks such as calculating attendance, then asks them to reflect on what they know about counting.

As we can conclude from the example of Hanita's classroom, seeing children as individuals with multiple intelligences does not mean that every child must be taught differently. Instead, individual variation among children requires using various teaching practices to be responsive to the abilities of all learners, including children whose development is well above the typical range, as discussed next.

 Application Exercise 5.1

Table 5.1: Gardner's Theory of Multiple Intelligences

 Application Exercise 5.2

Addressing Multiple Intelligences in a Project

Gifted and Talented Children

A small percentage of children may display highly specialized talents at a young age. Gardner's theory of multiple intelligences is helpful in adapting instruction for these children. What is giftedness? The National Association for Gifted Children (2010) defines it as: "Individuals who demonstrate outstanding levels of aptitude or competence in one or more domains." However, there is no universally accepted definition; giftedness, intelligence, and talent may look different in different contexts and cultures (Heward, 2014). Traditionally, giftedness was determined by a high IQ score, but today, broader conceptions are used to identify a child as gifted and talented. A child may be gifted in music, drama, or sports, for instance.

One way to identify young gifted children is to focus on a range of behaviors and characteristics that occur in daily activities as well as in school (Heward, 2014). Some common abilities of gifted young children include (National Association for Gifted Children, 2008):

- Curiosity and thoughtful questions about many things
- Solving problems in unique ways and using prior knowledge in new contexts
- Sustained attention span, willingness to persist on challenging tasks, and good memory
- Especially original imagination, wit, and humor
- Keen observation skills and rapid mastery of new learning
- Desire to work independently and take initiative
- Talent in making up stories and reading

However determined, for their talents to flourish, gifted children need challenging educational experiences and individualized instruction (Gadzikowski, 2013; National Association for Gifted Children, 2010). When interesting, engaging experiences are provided for all children, the needs of gifted children are more likely to be met in a regular classroom.

For example, Melvin's second-grade teacher, Ms. Dell, thinks he is "very precocious." He reads well above grade level and has a large vocabulary. One day, he announces to her that his brother is funny. She asks, "How so?" and he answers, "You know, strange, odd, peculiar." Melvin exhibits an intense curiosity, asking high-level questions such as, "Where does gasoline come from?" Ms. Dell modifies the curriculum to challenge him. She sets up a time for Melvin to read to preschoolers. She orders *National Geographic* to satisfy his voracious curiosity about geography. She is also patient with Melvin's persistent questioning that would bother most other adults.

Ms. Dell understands the importance of recognizing early signs of giftedness in young children—particularly in children like Melvin from low-income families, who are more often considered at risk than gifted—and nurturing the gift so that it may flourish (Coleman & Shah-Coltrane, 2015). She also understands that gifted children's development can be uneven in that they may have great strengths in many areas but still be at age level or below in others. For example, cognitively gifted children may be very good at articulating school rules and the reasons behind them but at the same time be less able to follow rules in action. A gifted child may also stand out from peers as being different and struggle to make friends.

✔ Check Your Understanding 5.3

🔺 Responsive Education for All Learners

In this section, we first describe how intentional teachers adapt their teaching practices in response to individual variation among all children. Then we describe a specific framework for systematically addressing the needs of all learners—Response to Intervention.

Differentiating Instruction

In every classroom, teachers need to differentiate instruction so that they support the engagement, interest, full participation, and success of every child (Tomlinson, 2014). Differentiated instruction refers to creating multiple paths so that children of different abilities, interests, and learning needs experience equally appropriate ways to achieve important learning goals. *Equally appropriate* does not mean the same or uniform. Nor does differentiated instruction mean that children receive their own assignments or that they receive a private, one-on-one lesson. Rather, it means that teachers provide interrelated learning opportunities that help facilitate children's mastery of new skills and content knowledge.

differentiated instruction The creation of multiple paths so that children of different abilities, interests, and learning needs experience equally appropriate ways to achieve important learning goals.

Differentiated instruction is a cyclical process that is illustrated in Figure 5.1. First, teachers must get to know each child in the classroom. They must also know the curriculum. Both of these components influence how teachers plan and differentiate instruction. Planning must take into account the learning environment and materials, the content, the teaching strategies, and the products that demonstrate what children have learned (Tomlinson, 2014), each of which is described next.

Plan the Environment The environment refers to the overall look and feel of the classroom. A differentiated environment provides various spaces throughout the classroom for learning to occur. For example, soft, cozy spaces allow some children to work alone. Other spaces are designed for intrapersonal learners to work together in small groups. A differentiated environment also provides a variety of materials. For example, a reading center includes books at different levels on various topics for children. A writing center might have sandpaper letters or plastic magnetic letters for tactile learners. Children who learn best while moving may have places to stand and work at tables.

Differentiate Content Differentiating the content involves meeting children where they are and focusing instruction on what they need to learn next. For example, a child who knows letters can begin to map letter sounds to the alphabet and is also ready to receive instruction on blending letters to make sounds. A child who is skilled at decoding words can focus on fluency and comprehension.

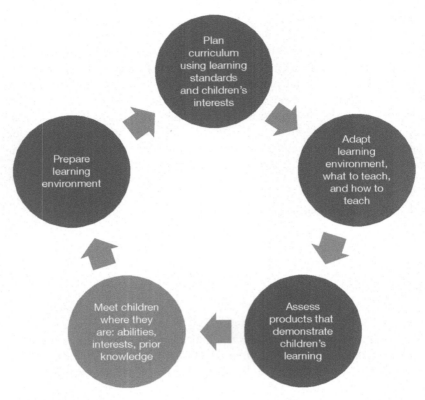

FIGURE 5.1　Model of Differentiated Instruction As illustrated here, differentiated instruction is a cyclical process that enables teachers to meet the needs and support the learning of each child.

Video Example 5.2:

Differentiating Instruction

In this video, a teacher implements a math lesson that takes the form of a game with dominos. How is this game an example of differentiated instruction?

Adapt Teaching Strategies Strategies are the ways teachers provide specific content instruction. The intentional teacher considers the child's abilities and interests when planning content instruction. For example, when teaching science, the teacher provides hands-on tools for children to observe, measure, and record their observations. A computer program or mobile app is motivating for many children. Other examples include providing information books for linguistic learners and cooperative learning activities for the intrapersonal learners.

Assess Learning Products The product that results from differentiated instruction is the demonstration of learning. When content and processes are differentiated for children, the products they produce will be different, too. Consider Josh Peters, a kindergarten teacher in an inclusive classroom. As he is reading a story, he stops occasionally to ask questions. The purpose of asking questions is so the children can demonstrate what they have learned (the product). He asks some children to recall the events of the story and others to predict what will happen next. One child may even be asked to simply point to an illustration of a character in the story. Josh takes each child's level of literacy into account and targets their engagement to successful participation and extending learning.

Response to Intervention

As we have seen, every early childhood classroom is composed of diverse learners—children of widely varying abilities and interests. Although every classroom teacher is responsible for differentiating instruction for the children in her class, in recent years, greater emphasis has been placed on preventing learning problems and intervening earlier for *all* children, rather than waiting until a child falls too far behind or is labeled as having a learning disability. To accomplish this goal, one frequently used approach is **Response to Intervention (RTI)**, a three-tiered, comprehensive framework for bridging assessment and instruction that is intended to prevent school failure, especially in the areas of reading and mathematics (Allington, 2009; National Center on Response to Intervention, 2010; National Professional Development Center on Inclusion [NPDCI], 2012).

Response to Intervention is *not* a special education framework or approach; when well implemented, it yields effective results for children with and without disabilities as well as dual language learners. Compared to differentiated instruction, RTI is a more systemic approach that is implemented by a program or school system. It requires collaborative participation by teachers, administrators, specialists, and families.

The three tiers of the RTI framework are:

1. Research-based curriculum, differentiated instruction, and ongoing assessment for all children (typically meets the needs of 80 percent of the children).

    Tier 1 of the framework provides a foundation of high-quality education for all children, including a comprehensive, evidence-based curriculum and intentional teaching. Tier 1 involves universal screening, assessment, and monitoring of children's progress to obtain information about each child and to determine whether a child would benefit from additional support.

2. Screening for learning difficulties, focused instruction, and ongoing progress monitoring for those who are not making expected learning progress (approximately 15 percent of children).

    Tier 2 provides developmentally appropriate, large- and small-group interventions for children who need more focused learning experiences. For example, some children may need regularly scheduled small-group reading to improve vocabulary and other literacy skills. To complement the more explicit activities and build on children's strengths and interests, teachers also embed learning opportunities in daily activities and routines. With these children, teachers monitor their learning progress more frequently and use the information to guide instruction.

3. Intensive instructional intervention for those children who need it (approximately 5 percent).

    Tier 3 focuses on the approximately 5 percent of children who do not make expected progress via the Tier 1 and Tier 2 interventions. At Tier 3, children receive intensive, individualized interventions. These include effective strategies to scaffold children's learning such as prompting and modeling (described later in this chapter). Progress monitoring and collaborative problem solving continue to guide decisions about the child.

Although it is a general-education model, RTI can bridge the gap between general and special education by ensuring that children with special needs fully access and participate in the regular curriculum. This framework looks at all students with the goal of preventing learning delays from becoming learning disabilities (Coleman, Roth, & West, 2009). It is

Response to Intervention (RTI) A three-tiered framework intended to prevent learning delays in primary grades from becoming learning disabilities.

important to note that children with already identified disabilities are expected to be found at all three tiers of the model. For children who show signs of struggling, this framework provides additional supports such as more focused time, content, scaffolding, and/or one-on-one attention.

Benefits of RTI   RTI is a framework that applies to all children. It is very important that RTI tiers are not misinterpreted or misused to categorize or label children. In reality, the tiers are flexible, and individual children move between them based on ongoing assessment of their progress.

Successful implementation of RTI depends on accurate, ongoing assessment of children, which can be challenging for teachers of dual language learners. An English language learner or a child who speaks a variation of English may have a well-developed vocabulary and understand many concepts, but may not be well understood at school (National Academies of Science, Engineering, and Medicine, 2017). In such a situation, it can be difficult to accurately assess either the child's competence or his or her needs, as illustrated in the *Language Lens* feature.

Language Lens
Accurate Assessment of Linguistically Diverse Children

Accurately assessing the abilities of children who speak a home language other than English or whose cultural background varies from the majority of children and teachers can be a challenging task. Cultural and linguistic diversity are *not* learning delays or disabilities. However, cultural and linguistic diversity can have a significant impact on identification and diagnosis of children's special needs, as the following example illustrates:

The student body of Rosa Parks Elementary School is about 30 percent Latino, 30 percent European American, and 40 percent African American. Scott James is an African American first-grade teacher. The school's speech therapist, Tess Brooks, is a white European American. Scott meets with Tess because he is concerned about two students, Reynoldo and Patrizia, who are behind in reading. Both children speak Spanish at home but speak both English and Spanish at school. Reynoldo is quite verbal; Patrizia hardly speaks at all. Scott thinks that Reynoldo's reading problem is related to a language delay but, because Scott doesn't speak Spanish, he can't be sure. However, the other children, even the Spanish-speaking children, don't seem to understand Reynoldo, either. As for Patrizia, Scott thinks she may have an undiagnosed hearing loss.

Scott's bigger concern is that the screening tools aren't very accurate for assessing language delays in Spanish, and Tess shares his concern. She thinks the best strategy is to get more information from Reynoldo's family about his communication at home. Using an interpreter, Tess and Scott meet with Reynoldo's mother. She is clearly alarmed. She tells the translator that these teachers think Reynoldo is stupid because he doesn't

speak English, but she knows that there is nothing wrong with her son.

Scott privately meets with Patrizia's grandmother, again using a translator. Her reaction is different from Reynoldo's mother's reaction: "I've been worried, too, because she hardly talks at home, either. But I understand her when she talks, and so does her brother."

In these situations, Scott and Tess must walk a fine line. They can easily make a mistake. In this case, Reynoldo's speech problems were real and not a product of learning a second language. Without an accurate assessment of the problem, Reynoldo did not receive therapy, and his language delay worsened. Patrizia, on the other hand, did not have a hearing loss. What her grandmother and Scott thought was a language delay was actually shyness.

When assessment tools aren't sensitive to language differences or when professionals do not understand a child's language, they can inaccurately diagnose a delay. In this case, a child may be mislabeled as "delayed," which can negatively affect teachers' and parents' expectations for him. On the other hand, if professionals assume that a language difference is the only cause, they can miss a real problem. The latter error has lasting consequences, because the child may not receive needed intervention services.

Source: Based on T. Bennett et al., 2001. *Cross-Cultural Considerations in Early Childhood Special Education* (Technical Report #14). Urbana-Champaign, IL: University of Illinois, Culturally and Linguistically Appropriate Services (CLAS). Retrieved April 20, 2018, from http://clas.uiuc.edu/techreport/tech14.html#4b.

The value of such prevention/intervention models is becoming more widely recognized. A growing body of research demonstrates the effectiveness of RTI in preventing and addressing learning disabilities (DEC, NAEYC & NHSA; 2014). The Individuals with Disabilities Education Act (IDEA) permits schools to use special education funds for RTI, which may reduce the number of children who are identified for special education. Nevertheless, there will always be a small percentage of children with identified disabilities and special needs, a topic we discuss next.

✓ Check Your Understanding 5.4

Individual Differences in Ability

For several reasons, all teachers must be prepared to work with children who have special needs. First, federal laws require that children with special needs be included in classrooms and programs where their typically developing peers are found, and that their learning progress be reported for accountability purposes. Second, effective practices exist that can positively alter the course of children's development and their success in life. Third, many of the strategies proven effective for children with special needs can be equally effective in addressing the individual variation among typically developing children. In short, early childhood educators who are familiar with the expertise of early childhood special education can be more effective teachers of all children.

To understand how to work with children with special needs, we next address the language of special education. In the sections following, we introduce principles that teachers should know about children with disabilities and describe the laws regulating special education and the benefits of serving children with disabilities in settings with their typically developing peers.

The Language of Early Childhood Special Education

One of the challenges for generalist early childhood educators is learning special education terminology. Because each field tends to have its own vocabulary, communicating effectively across these related fields requires a common vocabulary.

Defining Terms Children with special needs is a broad term used to describe children who may have multiple risk factors, specialized health care needs (such as asthma), mental or emotional health concerns, severe allergies, or physical and/or cognitive disabilities. The more specific term children with disabilities refers to children who have been identified as having a specific category of disability, such as autism or cerebral palsy. However, the terms *children with special needs* and *children with disabilities* are often used interchangeably.

Another all-encompassing, though less frequently used, term is exceptional children. This term is used to communicate inclusion of gifted and talented children as well as children whose development is below the expected range. In fact, the professional association for special education professionals is called the Council for Exceptional Children (CEC). Early childhood special education professionals are members of the Division for Early Childhood (DEC) of the Council for Exceptional Children. Table 5.2 lists and defines some of the most common categories of exceptionality.

© Pearson Education

Video Example 5.3:

Modifications and Accommodations

An early childhood special educator describes some examples of basic accommodations and modifications that can help every learner succeed. Why is it important for all teachers to be familiar with and use these practices?

children with special needs A broad term used to describe children who may have multiple risk factors, specialized health care needs, mental or emotional health concerns, severe allergies, or physical and/or cognitive disabilities.

children with disabilities Children who have been identified as having a specific category of disability, such as autism or cerebral palsy.

exceptional children An all-encompassing term used to communicate inclusion of gifted and talented children as well as children whose development is below the expected range.

Council for Exceptional Children (CEC) The national professional association for special educators.

Division for Early Childhood (DEC) Subdivision of the Council for Exceptional Children that is the national professional organization for early childhood special educators and early intervention specialists.

person-first language Language that recognizes that a child is a child first, whether or not he or she has a disability (e.g., saying "child with special needs" as opposed to "special needs child").

Using Person-First Language

A standard for professionals who work with individuals with special needs is that they use what is called **person-first language**. Person-first language recognizes that a child is a child first, whether or not he or she has a disability. Consider the difference between describing 4-year-old Zain as "a special needs child" and describing him as "a child with special needs." The former phrase emphasizes the disability, whereas the latter communicates that Zain is first and foremost a child whose special needs are only part of his identity.

By contrast, placing the adjective first modifies the entire noun to which it is referring; this can place undue emphasis on inability. For example, if you hear a traffic reporter describe a "disabled car," you think of a car that cannot be driven at all. Compare this to what you may think when you hear "a car with a flat tire." For similar reasons, we refer to a "child with Down syndrome" or "a child with autism" instead of saying a "Down's child" or "an autistic." A fundamental tenet of inclusion is that children are children regardless of disability status, and the use of person-first language reflects this principle.

Admittedly, using person-first language can sometimes feel cumbersome. But language matters. How we describe people and conditions communicates our attitudes about them. Currently, person-first terms begin with the word "individuals," thus emphasizing the uniqueness of each person regardless of an identified disability.

There is a recent movement among some adolescents and adults to reject person-first language because it denies an essential part of their identity. As one young woman stated, "I am autistic and it is part of every aspect of my life. When people say I 'have' autism, it

TABLE 5.2 Some Types of Exceptionality

Category	Definition
Attention deficit/hyperactivity disorder (ADHD)	Diagnosis describing children who display a pattern of severe inattentive, hyperactive, and/or impulsive behavior that interferes with the child's learning.
Autism spectrum disorder (ASD)	Condition in which the child has impairments in social communication and interactions and demonstrates restricted, repetitive patterns of behavior and interests.
Down syndrome (DS)	Condition in which extra genetic material causes the child to exhibit developmental delays and/or intellectual disability. Children with DS tend to share physical features such as a flat facial profile, an upward slant to the eyes, small ears, a single crease across the center of the palms, and an enlarged tongue.
Cerebral palsy (CP)	A neurological disorder that appears in infancy or early childhood and permanently affects the child's body movement, motor development, and muscle coordination.
Deafness and hearing impairment	A condition in which hearing is impaired, either permanently or temporarily, and negatively impacts a child's academic performance. Deafness is a severe hearing impairment that prevents a child from hearing and processing language and other sounds.
Visually impaired or blind	Condition describing loss or partial loss of vision.
Intellectual disability	Disability in which the child has limitations both in cognitive functioning and in social and adaptive behavior.
Developmental delay	Diagnosis describing a child whose development is behind expectations for his or her age group as measured by appropriate diagnostic instruments and procedures. Occurs in one or more areas of development: physical, cognitive, communication, social, emotional, or adaptive.
Gifted	Term applied to children with outstanding talent who perform or show potential for performing at remarkably high levels of accomplishment when compared with others of their age, experience, or environment.

sounds like an illness that needs to be cured." Given varying perspectives on this issue, it is wise to ask the individual or parent which terminology they prefer.

What Teachers Should Know about Children with Disabilities

Children with disabilities display a variation in skills beyond what is considered typical; as a result, in many instances, these children qualify for special education services. These services are provided by professionals and therapists who have specialized knowledge about childhood disabilities and disorders. Therefore, it is neither necessary nor reasonable for early childhood educators to know everything about every disorder that might affect a child. Yet, they do need to understand several key principles about children's disabilities (Wolery & Wilbers, 1994):

1. *Children with disabilities are diverse and distinct from one another.* All children have unique skills, interests, dislikes, and talents. Therefore, it is essential that teachers recognize each child as a distinctive individual. Children with disabilities share similarities with other children, but they may need more specialized and/or individualized instruction and care than children without special needs. However, it is vitally important for teachers to remember that no child is defined by his or her disability; children are diverse in countless ways, including culturally, linguistically, and socioeconomically.

2. *Some children may have more than one disability.* For example, a child with a hearing impairment may also have low vision or a seizure disorder. Moreover, children may develop additional disabilities as a result of their primary disability. For example, a child with a visual impairment may not be able to explore his environment and therefore develop motor or cognitive delays. Early identification and effective intervention can sometimes prevent secondary disabilities.

3. *A diagnosis rarely leads to specific educational interventions.* Educational practices and therapies, such as speech and language therapy, are not selected by the diagnosis. The selected interventions need to align with the child's current skills and abilities, family concerns, needs and resources, and what works best for the child. Teachers should not assume that a particular diagnosis will automatically respond to a specific intervention (Wolery & Wilbers, 1994).

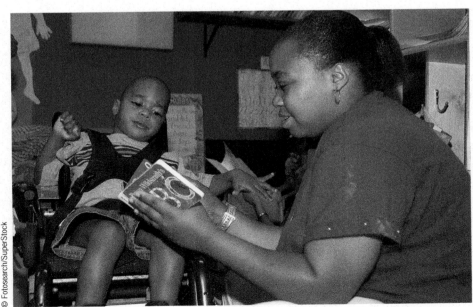

© Fotosearch/SuperStock

Inclusion means that every teacher must be prepared to work with children with disabilities and special needs in the regular classroom. The first step is for teachers to remember that children with disabilities are children first and are, like every child, unique.

Seeing Children with Disabilities as Individuals: The Case of Autism

autism spectrum disorder (ASD) Complex developmental disabilities that impact the normal development of the brain processes related to social interaction and communication skills.

Even with the same diagnosis, a great deal of individual variability exists, as in the case of **autism spectrum disorder (ASD)**, one of the fastest-growing serious developmental disabilities in the United States. The Centers for Disease Control and Prevention (Christensen et al., 2016) estimates that 1 out of every 68 children has been identified with ASD, and boys are almost five times as likely as girls to receive the diagnosis. Thus, early childhood teachers will likely encounter a child with autism at some point in their careers.

The first signs of autism often appear between 2 and 3 years of age. Young children with autism often have delays in language and communication, including nonverbal communication such as pointing and gesturing. They may display repetitive motor behaviors, and are often inflexible in their routines and play. For example, a child with autism may have a severe emotional reaction to a change in schedule or inability to find a favorite toy. The thinking and learning abilities of children with autism can vary—from gifted to a more significant intellectual disability. Consider the following examples:

> Jeffrey is 2½ years old with a head of curly brown hair. He does not talk yet, but if he wants something, he will pull an adult by the hand to what he wants. Sometimes it is easy for his teacher to guess what he wants, but lately he has started crying, screaming, and falling on the ground if she is not able to get him what he wants right away. He spends most of his time wandering around the classroom holding his favorite toy. When another child or teacher tries to play near him, he will quickly leave the area. He will often cry when changing from one activity to another, and once he starts crying, it is very difficult to calm him down. Other children and teachers are starting to avoid interacting with him, afraid it may trigger his crying.

> Nathan is 3 years old and can climb higher and faster than most other 3-year-olds. He has known his letters and numbers since age 2, and can read a variety of words and phrases. He cannot, however, consistently answer simple questions from adults, interact with children his own age, or tolerate changes to his routine. His parents are extremely concerned because they have been asked to stop bringing him to music lessons at the local community center. They were also told to find a "more appropriate" placement than the local co-op preschool. His grandparents wonder if there is anything "really wrong" with him or if his parents are simply overindulgent.

> Cherish is 30 months old and has beautiful blue eyes. Her parents report that she used to walk around the house, point to objects, label them, and laugh. She does not do that anymore. In fact, these days she rarely speaks except to request certain apps or preferred foods. She rarely looks at people or things unless she can find something that is spinning, and then she is mesmerized by it. Her parents cannot remember the last time they heard her laugh.

These children display some of the characteristics of ASD. Each child is a reminder that ASD is a spectrum disorder, which means that children who receive this diagnosis differ dramatically in their abilities, preferences, needs, and areas of delay. As Jeffery, Nathan, and Cherish remind us, there is no "typical" child with ASD. Every child and family brings a unique set of strengths and challenges that must be considered when planning an educational program. Early identification and intervention for children with ASD can dramatically improve educational outcomes (Hume, Turner-Brown & Boutot, 2016).

Often, the first adults to notice some of the early signs of autism are teachers and caregivers. It can sometimes be difficult for caregivers to articulate developmental concerns when autism is the question, because many of the behaviors associated with ASD can seemingly be explained by other factors such as "He just needs to be disciplined," "He is just like his father," or "It is a phase he or she is going through." As a result, teachers are often the first to recognize that a child's behavior may be a red flag for a more serious developmental delay, and may need to recommend that the family take action by seeking out a trained professional who can help. Red flags for autism in early childhood include:

- No big smiles or other warm, joyful expressions by 6 months or thereafter
- No back-and-forth sharing of sounds, smiles, or other facial expressions by 9 months or thereafter
- No babbling by 12 months
- No back-and-forth gestures, such as pointing, showing, reaching, or waving, by 12 months
- No words by 16 months
- No two-word meaningful phrases by 24 months
- Any loss of speech or babbling or social skills at any age

The foundation of any program for a child with autism should be the practices that are important for all children, including supportive, caring adults; activities that promote high levels of active engagement; and meaningful interactions with peers. While a common goal is for all children to have opportunities to interact successfully with children and adults, children with autism may require special supports and strategies to be successful in social interactions. Fortunately, researchers have identified many practices that work well for supporting learning and social development for children with autism; some of these practices are described later in this chapter (Wong et al., 2014). One of the most valuable of these strategies is using play to engage children with autism, as described in the feature *Promoting Play: Supporting Toddlers with Autism Using Play*.

In addition to understanding how to work effectively with children with special needs, all teachers must be familiar with special education laws. These laws are discussed in the next section.

What Teachers Should Know about Legal Requirements for Children with Disabilities

Federal laws govern how special education services are delivered in the United States. First, we describe the legislation generally. Then we discuss in more detail the requirements for individualized planning for children with special needs.

The Individuals with Disabilities Education Act

Many children with disabilities are eligible for early intervention and early childhood special education services. Both early intervention (EI) and early childhood special education (ECSE) are regulated under the Individuals with Disabilities Education Act (IDEA), formerly the Education of the Handicapped Act. IDEA was designed to provide protections for children to ensure their right to a **free appropriate public education (FAPE)**. The principle of the law is that children with disabilities should not be denied the same opportunities offered to everyone else. To receive specially designed instruction at no cost to parents and to meet the unique needs of a child with a disability, children must meet **eligibility guidelines** according to IDEA. These guidelines are determined on a state-by-state basis.

Part B of IDEA is a federal program that provides funds to states and local school districts to support education for children with disabilities from ages 3 to 21. The most relevant part of the law for early childhood teachers is Section 619 of Part B (also known as Early Childhood Special Education), which applies specifically to preschoolers with disabilities. To meet all children's individual needs, the law requires that a team of educators and family members create an individualized education plan for each student.

free appropriate public education (FAPE) Education for children with disabilities that is required by IDEA, so that children with disabilities are not denied the same opportunities offered to everyone else.

eligibility guidelines Guidelines established on a state-by-state basis according to IDEA that determine whether children may receive special education services.

© Pearson Education

Video Example 5.4:

Early Intervention

In this video, a parent describes her experiences with Early Intervention and Early Childhood Special Education services. In what ways have these services helped her daughter and supported her family?

Promoting Play

Supporting Toddlers with Autism Using Play

Play is an important learning activity for all children, and an important context for teachers to observe what and how children are learning. Play skills are associated with later language and social skills, self-regulation, and even reading skills. Toddlers learn to play and play to learn, exploring their environment using all of their senses. Toddlers who exhibit characteristics of autism often struggle learning to play. They prefer to play alone and often play repetitively, running a toy car back and forth, arranging dinosaurs and crashing them, or carefully constructing a toy train and running it on the track. They don't share much eye contact with adults or communicate their needs with pointing, gestures, or words. They struggle to copy motions or vary their play activities. Since play is such an important context for learning and development, teachers should carefully plan and support play activities and opportunities for all toddlers.

Play skills are excellent functional goals for children: they learn to play with peers in a natural setting, and can learn important cognitive and motor skills embedded in the context of play. They learn to communicate socially, problem-solve, and regulate their actions and emotions. Importantly, they learn to understand the perspectives of other people.

Teachers can support growth in children's play by encouraging interactive play. Teachers can make themselves needed in the child's play, such as by putting toys up high to encourage communication such as pointing, gesturing, or words. Max enjoys playing with trains, and his teacher, Alec, has noticed that he always uses the same cars to construct his train—the engine, the blue car, and the red car. Alec sits down to play with Max, holding the train cars in her lap. To use the cars, Max must indicate to Alec what he wants. Alec holds a car close to her face (encouraging eye contact) and asks Max, "Do you need the engine, Max?" Grabbing for the engine car, Max takes a quick look at Alec, who is smiling a warm smile. She hands the engine to Max. Each day, Alec inserts her play a bit more into Max's routine. One day, Alec takes the opportunity to encourage flexibility in play, and removes the blue car from the bin before Max arrives. Watching to make sure Max doesn't get too frustrated, Alec introduces a yellow train car, holds it up by her face to encourage eye contact, and offers Max the yellow train. She demonstrates that this yellow train makes a noise. Another day, she adds to their play routine by having a bridge fall onto the track, "Oh no, what shall we do?" Alec exclaims. Max laughs and moves the barrier, sharing some joy of play with his teacher.

Sources: C. S. Wong, 2013. A play and joint attention intervention for teachers of young children with autism: A randomized controlled pilot study. *Autism*, 17, 340–357; K. Hume, L. Turner-Brown, & E. A. Boutot, 2016. Play focused interventions for young children with autism. In E. Boutot (Ed.), *Autism spectrum disorders: Foundations, characteristics, and effective strategies* (2nd ed.), 169–180, Boston: Pearson.

Part C (Early Intervention) provides funds for states to provide services for infants and toddlers who have disabilities or developmental delays. Some states provide early intervention services for infants and toddlers who are *at risk* of developmental delay and their families. Early Intervention services are discussed in more detail later in the chapter.

individualized education program (IEP) A written plan designed to meet the unique needs of a child with a disability or special need; it is developed, reviewed, and revised by an IEP team during meetings for each child who is eligible for special education services.

Individualized Education Programs

When a child meets the disability requirements of the law and is identified as needing special education and related services, school districts are obligated to prepare and implement an **individualized education program (IEP)**, which is designed to meet the unique needs of the child. The IEP is a written plan for services that is developed, reviewed, and revised by an IEP team.

SAMPLE INDIVIDUALIZED EDUCATION PROGRAM (IEP)
Duration of Special Education and Related Services: From: 4/10/18 To: 4/9/19
Student: <u>Shuting Li</u>   DOB: <u>4/10/15</u>
School: <u>King Preschool</u>   Grade: <u>Preschool</u>
Primary Area of Eligibility* <u>Developmental Delay</u> **(*Reported on Child Count)**
Student Profile

> ***Student's overall strengths:*** Shuting is an active, independent little girl. She wants to communicate and interact with others. She shows excellent joint attention for shared looks, gives and interactions. She shows many emerging skills, and shows age-appropriate fine motor skills.
> ***Summarize assessment information:*** Shuting has wonderful communicative intent, and is very social. Her fine motor skills are age-appropriate, and she shows many emerging skills. Shuting is showing a greater than 30% delay at this time in her cognitive and communication skills.

> ***Parent's concerns, if any, for enhancing the student's education:*** Shuting's mother is concerned about her speech and that she only uses a few words.

Present Level(s) of Academic and Functional Performance

> Based on a recent Team Play-Based Assessment-2, home observation, and parent report: Shuting has emergent language skills and shows interest in play and peer interactions at home and in the preschool she attends. She has a short attention span for non-preferred activities. In order for Shuting to fully participate and learn from preschool activities, she needs to be able to follow the daily classroom routine, follow basic classroom directions, and remain in a designated area.
> Shuting shows excellent communicative intent with gestures, shared looks, and vocalizations. She is not consistently using words for getting her wants and needs met. In order to develop functional communication with others, Shuting needs to develop words for requesting a variety of nouns, actions, attention and help.

Annual Goal #1 - Given no more than 1 reminder, Shuting will follow the daily routine, follow classroom routine directions, and remain in a designated area in 4/5 opportunities, as sampled 1x weekly over 6 weeks.
_____ Academic Goal__X__Functional Goal
Benchmarks or Short-Term Objectives:

> Shuting will follow basic classroom routine directions (i.e., *come, sit, stop, throw away, clean up*) in 4/5 opportunities
>
> 1. given physical prompts
> 2. given verbal and visual prompts
> 3. given no more than 3 reminders

Describe how progress toward the annual goal will be measured: Teacher and therapist report, data collection
Does the student require assistive technology devices and/or services? ☒ Yes ☐ No
Visual supports (i.e., picture cues, visual schedule) Is this goal integrated with related service(s)? ☐ Yes* ☒ No

Annual Goal # 2– Given a variety of materials and pre-literacy activities, Shuting will name 5 new vocabulary items (including nouns, action words and modifiers) per marking period as sampled 1x weekly over 6 weeks.
_____ Academic Goal__X__ Functional Goal
Benchmarks or Short-Term Objectives:

> Shuting will name 5 new vocabulary items per marking period:
> a. with direct model
> b. with semantic/fill-in or phonemic cues/prompts

Describe how progress toward the annual goal will be measured: Teacher and therapist report, data collection

Does the student require assistive technology devices and/or services? ☐ Yes ☒ No

Is this goal integrated with related service(s)? ☒ Yes* ☐ No Speech/language therapy

Least Restrictive Environment

I. General Education Program Participation

General Education/Special Education Nonacademic Services & Activities	Supplemental Aids/Services Modifications/Accommodations Assistive Technology	Implementation Specifications (Example: Who? What? When? Where?)
Preschool child	Visual supports	As needed

Shuting attends a local inclusive preschool program and participates in all activities.

V. Specially Designed Instruction, Related Services, and Nonacademic Services and Activities

A. Anticipated Frequency and Location of Specially Designed Instruction

Special Education:	Sessions Per: Week Month	Reporting Period Year	Session Length:	Location:
Special Education	5		2 hours	General Education

B. Anticipated Frequency and Location of Related Services

☐ The IEP Team determined related services **are not required** to assist the student to benefit from special education.

☒ The IEP Team determined the following related services are required to assist the student to benefit from special education.

Related Service(s):	Sessions Per: Week Month Year	Reporting Period	Session Length:	Location:
Speech/Language Therapy	14		30 minutes	General Education

VII. Least Restrictive Environment Justification Statement

If the student will be removed from nondisabled peers for any part of the day (general education classroom, nonacademic services and activities), explain **why** the services cannot be delivered with nondisabled peers with the use of supplemental aids and services.

☒ N/A Student will not be removed from nondisabled peers.

X. Record of IEP Team Participation

Name	Position	Date
	LEA Representative	4/10/2018
	Parent	4/10/2018
	Parent	4/10/2018
	Speech/Language Pathologist	4/10/2018
	B-K Licensed Teacher	4/10/2018
	Early Intervention Service Coordinator	4/10/2018
	School Psychologist	4/10/2018
	Interpreter	4/10/2018
	Early Head Start Child Development Specialist	4/10/2018

Copy given/sent to parent(s): by ____LEA____ on __4/10/2018__.

An IEP must contain the following information:

1. A statement of the child's present levels of academic achievement and functional performance
2. A statement of measurable annual goals, including academic and functional goals designed to:
   - Meet the child's needs that result from the child's disability to enable the child to be involved in and make progress in the general education curriculum
   - Meet each of the child's other educational needs that result from the child's disability
3. A description of benchmarks or short-term objectives
4. A description of:
   - How the child's progress toward meeting the annual goals will be measured
   - When periodic reports on the progress the child is making toward meeting the annual goals (such as through the use of quarterly or other periodic reports, concurrent with the issuance of report cards) will be provided
5. A statement of the special education and related services and supplementary aids and services, based on peer-reviewed research to the extent practicable, to be provided to the child, or on behalf of the child
6. A statement of any individually appropriate accommodations that are necessary to measure the academic achievement and functional performance of the child on state- and district-wide assessments

The IEP Team The IEP is developed by a team that consists of educators, therapists and medical professionals, as well as family. By law, the team members must include:

- The child's parent(s) or guardian(s)
- The child's early childhood teacher
- The child's early childhood special education teacher
- A representative of the community program who has certain specific knowledge and qualifications
- An individual who can interpret the instructional implications of evaluation results (this may be one of the other listed members, such as an occupational therapist or speech language pathologist)
- Other individuals, who are chosen at the discretion of the parent or the agency, who have knowledge or special expertise regarding the child, including related services personnel such as the speech language pathologist or physical therapist, as appropriate

Early Intervention for Infants and Toddlers Children from birth to age 3 who have a developmental delay, a diagnosed condition, or in some states, are identified as at risk for developing a developmental delay may qualify for early intervention (EI) services. These children will have an **individualized family service plan (IFSP)**. An IFSP documents and guides the early intervention process for children with disabilities and their families. The IFSP contains information about the services necessary to support a child's development and enhance the family's capacity to facilitate the child's development. Some parents learn that their child has a disability before or immediately after birth, and the hospital may initiate EI soon after. For other children, delays or disabilities emerge later. In these cases, a parent, other family member, pediatrician, teacher, child care provider, or family friend initially may raise concerns about the child's development.

Children with developmental delays enter EI services following diagnostic testing or developmental evaluation administered in partnership with the family by a team of specialists. Through the IFSP process, family members and service providers work as a team to plan, implement, and evaluate services tailored to the family's unique concerns, priorities, and resources.

individualized family service plan (IFSP) Documents and guides the early intervention process for children with disabilities from birth to age 3 and their families; contains information about the services necessary to facilitate a child's development and enhance the family's capacity to facilitate the child's development.

According to IDEA, the IFSP, like the IEP, is a written plan that must contain specific information, including:

1. The child's present levels of physical, cognitive, communication, social or emotional, and adaptive development
2. The family's resources, priorities, and concerns relating to enhancing the development of the child with a disability
3. The major outcomes to be achieved for the child and the family; the criteria, procedures, and timelines used to determine progress; and whether modifications or revisions of the outcomes or services are necessary
4. Specific early intervention services necessary to meet the unique needs of the child and the family, including the frequency, intensity, and method of delivery
5. The environments in which services will be provided, including justification of the extent, if any, to which the services will not be provided in a *natural environment.* The *natural environment* refers to settings that are natural or normal for the child's same-age peers without disabilities.
6. The projected dates for initiation of services and their anticipated duration
7. The name of the service provider who will be responsible for implementing the plan and coordinating with other agencies and persons
8. Steps to support the child's transition to preschool or other appropriate services

Differences between IFSPs and IEPs   The IFSP and IEP are different processes and documents based upon the child's developmental needs and the family's role in the child's life. The IFSP:

- Revolves around the family, because the family is the constant in a child's life
- Includes outcomes for the family, as opposed to focusing only on the child
- Includes activities involving multiple agencies to integrate all services into one plan
- Names a service coordinator to help the family during the development, implementation, and evaluation of the IFSP
- Involves the notion of natural environments, which create opportunities for learning interventions in everyday routines and activities, rather than only in formal, contrived environments

The laws that dictate services for children with disabilities and special needs reflect research demonstrating the benefits of such services for children with special needs and the larger society. The laws also reflect underlying values about what life should be like for all children. However, laws and procedures related to services can be confusing for families. Community organizations, schools, and teachers are responsible for understanding and communicating to families how educational systems work for children with special needs.

© Pearson Education

Video Example 5.5:

Characteristics of IEPs and IFSPs

In this video, an early childhood special educator compares IEPs for preschoolers and older children with IFSPs for infants and toddlers. What are the primary differences between these important planning processes? Why do they differ?

Application Exercise 5.3

Requirements for IFSPs and IEPs

Embracing Natural Learning Environments and Inclusion

One of the primary goals of federal laws governing services for children with disabilities is to make sure that these children lead lives that are as similar as possible to those of children who do not have disabilities. To achieve this goal, professionals need to understand the rationale and embrace the values that led to the law being passed in the first place.

Benefits of Natural Learning Environments Part C requires that EI services be embedded in everyday routines and activities, and that they occur in the children's **natural learning environments**. Natural learning environments are settings where infants, toddlers, and their families would be spending time if the child did not have a disability, such as child care centers, parks, a neighbor's house, or the zoo. Natural learning environments are important, because for young children, learning occurs most effectively in the contexts where children will need to use the new skill (Dunst, 2011; Dunst, Hamby, Trivette, Raab, & Bruder, 2000).

So, what is *not* a natural environment? Places children go because they have a disability, such as hospitals, clinics, and therapy offices, are not optimal places for children to learn new skills. Young children, especially those under age 3, do not easily learn a skill in one setting and transfer it to another. Furthermore, just because a setting is natural does not ensure that a child with a disability will be able to access and benefit from what the environment offers. Teachers can use principles of **universal design** to plan for curriculum, assessment, and environmental adaptations to accommodate the

natural learning environments Settings that are natural or normal for the child's same-age peers without disabilities, such as child care centers, parks, a neighbor's house, or the zoo, as opposed to hospitals, clinics, and therapy offices.

universal design The concept that materials and environments need to be usable by everyone, including those with disabilities, to the greatest extent possible.

What Works

Universal Design

© Karen H Ilagan/Shutterstock

Universal design is the creation of products and environments that are accessible to all people—individuals with and without disabilities. Obvious examples of universal design are sidewalk curb cuts and ramps that are essential for people in wheelchairs. However, ramps also benefit travelers with roller-bag luggage, parents with strollers, elderly people, and even toddlers who haven't mastered steps. Examples abound in today's world, including Velcro, automatic doors, nonslip surfaces, closed captioning, and signs with universally recognizable symbols.

Planning environments based on principles of universal design from the beginning ensures that all children have meaningful opportunities to learn and prevents the need to modify at a later time. To implement universal design, early childhood teachers should think about learning as a continuum (rather than stages or categories), expect learning differences and adapt the curriculum for all children, and select a variety of materials and activities that allow children to demonstrate learning in multiple and different ways. Successful inclusion requires three major components: access to the learning environment and curriculum, participation in activities and routines, and adequate support for teachers—all of which are facilitated by attention to universal design. Intentional planning and implementation of universal design enables teachers to differentiate instruction for every child. Following are some examples of practices based on universal design principles:

- Provide toys and learning materials that offer a variety of sensory experiences, including textures, scents, sounds, and visual stimuli. For example, an assortment of balls of different colors, sizes, and textures (squishy, soft, or rubbery) facilitate engagement for children with sensory impairments. Some balls

make noise or light up as they roll or bounce, providing extra cues for children with special needs and making the toys more interesting for all children.

- Use open-ended materials that can be used in a variety of ways. Blocks are an excellent example, because there is no right or wrong way to play with them. Wooden unit blocks come in various shapes and sizes, enabling children to engage with them in multiple ways. Blocks that have textured sides and make noise add additional sensory clues as well as challenges for children.

- Provide materials that allow multiple ways for successful use. Play-Doh can be manipulated with fingers, cut with a plastic knife, or wrapped around another object. To make prints, finger paint can be applied to hands or feet, or applied to the feet of a dinosaur toy or car wheel for children who do not care for paint on their body.

- Provide experiences and materials that allow multiple ways to access. Books with easy-to-turn pages and various sizes of pictures and text facilitate children's independent literacy learning. Those with textures, cutouts, and sound effects engage children's interests. Sturdy board books make page turning easier. Books on iPad or audiotape help children with hearing disabilities participate in the language and literacy curriculum.

Sources: Based on L. Dinnebeil, M. Boat & Y. Bae, 2013. Integrating principles of universal design into the early childhood curriculum. *Dimensions of Early Childhood, 41*, 1, 3–14; National Center on Universal Design for Learning. *About UDL: What is universal design for learning?* Retrieved December 27, 2017, from www.cast.org/udl.

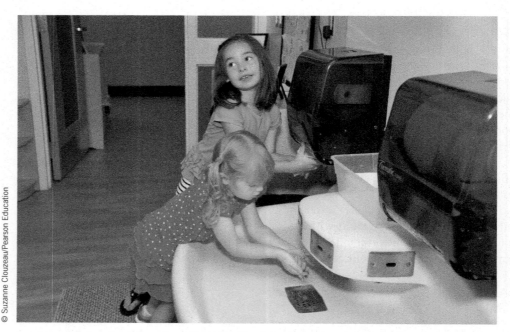

© Suzanne Clouzeau/Pearson Education

A universal design element, such as this automatic sink, eliminates a barrier for children who might have difficulty operating the handles while also achieving the goal of teaching proper hand washing and preventing illness for all children.

individual needs of all learners. Learn more about how early childhood teachers can use materials to accommodate the individual needs of all learners in the feature *What Works: Universal Design.*

Benefits of Inclusion

Inclusion is based on the same principle as natural learning environments—that children with disabilities need to be with their peers without disabilities. Although most images of inclusion involve school settings such as preschool or public schools, inclusion is also important in home and community environments such as parks, recreation, and faith settings.

Inclusion requires more than just access to settings; children need to participate as fully as possible and receive the supports they and their teachers need to ensure they make progress toward important learning goals (Division for Early Childhood [DEC] & National Association for the Education of Young Children [NAEYC], 2009). Successful inclusion means that *all* children in the classroom participate, learn, and thrive. Many, but not all, children with special needs will need individualized instruction to achieve positive learning and developmental outcomes in inclusive programs. But it is also important to cultivate a culture of inclusion that provides children with and without disabilities a sense of belonging and membership in the peer group (Brilliante, 2017).

It is important for teachers to understand that inclusion benefits all of society in addition to the children with disabilities. Children with disabilities develop opportunities to share in the daily life of their community, and they do as well or better than children in specialized programs, particularly with respect to social development (NPDCI, 2007). Children without disabilities benefit by developing positive attitudes toward individuals with diverse abilities. Families of children with and without disabilities benefit from developing strong, supportive relationships that enhance the quality of life. In the sections that follow, we describe what teachers need to do for children with special needs if inclusion is to be effective.

Intentional teachers foster friendships between children with special needs and their typically developing peers. What are some ways teachers can build positive relationships among children in inclusive classrooms?

Check Your Understanding 5.5

Effective Practices for Children With Diverse Abilities

The purpose of inclusion is to ensure that the individual needs of all children are being met in shared settings (Guralnick & Bruder, 2016). However, identifying what practices are best for children of varying abilities may be challenging for an early childhood teacher. The Division for Early Childhood (2014) has established a set of recommended practices designed to improve outcomes for children with disabilities ages birth to 5 years. They include practices associated with assessment, environment, family, instruction, interaction, teaming and collaboration, and transitions. All professionals who work with children with disabilities should be familiar with and adhere to this set of recommended practices.

Children with disabilities often "need more specialized practices that allow them to participate and engage meaningfully in their daily living routines and learning activities" (Division for Early Childhood, 2014, p. 3). The DEC Recommended Practices (DEC-RP) were developed to guide professionals working with young children with or at risk for disabilities and their families. While the DEC-RP recognizes that developmentally appropriate practice needs to be the foundation of any program (Copple & Bredekamp, 2009), DEC emphasizes practices supportive of inclusion and outcomes for children who may need more intensive supports to participate and learn. The recommended practices address the following topics:

- Leadership—including local and state leaders of early education
- Assessment—screening, service eligibility, individualized planning, progress monitoring, and measuring outcomes

- Environment—space, materials, equipment, routines, activities
- Family—family-centered, capacity-building, collaboration
- Instruction—"intentional and systematic strategies to maximize learning" (Division for Early Childhood, 2014, DEC-RP, p. 12)
- Interaction—sensitive and responsive practices supporting approaches to learning, communication, and cognitive development
- Teaming and Collaboration—practices that "promote and sustain collaborative adult partnerships, relationships and ongoing interactions to ensure that programs and services achieve desired child and family outcomes and goals" (Division for Early Childhood, 2014, DEC-RP, p. 15)
- Transition—practices that support child and family changes between environments and/or programs

specialized instruction Involves teachers matching an individual child's goals and objectives with appropriate teaching methods and materials, deciding what amount of assistance each child with special needs requires, providing the assistance, and then determining whether the instruction was effective.

Specialized instruction involves teachers matching an individual child's goals and objectives with appropriate teaching methods and materials. Teachers also decide what amount of assistance each child with special needs requires, provide the assistance, and then determine whether the instruction was effective. Most often, a team of specialists is available to help the teacher achieve these goals. Some practices to support children with special needs are described below: assessment, planning and implementing individualized strategies, and team collaboration.

Assess Young Children of Diverse Abilities

The effectiveness of individualized instruction for children with disabilities depends in large part on accurately assessing their needs and progress. Throughout this book, we address the topic of assessment as related to all children. In this section, we discuss types of assessment that are used to best accommodate children with special needs. Screening, diagnostic, and eligibility assessments are used by specialists to determine whether the child has a developmental delay or disability and is eligible for services. Curriculum-based assessments and routines-based assessments are the most appropriate and useful to early childhood teachers for planning what children with special needs should be learning.

functional skills The essential abilities needed to fulfill goals parents have for their children, such as communicating, making friends, and learning self-help skills.

Curriculum-Based Assessments

Curriculum-based assessments trace a child's progress along a continuum of functional skills within a developmentally sequenced curriculum organized by developmental domain. **Functional skills** are those that are useful and meaningful to children in their everyday lives. For example, it is generally useful for children to learn to use the toilet, feed themselves, communicate and play with peers, and count objects. A developmental domain is an area of development such as fine and gross motor skills, cognitive abilities, self-help capabilities, and social and communication skills. Curriculum-based assessments serve to link assessment, intervention, and evaluation, as the following example illustrates:

Corwin (age 3½) has experienced an eligibility evaluation for special education based on a recommendation from his pediatrician. According to the multidisciplinary team, he qualifies for early childhood special education because he has a moderate communication and social skills delay. Consequently, Corwin's parents are referred to the local preschool special education program near their house. After his parents observe the inclusive program, they enroll Corwin. During his first week at school, Corwin's teachers use a published curriculum-based measure to identify his needs and develop functional goals and objectives for his IEP. Test items list functional skills in predictable developmental sequence. The assessment is conducted within the context of the preschool routines and activities.

When Taiya Stoner, Corwin's teacher, observes him independently perform items that are on the test, these tasks are noted as "mastered" and listed as his current levels of performance on his IEP. For example, Corwin mastered one goal—uses simple problem-solving strategies—because he said "NO!" when a child took his crayon. Behaviors he had difficulty displaying or did not display over the course of a few observations, such as initiating play activities with another child, were considered targets for intervention and added as goals for his IEP. After his teachers and therapists provide instruction to Corwin on the identified goals, they administer the assessment again to determine whether their guidance was effective and to establish new goals for Corwin.

In this example, all of the steps of the linked system are in place. First, the teachers use the assessment to determine what the child needs to learn, then they teach the skills identified. Finally, the team reassesses, using the same tool to determine whether Corwin is making progress.

Routines-Based Assessment Another approach for determining goals for a child is called *routines-based assessment*, which is used to determine which functional skills a child should be taught. In a routines-based assessment, those who know the child well (e.g., family members, teachers) describe how the child participates in the typical routines of daily living (McWilliam, 2010). For example, Gwynneth's kindergarten teacher, Tamara Calhoun, is asked by the special education teacher to complete a routines-based assessment of Gwynneth's performance throughout the day to identify some functional learning goals for her. Tamara lists classroom activities in chronological order, such as arrival, circle time, centers, clean up, snack, and so on. She then observes Gwynneth's behavior during these routines and sets goals to work on with her, such as "Gwynneth will get off bus; walk to the classroom with group; put coat and backpack in cubby." Using routines-based assessment at home, her parents' list includes typical daily routines such as wake up, eat breakfast, and get dressed.

To ensure accurate information as well as follow-through, parents of children with special needs must participate in the assessment process. After the team gathers information to determine the child's functional goals, the next step is to plan for individualized instruction.

Monitor Progress The effectiveness of instruction depends on the team monitoring the child's progress to determine if the child has met a goal and is ready to move on to learning a new skill, or if the IEP needs modification. Information about children's progress can be collected in many ways. One data collection system used by many teachers is to observe and document the child's learning using a checklist of skills or a rating scale of the child's performance. A rating scale allows the teacher to indicate the level of a child's skill along a continuum. For example, the lowest level might be "child refuses to perform the skill" and the highest "child performs the skill independently," with several steps in between.

States must also monitor Early Childhood Outcomes (ECO) for children who receive services for special needs, whether through Part C (Early Intervention) or Part B (Preschool). They must report the percentage of infants and toddlers with Individualized Family Service Plans (IFSPs) or preschool children with Individualized Education Programs (IEPs) who demonstrate improved:

a. Positive social-emotional skills (including social relationships)

b. Acquisition and use of knowledge and skills (including early language/communication [and early literacy for preschoolers])

c. Use of appropriate behavior to meet needs

Because these outcomes apply to all children, they can help professionals and families communicate effectively regarding children's goal progress and needs.

Use Individualized Instructional Strategies

Every early childhood teacher needs a repertoire of teaching strategies to be effective with all children. Sometimes, however, in order to learn new skills, children with special needs require more explicit teaching than do typically developing children. In these instances, teachers use strategies that are carefully planned and implemented more frequently throughout the day. Individualizing instruction involves identifying specific goals, creating learning opportunities, providing teacher support, reinforcing children's learning, and monitoring their progress.

generative skills Skills that can be used across settings, people, events, and objects.

Identify Goals for Children
Either of the assessment approaches described previously can be used to determine learning goals. The ECSE teacher on the team can help write objectives that are functional and generative. Generative skills are those that can be used across settings, people, events, and objects. For example, one of the skills identified for Damon is "uses two fingers to pick up objects." To be generative, Damon needs to learn to use the skill across settings such as during mealtime to pick up Cheerios or in the bath to pick up the soap. He also needs to use the skill across objects, such as crayons or beads, and under various conditions, such as when the items are mushy or hard. If an identified skill is too limited, such as "uses a finger and thumb grasp to put beads into a bottle," it is difficult to create enough learning opportunities to be effective, and the skill is less likely to be useful in different situations.

Create Learning Opportunities
Effective teachers create learning opportunities in daily routines and activities that provide the child with multiple tools for learning a new skill (McWilliam, 2010). These opportunities may be more focused, but are not essentially different from those provided for every child. One strategy is to introduce unexpected events, as when the teacher says or does something that the child does not anticipate. These events may be funny or interesting things the adult says. For example, when teaching 6-year-old Miguel to use prepositions, his teacher walks over to where he is sitting and sits backwards next to him. Then she asks, "Miguel, where are you?" Miguel, giggling, says, "Right here." His teacher says "Right where? Are you *behind* me or *in front* of me?"

All children have different abilities and interests that teachers can use to help them meet learning goals. With minor adaptations, this teacher provides support for every child to learn early literacy skills.

Use Helping Strategies To help children learn skills, teachers use helping strategies called **prompts**. These are gestural, model, physical, pictorial, or verbal supports that help children use a specific skill (Neitzel & Wolery, 2009; Sandall & Schwartz, 2008):

- *Gestural prompts*. Movements that teachers use to let children know what behavior is expected. For example, when the teacher wants Julia to ask for more raisins, she waits and looks expectantly at Julia until Julia says, "I want more raisins."
- *Model prompts*. Involves the teacher saying or doing the behavior he wants the child to do. The teacher says "please" and "thank you" when he passes out food during lunchtime.
- *Physical prompts*. Gentle touching and guiding of children by the teacher to help the children accomplish a skill. When teaching Larisha to wash her hands, the teacher places her hands over Larisha's hands and helps her turn on the faucet, get soap, rub her hands together, dry her hands, and turn off the faucet with the towel.
- *Pictorial prompts*. Visual cues that help children accomplish a skill. To help Owen play independently at center time, his teacher places pictures of each center on a piece of construction paper, and Owen refers to a picture when he moves to another activity area.
- *Verbal prompts*. Teacher language strategies that help children accomplish a skill. When it is time for Dushawn to come to the group for story time, his teacher gives him a verbal prompt: "Dushawn, please come sit on your carpet square next to me." This may be enough for Dushawn to learn that he is expected to join the group.

> **prompts** Gestural, model, physical, pictorial, or verbal clues that elicit responses from children to assist them in using a specific skill.

 Application Exercise 5.4
Using Individualized Strategies to Manage Conflict

Reinforce Children's Learning When children receive positive reinforcement following performance of a new skill, they are more likely to try the new skill again. In educational settings, positive reinforcement can be very simple and natural. **Naturally occurring reinforcers** are consequences that are likely to occur *whenever* the child performs the skill, and are therefore highly effective. For example, when Raven puts on her coat independently, the teacher says, "Raven, you zipped up your coat all by yourself. Now you can go outside to play." Some examples of naturally occurring reinforcers include the child using the paint after making a request to do so; playing with friends after asking to join the group; and being acknowledged by a teacher for trying hard at a difficult task.

> **naturally occurring reinforcers** Consequences that are likely to occur *whenever* the child performs the skill and are, therefore, highly effective.

Teaming and Collaboration

Working collaboratively with a team is critical to the success of including young children with special needs in the classroom. Each member of the team has different expertise in areas such as early childhood, special education, motor development, and communication development. Additionally, all members possess specific knowledge about the particular child. The child's family plays an important role in the collaborative team. They (1) provide information about their child's strengths and needs, (2) help assess functional skills and develop the IFSP or IEP with the team, (3) implement intervention strategies at home and in the community, and (4) provide critical information about the effectiveness of interventions.

At the IEP or IFSP team meeting, professionals and family members collaborate to (1) identify and prioritize individualized goals, (2) determine if modifications to the

Becoming an Intentional Teacher

Individualizing in Large Group Time

Here's What Happened Halfway through the kindergarten year, there was a child in my class, Tasha, who continued to have difficulty with large-group instruction times. She would touch the other children, sometimes even leaning her whole body against them and touching their hair or faces. She was easily distracted, and stood up to look out the windows several times during story time. She also would leave circle time before it finished and wander around. Large-group time wasn't the only time we did learning activities, but it was an important context for introducing new concepts, so it was important that I find a way for her to be engaged.

I had learned about the DEC Recommended Practices and guidelines for instruction in my college class, so I decided to try some out for supporting Tasha. First, I decided to gather some data about Tasha's interests and what engages her. I asked her family about her interests (DEC-INS1), and observed Tasha during free play (DEC-INS3). Tasha's family shared that she loves to dance, and I noticed that she played with our class puppet, Whiskers, frequently during free play. I also suspected that visual strategies would work well in engaging Tasha and helping her follow directions, so I planned to use some cue cards developed by our speech therapist. Before implementing, I spent a few minutes showing Tasha the cue cards and practicing them with her: keep feet and hands to self; look and listen to the action; raise a quiet hand to ask a question. For the next large group time, I used Whiskers to call the group together, and began circle time with a dancing activity. I held up one copy of each cue card for children to see (I suspected the cards would help other children, too). Tasha had another set in her lap, and our classroom aide helped her choose the same card as a reminder.

Here's What I Was Thinking Tasha has difficulty attending in large groups, and is easily distracted. Young children in general can have difficulty remembering expected behaviors and directions. I also realized that Tasha wasn't as motivated as other children were to listen and participate at circle time. At first, I thought that perhaps I should let Tasha wander when she didn't want to be at circle time. But she is already 6 years old, and although she has some difficulties with attention, her parents and I believe that she can be successful at circle time. Starting with an active song helps get some energy out before sitting.

Using two sets of cards allowed Tasha to see what was expected of the group and of her, and the aide helped keep Tasha on task with expectations. Beginning and ending circle time with Whiskers, the cat puppet, motivates Tasha to come to circle right away and stay through the end. These easy-to-implement modifications help Tasha to learn more and spend more time with her peers.

Reflection Even though all children are not alike, teaching in whole group can be an efficient and effective strategy at times. Do you think it's fair that some children are treated differently during group times? What other strategies could the teacher use to engage all the children fully?

environment or curriculum are needed, (3) design specialized instructional strategies, and (4) monitor the child's progress toward the goals. Teamwork and collaboration goes beyond team meetings. Many people, including family members, teacher assistants, and community partners, work to facilitate children's learning beyond the classroom into home and community settings.

All early childhood teachers need to learn how to teach children with special needs in inclusive settings. In addition, when general early childhood educators learn some of the important skills of early childhood special education, they can apply these skills to teaching all children. In *Becoming an Intentional Teacher: Individualizing in Large Group Time*, read how a kindergarten teacher draws on the DEC Recommended Practices to individualize and provide specialized instruction to the children in her class.

Having explored the topic of individual differences among typically developing children as well as children with special needs, we now see that teachers can draw on a large body of effective practices to achieve their goals for all children. Successful inclusion of children with disabilities and special needs involves much more than the children's presence in the classroom. Teachers need to get to know all of the children and continually assess their learning and development. They must plan and implement individualized instructional strategies. Most important, teachers must create a classroom climate in which every child is valued and fully included.

Revisiting the Case Study

... Ms. Creighton's Classroom

At the beginning of this chapter, we met some of the children in Lindsay Creighton's preschool class and wondered how she could possibly meet the needs of these diverse children. Now that we have explored the topic of adapting for individual differences, we can see how Lindsay successfully teaches all of the children.

Lindsay's study of child development helps her understand that children's personalities and behaviors are the result of an interaction between their genetic makeup and their experiences in the environment. Therefore, she is aware of how important her work is in helping them achieve their full potential. Lindsay has high goals for each child's learning. But she realizes that because children are unique, she needs to use differentiated instruction to help them achieve the goals.

For Cal, whose grandmother does not speak English, Lindsay works with a translator as well as a team that includes a social worker. Lindsay recognizes that Rohan and Ruby, who both seem painfully shy, are also very different. They each have different interests and abilities. Because Rohan likes quiet activities and playing with one other child, Lindsay encourages him in that direction, and he gradually becomes more confident. Ruby is hesitant until she is assured that Lindsay will protect her from an allergic reaction. The other children soon become comfortable with that fact as they say, "Ruby's body was born not liking peanuts." They all embrace the need to protect Ruby's health.

Although at first Lindsay and the other children mix up the twins, Alex and Alice, they soon become aware that each is an individual. Lindsay focuses on working with each girl separately and engaging them in different activities so their uniqueness becomes evident to all. Carter's needs are more severe and specific. Working as a member of his IEP team and supported by his parents, Lindsay becomes more confident in her ability to teach Carter and to help him achieve his individualized goals.

After several months of working with this class, Lindsay decides that adapting for individual variation is the most interesting part of her work. At first, she was concerned when confronted with such diversity. But now, she finds that children's individuality is what makes her days most interesting and unpredictable. As she expands her repertoire of skills for working with diverse children, she finds that seeing individual children's progress is richly rewarding. ■

5 Chapter Summary

- Children differ from one another in many ways, including rate and timing of cognitive and language development, social skills and temperament, and interests. The transactional theory of development explains that development is influenced by *both* biology *and* experience, and how they interact with each other.

- Effective early childhood teachers understand the importance of knowing each child as an individual. One of the most useful frameworks for thinking about the variation among children is Gardner's theory of multiple intelligences.

- *Differentiating instruction* means to create multiple paths so that children of different abilities, interests, or learning needs experience equally appropriate ways to achieve important learning goals.

- All teachers need to be prepared to work with children who have special learning and developmental needs because federal law requires it, effective practices exist to alter the course of children's learning, and many of these practices can be used with typically developing children.

- Specialized instruction involves teachers matching an individual child's goals with appropriate teaching methods and materials, deciding what amount of assistance is needed by the child, providing the assistance, and determining whether the instruction was effective. Of equal importance to specialized instruction is cultivating a culture of inclusion, which provides children with disabilities with a sense of belonging and membership in the peer group.

Key Terms

- autism spectrum disorder (ASD)
- children with disabilities
- children with special needs
- Council for Exceptional Children (CEC)
- differentiated instruction
- Division for Early Childhood (DEC)
- eligibility guidelines
- exceptional children
- free appropriate public education (FAPE)
- functional skills
- generative skills
- individualized education program (IEP)
- individualized family service plan (IFSP)
- natural learning environments
- naturally occurring reinforcers
- nature
- nurture
- person-first language
- prompts
- protective factors
- resilience
- Response to Intervention (RTI)
- risk factors
- specialized instruction
- temperament
- theory of multiple intelligences
- transactional theory of development
- universal design

 Flash Cards 5.1

Readings and Websites

Brillante, P. (2017). *The essentials: Supporting young children with disabilities in the classroom.* Washington, DC: National Association for the Education of Young Children.

Division for Early Childhood of the Council for Exceptional Children. (2014). *DEC Recommended practices in early intervention/early childhood special education.* Available on DEC website.

Gadzikowski, A. (2013). *Challenging exceptionally bright children in early childhood classrooms.* St. Paul, MN: Redleaf Press.

Center for Response to Intervention in Early Children

Visit this website for more information and resources on differentiating instruction for young learners.

Division for Early Childhood (DEC) of the Council for Exceptional Children

On the DEC website, you can find numerous resources, and can also download and read *DEC recommended practices in early intervention/early childhood special education.*

Early Childhood Technical Assistance Center (ECTA)

This website at the FPG Child Development Institute offers resources about early childhood outcomes, universal design, Response to Intervention, early intervention, Preschool 619 services, and a variety of other topics.

National Professional Development Center on Inclusion

At this website at the FPG Child Development Institute, you will find research and resources for supporting the inclusion of children with disabilities in settings with peers.

Project Zero

View the Project Zero website at Harvard University to learn more about application and research studies related to multiple intelligences and learning.

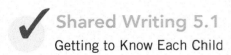

Shared Writing 5.1
Getting to Know Each Child

6

Embracing a Culturally and Linguistically Diverse World

Learning Outcomes

After studying this chapter, you should be able to

6.1 Define culture and explain how cultural contexts influence learning and development.

6.2 Describe a framework for thinking about culture.

6.3 Describe how your own cultural background influences your thinking and behavior.

6.4 Analyze why teachers need to understand and be sensitive to children's linguistic and cultural diversity.

6.5 Discuss how cultural competence is the key to effective teaching.

6.6 Apply principles of culturally responsive, effective practices for diverse learners.

Related NAEYC Professional Preparation Standards

The NAEYC Professional Preparation Standards (NAEYC, 2011) that apply to this chapter:

1: Promoting Child Development and Learning

Key elements:

    1a. Knowing and understanding young children's characteristics and needs

    1b. Knowing and understanding the multiple influences on development and learning

    1c. Using developmental knowledge to create healthy, respectful, supportive, and challenging learning environments

2: Building Family and Community Relationships

Key elements:

    2a. Knowing about and understanding diverse family and community characteristics

    2b. Supporting and engaging families and communities through respectful, reciprocal relationships

    2c. Involving families and communities in their children's development and learning

4: Using Developmentally Effective Approaches to Connect with Children and Families

Key elements:

    4a. Understanding positive relationships and supportive interactions as the foundation of their work with children

    4b. Knowing and understanding effective strategies and tools for early education

    4c. Using a broad repertoire of developmentally appropriate teaching/learning approaches

    4d. Reflecting on their own practice to promote positive outcomes for each child

Case Study

With her newly achieved associate's degree in early childhood education, Stacey Griffin is excited about her first job as a teacher of 18- to 30-month-old children in a child care center. Even though the center is located in a neighborhood close to where Stacey grew up, the population of the area has changed considerably in recent years. An influx of immigrants from Latin America is apparent in the number of families with young children who have replaced the elderly, White, European American, long-term residents, as well as in the goods available and language spoken in local markets. Despite these changes, Stacey feels confident that she knows enough about child development and early childhood practice to be a good teacher.

By the end of the first month, however, Stacey is feeling frustrated and less sure of herself. In the mornings, most of the families arrive late. They continue to carry their children into the classroom even though Stacey has informed them (gently, she thinks) that the children are capable of walking on their own and need to practice their developing motor skills. Similarly, she disapproves of the parents' continuing to spoon-feed the children rather than giving them finger food that they can manage on their own.

Mrs. Arguenta is unhappy that Stacey isn't cooperating in toilet training 18-month-old Ilsia. Stacey thinks Ilsia is too young because she can't verbalize her need to use the potty. Mrs. Arguenta says that Ilsia is already using the potty at home, and wants Ilsia to be dry. To make matters worse, Mrs. Arguenta sends Ilsia to child care wearing her best clothes and buckle shoes. Stacey thinks toddlers need to move about in comfort and should go barefoot to help them with their walking. Besides, the floor is carpeted.

Stacey tries to build a relationship with Mrs. Arguenta. She asks Mrs. Arguenta to call her Stacey instead of Miss Griffin, but Mrs. Arguenta ignores this friendly overture. Every time Stacey tries to meet with her to discuss Ilsia, Mrs. Arguenta is late or doesn't come. One day, Mrs. Arguenta sends Ilsia's 10-year-old sister to pick her up, which is a violation of center policies. Stacey can't understand why Mrs. Arguenta and the other families are being so difficult when she works so hard to communicate with them. ■

Some readers may think that Stacey's struggles as a new teacher are caused by the fact that she is working with difficult or uninterested parents. Others may think that Stacey is too inflexible to respond to legitimate concerns of families. In fact, Stacey and Mrs. Arguenta are operating from two different, albeit equally legitimate, cultural perspectives on appropriate child rearing. In the example above, we see the conflicts entirely from Stacey's perspective. But if the story were told from Mrs. Arguenta's view or that of other families, we might question Stacey's skills as a teacher; we might also question her sensitivity to the families' perspectives. In this situation, whatever appears to be happening on the surface, the underlying reality is an encounter between individuals from different cultural contexts.

The United States is becoming an increasingly diverse country. In the past decade, the number of white students in public schools decreased from 60% to 50%, and the Hispanic population of students increased from 17% to 26% (Annie E. Casey Foundation, 2017). Most early childhood programs serve children from diverse linguistic and cultural groups or will do so in the future. Therefore, it is essential for teachers to understand and embrace the realities of a culturally and linguistically diverse world.

But culture and its influences are subtle. Moreover, the majority cultural group of the United States—predominantly individuals of Anglo-European descent—tends to define culture and linguistic diversity as issues or challenges to be dealt with or solved. In fact, the word *diverse* means different, which raises the question—"Different from what?" The implication is that people whose cultural identity is not white European American or who are not native speakers of English are different from the norm.

In this book, we talk about the realities of culture and language because these forces influence the learning and development of all children. At the same time, we use the verb *embrace* when discussing culture and language to create a classroom climate that is culturally and linguistically supportive and responsive for *all* children. We believe that such a perspective is a precursor to helping all children achieve their full potentials.

In this chapter, we define the term *culture* and identify the basic principles of the role of culture in development and learning. We also describe a framework for thinking about contrasting cultural beliefs, values, and practices. We discuss effective teaching and learning strategies for working with all children, beginning with awareness of one's own cultural perspective.

Defining and Explaining the Influence of Cultural Contexts

The United States has always been a nation of immigrants, its diversity being a hallmark of American society. Recent waves of immigration and higher birth rates among certain groups have made the nation even more diverse. In many parts of the country, the majority of children are members of a so-called "minority" group. In the future, the concepts of majority and minority status are likely to become confusing if not meaningless.

Given the diversity of children and families served in programs, as well as changing demographics, every teacher will work with diverse groups of children and families. Even if differences are not outwardly apparent, individuals differ from one another in many ways: religion, national heritage, language, traditions, family structure, and many more. Therefore, all teachers must be committed to making it part of their ongoing education to learn about the diverse populations of their classrooms.

What Is Culture?

Culture refers to explicit and implicit values, beliefs, and patterns of behavior that are passed on from generation to generation (National Association for the Education of Young Children [NAEYC], 2009). Culture encompasses customs, rituals, beliefs, ways of interacting and communicating, and expectations for behaviors, roles, and relationships that are shared by members of a group (Allen, 2017).

To understand the concept of culture, it is crucial to understand that culture is a characteristic of *groups*, not an aspect of individual variation. Children learn the values, beliefs, and expectations for behavior from their cultural group. In Chapter 4, we learned how young children are similar to other children of the same age. In Chapter 5, we discussed how each child is unique and different from every other child. In this chapter, we describe how children share similar characteristics with other children of their cultural group. Although each of these three chapters focuses on a distinct principle of development, it is important to recognize that these principles are interrelated. All three of the following statements are equally true:

- Every child is like all other children in some ways.
- Every child is like some other children in some ways (those who are members of the same cultural group).
- Every child is like no other child.

Sometimes discussions of culture are limited, focusing on superficial characteristics such as those that can be observed. For example, we judge cultural origin based on the clothing that people wear, the holidays they celebrate, the accents with which they speak, or the music they enjoy. Although these external cues reveal something about children and their families, they neglect or ignore the deeper structures of culture—the values and rules—that truly influence behavior and decisions. Figure 6.1 illustrates the reality of culture, in which the surface characteristics are only the "tip of the iceberg" while the fundamental elements tend to be invisible.

The Role of Culture in Development

Why is culture so relevant for early childhood educators? The simplest answer to this question is that culture shapes and influences every child's

The population of young children in the United States is becoming ever more diverse. Effective teachers embrace the realities of cultural and linguistic diversity to help all children reach their full potentials.

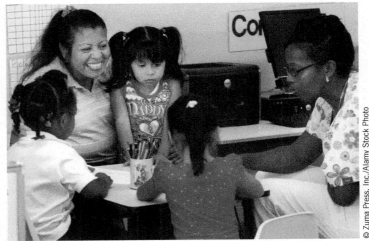

© Zuma Press, Inc./Alamy Stock Photo

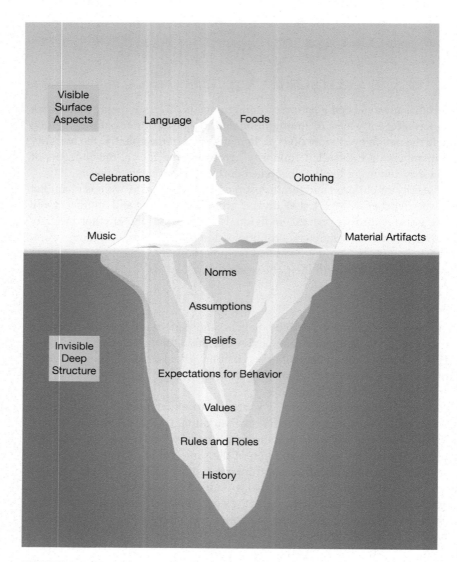

Visible Surface Aspects

Language   Foods

Celebrations   Clothing

Music   Material Artifacts

Norms

Assumptions

Beliefs

Invisible Deep Structure   Expectations for Behavior

Values

Rules and Roles

History

FIGURE 6.1 Model of Culture The complexity of culture is like an iceberg—the visible elements are only a small part while the deeper structures truly influence behavior and decisions.

Application Exercise 6.1

Figure 6.1: Model of Culture

development and learning (Banks, 2016; Bronfenbrenner, 1979, 2004). In fact, all aspects of human life are touched and affected by people's cultural contexts. This includes how people communicate, think, behave, solve problems, and organize communities and governments (Lynch, 2011).

Although the biological factors that influence maturation are similar for all human beings, culture has a huge influence on how children experience their growth and development—on how they are nurtured (Trawick-Smith, 2013). In general, cultural rules influence how children behave and how they make sense of their experiences.

acculturation The process whereby children learn expected rules of behavior.

Culture Influences Behavior Acculturation is the process whereby children learn expected rules of behavior. From their cultural group, children learn such critical lessons as how to show respect and how to properly greet an older or younger person, a friend, or a stranger (Rogoff, 2003).

Consider the range of child-rearing practices among various cultural groups. Are babies carried on mother's backs or pushed in strollers? Does the family remain silent during meals or talk openly? Do parents feel comfortable playing with their children or find this behavior embarrassing? Are mothers primarily responsible for a baby's care or is that care shared among different members of the extended family? These are only a few examples of the many ways cultural practices begin to shape children's development from the earliest moments of life.

Some cultural rules are explicitly taught, such as "hold the fork in your right hand and the knife in your left," or vice versa. In most countries, mixing up these rules would be of little consequence. By contrast, in Middle Eastern cultures, people eat with their right hand and use their left hand for toileting. Therefore, offering your left hand to someone is interpreted as a grave insult.

Children learn many cultural rules from adults or other children through modeling. From observation, children learn when to smile or look someone in the eye (Gonzalez-Mena, 2008). They also learn when to speak up and when to listen (Ramsey, 2015). They learn whether people shake hands or bow in greeting. In fact, what is considered *appropriate* behavior, thinking, or problem solving in a given situation is always culturally determined (Lynch, 2011). Consider how different cultural perspectives on appropriate child rearing come into play in the following situation:

> Patty Briggs is so excited because she has finally been approved to adopt a child from Costa Rica. She is prepared to stay there for several weeks to get to know her little boy, who is 1 year old, and for his foster family to get to know her. Even though Patty has studied child development and taken care of many young children, after a few days in Costa Rica, she starts to feel uncertain. Whenever she puts the baby down to crawl on the floor, the foster mother frowns and immediately picks him up. Patty is concerned because the baby is always so warmly dressed in a tropical climate. She finds that he has diaper rash, and wants to remove some of his warm clothing to help him heal. However, it's clear that the foster mother thinks he will get cold and become ill. During the time that Patty is in Costa Rica, she respects the foster mother's mode of caring for the baby, but also treats his diaper rash. After the adoption, she sends photos of him to his foster family to reassure them that he is well cared for. (P. Briggs, 1990, Personal Communication, Pearson Education)

Culture Creates Meaning Cultural rules determine the meaning attached to particular behaviors. Therefore, teachers need to be aware of how different experiences can carry different meanings for children. Consider the example of physical touch. Touch is an important aspect of human behavior, but different cultural groups attach different interpretations to the same kinds of touch (Lynch, 2011). In the United States, it is not unusual for opposite-sex couples to hold hands or lock arms as outward signs of affection. In other parts of the world, these behaviors between men and women might not be tolerated. Similarly, in some countries, members of the same sex walk arm in arm as a sign of friendship, but in the United States, same-sex public displays of affection are interpreted as a sign of sexual orientation. Accordingly, we see that the same behavior—holding hands or taking someone's arm—means something different, depending on the cultural context.

How does this concept affect teachers and children? When the same behaviors mean different things or different behaviors mean the same thing, mixed messages can result, as occurred in Stacey's classroom at the beginning of this chapter. Stacey thinks that using one's first name signals a positive relationship, whereas Mrs. Arguenta interprets it as a sign of disrespect.

How Culture Functions: Principles to Keep in Mind

As you continue your professional journey, you will probably find that the more you learn about culture, the more you need to know. This is not a comfortable position for most educators. While you may think that you should know all the answers, this is not realistic; the most effective stance is to acknowledge what you don't know and remain open to new learning. This will serve you well throughout your teaching career and in all areas of your professional journey.

In the meantime, it is useful to understand several key principles about how culture affects human development. These principles are listed and briefly described here (Day, 2006; Hanson, 2011):

1. *Everyone is rooted in one or more cultural groups.* This first principle is the foundation of all understanding about culture (Head Start, 2010b). Accepting this principle requires going beyond respecting diversity to deeper understanding; it requires that European American teachers reject the tendency to see white, European American children as exhibiting *ordinary* behaviors while thinking about children of other ethnic ancestries as exhibiting *cultural* behaviors (Day, 2006; Head Start, n.d.). Members of the majority cultural group in any country tend to have more difficulty recognizing that their cultural background influences their thinking and behavior.

2. *Cultures are dynamic.* Culture is not a fixed, static entity. Because it is born of traditions and historical experiences, intervening events can affect and change cultural rules. When groups immigrate, they take aspects of their culture with them; however, as they interact with members of other cultural groups, they may change. Similarly, the cultural traditions in the country of origin may diverge as a result of differing circumstances.

   New information and changing political situations may also challenge cultural assumptions, such as appropriate roles for men and women. In the 1960s, for instance, the women's movement and other political events led to rapid shifts in expectations for women and men in America. Similarly, female candidates for president and vice president of the United States altered perceptions about women as leaders, especially for young girls.

   Because culture is dynamic, teachers need to be careful not to make assumptions about students' and families' behaviors based on outdated information or even prior experience with members of a particular group. A teacher might assume, for example, that European American parents reject gender stereotyping, but change that assumption when families send in princess costumes for their daughters to play with.

3. *Culture, language, ethnicity, and race are aspects of experience that influence people's beliefs and values.* Culture is only one determinant, albeit a strong one, of people's values, beliefs, and behaviors. **Ethnicity** refers to the shared characteristics and experiences of a group of people, such as nationality, race, history, religion, and language. Ethnicity is usually connected to the geographic origin of a group, as with Greek or Chinese people. Additional factors, including socioeconomic status, education, occupation, ability/disability, sexual orientation, personality, and events in the larger society, influence how people behave and how groups function (Lynch, 2011).

   All of these factors interact to influence the values and behavior of various groups and of individuals within groups. History in particular plays a key role. For example, the history of slavery, racism, and discrimination in the United States and other countries has had a significant, differential effect on people's lives and opportunities, and continues to do so. Racism persists as new groups become its target, including Arabic people and immigrants from Spanish-speaking countries. In addition, LGBTQ people have been and continue to be discriminated against. Although considerable progress has been made toward equality of all groups of Americans, the struggle continues.

4. *Differences within a cultural group may be as great as, or greater than, differences between cultural groups.* Assuming that children who share the same culture or language are all alike is like assuming that all 3-year-olds are alike. Although there are some similarities, there are many differences in their skills, abilities, and behaviors. Likewise, children from the same cultural group share some attitudes, beliefs, and values, but there are many that they do not share. Children from one cultural group are both alike and different from children of another. African American children growing up in low-income, urban areas will share some but not all of

ethnicity The shared characteristics and experiences of a group of people, such as nationality, race, history, religion, and language.

the culturally determined behaviors of African American children whose families have been middle-class professionals for generations. Therefore, it is vitally important not to stereotype individuals who are members of particular groups even while learning some of the common practices, values, or beliefs of those groups.

5. *Culture is defined in terms of differences among groups and is complicated by issues of power and status.* Think for a minute about words such as *mainstream, dominant, majority,* and *minority.* In the United States, each of these words is used to describe group differences in relationship to White European Americans. But to members of other cultural groups such as Latinos, Native Americans, or African Americans, European Americans are the diverse group. When one group, such as European Americans, becomes the reference point against which other groups are compared, that group is the one with the most power and privilege in the society (Delpit, 2006; Lynch & Hanson, 2011).

Individual children within the same cultural group can be as different from each other as they are from those in other groups. In what ways might these children be similar to each other? How might they differ?

The practices of the cultural group that has the greatest power and status become the standard or norm against which other behaviors are judged (Lynch & Hanson, 2011). Cultural groups that have less status and power are perceived as deficient in some way (Delpit, 2006). Understanding how issues of power and privilege affect relationships and communication among cultural groups is critically important.

The election of President Barack Obama was hailed as a significant indicator of the nation's progress toward racial equality. Although that historical event did not negate the continued reality of racism and discrimination in many people's lives, it did challenge implicit assumptions about power and status in the society—not only for African Americans and other people of color, but for European Americans as well. There can be no question that, to some extent, the face of power was changed.

Relationship of Race and Culture An overview of the principles just discussed reveals that there is a complex relationship between race, ethnicity, and culture that knowledgeable teachers need to understand. Because race is a sensitive topic in the United States, the words *culture* and *race* are sometimes inaccurately used synonymously, but they are not the same thing (Gannon, 2016).

Scientists argue that a person's race cannot be determined by examining her or his biological makeup (Gannon, 2016). Nevertheless, race is associated with a person's biology and is determined by who their parents are, whereas culture is learned. As evidenced by how census data are collected, racial classifications are complex and, for the most part, politically determined (Banks, 2016). For example, the same person might be considered racially black in the United States, colored in South Africa, and brown in Brazil. Moreover, according to the 2010 U.S. Census, almost 5% of children are multiracial, mostly likely an underestimate that will change in the 2020 census.

Teachers need to understand that although a very limited number of racial categories, such as Asian or Caucasian, are identified based on skin color and other physical characteristics, hundreds of cultural/ethnic groups exist. Asian peoples include Chinese, Japanese, Koreans, Vietnamese, Hmong, and many others, some of which have been historical enemies (Wardle, 2008a). Similarly, Hispanic is not an actual racial, cultural, or even linguistic group, despite its designation as such by census takers. The term *Latino/a* is

Video Example 6.1:

Defining Culture

This video describes how experts currently define culture. What are some of the ways in which defining culture is a complex task?

currently used to refer to people of Mexican, Cuban, Puerto Rican, South or Central American, or other Spanish culture or origin (Derman-Sparks & Edwards, 2010). Given these complex realities, the increasing diversity of immigrants, and the growing number of biracial and multiracial children, it is essential that teachers not make assumptions about children and families' racial and cultural identities (Ramsey, 2015).

The most useful strategy is for responsive teachers to create a classroom climate in which it is safe to talk about and notice racial and cultural differences (Allen, 2017). Reading books such as *Colors Around Me* (Church, 1997) or *Shades of People* (Rotner & Kelly, 2010) can start a conversation about how people with different shades of black skin are part of the same race because their ancestors originally came from Africa. Providing different colors of paint for children to mix and match the color of their skin is another option.

In the previous sections, we described principles for understanding culture and how they interrelate. In the next section, we discuss similarities and differences among diverse cultures and how they influence various cultural groups' thinking and behavior.

✔ Check Your Understanding 6.1

A Framework for Thinking about Culture

To help you understand the role of culture in the lives of children and families, and in your own life, we examine a framework for thinking about values, beliefs, and practices among various cultural groups. In using this framework, it is important that you develop an awareness of similarities and differences among groups (Lynch, 2011).

Different cultural groups have different sets of values and beliefs, but beyond that, they have different ways of connecting with each other and functioning as a group. In some cultural groups, individual members put their needs first before those of the group; other cultures are group-oriented, putting the group's needs before their own individual needs. This framework classifies cultural groups in terms of two general orientations: (1) individualistic and (2) interdependent (Gonzalez-Mena, 2008).

Individualistic Cultural Orientation

individualistic cultural groups Cultural groups that focus on the needs of the individual, independence, self-expression, and personal property and choice.

The values of more individualistic cultural groups include focusing on the needs of the individual, independence, self-expression, and personal property and choice. In individualistic cultures, the primary goal is individual achievement and fulfillment. These cultures emphasize the rights of the individual over the rights of the group. With its history of individual rights and focus on personal achievement, this is the dominant cultural orientation in the United States.

Picture an individualistic-oriented classroom. All of the children have their own cubbies marked with their names in which to store their belongings. Developing independence in children is an important goal. The children's individual work is displayed and carefully identified. Children are praised for their achievements and graded in comparison to one another. When parents visit, they look carefully to find their child's contribution. The focus on individual children and their accomplishments is evident.

Interdependent Cultural Orientation

interdependent cultural groups Cultural groups that focus on the needs of the group rather than those of the individual, also called collectivist.

By contrast, interdependent cultural groups focus on the needs of the group rather than on those of the individual. Also called *collectivist*, these cultural groups value interdependence, cooperation and mutual assistance, shared property, and social responsibility. Interdependent cultures stress respect for tradition and authority over the rights of the individual. Among cultural groups that exhibit an interdependent orientation are Latinos, Asians, and people in West African and Middle Eastern countries. Because the United States is a nation of immigrants, many members of these cultural groups within this country, as well as Native Americans and African Americans, are oriented more toward interdependence than individualism (Hanson, 2011).

In an interdependent-oriented classroom, individual children do not draw attention to themselves. Children readily share their possessions with each other. Group work is displayed. A colorful mural representing the contributions of scores of children adorns the entrance to the school. These two classrooms are described in overly simplistic terms. Most classrooms would evidence both cultural orientations because in reality, they are not polar opposites but rather points on a continuum.

Continuum of Common Cultural Values

Instead of classifying cultural groups as *either* individualistic *or interdependent*, a more useful strategy is to think of values that are common across all cultural groups as varying along a continuum. Such a continuum is depicted in Figure 6.2.

Interdependent Orientation	Individualistic Orientation
Families value the welfare of the group—the extended family—over the achievements of individual members.	Families value the welfare of the nuclear family and its individual members.
Contributions to the community are valued.	Individual accomplishments are valued.
Respect for elders, traditions, and the past is a strong focus.	The future, youth, and technological advances are valued.
Respect for adult authority is expected; teacher-child relationships are formal.	Relationships with adults are relatively informal; children are encouraged to engage in conversation with teachers.
Time is flexible; people are more important than time.	Time is valuable; schedules are important. Being late or wasting time is considered disrespectful.
Extended families—grandparents, aunts, uncles, older siblings—care for and help raise children.	The nuclear family is primarily responsible for childrearing and may live far away from relatives.
Calling attention to oneself—standing out from the group—may be seen as selfish and rejection of family. Cooperation is valued.	Children's individual achievement and self-esteem are highly valued. Competition is encouraged.
Children are expected to contribute to the family functioning.	Children are expected to achieve on their own.
Children are encouraged to help each other, older ones help younger.	Children are encouraged to do things for themselves such as toileting, feeding, dressing at an early age.
Activity focuses on relationships, not objects; babies are carried and children engage in daily routines with family members.	Activities often focus on objects; children play on floor and with own toys and materials.
Ownership is shared.	Individual ownership is valued.
Children share family and community spaces, activities, and events.	Children have their own separate spaces (for example, their own rooms) and child-centered activities.
Gender and age determine rights and roles.	Individual freedom and rights are highly valued.

FIGURE 6.2 Continuum of Cultural Values

Source: Based on J. Bromer, K. Modigliani, and C. Callahan, no date. *Perspectives in childrearing values.* The Family Child Care Accreditation Project, Boston, MA: Wheelock College; E. W. Lynch, 2011. *Developing cross-cultural competence,* in E. W. Lynch and M. J. Hanson (Eds.), *Developing cross-cultural competence: A guide for working with children and their families* (4th ed). Baltimore, MD: Paul H. Brookes.

Individuals within cultural groups vary all along the continuum; families are more or less inclusive, just as they are more or less traditional rather than either traditional or not. In addition, the ends of the continuum can be seen from a *both/and* perspective. For example, in the United States, schools and society emphasize *both* individual achievement *and* cooperation, working together to solve problems and taking care of those in need.

Consider how misunderstandings can occur when teachers and family members operate from different points on the interdependent and individualist continuum, as in the following example:

Video Example 6.2:

Cultural Patterns

In this video on cultural patterns, notice some specific examples of the continuum of cultural values and its impact on children's behavior. How could teachers use this information to teach more effectively?

> Mr. Wu is late for a team meeting to discuss his son's IEP. The disabilities coordinator, Ms. Armstrong, impatiently taps her foot, repeatedly looks at her watch, and gets more and more irritated as minutes tick by. Ms. Garcia, the classroom teacher, seems less concerned. When Mr. Wu arrives, he doesn't apologize for being late, but he does tell Ms. Garcia that his mother is taking care of his son and that she has questions to ask about her grandson. Ms. Garcia understands that Mr. Wu's respect for his mother took precedence over arriving at the meeting on time.
>
> When the meeting ends, Ms. Garcia reviews her notes with Ms. Armstrong. She politely states, "I could see that you were concerned about the meeting running overtime. I know that you are very busy, but I believe that Mr. Wu did not intend to inconvenience us by being late. His greatest priority was to show respect for his mother, and I'm glad he consulted her, because with her input, we can do a better job of helping her grandson." In this way, Ms. Garcia did not tell Ms. Armstrong that her cultural views are wrong; instead, she clarified her own cultural views and those of Mr. Wu.

Applying the Continuum in Practice

Conceptualizing variations in cultural values along a continuum helps teachers in several ways: (1) It reduces the tendency to stereotype groups; (2) it reduces the likelihood that differences will be categorized as right or wrong, that is, an *us versus them* mentality; and (3) it has the potential to increase understanding and communication among teachers and families who may differ in their perspectives (Lynch, 2011).

Ultimately, cultures may tend toward one end of the continuum or the other, but the values of most people fall somewhere in between. All cultures value families, for instance, but they define family membership differently. Similarly, rigidly categorizing groups is likely to lead to inaccurate assumptions. For example, Japanese cultural values are typically viewed as traditional (on the interdependent end of the continuum) and yet Japan readily embraces new technologies.

Following is an example of what might happen during an encounter between members of individualist and interdependent cultural groups:

> To help children feel comfortable in their new surroundings, kindergarten teacher Alisha Watson created a bulletin board to display photos of children's families so that there would be something familiar to the children in the room. She asked for children to bring in pictures of themselves with their siblings and parents, and couldn't understand why some of the families never responded to her request. She thought perhaps families didn't have cameras or didn't want to participate in school activities. In frustration, she finally gave up the idea of the family bulletin board. Alisha never imagined that some parents weren't comfortable limiting the photo to just the immediate family. To many of them, the extended family, which includes neighbors and friends, is what matters. One mother was upset that grandparents would not be included, but didn't want to alienate the new teacher.

As we can see, Alisha's concept of "family" represents a more individualistic orientation than that of many families in her classroom. Alisha could have avoided the problem by respecting the families' own definitions of their members.

The continuum of cultural values (Lynch, 2011) is intended to help you concentrate on common values—how cultural groups are similar as well as different. At the same time, effectively working across cultural groups requires looking inward and analyzing your own cultural perspective, as we describe next.

 Check Your Understanding 6.2

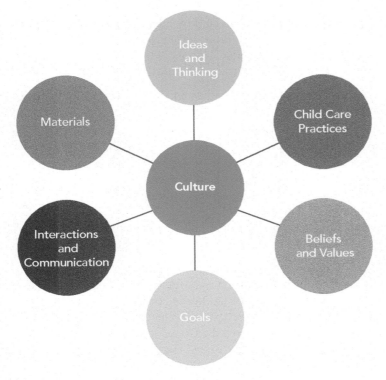 Understanding Your Own Cultural Perspective

As you read about interdependent and individualistic cultural values, how did you feel? Did you identify with one end of the continuum or the other? Did you find yourself judging people whose values and practices reflect the other extreme?

Teachers, like all human beings, view the world through their own cultural lenses. To be effective, you will need to overcome any potential biases about children's behavior in order to establish positive relationships, build on their prior knowledge and current levels of ability, and help children make sense of their experiences. The first step in accomplishing this goal is to examine your own cultural perspective. Figure 6.3 will help you focus your reflections.

FIGURE 6.3 Reflecting on Your Own Cultural Experiences

Source: Office of Head Start. *Multicultural principles for early childhood leaders.* Retrieved December 13, 2017, from https://eclkc.ohs.acf.hhs.gov/culture-language/article/multicultural-principles-early-childhood-leaders

 Application Exercise 6.2

Figure 6.3: Reflecting on Your Own Cultural Experiences

Become Aware of Your Own Cultural Experiences

Begin by reflecting on the origins of your family. Here are some questions to stimulate these reflections (Lynch, 2011):

- What stories have you heard about your ancestors or relatives living in other parts of the world?
- How do you identify yourself culturally? Do you feel a connection to your cultural background?
- Do you or does anyone in your family speak a language other than English? What language(s) do you speak?
- Are there rituals, traditions, or holidays that reflect your family's heritage?
- How does your family express affection or disapproval?
- How do your family members communicate? Are they more likely to listen and think before speaking, or do they jump into conversation eagerly, even talking over one another?
- Can you think of advice or sayings that guided behavior in your family?

Questions like these help you become aware of how your own values, beliefs, and practices affect your behavior. Now think about how your cultural perspective affects your views of appropriate child-rearing practices. Ask yourself the following questions and compare your answers with those of colleagues:

- What are your thoughts regarding infant feeding practices? Should the goal be for children to learn as toddlers how to independently feed themselves? Or do you believe that adults should feed babies as long as possible?
- What do you think are appropriate discipline techniques? Should children be given time-outs, spanked, or lose privileges when they misbehave? Should parents explain their reasoning to children?
- Should young children be directed by adults and their movements controlled? Or should they be allowed to explore and make choices?
- What behaviors are acceptable for girls? For boys?
- How should children behave around adults?

Finally, examine how your cultural beliefs and biases affect your behavior and emotions. Reflect on these questions:

- Have you ever felt uncomfortable or surprised in another part of the United States or in another country? What was the situation? Perhaps you felt that people invaded your personal space? Or weren't respectful of your possessions?
- Have you ever felt awkward or embarrassed by something you said or did when you were traveling or among another cultural group? Did you think about why you might have felt that way?
- Have you ever done or said something that was culturally inappropriate? For example, did you fail to offer an appropriate greeting? Did your behavior embarrass or offend other people?

Finding yourself in another group and experiencing what it feels like not to be certain of the rules is an excellent way to gain deeper understanding of your cultural views and those of other groups. I (the author) have had many such experiences when speaking about early childhood education throughout the United States and in other countries. I remember specifically telling a story about the struggles I encountered during my early days of teaching. I often said, "I knew that I was smart, but I also knew that I didn't know enough about teaching young children, and I had a lot to learn." Much to my surprise (and subsequent embarrassment), I later learned that some audiences were so stunned to hear me call myself smart that they couldn't hear anything else I said! Pointing out individual achievement even with self-deprecating humor is simply not considered appropriate behavior in many groups.

A part of reflecting on your own cultural experience includes comparing your perspective with that of other people. Therefore, the next step is to learn about other cultural groups and how your views and behaviors compare and contrast with theirs.

Learn about the Perspectives of Various Cultural Groups

To fully understand your own cultural perspectives, it is useful to learn as much as possible about how various groups think and respond to different situations and events. This knowledge will help overcome the tendency to impose your values and beliefs on the children that you teach and their families. To learn more about the values of various cultural groups:

- Read widely about children and families of diverse cultures and backgrounds.
- Seek out and read what has been written about diversity by researchers and theorists from a wide variety of cultural backgrounds.
- Identify key informants—family members, community elders, neighborhood leaders—who are willing to talk openly with you about their beliefs, values, and practices. To get as much accurate information as possible and to avoid stereotyping, don't rely on one person to be your cultural translator.
- Read books and magazines, watch movies, or search websites produced by members of diverse cultural groups.
- If possible, immerse yourself in another culture and experience the discomfort of not knowing exactly what to say or how to behave.
- Most important of all, observe carefully and listen closely to learn how various cultural groups communicate and nurture their young.

Learning generalities about cultural groups is a useful starting point, but it can easily lead to stereotyping—making assumptions that all children who appear part of a group share similar backgrounds. For example, a Cuban American father was dismayed to learn that his daughter's teacher kept telling her what she knew about the young girl's "Hispanic" culture and how the teacher was being responsive to it. None of the teacher's accommodations were meaningful to the little girl, whose family had lived in Minnesota for three generations.

Guard against Implicit Bias

In recent years, the term, *implicit bias* is more commonly heard and used, and has even become politically polarizing at times. Implicit bias refers to the attitudes or stereotypes that *unconsciously* affect people's thoughts, actions, and decisions. Talking about implicit bias can be difficult. Most people would never consider themselves prejudiced or bigoted in any way, nor would they want to be accused of such attitudes. But implicit bias consists of values, beliefs, or behaviors that we are unaware of and typically act on without prior thought. That is what makes implicit bias particularly risky.

implicit bias attitudes or stereotypes that unconsciously affect our thoughts, actions, and decisions.

Disturbing evidence of implicit bias was revealed in a well-designed study by Walter Gilliam and his colleagues at Yale University (Gilliam et al., 2016). In this study, a large group of preschool teachers watched a video of preschoolers (balanced by sex and race) who were engaged in typical classroom activity. The teachers were told to expect challenging behaviors although none were present, and their eye movements were tracked using sophisticated technology. The researchers found that, anticipating challenging behaviors, the teachers more closely observed Black children, especially boys. In another part of the study, teachers randomly received written vignettes about individual children's behavior identified by a child's name implying a Black boy, Black girl, White boy, or White girl. Again, when expecting challenging behavior, teachers gazed longer at Black children, especially boys. Implicit biases also varied by the teacher's race. When provided with family background information about the children, teachers responded less severely when their race matched that of the children, but more severely when their race did not. The researchers speculate that implicit bias such as revealed in their study may explain the large disparities in preschool expulsions and suspensions, described earlier (Gilliam, 2016), and at least in part, the achievement gap between Black and White children.

Therefore, awareness and avoidance of implicit bias is essential to ensure equity and excellence for all young children.

Now that we have discussed the complex concept of culture and identified several key principles that describe how culture functions in children's development and in our own experiences, consider how this knowledge can be applied to the classroom. How will this knowledge inform your teaching?

✔ Check Your Understanding 6.3

Teaching in a Culturally and Linguistically Diverse World

Imagine it is the first day of school. Parents who are dropping off their children are using various dialects and languages that you don't recognize. Some of the children are crying and clinging to their parents, while others, it is clear, have been told that crying is not allowed, so they are standing with quivering chins trying to hold it together. You are making the rounds, introducing yourself to the children and trying to get them excited about the day and the upcoming year.

You may have been through this before as a student teacher working in a culturally diverse classroom, but every year, the dynamic and the ethnic mix changes. It will be up to you to find a way to communicate with dual language learners, to be sensitive to the fact that the English language has many idioms that may be foreign to children who are mastering English, and to be sensitive to each child's home life, whether they live with their parents and siblings, live with their extended family, or are from a single-parent home. The key is to learn as much as you can about each of the children, to get to know their families, and to always be culturally and linguistically responsive in the classroom.

Why Does Culture Matter to Teachers?

Children from diverse language and cultural groups and those from low-income families (who are disproportionately linguistically and culturally diverse) are the very children who are not being well served in our nation's schools. In fact, federal education policy is often designed to hold schools accountable for educating every child and to close the achievement gap between groups of children.

The underlying causes and remedies for the achievement gap are complex, but part of the solution must be to recognize and build on the competencies that children bring from prior experiences (Oertwig, Gillanders, & Ritchie, 2014). To do so requires that teachers acquire cultural understanding. Without such knowledge, at least three problems can occur: (1) teachers can misunderstand children, (2) teachers can inaccurately assess children's competence, and (3) teachers can plan incorrectly to promote children's learning (Barbarin, 2011; Bowman, Donovan, & Burns, 2001).

Misunderstanding Children Failing to understand the influence of children's backgrounds on their development can lead to misunderstanding and miscommunication about children and their families, as the following example illustrates (based on Zepeda, Rothstein-Fisch, Gonzalez-Mena, & Trumbull, 2006):

> In Carey Foster's Head Start class, she tries to promote children's self-concepts and self-esteem by having them make "All About Me" books at the beginning of the year. The children draw pictures, and Carey writes down what they say about themselves.
>
> Four-year-old Antonia Rodriguez dictates, "My brothers are big and strong and help me and my mother."

Carey says, "But this book isn't about your brothers. It's about you. Let's say you have brown eyes and you can write your name."

Antonia doesn't respond. She feels unsure because she is proud of how her family helps each other, but her teacher doesn't seem to care about that. During the parent open house, Carey proudly displays Antonia's book for her mother, who doesn't look impressed. Carey doesn't realize that Antonia's mother thinks her daughter is becoming conceited and selfish in this school.

Carey's classroom activity was at odds with the interdependence valued by Antonia's family. Most likely, this situation would have turned out better if Carey had been sensitive to Antonia's discomfort initially. Instead of taking over for Antonia, Carey could have said, "Tell me more about your family." Listening would have helped Carey better understand the values of Antonia's family.

One area where cultural groups often differ is how they approach discipline. If teachers are unaware of these differences, they may be ineffective in guiding children's behavior. Furthermore, their methods may prove to be counterproductive. For example, time-out—removing children from the group for misbehavior for a period of time—is a discipline strategy that is widely used by parents and teachers. In general, the strategy is not effective, because it simply stops the children's negative behavior temporarily without teaching children what to do instead. Nevertheless, some teachers continue to use time-out. Let's consider time-out from a cultural perspective in the following example:

Mark Temple is a new teacher who is struggling to control his first-grade class for reading instruction. His school is in a close-in suburb of a major city, and some people call it the "little United Nations" because it serves so many cultural groups. Today, Mark is reading a story to the group, and Yao cannot keep still. He touches and sits very close to the other children, who pull away and are distracted by his behavior. After several warnings, Mark puts Yao in time-out for the duration of the story. Mark notices that Yao is sitting very quietly with his head bowed and a dejected look on his face, trying hard not to cry. Mark assumes that Yao is sorry for disrupting story time and that the time-out was effective.

Mark's interpretation of Yao's response to his time-out, however, is uninformed. Mark's ignorance of Yao's Chinese cultural values causes him to misunderstand Yao's behavior. Yao loves school and is excited by the opportunity to sit close to the other children. Being assigned to time-out means being isolated from the group where he feels most comfortable and happy. Yao feels ashamed and guilty, not because he didn't follow the rules, but because he has been separated from the others. Yao is humiliated because he thinks that the group has rejected him. Mark also fails to recognize that Yao's desire to belong is a strength that he can build on to engage Yao positively in the group.

Inaccurate Assessment of Children   Ignorance of children's culturally determined behavior can lead teachers to make inaccurate assessments of children's competence and ability. Language barriers can also lead to incorrect assessments of children's abilities. Cultural and linguistic differences can lead to errors in identifying and serving children with disabilities.

Assessing the learning of English language learners or children who speak a variation of English requires special tools and expertise. Too many English language learners are judged to be language delayed when they are actually demonstrating typical second language development (National Academies of Science, Engineering, and Medicine [NAS], 2017). No assumptions about children's competence should be based on measures in a language in which children are not fluent (Lopez, Hofer, Bumgarner, & Taylor, 2017). An English language learner or a child who speaks a variation of English may have a well-developed vocabulary and understand many concepts, but may not be well understood at school (NAS, 2017).

Including All Children
Cultural Diversity and Diverse Ability

Effective early intervention practices are supposed to be *family centered*, involving families both in decision making and in implementation. However, cultural differences can complicate communication and understanding between families and professionals. These differences can become a challenge in planning intervention strategies for children with disabilities, as the following example illustrates:

> Little Sparrow is a 3-year-old Native American child who was born with Down syndrome. Her family believes that such births are natural and that Little Sparrow's contributions to the community are important, however small. The community's goal is to maintain harmony among everyone. Little Sparrow is enrolled in Head Start on the reservation. Head Start program standards require that they provide early intervention services for children with disabilities. The teachers are members of the tribe, but they must work with the disabilities coordinator, who is not. Together, they help Little Sparrow improve her functional skills such as feeding and toileting, and she is making progress at school.
>
> The disabilities coordinator meets with the family to ensure that they will follow up on the effective strategies at home. But the family seems nonresponsive. They can't understand why the school is so concerned about changing Little Sparrow when they love her just the way she is. And they don't want to single her out for special attention among the other

children, which could upset the harmonious relationships in their community.

In this example, we see how a family's cultural perspective can be at odds with professional views. The professionals' intervention goals may not emphasize what is valued by the family, or the intervention may emphasize what they do not value. Such conflicting goals need to be negotiated if children's best interests are to be served.

In the case of Little Sparrow, the teachers worked with the disabilities coordinator to relinquish control of the situation and meet with elders in the community. They described their goals and how they thought that supporting Little Sparrow to do more would benefit everyone, actually bringing more harmony to the group. The elders decided that help for Little Sparrow would be shared by many adults and children in the tribe, and that in turn the little girl would help the others as best she could.

Sources: Based on M. J. Hanson and E. W. Lynch, 2004. *Understanding families: Approaches to diversity, disability, and risk.* Baltimore, MD: Paul H. Brookes; J. T. McCollum, T. Yates, M. Ostrosky, and J. Halle, 2001. Cross-cultural conceptions of child-rearing: Implications for reviewing/evaluating intervention practices, in T. Bennett et al., *Cross-cultural considerations in early childhood special education* (Technical Report #14), Urbana-Champaign, IL: University of Illinois, Culturally and Linguistically Appropriate Services (CLAS), retrieved December 16, 2017, from http://clas.uiuc.edu/techreport/tech14.html#4b.

One of the biggest mistakes that educators and the general public make is to equate cultural differences with disabilities. The fact is that children with disabilities cross all cultural groups. Likewise, cultural and linguistic diversity impact all dimensions of special education services. In a classroom of diverse learners, teachers may have a difficult time identifying students who have special needs. In addition, diagnosis and intervention planning for children with disabilities is a challenge when the child is of a different culture or language group than the professionals (Hanson & Lynch, 2004). Read the *Including All Children: Diversity and Diverse Ability* feature for an example of these challenges.

Failure to Promote Children's Achievement
Misunderstanding and inaccurate assessment of children's competence can lead to ineffective teaching that does not meet the needs of all students. If children's competence is acquired in a context that does not match that of the teacher or school, several potential problems can arise. Teachers can negatively judge children on the basis of their culturally influenced behaviors. Without accurate assessment, teachers' expectations for children's learning can be too low.

If teachers do not recognize what students already know—what they have learned from prior experiences—teachers cannot build on it (Oertwig, Gillanders, & Ritchie, 2014). For example, many early childhood programs encourage and expect children to speak up and share stories of their own experience or background. Yet this may not be a task that all students can do. Consider, for instance, that among many Native American tribes, children are expected to listen to older adults rather than speak themselves (Paradis, Genesee, & Crago, 2011).

If teachers do not understand these diverse communication styles, they may have trouble assessing what children already know. For example, researchers working with Inuit people in northern Canada (Native Canadians, called First Nations) assumed that children's language development was delayed because they spoke little in interactions with teachers. But in a play situation with interesting objects and toys and other children with whom they were comfortable, the children's vocabulary and grammar were far more complex than what they used with teachers (Paradis, Genesee, & Crago, 2011).

As we stated earlier, different cultural groups often make different meanings from the same experience. If new learning is to be meaningful, teachers must help children make connections between what they know and are able to do at home and in their community, and what is expected in school. Meaningful learning is more likely when teachers focus on the learning goal rather than on the specific means to the goal. For example, if the goal of a first-grade science curriculum is for children to understand life cycles, studying buffalo, which may be familiar to Native American children in the West, is as effective as learning about cows would be for children in the Midwest.

Misunderstandings, the roots of which are cultural in many cases, can have dire consequences. For example, cultural studies of African American children, boys in particular, find that *on average*, they tend to be more physically active and emotive than their European American peers (Barbarin, Murry, Tolan, & Graham, 2016; Woolfolk & Perry, 2015). Teachers may incorrectly judge this exuberance as aggression. As a result, the very behavior that is expected in their community may create challenges in school (Barbarin, 2015). When such negative responses persist, children may become discouraged and, perhaps, more disruptive (Ritchie & Gutman, 2014).

African American boys are disproportionately represented in special education and four times more likely to be expelled in preschool (Gilliam, 2016). The civil rights division of the U.S. Department of Education (2014) found that African American children represent 18% of preschool enrollment, but 42% of students had been suspended once, and 48% of the students were suspended more than once. To better understand this disturbing phenomenon, read the feature *Promoting Play: African American Children and Play*.

Promoting Play

African American Children and Play

Early childhood educators consider pretend play to be an integral part of developmentally appropriate practice and beneficial for children's development and learning. However, there are individual and cultural differences in how children play as well as how teachers view children's play that have important consequences for children, as revealed by recent research.

This study compared a large group of racially mixed preschoolers' pretend play and their adjustment (self-regulation and cognitive flexibility) as evaluated by outside observers in a laboratory setting with teachers' reports of children's social and educational adjustment. Teachers rated children's school readiness, peer relationships, and amount of teacher–child conflict.

The main finding of the study was that preschoolers' race affected how teachers viewed their play and how they rated their adjustment in the classroom, even after accounting for differences in individual children's age, IQ, family income, and gender. Moreover, even when the teacher and child were the same race and the teacher and child knew each other for the same length of time, these different evaluations of children based on their race held true. For Black preschoolers, teachers evaluated their imaginative

(Continued)

and expressive pretend play and rated them as less prepared for school, less accepted by their peers, and more prone to teacher-child conflict. On the other hand, comparable levels of imagination and expression in pretend play resulted in positive ratings of these same characteristics for non-Black children.

Children in all racial groups—Hispanic, Black, White, and bi/multiracial—played similarly in imaginative and expressive ways. But Black children's pretend play skills were evaluated negatively by teachers, while non-Black children with similar play behaviors were evaluated positively. Teachers also rated Black children who demonstrated more negative play behaviors as less prepared for school, less accepted

by other children, and involved in more teacher-child conflict than non-Black children whose play behaviors were equally negative.

This study raises significant concerns about teacher bias regarding the play of young African American children. Black children who are imaginative and expressive may be judged and treated differently in early childhood programs. Teachers need to become self-aware about the way they view children based on race and how those judgments can have lasting negative effects for children.

Source: T. M. Yates and A. K. Marcelo, 2014. Through race-colored glasses: Preschoolers' pretend play and teachers' ratings of preschooler adjustment. *Early Childhood Research Quarterly, 29,* 1–11.

In the previous sections, we saw how teachers' lack of cultural understanding can lead to several errors in supporting children's learning and development. In the next section, we focus on the realities of linguistic diversity and its interaction with culture in children's development and learning.

Embracing Linguistic Diversity

The primary goal of this chapter is to encourage you to embrace the realities of cultural and linguistic diversity. Although we have focused much attention on culture, language and culture are inextricably linked (Hamayan, Genesee, & Cloud, 2013). Language is the lens through which children make sense of the world, and it is a major vehicle for transmitting culture. Dual language learners are learning not only two languages, but also two cultures. Children must learn how to use each language in culturally meaningful and appropriate ways (Hamayan, Genesee, & Cloud, 2013).

If a concept does not exist in a culture, there is no need for a word to represent that concept. Consider a language without a word for *privacy*. What would that tell you about the culture's experiences and values? Most likely, the cultural group places greater value on the needs and rights of the group than on those of the individual. Also, personal space and private ownership may be less important.

How words are defined and used also reflects cultural differences. For example, in Italian, the verb *discutere* can mean "to discuss" but can also mean "to argue." Picture a group of Italians or Italian Americans all talking at once, with raised voices and many gestures. Arguing is just another form of discussion, and is much less threatening than in societies where English is spoken and where *arguing* has negative connotations.

Similarly, some languages may have many words to distinguish subtle variations in meaning that are important to the group. A large vocabulary for types of snow and ice is essential in the Arctic, but unnecessary in more temperate climates. What if English only had one word for *blue*? How could we communicate clearly without words such as *turquoise, navy,* or *periwinkle*? The inextricable link between language and culture means that one cannot be embraced without also embracing the other. Language is also strongly connected to emotions.

© Pearson Education

Video Example 6.3:

Language and Culture

This video describes the relationship between language and culture. What are some important ways that teachers can help dual language learners become bicultural and be successful in school? What "norms of school culture" might children need to be taught?

Words can trigger strong emotions in some cultures and not in others. For example, in Arab cultures, the word *crusade* carries a negative connotation dating back to the Middle Ages, while in the United States, we regularly have positive crusades to collect money for charity or fight disease.

The United States has always been a country in which many people are bilingual or multilingual. With increasing numbers of children speaking a language other than English at home, opportunity exists to help these children become bilingual. To do so, it is important that teachers support children's development and maintenance of their home language while helping them acquire proficiency in English. These children are dual language learners—learning two languages at once. In fact, many children are **multi-language learners** who are learning more than two languages.

All children in our society need to acquire English, but they can become proficient without giving up their home language (National Academies of Science, Engineering, and Medicine, 2017). The key is for teachers to support continued development of the home language and to inform parents that if they encourage their children to speak English both in the home and at school at a very early age, their children may lose their home language. Home language loss can harm children's long-term academic achievement (ibid.). In addition, if parents do not speak English well and their children lose the home language, serious communication and relationship problems between parents and children are likely to occur. In fact, Head Start's multicultural principles state that "Effective programs for children who speak languages other than English require continued development of the first language while the acquisition of English is facilitated" (Head Start, n.d.). Therefore, teachers should encourage families to speak to children in whatever language the parent is most proficient, usually their native tongue, to support children's educational achievement.

multi-language learners
Children who are learning more than two languages.

Application Exercise 6.3
Teaching Multi-Language Learners

In the previous sections, we discussed how educators often misunderstand, inaccurately assess, and fail to serve culturally and linguistically diverse children. One key to avoiding these pitfalls is for teachers to become more culturally competent, as we discuss in the next section.

Check Your Understanding 6.4

Cultural Competence: The Key to Effective Teaching

To accommodate diverse learners, teachers must integrate students' diverse backgrounds into the curriculum. A particular kind of ability is required to successfully use this type of effective practice in the classroom: cultural competence. Conflict may arise in situations where families and teachers do not have an inherent understanding of each other. Consider the following example:

Decatur Elementary School, which serves a wide range of cultural groups, has a lending library to encourage primary-grade children to read at home. After a few weeks, the library is bare because the families don't return the books. The European American teachers make insistent pleas for return of the books. The children begin to feel that their teachers are accusing them of stealing. But the children and their families don't understand; they assumed the books were meant for all the children in the neighborhood.

To resolve a conflict such as this, teachers must be well versed in effective cross-cultural communication. To provide the best education for all children, teachers need to become *culturally competent.*

cultural competence The ability to work respectfully and effectively with people of all cultures, languages, socio-economic classes, races, ethnicities, religions, and other aspects of diversity.

Cultural competence (also called *cross-cultural competence*) is the ability to work respectfully and effectively with people of all cultures, languages, socio-economic classes, races, ethnicities, religions, and other aspects of diversity. Cultural competence is not a set of skills but is instead a way of being—an openness to continual learning (Olsen et al., 2007). Although various characteristics demonstrate cultural competence, several are particularly applicable to teachers in diverse classrooms (Lynch, 2011; Lynch & Hanson, 2011). Some characteristics of cultural competence follow, along with the ways they apply to the teachers at Decatur Elementary School and the lending library situation:

- *An awareness of their own cultural perspectives.* Teachers reflect on their own feelings about losing the books. They are mystified and a little upset. They invested time and money in the library, and can't understand why it failed.

- *Appreciation and respect for individuals from other cultures.* Teachers do not prejudge children and families by their standards, realizing that more interdependent cultural groups view ownership of materials differently than do individualistic ones.

- *A belief that cross-cultural interactions should be viewed as learning opportunities rather than challenges.* Teachers decide to find out what might have caused the misunderstanding, rather than giving up in frustration.

- *An ability to identify and use cultural resources.* Teachers seek the advice of leaders in the community to help them understand what happened.

- *An appreciation for the integrity and value of all cultures.* Teachers realize that sharing the books more widely is a valuable although different way of achieving their goal of making reading material available to children.

- *Willingness to continue to try to understand other people's perspectives.* Teachers decide to talk regularly with older children, family, and community members to discuss school happenings.

- *Flexibility and a sense of humor.* Teachers look back and laugh at how naïve their expectations were and how rigid their reactions.

- *Comfort with uncertainty.* The main lesson the teachers learn is that they aren't going to be right all the time; there are no simple answers to complex situations.

This list of competencies is prerequisite for becoming a truly successful teacher. Encompassing all of these characteristics and behaviors is an attitude of *cultural humility*—the stance that one can "expect to be surprised, to be wrong, and (the need) to ask for help" (Sparrow, 2011, p. 14). Cultural humility assumes that one can never fully comprehend the perspective of another human being and requires the ability to put aside feelings of superiority and the tendency to judge.

Video Example 6.4:

Intercultural Competence

In this video, experts describe intercultural competence and communication. What skills are essential for intercultural competence? What strategies can teachers use to foster cross-cultural communication in the classroom?

Cross-Cultural Communication

The foundation of cultural competence is the ability to communicate effectively with members of diverse cultural groups (Lynch, 2011). To foster good communication, teachers must develop an understanding of how various cultural groups use verbal and nonverbal means of communicating. These communication styles are another example of a cultural continuum such as those described earlier in the chapter. In this case, the continuum extends from high-context cultures to low-context cultures.

High-Context and Low-Context Cultures* Awareness of different communication styles will help you better appreciate the competence of children whose cultural background is different from your own and avoid misunderstandings in communicating with parents.

Communication among those in **high-context cultures** relies less on words and more on contextual cues such as facial expressions, gestures, or other physical clues to convey meaning (Lynch, 2011). Examples of groups that are more attuned to nonverbal messages include Asian, American Indian, African American, Arab, and Latino groups.

In contrast, **low-context cultures** focus on direct, logical, and precise verbal communication (Lynch, 2011). Low-context cultural groups include European Americans, Germans, and Scandinavians. Members of low-context cultures often become impatient if the speaker does not come to the point quickly or the communication is not direct (Lynch, 2011). Similarly, low-context communicators may be confused when they miss the meaning of gestures or unstated emotions.

high-context culture Culture in which communication relies less on words and more on contextual cues, such as facial expressions, gestures, or other physical clues, to convey meaning.

low-context culture Culture that focuses on direct, logical, precise verbal communication.

Effective communication across these styles can be challenging. Shirley Brice Heath (1983, 1989) was one of the first to describe the consequences when children of high-context backgrounds encounter low-context schools. Her research identified situations such as the typical sharing time (show-and-tell), during which the teacher asks children what they did over the weekend. A low-context girl might chronologically describe events: "I went to my brother's soccer game. Then we went to McDonald's. Then my grandma came for dinner." This recitation meets the teacher's expectations of a clear, precise account. On the other hand, a high-context girl uses a more narrative, episodic style, which assumes that the listener can fill in the context. "My brother sang a funny song. Here's how it goes." When the child begins to sing, the teacher grows impatient, thinks the little girl's description doesn't make sense, and asks her to sit down. Think of the conflicting messages these children receive about the value of their experiences and their communication.

Culturally competent teachers are able to work effectively across all cultural groups. What knowledge, skills, and attitudes do teachers need to be culturally competent?

Difficulty communicating between low-context and high-context groups is not limited to teachers and children. Adults are even more steeped in their culture's ways of behaving than children are. Imagine the difficulties that can arise when a high-context teacher attempts to talk to a low-context parent about a child's behavior problem. Or think of involving a high-context parent in creating an IEP for a child with a disability, which requires very accurate communication.

Verbal and Nonverbal Communication A general description of high- and low-context communication styles only begins to describe the complexity of cross-cultural communication. Virtually every aspect of nonverbal communication can be misinterpreted. Of greater concern is that the failure to understand and respect cultural rules of behavior can offend and insult the very people with whom you are trying to communicate.

A number of nonverbal cues can lead to misunderstandings between people from different cultures. For example, allowing or not allowing for personal space, when and why we smile, when we make eye contact or touch, and how we use silence and view time are all culturally relevant (Gonzalez-Mena, 2008). We have already discussed some of these, but a few others may be surprising. Consider smiling. Most of us assume that smiling is a universal, human way of communicating—and it is. But like other behaviors, it can mean different things to different cultural groups. Russians, for example, smile when they are happy, not just to be friendly (Gonzalez-Mena, 2008). This could account for why

Russians are often depicted in American movies as unusually dour. Some Asian groups, on the other hand, smile more often than Americans, even when embarrassed or unhappy (Gonzalez-Mena, 2008).

Silence can communicate volumes, but it is also interpreted through a cultural lens. Some Asian groups pause before speaking as a respectful sign that they are really listening (Gonzalez-Mena, 2008). Some European Americans may interpret such periods of silence to mean that the other person isn't listening or doesn't have anything to say.

A full discussion of the typical ways of communicating among various cultural groups is beyond the scope of this book. Consult the resources listed at the end of this chapter to learn more about the practices, beliefs, values, and communication styles of various groups. As you encounter diverse, changing groups of children, you will need to continually update your knowledge to improve communication and avoid misunderstandings with children and parents. And, most of all, remember not to stereotype individuals based on such general descriptions of cultural expectations.

In the previous sections, we discussed the importance of becoming culturally competent. In the upcoming sections, we discuss how the curriculum for children should be culturally responsive. We also look at what kinds of practices are effective for teaching diverse learners.

Check Your Understanding 6.5

Culturally Responsive, Effective Practices for Diverse Learners

Every group of children is diverse on every conceivable dimension of development and learning, including their various cultural backgrounds and languages. It is important to remember that when we speak about teaching diverse learners, we really mean *all* learners. In the following sections, we discuss culturally and linguistically responsive teaching strategies, and anti-bias educational goals.

Culturally Responsive Teaching

Effective practices for working with culturally and linguistically diverse children are best practices for every child. For example, research on human learning demonstrates the critical importance of building on prior knowledge, which is naturally one of the most important principles of culturally responsive teaching. The challenge for teachers is to uncover children's culturally acquired prior knowledge and then use effective strategies to build on it. Read the *What Works: Making Education Culturally Compatible* feature for a description of such research-based practices.

Linguistically Responsive Teaching

Too often, educational discussions tend to lump children into categories such as "low income" or "children with special needs." This also happens frequently with dual language learners, despite the fact that there is great diversity among these children. Consider these 6-year-olds:

Rosalinda's father and mother are well educated and speak both English and Spanish fluently. Her parents have read and spoken to her in both languages since birth. The family lives in an upper-middle-class community, and they travel to Argentina at least once a year to visit her grandparents.

Manuel lives with his parents, four siblings, and other extended family members. They speak only Spanish at home. His family is very loving, and they tell wonderful,

What Works

Making Education Culturally Compatible

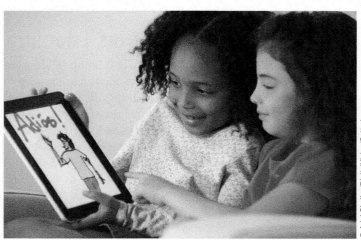

A body of research demonstrates that taking children's cultural backgrounds into consideration in curriculum and teaching is related to positive learning outcomes for students across age groups. These studies were conducted with elementary school children across many cultural groups: Puerto Ricans, African Americans, Native Hawaiians, Native American Indians, Mexican immigrants, Appalachian urban immigrant whites, Southeast Asian newcomers, Eskimos or Aleuts, and European American gifted and talented children. Based on this research, six key principles of effective, culturally supportive teaching were gleaned that are also congruent with several aspects of NAEYC's position on developmentally appropriate practices:

1. Teachers and students work together toward a common goal. Teachers participate with children in activities such as a nature walk near the school.
2. Teachers incorporate language and literacy learning throughout the day and in all areas of the curriculum. For example, children talk, read, and write about the life cycles of the animals they observe on their walk.
3. Teachers make learning meaningful by connecting school learning to children's lives. The conversation begins with what children already know about animals.
4. Teachers have high expectations for children, challenging their learning, and focusing on complex thinking. Teachers pose problems for children to think about, such as what would happen if the trees were cut down.
5. Teachers and children engage in instructional conversations, discussing the content they are learning. Children are grouped by interest, talk with each other, and meet with the teacher to discuss and share what they have learned and to identify new questions.
6. Teachers model language and actions, such as carefully handling a pet, so that children can learn through observation.
7. Teachers provide opportunities for child-initiated learning. Children generate learning topics or brainstorm solutions to problems.

These practices as well as providing more physically active learning opportunities have proven especially effective in teaching young Black children, and have great potential for closing the persistent achievement gap for all children of color.

Sources: R. Tharp and S. Entz, 2012. From high chair to high school: Research-based principles for teaching complex thinking. In C. Copple (Ed.), *Growing minds: Building strong cognitive foundations in early childhood*, pp. 131–136, Washington, DC: National Association for the Education of Young Children; D.R. Sullivan, 2016. *Cultivating the genius of black children: Strategies to close the achievement gap in the early years.* St. Paul, MN: Redleaf Press.

long stories, but they have few books in their home. They cannot return to the family's native country because of the political situation and also because they do not have the financial resources.

Clearly, Rosalinda's and Manuel's language learning experiences are different in many ways, including the language(s) spoken at home, the ages when they are introduced to English, the family's resources, and their verbal and written proficiency in either or both languages. In addition to primary and secondary language development, Rosalinda's and Manuel's capacities and interests differ in countless ways. For example, she loves to sing and paint, and her best subject is mathematics. Manuel loves soccer and animals, and his teacher soon discovers that he has great aptitude for reading. They and their families need to be treated as individuals with diverse strengths and needs.

Following are some effective, research-based practices that help dual language learners achieve at high levels in English (National Academies of Science, Engineering, and Medicine, 2017):

Linguistically responsive teaching provides the opportunity for all children to become bilingual if schools take advantage of children's innate ability to learn language and the affordable, technological resources now available.

- Directly instruct children on English vocabulary and certain aspects of literacy, such as pointing to objects or pictures as you say the word ("This book is about a bird. See the bird. Say bird."). Model the language for children, describing what the child is doing ("You put on your coat") or what you're doing ("I'm getting the red paint for you").
- Give lots of opportunities for children to practice the new language, such as during play and small-group times that require them to speak (rather than just point) to take a turn.
- Pair children with English-speaking peers for several activities. For example, ask a question in whole group and have children turn to a buddy to talk it over ("What do you plan to do outside today?").
- Support continued development in the home language, including teaching in that language as much as possible (at least learning key words and phrases), using qualified teachers, family members, or volunteers from the community who fluently speak the home language.
  - Collaborate with families to plan curriculum reflecting children's cultural backgrounds and language(s), such as rhymes, song, and books children can identify with to help them connect what they already know to what is taught at school.
  - Frequently review skills and concepts; do repeated reading.
  - Draw attention to similarities between English words and the word in the home language, called *cognates* (mucho/much).

© Pearson Education

Video Example 6.5:

Linguistically Responsive Teaching

In this video, two teachers plan a science lesson of sorting the different properties of rocks. What effective teaching practices for linguistically and culturally diverse learners do they use? How is this lesson culturally responsive?

Dual language learners are individuals. They need differentiated instruction to develop their English skills, maintain and further develop their home language, and achieve in school. Developing bilingualism is especially important because a large body of research now exists demonstrating that bilingualism is related to stronger executive function abilities, the most important of which is focused attention, which aids in academic achievement of all kinds (Bialystok, 2015).

Today's vast array of digital tools make individualizing instruction for multi-language learners much easier than in the past, as described in the feature *Language Lens: Using Technology to Teach Dual Language Learners*.

Awareness and responsiveness to all forms of diversity must be integrated across all areas of curriculum and teachers' relationships with children to ensure that all children succeed in school. But more than that, schools have a responsibility to provide today's children with the skills to function in a complex, global society. In short, they benefit from an anti-bias education, which we describe in the next section.

Anti-Bias Education

anti-bias education Learning experiences and teaching strategies that are specifically designed not only to prepare all children for life in a culturally rich society, but also to counter the stereotyping of diverse groups, and to guard against expressions of bias

The early childhood field has embraced the concept of an anti-bias education. Anti-bias education includes learning experiences and teaching strategies that are specifically designed not only to prepare all children for life in a culturally rich society but also to counter the stereotyping of diverse groups and to guard against expressions of bias (Derman-Sparks & Edwards, 2010; York, 2016). In this section, we discuss goals of culturally responsive, anti-bias education and ways of helping children achieve those goals. The overarching goal of anti-bias education is to help all children reach their full potential. To do so, anti-bias education focuses on four core goals for children (Derman-Sparks & Edwards, 2010; Teaching Tolerance, 2012):

1. *Identity.* Teachers foster and support children's self-awareness, confidence, and pride in their family and own identity.
2. *Diversity.* Teachers assist children to experience and value human diversity, and use accurate language for differences.

Language Lens
Using Technology to Teach Dual Language Learners

With growing numbers of dual and multi-language learners in our classrooms, all teachers need to be prepared to support English language acquisition while also promoting continued home language development. Using technology exponentially increases teachers' options to achieve these goals, as these examples illustrate:

Hai is a Chinese speaker who doesn't talk at all in preschool. He is isolated from the other children, who won't play with him. His teacher knows that without social interaction, his English skills won't develop. She loans his family an iPad, and with the help of a translator shows him a digital storytelling app to create a story about his family with photos and narration in both English and Chinese. When he shares the story with the other children, they realize that Hai has an interesting life, and several of them decide to use the app to create stories about themselves.

Kara's kindergarten includes speakers of four different home languages, some of whom are newly arrived immigrants. She relies on technology to create an accessible environment for all the children as they acquire sufficient English to navigate the school. Kara posts pictures and labels in various languages (in some cases with phonetic spellings) to help children learn routines and safety precautions. On the internet, she finds images, songs, and stories that accurately depict children's homelands, and uses these to spark conversations among small groups of children. She teaches all the children to use iTranslate on classroom tablets to aid communication and support burgeoning friendships. The class uses Skype to communicate with children's relatives in other parts of the country or world. Within a few weeks, all the children, including native English speakers, enjoy helping each other explore different languages and learn together.

Children all over the world speak multiple languages. The opportunity to become bilingual or multilingual awaits every child in America if schools take advantage of young children's inborn ability to learn language and the affordable, technological resources now available.

Sources: D. Bates, no date. *Digital story helps dual language learner connect with classmates.* Washington, DC: National Association for the Education of Young Children, retrieved August 27, 2014, from http://www.naeyc.org/technology/digital-story-helps-dual-language-learner; K. N. Nemeth and F. S. Simon, 2013. Using technology as a teaching tool for dual language learners in preschool through grade 3, *Young Children, 68*(1), 48–52.

3. *Justice.* Teachers help children recognize unfairness, stereotypes, and biases (negative expressions toward groups) and their harmful impact on people.
4. *Action.* Teachers help children to stand up, alone or with others, to counteract unfairness, prejudice, and/or discrimination against others.

Curriculum and teaching practices to help children achieve these goals need to be developmentally appropriate; that is, within the range of what is understandable and achievable for children. Let's look more closely at each of these goals.

Goal 1: Foster Children's Positive Identity within Their Own Group

One of your goals as a teacher working with young children is to foster a positive sense of identity and help them develop a sense of self-worth. **Identity** refers to the characteristics that individuals recognize as constituting a sense of self and belonging to a group. Consider how important your own name is—it represents you, and is a strong part of your identity. Teachers need to ensure that every child's name is spelled and, most important, pronounced correctly. Because membership in a cultural/ethnic group has such a strong influence on identity, it is important for teachers to be aware of and support children's connection to their group. Fostering children's identity may also involve their bicultural and/or biracial identity; it should not be assumed that these children or their families identify themselves with any particular ethnic, cultural, or racial group (Wardle, 2014).

In classrooms with children from multiple cultural or ethnic groups, teachers sometimes try to minimize the differences among students instead of acknowledging them.

identity The collection of characteristics that individuals recognize as constituting their sense of self and belonging to a group.

Culturally responsive curriculum and teaching promotes children's positive sense of their own identity, valuing of diversity, and critical thinking about stereotyping and bias.

In an effort to discourage prejudice in the classroom, they may state proudly, "We don't see differences among children. We're color-blind here." Such statements deny the reality that children plainly see and experience (Killen, 2012). Teachers may think that talking about differences draws unnecessary attention to them and leads to prejudices. But this attitude, although well intentioned, actually has the opposite effect by denying vitally important aspects of children's identity (Derman-Sparks & Edwards, 2010). Consider how you would feel if your significant other said, "I don't notice that you are a woman (or a man)."

One question European American teachers often ask is, "But what if all the children in the class are white?" This question itself reveals the confusion that exists between race and culture in our society, because "white" is not a cultural group, and white-skinned people are members of many different cultural groups. In addition, close examination of this question reveals the perspective, discussed earlier in this chapter, that the white, majority group somehow doesn't have a culture (Derman-Sparks & Ramsey, 2011). Thus, it is important to help all children become aware of similarities and differences between themselves and others. Society sends countless messages about the superiority of white European Americans. Therefore, in supporting a positive sense of identity among these children, teachers must avoid contributing to feelings of entitlement and superiority to others who are not of the majority culture.

To foster positive identity, teachers must make an effort to ensure that the learning environment is welcoming to *every* child and reflects the identities and cultures of every child in the class. They can use photos or drawings of children with family members and audiotapes and videos of family member's voices and activities, as well as books, music, and other materials that reflect children's cultural identity in a positive way.

Goal 2: Experience and Value Human Diversity Just as it is important to have a strong sense of self, it is important to value diversity in others. Related goals are the ability to respectfully ask about and comfortably adapt to differences (Derman-Sparks & Edwards, 2010). The following sections describe how teachers can help children acquire the knowledge and disposition to learn about the similarities and differences among people.

Video Example 6.6:

Sharing Home Language and Culture

In this video, a pre-kindergarten student spontaneously shares a traditional Cambodian dance that she learned from her mother, while singing in Khmer, the language of Cambodia. Notice how the teacher and other children serve as a respectful audience. How do you think this situation builds the little girl's self-confidence and pride in her own identity? What does it teach the other children?

Help Children Learn about Differences As our nation's history demonstrates, just exposing children to people of different races, cultures, abilities, or backgrounds is not sufficient to help them learn to value diversity. In fact, simple exposure can actually exacerbate negative reactions (Derman-Sparks & Edwards, 2010).

Research on inclusion of children with disabilities, for example, finds that teachers need to work with all of the children to help a child with special needs be accepted and included in the group (Sandall & Schwartz, 2008). Preschoolers may think that if they talk to or play with a child in a wheelchair, they won't be able to walk, either. Teachers need to actively support positive interactions among children and intervene when negative reactions occur. Teachers shouldn't deny differences with statements such as, "He's just like you." Instead, an honest explanation is best: "You and Justin both like to move around the classroom and playground. You walk and run, while Justin uses his wheelchair to get where he wants to go."

Similarly, teachers should not admonish children for noticing differences. A teacher who says, "It isn't nice to ask questions about other people?" leaves a child without the correct information she or he needs. A child might ask, "Why is Derrick's skin darker than Deion's?" A more helpful explanation might be, "Children usually look like their parents, and Derrick's parents also have dark skin."

Likewise, dismissing children's anxieties or fears about differences may lead to avoidance or contribute to the development of prejudices. Consider the situation where 5-year-old Ariel says, "I don't like Mashiko because she don't speak English." Her teacher responds, "Oh, yes, you do. We're all friends here." Such a patronizing comment may lead Ariel to avoid or dislike Mashiko even more. Instead, the teacher might say, "Mashiko can speak Japanese, and she's learning English. Maybe you can help her. And she can teach you some words in her language."

Avoid Tourist Curriculum In helping children understand and value diversity, teachers need to avoid the "tourist curriculum." A tourist curriculum (Derman-Sparks & Edwards, 2010) is one in which a culture is visited as though it were an exotic destination where people dress, talk, dance, and eat differently before returning to the "normal" place where we all live. Here are some signs of a tourist curriculum (Derman-Sparks & Edwards, 2010):

> **tourist curriculum** An approach in which a culture is visited as though it were an exotic destination where people dress, talk, dance, and eat differently before returning to the "normal" place where we all live.

- Trivializing by organizing activities around food or holidays
- Tokenism, such as having only one book about any cultural group
- Disconnecting diversity from the rest of the curriculum, such as having a one-week unit on a different culture or only discussing diversity on Martin Luther King Jr. Day
- Stereotyping groups, such as using Native American images only from the past or wearing traditional dress
- Misrepresenting groups, such as using only books about Africa to teach about African Americans

Integrate Diversity into the Curriculum Developing relationships with people from diverse cultural groups and engaging in authentic experiences is the best way to help children experience and value diversity. Such opportunities also help children understand that their perspective on the world is not necessarily the only or the best, but simply different. It is also important for children to understand that there are many languages in the world and that no language is better than others. Regardless of the composition of their class or school, children today are exposed to diversity through the media—for example, seeing an African American president on television or listening to a Latino news anchor. Their wider community may also be more diverse than the immediate neighborhood and serve as a source of study.

Cultural diversity can also be integrated throughout the curriculum (Souto-Manning, 2013). One way to help children experience and learn to value diversity is to teach overriding concepts that cut across cultural groups—we all need shelter, nourishment, friends, families, and exercise, but we meet these needs in various ways. In the primary grades, children begin to study history and the lives of people in their communities and beyond. Through oral histories and reading biographies and autobiographies, children can learn about their own ethnic group and others.

 Application Exercise 6.4

Fostering Positive Identity and Valuing Diversity

Building each child's positive identity and helping them appreciate and value diversity lays the foundation for them to think critically about fair treatment of all people. This is the third goal of culturally responsive teaching.

bias Negative feelings and expressions toward groups or individuals.

Goal 3: Foster Critical Thinking about Justice and Fairness
We live in a society in which great strides toward tolerance, understanding, and acceptance have been made; yet racism, classism, sexism, homophobia, ageism, and other negative expressions of bias and forms of discrimination persist. As a result, children will often experience these biases and at times express them. **Biases** are negative feelings and expressions toward groups or individuals. Understanding bias means recognizing that differences are not problematic, but negative reactions to differences are.

Countering bias and stereotypes is an area in which teachers must be ever vigilant. To achieve this goal, teachers must review books, videos, games, toys, and other curriculum materials to ensure that they do not perpetuate negative images of any group of people. Teachers must also pay attention to toys or materials that children bring from home.

In addition, teachers need to work with children to establish expectations for behavior that prohibit expressions of bias toward other people to ensure that race, gender, age, sexual orientation, appearance, and ability are never the subject of teasing or ridicule. This is an area where teachers must have a zero-tolerance policy. They should intervene immediately when such behavior occurs, reminding children of the rules for how children are treated in the classroom. They also need to offer comfort to the child who is the target of biased behavior: "Yolanda, it was unfair and unkind for Caleb to say you can't play because you have brown skin. Caleb, remember that we treat people fairly in this school."

Following are three important considerations when handling discriminatory or biased behaviors (Derman-Sparks & Edwards, 2010):

1. *Don't ignore.* Teachers need to address any signs of bias head on. Ignoring discriminatory behaviors implies that they are acceptable. Consequently, the victim feels unsafe and the perpetrator feels supported, the opposite of what is desirable. For example, Ms. Eli is busy helping her first-graders with math problems—when she hears Jasmine tell Hiroke that he has funny eyes. Ms. Eli contemplates saying nothing. Instead, she quietly says to Jasmine, "Everyone's looks are unique and different. Please remember that negative comments about people's appearance are hurtful, and we don't allow that here."

2. *Don't excuse.* Sometimes teachers will avoid an uncomfortable situation by saying things such as, "He didn't really mean it." Excusing expressions of bias teaches one child that the behavior is okay and the victim of that behavior that he or she will not be protected. Instead, the teacher could have said, "Calling other people names hurts them, but it also makes you look mean and not very smart. If you have bad feelings about someone's behavior, we need to learn better ways for you to express them."

3. *Don't be afraid to intervene.* Fear and ignorance are among the biggest impediments to confronting and eliminating discrimination in our society. Teachers may be afraid that they will say the wrong thing to children, or that parents will be upset if they talk about race, culture, language, or socioeconomic conditions. However, unless they are part of the solution to addressing bias and discrimination in society, teachers must accept the responsibility for being part of the problem. For example, two children in Mr. Pinto's second-grade class are living in a homeless shelter. The children are teased for coming to school each day wearing the same clothes. Mr. Pinto privately arranges for them to receive clothing donations. He also talks with the teasers about their feelings, and finds out that some of the most verbal children are actually afraid of losing their homes, too.

Goal 4: Take Action to Address Bias and Discrimination
Goal 4 builds on Goal 3. As children develop, they become more aware of others' feelings and ever more sensitive to the concept of fairness. How often have you heard a 4- or 5-year-old say, "That's not fair" in defense of their own rights? With teacher modeling and supports

as described in the previous section, children begin to care about others who are treated unfairly and to do something about it, including telling an adult. This work is essential to address the epidemic of bullying in schools.

In kindergarten and primary grades, children can problem-solve together ways to take action to address situations in the school or community. For example, one school in Washington, D.C., is having a lengthy discussion about the name of the local football team, the *Redskins*. Children's positions on changing the name tend to represent their parents' point of view; some think the name is offensive to Native Americans, while others think it is a tradition that honors them. The children read books about the history of Native Americans and current articles about why various people think the name should be changed. The children even explore what it feels like to be called "White-skin," "Blackskin," "Brownskin," or "Yellowskin." After much study, the class takes a vote on whether the name should be changed, with 15 *yes* votes and 6 voting *no*. Those who vote for changing the name decide to write letters to the team owner and the local newspaper advocating for a change. They also work together to think of alternative names to suggest.

The goals of anti-bias education do not need to be addressed as separate subject areas or topics of study. Instead, these goals should be integrated throughout the learning environment and curriculum, and in all aspects of teachers' interactions with children and their families (Kuh, Keenan, Given & Beneke, 2016).

As we saw in the chapter-opening scenario, contradictions may arise because what professionals think is good for children and what families believe and value might be very different. Finding a middle ground that balances what professionals consider developmentally appropriate practice with what families consider culturally appropriate is paramount to effective teaching.

Developmentally Appropriate and Culturally Responsive Practices

In this section, we address the sometimes controversial topic of the congruence of developmentally appropriate and culturally appropriate practices (Bredekamp & Copple, 1997; Mallory & New, 1994; NAEYC, 2009). Just as we are all products of our cultural upbringings, we are also products of our cultural environments, such as our schools, summer programs we might have attended, and jobs we have held. Professional organizations, including schools and child care programs, also have their own cultures.

When the culture—especially the rules for behavior—of the school or child care center is similar to that of children's families, their adaptation and ability to make sense of experiences is greatly eased. These children implicitly know much of what is expected even though they need to learn specific information such as the classroom routines. On the other hand, when there are cultural differences between the rules imposed at school and those imposed at home, children have greater difficulty adjusting. Not only do they have to learn the curriculum, but they also have to learn the implicit rules of discourse, such as "Respond promptly" or "Even though the teacher knows the answer, he will still expect you to answer the question."

For culturally diverse children to be successful in school, teachers must explicitly teach the rules of behavior that children of the majority culture already know. Lisa Delpit (2006), an African American education scholar and recipient of a MacArthur "genius" award, eloquently describes how the school culture is the "culture of power," and children who have access to its rules are more likely to succeed and gain access to the power in society. Delpit further describes how constructivist teaching, such as the developmentally appropriate practices advocated by NAEYC (2009), may leave children of diverse cultural perspectives at a disadvantage. In her view, constructivism and other progressive education approaches reflect the dominant European American cultural perspective. For children of other cultural backgrounds, success in school may depend on their ability to become *bicultural*, that is, to learn the rules of the school culture while holding on to the rules of the home culture.

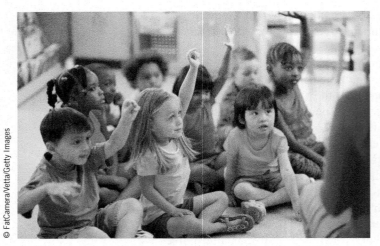

When there are cultural differences between what the school defines as developmentally appropriate and the expectations of the family, children are likely to have greater difficulty adjusting.

© FatCamera/Vetta/Getty Images

Like Delpit, many early childhood educators have questioned the cultural appropriateness of developmentally appropriate practice (Dahlberg, Moss, & Pence, 2007; Gonzalez-Mena, 2008; Graue & Delaney, 2011; Mallory & New, 1994; Sanders, Diehl, & Kyler, 2007). Let's think about this question in terms of what we've learned so far about culture.

The Culture of Early Childhood Education: Revisited Previously, we presented a framework contrasting individualistic and interdependent cultures. Even a cursory examination of NAEYC's guidelines for developmentally appropriate practice (NAEYC, 2009) or the association's accreditation standards (NAEYC, 2017) reveals the degree to which these documents reflect the individualistic cultural orientation. Goals such as promoting independence, self-concept and self-esteem, exploration, verbal communication, and child-initiated activity permeate the standards. Overall, a "child-centered" philosophy underlies the approach.

A clear example of this orientation is the role of play in early childhood education. Children are encouraged to play and explore the environment and materials, and to play with and talk to adults. On the other hand, in interdependent cultural groups, learning is directed by adults and depends more on observation of adults than on play, discovery, and child-chosen activity (Zepeda et al., 2006). In these cultures, objects such as toys are less important than social interaction, and play occurs mostly with siblings and other children. Consider that children from these diverse cultural orientations might gravitate toward peers in a free-flowing preschool classroom instead of making independent choices of materials as expected by the teacher.

Another standard focuses on the importance of warm, nurturing relationships among teachers and children (NAEYC, 2017). But the definition of "nurturing" behavior is also culturally influenced. For example, white European Americans might think that African American parents and teachers are harsh in the way they talk to or discipline their children (Hale, 1994). This "harshness" may reflect the need to help children of color navigate in a society that is often hostile to them (Killen, 2012). Consequently, those who observe this dynamic without this shared cultural perspective may not appreciate the love that is being conveyed. Similarly, African American teachers and parents may value children learning academics more than playing in preschool because they know these skills are essential for their children to succeed in school (Sanders et al., 2007).

To further illustrate how culturally determined our view of "best practice" is, consider an effort by Chinese researchers (Li, Hu, Pan, Qin, & Fan, 2013) to adapt a widely used American measure of high quality, the *Early Childhood Environment Rating Scale* (Harms, Clifford, & Cryer, 2014). The researchers found that the tool did not adequately reflect their Asian collectivist culture, especially in terms of their emphasis on group activities and whole-group instruction. They found it necessary to develop items measuring the quality of whole-group teaching, which they subsequently found to be highly related to children's learning outcomes. Another difference was in the way quality outdoor play is defined. Such play is far more restricted in their programs, perhaps due to overprotection by parents because most children are the only child in the family.

The point of this discussion is to acknowledge that the prevailing standards for good practice in early childhood education described throughout this book and taught in most teacher education courses reflect the dominant culture of society. At the same time, these standards require that programs be responsive to cultural and linguistic diversity. Given the diversity of children and families served today, teachers must help children become

bicultural, capable of operating successfully in both their home environment and the culture of the larger world. Accomplishing this goal requires teachers to resolve some of the inevitable contradictions that arise between what is considered developmentally appropriate and what is culturally appropriate.

bicultural Capable of operating successfully in both the home environment and the dominant culture of the larger world.

Resolving Contradictions   As you have seen, when you are caring for and educating other people's children, you are being relied on to do so in a way that adheres to other people's beliefs and values. In the case of infants and toddlers, for example, how feeding, sleeping, dressing, and toileting are handled is not consistent across cultures. Likewise, with preschoolers and elementary-grade children, teachers and families may disagree fundamentally on appropriate discipline as well as how and what children should be learning. Resolving these differences is an important part of working with children and families. Read the *Becoming an Intentional Teacher: Responding to Cultural Differences* feature for an example of how one teacher finds the balance between her ideas and family perspectives.

Professionals tend to think they know the right answers to situations that arise in the classroom. Yet in most situations, no one right answer exists. It is true that some practices, such as spanking children, are prohibited by law and others by licensing standards. In these cases, no compromise is possible. But more often, *both/and* solutions are more useful than *either/or* choices when such contradictions occur, as illustrated in the following real-life example (adapted from Bredekamp, 1997a, p. 47):

> Antonia Lopez was director of a program for Mexican American children and families in California. One of the program's primary objectives was to promote cultural

Becoming an Intentional Teacher

Responding to Cultural Differences

© Monkey Business Images/Shutterstock

Here's What Happened   Before the new group of 3-year-olds started in the fall, I let all of the families know that the children were welcome to bring from home any kind of "comfort object" they would like. Emma brought her favorite bear, Cookie. When she went to get him from her cubby at naptime, Cookie was gone, and when she searched for Cookie, she found Linh curled up and ready for her nap, holding the bear. I explained to Linh that the bear was Emma's, and gently took him from her and returned him to Emma. After this sequence of events repeated itself for several days, I talked to Linh's mother, Mrs. Pham, and asked for her help in getting her daughter to leave Emma's bear alone. Although she understands English fairly well, she looked at me with total incomprehension at this request. During the next few weeks, I talked with a few Vietnamese people who had lived in the community for a while. From our discussions, I saw the part of the picture I had been missing. In the Vietnamese and most other Asian cultures, the idea of individual ownership is not as important as shared ownership and enjoyment of objects.

I went back to Linh's mom to give her a sense of how Emma's experiences were different from Linh's. I also talked with Emma's mom about Linh's perspective. At her mother's encouragement, Linh brought in a toy animal that she and her siblings play with at home. After a few weeks, Linh and Emma sometimes would have their animals play together in the dramatic play area.

Here's What I Was Thinking   Getting the information from members of the Vietnamese community was very

helpful, as was my own research about "interdependent" cultures. Maybe I could have gotten to this eventually by talking with Linh's mother, but because I didn't understand the basis of her response, I didn't want to risk offending her as a result of my own ignorance. Once I had some understanding of interdependent and individualistic cultural values, I could talk with Mrs. Pham and see if we were communicating clearly. I felt it was important to go beyond just resolving the immediate conflict between the girls.

I think it is important for the families as well as the children to learn about the differences in cultural values and practices. After all, the Vietnamese children will experience the values predominant in European American culture throughout their lives in the United States, and ultimately the goal is for them to become sufficiently "bicultural" so that they can manage well in both worlds. At the same time, I was impressed with the way the Vietnamese children get along and share toys, which is a goal we have for all 3-year-olds. And the families who are natives to our area need to understand the new people who are joining our community, too. In fact, because Linh and Emma are so young, I thought their families might gain more cultural knowledge from this situation than they would.

Reflection   Rethink this situation from the perspective of a teacher whose own cultural values are interdependent. What might she have been thinking, and what would she have done?

congruity. As a relatively interdependent cultural group, Mexican Americans value cooperation over competition, and this value was encouraged in the program. Another accepted cultural practice is the giving of gifts to express respect and appreciation.

During the year, an uncomfortable situation arose. Parents began giving teachers gifts, and over time the gifts became more elaborate. The gift-giving escalated into a competition to see who could give the best gift, a direct contradiction of the program's goals. To resolve this dilemma, Antonia and her staff established two rules for dealing with the situation:

Rule 1) You can't accept the gifts.
Rule 2) You can't reject the gifts.

With these rules in place, the staff had to arrive at an alternative solution. They agreed that rather than teachers accepting gifts for themselves, gifts would be accepted on behalf of the school. Depending on the gift, it was shared by all the children or displayed in a place of honor for everyone to appreciate. Soon, families' gift-giving became less competitive and moved toward the goal of making the program a better place for everyone.

When teachers and families disagree on what is best for children, remembering Antonia's rules may be a good strategy. If teachers cannot accept the family's position for some reason, but they also cannot reject it, then they will have to work toward an alternative solution—one that might better serve everyone's interests.

Although it is true that all children are born ready to learn, it is equally true that their learning takes place within social and cultural contexts. Just as our cultural backgrounds influence our own development, behavior, and learning, developing an understanding of the role of each child's culture should influence what and how we teach young children. Although overall learning goals may be more or less the same across cultures, different teaching strategies may be required to help children achieve those goals.

To build successful relationships with children, you will need to take into account and learn about each child's cultural worlds, because their experiences and home language are integral components of their identity. As a teacher, you will need to demonstrate respect and support for children's language and culture. You must also help children make sense of their new experiences in school by making connections to their prior knowledge and experiences obtained in their own cultural contexts. Culturally and linguistically appropriate ways of teaching are not "add-ons"; they are integral dimensions of developmentally appropriate practice.

✓ Check Your Understanding 6.6

Revisiting the Case Study

... Ms. Griffin's Classroom

At the beginning of this chapter, we saw how Stacey struggled in her relationship with families during her first year of teaching. Now that we have explored the many ways culture influences thinking and behavior, we can revisit Stacey's situation and see how it could be improved for everyone involved.

Rather than giving up in frustration, Stacey attends a professional conference and takes workshops on cultural and linguistic diversity. This motivates her to do some reading and talking with the more experienced staff members at her center. These experiences cause Stacey to reexamine some of her prior assumptions and in turn change some of the ways she teaches.

Her first step is to alter her daily schedule so the beginning of the day is an informal time for her to talk and play with small groups or individual children. Before she calls for a group gathering to sing or tell the children the plans for the day, Stacey waits for all of the children to arrive. This schedule means that she is no longer frustrated if parents bring their children late.

Stacey reflects on the disagreements she has been having with families over carrying and dressing their children. She recognizes that these differences are quite minor. Consequently, she decides not to interfere with close family relationships by imposing her views of what is best for children's development.

Stacey explains to families that she doesn't always have time to feed each child individually, so at times she gives them finger food. In response to parents' concerns, however, she promises that she will help feed the children as much as possible. In general, she finds that once their families leave for the day, the children tend to model each other. In some ways, they function more independently, such as when they attempt self-help skills. In other ways, they function interdependently by helping each other often and waiting until Stacey tells them what to do.

In her conflict with Mrs. Arguenta, Stacey realizes that Mrs. Arguenta was showing respect by refusing to call her by her first name. Stacey comes to see that Mrs. Arguenta has a legitimate point of view about teaching Ilsia to use the toilet. She tries using the skills she learned for resolving conflict. She agrees to try Mrs. Arguenta's strategies, while Mrs. Arguenta agrees that they may not be entirely successful because Stacey has a group of children to supervise.

Finally, Stacey realizes that Mrs. Arguenta sent Ilsia's 10-year-old sister to pick her up because within their cultural group, older children naturally look after their younger siblings. Stacey respectfully explains to Mrs. Arguenta that because of licensing laws, the center can only release a child to an adult. This is an issue where compromise is not possible. Mrs. Arguenta presents a list of adult family members who have permission to pick up Ilsia.

As we see from the encounter between Stacey and Mrs. Arguenta, cultural competence and cross-cultural communication are key elements of effective practice in early childhood education. ■

6 Chapter Summary

- Culture can be defined as the values, beliefs, and patterns of behavior, both explicit and implicit, that are passed on from generation to generation. All learning and development occur in and are influenced by social and cultural contexts.

- A framework for studying culture is to understand that the beliefs, values, and behaviors that characterize cultural groups vary along a continuum from individualistic to interdependent.

- Teachers need to become aware of their own cultural perspectives and the risks of implicit bias as the first step toward becoming culturally competent.

- Knowledge of culture is important because without it, teachers can misunderstand children, inaccurately assess children's competence, and/or fail to promote children's learning.

- Cultural competence is the ability to work and communicate effectively, both verbally and nonverbally, with members of various cultural groups.

- Culturally responsive learning goals for children are to foster and support children's development and sense of identity within their own cultural group, to assist children to experience and value diversity, to foster children's critical thinking, and to counter stereotypes and biases (negative expressions toward groups).

- Given the diversity of children and families served today, teachers must help children become bicultural, capable of operating successfully in both their home environment and the larger world. Helping children become bicultural requires teachers to resolve some of the inevitable contradictions that arise between what is considered developmentally appropriate and what is culturally appropriate.

Key Terms

- acculturation
- anti-bias education
- bias
- bicultural

- cultural competence
- ethnicity
- high-context culture
- implict bias

- identity
- individualistic cultural groups
- interdependent cultural groups

- low-context culture
- multi-language learners
- tourist curriculum

 Flash Cards 6.1

Readings and Websites

Derman-Sparks, L., & Edwards, J. O. (2010). *Anti-bias education for young children and ourselves*. Washington, DC: National Association for the Education of Young Children.

National Black Child Development Institute. (2013). *Being Black is not a risk factor: A strengths-based look at the state of the Black child*. Washington, DC: National Black Child Development Institute. Retrieved from http://www.nbcdi.org/resource.

Nemeth, K. N. (2012). *Basics of supporting dual language learners: An introduction for educators of children from birth through age 8*. Washington, DC: National Association for the Education of Young Children.

York, S. (2016). *Roots and wings: Affirming culture and preventing bias in early childhood* (3rd ed.). St. Paul, MN: Redleaf Press.

Early Childhood Learning and Knowledge Center (ECKLC)

This website, sponsored by the Office of Head Start, provides online practical resources to guide any program serving culturally and linguistically diverse children and families, including tribal programs and refugee families from Iraq, Somalia, and Burma. Materials are available in Spanish and other languages.

National Association for Bilingual Education (NABE)

This website provides resources to improve instructional practices for linguistically and culturally diverse children, and to advocate for educational equity and excellence for bilingual and multilingual students.

Teaching Tolerance: A Project of the Southern Poverty Law Center

This website has a wealth of classroom resources, including sample lessons designed for different age groups on all aspects of diversity and anti-bias education.

 Shared Writing 6.1

Becoming Aware of Your Own Cultural Perspective

7 Building Effective Partnerships with Families

Learning Outcomes

After studying this chapter, you should be able to:

7.1 Describe contemporary families and their role in children's development.

7.2 Discuss reciprocal relationships with families and apply principles of family-centered practices.

7.3 Explain effective strategies for communicating with families.

7.4 Evaluate ways teachers can engage families in their children's care and education.

7.5 Apply a framework for building effective partnerships with families.

Case Study

Vilma Suarez has worked as a toddler teacher in an Early Head Start center for three years. She loves her job, but her days can be exhausting. Today was one of those days. Before the children even arrived, Vilma had a meeting with the early intervention team to discuss Aiya's individualized family service plan (IFSP). Aiya is deaf, and the team wants Vilma to begin signing with her. Aiya's mother is silent throughout the meeting. She is a new immigrant and feels threatened by this powerful group of professionals. Vilma is patiently working to gain her trust, beginning with being available to talk about other things besides Aiya's hearing impairment.

When Mrs. Vacaro drops 2-year-old Tomas off, he sobs and clings to her, and Mrs. Vacaro is clearly torn about leaving him. Vilma speaks softly to Tomas and gets his attention with his favorite stacking toy. Finally, Mrs. Vacaro is able to pry him loose and reluctantly departs. Vilma tries to call and text her during the day to reassure her, but Mrs. Vacaro attends school and must have turned off the sound on her phone.

The assistant teacher supervises the children's naptime while Vilma conducts a parent conference. The conference is difficult because she has to talk to Mr. Henderson about his son's recent biting of other children. Mr. Henderson responds defensively, saying, "He doesn't do that at home. He tried it once and I bit him back. That's what you have to do." Vilma explains that biting is actually very typical for toddlers, and that teachers cannot bite children or use any physical punishment in their program. Vilma continues that she is not worried, and will keep Mr. Henderson updated. She realizes that this situation will have to be negotiated carefully, and that it may take a while to help Mr. Henderson adopt positive behavior support with his son.

At 5:00 P.M., when Mrs. Vacaro comes in clearly dreading the worst, Vilma greets her with the news that Tomas had great fun today playing with his friends, ate well, and even said two new words. As Vilma reassures her about how well Tomas is doing, Mrs. Vacaro sighs and fights back tears. She stoops

© AndrewLilley/E+/Getty Images

to cuddle Tomas, and Vilma turns to talk with Marcy's grandmother and David's father, who have just arrived.

During her bus ride home, Vilma reflects on her day. She remembers that when she began her career, she was excited about working with very young children. Because she has three children of her own and helped parent her younger siblings, she felt confident working with babies and toddlers, and was relieved to have a job where she didn't have to work with adults. Vilma shakes her head, remembering how naïve she was. She now knows that working with children is only one part of her job. Working with their families is the bigger challenge. But doing so is also very rewarding. She understands that by learning from and with families, she doubles her impact as a teacher. Her contributions to children's lives will last long after they leave her classroom. ■

Whatever your age, if someone asked you to picture the most important people in your life, images of your family members would likely come to mind. Perhaps you would picture the people you grew up with, or your spouse/partner and children. Some of you might picture both your nuclear family of parents and siblings and your extended family of cousins, aunts, uncles, and grandparents. Families play essential roles in every aspect of human development through the life span. During early childhood, however, families are the primary context for children's development and learning, with child care and early education settings playing a secondary, albeit critically important, role. Given that these two contexts—families and early childhood programs and schools—are the two main environments in which children develop and learn, it is essential for teachers and parents to work in concert if children are to develop to their fullest potential.

Because young children are inherently connected to their families, early childhood teachers work with children *and* families. The younger the child, the stronger the connection to family and, therefore, the closer the relationship between teacher and parent must be. Most early childhood educators enter the field because of their interest in teaching young children; initially, they may not grasp the importance of developing skills to work with families. In fact, teachers report that working with families is among the areas where they feel least prepared, especially when it comes to implementing a strengths-based approach for all children and families (Baum & McMurray-Schwarz, 2004; Iruka, 2013). Throughout this book, we use the terms *families* and *parents* to mean those people who are primarily responsible for the children you teach, whoever they are—parents, stepparents, grandparents, guardians, foster families, or other household members.

This chapter describes how teachers establish effective partnerships with families. We begin by painting a picture of today's families, their exquisite diversity, and the challenges they face in providing for their children. Next, we describe the principles of family-centered practices as well as the nature of productive, reciprocal partnerships between teachers and families. We describe effective strategies for communicating with families and involving them in their children's education. We also acknowledge that some strategies are not effective in all situations; relationships with families are not always smooth. Therefore, the chapter provides a framework for building partnerships that is effective in resolving the inevitable conflicts that arise when working with families.

Contemporary Families and Their Role in Children's Development

One can hardly read a newspaper or watch a television program without hearing dire warnings about the state of the American family and the myriad threats it faces. Although it is true that families in the 21st century confront many challenges, it is equally true that the family is and has always been a dynamic, resilient, and effective institution for nurturing and acculturating each new generation.

What is a family? This may seem like a fairly easy question to answer, but it is not. Each of you, no doubt, has your own definition of family based on your own experiences. Throughout your career as a teacher, you will work with children who experience a wide range of family configurations, as discussed next.

Welcoming All Families

Louise's child care class consists of fifteen 3- to 5-year-olds. Four of the children live with their biological mothers and fathers; Blake and Debra are only children, Madeline is the youngest of four, and Stephen is the eldest of three. Five children live with their mothers only, but among them Joseph and Lauren are

Families today come in all shapes and sizes. How would you describe the membership in your family? How does it compare with the family your parents, grandparents or friends grew up in?

in shared custody arrangements and split days of the week living with their fathers. Both Joseph and Lauren have stepmothers as well as stepsiblings. Lauren also has a baby half-brother. Of the other three children who live with their mothers, Marin doesn't know her father at all, and Jackson has infrequent contact with his biological father. Jeanine's mom is serving in the military overseas. Marta lives with her two dads, and Logan lives with his two moms. Kim lives with his parents and siblings and also his paternal grandparents, aunt, and one cousin. David has lived with his grandmother and two brothers since his mother died, and his father is in prison. The diverse family configurations represented in Louise's class are typical of America today: two-parent, single-parent, families of divorce, blended/stepfamilies, LGBT (lesbian/gay/bisexual/transgender) families, and extended families.

Despite statistics and experience to the contrary, many people still think of the family as consisting of two first-time married parents and their biological or adopted children, known as the nuclear family. In looking at how children grow up today, however, as depicted in Figure. 7.1, we see that about two-thirds (64%) of *all* children live with two married parents, but considerable variation exists among those families. Mother-only

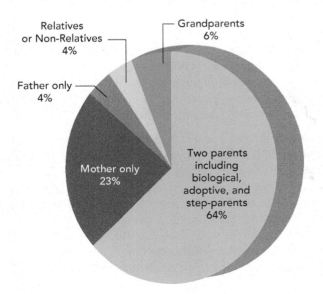

FIGURE 7.1 Living Arrangements for All Children Children's living arrangements vary widely depending on their family backgrounds, circumstances, and configurations.

Source: Family Structure, retrieved February 24, 2018, from www.childtrends.org/?indicators=family-structure.

families account for 23%, and 4% of children live with their fathers only (Child Trends, 2015). Another 4% of children live with neither parent but rather with other family members or nonrelatives. An increasing number of children live with grandparents, although many of those households include the child's mother.

Children's living arrangements vary dramatically by race and ethnicity. Almost half (49%) of African American children live with their mothers only, as do about 26% of Latino children (Child Trends, 2015). By contrast, only 15% of White children and 11% of Asian children live in mother-only households. In addition, more than twice as many African American children (8%) as non-Hispanic White children (3%) do not live with either parent (Child Trends, 2015).

Increasing numbers of children live in extended families, which are defined as a family unit where two or more generations of close family relatives live together in one household. Here again we see racial and ethnic diversity, with about 9% of White, 17% of African American, and 14% of Latino children living with at least one grandparent (Ellis & Simmons, 2014). Surprising to some, a quarter of children in the United States live in immigrant families, with at least one parent who is foreign-born (Annie E. Casey Foundation, 2016.

Contrary to popular belief, there has never been a "typical" or "traditional" family structure in America (Scully, Barbour, & Roberts-King, 2015). Various factors contribute to changing family structures over time. For example, until quite recently in history, women died in childbirth at alarming rates, and men also died young in wars or of disease. Therefore, although divorce was less common, many children grew up in single-parent families or blended families. Consider for a moment your own experiences of family, and those of your parents and grandparents. While some grow up in a "traditional" nuclear family with married parents of different sexes, many children grow up in single-parent, grandparent, or same-sex parent households. In fact, more than one-third of LGBT adults have children (Krogstad, 2014). Families form and re-form over time. At various times, children may live with only one or even no parents because of divorce, separation, remarriage, death, or other circumstances. Almost half (44%) of 18- to 29-year-olds have a step-sibling (Krogstad, 2014).

Regardless of your own family experiences or values, as a teacher you will encounter many different family configurations. To work successfully with families, it is important to accept the following assumptions:

- Families are diverse in many ways: composition, culture, religion, economic status, work, mobility, and sexual orientation.
- Families are not good or bad; they are different and unique.
- Almost all families want the best for their children, regardless of the difficult circumstances they may be trying to overcome.
- All families have strengths and resources as well as hopes and dreams for their children, just as all families face challenges.
- It is not your right to pass judgment on families. You do not need to agree with families at all times, but you cannot reject a child's family and at the same time successfully care for and educate the child.

In early childhood programs, conversations and curriculum often focus on children's families, but because families today are so diverse and changing, teachers need to foster an inclusive environment and not make assumptions (Paula & da Silva, 2014). Books, photos, posters and other media that depict the wide range of family types should be available, particularly children's own families. Teachers should use inclusive language (*families* rather than *parents*). Similarly, teachers should consult gay fathers and lesbian mothers regarding their preferences about what each is called by their children and others; use *husband, wife, partner* or *spouse* depending on individual preferences. Celebrate Family Day instead of Father's Day or Mother's Day. Better yet, make every day about the most significant adults in children's lives.

The important thing to understand is that all families are different, even in ways that are not easily apparent. As with understanding young children, the best strategy is to work hard to know each family well. The more you know about the intricacies of family functioning, the more likely you will be able to put these five assumptions into practice. In the next section, we describe the theoretical perspectives that help explain how families function and change.

Family Dynamics

Joelynn and Jeff Robeson already have 18-month-old twins when their third child, Eric, is born with spina bifida, a physical disability that requires repeated hospitalizations and considerable care. Just when Joelynn and Jeff are beginning to adjust to the strain on their marriage of caring for three young children, including one with special needs, the factory where Jeff works closes down, and he loses his job. Suffering from depression and alcohol abuse, Jeff leaves Joelynn without child support, forcing her to seek public assistance. After a while, however, the rules for continuing on public assistance require Joelynn to work full time, and she must leave her three young children in the care of her sister, who also has two preschool-age children. Joelynn suffers from the stresses of caring for her children and supporting them on her minimum wage salary.

As is true for every family, the development of each member of the Robeson family is affected by many different factors, both internal and external to the family. Two theoretical perspectives are helpful for thinking about families: Bronfenbrenner's ecological model of human development and family systems theory. Each of these frameworks helps explain the complex interactions known as family dynamics.

Bronfenbrenner's Ecological Model of Human Development As we learned in Chapter 4, ecological theory is a useful model for understanding the influence of social and cultural contexts on human development (Bronfenbrenner & Morris, 2006), and especially the important influence of family. At the center of Bronfenbrenner's model is the individual child, whose development is influenced by biology, and by the proximal processes of daily interactions in the family microsystem. In the Robeson family, Eric's disability at birth is a biological contributor to his development, but other variables also contribute to his development and mediate his disability. For example, Eric's personal characteristics, such as his above-average intelligence and lively personality, attract the positive attention of everyone he meets.

In the Robeson family, Eric was born into a family that was already caring for very young twins. His siblings' existence was part of the context into which he was born, but his birth and his disability dramatically changed the family's context. As a result, Eric's aunt provided child care; this event occurs within the microsystem in which experiences interact and affect each other. The interactions that Eric has with his parents, siblings, and extended family—proximal processes, or daily routines—bear the most influence on his development.

Other aspects of the systems surrounding Eric also matter for his development. Interactions between his family and his aunt, doctors, and early intervention professionals represent the mesosystems—the interactions among Eric's microsystems. For the Robeson family, the exosystem includes economic factors beyond its control that seriously affected the family. Jeff's unemployment led to the family's requiring public assistance. The laws governing eligibility for public support necessitated Joelynn's employment and the children's enrollment in child care.

Consider how changes in various elements of the exosystem could alter outcomes for the Robeson family and their children, especially Eric. With Jeff out of work and Joelynn working for minimum wage, the family's income is below poverty level, making them eligible for Early Head Start. This federal program provides child care for children from birth to age 3, early intervention services for Eric, and family support. The early intervention team helps Joelynn learn how to support Eric's development at home. They put Jeff in touch with mental health counselors to help him deal with his depression, and they also connect him to Alcoholics Anonymous and career retraining. Through the counseling offered by Early Head Start, Jeff gets a maintenance job while he attends computer school. Joelynn begins training as a nurse's aide, inspired by her newfound abilities to care for

Eric's health. The twins thrive in the social atmosphere at the child care center. The family reunites, and its emotional as well as financial security improves. The changes in Eric's family will have lasting benefits for his development as well.

When aspects of the child and family systems provide substantive supports outside of their home life, families have what they need to have positive interactions inside their home—and children benefit. Now that you have seen how various ecological systems interact to influence the family and children's development, we focus on family systems theory, which explains more about the internal workings of family dynamics.

Family Systems Theory   Understanding family dynamics is an important aspect of working with children of any age, but of young children in particular because they don't always have the language to describe their emotions and needs. Rodney may be angry because his father was just deployed, which makes his mother sad and nervous, and his big sister silent. To describe how this one event impacts the entire family, family systems theory views family members as interconnected parts, with each member influencing the others in predictable and recurring ways (Allen & Henderson, 2017). Family systems theory focuses on explaining family behavior—that is, why individual family members behave as they do in relation to one another and to those outside the family. Understanding how families function as systems can help teachers serve diverse children and build family partnerships more effectively.

Family systems theory describes some common characteristics of families, including boundaries, roles, rules, hierarchy, climate, and equilibrium (Christian, 2006). Each of these characteristics can be described on a continuum. For example, all families have rules regarding the acceptable behavior of members; some families operate according to strict and inflexible rules, whereas others have few rules or apply rules inconsistently. Table 7.1 presents characteristics of family systems, what they mean, and implications for effective teaching practice. Because each dimension of family functioning is particularly influenced by the cultural beliefs and practices of the family and community, teachers need to view family variability on these dimensions as differences rather than positives or negatives.

In the previous sections, we saw how families influence and are influenced by social, cultural, and political contexts. We also saw how different families' characteristics influence their behavior toward their children and in relation to teachers and school. In the next section, we describe some of the challenges confronting America's families today.

Family Circumstances and Challenges

Families face many challenges in providing the best care and education for their children. We regularly hear dire predictions about children *at risk*. This term is widely used, typically to refer to children who have characteristics (such as a disability) or life circumstances (such as poverty) that increase the likelihood that they will experience negative developmental and learning outcomes, such as dropping out of school. However, the term "at risk" has no consistent definition and often tends to stigmatize children, families, and/or communities by oversimplifying the strengths and challenges of children and families with a label that does not help address their needs (Moore, 2006).

Because families are the most influential setting for children's development, risk factors affecting families, such as poverty, single parenthood, and low levels of parental education (which tend to co-occur), are found to be related to poor outcomes for children. Other factors that place families at risk include family dysfunction, abuse, parental mental illness, chronic illness, and substance abuse, particularly the growing opioid crisis (U.S. Department of Health and Human Services [HHS], n.d.). Community risk factors create challenges for families as well; these include poverty, crime, unemployment, and high levels of teen parenthood.

Challenges for Families   The largest risk factor for poor child outcomes is poverty, which the federal government defines as less than $22,050 per year for a family of four. Because research shows that almost twice this income is required to adequately cover

family systems theory Views family members as interconnected parts, with each member influencing the others in predictable and recurring ways.

TABLE 7.1 Characteristics of Family Systems		
Dimension	**Explanation**	**Implication and Example**
Boundaries	Limitations on what or who is considered in or out of the family. Some families are open to new people and ideas, whereas others tend to be more closed and restrictive. Families at one extreme may share too much information about the private workings of the family, whereas extremely closed families may conceal information such as domestic violence or substance abuse.	Respecting a family's boundaries is an important skill of effective early childhood professionals. When the Robeson family enrolled in the Early Head Start program, the staff found that Joelynn was open to sharing her problems and seeking help, but Jeff at first felt the program was too intrusive into his personal business.
Roles	In every family, individual members have roles—the parts that individuals typically play in relation to others. Most of us readily remember our role in the family. Were you the baby, the peacemaker, or the rescuer?	These roles have powerful lasting effects on development that are often played out in school as well. For example, 7-year-old Deon's parents have addiction problems. From a young age, he has felt responsible for taking care of them and his younger sister. Deon's teacher values his serious attitude toward his work, but wishes that he didn't worry so much about his parents and could be more carefree.
Rules	The standards or traditions that dictate correct behavior in various situations and how we relate to one another. Defining and passing on rules for behavior is the major function of cultural groups; therefore, rules are, by definition, culturally determined.	Differences in teachers' and parents' expectations about rules often require negotiation. Deon's parents think he should act like a man and contribute to the family rather than play outside or spend time with friends.
Hierarchy	The decision making, control, and power within the family, who is in charge, and how power is distributed and used. Like rules, hierarchy is strongly influenced by culture. In some families, parents share responsibility equitably; in others, hierarchy is determined by gender, with fathers and mothers making decisions about different aspects of parenting. In some groups, power is vested in elders. Hierarchies change over time.	Teachers need to be aware of family hierarchy because so many interactions involve decisions, and effective family partnerships and family-centered practices require the sharing of power. In the Robeson family, Jeff was the one in charge during the early years of the marriage, but when he lost his job, power shifted to Joelynn as the breadwinner and single parent. Power shifts can also occur when a military parent is deployed.
Climate	The emotional and physical environment in which a child grows up. Emotionally close families can compensate to some extent for threatening physical environments.	The classroom climate needs to be emotionally safe and secure for all children. The Robeson family lived in a physically safe neighborhood, but the tensions between the parents created a hostile emotional climate in the home for a time.
Equilibrium	The sense of balance or consistency that family members experience. Growth and change, both positive and negative, are inevitable aspects of human development, but too much inconsistency creates confusion and resentment.	Teachers can help work with families during times of change to maintain stability and consistency. For example, at the Early Head Start center, the Robeson twins were kept in the same class with the same teachers for two years during the period of upheaval in their family. Then the staff worked with the Head Start program to transition the twins smoothly to preschool.

Source: Based on L. G. Christian, 2006. Understanding families: Applying family systems theory to early childhood practice. *Young Children,* *61*(1), 12–20.

expenses, the National Center for Children in Poverty (Koball & Jiang, 2018) estimates that 41% of children live in low-income families. In 2016, younger children are more likely than older children to live in poverty, with rates of deep poverty highest for children under three. While income alone is not responsible for child development problems, growing up in poverty creates risk of negative outcomes for children, including increased likelihood of abuse, neglect, school failure, delinquency, and violence.

Child poverty continues to grow despite the fact that most poor children live in working families (Children's Defense Fund [CDF], 2017). Moreover, a disproportionate number of children of color live in poverty (CDF, 2017). Compared to only 12% of White children,

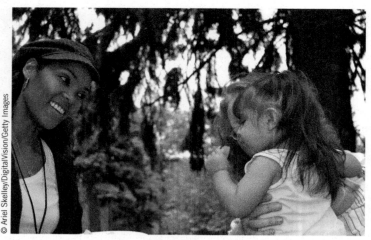

Programs such as Head Start and Early Head Start are designed to serve our nation's economically disadvantaged families. Early childhood teachers work closely with families, and can be resources to help strengthen and build resilience in families facing challenges.

34% of African American, 28% of Hispanic and Asian, and 35% of American Indian children under age 5 are poor (Koball & Jiang, 2018). Circumstances for children of immigrants are most dire. Over half are low-income, compared to only 38% of children of native-born parents.

Children living in poverty are at risk for poor physical and dental health, are more likely to experience hunger and malnutrition, and are less likely to have access to health care (CDF, 2017). The median income for African American, Hispanic, and American Indian families is roughly half that of White families. Although the number of children with health insurance is at an all-time high, 1 in 6 immigrant children are uninsured, compared to 1 in 20 children of U.S. citizens (CDF, 2017). Although decreasing, homelessness among families with young children remains a problem; over a third of homeless people are in families with children (CDF, 2017).

Cumulative risk factors increase the likelihood of poor outcomes for children. Poverty coupled with other factors such as low level of parent education (less than high school), single-parent family, or a teen parent multiplies risk. Economic stress also affects two-parent families. Almost 65% of mothers of children under age 6 are in the workforce (U.S. Bureau of Labor Statistics, 2017), which adds the high cost of child care for many financially strapped families.

Resilient Families Despite difficult family circumstances and challenges, it is important to note that poverty, neglect, and discrimination do not necessarily set children up for failure. Families' assets or strengths—their protective factors—can counter the potential negative effects of risks (Cabrera, 2013). Although public attention tends to focus on all that is wrong with the American family, compelling evidence exists that many families—including those living in the most difficult circumstances—have inner strengths that counter risk factors and predict positive results for children (Iruka, 2013).

Contemporary families have high levels of important family strengths: closeness, concern, caring, and interaction (Moore, Chalk, Scarpa, & Vandivere, 2002). Moreover, a positive, caring relationship with a parent can mitigate many risk factors (Center on the Developing Child, n.d.). Similarly, ongoing positive relationships with other adults, especially caregivers and teachers, are important protective factors (Driscoll, Wang, Mashburn, & Pianta, 2011).

Child Trends (2015) finds that about 10% of children growing up in two-parent, low-conflict families have problems, whereas 20% of all other children experience problems. Their conclusion is somewhat contrary to the popular images of at-risk children and families today: Most kids do fine. Some children with highly stable families will have problems; more children whose families experience several risk factors will struggle. The takeaway message with regard to risk and protective factors is that there are no guarantees. Poor outcomes are not inevitable for children placed at risk, just as "low risk" is not a guarantee of success in life. Given the critical role of families in children's development and learning, the simple conclusion is that anything we can do to strengthen families is a good idea (Child Trends, 2015). Later in this chapter, we discuss family-centered practices, which include research-based, effective strategies to support families.

Because they work directly with families as well as children, early childhood educators have the opportunity as well as the responsibility to strengthen families. In the next section, we address ways teachers can build reciprocal relationships with families toward the goal of achieving better outcomes for all children.

✓ Check Your Understanding 7.1

Reciprocal Relationships with Families and Family-Centered Practices

In her book on partnerships with parents, Janis Keyser (2017) describes her development as an early childhood professional as progressing through three stages of relationship with parents: save the child, save the parents, and draw on parents' expertise. These stages are identical to my own experience and that of many other early childhood teachers.

Like many others in the early childhood profession, Keyser chose this field because of her love of children. In the earliest days of her practice, when she encountered a child whose needs were great, she entered the first stage: "save the child." Inevitably there would be several children whom she thought if only she could save them from their parents, their lives would be better. She quickly realized the futility of this approach and moved on to the next stage of her development, which she calls "save the parents." Realizing that it would be impossible to save all of the children from their parents, she determined to fix the parents. She thought that if she taught them everything early childhood professionals know, they would become better parents. Soon, however, she realized that this notion fails to recognize that families bring **funds of knowledge**—experiences, traditions, goals, resources, strengths, and rich culture—to their roles (Gonzalez, Moll, & Amanti, 2005; Iruka, 2013). In fact, she concluded that families add unique value to the knowledge of early childhood teachers. In the third stage of development in her relationships with families, she rejected both goals of saving children and saving parents in favor of drawing on parents' expertise to work in partnerships with them in ways that were in the children's best interests.

Keyser's story about her own development as a teacher mirrors how the profession's views of parent–teacher relationships have evolved over time. In the past and even today in some educational settings, teachers thought that they could care for and educate children almost in spite of their parents. Today, however, the prevailing view of effective practice requires reciprocal relationships and partnerships between teachers and families (National Academies of Sciences, Engineering, and Medicine 2016). Reciprocal relationships are two-way relationships in which information and power are shared. Before describing the elements of effective partnerships, it is important to clarify the distinct roles of teachers and parents in the lives of young children.

funds of knowledge
Experiences, traditions, goals, resources, and rich culture that families bring to their roles.

Roles of Teachers and Parents

One of the challenges to building effective partnerships for early childhood teachers is that the younger the child in their care, the more blurred the lines become between families and teachers. Nevertheless, there are definite distinctions between the roles of parent and teacher. Children's relationships with their family members often last a lifetime. They view their children's development and learning more emotionally. Their relationships are often intense and culturally embedded. While family members are considered children's "first teacher," they typically have no training in how to care for and educate their child. While teachers' relationships with children are very important for their learning and development, they typically have short-term relationships with children and find it easier to be objective. Furthermore, teachers benefit from formal education related to supporting children's learning and development. These distinctions help explain why both perspectives are essential in providing high-quality care and education for each child (Keyser, 2017).

Young children are integrally connected to their families. Effective early childhood programs depend on positive relationships between teachers and parents.

Understanding these different but complementary roles reminds teachers of the important boundaries between their roles and those of parents. Children benefit greatly from the lasting unconditional love of at least one adult, usually a parent (Center on the Developing Child, n.d.). At the same time, children benefit from the more objective view that teachers can bring when they evaluate the children's needs and strengths. To help all of their students, teachers can draw on their experience from observing many children's development and knowing how to effectively support children's social and academic development in group situations such as that of the school or child care center. By contrast, parents are the most knowledgeable sources of information about their child's development and experience in settings outside the school. Moreover, parents are the most accurate, key informants about children's cultural and linguistic backgrounds. Once teachers are clear about what they and parents bring to the table, the opportunity exists to build reciprocal relationships with families.

Family-Centered Practices

Reciprocal relationships can develop only in an atmosphere of mutual respect, trust, cooperation, and shared responsibility. These are the elements of what is now called *family-centered care* or *family-centered practices* (Child Welfare Information Gateway, 2014).

family-centered practice
Providing resources and supports to families that promote children's development and learning while at the same time strengthen the competency of families in their role.

Family-centered practices is a term that originated in the early childhood special education community. According to special educators, family-centered practices elevate the family's individual needs and support families' ability to make decisions and act to promote children's development and learning. At the same time, such practices strengthen the competence of families in their roles and improve family well-being in the best interest of their child and family (Division for Early Childhood [DEC], 2014; DEC, 2016). Professionals focus on building family capacities and engaging in productive collaboration. Professionals may provide parent education to support parents' competence, confidence, and enjoyment of interactions with their child. To achieve these goals, professionals must actively involve families, be responsive to their requests, and treat them with dignity and respect.

Video Example 7.1:

Family-Centered Practices

An early childhood special educator discusses the active role of the family of a child with a disability. What are the legal requirements regarding the role of families of children with disabilities that should be applied to serving all children and families?

Considerable research documents the benefits of family-centered practices for children and families, especially for children with disabilities and special needs (Trivette, Dunst, & Hamby, 2010; DEC, 2014). Although family-centered practices have been at the heart of early childhood special education, they are also now recognized as essential elements of all high-quality early childhood programs (National Association for the Education of Young Children [NAEYC], 2016). The *Including All Children* feature demonstrates the value of family-centered practices for children and their families.

Regardless of the early childhood context, family-centered practices focus on building partnerships with families. These partnerships are characterized by several key principles: mutual respect and trust; regular, frequent two-way communication; collaboration, shared decision making and shared power; and negotiation of conflicts toward win-win solutions (Bredekamp, 1997a, 1997b). Iruka (2013) suggests that professionals employ a bi-directional approach when working with racially and ethnically diverse families. Such an approach integrates the families' culture and perspectives, and capitalizes on their strengths. What this means for teachers is that efforts to increase family engagement should include extensive, meaningful input from families on their routines, traditions, interaction preferences, and individual needs.

Including All Children
Family-Centered Practices

Teachers' skill in using family-centered practices is essential to the success of programs for children with disabilities. Family-centered practices reflect the understanding that supporting families' capacities will help children thrive, as we see in the following example.

Jennifer, a family service worker from the Beginnings Child Development Center, works with Carolyn and Mike's son, Ben. Three-year-old Ben is diagnosed with language and social skills delays and also struggles with self-regulation. Jennifer alternates her visits between Ben's preschool classroom and his family home. She visits Ben's home in the evening so Mike and Carolyn can both be there. At their last visit, Ben's parents shared that they struggled to know how to play with Ben. When she arrives at their home, Jennifer spies Ben behind a chair, kneels down, and pulls some cars from Ben's home toy basket. As Ben comes closer, Jennifer suggests to Mike that he might join in their play. Jennifer models how to provide a choice for Ben to engage him in the play. With a toy in each hand, Jennifer brings them close to her face and asks, "Ben, do you want the bus or the car?" Ben reaches for the bus, and Jennifer responds, "Show me, Ben, which one would you like to play with?" Ben points to the bus and Jennifer says, "Okay, here's the bus," handing it to Ben. She turns smiling to Mike and asks, "Want to try?" She moves to let Mike play with Ben. Jennifer understands that families need modeling and support to build their capacities around playing with their children.

Jennifer's tablet rings, and she answers a video call from Ben's teacher, Rashida, who would like to join Jennifer in her home visit but must be home in the evening. She—and Ben's family—are happy to meet with Rashida using Skype, and share successes and ideas for Ben's progress. Rashida has posted a video of Ben and another child playing at the sand table on their secure school website. She plays the video highlighting Ben's cooperative play, as the other child and Ben take turns pouring sand into a bucket and laughing together when they dump it out. Rashida points out how well Ben's social skills and friendships have developed, and they chat about some ideas for successful play dates outside of school. Before she hangs up, Rashida tells them to look for a surprise text the next day.

Carolyn notices Ben enjoying the cars, and comments on how he is using more words. Jennifer shows Carolyn how she can use a paper towel roll to make a "track" for small cars. Carolyn loves the idea, and decides to tape the track to the side of the refrigerator. "This way, he can play and we can talk while I am making dinner." Understanding the importance of working with families' routines, Jennifer is pleased because she knows dinnertime has been very stressful for Ben's family. Jennifer will check back in a couple of days to see how the new ideas are working. As she packs to go, Jennifer gives Mike information about the "dads' support group" he is interested in, and gives Carolyn a list of respite care providers.

The next day, Mike and Carolyn are surprised when they see that Ben used a tablet at school to take a picture of the big sand structure with cars around it. With Rashida's help, Ben sent the picture and a voice message "big garage" via text message. Mike and Carolyn find these text messages and Skype visits very valuable for keeping in touch with Ben's teacher. That day, Ben comes home from school with a printed picture of his "big garage," and they hang it on the refrigerator next to his tube track.

Jennifer spends only a little time interacting directly with Ben during this visit, because her primary goal is to provide supports to his family members that will enable them to be true partners in Ben's development and learning. She provides opportunities for teacher–parent connections using technology, and connects family members with resources such as support groups. Jennifer coaches the family on how to use learning strategies used in Ben's therapy sessions and preschool activities. By partnering with Ben's family and classroom teacher, Jennifer supports important relationships that will benefit Ben far beyond the one hour of her visit.

Mutual trust and respect develop gradually after numerous interactions. Although teachers and parents may initially disagree on certain issues, the goal is to recognize and respect one another's knowledge and expertise (Keyser, 2017). If parents feel respected, they are more likely to share information that teachers need to know.

Differences of opinion and goals are inevitable when working with other people's children. If mutual trust and respect are to be maintained and parents are to continue to be empowered, such conflicts must be negotiated toward win-win solutions (discussed later in this chapter). There are instances, however, when negotiation is not an option, such as in cases of suspected child abuse or neglect (discussed in Chapter 16). Policies regarding teachers' responsibilities for reporting child abuse should be clearly communicated to families as well as teachers (National Research Council [NRC], 2014).

Collaboration, shared decision making, and shared power can be difficult to negotiate for inexperienced teachers. Many early childhood educators fail to grasp the extent of their actual and perceived power in relationships with families. In addition, cultural differences may be a complicating factor in supporting family engagement in school community and activities. The *Culture Lens* feature describes research that sheds light on how Latino mothers may view engagement in their child's education differently than mothers of other cultural groups—and how building on funds of knowledge and strengths can support the family and child in the educational process.

If you, like many of your colleagues, think early childhood education involves just working with children, you might feel intimidated by the idea of developing reciprocal relationships with families. In the next section, we address the fundamental skill of two-way communication with families.

Video Example 7.2:

Serving Culturally and Linguistically Diverse Families

In this video, an elementary school principal talks about working with Hispanic and Hmong families. How does culture affect parents' relationships and communication with the school? What is done to support parents, teachers, and involve families?

Culture Lens

Developing Partnerships with Hispanic/Latino Families

Research shows that children develop and learn best when families are engaged in their children's education. However, teachers are sometimes frustrated when families don't participate in the parent involvement activities offered. Some families don't attend back-to-school night, rarely return paperwork, or fail to volunteer for school activities. Developing productive relationships and partnerships with families can be challenging. Just as with children, a teacher cannot assume a "one-size-fits-all" approach toward building family partnerships. When families' culture and language are different from the school culture, it can be even more challenging.

Families' cultural perspectives impact how they engage in the school community and in their children's educational activities. Taking a perspective of capitalizing on family strengths and funds of knowledge, Manica Ramos interviewed immigrant Latino mothers about how culture impacted their involvement in their preschool-aged children's education. Ramos found that Latino mothers were very invested in their children's education, and that they expressed this investment in ways that were similar to and different from non-Latino families. For example, Latino mothers in Ramos's study reported attending student–teacher conferences and reading to their children, similar to school expectations. However, they also discussed forms of involvement in their children's education that were more culturally specific to Latino families,

including *sacrificios* (sacrifices), *consejos* (advice), and *apoyo* (moral support).

Most mothers shared that they believed in making sacrifices (*sacrificios*) to support their children's education, and took great pride in working hard to support their children's education. They described how they gave advice (*consejos*) to their children to support their education, which for these Latino mothers included academic and social education. Finally, they described how they saw their role related to supporting their children's motivation to learn, morale and confidence, and respect (*respeto*) related to learning.

Ramos translated her findings to important implications for teachers working with immigrant families and non–European American families, in addition to Latino families. She recommends that teachers learn about the family cultures of the children in the classroom and school—from the families themselves. Ramos encourages teachers to think creatively about what constitutes family engagement opportunities and consult with families on how they would like to be engaged. To understand different family values and beliefs, Ramos recommends visiting families regularly in their homes to develop warm and productive relationships.

Source: M. Ramos, 2014. *The strengths of Latina mothers in supporting their children's education: A cultural perspective.* Bethesda, MD: Child Trends. Retrieved February 27, 2018, from www.childtrends.org.

Effective Communication with Families

Building relationships with families requires effective communication—one of the biggest challenges teachers face. Before we describe positive ways of communicating with families, we begin with considering some of the most common barriers to effective communication.

Barriers to Effective Communication

Effective communication between teachers and families means more than sharing information; it means developing shared understanding about who the child is, each party's goals, and how to achieve them. Early childhood education covers a broad age span—from birth through age 8. During the earliest years, children are most likely to be served in some form of child care while parents work. At the other end of the age continuum, children are in school and perhaps child care for part of the day. In each of these situations, communication problems can arise.

Communication Problems in Child Care Settings   In child care programs for infants, toddlers, and young preschoolers, deep emotions can consume parents as they leave their children in someone else's care, which can create tension with teachers. Following are examples of typical situations that arise over the care of young children and the feelings they may generate in parents:

- *Competition.* Parents may feel jealous if the child becomes attached to another adult. Three-year-old Madison has been in child care for one month. Her mother feels conflicted about it and threatened by the growing relationship between Madison and her teacher. She tells her husband, "I'm afraid Madison loves her teacher more than me. When I left the center, Madison called her teacher 'Mommy,' and I cried all the way to work."
- *Guilt and loss.* At times, parents feel a sense of loss over missed experiences. Jacob is 11 months old. His mother is torn between her desire to spend more time with him and her rewarding but demanding career. She worked very hard to earn her law degree, and her job is stressful. At the same time, she feels guilty about neglecting Jacob. She thinks, "I'm going to miss seeing my baby's first steps."
- *Differing child-rearing goals.* Disagreements between parents and teachers, both large and small, are inevitable. Child-rearing goals and practices are often culturally influenced. Tawanna, who is 4½ years old, enrolled in a new center recently, and her father has concerns about the informality and lack of emphasis on academic skills. He tells his wife, "I don't like Tawanna getting dirty at school. And I want her to learn to read to be ready for school, but they say that's not important yet. And they let the children call them by their first names in that school. I want Tawanna to learn good manners."
- *Power struggles.* Parents may feel that they are losing control over their child's upbringing. Sonya is turning 6, a milestone event in her family. Her grandmother is incensed, however, because she wants to hold a party at school, and the teachers won't let her control it. She tells her friend, "They say I can't send cupcakes for Sonya's birthday because they're not healthy food, but she wants cupcakes and so do I."

These parents' feelings illustrate that sharing their children with other adults is difficult and can be threatening to the close parent–child relationship. When other people have considerable influence over their children's lives, parents can feel powerless.

© P Deliss/Newscom

Infant/toddler teachers sometimes find that parents may feel threatened or unsure about sharing their child's care with another person. How can this teacher build a positive relationship that will benefit the baby and the family?

Communication Problems in School

Schools and parents can encounter a number of obstacles in their efforts to communicate. Following are examples of some common barriers to communication:

• *Confusion about regulations and policies.* Parents may lack the information they need about the school's goals, procedures, and policies. For example, Summit School has a policy that parents need to be alerted in the middle of first grade about whether their children's reading is below grade level so that an intervention plan can be set up. Shelley's mother becomes very anxious: "It's only January, and the teacher thinks that Shelley will have to stay back in first grade because she's not reading. I don't want my little girl to flunk, but what can I do?"

• *Lack of flexibility.* The school may not be sensitive to parents' individual needs and concerns. Mr. Jenkins is a concerned father who wants to be involved in his children's education, but he is frustrated: "That school always has meetings and events during the day, but I can't take off work."

• *Lack of attention to individual children.* At times, parents' concerns arise from fears that teachers don't really know and understand their children. Parents may feel that teachers' expectations for their children are too low because of the child's socioeconomic status, disability, or race, as in these examples:

- Seven-year-old Abigail has Down syndrome. Her two mothers believe that the teachers don't think Abigail can learn, so they don't teach her anything.
- Ms. Rice tells her mother, "I think that teacher is racist. She assigned all the black boys to the lowest reading group."

Communication problems can arise when parents don't understand how the school functions and how they can influence decisions. They may feel powerless to alter a policy or the teacher's perceptions about their child. Teachers may think they provide adequate information, but if the parent doesn't understand the message, considerable anxiety and confusion may result for the parents and the child as well.

At other times, power struggles can ensue due to conflicting goals. Some families have very high expectations for their children's success in school, so they may pressure teachers and children to ensure academic achievement. The term *helicopter parent* describes parents who "hover over" their children and try to control everything in their lives. Some parents will come forward and complain often, whereas others are too intimidated to voice even the gentlest concerns.

To address these communication problems openly and honestly, teachers can use a variety of strategies, discussed next, that will benefit both the child and the family.

Effective Communication Strategies

Communication is the basis of all relationships. Positive relationships begin when parents feel welcome in the school.

A Welcoming Environment On entering a school or child care center, parents can usually tell how welcome they are. The environment communicates messages about whether families are expected to be regular participants, infrequent guests, or simple agents of transmittal. Is there a sign greeting children and families? Do teachers greet them at the door? Is there an area where they can gather and visit with each other? Are there adult-sized chairs? Is there a bulletin board stocked with current information? Can parents easily find their children's work and space for their belongings?

The physical environment plays an important role in welcoming families. However, face-to-face communication between teachers and parents is more important.

Types of Messages Substantive communication is possible and more effective when it is built on a strong base of casual, routine conversation. Think of the messages that teachers need to send to parents as basically two kinds: tennis balls and slippery eggs (NAEYC, 1998).

Picture yourself tossing a tennis ball back and forth from hand to hand. **Tennis ball messages** are easily "tossed" and received. These messages help form the foundation of a relationship. Tennis ball messages constitute the everyday chitchat between teachers and parents. This kind of back-and-forth communication helps each party in the relationship to learn and become comfortable with the other's style.

> *Teacher:* Hello, Mr. Watkins, it's good to see Neil back at school today. I hope your family enjoyed the visit with his grandparents.
> *Parent:* We had a great time. They live so far away that Neil only sees them a few times a year. They had to leave this morning, so we are all a little down.

Now picture yourself tossing a slippery egg to another person. You would hold the egg carefully and toss it very gingerly, assuming that the other person is prepared to catch it with equal care. If the egg were tossed carelessly or too abruptly, a mess would result. The same is true of **slippery egg messages**. They are more difficult to toss and catch, and must be tossed gently to be sure that the catcher receives the communication as intended (NAEYC, 1998). Even the best of relationships requires slippery egg messages at times. Some relationships seem to consist almost entirely of slippery egg communications. How these messages are sent—the style of communication—determines how well they are received, as we see in the next section.

Communication Styles There are at least three styles of communication: passive, aggressive, and assertive (NAEYC, 1998). **Passive communication** is sensitive to the listener's feelings, but so vague that the message is easily misunderstood. The listener becomes confused about expectations and loses trust. **Aggressive communication** is truthful, but the delivery is hurtful. The listener feels angry and resentful, and the relationship is damaged. **Assertive communication**—telling the truth in a thoughtful and considerate way—is the most effective form of communication. Assertive communication strengthens relationships and increases the likelihood of successfully resolving problems.

The goal in sending a slippery egg message—the kind that is difficult to send as well as to receive—is to use assertive communication. Compared to passive or aggressive styles of communication, assertive communication succeeds in delivering the difficult message while also maintaining and perhaps deepening the relationship.

Following is an example of these three communication styles in action. First-grade teacher Julia Sykes is concerned that one of her students, Shawn Jameson, is not making progress in reading. Julia sets up a meeting with Shawn's mother to discuss the problem. They chat comfortably for a few minutes, but Ms. Jameson is clearly nervous, anticipating bad news. Here are three ways that Julia might present the situation:

- *Passive communication.* "I know you are worried about how Shawn is doing in school, and so am I: All the children take time to get settled and he'll come around as soon as he's ready." With such a passive statement, Julia demonstrates caring for the parent and child, but fails to convey the seriousness of the situation. Ms. Jameson is confused and a little angry because she doesn't understand why she took off work for this meeting.
- *Aggressive communication.* "We've got a problem with Shawn. He is so far behind in reading, he'll probably have to repeat first grade." Julia dreaded delivering this bad news, so she blurted it out with little concern for Ms. Jameson's feelings. Ms. Jameson immediately becomes defensive: "What do you mean? It's your job to teach him to read!"

tennis ball messages
Communications that are easily "tossed" and received and that help form the foundation of a relationship; they constitute the everyday chitchat between teachers and parents.

slippery egg messages
Communications that are difficult to "toss" (send) and "catch" (receive), and must be expressed gently to be sure that the "catcher" receives the communication as intended.

© Pearson Education

Video Example 7.3:

Building Positive Relationships

This video provides an example of the start of the school day in a typical preschool classroom. How do these teachers use everyday conversations to build positive, reciprocal relationships with families? What strategies do the teachers use to help the children transition from home to school? And how does the teacher help the little boy who is struggling to say goodbye to his mom?

passive communication
Speaking in a way that is sensitive to the listener's feelings, but so vague that the message is easily misunderstood.

aggressive communication
Speaking the truth in a hurtful way.

assertive communication
Telling the truth in a thoughtful and considerate way; considered the most effective form of communication.

- *Assertive communication.* "Ms. Jameson, during the first three months of school, I've found that Shawn isn't making the reading progress that he should be. We don't expect all the children to learn to read at the same time. But I'm concerned that if he falls further behind, he will really have a hard time catching up. What I'd like to do is have a reading specialist evaluate him to see if he would benefit from tutoring, which is provided free by the school. I wanted you to come in today so we could talk about how Shawn is doing at home and what options we have to help him." In this communication, Julia conveys caring for Shawn and his mother, but she also tells the truth—that there is a problem and there are possible solutions to work on together.

Assertive communication is often effective when the teacher is working with challenging situations and distraught or angry parents. As the *Becoming an Intentional Teacher* feature reveals, it is important to be open and really listen to parents' concerns and complaints. Teachers use many different vehicles to accomplish clear, honest, regular communication. In the sections that follow, we describe some of these strategies.

Becoming an Intentional Teacher

Responding to Parents: Welcoming "Complainers"

Here's What Happened   I taught 3- and 4-year-olds in an NAEYC-accredited child care center. Our program was well known in the community as a high-quality center. I taught there for 10 years, and we enjoyed good relationships with our families. One mother, Mrs. Mayer, became a constant complainer, however, when her little boy, Noah, kept getting sick. I knew that Noah had asthma, so I wasn't surprised when he missed days at the center. I was surprised, however, by how much Mrs. Mayer blamed me for Noah's repeated illnesses. At first, I tried to explain to her that increased illness is not unusual for children when they are in group care. When my explanation met with resistance, I started to become defensive. I assured Mrs. Mayer that our program was licensed and accredited, which means that we meet all required health standards.

One day, when Noah returned after an absence, his mother looked particularly weary. I asked my assistant teacher to take over the group while I spoke with Mrs. Mayer privately. She explained that she had spent the night with Noah in the emergency room. As we talked, I realized that due to Noah's chronic illness, colds and other seemingly innocuous childhood sicknesses are life-threatening experiences. I gave Mrs. Mayer a copy of our center's health policy handbook and asked her to review it and give me feedback. We set up a time to meet again.

Mrs. Mayer came back to me two days later with suggestions for ways we could focus everyone's attention on illness prevention. For example, to accommodate parents so they wouldn't have to miss school or work, we often allowed sick children to attend the center when perhaps they should have stayed home. We had a policy that required children to remain home when ill. When children arrived at school with symptoms of illness, our policy said we should take the child's temperature and exclude children who had a fever. We also had a policy that stated if children were heavily sneezing and coughing or required one-on-one care for their symptoms, that they should not attend the program until their symptoms remitted. And though our program worked

hard to teach and attend to staff and child handwashing, we didn't teach them to cough or sneeze into their elbows.

To address Mrs. Mayer's concerns and to figure out a reasonable solution, I spoke with our director and asked Mrs. Mayer to join me in speaking with staff and parents. At first, some of the other parents believed that we were enforcing policy changes to accommodate just one child; however, once they heard Noah's story, most parents were sympathetic. Together we agreed to enforce the policies in place and examine their effectiveness in reducing illness overall. After a few months, Noah's asthma attacks were much less frequent. In addition, other parents reported that their children were sick less often.

Here's What I Was Thinking   Months before school begins, I work hard to build a relationship with my children's families. I make home visits, hold open houses, and write letters or emails to families to introduce myself and the school—everything I can think of. When Mrs. Mayer began to complain about Noah's getting sick at school, I wondered if she was just a negative person or if she should find another program. As I spoke more with her, I came to realize that her complaints were evidence of her commitment as a parent. In meeting with Mrs. Mayer, I learned that her experience as the parent of a chronically ill child provided valuable knowledge and a perspective that could help our program be better. I realized that it wouldn't work if I was the only one who changed health procedures, so I had to get the other parents and staff involved. The outcome was improved health for all the children and for the teachers, too.

Reflection   What issues or situations in child care programs or schools might parents frequently complain about? In the above situation, the teacher almost automatically felt defensive and initially attributed blame to the "complaining" parent. How do you think you would feel if the same parent consistently complained about your teaching? What could you do in response?

Informal Communication In programs for infants and toddlers, families and teachers must communicate daily, both morning and evening, to ensure that children receive optimum care. Morning drop-off and afternoon pickup times are good for engaging in the kind of chitchat, or tennis ball back-and-forth, communication that builds relationships between teachers and parents.

For example, "How are you this morning, Ms. Kelly? I can see that Monique doesn't look too happy. Is there something I should know to help her get settled?"

Two-year-old Monique's mom might say, "She wouldn't eat her breakfast and I had to leave or I'd be late for work." "No problem. We'll feed her here, and don't worry or you'll be late," the teacher replies.

In another circumstance, Ms. Kelly looks distraught and responds, "Monique's father left last night and I've been up all night crying."

Here is an entirely different situation, calling for an entirely different response. "I can see you are upset. I'll take Monique now so you can go to work and I'll call to let you know how she's doing. If you would like, we can talk privately later."

Moments of informal conversation are so important for building trust and mutual respect. At the same time, teachers need to make sure that children are supervised during these conversations, and that it is clear who is responsible for this duty. Any confidential conversation should be scheduled for another time.

Following are strategies for ensuring that messages are delivered:

- *Information logs.* Daily messages must be relayed about children's eating, sleeping, toileting, signs of change in mood, and changes in developmental status. For example, last night baby Maggie stood up and tried to climb out of her crib—a first in her skill achievement. When her dad drops her off at child care, he needs to let the staff know about Maggie's new skill so they can take steps to prevent accidents and ensure her safety. Given that several different people are responsible for Maggie's care throughout the day, the staff keeps written logs about each child's needs and development, and pass them along to each other.
- *Daily notes "About My Day."* This message delivery system is important for all young children, but it is essential for babies and toddlers. Very young children can't communicate for themselves to families and teachers, so daily communication can't be left to chance conversations. Written notes, text messages, or emails that take little time to complete are essential. Ms. Evans sends a message to 2½-year-old Gabriel's mother: *Gabriel had a hard time waking up from nap this afternoon. He doesn't seem to be sick, but didn't eat as much as usual.*
- *Daily chitchat.* For teachers and parents of preschoolers, regular communication—the daily chitchat—is still important for building and maintaining the relationship. Teachers need to know about events at home that may affect a child, and parents love to hear about interesting or funny things their children have said or done. Teachers should be very careful to keep this informal conversation light and save talking about more difficult issues until private, scheduled times.
- *Weekly updates.* For preschoolers and older children, regular reporting of activities, such as the topic of study or upcoming events, is sufficient. Technology such as classroom websites or blogs greatly increases the opportunities for family communication and involvement.

Children's learning is supported best when schools and families work together. Traditional parent meetings can be combined with the latest technology to achieve goals of both teachers and families. For example, in the feature *Promoting Play: Playful Homework*, a primary-school teacher enlists families' support in reinforcing school learning in playful contexts at home.

✔ Application Exercise 7.1

Arrival: A Time to Engage Families

Promoting Play

Playful Homework

Rupa's energetic group of first-graders is learning to read, write, and solve math problems. She uses district-based curricula to teach, and works hard to keep her students engaged during the day. They are progressing well, but Rupa notices that by the end of the school day, her little learners are very tired. In her school district orientation, Rupa learned that homework is intended for two main purposes: 1) to provide practice and reinforcement for concepts and skills learned during the day, and 2) to inform and engage families regarding what children are learning in school. Rupa knows it is important to engage families in their children's learning, but a few parents shared at conference time that homework, usually worksheets or reading, has often ended in tears and tension. Rupa read about schools in Finland and how their world-class public schools support learning by increasing creative play and decreasing sit-down homework. She decided to give it a try. Here is her Rupa's note home to families:

Dear Families,

For the next few months, we are going to try a new homework routine, one that supports your child's learning practice and allows you to play with your child, reinforce learning, and keep your child interested in learning. I'll send home new ideas every week. Try these games, change them or expand them, and make them as active as you and your child like. But remember that the goal is to *KEEP LEARNING FUN!* I will invite children to share their playful homework experiences during class meeting every morning. Have fun, Ms. Rupa

- Shape Treasure Hunt. Search throughout your home for examples of all the different shapes you and your child can find. Practice describing the shapes with your child as you search, for example, "We are searching for a treasure of triangles. How many sides will it have? How many corners?" This

will support your child's geometric learning, especially the ability to describe *how* you recognize different shapes. Feel free to look up new shapes (such as parallelogram) on the internet at home or the library!

- Grocery Store Game. Using coins, have your child "purchase" food for dinner from your cabinets and refrigerator. Price each item and add up the cost of the dinner. Count aloud with your child, and talk about healthy food while you are at it. This will help your child practice counting and learn about how money works.

- Play consonant "I Spy Spelling," finding things in your home that begin or end with consonants. Keep track of your spy discoveries by writing the words in a notebook or piece of paper. Take turns writing with your child, and provide enough support that it is challenging but not too difficult. For example, "I spy something that begins with the letter *R.*" When you child guesses that it is the *rug,* write *rug* together on a piece of paper. Then give your child a turn to spy. This will help your child with spelling practice—be sure to reinforce efforts at spelling and worry less about perfection.

- Storytelling. Take turns making up sentences to a story. Encourage creative, silly or adventurous stories. You may want to record them on your phone or tablet and see what kinds of fun things you imagine together. Let your child take the lead on the topic, and follow along with the fun. This will help your child understand narrative, sequencing and increase vocabulary—all important for learning to read.

Source: A. Partenan, December 29, 2011. What Americans keep ignoring about Finland's school success. *The Atlantic.* Retrieved February 26, 2018 from www.theatlantic.com/national/archive/2011/12/what-americans-keep-ignoring-about-finlands-school-success/250564/

Use Technology

Technology has transformed all communication in the 21st century. Parents are more accessible than ever because of handheld mobile devices. Individual emails, texts, or voicemail messages can be used to share information about a child's daily activity or progress. Teachers, along with children, can create and maintain a classroom or school website where they post photos and samples of children's work. The potential is limited only by their imaginations and the technological resources available. Kaldor (2015) recommends many ways that teachers can use technology to strengthen relationships with families and increase family engagement in the school community, such as:

- Use video e-introduction before the school year begins. By posting on YouTube or a secure website and emailing the link, children and family members can see the classroom and learn about their child's teacher.
- Use video from the classroom to demonstrate daily routines and provide tips for transitions and guiding children's positive behavior.
- Use the Message from Me online feature. Children can use tablets and cameras to take photos or videos of classroom activities and send with an audio message to their family.
- Create e-books to share with families. Children can use photos, text, and audio recordings to document classroom experiences and produce e-books that can be shared online or printed, then read at home with family.
- Use messaging technology, such as instant message, Twitter, or WhatsApp to send messages and images (photos or videos) of special happenings during the school day.

Arguing that technology devices should be used responsibly and respectfully, Kaldor (2015) provides guidelines for how to do a BYOD (Bring Your Own Device) Night. Rather than leaving devices behind, families bring their devices, learn how to connect with their child's classroom and school, and see demonstrations of children's technology use in the classroom. Families learn how to respect boundaries around technological communication, and sign a digital contract.

Families may turn to early childhood professionals to learn about using technology with their children. Teachers can provide important information regarding how children use technology and how much they use it. Children under 3 years old should have few, short periods of screen time combined with lively interaction with family members (Lerner & Barr, 2014). Common Sense Media's website provides guidelines and ideas for families to use technology to enhance social relationships and learning.

Technology can make communication with families much more efficient. For example, listservs can be used to inform parents of logistical information such as reminders about school closings. Technology may help teachers communicate with families whose parents live in different homes, for example. Research shows that young parents and fathers rely heavily on technology to keep in touch with schools and engage in their children's development and learning (Grove, 2016). However, it is also important to recognize limitations of technology. For example, sensitive information should typically not be shared by text or email—telephone conversations or in-person meetings are much better for discussing behavior concerns and for problem solving (Kaldor, 2015). Teachers should set clear boundaries on communicating with families, and families' preferences for communication should be respected. For example, teachers may not be willing to answer emails in the evening while they are with their own family, but will answer the next day. These boundaries and expectations should be clearly stated in the digital contract.

Websites need to be password secured to limit access. Interactive sites are labor intensive, as they need to be checked and responded to regularly and monitored for inappropriate content. For families that do not speak or read English, teachers should be prepared to enlist the assistance of a bilingual colleague or an online translator application (Nemeth, 2015). Finally, email and especially texting may foster the use of incorrect grammar and

Video Example 7.4:

Engaging Parents in Programs and Schools

In this video, two preschool teachers discuss how they create and maintain relationships with parents and families. What specific strategies do they use? How do they use technology? And do you think they are effective at engaging families?

spelling. Teachers should always be accurate in written communication, electronic or otherwise.

Conferencing In addition to their everyday, routine communication with families, teachers and parents need to meet for more formal regular conferences. Traditionally, the purpose of parent–teacher conferences has been for teachers to report on children's progress. These conferences are usually a one-way communication, with teachers providing information to parents, who serve as the passive audience. With one-way communications, however, parents might feel as though the teachers are issuing a report card on their parenting.

More effective conferences promote two-way communication (Scully et al., 2015). Teachers not only provide parents with information about their child's progress but also listen to what parents say about their child's development and learning. In this setting, parents and teachers have a conversation and ask as well as answer questions.

Because families have diverse needs and schedules, arranging conference times can be tricky. Consider Noreen Hayes, a kindergarten teacher in a large urban school district. Three months into the school year, she is preparing for her first set of formal family conferences. Because many of the families work two jobs or odd hours, she is concerned that scheduling conferences will be difficult. To ease the stress for families, she offers a full week of times for them to sign up, including early morning, evening, and weekend hours. To make sure she can accommodate these families, she arranges for community volunteers to provide babysitting and translation services as needed. She also arranges for snacks to be available for parents arriving after work. She organizes the seating arrangement with adult-sized chairs comfortably facing each other. Before conferences, she carefully collects samples of drawings, writing, and photos of projects and other work to share with each child's parents. Consider this scenario:

> When Jillian's mother arrives looking nervous, Noreen offers her coffee. After they are comfortable, Noreen begins by saying, "Jillian is such a curious little girl. Every day, her questions keep me on my toes. Last week, before we visited the aquarium, she wanted to know how the fish breathe."
>
> Jillian's mother smiles and says, "She drives us crazy with her why, why, why."
>
> "Let me show you some of the things she's been learning," Noreen replies, "and how she's discovering ways to get answers to her questions."
>
> When Noreen describes some of the literacy goals, Jillian's mother says, "Oh, I know. At home, she is always rhyming words and retelling me the stories you read."
>
> Noreen makes a note about what she's learned from this parent because Jillian has not yet demonstrated these skills at school.

As children get older, three-way conferencing becomes more possible and desirable. Kia is a third-grader whose parents are surprised to find that during the "parent–teacher" conference, their role is primarily to observe while Kia and her teacher, Mr. Colbert, have a conversation about her work. Kia reports on how well she thinks she's doing and sets a goal for next term: to read eight chapter books. He then asks what she wants to be when she grows up. "A chef!" she replies. He asks her to pretend she is interviewing for a job and convince him that she would make a good chef. Kia proceeds to describe how she helps her mom cook, reads cookbooks, and makes up her own recipes—exhibiting her language and literacy skills, general knowledge, and reasoning ability as well as her confidence and competence. Kia's parents watch in wonder as their usually soft-spoken and shy daughter becomes increasingly animated.

Privately, her Dad questions Mr. Colbert about whether reading eight books will be too hard for her. "Trust her," replies Mr. Colbert.

These two examples include many key points to keep in mind when preparing and conducting conferences with families. Table 7.2 summarizes principles for planning and conducting family conferences. Formal conferences take considerable time to plan and carry out effectively. This time is well spent, however, when it is used to build partnerships and solve problems.

Home Visiting In **home visiting**, a teacher goes to the child's home on a regular basis to exchange information with parents. Home visiting has a long tradition in early

home visiting Visits made by a teacher to the child's home on a regular basis to get to know children and their families.

TABLE 7.2 Planning and Conducting Family Conferences

Principles of Effective Conferences	Strategies for Implementing Conferences
Prepare families in advance.	Notify families in writing about the purpose of the conference. Ask families to think about what goals they have for the conference and for their children, what information they want to share, and what questions they want to ask.
Schedule the conferences at times convenient for parents as well as teachers.	Accommodate parents' work schedules as much as possible. Set a specific time limit for the conference, 20 to 30 minutes, so parents can plan accordingly.
Provide appropriate space for the conference.	The space should be private to ensure confidential conversations. The furniture arrangement should communicate openness and comfort; use adult-sized chairs around a table or in front of a desk. There should be no physical barrier between teachers and families, such as a desk that sets up an artificial power relationship.
Collect children's portfolios or samples of their work.	Use examples of children's work as a springboard for discussion. Involve children themselves in this process.
Plan the conference agenda.	Make sure to include time to talk about children's progress and ask questions of each other.
Always begin on a positive note.	Begin your discussion about the child by sharing a specific comment about the child's strengths, interests, or abilities. An anxious parent can then relax, become less defensive, and be more able to listen and talk freely.
Plan in advance how to deliver a slippery egg message.	When you have difficult information or a problem to discuss, think in advance how you would phrase the concern and what suggestions or solutions you would offer. "Four-year-olds are just learning how to make friends. I have observed that Kenny often plays alone, and sometimes when he tries to join in, he gets aggressive. I thought maybe he could bring something interesting from home to get the other children's attention in a positive way. I'm also going to give him some phrases to say when he wants to play. I wondered if he has had any difficulty like this at home or in the neighborhood, or if you have any ideas for me to help Kenny make friends."
Give and receive information about children's progress.	Use open-ended questions as much as possible. Two-way communication, shared power, and collaborative decision making build true partnerships with families. "Reshia loves the construction center and is learning words for all the tools and equipment. What does she like to talk about at home?"
Set goals together for next steps.	Strive to identify a common goal and create a plan to work together. "I hear you saying that you want Garrett to learn to use the toilet on his own as soon as possible, before the new baby is born. That's a goal we share. But he hasn't shown any interest at the center yet. What's he doing at home? Maybe we could try to be consistent in how we work with him."

Source: Based on P. A. Scully & C.H. Barbour, 2015. *Families, schools, and communities: Building partnerships for educating children* (6th ed.). Upper Saddle River, NJ: Pearson; and J. Keyser, 2017. *From parents to partners: Building a family-centered early childhood program.* St. Paul, MN: Redleaf Press.

Video Example 7.5:

Parent–Teacher Conference

After studying Table 7.2, take note of the interactions between a parent and teacher in the parent-teacher conference featured in this video. What effective strategies does the teacher use to share information with Kayla's mother? How do you think Kayla's mother is feeling during the conference? How does the teacher learn new ways to work with Kayla in the classroom?

childhood education. For example, the model early childhood programs that demonstrated lasting effects, such as the Perry Preschool Project and the Abecedarian Project, included weekly home visits. Since its inception, Head Start has required home visits. Currently, Head Start requires at least two home visits per program year. Two types of home visiting exist—teacher home visits and home-based programs.

Teacher Home Visits Home visits are an excellent way for every teacher to establish more comfortable relationships with families, and children usually love the idea of their teacher visiting them at home. Conferences are typically held at school or in the child care center—on the teacher's turf. As a result, a disproportionate amount of power is attributed to the professionals, putting parents at somewhat of a disadvantage. Home visits by teachers can be effective in creating a more reciprocal relationship and enhancing children's learning. Even middle schools are now discovering the power of home visiting to increase student achievement and motivation. Following are some guidelines for successful home visits:

•   Be available for a home visit. Let families know that you would like to visit the children at home to make them more comfortable with you and to learn more about their interests. Do not be offended if families decline the opportunity.

•   *Set a time for the visit and stick to it.* Visits should last from 15 to 30 minutes.

• *Reassure families in advance about the visit's purpose.* Families need to know that you do not expect them to entertain you, feed you, or clean up for your visit. Nevertheless, teachers should be respectful of diverse cultural perspectives; for example, some cultural groups would be hurt or insulted if a guest refused food.

• *Include the child in the visit.* Ask children to share something they like to do at home or in the community.

• *If you take a photo, ask permission first, and perhaps pose the family together at the front door to protect their privacy.* Show the family the photo on your digital camera that you will display at school.

Home-Based Programs Child development programs based on visits to families—**home-based programs**—are designed to support parents in the parenting role, fully involve them in their children's education, and help them achieve their own life goals. About 35% of Early Head Start programs are home-based (Head Start, 2016). Considerable research demonstrating the lasting benefits of home-visiting programs for expectant and new parents, infants, and toddlers has led to significant expansion and increases in funding (HHS, n.d.). Home-visiting programs enhance mother and child health, strengthen parenting skills, reduce child abuse, increase children's achievement, and have lasting economic benefits for parents by decreasing unemployment and welfare dependence (Novoa & Taylor, 2017).

The most effective home-visiting programs employ qualified early childhood professionals who actively engage parents with their children. Parents stay in close proximity to the child and home visitor, interact and play with their child, and learn how to use daily activities of life to promote children's development.

Meeting on Neutral Ground In recent years, teacher home visits have become more challenging for several reasons. They are time consuming, and union contracts may discourage them. Because children do not live in self-contained communities and take transportation to school, home visits become logistically difficult. Teachers may feel unsafe visiting communities where there have been incidents involving violence or drugs. Likewise, some families may be uncomfortable about teachers' visiting for reasons of

home-based programs
Programs based on visits to families designed to support parents in the parenting role, involve them in their children's education, and help them achieve their own life goals.

poverty, differences in language and cultural background, or simply wanting to protect their privacy.

Given that home visiting and conferencing at school can be threatening or difficult, some teachers find that meeting families on neutral ground such as a local coffee shop or fast-food restaurant may be the best strategy (Powell, 2013). Talking in a less formal setting over a cup of coffee, parents and teachers may be more relaxed and able to work out solutions to difficult problems.

Early childhood education is most effective when there is regular two-way communication between families and teachers. Truly effective programs go beyond communication to active engagement of families in their children's education, a topic addressed in the next section.

✓ Check Your Understanding 7.3

Family Engagement in Programs and Schools

More than 40 years of research confirms that family engagement has a positive impact on children's achievement in school (Dearing, Sibley & Nguyen, 2015). The benefits are so well established that they are written into public law. For example, the Head Start program requires parent involvement at all levels, from classroom interaction with children to representation on policy-making boards. Special education laws also dictate specific roles for families as decision makers about services for their children. In the sections that follow, we examine research on the benefits of family involvement and then describe ways to engage families meaningfully in their children's education.

Benefits of Family Engagement

A thorough review of research (Dearing, Sibly & Nguyen, 2015) summarizes the impact of family engagement on children's achievement in school. When families are more intensely engaged in their children's early learning experiences at home and school, children:

- Demonstrate higher achievement
- Have more positive feelings toward learning and school
- Are more motivated in their learning
- Have better problem-solving and study skills

Further, engaging families can reduce family risk, increase resilience, and be an especially effective deterrent to child abuse (Lim, 2012). Research shows that children prosper when families of all income and education levels and of diverse cultural backgrounds support their children's learning at home (National Academies of Sciences, Engineering, and Medicine, 2016).

Family engagement in school has the greatest benefit for children at risk of school failure (Sheridan, Holmes, Smith & Moen, 2016). When low-income families become more involved in school from kindergarten to fifth grade, children's literacy performance increases significantly (Dearing et al., 2015). Typically, there is an achievement gap in literacy performance between children of more- and less-educated mothers, but this gap is nonexistent when family engagement levels are high (Dearing, Kreider, Simpkins, & Weiss, 2007). Therefore, schools need to make an extra effort to involve all families because this would be an effective way to address the achievement gap between children of color growing up in poverty and their more affluent, White peers.

Opportunities for Meaningful Family Engagement

As we have seen, the benefits of family involvement for children's success in school and life are well documented (National Academies of Sciences, Engineering, and Medicine, 2016) and are centered on supporting positive parenting by building relationships between school and families' home lives. Family engagement also has significant benefits for schools, including increased job satisfaction among teachers and principals, despite the necessary additional work (Lim, 2012). Some effective strategies for engaging families in centers and schools are described in Table 7.3.

Meaningful family engagement requires effort on the part of teachers and parents. For instance, volunteering is one of the most common ways of involving parents. Sometimes, however, volunteers are used only to wipe tables, clean playgrounds, or bake cookies for bake sales. These may be necessary tasks, but more meaningful opportunities are available. If the school prepares parents in advance, classroom volunteers can provide one-on-one conversation or small-group reading for young children. If families engage in such learning experiences with children at school, they are more likely to do these things at home with their children.

Application Exercise 7.2
Meaningful Family Engagement

TABLE 7.3   Strategies for Engaging Families

Type of Engagement	Effective Strategies
Relationship building and communication	Families and early childhood teachers use frequent communication and sharing of information, emphasizing respect and sharing of responsibility.
Cultural sensitivity	Schools and teachers learn about families' cultural values and interaction styles, respecting families' values and priorities for their children, and focusing on family strengths as opposed to deficits.
Intentional and collaborative	Families and schools engage in collaborative goal-setting, working as partners to develop children's educational plans and objectives.
Developmentally responsive and strengths-based	Schools support families' understanding of children's developmental needs and emphasize children's and families' interests and abilities.
Support understanding of school expectations among families and communities	Schools and teachers welcome families and community members to classroom settings and share accessible information about child development and learning. These resources may include presentations, literature, videos, and interactive websites.
Decision making and advocacy	Families participate in decisions affecting their children and assume leadership and policy-making roles in the school. Families act as advocates to improve children's educational and life experiences.
Support families' engagement with children's transitions	Schools support parents as they transition their children to new learning environments from preschool to kindergarten through elementary school. They connect families to community resources, services, and to other families, to enhance families' social networks.

Sources: Office of Head Start. *Parent, family, and community engagement interactive framework.* Retrieved February 28, 2018, from https://eclkc.ohs.acf.hhs.gov/school-readiness/article/pfce-interactive-framework; and M.S. Sheridan et al., 2016. Complexities in field-based partnership research: Exemplars, challenges and an agenda for the field. In M.S. Sheridan and E. Moorman Kim (Eds.), *Family–school partnerships in context,* 1–23. Cham, Switzerland: Springer International.

Engaging Fathers

Too often, "parent" engagement is based on the assumption that the engaged parent will be the mother. However, there are distinct benefits to fathers' engagement in children's education (Minnesota Fathers & Families Network, 2013).

Fathers play a critical role in the healthy development of young children. When fathers are involved in their children's education, children of all ages perform better academically, demonstrate more empathy, and exhibit healthier behavior. Although some research has focused on how fathers and mothers parent differently and have different effects on their children's achievement, recent research suggests that mothers and fathers have grown more similar in their daily family roles and that their impacts on children's learning and development are quite similar (Fagan, Day, Lamb, & Cabrera, 2014). However, fathers, especially those from low-income backgrounds, are less likely to be engaged in schools than are mothers and therefore need more targeted encouragement (Levine, Kaufman, Hammar, & Fagan, 2015). In response, the Head Start Program Performance Standards require programs to implement "specific strategies for father engagement."

While a traditional barrier to fathers' involvement consists of time and work schedules that conflict with school hours, mothers are also heavily involved in the workforce, and many schools and programs have adapted to employed parents. But subtle barriers to fathers' engagement can be even more powerful. Fathers may perceive that engagement in school is not part of their role, but rather the mothers' job. They may feel awkward and unwelcome entering a female-dominated environment. Female teachers may hesitate to encourage father engagement for fear their actions will be misinterpreted. Because a large number of children do not live with their fathers, programs are often hesitant to promote father engagement for fear of harming children's self-esteem or offending single mothers and lesbian mothers. In addition, programs may be legitimately concerned about perpetuating gender stereotyping or disrespecting cultural groups for whom the *machismo* role of fathers is particularly important.

Although these barriers are justifiable, they need not be insurmountable. Research shows that the following *father-friendly practices* not only increase father involvement in schools but also improve family functioning and relationships as well as outcomes for children (Hennon, Palm, & Olsen, 2012):

- Make father involvement a priority by designating a male teacher, administrator, community leader, or parent volunteer to organize a father initiative. Fathers are more likely to participate when they see other men doing so.
- Be clear that your definition of "father" includes non-resident fathers as well as father figures such as grandfathers, uncles, older siblings, foster fathers, or mother's boyfriends.
- Be sensitive and responsive to two-father families.
- Create a father-friendly school environment. Greet fathers with a sign, "Dads Welcome Here!" Post pictures of positive images of diverse men engaged in various occupations and activities with and without children.
- Invite fathers explicitly and personally to participate in school so they know they are welcome and expected. Often, fathers don't feel that invitations to "parents" apply to them.
- Be responsive to cultural values. For example, Hispanic groups value *familismo* (relationships and distinct gender roles) and *respeto* (respect for elders and extended family).
- Provide bigger chairs!

Most important is to focus on fathers' strengths. Too often, fathers are portrayed in a negative light as absent or irresponsible. Every father has unique strengths and abilities. Engaged fathers are likely to be major contributors to the well-being of all children, schools, and communities.

Engaging fathers in programs and schools has a positive impact on children's educational outcomes and teacher-parent communication and relationships.

Many communities, school districts, and teachers have come to realize that opportunities for engaging families may be missed if we wait until children attend school. Another missed opportunity exists when programs and schools focus solely on children's needs and don't incorporate families' needs, priorities and goals. Programs that intentionally address both family and child needs at the same time are called *two-generation approaches*. A growing body of research documents the value of these approaches for supporting child learning and development and family wellbeing. The *What Works* feature describes how one community uses a two-generation approach to reduce family stress and increase children's attention and self-regulation.

Community Partnerships

One effective form of family engagement is community collaboration. Just as partnerships between teachers and families contribute to positive outcomes for children, early childhood programs and schools function most effectively

What Works

Two-Generation Approach to Support Children's Self-Regulation

Many families experience high levels of stress. Such stress can lead to more negative interactions in the home and fewer positive experiences, potentially interfering with healthy brain development. Children who live in highly stressful homes and communities are prone to poorer attention, emotion regulation and memory. To help address this challenge, many programs have been developed that simultaneously support both young children and their families. These programs are known as two-generation approaches.

One such program is Parents and Children Making Connections—Highlighting Attention (PCMC-A) in Oregon. In the PCMC-A program, families enrolled in Head Start engage in eight two-hour sessions designed to help parents and children increase their resilience in the context of stress. PCMC-A employs the following strategies to achieve these gains:

- Child activities are focused on increasing positive social interactions, cognitive awareness, self-regulation, attention and dealing with distractions. For example, children practice increasing their focused attention by participating in games. Program teachers lead children in activities in which children do a task (such as coloring) while their peers try to distract them with bouncing balloons. The children take turns being the colorers and bouncers. Over time, the tasks become more difficult, allowing children to develop important attention skills and resist distractions.
- Teachers also engage children in games to support emotion literacy and activities to support calming strategies focused on

breathing. A key feature of the program is that children are first taught to de-escalate (calm themselves), before learning to apply attention strategies.

- Adult activities support parents' stress reduction by enhancing their positive interactions with children, responding to stressful situations, and supporting children's learning and development. Parent–child communication is central to the program's activities. Parents receive information, practice strategies for child guidance and interactions, and learn the activities that children are using in their group sessions.

In the evaluation of PCMC-A, parents who participated experienced reduced stress and increased the quality of their language interactions with children. Impressively, children who participated showed increased selective attention in brain scans, improved language and cognitive development, and decreased problem behaviors.

PCMC-A is one of the many effective two-generation approaches that communities, school districts, and early childhood programs can use. They are all based on the understanding that when we support families well, we also support children.

Source: E. Pakulak, M. Gomsrud, M. M. Reynolds, T. A. Bell, R. J. Giuliano, et al., 2017. Focusing on families: A two-generation model for reducing parents' stress and boosting preschoolers' self-regulation and attention. *Young Children, 72*(2), 25–37.

when they build reciprocal partnerships in the broader community. For example, a Head Start program, with its comprehensive services for families, may serve as a focal point for positive change in the community. Likewise, a community organization might adopt a neighborhood school, clean up and equip its playground, or provide literacy volunteers and other services that improve school performance.

Teachers, especially beginning teachers, may feel overwhelmed by the idea of building partnerships with communities in addition to carrying out their other responsibilities. However, community linkages can enhance their work and make it more effective. All communities have unique individuals with talents to share. A local orchestra might have musicians who are willing to visit and perform for the children. Artists of all kinds can enrich children's experiences with demonstrations and skill instruction. Doctors, nurses, dentists, or hygienists can demonstrate healthy practices for children. One preschool has an annual Truck Touch as a community experience and fundraiser in which the nearby International Harvester company lends giant tractor trailers for the children to see and explore under careful supervision. The Truck Touch is open to all children in the community for free, and an accompanying snack bar raises funds for the preschool's library.

Schools can also inform families about child-related events or activities in the community such as concerts, puppet shows, museum exhibits, storytelling, and the like. Connecting families, including siblings, through such community events can help create a network of family support, which is especially helpful for single or teen parents. Such a network can serve as a protective factor for families in low-resourced communities (National Academies of Sciences, Engineering, and Medicine, 2016).

In addition, teachers can use knowledge of the community in planning curriculum. For example, a town has an ongoing project to clean up the environment around a creek area that was once a beaver dam. Each class in the local primary school takes on an aspect of the project and expands its study of ecology over several years. When early childhood programs fully integrate into the community by inviting participation and taking advantage of what the community has to offer, positive outcomes result for everyone involved.

Throughout this chapter, we have discussed the importance of relationships with families. In the next section, we provide a conceptual framework—a "how to" guide—for building partnerships with families and describe specific skills for negotiating conflicts.

✔ **Check Your Understanding 7.4**

🔺 A Framework for Building Effective Partnerships with Families

Denyce Lyons is nearing the end of her first year teaching 4-year-olds in Head Start. She has enjoyed the children, but continues to struggle at times in her relationships with parents. Now she's facing one of the biggest challenges of the year. The program in which Denyce works traditionally holds a graduation ceremony, complete with caps, gowns, diplomas, and lengthy performances by the children to mark the year's end. Denyce feels strongly that such programs are not developmentally appropriate. She also thinks they are a waste of time and money that could be used more effectively. When she announces that there will be no graduation ceremony this year, several parents become very angry and go to the director, who threatens to fire Denyce if she doesn't change her mind. Such drastic breakdowns in relationships between teachers and families are all too common in programs for young children. In this section, we present a framework for building effective partnerships with families. This framework is designed to prevent crises such as Denyce's and to address them when they do arise.

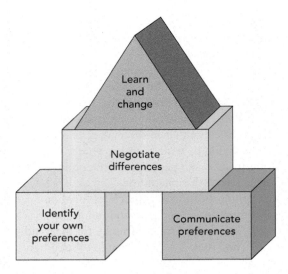

FIGURE 7.2 Framework for Partnerships with Families Effective partnerships with families involve four key strategies that connect to and build on each other, as depicted in this framework.

Effective partnerships with families involve four key strategies: clarity about preferences, ability to communicate, ability to negotiate, and willingness to learn and change (NAEYC, 1998). Figure 7.2 presents this partnership model visually. Each of these building blocks of partnership is described in the sections that follow and then used to address Denyce's graduation ceremony dilemma.

Clarify Preferences

Teachers and families have preferences about all aspects of children's learning and development. Sometimes these preferences are shared. For example, most people prefer that children dress warmly in cold weather. However, in other cases, parents and teachers may have conflicting preferences in their child-rearing practices or educational goals. Areas where teacher and family preferences may be strong and at odds include napping, snacking and meal structure, tasks children should do for themselves, learning to use the toilet and bathroom habits, talking and listening, cleanliness, discipline techniques, roles of girls and boys, and traditions and holidays. There are various sources and reasons for these different preferences:

- Cultural backgrounds
- Personal experiences as members of families, both as children and as parents
- Outside influences such as information gained from the media
- Education and training

Teachers as well as parents are influenced by all of these factors. To understand and negotiate these differences, teachers must clarify their preferences and reflect on the sources of their beliefs. Is a strong preference for children learning to feed themselves at an early age the result of studying child development or being the mother of five children? Does a teacher believe that children should take turns based on research about social skills or a cultural judgment about good manners?

Revisiting the graduation dilemma presented earlier, Denyce needs to reflect on why she feels so strongly about preschool graduation ceremonies. She recalls that one of her professors at the community college stated unequivocally that requiring preschoolers to perform for adults is not developmentally appropriate. Denyce reasons that such events are inappropriate because they last too long, straining children's attention spans and self-control. She also objects to a few children being singled out for "star" treatment. She thinks that valuable class time is spent unproductively in rehearsals and teaching children how to march in line. Upon reflection, Denyce believes that the money spent on props such as caps and gowns would be better used to buy books or other educational materials for the school. Denyce also recognizes that she is worried that the children will misbehave and she will be judged a poor teacher. On closer analysis, Denyce has to admit to herself that she thinks graduating from preschool is not much of an accomplishment, and that the ceremonial trappings should be saved for greater achievements such as high school graduation.

Communicate Preferences

The next step in building partnerships is communicating with families about preferences. In situations such as Denyce's where a difference of opinion exists, clear and honest communication is vital. Denyce needs to begin by listening to parents' preferences for holding a graduation ceremony. She does this by organizing a meeting to which she invites the disgruntled families. Rather than beginning with her viewpoint, Denyce encourages parents to air their concerns:

"We've always had graduations here. My two older kids have their diplomas, and I want this for Dedra, too," says one mother.

"We want to have this big party so we can let the kids know how proud we are," says one of the fathers.

After several parents express their feelings, a grandmother sighs and says, "This may be the only graduation I get to go to. My other grandkids dropped out of school."

Having listened carefully and respectfully to each one's concerns, Denyce states her interpretation of what the parents have said. "I think you want me to understand how much you value your children's accomplishments in Head Start, and how important this experience has been for the children and for you. I can tell from your comments that you really value education, and it sounds like you think it's a really important thing to celebrate." Several parents nod, and agree that Denyce's summary reflects their feelings.

Denyce then explains her own concerns about the graduation. "I value learning, too, but I am concerned that spending time getting ready for the ceremony will take away time that the children could be learning skills they'll need in kindergarten. I also think that the money we spend could be used for classroom supplies such as books that would last longer."

This opportunity to communicate identifies differences in the parents' and Denyce's perspectives. If Denyce continues to insist she is right, the parents will probably feel disrespected and lose power in the relationship. The children will see their parents' anger at the teacher. If the parents "win" and the director forces Denyce to hold graduation, she will do so begrudgingly and the children will sense her lack of commitment. In both cases, whether teachers win and parents lose or parents win and teachers lose, the real losers are the children. The next step to build and maintain a partnership is to negotiate the conflict toward a win-win solution (Fisher, Ury, & Patton, 2011).

Negotiate Successfully

Collaborating and sharing power with families requires negotiation skills. There are certain characteristics of power relationships that determine successful or unsuccessful negotiations. Figure 7.3 illustrates these characteristics and shows that neither exercising power unilaterally nor avoiding a power struggle results in a positive outcome.

The Five-Step Negotiation Process Shared power requires win-win negotiation. Successful negotiations that result in a win-win solution to a conflict involve several steps (Fisher et al., 2011). Figure 7.4 depicts the five-step negotiation process, which is described next and illustrated using the conflict over the graduation.

No Power or Avoidance	Shared Power or Negotiation	Power or Fighting
Characterized by:	Characterized by:	Characterized by:
Walking away	Talking about the problem	Put downs
Giving up	Communicating	Threats
Holding in feelings and opinions	Seeking solutions	Punishment
Changing the subject		Arbitrary action
Gets these results:	Gets these results:	Gets these results:
Problem is still there	Both sides can win	One winner
No one is satisfied	Real solutions	Doubts and fears
Ongoing discomfort	All are satisfied	Revenge

FIGURE 7.3 **Understanding Shared Power** Understanding power relationships is essential for successful collaboration and negotiation of differences.

Source: Reprinted with permission from the National Association for the Education of Young Children (NAEYC). www.naeyc.org.

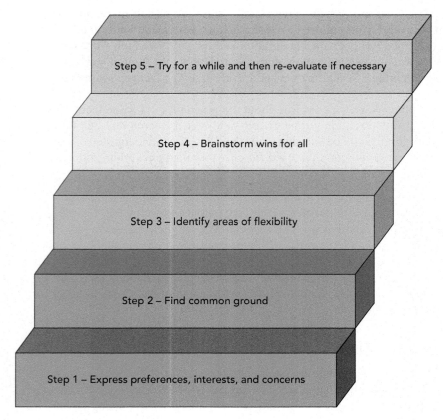

Step 5 – Try for a while and then re-evaluate if necessary

Step 4 – Brainstorm wins for all

Step 3 – Identify areas of flexibility

Step 2 – Find common ground

Step 1 – Express preferences, interests, and concerns

FIGURE 7.4 **Five-Step Negotiation Process** This five-step negotiation process is designed to ensure a win-win resolution to the inevitable conflicts that arise between teachers and families.

Step 1: Express preferences, interests, and concerns. As a teacher, when you are expressing preferences, you will find it useful to focus on what you value rather than taking a rigid position. Denyce might have stated her strongly held position: "I'm against graduations for young children because they're developmentally inappropriate." Instead, Denyce expressed her preferred value for her students: "I would like to use the money for classroom materials and I don't want to take time away from teaching." Similarly, the families made their interests known by pointing out that they value education and that graduation marks an important milestone in their children's lives.

Step 2: Find common ground. Successful negotiation requires compromise. Sometimes people view compromise as a loss, a sign of weakness, or as giving in. Compromise is actually an effective strategy for achieving a win-win negotiated solution to a conflict. To achieve a satisfactory compromise, parties need to identify their common ground: their fundamental agreements, as well as the areas where they disagree. Denyce and the parents agree on the value of education and their desire to communicate their pride in the children. The areas they don't agree on are wearing caps and gowns and allowing time for rehearsals and a ceremony.

Step 3: Identify areas of flexibility. The next step in the negotiation process is to identify areas of potential flexibility. These might include ways of varying timing, frequency, or quantity. For example, the time designated for preparing for graduation and for the performance are negotiable areas. In addition, the amount of money available and how it is used are areas that could be flexibly negotiated. The parents' expectations of the ceremony could also be negotiable.

Step 4: Brainstorm wins for all. Having identified areas of flexibility, Denyce and the parents can brainstorm possible solutions that would be agreeable to all concerned. One possible solution is having a party for everyone, during which the children sing some of the songs and recite some of the poems they have learned this year. Other possibilities include using the money that would have been spent on caps and gowns to buy books for the center and creating "diplomas" on the computer rather than buying them. Other suggestions are that parents provide refreshments and that all of the children wear white shirts during the party.

Step 5: Try for a while and then reevaluate if necessary. Negotiated solutions should be tried and evaluated to make sure that all parties are satisfied. During and after the "graduation" party, Denyce talked with the parents to get their reactions. Some of the parents still missed the caps and gowns, but they were pleased when the children took such interest and pride in the new books. Several parents thought the program was actually more fun because it was less rehearsed and funnier than in previous years. One parent pointed out that he was glad that there weren't any stars of the show and all the children performed the same thing. Perhaps because the program was only 20 minutes long, none of the children misbehaved and all seemed to enjoy themselves, including Denyce. Because some parents didn't like the white shirts and wanted their children to dress up in their best clothes, Denyce agreed to try that idea next year.

 Application Exercise 7.3

Figure 7.4: Five-Step Negotiation Process

The final building block of successful partnerships is the willingness to learn and change, described next.

Demonstrate Willingness to Learn and Change

We can see from the negotiation between Denyce and the families in her classroom that effective partnerships depend on the willingness to learn and change. In Denyce's case, she was willing to listen to the parents' concerns respectfully, and as a result, she learned how much they value education for their children and why the graduation ceremony was meaningful for them. On the other hand, the families learned about Denyce's concerns for their children's readiness for kindergarten, and hence were willing to change their expectations regarding appropriate ways to celebrate the children's achievements. True partnerships occur only when teachers as well as families are willing to learn from one another and to grow and change as a result.

The five-step negotiation process outlined here does not involve a quick fix; it requires time and respect for the other parties' interests, strengths, and abilities. Win-win negotiation depends on appreciating the importance of everyone's interests, particularly parents' perceptions about what is important for their children. Denyce could easily have erred by trivializing the parents' desire to see their children "graduate." Instead, she accurately perceived that graduation represented an underlying value of education rather than the actual ceremony.

As we have seen, teaching young children requires working with families, which requires good communication and negotiation skills. Throughout this chapter, we examined the various aspects of building effective partnerships with families and communities. These include establishing reciprocal relationships, communicating effectively, and negotiating conflicts. We conclude with a return visit to Vilma Suarez's Early Head Start program where we began.

✔ **Check Your Understanding 7.5**

Revisiting the Case Study

… Ms. Suarez's Classroom

Now that we have explored the many ways in which teachers build effective partnerships with families, we can see how well Vilma Suarez fulfills this important responsibility. She plays a key role in implementing Aiya's IFSP plan, but she also respects and supports Aiya's mother, and works to gain her trust. She helps Tomas and Mrs. Vacaro through difficult daily transitions and takes time to communicate with her throughout the day.

Her biggest challenge will be resolving the conflict with Mr. Henderson over his son's biting. She needs to employ all of her skills of effective communication and negotiation. She begins by saying, "Mr. Henderson, I know how upsetting it is when children bite, but I cannot use physical punishment of any kind. I would like to talk with you about other ways we can work together on this problem." Thus begins the complex negotiation process that Vilma knows from experience may take one meeting or many.

As the families arrive the next morning, Vilma notices that Mrs. Vacaro is even more anxious than she was the night before when she picked up Tomas. Feeling that she has gained Mrs. Vacaro's trust over the many months they have known each other, Vilma carefully asks, "Is everything all right?" Mrs. Vacaro's eyes well up and she whispers, "I'm pregnant again, and I don't have health insurance."

Vilma calmly replies, "Tomas will make a wonderful brother. He's so loving. I'm sure you're feeling a lot of stress. But our Early Head Start program can help you. With your permission, I'll check with the director during the day about the resources we have to offer you and the help we can find in the community. If you have time, we can meet this evening or I'll phone you at home." Mrs. Vacaro exhales with relief and promises to check back at the end of the day. She calls goodbye to Tomas, who is already eating his breakfast with the other children. ■

7 Chapter Summary

- Families are diverse in many ways: composition, culture, religion, economic status, work, mobility, and sexual orientation.

- Along with reciprocal relationships and partnerships between teachers and families, family-centered practices are characterized by several key principles: mutual respect and trust; regular, frequent two-way communication; collaboration, shared decision making and shared power; and negotiation of conflicts toward win-win situations.

- Effective two-way communication is the basis for positive relationships with families. Communication strategies include teachers' creating a welcoming environment; informal conversation; sharing important information on a daily and/or weekly basis, depending on the age of the child; using an assertive communication style, especially when discussing delicate issues; conferencing; home visiting; and using technology.

- A large body of research confirms that family engagement in schools and early childhood programs has a positive impact on children's success in school and life.

- Effective partnerships with families involve four key strategies: clarity about preferences, ability to communicate, ability to negotiate, and willingness to change and learn.

Key Terms

- aggressive communication
- assertive communication
- family-centered practice
- family systems theory
- funds of knowledge
- home-based programs
- home visiting
- passive communication
- slippery egg messages
- tennis ball messages

 Flash Cards 7.1

Readings and Websites

Ernst, J. D. (2014). *The welcoming classroom: Building strong home–school connections for early learning.* Lewisville, NC: Gryphon House.

Gonzalez-Mena, J. (2014). *50 strategies for communicating and working with diverse families* (3rd ed.). Upper Saddle River, NJ: Pearson.

Keyser, J. (2017). *From parents to partners: Building a family-centered early childhood program* (2nd ed.). St. Paul, MN: Redleaf Press.

Head Start Parent, Family, and Community Engagement Framework (PFCE)

On the ECLKC website of Head Start, the PFCE interactive framework offers many resources for engaging families in their children's learning, engaging fathers, and videos of effective practices.

National Center for Families Learning (NCFL)

NCFL provides resources and services to benefit all families, with a primary focus on empowering and improving literacy and language skills of parents and children living in poverty. Their website offers information about innovative two-generation programs and practices.

National Black Child Development Institute (NBCDI)

Among a variety of helpful resources for engaging with families of color, the NBCDI website offers a Classroom Family Engagement Rubric link that teachers can use to identify their strengths and needs related to engaging families around children's learning and development.

The Global Family Research Project

The Global Family Research Project is an independent, nonprofit organization that supports all families and communities in helping children find success in and out of school and offering a worldwide exchange of ideas.

Shared Writing 7.1
Building Partnerships with Families

8 Creating a Caring Community of Learners: Guiding Young Children

Learning Outcomes

After studying this chapter, you should be able to:

8.1 Explain the value of a caring community of learners and the Teaching Pyramid model.

8.2 Review ways teachers can build positive relationships with young children.

8.3 Discuss how high-quality supportive environments support children's positive behavior.

8.4 Outline strategies for teaching social–emotional competence and guiding behavior.

8.5 Describe the use of intensive individualized interventions.

8.6 Apply the Teaching Pyramid model in practice.

Related NAEYC Professional Preparation Standards

The NAEYC Professional Preparation Standards (NAEYC, 2011) that apply to this chapter:

1: Promoting Child Development and Learning
Key elements:
    1a. Knowing and understanding young children's characteristics and needs
    1b. Knowing and understanding the multiple influences on development and learning
    1c. Using developmental knowledge to create healthy, respectful, supportive, and challenging learning environments
2: Building Family and Community Relationships
Key elements:
    2b. Supporting and engaging families and communities through respectful, reciprocal relationships
    2c. Involving families and communities in their children's development and learning
3: Observing, Documenting, and Assessing to Support Young Children and Families
Key elements:
    3b. Knowing about and using observation, documentation, and other appropriate assessment tools and approaches
    3c. Understanding and practicing responsible assessment to promote positive outcomes for each child
    3d. Knowing about assessment partnerships with families and with professional colleagues
4: Using Developmentally Effective Approaches to Connect with Children and Families
Key elements:
    4a. Understanding positive relationships and supportive interactions as the foundation of their work with children
    4b. Knowing and understanding effective strategies and tools for early education
    4c. Using a broad repertoire of developmentally appropriate teaching/learning approaches
    4d. Reflecting on their own practice to promote positive outcomes for each child

Case Study

Today is the first day of school for Sue Brady, a teacher of 20 4-year-olds in a child care center. She and her co-teacher, Elly Donahue, are both inexperienced teachers responsible for a group of children for the first time. Sue and Elly spent the last week preparing their classroom. They are a little worried that there are not enough toys to keep children's interest, and have requested more from the director. The room has a sink, but it is located in the pathway from the front door to the closet, so it is not possible to put the paint easels near it. There is no book rack, and the books are stacked on an open shelf near the blocks. There is one large open area with a rug that they plan to use for group time and block building next to a table for toys. Tables are lined up along the far side of the room.

As soon as the children begin to arrive, things go wrong. Playtime becomes disorganized, and the children dump materials all over the floor rather than use them constructively. The teachers give so much attention to the children who are out of control that they neglect the others who are behaving well, such as Edie, who is absorbed in her painting. Over the course of the day, the teachers' voices become louder as they try to restore order while the noise level in the room becomes almost unbearable. No one cooperates during cleanup time.

At lunch, Ricky blows milk at his friends through his straw, and the others soon emulate his skill. Sue asks Paula and Aimee, "Would you like to go outside now?" and they simply say, "No," leaving her unsure about what to do, since she can't leave them alone inside. On the playground, Booth punches Elijah hard in the stomach, seemingly for no reason. Furious but feeling totally incompetent, Sue grabs Booth by the arms and repeatedly says, "Say you're sorry!" while Booth just smirks and Elijah cries loudly. Both teachers can't wait for naptime, but when they turn out the lights, the ensuing chaos becomes overwhelming. Children refuse to stay on their cots, grab toys off the shelves, talk loudly, and make it impossible for even the most exhausted to sleep. Sue will remember this day vividly, because it is one of the longest days of her life. Unfortunately, the next day will be all too similar. ■

This glimpse into Sue's classroom is not a fictional account. It is actually what happened to me on my first day of teaching many years ago. I learned very quickly that teaching young children is hard work. I also discovered that there was a lot more I needed to know to become an effective teacher.

The goal of this chapter is to help ensure that you and the children you teach do not experience days like the one described In the case study. This chapter describes research-based practices—ways of creating a caring community of learners—that make teaching young children more effective and enjoyable. To help you learn how to promote children's social competence and address challenging behaviors, we will describe a conceptual framework—the Teaching Pyramid (Center on the Social and Emotional Foundations of Early Learning, n.d.; Hemmeter, Snyder, Fox, & Algina, 2016). Applying this framework will help you create a caring community of learners in which young children thrive. Using these research-based, positive guidance strategies will not prevent all of the challenges you will face as a teacher, but it will help you become more calm, confident, and effective in your work with all children.

A Caring Community of Learners: The Teaching Pyramid Model

caring community of learners A group or classroom in which children and adults engage in warm, positive relationships, treat each other with respect, and learn from and with each other.

A **caring community of learners** is a group or classroom in which children and adults engage in warm, positive relationships; treat each other with respect; and learn from and with each other. The late Jim Greenman (2017), one of the foremost experts on children's environments, described early childhood programs as "caring spaces, learning places." This phrase is apt because it emphasizes a fundamental principle of early childhood education: Children's care and education are interrelated.

Wherever children are served, they are always learning and being cared for. In other words, *both/and* thinking is required. Effective early childhood programs provide *both* nurturing, responsive relationships *and* stimulating, interesting educational experiences. If children's needs for either care or learning are neglected, the program will be ineffective.

The Value of a Caring Community of Learners

Children learn and develop best in the context of a caring community of learners. Research provides strong evidence that this is the case. As we have seen, a well-known tool for evaluating the quality and effectiveness of programs is the *Classroom Assessment Scoring System* (CLASS), which assesses the social–emotional climate and the instructional climate of preschool or primary-grade classrooms through detailed observations of teachers' behaviors (Pianta, La Paro, & Hamre, 2008). Research using the CLASS has found that high-quality emotional and instructional classroom climates uniquely predict children's academic achievement and improve social and emotional outcomes (Perlman et al., 2016). Teachers who provide high-quality emotional support are aware of and respond to children's individual needs, rarely display intense negative emotion, and engage in positive, respectful interactions with children (Hamre, 2014). This chapter is dedicated to providing information for how teachers can ensure classroom climates that support children's emotional and social development.

Equally important, if not more so, is that the emotional climate *not* be negative—that there is little or no aggression or hostility among children and teachers (Hamre, 2014). Most of us have observed classrooms or been students in them in which it is obvious which children are the "bad kids." They may be sitting at a desk by themselves, or their names may be the ones you hear over and over. They may be waving their hands in the air while the teacher continues to ignore them. Young children are very perceptive. They know whether teachers like them and which kids are the favorites (Janson & King, 2010). Imagine figuring out within a few days after school starts that your teacher doesn't like you very much and facing nine months of being in that person's control with no choice to stay home or switch to another teacher. Children soon begin to act the way they are perceived and live up to low or negative expectations.

Building a caring community of learners requires effort on the part of teachers and children, but the effort pays off in short- and long-term benefits. In the present, the classroom will be a more harmonious, pleasant environment in which children are more likely to learn successfully. In addition, experiencing a caring community helps achieve three essential, long-term goals for children:

1. To develop positive social skills and emotional self-regulation, which are essential tasks during the first 5 to 8 years of life
2. To prevent future social and behavioral difficulties, which is more efficient, effective, and humane than later remediation
3. To build a foundation of learning for later success in school and in life.

Develop Social Skills and Self-Regulation Think back to your school days when you were really excited to give an answer, and had to sit quietly, raise your hand, and wait before speaking. Remember the playground where you played tag without getting too rough or walked away when someone made you feel mad? That was self-regulation at work. A major developmental accomplishment of the first 5 years of life is the development of self-regulation in all areas of behavior. Self-regulation in its broadest sense represents the ability to willfully plan and, as necessary, control one's behavior to meet their needs. This process begins early as babies learn to regulate their sleeping, crying, and other behavior patterns, and expands during the preschool years to more complex self-regulation.

Research indicates that between ages 3 and 7, a qualitative shift in self-regulation may take place when children typically progress from reactive behavior to more advanced, cognitive–behavioral forms of self-regulation that likely require the integration of many skills, such as executive functions and language skills (Cole, Armstrong, & Pemberton, 2010). During these years, children develop the ability to control emotions, to learn to delay gratification, and to build relationships with other people—all key factors essential for healthy development (Montroy, Bowles, Skibbe, McClelland, & Morrison, 2016). A core aspect of self-regulation is effortful control (Rueda, 2015).

Effortful control is an individual's ability to act purposefully, including controlling thoughts, emotions, and behaviors. For children growing up in poverty or in stressful situations, development of effortful control can be compromised (Lengua, 2012). These early disruptions can have long-term and wide-spread effects on a child's academic, social, and emotional outcomes reaching into adulthood. Early childhood is a key developmental period

effortful control Children's ability to act purposefully including controlling thoughts, emotions, and behaviors.

to learn effortful control. During this time, parents, families, educators and school settings can play central roles in promoting the development of effortful control and self-regulation.

Children's ability to regulate their emotional responses is associated with successful learning and social relationships (Durlak, Weissberg, Dynmicki, Taylor & Shellinger, 2011). Children who regulate their emotions can work collaboratively, play with others, seek help, and offer help to others. Children who have difficulty regulating their emotions exhibit more frustration in school and often have trouble focusing their attention, completing tasks and working with other children (Blair & Raver, 2015). Because learning to regulate one's emotions involves acquiring a complex set of skills, children need support from adults to be successful.

Other important goals of the early years are the development of self-concept and self-esteem. Self-concept, which forms rapidly during the preschool years, refers to children's stable perceptions about themselves despite variations in their behavior. Children's self-esteem, or perception of their own worth, is also in its formative stages during these years, and can be fragile. Similarly, children gradually acquire a sense of efficacy, a belief in their own abilities to accomplish what they set out to do. Positive self-concept, self-esteem, and feelings of efficacy don't develop by people telling children how special and talented they are, but rather as children take initiative and master challenges with a lot of adult encouragement (Galinsky, 2010).

self-concept Children's stable perceptions about themselves despite variations in their behavior.

self-esteem Children's perception of their own worth.

efficacy Children's belief in their own ability to accomplish what they set out to do.

Prevent Social and Behavioral Difficulties   Teachers today report a larger percentage of children who exhibit extremely challenging behaviors, such as excessive aggression, anger, and hostility (Kaiser & Rasminsky, 2017). These children take up most of the teacher's attention, yet fail to improve. In worst case scenarios, some children may be expelled from child care or preschool, experiencing failure before their educational experiences have even begun (Gilliam, 2016; Vinh, Strain, Davidon, & Smith, 2016). During the last few decades, since federal laws began requiring child care programs and schools to fully include children with disabilities and special needs, the number of children with challenging behaviors may have increased. Some disabilities such as attention deficit/hyperactivity disorder (ADHD) or autism may adversely affect children's social behavior (Gregg, 2017; Stadnick, Nicole, Chlebowski, & Brookman-Frazee, 2017). To successfully teach in these increasingly complex classrooms, teachers must have knowledge of effective, research-based, early intervention strategies before they encounter these difficult situations. Children who exhibit persistent challenging behaviors are those most in need of good teaching.

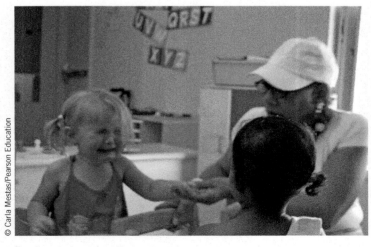

Building positive social skills and healthy emotional relationships during the early years is more effective than trying to remedy problems later. Research demonstrates that preschool children who lack self-regulation and/or fail to develop positive relationships with peers are likely to encounter significant difficulties in school and in life. A recent study of children entering kindergarten found significant relationships between social and behavioral readiness in kindergarten and school outcomes. Specifically, by third grade, students assessed as not socially and behaviorally ready in kindergarten were significantly more likely to be retained in grade, receive services and supports through special education, and be suspended or expelled (Bettencourt, Gross & Ho, 2016). Children who don't acquire minimal social competence and thus are unable to make friends are at significant risk of dropping out of school, becoming delinquent, or experiencing mental health problems in adolescence or adulthood (McCoy et al., 2017; Moffitt et al., 2011).

Teachers today report that more children are exhibiting challenging behaviors than in the past. Why might this be true? What might account for this perception?

Even when children are 3 or 4 years old, it is possible to observe which children are socially isolated and do not make friends easily (Waller et al., 2016). Even adults

© Carla Mestas/Pearson Education

sometimes find these children difficult to interact with, and may want to avoid them. Yet teachers must recognize that socially isolated children need their help the most. With systematic support and intentional teaching, teachers can promote children's development of social competence.

If children's problems are ignored or set aside because teachers hope "they'll grow out of it," the problems only get worse as children get older. Teachers can instead adopt a proactive approach, such as this one:

> Preschool teacher Karen Hagey observed that every time 3½-year-old Marcus tried to push his way into the block corner, the other children shouted, "Get out, Marcus! You can't play." She thought about forcing the children to accept Marcus, but realized they would resent him, and he would be humiliated by her interference. Instead, Karen quietly coached Marcus on strategies for entering play: "Let's sit next to Jason and see if you and I can build a tall tower." Marcus's tower soon eclipsed that of his peers, who started to pay attention to his skill. After a few days of this kind of assistance from Karen, Marcus entered the play area more calmly and Jason said, "Hey, Marcus, help me make my building as tall as me."

Promote Academic Success   Social–emotional competence is clearly linked to academic success throughout all the years of school (Curby, Brown, Bassett, & Denham, 2015; Bettencourt, Gross & Ho, 2016). Children in preschool and the primary grades perform better on measures of academic achievement, language, and social–emotional development when they have positive, sensitive, trusting relationships with their teachers (Hamre, 2014). Relationships with teachers predict children's later relationships with their peers, self-regulation, behavior problems, school satisfaction, and learning (Brock & Curby, 2016; Graziano, Garb, Ros, Hart & Garcia, 2015; Williford et al., 2017).

Vygotsky's theory of learning as a social construction of knowledge emphasizes that much of our understanding occurs as we talk with and listen to other people's ideas. This give and take of conversation and debate with other people plays a major role in learning. Promoting social construction of knowledge requires that children learn not just as individuals but also in the context of small and large groups—as part of a community of learners. We now have a large body of research to guide teachers in this important work.

The Teaching Pyramid Model

The Center on the Social and Emotional Foundations for Early Learning (CSEFEL) and the Technical Assistance Center on Social Emotional Intervention for Young Children disseminate resources to teachers that translate research on social–emotional development into best practice. CSEFEL developed a model—the *Teaching Pyramid*—for promoting social competence and preventing challenging behavior in young children, which is depicted in Figure 8.1. **Challenging behavior** is defined as "any behavior that interferes with children's learning, development, and success at play; is harmful to the child, other children, or adults; and/or puts a child at high risk for later social problems or school failure" (Kaiser & Rasminsky, 2017).

challenging behavior Any behavior that interferes with children's learning, development, and success at play; is harmful to the child, other children, or adults; or puts a child at high risk for later social problems or school failure.

Pyramid Components   The Teaching Pyramid is composed of four parts: (1) positive relationships with children, (2) high-quality supportive environments, (3) social and emotional teaching strategies, and (4) intensive individualized interventions. The base of the pyramid is the largest portion because it represents the foundation of positive relationships on which everything else depends. Each subsequent topic on the pyramid builds on the ones below and represents a proportionately smaller amount of teachers' time and effort. This model indicates that if teachers effectively provide these supports, children will learn social competence, their positive behaviors will increase, and challenging behaviors will diminish.

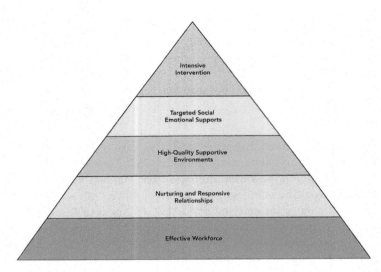

FIGURE 8.1 Teaching Pyramid Model for Promoting Social and Emotional Competence in Infants and Young Children The Teaching Pyramid is a research-based, effective framework to help teachers support children's social–emotional learning and reduce challenging behaviors in the classroom. Reprinted with permission from Promoting Social and Emotional Competence in infants and Young Children. Developed by the center on social emotional foundations for earth learning at Vanderbilt University, www.vanderbilt.edu/csefel.

 Application Exercise 8.1

Figure 8.1: Teaching Pyramid Model for Promoting Social and Emotional Competence in Infants and Young Children

When teachers encounter children who exhibit negative behaviors such as aggression or hostility, their first inclination is to try to "fix" that child. As teachers, we naturally assume that if we could just quickly change that child's behavior, everything would be well and our job would be so much easier. The truth is that there are no quick fixes; in fact, the more effective strategy is not to try to fix the child at first. It is always more difficult to change another person's behavior, even if that person is only 3 years old, than to change our own behavior.

The Teaching Pyramid turns our prior assumptions on their head. Rather than trying to change children first, we begin by changing ourselves—that is, we examine our behavior to focus on establishing a positive relationship with each child. We recognize that more difficult children will take more effort, but we also acknowledge that the effort will pay off greatly. Next, we evaluate teaching environments and routines, and determine what changes need to be made to support children's positive behavior. How can we support routines that help children do their best? How can we teach social skills and emotional self-regulation? By asking these questions and exploring solutions, we attempt to directly address individual children's challenging behaviors.

The Pyramid's Effectiveness Research demonstrates that when teachers consistently apply the strategies described in the Teaching Pyramid model, positive social interactions among children increase and behavior problems decrease (Hemmeter, Snyder, Fox, & Algina, 2011, 2016; Hemmeter, Hardy, Schnitz, Adams, & Kinder, 2015). Research suggests that fewer than 4% of children require the more intensive level of interventions (Fox, Dunlap, Hemmeter, Joseph, & Strain, 2003). In a group of 20 children, that equates to only one child. In a center serving 100 children, about 4 children might require this level of intensive assistance. In the following sections, we discuss each level of the Teaching Pyramid and provide examples of effective teaching practices.

 Check Your Understanding 8.1

Building Positive Relationships with Children

A key premise of the Teaching Pyramid is that the most fundamental way to promote healthy development and learning in young children is for teachers to build and sustain positive relationships with children.

The Importance of Relationships

From the earliest moments of life, children's development—who they become—is influenced by the nurturance and care that they receive from adults—first their parents, then members of the extended family and other caregivers. In the next sections, we describe the importance of relationships in the family, then with teachers and other children.

Family Relationships: Attachment Theory Decades of research on mother–child interactions support the concept that children's ability to learn depends on their developing trusting relationships with caregivers—called **attachment theory** (Bowlby, 1969/2000). Much of the research was conducted by Mary Ainsworth and her colleagues (1978). They observed how young children interacted with their mothers when they were brought into a novel or strange situation (such as being presented with new or unusual materials to explore). They identified kinds of attachments between mothers and children that have varying effects on children's development. It is important to note, however, that attachment is influenced by cultural contexts and will look and mean different things to diverse cultural groups.

> **attachment theory** The theory that children's ability to learn depends on their developing trusting relationships with caregivers.

Secure Attachment All children develop attachments to their primary caregivers. They rely on their caregivers' protection and nurturing, and base their understanding of relationships on their early experiences. Based on the quality of care infants receive from caregivers, they develop secure or insecure attachments. According to attachment theory (Ainsworth et al., 1978; Bowlby, 1969/2000; Scroufe, 1996), when children's caregivers are responsive and sensitive to their needs, children develop **secure attachment relationships**. Securely attached children rely on their caregivers for support, yet comfortably explore their surroundings. Children who are securely attached to their caregivers have a strong foundation not only for building relationships with other people, but also for school success (Sagi-Schwartz, 2016). Research suggests that kindergarteners who were more securely attached to their mothers in toddlerhood show better self-regulation, and are considered by their teachers to present fewer problems in everyday school situations (Bernier, Beauchamp, Carlson, & Lalonde, 2015).

> **secure attachment relationship** A responsive and sensitive relationship with caregivers that allows children to venture forth and comfortably explore and learn about the world.

What does secure attachment look like? Consider Matthew, a 2½-year-old who enjoys a warm, loving relationship with his mother. When his mother enrolls him in a child care center, she stays with him for almost an hour while he becomes acclimated. At first, he clings to her leg and eyes the toys and other children. Gradually, he ventures a few steps toward an enticing ramp that the other kids are sliding down, but quickly runs back to his mother. After a few more attempts, he hesitantly joins in the fun by rolling a ball down the incline, all the while seeking regular eye contact with his mother. After a while, he begins to explore the classroom, occasionally returning to her side for reassurance. Matthew relies on his mother as a **secure base** from which to explore his new environment. During the next few days, his mother stays with him for shorter periods of time, until one day he joyfully waves goodbye to her at the door. He no longer needs her actual presence as a physical base from which to explore because he has internalized the sense of trust and confidence that she provides. Teachers can help children make such transitions from the secure attachments of home to child care settings, as described in the following example:

> **secure base** An attachment figure (mother or caregiver) who serves as an anchor for children to rely on and from which children can safely venture out and explore.

A month before a new group of 1- and 2-year-olds entered the child care center, their teacher, Durrell, contacted the families to learn about the daily routines at home.

He encouraged the parents to have the child bring a favorite blanket or toy to the center. He asked if there were snapshots of family members or of pets that they could share so he could make a little photo book for each child. Durrell also suggested to parents that children stay for a shorter time for a few days rather than a full day if the parents' work schedules allowed it.

On the first day, Sasha's mom whispered to Durrell that she was going to sneak out so her 2-year-old son wouldn't get upset at seeing her go. Durrell told her that it would help Sasha if she said goodbye and told him when she would be back.

Parents sometimes want to leave without saying goodbye, and that's understandable. They think the child will be less upset, and that this may be less stressful for teachers. However, sneaking away actually creates mistrust in children; it sends the message that the child cannot rely on the parent. One- and 2-year-olds fare better when a parent tells them, "I'm leaving now and I'll be back after you eat lunch." Durrell tries to reassure the parents and tell them not to worry or feel guilty if their children are crying and having difficulty with the separation for a while. It means their children feel a bond and are learning to cope with strong emotions. During the day, he also tries to call or text parents to ease their anxiety.

From 10 months to about 2 years of age, the typically developing child learns that separations from parents are not permanent, and begins to cope with short periods of time apart. The child's increasing representational abilities—remembering people and situations—help this understanding develop. Thus, bringing a favorite toy or photo from home often provides comfort and reminds the child that home is still a part of his day. Transitioning to the program with a shorter day also allows children to hold on to the idea that a parent is coming back and then gradually extend that to a longer period of time.

Insecure Attachment By contrast, some children grow up in families that, for a variety of reasons, are unable or unwilling to provide reasonably consistent, sensitive, responsive care. Mothers or other caregivers may be depressed, ill, or stressed by economic or other conditions that lead them to be neglectful, punitive, or hostile to their young children. Some children grow up in very difficult circumstances in which they may have been abused, neglected, or exposed to drugs and violence. Children growing up in such an environment may be unable to trust caregivers to keep them safe, and as a result, develop poor social skills. Such *insecurely attached* children may often have difficulty developing positive social relationships, and may exhibit disruptive behavior in child care centers or schools (Ainsworth et al., 1978).

Various patterns of insecure attachment exist, depending on children's experiences, which are related to different patterns of behavior (Ainsworth et al., 1978; Bowlby, 1969/2000). Children who have experienced rejection and insensitivity from adult caregivers may demonstrate **insecure–avoidant attachment**. These children tend to turn away from or avoid adults and do not seek their comfort; in fact, they may become hostile in order to avoid rejection before it occurs.

Other insecurely attached children who have experienced confusing and inconsistent nurturing from adults are said to be experiencing **insecure–ambivalent/resistant attachment**. Because they are unsure whether adults will be there for them, these children may appear to seek comfort but then reject it when it is offered. They may be irritable and fussy, easily frustrated, and difficult to manage in a group.

In more extreme circumstances, when children have experienced neglect, abuse, or violence in the home, they may exhibit **disorganized/disoriented attachment** (Main & Solomon, 1990). Because their past experiences with adults have left them without secure attachments, they have not developed useful strategies for seeking comfort or attention or for handling difficulties. Their behavior can be very unpredictable and confusing to teachers, and can negatively affect the children's ability to learn.

Attachment to Teachers Although earlier attachment studies focused on mother–child attachment, current research also applies the theory to teacher–child relationships

---

insecure–avoidant attachment Rejection and insensitivity from adult caregivers that causes children to turn away from or avoid adults and not seek their comfort.

insecure–ambivalent/resistant attachment Children's inability to trust adults to keep them safe due to neglect, abuse, or other difficult circumstances that results in a lack of social competence.

disorganized/disoriented attachment Seen in children who lack secure attachments with adults due to having experienced neglect, abuse, or violence in the home and who have not developed useful strategies for seeking comfort or attention or handling difficulties.

(Hamre, 2014; Howes & Ritchie, 2002). This research demonstrates that across the full age span of infancy through the primary grades, a caring, sensitive relationship with a teacher is related to positive social and academic development. For example, in one study, first-graders who were at high risk for school failure but had emotionally supportive teachers had achievement scores and relationships with teachers comparable to those of children who were not at risk (Hamre & Pianta, 2005). By contrast, children whose teachers were not emotionally supportive had lower achievement and more conflict with their teachers and peers. Other studies demonstrate that when teachers have positive relationships with children and are sensitive to their needs, children develop better self-regulation and social skills (Johnson, Seidenfeld, Izard, & Kobak, 2013; Williford, Vick, Whittaker, Vitiello, & Downer, 2013).

In addition, attachment relationships with parents may not predict attachment relationships with teachers (Howes & Ritchie, 2002; Beckh & Becker-Stoll, 2016). Just as a child who is securely attached to parents may be insecurely attached to teachers, a child who is insecurely attached to parents may develop a secure attachment to a teacher (Buyse, Verschueren & Doumen, 2011). Teachers serve attachment needs when the parent is not present. In this way, teachers know that they can make a positive difference for all children, even those who have troubled family relationships.

Although building relationships with insecurely attached children can be challenging for teachers, these children are most in need of such support if they are to succeed in school and life. Research shows that teachers tend to have more conflict in their relationships with children with behavior challenges, with boys, and with children of color (Gallagher, Kainz, White, & Vernon-Feagans, 2013). Therefore, it is vitally important for teachers to be aware of how their own potential biases may affect their behavior.

Responsive teachers observe children carefully and notice when children need extra attention or support, and children respond by growing in their social and academic competence (Hamre, 2014). Although the attachment literature tends to focus on individual relationships between parents or teachers and children, it does not focus on children's roles as members of groups, which we discuss next.

Video Example 8.1:

Teacher-Child Relationships

An elementary school teacher describes her views on teacher-child relationships. In what ways do teachers' relationships with children differ from those with their families? Why do such relationships matter for children's learning?

© Pearson Education

Relationships with Other Children

Across the age span of birth through age 8, teachers create a caring community by promoting positive interactions among young children. Such a community is essential not only for social–emotional development but for learning in every area. Teaching that supports children's peer relationships depends in part on the age of the children served.

Infants and Toddlers

Building relationships with babies and toddlers takes time, sensitive touch, talking, and playful learning experiences (Raikes & Edwards, 2009). Teachers create a climate of respect by listening and responding to babies' verbal and nonverbal cues, such as their cries or coos, facial expressions, and body movements. These behaviors send signals about the baby's wants and needs, such as "I'm hungry" or "I'm bored and want to do something else." When adults respond appropriately to their cues, babies begin to develop a sense of trust and efficacy.

Toddlers in child care can show the same patterns of attachment and exploration behavior that were described for parental attachments. In order to engage actively in exploration, play, and learning while enjoying the stimulating environment, toddlers need to feel confident about their relationships with non-parental caregivers. Thus, providing a secure base for exploration and a haven of safety to which the children can return when needed is a critical task for toddler teachers. Think about what this might mean for room arrangement, and where teachers position themselves in the classroom.

Teachers also model the kind of warmth and caring that they want children to develop. Even very young infants and toddlers demonstrate empathic behaviors toward their peers (Raikes & Edwards, 2009). Teachers can promote empathy by labeling children's feelings and helping them comfort one another (Giménez-Dasí, Fernández-Sánchez, & Quintanilla, 2015). For instance, "Claudia is crying and is feeling frustrated because she dropped her binky. Let's help her." Finally, teachers can engage in conversations with infants and toddlers that focus on discussions of their peers. They can point out to Felix that Anna chose the same color for her painting, and that Amir is waiting for them to finish painting for his turn. To Amir, the teacher can say, "Look, Felix and Anna are painting with green; I wonder what color you will choose when it is your turn."

Preschoolers and School-Age Children During the preschool years, attachment behavior seems to shift from the need for continual guidance and security towards instrumental support (Sroufe. 2005). Specifically, the role of preschool teachers changes gradually towards instructional support, guidance and limit setting, encouragement of deeper thinking, and support in interactions with other children, such as problem solving. Nonetheless, close relationships with preschool teachers continue to play an important role for development and learning, which can be best characterized by a sense of warmth, responsive support, and trust, all of which promote self-regulation, independence and secure exploration in older children.

As children get older, their understanding of relationships and need of friendship increases. Teachers set the tone for a harmonious classroom by organizing cooperative learning experiences so that children can play and work together on projects or in small groups. In preschool and even more so in the primary grades, achieving a harmonious classroom involves the entire group working together (Durlak et al., 2011). To foster such harmony, encouraging children to talk about potential or actual social problems, offer solutions, and reflect on the outcomes during class meetings can be effective (Vance, 2013). In the *Promoting Play: A Member of the Class* feature, learn how Tasha creates a context for children to build a strong community.

Beyond focusing on children's social "skills," teachers need to promote positive interactions among children and be attentive to supporting children's close, reciprocal friendships (Gallagher, 2013). Teachers can identify potential friends for children and arrange for them to work together on a project or be placed at the same table. Teachers can make cooperative games part of their learning centers and assign classroom duties to pairs of children. They can include families in their planning and suggest play dates or shared activities after school. Teachers can make a point of communicating with parents about relationships among children as they emerge, and share photos or stories of children sharing each other's company.

Emerging research also suggests that teaching young children about the characteristics of good friends can influence their efforts at making and sustaining positive relationships with peers. In a study of third-graders, researchers found that children who had higher "friendship expectations" exerted more friendship efforts, which resulted in having more friends and feeling less lonely (MacEvoy, Papadakis, Fedigan, & Ash, 2016). Characteristics of good friends include sharing and taking turns, helping, listening, keeping promises, demonstrating care, being nice and respectful, spending time, having fun, and apologizing when necessary. Although this research was conducted with children in middle childhood, children had formed "friendship expectations" by third grade, implying that early childhood teachers can play a role in teaching children friendship expectations. For example, preschool teachers could role-play different scenarios with puppets that illustrated good and poor friendship skills, and ask the children to give a thumbs-up if they thought the puppet was acting like a good friend or a thumbs-down if not.

Children need to share space and activities with all the children in their group; however, only a few of the children may actually be chosen as friends. Friends are a type of relationship that is special and intimate—and chosen by the child. There is a current trend in early childhood to refer to all children in a group as "friends" and to call and refer to children as "friends" (as when a teacher says, "Your friend is waiting for her turn."). However, teachers should be mindful of the use of the word "friend." While all children can play, only children can choose with whom to be friends. Labeling all children in a classroom as "friends" could also serve to diminish the understanding of the characteristics of good friends.

Promoting Play

A Member of the Class

Beth teaches in an inclusive preschool classroom in a diverse urban school. The children in her classroom enjoy a schedule that includes a lot of time to explore and play in the classroom and outside. An intentional teacher, Beth has mindfully prepared the classroom and schedule to meet children's group and individual needs. She helps children plan their choice time, and teaches emotional literacy and social skills as part of her curriculum. So, Beth feels surprised and dismayed when she realizes a group of children has created a sort of "members-only club" in the class. They have been excluding a small group of children from their play and after-school activities, such as play dates and party invitations. This is brought to her attention by Tim, who is the father of Jonah, a child in her classroom. Tim described feeling sad for Jonah over the weekend, who realized he was the only one not invited to a classmates' party.

Beth feels sad to hear this report, and starts paying more attention to play behavior in the classroom and outside. She notices that certain peers are often excluded from play. In addition to Jonah, a child with cerebral palsy, the class tends to exclude Ikran, a recent immigrant who speaks little English, and Nevaeh, a shy child who wears the same clothing almost every day.

Beth shares her concerns with a colleague, who says she learned about "membership" at a recent in-service on inclusion. A key feature and goal of true inclusion, membership encompasses such terms as belonging, acceptance, and positive relationships with other members of the classroom community. Perhaps the best way to describe being a member of the class is when the child is described as "just one of the kids." Her colleague shares some of the strategies she learned to increase "membership" in the inclusive classroom, including creating shared experiences, fostering a sense of classroom community, and supporting peer interactions.

To create more shared experiences, Beth makes sure that everyone gets assigned classroom jobs (she realizes she wasn't giving Jonah as many opportunities), and finds ways for all children to participate fully in activities. For example, it was difficult for Ikran to make choices about which song to sing or which book to read at circle time because she was just beginning to learn English. Beth created picture cards representing songs so that Ikran could point to them when given a chance to select the hello song. All the children seemed to enjoy using the pictures.

To foster a sense of classroom community, Beth started referring to the classroom by name, "Room 3," and when doing attendance, the class named everyone who was in Room 3 and noted when some children were absent. Beth also took and posted a lot of pictures of all the children doing Room 3 activities, such as the recent field trip to the sculpture garden. At circle time, she brought out a beloved puppet, Friendship Franklyn, who professed to love the words "everyone" and "all." To the children's delight, Beth made a big deal of it whenever she heard them use Franklyn's favorite words.

To foster peer interaction, Beth started planning more collaborative art activities at small group; put out more toys that required two children use them together (such as a wooden rocking boat, a tandem tricycle, and a teeter-totter); and started embedding peer interactions into songs and finger plays. Instead of singing, "if you are happy and you know it, clap your hands," she sang, "if you feel happy and you know it—give a high five!" She also assigned children to the same small group and snack tables, and kept the same children together for a few months.

Eventually, Beth noticed that children started increasing peer interactions and inclusion of all children in the classroom. During her spring conferences, she was delighted to learn from Tim that Jonah was being invited often to play dates and birthday parties.

Teachers play an important role in children's relationship development at all ages, and they can play an essential role in making sure that children develop friendships (Gallagher, 2013; Gallagher & Sylvester, 2009). Friendships are a specific and complex type of relationship, and are important for lifelong health and well-being. When children are mutual friends, they share interests and affection for each other. When teachers learn how important friendships are for children's well-being, they can use the Teaching Pyramid to organize classroom environments, routines, and experiences to support children's friendship development (Gallagher, 2013). A teacher can pair preschoolers with similar interests. She can teach them how to enter group activities by observing and commenting on the play. Elementary-school teachers can use board games (with some adult guidance) and games that require teamwork. American classrooms often emphasize the importance of independence, but children fare much better socially and academically when we shift our attention to relationships and interdependence in the classroom.

✔ Application Exercise 8.2
Play Among Friends

Effective Strategies to Build Positive Relationships

Teachers who have positive relationships with children are significantly more likely to influence their behavior because children pay more attention to responsive, caring adults (DeMeulenaere, 2015). In addition, caring relationships help children develop positive self-concept, confidence, and a sense of safety, which in turn reduces the incidence of challenging behavior. In fact, "the time spent building a strong relationship is probably less than the time required to implement more elaborate and time-consuming strategies" to address challenging behaviors (Fox et al., 2003, p. 49).

A sage piece of advice comes from Kaiser and Rasminsky (2017): "Start fresh every day." This seems simple, but sometimes teachers find themselves storing up grievances against children for past transgressions, creating resentment in both parties. One proven effective strategy is called "banking time" (Driscoll & Pianta, 2010). Just as saving money for unexpected expenses helps in an emergency, taking 5 to 15 minutes a week to focus individually on each child—playing with him or her or talking about something interesting unrelated to academics or the child's behavior—can pay dividends in building a relationship.

Effective teachers develop warm, responsive, positive relationships with each child. From infancy through primary grades, the quality of teacher–child relationships is related to positive learning and developmental outcomes for children.

Reducing Teacher Stress: Mindfulness and Thought Interruption   An important but often overlooked aspect of creating a caring community of learners is the health and well-being of the leaders of the classroom—the teachers. Just as healthy parents raise healthy children, well teachers create and support a high-quality social–emotional climate. Teachers who experience more work stress have more conflict in their relationships with children (Neuenschwander, Friedman-Krauss, Raver, & Blair, 2017). In order to calmly and effectively respond to the demands and stresses of working daily and intensively with young children and their families, effective early childhood teachers find it necessary to practice self-care. Teachers can do this by taking care of their physical health (eating well, sleeping, and exercising) as well as making sure to stay socially connected. Friendships are important for teachers, too. Some teachers find that practicing **mindfulness**, or noticing present moments without judgment, helps them regulate their emotions and respond to stressful situations more effectively (Hartigan, 2017).

Mindfulness-based stress reduction strategies can be very helpful for teachers to become and stay resilient through the rewarding but challenging profession of being an early childhood educator. Noticing and interrupting negative thinking is another strategy that teachers find helpful in reducing stress and negativity and increasing effectiveness (Cook, Miller, Fiat, Renshaw, Frye, & Joseph, 2017). One strategy for noticing and interrupting negative thinking is called *red light and green light thinking*. This strategy is based on the fact that our thoughts, feelings and behavior are intertwined. How we think about a situation can influence how we feel, which will influence how we behave. When we get stuck in our negative thinking, we start to feel bad, and then our behavior is often negative or at least unhelpful. For example, imagine you were trying to save some money and managed to save a little. However, you received an unexpected bill to pay and had to use your newly saved money toward the bill. You think to yourself, "This is useless! I'll NEVER be able to save any money!" Then you start feeling depressed and hopeless.

mindfulness The practice of purposefully and nonjudgmentally noticing sensations (bodily, mentally, emotionally) in the present moment.

Becoming an Intentional Teacher

Am I Stuck at a Red Light?

Here's What Happened   My supervisor came by to complete an observation of my teaching. She observed for most of the morning and had to see another teacher's classroom. She said she would come back after school to meet about her observation, but she left her notes. During her observation, one boy, Oliver, was acting out at circle time and small group. He was yelling out phrases from a favorite cartoon, standing up when the children were supposed to be sitting down, and trying to get the other children's attention. Several times, I stopped reading the story and asked Oliver to sit down and to have a quiet mouth so that I could read. I could feel my body tensing up. I started thinking, "I am the worst teacher." Then I started feeling sad and discouraged. My energy started going down. When the music teacher took the children to music class, I took a quick break, and when my colleague said "hello" to me in the hallway, I made a snide remark. When I walked back into the classroom, I took a deep breath, smiled, finished the day with energy, and spent a few extra minutes reading with Oliver in the book corner. We had a nice interaction, and I felt better and more hopeful about my teaching. I decided to ask my supervisor for some tips on how to redirect Oliver.

Here's What I Was Thinking   I realized that I was stuck in red-light thinking after my poor interaction with my colleague. I knew that this type of thinking was ultimately not helpful and certainly wasn't making me feel better or become a better teacher. So, I took a deep breath and thought about the situation another way. I thought to myself, "That was a stressful moment and I had trouble redirecting Oliver, but I did other things well—like reading a book with enthusiasm and coming in extra early to prepare a special small group activity." I started feeling more positive about my teaching and more hopeful about the debrief meeting with my supervisor.

Reflection   Teaching can be stressful. When we aren't feeling our best or paying too much attention to negative thoughts, it can feel even more stressful, and we can become less effective. Are there times when you have experienced "red-light" thinking? How could you have adjusted your thinking to be more realistic and positive? How might this have affected the way you were feeling and behaving?

© Monkey Business Images/Shutterstock

And you stop trying to save in the future. But you can interrupt the negative thinking and start a very different, more positive cycle. In the same situation, you think, "Well, this is a setback. But I'm so glad I had some savings so that I could pay this bill." Then you feel a little more hopeful about the future and decide to keep on your saving track along with implementing a reminder for bills. For an example of this strategy, read the feature *Becoming and Intentional Teacher: Am I Stuck at a Red Light?*

The effectiveness of any strategy will vary with individual children. For this reason, it is important for teachers to have a large repertoire of strategies to use as they build relationships with each child. Table 8.1 describes a caring community from the points of view of both the children and the teachers.

Human relationships are complex, two-way interactions, and children's behavior influences adults' reactions and behaviors just as much as adults influence children. Therefore, it is important for teachers to spend time reflecting on the basis for their expectations and judgments about children's behavior.

Personal, Family, and Cultural Views of Children's Behavior   Each of us has her own views about the acceptability of specific behaviors in children based on personal, family, and cultural experiences (Kaiser & Rasminsky, 2017). For example, some adults welcome children's exuberance, whereas others see rambunctious play as misbehavior. Some children are hypersensitive to touch. With 3-year-old Shisuko, pats or hugs

---

TABLE 8.1   What a Caring Community Looks Like

To create a true caring community of learners, teachers need to consider the child's point of view as well as their own, as described in this table.

From a Child's Point of View	From a Teacher's Point of View
My teacher cares about me, really listens to me, and likes me.	Shows respect and warmth to all children through physical affection, using a soothing tone of voice, smiles, and laughter. Listens carefully to children's feelings and ideas with attention and respect.
My teacher knows me well—my abilities, strengths, interests, and needs.	Engages in individual conversations with children throughout the day. Gets to know children by carefully observing them and developing a relationship with their families.
I feel safe, secure, and happy.	Holds a child's hand, smiles, or pats a child lightly on the shoulder.
I'm not scared; no one bullies me.	Is sure to protect every child, and has zero tolerance for bullying.
I feel like I belong. My identity, language, and culture are valued.	Greets children personally each day when they arrive, calls each child by his or her name, and talks with children at their eye level. Learns key phrases in the child's home language.
I feel proud of my family, and they are welcome in my school.	Greets families warmly. Displays family photos. Conducts home visits or, if parents prefer, meets privately with them at a comfortable site such as a library or local community center.
I have friends.	Helps children who are isolated or lonely connect with at least one other child.
I am challenged, and I am learning.	Expects children to succeed. Acknowledges effort and accomplishments with nods, smiles, hugs, high-fives, or thumbs-up.
My teacher understands what I am facing outside of school.	Pays attention to what the children "wish" their teachers knew about their life circumstances—such as, "I didn't have food for breakfast," "I miss my mom because she is in rehab," or "My dad has been deported."
My teacher still likes me even if I don't always remember the rules or if I sometimes do the wrong thing.	Acknowledges and supports children's positive behavior, especially those children who tend to demonstrate challenging behavior. Takes time to nurture individual relationships each day.
I experience joy.	Begins each day anew, genuinely enjoys children, and delights in their accomplishments.

Source: Based on Inventory of Practices for Promoting Children's Social-Emotional Competence, by the Center on the Social and Emotional Foundations for Early Learning and WestED San Marcos, 2011. Retrieved from http://cainclusion.org/camap/pdfs/CACSEFEL/InventoryOfPractice_AUG11.pdf.

would not be welcome, but sitting nearby and talking quietly would. Relationship building, like all other aspects of teaching, requires individualizing.

Because what is considered acceptable behavior in one family, community, or cultural group may be frowned on or prohibited in another (Kaiser & Rasminsky, 2017), teachers should help children learn the kinds of behaviors that predict success in school. In doing so, they can help young children learn that there are different rules of behavior for different environments. Children make these distinctions all the time. Early on, they learn that what is accepted and safe behavior in their own home is not acceptable behavior in the neighborhood. Read the *Culture Lens: Helping Each Child Adapt to School* feature for an example of what teachers can do to help children feel comfortable at school.

Examine Your Own Attitudes and Biases about Challenging Behavior An essential part of your development as a teacher is to examine your own attitudes toward children's challenging behavior. These attitudes are based in your own upbringing, personal values, cultural practices, and many other aspects of your prior experiences. Which behaviors do you find most unacceptable? Which behaviors "push your buttons"? Spitting, hitting,

Video Example 8.2:

Creating a Caring Community

Two kindergarten teachers discuss how they encourage children to build and maintain a caring community in their classroom. Which of their specific strategies do you think would be most effective in achieving their goals? From a child's point of view, what would it be like to be in their class?

Culture Lens
Helping Each Child Adapt to School

Children from diverse cultural backgrounds may face challenges adapting to unfamiliar environments, and school can be the most daunting. On the first morning of kindergarten, Miguel Hernandez sets in motion a plan to build a sense of community among the children. His class includes children from many different countries and cultural backgrounds. Miguel greets the children, most of whom arrived by bus, at the door. He hasn't had a chance to meet their families.

He begins the day with a morning meeting, and wants the children to introduce themselves. Quickly, however, he changes his plan. In gathering the group and observing them, he realizes how uncomfortable and awkward many of the children would feel if he asked them to speak up in the group. Instead, he introduces himself and reassures them by talking briefly about what will happen today and what they can expect.

Even though Miguel has lived and worked in many different contexts in his life, he remembers vividly his first day of kindergarten. His mother gave him some last-minute instructions so that he would be successful in school. She told him to do three things: stand tall, show respect to his teacher, and speak only in English. When he arrived at school, the teacher said, "Look at me. Now what's your name?" He was nervous and confused, because he wanted to do what the teacher told him, but he also wanted to follow his mother's instructions. He knew that looking into the teacher's

eyes would be disrespectful, and he was unsure of how to say his name in English. On his first day of school, differing cultural expectations clashed, and he was caught in the middle.

Fortunately for the children in Miguel's class, he knows not to make assumptions, and is sensitive to their needs. He will continue to work toward his goal—to create a caring community of learners—but he also knows that to achieve it, he will have to learn as much as possible about the children's families, their values, and their behavioral repertoires. Although it would have been better for this to happen before the first day, he will find ways to talk with families to discover areas where school and home expectations might differ. Once these are revealed, he will be able to propose some options to make things easier for each child and to offer a chance to talk about the differences. For example, "At home, you remove your shoes before entering the house. At school, we keep shoes on."

Teachers can use the same principle when problems arise over differing expectations about appropriate behavior that may be more sensitive to discuss with parents, such as the use of profanity. Children may hear and use language at home that is prohibited at school. Helping children adapt to the expectations of school without criticizing their family or community can be a tricky balancing act for teachers, but is likely to be in the child's best interest.

name-calling, bullying? Are they equally unacceptable? Do you see challenging behavior as characteristic of the child or something that is learned?

It is also important to consider how implicit bias might impact your perception, interactions, behaviors, and feelings toward others in an unconscious way (Allen & Steed, 2016). There is evidence that harsh disciplinary practices that disproportionally impact some groups of children are influenced by teacher's responses to behaviors that are based on unconscious and implicit bias (McIntosh, Barnes, Eliason, & Morris, 2014). For example, a teacher who views a child of color as disrespectful is more likely to use punishment such as time-out, suspension, or even expelling the child from school.

To effectively decrease implicit bias, teachers can engage in learning opportunities and self-reflection activities that make them more aware of the prevalence of bias, stereotyping, prejudice, and systemic racism in society. Additionally, collecting data on when and with whom teachers are using more harsh discipline can help identify when teachers need more support.

It is also important for you to consider your personal beliefs about the causes of specific types of unacceptable child behavior. Do you attribute motives to certain children but not to others? Do you find yourself thinking that a particularly aggressive child is mean-spirited, or do you think that she wants your attention and is willing to get it any way she can?

Mistaken Behavior, Not Misbehavior

mistaken behavior Alternative term for children's misbehavior, recognizing the fact that young children are still learning acceptable behavior and that they are bound to make mistakes.

Considering the causes for children's behavior is an important part of the reflection process. Dan Gartrell (2011), an expert on guiding children's behavior, prefers the term mistaken behavior to *misbehavior*. Young children are still learning acceptable behavior and are bound to make mistakes, just as they make mistakes when learning to tie their shoes or write their names. We not only tolerate, but we expect mistaken behavior as part of the learning process. Why, then, are we so much less tolerant of mistakes in children's social behavior?

Some aspects of children's behavior that disturb adults are actually reflections of children's typical development. For example, toddlers come to love and overuse the word *no,* and may accompany their insistent "No!" with temper tantrums. These behaviors demonstrate children's growing independence from adults, their beginning knowledge of the power of language, and frustration over not being able to do everything they would like. Most of the time, children grow out of these oppositional behaviors if given appropriate support and nurturance.

Behavior Is Functional

All behavior is a form of communication; it serves a function (Kaiser & Rasminsky, 2017). Teachers need to understand that even challenging behaviors—those behaviors that are potentially harmful in the short or long term—are conveying some type of message. Experts who study children's behavior have found that most challenging behavior serves one of three functions: It helps children get something, avoid something, or change the level of stimulation (Kaiser & Rasminsky, 2017). For example, Brian wants Tonia's truck, so he pushes her down. Tray doesn't want to clean up, so he throws the toys at Emma. Lala is bored waiting in line for the bathroom, so she pinches Mona. As undesirable as these behaviors may be, to effectively handle the children's frustration, the teacher must determine what each behavior is conveying, and provide the appropriate support and guidance.

If teachers think about children's challenging behavior as either a mistake on the path to learning or a message they are trying to send, it is likely that their attitudes toward challenging behaviors will change. Instead of blaming children or rejecting them, teachers are more likely to embrace these challenges as problems to solve. Of course, the most effective strategy is to prevent problems in the first place, which is the second step on the Teaching Pyramid.

⬆ High-Quality Supportive Environments and Children's Positive Behavior

The quality of the learning environment is also very important in creating a caring community of learners and enabling children to do their best. Teachers' work begins before they meet the children in their groups. The physical environment; the schedule, including use of routines and transitions; and the curriculum plan are all important factors in promoting children's positive outcomes, preventing negative behaviors, and creating a caring community. As discussed in Chapter 3, the arrangement of the physical space and materials provides the framework to support children's positive behavior. When the classroom is well organized and predictable, children's behavior reflects that. In addition, the classroom literally communicates to children what is acceptable. In a wide-open space, children may become boisterous or unruly, as compared to a quiet, cozy nook where they are more likely to calmly peruse a book.

Environments send messages to children about what behavior is acceptable and what is valued. What messages does this classroom environment send to children?

To ensure the best possible outcomes, teachers need to plan engaging daily routines with smooth transitions. Teachers can establish clear expectations for classroom behavior and make sure supports are in place so that children can develop warm relationships, demonstrate their best behavior, and engage productively in learning.

Ensure Smooth Transitions

Young children's care and education involves numerous changes in activity and relocation of their physical space. They move from group time to learning centers, eat regularly, wash their hands, use the bathroom, take naps, and go outdoors and return. Primary-grade children move between special classes such as music, art, or physical education in addition to lunch and recess, or switch subject matter teachers. Each of these situations involves transitions.

transitions Changes from one activity or place to another.

Transitions are the changes from one activity or place to another. Although inevitable, transitions can be difficult for young children who are not particularly good at waiting or who do not adapt well to change. Children who exhibit challenging behaviors tend to display oppositional behavior during transitions. Following are principles to keep in mind to ease transitions:

Video Example 8.3:

Choosing a Learning Center

A pre-kindergarten teacher manages the transition from group time to intentional play in learning centers. What does the teacher do to prepare the children for the transition? How does she facilitate their decision making?

- Prepare ahead of time for the next activity so children do not spend excessive amounts of time waiting. For instance, have several children set up for snack while the others clean up centers so the transition to snack time is smooth.
- Give children a 5-minute warning before a transition happens, such as, "Five more minutes 'til cleanup time." Point out the numbers on a digital clock (which becomes a math/addition learning experience) or the hands of the clock to help children grasp the concept of 5 minutes.

- For those children who have particular difficulty with transitions, give them an individual warning and explanation of what is to come, or perhaps a pictorial cue.
- Make transitions learning experiences by singing songs, reciting rhymes or poems, counting steps, following the leader's motions, doing movement exercises, or following specific directions such as, "If your name starts with a K, get your coat."
- Minimize the number of transitions between activities and the amount of time children spend in transitions.

Use Engaging Routines

The early childhood day is governed by routines of daily living, which, if planned well, can provide children with excellent learning experiences. A large-scale study of 652 pre-kindergartens in 11 states found that, on average, children spent more than one-third of their time in routines and transitions, but during 87% of that time, they were waiting idly and/or uninvolved in any learning activity (Early et al., 2010). These regular, informal moments of the day provide valuable learning opportunities that should not be wasted.

Routines—snacks and mealtimes, cleaning up, washing hands, napping, dressing for outdoors—all provide opportunities for children to practice newly acquired skills and engage in conversation essential for developing language. In addition, teachers can use routines as times for individual interactions such as sitting and talking with children during snacks and meals.

Teachers should establish routines that allow children to do as much as possible themselves. When adults do things for children that they can already do themselves, they rob children of important learning experiences. Routines such as dressing or cleaning up also provide many chances for children to practice fine motor skills as well as cognitive abilities such as categorization (for example, the long blocks go together and the short blocks go together).

© Pearson Education

Video Example 8.4:

Engaging Routines

This video provides an example of a preschool napping routine. Teachers often struggle with guiding children's behavior during routines and the difficult transition to naptime. How does the teacher in this video turn a daily routine into a learning opportunity?

Use a Staff Schedule and Zoning Chart

Using a staff schedule and zoning chart is an effective practice to help children be active participants in the classroom activities. This is also called engagement. Staff schedules organize classroom staff by assigning specific roles and duties for the day. It helps the classroom run smoothly, allows the teachers to be responsive to the children at all times, and decreases the amount of time children wait during transitions between activities. With a staff schedule and zoning chart, all classroom team members know where they should be and what they should be doing. Children are not left to wait while the adults try to organize their roles, and staff can work more efficiently as a team when everyone knows where they need to be and who handles any unexpected events. Figure 8.2 is an example of a staff schedule and zoning chart.

Activities/ Transitions	Staff Person A	Staff Person B	Staff Person C
Arrival	Greet children and parents	Help children put away backpacks	Get tables ready for breakfast
Breakfast	At red table	At blue table	At green table
Transition to outside	Signal transition/blow bubbles	Clean up breakfast tables	Help children transition
Outside	At big toy	In the field	Clean and sanitize tables
Transition to classroom	Help children transition to circle time	Signal transition	Help children wash hands
Circle time	Support children at circle	Lead circle	Break
Centers	Zone 1	Zone 2	Zone 3

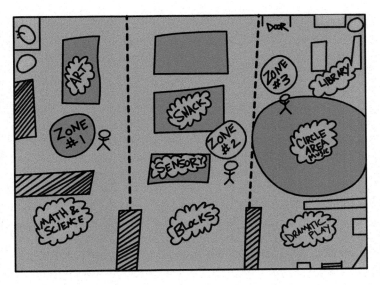

FIGURE 8.2 Staff Schedule and Zoning Chart

To develop a staff schedule and zoning chart, the first step is to create a daily schedule of all the activities and routines (including transitions) throughout the day. This helps keep the day predictable for all members of the classroom community. Then create a chart that specifies which teacher is in charge of which area/activity, as well as what individual duties are during the transitions before and after the activity. When a teacher is "zoned" to an area, she positions her body so that she is always able to see the children. If teachers are on their knees in the classroom, they need to be sure they can see over the shelving units and are aware of the children's whereabouts at all times. They must scan their assigned area and the rest of the classroom at all times. This allows teachers to be constantly aware of what is happening in the classroom. They need to talk to the other staff members in the classroom throughout the day and highlight children's positive behaviors, such as, "Look at these children trading toys so nicely," as well as address any issues that may arise, such as, "Ms. Teri, I need to help Oscar wash his hands, can you cover my area?"

Application Exercise 8.3

Transitions as a Learning Experience

Establish Clear, Consistent, Fair Rules for Behavior

Just as children thrive in predictable physical and temporal environments, they also thrive when the expectations for behavior are clear and predictable. Therefore, it is essential that teachers involve children early on in establishing clear rules, limits, and consequences for behavior. It is equally important that teachers consistently and fairly enforce these rules in order for children to feel safe and secure.

In establishing classroom rules or *guidelines* for behavior, as Gartrell (2011) calls them, teachers need to engage children in discussing and enforcing a manageable number (three to six) of positively stated classroom rules. These discussions should take place during times of calm and quiet reflection. Some teachers may be tempted to focus children's attention on what not to do—don't hit, don't throw toys. However, a more effective approach is to positively state what children *should* do. Virtually all situations can be covered by these three rules:

1. We take care of ourselves.
2. We take care of other people.
3. We take care of our school.

When we say "don't run" to young children, their brains might process only the word *run*; they don't process the prohibition. Therefore, it is always more effective to state behavioral expectations clearly and positively: "Keep the food on the table" or "Walk inside." It is also important to provide reasons for the expected behavior: "If you run, someone might get knocked over." Children are more likely to be successful and to follow the rules and expectations if the teacher provides the behavioral expectations in advance. For example, as soon as children join storytime, the teacher says, "It is time for story. Remember to keep your eyes on the action, your ears listening, your voice is quiet, your hands and feet are to yourself," instead of waiting for a child to shout out or poke his or her friend. Some teachers find it helpful to provide a visual cue of the behavioral expectations in advance. Using "Show Me Five" is a strategy to teach children the behavioral expectations of group time. The teacher teaches each behavioral expectation through modeling and role play and then can start to simply say, "Show Me Five" to gain (or regain) the students' attention. Figure 8.3 is an example of a "Show Me Five" visual.

Support Children to Do Their Best

Earlier, we identified several reasons why children behave as they do: to get something, to avoid something, or to change the level of stimulation. When it comes to "getting something," the object of desire is usually the teacher's attention. Children are willing to do almost anything to attract adults' attention, and they tend not to discriminate between positive and negative attention. To guide children toward using positive strategies to attract attention, teachers must keep in mind that because they have the power to control only their own behavior, they can determine which behaviors of children they give attention to and when. Teachers can ignore mistaken behavior, redirect behavior, and give positive feedback and encouragement.

Ignore When Appropriate Behaviors that are not reinforced will be extinguished or eliminated. If the reinforcement that children are seeking is the teacher's attention—and they are behaving inappropriately to receive that attention—then ignoring the inappropriate

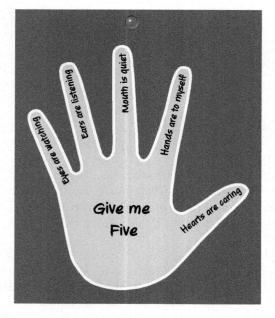

FIGURE 8.3 Show Me Five "Show Me Five" is a strategy to teach and remind children about the behavioral expectations of group time.

behavior can be an effective way of extinguishing it. When teachers react to these behaviors, they continue.

Consider, for example, 3½-year-old Curt, who has daily temper tantrums and lies on the floor kicking and screaming. His teacher, Janine, knows that he is too old for this behavior and believes that it is a cry for her attention. She decides to ignore the tantrums by physically removing herself to the other side of the room, but as soon as Curt tires from his explosion and quiets, she returns and invites him to sit by her and read a story. It takes several days, during which she has to remind the other children not to pay attention to Curt during these episodes, but gradually Curt's tantrums disappear.

To be effective, teachers must be careful to give more attention to children's positive behaviors than to their negative ones. Teachers can identify a select few negative behaviors to ignore and also identify prosocial or positive behaviors to acknowledge that are the opposite of the ones they are trying to ignore. It may also be necessary to teach the other children to ignore a peer's undesirable behavior, since the child may desire the attention of his or her peers as well as the teacher's.

Focus on Desired Behavior It is usually easier for teachers to think about what child behaviors they want to see less of than what they want to see more of. However, focusing on desired outcomes is an important step to help children increase positive behaviors and decrease challenging behaviors. It is helpful for teachers to think what they want to see less of, what they want the child to do instead, and how they will provide attention and feedback when the child is engaged in the appropriate behavior, as illustrated in Table 8.2.

Redirect Behavior Another strategy for supporting children to do their best is redirection, which is the drawing of a child's attention or behavior toward a more desirable alternative. Redirection is especially effective with very young children whose attention is easily distracted. For instance, 18-month-old Jamie appears ready to bite Erika because she has the toy train he covets. His teacher has anticipated this situation, and heads it off by offering him an identical engine and turning his attention toward her and away from where Erika is playing.

redirection Drawing a child's attention or behavior toward a more desirable alternative than the one on which the child is currently focusing.

Redirecting children toward more productive activities is a useful strategy for toddlers who have yet to learn language or other problem-solving strategies and for children who are wandering or withdrawn. As children get older and become more competent problem solvers, adults should rely less on redirection and more on intentionally teaching children to get along with others. Because adults won't always be available to redirect behavior, it is important to use this strategy sparingly.

TABLE 8.2 Focus on Desired Behaviors

Behaviors I want to see less of	What I want them to do instead	What will I say in advance?	What I will say or do when they engage in the desired behavior
Grabbing materials from peers	Request a turn	"We only have two glitter bottles and six artists. If you would like to use some glitter and someone has it, you can say, 'Can I have the glitter?'"	"Samantha, you used your words to ask for the glitter. Kyle is giving you the glitter. It is so sparkly!"
Running down the hall or in the classroom	Walk inside	"Room 3, we are going to the gym! We need to use our walking feet in the hallway until we get there."	"Eugenie, you are using your walking feet and keeping everyone safe in the hallway!"
Yelling out answers at large group time	Raising a quiet hand and waiting to be called on to answer	"I have a mystery box, and I am looking for someone raising a quiet hand to have a turn and guess what is inside."	"Arlo is raising a quiet hand. Arlo, what do you think is in the mystery box today?"

Give Positive Feedback and Encouragement   One of the most powerful ways teachers can support children's prosocial behavior is to give positive attention when children behave in desirable ways. When teachers use positive feedback and encouragement related to children's appropriate behavior, children feel supported, and are more likely to continue to behave acceptably.

If a teacher wants a behavior to continue, it is necessary to provide positive feedback or encouragement. It is important for teachers not to give empty praise such as "good girl" or "nice job," but rather to enthusiastically encourage and describe the desired behavior or acknowledge the effort. "Heath, thank you for telling me why you were feeling angry," says his teacher, Jane. "Next time, I'll make sure you get a turn on the balance beam." At times, encouragement will be nonverbal, such as offering a child a smile, a nod, or a thumbs-up for an achievement.

For positive feedback and encouragement to be effective, teachers need to recognize that there are individual differences in the forms of acknowledgment that children find positive. Communicating with families about what kinds of feedback work for their children may be necessary. One might prefer to sit by the teacher, while another prefers to be given a task to do. When teachers frequently give positive support for appropriate behavior, children will often pick up on their lead by giving positive feedback to each other. Repeating words she has heard her teacher use, 5-year-old Karena says to her friend Darla, "Thanks for helping me clean up this mess. I'll help you next time."

Intentional teachers encourage young children's positive behavior. This is sometimes called *behavior approving interactions*, and research suggests that when teachers spend more of their day engaged in behavior approving interactions versus behavior correcting interactions, children have better social emotional and academic outcomes (Fuhs, Farran & Nesbitt, 2013). Sometimes, just a smile or nod is enough to communicate that you noticed a child's effort or success.

Let's think about how a teacher might use all of these ways of supporting children to do their best when confronted with a challenging situation. Andy picks his nose, and it definitely irritates his teacher. She finds this behavior disgusting, but realizes after reflection that she overreacts every time he does it, and the frequency of the behavior is actually increasing, especially during snack times. She decides to encourage more appropriate behavior by giving him his own box of tissues and reminding him in advance how to use them. At first, Andy's nose picking increases, but his teacher decides to ignore it. Instead, when he does anything with the tissue box, even if he simply picks it up, she gives him attention and encouragement. She also gives him positive attention unrelated to the negative behavior: "Andy, thanks for helping me bring the tricycles inside." Over time, his teacher finds much to enjoy in Andy, and the nose picking becomes a rare event.

As we have seen, there are many effective strategies teachers can use to support children to do their best and prevent problem behaviors. In addition to preventing negative behaviors, however, adults have key roles to play in teaching children appropriate behavior, which we examine next.

© Pearson Education

Video Example 8.5:

Encouraging Cooperation

A group of kindergartners work alongside one another as they play and build with blocks creatively. What does the teacher do to promote cooperation among them? And how does she diffuse potential conflict?

✔️ Check Your Understanding 8.3

🔺 Teaching Social–Emotional Competence and Guiding Behavior

Children aren't born with the ability to get along well with other people and regulate their own strong emotions. These social and emotional skills are learned gradually over the first years of life, and they are among the most important accomplishments of children's lives.

Guiding children to function well in a caring community of learners, however, depends on three key aspects of teaching practice: fostering emotional literacy, teaching social skills, and teaching conflict resolution. Before addressing each of these dimensions of teaching practice, it is important to clarify the distinction between guidance and punishment.

Guidance and Punishment

When children display unacceptable or inappropriate behavior, which is a natural part of growing up, adults' automatic response is often to discipline them. Consider that the word *disciple* means "to learn." Often when teachers and adults discipline, however, they do so not to teach, but rather to punish. However, children do not learn positive behaviors from punishment. Although punishment may stop a negative behavior temporarily, it does not teach the child what to do instead. Consequently, teachers may find that using the same punishment repeatedly with a child (which they often do) doesn't deter the negative behavior.

One discipline strategy teachers and parents too often use is time-out. **Time-out** is removing a child to a specified chair or area of the room for a period of time following an unacceptable behavior. Many adults think that time-out is a good way to get children to stop their unacceptable behavior. Removing a child from a situation for a period of time, however, can be a form of punishment, and if so, it is unlikely that the child is reflecting on righteousness in this situation. Time-out does not teach the child what to do instead of the negative behavior; in fact, it may achieve the child's purpose by removing him from the situation he sought to avoid, such as helping to clean up. On the other hand, occasionally giving children a brief time away to calm down *before* negative behavior escalates may be helpful if the child feels supported by the teacher in this situation and if the child's culture does not consider isolation from the group as humiliation (Kaiser & Rasminsky, 2017).

Guidance is the process of teaching children the life skills they need to function productively. Instead of punishments, children need adults to actively teach them positive behaviors to replace negative, ineffective behaviors. Children must be taught important life skills—such as appropriate expression of negative emotions, getting along with others, and conflict resolution—through a variety of developmentally appropriate learning experiences and teaching strategies. In the busy classroom atmosphere, teachers often guide children's behavior very publicly, calling attention to children who struggle more with self-regulation. For Micah, hearing that the teacher "likes the way" other children are sitting and hearing his name called out by the teacher, "We're waiting for you, Micah," convinces Micah over time that he is not very good at keeping up with the demands of school.

Sometimes teachers adopt shortcut techniques that seem to simplify child guidance in the classroom, such as the often used "Traffic Light" technique. In this method, each child has three cards: green (for positive behavior), yellow (for a "warning") and red (for challenging behavior). The teacher assigns colors to individual children based on their behavior, often publicly displaying children's traffic light status. For children who struggle, and whose cards are often yellow or red, this technique can bring shame and frustration. Sadly for those children, there's no card for trying hard. The Traffic Light behavior control method is frequently used school- or district-wide, which is surprising given that it is not an effective strategy for teaching children positive behavior. The same children receive a red card repeatedly and, as is true of punishment in general, their behavior often worsens. In the next sections, you'll learn strategies for supporting children's positive behavior and responding to their challenging behavior in respectful ways.

Teach Emotional Literacy and Social Skills

When children grapple over a toy, hit, or bite, teachers often suggest, "Use your words." This is an effective strategy if, and only if, children have the vocabulary to describe their emotions and the language proficiency to articulate their wants and needs. **Emotional literacy** is "the ability to identify, understand, and respond to emotions in oneself and others in a healthy manner" (Joseph, Strain, & Ostrosky, 2006). Children who have a strong foundation in emotional literacy are more likely to tolerate frustration and fight less, and are

time-out Removing a child to a specified chair or area of the room for a period of time following an unacceptable behavior.

guidance The process of teaching children the life skills they need to function productively with other children.

emotional literacy Children's ability to identify their own and others' emotions, to express emotions in a healthy way, and to self-regulate their feelings.

less lonely and impulsive. They also are more focused and have greater academic achievement. Developing a vocabulary for expressing feelings is an essential aspect of emotional literacy because the larger a child's emotional vocabulary, the finer the distinctions she can make when expressing her feelings to other people (Kusché & Greenberg, 2012).

Think about the number of words you know related to feeling bad: *angry, mad, furious, upset, anxious, unhappy, distraught, disturbed, disappointed, depressed, disgusted, dismayed, frustrated*—we could empty a thesaurus. The same could be said for other emotional states. Feeling frustrated, however, is not the same as feeling furious. Children's behavior may be communicating frustration or fury and, without knowing which, we may be more or less effective in helping them.

When fostering emotional literacy with young children, teachers need to try using "I feel" versus "I am" language. Imagine saying, "I am stupid, depressed, irritated" versus saying, "I feel stupid; I feel depressed; I feel irritated." It is subtle, but it significantly changes the energy of the sentence. The first sentence defines you. The second is simply a description of your emotions and how you are feeling in the moment. Expressing emotional literacy with "I feel" acknowledges that this situation is just temporary and that you have some ability to change it.

An important aspect of emotional literacy is being able to reflect on one's own emotions. Read the *What Works: Teaching Emotional Literacy* feature for examples of effective strategies to promote emotional literacy in young children.

What Works

Teaching Emotional Literacy

Teaching emotional literacy is a proven strategy for promoting children's self-regulation and social skills and preventing challenging behavior. Here are some research-based ways teachers can help children become more emotionally literate.

- Express your own feelings. "I feel frustrated because this is the third time I tried to open the paint jar and it's stuck. I'm going to take a deep breath and then try again."
- Label children's feelings and your own emotions. "You look like you might feel disappointed that Micah didn't come to school today. I miss him, too."
- Help children talk about their own and others' emotions and discuss acceptable ways of expressing strong feelings. "I think you and Rashid feel angry because you both want to paint. Can you ask how much longer it will be before you can have a turn at the easel?"
- Use or adapt songs and rhymes, games, and stories that introduce and expand feeling words. "If you feel happy and you know it, clap your hands. If you feel excited and you know it, jump up high. If you feel frustrated and you know it, take a breath."
- Narrate and describe ongoing interactions to help children develop vocabulary related to prosocial behaviors. "Gregory and Keisha, you are working so well together at the computer. You look pleased and feel proud of the book you've created."
- Draw children's attention to the feelings or experiences of others, at times using pictures or photos of people's faces. "Look at this face. Can you tell how this person might be feeling?"
- Help children develop empathy by reminding them of their own similar feelings or experiences. "You know what it feels like when someone says you can't play."

- Model caring, positive regard for others. When a child is sick, have children make cards or send emails.

Emotional literacy helps children calm down when they are feeling very strong emotions. Teachers can use an emotion thermometer to help children monitor their own feelings. The children decorate the thermometer with pictures of feeling faces from "happy," "calm," and "relaxed" in the blue, cool section of the thermometer all the way up to "angry" or "stressed out" in the red, hot section of the thermometer. The teacher then asks children to describe a recent conflict, and together they retrace the steps that led to the angry outburst. Then the teacher discusses with the child the thoughts, actions, and words that the child can use to reduce her anger.

As the teacher retraces the steps of the angry outburst, the children identify the time or situation that began the episode. This is marked as the "Danger Point" on the thermometer. Once children have established their danger points, they name the zone, such as "Think Calm Thoughts," "Cool Down," or "Code Red." Then the teacher and children can use this code word as a signal that anger or stress has reached the threshold. This in turn can trigger the use of a calming strategy, such as taking three deep breaths or visualizing happy and calming places.

Sources: Based on G. Joseph, P. Strain, & M. M. Ostrosky, 2006. *Fostering emotional literacy in young children: Labeling emotions* (What Works Brief 21). Urbana-Champaign, IL: Center on the Social and Emotional Foundations for Early Learning; and G. E. Joseph, C. Webster-Stratton, & M. Reid, 2006. *Fostering social and emotional competence: Implementing Dina Dinosaur's social skills and problem solving curriculum in inclusive early childhood programs* Seattle, WA: The Incredible Years.

Just as children need adults to teach them how to regulate and express emotions constructively, children need adults to explicitly teach them social skills such as cooperation, social problem solving, and interacting with peers. In addition, children with disabilities may need particular help from adults in forming friendships with typically developing peers (Joseph & Strain, 2003a, 2003b).

One important decision facing teachers is when to teach social skills. Some moments in time are more effective than others to teach social skills. Teachers often try to teach problem solving in the middle of a crisis situation, when intervention is least effective. Read the *Including All Children: When to Teach Social and Emotional Skills* feature to learn timely ways to teach social skills.

Including All Children
When to Teach Social and Emotional Skills

The figure below illustrates the cycle of challenging behavior as it typically occurs in early childhood settings. It depicts the point at which teachers are most effective in supporting children's social–emotional development and in preventing challenging behaviors. Consider how the cycle unfolds in the following scenario.

At choice time, Jessie moves to the block corner, sits down, and begins constructing a boat with the unit blocks. He is serious about his project, but calm and content. His teacher, Sarah, looks around the room and notices that all of the children are happily playing and learning. A few minutes pass, and more children are now in the block corner. There are fewer blocks to go around, and it is getting crowded. Still, Jessie is busy concentrating and enjoying his creation.

Fifteen minutes later, Jessie has an idea and searches for the Y-shaped block. He sees a child using it and demands it with angry words, but the other boy continues to claim it.

Sarah hears a scream and rushes to see what happened. Jessie has attacked the boy with the Y-shaped block, who is badly hurt and cries loudly.

At precisely this point—marked by the red arrow—many teachers try to teach Jessie a social skills lesson. For example, teachers might say any of the following: "Use your words!" "Hitting is not okay." "We share

our toys." "Say you're sorry!" "You need to calm down. Go to the thinking chair."

It is true that preschoolers need to use words to resolve conflict, to understand that aggression is not okay, to share materials, to know how and when to use an apology, and how to regulate their emotions. However, teaching these skills is ineffective if teachers try to do so at the wrong time. The crisis moment (red arrow) is not a teachable moment for several reasons: (1) The challenging behavior has already occurred. (2) The child who engages in aggression is likely to be upset and agitated, and not responsive to a lesson highlighting his or her mistakes. (3) The time and attention the teacher spends trying to teach the child what to do instead (even if it is negative attention) may serve to reinforce the challenging behavior. (4) If the teacher uses these crisis moments only as times to teach social–emotional skills, the child will never receive enough positive learning and practice opportunities to effectively alter his or her behavior.

The most effective teachable moments happen *before* problems occur, when the teacher and children are calm and engaged in appropriate behavior—green arrows. At these times, teachers can build positive relationships and teach key social–emotional skills, such as identifying emotions and resolving conflict.

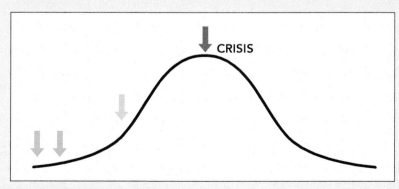

Cycle of Challenging Behavior

Source: Based on G. E. Joseph, 2002. *Center for social and emotional foundations for early learning preschool training module 2.*

Video Example 8.6:

Peaceful Conflict Resolution

This video discusses conflict resolution. Young children often need guidance and support to learn how to get along with other people. What are some of the strategies the teacher in this video uses to help the children resolve their conflicts and avoid future conflicts?

Helping children learn conflict negotiation skills takes time and practice. Sometimes a conflict does not warrant a full-scale negotiation because one child is not as vested in the issue. But equipping all children with conflict negotiation skills helps ensure that rules are fairly and equitably applied, and that the classroom is truly a caring community of learners.

Conflict Resolution

Organizing the environment and routines and establishing classroom expectations and structure around respect will prevent much classroom conflict. However, conflict is an inevitable part of social interaction, especially with young children who are just developing their ability to get along with other people. In fact, episodes of conflict should be considered learning opportunities. Teaching children specific steps in conflict resolution before problems occur and trusting them to solve their own problems are important steps in children's social–emotional development.

When teachers remain calm and in control of their own emotions during conflicts between students, children feel assured and safe. It is important to acknowledge children's strong feelings and help them learn to describe their feelings and perceptions of the conflict to each other. Rather than asking a question that children will not be able to answer, such as "How do you think that made him feel?" ask the child, "What happened? How do you feel?" Like adults, children experiencing strong negative emotions are less able to "use their words" or use perspective-taking to think about how other children feel. Think about the last time you were very angry, and how effectively you were able to describe your feelings or consider the other person's perspective. By giving each child the opportunity to offer solutions to the conflict and by offering their own only if needed, teachers help children become better negotiators and communicators. Table 8.3 describes strategies for teaching conflict resolution.

TABLE 8.3   Strategies for Teaching Conflict Resolution

Effective strategies exist for teaching children to solve their own conflicts, as illustrated here in the examples.

Strategy	Example
Acknowledge, accept, and validate all children's feelings and perceptions of the conflict.	Use "I messages"—sentences that describe your own observations or perceptions about a situation, such as "Katie, I think you are angry because Ally took the blocks you wanted."
Help children verbalize feelings and desires to each other and listen to one another. Use *active listening*, which reflects what you are hearing so the child can agree or disagree.	The teacher says, "Katie, it sounds like you wanted all the big blocks for your bridge." Katie responds, "No, I just want the two biggest, and Ally took them."
Clarify and state the problem.	"Katie and Ally, you both want the two biggest blocks."
Give children the opportunity to suggest solutions.	The teacher says, "How could we solve this problem?" Katie says, "I get to have the blocks because I was here first." Ally says, "You have been playing with them the whole time. I want a turn." Katie replies, "I could play with them today and you can have them next week." Ally ponders for a while and says, "Okay, but only if you promise."
Propose solutions when children do not have ideas or if their ideas are too extreme or punitive.	"Next week seems like a long time away," the teacher says. "Maybe tomorrow would be a fairer solution."
Uphold the value of mutual agreement and give children the opportunity to reject proposed solutions. That is, both parties in the conflict must mutually agree on the solution. When both children lose interest in the conflict, do not pursue it.	"Do you both agree that tomorrow Ally can have the two biggest blocks? If so, we'll write it down so we remember."
Help children recognize their responsibility in a conflict situation.	"Ally, I know you wanted the blocks, but Katie got angry when you took them without asking."

TABLE 8.3 Strategies for Teaching Conflict Resolution (*Continued*)

Effective strategies exist for teaching children to solve their own conflicts, as illustrated here in the examples.

Strategy	Example
Help children repair the relationships, but do not force children to be insincere.	"Ally, you usually like to build with Katie. And I know Katie is your friend."
Encourage children to resolve their conflict by themselves.	"Katie, I know that you and Ally built a hospital together last week, so I think you can solve this problem together."

Sources: Based on D. Gartrell, 2006. Guidance matters. In *Beyond the Journal: Young Children on the Web.* Retrieved from www.naeyc.org/files/yc/file/200603/GuidanceBTJ.pdf; R. DeVries & B. Zan, 2012. *Moral classrooms, moral children: Creating a constructivist atmosphere in early education* (2nd ed.). New York: Teachers College Press; and E. Wheeler, 2004. *Conflict resolution in early childhood: Helping children understand and resolve conflicts.* Upper Saddle River, NJ: Pearson.

Application Exercise 8.4
Resolving Conflicts

Applying the first three parts of the Teaching Pyramid—establishing positive relationships, organizing high-quality supportive environments, and teaching social and emotional skills and positively guiding behavior—will go a long way toward creating a caring community of learners. Nevertheless, a few children will require more individualized interventions to successfully navigate the classroom and learn optimally, as we discuss next.

Check Your Understanding 8.4

Intensive Individualized Interventions

In most classrooms, it is likely that there will be a few children who demonstrate persistent challenging behaviors. To effectively reach these students, it may be necessary to use **individualized intervention**, which is a systematically planned and implemented set of actions designed to alter the course of a child's development or learning.

Research demonstrates that **positive behavior support (PBS)** is a highly effective, humane intervention approach for working with children with severe and persistent challenging behaviors (Caldarella, Williams, Ahnsen & Willis, 2015; Kaiser & Rasminsky, 2017). Positive behavior support is a method of identifying the causes and functions of problem behaviors in order to develop support strategies that prevent such behaviors and teach new, more appropriate skills. In the following sections, we identify and describe challenging behaviors and then explain each of the elements of positive behavior support.

individualized intervention A systematically planned and implemented set of actions designed to alter the course of a child's development or learning.

positive behavior support (PBS) A method of identifying the causes and functions of problem behaviors in order to develop support strategies that prevent challenging behaviors and teach new, more appropriate skills.

Understand Challenging Behaviors

A formal definition of *challenging behaviors* is "any repeated pattern of behavior ... that interferes with or is at risk of interfering with the child's optimal learning or engagement in pro-social interactions with peers and adults" (Division for Early Childhood, 2017). However, each of us defines *challenging behaviors* according to our own values, experiences, and cultural perspectives. Strain and Hemmeter (1999) take a more pragmatic view in their definition: "Challenging behavior is any behavior that is disturbing to you and you wish to see stopped" (p. 17).

Conflicts are inevitable when children are together in group situations. Effective teachers do not solve problems for children. They teach children the skills they need to resolve their own conflicts.

Strain and Hemmeter (1999) also offer some timeless wisdom for anyone working with children with challenging behaviors (and that's everyone who works with children!). They advise early childhood professionals to become more "comfortable" with challenging behavior; they emphasize how important it is to recognize that when feeling stressed, embarrassed, disturbed, or hopeless, it is difficult to be effective. They suggest that teachers need to acknowledge these feelings and serve as mutual support for each other. Then, if a child loses control and a teacher begins to feel herself losing control as a result, she can seek help from a colleague. These researchers (Strain & Hemmeter, 1999) also suggest that teachers avoid blaming parents or other uncontrollable events and focus on small successes. For example, instead of lamenting that Andy picks his nose, celebrate that he picked his nose only once today instead of 10 times.

Positive behavior support involves several steps. The first, and perhaps most important, is determining the function of the child's behavior.

Assess and Address the Function of the Child's Behavior

functional behavioral assessment The process of determining why a child is behaving a certain way, based on the principle that all behavior serves a function or purpose.

Functional behavioral assessment, sometimes referred to as FBA, is the process of determining why a child is behaving a certain way. "Any challenging behavior that persists over time is 'working' for the child" (Strain & Hemmeter 1999, p. 19) and is an attempt to communicate a message such as "You're asking me to do something that is too difficult" (e.g., when a teacher expects preschoolers to sit still for a 30-minute group time) or "I'm bored; pay attention to me."

Acknowledging that children's behavior serves a function and communicates a message helps teachers focus on teaching alternative ways of interacting with other people. Remember Tray, who didn't want to clean up and threw the toys at Emma? If his teacher puts him in time-out, Tray will most likely throw toys again tomorrow because he succeeded in avoiding cleanup time.

Functional assessment is a process of systematic observation and documentation of children's behavior over time involving three steps that are easily remembered using the letters A, B, and C (Kaiser & Rasminsky, 2017):

- *A = Antecedents.* This step is observing what usually occurs before the negative behavior or what conditions trigger the behavior, such as a whole-group time.
- *B = Behavior.* During this step, teachers systematically document what the behavior is and how frequently it occurs.
- *C = Consequences.* During the third step, the teacher or child care provider attempts to determine the function the behavior serves; that is, what does the child get, avoid, and/or change as a result of the behavior?

Identify Antecedents   Assessing the antecedents (A) of the behavior requires a teacher to carefully observe to determine the conditions or situations that most often trigger the behavior. By identifying key triggers, the teacher can change the conditions to prevent the behavior or redirect the child before the occasion arises. For example, observing that Lala's behavior usually deteriorates during transitions, such as when she pinched Mona while standing in line, her teacher uses a rhyming game to keep her engaged.

Document Behavior   The next step is documenting the behavior (B). In using functional assessment, it is important to carefully define and count the frequency (how often) of the behavior to be changed. For example, in the midst of working with a particularly disturbing behavior such as spitting or biting, sometimes teachers lament, "He spits constantly," or "He bites all the time." In fact, a child could not spit or bite "all the time"; even the most avid spitter or biter must come up for air occasionally. Systematic observation and recording of the actual number of unacceptable behaviors is required for successful intervention. In doing so, Andy's teacher finds that he picks his nose 10 times a day, and sets out to intervene to decrease this behavior.

Observe Consequences   Objectively observing the consequences (C) of the behavior is essential to form a hypothesis about the function of the child's behavior. What usually happens after the behavior occurs? Does Hans get the Legos after pushing Natasha away from the table? Does Manny avoid reading group because he cries and insists he has a stomachache?

Once antecedents, behavior, and consequences are documented, teachers can assess possible functions that the behavior is serving. What does the child appear to be getting or avoiding? Children most often exhibit challenging behavior to get attention from adults or peers. At times, however, a child wants *power*, the ability to control what is happening to him or others. This may be the case for a child who is experiencing some kind of disruption that is beyond his power to control, such as his parents' divorce or an abusive relationship. Avoiding power struggles with children is always advisable. Adults often lose, and there is nothing scarier to a child than having too much power. If a child is trying to get power, it is best to give him choices and power over manageable things, such as what book to read or who to play with and where.

Objective documentation describes behaviors without adding judgmental comments. Using a form such as the one shown in Figure 8.4 facilitates a teacher's objective documentation of an ABC analysis. With children whose challenging behaviors are severe and persistent, it is especially important to involve a team of people in the process of functional assessment and developing a plan.

Team with Families and Professionals to Implement Individualized Plans

Too often, teachers, especially new teachers, feel alone and helpless when confronted by children who display challenging behaviors. They can find strength and knowledge in a team for several reasons. Children benefit from consistent, clear messages about expectations for their behavior from the significant adults in their lives. Teachers and parents need support to both endure and transform children's challenging behavior. Finally, some children have problems that are more serious and need the support of a mental health specialist. Although this can be difficult for family members to understand and accept, addressing serious problems early on prevents much more serious difficulties later.

Intervention is more likely to be successful if family members are engaged. Understanding how children behave at home and communicating to parents how their children behave in school is an essential part of the process.

Creating and implementing individualized intervention plans require the expertise of professionals beyond classroom teachers. Early childhood special educators, mental health professionals, social workers, and therapists play key roles in developing the plan. Every state has such resources available to families and child care programs through its public school system, and is required by law to provide this assistance to children with disabilities and special needs.

Use Positive Behavior Support

Once a team has been established and a functional assessment completed, the next step is to develop and implement a **behavior intervention plan**, which describes the behavior to be changed and the strategies adults will use to prevent the negative behavior and teach more acceptable behavior. For example, once a teacher better understands what triggers the behavior, she can prevent or redirect the child before events escalate. In addition, understanding the consequences of a behavior enables the teacher to ensure that the behavior is not effective in achieving its goals.

behavior intervention plan Describes the strategies adults will use to prevent a child's negative behavior and to teach more acceptable behavior.

Child: Rachel **Date**: 10/15

	Antecedent	Behavior	Consequence	Perceived Function
9:15	Teacher begins to collect the instruments from the children.	Rachel hides her maracas behind her back and refuses to give them to the teacher. Rachel is giggling.	The teacher keeps asking for the instruments and tries to grab them from Rachel. Rachel squeals with delight.	Getting attention
9:45	The children are told to brush their teeth after breakfast.	Rachel grabs another child's toothbrush and starts running around the classroom.	The child screams and tells the teacher. The teacher tells Rachel to bring the toothbrush back, then proceeds to chase her.	Getting attention
10:30	The children are on the playground. A small group of children is playing with a ball on the field.	Rachel runs up to one of the girls on the field and pushes her, then laughs and runs.	The children run to the teacher to tell on Rachel.	Getting peers' attention
11:00	Children are at centers for free choice time.	Rachel approaches the child at the computer center and pushes her body onto the child's chair.	The teacher tells Rachel she needs to use her words, but allows her to stay.	Getting to use the computer
11:20	The teacher tells the children it is time for cleanup.	Rachel drops to the floor and pretends to sleep.	The teacher approaches Rachel, insists it isn't nap time, and attempts to help Rachel up.	Avoiding cleanup; getting the teacher's attention

FIGURE 8.4 Functional Behavioral Assessment for 4-Year-Old Rachel A form such as this is useful in conducting a functional behavioral assessment of a child's behavior—the first step in implementing a positive behavior support plan.

replacement behaviors
Desirable prosocial behaviors that replace problem behaviors.

Although one goal of the behavior plan is to diminish negative behaviors, a more important goal is to teach **replacement behaviors**, which are the prosocial behaviors you want the child to exhibit instead of the problem behaviors that meet the same needs. To replace negative, challenging behaviors with prosocial behavior, teachers can use the teaching strategies described previously in this chapter as well as more explicit instruction and reinforcement of acceptable alternatives. Replacement skills should be taught throughout the day, particularly during times when the problem behavior is not occurring. It is also critical that the child is provided with encouragement whenever he uses the new replacement skill, and that the challenging behavior is largely ignored.

The last stage of the behavior plan is to carefully monitor and document the child's progress and make adjustments as needed. Teachers should not become discouraged if results are not immediately positive. The fact is that when interventions are first initiated, children's behavior often gets worse before it improves. As a result, teachers or parents often abandon the intervention too soon. Teachers and team members must continue to observe children's behavior over time and change strategies that are not successful.

Working with children with challenging behaviors can be a humbling experience, but the ultimate result can be tremendously rewarding for everyone involved, particularly the child. In the following sections, we demonstrate how to apply the Teaching Pyramid in specific circumstances that teachers are likely to encounter in practice.

✔ Check Your Understanding 8.5

Applying the Teaching Pyramid Model

Using the Teaching Pyramid to guide teaching practice every day will improve the quality of the educational experience for all children and teachers. In this section, we illustrate how the Teaching Pyramid can be used to teach more effectively in commonly encountered situations—teaching boys, working with children who bite, and preventing and responding to bullying.

Apply the Pyramid Model to Teaching Boys

> Darlene is the sole kindergarten teacher in a group of 23, 15 of whom are boys. During center time, a fight breaks out in the block corner. When Darlene tries to intervene, Jamie screams at her, "You're stupid!" and the other four boys cover their ears and laugh. For 20 minutes at a time, four of the girls happily play in the grocery store Darlene has set up, but Darryl and Jason rush in and knock over the food stands as they race with the shopping carts. At story time, a group of boys start tickling each other or pushing one another over while Darlene tries to read. Despite years of experience as a teacher, Darlene finds herself struggling to control her emotions, speaking harshly to the boys and putting them in time-out repeatedly—but to no avail.

Perhaps fearing the label of *gender biased*, many educators avoid discussing boys' behavior in the classroom. However, many teachers, who are often female themselves, may find active, energetic boys difficult to manage. Denying this fact does not help teachers any more than it helps boys function more successfully in school. One could speculate that increasing the presence of male teachers in early education might alleviate the problem because males might be more understanding and tolerant of boys' typical behavior. However, according to the U.S. Bureau of Labor Statistics, as of 2015, just 3.2 percent of preschool and kindergarten teachers were men.

We realize that addressing the behavior of boys as a group runs the risk of stereotyping. Of course, all boys are not alike any more than all girls are alike. Most boys do not exhibit challenging behaviors, and many girls do. However, there are some observable gender differences, such as more rough-and-tumble play among boys. At the same time, there is an intersection of race and gender in judgments about children's behavior. Black children—both boys and girls—are suspended or expelled at disproportionately higher rates than White children. Black boys make up 19% of the preschool male population and account for 45% of male suspensions/expulsions; Black girls make up 20% of the preschool female population but make up 54% of the female suspensions/expulsions (Gilliam, 2016).

In general, boys are described as socially immature and developmentally young more often than girls are. As a result, boys are more likely to be held back in preschool or kindergarten. In addition, boys are disproportionately labeled as having ADHD, are assigned to special education, and/or are expelled from school, especially African

Effective teachers can apply the Teaching Pyramid to help active boys succeed in school and prevent challenging behaviors. These same strategies will work with girls as well.

© David Kostelnik/Pearson Education

American boys (Barbarin, 2013; King & Janson, 2010; U.S. Department of Education Office of Civil Rights, 2014). In fact, there is some evidence that African American boys are more often stigmatized as troublemakers and singled out for harsh punishment (Barbarin, 2013). While prekindergarten teachers are likely to describe African American and Latino boys as socially competent as White boys, by the time they reach second grade, teachers describe them as less socially and academically competent. Do boys' social–emotional skills decrease during this time? Not likely, but the contexts of early elementary classrooms and expectations may be a poor match for the strengths of boys of color (Barbarin et al., 2013).

In the sections that follow, we discuss strategies from the Teaching Pyramid model to build positive, encouraging relationships with boys; rethink the environment and routines to prevent boys' challenging behaviors; and adapt teaching and intervention strategies for boys.

Build Positive Relationships with Boys

All children need nurturing to thrive. This statement is no less true for boys than for girls. Because girls tend to be more verbal, less active, and more comfortable with emotional expression, teachers may find it easier to establish warm, positive relationships with them. Boys need physical affection, kind words, and emotional support just as much as girls do. However, preschool boys may be more likely to demonstrate warmth by jostling a teachers' leg or climbing over her back than curling in her lap—behaviors that some female teachers may misinterpret. And primary-grade boys may feel the need to demonstrate their "manliness" even if it manifests as emotional withdrawal.

Relationships enable teachers to get to know boys as individuals and to learn their abilities and interests, whether insects or robots. This information is especially important for teachers to use in planning the environment and activities to prevent problem behaviors in boys.

Rethink the Environment for Boys

The following classroom modifications, based on research and observations of the activity level of boys, are designed to prevent problems and support boys to do their best (Barbarin, 2011; King & Gartrell, 2004; King & Janson, 2010):

1. Increase indoor and outdoor large-motor and whole-body experiences, such as allowing rough-and-tumble play and regularly alternating active and quiet learning experiences.
2. Provide opportunities for children to communicate and interact through movement rather than rewarding only verbal communication.
3. Add sensory exploration and experimentation, such as digging a garden or science investigation, both indoors and outdoors.
4. Provide active experiences and technology that use larger muscles as an alternative to quiet seatwork requiring fine motor skill and focusing on handwriting.
5. Enlarge and enrich construction and block-building areas with props such as hard hats, and add a woodworking center with real tools, lumber, and safety goggles.
6. Increase variety by adding novel dramatic play experiences, such as space travel and boating.
7. Use materials such as books, comic books, and games on topics of interest to boys, such as sports, dinosaurs, or space travel, and those that include male role models.

Rethinking the environment with boys in mind will go a long way toward preventing many of the challenging behaviors of boys, especially those that result from their trying to change the level of stimulation. Boys who are engaged in stimulating activities are less likely to be bored and uninvolved, and thus less disruptive. The next two levels of the Teaching Pyramid—teaching social and emotional skills, and individualized interventions—should also be adapted to ensure successful experiences for boys.

Adapt Teaching and Intervention Strategies for Boys   The Teaching Pyramid strategies described earlier apply to all children; however, researchers who study boys' behavior in school offer several adaptations to increase the likelihood of their success (Barbarin, 2013; Gartrell, 2011; King & Janson, 2010; Sprung et al., 2010). These suggestions are based on the fact that boys tend to have a strong sense of justice and fair play, and may feel humiliated or unfairly treated by a teacher. With boys, what teachers *don't* do may be more important than what they do. Table 8.4 lists effective as well as ineffective teaching and intervention strategies for boys. It is important to note that these strategies are important for working with boys *and* girls.

With these adaptations for boys in mind, kindergarten teacher Darlene rethinks her classroom environment:

> Darlene realizes that with so many boys trying to build, the construction area is too small. By removing some of the puzzles and other table toys that are not used, she creates more space for building. She also obtains additional blocks from one of the other kindergartens where they are not being used. Darlene teaches prosocial behaviors and steps to conflict resolution. "If someone takes the block you're using, Jake, what could you say to him?" When Jake and the other boys suggest silly things like "Tell him he's

TABLE 8.4   Effective Teaching and Intervention Strategies for Boys

These teaching strategies and examples support positive behavior and school success in boys, but are also effective for girls.

What Works	What Doesn't Work
Speaking privately before or after a difficult situation or conflict arises	Publicly shaming, humiliating, or embarrassing a boy
Observing carefully and downplaying a conflict before it happens ("Rodney didn't mean to knock over your building. It was an accident.")	Waiting until a situation escalates out of control
Providing a space for "time away" where a child can calm down before a situation escalates	Separating the boy from the group by putting the child's desk in a corner or frequently using time-out
Reflecting on your own behavior and how it may be perceived by the boy and the other children	Stigmatizing to the point that the other children in the group can readily identify the "bad boy" or the troublemaker
Appealing to boys' sense of justice and fair play	Issuing threats that create a power struggle
Following through with logical consequences ("If you throw the sand, you have to leave the sand table.")	Inflicting harsh discipline or punishment ("If you throw the sand, you can't go out to recess.")
Offering boys' choices to help them feel in control	Attempting to overly control boys' impulses
Teaching boys to think before they act and offering them alternatives to physical aggression.	Waiting until boys behave impulsively and punishing them afterwards
Allowing for movement during all learning activities: fidget toys for group time, standing to do writing and fine motor activities.	Punishing boys for fidgeting or requiring them to sit "criss-cross applesauce" for more than a few minutes.
Encouraging boys to move without disturbing other children; teaching all children to have a little extra "body space" in group activities, lines, and circle time.	Publicly chastising boys for touching others, bumping in line or getting too close to peers.

Sources: Based on M. King & D. Gartrell, 2004. Guidance with boys. In D. Gartrell (Ed.), *The Power of guidance: Teaching social–emotional skills in early childhood classrooms.* Clifton Park, NY: Delmar Learning; B. Sprung, M. Froschl, & N. Gropper, 2010. *Supporting boys' learning: Strategies for teacher practice, pre-K–grade 3.* New York: Teachers College Press; and R. H. Morhard, 2013. *Wired to move: Facts and strategies for nurturing boys in an early childhood setting.* Lewisville, NC: Gryphon House.

Video Example 8.7:

Managing Challenging Behavior

An early childhood special educator discusses how she manages challenging behaviors. What elements of the Teaching Pyramid model does she apply? Why is her approach effective?

a butthead," Darlene laughs with them. She calmly says, "That sounds funny now, but I don't think Marco will laugh. What else could you say?"

Darlene also finds the boys are interested in playing ambulance, so she transforms the grocery store into a hospital, which the girls enjoy as well. Instead of reading to the whole group, which invites the boys to act up, Darlene, in smaller groups of eight, reads more books with male characters to actively involve all of the children in talking about the story or acting it out.

Having applied the Teaching Pyramid to working with boys, in the next section we demonstrate its applicability to one of the most common but challenging behaviors teachers confront that cuts across gender lines—biting.

Apply the Pyramid Model to Address Biting

Experienced teachers of toddlers tend to think of dealing with biting as one of the occupational hazards of group care for this age group. Biting is viewed as an aspect of typical development in all children, like separation anxiety or oppositional behavior. Nevertheless, biting is a very emotional experience for the biter, the victim, their parents, and their teachers (Greenman, Stonehouse, & Schweikert, 2007). Parents of children who are bitten often become very upset and demand better supervision of their children. Parents of biters may feel they are somehow responsible and fear that if the situation continues, the child care center will demand they remove their child.

As we learned from the Teaching Pyramid, teachers in groups where biting occurs need to assume responsibility for the safety and nurturance of all of the children while also taking steps to prevent biting, teach alternative behaviors, and intervene when it persists. Biting is not a behavior to ignore; once biting starts in a group of toddlers, others may imitate the behavior, leading to an epidemic of biting that is very hard to control. Biting, like other challenging behaviors, serves a function. There are actually two kinds of biting. The first is a communication strategy, which usually responds to prevention strategies. The second occurs when a child persists in using biting because biting is successful in getting the child what she wants. The persistent form of biting requires systematic intervention.

Prevent Biting Applying the levels of the Teaching Pyramid to biting begins with making sure that toddlers feel nurtured, loved, and cared for. Having close relationships with very young children and their families enables caregivers to be aware of situations that may contribute to biting, such as the stress of a new baby or divorce, or a developmental transition such as beginning to eat solid food. Children tend to treat others the way they are treated. Therefore, it is important for caregivers to speak softly and be gentle and kind.

One theory relates biting to children's sensory and oral development (Ramming, Kyger, & Thompson, 2006). During the earliest years of life, "the mouth is the quickest route for providing sensory information to the brain" and children are literally hungry to experience and make sense of their world (Ramming et al., 2006, p. 21). The hypothesis is that biting may occur because the foods children are offered do not meet their needs for tactile stimulation and do not sufficiently stimulate their senses.

To prevent this type of biting, researchers recommend that caregivers offer toddlers foods with a variety of textures, tastes, and temperatures to suck, gum, munch, or crunch and chew (Ramming et al., 2006). Of course, caregivers must supervise children while the children are eating and make sure foods are the right size to prevent choking. Varying the textures and types of foods, as well as when children are fed, is found to be effective in reducing biting in child care settings (Ramming et al., 2006).

Most biting is preventable if children are closely supervised. When child care groups are too large (as happens when licensing standards are weak), or classrooms are very small, it is more difficult to prevent biting. In such cases, teachers should separate the large group into smaller groups as much as possible, especially if there is a second adult. In a smaller group, a child is less likely to bite when a peer invades his space. The teacher also has more opportunity to play and talk with children and redirect those who frequently have conflicts.

One of the best ways to prevent biting is to minimize frustration. Programs need to provide enough developmentally appropriate toys so children do not fight over them and do not become frustrated if the toy requires skills they do not yet have. For example, large cardboard blocks are lightweight and easily moved by toddlers, whereas smaller toys may be too difficult to manipulate.

Teach Alternatives to Biting   Because most children who bite are under the age of 3 and have not yet developed language, biting is often used as a powerful form of communication. The biter may be saying, "You are too close to me," "I want that toy," or "I'm tired." Biting may occur as a self-defense mechanism by the child who feels threatened.

Biting may occur more frequently when children are feeling stress due to changes in their development or the environment, or lack of attention from caregivers (Greenman et al., 2007). When children are undergoing periods of rapid development, such as when they first learn to walk or talk, they can easily become frustrated if their emerging skills do not match their desires for locomotion or communication (Greenman et al., 2007). Some toddlers begin to bite when their family (often at the recommendation of the pediatrician) weans them from their pacifier. Others begin biting after the birth of a sibling. It is common to see biting among children who develop language more slowly than their peers; it must be very frustrating to want to communicate but unable to generate the words. Initially, biting may relieve the stress or enable the child to get what she wants.

An important dimension of responding to biting is to teach children how to express their feelings and desires. In working with very young children who are just learning language, it is important to give them the words or to use signs or visual images to support their communication. Teachers should model specific language: "Say 'I want it,'" rather than an unhelpful phrase, such as "Use your words."

It is very important that teachers and families respond to this biting in ways that do not escalate the biting behavior. This is difficult, because biting is seen as a dangerous behavior; a bite that breaks the skin of the victim can have serious health consequences. But biting needs only a little reinforcement to become a big problem. When a bite occurs, the victim should quietly and quickly be attended to and comforted. The biter should be quickly and quietly redirected to an activity. Remembering that there often was a perceived offense that preceded the bite ("You're too close to me" or "You took my toy"), direct the offender to another activity (not the toy he was trying to get) with a reminder such as "We need to be gentle." When a teacher or parent exclaims, "No, we don't bite our friends" or places the child in time-out, it practically guarantees a repeat of the behavior.

Teachers can be very helpful in sharing this information and strategy with parents. Once a child has bitten another, it is a good idea to increase the level of prevention. Teachers should observe when and under what circumstances the toddler tends to bite, and increase teacher presence during those times. Many teachers find it helpful to use books with children about biting (and hitting)—but not close to the time the biting has occurred.

Intervene with Persistent Biters   If biting persists over time or if children continue to bite beyond the toddler years, the behavior is working for them in some way. In this situation, caregivers need to apply the fourth level of the pyramid and use functional assessment to determine what conditions tend to trigger the behavior and what function biting is serving for the child. Then a behavior plan can be implemented involving parents and other staff members to eliminate the biting and replace it with more socially acceptable behaviors.

We have seen how the Teaching Pyramid relates to addressing the common phenomenon of biting among young children in groups. In the final section, we apply the framework to one of the most disturbing and potentially destructive of all challenging behaviors—bullying.

Apply the Pyramid Model to Alleviate Bullying

bullying Occurs when a person repeatedly commits aggressive acts that intend to harm, and an imbalance of power makes it hard for the victim to defend himself or herself.

Tragic events such as high school shootings and teen suicide have drawn public attention to an age-old societal problem—bullying. **Bullying** occurs when a person repeatedly commits aggressive acts that intend to harm, and an imbalance of power makes it hard for the victim to defend himself or herself (Kaiser & Rasminsky, 2017). Despite media attention that would suggest the contrary, bullying among children in the United States is not epidemic, and is harmful for both bully and bullied (Temkin, 2014). In recent years, school personnel and mental health experts have become much more attuned to the long-term damage that bullying can inflict on bullies and their victims, as well as on the bystanders who may assist or incite bullying behavior. At the same time, a new challenge has arisen—cyberbullying, the roots of which may be evident in early childhood even though it is not yet practiced.

Every teacher needs to be alert to the existence of bullying, take steps to prevent it, and intervene immediately when bullying occurs. Although bullying usually begins to appear during the primary grades of school, there is evidence that the roots of bullying behavior are evident during preschool. However, little research has addressed bullying with young children (Lawner & Terzian, 2013). Earlier in this chapter, we cautioned teachers to be alert for children who are socially isolated or neglected by peers, as these children may be more likely to bully or be bullied.

Prevent Bullying

Bullying is a learned behavior, and can be minimized and prevented (Kaiser & Rasminsky, 2017a). As with other, less volatile aspects of challenging behavior, solutions to bullying can be found in the framework of the Teaching Pyramid, beginning with the foundation level of relationships.

Research suggests that programs using a whole-school awareness approach that involves teachers, administrators, children, counselors, and families have the most impact in reducing bullying and its effects in school settings (Lawner & Terzian, 2013; Saracho, 2017b). The goal is to prevent bullying by restructuring the environment so that there are fewer opportunities for bullying to occur, more reinforcement of positive behavior, and assurance of protection for all children.

Intervene in Bullying

Research on specific programs targeting bullying in early childhood suggests that no quick-fix curriculum can be used to solve the problem (Lawner & Terzian, 2013). Preventing and addressing bullying relies on establishing the high-quality environment and supports that have been addressed throughout the chapter. Responding to bullying would be an example of the more intensive strategies discussed earlier. Among the most important and effective tools that teachers, families, and schools can use are (Kaiser & Rasminsky, 2017):

- A school-wide commitment to Positive Behavior Support
- Integrating anti-bullying content into the curriculum, including the important roles that bystanders play
- Sensitive, responsive, and involved relationships with children
- Clear rules about unacceptable behavior
- Close monitoring and supervision, including secluded areas where bullying is likely to occur
- Modeling the positive use of power and problem-solving techniques
- A cooperative classroom climate—what we call a caring community of learners

Children who need intensive, individualized intervention for persistent, challenging behaviors benefit from a team approach. In these situations, it is essential to involve not only teachers and other professionals but family members as well.

Regular class meetings are an effective strategy to involve children in setting limits and establishing clear rules: Don't bully other children, help children who are bullied, and include children who are left out (Kaiser & Rasminsky, 2017). Children can discuss and analyze complex topics such as empathy, peer pressure, courage, and the difference between teasing and bullying.

Children also need to learn the difference between *tattling*, the purpose of which is to get someone in trouble, and *telling* to get someone out of trouble, which is necessary when bullying is observed or experienced. Useful strategies include helping children report where they don't feel safe and, in primary grades, providing a box for anonymous reporting of bullying. Meeting times can then be used to discuss prosocial skills, such as cooperation, and to practice responses.

In this chapter, we discussed the importance of creating a caring community of learners, as well as strategies for positively guiding children's behavior and promoting their social and emotional development. With this information in mind, we return to Sue and Elly's classroom, where we began this chapter.

 Check Your Understanding 8.6

Revisiting the Case Study

... Ms. Brady and Ms. Donahue's Classroom

At the beginning of this chapter, Sue, Elly, and the children in their classroom were having a very bad day. The director of their program worked with them to help them learn about the Teaching Pyramid—encouraging them to start with the foundation of their classroom and integrate practices that supported creating a caring community of learners. Let's revisit their classroom now that these two teachers have begun to implement many of these research-based strategies.

The day begins with Sue and Elly greeting each child individually and talking briefly with their family members. The two teachers have been doing home visits and making phone calls to parents so that they could get to know the children and their interests much better. In addition, they have put practices into place that support building warm, nurturing relationships with each child in the class (level 1 of the pyramid). They make sure to touch base with each child every day, even if for only a moment. They create a safe environment for children by arriving each day rested, healthy, and mindful that their interactions with children are important for children's well-being.

They reorganize their classroom to support positive behavior by making signs, labeling bins, organizing shelves, and designating specific areas where materials belong. They also create learning centers where children can comfortably work and play. They've been holding group meetings each morning to talk with children about the class routines and making choices during Center Time, and the children are playing more productively.

Sue and Elly also remember to use calm and quiet voices themselves at all times; when they really want to be heard, they whisper. The noise level is now much more tolerable. When it's time to go outside, they offer Aimee and Paula the choice of what they'd like to carry. The teachers focus a lot of attention on transitions, such as preparing for naptime and cleanup because these are times when children have struggled in the past. They now give warnings before transitions and assign children different responsibilities at cleanup time. At naptime, they play soothing music, turn out the lights, and rub the backs of children who are slow to relax. These changes to the environment and adult–child interactions have made a world of difference for the teachers and children because they are preventing many problems and helping children to do their best (level 2).

Sue and Elly also teach social skills and emotional self-regulation to all the children. For those children who need extra help, however, they use more individualized instruction. For example, Ricky so wants to have friends that he will do anything to get the children's attention. Sue and Elly coach him in acceptable ways to play with others and strategies for joining in a group. Ricky likes Aimee, and she has a calming effect on him, so the teachers encourage the two of them to play together. They also suggest to his mother that he bring something interesting from home to gain attention from the other children in a positive way (level 3).

Having attended to the first three levels of the Teaching Pyramid, Sue and Elly have solved almost all of their behavior challenges. However, Booth's physical aggression and unprovoked attacks continue to be a serious problem. The director is aware of the federally funded early intervention services provided by the state. She contacts the school district, which coordinates mental health consultation to child care centers. The director and Sue initiate a meeting with a consultant and Booth's family to develop an individualized intervention plan (level 4). Sue and Elly are pleased to see that the consultant uses strategies that include the Teaching Pyramid ones that they have become familiar with. The consultant helps them organize their interactions to support Booth. Sue and Elly now realize that although there are no quick fixes to children's challenging behavior, there are many effective ways to create a caring community of learners. ∎

8 Chapter Summary

- A caring community of learners is a group or classroom in which children and adults engage in warm, positive relationships; treat each other with respect; and learn from and with each other.

- Teachers have a significant role to play in promoting children's social competence, helping them acquire emotional and cognitive self-regulation and preventing later difficulties.

- The Teaching Pyramid is a research-based framework for promoting social competence and addressing children's challenging behaviors.

- The foundation level of the Teaching Pyramid is teachers' positive relationships with children. Young children learn best when they experience warm, positive, responsive relationships with adults—parents, teachers, and caregivers.

- Level 2 of the pyramid describes high-quality supportive environments that help promote positive

outcomes for children and prevent challenging behaviors, including the physical space and organizing routines and schedules. A critical aspect of high-quality supportive environments is how teachers support children's engagement in play and learning.

- Level 3 of the pyramid describes positive ways to guide children's behavior and effective strategies such as teaching emotional literacy, social skills, and conflict resolution.

- Level 4 describes intensive individualized interventions to address persistent, severe, challenging behaviors. Intervention includes functional behavioral assessment, a team approach involving families and specialists, and a behavior plan that includes prevention strategies and teaching replacement skills.

- The Teaching Pyramid can be applied to more effectively teach in many diverse situations including teaching boys, addressing biting, and alleviating bullying.

Key Terms

- attachment theory
- behavior intervention plan
- bullying
- caring community of learners
- challenging behavior
- disorganized/disoriented attachment
- efficacy
- effortful control
- emotional literacy
- functional behavioral assessment
- guidance
- individualized intervention

- insecure–ambivalent/ resistant attachment
- insecure–avoidant attachment
- mindfulness

- mistaken behavior
- positive behavior support (PBS)
- redirection

- replacement behaviors
- secure attachment relationship
- secure base

- self-concept
- self-esteem
- time-out
- transitions

 Flash Cards 8.1

Readings and Websites

Forrester, M. M., & Albrecht, K. M. (2014). *SET for life: An early childhood teacher's guide to supporting strong emotional foundations and successful social relationships*. Houston, TX: Innovations in ECE Press.

Humphries, J., & Rains, K. (2017). *A fighting chance: Supporting children experiencing disruptive change*. St. Paul, MN: Redleaf.

Kaiser, B., & Rasminsky, J. S. (2017). *Challenging behavior in young children: Understanding, preventing, and responding effectively* (4th ed.). Upper Saddle River, NJ: Pearson.

Morhard, R. H. (2013). *Wired to move: Facts and strategies for nurturing boys in an early childhood setting*. Lewisville, NC: Gryphon House.

Webster-Stratton, C. (2012). *Incredible teachers: Nurturing children's social, emotional, and academic competence*. Seattle, WA: Incredible Years.

Center on the Social and Emotional Foundations of Early Learning

This website offers a variety of resources for supporting children's positive behavior and relationships and implementing the Teaching Pyramid model.

Collaborative for Academic, Social, and Emotional Learning

This website offers research and resources for supporting social and emotional learning for children in elementary school.

Devereux Center for Resilient Children

This website offers resources for supporting children's social development and building resilience, and for the social–emotional well-being of the adults who care for them.

Head Start Center on Inclusion

Successful inclusion involves more than children "just being there." This website provides information and resources to ensure the full and active participation of young children with disabilities in everyday settings.

 Shared Writing 8.1

Applying the Teaching Pyramid Model

9

Teaching to Enhance Learning and Development

Learning Outcomes

After studying this chapter, you should be able to:

9.1 Discuss ways in which teaching is both a science and an art.

9.2 Identify research-based, effective teaching strategies for young children.

9.3 Explain strategies that help children make meaning, develop concepts, acquire higher-order thinking skills and executive function.

9.4 Demonstrate how effective teachers use grouping as an instructional approach.

9.5 Analyze how teachers use play as a context for teaching and learning.

9.6 Evaluate effective ways of teaching with digital media.

Related NAEYC Professional Preparation Standards

The NAEYC Professional Preparation Standards (NAEYC, 2011) that apply to this chapter

1: Promoting Child Development and Learning
Key elements:
    1a. Knowing and understanding young children's characteristics and needs
    1b. Knowing and understanding the multiple influences on development and learning
    1c. Using developmental knowledge to create healthy, respectful, supportive, and challenging learning environments
4: Using Developmentally Effective Approaches to Connect with Children and Families
Key elements:
    4a. Understanding positive relationships and supportive interactions as the foundation of their work with children
    4b. Knowing and understanding effective strategies and tools for early education
    4c. Using a broad repertoire of developmentally appropriate teaching/learning approaches
    4d. Reflecting on their own practice to promote positive outcomes for each child
6: Becoming a Professional
Key element:
    6d. Integrating knowledgeable, reflective, and critical perspectives on early education

Case Study

Sally Hanson is a kindergarten teacher in a large urban school district. Her class of 23 children includes several children whose home language is not English and two children with IEPs. Some of the children have been in child care since they were infants, but five did not attend any early childhood program before entering school. The children's skills and abilities are at different levels. In short, Sally's class is typical, with a wide range of individual variation in the children's development and learning, and in their preparedness to tackle the demands of the curriculum.

Sally's school district uses the English Language Arts standards based on the Common Core. Among the goals for kindergartners are: "with prompting and support, ask and answer questions about key features in a text; retell familiar stories; and identify characters, settings, and major events." Children also need to "know all upper- and lowercase letters, and use a combination of drawing, dictating, and writing to express an opinion about a topic or a book they are reading, e.g., *My favorite book is ..."* (Common Core State Standards Initiative, 2011a).

Sally has been teaching for many years, and was concerned at first that these standards were not developmentally appropriate for kindergarten. As she began working with the standards, she found that most of the children were capable of achieving the goals through a combination of her integrated curriculum and diverse teaching strategies.

When the children arrive each morning, they immediately go to the library area and choose a book to look at or read, depending on their skills. Children often choose to revisit books that Sally has read previously to the group. Elena has only recently arrived from Guatemala and speaks little English. Sally kneels next to her and offers an e-book that has print and audio versions of the same story in Spanish and English. Soon they are joined by the other children whose home language is Spanish. Sally then encourages Lucy, who has Down syndrome, to find the book that Sally made for her with photos and words about her family. Sally says, "Lucy, I see you found the *L* in your name."

Logan's reading skills are advanced. He picks up a book that he hasn't seen before and begins to decode it himself along with his friend Gabe. When they finish, Sally asks, "Logan, why did you pick this book?" Logan explains, "It's about pirates, and the story was scary." She turns to Gabe and says, "I haven't read this book yet; can you tell me what happened in the story?"

Marguerite is still working on identifying letters. She has a long name, struggles to remember the order of the letters, and usually forgets the *E* in the middle. Sally gives her a name card with the middle *E* written in red to draw her attention to the correct order of the letters. With this assistance and reminder, Marguerite spells her name correctly. Some children are not interested in reading, so Sally directs them to their journals to begin drawing and writing about the books they read yesterday. A few children need more direct instruction and practice in writing letters. "Tommy, when you write your *T*, make a straight line down. That's right." Pointing to the left side of the paper, Sally says, "Now begin on the left and draw a shorter line across the top." Because Amanda needs practice on letter sounds but is easily distracted, Sally suggests several letter-learning apps on the tablet. Sally sits with the children, offering assistance as needed and using strategies adapted to each child's skill level. ■

As we see in Sally's interactions with each child in her classroom, the early childhood teacher's role is complex. Engaging in developmentally appropriate practice involves knowing the learner, knowing what to teach, and knowing how to teach. Teachers are always teaching *something* to *someone*. In this chapter, we focus on knowing *how to teach* to help children reach challenging and achievable learning goals. Becoming an intentional teacher requires an understanding of the range of effective teaching strategies, and how and when they are most useful. Armed with this knowledge, teachers can intentionally choose the strategies that work best with each learner or group of learners in a given situation.

Because many teaching behaviors in early childhood classrooms are subtle or take place in the context of play or child-initiated learning, the novice may be uncertain of what "effective teaching" entails and how to do it. Without knowledge of research-based teaching practices, inexperienced or ill-informed teachers may be too passive and miss important opportunities to promote children's learning (Goble et al., 2016). On the other hand, they may err in assuming that the only time they are "teaching" is when they are talking. The fact is that good teaching is a complex interplay of both science and art.

pedagogy What a teacher says or does that engages children and contributes to their learning and development.

effective teaching The use of approaches that are proven to be successful based on scientific evidence and that have a high probability of enhancing children's learning and development.

Teaching: Both a Science and an Art

This chapter is about teaching—also known as **pedagogy**—which is what a teacher says or does that engages children and contributes to their learning and development. In this book, we emphasize **effective teaching**, which is the use of an approach that has proven to be successful based on research evidence and that has a high probability of enhancing student achievement (Marzano, 2017). Using knowledge of research to inform planning and decisions about practice is essential to becoming an intentional teacher.

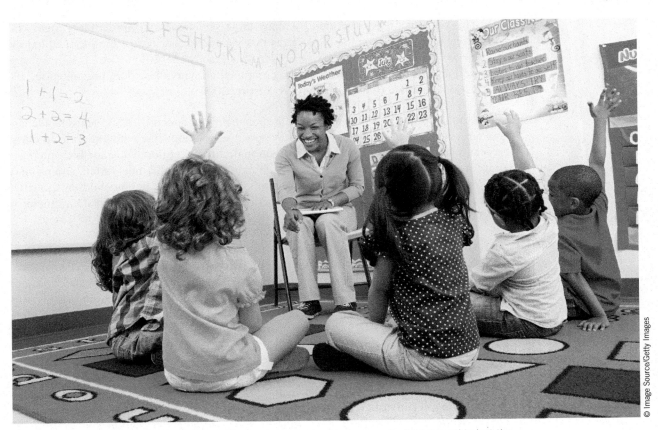

Intentional teachers use research-based teaching strategies and get to know each child to provide just the right kind and amount of assistance.

The Science of Teaching

In recent decades and in response to federal laws including the Every Student Succeeds Act (ESSA), the emphasis in education has been on evidence-based practice (Boyd, Kucharczyk, & Wong, 2016; IOM & NRC, 2015; U.S. Department of Education, 2016). Such practice is informed by at least three areas of research: the science of child development, including neuroscience; cognitive science, or the study of how people learn; and research on effective instructional strategies and contexts.

Scientific Research Research is used to answer two sets of questions: (1) What skills and abilities predict children's later outcomes in important areas such as reading, mathematics, and social relationships? (2) What teaching behaviors, curriculum, and other educational interventions contribute to or inhibit gains in children's skills and abilities in these areas? Reviews of research by experts, such as the Institute of Medicine (IOM) and the National Research Council (NRC) (2015), the National Reading Panel (National Institute of Child Health and Human Development [NICHD], 2000), the National Early Literacy Panel (2008), and the National Committee on Early Childhood Mathematics (National Research Council [NRC], 2009) have been particularly influential.

Classroom Research Although debate is ongoing about various aspects of practice, the strong consensus is that the daily interaction among teachers and children and the quality of instruction are the most important determinants of the effectiveness of programs from infancy through primary grades (Burchinal, 2017; Burchinal, Zaslow, & Tarullo, 2016; Teachstone, 2017). Regardless of the specific curriculum used or the materials in the environment, everything that happens in the classroom is influenced by the teacher's interactions with children.

This conclusion is supported by many large-scale studies of prekindergarten, kindergarten, and primary-grade classrooms that used a teacher observation tool called the *Classroom Assessment Scoring System* (CLASS) (Teachstone, 2017). The CLASS assesses three dimensions of classroom quality: emotional climate, classroom organization, and instructional climate (Pianta, La Paro, & Hamre, 2008).

Emotional Climate A high score on emotional climate on the CLASS means that teachers are sensitive and responsive, and have positive relationships with children. In classrooms where teachers score high on emotional climate, children's academic outcomes improve and they have fewer behavior problems in preschool, kindergarten, and primary grades (Hamre et al., 2014). Teachers' emotional support also builds children's positive approaches to learning and executive functions such as inhibitory control and memory (Teachstone, 2017).

Classroom Organization In well-organized classrooms, teachers use positive strategies to guide children's behavior. They are well prepared in advance and manage time productively, maximizing opportunities for learning. For example, they don't waste children's time during routines or transitions. Teachers who score high on classroom organization also use a variety of materials, teaching strategies, and learning formats to engage children and activate their interest.

Instructional Climate The CLASS instructional climate score indicates how well teachers use a variety of teaching strategies to promote children's language, concept development, and higher-order thinking. The classroom's instructional climate has been found to be the strongest and most consistent predictor of children's learning over time (Teachstone, 2017). Researchers have found that children gain more when instruction is intentional and high quality (Burchinal, Zaslow, & Tarullo, 2016). Children benefit most when a teacher interacts with them in an intentional way with a learning goal in mind or supports children's learning during play and other child-initiated activity (Fuller et al., 2017; Goble & Pianta, 2017).

Research Results Research on the emotional climate of early childhood classrooms finds that on average, they are generally positive, supportive environments for children (Early et al., 2010; Head Start, 2016). However, researchers also tend to find low-quality instructional climates in early childhood classrooms studied, with an average score of about 2 on the 7-point scale. Teachers in these classrooms either provide very little instruction at all or tend to rely on worksheets or whole-group repetitive lessons.

Head Start uses the CLASS in all 30,000 classrooms to improve the quality of teaching and evaluate the effectiveness of its programs. From 2012–2015, the average Emotional Climate CLASS score was 6.0 and the Organizational score was 5.9, averaging in the high range (Head Start, 2016). On the other hand, Instuctional Climate scores averaged 2.9 across the four years. This is a higher score than typical early childhood programs but still below the quality of teaching needed for more positive learning outcomes for children (Burchinal, Zaslow, & Tarullo, 2016).

Large-scale studies have examined how children spend their time in school. In prekindergarten, almost 30% of children's time is spent in free choice and about 37% engaged with a teacher-assigned activity (Early et al., 2010). However, observers found that no specific learning activity occurred during 19% of free choice time, 23% of teacher-assigned time, and 87% of meal and routine time (Early et al., 2010). Therefore, almost half of the preschool children's day did not involve experiences to promote their social or academic learning. The researchers concluded that most of these classrooms were pleasant places in which there were many missed opportunities for learning. Moreover, classrooms with higher percentages of Latino and African American children were less educationally stimulating.

These studies provide a window through which we can assess the quality of teaching practices in early childhood classrooms today. In Chapter 8, we described how you as a teacher can provide a positive emotional climate in your classroom. The goal of this chapter is to prepare you to create an effective instructional climate to help all children achieve their learning potential.

The Limits of Research   Early childhood education has a large and growing research base to guide practice. Where research evidence is strong, teachers have a professional responsibility to adhere to its guidance. However, research on effective teaching is an evolving science. Although a great deal of work has been done, we still need answers to questions about which practices work best with which learners.

With classrooms increasingly serving children with diverse language and cultural backgrounds, teachers need to adapt for variation of all kinds. Consequently, valid research is not always available to guide practice. In these instances, teachers need to supplement the evidence base with practical wisdom and information obtained from families (Keyser, 2017; Sullivan, 2016). Even when research is available, applying evidence-based practice in unique classroom situations with diverse groups of children requires considerable skill. Teachers need to respond to situations as they happen, which often requires creativity—more art than science (Marzano, 2017).

The Art of Teaching

Although effective teaching is informed and guided by research, teaching is also an art in that it requires vision, creativity, and decision making. What makes good science is controlling as many variables as possible to be able to determine cause and effect. But in classrooms, there are simply too many variables to control. Effective teaching requires creatively adapting to individual children and to the situations that arise (Beneke & Ostrosky, 2013; Gadzikowski, 2013).

Consider the following analogy, which compares the work of a painter to the work of a teacher: Skilled painters are knowledgeable about theories of art, composition, color, and perspective. But each artist, like each teacher, applies her or his knowledge in creative ways. One of the painter's most powerful tools is the use of color and knowledge of how the myriad colors in nature can be created by mixing a few basic colors. For example, given the three primary colors—red, yellow, and blue—a skilled painter can create virtually every color of the spectrum. Think of those basic colors as the basic strategies from which teachers create innumerable variations in interactions with individual children and groups. If we add to the color wheel the many gradations of gray—ranging between white and black—and mix these with our primary colors, we have an almost infinite variety of options from which to "color" the world of experiences for children.

We begin our exploration of the science and art of teaching by examining research-based teaching strategies. This discussion will demonstrate how art and science can coexist to create an enriching classroom filled with color, creativity, and a variety of options for teachers as well as children.

© Suzanne Clouzeau/Pearson Education

Effective teaching is both an art and a science. Intentional teachers ensure that children's experiences in the classroom are as creative and colorful as the world around them.

✔ Check Your Understanding 9.1

Research-Based, Effective Teaching Strategies

The most effective teachers have a large repertoire of teaching strategies that they use as situations present themselves. Teachers must first become familiar with the many options. In practice, there is no one teaching strategy that will address all situations.

Children's development and learning are complex processes. Therefore, the more strategies teachers know how to use, the more ways they will be able to meet the needs of diverse learners. Throughout your career as a teacher, you will continue to add to and refine your repertoire of effective teaching tools.

What Are Teaching Strategies?

teaching strategy A behavior or activity that a teacher deliberately selects and flexibly applies to help students construct meaning.

A **teaching strategy** is a behavior or activity that a teacher deliberately selects and flexibly applies to help students construct meaning (Mehigan, 2005, p. 557). Applying teaching strategies demands conscious thought and flexible decision making, which are the essence of intentional teaching. Earlier, for example, we saw how Sally Hanson encouraged some of the children to practice their writing but also demonstrated how to write a letter for those who needed more help.

learning strategy How children construct meaning in any context or situation.

Because the processes of teaching and learning are linked, the most effective teaching strategies parallel learning strategies. A **learning strategy** refers to how children construct meaning in every context or situation. As later examples illustrate, some of the most effective teaching strategies are designed to develop students' own learning strategies.

Strategies as Tools   Education is often plagued by *either/or* debates that pit one practice against another, or that dichotomize complex decisions into either/or choices, such as "Which is better, direct instruction or active learning?" As teaching becomes more scientific, we realize that these are the wrong questions. Asking which teaching technique is best is like asking whether a hammer is better than pliers. The answer, of course, depends on what the carpenter needs to do. In teaching, as in carpentry, the selection of tools depends on what the teacher is trying to accomplish and with which child; there is no one best teaching practice (NRC, 2018).

The Right Tools   You may have heard the statement—in fact, I've written it myself—that young children are not miniature adults, and do not think and learn the way adults or older children do. Although this statement is essentially true, it is equally true that some practices that are inappropriate for young children, such as listening in a whole group for an extended period of time, are not effective for older students either (NRC, 2018).

In fact, many of the most effective teaching practices for young children—such as connecting new learning to what students already know and can do—are also effective with college students. The particular strategies teachers use to help children build on prior learning will vary with the age and ability of the learner (that is, if the strategies are developmentally appropriate). All of these strategies can be used in the context of teacher-initiated or child-initiated experiences, which we discuss next.

teacher-initiated experiences Learning experiences in which teachers take the lead by providing explicit information and modeling or demonstrating a skill, as determined by the teacher's goals and direction.

Teacher-Initiated *and* Child-Initiated Experiences

Early childhood practices are often described as either teacher-initiated or child-initiated experiences. However, both contexts are effective for learning and should be used concurrently depending on the teachers' goals (Goble & Pianta, 2017; Hirsh-Pasek & Golinkoff, 2011; Hong & Diamond, 2012). During teacher-initiated experiences, teachers take the lead by providing explicit information and modeling or demonstrating skills. Teacher-initiated learning experiences are determined by the teacher's goals and direction, but children should be actively engaged (Epstein, 2014). Under these conditions, focused, teacher-guided instruction can contribute significantly to children's learning (Fuller et al., 2017; Hong & Diamond, 2012).

By contrast, during child-initiated experiences, children acquire knowledge and skills through their own exploration and interactions with objects and other children (Weisberg et al., 2016, 2017). Child-initiated experiences grow out of children's interests. However, teachers organize the environment and materials, and provide the learning opportunities from which children make choices. Teachers observe children during child-initiated activities and interact with them to support their continued learning and development. During child-initiated experiences, teachers as well as children should be actively involved.

child-initiated experiences Experiences that allow children to gain knowledge and skills through their own exploration and interactions with objects and other children.

Using an Array of Teaching Strategies

Many different strategies are effective in supporting children's learning and development. Understanding when and how to apply each strategy gives teachers the tools necessary to be thoughtful, purposeful, and intentional (Copple & Bredekamp, 2009; Heidemann, Menninga, & Chang, 2016).

Note, however, that in practice, strategies are used in combination. Observe a skilled teacher at work and you will find it almost impossible to isolate an example of a teaching strategy—even explicit instruction—that doesn't also include some other strategy such as encouragement, modeling, or questioning. For example, a preschool teacher may acknowledge a child's accomplishment by saying, "Luca, you found the two shapes that match." Then she immediately provides specific information, "They have eight sides and they are called octagons," while quickly adding challenge to the task, "Can you find another octagon in our room?"

One particularly effective strategy, *scaffolding*, draws on many different strategies at once; therefore, we discuss it following our description of the individual strategies. In the sections that follow, we define and give examples of a variety of teaching strategies, which are listed in Table 9.1.

Acknowledging and Encouraging Acknowledging is the positive attention a teacher gives to a child that tells the child the teacher noticed what the child did. Teachers often use this strategy without conscious awareness. Acknowledging is particularly effective in keeping children engaged in desirable behaviors. For example, after observing 3-year-old Keily while she serves as the snack helper, her teacher says, "I see you gave each person a napkin, Keily. Now we're ready for our snack." Noting 2-year-old Bailey's empathic behavior, her teacher says, "Thank you, Bailey, for sitting with Kayla. She was sad that her mommy left." By understanding the power of their acknowledgment of children's competence and performance, teachers are able to influence children to demonstrate desired behaviors.

acknowledging Giving positive verbal or nonverbal attention that promotes the child's persistence and effort.

Encouragement can be conveyed through verbal comments or nonverbal signs such as pats or high fives that promote the child's persistence and effort. Although encouragement doesn't directly enhance a child's understanding or skill, it is most valuable in helping children realize that effort is necessary for mastering skills, completing tasks, and solving complex problems. For example, second-grader Jushawn struggles with writing a funny story about his dog. His teacher encourages him to persist by making comments such as, "I really laughed when you told me how he spilled his food." When Jushawn finishes, she points out, "You worked hard writing your story and I enjoyed reading it, and I laughed again at your dog's antics."

encouragement Verbal comments or nonverbal signs such as pats or high fives that promote the child's persistence and effort.

TABLE 9.1 Effective Teaching Strategies

Effective teachers have a large repertoire of teaching strategies to use depending on their goals for children, as described and illustrated in this table.

Teaching Strategy	Definition	Most Effective Uses
Acknowledging and encouraging	Giving positive verbal or nonverbal attention that promotes a child's persistence and effort	Teachers influence children to stay engaged; demonstrate desired behaviors; and help children master skills, complete tasks, and solve complex problems.
Giving quality feedback	Providing specific information on a child's performance or responding to questions and comments	Teachers expand learning and understanding (how children come to solve a problem) rather than focusing only on the correct answer or end product.
Modeling	Displaying or showing children a skill or desirable way of behaving or speaking	Teachers portray positive social skills and self-regulation. Teachers model language—repeating and extending children's verbal responses, describing their own and children's actions, and using advanced vocabulary.
Demonstrating	Showing the correct way to perform a skill or procedure while children observe the outcome	Teachers teach skills that require particular steps in a certain order.
Giving cues and hints, and offering assistance	Reminding children of what they already know and can do, and helping them use that knowledge for new learning	Teachers help children build on prior knowledge to gain new skills and understanding.
Creating and adding challenges	Making learning situations harder by generating a problem or adding difficulty to a task so that it is a bit beyond what children have already mastered	Teachers add challenges to interest children and motivate them to learn, but not so much that they become frustrated or repeatedly fail. Children continue to make learning and developmental progress.
Questioning	Eliciting different types of responses and promoting different types of thinking	Teachers ask open-ended questions that require children to analyze information or engage in higher-order thinking.
Co-constructing	Thinking with different points of view; working collaboratively to solve a problem or clarify a concept	Teachers and children think and talk together during a joint activity such as a project, and both parties learn from the exchange.
Giving direct or explicit instruction	Explicitly giving directions for completing a task; providing facts, verbal labels, or other specific information; or providing instructions for a child's action or behavior	Teachers transmit knowledge that can be learned only from one person telling another, that is, social-conventional or procedural knowledge.
Scaffolding—using the above strategies in combination	Supporting children's ability to accomplish learning tasks that they could not otherwise accomplish independently; using strategies such as cues, hints, assistance, questions, and so on to help children work "on the edge" of their current level of competence.	Teachers adapt instruction for individual children of different skill levels, cultural backgrounds, personalities, and talents toward new, achievable goals. Teachers help children acquire the skills to eventually achieve the same task independently.

Sources: Based on C. Copple and S. Bredekamp, 2006. *Basics of developmentally appropriate practice: An introduction for teachers of children 3 to 6.* Washington, DC: NAEYC; and C. Copple and S. Bredekamp (Eds.), 2009. *Developmentally appropriate practice in early childhood programs serving children from birth through age 8 (revised edition).* Washington, DC: NAEYC.

Giving Quality Feedback Feedback, in which teachers provide specific information on a child's performance or respond to questions, helps focus the child's attention on the process of learning. Effective feedback helps children expand their learning and understanding, rather than focusing on correct answers (Pianta et al., 2008). Research finds that such instructional feedback helps improve literacy and language in preschool and kindergarten children (Howes et al., 2008) and helps close the achievement gap for children in first grade and up (Hamre & Pianta, 2005).

Effective feedback often involves back-and-forth exchanges between teachers and students. This exchange is called a feedback loop and involves a teacher and a child or small group of children communicating in an effort to reach deeper understanding. Consider the following example of a feedback loop that occurred in a preschool class where the teacher and children were discussing a book about shadows:

> *Teacher points to a picture in book:* What do you think made this shadow?
> *Various children call out:* An animal. A dog. A cat.
> *Teacher:* Kami, why do you think it's a cat?
> *Kami:* The tail.
> *Teacher:* What makes you think that it's a cat's tail?
> *Kami:* Well, it looks like a long tail.
> *Connor:* But dogs have tails, too. It could be a wolf.
> *Teacher to class:* What do you notice about the tail?
> *Kami:* It's a cat's tail. It's skinny, and it has a curl on the end.
> *Teacher:* Oh, so you're sure it's a cat. Let's find out.

Positive feedback provides children with specific information and helps focus their attention. Back-and-forth exchanges in small groups help everyone learn more.

feedback loop Back-and-forth communication between a teacher and a child or small group of children in an effort to reach deeper understanding.

Modeling Teachers are especially powerful models for children with whom they have built positive relationships. Modeling is a technique teachers use to show children a skill or desirable way of behaving or speaking.

Language modeling is among the most effective instructional strategies teachers can use. A large body of research demonstrates that teacher's language modeling strongly predicts children's achievement in all areas of learning and development (Beck, McKeown, & Kucan, 2013; Neuman & Wright, 2013). Effective *language modeling* includes:

modeling Showing children a skill or desirable way of behaving or speaking.

- Engaging children in frequent, extended, one-on-one conversations—called "serve and return" as in a tennis game, where teachers and children take turns speaking in response to what the other has said
- Listening carefully, waiting for a response, minimizing questions, and gauging comments to children's remarks
- Using open-ended questions to stimulate and extend discussions, such as "What do you think will happen if …? Why do you think that?" and "How did that happen?"
- Repeating and expanding on what children say
- Using new and advanced words that children may not know or use in everyday speech
- Supporting children's conversations with each other

Adult–child language interactions are especially important because the most competent language user in the classroom is the teacher. One of the most effective strategies for developing young children's language is to engage them in conversations during their play without being too intrusive (Dickinson, 2011; Meacham, Vukelich, Han, & Buell, 2014). In the following example, preschool teacher Ms. Lawry models language with children who pretend to cook in the dramatic play center:

> *Child:* Here's your dinner. It's hot.
> *Ms. Lawry:* Thank you. This soup must be boiling hot. I think I can see steam rising up. I'll just sip it slowly. I don't want it to scald me.
> *Child:* Huh? Scald?
> *Ms. Lawry:* Yes. I don't want it to burn my lips.

During this pretend scenario, the teacher modeled advanced vocabulary words such as *boiling*, *rising*, *sip*, *steam*, and *scald*, and introduced some science concepts at the same time. In some respect, teachers are always engaged in modeling because children pay attention to what teachers do as much as to what they say.

Demonstrating An effective strategy for teaching skills that require performing particular steps in a certain order is demonstrating. When teachers show the correct way to perform a skill or procedure, children are able to observe the outcome. Similar to modeling, demonstrating is more formal and directive, with the adult drawing children's attention to the correct steps necessary to complete a task, as in the following examples:

demonstrating Showing the correct way to perform a skill or procedure while children observe the outcome.

> Irene demonstrates for her 3-year-olds how to wash their hands thoroughly to prevent the spread of infection. As she washes her own hands, she says, "See? Now I'm drying my hands with the paper towel. Before I throw the towel away, I use it to turn off the faucet. That way, my hands stay really clean. Now you try it."

> In the art area, kindergarten teacher Max introduces potter's clay to the group. As he demonstrates, he says, "Watch how I pinch off a little piece of clay and use a small amount of water to make the little piece stick to the bigger piece."

apprenticeship The process of children learning by observing adults and more accomplished peers performing tasks and by practicing the skills themselves with adult guidance and support.

Children often learn by observing not only adults but also more accomplished peers performing tasks. Such learning has been called apprenticeship, and researchers have observed it across cultural groups (Rogoff, 1990, 2003). When young children watch others perform basic skills of living such as dressing, feeding, or tying shoes, they gradually learn how to accomplish these skills themselves. For demonstrating to be effective, children's observations must be followed by opportunities for them to practice the skills themselves with adult guidance and support.

Giving Cues, Hints, and Assistance Giving *cues* or *hints* are ways of reminding children what they already know and helping them use that knowledge to build new skills. For example, when a child is reading and is stuck on a word, the teacher may say, "That word has 'ch' at the beginning like another one you know." In this case, the teacher is cueing the beginning reader to compare the new word to one she already knows.

facilitating Providing short-term, temporary assistance to help a child achieve the next level of functioning.

Other common teaching strategies fall in the general category of facilitating or supporting learning. When teachers *facilitate*, they provide short-term, temporary assistance to help a child achieve the next level of functioning, such as when the teacher gently holds a preschooler's hand as he walks across the balance beam. When teachers *support* learning, they provide a more fixed-form of assistance such as providing a word wall (displaying frequently used words) for kindergartners to refer to as they work in their journals. In both facilitating and supporting learning, the teacher provides assistance that helps the child accomplish a difficult task by making it easier.

supporting Providing assistance that helps the child accomplish a difficult task by making it easier.

Creating and Adding Challenges

Although cues, hints, and other assistance make children's learning tasks easier, effective teachers also intentionally make learning situations harder at times by creating challenge, generating a problem, or adding difficulty to a task so that it is a bit beyond what children have already mastered. For example, Hiroki is especially adept at doing puzzles and quickly completes all that are available in his preschool classroom. His teacher, Keith, brings in an alphabet puzzle with 26 pieces, one for every letter, challenging Hiroki's skill with puzzles to help him learn the alphabet.

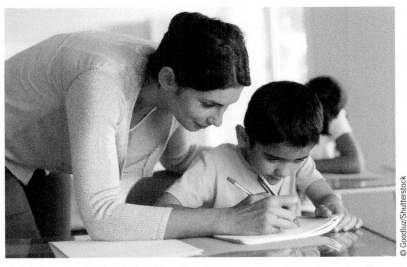

In her second-grade classroom, Catarina determines that although most of the children are reading at or below grade level, two of them are much more advanced. She provides fourth- and fifth-grade-level reading materials to ensure they are challenged to continue their reading growth. In addition, she adapts her writing assignments to add challenge. For example, if the other children's assignment is to describe their own experiences over the weekend, to add challenge for the more advanced children, Catarina asks them to write a different ending for a story they've read, requiring higher-level comprehension and analysis.

Effective teachers have a large repertoire of strategies to use in different situations. When there is a specific skill that children need to learn, a teacher may intentionally demonstrate it for children.

Questioning One of the most frequently used teaching strategies, **questioning** is used to elicit different types of responses and promote different types of thinking. Research on questioning finds that higher-level, **open-ended questions**—those that require children to analyze information in some way—are more effective learning tools than lower-level questions (Meacham et al., 2014; Strasser & Bresson, 2017). Lower-level or **closed questions** have one right answer, usually requiring children to recall information or facts. Closed questions, which are often the type used on tests, may reveal what a child knows, but they do not propel further learning. Open-ended questions, on the other hand, have many possible answers. Indeed, a truly open-ended question is one for which the teacher does not have an answer in mind.

To understand how different types of questions elicit different types of responses, compare the following two questions, asked after a reading of Beatrix Potter's *The Tale of Peter Rabbit*:

> *Question 1:* Where did Peter Rabbit get lost?
> *Question 2:* How would you feel if you were lost like Peter?

Question 1 has one right answer—Mr. McGregor's garden. This question offers little opportunity to generate further conversation. Conversely, Question 2 would most likely evoke many different responses from children with various adjectives describing feelings—*scared, nervous, afraid, unhappy, sad, tired,* or *hungry*—as well as opportunities for follow-up questions that would extend the conversation. For example, "What would you do?" or "How could you get help?" would elicit a host of responses. Even more beneficial, the open-ended questions would enable children to connect the story to their own experiences beyond the classroom, making the reading even more meaningful—"Have you ever been lost?"

Questions That Promote Problem Solving Teachers often use questions as ways to cue or prompt children to take the next step in solving a problem or performing a skill. In addition, they may use questions to remind children of what they already know before introducing new information, as well as to focus their attention and thinking in advance.

Video Example 9.1:

Teaching Strategies

In this kindergarten writing center, the teacher helps a student plan and write his own treasure map and then goes on to help other students develop their own individualized projects. What teaching strategies does she use? What other ways could she support and also challenge the children's learning?

questioning Eliciting different types of responses and promoting different types of thinking.

open-ended questions Questions that require children to analyze information in some way and that have many possible answers.

closed questions Lower-level questions that have one right answer and usually require children to recall information or facts.

In the following example, before reading *Caps for Sale* by E. Slobodkina to a group of preschoolers, Carole holds up the book cover and begins a conversation with a question:

Teacher: What do you see in this picture?
Mark: A man with lotsa hats on his head.
Tory: He looks funny. The hats are all different colors.
Teacher: So you think this will be a funny story, Tory?
Tory: I don't know. How can those hats stay on his head? I bet they fall off.
Teacher: Let's read the story and find out.

By asking questions before she reads the book to the children, Carole engages their interest. As soon as Carole begins reading, the children are observing and analyzing the pictures and making predictions about the story. After the story, Carole and the children will discuss whether their predictions were correct.

Quality of Questioning Research on questioning demonstrates its effectiveness as a teaching strategy. However, research also finds that although questions are by far the most frequent verbal interaction among teachers and children, teachers most often ask low-level questions (Justice, Mashburn, Hamre, & Pianta, 2008; Meacham et al., 2014). One large-scale observational study of preschool classrooms in England (Sylva et al., 2011) found that even in good programs, only about 5% of teachers' questions were open ended. More than 34% of their questions were closed (one-right-answer, low-level questions), and more than 60% were related to controlling behavior and not directly related to pedagogy.

Despite the scarcity of open-ended questions, however, when open-ended questions were asked, they provoked rich conversations and thoughtful speculation, and extended children's imaginations. The researchers concluded that given their potential effectiveness, increasing the use of open-ended questions could greatly improve outcomes for children, especially those who are at risk of school failure (Sylva et al., 2011).

wait time The length of time that a teacher waits for a response after asking a question or responding to a comment.

Wait Time An important aspect of questioning is wait time, the length of time that a teacher waits for a response after asking a question. Research reveals that when teachers pause or wait briefly—about 5 seconds—for responses from children, it increases the frequency and depth of children's responses (Cohrssen, Church, & Tayler, 2014; Tharp & Entz, 2012). Wait time is especially valuable for young children who are just beginning to master verbal communication and for children who are learning a second language (National Academies of Science, 2017).

Wait time helps extend conversations with children and among groups of children. Sometimes, when children do not immediately respond to adult questions or comments, adults might impatiently talk for them or over them. For teachers who are patient and recognize the beauty of wait time, however, it becomes a highly useful strategy to add to their repertoire.

Application Exercise 9.1
Questioning Strategies

Co-Constructing Learning and Understanding One of the most important ways children learn is by constructing their own understanding of concepts as they actively try to make sense of their experiences. The process of co-construction often happens when children work collaboratively with teachers and/or other children on a joint project or activity (Tharp & Entz, 2012). This strategy of working collaboratively to solve a problem or clarify a concept is called *co-construction*, because both parties in the task think and talk together, and each learns from it. The value of this strategy was demonstrated in a

Activities such as a digital table provide rich opportunities for children and teachers to talk and think together—what is called co-construction.

large-scale observational study in England. The researchers found that in the most effective classrooms, teachers encouraged co-construction during children's play activities, which they called *sustained shared thinking* (Sylva et al., 2011), as in this example:

> Four-year-old James is watching various objects floating in the water table. "Look at the toys. The blocks are sinking. I don't like that," he observes. Modeling curiosity and extending the interaction, his teacher says, "Why do you think they're sinking?" James responds, "Because they're too big." The teacher picks up a bigger block and shows the children how two blocks compare in size. Another child, Kathy, says, "That's going to sink too." When the block floats, the children look astonished. The teacher asks, "Why do you think that happened?" and the children begin to share many different explanations.

This process of co-construction, or sustained shared thinking, proved to be so predictive of positive outcomes for young children that the researchers concluded it is a prerequisite of effective preschool education. Co-construction is one of the most frequently used strategies in the schools in Reggio Emilia, Italy. Although open-ended questioning is one way to initiate co-construction during children's play, teachers need to sustain the back-and-forth conversation and think along with the children to help them construct their understanding of new concepts.

Giving Direct or Explicit Instruction **Direct instruction**, also called didactic instruction, occurs when a teacher gives explicit directions for completing a task; presents facts, verbal labels, or other specific information; or provides instructions for a child's action or behavior. Direct or explicit instruction is used for transmitting knowledge that can be learned only from one person telling another the culturally agreed-on labels for objects, events, and experiences, which is called *social-conventional knowledge*. For example, the days of the week, letters, or punctuation symbols have conventionally agreed-on names that children learn more easily and efficiently through direct instruction. Writing a question mark on chart paper, first-grade teacher Lydia uses direct instruction when she points out, "This is a question mark, and we write it at the end of a sentence that is asking a question or making a request."

direct instruction Explicitly giving directions for completing a task; providing facts, verbal labels, or other specific information; or providing instructions for a child's action or behavior.

Teachers also use direct instruction during child-initiated activities and when working with small groups. For example, when working with a group of 4-year-olds building with blocks, the teacher points to a block and says, "This rounded block is called a cylinder. You used four cylinder blocks to hold up your bridge."

Direct instruction is the easiest way to present new knowledge, such as agreed-on names for tools, and some skills, such as tying shoes. However, this type of instruction is only one part of helping children learn concepts. For example, children can learn aspects of mathematical computation through direct instruction, but they need many additional experiences to understand the complex concepts of numbers and operations.

Direct instruction can be the most efficient and effective way of conveying information and introducing new concepts, procedures, or vocabulary. However, it should not be overused. Despite this caution, whole group direct instruction is the most frequently used strategy in primary grades, and increasingly so in kindergarten and even preschool (Riley-Ayers et al., 2017).

Although the list of teaching strategies presented so far is not exhaustive, it provides a basic overview of options teachers can use to become intentional, effective teachers. Next, we turn to a particularly effective teaching strategy, scaffolding, that draws on the strengths of several different strategies at once.

The Power of Scaffolding: An Integrated Approach

We have now discussed a number of effective strategies that will help you create an effective classroom. Yet how do you best guide children of different skill levels, cultural backgrounds, personalities, and talents toward new, achievable goals? Scaffolding is the most effective teaching strategy for such a challenging task.

What Is Scaffolding? Scaffolding is a metaphor for a series of teacher behaviors that support children's ability to accomplish learning tasks or solve a problem that they could not otherwise accomplish independently (Wood, Bruner, & Ross, 1976). This strategy not only allows children to progress toward challenging goals but also gives them the skills to eventually achieve the same task on their own. Scaffolding may be such an effective teaching practice because it actually draws on the strengths of many of the other teaching strategies all at once.

Literally, scaffolding is a temporary structure, usually an elevated platform, that builders or painters stand on to reach otherwise inaccessible parts of a building. Like the painter's platform, the scaffold used in the classroom is the right amount of teacher support for the learner to achieve a task or accomplish an objective that would be beyond his or her reach without the assistance.

Scaffolding assists a child to work in his or her *zone of proximal development*—the area just beyond a child's current level of understanding or ability to achieve (Vygotsky, 1978). What makes scaffolding effective is that it presents learners with just the right amount of challenge—enough so they don't give up or fail, but not so much that they aren't solving the problem themselves (Clark & Graves, 2005). Scaffolding also gives children the opportunity to practice skills they couldn't do on their own. Despite the demonstrated effectiveness of scaffolding as a teaching strategy, it is used all too seldom. In a large-scale prekindergarten study, teachers supported children's learning by scaffolding less than 10% of the time (Early et al., 2010). Nevertheless, scaffolding is the most effective strategy in any teacher's tool box (Burchinal, 2017).

The Teacher's Role The process of scaffolding, which is depicted in Figure 9.1, begins with the teacher having responsibility for the learning and gradually releasing more and more of it to the learner until the child is capable of assuming full responsibility for the task. At that point, a new zone of proximal development is created and a new challenge can be presented, starting the process once again. Alternatively, scaffolding may occur in a situation in which a child is close to mastering a task and therefore the

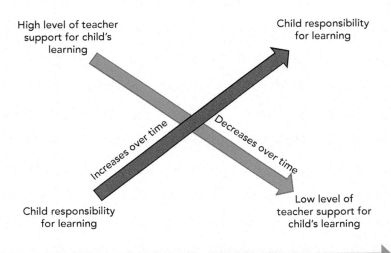

High level of teacher
support for child's
learning

Child responsibility
for learning

Increases over time

Decreases over time

Child responsibility
for learning

Low level of
teacher support for
child's learning

Teacher uses a variety of strategies with individual children over time

FIGURE 9.1 **Scaffolding in Action** Scaffolding involves using multiple teaching strategies to assist children to move from learning with assistance to learning on their own.
© Pearson Education

teacher provides just a little assistance. For example, 7-year-old Barry loves jigsaw puzzles, but he is working on a very difficult one. He has completed the outside border but is struggling with the middle. His family child care provider suggests that he put all the pieces that are the same color together and match the colors first, then try to match the shapes. He finds this suggestion works well, and is able to complete the puzzle on his own.

The process of scaffolding comes to life in the following example, in which Ms. Riley, a kindergarten teacher, gradually releases responsibility for learning to the students as she teaches writing and social studies content.

During morning meeting, after a visit to the classroom by a local dentist, Ms. Riley leads a discussion of what the children learned. Ms. Riley writes their ideas on chart paper as they watch. Then she suggests that the children write thank-you notes, and models for them how to begin a letter. "Dear Dr. Martinez," she writes, pointing out how she uses capital letters for the dentist's name and a period after "Dr." During choice time, children visit the writing center and work on writing their thank-you letters. Ms. Riley sits down with a small group. She prompts their memories about the visit. They were impressed by the big brush, set of teeth, and the kinds of food, such as apples, that help clean teeth. Ms. Riley places the chart that the children dictated where they can see it for reference. With Ms. Riley's help, the children take turns copying some of the words on the chart. She is available as they use their own developmental spelling to sound out the words they want to write. Occasionally she draws attention to the correct spelling of Dr. Martinez's name. Gradually, the children take more responsibility, creating drawings to include in their letters. On their own, some children make a chart with pictures and words of how to brush teeth, which they post in the bathroom.

In the previous sections, we described an array of research-based effective strategies. In the following section, we illustrate how intentional teachers apply these strategies in practice to help individual children reach developmentally appropriate goals.

Video Example 9.2:

Scaffolding in Action

Teachers use a variety of strategies to guide children's learning about different kinds of birds. How do these intentional teachers artfully scaffold children's learning? What specific strategies do the teachers use?

Helping Children Make Meaning, Develop Concepts, and Acquire Executive Function and Higher-Level Thinking

As you are starting to see, various teaching strategies accommodate different types of knowledge and ways of learning. Teachers, therefore, must always be open to different ways of teaching. In the classic volume *Eager to Learn: Educating Our Preschoolers* (Bowman et al., 2001), experts reviewed the research on young children's cognitive development and its implications for teaching. They identified three key principles of early childhood teaching and learning:

1. Effective teachers make learning meaningful by building on what children already know and can do.
2. Effective teachers develop children's conceptual understanding by teaching topics in depth, using many examples, and making connections to children's everyday experiences. For example, learning knowledge and skills (such as identifying letters and numbers) must be framed within the larger, key concepts involved in each domain of learning (such as the written language system in literacy or the concept of quantity in mathematics).
3. Effective teachers promote children's higher-level thinking and problem solving. They encourage development of children's metacognitive skills such as reflecting, predicting, questioning, and hypothesizing.

The above three principles of learning apply to people of all ages (NRC, 2018). Consider what these three principles mean to you as a college student or as a professional who is expanding your knowledge of teaching.

Reflect on Your Own Learning

During the course of your schooling and from your work experiences, you have probably identified subjects that you are more interested in than others and that you are likely to pursue as a major or minor. Whenever you take an additional course in your major or in an area you have studied thoroughly before, it becomes easier for you to understand and learn the material, because you already know a great deal about the subject. In short, you begin by activating your prior knowledge by connecting new learning to what you already know. An additional advantage to you as a learner is that in your preferred subject area, you are gradually building conceptual frameworks, or mental models, to which you can integrate new information, thereby deepening your understanding.

conceptual frameworks
Mental models that connect new learning to prior knowledge, enhance memory, and deepen understanding.

These types of **conceptual frameworks** serve as memory aids when you need to recall something you've learned or apply knowledge to a new situation. In fact, the more you know about a topic, the more necessary these mental models become in helping you organize, retrieve, and use your knowledge. Finally, when you have that level of understanding, you can begin to analyze your thinking, engage in metacognitive strategies such as reflecting on what you know and don't know, and apply your knowledge to solve new problems.

By contrast, consider some of the general electives you were required to take. You might have very little prior knowledge about those subjects—and perhaps even less interest. If you are like many other students, you may resort to memorizing the facts for a test without developing a deep understanding. Without a mental framework of concepts to which you can connect and therefore retain new information, you soon forget everything you have "learned." In addition, you cannot engage metacognitively in this subject area because you don't know enough about what you know to reflect on it, analyze it, make predictions about it, or evaluate your own thinking in regard to it.

Now that we have introduced teaching strategies and discussed the importance of accommodating each child's needs, we will show how teachers can use these strategies to make learning meaningful for children, to help them develop conceptual understanding, and to build higher-level thinking, problem-solving skills, and executive function.

Strategies That Make Learning Meaningful

According to the principles identified previously, effective teaching draws out and builds on children's preexisting understandings (NRC, 2018). Several strategies are effective in activating and building on children's prior knowledge, including cueing, questioning, and using some form of advance organizer (Ausubel, 1978; Cameron & Morrison, 2011).

Cues and Questions Straightforward ways of activating children's prior knowledge are to provide cues that will spark a connection or to ask questions. For example, before reading *Caps for Sale*, Carol continues to engage children's prior knowledge to help make the story meaningful:

> *Teacher:* Our story is called *Caps for Sale: A Tale of a Peddler, Some Monkeys, and Their Monkey Business*. You already know what caps are, don't you Jason?
> *Jason:* Yeah. I wore a baseball cap to school today.
> *Teacher:* That's right. It's a kind of hat.

Pressing on with more pointed questions, the teacher continues:

> *Teacher:* What do you think the author means when he says the story is about "monkey business"? Have you ever heard that before?
> Most of the children shrug or say no. Marly raises her hand:
> *Marly:* When my grandma babysits us, she always says she won't allow any monkey business, but she is smiling when she says it.
> *Teacher:* So what is Marly's grandma talking about, do you think?
> *Ricardo:* I guess she means she won't let anybody act silly.

Prior to reading the story, the teacher used cues and questions to tap into what the children already know and understand. As she reads the story, she connects the antics of the monkeys to children's ideas and effectively builds on their prior knowledge.

Advance Organizers Another way teachers help children build on their background knowledge to engage new learning is to use advance organizers. **Advance organizers** are used before introducing new information, and serve as a bridge between what the student already knows and the new learning (Ausubel, 1978; Dean et al., 2012). A widely used advance organizer strategy is known as **K-W-L** (Ogle, 1986), an example of which appears as Figure 9.2. In using K-W-L, teachers first ask children what they already *know* (K) about the topic of study. Then they ask children what they *want* (W) to know or what questions they have about the topic. One early childhood educator uses the "W" to stand for "What I wonder about ..." (McDermott, 2012). After the study is complete, these responses are compared to the answers children provide to the third question, "What did you *learn* (L)"? Sometimes teachers use a K-W-H-L chart, with H standing for "How will I find information?" In other words, which resources, websites, books, observations, or people will I consult? Other teachers use a similar advance organizer: "I notice ... I wonder."

advance organizers Ways of introducing new information that serve as a bridge between what the student already knows and the new learning.

K-W-L An advance organizer strategy in which teachers ask children what they already know (K) about the topic of study, what they want (W) to know, and then what they learned (L).

K	W	L
What do I <u>know</u>	What do I <u>want</u> to find our?	What did I <u>learn?</u>
Eggs are white.	Why do animals lay	Eggs come out of a
my mommy cooks eggs.	eggs?	chicken's behind.
I like eggs sometimes but	What other animals come	It pops out of the bird.
not when the yellow part	from eggs?	You have to wash your
is runny.	Do butterflies lay eggs?	hands after holding or
We get eggs at the store.	How long does a chicken	touching an egg.
We play with egg	have to sit on an egg to	Eggs are oval like a
cartons.	make it crack open with a	head.
Chickens lay eggs.	little chick inside?	Eggs are white, oval,
A robin made a nest with	How do you cook eggs?	hard outside.
eggs in it.	What shape is the egg?	Cracked eggs are yellow
Birds hatch out of eggs.	Are eggs good for you?	and wet inside.
		If you drop eggs, they
		break.
		Birds lay them in the nest
		& sit on them to keep
		them warm.
		A chick comes from
		eggs.
		Eggs come from
		crocodiles, fish, and
		turtles.
		Snakes and frogs lay
		eggs.
		Cats don't lay eggs.
		I like to eat eggs.
		I can share them with my
		family.
		You can crack thm to
		make scrambled eggs

FIGURE 9.2 Example of K-W-L Chart This K-W-L chart from an egg-hatching project reminds children of their prior knowledge and encourages them to reflect on what they have learned.

K-W-L is a useful strategy to build reading comprehension or to organize learning about a science or social studies topic. Consider the following example:

In his second-grade classroom, Mr. Ivey uses K-W-L to launch a study on wolves with a small group of children:

Mr. Ivey: Today, we're going to read a book about wolves. What do you already know (K) about wolves?

Children's responses include these: They live in the forest. They kill other animals. They are scary.

Mr. Ivey: What do you want to find out about wolves? (W)

The children raise many questions: What do they eat? Where do they sleep? Do they sleep all winter like bears? How big do they grow? How do they take care of their babies? Mr. Ivey writes each question on chart paper.

Mr. Ivey: Let's read this book, and afterward, we'll write down what we've learned.

Following the reading, the children have learned many facts about wolves, but they still don't know if they hibernate.

> *Mr. Ivey:* How could you find out if wolves hibernate?
> *Melinda:* We could Google it or we could email the zookeeper.

This process of building on prior knowledge is easier when teachers and children share a common language and similar cultural background. When children's prior knowledge is acquired in a language and/or cultural context that is different from that of the teacher, the task of building on the children's prior knowledge becomes more difficult but perhaps more important. Teachers of dual language learners must become aware of children's abilities and how to build on them.

Cueing, questioning, and using advance organizers are all effective approaches to activate children's prior knowledge, which in turn enhances their understanding and retention of what they learn (NRC, 2018). Next, we identify some strategies for building concept development.

Strategies That Develop Concepts

The second principle of teaching and learning emphasizes the need for children to learn topics in depth rather than amassing a large number of unrelated facts. Such understanding is enhanced when children's factual knowledge is organized into conceptual frameworks with many examples and apparent connections. To help children build conceptual frameworks, teachers can engage them in classification and representation activities.

Classify and Identify Similarities and Differences Teachers can help children build concepts by engaging them in forming **classification systems** that identify similarities and differences or compare and contrast objects and ideas (Strasser & Bresson, 2017). These cognitive activities begin early for young children.

When interacting with babies, adults continually use comparative language: "Look how big you are! You're bigger than the teddy bear now, but Scruffy is the biggest." Likewise, children learn many mathematical concepts through building classification systems. With her group of 2- and 3-year-olds, Jeanne helps the children learn the concept of the number *2* by matching pairs of shoes and socks. They soon apply this new concept to their body parts, singing a song while pointing out their two feet, two hands, two legs, two ears, and on and on.

classification systems Systems teachers use to help children build concepts by identifying similarities and differences or by comparing and contrasting objects and ideas.

Create Graphic Representations "A picture is worth a thousand words" may be a hackneyed cliché, but when it comes to developing children's conceptual understanding, the phrase is true. In fact, it is also true for college students. You've probably experienced seemingly endless pages of text or hours of lecture that become clear to you only after you've seen a chart, graph, or Venn diagram. This teaching strategy, called **graphic representation**, is the process of depicting thoughts and ideas through drawing, modeling, or using other media.

Teachers can use representation in many ways. For instance, when learning about "quantity," first-graders create a graph showing their preference: basketball or soccer. The higher bar, soccer, is the one with "more" votes, providing a visual representation of the concept for the children. They then create a graph comparing the votes of boys and girls.

Teachers' use of graphic representations is an effective way to teach concepts and engage children. Another powerful use of representation is to engage children in creating their own representations. This activity is a defining characteristic of the Reggio Emilia approach and one of its many contributions to the knowledge base of early childhood.

Loris Malaguzzi (1998) described the purpose of representation as clarifying children's understanding. George Forman, one of the earliest disseminators of the Reggio approach in America, described children's use of graphic representation in Reggio as "not learning to draw, but drawing to learn" (Forman, 1994). Reggio educators (Edwards, Gandini, & Forman, 2012) view graphic representation as a communication tool that is simpler and clearer than words, and is therefore an invaluable way to help children clarify and extend their thinking—that is, deepen their conceptual understanding. Because

graphic representation The process of depicting thoughts and ideas through drawing, modeling, or other media.

children are trying to communicate with others through their drawings, clay models, or other representations, they often pause to clarify their ideas before putting them down on paper and making them visible to other people. Important thinking is going on at such moments.

One classic example of how representation reveals and challenges a child's thinking is related to a study of rain (from the *Hundred Languages of Children* exhibit, Commune of Reggio Emilia, Italy, cited in Landry & Forman, 1999). After many days of rain, teachers asked children, "Where do you think rain comes from?" Children expressed various theories, such as "the Lord makes the rain." But Simone, age 5½, explained, "The sun heats the rain that has fallen and that's how it goes away afterwards. It goes back into the clouds and then it starts to rain again." From his explanation, it seems that Simone has a good understanding of the rain cycle.

After writing down (representing) children's theories in words, their teacher asked them to draw pictures of where the rain comes from. Simone's detailed drawing included pipes or tubes going up from the ground to the sky to convey the water. Thus, when asked to represent his theory, the child had to further elaborate on it. By engaging children in graphic representation of their theories, the teacher got a much clearer picture of Simone's understanding—somewhat different from his seemingly accurate verbal representation. Additionally, other children might challenge his theory—"Look outside, I don't see any pipes"—causing him to reflect on and probably rethink his ideas.

Strategies That Promote Higher-Level Thinking and Problem Solving

Strategies that are effective in building higher-level thinking and problem solving are those that integrate teaching of metacognitive skills. Metacognitive activities engage children in thinking and reflecting about their own learning. Early childhood education has a long tradition of incorporating these strategies in effective ways (Bodrova & Leong, 2007; Epstein & Hohmann, 2012). We next describe three strategies that not only engage children's metacognition but also contribute to their achievement in school and life.

Planning and Reflection Many early childhood programs offer children choices during center time, but planning is more than making choices. Planning requires children to make intentional choices and encourages them to identify their goals, consider the options for achieving them, make predictions, and anticipate consequences (Epstein, 2012).

Reflection is remembering with analysis, which is more than just memory and recall of events (Epstein, 2012). Teachers help children go beyond remembering what they did to becoming aware of what they learned, what was interesting, how they felt about the experience, and what they can do to build on and extend the experience. Planning and reflection promote intentionality and metacognition among teachers as well as children.

Reciprocal Teaching One of the best-researched strategies available to primary grade teachers is reciprocal teaching (Palincsar & Brown, 1984). Reciprocal teaching involves teachers working with groups of children to enhance their reading comprehension (Oczkus, 2010). The learning strategies that children develop make them better readers but can also be applied to other areas of the curriculum such as social studies or science, and with dual language learners.

Reciprocal teaching engages children in summarizing, questioning, clarifying, and predicting—all metacognitive strategies and higher-level thinking skills. Reciprocal teaching is a good example of scaffolding because at first, the teacher models the use of effective strategies, such as summarizing a passage

---

metacognitive activities Activities that engage children in thinking and reflecting about their own learning.

planning Requires children to make intentional choices and encourages them to identify their goals, consider the options for achieving them, make predictions, and anticipate consequences; helps build children's higher-level thinking and problem solving.

reflection Teaching strategy in which teachers help children go beyond remembering what they did to becoming aware of what they learned, what was interesting, how they felt about the experience, and what they can do to build on and extend the experience.

reciprocal teaching A strategy that promotes children's reading comprehension and higher-order thinking by engaging them in summarizing, questioning, clarifying, and predicting.

© Pearson Education

Video Example 9.3:

Promoting Higher-Level Thinking

A kindergarten teacher and her students discuss their quilting project based on the prior brainstorming that they did with an idea map. Notice examples of planning and reflection in the video. How does the experience build on what the children already know about shapes, patterns, and safety procedures?

that is read and asking questions, and then gradually turns over those tasks to individual children, as seen in the example that follows.

Ms. Leon, a second-grade teacher, works with five children as they read the tale *The Emperor's New Clothes*. Having previously modeled the strategies of summarizing, questioning, clarifying, and predicting, Ms. Leon chooses a student leader to take on these tasks with the group.

Summarizing: After the children silently read a short passage, she asks Christopher, acting as the student leader, to summarize what they read. Christopher says, "The emperor is like the king of the country. He's kind of ugly, but he always wants to look good by getting new clothes." Ms. Leon gives cues to help Christopher elaborate on the story: "What did the emperor do to get new clothes?" "Oh, yeah, he hired some tailors," Christopher says.

Questioning: Next, the student leader asks the other children some questions to identify important information in the passage. Christopher asks, "Were those guys really tailors?" The other children try to answer the question based on their recollection of what they read.

Clarifying: Then the student leader tries to clarify confusing parts in the passage or asks the other children for clarification. "How did the tailors trick the emperor?" Ermalinda answers, "They weren't really tailors, and they just pretended to sew new clothes to cheat the emperor."

Predicting: The student leader asks the other children to predict what will happen in the next section: "What do you think will happen when the emperor walks down the street in his underwear?"

From this brief example, we see that reciprocal teaching engages children in assuming the role of teacher, and involves them in higher-level thinking processes and metacognitive strategies.

Generate and Test Hypotheses Tisha, a second-grader, stares up at the sky for a long time and announces, "I think we're going to have a bad storm. It was hot but now it's cold, and see those cumulus clouds." Impressed, her grandma asks her where she learned all that. "We're studying weather all year in my class. We go outside every day."

At least once a week, Tisha's class looks at the weather map online, discusses what has been happening during the last 24 hours, then goes outside and observes the sky in the morning and again in the afternoon. The children make predictions about what they think will happen before the next school day, explaining the reasoning behind their predictions. The next morning, they discuss their hypotheses and the extent to which they were correct. If their predictions were accurate, they identify the observations that were the most helpful. If their predictions were not accurate, they try to figure out what they missed or misunderstood (adapted from Marzano, Pickering, & Pollock, 2001, p. 103).

In Trisha's classroom, her teacher uses a strategy that draws on children's metacognitive abilities. **Hypothesis generating and testing** is the strategy of applying previously acquired knowledge to a new situation by making a prediction and then observing and reflecting on the outcome. Using this strategy, learners activate prior knowledge, gather new information, and expand and deepen their understanding of concepts. The greatest benefit of hypothesis testing comes when learners explain their thinking, which deepens understanding (Dean et al., 2012).

Hypothesis testing is used in science curricula because it actively engages children in applying the **scientific method**: Begin with a hypothesis, test it with an experiment, make observations and gather data, and confirm or disconfirm the initial hypothesis. However, hypothesis testing is not exclusively used for science; in fact, it is used in all kinds of problem-solving situations, such as those encountered in teaching mathematics or social studies, or

hypothesis generating and testing Applying previously acquired knowledge to a new situation by making a prediction and then observing and reflecting on the outcome.

scientific method Method of beginning with a hypothesis, testing it with an experiment, making observations and gathering data, and then confirming or disconfirming the initial hypothesis.

when negotiating social problems among peers. Consider how hypothesis testing is used in the following example:

A small group of preschoolers wants to construct model cars to use on the race track they have built. Their teacher asks them to hypothesize about what kinds of materials they could use to get the wheels to turn, and the children offer suggestions:

Mary: Straws with buttons glued on the ends.
Damon: Donuts. (Several children laugh.)
Teacher: Why do you think donuts wouldn't work?
Gina: We'd eat them before we finished the car!
Damon: But maybe something like a donut, because a wheel needs to have a hole in the middle.

Damon and his friend Jaleel search for objects among the collage art materials that might work to test their hypothesis, while Mary and her friend glue the buttons. Later, the teacher and children describe what happened with their experiments and whether their hypotheses were accurate. The girls admit that although the buttons are round, the glue makes them stationary and therefore not very good wheels.

In the previous sections, we described an array of effective strategies to make learning meaningful for children, help them learn concepts, and engage them in higher-level thinking—all of which relate to children's executive function capacities. Read the feature *What Works: Strategies to Build Executive Function* for additional examples. To be an effective teacher, you will need to have all of these strategies in your repertoire, and know when and how to use them.

What Works

Strategies to Build Executive Function

As discussed previously, *executive function* (EF) refers to cognitive capacities that enable children to remember, think flexibly, and focus attention. These capacities are the foundation for higher-order executive functions that include planning, problem solving, and reasoning. Following are examples of specific strategies that are effective in building all these higher-order executive functions.

1) Ask children what they remember about an experience. Deliberate "demands" for memory promote EF. For example, after a trip or visit from an expert or community member, ask the children to describe what they remember, write a story, or draw a picture of it.

2) Have children reflect on their own memory processes. Reflecting on their memory is a metacognitive process—How did you remember that? What could you do ahead of time to help you remember?

3) Use *Wh* questions such as *Why?* and *What if?* These questions call children's attention to details. *Wh* questions promote executive function, because they rely on and deepen children's flexible thinking and memory capacity.

4) Connect to children's interests. Children are always more motivated to engage deeply in an experience if the content is interesting to them. Deep engagement is both a characteristic of executive function and a contributor to this important capacity.

5) Help children think about and plan their experiences in advance. Mentally prepare children to make choices by orienting them to options or how to use new materials and tools.

6) Following a learning experience or choice time, ask questions, such as: What did you do? Why did you choose to do that? What did you learn? How did you learn that? How do you know?

7) Ask children to compare, contrast, and evaluate specific events and experiences—Which story did you like better? Why?

Sources: P. A. Ornstein, J. L. Coffman, & J. K. Grammer, 2009. Learning to remember. In O. A. Barbarin & B. H. Wasik (Eds.), *Handbook of child development and early education: Research to practice*, 103–122; and C. E. Cameron & F. J. Morrison, 2011. Teacher activity orienting predicts preschoolers' academic and self-regulatory skills. *Early Education and Development*, 22(4), 620–648 New York, NY: Guilford.

Grouping as an Instructional Approach

In Chapter 8, we described how the environment influences children's behavior and helps teachers create caring communities. At the same time, the environment provides a powerful context for learning. Environments communicate messages to children about what kind of learning is valued and what their role is in the process. For example, a classroom with rows of individual desks and the teacher's desk in the front sends the message that children work only as individuals and teachers control the dissemination of knowledge.

On the other hand, a classroom with tables that encourage small groups of children to work together, an open space for class meetings and discussions, and learning centers for children to choose where they will work and play sends an entirely different message. In the latter environment, the expectation is clear that the teacher and children will work together in various contexts—whole group, small group, individually, and learning centers.

As we will see, each of these configurations has different benefits for children. However, studies of children's experiences in the school have found that whole group, direct instruction is by far the most frequently used teaching context (Riley-Ayers et al., 2017). Whole group, direct teaching is used much more often in kindergarten than in preschool. In preschool, on average, children spend 24% in whole group and 37% of their day in choice time. By contrast, in kindergarten, choice time is barely existent (6%), and time spent in whole group increases to 40% or more of a child's day (Holland, Crawford, Ritchie, & Early, 2014). There is little variation in the use of time from kindergarten through the primary grades. In the primary grades, most of the time is spent in whole group lessons, 25% working individually, and 16% in transitions, with little or no choice time at all (Riley-Ayers et al., 2017).

> **Video Example 9.4:**
>
> **Grouping as an Instructional Strategy**
>
> A first-grade teacher effectively uses different grouping configurations and various instructional strategies to teach important content and skills. What do you notice about the the environment and the children's engagement in each context? What are the benefits for children's learning of using different ways of grouping for instruction?

Learning in the Whole Group

Whole group, which is also called *circle time* or *class meeting time,* provides a valuable context for class discussions, music and movement, planning for the day or for special experiences such as visitors or field trips, and for children to share their experiences and ideas. Whole group is a time to build a sense of community and shared purpose.

Children benefit most from whole group time when a teacher uses it to orient them to upcoming activity that will occur during center time or projects. One research study found that, although rarely done, when preschool teachers model or demonstrate an activity in advance and explain the rationale for it, children's general knowledge, mathematics, literacy, vocabulary, and self-regulation significantly improved (Cameron & Morrison, 2011).

Research with preschoolers demonstrates that during large group times, teachers' explanations and use of challenging vocabulary is related to improving learning outcomes for children (Dickinson, 2001), as in this example:

> Prior to a visit by a local police officer, Margo gathers her whole class of preschoolers on the rug. She explains, "Officer Gardner is coming tomorrow. She will be wearing her uniform and her badge that identify her to everyone as a police officer. She wants to tell you some ways to stay safe because keeping people safe is the main job of the police. I'll write on our chart some questions you want to ask her." During this brief introduction, Margo provided the children with a concise explanation of what to expect. She also clarified the meanings of the vocabulary she used, such as *uniform, badge,* and *identify.*

Teachers may also engage the whole group in discussion, using questions to prompt and sustain the interaction. For example, a teacher might have her third-grade children working in small groups on an investigation of batteries and electricity. Each group will share their theories about how electricity works with the rest of the class.

If children are actively engaged in a large group, mentally and/or physically, this setting can be an effective learning context where children have the opportunity to express themselves, to hear the opinions of others, and to feel part of the larger learning community. The important caveat is that teachers need to take their cue from the children. If interest wanes during whole group, it is best to bring the group time to a close and move on to another activity setting or actively engage all the children in singing or movement.

In general, the younger the child, the shorter the length of time she or he should spend in whole-group experience. Children are most distracted and inattentive during whole group and individual seat work, which is usually work sheets (Crawford, Cobb, Clifford, & Ritchie, 2014). By contrast, they are most attentive and engaged during center choice times. One study found that kindergarten children demonstrate higher levels of social engagement and self-regulation during play and small group time compared to whole group, teacher-directed settings (Timmons, Pelletier, & Corter, 2016).

Learning in Small Groups

Small groups, usually composed of four to six children, are especially valuable learning contexts for two reasons. First, they provide the opportunity for more focused attention and individualized instruction from the teacher. Teachers can give children immediate, high-quality feedback and also evaluate their performance more accurately. Second, small groups give children the opportunity to interact with and learn from peers and also engage in hands-on experiences. Teachers also use small groups for a focused learning experience, such as introducing a new skill or concept.

Small groups are highly effective for learning vocabulary, literacy, and mathematics (NRC, 2009; Timmons, Pelletier, & Corter, 2016). Reading a story to a small group makes it easier for teachers to engage children in conversation before, during, and after reading, which has been found to be especially beneficial for building vocabulary and other literacy skills (Gonzalez et al., 2014; Whitehurst & Lonigan, 1998). Despite a great deal of research supporting the positive effects of small group instruction, young children from preschool through primary grades spend little time in small group interaction (Riley-Ayers et al., 2017).

One of the greatest benefits of small groups consists of the back-and-forth exchanges among children, which can scaffold children's learning just as teacher interactions can. Small groups also provide the opportunity for active engagement in the learning experience. Without such active involvement, the benefit of small groups goes unrealized. Children should have the opportunity to participate in more than one small group each day, depending on the instructional goals, and should work with peers of varying ability levels (Bates, 2013). For an example of this effective teaching strategy, read the feature *Becoming an Intentional Teacher: Working in Small Groups.*

© Pearson Education

▶

Video Example 9.5:

Small Group Instruction

Third-graders engage in a small group reading lesson. What teaching and questioning strategies does the teacher use? How does she use the small group to assess the children's learning? How might the children benefit from this small group instruction as compared to whole group?

Teaching in Learning Centers

Effective early childhood classrooms provide an extended period of time, from 45 to 90 minutes, for children to engage in child-initiated experiences in learning centers (Epstein, 2014). These defined areas of the classroom have particular purposes. The library area promotes book reading and listening. A block area provides for building, pretending, and learning mathematics and engineering concepts. Art and writing centers promote creative expression, symbolic representation, and development of fine-motor skills. Manipulative toys such as peg boards, beads, and Legos offer opportunities to practice fine-motor skills and solve problems. The dramatic play area promotes symbolic pretend play, self-regulation, language and social interaction.

Becoming an Intentional Teacher

Working in Small Groups

Here's What Happened In my kindergarten class, I have a 45-minute small group mathematics block three times each week. Prior to the block in whole group, I explain the available options and may introduce a new concept. There are three small group alternatives, and children circulate among them. In one group, children played a board game that requires rolling dice and counting. In another group, children worked with tangram-shaped blocks to replicate or create complex patterns. They tried stumping each other with increasingly difficult patterns. I worked with the third group on word problems. In my group, I helped each child read a word problem that one of their classmates had written, such as, "Odella has 9 cookies and Tomas has 5, how many do they have altogether?" I provided different kinds of materials, including manipulatives, markers, and erase boards, for them to use different strategies to solve their problems. Latesha was excited to get this problem, because Odella is her best friend. Her first idea was to draw 9 dots and 5 dots. Then she counted them and came up with 15. Tomas suggested she try using the Unifix cubes, which helped her count each object more easily and arrive at 14. Dora explained that she used regrouping to solve the problem—adding 1 to 9, taking away 1 from 5, then adding 10 and 4 to get 14.

Here's What I Was Thinking I plan the small group times for several reasons. When each child can participate more actively in investigating, predicting, and recording, they care more about the outcome. They pay attention and get ideas from each other, and are more motivated because it is a meaningful problem involving their friends' own names.

Small groups allow the children to participate and at the same time allow me to observe what each child does and does not understand and engage each child in the learning experience at his or her own level. I formed groups that were mixed with respect to the children's developmental levels, or what I thought their ability would be on this task. Some children are still counting on fingers, while others like Dora are mentally solving the problem and writing the algorithm ($9 + 5 = 14$).

I encourage children to explain their strategy to the others because it helps them get a firmer understanding of the concepts. And the less advanced children get exposure to new strategies for solving an addition problem.

Reflection A large body of research supports the benefits of teaching children in small groups, yet most teachers rarely use this approach. Why do you think this is so? What conditions might make teachers more likely to decrease time spent in whole group instruction and increase small group experiences for children?

During learning center time, children have opportunities to plan, initiate, and make choices and to practice their developing skills, which is essential for mastery. Learning centers provide natural laboratories for children to work out social problems with other children and to practice their language. Center time also promotes decision-making skills because children make choices about how they will spend their time, what they will do, and with whom they will play. Research shows that time spent in free choice contributes to the development of inhibitory control and self-regulation as long as teachers' interactions are supportive (Goble & Pianta, 2017).

Effective teachers use center time to engage children in one-on-one, extended conversations (Cabell et al., 2013, 2015). During this period in which children are engaged with various tasks, such as writing, doing a puzzle, or pouring water, teachers are available to scaffold individual children's learning as needed. Such effective teacher-child interactions during center time are positively related to gains in language development and early literacy skills (Dickinson et al., 2013; Goble & Pianta, 2017). Finally, center time provides an excellent opportunity for teachers to observe and assess children's developing capabilities in various contexts.

All of the grouping approaches described previously—large group, small groups, centers, and individual activities—provide excellent opportunities for teachers to support dual language learners. Read the *Language Lens: Teachable Moments with Dual Language Learners* feature for suggested strategies.

In the previous sections, we described the various contexts commonly found in early childhood classrooms: whole group, small group, and learning centers. Center time is an excellent opportunity for children to engage in their favorite activity—play (Wiltz & Klein, 2001). Play is also a highly effective context for learning and teaching, as described next.

Language Lens
Teachable Moments with Dual Language Learners

For children who are learning English, every moment in the classroom is a teaching and learning opportunity. They may be wearing winter clothes for the first time, riding a school bus, and meeting people who do not look or sound like them. Learning a new language takes time, effort, and intentional teaching. Teachers need to take advantage of every teachable moment. Here are some points for teachers to keep in mind:

- As a role model of the language, speak slowly but not loudly, simplifying your vocabulary and sentence structure as you might for a younger child. Over time, work toward more challenging vocabulary, sentences, and short conversation.
- Use your body and facial expressions to communicate. For instance, to emphasize words such as *under, through, around,* or *on top,* play with children around a table to physically demonstrate these words and concepts.
- Use repetition. Be as clear as possible in pronunciation and diction, which may mean opening the mouth wider because children look for facial clues.
- Use large group time to engage children in the joy of group movement and exercise, singing and choral repetition, preparing children in advance for upcoming activities.
- Use small group time, which is especially effective for dual language learners because it allows for active participation, individual attention, and experiences with objects. For example, if children are learning about vegetables, have real broccoli, carrots, and squash for them to see, touch, and taste.

- Use small groups of children with the same home language to introduce new concepts in the home language first.
- Vary the composition of groups, at times bringing together learners who speak the same language and at other times children from two or more language groups.
- Provide a visually rich environment with pictures and words in multiple languages.
- Organize centers with language learning in mind, including spaces for individuals such as a listening center with tapes in the home language, tablets or smartphones with translation apps, or a computer with programs in both languages.
- Provide private, quiet spaces for children to de-stress—being surrounded by an unfamiliar language for long periods of time can be overwhelming for anyone.
- Outdoor playtime is a great venue for children to learn new English words for physical actions and social interactions. Create games that repeat words, such as *run, kick, walk, jump, throw over,* or *throw under.* Making friends and playing together motivate children to learn a new language.
- Give special attention to particular sounds that may not exist in the child's home language. For some Spanish-speaking children, it may be the /ch/ or /sh/ or /w/ pronunciations; for some Asian children, it may be the /r/ or /th/ sounds.
- Encourage children's efforts at speaking the new language; avoid correcting children by simply rephrasing and repeating.

✔ Check Your Understanding 9.4

▲ Play as a Context for Teaching and Learning

The word *play* is used to describe different types of activities, including constructive play and games with rules as well as pretend play. In the previous discussion of learning centers, we saw how teachers' behaviors support learning during various forms of play. In this section, we explore teachers' roles during sociodramatic play, a particularly effective form of play for developing children's self-regulation, problem solving, and language and literacy skills (Bodrova & Leong, 2015; Weisberg et al., 2015, 2016).

Rarely is play thought of as a teaching strategy. Researchers define play as child-initiated experience, and in fact, children themselves see play as something they control (Johnson, Eberle, & Hendricks, 2015; Weisberg et al., 2016). Nevertheless, decades of research on play demonstrates that teachers have important roles in children's play and can help play achieve its full potential as an effective learning experience for children (Weisberg et al., 2015, 2016). The key is not to take over or turn play into a formal lesson.

During sociodramatic play, children pretend, create a theme, use props, develop roles, and follow rules related to the roles. Moreover, sociodramatic play involves language interaction (Bodrova & Leong, 2007), as we see in this example:

> In her Head Start classroom, Marita Lewis sets up a grocery store with food boxes, plastic fruit and vegetables, shopping carts, a cash register, and a check-out counter. She adds paper and pencils for writing shopping lists, play money, and paper receipts. As 4-year-old Carey pushes her cart up to the counter, the "cashier" Angela, her classmate, asks, "Paper or plastic?" After Carey selects, "Paper," Angela continues to recite the script of a cashier to the best of her recollection, "Credit card or money?" Meanwhile, sitting nearby, Marita is approached by LaToya, who needs help writing her shopping list. She wants to add bananas. Marita says, "BBBBananas," drawing out the /b/ sound at the beginning of the word. "What letter does it start with?" "B!" shouts LaToya, who quickly starts to write a B on her list.

Teachers' Involvement During Play

Research reveals that teachers play a variety of roles during children's play that can be placed on a continuum from minimal to maximum teacher involvement (Jones & Reynolds, 2011). Figure 9.3 depicts the continuum of teacher roles in play (Johnson, Christie, & Wardle, 2005). As the figure illustrates, the effective *facilitating* roles are the ones in the middle of the continuum.

The two extremes of teacher behavior, either *uninvolved* or *overly directive*, have a negative effect on play. If teachers are uninvolved and ignore children during play, using playtime to do paperwork or housekeeping tasks, children's pretend play tends to become simplistic, repetitive, and raucous, featuring themes like monsters and superheroes (Johnson et al., 2005). In these situations, the play often turns into a disciplinary situation with the teacher only stepping in to police behavior. Consequently, the learning potential of play is lost.

At the other end of the continuum, teachers are ineffective if they take too much control of children's play, either by trying to direct what children do from the sidelines or by redirecting the play away from what the children are doing toward the teacher's goal. Situations in which teachers are maximally involved cease to be child-initiated play, and most of the time, children will simply withdraw mentally from the pretend scenario or leave the scene entirely.

FIGURE 9.3 Continuum of Teacher Roles in Play Teachers can use various strategies to support children's play—from minimal to maximum involvement—as depicted on this continuum.

Source: From J. E. Johnson, J. F. Christie, & F. Wardle, © 2005. *Play, development and early education.* Reprinted and electronically reproduced by permission of Pearson Education, Inc., Upper Saddle River, NJ.

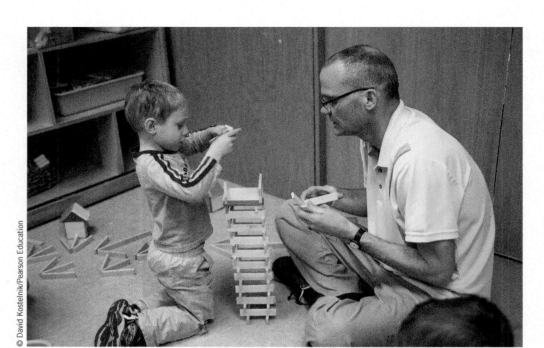

Play is a valuable context for children's learning. But children don't automatically play productively. How can teachers support play to benefit children without taking over?

So we see that using play as a context for teaching and learning requires teachers to walk a fine line between doing too little and doing too much. Next, we discuss several effective roles of teachers during play.

Teachers' Role During Play

The four roles in the midrange of the continuum are onlooker, stage manager, co-player, and play leader. These roles are all effective in helping children get involved and stay engaged in play situations. In each of these roles, the teacher becomes more involved in the play scene. At the same time, the teacher adapts her role as the children play, depending on their interests and needs.

onlooker Teachers act as the audience for children's play.

Onlooker   In the onlooker role, teachers act as the audience for children's play. They position themselves nearby, acknowledging and encouraging children's play by nodding, smiling, or making positive comments. The onlooker role lets children know that play is valued and important, and encourages them to persist. In the onlooker role, teachers observe and assess children's competencies exhibited during their play interactions. Based on these observations, the teacher intentionally decides whether and how to become more involved in the play (Jones & Reynolds, 2011).

stage manager Teachers set the stage for children's play by providing the props and theme and being available to respond to children's requests.

Stage Manager   As the name implies, stage managers do not actively enter the play; they instead set the stage by providing the props and theme. They are also available to respond to children's requests for materials or assistance. In the grocery store play described previously, Marita acted as a stage manager, having prepared the setting, which encouraged children's involvement. Stage managers scaffold children's learning, as when Marita helped LaToya with her shopping list. Teachers as stage managers also make suggestions to help extend the play. For example, if LaToya begins to lose interest, Marita might ask, "What else do you need for your dinner tonight?"

co-player Teachers actually join in and take an active role in children's play.

Co-Player   As co-players, teachers join in and take an active role in the play. Co-players are equal play partners with children, but it is best if teachers take the subordinate role in the drama, such as the patient in the doctor's office or the passenger on the airplane, leaving the prime roles of doctor or pilot for the children. As a co-player, the teacher is careful to let the children take the lead. This role provides ample opportunity, however, for the teacher to model play skills, including pretending with objects and roles, turn-taking, ways to enter an ongoing scene, and vocabulary (Johnson et al., 2005, p. 272). Consider how the teacher accomplishes all of these goals in the following play situation:

> In Sascha Britt's preschool classroom, the children are playing pet store as part of their study of domestic animals. Sascha arrives cradling a stuffed dog and says, "I just got a brand new puppy. I don't know what I'm going to need to take care of him. Can you help me?" The children scramble about looking for supplies on the shelves of their store. Martha says, "He'll be hungry. Here's some dog food." Dominic chimes in, "He has to take walks. You better get him a leash." "I think he needs a nice soft bed," says Emory, who looks around but can't find anything to fit the bill. Instead, he picks up the pillow off the doll bed and hands it to his teacher. Sascha replies, "I'm glad I came to this store. You have lots of supplies. How much will this cost?"

Video Example 9.6:

Scaffolding Play

This video provides an example of an evolving pretend play scenario. What roles does the teacher play? How does her behavior affect the children's play?

Play Leader This role involves teachers' direct participation in children's play, but exerts more influence than the co-player's role. As the **play leader**, the teacher deliberately attempts to enrich and extend the play episode, suggesting a theme and introducing new props or plot elements. Teachers become play leaders when children have difficulty beginning sociodramatic play or when play breaks down:

> After several days playing in the grocery store, the children's play becomes repetitive and fewer children choose to play there. To spark some interest, Marita puts herself in the role of store manager.
>
> *Marita:* This store is losing business. I think it needs some new attractions for shoppers.
>   What if we reduce the prices on everything and have a sale?
> *Josh:* We'll have to change all the signs.
> *Marita:* What else could we do to get more customers?
> *Toby:* We could put in a McDonald's like they have at the mall.
>
> The children quickly embrace Toby's idea. Josh starts to draw a big "M" for the McDonald's sign, while other children start gathering props for the food. Toby's suggestion leads to many changes in the dramatic play episode with new roles such as cook that extend the play over several days.

play leader Teachers participate in children's play; includes making deliberate attempts to enrich and extend the play episode.

Because sociodramatic play is such an effective learning context, teachers need to be aware of and use the full range of roles and strategies available to them in supporting children's make-believe play. Although some educators believe that pretend play comes naturally to children and that adults are not needed, this is a misperception. In fact, children who are skilled "players" during preschool most likely had parents or caregivers who played with them beginning as babies and toddlers (Elias & Berk, 2002).

Today's teachers report that many children, from both low-income and middle-income backgrounds, are unskilled at pretend play when they come to early childhood programs. Their play tends to be repetitive and immature. In situations such as these, teachers in the role of stage managers can coach children from the sidelines to improve play behaviors or, as co-players or leaders, they can model and scaffold appropriate play behavior (Bodrova & Leong, 2015).

 Application Exercise 9.2

Teachers' Roles in Play

Research demonstrates that participation in sociodramatic play has positive effects on children's self-regulation, language, literacy, and mathematics ability (Blair & Raver, 2014). To be effective, however, teachers must be intentional in their roles in children's play. Play has a long tradition in early childhood programs as well as a thorough, although sometimes contradictory, research base—most likely because there are so many different types of play. Read the feature *Promoting Play: Guided Play* to learn more about current research on play.

Promoting Play

Guided Play

Too often, early education is presented as a dichotomy—play vs. academics. A new and more effective approach is the concept of *guided play,* in which a curriculum-centered preschool uses play as a developmentally appropriate teaching strategy. Guided play is not "free play," which is both child-initiated and child-directed. Research demonstrates that free play is essential for healthy development, and benefits children's social skills and self-regulation. However, free play is less valuable in promoting specific curriculum goals such as literacy and mathematics. Proponents of guided play suggest that it is the best way to protect the joys and benefits of play in school while also ensuring positive learning outcomes for children. Guided play is a blend of teacher-initiated and child-directed experience.

During guided play as in all true play, children are in control. This is important, because as we've said previously, if adults co-opt play, children disengage. Teachers carefully prepare the environment and then scaffold children's activity as the play evolves. During block play, a teacher might say, "I wonder what would happen if you added this?" The child has a choice to follow the teacher's suggestion or pursue his own.

Guided play involves exploration in a structured environment. One study compared three situations for children's learning about triangles: 1) a guided play activity in which the teacher explored the properties of triangles with the children using bendable sticks and picture cards; 2) teacher-direct instruction demonstrating the materials; and 3) free play in which children could do whatever they wished with the materials. Afterward, children were asked to choose the "real" triangles. Children learned basic properties of triangles better in both the teacher-directed and guided play situations than in free play. However, children who engaged in guided play were better able to transfer the knowledge to new situations and identify atypical shapes. Children's active discovery plus adult scaffolding led to deeper understanding about the features of shapes.

Sources: D. S. Weisberg, A. K. Kittredge, K. Hirsh-Pasek, R. M. Golinkoff, & D. Klahr, 2015. Making play work for education. *Phi Delta Kappa International, 26*(8), 8–13; and B. Hassinger-Das, K. Hirsh-Pasek, & R. M. Golinkoff, 2017. The case of brain science and guided play: A developing story. *Young Children, 72*(2), 45–50.

In the next section, we discuss a more recent and yet pervasive educational phenomenon: digital media in schools and child care programs.

Check Your Understanding 9.5

Effective Teaching with Digital Media

Ninety-eight percent (98%) of children under age 8 now have mobile devices in their homes, and most use them daily for relatively long periods of time (Rideout, 2017). In fact, most children are expert users of every type of technological device and application—smartphones, touch tablets, e-books, social networking, whiteboards, video games, computers, internet, digital cameras, and video camcorders. As these words are written, new and emerging technologies are being developed at lightning speed. Children are no longer just consumers of media; they are creators.

Digital media for education, communication, social networking, and user-generated content have transformed every aspect of children's lives, including how teachers use technology in the classroom and how teacher education is delivered. The early childhood technology market is booming, with tens of thousands of apps designed for preschoolers and primary-grade children (Vaala, Ly, & Levine, 2015).

Professional Decision-Making

Bombarded by an ever-changing technological landscape, teachers must make informed decisions about effective uses of technology and also teach children to be critical thinkers and consumers of media. NAEYC and the Fred Rogers Center for Early Learning and Children's Media (2012) take the position that "technology and interactive media are learning tools that, when used in intentional and developmentally appropriate ways and in conjunction with other traditional tools and materials, can support the development and learning of young children" (p. 1). (This statement focuses on interactive media, not television.)

In the past, conversations have focused on how much time children should spend with screens, which remains a critical issue. But the NAEYC–Fred Rogers Center position raises the most challenging question for early educators: What is developmentally appropriate digital media, and how can it contribute to children's learning?

Enormous growth and change in children's technology have occurred since the 2012 statement. Nevertheless, consensus exists about what matters most in using technology with children. NAEYC, the Fred Rogers Center, the American Academy of Pediatrics, the U.S. Department of Education, the RAND Corporation and other prestigious groups agree on the following considerations (Donahue & Schomburg, 2017; Hirsh-Pasek et al., 2015):

- Technology should promote relationships, interaction, collaboration, and communication among children and with adults.
- Parents or teachers should co-view with children to promote languge and connect experiences to other learning at home or school.
- Content, context, and quality matter. The quality of what is on the screen is more important than screen time.
- Apps and other software should promote engagement, creativity, curiosity, initiative, problem solving, and other positive approaches to learning. Technology should promote active experiences rather than sedentary activity.
- Devices should be sturdy and easy for children to operate and manipulate; for example, tablets can be adapted to help develop fine-motor skills.
- Digital media should not replace essential early childhood experiences such as imaginative and outdoor play, conversation, and exploring the world firsthand.
- Technology should be well integrated into the larger curriculum, with clear educational goals that are achievable by children in the targeted age group.

Classroom Practices

Just as digital media has created limitless options for social interaction and information dissemination, the use of technology in classrooms has endless possibilities. These possibilities are achieved only if intentional teachers make good choices about developmentally appropriate interactive media and teach children how to use these resources well. Interactions with media should be playful and creative, promoting exploration, problem solving, pretend, physical activity, and social interaction (Puerling, 2018). The key is for children and teachers to jointly engage with media. All experts in children's digital media agree on one major criterion—to the extent possible, children themselves should be in control of the medium (Donohue & Schomburg, 2017).

Effective teachers integrate interactive media into curriculum and instruction throughout the day. Children use e-books independently and do online research for projects or research on topics of study. Both teachers and children use digital cameras regularly to document children's work products. Children can use a program to create their own stories by clicking on the characters and events of their choosing. The internet allows communication with other children or adults, such as favorite authors, in other cities, states, or countries. Through technology, a second-grade class can take an electronic field trip and regularly monitor the growth of the baby panda at the National Zoo via the zoo's website. In turn, during an actual field trip to the zoo, children can use a mobile device to view the native environments of pandas in China and access information about other species of bears.

Numerous digital media resources are available that make learning meaningful; promote literacy, STEM, and concept development; and engage children in higher-level thinking and problem solving. For example, the International Children's Digital Library provides access to children's books in diverse languages, including Spanish, Arabic, Swahili, Chinese, Thai, Farsi, and many more. The digital format makes it possible for books to be projected onto white boards for whole group reading or by an individual child to build on home language and culture. Imagine the pride on children's faces upon seeing their home language shown so much respect.

Other software is designed primarily for children to practice basic skills such as phonics or counting. A teacher might introduce a concept such as rhyming in whole group time, then the children can play a rhyming game on a tablet or laptop during center time. Choosing appropriate digital media is like choosing books or any other educational resource: Educators making decisions about technology need to carefully evaluate the philosophy and purpose as well as the developmental, individual, and cultural appropriateness of the resource. For example, providing bilingual software may be an excellent decision.

Mobile devices should support, not supplant, other activities. Fortunately, technology can be incorporated in children's play if apps or tools are engaging and children play together. "The most innovative apps empower children to take charge of their learning" (Bailey, 2017).

Research on Digital Media

Digital media is ubiquitous in children's lives. A survey by Common Sense Media (Rideout, 2017) found that increasing numbers of children use mobile devices at younger and younger ages, and for longer periods of time. In 2011, only 4% of children's media use involved a mobile device, compared with 35% in 2017 (Rideout, 2017). And in that same period, the average time spent with devices tripled.

Although a digital divide continues to exist, it is much smaller than in the past (Rideout, 2017). Children in lower-income families are less likely to have tablets in the home compared to higher-income families (61% to 85%), but virtually all families now have smartphones. And approximately the same numbers of lower- and higher-income parents download educational apps for their children.

Although we know that young children spend a considerable amount of time using mobile devices, research on the effects on their development is relatively slim (Paciga et al., 2017). One study examined preschoolers' use of iPads and three types of apps—*gaming* apps that children often enjoy and master quickly, *creating* apps with which children can build or draw something, and *e-books* (Cohen Group, 2011). The researchers found that children embraced the apps that share characteristics with most effective early childhood experiences: learning by doing, building on interests and prior skills, self-pacing, and offering "a no-fail environment and endless possibilities and outcomes" (Cohen Group, 2011, p. 2).

Although more research on the effects and benefits of mobile digital media is needed, studies demonstrate that they can be highly effective in promoting children's learning as long as software is developmentally appropriate and children are in control

(Paciga et al., 2017). Unlike adults, who tend to work on computers in isolation, preschool and primary-grade children willingly seek peer involvement and conversation if the device and software are engaging and interactive. Placing two seats in front of a laptop or having two or more children share a tablet encourages interaction. Using a digital microscope can engage an entire classroom in excitedly observing the wonder of a butterfly's wings or the skin of an orange.

Using technology in early childhood programs is not without controversy. Much of the concern focuses on the negative effects of passive television viewing; promotion of violence, sexuality, and commercialism; and the importance of limiting children's screen time for their physical health and overall development (Rideout, 2017). The debate becomes complicated, however, because all "screens" are not equal (Donahue & Schomburg, 2017). Television often becomes background noise that harms language development and social interaction (ZERO TO THREE, 2014). The quality of television content also matters. For example, decades of evidence demonstrates the educational benefits of programs such as *Sesame Street* and *Super Why!* (Linebarger, McMenamin, & Wainwright, n.d.). An analysis of 24 studies on the effects of international co-productions of *Sesame Street* involving over 10,000 children in 15 countries found significant positive effects on literacy and mathematics; world knowledge; health and safety; social reasoning; and attitudes toward diverse people. The effects occurred in both low-, middle-, and high-income countries (Mares & Zan, 2013).

Use of assistive technology may be part of a child's IEP. Well-designed assistive technology can be valuable for children with and without disabilities.

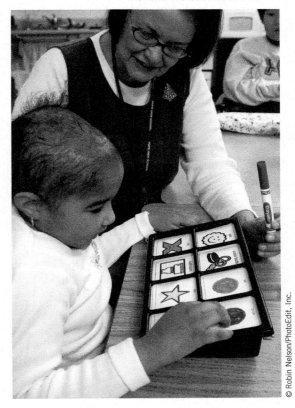

© Robin Nelson/PhotoEdit, Inc.

Assistive Technology for Children with Diverse Abilities

One of the most valuable uses of technology is that it can empower children with disabilities to participate more fully and successfully in inclusive classrooms. The Individuals with Disabilities Education Act (IDEA) defines assistive technology as "any item, piece of equipment, or product system whether acquired commercially off the shelf, modified, or customized, that is used to increase, maintain, or improve functional capabilities of individuals with disabilities."

assistive technolog A piece of equipment or product that is used to increase, maintain, or improve the functional capabilities of individuals with disabilities.

Assistive technology incorporates a wide range of options designed for many different purposes, offering various benefits. For example, a child with cerebral palsy can use a device that supports him to stand at an easel or another device to help him grip a pencil. Technology can be essential for successful inclusion by not only ensuring children access to a setting, but facilitating their participation and providing the supports they need (DEC & NAEYC, 2009). Read the *Including All Children: Technology for Children with Special Needs* feature for examples of how technology can be used to help children with disabilities or any child who is not making expected progress.

If necessary and appropriate, the use of assistive technology will be part of a child's individual education plan (IEP). Teachers working in inclusive settings need to be prepared to use whatever technology is required to successfully include all children and help them achieve individualized learning goals.

Assistive technologies help children function independently and support their inclusion in classrooms with their peers. Such technology is valuable for children without disabilities as well. The options are considerable, depending on the creativity of individuals and the resources available.

© Pearson Education

Video Example 9.7:

Assistive Technology

This video provides an example of assistive technolgy in a second grade class. The teacher uses "I notice, I wonder" as an advance organizer for this science lesson. How does the assistive keyboard enable Jeffrey to fully participate in the learning experience? What do you observe about the role of assistive technology in supporting inclusion?

Including All Children
Technology for Children with Special Needs

For children with learning differences, vision or hearing loss, autism, or other special needs, technology can make a huge difference. Apps, games, websites, and mobile devices can support access, participation, and inclusion for all children. Perhaps most important, technology helps children use their abilities and strengths to overcome their challenges.

Tools are now available and effective to help children develop self-regulation, communication and social skills, organization, literacy, and mathematics. Devices range from low-tech toys to complex communication systems. For example, children who lack the physical ability to write can use voice-activated software to express their ideas and feelings. Writing requires both working memory and control over fine motor skills. Either or both can present a challenge for some children. A speech-to-text program can turn a storyteller into a story writer. A child is less likely to forget the narrative if not struggling to form letters on the page. Children who cannot speak can use communication boards that they touch with a hand, foot, or other body part to activate a voice that speaks for them.

A girl with attention deficit disorder can use headphones at a computer to decrease distractions from the classroom. Apps are available to help children with autism spectrum disorder identify emotions in others and in themselves. Some apps support mindfulness and help children calm down and manage anger.

In 2017, *Sesame Street* introduced Julia, a little girl with autism who doesn't like loud noises and doesn't always make eye contact. Elmo explains that it doesn't mean she doesn't want to be a friend. When Big Bird tries to meet her, Julia doesn't respond, and Abby explains, "My friend Julia has autism." Adding Julia to *Sesame Street* provides opportunities to explain differences and model understanding, inclusion, and acceptance. Julia's character is valuable for children with and without autism, and has been embraced by parents.

Sources: W. Kane, April 4, 2017. Meet Julia, Sesame Street's new character. www.commonsensemedia.org/blog/meet-julia-sesame-streets-new-character; and Common Sense Media, n.d. Special needs and learning disabilities. www.commonsensemedia.org/special-needs.

 Check Your Understanding 9.6

Revisiting the Case Study

… Ms. Hanson's Classroom

In this chapter, we provided a conceptual framework that enables teachers to build a repertoire of effective teaching strategies. We also cited research demonstrating that current practices in preschool and primary-grade classrooms could be improved to reflect what is known about effective teaching. At the outset, we visited Sally Hanson's kindergarten class, where she used various strategies to help the children achieve literacy goals. Having now explored the array of effective strategies that make up a teacher's repertoire, we can analyze what Sally was doing and why.

Sally's goal was for all of the children to make progress on some of the English Language Arts standards. Because the children have differing skill levels and prior knowledge, she adapted her teaching to match their needs. She used *encouragement, cueing,* and *questioning* as needed for different children. She provided *scaffolding* for Elena and Lucy, adapting her instruction to help them do tasks that they could not do independently. Homemade books and posted words helped several children function with less of her direct support. Sally provided a more fixed form of *support* for Marguerite to focus her attention on the order of the letters in her name. Sally *activated prior knowledge* for Logan and Gabe, and *added challenge* to extend their learning. She used *direct instruction* with Tommy, who was struggling to form the letter *T*. Any one of these strategies would have been less effective if used with every child.

Intentional teachers know the children in their classrooms as well as their curriculum goals. They flexibly draw on their professional knowledge of teaching strategies to effectively promote children's learning and development. ■

9 Chapter Summary

- Effective teaching is a science informed and guided by research. Teaching, however, is also an art because it requires vision, creativity, and decision making.

- The most effective teachers have a large repertoire of research-based teaching strategies, including acknowledging and encouraging, giving quality feedback, modeling, demonstrating, giving cues and hints, adding challenge, questioning, co-constructing learning, direct instruction, and scaffolding.

- Children learn best when teaching strategies build on their prior knowledge (make learning meaningful), build conceptual understanding, and promote higher-order thinking, problem solving, and executive function.

- An intellectually engaging learning environment provides various contexts that offer different opportunities for learning and types of teacher–child interactions: individual interactions, whole-group meetings, small groups, center choice time, and opportunities for play.

- Teachers use play as a teaching strategy by taking on various roles—onlooker, stage manager, co-player, and play leader—to help children get involved and stay engaged in play situations. Guided play is an effective way to engage children in playful learning of curriculum goals.

- Many types of digital media can be effective in supporting all children's learning and development. Assistive technology can enable children with and without disabilities to participate more fully and successfully in inclusive classrooms.

Key Terms

- acknowledging
- advance organizers
- apprenticeship
- assistive technology
- child-initiated experiences
- classification systems
- closed questions
- co-players
- conceptual frameworks
- demonstrating
- direct instruction
- effective teaching
- encouragement
- facilitating
- feedback loop
- graphic representation
- hypothesis generating and testing
- K-W-L
- learning strategy
- metacognitive activities
- modeling
- onlooker
- open-ended questions
- pedagogy
- planning
- play leader
- questioning
- reciprocal teaching
- reflection
- scientific method
- stage managers
- supporting
- teacher-initiated experiences
- teaching strategy
- wait time

 Flash Cards 9.1

Readings and Websites

Heidemann, S., Menninga, B., & Chang, C. (2016). *The thinking teacher: A framework for intentional teaching in the early childhood classroom.* Redmond, WA: Exchange Press.

Dombro, A. L., Jablon, J., & Stetson, C. (2011). *Powerful interactions: How to connect with children to extend their learning.* Washington, DC: National Association for the Education of Young Children.

Epstein, A. S. (2014). *The intentional teacher: Choosing the best strategies for young children's learning* (rev. ed.). Washington, DC: National Association for the Education of Young Children.

Strasser, J. & Bresson, L. M. (2017). *Big questions for young minds: Extending children's thinking.* Washington, DC: National Association for the Education of Young Children.

Children's Technology Review

Edited by Dr. Warren Buckleitner, an expert on early education and technology, CTR is both a website and an annual e-book publication that provides detailed reviews of thousands of apps as well as reviews of new technological devices and their utility for young children.

Common Sense Media

Go to this website and click on "Best Apps and Games" for up-to-date reviews of apps by age group. The criteria these experts use to rate apps are useful lenses for teachers to use in selecting apps on their own. The organization also conducts and disseminates research on educational media.

National Center on Early Childhood Development, Teaching, and Learning (NCECDTL)

Sponsored by the Office of Head Start, this center's website provides a wealth of resources on effective instructional practices, webinars, and a library of visual supports and classroom activity suggestions based on the latest research.

TEC Center at Erikson Institute

On Erikson's Technology in Early Childhood website, you will find videos, webinars, and other resources on the most effective, current practices for using technology to teach young children.

Shared Writing 9.1

Using a Variety of Teaching Strategies to Meet Learning Goals

10 Planning Effective Curriculum

Learning Outcomes

After studying this chapter, you should be able to:

10.1 Define curriculum.

10.2 Describe the components of an effective curriculum.

10.3 Explain the role of standards in planning curriculum.

10.4 Evaluate various approaches to curriculum planning.

10.5 Compare various research-based early childhood curriculums.

10.6 Apply a model for planning effective curriculum.

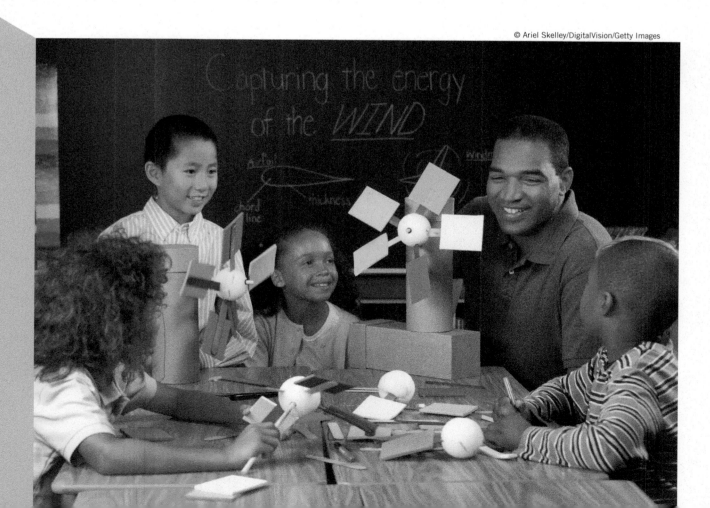

Case Study

This is an exciting week at Ross Elementary School, a public school serving prekindergarten through fifth-grade students. All the classes are engaged in a schoolwide project called *Career Explorations: What Do I Want to Be When I Grow Up?* The project is designed to help children achieve the following goals: learn about a variety of careers and occupations; build their self-concepts about the world of work; understand that what they are studying now is preparing them for their future careers; connect character and careers; and set high expectations and goals for themselves.

To begin the project, parents and community members are invited to spend about 30 minutes in each of the classrooms explaining their work. The younger children eagerly await their visits with a police officer, doctor, and veterinarian. The primary-grade classes are thrilled to meet a real pilot. Among their other visitors are a librarian, chef, author, and artist/illustrator. Prior to the visits, teachers prepare the students by asking them to come up with six good questions for the experts. Plus, the children ask the experts how they use what they learned in school in their jobs or in their everyday lives—whether science, social studies, math, or any other subject. Most visitors are asked, "Why did you choose this job?" and "What is the best part of it?" Their answers cause the children to reflect on the type of character needed to perform each job and whether they are suited for it. For example, 5-year-old Maisie changes her mind about being a veterinarian when she realizes that the vet may be there when the dogs die. She decides to be an author instead.

Beyond the presentations by parents and community volunteers, children explore the world of potential careers via technology. Working in class sessions with their teachers or using individual time to explore on computers or tablets, they visit an interactive career website that has information, games, and apps related to about 100 career options. *Kids Search* allows them to click on their interests, such as sports, computers, and traveling, or their favorite school subject, perhaps music or geography, and learn how it applies to real jobs. The older children seek out the section devoted to unusual occupations such as aerial cinematographer, digital artist, forensic crime scene investigator, toy designer, highway worker, landscaper, or language translator. As children became more interested, they conduct more research and connect via email with other career experts such as zookeeper, Army captain, scientist, secret service agent, inventor, professional soccer player, and even an astronaut.

After the information-gathering portion of the project, children create posters and write essays and poems addressing the question, *What do I want to be when I grow up?* that are displayed in the school hallway. There's also a career dress-up and hat day, when everyone dresses as their favorite job. The project culminates with a poster and essay contest voted on by the children in each class. The majority vote for the astronaut as favorite poster, which appears in Figure 10.1. ■

Even the most uninformed visitor to this school could not fail to observe the content of the curriculum during this brief visit. Clearly, the curriculum is focused on a social studies topic—the career awareness study—into which other subjects are integrated. But the curriculum also incorporates state learning standards related to character development, communication, collaboration, and making connections. The children are speaking and listening, reading and writing about a topic of interest, and learning new vocabulary words and concepts. Skills such as using technology, planning, and researching are also addressed. The theme is literally "played out" on dress-up day, during which children use the language they are learning as well as their social skills. The curriculum is so rich and engaging that there are very few discipline problems; the school hums with children's happy voices, smiles, and laughter.

The goal of this chapter is to help you understand the complexity of planning effective curriculum and the intentional teacher's roles in working with curriculum. We begin by defining the term *curriculum* and describe ways of organizing curriculum plans. We discuss the early childhood profession's indicators of effective curriculum and the role of standards. Next, we describe some frequently used curriculum models. Finally, we present a model for planning curriculum that demonstrates the connection between discipline-based content and child development knowledge.

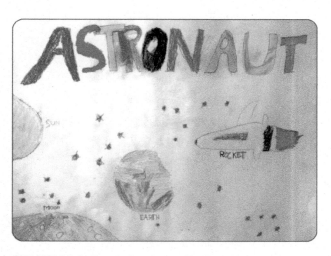

FIGURE 10.1 Career Awareness Poster The schoolwide career awareness project engaged children's interests while also addressing several state learning standards.

Defining Curriculum

Curriculum is usually thought of as the "what"—the content that children are learning—while teaching is the "how." In early childhood education, it is especially difficult to separate curriculum from teaching. There is no one agreed-on understanding of curriculum that is a comfortable fit for this diverse field. In this chapter, however, we present our vision of early childhood curriculum and its contributions to children's learning.

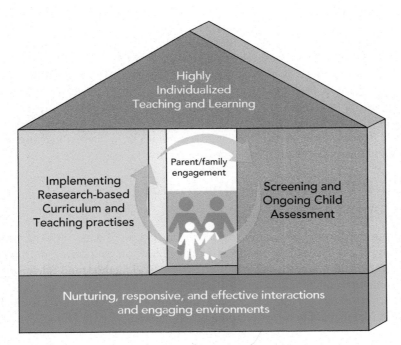

FIGURE 10.2 Framework for Effective Practice Choosing and implementing a strong curriculum is one of the pillars of effective practice—depicted as a house in this model developed by the Head Start National Center on Early Childhood Development, Teaching, and Learning.

Source: National Center on Early Childhood Development, Teaching ,and Learning. (2017). *Framework for effective practice.* Retrieved February 9, 2018, from https://eclkc.ohs.acf.hhs.gov/teaching-practices/article/framework-effective-practice.

Application Exercise 10.1

Figure 10.2: Framework for Effective Practice

We begin by illustrating the relationship of curriculum to other aspects of the complex role of the teacher. Figure 10.2 is a visual representation of the elements of effective practice that foster children's learning and development, depicted as a house (NCECDTL, 2017b). The foundation is an engaging environment and nurturing, responsive, and effective interactions that create a caring community. The two pillars that support the structure are (1) implementing developmentally appropriate, research-based curriculum and teaching practices and (2) screening and ongoing child assessment. Each of these pillars supports the roof—highly individualized teaching and learning experiences that ensure each child's progress. At the core of the structure is parent/family engagement in a circle indicating the connectedness of all parts of effective practice.

Although in reality these structural components of practice are integrally connected, in this book we address each in a separate chapter. In Chapter 7, we discuss family engagement; in Chapter 8, we describe the foundation of a caring community; Chapter 9 presents evidence-based teaching strategies; Chapter 11 discusses ongoing assessment of child progress; and in this chapter we describe research-based curriculum.

What Is Curriculum?

Curriculum is a written plan that describes the goals for children's learning and development and the learning sequences, experiences, materials, and teaching strategies that are used to help children achieve those goals. The goals include the knowledge, skills, and approaches to learning that we want children to achieve.

Curriculum content—*what* children are learning about—is vitally important. One of the strongest predictors of preschool children's later academic success is their general

curriculum a written plan that describes the goals for children's learning and development and the learning sequences, experiences, materials, and teaching strategies used to help children achieve those goals.

understanding of the world—what's happening in nature and what people do and say (Grissmer, Grimm, Aiyer, Murrah, & Steele, 2010). The achievement gap in our schools is a product of inequitable opportunity to learn. Lack of opportunity leads to inexposure to the background knowledge needed to build on for school success. Moreover, young children *want* to learn. They are curious about their world, and everyone and everything in it. As 4-year-old Ryan said when asked what he likes about preschool, "I learn stuff!"

The word *curriculum* is often used in relation to various models, approaches, or frameworks. Because these general terms are sometimes used interchangeably, we provide definitions and examples of each in the next sections.

Curriculum Models, Approaches, and Frameworks

curriculum model A research-based, idealized version of what and how teaching and learning should occur.

A **curriculum model** is a research-based, idealized version of what and how teaching and learning should occur. Widely used early childhood curriculum models include the HighScope Curriculum, Creative Curriculum, Montessori method, and Bank Street, which are based on theories of child development and learning. To ensure **fidelity**, that is, faithful implementation of the curriculum model, developers typically provide professional development for teachers in how to implement the model.

fidelity Faithful implementation of a curriculum model.

curriculum approach Describes the main elements or direction of a program; is less detailed than a curriculum model.

A **curriculum approach** describes the main elements or direction of a program (Roopnarine & Johnson, 2013) and is less detailed than a model. For example, Reggio Emilia educators purposely call their work the Reggio Emilia *approach* and reject the word *model*. They do not see their work as a model to be imitated or adopted, but rather as a set of principles to be applied in various contexts with diverse children, families, and teachers (Cagliari et al., 2016; Edwards, Gandini, & Forman, 2012). Similarly, the project approach (discussed later in the chapter) is not a curriculum, but a method of engaging children with curriculum content.

curriculum framework A guide for designing or choosing a curriculum.

Curriculum is sometimes defined as a framework; however, a **curriculum framework** is more precisely defined as a guide for designing or choosing a curriculum. For example, most state departments of education write curriculum frameworks that influence or determine which commercial curriculum packages school districts purchase. A state reading framework would include ways of grouping for and differentiating instruction, and how much time should be devoted to language arts. A published curriculum that did not address the standards would not be used in that state.

Written Curriculum Plans

Different types of written plans can be used to guide instruction and meet the needs of specific groups of children. These include research-based curricula, teacher-developed and locally developed plans, and published curriculum resources.

validated curriculum Curriculum that has been evaluated and its effectiveness demonstrated.

Research-Based Curriculum Current trends place increasing emphasis on formal, research-based curriculum in early childhood education. In an effort to increase accountability, public schools as well as Head Start programs are required to use evidence-based curriculum. Such curriculum is based on solid research about child development and learning, what kinds of learning outcomes relate to later achievement, and what types of teaching and learning experiences help children achieve those outcomes (NCECDTL, 2017c). **Validated curriculum** has been evaluated, and has demonstrated its effectiveness in producing desired learning outcomes. A growing number of validated early literacy, mathematics, and social-emotional curricula have been developed for preschool and primary grades (Jenkins & Duncan, 2017; CASEL, 2013). Despite the current emphasis on research-based curriculum, the early childhood field has a long history and comfort with teacher-developed and locally developed plans.

Teacher-Developed Plans Because teachers know individual children best and are most familiar with the context in which children live, teachers often prepare their own curriculum plans. For example, Dominique and Tami teach a group of 2-year-olds. Their child care center has goals for the children such as fostering their language and helping them learn about the physical world. Each week, Dominique and Tami meet to prepare written plans that help them think in advance about their goals and the kinds of experiences and materials they need to prepare. Such advance planning frees them to focus their attention on the children. This week, the group is exploring water by playing in the water table, splashing in a wading pool outside, and blowing bubbles. Tami suggests putting ice cubes in the water table to encourage new words, such as *freezing*, *melting*, and *floating*. Dominique thinks of adding food coloring to create more interest and challenge.

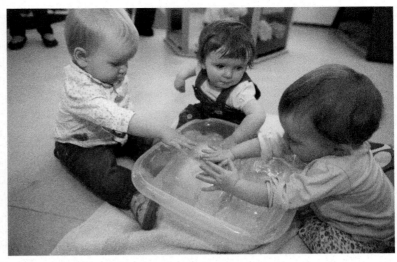

Curriculum for very young children is often developed by teachers. Even for toddlers, having a curriculum plan helps teachers prepare engaging learning opportunities.

Locally Developed Plans In other cases, an agency such as a child care program or a school district develops a written plan. In these situations, a curriculum specialist and team of teachers develop a plan that is designed to achieve the school or program's goals for children. For example, Frankie Sanders's job is education leader for a chain of employer-supported child care centers. To ensure consistency across the 10 centers in the agency and meet the parents' goal that their children will be prepared for kindergarten, she develops, with input from the teachers, the curriculum based on the state early learning standards. The teachers use the plan flexibly, but its existence helps keep them focused on important goals for children and prevents missed opportunities for learning.

Published Curriculum In the primary grades, more than 80% of teachers use some form of published curriculum (Shanahan, 2006). These decisions may be made at the state, district, or school level. In such situations, a committee, which usually includes teachers, reviews the available options and makes a decision about which curriculum resource to adopt. Periodically, state departments of education review new editions of primary-grade curricula in subject areas such as reading, mathematics, and science, and identify a list of approved programs from which schools may choose.

The universal pre-K movement has led to greater involvement of public schools in preschool as well as calls for alignment of pre-K with K–12 curricula. As a result, all major publishers of K–12 curricula now publish curricula for 3- and 4-year-olds. The greater availability of published curricula for preschoolers adds another factor to the curriculum decision-making process at that level (NCECDTL, 2017c).

Written curriculum plans, including those that are commercially published and used in primary grades, are by no means uniform. Some curricula provide an organizing structure and require a lot of initiative on the part of the teacher and children. Others provide goals, suggested activities to help children achieve those goals, and recommended teaching strategies. Usually, curriculum packages include teacher's guides with many options for learning experiences, strategies, and resources, from which teachers choose those that fit their goals for children. In other cases, the curriculum is more prescriptive, and less choice is available or expected.

Advantages of Written Curriculum Plans Whereas critics of written plans believe that they limit teachers' creativity, decision making, and responsiveness to individual children, this is not necessarily true. One advantage of written curriculum plans is that they can be evaluated. Written plans make it possible for administrators, teachers, families, funders (such as taxpayers, parents, or contributors), evaluators, and other interested parties to review, debate, and potentially revise the program's goals, expectations, and learning opportunities for children. Written plans can also be evaluated for their responsiveness to cultural and linguistic diversity, and to community values.

Putting expectations for children in writing also means that teachers can evaluate whether they are developmentally appropriate. For instance, if the kindergarten curriculum calls for all children to learn to read, teachers who know the children can determine that this expectation is too high for most but may be appropriate for some.

The Teacher's Role

Among teachers' most important responsibilities is planning and implementing intentional curriculum. With increasing calls for accountability and rising expectations, providing teachers with thoughtfully planned, research-based curriculum resources can free them to focus on adapting their teaching for individual children's abilities, needs, and interests. Instead of using all of their time preparing lessons and locating related resources, teachers can instead spend their valuable time observing and assessing children's learning and adapting their teaching. In cases such as these, the written plan serves as a scaffold for teachers, providing them with the support they need to go beyond and do more on their own (Kauffman, Johnson, Kardos, Liu, & Peske, 2002).

Curriculum plans do not take the place of teacher creativity or decision making. Early childhood leaders frequently use pejorative terms such as "curriculum in a box" or "canned curriculum" to describe any published curriculum resource (Jones & Nimmo, 1994). These terms imply that such products are by definition less desirable than teacher's "homemade" curriculum. Terms such as "canned," "in-a-box," and "homemade" are analogous to food preparation. There was a time when all food preparation was from scratch, and the only good cooking was completely homemade. Some people still look back on this time with nostalgia. But in an age of microwave and prepared foods, even the best cooks don't make everything from scratch, such as homemade pasta. The analogy is offered not to justify commercial curricula, but to acknowledge that good teachers can produce high-quality educational experiences using either emergent curriculum or published curriculum resources. Similarly, published curriculum does not automatically produce poor teaching.

Research shows that no curriculum is teacher-proof and that teachers' qualifications as well as how they teach content matter (IOM & NRC, 2015). Teacher-proof curriculum is the concept that curriculum can be designed to control for variations in teacher behaviors and professional preparation. The concept is talked about a lot, but it is a myth. There is no such thing as teacher-proof curriculum. Teachers matter, regardless of the type of curriculum they are given.

Rather than dichotomize curriculum as *either* completely teacher-planned and emerging from children's interests *or* commercially published and scripted, consider a more complex range of curriculum options. Table 10.1 describes a continuum of types of curricula available and the impact on the teacher's role. The primary-grade examples illustrate various approaches to teaching reading (Commeyras, 2007).

In Table 10.1, we suggest a way of conceptualizing curriculum plans while at the same time thinking about the teacher's role in relation to those plans. Two basic points should be clear: (1) in some cases, curriculum is developed very close to the classroom and is highly open-ended, flexible, and responsive to individual children. Teachers plan instruction to fit the needs of individual children and the class as a whole, building on and responding to children's interests, motivation, and understanding. (2) In other cases, curriculum is developed at a distance from the classroom and is highly

© Pearson Education

Video Example 10.1:

Teachers' Roles in Curriculum

A second grade teacher describes her role in helping students achieve science standards. How does she adapt for individual student's interests and needs? How does she connect science to learning in other areas of the curriculum?

TABLE 10.1 Continuum of Curriculum Approaches and the Teacher's Role		
Rather than dichotomize curriculum as *either* emergent *or* scripted, this table describes a continuum of types of curriculum and the impact on teachers' roles.		
Type of Preschool Curriculum	**Type of Primary-Grade Curriculum**	**Teacher's Role in Curriculum Implementation (in collaboration with other teachers and families)**
Emergent curriculum, e.g., Reggio Emilia approach, or curriculum based on children's interests	A teacher-developed literacy lesson	Identify developmental and learning goals. Know hierarchy of skills and knowledge in each curriculum area. Observe and assess children's interests and progress. Prepare the environment and obtain resources. Plan interest-based curriculum with children to help achieve goals. Adapt teaching to help individuals make progress.
Curriculum model with linked assessment tools and professional development, e.g., Creative Curriculum, HighScope, Tools of the Mind	A guided reading lesson using leveled readers as defined by Fountas & Pinnell (1996).	Observe and assess children's interests and progress. Prepare the environment and plan learning experiences within the suggested framework. Use intentional teacher-guided and child-guided strategies. Use program's assessment tools and adapt teaching to help children make progress toward identified goals.
Published curriculum with teacher's guide, e.g., Pearson's Opening World of Learning (OWL) or DLM Early Learning Express	A basal reading program from a major publisher, e.g., Pearson Scott Foresman	Observe and assess children's interests and progress. Reference teacher's guide to identify scope and sequence. Make decisions about how to use or adapt suggested learning plans. Adapt teaching, including lessons, scripts, or prompts, to help individuals make progress.
Prescribed/scripted curriculum, e.g., Open Court or Direct Instruction	A scripted lesson from Reading Mastery (formerly DISTAR)	Implement prescribed curriculum closely to ensure fidelity to program. Use program's assessment tools to track children's progress. Maintain children's attention through positive responses. Remain sensitive to children's responses and plan for needs. Adapt teaching as much as possible to engage children and help them make progress.

prescribed. Teachers pace instruction to ensure the curriculum scope and sequence is covered so that children are exposed to and learn concepts that prepare them for formal assessment and learning goals and expectations. In reality, curriculum is usually somewhere in between these two extremes.

The complexity of the roles of teachers is only alluded to in Table 10.1. Nevertheless, even this cursory description reveals the relationship of curriculum and teaching. At one extreme, teachers have huge responsibilities and are expected to create almost everything while at the same time ensuring that children achieve important learning outcomes. At the other extreme, teachers' expertise is underestimated and undervalued, especially if principals or supervisors do not permit them to deviate from a prescribed script, a growing concern of early educators.

Regardless of the type of curriculum used by a program or school, teachers need to apply their professional expertise. For this reason, all along the continuum, we acknowledge that teachers must observe and assess children and adapt their teaching to help individuals make progress. That adaptation may take many forms, such as adjusting student groupings, daily schedules, the nature of teacher–child interactions, or the amount and kind of scaffolding provided.

The feature *Becoming an Intentional Teacher: Adapting Scripted Curriculum* describes one teacher's thinking as she uses the school's prescribed curriculum and adapts for individual children.

Becoming an Intentional Teacher

Adapting Scripted Curriculum

Here's What Happened   I've been teaching first grade for four years now. This year, the district adopted a new, much more scripted K–2 curriculum than the one I've been using. Our principal expects us to stick closely to the published curriculum. In the past, I had more freedom to develop my own lessons, and incorporated projects and more playful activities at times.

My first step was to carefully evaluate the curriculum's strengths. The scope and sequence was helpful, especially in math, which is not my strength. And the goals were within an achievable range for most of the kids. I use the teacher script as a scaffold for me in asking questions and identifying prompts to scaffold the children's learning. My most successful strategy has been to implement the curriculum by using grouping as much as possible. I do less whole group instruction than the curriculum calls for and more work with small groups and individual students. The packaged curriculum includes a lot of worksheets, but I use them only when children need to practice a specific skill to mastery. So far, my principal has agreed to my modifications as long as I make a good case for them and the children are achieving goals.

Here's What I Was Thinking   I agree with the principal's goal to have all the first graders make consistent progress and be ready for second grade. When I use small groups for instruction, there's always a good reason. Similarly, if I change the order of lessons for an individual child, I have to be sure that I assess accurately. I have to consider whether

the change will affect the way the child's learning proceeds and whether there are any related skills where the learning path would be negatively affected. I use the worksheets as little as possible because they are more a test of what children already know than a teaching tool. I evaluate each one to see if it is a worthwhile use of children's time.

I sometimes adjust the pace of the curriculum plan. I may see that we need a detour or to slow down to work on a skill the children must master before going on. In other cases, some children may be ready for more challenge, and I want to keep them engaged. Sometimes it's just a few children who need these kinds of adaptations; sometimes it's the class as a whole.

The most important thing I've done is to continue to focus on positive relationships in the classroom. I always encourage children's efforts and recognize their progress. I also help them connect whatever we are studying to their own interests and experiences out of school so it is more meaningful. Every day, I think of a new surprise, song, or story to make school "serious fun." Most of all—I work to keep joy in my classroom for the children and also for myself.

Reflection   In what other ways might this teacher adapt the scripted curriculum plan for the group as a whole? What could the teacher do if a few children showed no interest in the lesson? What problems might arise when a teacher changes the order or pace of a schoolwide curriculum?

✔ Check Your Understanding 10.1

Video Example 10.2:

Adapting Curriculum for Dual Language Learners

A kindergarten teacher describes how she adapts her curriculum and teaching for the dual language learners in her English-immersion classroom. What strategies does she use? How would these strategies help the children understand complex scientific concepts?

🔼 Components of Effective Curriculum

Now that we have established a common vocabulary with which to discuss curriculum, we turn to a discussion of indicators of effective curriculum. Such a curriculum should engage, interest, and challenge children to think deeply about rich content, lead to positive learning and developmental outcomes, and be developmentally appropriate as well as culturally and linguistically responsive (NCECDTL, 2017c).

With the proliferation of options available today, making decisions about which curriculum to choose can be daunting. To assist with this task and to help professionals evaluate whether a specific curriculum is effective, the Office of Head Start (NCQTL, 2015) developed consumers' guides. Listed in Table 10.2, the criteria apply to planning, developing, and implementing effective curriculum.

TABLE 10.2   Components of Effective Curriculum

Curriculum Component	Key Considerations
Based on current knowledge of child development	Are essential principles of how children develop and learn reflected in the curriculum philosophy and planned experiences?
Is research-based	Has the curriculum been rigorously evaluated? Is there evidence of its effectiveness with diverse groups of children—in terms of ethnicity/race, language, and socioeconomic background?
Shows positive effects on child outcomes	Do children who experience the curriculum demonstrate positive learning and developmental outcomes?
Is comprehensive across learning domains or incorporates aligned domain-specific curriculum	Does the curriculum address "the whole child"—all domains of development (cognitive, social, emotional, and physical)—and all content areas such as literacy, mathematics, science, social studies, health and physical education, and the arts? Do domain-specific curricula such as focused literacy or mathematics programs align coherently?
Covers content and learning domains in depth	Is there an organized scope and sequence in each of the learning domains that describes progressive steps and individual learning experiences? Does the curriculum build on prior learning and experiences?
Clearly defines specific developmentally appropriate learning goals	Does the written plan address important goals such as the standards of the disciplines (mathematics or literacy)? Are the goals reasonable expectations for most children within the age range for which the curriculum is designed?
Includes well-designed learning experiences	Does the curriculum provide opportunities for children to be active and engaged both mentally and physically?
Emphasizes responsive teaching	Do learning experiences include both child-focused exploration and investigation and teacher-guided instruction? Is the curriculum responsive to children's interests? Does it promote positive interactions among teachers and children?
Supports individualized instruction	Is the curriculum flexible enough for teachers to adapt to individual variation in children? Can the curriculum be adapted for children with special needs?
Is culturally and linguistically responsive	Does the curriculum promote children's cultural identities and home languages and also recognize and build on their competence?
Includes ongoing assessment tools and strategies aligned with goals and experiences	Is there support for teachers to collect, analyze, and use assessment results to adapt and individualize instruction, and to help children make continued progress?
Provides professional development	Are there initial and ongoing professional learning opportunities to ensure that teachers implement the curriculum with fidelity?
Supports family involvement	Are materials and strategies provided for families to extend children's learning at home?

Source: Based on Guidance on comprehensive and domain-specific preschool curriculum consumer reports by National Center on Quality Teaching and Learning (NCQTL), 2015. Retrieved February 10, 2018, from https://eclkc.ohs.acf.hhs.gov/sites/default/files/pdf/curriculum-report-guidance.pdf.

In evaluating effective curriculum, it is important to consider the challenge of providing culturally and linguistically responsive curriculum. Several different curriculum approaches are used to accommodate dual language learners (National Academy of Science, Engineering, & Medicine, 2017). Read the *Language Lens: Curriculum Approaches for Dual Language Learners* feature and consider the potential strengths and weaknesses of each approach.

This brief examination of indicators of effective curriculum demonstrates the role of standards on current thinking about curriculum. The connections between learning standards and curriculum are becoming increasingly important and powerful in education, as we discuss in the next section.

Language Lens
Curriculum Approaches for Dual Language Learners

Schools serve increasing numbers of dual and multi-language learners, with most speaking Spanish as a home language. Many of these children are growing up in homes below the poverty level and need excellent educational experiences to ensure they have equitable opportunities to learn. The following are brief descriptions of commonly used approaches for educating dual language learners:

- *English immersion.* All the instruction is in English throughout the child's school career. Students may receive assistance from specialists in English as a second language, but the classroom teacher uses English only.
- *English-Plus-Spanish.* Programs use English and Spanish in a wide range of formal and informal teaching and learning experiences. For example, instruction might be in English, but teachers or teacher assistants use Spanish to explain, clarify, or ask questions to assess children's understanding. Teacher–child conversations occur in both English and Spanish. Sometimes children are taught academic subjects in Spanish until their English is sufficiently developed.
- *Two-way dual immersion approach.* In these programs, half of the instruction takes place in English and the other half occurs in the second language—usually Spanish, but perhaps a Native American language or other language such as Mandarin. The goal is for *all* the children to become bilingual and biliterate and achieve academic standards.

Consider each of these approaches and how they might affect Antonia Zapeda, who is starting kindergarten:

Antonia's family came to the United States from Mexico two years ago and want very much for their children to succeed in school, but they are struggling to learn English themselves. Antonia's language development in Spanish is advanced; however, she tends to be shy in new situations, relying on her brothers to pave the way for her.

Put yourself in Antonia's shoes as she encounters school for the first time. What would her experience be like? How would she feel about her home language and family?

What will she be learning? How successful will she be in mastering curriculum content? The school district's curriculum approach for dual language learners like Antonia is likely to have a significant impact on her later success in school and life, depending on the type of approach used. For example, in an English immersion situation, she is likely to struggle both emotionally and academically despite her competence and knowledge in her home language. In fact, research finds that English immersion is not an effective approach. An English-Plus-Spanish program would be much more likely to build her confidence, competence, and English proficiency.

By contrast, consider what Antonia's experience might be like in a *two-way dual language* program:

In the morning, Ms. Cafritz does all of the teaching in English, and in the afternoon, Mr. Jimenez teaches in Spanish, or vice versa. All of Antonia's friends at school are learning both English and Spanish. Her new best friend, Joy, speaks English at home and has trouble with some of the sounds in Spanish, so Antonia helps her when they are on the playground. They laugh together about how funny each other sounds. During Spanish instruction time, Antonia knows most of the answers to the teacher's questions and often speaks up, while Joy listens more. After several months, Antonia becomes more confident in English, mixing languages on the playground with her friends but trying to answer the teacher's questions in English. Her parents are proud when she begins to read in English as well as Spanish. They are impressed that she is learning so many new Spanish words while also learning English.

In your career as a teacher, you are likely to work in situations with different policies regarding dual language learners. As you do, remember Antonia. Be intentional in your approach, considering children's best interests and respecting the languages and cultures of the families.

Source: L. Espinosa, 2015. *Getting it right for children from diverse backgrounds: Applying research to improve practice with an emphasis on dual language learner*s. Upper Saddle River, NJ: Pearson.

✓ Check Your Understanding 10.2

The Role of Standards in Curriculum Planning

One of the most influential trends in education today is the standards movement. By the beginning of the 21st century, each of the discipline-based content organizations had developed standards for what students should know and be able to do at various grade levels, which in turn influenced the content of state standards. Also highly significant was the development of K–12 Common Core standards for Englisg language arts (reading, writing, speaking, and listening) and mathematics (Common Core State Standards Initiative, 2011a, 2011b). This initiative is designed to prepare all students for college and careers by bringing greater consistency and higher expectations to school curriculum across the country. By 2018, 42 states and the District of Columbia adopted the Common Core as the framework for their school standards.

Similarly, Next Generation Science Standards (NGSS Lead States, 2013) were developed by a consortium of 26 states, the National Science Teachers Association, the American Association for the Advancement of Science, and other organizations to elevate science teaching, ensure that students deeply understand concepts and processes, and add coherence to the science curriculum. As of 2017, the NGSS were adopted by almost half the states.

An exciting development in "standard-setting" is the P21Partnership for 21st Century Learning (2011), a collaborative group of education, business, community, and government leaders whose goal is to ensure that all learners acquire the knowledge and skills needed to thrive in an ever-changing world. Their *P21 Framework of 21st Learning* goes beyond the traditional subject matter content to include interdisciplinary themes such as global literacy and 4Cs— communication, collaboration, critical thinking, and creativity— essential for lifelong learning and adaptation in our rapidly changing world.

learning standards
Expectations for student learning.

content standards Describe what students should know and/or be able to do within a particular discipline such as math or science.

performance standards Describe the knowledge or skill that students should acquire by a particular point in their schooling, usually tied to grade or age level; also known as *benchmarks*.

What Are Standards?

Every state has standards for K–12 schools, 49 states have developed early learning standards for preschool, and many have infant/toddler standards (Scott-Little et al., 2015). To understand the relevance and impact of the standards movement, it is important to understand the language of standards.

- **Learning standards** are expectations for student learning.
- **Content standards** describe what students should know and/or be able to do within a particular discipline such as math or science.
- **Performance standards**, or *benchmarks*, describe the knowledge or skill that students should acquire by a particular point in their schooling, usually tied to grade or age level.

How Do Standards Affect Curriculum?

Standards are not curriculum; nevertheless, they have a powerful influence over curriculum development. Today, curriculum is often designed for the express purpose of helping children achieve standards (Jacobs & Crowley, 2014; Kagan, Castillo, Gomez, & Gowani, 2013). Similarly,

A major portion of the day in primary grades is devoted to reading and writing instruction using published curriculum. Intentional teachers know that regardless of the source of the curriculum, their role is to be responsive to individual children.

© Jules Selmes/Pearson Education

assessment of learning is linked to achieving standards. Ideally, the goals of a curriculum include, but are not necessarily limited to, the relevant early learning standards. As teachers implement curriculum, they should regularly assess children's learning and adapt the curriculum and their teaching to ensure that children make progress toward the standards. In such a scenario, standards *guide* but do not determine or standardize the curriculum (Bredekamp, 2009).

Because curriculum is influenced by standards, it is essential that standards be comprehensive as well as developmentally and culturally appropriate. Yet, this is often not the case. Evaluations of state early learning standards find uneven attention to all areas of child development and learning, especially for dual language learners (Espinosa & Calderon, 2015; Scott-Little et al., 2015). For example, although every state addresses the areas of language and cognition, less consistent attention is paid to social–emotional development, physical health and development, and approaches toward learning, such as curiosity and persistence. In some cases, standards may underestimate children's competence, such as the standard of counting only to 10 in kindergarten (National Research Council [NRC], 2009). In others, they overestimate it, such as expecting kindergartners to read (Carlson-Paige, McLaughlin, & Almon, 2015).

Alignment of Standards and Curriculum Across Age Groups

A major trend in education is the move to align standards and curriculum from birth through age 8 and beyond. Alignment means that standards and curriculum are designed to progress as children get older so that they acquire the foundations of skills and knowledge to continue to achieve (IOM & NRC, 2015). Alignment also reflects the fact that many curriculum areas such as mathematics are sequential, with later understandings built on earlier ones. Further, if done well, alignment should support developmentally appropriate practice, because the expectations for an older age group may not be appropriate for younger children.

Even with alignment, in each of the broad age periods of early childhood—infants/toddlers, 3- through 5-year-olds, and primary grades—standards and the curriculum take a different form with different emphases. The *focus* of curriculum changes at each period of the early childhood age continuum, as described next.

Curriculum for Infants and Toddlers

A thoughtfully planned, challenging, and engaging curriculum for infants and toddlers focuses on (Head Start, 2017; Wittmer & Petersen, 2017):

- Relationships that promote a sense of identity, security, and social interaction
- Language development
- Exploration of the physical world and play

Most states now have early learning guidelines for infants and toddlers. These standards are usually organized around developmental domains and by age spans such as young infants (0 to 8 months), mobile infants (about 6 to 18 months), and toddlers (16 to 36 months). In addition to developmental domains such as physical and social, the guidelines may include precursors of learning in subject areas such as early literacy, science, and mathematics. An added feature of guidelines for very young children is that they usually include suggestions for what adults can do to promote children's ongoing progress. As illustrated in Figure 10.3 from the Head Start ELOF for infants and toddlers which, as you can see, includes approaches to learning and executive function.

Effective curriculum for babies and toddlers is highly individualized and responsive to children's needs and interests, while also extending their language and learning (Wittmer & Petersen, 2017). High-quality programs for babies and toddlers usually use an **emergent curriculum** process, in which learning experiences are responsive to children's interests. Teachers observe children, assess their capacities, and respond by enriching and extending the play or by adding novelty and complexity.

emergent curriculum
Curriculum that develops in an educational environment in response to children's interests and needs rather than according to predeveloped plans.

Cognitive Self-Regulation/Executive Function

- *Maintain focus and attention*: Child maintains focus and attention with support. Shows increasing ability to attend to people, objects, and activities in order to extend or complete an activity, or to join others in common focus.
- *Shows persistence*: Child develops the ability to show persistence in actions and behavior. Shows willingness to repeat attempts to communicate or to repeat actions to solve a problem even when encountering difficulties.
- *Demonstrates flexibility*: Child demonstrates the ability to be flexible in actions and behavior. Shows ability to shift focus in order to attend to something else, participate in a new activity, or try a new approach to solving a problem.

FIGURE 10.3 Example of Head Start Early Learning Outcomes for Child 8 to 18 Months—Approaches to Learning

Source: From *Head Start Early Learning Outcomes Framework*, 2017. Washington, DC: U.S. Department of Health and Human Services.

Curriculum for Preschoolers Thoughtfully planned curriculum for 3- through 5-year-olds addresses the development of the whole child, including physical well-being and motor development, social and emotional development, approaches to learning such as curiosity and persistence, language development, and cognition and general knowledge. At the same time, the curriculum builds knowledge and skill in literacy, mathematics, science, social studies, and the visual and performing arts.

In preschool, integration across subject matter areas is the primary planning strategy, although at times the curriculum will focus on one area such as math or early literacy (Jenkins & Duncan, 2017). Play and projects are valuable ways of bringing curriculum content to this age group. In fact, research shows that in content-rich classrooms with engaging social studies and science, children play in more complex and high-level ways (Nayfeld, Brenneman, & Gelman, 2009).

Forty-nine states have early learning standards for preschoolers. The Head Start Early Learning Outcomes Framework (ELOF) (Head Start, 2017) has had a major impact on the field. The ELOF addresses all areas of development and learning, including English language development for dual language learners, and includes examples of effective teaching practices. Figure 10.4 is an example from the preschool ELOF of Approaches to Learning standards.

Cognitive Self-Regulation/Executive Function

- *Demonstrates an increasing ability to control impulses*: Frequently engages in impulsive behaviors but inhibits them when directly supported by an adult.
- *Maintains focus and sustains attention with minimal adult support*: With adult support, focuses attention on tasks and experiences for short periods of time, despite interruptions or distractions.
- *Persists on preferred tasks when presented with small challenges with or without adult support* (e.g., continuing to try to build a tall tower with blocks even when some pieces fall).
- *Holds information in mind and manipulates it to perform tasks*: Holds small amounts of information in mind (e.g., two-step directions to successfully complete tasks).
- *Demonstrates flexibility in thinking and behavior*: Demonstrates flexibility, or the ability to switch gears, in thinking and behavior when prompted by an adult (e.g., trying a new way to climb a structure when the first attempt does not work).

FIGURE 10.4 Example of Head Start Early Learning Outcomes for Children Ages 36 to 48 months—Approaches to Learning

Source: From *Head Start Early Learning Outcomes Framework*, 2017. Washington, DC: U.S. Department of Health and Human Services.

Each of the broad goals in the Head Start framework include a continuum of benchmarks that describes widely held expectations across the age range. A curriculum designed to help children achieve early literacy goals would provide materials, time, and opportunities to engage in writing. A science curriculum about eggs hatching provides ample opportunities for children to draw and write about their observations of an incubator and chicks. Such a project addresses one of the science reasoning outcomes: "Uses the five senses to observe objects, materials, organisms, and events. Provides simple verbal or signed descriptions. With adult support, represents observable phenomena, such as draws a picture." These are a few examples of how curriculum is designed to help children meet learning standards, and how standards guide curriculum development.

Curriculum in Kindergarten and the Primary Grades

In primary school, the curriculum focus shifts to knowledge and skills in the subject matter areas. These include language, literacy, mathematics, science, social studies, health, physical education, and the visual and performing arts. Goals should continue to address the importance of social–emotional development and approaches to learning, including motivation, curiosity, creativity, and initiative, although these areas are rarely included in state standards. And as we have discussed, essential goals include self-regulation and executive function abilities, such as problem solving, planning, focused attention, and persistence.

Challenging and engaging curriculum for this age group helps children develop and use oral and written language, mathematical and scientific thinking, and investigation skills across the disciplines. Curriculum in the primary grades should help children develop a sense of their own competence and confidence—Erikson's notion of mastery. The overarching goal of the primary grades, however, is learning to read. As described previously, many states now use the Common Core standards. Figure 10.5 is a Common Core writing standard for kindergarten through second grade. Consider how this standard is designed to promote alignment of curriculum across grade levels.

During your career as a teacher, you will confront many decisions about curriculum that will be related to standards. Having discussed indicators of effective curriculum and the role of standards, we now turn to a discussion of general approaches to planning curriculum. These approaches share the goal of making curriculum meaningful and interesting to children, and therefore more effective.

Kindergartners	Grade 1 Students	Grade 2 Students
Use a combination of drawing, dictating, and writing to compose opinion pieces in which they tell a reader the topic or the name of the book they are writing about and state an opinion or preference about the topic or book (e.g., *My favorite book is . . .*).	Write opinion pieces in which they introduce the topic or name the book they are writing about, state an opinion, supply a reason for the opinion, and provide some sense of closure.	Write opinion pieces in which they introduce the topic or book they are writing about, state an opinion, supply reasons that support the opinion, use linking words (e.g., *because, and, also*) to connect opinion and reasons, and provide a concluding statement or section.

FIGURE 10.5 Example of Common Core English Language Arts Standard Common Core State Standards are not a curriculum. They are designed to promote consistent high learning standards across states and alignment across grade levels.

Source: Common Core State Standards Initiative, 2011. *Common Core standards for English Language Arts.* Washington, DC: Council for Chief State School Officers and National Governors Association. Retrieved February 2018 from www.corestandards.org/ELA-Literacy/ All rights reserved.

 Check Your Understanding 10.3

Approaches to Planning Curriculum

A plan helps guide teachers in making decisions about what, when, and how to teach. In other words, curriculum is not a set of random activities that children might find enjoyable; instead, the experiences must be connected in a coherent way to content goals and teaching strategies. There are several ways of planning a coherent curriculum. These include emergent curriculum, integrated curriculum, thematic curriculum, webbing, the project approach, and scope and sequence.

Emergent Curriculum

Early childhood education has a strong tradition of emergent curriculum. According to this perspective, the focus should be on children, not on curriculum. Emergent curriculum is "what happens in an educational environment, not what is rationally planned to happen but what actually takes place" (Jones & Nimmo, 1994, p. 12). Advocates of emergent curriculum believe that children's interests and needs, rather than a predetermined plan, should determine what goes on in a classroom. They assume that a written curriculum plan may be too rigid to be responsive to children's individual and cultural variation.

Although emergent curriculum places considerable emphasis on following children's interests, it does not mean that nothing is planned and that everything emerges solely from the children. Elizabeth Jones, one of the foremost proponents of emergent curriculum, describes it as a *planning process* in which teachers work from children's interests, creating webs of possibilities that become tentative plans for experiences (Jones & Nimmo, 1994). What follows depends on children's responses, with the teacher observing what happens and evaluating and adjusting the plans as needed:

Monday morning in John and Bettina's preschool class begins with a class meeting in which children talk about their weekend experiences.

Courtney: "My dad took me and my cousins to a museum, and we saw dinosaur bones. They were humongous."

Shauntae: "I went there. My mom only came up to the dinosaur's knee."

The discussion continues, with children becoming more animated by the minute. John and Bettina look at each other and smile. Their plan was to introduce a discussion about families. They don't think that dinosaurs are the best topic of study because young children can't grasp concepts of historical time and extinction. At the same time, the teachers recognize that young children are drawn to dinosaurs because they are "manageable monsters." They decide that with this much enthusiasm generated, following the children's interest could open up new possibilities.

Bettina: "It looks like you want to learn more about dinosaurs. Let's start by thinking about everything we already know and writing down what we want to find out."

Later, Bettina and John meet to map out how a study of dinosaurs can help them meet the goals of their original plan. They decide that it will be a novel way to help children learn math concepts, including classification and measurement, and some of the "big ideas" in science, such as change and living/nonliving things.

Video Example 10.3:

Impact of Standards on Curriculum

In this video, first-graders are engaged in an integrated English Language Arts lesson. How did standards impact the curriculum and other aspects of teaching and the children's learning? What do you think the teacher did during the planning phase to present a coherent and organized curriculum?

Within a broad topic of study such as transportation, teachers build children's language and other skills. This child learns accurate terms for vehicles and motions in the context of an exciting real-life experience.

© Pearson Education

Video Example 10.4:

Emergent Curriculum

This video summarizes an in-depth curriculum study on the hospital that emerges from a preschool teacher's personal experience. What do you notice about the teacher's planning and role in the study? How do children's interests and curiosity influence the decisions, and what learning goals are being addressed?

thematic curriculum Way of integrating curriculum in which a broad topic of interest or a "big idea" provides the basis for making connections across learning goals.

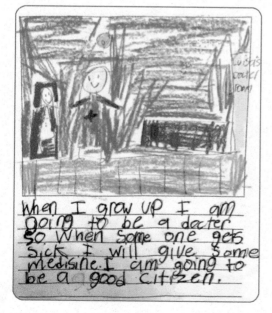

When I grow up I am going to be a dacter so when some one gets sick I will give some medisine. I am going to be a good citizen.

FIGURE 10.6 First-grader's Career Awareness Poster This first-grader's career awareness poster illustrates how the project addressed several learning standards at the same time, including social studies, literacy, and art.

One of the goals of this chapter is to address the tendency in the field to view emergent curriculum and written curriculum as complete opposites. To be effective, curriculum planning needs to be intentional while at the same time responsive to children's interests and needs. In other words, goal-directed written curriculum must be flexible and adapt to children's interests and needs, and emergent curriculum must use children's interests to help them achieve important learning goals. Whichever approach a program chooses, to be effective, children must benefit. One way to help children achieve important goals while also responding to their interests is to use an integrated curriculum, defined next.

Integrated Curriculum

A curriculum can be focused on one subject area, such as mathematics or science, or it can be comprehensive, addressing all learning goals for a specified age or grade level. It may also focus on various developmental domains, such as cognitive, physical, language, and social–emotional. Integrated curriculum addresses learning goals across multiple areas of curriculum at the same time. For example, it might address literacy and social–emotional goals within a single experience or lesson, such as when a preschool teacher reads books about feelings or making friends. A third-grade reading curriculum may include biographies of historical figures such as Harriet Tubman or Abraham Lincoln. In this way, children acquire knowledge of both history and literacy in the same experience.

Integrated curriculum is useful for several reasons. First, it helps address the challenge of covering many learning goals in a limited period of instructional time. Recall our visit to Ross Elementary School in the opening vignette of this chapter. The schoolwide project integrated various subject areas, such as social studies and literacy. The children engaged in reading and writing about a topic of interest—what they want to be when they grow up. At the same time, the children learned concepts about the world of work and the relevance of education, symbolic representation, and technological skills. Figure 10.6 shows how a first-grader's career awareness poster demonstrates her achievement of these goals.

Integrated curriculum helps children make connections between skills and knowledge in various domains and decreases wasted time when no learning occurs. Integrated curriculum is usually organized around a topic of study or theme, which we discuss next.

Thematic/Conceptual Curriculum

Another advantage of integrated curriculum is that curriculum can be organized around topics (sometimes called *units*) that children find interesting or engaging. This type of integrated curriculum is called a thematic curriculum, in which a broad topic of interest, or a "*big idea*" or concept, provides the basis for making connections across learning goals. For example, the life cycle of birds or the concept of categorizing can be the organizing structure for several weeks or longer.

Thematic curriculum not only motivates children but also builds deeper conceptual understanding (National Research Council, 2018). For example, a predictable interest of preschool children—building with blocks—provides a basis for curriculum around the concept of construction. Children's interest in building structures becomes a vehicle for teaching physical science and engineering, such as how buildings stand up or how roofs are constructed to make enclosed spaces. A construction study helps children understand math concepts such as counting, measuring, and classification, which they will need when they decide how to balance a skyscraper. Children also learn vocabulary words related to building. Books, such as *Alphabet under Construction* by D. Fleming (2006), can bring in literacy skills. A neighborhood walk to see architecture, historical structures, or civic buildings addresses social studies standards.

For thematic curriculum to be effective, however, it is important that teachers select truly "big" ideas—concepts that are rich enough to be studied in depth and lead to new learning. Consider the difference between a unit on teddy bears and a study of living bears—there is no comparison in terms of the concepts that can be explored. Yet children love teddy bears, so a teacher might be tempted to pursue that interest despite its shallow nature. How then do teachers decide whether a topic is sufficiently rich to pursue? One strategy is to use webbing, discussed next.

Webbing

In Chapter 9, we discussed teaching strategies that build children's understanding. These included using advance organizers and graphic representations, such as K-W-L and *I notice, I wonder,* which are effective ways of engaging children in curriculum studies.

✓ **Application Exercise 10.2**

I Notice, I Wonder

Idea webbing, or *concept* webbing, is another example of an advance organizer, and is also an effective planning tool to organize curriculum content around topics and concepts. Webbing serves many valuable functions in early childhood curriculum. It helps teachers plan in advance and acts as a conceptual organizer for children's thinking and learning. Webbing graphically represents the connections children make among facts and larger concepts, as depicted in the photo on page 362 of a web created for a project about Hands. Figure 10.7 is an example of a web of ideas, which children generated at the beginning of a project on drawing.

Idea webbing (also called webbing or concept webbing) a planning tool that teachers and children create together to organize curriculum content.

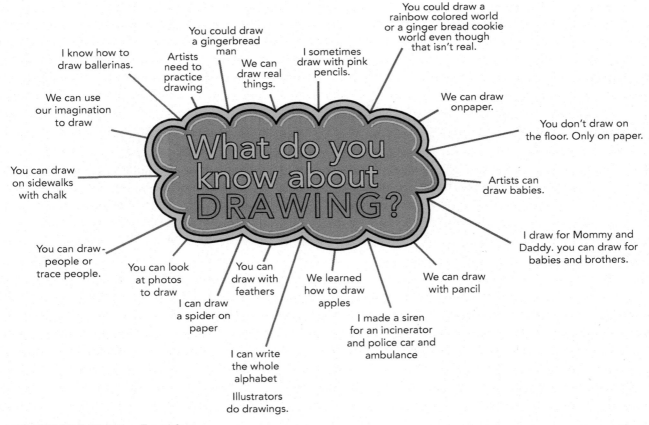

FIGURE 10.7 Webbing Example

Webbing is a useful tool for all the ways of organizing curriculum discussed thus far: emergent, integrated, and thematic/conceptual. But it is particularly valuable as a core component of the project approach, a topic to which we turn next.

The Project Approach

project An in-depth investigation of a topic worth learning more about, usually involving a small group but occasionally the whole class.

Engaging children in projects or investigations, a concept going as far back as John Dewey and an integral part of the Bank Street approach, continues to be one of the most popular activities among early childhood teachers and children (Helm & Katz, 2016). A **project** is an in-depth investigation of a topic worth learning more about, usually involving a small group but occasionally the whole class. The key feature of a project is that it is a research effort focused on finding answers to questions posed by the children, the teacher, or the teacher working with the children (Helm & Katz, 2016).

project approach Strategy for conceptually organizing curriculum by engaging children in in-depth investigation of a topic, focused on finding answers to questions posed by the children, the teacher, or the teacher working with children.

Benefits of Projects   The **project approach** is not a curriculum; rather, it is a way of *engaging children's minds* with curriculum content and processes (Katz & Chard, 2000). In the project approach, teachers guide children through in-depth studies of real-world topics of interest to children. When teachers implement the project approach well, children can be highly motivated, feel actively involved in their own learning, and produce high-quality work.

Well-planned and implemented projects engage children's interests and eagerness to learn, focus their attention, and are lots of fun. More important than simple enjoyment is the fact that projects or investigations are effective ways of integrating curriculum content and promoting children's understanding and thinking. Consider the following example of a project that integrates social studies and other areas of the curriculum, shared by Gail Joseph:

One morning at the Active Learning Center, the organic milk delivery service mistakenly left chocolate milk. Before she notices, the teacher, Diane, asks Lamont and Sara to bring it to the kitchen because they have the "milk deliverer" job today. Lamont and Sara shriek as they carefully lift a glass bottle filled with chocolate milk out of the box. They head for the classroom to find Diane, but along the way they tell each child in the class about the yummy mistake: "We got chocolate. It's brown!"

By the time they reach Diane, there is a line of children asking if they can have the chocolate milk with their snack. After Diane agrees, a more dedicated line of inquiry ensues. "Who left this for us?" "How do they make it brown?" "Does it cost more money?" "Can we have it again?" Diane sees that the milk mistake has the potential for an interesting project.

At group time, Diane asks the children to list what they know about chocolate milk and what else they want to find out. She records their ideas on chart paper. During the next two weeks, the children learn a lot about chocolate milk. They write stories about the "chocolate mistake" in the writing center. They write letters to the milkman thanking him for the mistake. They examine the price list to compare the cost of chocolate and plain milk. They make chocolate milk and graph how many children like chocolate versus plain milk (a skewed distribution for sure!).

The milk investigation goes into greater depth when the children take a field trip to the dairy and learn about "organic" milk, and why people might prefer it to nonorganic. They observe dairy cows and see milking machines. The children also learn how the milk is transported to the customers and why they use glass bottles. On the trip, they discover that the empty bottles are recycled, which prompts one of the children to propose a "recycler" job in the classroom. The children learn that not all people drink milk, and the reasons why. They learn why regular milk is healthier than chocolate.

During the last week, the children decide to have a "chocolate milk celebration" with their families. They make invitations, propose and vote on the menu, and help develop displays documenting their field trip and what they've learned. They also offer a book signing for the class book, which they title *The Chocolate Mistake*.

At the end of the project, Diane revisits the chart created a few weeks ago and asks the children what they have learned. It is clear that they thoroughly enjoyed the project and learned a lot about chocolate milk. But they learned much more about social studies, including concepts about culture, health, community, the environment, diverse beliefs, production of goods and services, and economics, and they also engaged in reading, writing, mathematics, and science.

Video Example 10.5:

The Project Approach

In this video, two preschool teachers discuss how they use the project approach to teach concepts in-depth, integrate curriculum, and meet standards. How do they use an idea web? Why do you think this is an effective curriculum approach for young children? And what do teachers need to know and do to implement the project approach well?

Phases of a Project The previous example illustrates the phases of a project:

- *Phase 1: Beginning a project.* The beginning phase occurs when a possible topic emerges either from the children's interest or from an idea initiated by the teacher. During this phase, the class might create a K-W-L list or web of what they know and what they want to find out. At this stage in a project, the teacher needs to decide whether the topic is appropriate, practical, and consistent with the goals of the curriculum (Helm & Katz, 2016). In the scenario above, Diane recognizes that the children are very interested in the chocolate milk, although the interest was a fortuitous mistake. Other ways to discover or cultivate children's interest could be through bringing something into the classroom, such as a musical instrument, or through a story. The key is to notice what children are interested in and to follow it. The next step is to develop a web of children's thoughts and questions about the topic.
- *Phase 2: Developing a project.* In this phase, children begin to think about and engage in an investigation of the topic. The questions children want answered should be broad enough to allow for substantive research. They might take a field trip as Diane's class did when they went to the dairy, hear from visiting experts to learn more about the topic, or conduct experiments.
- *Phase 3: A culminating event.* An event can be arranged that involves communicating, sharing, and presenting the work of the project to others. Diane's class held a chocolate milk celebration to share with their families all they had learned.

The project approach draws on and cultivates children's interests as it builds their motivation to learn. But more important, it engages children in thinking and problem solving, finding answers to their questions, and building content knowledge and skills. Research on the project approach finds that although it is challenging to implement, it is most effective when teachers have content knowledge themselves (David, 2008).

In previous sections, we described several well-known approaches to organizing curriculum content in early childhood settings. Next, we turn to a different approach, organizing curriculum sequentially.

Scope and Sequence

In recent years, research on early learning has provided greater insight about which skills are foundational in content areas such as reading and mathematics (IOM & NRC, 2015; National Early Literacy Panel, 2008; NRC, 2009). This knowledge is useful in developing the *scope* and *sequence* of a curriculum, especially in areas where sequential learning is particularly important. In mathematics, for example, children need to have a basic understanding about numbers before they can tackle number operations such as adding and subtracting. Scope refers to the focus of the curriculum—breadth and depth—at a given point in time; that is, how much of a larger content area will be addressed (NCECDTL, 2017a). Sequence, as the word implies, is the order in which knowledge and skills will be taught.

Scope and sequence are familiar terms in elementary education, where the curriculum is more closely linked to teachers' guides and textbook series for children, but is relatively

scope The particular focus of the curriculum at a given point in time; that is, how much of a larger content area will be taught.

sequence The order in which knowledge and skills will be taught.

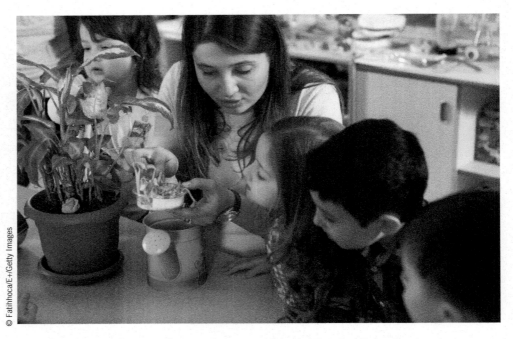

© Fatihhoca/E+/Getty Images

The project approach is an excellent way to engage children's interest while meeting learning goals. Projects have three phases: cultivating children's interest, preparing for and conducting the investigation, and a culminating event.

new in the preschool world (NCECDTL, 2017a). Scope and sequence curriculum provides teachers with guidance about what to teach and when. For example, learning to read involves many different abilities that children acquire over time. A primary-grade reading curriculum identifies the expectations for children's reading achievement at each age level (the scope of what is to be learned) and suggests an order in which reading skills should be taught as well. However, because children's acquisition of skills and knowledge does not occur in a predetermined order and because many skills are acquired simultaneously, curriculum sequences should not be applied rigidly.

In the previous sections, we described several ways of planning curriculum: emergent, thematic, integrated, webbing, the project approach, and scope and sequence. Earlier, we described types of plans, from teacher developed to commercially published. All of these curriculum approaches can be used from preschool through primary grades. For example, although a second-grade teacher is highly likely to use a published reading program with a predetermined scope and sequence, she may also use an integrated science curriculum and the project approach to teaching social studies.

Having defined curriculum and explored indicators of effective curriculum, next we go deeper into the concept of curriculum models. In the following section, we describe well-known, though somewhat different, models of early childhood curriculum.

✔ Check Your Understanding 10.4

🏠 Research-Based Early Childhood Curricula

Effective early childhood curriculum focuses on both the process of teaching and the content of what children are learning. Two types of early childhood curricula exist: (1) comprehensive models that address the whole child, and (2) focused curricula that target one or more content areas such as science and mathematics or a developmental domain such as social–emotional.

Comprehensive Curriculum

Several research-based comprehensive curriculum models are widely used—HighScope, Creative Curriculum, Core Knowledge, and Tools of the Mind. In this section, we discuss the key components of each of these models.

HighScope Curriculum The HighScope curriculum was first developed by David Weikart and his colleagues, who launched the Perry Preschool Project in the early 1960s. HighScope is a *validated curriculum* because research has demonstrated that using it has lasting positive effects on children's long-term success in school and in life (Garcia et al., 2016; Garcia, Heckman, & Ziff, 2017; Schweinhart et al., 2005).

HighScope emphasizes that children need to be engaged in active learning—direct, hands-on experience with people, objects, events, and ideas. Both teachers and children play an active role, functioning as partners in learning. A key element is the *plan-do-review process* that begins with a small group time, during which children plan what they want to do during work time—that is, the area they plan to visit, the materials they will use, and the peers they will play with. The children then have a work time of about an hour for carrying out their plans. Following this period is another small group time for children to review and recall with the teacher and the other children what they have done and learned. The HighScope curriculum intentionally promotes use of higher-order thinking skills and executive function (Heckman, Pinto, & Savelyev, 2013). Many early childhood programs offer children choices during play time, but planning is more than making choices.

The content of the HighScope preschool curriculum consists of a set of 58 key developmental indicators that describe goals across 10 child-development areas. For example, there are two key indicators for the goal area "Approaches to Learning": (1) making and expressing choices, plans, and decisions, and (2) solving problems encountered in play. An online assessment system, the COR Advantage is an 8-point rating scale that can be used by any program serving infants through kindergarten. HighScope also provides professional development to implement the curriculum at a high level.

Creative Curriculum Creative Curriculum® Solutions is a comprehensive set of curriculum and assessment tools originally developed by Diane Trister Dodge and her colleagues at Teaching Strategies. The program addresses all areas of child development, early literacy, and mathematics for infants through kindergarten. The curriculum identifies intentional teaching strategies and learning sequences, and includes kits of materials to accompany investigations of topics such as clothing, building, trees, and recycling. Creative Curriculum's goals are described in a developmental continuum that guides teachers' observations and assessment of children's progress and their planning, called GOLD®. This assessment tool is widely adopted for state prekindergarten programs. Materials are available in English and Spanish.

Creative Curriculum strongly emphasizes the learning environment, children's play, and child-initiated activity. The learning environment is the organizing framework of the curriculum. Teachers use children's involvement in centers in the classroom, including blocks, dramatic play, toys and games, art, library, discovery (science center), sand and water, music and movement, cooking, technology, and outdoors, to foster development and learning (Dodge et al., 2010).

The Creative Curriculum has evolved over the years, drawing on the work of several learning theorists, including Maslow, Erikson, Piaget, Vygotsky, and Gardner. These influences have contributed to the teacher's role as observing, reflecting, and responding to children in their environment in order to facilitate and scaffold their development and learning. Both HighScope and Creative Curriculum are child-centered curriculum models that focus on the goals as well as the process of how children learn and develop. HighScope's distinguishing characteristic is the plan-do-review learning process, whereas Creative Curriculum emanates from the learning environment.

Tools of the Mind Developed by Deborah Leong and Elena Bodrova, the Tools of the Mind curriculum is based on Vygotsky's sociocultural theory and current neuroscience (Bodrova & Leong, 2007). Dr. Bodrova came to the United States from Russia, where she worked with students and colleagues of Vygotsky. Tools of the Mind is a comprehensive curriculum for preschool through second grade that provides teachers with ideas and strategies to support children's development of executive function, self-regulation, and academic skills. The curriculum emphasizes the teacher's role in scaffolding children's learning along with child-directed experiences and teacher-supported socio-dramatic play. Teachers engage in ongoing assessment of children's development to provide individualized scaffolding in which they increase or decrease their level of support depending on the degree to which children independently perform specific skills. The curriculum is designed to achieve two main interrelated goals (Blair & Raver, 2014; Diamond & Lee, 2011):

1. Development of foundational cognitive abilities that include self-regulation of behavior, emotions, and cognition; memory; and focused attention.
2. Learning academic skills aligned with the Common Core standards, such as literacy, mathematics, and science.

The central element of Tools of the Mind is using high-level, mature socio-dramatic play to develop children's self-regulation. Such mature play includes a theme, roles with rules, language, and symbolic props, such as using a rhythm stick for a magic wand.

To make play a more effective learning experience, teachers engage children in play planning before and during the play. Children produce their own play plans, which include written and graphic descriptions of what they intend to do during the play. By writing and/or drawing their plans, the children's writing abilities improve over time, a process called *scaffolded writing*. Children state their plans verbally, and the teacher draws lines on the paper for each spoken word. This serves as a short-term memory scaffold as children write and draw their plans. Over time, teachers help children make more complex plans, encouraging two or more children to plan together to build friendships and collaborative learning.

To enhance the quality of the play, teachers also provide children with relevant experiences that will inform their play. For example, a trip to the fire station helps children learn about the roles and scenarios that occur there. But teachers do not leave the learning to chance. They ask the firefighters and other workers to demonstrate for children what they actually say before and after the fire bell goes off. Such experiences expand children's vocabulary and use of complex language, which they then practice during play.

One of the key aspects of Tools of the Mind is that it is based on the assumption that if children lack underlying cognitive skills such as self-regulation, trying to teach them academic skills is more difficult and inefficient. As a result, activities in Tools of the Mind promote these abilities simultaneously. Teachers organize the classroom routines to eliminate or minimize situations that tend to interfere with the development of self-regulation, such as long periods of whole-group instruction or lengthy waits for a turn.

Teachers embed self-regulation practice in all activities. For example, a preschool teacher might use props to scaffold children's practice of conversation turn-taking. After the teacher explains what to do with the props, Kesharia holds a cardboard ear to prompt her to listen, while Ashanti holds a cardboard mouth assigning him the role of speaker. Then they switch roles.

Read the feature *What Works: Using Tools of the Mind to Promote Executive Function* to learn the results of a rigorous evaluation of the curriculum and its lasting impact on kindergarten children's self-regulation and academic skills.

Core Knowledge Another approach to curriculum development focuses on content: what children should know and be able to do. This is the key component of the Core Knowledge curriculum. Founded in 1986 by E. D. Hirsch Jr., professor at the University of Virginia, the Core Knowledge Foundation is a nonprofit organization that promotes greater excellence and fairness in education. The premise of Core Knowledge is that equal educational opportunity can be guaranteed for every child only by explicitly identifying the knowledge that all children should acquire, because knowledge is key to reading

What Works

Using Tools of the Mind to Promote Executive Function

The Tools of the Mind curriculum is based on the premise that developing young children's executive functions—flexible thinking, focused attention, and working memory—and self-regulation of emotions and behavior are key to their later academic success and social competence. Neuroscientists and child development researchers are finding strong support for the effectiveness of the curriculum in achieving this objective.

A well-designed evaluation study involving 29 schools, 79 kindergarten classrooms, and 759 children compared the impact of Tools of the Mind to the traditional curriculum. What was unique about this study was that it not only assessed children's executive function abilities and academic skills, but it also tested saliva samples to compare children's stress levels.

At every grade level, Tools of the Mind has the same overarching goals, but the teaching strategies and learning activities vary by age group. At the kindergarten level, children meet with teachers to create and implement weekly learning goals and plans. Instead of the strong emphasis on sociodramatic play that occurs in preschool, Tools of the Mind kindergartens use dramatization. Children "play out" the stories that they are learning to read, beginning with fairy tales and moving to chapter books, rather than pretending about everyday experiences. This intentional pretend play develops language, vocabulary, reading, and creativity. By contrast, the traditional, academically focused kindergarten classrooms typically allow only 10 to 15 minutes of play during free choice time, and have no materials to support pretend play or connect it to literacy learning.

Another major difference between Tools of the Mind classrooms and the traditional kindergartens is the emphasis on peer interaction and teacher scaffolding to support higher-order thinking and promote social competence and intrinsic motivation. Children talk with teachers, question, and reflect on their own understanding. Mistakes become learning opportunities.

The study found that children in Tools of the Mind classrooms performed better on neurologically based executive function tasks such as focusing attention, ignoring distractions, and working memory. Children's reading, vocabulary, and mathematics also improved at the end of kindergarten, and even better reading and vocabulary results were achieved in first grade. Significantly, these differences were greater in schools serving children in poverty.

One of the most encouraging aspects of the study is the neurobiological findings. Children in the Tools of the Mind kindergartens demonstrated lower levels of stress. Given the heightened academic demands of kindergarten resulting in increased stress for all children coupled with the toxic stress associated with poverty, lowering stress is essential. Children cannot learn effectively if they are anxious, worried, or unable to focus. This study demonstrates that through teacher-scaffolded support of executive function and self-regulation, Tools of the Mind can benefit children in high-poverty schools academically, physically, and emotionally, and has the potential to close the achievement gap.

Source: Based on "Reaching Individual Potentials through Transformational Curriculum," by T. Rosegrant and S. Bredekamp, 1992, pp. 66–73, in Reaching Potentials: Appropriate Curriculum and Assessment for Young Children, Vol. 1, edited by S. Bredekamp and T. Rosegrant, Washington, DC: NAEYC. Reprinted with permission from the National Association for the Education of Young Children (NAEYC).

comprehension. Hirsch believes that the achievement gap in American schools is actually a result of inequity in exposure to content knowledge. This belief led the Core Knowledge Foundation to develop a curriculum sequence for prekindergarten through eighth grade, which is available for free online.

The Core Knowledge sequence (Core Knowledge Foundation, 2013) is designed to be a coherent, content- and language-rich curriculum that offers a progression of skills and knowledge across all areas of development as well as mathematical reasoning and number sense, orientation in time and space, scientific reasoning and the physical world, music, and visual arts.

These areas of skill and knowledge are similar to those included in the other curriculum models described previously. However, the Core Knowledge preschool sequence differs from those approaches in at least two ways:

- *Specificity regarding content.* The preschool sequence identifies specific experiences, knowledge, and skills for all children, including particular stories, fables, legends, nonfiction books, songs, rhymes, and poems. A month-by-month planning guide promotes the concept of a sequence of knowledge and competencies building on one another.

Although the program is flexible, it establishes expectations that all the content and language should be incorporated to prepare children for the next level of curriculum.

- *Lack of specificity regarding pedagogy.* The Core Knowledge sequence specifies *what* to teach, not *how* to teach. It does not advocate any particular approach, but rather a wide range of strategies that includes teacher-directed, large and small group experiences as well as children's play and discovery learning.

Connect4 Learning   A more recently developed research-based comprehensive preschool curriculum is Connect4 Learning (Sarama et al., 2016). Funded by a five-year grant from the National Science Foundation, Connect4 Learning is an interdisciplinary curriculum with a strong focus on content in four key areas: science, math, literacy, and social-emotional. Sequences of learning and development are integrated in each of these domains around five units of study: connecting with school and families, our environment, how structures are built, growing our garden, and how we've grown. The curriculum's supplementary materials include books, computer games, lessons, assessment tools, and an online portal for teachers, administrators, and families.

A defining characteristic of Connect4 is its strong emphasis on a scope and sequence of subject matter content. For example, although learning centers are incorporated, they are organized by content areas such as the math center. In this way, Connect4 Learning bridges the two commonly used approaches in early education—comprehensive and content-area focused curriculum, the latter of which we discuss next.

Focused Curriculum

Historically, in early childhood education, comprehensive curriculum has been essentially the only approach. Recently, however, there has been an explosion in curriculum development among researchers as well as publishers, much of which focuses on a single area such as literacy, mathematics, or social–emotional development. Perhaps because these curricula are targeted to relatively specific goals, such focused curricula have been found to be more effective in improving children's outcomes than comprehensive approaches (Jenkins & Duncan, 2017; Yoshikawa et al., 2013). We discuss some of these curricula in later relevant chapters on literacy, STEM, and social-emotional development.

One highly effective example of focused curriculum is in Boston Public Schools (BPS). In an effort to improve the quality and consistency of preschool and kindergarten classrooms, the school district implemented systemwide a literacy curriculum, Opening the World of Learning (OWL) (Schickedanz & Dickinson, 2011), and a mathematics curriculum, Building Blocks (Clements & Sarama, 2007a). An evaluation of the program found significant positive effects on children's literacy, language, early math, and executive function abilities (Weiland & Yoshikawa, 2011). The researchers concluded that using a uniform curriculum and intentional teaching strategies with professional development for teachers made the difference. The effects on executive function were especially important because these abilities are vital for later success.

Subsequently, the district developed its own curriculum for preschool through second grade—Focus on Early Learning, a rare example of "push-up" curriculum. At each grade level, there is a broad theme, such as globalization in first grade, and in-depth units of study. Participation in the BPS Pre-K program was found to close kindergarten racial and income achievement gaps. African American and Hispanic/Latino students who participate in the BPS preschool *outperform* White students who do not participate (Weiland & Yoshikawa, 2013). Materials are available online.

Similarly, one study (Wilson, Dickinson, & Rowe, 2013) found that the OWL curriculum produced large improvements in literacy and language outcomes for all children but especially for dual language learners. These children performed nearly as well or better than native speakers at kindergarten entry, and reached national norms on standardized tests. Dual language learners in OWL classrooms performed better on expressive and receptive vocabulary than those who did not experience the curriculum.

Promoting Play

Playful Mathematics Curriculum

During morning meeting, preschool teacher Akimi Quang plays a counting game with the children. When she holds up one finger, they jump once; then two fingers, two jumps, and so on to 10. That gets the wiggles out, and they settle on the rug. Then she says, "Before we go to centers, let me tell you what the options are. In the math center, there is a fun card game for four children. In the computer center, two children can play the matching shape game we learned yesterday." She goes on to describe the other centers. Then she says, "Think before you raise your hand. Four people can go to the math center." Hands shoot up, and the children look around to count how many. "That's six!" says Emanuel. "You're right," Akimi says, "What should we do?" Harmony immediately answers, "Two people have to choose something else."

As you can see, Akimi infuses playful math throughout the day, including whole group time and transitions. But the curriculum also includes playful math experiences related to specific learning goals. A characteristic of research-based mathematics curricula consists of learning trajectories that provide the scope and sequence. This is important, because math is a sequential discipline—later learning builds on earlier understanding. But scope and sequence doesn't preclude playful activities.

Effective curriculum and instruction involves a variety of strategies. Overuse of any one strategy or context—whether it's whole group, small group, or play in centers—would not achieve all the necessary learning goals. Children learn through teacher-supported play, but in the absence of teacher-planned and guided experiences, there would be too many missed opportunities for learning. The curricula described here incorporate both play and intentional teaching to achieve goals.

Whether comprehensive or content-area focused, one thing these curricula have in common is that they incorporate play and playful experiences in various forms. For an example, read the feature *Promoting Play: Playful Mathematics Curriculum*.

 Application Exercise 10.3

Playful Science Curriculum

The Reggio Emilia Approach

The internationally known schools of Reggio Emilia, Italy, have been called "the place theory and practice touch like the magic moment when night becomes day" (quoted in Bredekamp, 2008, p. 49). Since the approach was first introduced in the United States, it has inspired teachers throughout the world and made major contributions to the knowledge base (Baldini, Cavallini, Moss, & Vecchi, 2012; Edwards, Gandini, & Forman, 2012).

The Schools of Reggio Emilia, Italy Loris Malaguzzi, considered the founder of the approach, used the metaphor "the hundred languages of children" to connote the complex elements of the approach. First and foremost, the metaphor communicates the inherent genius of every child. Secondly, the "hundred languages" stand for the processes of children's learning as well as how they demonstrate it. In addition, "languages" are various forms of media—drawing, sculpting, writing, photography, video, music, dance, words, numbers, and so on—that are used to promote and display children's understanding of the world. By focusing attention on what children are capable of doing, the Reggio approach has made young children's amazing competence visible to the world.

The Reggio Emilia approach is not a curriculum, nor is it a model. It draws on several theories in an integrated fashion, but also goes beyond them. For example, a visitor to the schools would see evidence of Vygotskian sociocultural theory in the collaborative project work among small groups of children and also in the co-construction of knowledge between teachers and children. In addition, teachers and peers place themselves in zones of proximal development, continually scaffolding each other's learning. Teachers often act as provocateurs for children, deliberately creating what Piaget termed *disequilibrium*, to drive children's learning.

Principles and Values of the Reggio Emilia Approach The Reggio Emilia approach is based on a set of core values and principles (Gandini, 2008). However, the complexity and uniqueness of the approach cannot be reduced to a list of principles. Anyone attempting to implement a Reggio-inspired program should devote considerable study to the intricacies of its cultural origins and theoretical underpinnings (Rinaldi, 2006; Vecchi, 2010). A brief summary of its core components follows.

The Image of the Child The foundation of the Reggio Emilia approach is the *image of the child* as rich in potential, strong, and powerful, with rights as a citizen and contributing member of the community. In Reggio, children with special rights (what Americans call *children with special needs*) are given precedence in school enrollment.

Children's Relationships and Interactions Malaguzzi (1993) called the approach "an education based on relationships." Teachers stay with the same group of children for three years and focus on reciprocal relationships among children (often in small groups) and the community.

The Role of Parents Malaguzzi often said that the school has three protagonists without which schools do not exist: children, teachers, and parents. The active participation of parents is essential to the operation of the schools; parents are deeply involved in the learning activities of the children.

The Role of Space: An Amiable School The environments convey the message that "this is a place where adults have thought about the quality and the instructive power of space" (Gandini, 2008, p. 25). Americans are struck by the aesthetic beauty of the schools, but each element is designed for a purpose, such as to promote small group interaction, demonstrate respect for children, or display evidence of the process of children's learning.

© Erika Landorf-Kelly/Pearson Education

The Reggio Emilia approach has inspired schools in the United States to rethink the environment and children's representational ability. What does this Reggio-inspired learning environment communicate about and to children?

Teachers and Children as Partners in Learning Although highly knowledgeable, teachers do not consider themselves experts who impart knowledge, but rather partners with children in the journey of discovery. They act as a resource to children, asking provocative questions, exploring children's thoughts and hypotheses, and learning along with them.

Curriculum as a Process of Inviting and Sustaining Learning There is no preset curriculum in Reggio schools. Teachers prepare a declaration of intent about possible learning experiences they will offer to children, but the curriculum emerges from children's interests in topics or questions and their desire to find out more or to solve a problem. However, teachers do have goals, and plan in advance for possible directions the work will take. They listen carefully to children, and regularly meet to discuss how to further children's involvement and deepen their understanding.

The Many Languages of Children Each school has a special teacher, called an *atelierista*, who is knowledgeable about the visual arts and works closely with the other teachers and children. Each preschool has an *atelier*, a specially equipped studio that contains a wide range of materials and resources that are used by children to represent their ideas and thinking and in projects.

In the United States, the Reggio Emilia approach is sometimes described as an art program. However, the Italians see the children's work as symbolic representation that is an integral part of learning. When children represent the same concept using different media, their understanding deepens. For example, drawing a horse in two dimensions conveys a partial concept of the animal. Constructing a three-dimensional model of a horse in clay requires thinking about how the horse stands up and how it runs.

Learning through Projects Short- and long-term projects are a major teaching and learning strategy in Reggio schools. Facilitated by teachers, children work in small groups on a topic or a problem of interest to them. Ideas for projects great and small grow out of children's experiences or chance encounters. An invitation from the town to design a theater curtain for the opera house led to a lengthy project that included generating artistic designs, making computer models, painting large murals, and exploring cloth production. The project culminated in a celebratory unveiling (Vecchi, 2002).

The Power of Documentation The growth in children's thinking that occurs through project work is captured in one of the most compelling and unique aspects of the approach: documentation. As a project proceeds, teachers and the *atelierista* carefully arrange and display transcripts of children's discussions, photographs of them at work, and representations of their thinking and learning in various media (drawings, sculptures, and constructions). These documentations can be interpreted as assessments, but they are more like records of the processes of learning and problem solving in groups of children. What goes on in children's minds cannot be seen, but documentation *makes learning visible* (Reggio Children & Project Zero, 2001). Documentation powerfully communicates the competence of children to parents, community members, and policy makers. Teachers use documentation to help children revisit their experiences, remember and analyze their thinking, and deepen their understanding.

Finally, play is a vital part of Reggio schools, although most written accounts or presentations about Reggio in the United States fail to talk about play. One must observe in the schools to see that play is as important to the Reggio Emilia approach as it is to developmentally appropriate practice.

The Influence of the Reggio Emilia Approach One of the most important contributions of Reggio Emilia is the deeper understanding of how *representation* not only reflects what children know and can do but also changes it (Vecchi, 2010). Other practices that have expanded theoretical understandings are the role projects and documentation can play in higher-order thinking and memory, and the effectiveness of collaboration and co-construction as teaching and learning strategies. Although these practices are not new to the United States, the quality of implementation in Reggio is beyond what is usually seen here, with few exceptions.

The Reggio Emilia approach is deeply rooted in the sociocultural context of its region and town in Italy. Therefore, it cannot be successfully imitated in a different cultural milieu. Instead, many American educators learn from and with Reggio educators, and are inspired by the possibilities inherent in their work. A large number of these educators are members of the North American Reggio Emilia Alliance (NAREA), which offers conferences, publications, and other opportunities to exchange inspirations and experiences.

Research on Preschool Curriculum

The irony of mandates for research-based curriculum is that there has been a limited body of well-designed research on the comparative effectiveness of preschool curricula. However, as we see from the studies cited previously, this situation is changing

(Bierman, 2011; Fantuzzo et al., 2010; Yoshikawa et al., 2013). In the past decade, expansion of publicly funded preschool has increased demand for accountability. As a result, research has increased as well.

In the past, much of existing research compared the effectiveness of teacher-directed instruction and more child-initiated, play-oriented approaches to curriculum. In fact, these studies were more about particular teaching strategies than evaluations of curricula.

Ample evidence exists that a well-planned, focused, research-based curriculum is an essential element of an effective early childhood program (Burchinal, 2017; Jenkins & Duncan, 2017). The bottom line is that to be most effective, teachers need *both* good curriculum knowledge *and* understanding of child development (IOM & NRC, 2015). Teachers who have this knowledge possess the fundamental resources for planning and implementing an effective curriculum, which is described in the next section.

✔ Check Your Understanding 10.5

A Model for Planning Effective Curriculum

In this section, we present a model for planning effective curriculum that applies across the full age range of early childhood as well as in diverse settings. This model for developing and planning curriculum is shown in Figure 10.8 (Bredekamp & Rosegrant, 1995; Rosegrant & Bredekamp, 1992). In the sections that follow, we briefly describe the sources of knowledge that are brought together in a coherent curriculum, then we provide examples of applying the planning model in action. All good early childhood curriculum needs to focus first on children, as we discuss next.

FIGURE 10.8 Model for Planning Effective Curriculum Based on "Reaching Individual Potentials through Transformational Curriculum," by T. Rosegrant and S. Bredekamp, 1992, pp. 66–73, in Reaching Potentials: Appropriate Curriculum and Assessment for Young Children, Vol. 1, edited by S. Bredekamp and T. Rosegrant, Washington, DC: NAEYC. Reprinted with permission from the National Association for the Education of Young Children (NAEYC).

Figure 10.8: Model for Planning Effective Curriculum

The Child in the Sociocultural Context

Early childhood curriculum is often called *child centered*; accordingly, this model places the child at the center of curriculum planning. In a child-centered curriculum, learning is an interactive process—children change from exposure to the curriculum, and the curriculum changes in response to the learner's progress. Teachers involve children in planning by determining what they already know, as well as what they want and need to know. As curriculum is implemented, teachers continually assess children's abilities and adapt the curriculum and teaching in response.

However, children do not grow and learn in isolation; in early childhood classrooms, children are part of a group. The group, in turn, exists in a larger context of a program or school, a community, state, and nation. Therefore, the model situates the child in a sociocultural context that influences what is included in the curriculum (Bronfenbrenner & Morris, 2006).

The cultural values of families and the community always influence curriculum decisions. For example, a faith-based private school may include religious study in its curriculum, whereas a public school may avoid reference to religious activity of any kind. Similarly, if the program serves a cultural community that values interdependence over independence, a focus on the individual child at the center of the curriculum may not be appropriate. Most likely, families would prefer a model with children as part of a cultural group as its focus.

In this model of curriculum planning, culture is not viewed as a separate source of curriculum, but rather as the context within which all curriculum decisions are made. Therefore, culture influences all aspects of curriculum planning, as we describe in the sections that follow on each dimension of the model.

Sources of Curriculum

As illustrated in Figure 10.8, curriculum planning draws on four sources:

1. *The content of the disciplines.* Much of the curriculum comes directly from the subject-matter disciplines: what children need to know and be able to do in science, mathematics, language arts, health, social studies, and the arts. Such content gives curriculum intellectual integrity; that is, it teaches accurate information about how the world works and how to obtain new knowledge. However, the content of the disciplines can be abstract and removed from children's direct experiences. Therefore, early childhood curriculum needs to be conceptually organized.
2. *Conceptual organizers.* We have already discussed several approaches to conceptually organizing curriculum. Conceptual organizers make content knowledge more meaningful, interesting, and understandable for young children. For example, children can learn key scientific concepts by planting a garden or studying the effects of light on shadows.
3. *Child development knowledge.* Knowledge of how young children develop and learn is critical in planning curriculum that will reach all children. Research on children's cognitive, language, social, emotional, and physical development allows teachers to anticipate whether curriculum goals will be achievable and challenging (that is, developmentally appropriate).
4. *Developmental/learning continuum.* A developmental continuum is a predictable, but not rigid, sequence of typical developmental accomplishments within age ranges (McAfee, Leong, & Bodrova, 2016). A learning continuum (also called a learning trajectory or learning path) is similar to a developmental continuum but focuses on sequences of knowledge or skill in a content area such as mathematics or physical education, with each level more sophisticated than the last (IOM & NRC, 2015). (The terms *developmental continuum* and *learning trajectory* are often used interchangeably.) Research-based developmental and learning continua are the basis for planning the scope and sequence of a curriculum. Teachers use a continuum of

conceptual organizer Ways of organizing curriculum, such as the project approach, that make content knowledge more meaningful, interesting, and understandable for children.

developmental continuum A predictable, but not rigid, sequence of typical accomplishments within age ranges that is used to plan curriculum; also an effective assessment tool used to focus teacher attention on what is important to assess—what children can do—and to identify goals for continued progress.

learning continuum, learning trajectory, or learning path Similar to a developmental continuum, but focuses on sequences of knowledge or skill in a content area.

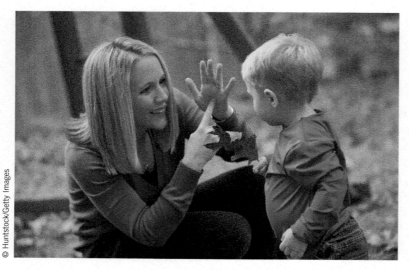

development and learning in a curriculum area to determine when, where, and how to provide individual instruction and scaffolding.

This model illustrates how both content knowledge and child development knowledge must be considered in planning effective early childhood curriculum. If state learning standards are well done, they should play a role in guiding discipline content and the developmental/learning continua. The goal of this planning model is for programs and schools serving children from birth through age 8 to teach the *whole child*—the thinking, feeling, moving, expressing, creating, problem-solving, interacting human being.

Applying the Curriculum Model in Practice

In the following example, we see teachers putting the planning model into practice.

Jamie, who is hearing-impaired, is a 4-year-old in Kathleen and Cheryl's classroom. Before school started, Kathleen took a brief course in American Sign Language to ensure that she could communicate with him and to teach the other children some essential signs.

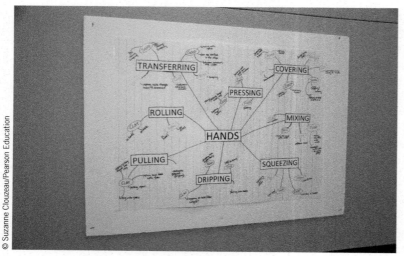

Intentional teachers can use children's interests to plan curriculum that meets many learning goals. One child's use of American Sign Language can lead to a project about hands, as evident in this preschool concept web.

On the first day of school during morning meeting, the children become fascinated by Jamie and Kathleen's ability to talk with their hands, and want to learn signs themselves. Jamie begins to feel comfortable and make friends. Kathleen and Cheryl soon observe the children's fascination with the power of communicating with hands, and launch a curriculum project about hands.

The project begins with the children generating a concept web about all the things that they do with their hands, using materials such as sand and clay—squeezing, covering, pressing, and transferring. The concept web introduces many new vocabulary words as well as new signs to practice with Jamie. The teachers decide to set up two play areas to extend the interest in hands. One is a clothing store that includes props such as gloves and mittens of various colors and fabrics as well as clothing that requires zipping, buttoning, or other fine-motor skills. They also set up the woodworking table for carpentry, which requires eye-hand coordination skills and creativity.

Angelique: I'm going to visit my grandma in Alaska, so I need a heavy coat and warm gloves.

Mitchell, the store manager: What kind?

Angelique, pointing to her hands: I want pink ones.

Mitchell sorts through his boxes and replies: We got red, green, and blue gloves. I got pink mittens. They'll be warm.

Angelique: No, they won't. Gloves are better. I'll look online.

Overhearing their conversation, Kathleen raises the question at group time—which is warmer, gloves or mittens? The children vote and make a graph of their answers. Most choose gloves. They begin an experiment to see which is actually warmer and explore the larger question of how people stay warm.

In large group, the children also enjoy fingerplays and songs such as "Where Is Thumbkin?" and "I Have a Family in My Hand." At small group time, Cheryl reads *The Mitten* to four children. Kathleen plays a math game with several others, challenging them to find everything in the classroom that comes in pairs like hands. After looking everywhere and feeling stumped, Ross shouts with glee, "Ear lobes!"

Over time, the study expands to investigate the type of jobs that require working with hands: some requiring strength and others finesse, such as musicians, painters, computer scientists, and many others.

Video Example 10.6:

Implementing A Content-Rich, Child-Centered Curriculum

In this video of a preschool classroom, how are all the elements of the child-centered curriculum planning model used during the in-depth study of birds? What content goals are being addressed? And what do you notice about the children's engagement and approaches to learning?

This glimpse into Kathleen and Cheryl's classroom finds happy children laughing and playing together. What is not immediately apparent, however, is the planning that has gone into the curriculum. To begin, the teachers identified the topic of hands as a conceptual organizer for several reasons. They had observed how much interest the children showed in Jamie's capacity to communicate with his hands and how they could do it, too. Thus, Jamie became a leader in the study. Also, the teachers could predict that preschoolers are generally interested in their own bodies and mastering new skills, in this case zipping, tying, or keyboarding.

Next, the teachers considered how well the topic promotes child development. They agreed that it would provide opportunities to build cognitive processes such as matching, describing, organizing, and categorizing by size, color, and function (dress-up, carpentry, inclement weather). The topic promotes physical development such as practicing fine-motor skills and eye-hand coordination. The clothing store and other activities, such as modelling with clay, encourage social interaction and turn-taking as well as language development.

As for content knowledge, the study supported children's learning in every discipline area listed below.

Mathematics: counting by ones and twos; measuring and ordering by size (hands are different sizes); learning about patterns and relationships (clothing designs are in patterns; hands have similarities and differences)

Science: learning technology about tools and materials we use with our hands; physical properties (some gloves are water repellant, others are not); learning about body warmth

Language and literacy: vocabulary (nouns such as *fist, tight, loose,* and verbs such as *transfer, squeeze, grab, pinch*); books, songs, and fingerplays; nonverbal communication using gestures, body language, and signing

Social studies: economics of buying and selling clothing; cultural differences related to when and what kind of clothing to wear or what jobs people do

Health: gloves and clothing for protecting hands from injury and weather

As the model indicates, the socio–cultural context impacts every dimension of curriculum. Read the feature *Culture Lens: Culturally Appropriate Curriculum* for some real-life examples of this phenomenon.

Adapting for Individual Differences

One important criterion in planning curriculum for every age group is the need to adapt for individual differences in children, including children with special needs. The final element of the curriculum model is that teachers need to know the continuum of development and learning in each area so they can adapt the curriculum to accommodate individual differences in children. Although we raise this issue at the end of the chapter, it is the most important aspect of implementing an effective curriculum. The following example illustrates how a teacher uses her general curriculum goals as a framework to adapt for individual children.

In Kiara's Head Start classroom of 14 3-year-olds, three of the children, Nikki, Devren, and Theo, have individualized education programs (IEPs). Once a month, Kiara meets

Culture Lens
Culturally Responsive Curriculum

One of the key components of effective curriculum is that it be culturally appropriate. To achieve this goal, it is vital that families and members of cultural communities be involved and that their values are reflected to the degree possible. This process can take time, but is likely to result in greater commitment by parents, teachers, and children. Following are some examples.

One such example is *CIRCLES: A culturally appropriate curriculum for American Indian preschool children.* Based on nearly three decades of work, the National Center for Families Learning developed this evidence-based curriculum with a strong focus on Native culture and language preservation. The child is the center of the framework surrounded by four key elements: Home (parents and family), Community (culture and language), School (learning community, routines, and materials), and Approaches to Learning. The curriculum includes a scope and sequence of literacy, mathematics, and other key preschool activities, but frames them in American Indian values: community and family, knowledge and wisdom, strengths and introspection, and communication and creativity.

The Office of Head Start assists American Indian and Alaska Native (AIAN) Head Start programs to teach their languages and cultures while meeting Head Start standards. In 2018, OHS released *Making It Work! Connecting Cultural Learning Experiences in American Indian and Alaska Native Classrooms and Communities with the Head Start Child Development and Early Learning Framework.* A wide array of materials is available online to help programs align school expectations with traditional cultural skills, values, beliefs, and life ways, including examples of cultural lessons.

Culturally appropriate curriculum approaches have also been developed in Hawaii, the nation's most diverse state. *'Ohana Math* is a program developed to draw on cultural strengths of families in order to promote learning for their children from infancy through preschool. Parents are encouraged to help their children learn concepts such as patterns by using native materials

and crafts, such as creating a lei. As with CIRCLES, the approach draws on the cultural funds of knowledge of children's extended families, including aunties, uncles, grandparents, and others.

Other countries share many similarities with American approaches to early childhood education. However, their curriculum frameworks always reflect the cultures and languages of their countries. For example, New Zealand has had a world-renowned national curriculum framework, *Te Whāriki,* for more than two decades that is a powerful reflection of its bilingual, bicultural society of Native Maori and White Europeans. The framework reflects the values of preserving and promoting identity, language, and culture, and a balance of mind/body/spirit. The words *Te Whāriki* means "a woven mat," which is used as a metaphor for the curriculum. The mat consists of four principles—empowerment, holistic development, family and community, and relationships—which are interwoven with strands—well-being, belonging, contribution, communication, and engagement.

One of the New Zealand learning outcomes is: "Recognizing mathematical symbols and concepts and using them with enjoyment, meaning and purpose" (p. 25). This focus on joy is a reflection of the culture, as is a strong emphasis on connections to and respect for the natural environment. These types of outcome statements are not likely to be found in an American state's early learning standards.

Sources: Head Start, 2018. "*Making it work! Connecting cultural learning experiences in American Indian and Alaska Native classrooms and communities with the Head Start Child Development and Early Learning Framework*". Online at https://eclkc.ohs.acf.hhs.gov. National Center for Families Learning, 2018. *CIRCLES: A culturally appropriate curriculum for American Indian preschool children.* Louisville, KY; L. S. Muccio, R. Kuwahara-Fujita, & J. J. Y. Otsuji, 2014. 'Ohana math: Family engagement to promote mathematical learning for Hawai'i's young children. *Young Children, 69*(4), 24–30; and New Zealand Ministry of Education, 2017. *Te Whāriki: Early childhood curriculum.* Wellington, NZ.

with the children's IEP team to brainstorm ideas for addressing their individual goals in the context of the general curriculum and daily routines. First, the team considers the current IEP objectives for each child:

- *Nikki:* Improve fine motor skills such as holding writing instruments and cutting; identify colors and shapes; demonstrate one-to-one correspondence.
- *Devren:* Make requests; initiate interactions with his peers; watch, listen, and participate in large-group settings.
- *Theo:* Ask for help when needed; label objects; share toys and materials.

During the meeting, the team considers these individual goals along with the curriculum plan for the entire class, which at the moment is a study of transportation. With this approach, the children with special needs do not need to be segregated from their peers for one-on-one direct instruction, and they have many opportunities to learn and practice skills. Because the topic is interesting and motivating, learning occurs more quickly for children with special needs.

To ensure sufficient practice opportunities throughout the day, Kiara prepares the activity matrix that is depicted in Table 10.3. It describes the opportunities to embed the children's learning goals in the daily schedule and lesson plans.

Classroom teachers and early childhood special educators can collaborate to create fun, meaningful curriculum that provides powerful motivation for children, both with and without special needs, to practice important skills throughout their day.

Effective curriculum planning involves several key steps, whether the curriculum is locally developed or purchased. If teachers use a published program, they need to use it flexibly and adapt it in response to children's cues and information obtained from ongoing assessment. Similarly, if teachers develop their own curriculum plans, they need to ensure

TABLE 10.3 Individualizing Instruction with an Activity Matrix

	Nikki	Devren	Theo
Arrival	Have Nikki "sign in" for the day holding an adaptive marker.	Have Devren be the greeter and ask children if they would like to sign in.	Have Theo be in charge of the dry erase markers for sign-in time so that he has opportunities to share.
Breakfast	Nikki will be the helper who sets out plates and utensils at each place mat. She will help "take orders" by making a mark on her paper for each child who wants milk.	Serve some of Devren's favorite foods at mealtime to encourage him to verbalize his requests.	Provide Theo's favorite snack (crackers) inside a jar with a lid and wait for a request for help to open and provide the snack. Put the lid back on when done so that Theo will ask for help again.
Group time	Have Nikki hand out colored bus circle time props (she waits for peer to request a specific color). Sing modified version of "Wheels on the Bus," i.e., "The red bus goes ..."	Have Devren collect circle time props, initiating to each peer, " ___ , please hand me your bus."	Have Theo label the color pattern of the bus props that the children use: red, green, blue.
Free choice/centers	Provide colored train tickets to correspond with colored train car. Ask Nikki to identify the colors of both.	Devren can be the engineer and request tickets from peers. At art, keep glitter in sight but out of reach, and have Devren request to use it.	Have train engineer clothes available for dramatic play. Prompt Theo to ask for help with dressing.
Outdoor play	Take colored sidewalk chalk outside. Have Nikki draw and identify chalk colors.	Put teeter-totter and Sit 'n Spin (Devren's favorites) outside to increase initiations with peers.	Make a scavenger hunt of transportation objects outside. Have Theo label the items as he finds them.
Small group/tables	Make trains out of shapes. Have Nikki identify different shapes.	Put peer in charge of highly preferred art material. Devren has to initiate with a peer to make a request.	Close lid on glue after each use. Prompt Theo to ask for help.
Story	Ask questions about the colors and shapes in the book.	Let Devren sit close to teacher and hold favorite item during story to increase engagement.	Ask object identification questions after reading the story to Theo.
Departure	Have children identify a shape and color before leaving to get their coats.	Have children identify a shape and color before leaving to get their coats.	Have children identify a shape and color before leaving to get their coats.

that those plans reflect the most current knowledge from the disciplines as well as research on child development and learning.

Teachers must take into account that children vary enormously on practically every dimension of development and learning. These differences are manifest in rates of development; prior experiences, which greatly influence learning; diverse cultural and linguistic backgrounds; and the existence of specific abilities and disabilities. Understanding students' diverse abilities is critical in implementing curriculum and adapting for individual variation. Regardless of the type of curriculum used, teachers need to apply their professional expertise.

✔ **Check Your Understanding 10.6**

Revisiting the Case Study

... Ross Elementary School

In this chapter, we described indicators of effective curriculum and provided a model for planning curriculum that draws on both content knowledge and knowledge of child development while also placing children at the center of the planning process. At the outset, we saw a career awareness project involving all the children from pre-K to fifth grade. Now we can revisit the school and think about the project in relation to what we have learned about curriculum.

To implement the principles of effective curriculum, the teachers thoughtfully planned what they wanted children to think about and learn during this study, and also considered the relevant learning standards. Although it was a schoolwide project, the activities varied by grade level to be developmentally appropriate, and connected to children's predictable interests.

Children were active and engaged as they interacted with the visiting experts, drew pictures for their posters, and wrote essays and poems. They used various forms of technology for research and to communicate with other experts. The project addressed several state learning goals, including English language arts and social studies. But children also learned about other disciplines, new concepts, and vocabulary in their discussions with professionals—such as how they use math and science in their work. The study drew on children's interests, connected what they are learning in school to the real world, and motivated them to continue learning. This activity illustrates integrated curriculum in action, with children's experiences contributing to different areas of their development and learning at the same time.

With regard to the planning model used in this classroom, the curriculum is based in the discipline of social studies, but content is made accessible to children through a topic that fascinates them: their own lives and future careers. At the same time, children are learning the key concepts and tools of inquiry used by researchers. For example, they investigate using the internet and interview experts. They enhance their language and literacy as they learn new words and concepts related to the occupations they are studying.

Child development knowledge is reflected in providing developmentally appropriate experiences, including play and book reading. At the same time, teachers assess each child's progress in relation to learning goals and support their developing abilities, as when they evaluate their writing, observe their symbolic representation ability in drawings, and listen when they engage in conversation with experts and peers. As this schoolwide project demonstrates, effective early childhood curriculum is not only motivating and engaging but also intellectually challenging for children and teachers. ■

10 Chapter Summary

- Curriculum is a written plan that describes the goals for children's learning and development, and the learning experiences, materials, and teaching strategies that are used to help children achieve those goals.

- Scientifically based curriculum derives from research evidence about what kinds of learning outcomes relate to later achievement and what types of teaching and learning experiences help children acquire those outcomes. Research-based curriculum has been evaluated, and it has demonstrated its effectiveness.

- Effective curriculum is thoughtfully planned; challenging, engaging, and developmentally appropriate; culturally and linguistically responsive; comprehensive; and likely to promote positive outcomes for all young children.

- Learning standards define what is to be taught and what kind of performance is expected. Standards provide guidance to curriculum developers and teachers about what and when to teach particular content.

- Effective approaches to planning early childhood curriculum include emergent curriculum, integrated curriculum, thematic/conceptual curriculum, webbing, the project approach, and scope and sequence.

- Curriculum models are idealized versions of what and how teaching and learning should occur. Frequently used comprehensive models include HighScope, Creative Curriculum, Core Knowledge, Tools of the Mind, and Connect4 Learning. Several focused curricula that address one content area or developmental domain have been found to be highly effective.

- The Reggio Emilia Approach originating in Italy is a comprehensive approach to early education, including key tenets, the Image of the Child, and 100 Languages of Children, that has inspired programs throughout the world.

- A child-centered model of curriculum planning draws on content knowledge, conceptual organizers, knowledge of child development, and developmental and learning continua. All four dimensions of the model occur in and are influenced by sociocultural contexts.

Key Terms

- conceptual organizer
- content standards
- curriculum
- curriculum approach
- curriculum framework
- curriculum model
- developmental continuum
- emergent curriculum
- fidelity
- idea webbing
- learning continuum, learning trajectory, or learning path
- learning standards
- performance standards
- project
- project approach
- scope
- sequence
- thematic curriculum
- validated curriculum

Readings and Websites

Helm, J. H., & Katz, L. G. (2016). *Young investigators: The Project Approach in the early years* (expanded 3rd ed). New York: Teachers College Press.

Collick, H. B., Bohart, H., & Charner, K. (2016). *Spotlight on young children: Teaching and learning in the primary grades*. Washington, DC: National Association for the Education of Young Children.

Moravcik, E., & Nolte, S. (2018). *Meaningful curriculum for young children* (2nd ed.). New York: Pearson.

Puerling, B. (2018). *Teaching in the digital age for preschool and kindergarten: Enhancing curriculum with technology*. St. Paul, MN: Redleaf Press.

Common Core State Standards Initiative

On this website, you will find complete copies of the Common Core standards, an interactive map of state adoptions, answers to frequently asked questions, and responses to commonly-held myths about the initiative.

Edutopia

Sponsored by the George Lucas Educational Foundation, Edutopia's website contains innovative resources to implement project-based learning, social and emotional learning, comprehensive assessment, integrated curriculum, and effective use of technology.

Head Start Early Childhood Early Learning and Knowledge Center (ECLKC)

This website provides a wealth of resources on research-based curriculum and teaching for young children, including videos, webinars, and curriculum alignment with the Head Start Early Learning Outcomes Framework (ELOF). An outstanding app, ELOF2Go, is available with examples of teaching practices.

Project Approach

Visit this website, directed by Sylvia Chard, to find resources for using the project approach, including rich project examples for pre-K to grade 12 and a free downloadable study guide.

Reggio Children

Reggio Children—International Center for the Defense and Promotion of the Rights and Potentials of All Children, is the official organization in Reggio Emilia, Italy, that manages educational and cultural exchange between the early childhood institutions of Reggio Emilia and educators and researchers around the world. Its website provides access to publications and other resources produced in Italy and information about visiting delegations.

Shared Writing 10.1

Developing Effective Curriculum

11

Assessing Children's Learning and Development

Learning Outcomes

After studying this chapter, you should be able to:

11.1 Define the language of assessment.

11.2 Identify purposes for assessing young children.

11.3 Describe the most important indicators of effective assessment.

11.4 Apply effective strategies for gathering and recording evidence to support learning and development.

11.5 Explain and evaluate standardized testing.

Related NAEYC Professional Preparation Standard

The NAEYC Professional Preparation Standards (NAEYC, 2011) that apply to this chapter are:

3: Observing, Documenting, and Assessing to Support Young Children and Families
Key elements:
3a. Understanding the goals, benefits, and uses of assessment
3b. Knowing about and using observation, documentation, and other appropriate assessment tools and approaches
3c. Understanding and practicing responsible assessment to promote positive outcomes for each child
3d. Knowing about assessment partnerships with families and with professional colleagues

Case Study

First-grade teacher Bonnie Kinsela begins every day with group meeting. She reads a story and calls on children to check their understanding of the story. Then she and her students discuss their day. Today, Bonnie makes short notes and a few checkmarks on her clipboard as the children transition to their literacy centers. She notes that Alexi and Nassim are able to answer questions about key details in the story. This is one of the Common Core standards, and Alexi and Nassim have not previously demonstrated this ability. She is pleased, and wonders if this is because they followed this particular story or if their listening comprehension has improved. She makes a note to observe this skill again.

Literacy block follows. Bonnie finds herself intensely engaged in a cycle of assessment and instruction, working with some children individually and others in small groups. Bonnie takes notes about each child as she observes one group writing a play. She uses her iPad to take photos of an in-progress poem that Ariana is writing, uploads it to the online assessment site, and shares it with Ariana's parents via an information sharing app. She'll use this example for Ariana's portfolio and share it at the next Professional Learning Community (PLC) meeting. The kindergarten teachers requested examples of the kinds of creative writing the first-graders are doing to help them adapt some experiences for their writing centers.

Approaching the listening center, Bonnie notices that Bella and Cal are arguing over the headphones. Cal becomes angry, unplugs the headphones, and raises them over his head, about to throw them. He then lowers them and looks to Bonnie for assistance. She draws the children's attention to the visual schedule in the center and helps them plan when each has a turn. Both children calm down. Bonnie is grateful that their school district has integrated social–emotional assessment scales into ongoing assessment tools. Cal has made great progress in developing emotion regulation and executive function skills, including impulse control. The assessment scale has helped Bonnie understand the gains he has made and how he can continue to grow in this regard. She jots a note that Cal resisted the urge to throw the headphones and instead looked for help in this situation. Bonnie will later enter this anecdotal note about Cal's executive function skills into his assessment profile and send a message about his progress in managing his impulses to his parents through the information sharing app on her phone.

After listening to two groups in guided reading, Bonnie calls Devin and Egan over for reading. Devin has a diagnosis of autism spectrum disorder (ASD) and has an IEP to help meet his educational needs. Devin sounds out words and reads aloud well; however, he has trouble comprehending meaning in the text. Egan is his best friend, and Devin listens well and follows Egan's lead for reading time. Devin's annual IEP review meeting is approaching, and Bonnie wants to make certain she has data that represents Devin's literacy progress and ongoing needs. Last week, she used a standardized tool to assess Devin's reading comprehension, but now she wants to assess his supported level of comprehension. She suspects that Devin will demonstrate better comprehension when reading high-interest content with a supportive peer. Using her iPad, Connie tapes the session to share a clip with his parents before the IEP meeting. The boys have a great interactive reading session, and Devin demonstrates higher-level skills than on the standardized measure. Both are valuable data, but Bonnie is pleased that she is able to show the higher edges of Devin's ability.

Over the course of the literacy block, children engage in rhyming games at the writing center. Although their interactions are sometimes silly and need a bit of redirection to complete their work, Bonnie observes that the children produce some high-level rhyme and rhythmic patterns. Her poetry unit is scheduled for later in the year, but it seems as though the children's interest is peaked now. Bonnie decides to modify her teaching plan to capitalize on children's interests.■

B onnie's school is in its second year using the Common Core to guide instruction. This means making sure that all her first-graders meet literacy standards for reading, writing, and language. Sometimes the work related to tracking and addressing the standards can seem overwhelming. However, Bonnie also finds that the structure helps her ensure that she is addressing all of the important literacy needs of first-graders.

Accurate assessment of children's learning and development is a vital component of effective practice in early childhood education. The profession has a long history of studying children, and observation of young children is essential to providing developmentally appropriate practice (Cohen, Balaban, Gropper & Stern, 2016). To a large extent, early childhood education has grown because research based on assessments of children's learning has found that high-quality programs have positive, lasting effects on children's development. The closely related field of early intervention is steeped in the necessity for and value of assessment for educating children with special needs. The school accountability movement and federal policies, including the Every Student Succeeds Act, place considerable emphasis on testing in the early years of school to ensure all children achieve reading and mathematics skills.

The goal of this chapter is to prepare you to achieve the most important purpose of assessment: to improve children's learning and development. If children are to benefit fully from early childhood programs, intentional teachers must know why, what, and how to assess. Like many other areas of education, assessment has its own—sometimes bewildering—vocabulary and jargon. We begin by helping you learn the language of assessment. Then we discuss four fundamental purposes of assessment and connect these to various tools and procedures. We present indicators of effective assessment. The chapter concludes with a discussion of appropriate and inappropriate uses of standardized tests and of program evaluation and accountability.

Learning the Language of Assessment

The first step in understanding and using assessment appropriately and accurately is for teachers to acquire the vocabulary of assessment. As teachers become more experienced in using various assessment methods and tools, their knowledge of assessment—their *assessment literacy*—grows and deepens. Broadly defined, assessment is the ongoing process of gathering evidence of children's learning and development, then organizing and interpreting the information in order to make informed decisions about instructional practice (McAfee & Leong, 2015). Evidence is an outward sign or indication of children's learning, such as their response to a question or their solution to a problem (McAfee & Leong, 2015). Therefore, assessment involves using multiple sources of evidence systematically collected over time, from which professionals make judgments about specific actions to take on behalf of children.

> **evidence** An outward sign or indication of children's learning, such as their response to a question or their solution to a problem.

Each of the many different types of assessment has various implications for how and when it is conducted. We begin by describing assessment in its broadest terms—formative and summative—and then describe more specific types of assessments.

Formative and Summative Assessment

Formative assessment is the process of gathering information about children and using it to plan effective and individualized instruction (Mindes & Jung, 2015). The information obtained from formative assessment helps *form* the next steps in the teaching and learning process. In practice, formative assessment is so closely linked to teaching and curriculum that teachers may not even recognize it as assessment.

> **formative assessment** The process of gathering information about children and using it to plan effective and individualized instruction.

At the end of an educational experience, student progress is assessed using a summative assessment, which *sums up*, or evaluates, the effectiveness of an experience after it concludes. Evaluation is the process of making a judgment about assessment results, and is frequently considered the last step in assessment (McAfee & Leong, 2015). In a college English course, for example, the instructor's feedback on student essays is formative assessment, whereas the final exam is summative. In Bonnie's classroom, the assessments she completes to determine Devin's reading level is formative. She and the IEP team will use it to determine how to tailor reading instruction for him. Bonnie will complete an additional summative assessment at the end of the school year for Devin when she completes the end-of-year progress.

> **summative assessment** Assessing student learning at the end of an educational experience to evaluate the effectiveness of the experience.

> **evaluation** The process of making a judgment about assessment results; frequently considered the last step in assessment.

Informal and Formal Assessments

Assessments are often identified as informal or formal. Informal assessment refers to information that is gathered for teachers' use to make everyday classroom decisions or adjustments to teaching (McAfee & Leong, 2015). For instance, while reading a storybook to her preschool class, Abby Cosgrove observes that some children are listening intently while others are clearly uninterested and not following the story. She uses this informal observation of children's cues to quickly adapt her behavior. "This is a very long story," she says. "I will finish reading it during choice time if you want to hear the rest. Right now, let's all reach for the sky … turn around … touch the ground … and sit down." As Abby slowly gives each direction, all of the children become engaged in the physical movement and return their attention to her. "Now who has a song for us to sing?" In this example, Abby used her informal assessment of the children to adapt her teaching and engage them in the learning process.

> **informal assessment** Gathering information for teacher's use to make everyday classroom decisions or adjustments to teaching.

formal assessment Assessment that follows a specific procedure and uses a specially designed instrument or tool.

curriculum-embedded assessment Formative assessment that is integrated into the curriculum; this assessment does not occur as a separate procedure.

A formal assessment is an assessment that follows a specific procedure and uses a specially designed instrument or tool. Teachers often use such assessments to report results to others, especially when reporting current skills levels and progress during IEP meetings. Formal assessments include structured child observations or assessments that produce specific scores. In contrast to informal assessment, the formal assessment is also used to describe any method of gathering information that is standardized, a topic discussed later in this chapter.

Observation

Observation of children's behavior and development is the most important and frequently used assessment strategy. Observation can be used for both formative and summative evaluation, informal or formal. Teachers observe informally on a daily basis as part of the instructional process, and they also assess children formally using rigorously designed observational tools. Bonnie utilized a variety of strategies to record observations throughout the vignette, including taking notes, photographs, and work sampling.

One type of formative assessment is curriculum-embedded assessment, which is based on teacher observation that is integrated into the curriculum and not conducted as a separate procedure. The teacher assesses the children while teaching using the classroom activity itself—for example, when a teacher listens to children describe their reasoning or watches them write. A similar formative assessment strategy is play-based assessment, in which the context for observing and interacting with children is the children's play. Most infant and toddler and some preschool assessments, such as the *Hawaii Early Learning Profile* (Parks & Vort Corporation, 1994) take place while the child plays and the assessor observes which skills the child demonstrates.

Performance Assessment

Performance assessment, also known as authentic assessment, is used to determine what children know and can do from their demonstration of a skill or their creation of a product. Consider, for instance, how figure skaters are judged on the basis of their skating *performance*, not on whether they can draw a skating maneuver or write a description of how to do a triple axel.

For children, authentic assessment engages them in tasks that occur in real-life contexts, whether in the classroom or on the playground, or in situations as close as possible to that context. For example, to assess children's reading ability, a teacher listens to them read aloud rather than giving them a multiple-choice test. Assessments such as this, which call for a child to produce a response rather than select from a list of possible responses, are also called alternative assessments.

Dynamic Assessment

Based on Vygotsky's concept of the zone of proximal development, dynamic assessment analyzes a child's performance not just in terms of what the child can do independently, as most assessment procedures require, but what the child can do with the assistance of a teacher or peer (Mindes & Jung, 2015). A teacher may provide prompts, cues, hints, or questions that elicit a child's response. Analyzing the amount and kind of assistance the child needs to perform a task provides information about the child's current level of understanding and skill, and also guides the next steps in teaching (McAfee & Leong, 2015). Bonnie engaged Devin in a kind of dynamic assessment while he engaged in a reading task with his best friend, Egan.

Video Example 11.1:

Assessing to Meet the Needs of All Learners

In this video, a curriculum specialist discusses how to meet the needs of all learners by using formative assessment, a screening tool, and strategic use of classroom materials. Why do you think a comprehensive approach to assessment such as this is valuable? What is the role of families in this process?

play-based assessment Similar to curriculum-embedded assessment, but the context for observing and interacting with children is the children's play.

Accurate assessment is essential for effective practice. Intentional teachers observe children and gather information about their learning and development to plan curriculum and adapt their teaching.

Standardized Testing

Many people hear the word *assessment* and automatically think of testing. Standardized assessment refers to the assessment of all children, using the same procedures and performing the same task under the same conditions. The thought behind standardizing procedures is that it leads to less biased and more objective results.

Although assessment is sometimes used as a synonym for testing, testing is only one part of the larger concept of assessment. Testing is a systematic procedure for evaluating a child's behavior and knowledge, which results in the assignment of a score (McAfee & Leong, 2015). Therefore, a test is a snapshot of a child's performance or knowledge that is administered to an individual or group under controlled conditions. Some tests are teacher developed, whereas others are developed by researchers or test publishing companies. Some, but not all, commercially published tests are standardized.

Standardized testing uses prescribed methods for administering and scoring, and needs to meet technical standards for educational and psychological testing (American Educational Research Association, American Psychological Association & National Council on Measurement in Education, 2014). These standards are designed to ensure that tests have high levels of reliability and validity.

Reliability Reliability is the extent to which the results obtained from a test are accurate and consistent over time. A test is said to be reliable if the tool is likely to get the same or similar results when used by different people or on different days. To understand the concept of reliability, consider an example unrelated to education: measuring cooking ingredients. If a recipe calls for 1 cup of flour, even a beginning cook would reach for a standard, 8-ounce measuring cup. If one cook used a demitasse cup, another chose a giant-size coffee mug, and another filled a tea cup half full, the final results would vary considerably. The standard measuring cup, therefore, is reliable, whereas the other cup selections are not.

Validity Validity means that the instrument measures what it purports to measure. For example, a test designed to measure children's physical skills should not depend on children's ability to understand verbal directions; in such a case, the test is really a measure of the children's language.

In revisiting our cooking example, suppose we are trying to measure volume. There are a number of ways to measure volume, such as using a liquid measuring cup or an 8-ounce standard cup, which would yield an equally accurate amount of flour for a recipe. However, if we tried to measure flour with a yardstick, which is for measuring length, the results would be not only messy but also inaccurate and therefore lacking validity. If a standardized test lacks reliability or validity, the results it yields are meaningless.

Types of Standardized Tests

In addition to reliability and validity, standardized tests involve one of two ways of scoring. They may be either norm referenced or criterion referenced.

Criterion-Referenced Tests Criterion-referenced tests compare a person's score to a predetermined level of performance. They are designed to measure how well an individual has learned a specific body of knowledge and skills (Mindes & Jung, 2015). Third-grade standardized achievement tests administered by state departments of education are criterion-referenced tests. The criterion for passing is a preset number of correct answers, which presumably represents how much a child has learned. Similarly, the SAT test is a criterion-referenced test, with different colleges setting the cut-off score, or criterion, needed for admission.

performance assessment or authentic assessment Determines what children know and can do from their demonstration of a skill or their creation of a product.

authentic assessment Determines what children know and can do from their demonstration of a skill or their creation of a product.

dynamic assessment Analyzes a child's performance not just in terms of what the child can do independently, but what the child can do with the assistance of a teacher or peer.

standardized assessment Assessment of all children using the same procedures and performing the same task under the same conditions.

testing A systematic procedure for evaluating a child's behavior and knowledge that is then assigned a score.

standardized testing Uses prescribed methods for administering and scoring.

reliability The extent to which the results obtained from a test are accurate and consistent over time.

validity The degree to which an instrument measures what it purports to measure.

criterion-referenced tests Tests that compare a person's score to a predetermined level of performance.

norm-referenced tests Tests that compare an individual's score to that of other test takers.

Norm-Referenced Tests By contrast, **norm-referenced tests** compare an individual's score to that of other test takers—who knows the most and who the least? Scores are reported by percentage rank, with half scoring above and half scoring below the midpoint or average (Great Schools Partnership, 2015). Many school-administered tests are norm referenced. For example, screening or diagnostic tests used in the process of identifying children's special needs compare children's scores to that of other children to determine if their development is within the typical, or "normal," range.

Norm-referenced tests are developed by giving the tests to large numbers of children and comparing their scores. These tests result in a distribution of scores that look like a bell, or **normal curve**, with most people scoring at the midrange and fewer scoring at the higher and lower ends. For example, on a hypothetical vocabulary test of 4-year-olds, most children's vocabulary might average about 1,200 words, whereas some know as many as 2,500 and others know as few as 400.

normal curve A distribution of scores that looks like a bell shape, with most people scoring at the midrange and fewer scoring at the higher and lower ends.

In administering a norm-referenced test, it is essential to know the characteristics of the group used to develop the norms—that is, the *norming group*. In the vocabulary test example, the norming group consists of the thousands of 4-year-olds whose vocabularies were measured. If a norm-referenced test is used, the administrator needs to consider the composition of the norming group in terms of gender, ethnicity, age, socioeconomic background, culture, language, and inclusion of children with disabilities. If the norming group differs a great deal from the group of children with whom the test will be used, the results may not be accurate or reliable. For example, if a vocabulary test designed to identify language delays were given to a child who is learning English, the result might indicate a learning problem where none actually exists.

The language of assessment is complex. In practice, terminology is often misused or used inconsistently. Teachers need to be clear about the concepts underlying the words; they need to become assessment literate. Now that we have established a common vocabulary with which to discuss assessment, in the next section, we describe fundamental purposes of assessment.

✔ Check Your Understanding 11.1

Purposes of Assessment

Before engaging in any form of assessment, teachers need to ask, "What is the purpose of the assessment?" The answer to this question determines all aspects of how the assessment will be conducted, including:

- Who is to be assessed
- What is to be measured and with what tool
- Who will conduct the assessment and when
- What technical requirements are needed for the assessment
- How the results will be interpreted and used

In early childhood programs, the four basic purposes of assessment are (1) to improve teaching and learning, (2) to identify children with special learning or developmental needs, (3) to evaluate programs, and (4) to demonstrate accountability (National Research Council [NRC], 2008). First, we discuss these purposes, then we give examples of informal and formal assessments related to them.

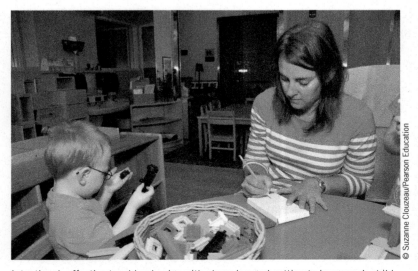

Intentional, effective teaching begins with observing and getting to know each child.

© Suzanne Clouzeau/Pearson Education

Assessing to Improve Teaching and Learning

Effective teaching cannot occur without ongoing assessment. The first step in developmentally appropriate practice—*meeting the learner,* or monitoring children's progress—requires assessment. Consider the following examples of how teachers use the information they gather to make decisions about curriculum planning and teaching:

> In David Billings's preschool class, there is a curricular focus on social–emotional learning and developing beginning executive function skills. David observes the children while they play together in learning centers. He notices that many children are not yet able to articulate when they need help with a task, so they flit from learning center to learning center instead of persevering through challenges such as a falling block tower. David adjusts his lesson planning to include opportunities to explicitly teach how to ask for help and problem-solving strategies with his students.
>
> Margie Wasky regularly monitors whether her second-graders comprehend what they read. She discovers a few children who read fast but can't accurately answer questions about the passages they read. She has these children read aloud to each other in pairs, and finds that reading more slowly with expression to a partner improves their understanding of what they've read.

In these examples, we see that planning and adapting curriculum and teaching practices requires ongoing assessment. These teachers assessed children's learning by observing and documenting, and then reflecting on and interpreting the information. They then adapted their teaching and planned curriculum accordingly. Although we address teaching, curriculum, and assessment in separate chapters in this book, in reality, they are integrally connected. What happens in one area influences and is influenced by what happens in the others, as depicted in Figure 11.1.

 Application Exercise 11.1

Figure 11.1: Cycle of Assessment, Teaching, and Curriculum

Many schools use systematic, ongoing assessment as an integral part of three-tiered-models of instruction, such as Response to Intervention (RTI), which we describe in Chapter 5. In this framework, children's learning is assessed regularly and teaching adapted accordingly. Based on assessment data, some children receive more individualized instruction in reading and mathematics or other areas; a few children receive highly individualized interventions (McInerney & Elledge, 2013).

Teachers are the primary assessors as well as the primary audiences for classroom assessment. In early childhood, much classroom assessment is informal and performance-based, relying heavily on teacher observations. Because everyday decisions are not high-stakes and are easily corrected, classroom assessment does not need to meet technical standards for reliability and validity. For instance, after David teaches small group lessons about asking for help, he observes that Jamal and Sarah still aren't using words to ask for help. David works with them one on one in learning centers throughout the

FIGURE 11.1 Cycle of Assessment, Teaching, and Curriculum
Effective curriculum and teaching depend on systematic, ongoing assessment, as depicted in this cycle.

week, coaching them on how to ask for help when Sarah's tower falls down and she leaves the block area, and when Jamal gets stuck trying to put on the mail carrier costume in dramatic play.

Nevertheless, teacher observations and judgments can be unreliable, invalid, or biased. This is why teachers need to use many sources of information. They should observe children in different situations over time, rather than base their conclusions about children's ability on one encounter. Intentional teaching depends on accurate assessment tools, which we discuss later in this chapter.

Identifying Children with Special Learning or Developmental Needs

screening tests Tests administered to all children, usually in preschool or kindergarten, as the first step in a process to determine which children are at risk of a possible disability or learning problem; also called *developmental screening.*

This purpose of assessment encompasses routine checks for vision, hearing, and immunization to ensure healthy development as well as identification of physical, cognitive, or emotional disabilities. Regular health checks by physicians beginning at birth may also uncover possible disabilities or special needs. If undetected, vision and hearing problems can have long-term consequences for children's learning, so early health screenings are essential for every child.

Because the benefits of early intervention are well established, professionals have an ethical as well as a legal responsibility to accurately identify young children with special needs and help them access appropriate services (Division for Early Childhood [DEC], 2014). These decisions have lasting consequences for individual children; therefore, the instruments used need to meet high standards of reliability and validity (McAfee & Leong, 2015). Screening and diagnostic tests are used as part of a two-step process of identifying children who may have disabilities or special learning or developmental needs.

Screening Screening tests, also called *developmental screening*, are administered to all children, usually in preschool or kindergarten, as the first step in a process to determine which children are at risk of a possible disability or learning problem. Teachers or other professionals administer these brief tests, which include general items on motor development, perception, language, and cognitive development. A screening test is like the toy screen used in a sandbox; most of the grains of sand will pass through readily, but a few will be left for closer inspection. In many preschools and child care programs, screening is a well-established rite of fall. Sometimes, the need arises to screen a child based on a particular set of concerns. For example, The *Modified Checklist for Autism in Toddlers, Revised with Follow Up* (M-CHAT R/F (Robins, Fein, & Barton, 2009) is an open source (i.e., freely available on the internet) list of questions that screens for autism symptom disorders in toddlers.

The process is not foolproof, and some children may have problems that go undetected. Therefore, teachers and families play a critical role in contributing information to the screening and identification process. Information on a child's functioning should be drawn from multiple sources and include family members in

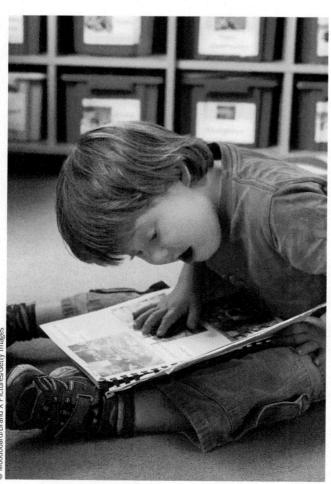

One of the most important purposes of assessment consists of screening and identification of children with special needs. To ensure accurate diagnosis and services, valid and reliable measures must be used along with information from parents and teachers.

the screening process (DEC, 2014). As teachers assess children's progress on a daily basis, they may obtain information that raises concerns that formal screening may confirm or deny. Those few children who do not pass the initial screening may or may not have a more serious condition; to make this determination, diagnostic testing is required (DEC, 2014).

Diagnostic Testing Diagnostic tests are designed to gather information to identify the specific learning or developmental delays a child may have and to plan educational interventions. The second part of the two-step process is a complete diagnostic evaluation designed to identify the child's areas of need and strength, to prepare individualized goals, and to plan activities and supports. Multiple sources of information are used, such as medical evaluations, standardized tests, and teacher and parent observations in authentic contexts. The Division for Early Childhood (2014) recommends that assessment for children with disabilities include input from the family and address children's interests, needs, and personal characteristics in addition to intellectual and ability testing. Furthermore, testing should be done in the child's dominant language, and should consider other cultural factors. Diagnostic tests require specialized training to administer and interpret, and are therefore given by developmental pediatricians, neurologists, psychiatrists, neuropsychologists, school psychologists, speech pathologists, and/or therapists.

> **diagnostic tests** Tests designed to identify the specific learning or developmental problems a child has and to plan interventions; must be administered by specially trained professionals.

For the first two purposes of assessment—to support learning and identify children with special needs—the target of assessment is the individual child. Next we turn to assessment purposes, for which information is gathered on groups of children.

Evaluating Program Quality

Program evaluation is the process of gathering information about the quality of the classroom and its effects to determine whether the program is achieving its goals and objectives. Observational instruments that are often used to evaluate the quality of children's experiences are the *Early Childhood Environment Rating Scales* for infants, toddlers, preschoolers, and school-agers (Harms, Clifford, & Cryer, 2014) and the *Classroom Assessment Scoring System* for infant and toddler classrooms through primary grades (Pianta, La Paro, & Hamre, 2008; Hamre, La Paro, Pianta & LaCasole-Crouch, 2014). These tools are frequently used to evaluate the quality of programs as part of state Quality Rating and Improvement Systems and in Early Head Start, Head Start, and public prekindergarten.

> **program evaluation** The process of gathering information about a program's quality and effectiveness.

Some types of program evaluation such as licensing or accreditation may not require information about children's performance. Increasingly, however, program evaluation includes data on child outcomes—how well the group of children as a whole is achieving the goals of the program. The results of assessment for program evaluation are usually *aggregated*; that is, they are combined and reported as total scores for the group rather than scores attached to individual children.

The audience for program evaluation data is usually policy makers or funders who want to know if a program represents a cost-effective use of public or private dollars. Although stakeholders need accurate program evaluation data for future decision making, the stakes for such assessment are not as high as for accountability assessment.

Video Example 11.2:

Identifying Children with Special Needs

In this video, an early childhood special educator discusses assessment of children for the purpose of identification and referral to diagnostic services. What key components does she emphasize? And how do these processes differ from assessment for other purposes?

Assessing for Accountability

Closely related to program evaluation, assessment for accountability is, by definition, high-stakes testing. Accountability is "holding teachers, schools, or programs responsible for meeting a required level of performance" (McAfee & Leong, 2015).

Accountability requirements often specify what children should know and be able to do based on state learning standards. The audiences for accountability data include federal, state, and local policy makers; parents; administrators; and the general tax-paying public.

As we discussed earlier, the stakes attached to accountability testing are high. By the same token, holding schools accountable can lead to more attention being focused on the children who need it and on improvements in teaching and learning; however, this has not always been the outcome (Au, 2007). The standards for accuracy of accountability testing must be extremely rigorous because scores are attached to individuals—children and teachers—rather than a group or program (NRC, 2008).

Connecting Purposes and Types of Assessment

As we have seen, each of the four purposes of assessment demands various types of tools and procedures. Given that all effective assessment decisions require multiple sources of information, teachers need to know which kinds of assessment are most effective for which purposes. Table 11.1 provides examples of formal and informal assessment tools appropriate for each of the four purposes.

Using assessment tools for the right purpose is essential. However, other important indicators of effective assessment exist and are described in the next section.

TABLE 11.1 Matching Purpose and Types of Assessment

Each type of assessment has specific purposes. To yield accurate results, assessment tools must be used for the purposes for which they were developed.

Purpose	Types of Assessment	
	Formal	Informal
To monitor children's progress and make decisions about teaching and learning	Published, validated observation tools and rating scales; criterion-referenced achievement tests	Observation; interviews, analysis of work samples; teacher-made tests and procedures
To identify children who may have special needs	Developmental screening tests to be followed by diagnostic evaluation for those identified; norm-referenced standardized tests with high reliability and validity	Structured observation of behavior and performance by teachers; information from parents
Program evaluation	Validated observational measures of classroom quality and teacher–child interactions; criterion-referenced tests for samples of children keyed to program goals	Surveys of children, teachers, and parents; data collected by teachers from informal classroom assessments including observations, performance assessments, and portfolios
Accountability	Criterion-referenced standardized achievement tests	Data collected by teachers from informal classroom assessments including observations, performance assessments, and portfolios

Source: Adapted from T. W. Hills, 1992. Reaching potentials through appropriate assessment, 43–63, in S. Bredekamp and T. Rosegrant (Eds.), *Reaching potentials: Appropriate curriculum and assessment for young children, Vol. 1.* Washington, DC: NAEYC. Reprinted with permission from the National Association for the Education of Young Children.

Check Your Understanding 11.2

Indicators of Effective Assessment

According to the NAEYC and the National Association of Early Childhood Specialists in State Departments of Education (NAECS–SDE) (2003), ethical, appropriate, valid, and reliable assessment is a central part of early childhood education. These professional associations call for assessment methods that are "developmentally appropriate, culturally and linguistically responsive, tied to children's daily activities, supported by professional development for teachers, inclusive of families, and connected to beneficial purposes" (NAEYC & NAECS–SDE, 2003, p. 2). NAEYC's Code of Ethical Conduct (2011) states that the goal of assessment should be to benefit children by making sound decisions about teaching and learning, providing access to intervention services, or improving the quality of the program.

Early childhood professional organizations have established guidelines for effective assessment and evaluation (DEC, 2014; NAEYC & NAECS–SDE, 2003). Key indicators of effective assessment practices are described in Table 11.2. To implement these assessment practices, teachers need to understand the implications for assessing very young children, Dual language learners, and children with special needs, discussed in the sections that follow.

Developmentally Appropriate Assessment

Most parents, grandparents, and teachers would agree with the statement, "Young children are not good test takers." But why is this statement a truism? Sound assessment of young children is difficult for several reasons: (1) the nature of typical child development, (2) children's sensitivity to context, and (3) their lack of motivation, as well as (4) their inability to perform many of the tasks required by traditional assessments (McAfee & Leong, 2015). For assessment to be developmentally appropriate, each of these factors must be taken into consideration.

The Nature of Child Development Many of the characteristics of young children make it difficult to obtain trustworthy assessment information. Children's development is rapid, uneven, and embedded in their own cultural and linguistic contexts (Arnett & Maynard, 2017). For example, 2½-year-old Brian barely said a word at child care, and then one day he got so excited about the new set of trucks that he couldn't stop talking. Four-year-old Wyatt spent all day showing off how he could balance on one foot, but when his aunt arrived to pick him up, he refused to demonstrate this newly acquired skill.

Young children's development and learning is marked by spurts and plateaus (McAfee & Leong, 2015). For months, 6-year-old Aura struggled during language arts period. Then in March, she seemed to have an "ah-ha" moment. She stopped guessing at words she didn't know and began really reading for the first time. At times, children's development may even go backward. Three-year-old Jacob seemed to have thoroughly mastered the potty until his baby sister was born, then he started having accidents every day.

Children's progress is also uneven across different developmental areas. Five-year-old Claudio has the vocabulary of an 8-year-old and can read at the second-grade level, but he struggles to regulate his emotions and is aggressive when frustrated. If only Claudio's reading skills were assessed, we would have a skewed picture of his school performance.

Language development is also a work in progress during early childhood. Most types of assessment require that children understand directions, know particular vocabulary words, or be understood by an adult, perhaps even a relative stranger. Limited language skills can easily interfere with obtaining an accurate picture of children's competence. Accurate assessment of children who are learning two languages raises an additional set of concerns, which are addressed later in this chapter.

TABLE 11.2 Effective Assessment Practices

Due to the power of assessment results to effect children's lives, assessment practices must meet high professional standards, as described in this table.

Indicators	Key Considerations
Ethical principles guide assessment practices.	Children should never be denied opportunities or services on the basis of assessment. Decisions should never be made on the basis of a single assessment or test score. Assessment findings should remain confidential.
Assessment instruments are used for their intended purposes.	Using a measure for a different purpose inevitably invalidates the results. For example, a developmental screening test should be used as the first step in an identification process, not as a measure of kindergarten readiness.
Assessments are appropriate for the ages and other characteristics of children being assessed.	Assessments should be used with groups of children who are similar to the group with which the measure was validated in terms of age, culture, home language, socioeconomic status, and abilities and disabilities.
Assessment instruments comply with professional criteria for quality.	Test development must meet technical guidelines for reliability and validity.
What is assessed is developmentally and educationally significant.	Because assessment takes up considerable time and resources, it should address the important learning goals and standards that are emphasized in the curriculum.
Assessment evidence is used to understand and improve learning.	Good assessment teaches teachers about children. That knowledge is used to individualize instruction or adapt curriculum; otherwise, teachers' and children's time and effort are wasted.
Assessment evidence is gathered in realistic settings and situations that reflect children's actual performance.	This indicator calls for authentic performance assessment based on the results of teachers' observations of children in context, in interviews, and on collections of children's work.
Assessments use multiple sources of evidence gathered over time.	Repeated, systematic observation, documentation, and other forms of criterion- or performance-based assessment are needed to accurately assess young children.
Screening is always linked to follow-up.	When screening or informal assessment indicates a possible problem, referral to specialists for diagnostic assessment follows. Labeling a child as having a disability is never made on the basis of a brief screening or one-time assessment.
Use of individually administered, norm-referenced tests is limited.	Formal, standardized, and norm-referenced tests are beneficial as part of the process of identification and diagnosis of special needs.
Professionals and families are knowledgeable about assessment.	Teachers as well as families see assessment as a tool to improve outcomes for children. Parents are not simply audiences; they are important sources of information about children's capabilities at home and in the community.

Source: National Association for the Education of Young Children and National Association of Early Childhood Specialists in State Departments of Education, 2003. *Early Childhood Curriculum, Assessment, and Program Evaluation: Building an Effective, Accountable System in Programs for Children Birth through Age 8.* Joint Position Statement. Washington, DC: NAEYC. Reprinted with permission from the National Association for the Education of Young Children (NAEYC). www.naeyc.org.

Children's Sensitivity to Context The context in which an assessment takes place, either informal or formal, can affect children's performance. Context includes the physical setting, whether in the classroom, home, or on the playground, and the social setting: one on one, small group, or whole group. A familiar context can serve to make children comfortable and relaxed, and more likely to perform naturally and do their best.

A strange or unfamiliar context, either in terms of the place or the people, can be distracting or even stressful. Consider Hugo, who is a relatively fearless 5-year-old. Because Hugo usually charges into new situations head first, his mother wasn't concerned about taking him to the community center for kindergarten readiness testing. But Hugo became so interested in seeing the other children and examining the lines on the floor of the basketball court that he didn't attend at all to the tasks the kindergarten teacher asked of him.

Context influences not only children's attention to the assessment task but also their actual performance. Young children behave differently at home than at family child care, the child care center, or school. Five-year-old Dolly goes to gymnastics with her mom and can do backflips and cartwheels, but when her teacher at school asks her to skip, Dolly says, "I don't know how." Perhaps Dolly didn't demonstrate her advanced physical skills at school because she didn't want to be different from the other children, but maybe she just wasn't interested in skipping. Motivation as well as context is a big factor in obtaining accurate assessment of young children.

The Role of Motivation   Assessment is "an adult's agenda" in which young children have little interest (Hills, 1992). Children are most likely to be motivated in situations that appeal to their interests and cultivate their curiosity, that offer choices of activities and materials, and that provide active involvement with other people. Many formal assessment procedures do not allow for any of these conditions. Young children are not interested in being assessed. They may be removed from the usual activity setting, and their movement, talk, and expression of feelings may be restricted (Hills, 1992). To counter these issues, play-based assessments are excellent assessment strategies for assessing young children's skills.

As children get older, they can reflect more on their performance and competence, and can be encouraged to do their best in an assessment situation (Hills, 1992). For some children, demonstrating their competence will become intrinsically motivating. In general, however, results will be more accurate if children's interests are taken into consideration. For example, second-grader Laticia loves stories about horses and reads these stories with more expression than she does other books.

A final developmental constraint on assessment is children's ability to perform the tasks required. Group-administered, paper-and-pencil tests are especially challenging for children before third grade (NAEYC & NAECS/SDE, 2003). They may not be able to follow the directions, and may not understand why the teacher can't help today. Some children may not have the fine-motor skill to fill in the bubble carefully, may generally operate at a slower pace than the others, or lack the executive function skills required to follow test directions or complete the test.

Characteristics of Developmentally Appropriate Assessment   Even a cursory discussion of typical child development characteristics leads to the conclusion that the younger the child, the more difficult it is to obtain an accurate assessment (Mindes & Jung, 2015). Therefore, assessment can be considered developmentally appropriate when it:

- Draws on multiple sources of evidence, especially observations by teachers and parents who can observe children's performance in various contexts over time. The NAEYC Code of Ethical Conduct (2011) holds the use of multiple sources of information as an ethical ideal.
- Occurs in a variety of situations representing children's typical range of activities, in the regular classroom or at home.
- Makes children feel comfortable, which means that they are assessed by familiar adults, or that parents or other known adults can stay with them.
- Accommodates children's rapid developmental changes. This doesn't mean that assessment consumes other important teaching and learning experiences, but rather that it occurs frequently and is embedded in children's ongoing experiences.
- Engages children's interest and is within their range of ability. For example, instead of requiring a child to circle the picture of four kittens, the item requires the child to count four toy plastic kittens, one for each of her friends.

© Pearson Education

Video Example 11.3:

Influences on Assessment

In this video, a first grade teacher provides an excellent example of factors that affect children's performance on assessments. What other issues might be at play? And what else could this teacher do to obtain accurate assessment information?

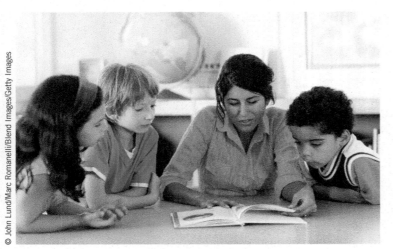

Accurate assessment of children whose home language is not English is difficult. Standardized tests are often not reliable. How can teachers get accurate information about the abilities of dual language learners?

Culturally and Linguistically Responsive Assessment

Developmentally appropriate assessment must be culturally and linguistically responsive (Regenstein, Connors, Romero-Jurado, & Weiner, 2018). One of the biggest challenges is serving the needs of dual language learners because, to some extent, all assessments of children are fundamentally measures of language ability (Espinosa, 2015; Michael-Luna, 2013). Children's ability to demonstrate their learning depends a great deal on their language capacity, both to understand the demands of the task and to respond either to a teacher's question or a written test. Although the role of language in assessment is relevant for all children, it is of special concern for children whose home language is not English.

In many instances, the only way to get a fully accurate picture of children's learning is to assess them in their home language. But even if valid and reliable assessment tools were available in multiple languages, which they are not, such assessments are not a foolproof solution. All languages, including English, have dialects, so translations do not always solve the problem. A child from Mexico and one from Peru may not understand the same Spanish translation of a test. Nonetheless, children should be assessed in their dominant language (usually home language for young children) and in other languages they are learning, Often, their language competence is found in the combination of their capacity in each language (Espinosa, 2015).

Determining whether a child is sufficiently proficient in English for accurate testing is also difficult. Academic language used in schools is quite different from the conversational language children use on a daily basis. Linguists estimate that it takes four to seven years to acquire proficiency in academic English (NASEM, 2017). A child may speak English well on the playground or in casual conversation, yet struggle with the language of an assessment. Because of this, it is especially important to include families in assessment of dual language learners. Some research suggests that parents are often more reliable reporters of their children's vocabulary learning than are teachers (Michael-Luna, 2013). The importance of linguistically appropriate assessment is illustrated in the feature *Language Lens: Involving Parents in Assessment of Dual Language Learners*.

Accurate assessment of dual language learners poses difficult challenges for teachers and educational leaders (Czik & Lewis, 2016). Children's language and prior knowledge are closely tied to their culture, yet assessment materials do not take into account culturally influenced variations in knowledge and skills. For example, a language assessment may ask children to identify items that are unique to U.S. culture, such as a hamburger. Inclusion of many such culturally biased items in a measure biases the outcome for individual children and misrepresents their abilities. High-stakes standardized testing is particularly problematic, as the following examples demonstrate.

Children's learning is a product of their experiences, which occur in cultural contexts. For example, a standardized test asks where to find a lion, and 4-year-old Omari replies, "In the park." His answer, accurate in his native Kenya, is marked incorrect because the correct answer in the test manual is "in the zoo." Such cultural influences exist within the United States as well. Consider a test item that asks children to point to a picture of a *swamp*. Imagine the blank stares of children living in New York City or rural Nebraska

Language Lens
Involving Parents in Assessment of Dual Language Learners

The only way to obtain an accurate, meaningful assessment of dual language learners' competence is to draw on many different sources of information. Teachers' observations and conversations with children are invaluable, but information gleaned from families is essential in determining dual language learners' proficiency in each language.

Most parents are good judges of their children's language ability, but many teachers are unsure of how to efficiently obtain the needed information. Following are interview questions for teachers to ask of parents to effectively involve parents in assessing their child's language. The interview would need to be conducted in the parents' home language or translated for them. Here are some of the important questions to include:

1. What name do you use for your child? How did you decide to give your child this name? Does this name have a particular meaning or translation?
2. What language(s) do you use to talk to your child? Who else does your child spend time with, and what language do they use?
3. Tell me your opinion about how well your child speaks each language. (The same questions would be asked about the home language and English.)
   (0) My child cannot speak (e.g., Spanish, Tagalog, etc.), has a few words or phrases, but cannot produce sentences (e.g., "I want cookies"). My child understands only a few words.
   (1) My child cannot speak _____, has a few words or phrases, but understands the general idea of what is being said.
   (2) My child has limited proficiency in _____ with grammatical errors and has limited vocabulary, but understands the general idea of what is being said.
   (3) My child has good proficiency in _____ with some grammatical errors, has some social and school vocabulary, and understands most of what is said.
   (4) My child has native-like proficiency in ____ with few grammatical errors, has good vocabulary, and understands most of what is said.
4. How much does your child use each language?
   (0) Never speaks (e.g., Spanish, Tagalog, English, etc.), never hears it.
   (1) Never speaks _____, hears it very little.
   (2) Speaks _____ a little, hears it sometimes.
   (3) Speaks _____ sometimes, hears it most of the time.
   (4) Speaks _____ all of the time, hears it all of the time.

Of course, there is much more teachers need to learn from parents about their children, such as their interests, routines, cultural preferences, and much more. But conducting an interview such as one described here, whether during a home visit before the school year begins or in writing, is an essential first step in getting to know a child who is learning more than one language and becoming the best possible teacher for that child.

Source: Based on P. O. Tabors and L. M. López, 2005. How can teachers and parents help young children become (and stay) bilingual? 14–16; V. F. Gutiérrez-Clellen, 2005. Assessment of English language learners: Challenges and strategies, 47–51. Both in *Head Start Bulletin: English Language Learners, Vol. 78*, Washington, DC: Head Start Bureau, Administration on Children, Youth and Families, U.S. Department of Health and Human Services.

when presented with such a request, compared to the nodding heads of those from parts of Florida or Louisiana. Omari's experience and its consequences are powerful reminders not only of the importance of using linguistically appropriate assessment tools but also the risks of high-stakes testing.

Individually Appropriate Assessment for Children with Special Needs

Young children with disabilities or special needs face a lifetime of being assessed. Federal laws govern how, when, and under what conditions children with disabilities are to be assessed, and how assessment information should be used by teachers in implementing individualized education plans and individualized family service plans. Furthermore, the Council for Exceptional Children's Division for Early Childhood (2014) has established recommended practices for screening, establishing eligibility for special education services, individualized planning, monitoring child progress, and assessing child outcomes for reporting. Ensuring that assessments are *individually appropriate* for all children may require accommodations or modifications to the tools or procedures used.

accommodations Changes in assessment procedures, materials, or setting to eliminate barriers related to the child's disability that might keep children from demonstrating their full capabilities.

Accommodations are changes in assessment procedures, materials, or setting to eliminate barriers related to the child's disability that might keep children from demonstrating their full capabilities (Batshaw, Roizen, & Lotrecchiano, 2013). Assessments for children with disabilities should take child's age and developmental level into account (DEC, 2014). A child with a physical disability might be allowed to answer questions verbally rather than in writing. A child with attention deficit/ hyperactivity disorder (ADHD) might be given more time or allowed to take a test in a separate place away from distractions.

modifications Changes in an assessment that alter what the assessment measures or what the results mean.

Modifications are changes in the assessment that alter what the assessment measures or what the results mean (Batshaw, et al, 2013). For example, rather than asking Jade, a child with special needs, to point to pictures of objects to measure her receptive vocabulary, her teacher talks with Jade as she plays with real toys and makes notes of which ones Jade names correctly.

The process of identifying children for special education services requires the use of many different sources of information, including standardized, norm-referenced tests. Even with these various sources, however, the wide use of standardized tests with children who have special needs is fraught with problems (McLoughlin, Lewis, & Kritikos, 2017). Because standardized tests are based on norms of typically developing children, the results are often not relevant or useful to the goals for a child who has a disability. It is important to use tools that are very sensitive to identify children's progress, as changes are sometimes small (DEC, 2014). Moreover, considerations needed to make assessment developmentally appropriate and authentic are even more important for children with special needs, such as learning about their functioning in multiple environments, including home, school, child care, and community (DEC, 2014).

Early childhood special educators strongly advocate a play-based approach to assessment that focuses on children's functional skills, the essential abilities needed to fulfill goals parents have for their children such as communicating, making friends, and learning self-help skills (Macy & Bagnato, 2010). Some assessment checklists for young children with developmental delays, such as the *Hawaii Early Learning Profile,* allow for parent and caregiver reports as well as direct observation and assessment tasks as potential sources of data for the assessment. As described earlier in this chapter, play-based assessment involves systematic observation of children's behavior and skills in the context of their play. The feature *Including All Children: Individually Appropriate Assessment Practices* discusses assessment practices for children with special needs.

With increased demands for demonstrating program effectiveness and accountability, teachers must be knowledgeable consumers of assessment information. It is usually the classroom teacher who must explain the results of testing to parents or children, and teachers themselves most often feel the pressure of testing and assessment. Nevertheless, teachers' most important use of assessment is to improve learning outcomes for children, as discussed next.

Including All Children
Individually Appropriate Assessment Practices

Individually appropriate assessment of young children with special needs requires that professionals and family members work together and respectfully share useful information. In the following contrasting scenarios, we see how important individually appropriate assessment practices are for children as well as their families:

The O'Briens' 4-year-old son, Dan, has been diagnosed as having developmental delays in language, cognitive, and social development. During a conference with his teacher, Ms. Blako, about Dan's progress, Mrs. O'Brien becomes increasingly discouraged as she is told once more what her child cannot do and that he is functioning at the 24-month level on a norm-referenced test. Ms. Blako explains that they will continue to work with Dan on colors, writing his first name, and counting to 20. Mr. O'Brien is frustrated because these are the same skills Dan has been working on all year. Mrs. O'Brien is concerned that Dan still isn't potty trained and doesn't seem to have friends. Ms. Blako smiles and suggests some good books on toilet training. The O'Briens leave feeling belittled, apprehensive, and concerned about Dan's remaining preschool year and pending transition to kindergarten.

In contrast, consider the conference between Larisha's mother, Tina, and the preschool teacher, Stephanie. Larisha, who has cerebral palsy, attends an inclusive preschool. The meeting is attended not only by Tina and Stephanie but also the physical therapist, speech-language pathologist, and psychologist, who all know Larisha and her family well. The purpose of the conference is to discuss what Larisha does well at home and at school, and to establish new goals for her. Stephanie shares the results of her observations of physical, language, social, and emotional skills that Larisha displayed during the last several months. Tina shares what she has observed Larisha doing at home. The team agrees that Larisha is showing impressive growth and is making progress toward full participation in all aspects of the

preschool day. They identify target skills in functional and pre-academic areas to work on with her over the next few months:

1. In the morning, sign in by writing her initials on the attendance board and put her things in her cubbie.
2. Initiate play with peers, not just her cousins at home.
3. Watch, listen, and participate in small and large group times, including singing songs and answering questions about stories and lessons. Larisha can sit in a supportive chair to stabilize her trunk (rather than on the carpet).
4. Pedal and steer a tricycle. The physical therapist agrees to modify the trike so Larisha can reach the pedals and grasp the handles better.
5. Recognize when she needs to use the restroom, notify the teacher, and complete toileting activities independently. Stephanie will provide information for how to work on this at home as well.

Tina says that her number-one priority is for Larisha to have friends, and the team agrees to include this as an area of focus. Tina leaves the conference feeling heard, valued, and inspired about Larisha's progress and her future skill development.

The difference between these two assessment scenarios is profound. Dan's parents were passive recipients of information. Dan's assessment focused solely on traditional academics rather than his overall development. This led to underestimating his skills as well as to setting goals that are of questionable value to his family.

In sharp contrast, Larisha's family is part of the team, providing valuable information about her development. Her teacher uses observational assessment, focusing on skills in all developmental domains—the skills that Larisha needs to function well in the classroom, on the playground, or at home. Both her teacher and her mother can use the assessment information to identify goals for Larisha's further development.

 Check Your Understanding 11.3

Video Example 11.4:

Learning to Observe

In this video, a teacher observes children at play regularly and intentionally. How might her observations influence her assessments of the children's learning progress and her planning for future instruction?

⬆ Observation and Recording to Improve Learning

Like every other aspect of intentional teaching, assessment engages teachers in professional decision making. They must decide what evidence is important to collect, as well as how and when to gather information. The process of gathering evidence of children's learning is also called *documenting,* and involves two kinds of decisions: (1) how to gather information about children, and (2) how to record the findings (McAfee & Leong, 2015). Thinking of these processes separately opens up more options for assessment, or more "windows" into children's learning (McAfee & Leong, 2015).

Observation is the most frequently used method of gathering information. However, there are many ways of recording findings from observation—among them, *anecdotal records, checklists,* or *rating scales*—that increase teachers' options for learning about children. In the sections that follow, we describe ways teachers can observe and collect information about children, then we describe various ways to record or document the information for later reflection and analysis.

Observing and Gathering Evidence

The most effective classroom assessment procedures need to be part of every teacher's repertoire. These include systematic observation, eliciting responses from children, collecting work products, and gathering information from family members and other adults (McAfee & Leong, 2015). We begin with observation, which is the foundation of effective, developmentally appropriate practice.

Keen observation skills are the most important assessment tool a teacher can develop and use. Effective teaching requires positive relationships and building on children's prior learning. Therefore, teachers must know as much as possible about children's strengths, needs, interests, temperament, typical behavior, and much more. Careful observation is the best way to get to know individual children, especially infants, toddlers, and young preschoolers who have limited ability to create products and communicate verbally. During preschool, kindergarten, and the primary grades, teachers continue to regularly observe children's interests, interactions, and performance of tasks to assess their skills and understanding as part of an overall assessment plan (Mindes & Jung, 2015). Since play is so central to young children's experiences, it is also an important context for assessing children's interests, interactions, and skills. In the feature *Promoting Play: Play as an Assessment Context,* read how one teacher uses play to assess and document children's progress, and applies the information to inform her teaching.

Accurate, objective observation can be quite difficult. Consider the fact that eyewitness accounts of events tend to vary considerably. Likewise, even everyday experiences may be described differently by different participants. For instance, a teenager's view of a holiday gathering she didn't want to attend would be quite different from her grandmother's, who savored seeing the whole family together. Similarly, if two teachers observe the same preschooler's boisterous behavior, one might see happiness where the other might see rowdiness.

Learn to Observe   Systematic observation means that teachers focus their attention on individual children or groups, watch what children do as they work and play together, and listen carefully as they speak. Table 11.3 lists the important skills of systematic observation that every effective teacher needs and why.

At times, teachers stand back and observe children as they engage in the ongoing life of the classroom or on the playground. Who does Marcus play with and for how long? Does he play alone or with a friend? At other times, teachers arrange specific tasks or activities and observe children's performance. First-grade teacher Ms. Victor adds frequently used words to the "word wall" each week and observes which children refer to them as they are writing. In most

Video Example 11.5:

Eliciting Responses to Assess Learning

Observing children's behavior is important, but it doesn't reveal what children are thinking. In this video of a primary grade math lesson, how does the teacher elicit information from the student? And how does this interaction enable the teacher to assess a child's understanding more accurately?

Promoting Play

Play as an Assessment Context

Adele understands that schools have increased expectations of kindergarteners' academic performance over the years. But her professional education convinced her that much of young children's learning happens in the context of play. Adele uses intentional, short periods of direct instruction, and includes longer periods of supported and free play for children to learn and practice. However, Adele also knows that play is where children's learning and development is demonstrated, and she takes full advantage of play as an assessment context. Because she often uses the project approach, Adele engages children in the assessment process as well.

All of Adele's centers are stocked with reading and writing materials and appropriate learning equipment. Children are encouraged to experiment and imagine. Problem solving and socio-dramatic play are valued equally. As part of their "food" study, children play and demonstrate learning in a grocery store center. Food items are sorted and priced, and children add and subtract pennies to spend their grocery money and fulfill their planned grocery lists. At the garden center, children plant different seeds and nurture their growth. They compare different types of plants as they grow, writing descriptions and recording plant growth. They use a classroom iPad to take photos and record oral descriptions of their garden progress. Children compare how carrots grow in soil that is fed different ways. They have conversations about the weather, pretending to be farmers, and consult a website called "Old Farmer's Almanac for Kids."

Everywhere in Adele's classroom, children are engaged, exploring, and producing products that provide evidence of powerful learning. For each project, children create vocabulary lists that they use in their writing and work together to produce a class book. The book becomes part of their classroom library.

Adele uses video, audiotape, photographs, and work products to document children's learning. After collecting and uploading artifacts, she consults her online assessment tool, identifies the area of evidence, and rates the products according to proficiency. She meets with each child every two weeks for portfolio review, and helps children set learning goals for the upcoming weeks. Adele uses an app on the classroom tablet to share updates to children's portfolios and their goals with families. Children's learning goals are posted on the online assessment tool, which parents can access. Using play as a context for learning and assessment keeps Adele focused on children's development while also addressing learning standards. All the while, children are motivated to learn and take responsibility for their learning.

situations, teachers are participant-observers who converse with children, listen carefully, and assess while they teach individuals as well as small and large groups.

Observation is most effective if teachers think in advance about what they want to observe while remaining flexible to observe events as they proceed. Janice planned to observe the babies in her care during feeding time to see how their fine-motor skills were developing. She observed that two of the 13-month-olds, Josie and Ana, could pick up the cereal on the highchair tray. However, 15-month-old Tania became frustrated and started to cry. Janice watched to see whether and how soon Tania would calm herself before she had to intervene. In this case, an observation of fine-motor skill turned into an observation of emotional self-regulation, an example of the kind of shift that occurs constantly in early childhood programs.

Elicit Responses from Children   Aspects of children's learning and development that cannot be directly observed, such as their conceptual understanding or reasoning, can be elicited from children through questioning, conversation, or other informal teacher–child interactions. Eliciting children's responses—drawing out their ideas or reflections—is an efficient way of gathering information; this way, teachers do not have to wait for behaviors or responses to occur spontaneously (McAfee & Leong, 2015).

TABLE 11.3 Learning to Observe

Effective teachers must be skilled observers in order to assess children's learning and development accurately, as described in this table.

Effective Observation Practice	Explanation
1. Describe behavior objectively and avoid judgmental labels	An objective statement ("During clean-up time, David ran from one center to another for 10 minutes making siren sounds") provides specific information that can be interpreted accurately. A judgmental statement ("David is hyperactive") may be meaningless or inaccurate, and can lead to false assumptions and ineffective interactions with a child.
2. Observe in different contexts	Children's behavior varies depending on the context, their engagement, and interest. David loves center time and will engage with table toys for extended periods of time, but often acts out during cleanup. Observing his behavior in only one context would be misleading.
3. Observe at different times of the day	Children's behavior and learning are affected by many variables such as fatigue, hunger, boredom, exhilaration, fear, and anxiety. Accurate interpretation of behavior and effective teaching depends on having the most complete information.
4. Observe children as individuals and in groups	Children learn and display their learning, both as individuals and as members of groups. Obtaining the most complete picture of a child's abilities, such as their language, social skills, and problem solving, requires observing their interactions with other children.
5. Plan to observe each child during a given time period each week	Teachers' time is limited by many conflicting demands. Too often, some children receive most of the teachers' attention while others are overlooked. To guard against this natural tendency, teachers need to set aside specific times weekly to systematically observe each child, if only for 10 minutes.
6. Devise a system for recording information that works for you	Every system for observing and recording assessment evidence places demands on teachers' time and energy. Teachers need to experiment with and adopt strategies that work for them, whether using sticky notes, strategically placed clipboards, iPads, laptops, digital cameras, or handheld devices.
7. Be aware of and avoid individual and cultural biases	The same behavior may be interpreted differently depending on a teacher's personal or cultural perspective. Such bias can never be completely eliminated but requires that teachers become self-aware and strive for understanding of others' points of view.
8. Gather information from other teachers and parents	The eye of the beholder always influences what is observed and how it is interpreted. To avoid misinterpretation and inaccurate conclusions, gather information from as many people as possible. Family members are essential informants about what children know and are able to do outside of school.

interviews Teacher-created, predetermined questions that are designed to reveal what children understand.

Teachers can have interviews and conferences to elicit children's ideas, problem-solving strategies, and feelings (McAfee & Leong, 2015). Interviews usually involve the teacher asking predetermined questions that are designed to reveal what children understand. For example, rather than asking a closed question such as "How many is 9 + 5?" the teacher might ask, "How would you figure out what 9 + 5 is?" Such an open-ended question is valuable because it requires an extended response that reveals more about children's thinking and understanding.

Conferences engage children in reflecting on their own work. Second-grade teacher Ernestine Cunningham holds regular writing conferences with her students to discuss their writing samples and identify ways to edit or improve them.

Small group discussions provide opportunities to elicit children's thinking in collaboration with other children. At the end of each science unit, rather than giving a multiple-choice test to see what facts children remember, third-grade teacher Devon Kerns meets with small groups of children and asks them to discuss the phenomenon they have been studying. During one such discussion, Mr. Kerns begins this way: "We've been learning about sinking and floating. So why don't giant ships weighing several tons sink?" The children's responses reveal varying degrees of understanding of the concept of displacement. Barry stays silent until the end when he admits, "I think there's something magic going on."

Collect Work Products Much of children's work and play produces a product such as a drawing, a painting, a construction in a particular medium, a piece of writing, a dramatic performance, or speaking in a group. These products, if systematically collected over time, provide evidence of changes in children's development and learning. Examples of individual work might be one child's journal or an art project. When maintaining web-based portfolios, teachers can take a photo of work products or video of intangible products such as skits.

Teachers may also collect or evaluate the work of a group, such as a mural, or a compilation of children's observations from a field trip, such as a PowerPoint presentation with digital photos. Portfolio assessment, which is discussed later in the chapter, is one strategy for systematically collecting and analyzing children's work samples.

Gather Information from Family Members Parents are often thought of as the audience for assessment information, passively receiving report cards or listening attentively during parent–teacher conferences. However, teachers must not only *give* information *to* parents, they must *get* information *from* parents as well. Parents can provide insights about children's behavior and capabilities outside the school or child care center. They can also serve as key informants about children's culture and language. Family

TABLE 11.4 Methods of Gathering Assessment Information: Advantages and Disadvantages

Teachers can gather assessment information in several ways, but they should consider the advantages and disadvantages of each method.

Method	Advantages	Disadvantages
Observation	• Truly authentic assessment • Best way to obtain information about children's behavior • Can observe without interfering with the ongoing activities in the classroom • Can see children's performance in relevant context (play, routines, group projects, outdoors)	• Time consuming • Children's thinking and/or problem solving cannot be directly observed • Can distract teachers from interacting with children • Can be affected by individual and cultural biases
Eliciting Responses from Children (interviews, conferences, and discussions)	• Saves time • Provides insight into children's thinking and learning that cannot be directly observed • Engages children in thinking and reflecting about their own learning—important metacognitive processes that contribute to further development • Demonstrates a child's ability in interaction with other children and adults	• If children do not respond, teachers may inaccurately assume that they don't know the answer • Wording of questions may influence the child's response • Cultural or emotional factors such as lack of self-confidence may inhibit child's response
Collecting Work Products	• Gathered over time • Provide multiple sources of information • Can be used to evaluate children's progress and analyze where help is needed • Concretely demonstrate children's progress to parents and to children themselves	• Teachers may not be sure which products to keep, how many to save, and how to evaluate them • Organization and storage can be difficult
Information from Family Members	• Provide insight into children's cultural and linguistic backgrounds • Describe children's abilities in familiar context • Required for children with disabilities and special needs	• May be intimidating or threatening to families • Language and/or cultural differences may create communication barriers • May not be reliable

Source: Based on O. McAfee , D. Leong, and E. Bodrova, 2015. Assessing and guiding young children's development and learning (6th ed.). Upper Saddle River, NJ: Pearson; J. J. Beaty, 2013. Observing development of the young child (8th ed.). Upper Saddle River, NJ: Pearson.

involvement is so necessary to valid assessment of children with disabilities and special needs that it is legally required (DEC, 2014). Each of these methods of gathering assessment information has advantages and disadvantages, which are summarized in Table 11.4.

Effective assessment systems—those that provide valid, reliable, and useful information for decision making—use all the ways of gathering evidence discussed in previous sections. Intentional teachers regularly gather evidence and then use it to inform their teaching decisions about individual children. In the feature *Becoming an Intentional Teacher: Using Assessment to Inform Teaching*, we see this process in action for one teacher.

What Children Know and Can Do

Observation, eliciting children's responses, collecting work samples, and other authentic assessment procedures are generally informal and therefore not subject to the technical requirements of standardized testing. Nevertheless, for informal assessment results to be accurate and useful, they need to be as objective and nonbiased as possible. Various methods of documenting assessment are designed to increase the likelihood of gathering reliable and valid information. We turn now to a description of the most commonly used methods of documentation. These methods include descriptive records, frequency counts, checklists, rating scales and rubrics, and portfolios.

narrative records Teachers' attempts to record detailed descriptions of children in a situation or event that is the focus of the observation.

Descriptive Records *Narratives* are stories in which the narrator stands outside the experience and describes the people, situation, and events that occur. The same is true of narrative approaches to observation. **Narrative records** are teachers' attempts to record

Becoming an Intentional Teacher

Using Assessment to Inform Teaching

© Monkey Business Images/Shutterstock

Here's What Happened Four-year-old Moses is a gentle boy who plays alone and rarely speaks up. I made a point of observing Moses with other children during center time and when we were doing things that interested him. I also spoke with his mother.

One morning, I recorded a short video of Moses in the block corner with two other boys for 7 minutes. Buddy and Eugene were building a house and kept up a running conversation about what they were doing. Buddy: "This is the bathroom right here. This is the bathtub and toilet." Eugene, picking up a block: "This is the frigerator." Moses sat silently right next to them, frowning, and watching every move they made. After 6 minutes, Moses went to the shelf, picked up three plastic people, and said, "This is fun, too." Buddy grabbed the people from Moses's hands, put them in the house, and said, "This is my family, my mommy and daddy." Frowning, Moses quietly sat down and continued to observe. He then picked up the bin of plastic people figures and went to the table to play with them alone.

Here's What I Was Thinking Before I can take action to help a child, I need to know as much as possible about the child's skills, abilities, and needs. That's where assessment comes in. Maybe Moses did not successfully join the play because he was intimidated by Buddy, in which case I would focus attention on helping him become more comfortable expressing himself. Or maybe he was behind in language and vocabulary development, so I should work on that. Observing him in different situations was the key. I also needed to ask Moses open-ended questions about how he felt about the experience. It could have been that his sad face and frown meant that he longed to join in the play, or he could have been patiently but unhappily waiting a turn to play alone with the blocks.

I shared the video with Moses's family and spoke with his grandmother about what she thought about the interaction. From my observations and conversations with Moses's family, I now have a working hypothesis. It seems likely that not participating in cooperative play is related to his limited vocabulary and lack of experience interacting with other children because he is an only child. To help Moses with both of these issues, I will set up situations to encourage his ease when talking with others. I will also plan some activities that work directly on his social skills. This observation also gave me insights into Buddy's and Eugene's behaviors, and I plan to work with them on their skills at making friends.

Reflection How else might the teacher have interpreted her observations of Moses's behavior during the play sequence? What other tools could she use to assess his social skills and then plan accordingly?

detailed descriptions of children in a situation or event that is the focus of the observation (McAfee & Leong, 2015). It is important for narrative records to focus on the observed behavior rather than implying judgment. "Kery kicked over Stan's building, threw the sand toys on the floor, and pushed Mimi down" is much more informative and useful later than "Kery was disruptive at school today."

Teachers use various methods of collecting anecdotal records for later reflection and analysis. They may take brief notes while observing children in action or as soon as possible, adding more detail later. After documenting their observations, teachers reflect on and interpret their records and plan how to improve teaching and learning. Anecdotal records should include the date and time of observation, names of children observed, location of the incident such as lunch table or hallway, and what the children said and actually did (Mindes & Jung, 2015). Photographs may accompany anecdotal notes. Figure 11.2 presents contrasting examples of anecdotal records about the same situation. A teacher would have difficulty interpreting the first example because it is too general and judgmental to be helpful. By contrast, the second example lends itself to deeper reflection and more effective intervention.

Here are some types of narrative records:

- A **running record** is a chronological record, much like a diary, of an individual child's behavior that helps teachers better understand that behavior (Wortham & Hardin, 2015). The diary format allows the teacher to compare and analyze a child's behavior and development over time. Ms. Dollan worries about Jennifer's shyness and is concerned that it is interfering with her ability to become involved and learn in kindergarten. She keeps a running record for one week, noting as many of Jennifer's social interactions as she can observe. At the end of the week, Ms. Dollan is surprised to find that Jennifer engages much more than she thought; Jennifer just tends to wait and observe before she gets involved.

  running record A chronological record, like a diary, of an individual child's behavior that helps teachers better understand that behavior.

- **Anecdotal records** are short descriptions of incidents, or anecdotes, involving one or more children (McAfee & Leong, 2015). "Monday 5/8—When I read *Hansel and Gretel* to 5 children, Sam (a child with special needs) sat up front and counted the pebbles on the page. He kept his eyes glued to the story for 15 minutes. He frowned when the children were lost and smiled at the ending. He picked up the book on his own afterward." When his teacher, Joanne, reflects on her anecdotal record about Sam, she realizes that previously she underestimated Sam's attention span. Sam's attention during whole group wanders, but she had never assessed it in the small group context before. Joanne is looking forward to sharing this newly found strength with Sam's dad.

  anecdotal records Short descriptions written by teachers and based on observations of incidents or anecdotes involving one or more children.

- *Videotapes, audiotapes,* and *digital photography* are tools for capturing ongoing streams of behavior or performances that are difficult to document in writing.

Example 1

Child's Name: <u>Ledo</u>
Date: <u>July 15, 2018</u>
Setting: <u>Classroom</u>
Activity: <u>Reading Group</u>
<u>Book: Frog and Toad Are Friends. He is really strug-</u>
<u>gling to read this book. It's Level 2 - he's way</u>
<u>behind. No fluency, Loses attention.</u>

Example 2

Child's Name: <u>Ledo</u>
Date: <u>July 15, 2018</u>
Setting: <u>Reading Group with Moria and Devonne</u>
Activity: <u>Frog and Toad Are Friends – 2 pages each Ledo</u>
<u>got excited that it's a Frog and Toad book – he likes</u>
<u>these characters. He stopped at p.1 – no picture clue</u>
<u>for him. First word – Spring, he used structure and</u>
<u>visual cues. He made 15 errors on the page. Self-cor-</u>
<u>rected 5 times. When turned page and saw picture of</u>
<u>Toad Knocking – went back and changed (smiled) his</u>
<u>expression-"I got that right."</u>

FIGURE 11.2 Contrasting Examples of Anecdotal Records Compare these examples of anecdotal records. Which one provides more useful information for the teacher?

Doreen videotaped a small group of 5-year-olds as they discussed how they would build a replica of the zoo's panda house in their classroom. When she played back the tape with the children, she discovered that the group really listened to each other's ideas, abandoned some, and agreed on others, which she later helped them implement.

 Application Exercise 11.2
Observation and Recording to Improve Learning

The benefits of such detailed observations are that they are open-ended, flexible, and provide a wealth of information. Children can be assessed in the context of regular classroom routines and activities so their behavior is most natural and authentic. The primary disadvantage of narrative records, on the other hand, is that they are time consuming to both record and interpret. However, using technology can increase the ease of collecting and evaluating narrative data. Other assessment tools and methods are available that essentially count or tally what is observed.

Frequency Counts   In some cases, teachers need to know how often a behavior occurs—the *frequency*—and/or how long it lasts—the *duration*. For example, to intervene with a child who hits, teachers begin by keeping track of how often the negative behavior occurs. Then, once an intervention plan is in place, they can use a frequency count to evaluate its effectiveness.

Teachers use **frequency counts**, also called event sampling, to tally each time a specific behavior occurs. The teacher simply makes a mark whenever a child demonstrates a behavior or participates in an activity, as shown in Figure 11.3. For example, the teacher was concerned about Avery's continued crying after several weeks of school, but her mother dismissed it as a phase. Based on the frequency count, the teacher decided to keep more detailed narrative records of the child's behavior and convinced Avery's mother to work with her to ease her adjustment to school.

frequency counts Method used by teachers to keep track of how often a behavior occurs.

Child's Name: Avery Lucas
Date: 10/1 to 10/4
Time: 9.00 to 10:30
Setting: Classroom
Behavior: Crying

Date	Frequency	Day Total
9/21	ℋℋℋ /	6
9/22	///	3
9/23	ℋℋℋ	5
9/24	ℋℋℋ	5
Total		19

FIGURE 11.3 Sample Frequency Count Chart A frequency count chart such as this is simple to use, and can provide teachers with helpful information about children's behavior.

Source: McAfee, Oralie; Leong, Deborah J., Assessing and Guiding Young Children's Development and Learning, 5th ed., © 2011. Reprinted and electronically reproduced by permission of Pearson Education, Inc., Upper Saddle River, New Jersey.

Frequency counts serve a valuable but limited function. They are easy to use and help teachers quickly gather general information about children's participation and experience. However, they do not provide contextual information about what occurs before and after a specific behavior. For that evidence, teachers need to supplement frequency tallies with narrative records or checklists, addressed next.

Checklists   One of the most commonly used recording methods, checklists, are practical and versatile tools for gathering assessment information about almost any aspect of children's behavior, skills, or attitudes (McAfee & Leong, 2015). They can be based on learning standards in literacy or mathematics, or on sequences of development such as physical or social skills. Some checklists are designed by teachers; others are commercially published.

Some checklists require marking only "yes" or "no" as to whether a child engages in a behavior (such as, "follows two directions"). Other, more open-ended checklists require the teacher to make a judgment of the degree to which a child has mastered a skill. Teachers may make notes while observing children and then use those notes to complete the checklist at a later time. One of the strengths of checklists is that they focus teachers' observations; in effect, checklists tell teachers what to look for and which skills are important. Checklists can provide data that can be analyzed and compared over time and also aggregated for a group of children. Their limitation is that no checklist can adequately capture the complexity of an individual child's competence.

Rating Scales and Rubrics   *Rating scales* and *rubrics* record teachers' judgments about how a child's performance compares to that of peers or to a predetermined standard (McAfee & Leong, 2015). Ratings should be based on sound assessment evidence collected over time. **Rating scales** require the assessor to evaluate an individual on a characteristic and then rank the individual's ability on a continuum from low to high frequency or quality (McAfee & Leong, 2015). For example, a frequency scale might rate whether a child performs a skill "usually," "sometimes," "seldom," or "never." A scale designed to rate the quality of a child's performance might be "exceeds standard," "meets standard," or "making progress toward standard."

Rubrics are descriptive rating scales that include clear descriptions of each point on the scale or guidelines for making judgments about a rating (McAfee & Leong, 2015). Figure 11.4 shows a sample rubric of an approaches to learning item from *COR-Advantage*, the revised Child Observation Record, developed by the HighScope Educational Research Foundation (Epstein, Marshall, & Gainsley, 2014). *COR-Advantage* articulates eight levels of development or learning because it is designed for children from infancy through age 5. Note that in this instrument, all eight levels of the rubric are described. This specificity helps teachers make more accurate ratings and increases reliability between teachers. The tool also includes additional descriptions of what behaviors to observe as well as examples of anecdotal observations that would lead teachers to make their ratings.

checklists Practical and versatile tools for gathering assessment information about children's behavior, skills, or attitudes.

rating scales Method of recording teacher's judgments about how a child's performance compares to that of peers or to a predetermined standard.

rubrics Descriptive rating scales that detail the qualities related to each rank on the scale; includes clear descriptions of each point on the scale or guidelines for making judgments about a rating.

Level 0	Level 1	Level 2	Level 3	Level 4	Level 5	Level 6	Level 7
Child indicates he or she wants something to happen again.	Child returns to where something he or she previously played with was located.	Child points to or shows something he or she played with.	Child says one thing he or she did some after the event.	Child recalls three or more things that he or she did and/or details of something that happened.	Child recalls, without prompting, the sequence of three or more things he or she did or that happened.	Child says the reason why the experience happened to him or her as it did and what he or she would do the same or differently next time.	Child recalls another person's experience and uses what he or she observed in a similar situation.

From: "COR Advantage Scoring Guide" by A. S. Epstein, B. Marshall, and S. Gainsley. Ypsilanti, MI: HighScope Press, pp. 8–9.©2014 HighScope Educational Research Foundation. Used with permission.

FIGURE 11.4 Rubric Example from HighScope's COR-Advantage Rubrics are valuable assessment tools because having specific descriptions for each point on the scale helps teachers make more accurate and reliable ratings.

Rating scales and rubrics are relatively quick and systematic ways of keeping track of children's progress, and they assist teachers by focusing their observations and evidence collections. Rubrics are more reliable than rating scales because the guidelines for rating are explicit, which helps teachers make more accurate judgments. Rating scales and rubrics also help teachers identify where children are in relation to program objectives, and help guide curriculum planning and teaching. Some commercially published authentic assessment tools that use rating scales and/or rubrics have been validated (i.e., they meet standards for reliability and validity).

portfolios Systematic and organized collections of children's work and demonstrations of their progress relevant to the goals of the curriculum.

Portfolios

Portfolios are systematic and organized collections of children's work and demonstrations of their progress relevant to the goals of the curriculum (Mindes & Jung, 2015). They can be paper-based and stored in binders or cabinets, or web-based and stored in cloud drives. Portfolios have several benefits. They focus on how individual children change over time, rather than comparing children to each other. Teachers create portfolios to document how well children are learning the content of the curriculum. In addition, portfolios provide concrete and meaningful information about children's progress to share with parents, other teachers, administrators, specialists, and even the general public.

The materials contained in a portfolio provide teachers and children with the opportunity to reflect together on children's progress. Most teachers involve children in selecting work to be included in a portfolio. This requires children to think about which of their products are worth keeping and evaluate the quality of their own performances, an example of which appears in Figure 11.5. Jocelyn, a second-grader, created an elephant in art class that she wanted to include in her portfolio. Jocelyn's teacher, Ms. Stephenson, guided the students in her class to write narratives explaining why they picked certain pieces to include in the portfolio and the learning that each work sample demonstrates. Jocelyn's narrative addresses the Common Core English Language Arts standards and provides some insight into her social–emotional learning and math skills. The elephant is evidence of a beginning understanding of symmetry as well as the executive function skills required to make a plan and follow through to complete a project over multiple art class sessions.

The contents of portfolios can vary, but they need to be consistent among children in a group. Generally, portfolios include dated samples of children's work representing at least the beginning, middle, and end of a school year. These samples should include teacher notes about context or children's verbal comments made about the work. A portfolio may also include anecdotal or other narrative records plus observational checklists related to curriculum goals. One widely used, validated portfolio assessment system that includes all these elements is the ©*Work Sampling System*, designed for children from preschool to grade 6 (Meisels, Marsden, Jablon, & Dichtelmiller, 2013).

FIGURE 11.5 Sample Contents of a Second-Grade Child's Portfolio The contents of a child's portfolio serve as important evidence of children's learning over time.

Documentation as Dynamic Assessment   Earlier in this chapter, we defined documenting as the process of collecting and recording evidence about children's learning and development. The word *documentation* is often used to refer to the recorded evidence that is then analyzed and interpreted. However, the influence of the Reggio Emilia approach on early childhood practice (Quinn & Parker, 2015) created a new, expanded definition of documentation.

Teachers can assess children's learning by documenting a project or activity through note-taking, photography, audiotaping, videotaping, and collecting samples of student work. Through the children's verbal expression, writing, drawing, and construction, researchers and teachers are able to see what the children understand and how they convey their ideas and knowledge.

From carefully studying the children's work and tapes of their discussions, teachers are able to see what misconceptions and areas of incomplete knowledge the children have, as well as in their writing, communication skills, and pictorial representation. This information guides their planning of what additional experiences and instruction to provide next. Characteristics that make documentation a unique assessment tool include the following (Helm, Beneke, & Steinheimer, 2007; Reggio Children & Project Zero, 2001):

- Involves teachers intensely observing and recording, using all forms of technology and displaying children's processes of thinking and problem solving as they work together on projects.
- Captures the collaborative interaction that occurs among teachers and children, and depicts the process of learning rather than any one product.
- Encourages children to revisit and remember their experiences as they examine the documentation, which extends and deepens their learning.
- Draws parents into the life of the school through compelling, visual evidence of their children's competence.
- Serves as research on children's thinking and learning processes that contributes to teachers' professional development.
- Provides evidence of children's competencies that cannot be measured on more formal tests, such as their ability to collaborate with other children.

Video Example 11.6:

Using Documentation for Assessment

The teachers in this video are in a Reggio-inspired classroom using documentation as evidence of learning and development for children's portfolios. How do the teachers use this information to inform the curriculum? What are some strengths of using this approach?

As we saw with ways of gathering assessment information, every method teachers use to record assessment information has strengths but also limitations, which are described in Table 11.5. As previously noted, ethical, intentional teachers collect assessment data from myriad sources.

 Application Exercise 11.3

Gathering and Evaluating Evidence of Learning

Interpreting and Using Evidence to Improve Teaching and Learning

So far, we have described two major steps in classroom assessment: (1) gathering evidence of children's development and learning, and (2) recording the findings. The next step is interpreting and using the evidence to plan curriculum or adapt teaching strategies.

Accurate interpretation and effective use of assessment evidence depend on how well teachers know what children should accomplish at developmental junctures and when those junctures occur. This means that every teacher needs to be familiar with the continuum of development and expected learning sequences relevant to the age range he or she teaches. Given the wide range of individual variation, in fact, early childhood teachers should be familiar with the full range of development from birth through age 8.

TABLE 11.5 Methods of Recording Assessment Information: Advantages and Disadvantages

Teachers need to use various ways of recording assessment information but they should consider the advantages and disadvantages of each, as described in this table.

Method	Advantages	Disadvantages
Descriptive records (narrative, running, anecdotal)	• Provide rich, detailed information about children's behavior in context • Can be objective • May assess individuals or groups	• Time consuming and difficult to record streams of behavior • May be judgmental • May be difficult to interpret
Frequency counts (event sampling)	• More objective because focuses on specific behavior • Document how often behavior occurs • Show change in behavior over time • Not time-consuming • Efficient	• No description or information about behavior and context • May lead to biased view of child because often focuses on one negative behavior
Checklists	• Efficient way of gathering information • Helps teachers know what to observe • Can be completed quickly and easily • Data can be analyzed and compared over time • Can be scored for individuals and groups	• No information provided about context • Can't capture the complexity of a child's performance • Provide limited guidance for teachers' decisions
Rating scales and rubrics	• Focus teachers' observations on specific goals • Help teachers understand development and learning progressions • Relatively quick and easy to use • Can assist curriculum planning and teaching • Data can be analyzed and compared over time • Can be scored for individuals and groups	• Limited information about context • Ratings may not be reliable across teachers or children • Scores can oversimplify complex behavior and ability
Portfolios	• Demonstrate an individual child's progress over a long period of time • Include multiple sources of information (photos, videos, work samples, teacher's and parents' observations) • Can be passed along to next teacher (with parents' permission)	• Difficult to organize, store, and access easily • Teachers may not be sure which products to keep, how many to save, and how to evaluate them
Documentation as dynamic assessment	• Makes learning visible to children, teachers, and families • Uses multiple sources of information (videos, audio recording, photos, observations, work samples) • Displays children's thinking and problem solving as they work together on projects • Helps teachers assess children's understanding and misconceptions • Illustrates both individual and group learning	• Time consuming to collect information and create display panels • Requires large amount of space • Does not identify their individual child's work, which may frustrate parents

Sources: Based on O. McAfee and D. J. Leong, 2015. *Assessing and guiding young children's development and* learning *(6th ed.)*. Upper Saddle River, NJ: Pearson; J. J. Beaty, 2013. *Observing development of the young child (8th ed.)*. Upper Saddle River, NJ: Pearson.

A developmental continuum is a predictable, but not rigid, sequence of typical accomplishments within age ranges that is used to plan curriculum. A developmental continuum is an effective assessment tool because it helps teachers focus attention on what is important to assess—what children can do—and identify goals for continued progress (McAfee & Leong, 2015; Arnett & Maynard, 2017). When teachers are familiar with predictable sequences of learning and development, they can use these to assess where children are in the sequence and adjust their teaching to help them progress.

Learning standards set curriculum goals for what a child should know and be able to do. They also guide the development of assessments. Effective teachers interpret and use the assessment information they have gathered and recorded in relation to learning standards. For instance, Micah observes that at the midpoint of the year, most of the children in his preschool class can recognize the first letter in their names and maybe one other letter. Is this good or bad? Unless Micah is familiar with early learning standards in the area of literacy, he can't make a judgment about whether his children are achieving at an acceptable rate. Similarly, four of the children in Micah's class do not speak in complete sentences. Because Micah is familiar with the developmental continuum of language, he realizes these children are significantly behind their peers in language. He adds book reading and additional one-on-one conversation time to his teaching plan, continues to observe and record their language, and seeks out the speech pathologist to consider systematic evaluations. Effective solutions to these challenges are available through the use of technology.

Using Technology to Assess Learning

Teachers can be overwhelmed at the prospect of recording their observations, keeping track of all the data they collect about children's progress, and compiling portfolios of children's work. Fortunately, technology including smartphones, digital cameras, tablets, and laptops can minimize these disadvantages and support teachers to reliably assess and document children's learning.

One such example is the 36-item online *COR-Advantage*, an authentic assessment tool for evaluating the development and learning of children from birth through age 5 developed by the HighScope Educational Research Foundation (Epstein, Marshall, & Gainsley, 2014). *COR-Advantage* can be in any early childhood program, not just those using the HighScope curriculum. A similar online system is ©*Teaching Strategies GOLD,* which is aligned to the ©Creative Curriculum and offers a process to ensure reliability among observers. Both systems enable teachers to use the internet and a smartphone or tablet to record and store anecdotal records and to generate scores, charts, and graphs of children's progress as well as narrative reports for individuals and the group. The data can be aggregated to meet reporting requirements of school districts or Head Start. Children's files can be easily updated with new information. Scanned artwork, photographs, sample writing, or video clips may also be included. *COR-Advantage* allows families to access their child's online community, view uploaded attachments, and participate in the assessment process. *Teaching Strategies GOLD* provides the option to share portfolios with families, special education providers, and school districts (with the family's permission).

A variety of apps, including *Transparent Classroom* are also available to educators. Developed by Montessori teachers, *Transparent Classroom* allows teachers to quickly type anecdotal notes tagging multiple students, upload photos and complete developmental checklists. Settings in *Transparent Classroom* allow for real-time email or text sharing with families. Apps such as *Transparent Classroom* are not tied to specific curriculum, and can be utilized across infant and primary grade classrooms.

Many educational software companies provide electronic portfolios that can be used to create, preserve, and store children's work using digital technology. With smartphones and tablets that allow teachers to photograph, scan, and record video and audio products, the possibilities for storing work samples and performances are almost endless. The long-term storage capabilities make it possible to continue to track children's progress across grades and to produce a permanent record for children's families. For teachers looking for cost-free technology options, apps such as *Notability, Dropbox,* and *Evernote* can be helpful. Teachers should ensure that any online app or web-based storage is compliant with the Family Educational Rights and Privacy Act (FERPA).

These and other technology-based assessment systems help teachers assess, and are designed to be connected to curriculum goals. They provide suggestions for individual and group learning experiences and intentional teaching strategies. Thus, technology not only lightens the time-consuming demands of gathering assessment information but also links results to improving teaching and curriculum.

Effective assessment systems—those that provide valid, reliable, and useful information for decision making—gather evidence from many sources. An example of such a system designed for children from birth to 3½ years, a notoriously difficult age group to accurately access, is the *Ounce Scale* (Meisels, Marsden, Dombro, Weston, & Jewkes, 2003). The tool includes an observation record, an album for gathering the family's responses, and developmental profiles and standards to use in completing the observation and analyzing the evidence.

The role of authentic assessment in effective practice for children from birth to age 8 is now widely accepted. At the same time, educational policy and practice in elementary schools has become increasingly dominated by standardized testing, a controversial topic that is discussed next.

✔ Check Your Understanding 11.4

🔺 Standardized Testing of Young Children

Anyone who has attended school in the United States in the past half century is intimately familiar with the regular rituals of standardized testing. The Every Student Succeeds Act (ESSA) requires that states begin administering standardized tests in third grade. We have all taken some form of state-mandated achievement test at some time during our educational careers. Passing a standardized test is often required to become a certified teacher or for other professions such as nursing. Despite educators' concerns and increasing doubts expressed by the general public, standardized testing is inescapable in today's political climate. Therefore, teachers must be more knowledgeable than ever about the content that will be tested as well as the appropriate and inappropriate uses of standardized tests.

achievement tests Tests designed to measure what children have learned in general or in a content area such as reading or mathematics.

Types of Standardized Tests

There are many types of standardized tests. Most standardized tests can be categorized as achievement tests, aptitude or ability tests, readiness tests, or screening and diagnostic tests (McAfee & Leong, 2015).

Achievement Tests One of the most familiar types of standardized tests are achievement tests such as the SAT, the Iowa Test of Basic Skills, or the California Achievement Test. Achievement tests are designed to measure what children have learned in general or in a content area such as reading or mathematics. The test items are a sample of the curriculum

Portfolios are a valuable alternative to standardized testing. ESSA includes a provision to allow states to utilize portfolio assessments as part of overall performance data that schools collect and report.

content, and children's responses are an indication of what they have learned. Recent examples of achievement tests are those administered to meet federal requirements or state learning standards.

Aptitude or Ability Tests   Aptitude tests are presumably designed to measure not what children have already learned, but their potential for learning in the future (McAfee & Leong, 2015). Consequently, scores on aptitude tests are intended to predict future performance. As such, they are sometimes used to identify children for gifted and talented programs.

> **aptitude tests** Tests designed to measure children's potential for learning in the future.

In education, intelligence or IQ tests such as the Stanford–Binet or the McCarthy Scales of Children's Abilities are aptitude tests. Such tests are controversial because children's scores will naturally be influenced by their prior experience. If children do not perform well on such tests, it may be because they have not had the opportunity to learn rather than because they are incapable of learning.

Readiness Tests   School readiness tests are typically administered before entrance to kindergarten (Snow, 2011). Some norm-referenced readiness tests are considered aptitude tests because they purport to predict whether children are sufficiently developed to benefit from kindergarten instruction. These tests are especially problematic because the younger the child, the more difficult it is to obtain an accurate assessment of what she or he has learned, much less what the child is capable of learning in the future.

> **readiness tests** Achievement tests administered to children at entry to kindergarten.

The fact is that children's scores on readiness tests actually reflect their past experiences and opportunities to learn, and hence are more accurately categorized as achievement tests (Snow, 2011). The use of readiness tests to keep children out of kindergarten is considered inappropriate by NAEYC and other early childhood professional organizations because it denies children what they need most: the opportunity to attend school (Snow, 2011).

Increasing recognition of the importance of promoting children's executive functions has naturally raised the issue of how to assess these capacities. Many circumstances including premature birth, parental mental illness, lead paint exposure, sleep disturbances, and trauma can impair executive function development (Ackerman & Friedman-Kraus, 2017). Therefore, accurate assessments are important because executive functions provide the foundation for academic success and are amenable to intervention (Fuhs, Farran, & Nesbitt, 2015). Of course, it is much more difficult to assess children's approaches to learning than the basic skills of literacy or mathematics that typically appear on achievement or readiness tests. Nevertheless, a growing number of researchers are developing valid and reliable measures of children's executive function, as described in the feature *What Works: Assessing Executive Function*.

Appropriate Uses of Standardized Testing

Before addressing the controversies and concerns about standardized testing, it is important to recognize the benefits and well-intended purposes for using standardized tests. Standardized tests are not inherently good or evil. Although some published tests do not meet technical requirements for reliability and validity, many others are technically sound. As described earlier in this chapter, standardized tests have particular characteristics and specific purposes for which they have been developed. When used for these purposes, they can have utility; that is, they can be used to benefit children, especially those enrolled in third grade or higher. The most positive uses of standardized tests are: (1) to help identify and diagnose children with special needs, (2) to serve as a source of information for assessing children for instruction, and (3) to provide information for program evaluation and accountability. Tests are often used to gather comparative data for the purpose of addressing inequities among genders, socioeconomic groups, and racial/cultural groups. Tests are also used for research purposes.

> **utility** Used to benefit children.

Standardized testing has appropriate uses as long as the instruments are technically sound, unbiased, and used for the purposes for which they were designed, to benefit

What Works

Assessing Executive Function

Children with age-appropriate executive function demonstrate higher math and literacy outcomes in preschool and beyond. To focus on classroom learning, children need to activate their abilities to pay attention, inhibit distracting behaviors and thoughts, and engage in the use of mental flexibility and working memory.

One measurement tool is the *Minnesota Executive Function Scale* (MEFS). MEFS assesses these skills through a quick, tablet-based sorting game. This standardized test helps identify students who need targeted instruction around working memory, inhibitory control, and mental flexibility while they participate in sorting tasks that asks children to first sort the cards by color and then shape. Another measure, *Head-Toes-Knees-Shoulders*, quickly assesses executive function skills during a modified game of Head, Shoulders, Knees and Toes. An assessor follows a short script leading the activity and changes the order of body parts to touch as the game progresses. Children use working memory to recall the instructions and inhibitory control to keep from touching the "wrong" body part. This test is available in 15 languages and easily accessible for teachers.

Another measure of executive function that has been in existence much longer is the *Child Behavior Rating Scale (CBRS)*. The results are based on teachers' ratings of their perceptions of

a child's classroom behavior. Observing and rating executive function skills in a classroom setting is a way to authentically assess these skills and help teachers target their instructional interventions to the child's existing skills and areas for growth. When completing the *Child Behavior Rating Scale*, teachers must take care to be unbiased in their answers to ensure accurate results.

Early childhood teachers can facilitate the development of executive function skills through positive, nurturing relationships, thoughtful construction of learning environments and intentional instructional planning. (Fuhs, Farran, & Nesbitt, 2015; Blair, McKinnon, & Family Life Project Investigators, 2016). Therefore, accurate assessment of children's executive function is especially important.

Sources: M. B. Bronson, B. D. Goodson, J. L. Layzer, & J.M. Love, 1990. *Child Behavior Rating Scale.* Cambridge, MA: AbtAssociates; S. M. Carlson & P. D. Zelazo, 2014. *Minnesota Executive Function Scale: Test manual.* St. Paul, MN: Reflection Sciences; M. M. McClelland, C. E. Cameron, R. Duncan, R. P. Bowles et al., 2014. Predictors of early growth in academic achievement: The Head–Toes–Knees–Shoulders task. *Frontiers in Psychology, 5,* Article 599.

---

children, and in conjunction with other sources for decision making. Throughout your career as a teacher, you will face decisions about using standardized tests. Although there are appropriate uses for standardized testing, there are controversies and concerns that surround their use, which we discuss next.

Concerns about Standardized Testing

high-stakes testing Using standardized test scores to make decisions about individual children, teachers, or schools that have potential long-term consequences.

High-stakes testing refers to the use of standardized test scores to make decisions that have potential long-term consequences for individual children, teachers, or schools. Today's school accountability movement has increased the amount of high-stakes testing. Test results can lead to children being retained in grade, a decision with lifelong consequences. School districts use children's test scores in teacher performance evaluations and even for decisions about teacher pay. Schools are ranked on websites according to test scores. When the stakes surrounding testing become so high, unintended consequences may result, such as narrowing the curriculum to teach only what is tested; cheating by giving children assistance or changing the conditions under which a test is administered; and an increase in educational inequity for people of color and lower socioeconomic status. (Au, 2007; 2014).

High-stakes accountability testing can have adverse consequences for teaching practices in primary grades that trickle down into kindergarten and preschool. Among the major concerns about standardized testing are potential for bias and negative effects on curriculum and teaching.

Bias in Standardized Tests   One of the biggest fallacies of standardized tests is that they are completely fair and objective (Santos, 2004). Although objectivity is the intent behind standardization, that goal has not been reached. The only truly objective part of standardized tests is the scoring, often done by machine The choice of test content, wording of items, and determination of the correct answer is decided by human beings who have their own subjective perspectives (FairTest, 2012). As a result, it is virtually impossible to develop a truly objective test that is free of all cultural and other forms of bias.

Although standardized tests are seen by policy makers as objective measures of student performance, this is not always the case. For example, students who do not eat breakfast before taking a standardized test demonstrate much lower performance than those students who eat before school (Au, 2014). This difference can lead to characterization of students living in poverty as lower achieving. Additionally, many standardized tests are based on content knowledge reflective of the dominant, White, middle-class culture, which creates a test bias in the favor of students in this group and results in lower scores for students outside this group (Au, 2014). In the United States, where high-stakes testing can impact school funding, schools serving high proportions of African American and Hispanic students are much more likely to be labeled "underperforming" due to lower than average standardized test scores on potentially culturally biased tests.

Negative Effects on Curriculum and Teaching   The power of paper-and-pencil, multiple-choice tests to drive what happens in schools is well documented (Ravitch, 2010). Although testing was a controversial issue before federal laws such as the Every Student Succeds Act and its predecessors, No Child Left Behind and Race to the Top, were introduced. Since these policies went into effect, schools report narrowing the curriculum to put more focus on the content that is being tested, especially reading and math. This means that other areas of the curriculum such as physical education, the arts, and even academic subjects such as social studies are sacrificed. Some schools have even taken away recess to allow more time for reading practice and test preparation.

Another negative effect of standardized testing is on instruction itself. Because multiple-choice tests tend to measure basic skills and factual knowledge, instructional practices are adversely affected (Ravitch, 2010). Instead of using effective teaching practices that emphasize learning as a socially constructed process, direct instruction on the basic skills that will be tested takes precedence in many classrooms. The "one right answer" format fails to reveal children's true competence. Consider 4-year-old Lulu's experience during such a test (G. Joseph, personal communication, 2011):

> *Tester:* "What do you do when you're cold?"
> *Lulu:* "I start to shiver" [which is not the "correct answer" in the test booklet].
> *Tester:* "What else do you do?"
> *Lulu:* "The hair on my neck starts to stand up."
> *Tester, in somewhat frustrated voice:* "What do you do if you *don't* want to be cold?"
> *Lulu, with a slightly disdainful look:* "I put a coat on" [which is seemingly the only "correct" answer to the question].

Without the extended conversation, the tester would judge Lulu to be incorrect, and her rich language expression would have been missed.

Perhaps the biggest problem with large-scale standardized testing for accountability is that it often fails to achieve its well-intended purpose, which is to improve learning outcomes for individual children (Ravitch, 2010). Test scores become available *after* children have moved on from the classroom that is being evaluated. More important, the results of such tests are not useful for informing curriculum and teaching. A single score in no way describes the complexity of children's achievement, as the following example demonstrates.

A classic study that analyzed the results of children who failed the state fourth-grade reading test shows the ineffectiveness of large-scale testing in improving teaching (Valencia & Buly, 2004). The researchers wanted to understand why these children were experiencing reading difficulty. Among the students in their study, they identified six very different clusters of reading problems. For example, one group of children could read fast but didn't understand what they read. Another group of children had good comprehension skills but slow decoding ability, which interfered with their comprehending what they read. In addition, the researchers found considerable variance among individual children that would call for different kinds of reading support. Some of the children failed the test by only one or two points. Fewer than 10% of the children were identified as "disabled" readers. These few children are what we picture when we hear that large numbers of children failed the state tests.

As the researchers concluded, the standardized test score alone does not begin to describe the complexity and diversity of the reading difficulties children face. Neither is it useful in helping teachers address children's individual problems. Although their conclusion could extend to other areas of the curriculum as well, it is particularly ironic here, since improving reading achievement is the primary goal of so many accountability efforts.

Currently, the Common Core State Standards and the Kindergarten Readiness Assessments standards are generating the most heated discussion and controversy related to assessment for children, teachers, schools, and districts. These issues are described in the sections that follow.

Assessment and the Common Core

The Common Core State Standards (CCSS) have changed the landscape of child assessment—directly in kindergarten and higher grades, and indirectly in preschool. Many states are simultaneously interpreting the standards for curriculum while attempting to assess what children are learning and how well teachers and schools are teaching. In order to manage the large task of integrating standards and to align curriculum and assessment, states formed consortia to establish guidelines and develop products. Two such consortia are the Smarter Balanced Assessment Consortium and the Partnership for Assessment of Readiness for College and Careers (PARCC). Both groups developed assessment approaches aligned to the CCSS in English language arts and mathematics.

Because the Common Core standards focus on higher-level competencies such as problem solving, analyzing, and interpreting evidence, the assessments differ from other large-scale testing efforts that rely on machine-scored, low-level, multiple-choice questions. For example, Common Core assessments require written responses to open-ended questions and keyboard skills. Many are uncomfortable with several aspects of the assessments, including the increased difficulty and developmental appropriateness of the grade-level content, the new types of testing needed, new testing formats, and the difficult task of scheduling test administration. Some states developed formative assessments for K–3 in an effort to be more developmentally appropriate. However, the ultimate test will be whether CCSS and its aligned curricula and assessments are able to enhance learning for *all* children.

Kindergarten Readiness Assessment

While early childhood teachers are being educated to be keen observers and skilled at formative assessment, 40 states have adopted Kindergarten Readiness Assessments (Bornfruend & Sillers, 2017). The U.S. Department of Education's 2009 Race to the Top—Early Learning Challenge (RttT-ELC) stimulated this trend of Kindergarten Readiness Assessments (KRAs). Definitions of kindergarten readiness vary from state to state but generally address a child's general knowledge of concepts including shapes and letters, language and literacy skills, motor development, social emotional skills, and some executive function skills including the ability to maintain attention (Regenstein, Connors, Romero-Jurado, & Weiner, 2017). Appropriate uses of KRA data include:

- Assess the extent to which the state's children are "ready" for formal schooling.
- Identify and target populations of children that require extra educational effort.
- Guide kindergarten teachers in their efforts to support children's development and learning.
- Inform and engage parents in their children's development and learning.
- Provide information about needed professional development for teachers.

Early Learning Challenge grants emphasize that KRAs are not designed or intended to function as high-stakes assessment and should adhere to the NRC's recommendations on assessment in early childhood (NRC, 2008). The Ounce (Regenstein, et al, 2017) and NAEYC (Snow, 2011) echo these recommendations and assert that KRAs can have value for identifying children with special educational needs and targeting effective interventions, but caution that the tools used must have strong psychometrics (reliability and validity) and be administered in ways consistent with developmentally appropriate practice.

For dual language learners, assessments should be linguistically and culturally appropriate, include the child's family in the process, and be administered by someone who has linguistic and cultural competence that aligns with the child's experience (NASEM, 2017). Although these standards may be difficult to achieve, they are necessary conditions to increase the validity of assessment for dual language learners. Used properly, KRAs could prove to be a valuable tool for states and school districts in determining what supports are needed for early childhood programs, and for teachers in planning the kindergarten curriculum and adapting for individual children.

Despite the challenges and controversies surrounding testing of young children, accurate assessment of young children's development and learning is an essential component of developmentally appropriate practice. Intentional teachers use the effective assessment strategies described in this chapter to meet children where they are in order to plan curriculum and adapt their teaching to help children achieve challenging goals.

✔ **Check Your Understanding 11.5**

Revisiting the Case Study

... Ms. Kinsela's Classroom

At the outset of this chapter, we met a first-grade teacher, Bonnie Kinsela. During the course of a two-hour literacy block, Bonnie's work demonstrates the positive power of informal as well as formal, authentic assessment to improve teaching and learning outcomes for young children and communicate children's progress with their families in real time. Bonnie smoothly embeds assessment in her curriculum and teaching as she helps children document their work. She uses technology to keep track of her observations, narrative records, ratings of children's performance, and portfolios, and to share these artifacts with families. The children in her classroom clearly benefit from their district's emphasis on using assessment to support the progress of all children.

Bonnie's experiences expanded her thinking about assessment. She knows the benefits of using standardized measures for screening and diagnosing children's special needs, and for documenting IEP progress. At the same time, she realizes that using observation and other tools to formally and informally assess children's learning and development provides her with essential information to make good decisions about her teaching. Most important, she now believes that assessment is not an add-on to her job but rather an integral aspect of her role as an intentional teacher. Using assessment wisely and accurately is essential if children are to benefit from their school experiences. Based on Bonnie's ongoing assessments of her students, she decided that beginning her poetry unit now rather than later in the school year will maximaize student interests and learning.

Assessing children's progress on specific literacy goals helps Bonnie see the need to adapt and individualize her teaching. The families she works with are integrally involved in the assessment process, examining online portfolios, sharing anecdotes, and marveling at their own children's competence. In Bonnie's program, assessment meets the ultimate test—it benefits children and their families. ■

11 Chapter Summary

- Assessment literacy is teachers' understanding and using the vocabulary of assessment and testing.

- Assessment is the ongoing process of gathering evidence of children's learning and development, and then organizing and interpreting that information in order to make informed decisions about instructional practice.

- Early childhood programs have four basic purposes for assessment: (1) to inform teaching and promote learning, (2) to identify children with special learning or developmental needs, (3) to evaluate programs, and (4) to demonstrate accountability.

- Indicators of effective assessment include (1) using multiple sources of evidence; (2) using assessments only for the purpose for which they are reliable and valid; and (3) considering what is developmentally appropriate, culturally and linguistically responsive, and individually appropriate for all children, including children with special needs.

- The most effective methods for collecting evidence to improve learning and development are observing children's behavior and performance, eliciting responses from children, collecting work products, and gathering information from family members.

- Accurate interpretation and effective use of assessment evidence depend on teachers' knowing what and when children should be accomplishing certain developmental tasks and learning skills.

- Benefits of standardized tests include: (1) they help identify and diagnose children with special needs, (2) they serve as a source of information for assessing children for instruction, and (3) they are one source of information for program evaluation and accountability.

- High-stakes accountability testing can have adverse consequences for teaching practices in primary grades that trickle down into kindergarten and preschool, including biased results and negative effects on curriculum and teaching.

Key Terms

- accommodations
- achievement tests
- anecdotal records
- aptitude tests
- authentic assessment
- checklists
- criterion-referenced tests
- curriculum-embedded assessment
- diagnostic tests

- dynamic assessment
- evaluation
- evidence
- formal assessment
- formative assessment
- frequency counts
- high-stakes testing
- informal assessment
- interviews
- modifications

- narrative records
- normal curve
- norm-referenced tests
- performance assessment or authentic assessment
- play-based assessment
- portfolios
- program evaluation
- rating scales
- readiness tests
- reliability

- rubrics
- running record
- screening tests
- standardized assessment
- standardized testing
- summative assessment
- testing
- utility
- validity

Flash Cards 11.1

Readings and Websites

Cohen, D. H., Stern, V., Balaban, N., & Gropper, N. (2016). *Observing and recording the behavior of young children*. New York: Teachers College Press.

Curtis, D. (2017). *Really seeing children: A collection of teaching and learning stories*. Redmond, WA: Exchange Press.

Curtis, D., & Carter, M. (2013). *The art of awareness: How observation can transform your teaching (2nd ed.)*. St. Paul, MN: Redleaf Press.

Mindes, G. & Jung, L.A. (2015). *Assessing young children (5th ed.)*. New York: Pearson.

Fair Test: National Center for Fair and Open Testing

This organization's website provides resources to end the misuses of standardized testing and to ensure fair evaluation of students, teachers, and schools.

Early Learning Challenge Collaborative

This website has valuable information about Kindergarten Entry Assessments and discussion points for using with colleagues and families.

Smarter Balanced Assessment Consortium and Partnership for Assessment of Readiness for College and Careers

These websites describe states' efforts to collaborate on the development and implementation of state-level assessments designed to measure students' progress on meeting Common Core State Standards.

Understanding ESSA (Every Student Succeeds Act)

This website describes the Every Student Succeeds Act of 2015 and provides accurate information about how ESSA requirements are being implemented state by state.

 Shared Writing 11.1

Reflecting on Your Own Experiences with Assessment

12 Teaching Children to Communicate: Language, Literacy, and the Arts

Learning Outcomes

After studying this chapter, you should be able to:

12.1 Describe the continuum of language development from birth to age 8.

12.2 Identify effective strategies to scaffold children's language learning.

12.3 Explain effective strategies for teaching dual language learners.

12.4 Analyze effective teaching strategies to promote early literacy skills.

12.5 Discuss the components of effective literacy instruction in the primary grades.

12.6 Demonstrate how children learn to communicate through the arts.

Related NAEYC Professional Preparation Standards

The NAEYC Professional Preparation Standards (NAEYC, 2011) that apply to this chapter:

1: Promoting Child Development and Learning

Key elements:

    1a. Knowing and understanding young children's characteristics and needs

    1b. Knowing and understanding the multiple influences on development and learning

    1c. Using developmental knowledge to create healthy, respectful, supportive, and challenging learning environments

4: Using Developmentally Effective Approaches to Connect with Children and Families

Key elements:

    4a. Understanding positive relationships and supportive interactions as the foundation of their work with children

    4b. Knowing and understanding effective strategies and tools for early education

    4c. Using a broad repertoire of developmentally appropriate teaching/learning approaches

    4d. Reflecting on their own practice to promote positive outcomes for each child

5: Using Content Knowledge to Build Meaningful Curriculum

Key elements:

    5a. Understanding content knowledge and resources in academic disciplines

    5b. Knowing and using the central concepts, inquiry tools, and structures of content areas or academic disciplines

    5c. Using their own knowledge, appropriate early learning standards, and other resources to design, implement, and evaluate meaningful, challenging curricula for each child

6: Becoming a Professional

Key element:

    6d. Integrating knowledgeable, reflective, and critical perspectives on early education

Case Study

Thurgood Marshall Early Learning Center is a public school serving prekindergarten through second grade. In April, the whole school faculty plans to focus on art appreciation and communication. Each class takes a field trip to the local art museum. In preparation, the kindergarteners take a virtual tour on the museum's website and identify artists and pictures of their work they'd like to see. The teacher, Ms. Barker, ensures that the children examine the work of many different artists, including women and people of color such as Frida Kahlo, Mary Cassatt, Romare Beardon, and Jacob Lawrence. She prints copies of their favorites to focus the children's attention. Each group of four children chooses a picture such as one of Romare Beardon's collages of jazz musicians or one depicting bright sunflowers by Vincent van Gogh. Meeting with each small group, Ms. Barker stimulates their conversations with open-ended questions such as "What do you see? What do you think the artist was feeling/thinking?"

After their discussions, each group tries its hand at producing artwork on the same theme as the artist. Using their own attempts at spelling, children write about or dictate to the teacher descriptions of their pictures and how they compare to the original: "I drew a trumpet and a man who looks like my daddy," says Jenice. "I painted yellow flowers, too, but mine are little," explains Elijah.

Before the visit, the teacher projects pictures by each of the artists on the interactive whiteboard for the whole group to compare subjects, styles, and colors. At the gallery, the groups look for their "own" pictures and the teacher asks if they are surprised by what they see.

Jenice [after carefully studying the Beardon]: It's not a painting at all. It's a collage like we made in pre-K! And I can almost hear music."

Ms. Barker: "Yes, it is a collage. What materials can you identify? Why do you think it makes you hear music?"

Camden [upon encountering the Van Gogh]: It looks rough!

Ms. Barker: How a painting feels is called texture. The painter used thick layers of paint.

Marion [pointing to the copy in his hand]: But here it looks smooth.

Ms. Barker [reinforces the new word]: That's true. The texture of the copy isn't rough. It's smooth.

Tallulah: The sunflowers are so yellow. They almost hurt my eyes.

Ms. Barker: The color in the painting is brighter and more intense than in the copy.

After the trip, children discuss and write about what they observed and create their own art. Their creations and the words they use to describe them are far more detailed than before their visit. The field trip stimulated a new interest, which leads to playing *Museum Mix-Up* on iPad, a game developed by the Fred Rogers Center to help children discover great works of art.

Similar experiences occur in other classes, and the teachers set up a gallery in the hallway. Children display their art next to the posters of the great artists' works that inspired them. In the first and second grades, the children conduct Internet research and read short biographies of the artists. The first-graders are surprised to learn that many famous artists painted outside. The teachers set up easels outside so children can paint the views from their school. Their vocabulary for colors expands as they try to mix new variations to match what they see such as *lavender, chartreuse,* or *magenta.*

The art study lasts several weeks, during which children increase their language and literacy skills. They sharpen their observation skills, learn descriptive vocabulary, and broaden their understanding of how art is used for communication and expression. ■

In this chapter, we address fundamental areas of the early childhood curriculum: language and literacy development. Speaking and understanding, reading, and writing are the foundation of all other learning in school, and are essential for success in life. Also in this chapter, we address the arts, a content area that, in contrast to literacy, is often seen as expendable. Today's emphasis on reading and test scores now drives the curriculum to a large extent. Some schools have eliminated the arts altogether; others use them only as a reward for good behavior. This chapter views the arts as an essential means of communication for young children and demonstrates their connection to other areas of communication: language and reading. Although we describe the integration of the arts, we also believe in art for art's sake, especially for young children, for whom art experiences contribute to development in so many ways.

First, we address the all-important area of language development—how both first and second language develops and ways that teachers can scaffold children's language learning. Next, we discuss the foundations of literacy from birth through age 5, as well as the key components of reading instruction in the primary grades. We then turn to the creative arts, describing goals for art education and teaching strategies to enhance children's enjoyment and engagement in the arts.

Children's Language Development

After three months of separation, 4-year-old Liam is excited to see his Nana. He talks and talks as she tries to quiet him for bedtime. Finally, in exasperation, he says to her, "But I have so many words for you, and they never get tired."

Seeing their language skills blossom is one of the most delightful aspects of teaching young children. Perhaps the most important task of the first five years of life is development of language, because it supports learning in so many other areas. Language is a strong predictor of later success in learning to read and write (National Institute of Child Health and Human Development [NICHD], 2000; Neuman & Wright, 2013). Likewise, children who are skilled communicators demonstrate better social competence and emotional self-regulation.

The Critical Importance of Language Development

Because children seem to learn language naturally, adults often assume that it is simply the product of maturation, like learning to walk. But it is not. Biology primes humans for language, but the language children speak is learned over many years through verbal interaction with adults and other children (IOM & NRC, 2015). By the time they reach preschool, children are experienced users of language. However, the amount and type of language they use may differ from the language used in the school, because children's speech is acquired in the context of their homes and cultural and linguistic community.

Language learning is far from complete when children enter kindergarten or even finish elementary school. Human beings learn language throughout school and life. Undoubtedly, as a college student, you continually add new words to your vocabulary. As a teacher working with a diverse population of children and their families, you will find that your vocabulary will continue to expand.

Types of Language

There are basically two types of language: receptive and expressive. **Receptive language** is the ability to understand what is being said. **Expressive language** is the ability to communicate through use and knowledge of spoken language. Receptive language skills—listening and understanding—develop earlier than the expressive abilities of speaking and communicating. At any point in time, children understand more words and more advanced sentence structures than they use.

Vocabulary Vocabulary is a combination of receptive and expressive language—that is, the number of words a person knows and uses when listening or speaking (Morrow, 2015). An important goal of all teaching is to increase both the quantity and quality of children's receptive and expressive vocabulary. It is not enough that children speak a lot. We must pay attention to the range of words they understand and use—the use of verbs, pronouns, adverbs and adjectives, and other elements of speech (Hirsh-Pasek et al., 2015).

Vocabulary words are the labels children use for concepts they are learning, as well as for those they already know and understand. Consequently, the more limited

receptive language The ability to understand what is being said.

expressive language The ability to communicate; use and knowledge of spoken language.

vocabulary A combination of receptive and expressive language; the number of words a person knows and uses when listening or speaking.

the vocabulary, the more limited the child's understanding of the world (Neuman & Wright, 2013). A child who knows the words *mail, stamp, envelope, address, package,* and *delivery* has a more refined concept of the postal system than a child who refers to all of those concepts as *mail.*

syntax Grammar and sentence structure.

Grammar   Another important element of language development is the complexity of sentence structure that children use, referred to as syntax or grammar. As children become more skilled users of language, their syntax becomes more complex. For example, a toddler may say "me go" to indicate he wants to play outside. But a preschooler will use a more conventional sentence structure such as "I wanna go to the playground and climb the ladder swing."

script language The typical ways that people communicate in different contexts or settings.

academic discourse The language of school, which is important for school success.

A related goal is for children to begin to acquire script language—the typical ways that people communicate in different settings. For example, what the doctor says is different from what the grocery clerk says. Similarly, the way one talks at school is different from the way one talks at home or on the playground. Learning the language of school, what is called academic discourse, is important for school success, and it is not an automatic process. For example, if you have ever seen children "play school," you have seen how they rehearse the script that teachers use (and it is not always comfortable for adults to watch their behavior played back for them).

Language Differences in Children

During the preschool years, language develops far more rapidly than at any other time, but there are enormous individual differences (Hart & Risley, 1999). Of particular concern is that differences in children's language abilities exist between socioeconomic groups as early as 18 months of age (Fernald, Marchman, & Weisleder, 2013). Not only does the size of very young children's vocabularies differ, but also how quickly they process and respond to language. These differences become greater over time and contribute to the persistent achievement gap in our country (Neuman & Wright, 2013). Therefore, programs serving children from low-income families and children from diverse linguistic backgrounds must take on the challenge of accelerating children's language progress.

Effects of Early Language Experience   A classic study of early language acquisition found that socioeconomic advantage was a major factor affecting young children's language development (Hart & Risley, 1995). The researchers videotaped language interactions between parents of different income levels and their children from infancy to age 3. The study found that, over the course of a year, children of parents who were professionals were exposed to more than 11 million words. In contrast, children whose families were receiving public assistance were exposed to only 3 million words.

Researchers estimated that during the first four years of a child's life, an average child in a professional family would have accumulated experience with almost 50 million words, whereas an average child living in poverty would have been exposed to 13 million words (Hart & Risley, 1995). Consequently, children's vocabulary growth reflected their experience. By age 4, children from more affluent homes had vocabularies approximately three times as large as those of children living in poverty. The large vocabulary difference between income groups has come to be called "the 30 million word gap" (Hart & Risley, 2003).

It is important to note that Hart and Risley (1995) found economic advantage to be the *only* factor related to language differences. Race/ethnicity, gender, or birth order of the child made no difference. The researchers also cautioned about negatively judging the parents, who are coping with the many stresses of poverty. Additionally, the Hart and Risley study involved a very small number of families. SES may no longer be as influential a factor, because many of today's economically advantaged parents spend more time on handheld devices than in conversation with their children.

Recently, concerns have been raised about the interpretation of these findings. Focusing on the "word gap" has led to people assuming that what matters is somehow filling the gap with more words. However, researchers now emphasize that just increasing the number of words children hear is not enough; more important is the complexity and variety of language interactions that children experience. (Hirsh-Pasek et al., 2015). For example, learning nouns is relatively simple compared to the task of learning verbs, which convey the action in a sentence and therefore its meaning (Hirsh-Pasek et al., 2015). For example, a child may know the words *car* and *mommy*, but consider the myriad of actions that can link those words. Mommy drove the car, parked it, crashed it, bought it, washed it, and so on. Today, we could even say, "Mommy's car is parking."

To promote all children's language development, teachers must first understand how language typically develops. Teachers must also be aware that various types of disability affect communication; some individual children will need access to assistive technology—*augmented communication devices* and/or sign language.

Developmental Continuum: Oral Language

Language development follows a relatively predictable sequence, but there are individual differences that are well within the range of normal (Hart & Risley, 1999). In addition, as we saw in research cited earlier, if children have many opportunities to speak and be spoken to, they are likely to develop richer, more complex language. The *Developmental Continuum: Oral Language* feature provides an overview of the typical progression of language development and how children of different ages communicate.

Developmental Continuum
Oral Language

cooing Vocalizing vowel sounds.

babble Produce consonant/ vowel sounds such as "ba ba."

Age of Child	Developmental Expectations
Birth to about 8 months	• Communicate through behaviors rather than words; signal distress by crying. Caregivers need to interpret babies' sounds and gestures. • Smile or vocalize if they want someone to pay attention or play. • Begin vocalizing vowel sounds called cooing. Soon after, they begin to babble, producing consonant/vowel sounds such as "ba." • Continue to babble using all kinds of sounds, and will play with sounds when alone. • Begin to understand familiar names such as those of siblings or pets. • Laugh and appear to listen to conversations.
Between 8 and 18 months	• Become more purposeful in their communications. • Use facial expressions, gestures, and sounds to get their needs met. (If a bottle falls from a high chair tray, instead of just crying, the 14-month-old may grunt and wave at the floor.) • Understand many more words than they can say. • Speak in long, babbled sentences that mirror the cadence of conventional speech. • Soon start to shake their head "no" and begin to use the word *me*. • Usually crack the language code and begin to use their first words between 12 and 18 months.

(Continued)

Age of Child	Developmental Expectations
From 18 to 24 months	• Experience a burst in vocabulary and begin to combine words into two-word utterances called telegraphic speech. Like old-fashioned telegrams, they waste no words in communicating their message: "No nap."
Ages 2 to 3	• Progress from using two-word combinations ("my truck") to three- and four-word sentences with words in the correct order more often ("Where's my truck?"). • Speaking vocabulary may reach 200 words. • Use adjectives and adverbs. ("Give me my blue truck now.") • Most children's speech becomes more understandable. Constantly ask "Wassat?" as they seem to want to name everything.
Ages 3 to 6	• By age 4, receptive vocabulary of about 1,500 words and expressive between 600 and 1,000. • Although some may still have difficulty, most are better able to articulate some of the more difficult sounds such as *s, th, z, r,* and *l.* • Can initiate and engage in more complex conversations. • Use 1,500 to 2,000 words as vocabulary expands rapidly during kindergarten. • Usually speak clearly and are lively conversation partners with adults and other children.
The primary grades	• Language development continues at a rapid pace. • During these years, children need a large vocabulary to learn to read and to comprehend what they read. Explicit teaching of vocabulary needs to be an instructional goal. • At the same time, the more children read, the more words they learn, because the language of books is more elaborate than everyday conversation. Some researchers estimate that children need to learn 3,000 words a year throughout the elementary school years.

Sources: Based on O. McAfee & D.J. Leong. 2016. *Assessing and guiding young children's development and learning* (6th ed.). Upper Saddle River, NJ: Pearson; Zero to Three, 2016a. *Your child's development: Age-based tips from birth to 36 months.* Online at zerotothree.org/early-development.

telegraphic speech Combining words into two-word utterances.

Impact of Common Core Speaking and Listening Standards

The Developmental Continuum provided here describes widely held expectations for typical language development. However, the K–3 Common Core Speaking and Listening standards (2011) establish specific expectations by grade level. For example, kindergartners need to participate in collaborative conversations in small and large groups and confirm their understanding of a read-aloud book by asking and answering questions. Standards at each grade level build on earlier abilities and become progressively more challenging. For example, kindergartners need to have back-and-forth conversations; first-graders' conversations need to build on what the other person says through questions and comments; and second-graders need to have multiple exchanges that link what they say to the other person's comments. Obviously, these standards directly affect how teachers teach. Teachers have to move beyond "yes or no" questions to provoking more intellectually engaging, stimulating conversations among children.

In the previous sections, we described the critically important role of early experience to language development and expectations across the period from birth to age 8. Next, we describe what adults can do to help develop children's communication skills.

 Check Your Understanding 12.1

Scaffolding Children's Language Development

As we have seen, public reports about the "30 million word gap" have garnered considerable media attention that can lead to inaccurate information about how to help children develop language. The quality and complexity of children's language experiences matter most (Hirsh-Pasek et al., 2015). However, effective teaching strategies differ based on the age of the children. Next, we discuss developmentally appropriate ways of promoting language in each age group.

Supporting Language Development in Babies and Toddlers

Depicting language development as a progression may imply that it happens automatically. Although very young children learn to talk without formal instruction, adults play a critical role in supporting that process.

Talk to Babies and Toddlers The role of conversational partner is especially important for teachers working with babies and toddlers, because the first three years of life are prime time for developing language and laying the foundation for social interaction (Golinkoff et al., 2015; Hirsh-Pasek et al., 2015). Nevertheless, some teachers and parents of very young children persist in the view that there is no reason to talk to children who can't talk back. The opposite is true. From the earliest moments of life, babies are trying to communicate. Teachers need to talk as if the child can talk back and respond to almost any attempt to communicate.

If you are like most adults, your interaction with a baby may sound like a high-pitched voice saying this: "Hi, Jesse. How are you this morning, baby?" You pause. The infant moves his mouth, waves his arms, or just looks at you intently. And now you say, "Oh, you had a good sleep, did you? Are you ready to have some fun today?" When the baby gurgles, you say, "You are ready, aren't you? Jesse's ready to play!"

Adults (and even older children) talk to babies differently than they do to each other. The high-pitched tone of voice and exaggerated vowel sounds ("youuuu are sweeet") that adults tend to use naturally with babies is called **parentese** or *motherese*, and researchers have observed its use around the world. What's more, using parentese in context (as when feeding or bathing) predicts speech development (Ramirez-Esparza, Garcia-Sierra, & Kuhl, 2014). And babies like it. Infants consistently prefer hearing parentese to adult conversation. In laboratory studies, they show this preference by turning their heads one way to trigger a tape of parentese more often than they turn it the other way to hear a tape of adult-to-adult conversation.

Effective communication begins as babies pay attention and respond. When the child initiates, teachers need to respond enthusiastically and then wait for a response. They interpret what babies are trying to communicate and expand on the message with words. Teachers shouldn't pressure young children to talk. Communication needs to be meaningful; it should not test children with obvious questions such as "What are you doing?" or direct them with comments like "Put the car on the road" (Greenberg &

parentese The high-pitched tone of voice that adults and even children tend to use naturally with babies; also called motherese.

© Carla Mestas/Pearson Education

Infants and toddlers are learning language and literacy skills from birth. What do you think these children are learning from examining this cardboard book?

Weitzman, 2014). Instead, the teacher might say, "Your car is going fast." If the comment sparks the child's interest, the child might respond, "Fast." Then it's the teacher's turn: "You're making the car go very fast."

Describe Their Experiences

play-by-play language
Language that describes what is happening during routines and social interactions with babies and toddlers; also called running commentary.

Describe Their Experiences   One of the most effective ways of building language in babies and toddlers is to use play-by-play language or *running commentary* during routines and social interactions with babies and toddlers. Think of watching a sporting event on TV. A play-by-play announcer describes the action even though you're seeing it before you. This sort of commentary connects actions and objects with words, and familiarizes babies with the cadences of speech. Here's an example of play-by-play during a typical routine, with the words tied to each action: "Let's change your diaper now. I need to pick you up. You're such a big boy. Let's lie down on the changing table. You can hold your horsie. We need to put on some dry pants," and on and on.

Finally, to promote language in babies and toddlers, two very important points must be kept in mind. First, children need a lot of opportunities to play with different kinds of toys, to touch real objects, and to move around. Think of the many different words a child could learn from playing in water, eating applesauce, climbing on a low ramp, rolling a ball, or looking at a cardboard book. Secondly, in each of these situations, teachers need to supply the words. While children play on a ramp, the teacher can introduce verbs such as *slide, roll, climb, push,* and many more.

As children's understanding and language use improves, teachers need to adapt their language by using longer, more complex comments and more sophisticated vocabulary. Many of these same strategies apply to promoting language with preschoolers, discussed next.

Scaffolding Preschoolers' Language Development

Research demonstrates that several strategies are particularly effective in promoting preschooler's language acquisition (Dickinson, 2011; Neuman & Wright, 2013). These strategies include modeling language, conversation, listening, decontextualized speech, and intentional teaching of new words.

Model Language and Complex Vocabulary   Teachers do a lot of talking, and are important role models for children. Therefore, they need to use standard grammatical speech. They also need to recognize that many of the grammatical errors children make, such as *I goed to the store* or *three sheeps,* show their efforts to learn a language rule. As they learn the rule, like using *s* to indicate plural, they overgeneralize it. Instead of pointing out the mistake, a more effective approach is to pick up on what the child says and say it correctly. A child might say, "I gots two foots," to which the teacher replies, "Yes, you have two feet, so you need two socks."

Similarly, if children speak a dialect or African American language (AAL), teachers should not correct or prohibit their speech. Doing so tells children that the speech of their family and cultural group is inferior. This negative message may inhibit children's attempts to communicate (Boutte, 2015). Instead, teachers need to recognize that African American language is a systematic, rule-governed, parallel form of English. For example, the verb "to be" is used in a particular, consistent way in the language. In supportive classrooms, children who speak AAL become essentially bilingual, speaking both standard English and the language of their family and community. A teacher can use strategies such as acknowledging the child's statement and restating it in standard English. Books can also be a valuable resource such as the story *Flossie and the Fox,* in which Flossie speaks AAL as she outwits a clever fox who speaks standard English (McKissack, 1986).

Engage in One-to-One Conversation   One of the most effective strategies for promoting children's language development is engaging them in one-to-one conversations (Dickinson, 2011; Neuman & Wright, 2013). When children are served in groups, the task of supporting each child's language acquisition and understanding what they are trying to say can be daunting. Too often, the children whose language is most advanced are spoken to more often. This leads to a vicious cycle where those children who are lagging behind get less language interaction than they need, while those who need less actually get more.

Extend Conversation One of the best ways to build children's vocabulary is to increase the amount of talk in the classroom and to intentionally extend conversations. **Extended discourse** occurs when adults talk with children in ways that build on and expand what the children say. Such conversations with open-ended questions and many back-and-forth exchanges improve children's vocabularies and self-regulation (Cabell et al., 2015; Farran et al, 2017; Strasser & Bresson, 2017). Head Start calls these "thick" conversations as opposed to "thin" ones. In short, teachers need to use fewer conversation closers and more conversation stretchers, as described in Table 12.1.

> **extended discourse** Talking with children in ways that build on and expand what they say.

Build Listening Comprehension Conversation involves turn-taking. One person speaks and the other person listens. Listening is critical to understanding what is said. In addition, listening comprehension prepares young children for later reading comprehension (Jalongo, 2008). As important as listening is, most teachers do not treat it as a skill to be taught. When adults tell children to "listen," they often mean "behave" or "do as I say." No wonder children often tune out the word.

TABLE 12.1 Improving Teacher–Child Conversations

The examples in this table help teachers become more aware of how they can encourage and extend conversations with children or unwittingly close off communication.

AVOID Conversation Closers—Types of Teacher Talk That Cut Off Conversation with Individual Children

Conversation Closers	Examples
Answering own questions—talking for children or over children	Teacher speaking without waiting for a reply: "How did you like our trip to the firehouse, Jack? I bet you liked hearing the fire bell. I saw you looking at the pole. That was neat."
Moralizing	Jack: "I wanna ring that bell." Teacher: "You can't ring the bell. It's not allowed."
Using empty praise or phrases	Teacher: "That's nice, Jack." "Good boy."
Time-passing remarks	Jack: "Can we drive the truck?" Teacher: "We'll be going pretty soon."
Focusing on safety and rules	Jack: "Look, I found a caterpillar." Teacher: "You'll have to wash your hands now."

INCREASE Conversation Stretchers—Types of Teacher Talk That Extend One-to-One Conversation and Contribute to More Turn-Taking

Conversation Stretchers	Examples
Focusing on and adding details	"The firefighter's boots are tall. Let's see how big they are compared to your shoes, Jack. They're gigantic. Why do you think they have these handles?"
Expanding and asking questions	"It sounds like you want to build a firehouse out of your blocks with a pole. What materials will you need?"
Repeating important words	"Here's the fire extinguisher. We have a fire extinguisher like this at school. Who remembers where we keep the extinguisher?"
Sharing own experiences	"When I was on my way to school, I heard an ambulance siren. It startled me."
Explaining terms	"A false alarm. *False* means it is not real. So a false alarm means there isn't a real fire."
Wondering aloud	"I wonder what it would be like to work in a fire station …"
Using wait time	Giving 5 to 10 seconds for children to respond. The other children and you will learn that waiting for a less verbal child can sometimes yield keen insights.

Source: Based on K. A. Roskos, P. O. Tabors, & L. A. Lenhart, 2009. *Oral language and early literacy in preschool: Talking, reading, and writing* (2nd ed.). Newark, DE: International Reading Association; E. Weitzman & J. Greenberg, 2002. *Learning language and loving it: A guide to promoting children's social, language, and literacy development in early childhood settings* (2nd ed.). Toronto: The Hanen Centre.

listening The process of taking in information through the sense of hearing and making meaning from what is heard.

Young children need to listen in order to learn; therefore, they need to learn to listen (Jalongo, 2008). Because teachers or parents tell children, "be quiet, sit still, and listen," listening may seem a passive activity. However, effective listening is an active process. Listening is "the process of taking in information through the sense of hearing and making meaning from what was heard" (Jalongo, 2008, p. 12).

To promote listening and understanding, teachers should model good listening for children. Children whose teachers spend more time listening to them exhibit stronger literacy and math abilities (Farran et al., 2017). Teachers can use the conversation stretchers and avoid the conversation closers listed in Table 12.1 and depicted in the following example:

> Ms. Abell's kindergarten class gathers around her for meeting time. The children become excited when they spy the "mystery box," which signals that they are going to play one of their favorite games.
>
> *Ms. Abell, putting her hand inside the box:* I'm touching something that is hard and has points on one end.
> *The children take turns guessing:* A pencil…. a knife…. a carrot.
> *Ms. Abell:* Listen to my clue. I said points.
> *Ashley:* I know. It's scissors. (The other children nod and agree.)
> *Ms. Abell, feeling in the box:* "That's close, but it has four points, called prongs."
>
> Because *prongs* is a new word for them, the children need other clues. Ms. Abell says, "Who can remember all the clues?" After Dorsey lists the clues so far, Ms. Abell adds another one: "You use it at lunchtime." Soon, Robin figures out that the mystery item is a fork.

This game is only one of the ways in which Ms. Abell promotes listening skills. During center time, a group plays a matching sounds Lotto game. Two children from Cambodia listen to a story on tape in their home language. Ms. Abell sets up a treasure hunt in which children must listen and follow a series of directions to find the surprise.

decontextualized speech Talk about events, experiences, or people that are beyond the here and now or that inhabit children's imaginations.

Use Decontextualized Speech One of the most effective ways to expand children's language is to use decontextualized speech. This is talk about events, experiences, or people that are beyond the here and now or that inhabit children's imaginations. Such interaction requires children and adults to use more complex and varied vocabulary in explanations, descriptions, dialogue, and pretend talk.

Decontextualized speech can be complicated, because the speaker and the listener can't rely on cues from the context to understand the communication. When children talk about the here and now, the context permits using words such as *this, that, there, here,* and *it*. These are words that children already know. Such conversation doesn't require or challenge them to use more descriptive language to be understood.

Furthermore, decontextualized speech is valuable preparation for reading (Snow et al., 1998). In spoken communication, lots of cues such as gestures, facial expressions, physical space, and objects are available. If someone says, "Take your seat," the listener quickly understands that he is being told to sit down. But if the same sentence appears in writing, the reader would have to figure out whether it means *sit in a chair* or *pick up a cushion*. This is just one example of the important connection between speaking and reading.

Teach New and Rare Words Four-year-old Liam has a new baby brother named Ryan. Liam decides that the baby should be named Nathan, after his best friend at preschool. The first few days after Ryan comes home from the hospital, Liam persists in calling him Nathan. His parents don't correct him, but they keep calling the baby *Ryan*. Sitting next to his mom and Ryan on the couch one day, Liam thoughtfully says, "We can call him Rynathan. That will be a compromise."

Liam's advanced vocabulary, which also includes words such as *actually, amazing, entertaining,* and *nocturnal,* did not develop by chance. His parents and teachers talk with him, use these words regularly, and explain and show what they mean.

Learning new words occurs through repeated exposure to the words in a context where the meaning becomes clear. Liam's parents undoubtedly negotiate with him rather than get into power struggles. For example, if he wants to watch TV and his mother wants him to go outside, she might say, "Let's compromise. You can go outside while it's still light, and we'll record the program so you can watch it later." After hearing and using this word several times, Liam begins to use it himself.

Teachers need to use explicit instruction to expand children's vocabulary, and should intentionally introduce new and **rare words**—multisyllable, sophisticated words that are not typically part of a child's vocabulary (Neuman & Wright, 2013). For example, in *The Tale of Peter Rabbit*, Peter's coat gets caught in the fence and the birds *implore* him to *exert* himself. Before reading the book, the teacher introduces these words with simple definitions: "*Implore* means to ask someone to do something you really want them to do" and "*Exert* means to try really hard." During the reading, she pauses at the sentence to ask the children what it means. Later, she reinforces the learning by using the new words repeatedly, sometimes jokingly—"I implore you to get your coats on"—and encouraging children to use them.

rare words Multisyllable words that are not typically part of a young child's vocabulary.

Use Interactive Book Reading One of the most effective ways to promote children's language and increase their vocabulary is to engage in interactive book reading (Zucker et al., 2013). In many classrooms, storybook reading is the favorite activity of teachers as well as children. However, teachers usually read books only to the whole group (Dickinson, 2011). At times, reading is seen as entertainment only; at other times, teachers use it as a transition activity, with children taking turns to go wash their hands while the teacher reads. These practices are missed opportunities for learning. Instead, interactive book reading can serve many valuable purposes for individual children, as we see in the following example (based on Connect Module—Embedded Interventions, 2010):

> Four-year-old Tristan eagerly joins a group of friends in his Head Start classroom during choice time. At least 10% of Head Start children have identified disabilities, and like the majority of those children, Tristan has a speech and language delay. His teacher, Ms. Freedman, uses interactive book reading to help meet Tristan's speech therapy goals and also to build all the children's language development. As she reads a book specially made by Tristan's therapist to a small group of five children, all the children respond to the language prompts. The children love it when Ms. Freedman passes around a mirror and they see how to put their lips together to make the /m/, /b/, and /p/ sounds. In this inclusive classroom, Tristan receives peer support to improve his speech articulation, and the other children serve as language models for him.

Wordless picture books are another way to support children's language. If teachers discuss the pictures *with* children, their verbal interactions are more lengthy and complex (Chaparo-Marino, Reali, & Maldonado-Carreno, 2017).

Read in Small Groups The power of reading is not in the book alone, but in the conversation about the book among teachers and children before, during, and after reading (Gonzalez et al., 2014). This type of interaction is more likely to occur in a small group than in the whole group or even in a one-on-one reading situation (Bates, 2013; McGee, 2013). Reading in small groups and rereading the same book are especially effective strategies for dual language learners and children from low-income families (International Literacy Association [ILA], 2017a&b; Schickedanz & Collins, 2013).

Small groups make it possible for each child to see the pictures, follow the print, participate in a discussion, and comprehend the story better. Small-group reading makes it more feasible for teachers to interact with children before, during, and after reading. This is particularly valuable when the book has a complex narrative and rare words. A **narrative** is a story with a beginning, middle, and end; characters; dialogue; and a plot with a problem to solve or a dilemma to be resolved. Interactive, shared book reading is a highly effective strategy for expanding children's language and listening comprehension.

narrative A story with a beginning, middle, and end; characters; dialogue; and a plot with a problem to solve or a dilemma to be resolved.

Research on early literacy has led to considerable emphasis on shared book reading to promote children's understanding of narrative and language. Such emphasis on the written word fails to harness the power of oral storytelling traditions in various cultural groups, as described in the feature *Culture Lens: The Power of Storytelling*.

Culture Lens
The Power of Storytelling

A new study involving more than 6,000 children nationwide demonstrated for the first time that African American preschoolers' storytelling abilities are positively related to the development of their early reading skills in kindergarten. The researchers found that preschool oral narrative skills predicted early literacy for both poor and non-poor African American kindergartners. They did not find this relationship for other children in the study, *only* for the African American children.

Previous research has found that African American children are skillful at telling many different types of complex stories, which may explain this study's results. African American children tend to flexibly vary the narrative according to context. Such storytelling ability may benefit the children as they move from oral language to "real" reading in school, which requires decoding and comprehending written text.

Oral storytelling is an especially rich aspect of African American culture. It is also an important part of the histories and present-day life of children of other ethnicities. This study has important implications for schools looking to connect with and improve the reading achievement of all children—particularly children of color, who come from a culture in which oral storytelling skills are esteemed and treasured. Teachers need to view children's storytelling as a strength and use it to help all children become proficient readers and writers.

Source: N. Gardner-Neblett & I. Iruka, 2017. Viewing African American children's oral language skills as a strength. In I. U. Iruka, S M. Curenton, & T. R. Durden (Eds.), *African American children in early childhood education (Advances in race and ethnicity in education, Vol. 5).* Emerald Publishing Limited, 123–141.

Use Dialogic Reading One of the most effective ways to build children's language and literacy skills is **dialogic reading**, an interactive, shared picture book reading (Institute of Education Sciences, 2007). During the shared reading practice, the adult and child gradually switch roles so that the child learns to become the storyteller with the assistance of the adult, who plays the role of active listener and questioner.

dialogic reading Interactive, shared picture book reading during which the adult and the child gradually switch roles so that the child learns to become the storyteller with the assistance of the adult, who plays the role of active listener and questioner.

Teachers can use dialogic reading with children individually or in small groups. While reading books with the children, the teacher uses five types of prompts or questioning strategies to stimulate children's language interaction. Prompts are used by the adult in a reading technique called PEER:

Prompts the child to say something about the book.
Evaluates (listens to) the child's response to decide how to respond.
Expands the child's response.
Repeats the prompt.

As the child becomes increasingly familiar with a book, the adult reads less, listens more, and gradually uses more high-level prompts to encourage the child to go beyond naming objects in the pictures to thinking about what is happening in the pictures and how this relates to the child's own experiences.

Research on dialogic reading demonstrates that it enhances the language skills of children from middle- and upper-income families more than typical picture book reading. More important, studies conducted with children from low-income families and children with disabilities found substantial positive effects on language (Towson, Gallagher, & Bingham, 2016).

A handy mnemonic device to remember the five prompts is the word *CROWD*. Table 12.2 lists the prompts with examples of questions from a reading of *The Tale of Peter Rabbit* by Beatrix Potter.

Application Exercise 12.1

Table 12.2: Dialogic Reading CROWD Prompts

TABLE 12.2   Dialogic Reading CROWD Prompts

Prompt	Description	Example
*C*ompletion prompt	Child completes an incomplete sentence.	Teacher: "Peter Rabbit got stuck in _____ ."
*R*ecall questions	Teacher asks specific questions about the book the child has read.	Teacher: "What did Peter lose in the garden?"
*O*pen-ended questions	Teacher encourages child to describe what is happening in a picture.	Showing the picture of Peter caught and the birds flapping their wings, the teacher asks: "How are the birds helping Peter?"
Wh-questions	Teacher asks *Wh-* questions about the book that help children think about a character's motives or feelings.	Teacher: "Why do you think Peter went in the garden even though his mother told him not to?"
*D*istancing questions	Teacher relates pictures and words in the book to children's own experiences outside of the book.	Teacher: "Have you ever been scared like Peter? What happened? What did you do?"

Source: Based on Dialogic Reading (What Works Clearinghouse Intervention Report), by Institute of Education Sciences, 2007, Washington, DC:U.S. Department of Education.

Reading to the Whole Group   The effectiveness of small-group reading does not mean that teachers should never read to the whole group. If the book is relatively short and involves children's active participation and *predictable* text, whole-group reading may be the best choice. **Predictable books** use parallel text structures that become familiar to children, such as those in Bill Martin's *Brown Bear, Brown Bear* or Dr. Seuss's *Hop on Pop*. The whole group can chime in during Eric Carle's *The Very Hungry Caterpillar*, with predictable text such as "But he was still hungry."

Throughout life, children develop language and literacy skills simultaneously, and the two are interrelated (ILA, 2018; Zero to Three, 2016b). Reading to children enhances their language, because the structures and words used in books are more complex than those used in everyday speech. Knowing more words, in turn, helps children make sense of print and find what they read more meaningful and interesting. Talking with children about what is read further boosts vocabulary and comprehension. But what about children who don't speak the language of the classroom? Next, we discuss the timely topic of learning in two languages.

© Pearson Education

Video Example 12.1:

Language and Early Literacy

This video provides an example of an outstanding first grade lesson based on the story of the *Three Bears*. What do you notice about the children's language and literacy skills, comprehension, and motivation to learn? How does the teacher support dual language learners?

 Check Your Understanding 12.2

> **completion prompt** A prompt that requires the child to verbally complete the end of a sentence.
>
> **recall questions** Questions asked by the teacher about a book to see what children remember.
>
> **Wh-questions** Questions that begin with "why" or "what" to get children thinking about characters' motives or feelings.
>
> **distancing questions** Questions that relate pictures and words in the book to children's own experiences beyond the book.
>
> **predictable books** Books with controlled vocabulary using parallel text structures that become familiar to children.
>
> **dual language learning** Simultaneously learning two languages: the home, or first, language and English or another second language.

Teaching Dual Language Learners

Consider these two phrases: *English language learners* and *dual language learners*. The first communicates that the focus is on children learning English. In contrast, **dual language learning** conveys that children are learning two languages—their home, or first, language as well as English or another second language. Effective teachers understand the process by which children acquire a second language and how best to support children as they learn two languages.

How Children Learn a Second Language

Acquiring two or more languages is a complex process that doesn't happen as easily for young children as some people think. Generally, children take one of two paths to

simultaneous acquisition
Learning two languages at the same time during the earliest years of life.

becoming bilingual—either simultaneous or sequential (National Academies of Science, Engineering, and Medicine [NASEM] , 2017). When children learn two languages at the same time during the earliest years of life—simultaneous acquisition—their dual language development is similar to that of monolingual children, those who are learning only one language. All over the world, children grow up in homes learning multiple languages from birth. Sometimes, one language will become more dominant depending on the context. Similarly, it is normal for vocabulary development in each language to be uneven (NASEM, 2017).

sequential language learning
Learning a second language *after* the first language is relatively well established.

By contrast, many children, especially in the United States, are sequential language learners. They learn a second language *after* their first language is relatively well established (NASEM, 2017). Learning two languages sequentially is a more complicated, highly individual process that varies with children's personality, experience, and other factors, but tends to follow a relatively predictable pattern, which is described in the next section.

Developmental Continuum: Dual Language Acquisition

The sequence of second language acquisition is described in the feature *Developmental Continuum: Second Language Learning*. The length of time individual children spend at each level varies, and unlike learning their home language, learning a second language is a conscious process that requires effort.

Developmental Continuum
Second Language Learning

Stage	Description	How Teachers Can Help
Stage 1: Home Language Use The child speaks the home language only.	Even though other people are speaking English, children may not realize or understand that the two languages differ. At first, they try to use their home language, but soon learn that this isn't working. At some point, this becomes frustrating and they stop trying, leading to the second stage.	Teachers provide cues to help children make sense of words by pointing to and labeling objects. At lunchtime, Rachel sits with a group of Spanish-speaking 4-year-olds. As they eat, she labels the utensils and food, speaking slowly and distinctly. "Spoon," she says as she picks up her own. "Here's your spoon for your soup," as she guides Carlos to follow her directions.
Stage 2: Nonverbal, Observational Period After children stop trying to speak in their first language, they enter a period where they may not talk at all, but rather listen and observe.	This period can last for a long time or can be relatively brief, depending on the individual. This stage is sometimes called the silent period, but a better name is the nonverbal period. Silent implies that no communication occurs. Actually, during this period, children are learning a lot about the new language by listening and observing, but they are not verbal themselves. Children may not be talking, but that does not mean they are not communicating.	Teachers should not force children to speak. Children may try to communicate nonverbally to get help from adults or other children. They may point to the object they want or smile when their request is granted. Gradually, they begin to rehearse the new language by speaking some words quietly to themselves or playing with the sounds. A child says "Paint paper," and the teacher interprets whether the child wants to paint or take her picture home.
Stage 3: Telegraphic and Formulaic Speech Children have a small, working vocabulary in the second language and begin to use it out loud.	Children speak in one- or two-word utterances and repeat routine phrases without understanding what they mean. At story time, Carlos automatically says "It's circle time" because he has heard these words in this context many times.	Teachers give simple choices that require "yes" or "no" or one-word responses, such as "Do you want to play with blocks or paint?" Children can also answer simple *who*, *what*, or *where* questions.

(Continued)

Stage	Description	How Teachers Can Help
Stage 4: Productive Language Children begin producing the new language. This stage can take 1 to 2 years, during which children gradually produce longer sentences.	Listening comprehension improves as receptive language increases. Children use the social language of the classroom or playground, such as "My turn now" or "Be my friend." They begin to apply the grammar rules of the new language, but not consistently. Children are better able to participate in academic learning.	Rather than correcting "errors," teachers strive for communication. Carlos might say, "I like my school big" rather than "I like my big school." His teacher responds, "I'm glad you like our big school." Teachers ask *how* and *why* questions that require short responses: "How did your shoes get wet?"
Stage 5: Fluent Second-Language Production Moving from emergent to fluent language production can take 1 to 2 years.	Children can understand what is said in the classroom and begin to understand written communications.	Teachers use open-ended questions that engage children in producing more complex sentences. Second language learners will probably need extra help in the early grades, where the curriculum focuses on learning to read. Teaching reading in the home language is most effective.
Stage 6: Advanced Language Proficiency	Children have developed understanding of specialized, content-related vocabulary. It can take 5 to 7 years for children to master this level of cognitively demanding language.	Teachers intentionally teach the vocabulary and language skills required for academic achievement in school. For example, mathematics requires knowing words such as *addend* or *double-digit multiplication* that are not used in everyday speech.

Sources: Based on L. Espinosa, 2015. *Getting it right for children from diverse backgrounds: Applying research to improve practice with an emphasis on dual language learners* (2nd ed.). Upper Saddle River, NJ: Pearson.

Young children who are learning a new language will often alternate between the two languages even within the same sentence. When children understand and use elements of both their home language or dialect and English, they **code switch**, also called language mixing. Teachers aren't always sure what to do about it. Code switching is a well-developed skill in most bilingual, bicultural individuals, and it contributes to their ability to think and analyze complex problems and express emotions (NASEM, 2017). To learn more about this skill and how teachers should respond to it, read the feature *Language Lens: Understanding and Responding to Code Switching*.

code switch The ability to understand and use both the mainstream version of English and the home dialect or language.

Teaching Dual Language Learners

Several myths about teaching dual language learners continue to persist despite research to the contrary. Some of the most common myths are that children must learn one language before they can learn another, that learning a second language delays or interferes with learning the first, or that learning more than one language harms brain functioning (Espinosa, 2015). In fact, learning two languages does not confuse or overwhelm children, nor does it unduly delay their English acquisition.

Research demonstrates that beginning at birth, all children have the capacity to learn any of the world's languages, and the younger the child's brain, the greater its capacity to learn more than one language (Rivera-Gaxiola, Silva-Pereyra, & Kuhl, 2008). Moreover, bilingualism in children ages 4 to 8 has long-term positive effects on cognitive development and executive function, including the ability to think flexibly and solve problems that require taking different perspectives (Bialystok, 2015). This may be because bilingualism regularly requires children to mentally shift between two language systems.

Some non-English-speaking parents are so concerned that their children learn English that they avoid speaking their native language, and want early childhood programs to do the same. In these cases, teachers need to help parents understand that it is important for children to have a strong foundation in their home language. Maintaining and developing the home language is vital for nurturing family relationships and cultural values (Espinosa, 2015).

Video Example 12.2:

Teaching Dual Language Learners

A primary grade teacher, Ms. Gomez, explains why she teaches in both English and Spanish. How do her students benefit academically from such bilingual instruction? What impact does the teacher's use of both languages have on the children's social-emotional development?

Language Lens
Understanding and Responding to Code Switching

Code switching is the ability to understand and use both the commonly accepted version of English and the home language or dialect. When children are learning a second language, they often code switch, usually beginning a sentence in one language and then switching to the other, as in: "I drew a picture de mi madre" or "Mi mano es dirty." Code switching is not limited to children. In fact, bilingual people of all ages alternate between languages depending on the setting and the topic of conversation. Many bilingual individuals find that they can best express their feelings and personal thoughts in their native language.

In the past, it was assumed that code switching meant that children were confused or incompetent. But now we know that the opposite is true: Children are able to separate the languages in their brains and apply the different rules of grammar of each language. Code switching is actually a sign of children's growing communicative competence. They are using all they know to communicate as clearly as they can.

So what should teachers do about code switching? First, they should expect code switching as a normal aspect of dual language learning. The most important thing is *not* to correct children when they mix languages. Correcting children's language attempts sends a signal that they've done something wrong. They may stop trying to communicate in order to avoid making the "mistake" of code switching.

Instead of focusing on a child's "errors," teachers should focus on understanding the child's message. They should view code switching as a strength. As always, teachers should be good language models themselves, using the same strategies that promote language learning in all children: listening and responding in a meaningful way, using real objects and nonverbal cues, intentionally teaching new words, and extending conversations with questions and ideas.

Sometimes, bilingual teachers think they can support dual language learning by alternating languages themselves. Again, the opposite is true. Children's brains will automatically listen and respond to the language they know best and tune out the other one. To promote dual language development, bilingual teachers can read books in each language, but should do so at separate times.

Encouraging children to code switch and responding positively honors the language system that they already possess and helps them adapt to different communication requirements in different situations. It also respects and supports their cultural identity, because language and culture are inextricably linked. Teachers should always create a warm, positive classroom climate in which children feel safe to express themselves. Capable code switchers acquire the ability to think about their own use of language, which serves them well in other learning situations and has long-lasting positive effects on language, executive function, and social development.

Source: National Center on Cultural and Linguistic Responsiveness, n.d. *Code switching: Why it matters and how to respond.* Washington, DC: U.S. Department of Health and Human Services, Office of Head Start. Retrieved February 21, 2018, from http://eclkc.ohs.acf.hhs.gov/hslc/tta-system/cultural-linguistic/fcp/docs/code-switching.pdf.

As for school achievement, the more words and concepts children know in their first language, the more likely that knowledge will transfer as children become proficient in English (Espinosa, 2015). Learning to read is also more effective when instruction occurs in the home language (NASEM, 2017). Children who receive content instruction in their home language perform better academically later in school than those enrolled in programs designed primarily to teach them English (ILA, 2017a; ILA, 2017b). The reality of so many dual language learners in today's classrooms means that teachers have a special responsibility to help children make progress in understanding and speaking *both* English *and* their home language.

In the previous sections, we described how children learn both their first and second languages and ways to promote language development from birth through primary grades. Next, we turn to the related topic of how children become literate.

✔ Check Your Understanding 12.3

 Promoting Early Literacy: Birth through Age 5

Young children begin the process of learning to read and write long before they enter formal school. Decades of research shows that children who enter kindergarten with specific kinds of knowledge and skills are more likely to become successful readers and writers (National Early Literacy Panel [NELP], 2008; Shanahan & Lonigan, 2013).

Developmental Continuum: Early Literacy Learning

Some of the widely held expectations for children's literacy development from birth through age 5 are presented in the *Developmental Continuum: Early Literacy* feature. Accomplishing these goals assumes that children have had good learning opportunities. Individual children's progress will vary depending on their prior experiences with written language and other factors.

 Developmental Continuum
Early Literacy

Age Range	Widely Held Expectations
Most babies (about 6 to 12 months)	• Play with books, so books should be made of sturdy cardboard • Put them in their mouths, chew them • Open and close them • Bang on them • Look at the pictures briefly • Will look at the book with an adult for a short time
Most toddlers (about 12 to 24 months)	• Love to look at the same book again and again • Point out pictures to the adult and label pictures with names • Like to turn the pages (though not in order) • Sit for a few minutes to look at a book • Pretend to read by turning the pages and babbling • Connect the pictures to real objects (point out a doll after seeing the picture of a doll) • Take books off the shelf • Like books with textures or sounds
Most 2-year-olds	• Recognize favorite books by their covers • Listen to short stories and enjoy book-reading routines such as lap book reading • Label objects pictured in books • Begin to pay attention to print, especially the first letter of their names • Play with sounds and enjoy rhymes and songs • Scribble and gradually produce increasingly controlled scribbles with some letter-like forms (circles and lines)

(Continued)

Age Range	Widely Held Expectations
Most 3- and 4-year-olds	• Enjoy listening to and talking about age-appropriate story books and information books • Understand that print carries a message • Can follow the sequence of events in a story and answer questions that demonstrate listening comprehension • Pretend to read and attempt to write • Recognize familiar labels and environmental print (signs for stores, street signs) • Understand concepts of print and directionality (English is read left-to-right and top-to-bottom) • Attend to chunks of sound in spoken language, identify rhymes and alliteration (silly Susie), clap syllables • Recognize many letters, especially those in meaningful words • Make some letter-sound matches (as when attempting to write words) • Use known letters and letter-like symbols to represent written language

Sources: Based on O. McAfee & D.J. Leong 2016. *Assessing and guiding young children's development and learning* (6th ed.), and L. M. Morrow, 2015. *Literacy development in the early years: Helping children read and write* (8th ed.). Upper Saddle River, NJ: Pearson.

© Pearson Education

▶ **Video Example 12.3:**

Print Rich Environment

This video features an early childhood program. How does a print-rich environment contribute to children's early literacy learning? What should an intentional teacher do to ensure that children learn optimally in such an environment?

Teachers need to be intentional in promoting children's language and literacy learning. This means that they thoughtfully plan and prepare in advance but are also playful. Children need to playfully explore and engage in activities involving reading, writing, and learning letters and sounds. These opportunities are more likely to occur in a literacy-rich environment.

Literacy-Rich Environments

Some children grow up in homes where they observe family members reading books and magazines, writing lists, browsing the internet, or answering email. But access to literacy and technology is unequal in our society. Affluent American children may have as many books in their bedrooms as poor children have in their entire neighborhoods. Many low-income communities have so little access to books and print that they have been called "book deserts" (Neuman & Moland, 2016).

Children learn whether literacy is valued and important from their environment. Therefore, every classroom needs to be rich in literacy-enhancing materials and experiences. To picture a literacy-rich environment, consider the following example:

A look into Ms. DeSoto's preschool room reveals the many ways she creates an environment that communicates the value of literacy to children and teaches them important skills. In strategic places, she posts signs, labels, and other print materials that have real purposes, such as the names of today's helpers, classroom attendance, message boxes, menus, and directions. But she is careful not to clutter the classroom, because too much print on the walls becomes as meaningless to children as wallpaper. Instead, she engages children in creating and using the print and calls children's attention to it, as when she points to the written schedule on the wall and says, "Let's look at the schedule and see what we will do after lunch."

One of the children's favorite spots is the cozy, well-lit library area with its comfortable, child-size furniture and pictures of favorite story characters. Books are attractively displayed on open shelves, accessible to children and inviting their interest, much as bookstores do when they attractively display covers of new titles. The classroom library is well stocked with at least five books per child, with two to three per child on display at one time. The collection includes culturally and developmentally appropriate storybooks, information books, wordless picture books, and poetry. There are also iPads with e-books and apps in multiple languages.

Ms. DeSoto places books and writing tools in centers where they are relevant, such as a book on construction in the block area and paper and markers to make signs. Even a casual observer notices that books are in children's hands throughout the day, not just in the teacher's hands during story time. Shelves are stocked with games, toys, and equipment that promote knowledge of letters and sounds such as alphabet blocks, magnetic letters, and an alphabet puzzle. Handheld digital devices are available with apps for children to practice letters and phonological awareness as well as more sophisticated apps with which children practice writing and creating their own stories.

early literacy Skills and knowledge that come before and lead up to (forerunners) conventional reading and writing.

predictors Set of early literacy skills and knowledge that increase the likelihood of later success in learning to read and write.

Early Literacy from Birth to Kindergarten

Early literacy is the knowledge and skills that are the forerunners of conventional reading and writing. Research demonstrates that specific early literacy skills predict later success in learning to read and write (Shanahan & Lonigan, 2013). These **predictors** do not guarantee success, but they do increase the likelihood of success. More important, without these abilities upon entrance to kindergarten, children are more likely to encounter difficulties in learning to read (Snow et al., 1998).

Research-based early literacy skills include phonological awareness, alphabet knowledge, print awareness, and oral language (Shanahan & Lonigan, 2013). Other important skills that contribute to later reading include writing (specifically, name writing), listening comprehension, and motivation to read. Because these abilities are essential predictors of later reading success, Head Start provides a consumer's guide to evidence-based language and literacy curricula that are designed around these goals (National Center for Quality Teaching and Learning, 2015). In the following sections, we define and describe each of these skills and ways teachers can promote children's literacy learning. (In the previous sections, we described numerous strategies for building vocabulary.)

Literacy-rich environments help children experience the pleasure and power of reading and writing. In classrooms such as this one, children use print for real purposes. What would children learn about literacy in this environment?

Phonological Awareness and Letter Knowledge Written language is a symbol system—a code that children need to learn. This code may seem abstract and beyond young children's capacity. However, children are constantly exposed to abstract symbols, including *walk/don't walk* symbols, computer icons and emojis, pictures to signify restrooms—the list is endless.

Precisely because written language is a complex symbol system, children need practice playing with it over many years to become proficient users (Morrow, 2015). At preschool, the two important skills for learning the code are phonological awareness and learning the alphabet (Shanahan & Lonigan, 2013).

Understanding Phonological Awareness **Phonological awareness** is the consciousness that the stream of spoken language is made up of smaller units or chunks of sound (Schickedanz & Collins, 2013). Phonological awareness develops along a continuum, from recognizing the larger units of sound such as **rhymes** (two words ending with the same sound) and **alliteration** (two words beginning with the same sound), to the smaller units such as syllables. A more complex level of phonological awareness involves awareness of parts of syllables.

phonological awareness Consciousness that the stream of spoken language is made up of smaller units or chunks of sound.

rhymes Two words ending with the same sound.

alliteration Two words beginning with the same sound.

phonemic awareness Recognizing that spoken words are made up of individual sounds that can be manipulated.

phonemes The individual sounds of spoken language; changing one in a word changes the meaning of the word.

The most difficult level is phonemic awareness, or recognizing that spoken words are made up of individual sounds called phonemes. English has approximately 44 phonemes that are represented by the 26 letters of the alphabet either alone or in combination. The letter *m* stands for a sound, while the letters *th* stand for another sound. The word *bat* is made up of three phonemes: /b/, /a/, and /t/. If one phoneme is changed—using /m/ instead of /b/—the meaning of the word is changed. Phonemes are important to later reading, because written language represents these sounds.

Teaching Phonological Awareness As with virtually every other early literacy skill, children do not automatically acquire phonological awareness. Teachers need to intentionally plan experiences that help children make progress on the phonological awareness continuum, beginning with the bigger chunks of speech (words) and eventually moving to the smallest ones (individual phonemes). Some preschool teachers provide limited experiences or continue rhyming activities (although children have acquired this skill) rather than moving on to more complex abilities (Pelatti, Piasta, Justice, & O'Connell, 2014). On the other hand, in some classrooms too much time is spent drilling children on phonological awareness, even though it is estimated that learning the skills requires only about six minutes of instruction a day (Morrow, 2015). But these learning activities need to be fun and playful to ensure children's participation, motivation, and interest.

Learning the Alphabet The ability to read and write depends on mastering the alphabetic principle, the understanding that there is a systematic relationship between letters and sounds, and that all spoken language can be represented by a set of agreed-on symbols called *letters* (Snow et al., 1998). Children will not master the alphabetic principle in preschool, but knowing the alphabet at kindergarten entry is the strongest predictor of success in reading during first grade (Jones, Clark, & Reutzel, 2012). *Knowing letters* means remembering their shapes, names, and sounds (Morrow, 2015). Because the names of many letters mirror the sounds they represent, learning letter names is an important skill.

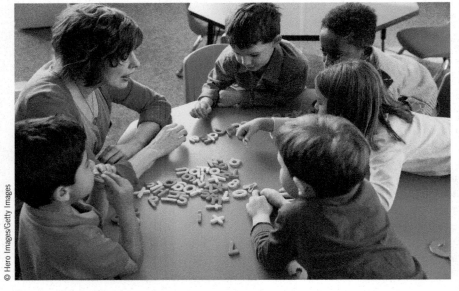

© Hero Images/Getty Images

Knowing the alphabet is one of the best predictors of later success in learning to read. What are some developmentally appropriate ways to teach letters to young children?

alphabetic principle The understanding that there is a systematic relationship between letters and sounds, and that all spoken sounds and words can be represented by a limited set of agreed-on symbols called *letters*.

Teaching the Alphabet Katya, age 3, and her dad drive to Kmart to buy some clothes. Her dad points to the large sign and says, "Look, Katya, there's your K." Katya wonders, "This is my store. Why are these people here?"

Like many children her age, Katya has discovered her letter, and she feels personal ownership. But how did this important discovery occur? As her father demonstrated, Katya's parents helped her learn the first letter in her name. As with phonological awareness, children need adult support to learn the alphabet.

The alphabet is a set of arbitrary symbols with preset names that require instruction. Teaching the alphabet is necessary, but how it is taught is also important. Because adults clearly value this skill, most children are motivated to learn the letters. However, teachers need to make learning the alphabet meaningful. Teaching one letter a week or teaching letters without any connection to sounds and words is not effective (Jones, Clark, & Reutzel, 2012). Letters are not "equal." Some letters, such as M and S, are easily mastered because the letter name and sound are very similar; while others such as Y and C are much more difficult. Focusing on a letter a week gives too much time to some and not enough to others; it doesn't help children compare and see relationships among letters or review previously learned letters.

As Katya did, children first focus on the letters in their own names, which is perhaps the most effective strategy for teaching letters (Morrow, 2015). If they frequently see their name in writing, at some point between about 18 months and age 3, they will identify the first letter as their own. A child may be affronted if someone else claims the letter too. Toddlers love to sing the alphabet song, play with alphabet blocks, and look at alphabet books.

In the classroom, letters should be where children can see, touch, and manipulate them, such as magnetic or sandpaper letters (Morrow, 2015). Name writing is an important ability that helps build all other early literacy skills (Puranik & Lonigan, 2012). Children need to see uppercase as well as lowercase letters and different fonts of the same letter. This way, children learn the "essence" of the letter symbol rather than only one representation of it. For a description of how to effectively teach letters and sounds, read the feature *Becoming an Intentional Teacher*.

Becoming an Intentional Teacher

Teaching the Alphabet and Phonological Awareness

Here's What Happened   I teach 4-year-olds in a Head Start program. Our literacy goals include alphabet knowledge, phonological awareness, print concepts, early writing, and book appreciation. Most of my children have had limited exposure to books in their homes, so I take every opportunity to integrate literacy learning throughout the day. Fortunately, our program is well equipped with both traditional reading and writing materials and various digital devices, including touch-screen tablets and an interactive whiteboard.

At the beginning of the year, I found that most children could identify only one or two letters. I began to set aside a short time each day (a total of about 10 minutes) to focus on teaching letters and phonological awareness together, in large or small group activities. For example, during morning meeting, I may use the interactive whiteboard to introduce a new letter—perhaps the beginning letter of a child's name or a special day such as Valentine's. The children can trace letters and move images around on the whiteboard. We also play active games like making the letter in the air or with our bodies. Another activity is for children to go on a hunt to find the letter in the classroom or in a book, or to find an object that begins with the letter.

The children especially enjoy focusing on how their mouth feels when they form letter sounds, which inevitably makes them laugh. I also demonstrate both the uppercase and lowercase versions of a letter, starting with those that look most alike and later moving on to the more difficult ones.

At the end of a week, we review the letters and sounds we've learned. Children may also independently practice their letter skills on the tablets, which I've loaded with educational apps for basic skills such as *Elmo Loves ABC* and others that promote vocabulary, writing, and comprehension. I also have Spanish language apps so that children can learn these skills in Spanish, which will later to transfer to English.

I find that children's writing is especially effective in building their letter-sound knowledge and motivation to learn letters. Working in small groups primarily, we begin with the letters in children's names. Falicia, Bode, Keira, and Marcus picked up their beginning letters right away, while Phillip took longer to learn the letter P but caught on more quickly to L.

Here's What I Was Thinking   Previously, I thought that learning the alphabet was a relatively easy skill that children would pick up from reading books and seeing print in the classroom. But after I systematically assessed children's letter knowledge, I realized that I needed to explicitly teach letter-sound relationships—always in a fun and engaging way—as well as embed letter-sound learning in read-alouds, writing, and other literacy experiences. Given the children's lack of prior alphabet knowledge, I found that they needed repeated opportunities to play with and practice letters and sounds.

Integrating digital media was highly motivating for the children and me. My two biggest challenges have been to identify high-quality apps and to find time to scaffold individual children's engagement. But almost all the parents have smartphones and many have tablets, so I recommended some free apps for children to practice with at home or in the car. And I talked to parents about how they could play along with their child.

Reflection   This teacher intentionally used whole group, small group, and individual instruction as well as print and digital media to promote literacy skills. She provided opportunities to practice and more complex experiences as children mastered new ones. What other ways could she have taught letter-sound relationships, language, and early literacy?

Source: K. A. D. Stahl, 2014. Research into practice: New insights about letter learning. *The Reading Teacher, 68*(4), 261–265; C. D. Jones, S. K. Clark, & D. R. Reutzel, 2012. Enhancing alphabet knowledge instruction: Research implications and practical strategies for early childhood educators. *TEaL Faculty Publications*, Paper 404. Retrieved from http://digitalcommons.usu.edu/teal_facpub/404.

print awareness Beginning knowledge about written language.

Print Awareness

Print awareness is beginning knowledge about written language. Various purposes of print include communication, expression, explanation, direction, and information. Concepts and abilities related to print awareness include (Schickedanz & Collins, 2013):

- Understanding that print performs a variety of functions and purposes
- Recognizing print in the environment (such as in signs or labels)
- Knowing that print, not pictures, carries the message in the story
- Understanding the concept of *word*—that is, that specific clusters of letters on the page with spaces between them represent the words said by the reader
- Realizing that print represents speech or thought that is written down
- Realizing that print in English is read left to right, top to bottom

concepts of print Beginning understandings about the forms and functions of written language, such as that words carry messages.

The skills listed above—also called **concepts of print** or *print conventions*—are important elements of literacy learning (Schickedanz & Collins, 2013). These developmentally appropriate outcomes are challenging but achievable for preschool children if they have good teaching and planned learning experiences.

Early Writing

Encouraging young children to write is an effective way to help them learn to read (Schickedanz & Collins, 2013). Research demonstrates that talking, reading, and writing are developing simultaneously, and that progress in one area supports learning in the others (Shanahan & Lonigan, 2013; Snow et al., 1998).

Continuum of Early Writing As children try to write on their own, the writing process promotes print awareness as well as many other early literacy skills (Schickedanz & Collins, 2013). Children's writing is another area that tends to follow a developmental progression, as depicted in the examples in Figure 12.1.

 ## Application Exercise 12.2

Figure 12.1: Progression of Children's Writing

At first, they do not distinguish drawing and writing. But over time, they learn the difference and will label scribbles that are indistinguishable to adults as one or the other. Figure 12.1a is a typical 2-year-old's scribble writing. Gradually, children's scribbles become more deliberate and controlled. Between the ages of 3 and 4, children incorporate letter-like shapes or symbols (circles and straight lines) and random strings of letters. Typically, the first recognizable word children produce is their name, followed by names of friends, as we see in the love letter Ryan received in preschool (see Figure 12.1b).

Often, children begin to identify sounds within words, and 4-year-olds begin to use *invented spelling*, at least with initial consonants in English, as seen in Figure 12.1c. Spanish-speaking children tend to use vowels first (Snow et al., 1998). With practice and support, primary-grade children's writing becomes more conventional, as in Figure 12.1d.

invented spelling Developmental or phonetic spelling that represents children's initial attempts to associate sounds with letters.

Temporary **invented spelling**, also called *developmental*, *temporary*, or *phonetic spelling*, represents children's initial attempts to associate sounds with letters, as when a 4-year-old writes "Mk" for "Mike." This process of trying to figure out how to write words is an important step on the way to learning conventional spelling. Observing and talking with children as they produce these spellings enables teachers to monitor children's understanding of letter-sound relationships. For example, 6-year-old Cora writes: "Good moraning. We are going to be bise [busy]. We are genu go to the postofs [post office]."

Using invented spelling does not interfere with learning conventional spelling. In fact, the opposite is true. Invented spelling actually accelerates children's later development of phonemic awareness and conventional spelling when it is taught in the primary grades (Snow et al., 1998).

FIGURE 12.1 Progression of Children's Writing (a) Scribble-writing (b) Name writing (c) 5-year-old writing and drawing (d) First grader drawing and writing These figures illustrate the predictable progression of children's writing skills—from scribbles, to letter-like forms, to recognizable letters and words, and then to complete sentences.

FIGURE 12.2 Museum Sign

Teaching Early Writing Skills When children see adults writing, they want to write, too. To encourage and scaffold writing, teachers need to reinforce children's sense of competence (Graham & Harris, 2013). Curriculum should expose children to various types of writing. A cooking project requires them to attend to a recipe. Science experiments require data collection. Children's desire to communicate a message to the entire group motivates them to write a sign, such as the one in Figure 12.2 posted by a child to invite the whole school to visit the museum his class created as the culmination of their photography project.

It is important that teachers do not focus too much attention on children's handwriting, because that approach is likely to be less meaningful and potentially frustrating for children. Teachers and parents should not be alarmed when children reverse letters or even write words as if in mirror-image. These "errors" are normal at this age (Schickedanz & Collins, 2013). If children persist in writing letters backwards, however, teachers scaffold correct production. For example, 4½-year-old Franklin tends to write his name backwards. Mr. Gandini notices that he starts writing on the right-hand side of the page and usually runs out of room, so he continues toward the left. He simply says, "Franklin, why don't you start your name up here in the left-hand corner of your paper, the way I write people's names on their paintings. Then you have plenty of space."

 Application Exercise 12.3

Early Writing

Book Appreciation and Motivation to Read Children who are motivated to read show interest in books and reading, connect reading events to real life, and experience the pleasure and power of reading (Wigfield, Gladstone, & Turci, 2016). All children can come to appreciate books and find that reading is enjoyable, especially if they are exposed to books at a very early age.

Reading with Babies and Toddlers Earlier in this chapter, we described how interactive book reading facilitates language development. Reading aloud is especially valuable for promoting children's literacy skills and motivation to read. Like so many other aspects of teaching, appropriate use of books varies with the age of the child.

Babies and toddlers explore and "play" with books. This is why publishers sell board books and cloth books that can stand up to the onslaught of a baby's interest. Teachers should sit with a child on their laps or close by a few children to feel an affectionate connection. They shouldn't expect children to sit still, nor should they try to read a book word for word or beginning to end. Instead, they should describe what they're doing— "I'm going to open the book. Now let's turn the page"—and use simple words to talk about the pictures: "The fish is swimming. Splish, splash." Exploring books with babies and toddlers builds their interest and enjoyment, which is further developed during the preschool years.

Reading Aloud with Preschoolers One of the most important goals of all early literacy experience is to get children excited about books and eager to learn how to read. In fact, young children who love books ask for them to be read over and over, memorize them, and proudly announce that they are reading. For a variety of reasons, however, not every child has these wonderful early experiences with books. Therefore, preschool teachers must actively make reading pleasurable and fun, and build children's appreciation for books and motivation to become literate. To build children's motivation to read, effective teachers (based on Head Start, 2003):

- Hold children on their laps or snuggle with them in small groups so their children can see and touch the book, helping to develop positive feelings about reading.
- Hold the book and turn the pages so children can always see the pictures.
- Read with expression and enthusiasm, using different voices for characters in the story. Overdramatizing distracts children from attending to the book.
- Occasionally pause to build suspense, to ask children to predict what will happen next, or to increase their interest ("Uh, oh. Here comes the big bad wolf!"). They pause briefly to clarify the meaning of an unknown word if it is crucial to understanding the story.
- Make sure that books reflect children's culture, home language, and identity.
- Plan times during the day when children select their own books to look at alone or with a friend. Then allow children to take books home or receive books to keep.
- Read to children several times a day, every day, expressively and enthusiastically.
- Read favorite books repeatedly when requested. Talk with children about their favorite books and authors, and encourage children to write or email them and use the internet to get more information about authors' lives and work.

For nearly every child, the process of learning to read becomes difficult at some point, whether in first grade, when decoding becomes the focus of instruction, or in third grade, when comprehension takes center stage. Children who are motivated to read are more likely to persist when they encounter these challenges (Wigfield et al., 2016). Motivation is also important, because the more a child reads, the better reader he or she becomes (Stanovich, 1986). Children who like reading and therefore choose to read are almost always good readers.

Literacy and Background Knowledge Early literacy experiences are now a key part of every good early childhood program, but they should not become the whole curriculum. Because the curriculum lends itself to integration, many teaching strategies are effective for multiple goals. For example, book reading promotes listening and understanding, vocabulary development, phonological awareness, alphabet knowledge, print awareness, knowledge in a subject area such as science, and even social problem-solving skills. Learning curriculum content builds all-important background knowledge, concepts, and basic information about how the world works (Duke, Halvorson, & Knight, 2012; Pinkham, Kaefer, & Neuman, 2012).

background knowledge
Concepts and basic information about how the world works that is essential for reading comprehension.

Background knowledge is essential for reading comprehension. Information books are especially valuable sources of such knowledge. As a result, the Common Core standards call for a 50-50 balance between fiction and nonfiction reading in kindergarten. Information books are more cognitively challenging than stories. However, teachers tend to talk less when reading them, which is a missed opportunity to enhance their value (Price, Bradley, & Smith, 2012). Exposure to information books and academic vocabulary in the early years helps prepares children for the texts they will later encounter in elementary school.

Play and Literacy Children's play provides an excellent and highly motivating context to learn literacy and language. Various types of play can be employed to help children develop these important skills. Read the feature *Promoting Play: How Play Supports Language and Literacy Development* for some examples.

Promoting Play

How Play Supports Language and Literacy Development

Next year, Ms. Keegan's preschoolers will attend kindergartens in which the curriculum is designed to meet Common Core standards. She knows how important it is to prepare them for the rigorous expectations. But she also understands the value of play for children's development and learning, and provides various types of play to help meet her language and literacy goals.

To build children's speaking and listening skills, she uses several strategies. She identifies a topic or project that children are interested in and key vocabulary words that are connected to it. She intentionally teaches new words, frequently repeats them, and engages children in extended conversations using the words. Much of this "instruction" happens during their play, as we see in the following example.

After a visit to the local airport, Ms. Keegan's preschool class wants to take an airplane ride. She helps them set up an airport and airplane that includes lots of literacy opportunities: a computer to make plane reservations; paper and markers to write tickets, baggage tags, and signs for departures and arrivals; and magazines and iPads to read on the plane. They organize chairs into the two aisles of the plane and choose roles. Two children are the pilots, three are the flight attendants, one is the ticket agent, another is the baggage handler, and the rest are passengers. In preparation, one group writes tickets while another sets up a beverage cart.

As the plane loads, Grayson, the flight attendant, greets each passenger with a "welcome aboard" and tells the assembled group to fasten their seat belts. The pilots announce that the plane is going to Disneyland. Most children get deep into the scenario and stay with it for 20 minutes or more. The play is repeated for several days, with children exchanging roles and practicing the language of air travel.

After a few days, Ms. Keegan invites a real pilot to visit. She explains her job and introduces new words. She also describes how pilots read and write every day. After the visit, children consult Google maps and other geography apps to identify and practice writing flight plans.

One of the defining characteristics of sophisticated socio-dramatic play is the use of language. During such play, children try to imitate adults, and their language becomes more complex and sophisticated. Similarly, when children play out roles in pretend contexts, they adapt their speech style and employ the familiar scripts common to those settings. For instance, the airport, office, and restaurant are different contexts, each with its own vocabulary and script.

To stimulate language, teachers may need to take a role in play to get it going or to extend it to include more language. For instance, Ms. Keegan might arrive at the airport and say, "I almost missed the plane. Can you tell me what to do in case of emergency? How does the oxygen mask work?" Play provides many opportunities to practice such verbal interaction with other children and occasionally with adults.

Ms. Keegan used play to support children's use of sophisticated language and extended conversations. The play also provided many opportunities for the children to express their ideas and extend their knowledge of letter-sound relationships through writing.

Sources: L. M. Morrow, S. B. Berkule, A. L. Mendelsohn, A. L. Healey, & C. B. Cates, 2013. Learning through play. In D. R. Reutzel (Ed.), *Handbook of research-based practice in early education*. New York: Guilford Press; S. B. Neuman and T. S. Wright, 2013. *All about words: Increasing vocabulary in the Common Core classroom, preK–2*. New York: Teachers College Press.

The predictors described in the previous sections are the forerunners of successful reading and writing. We now turn to the topic of the formal teaching of reading in the primary grades.

 Check Your Understanding 12.4

Literacy Instruction in the Primary Grades

In this section, we introduce some of the key terms and issues in teaching reading. We revisit the reading and writing developmental continuum. Then we describe the components of an evidence-based reading program and the importance of digital literacy. We conclude with a discussion of the Common Core English Language Arts (ELA) standards.

Learning to Read

Conventional reading is reading in which the reader gains meaning from unfamiliar text. This is what we think of when we talk about being literate—the ability to read without conscious effort, the way adults and older children read. English is an alphabetic language, as are Spanish and many other languages. In these languages, we translate or **encode** speech sounds into symbols—the letters of the alphabet—to create writing. Reading requires the ability to **decode**—that is, to figure out what those symbols represent.

Basically, reading involves two processes:

1. **Word identification**: the process of decoding unfamiliar words and recognizing high-frequency (both regularly and irregularly spelled) words by sight, such as *the*, *with*, *that*, *house*, *dog*.
2. **Comprehension**: the ability to understand what is read and to interpret and analyze the author's meaning.

For many decades, there have been heated debates about which of these processes is more important and needs more attention when teaching beginning reading. Today, researchers agree that effective reading instruction helps children master the alphabetic principle *and* acquire meaning from text—what is called a **balanced approach** (International Reading Association [IRA] & National Association for the Education of Young Children [NAEYC], 1998; Kim, 2008; Snow et al., 1998). Such an approach is more likely to be meaningful and motivating for children and therefore more likely to help them become successful readers.

Learning to read is an example of a *both/and*, not an *either/or* choice—both decoding and comprehension are required. Teachers need to realize that it is impossible to understand what you cannot decode, but it is possible to decode what you cannot understand. Those of us who have never studied physics, for example, would probably be able to "read" (that is, decode) the words in a physics textbook, but would have no idea what we've read.

Developmental Continuum: Literacy in Kindergarten and Primary Grades

The *Developmental Continuum: Literacy in Kindergarten and Primary Grades* feature describes reading and writing expectations for this age group. Being familiar with such a continuum is useful for teachers, because it identifies the goals for literacy instruction at each age level and helps them assess children's progress toward those goals (McAfee & Leong, 2016).

---

conventional reading Reading in which the reader gains meaning from unfamiliar text.

encode Translating speech sounds into symbols—the letters of the alphabet—to create writing.

decode The ability to figure out what written symbols—letters of the alphabet—represent.

word identification The process of decoding unfamiliar words and recognizing high-frequency (both regularly and irregularly spelled) words by sight.

comprehension The ability to understand what is read and to interpret and analyze the author's meaning; the ability to make sense of what is read.

balanced approach Effective reading instruction that helps children master the alphabetic principle *and* acquire meaning from text.

Video Example 12.4:

Integrated Language and Literacy Instruction

This video features an example of a first-grade class writing a classroom guide for incoming kindergartners. Note what the teacher does to integrate reading, writing, and language instruction. How does she use a balanced approach? How does this lesson build children's thinking, reasoning, and vocabulary learning?

Developmental Continuum
Literacy in Kindergarten and Primary Grades

Age/Grade Level	Widely Held Expectations
Most kindergartners	• Enjoy being read to, retell stories and what they've learned from information books • Experiment with and use early literacy skills • Respond to open-ended questions that require inferences about a story and connections to events beyond the story • Begin to track print when listening to book • Use language to describe and explain what is read • Recognize and name all upper- and lowercase letters automatically and make most letter-sound matches • Demonstrate phonemic awareness, blend and segment syllables in words, and blend and segment onsets and rimes • Write letters and high-frequency words • Recognize some words by sight, including common ones (a, the, me, you, is) • Use phonemic awareness and letter knowledge to write with invented spelling • May read emergent literacy texts conventionally by the end of kindergarten
Most first-graders	• Make the transition from experimental to "real" or conventional reading • Read aloud accurately and with reasonable fluency texts appropriate for beginning grade 1 • Use letter-sound associations, word parts, and context to decode and identify new words • Use strategies when comprehension breaks down (picture and context clues, rereading, predicting, questioning) • Use reading and writing for various purposes on their own initiative ("I want to write a Valentine for my mom.") • Sound out and represent all substantial sounds when spelling a word • Identify an increasing number of words by sight, including common irregularly spelled words such as said, where, and two • Write various kinds of texts about meaningful topics (journals, stories) • Use some punctuations and capitalization correctly
Most second-graders	• Read more fluently and write various text forms using simple and more complex sentences • Use word identification strategies to figure out unknown words • Use strategies to aid comprehension more efficiently, such as rereading, questioning, and using context • Read with greater fluency • Identify an increasing number of words by sight • Write about a range of topics for different audiences • Use common letter patterns to spell words • Punctuate basic sentences correctly and proofread their writing • Read daily and use reading to get information on topics of study
Most third-graders	• Read fluently and enjoy reading • Extend and refine their reading and writing for various purposes and audiences • Use a range of strategies to make meaning from unfamiliar text • Use word identification strategies appropriately and automatically when encountering unknown words • Recognize and discuss elements of different text structures • Write expressively in various forms such as stories, reports, and letters • Use a rich vocabulary and complex sentence structure • Revise and edit their writing during and after composing • Spell words correctly in final drafts

Sources: Based on O. McAfee & D.J. Leong, 2016. *Assessing and guiding young children's development and learning* (6th ed.). Upper Saddle River, NJ: Pearson Common Core State Standards Initiative, 2011. Common core standards for English language arts. Washington, DC: Council for Chief State School Officers and National Governor's Association.; and C. E. Snow, M. S. Burns, & P. Griffin (Eds.), 1998. *Preventing reading difficulties in young children*. Washington, DC: National Academies Press.

Children's progress along the continuum depends to a large extent on their earlier experience. Children will arrive at kindergarten and first grade with very different abilities. Some will already be reading; others may know only a few letters. Therefore, teachers must adapt their instruction to start where children are and help them make continuing progress.

Evidence-Based Reading Instruction

Given the current understanding of research, the National Reading Panel identified five components of an evidence-based reading program that are widely used in planning and evaluating curriculum (NICHD, 2000). Each of these components—phonemic awareness, phonics, fluency, vocabulary, and comprehension—is described in the sections that follow.

Phonemic Awareness   Phonemic awareness is one of the strongest predictors of success in reading (Strickland & Schickedanz, 2009). Without it, later instruction in phonics doesn't make sense. However, although research has found that phonemic awareness is absolutely necessary for success in reading, it is not by itself sufficient; there is much more to beginning reading than the spoken sounds of words (NICHD, 2000).

Phonics   Phonics is a system of teaching the correspondences between letters or groups of letters and the sounds they represent. Although the use of phonics to teach reading has been hotly debated, the value of phonics has long been established as a necessary component in an effective, research-based program (Strickland, 2011; Taylor, Davis, & Rastle, 2017). The major issue concerning phonics instruction is not whether to teach phonics and other skills such as spelling, but how to teach them in engaging ways that support children's continued reading development as well as their motivation to read. Whereas some children need extensive help with phonics, other children do not (Strickland, 2011).

phonics A system of teaching the correspondences between letters or groups of letters and the sounds they represent.

fluency Rapid, efficient, and accurate word recognition skills that permit the reader to comprehend the meaning of text.

Fluency   Fluency refers to rapid, efficient, and accurate word recognition skills that permit the reader to comprehend the meaning of text (Rasinski, 2012). Fluency is first apparent when children are able to read out loud quickly, accurately, and with appropriate expression. This ability then leads to their ability to comprehend what they read silently.

Fluency is like the bridge between phonics and comprehension (Rasinski, 2012). If children's decoding skills are inadequate, they must slowly sound out and stumble over each word. By the time they've reached the end of the sentence, they've forgotten the words they've read, and as a result, the sentence doesn't make sense. Fluency requires practice and careful matching of texts to children's approximate reading ability.

How do children become fluent readers? One way is for teachers to read aloud to children, modeling the elements of fluent reading such as reading with expression (Rasinski, 2012). Fluency requires practice. Children can read short passages with the teacher and to each other in pairs. Even after children in the primary grades become fairly competent readers, teachers should continue to read to them, using more sophisticated chapter books than students can read independently.

© Rebecca Emery/Stockbyte/Getty Images

Reading aloud in primary grades helps build word identification skills, background knowledge, and fluency. All are needed for reading comprehension.

Vocabulary   As described earlier, vocabulary knowledge is perhaps the strongest predictor of reading comprehension (NICHD, 2000). Children who understand and use more words to begin with are more likely to recognize these words in print. When they encounter unknown words in their reading, they can figure them out based on what they already know (Snow et al., 1998).

Because children in the primary grades need to grow their vocabularies by about 3,000 words per year, they need to learn about 15 words per day (Beck, McKeown, & Kucan, 2013). Consequently, vocabulary instruction needs to be intentional and explicit during these years, especially for children who are behind in vocabulary development at school entry (Neuman & Wright, 2013).

Reading Comprehension   *Reading comprehension* is the construction of meaning from unfamiliar text—the ability to make sense of what is read. A prerequisite for high levels of reading achievement is a rich amount of background and content knowledge. The content that children learn in social studies, science, and other areas provides essential background knowledge to comprehend what they read. For this reason, children need a great deal of experience with information (nonfiction) texts in the primary grades and before (Duke, 2014).

A solid base of knowledge is essential for becoming a skilled reader and succeeding in school (NICHD, 2000). By third grade, the curriculum shifts from a focus on learning to read to an expectation that children read to learn as they encounter increasingly more complex textbooks. In fact, the fourth-grade reading slump that typically occurs in American schools may be caused in part by children's lack of content knowledge from which to make sense of more challenging texts (Duke, 2014; Hirsch, 2007)

Video Example 12.5:

Evidence-Based Reading Instruction

Notice the many ways this teacher effectively uses learning centers to implement a research-based and balanced approach to teaching reading with her primary-grade students in this video. How does this teacher address each of the five components of evidence-based reading instruction—phonemic awareness, phonics, fluency, vocabulary, and comprehension?

Impact of the Common Core State Standards

In the past, reading instruction in kindergarten and the primary grades focused on basic skills such as phonics and word identification. Concerns about uneven, low educational standards and poor academic achievement in many states led to the Common Core State Standards initiative (2011). Common Core standards are designed to ensure that all children are prepared for college and careers in reading, writing, speaking, listening, and language, and they significantly raise the bar across all grades.

The Common Core English Language Arts (ELA) standards begin at kindergarten, but because they are so rigorous, they have had a significant impact on prekindergarten as well. Many educators are seriously concerned that the standards are developmentally inappropriate and that implementing them is harming children (Carlson-Paige, McLaughlin, & Almon, 2014). Most worrisome is the expectation that kindergartners should "read emergent-reader texts with purpose an understanding." Common Core includes examples of what is meant by *emergent-reader* story books, such as *Are You My Mother?* by P. D. Eastman and *Green Eggs and Ham* by Dr. Seuss, and information books such as *My Five Senses* by Aliki.

To help children achieve the overarching goals of comprehension, critical thinking, communication, and creativity, the ELA standards (Common Core State Standards Initiative, 2015) emphasize the following:

- *Complexity.* Students are expected to comprehend complex texts and learn academic vocabulary that is used in a variety of content areas such as science or social studies.
- *Evidence.* Students are required to provide evidence—gleaned from literature and information books—to support their opinions and conclusions, both verbally and in their writing. For example, instead of simply asking children if they liked the story or how it made them feel, the teacher would ask, "What in the story made you feel

(that emotion)?" or "What motivated a character to behave in a certain way? Explain your thinking.".

- *Background knowledge.* To build content knowledge, the K–third-grade standards call for a 50-50 balance between fiction and nonfiction books.

Common Core also stresses that literacy involves using, communicating, interpreting, and evaluating digital media sources. For example, Common Core assessments are delivered on computers or tablets requiring students to have technological aptitude and keyboard skills.

The Common Core standards have become a political hot button. Abolishing them is part of political candidates' platforms as well as parents' and some teachers' agendas. Nevertheless, the Common Core standards have had a significant impact on the way that literacy is defined and the expectations for teaching and learning.

Digital Literacy

In 2015, the International Reading Association officially changed its name to the International Literacy Association (ILA) to reflect the fact that reading is only part of literacy. Children of every age must learn to use technology and digital media to enhance all their communication skills—reading, writing, speaking, and listening. Across the curriculum, they need to seek information online and connect that knowledge with what they learn offline. Children also need to learn the strengths and limitations of various technological tools and media, and choose those that are suited to their communication goals.

Life in our technological society requires more than reading; it requires **digital literacy** or *media literacy*, the ability to locate, understand, interpret, and evaluate information from multimedia digital sources (Rogow, 2015). Perhaps the biggest

digital literacy The ability to obtain, use, interpret, and evaluate information available through multimedia digital sources.

What Works

Using E-Books Effectively

© Karen H Ilagan/Shutterstock

Early childhood educators are understandably concerned about the proliferation of technology in children's lives and question the efficacy of using e-books compared to "real" ones. So do e-books harm children's reading development? Are there any benefits in using e-books?

The most important consideration is always how the technology is actually used. The primary risk of any digital device is that it often interferes with adult-child interaction. As we have seen in reading print books aloud, it is the conversation around the book that matters most, and this is also true with digital storybooks.

The best technology has multiple "affordances" or various ways it can be used. Affordances support creativity and put power in the hands of the child. Based on a review of the research on e-books, experts Lisa Guernsey and Michael Levine conclude that well-designed digital storybooks coupled with responsive adult-child interactions can enhance children's learning as much as print books.

There are basically two kinds of digital story books—educational and commercial. Commercial ones include many interactive "bells and whistles" that are not directly related to the story such as games, puzzles, or hotspots. These have been found to

distract children's attention and interrupt the narrative—outcomes that undermine children's self-regulation and are detrimental to literacy learning.

By contrast, educational e-books offer various affordances that may include audio narration to read the story to the child or demonstrate how to pronounce unknown words, text highlighting along with the audio that supports tracking print, real-time definitions for new or difficult words, and translations. These affordances support children's engagement and effortful control. For children who need help building fluency, narration can be valuable as long as children also practice reading aloud themselves.

What's more, educational apps such as *Book Creator* and *My Story* really put children in charge of the creative process by allowing them to create, write, illustrate, print, and even publish their own work online.

Sources: L. Guernsey & M. Levine, 2016. Getting smarter about e-books for children. *Young Children, 71*(2); W. Buckleitner, 2017. *Inspiring and empowering young children: Exploring innovative uses of exciting new digital tools.* NAEYC Annual conference presentation, Atlanta, GA.

Digital literacy is essential, as children must learn to find, use, interpret, and critically evaluate information from print and nonprint sources.

challenge is determining which information sources are accurate and trustworthy. Another challenge teachers face is choosing among the vast number of educational apps that purport to teach children to read. Despite lofty claims, most of these apps focus on very basic skills—letters, sounds, phonics, and word identification (Guernsey & Levine, 2015). Only about 10% address higher-level abilities such as vocabulary, comprehension, and storytelling. Similarly, teachers must make decisions about whether and how to use e-books, a topic discussed in the feature *What Works: Using E-Books Effectively.*

In previous sections, we discussed the development and learning of verbal and written communication skills. In the final sections, we address another dimension of human communication—the creative arts.

✓ Check Your Understanding 12.5

🔺 Communicating Through the Arts

We began this chapter with a visit to a primary school where teachers used children's art production and appreciation to teach language, reading, and writing. In previous sections, we focused on two dimensions of communication: language and literacy. Although it is true that speaking, listening, reading, and writing skills are essential for school success, they are not the only ways of communicating and learning, as Gardner's theory of multiple intelligences states.

Young children, who tend to be less inhibited than older children and adults, use their entire bodies to express their ideas and emotions. If encouraged and provided a range of interesting materials, they can be incredibly creative in representing their world through traditional and digital media. Children's enjoyment and accomplishment in the creative arts depend in part on teachers providing adequate materials, time, and instruction in specific art techniques.

The Value of Creative Arts

The creative arts include visual arts, music, movement, dance, and drama. *National Core Arts Standards* for pre-K through grade 12 address all these areas plus media arts (National Coalition for Core Arts Standards, 2014). The overarching goals of the standards are that children create art; perform, present, and produce art; respond to art (interpret, evaluate, and find meaning in it); and connect art to their lives and the larger culture. The media arts standards address how all forms of art are created and presented using technology and digital media. The Core Arts standards are designed to align with the Common Core and also elevate the value and importance of the arts in education.

Each type of creative art supports children's imaginative thinking and expression of their ideas and emotions (Isenberg & Jalongo, 2018). Participation in the arts achieves several goals for children: enhanced cognitive development, promotion of symbolic representation, support for creativity, and engagement of children from all cultural and linguistic backgrounds.

As we saw in the case study at the opening of this chapter, the arts also provide an excellent basis for integrating curriculum. In fact, one study of an arts-enriched integrated curriculum in a preschool serving low-income children found that engaging children in music, creative movement, and visual arts improved their school readiness skills (Brown, Benedett, & Armistead, 2010). Research demonstrates that involvement in the arts enhances development and learning throughout schooling (Munsen, 2013; Ruppert, 2006). Such research contradicts the tendency today to minimize the arts in order to spend more time supposedly preparing children for academic success.

Creative Arts and Cognitive Development The creative arts contribute to children's development in many ways. Engaging in the arts helps children reflect on their own thinking, which becomes more complex as a result. The following example illustrates this relationship between the arts and cognition:

> Karen Spitzer's kindergarten class is involved in a yearlong study of plants and growing things. In the early days of spring, the children become very excited by the flowers bursting forth on the grounds surrounding their rural school. Karen guides the children to observe several types of roses closely. The children take sketch pads outside and draw the roses, and also take digital photos. When they return to the classroom, Karen reads an information book about flowers and projects their photos on the whiteboard. Then she instructs them to "use your poet's eyes (It's like …) instead of your scientist's eyes (I see and I describe specifically)." The children write short poems or sentences about how the flowers make them feel. Next, they create pictures using various media such as tempera paint, watercolors, colored pencils, and chalk. Then the children examine and critique each other's pictures:

> *Kehembe:* I wanted my roses to be pink, but they look too red.
> *Chrystal:* Yeah. Maybe you could add more white next time.
> *Tyree:* Why don't you try the chalks? They come in more shades than the watercolors. Or try the paints, because they're easier to mix colors.

> The next day, Karen brings in a dozen roses. She places them in water near the art area and then gives each child one to hold.

> *Karen:* Now look very carefully at your flower and compare it to your picture. What do you see?
> *Chrystal:* Ouch! I forgot about the thorns. I'm going to put some in my painting.
> *Kehembe:* My rose isn't just one color. Even though it's mostly light pink, there's white and some darker pink, too. And the stem is way longer than I thought.
> *Tyree:* I'm going to try making a rose from wire and colored tissue paper so it will look more like a real one, not flat like my drawing and the photos.

Karen also projects different images of artists' depictions of flowers. The ensuing class discussion leads the children to conclude that there isn't a "right" way to represent an object—every artist has their own interpretation. In this example, many important things are going on. Children are having fun creating art. But even more important, they are developing key abilities: *symbolic representation* and *visual literacy* (discussed later in this chapter), which support language and literacy as well as thinking in all areas.

Symbolic Representation Symbolic representation is the process of mentally using one thing to stand for something else. When children engage in the visual arts, they are using various media to represent their concepts of the real world (Thompson, 2013). Language is a representation of objects, experiences, feelings, and concepts. For example, in English, we use the word *chair* to represent an object with four legs that we sit on. Other languages use a different word for the same object. Written language is also an example

symbolic representation
the process of mentally using one thing to stand for something else

© Pearson Education

Video Example 12.6:

Learning through Visual Arts

In this video a preschool class is engaged in an integrated curriculum study about birds. How are the visual arts used to promote symbolic representation, creativity, appreciation for the beauty of nature, children's observation skills, and content learning?

of symbolic representation. The letters of the alphabet are symbols to represent the sounds of the spoken language. Developing symbolic representation is essential to speaking and reading.

Consider how, in the previous example, Karen Spitzer uses the arts to build symbolic representation in her kindergartners. The children represented the flowers in their initial drawings, in verbal descriptions, and in writing, and they read about them in books. Using different media such as paint and sculpture tools, they again represented the roses. Then they observed real roses closely and discussed their pictures, reflecting on each other's representations. Finally, they were able to add more realistic detail, representing their more accurate concepts of a rose. The processes that Karen used with her class promoted their creativity, artistic ability, and symbolic representation skills. The activities were part of a science unit that also integrated language and literacy skills.

Supporting Creativity Individuals are *creative* when they take existing objects or ideas and combine them in different ways for new purposes. Creative individuals use their ever-growing body of knowledge to generate new and useful solutions to everyday challenges (Isenberg & Jalongo, 2018). Therefore, creativity applies not only to the arts but to all aspects of children's experience.

To support children's involvement in the creative arts, effective teachers need to understand their role. Teachers can err in doing either too little or too much (Isenberg & Jalongo, 2018). Some teachers are too passive, providing no help with art techniques. They merely provide materials and stand back. The commonly heard phrase "It's not the product, it's the process" relates to this view of creativity. The assumption is that whatever children produce is unimportant compared to their creative use of materials.

By contrast, some teachers are too controlling, overemphasizing the finished product. These teachers may assume that parents want children to color within predrawn lines or produce art that conforms to adult-made models. Envision a classroom wall decorated with a series of rabbits that look like they came off an assembly line. The rabbit ears and other parts were obviously cut out by the teacher.

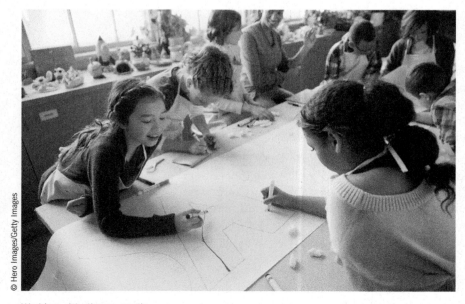

© Hero Images/Getty Images

Working with diverse media helps build children's symbolic representation ability. What abilities do you think children gain by working on a group art project?

Cultural differences also exist in how adults view and support children's creativity. For example, one study found that Chinese American parents and teachers believe that children need formal art instruction first and then creativity will follow, while European Americans tend to assume that children's creativity will emerge naturally (Huntsinger, Jose, Krieg, & Luo, 2011). In this study, Chinese American children's drawing skills from ages 5 to 9 were more mature and creative than those of the European American children who had received less instruction.

This phenomenon has been observed countless times by American visitors to Reggio Emilia, Italy, where young children's artistic representations appear to be much more advanced than those of comparable age American children. It isn't that Reggio children are inherently more creative and artistic but rather that they have instruction and experience in symbolic representation of all kinds from an early age (Vecchi, 2010). And they live in a country and a culture in which the arts and artists are highly valued.

The best approach is for teachers and children to value *both* the process *and* the product. Teachers need to understand that the process of producing art is more satisfying and educationally valuable if children have been taught some techniques (Thompson, 2013). Children will enjoy the art more and become less frustrated. At the same time, they will feel prouder about the products they produce.

Teachers can also encourage creativity and learning through the arts by introducing children to excellent examples of art. As the teachers from the Thurgood Marshall School did at the beginning of the chapter, they can involve children in noticing, thinking about, and discussing the work of other artists. Then, to promote discussion, teachers use complex questions that invite children to observe, critique, evaluate, and develop their own aesthetic preferences (Strasser & Bresson, 2017).

Engage Every Child   All areas of the arts can involve and engage all groups of children. It is always important to adapt materials and experiences to ensure that children with disabilities can fully engage in the creative arts.

Art, music, and movement are areas where dual language learners can be included without needing to rely on their English language skills. All children can enjoy learning a song in either English or another language. In addition, when singing, there is a clearer distinction between each word than in speaking. With her 3-year-olds, Derry sings, "Head, shoulders, knees, and toes … and eyes, and ears, and a mouth and nose," touching each body part as she sings. Such a rhyme or song helps dual language learners by connecting physical movements with words.

Every cultural group has its tradition of artistic expression. Consider origami in Asian cultures or African masks. Children of every background find meaning through exploration of diverse artistic traditions (Eckhoff, 2017). Teachers can involve families by inviting them to share art forms from their culture. Exploring children's cultural diversity should not be limited to examining such artifacts, but including them is important.

Even at an early age, some children will say, "I can't draw." They've already learned that the broader culture values particular ways of representing the world. Digital media is a great way to motivate reluctant artists as well as those who happily embrace their creative selves (Puerling, 2018). Engaging art production apps abound, such as *MoMA Art Lab* from New York's Museum of Modern Art.

In the following discussion, we describe and give examples of effective teaching strategies in each area—visual arts, music, movement, dance, and drama.

Visual Arts

The **visual arts** are creative processes and products that involve drawing, painting, sculpting with clay, or making models of objects using a variety of materials. Art experiences allow children to convey their ideas, feelings, and knowledge in visual forms. Individually and in groups, children use materials such as crayons, markers, paint, Play-Doh, clay, wire, found objects, glue, tape, and paper, along with tools such as scissors, brushes, rolling pins, and cookie cutters. Developing an appreciation for and an aesthetic awareness of art is another important element. Including art forms, materials, and techniques from children's home cultures can increase their motivation and interest in art.

visual arts Creative processes and products that involve drawing, painting, sculpting with clay, or making models of objects using a variety of materials.

Artistic Development and Learning   The arts are part of the curriculum and therefore are influenced by children's development and learning just like literacy or mathematics. To plan and implement a challenging arts curriculum, teachers need to understand how children make progress in drawing and painting ability. However, children's progress is not as tightly linked to age as assumed in the past; instead, it is strongly influenced by their experiences with various media and adult scaffolding, and these experiences are culturally determined. Art itself is a cultural artifact (Eisner & Day, 2004; Thompson, 2013). Current thinking reflects Vygotsky's theory that learning leads development instead of the other way around. Figure 12.3 provides some examples of young children's art production.

FIGURE 12.3   Progression of Children's Drawing (a) 2-year-old's painting (b) Stick figure drawing (c) Preschooler's drawing (d) Kindergartner's drawing (e) Second grader's drawing These figures illustrate a progression of children's drawing from scribbles to stick figures, to more detailed and recognizable representations.

Application Exercise 12.4
Figure 12.3: Progression of Children's Drawing

When young children begin to draw, they first make random scribbles, lines, zigzags, and circles that may cover the whole paper (see Figure 12.3a). As they gain experience, children begin to produce shapes such as crosses, squares, and rectangles. Then they combine shapes, making sun-like objects using circles and lines. Soon, children make figures that look like humans, beginning as stick figures that gradually get more features, as well as animals, houses, and trees (see Figures 12.3b & 12.3c).

With experience and adult scaffolding, children's artwork becomes more and more representational over time. They talk about the process they used and what the product represents. Increasingly, they plan what to create and decide which materials and techniques they will need. Their work becomes more sophisticated, as in the page from a kindergartner's journal about the photography project (Figure 12.3d) and in a first-grader's action-packed firefighter scene in Figure 12.3e.

Understanding children's artistic development and learning helps teachers know what kinds of materials and experiences will be safe, interesting, and challenging for each age group. For example, with a group of toddlers, it is unrealistic to expect representational drawing, but teachers can expect preschoolers to increasingly present more recognizable objects in their work, especially if the teachers provide scaffolding as Karen Spitzer did in the earlier example of drawing flowers.

Artistic skills are related to physical development. When finger painting or sculpting with wire, Play-Doh, or clay, children use their senses, explore the properties of the materials, build fine-motor skills, and practice eye-hand coordination. Children build the same muscles and skills they need for writing. Fine-motor skills are a strong predictor of later achievement because they enable children to have more diverse and challenging experiences that promote their cognitive development (Grissmer, Grimm, Aiyer, Murrah, & Steele, 2010).

Scaffold Artistic Development and Learning Many people think that creativity is inborn. Actually, children's ability to be creative depends in large part on their skills in producing art. Children who lack the skills to model with clay, for instance, may continue to roll clay into balls or make "snakes," but they won't advance to sculpting objects. Soon, they may lose interest in working with clay altogether.

When teachers provide adequate materials, time, instruction in specific techniques, and assistance when needed, children's skills continue to develop (Thompson, 2013). For example, after observing the art center in her kindergarten, Lara Mann sees that Duane has a tendency to use too much water, sopping the paper that he inevitably wads up and tosses away. With a little instruction in how to use watercolors effectively, Duane produces a painting he wants to take home.

Specific art skills that can be taught can be as simple as tapping the paint on the side of the can to get a more controlled stroke and as complex as using potter's clay to make elaborate and durable sculptures. Effective teachers encourage children by making positive, specific comments rather than by giving compliments. Instead of saying, "What a beautiful picture," they say, "I see you've made a pattern—two red stripes, two blue stripes, two red stripes, two blue stripes." The following example illustrates how important teacher scaffolding can be to maintaining children's enjoyment of art:

Three-year-old Emily, a budding artist, loves to paint. She often spends long periods of time at the easel, layering colors of thick paint until her paper is wet through. After weeks of this activity, she tells her teacher, Lelia, that she doesn't want to paint anymore. When Lelia asks why, Emily says, "It always comes out brown." At this point, Emily's teacher has a choice. She can smile and ignore Emily's problem, or she can see the situation as a teachable moment.

Lelia begins by asking: Emily, let's think about why your pictures turn brown.
What color do you put on first?

Emily: I like red best. And I like blue and yellow, too.
Lelia: Those are all pretty colors. Let's mix them together and see what color we get.
As Lelia and Emily mix the colors, Emily's eyes get very wide.
Emily: It makes brown! Let's try it again.

After they mix the color brown over and over, Lelia asks, "What could you do next time you paint a picture so it won't come out brown?" With such minimal assistance, Lelia supports Emily to find the solution of separating colors on her paper instead of continually painting over the same spot, and renews Emily's enthusiasm for painting.

To effectively support children's artistic development and creativity, teachers need to organize the environment to provide sufficient space and materials for messy activity, cleanup, and storage of children's work and work-in-progress. Also critically important is for teachers to treat children's work with respect. To do so, teachers display children's work with their permission. They can also mat or frame selected works for each child to display and keep. Teachers encourage children to take art home to share with families. In preschool and in kindergarten and the primary grades, children can evaluate their own artwork and decide which products they judge worthy of keeping. Digital cameras and scanning extend the life of children's creations.

Video Example 12.7:

Easel Painting

In this video children are painting in an easel center. What specific art skills do you observe? How does easel painting support creativity? And what does this environment communicate to children about the importance and value of their work?

visual literacy Ability to create visual messages and to interpret messages contained in visual communications.

Promote Visual Literacy   All of the experiences described previously contribute to the development of children's visual literacy. **Visual literacy** is the "ability to create visual messages and to 'read' messages contained in visual communications; to perceive, understand, interpret, and evaluate the visual environment" (Johnson, 2008, p. 74). To build children's visual literacy experiences, teachers engage them in talking about art, extending their thinking about art, and reflecting on art (Johnson, 2008). These processes are similar to the connections that exist among speaking, reading, and writing.

Teachers engage children in talking about their art by commenting on colors, textures, techniques, and patterns. They also lead children through thinking and problem solving by asking open-ended questions such as "What materials did you use to make this flower sculpture?" and "How can you make a door in your house structure? What will you need? What could you do first?"

As in the case study that opened this chapter, teachers can help children observe, compare, and respond to the properties of artistic works. With a teacher's guidance, children can discuss the artist's use of color, shape, line, pattern, texture, and more. Typical comments might include "Look at the big blocks of color in the Mondrian painting." "Look very closely. Can you see how the people in this picture by Seurat are painted with tiny dots of color?" "See how the Romare Bearden picture is a collage like we make." To bring art closer to children's firsthand experience, local artists can share and discuss a work-in-progress or display their work in the classroom.

✓ **Application Exercise 12.5**
Visual Literacy, Reading, and Writing

Music, Movement, and Dance

On the first day of school for her preschool class, Yasmine gathers the children on the rug and begins to sing a simple song with corresponding hand gestures: "Open, shut them. Open, shut them. Give a little clap. Open, shut them. Open, shut them. Put them in your lap. Creep them, creep them. Creep them, creep them, right up to your chin. Open wide your little mouth ... but do not let them in!" The children are enchanted, and their attention is fully engaged. They beg for her to do it again. Many of them begin following her movements and mimicking the words immediately. Right from the start, the children learn that music will be a fun and active part of every day in Yasmine's room.

Developmentally appropriate music and movement experiences involve creating, performing (singing, making and moving to music), listening and responding, and connecting music and movement to interests, ideas, and knowledge (National Coalition for Core Arts Standards, 2014). Music and movement should be a primary focus of the curriculum, and should also be used to accomplish other learning goals. Every day, teachers can provide opportunities for children to sing favorite songs, learn new ones, and make up their own. Children should also use simple rhythm instruments to create music or to accompany live or recorded music.

Music in the Lives of Young Children Children's experiences and connections with music begin at birth, when they are comforted by lullabies or the soft humming of their mothers' voices. Some families make music an integral part of their lives. By the time they reach the toddler years, many children have favorite songs and musical pieces. They listen attentively, sing along with a familiar chorus, move to the music, and begin making their own music by shaking a tambourine or banging on a pot or drum. As language skills develop, toddlers begin making up their own songs. If they have had many opportunities to listen to and talk about music, they can identify the sounds made by specific instruments such as a trumpet, drum, or violin.

Music experiences play an important role in children's lives. Music and dance influence children's identities, connect them to their cultural group and the larger society, help them experience and express emotions and ideas, and support their learning across the curriculum. Moreover, music and dance can be lots of fun.

Every cultural group and family has a musical tradition. As communities connect within a broader culture, these musical traditions are shared and influence each other. Rock 'n' roll began as a blending of several musical forms, including the blues and gospel. This is what makes music a part of children's identities and why it is important to incorporate the music of children's cultures and home languages into the curriculum. If children don't know the songs, they can sing along with a recorded version of a song, such as "Abiyoyo," until everyone learns the words. An iPod can be loaded with literally hundreds of selections. Teachers can also introduce real or homemade versions of instruments that are typical of children's cultures.

Memory and sequencing are required to coordinate music and movement, and both require children to follow directions. There is some research evidence that music education strengthens academic achievement, phonological awareness, and word decoding (Hetland & Winner, 2004). Overall, the skills and knowledge that children gain from participating in music and dance include:

- Listening, as when children try to identify the words in a lyric or sounds made by different instruments
- Responding by clapping to the beat or marching around the room
- Creating music by exploring the sounds made by different instruments and making up a new song or verse for a familiar song, sometimes a silly one
- Understanding, such as whether a piece of music has a slow or fast beat
- Playing music, such as when they use bells or rhythm sticks to accompany a song
- Moving and dancing with or without music—swinging, rotating, twirling, twisting, or shaking their bodies.

Music and Movement in the Classroom Exposing children to all kinds of music provides many different opportunities for learning. First-grade teacher Malique is an amateur guitarist and music lover. Even though he doesn't sing very well, he never lets that stop him from singing with the children. He knows that children don't mind as long as they can sing along, too. Malique introduces a different kind of music each week and provides follow-up activities. To launch this music appreciation curriculum, Malique invites sixth-grade band members to bring their instruments and demonstrate the sounds. The children love seeing the instruments up close and learning how to care for them. Then he plays a recording of portions of *Peter and the Wolf* and asks children to listen to how the instruments sound like animals.

Whatever music Malique uses in his classroom, he involves children in thinking and talking about their experiences. He asks questions such as "What do you like or dislike about it?" "How is it similar to and different from other music you have heard?" "What instruments do you hear in different pieces of music?" In this way, children can become critical thinkers about music as well as music appreciators.

Drama

Pretend play and dramatization involve creative production and demonstration. We have already discussed the benefits of socio-dramatic play for language and early literacy skills. Dramatization, however, is more closely tied to a specific story or script, and has been found to positively impact children's verbal skills (Hetland & Winner, 2004). Children in primary grades are more likely to engage in dramatization than younger children, although preschoolers do act out favorite stories. Children can also dramatize traditional stories from their own cultures.

Teachers can structure a drama session to promote literacy skills in story sequence, character development, and plot. Many dramatizations, both child-initiated and teacher-guided, involve retelling familiar stories. After reading *Three Billy Goats Gruff* to her class of 4-year-olds, Marissa Reese helps them act it out. First, she encourages their recall and story sequencing skills by asking them to tell what happened: "How did the story start?" "What happened next?" She helps them identify emotions or problems that surface in the dialogue: "How did the little billy goat feel?" As the children practice acting out the different roles, they get an opportunity to play with dialogue, changing their tone of voice and expression to fit the character of each goat or the troll.

Scaffolding dramatization requires providing different kinds and the right amount of support for different children, including exposure to stories and real-life experiences (Bodrova & Leong, 2015). Providing props of varying realism can meet the needs of inexperienced as well as capable players. Some will need realistic props to get into character, such as a variety of dress-up clothes or the actual props used by characters in a story. For example, after reading *The Little Old Lady Who Was Not Afraid of Anything* (Williams, 1988), a kindergarten teacher gives children props to act out the story—shoes, pants, shirts, and a hat—and create a scarecrow at the end. Other children can take on a creative role with more open-ended objects such as cardboard tubes, unit blocks, or pieces of cloth. Videotaping the production and sharing it on a class website or on YouTube encourages children to do their best work.

Seeing the Arts with New Eyes

Pablo Picasso once said that every child is an artist. But given the current emphasis on the basics of reading, writing, and mathematics in early schooling, time and resources for arts education are diminishing. Many children today have less opportunity to experience the arts. However, all forms of art offer new ways in which children can build language and literacy skills, develop cognitive and social skills, and learn about their own and other cultures (Eckhoff, 2017). Each of the creative arts can enhance learning in other areas. For example, children might count musical beats, draw or construct a model of the Earth, analyze the message in a painting, or write dialogue for a drama.

Creativity and abilities developed in the arts at an early age positively impact other areas of learning (Isenberg & Jalongo, 2018). However, arts education should *not* have to be justified by its relationship to other disciplines; instead, children should engage in the creative arts, because in doing so, they participate actively in diverse cultures and gain knowledge, confidence, and competence in the arts themselves (Winner, Goldstein, & Vincent-Lancrin, 2013). The possibilities are endless. As 5-year-old Chandra confidently states, "You could draw a rainbow-colored world or a gingerbread cookie world even though that isn't real."

Given the power of the creative arts to promote children's learning and enrich their lives, teachers can use all forms of art in their teaching to keep students engaged and excited about learning. State standards and program goals for early education always include language and literacy. Reading proficiency has become the overarching purpose of primary grades. Teachers who know and love young children, however, never lose sight of the long-term goal: learning to communicate creatively in all forms of the arts.

✔ Check Your Understanding 12.6

Revisiting the Case Study

… Thurgood Marshall School

At the beginning of this chapter, we visited a primary school where a school-wide art project was occurring. The curriculum at Thurgood Marshall, as at every other school in the United States, is full to the brim. Teachers need to be creative to cover the breadth of the curriculum while helping children gain depth in important subject areas. The art study was an excellent example of how teachers can integrate curriculum in meaningful ways. Teachers didn't miss an opportunity to infuse language and literacy throughout the day in all areas of study.

Having examined how children acquire language and become literate, we can now see how the art project promoted these skills. Children learned new vocabulary words and used language in conversation and analysis. They also used digital media and read books on topics of interest, thus promoting their motivation to read. They produced their own art and learned to appreciate and evaluate the work of diverse artists. These experiences developed symbolic representation ability and visual literacy. Firsthand experience with art sharpened children's observations and critical-thinking skills. All of these experiences motivated the children to become more competent and confident readers, writers, speakers, and artists. ■

12 Chapter Summary

- Children gradually learn language over many years from verbal interaction with adults and other children. Language development follows a relatively predictable sequence, but there is a wide range of individual variation that is well within the range of normal.

- Research-based vocabulary-building strategies include one-to-one and extended conversations, listening, decontextualized speech, intentional teaching of new and rare words, interactive book reading, and play.

- The developmental sequence of second language acquisition is similar but not identical to first language learning. To help children acquire English while also maintaining and further developing their home language, teachers must work effectively with parents and use proven classroom strategies, including play.

- Literacy is the result of many cumulative, interrelated experiences beginning at birth. Research demonstrates that there is a specific set of early literacy skills and knowledge that predict later success in learning to read and write: phonological awareness, alphabet knowledge, print awareness, and vocabulary. Other important skills that contribute to later reading ability

include early writing, listening comprehension, motivation to read, and background knowledge.

- Conventional reading is the ability to gain meaning from unfamiliar text. The most effective reading instruction helps children master the alphabetic principle *and* acquire meaning from text in what is called a balanced approach. Components of an evidence-based reading program include phonemic awareness, phonics, fluency, vocabulary, and comprehension. Motivation is key to reading achievement.

- Common Core English Language Arts Standards emphasize students' developing higher-order thinking skills by reading complex texts with academic vocabulary, analyzing evidence, and gaining content knowledge from information books.

- Children learn to communicate through the creative arts: visual arts, music, movement, dance, drama, and media arts. The arts promote the development of symbolic representation, creativity, and visual literacy. Children's enjoyment and accomplishment in the creative arts depends on teachers' providing adequate materials, time, and instruction in specific artistic skills.

Key Terms

- academic discourse
- alliteration
- alphabetic principle
- babble
- background knowledge
- balanced approach
- code switch
- completion prompt
- comprehension
- concepts of print
- conventional reading
- cooing
- decode

- decontextualized speech
- dialogic reading
- digital literacy
- distancing questions
- dual language learning
- early literacy
- encode
- expressive language
- extended discourse
- fluency
- invented spelling
- listening
- narrative

- parentese
- phonemes
- phonemic awareness
- phonics
- phonological awareness
- play-by-play language
- predictable books
- predictors
- print awareness
- rare words
- recall questions
- receptive language
- rhymes

- script language
- sequential language learning
- simultaneous acquisition
- symbolic representation
- syntax
- telegraphic speech
- visual arts
- visual literacy
- vocabulary
- Wh-questions
- word identification

✔ Flash Cards 12.1

Readings and Websites

Chen, J. J. (2016). *Connecting right from the start: Fostering effective communication with dual language learners*. Boston, MA: Gryphon House.

Ellery, V. A., Oczkus, L., & Rasinski, T. V. (2015). *Literacy strong all year long: Powerful lessons for K–2*. Newark, DE: International Literacy Association.

Isbell, R., & Yoshizawa, S. A. (2017). *Nurturing creativity: An essential mindset for young children's learning*. Washington, DC: National Association for the Education of Young Children.

Jalongo, M. R. (2015). *Literacy for all young learners*. Boston, MA: Gryphon House.

Schickedanz, J. A., & Collins, M. F. (2013). *So much more than the ABCs: The early phases of reading and writing*. Washington, DC: National Association for the Education of Young Children.

International Literacy Association (ILA)

This organization's website offers a wealth of resources for teaching language and literacy from pre-K through third grade.

National Core Arts Standards

On this website, you will find the most recent comprehensive set of national learning standards for dance, music, theatre, visual arts, and media arts.

Tap, Click, Read

Visit this website for the most up-to-date information and resources to effectively use digital tools to build children's literacy, including tip sheets for selecting apps and ways to use media to support home language.

Reading Rockets

Reading Rockets, a national multimedia project funded by the U.S. Department of Education and PBS, provides a wealth of strategies, lessons, book lists, and other resources for parents and teachers to help young children learn how to read and to assist struggling readers.

✔ Shared Writing 12.1
Teaching Children to Communicate

13 Teaching Children to Investigate and Solve Problems: Science, Technology, Engineering, and Mathematics (STEM)

Learning Outcomes

After studying this chapter, you should be able to:

13.1 Explain why STEM learning is important in the early years.

13.2 Describe the continuum of cognitive development.

13.3 Apply effective teaching strategies and curricula to help children learn mathematics.

13.4 Apply effective teaching strategies and curricula to help children learn about science and engineering.

13.5 Describe what children need to know about technology and how it can be used to teach effectively.

13.6 Analyze the role of play in learning and teaching STEM.

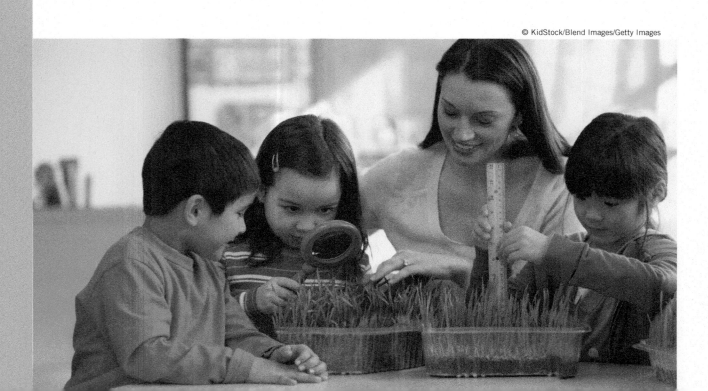

Related NAEYC Professional Preparation Standards

The NAEYC Professional Preparation Standards (NAEYC, 2011) that apply to this chapter:

1: Promoting Child Development and Learning
Key elements:
   1a. Knowing and understanding young children's characteristics and needs
   1b. Knowing and understanding the multiple influences on development and learning
   1c. Using developmental knowledge to create healthy, respectful, supportive, and challenging learning environments
4: Using Developmentally Effective Approaches to Connect with Children and Families
Key elements:
   4b. Knowing and understanding effective strategies and tools for early education
   4c. Using a broad repertoire of developmentally appropriate teaching/learning approaches
5: Using Content Knowledge to Build Meaningful Curriculum
Key elements:
   5a. Understanding content knowledge and resources in academic disciplines
   5b. Knowing and using the central concepts, inquiry tools, and structures of content areas or academic disciplines
   5c. Using their own knowledge, appropriate early learning standards, and other resources to design, implement, and evaluate meaningful, challenging curricula for each child

Case Study

The kindergartners in Celinda Duncan's class are especially excited today because it is the 100th day of school. They have been counting and marking off the days since the beginning of the year. The number 100 is the focus of each learning center. Four children are working to string 100 small beads to make necklaces. Celinda is impressed by their perseverance and concentration. The task requires well-developed fine motor skills and eye-hand coordination. More important, the children first have to count 100 beads and then demonstrate a high level of focused attention and persistence to complete the task. Beatrice is almost half-way finished when her string slips out of her hand. Celinda calmly helps her pick up the beads and says, "I know that was frustrating after all your hard work. But you already counted the 100 beads. You may want to take a break from stringing the beads and try one of the other activities."

Beatrice quickly moves on to the self-serve snack table where the children are creating 100-piece snacks by counting small foods—raisins, dried cherries, goldfish, almonds, and the like. Currently, the class is engaged in a science study of the human body. They've begun to think critically about healthy foods so they are comparing the nutrition information on the packages of the food. Paolo is excited to see that some of the calorie portions are 100.

In another area of the room, children are creating and measuring the lengths of stacks of 100 unifix cubes. Porter is working on a 100-piece puzzle. A group of four children demonstrate that they can write 100 words on large sheets of paper, a task which demands memory as well as language and writing skill. Another small group is using grid paper with 100 numbered squares representing the 10's columns. The children are using the grids to practice counting by 1s and 10s. Asher and Enzo are creating their own math games using the grid. They toss the dice and move their markers. They keep track of how many tries it takes to get to 100—the person who gets there in fewer tries, wins! Another small group of children write and illustrate stories based on the prompt: "When I am 100 years old..."

Leann, Edna, and Oscar study the blueprint they made earlier of a skyscraper model that they want to be 100 inches tall. They worked on the computer to design the model but aren't sure how to represent it in real life. In the art area, they begin tinkering with various materials to bring their plans to fruition.

Celinda's school district uses the rigorous Common Core Mathematics Standards and also the Next Generation Science Standards. By the end of kindergarten, children are expected to count to 100 by 1's and 10's. They also need to be able to compose and decompose numbers from 11–19 into 10 ones plus the correct number of additional ones. At the beginning of the year, Celinda was skeptical about the children's ability to accomplish these goals. But on the 100th day of school, she is feeling much more confident. ■

This chapter addresses separate but interrelated aspects of the curriculum: mathematics, science, and engineering. We also address technology, which applies across content areas. *STEM* is the abbreviation commonly used for these learning goals. (Early childhood educators sometimes use the term, *STEAM*, because the arts can be integrated as well.) The four curriculum areas are certainly connected. However, *STEM* does *not* communicate priority; mathematics learning in the early years is the most important area of focus despite the fact that it appears last in the acronym. And too much emphasis on integrated curriculum can diminish necessary focus on key learning goals.

First, we discuss the importance of mathematics and science learning. Then we present the continuum of cognitive development that underlies these curriculum areas and applies across all aspects of learning. Next, we discuss effective math curriculum and teaching strategies that lay the foundation for later school mathematics as well as describe the science and engineering curriculum and how teachers can engage children in the scientific process. We describe how children learn with and about technology, and how children learn STEM through play. A key goal is to raise awareness of the importance of math and science for *all* children. We particularly focus on the need to narrow the persistent achievement gap in mathematics between children from low-income families and their more affluent peers. The "achievement gap" is actually a gap in opportunity to learn, both at home and in school.

The Importance of Mathematics and Science

Mathematics and science education generate considerable interest for several reasons. The first is widespread concern about the nation's ability to produce a workforce qualified to compete in the global economy. Second is the issue of equal educational and economic opportunity for all citizens.

With so many competing goals in early childhood programs, why is mathematics important? Preschool math matters because it is highly related to later math achievement and because effective curriculum and teaching can narrow the knowledge gap early on (Duncan et al., 2007; Nguyen et al., 2016). Research demonstrates that young children are capable of learning important mathematics concepts, but they are usually not given the opportunity to do so (Engel, Classens, Watts, & Farkas, 2016; Farran et al., 2017).

The Need for an Educated Workforce

In today's global economy, a large number of jobs require mastery of STEM. However, in international comparisons of mathematics achievement, children in other nations regularly outperform American children (Mullis, 2016). Similarly, fourth grade science achievement in Russia, Kazakstan, and Poland as well as seven other countries exceeds that of children in the U.S. (Martin, 2016). Moreover, these differences in mathematics knowledge are apparent as early as age 4 or 5 (Starkey & Klein, 2008).

Although achievement in science and technology is important, understanding mathematics is strongly connected to both of these areas. As a result, more emphasis is needed on children developing a firm foundation in mathematics during the early years of school. In 2009, the National Research Council issued a seminal report on early childhood mathematics that outlined recommendations for improving mathematics teaching and learning for all children ages 3 to 6.

The Mathematics Achievement Gap

Significant gaps exist not just between our country and others, but within our country. As in reading, a mathematics achievement gap of as much as three years exists between children growing up in middle income versus low income families (Friedman-Krauss, Barnett, & Nores, 2016). Kindergarten math achievement scores predict eighth grade achievement and the gap gets wider over time (Franke & Stipek, 2017).

Mathematics Predicts School Success Although reading has received much more attention, research now demonstrates that math skills at kindergarten entry are the *strongest* predictor of later school achievement and executive function (Duncan et al., 2007; Nguyen, 2016). In an analysis of six large-scale longitudinal studies in the United States, Great Britain, and Canada, researchers found that early math skills predicted not only later math ability but also success in reading (Duncan et al., 2007). By contrast, early literacy skills were related only to later reading. Apparently, the cognitive abilities employed in mastering mathematics apply broadly to other content areas.

Mathematics knowledge in preschool is a strong predictor of executive function and later success in learning both math and reading.

Children who struggle with math are much less likely to graduate from high school and attend college (Szekely, 2014). Mathematics is a cumulative topic of study. Later understanding not only builds on earlier concepts but *depends* on them. Many adults who disliked math in school did not have a firm foundation on which to build. As a result, in later grades, more complex math didn't make sense and they began to feel less competent. Early education can narrow the gap. Research in the United States and other countries demonstrates that using a math-focused curriculum can significantly improve math achievement for all children (Mongeau, 2017; Presser, Clements, Ginsburg, & Ertle, 2015).

International Research Can Inform U.S. Instruction   One international study compared mathematics learning among preschoolers of high and low socioeconomic status (SES) in China and the United States (Starkey, 2007). Two findings were noteworthy. First, Chinese 3-year-olds started out knowing more about math than their American counterparts regardless of their SES status. In fact, the low-SES Chinese group knew more math than the high-SES Americans. Nevertheless, a knowledge gap between socioeconomic groups existed in both countries at age 3. But by the end of preschool, the gap between the two groups had narrowed considerably for the Chinese youngsters but had actually widened for the Americans. What accounts for these differences? There are two feasible explanations:

1. Teaching mathematics in preschool and promoting mathematics at home is a higher priority in countries like China and Japan than in the United States. The studies demonstrate that when young children, even those growing up in poverty, are taught more focused math, they learn it and carry it into later schooling (Mullis et al. 2016; Starkey & Klein, 2008).
2. A fundamental cultural difference seems to exist in the value these countries place on mathematics and their beliefs about what it takes to succeed. In the United States, we tend to assume that mathematics achievement results from having talent or innate ability; by contrast, in Eastern countries, the assumption is that students can achieve in mathematics if they work hard enough (NRC, 2009).

In the previous sections, we presented the case for teaching and learning mathematics in the early years. To truly understand the learning process, it is important to be aware of the cognitive foundations that underlie mathematics and science learning.

✔ Check Your Understanding 13.1

🔺 The Cognitive Foundations of Early Learning

The word *cognition* generally means "to know." In education, *cognitive development* refers to mental processes such as attention, remembering, language, and problem solving. These processes are essential for all learning to take place. However, in discussing one domain such as cognition, it is important to remember that children's development cannot be separated neatly into compartments. Cognitive, social, and emotional development are highly connected.

In this section, we delve into the domain of cognitive development. We begin by describing the continuum of cognitive development and then discuss several mental processes that are the foundations of all early learning, especially children's understanding of mathematics and science. These processes include executive function, concrete and abstract thinking, and language (Clements, Sarama, and Germeroth, 2016)

The Continuum of Cognitive Development

Children's cognitive abilities such as their attention, memory, thinking, reasoning, and problem solving develop over time as their experience increases and becomes more complex and their brains mature. For a description of these processes in children from birth through age 8, read the *Developmental Continuum: Cognitive Development* feature.

Developmental Continuum
Cognitive Development

Approximate Age	Widely Held Expectations
Birth to about 9 months	• Learn through their senses (especially taste, touch) • Gain increasing control over their bodies • Increasingly able to remember people, objects, and favorite toys • Focus attention for short time • Gradually learn about cause and effect (3-month-old turns to noise; 6-month-old bangs toy to make noise) • Intentionally act on objects (kicks to move the mobile) • Enjoy solving simple problems, such as taking objects in and out of containers, and discovering consequences of actions • Develop object permanence (remembers that out-of-sight objects are still there)
About 9 to 18 months	• Increasing memory for games, toys, and people from previous days • Enjoy doing things over and over such as carrying and dumping • Use trial and error to solve problems • Observe and imitate others' actions • Begin to understand symbols (*M* for McDonald's) • Play with objects
About 18 to 36 months	• Begin to solve problems mentally (think before acting) • Develop memory and problem solving • Understand basic cause and effect • Begin to sort by categories (blue or red), compare size and shape • Complete simple puzzles accurately • Follow two-step directions • Pretend with objects
3- to 6-year-olds	• Experiment with and begin to understand cause and effect • Increasingly able to plan ahead, predict, and carry out an activity • Engage in socio-dramatic play with other children • Can generate more than one solution to simple problems • Can reason, but logic may be flawed ("The food goes into your legs and makes them grow.") • Increasingly able to focus attention, persist at tasks, self-regulate behavior and emotions • Able to compare and contrast, quantify (find out how many), put objects and events in order or sequence, understand spatial relationships • Has basic sense of present, past, and future
6- to 9-year-olds	• Can symbolically represent thoughts and ideas in many ways (drawing, writing, speaking, modeling) • Memory capacity increases considerably • Can take multiple perspectives (teachers, book authors) • Aware of patterns and part-whole relationships • Can make accurate predictions • Thinking and problem solving become more flexible • Can categorize and think conceptually • Play more complex games with rules, understand fairness • Solve concrete problems easier than abstract problems

Executive Function

As we've discussed throughout this book, perhaps the most significant cognitive achievement of childhood and adolescence is the development of executive function—the brain's "air traffic control system" (Center on the Developing Child at Harvard University, 2011). Imagine the coordination it takes to ensure that hundreds of airplanes fly to the right places at the right times and don't collide with one another during takeoff and landing. Similar to the job of the air traffic controller, executive function coordinates essential abilities that make all other learning possible (Diamond, 2012). These include at least three key abilities: working memory, inhibitory self-control, and cognitive flexibility (Center on the Developing Child at Harvard University, 2011).

These executive functions are vital for all learning. Memory is essential for new learning to take place and for previous learning to be retrieved when it is needed. Working memory is the ability to hold information in our heads for a short period of time, such as a phone number or where we laid down a sock. Working memory is necessary for children to follow multistep directions such as "go to the writing center, choose paper and markers, and draw a picture of yourself." Inhibitory control (also called *cognitive self-control*) is the ability to think before we act, which is very difficult for young children to do. In school, many tasks require mental self-control, such as waiting to be called on. Self-control requires focusing attention on what is necessary, such as the reading lesson, and ignoring irrelevant information, such as the fly on the wall. Cognitive (mental) flexibility involves finding new solutions or revising plans in response to changing circumstances.

Consider how children practice these executive functions when they engage in an activity such as socio-dramatic play. If a group of preschoolers plays airport, they have to remember their role (pilot, passenger, or flight attendant), inhibit their actions (not jump out of the seat while the plane is flying), and think flexibly (adapt to the twists and turns of the plot, such as the plane being delayed).

Just as the air traffic control system integrates many complex parts working simultaneously, executive functions are interrelated. These abilities, which develop over time, are particularly important for reasoning and problem solving in mathematics and experimenting in science (Klahr, Zimmerman, and Jirout, 2011; Nayfeld, Fuccillo, and Greenfield, 2013) as described in the feature, *What Works: Mathematics, Science, and Executive Function.*

working memory The ability to retain information for a short period of time, which enables transfer to long-term memory.

inhibitory control (also called cognitive self-control) The ability to think before we act and to focus attention on what is necessary.

cognitive (mental) flexibility The ability to find new solutions or revise plans in response to changing circumstances.

Children's Thinking

Three-year-old Levi was walking with his mother when he asked why she wasn't talking to him (N. Karp, 2011, personal communication). His mom, Gail, replied, "I'm thinking about the work I have to do." Levi got all excited and replied, "I'm thinking, too! I'm thinking about numbers. I love numbers. I love the way they look, I like the shapes, I like the names, and I love to count. I just like to think about numbers!" Like Levi, most young children have a natural interest in mathematical and scientific ideas, spontaneously count, and love big numbers (Ginsburg et al., 2008).

Competent and Capable In the past, Piaget's theory dominated early childhood educators' thinking about children's capacity to learn mathematics. Based on his observations of children's inability to perform conservation tasks, Piaget theorized that children from about age 2 to 7 were not capable of abstract thought, and, therefore, had little capacity to learn mathematics or think scientifically. As a result, teachers often considered it developmentally inappropriate to teach math (Ginsburg et al., 2008).

In the intervening years, a growing body of research demonstrates that children are more competent than previously thought and capable of sophisticated reasoning and problem solving (Gelman & Gallistel, 1978; McClure, 2017; Whittaker, 2014). For example, we now know that children can perform conservation tasks at earlier ages, depending on how an adult asks the question or alerts children to events they might not have focused on. The key is teaching in developmentally appropriate ways and matching the task to their current understanding (Clements, Fuson, and Sarama, 2017b).

What Works

Mathematics, Science, and Executive Function

An ever-expanding research base demonstrates that preschool children's executive function (EF) abilities are related to their math achievement in kindergarten and beyond. We know that early math ability predicts later achievement in both math and literacy. Given this strong relationship, it is important to provide experiences that support learning both math and EF. Although less research has been conducted, a similar relationship exists for science. Apparently, doing science activities builds math and literacy competencies by increasing executive functioning as well.

Why do experiences in mathematics develop EF? Consider what seems to be a relatively simple math problem: *How many different ways can you add two numbers to make 10?* Answering the question is not simple. The child must focus and shift attention to understand the question and consider possible solutions. The problem demands working memory about quantity as well as holding in mind which combinations of numbers have already been tried.

Similarly, active science experiences engage children's higher-order thinking skills: questioning, comparing, reasoning, and problem solving. A first grade class is studying the life cycle of plants. They wonder what plants need to grow and why some plants only grow in certain places. They set up experiments with seeds and seedlings in different conditions—varying sunlight, water, soil, and so on. A "what happens if" science experiment requires children to observe carefully (focus attention), think flexibly (reject or accept prior hypotheses), and use working memory—all of which draw on and at the same time develop executive function.

Sources: D.H. Clements, J. Sarama & C. Germeroth, 2016. Learning executive function and early math: Directions of causal relations. *Early Childhood Research Quarterly, 36*(3), 79–90; and I. Nayfeld, J. Fuccillo & D.B. Greenfield, D.B., 2013. Executive functions in early learning: Extending the relationships between executive functions in school readiness to science. *Learning and Individual Differences, 26*, 81–88.

Children's minds are not simple, however. Compared to adults, children are *both* concrete *and* abstract thinkers (Ginsburg et al., 2008). And from an early age, they spontaneously demonstrate math interest and ability well before entering school.

Concrete and Abstract Even 3-year-olds can look at a small set of objects (four or fewer) and know how many there are without counting, a skill called **subitizing**, a necessary precursor to later math competence (Clements, Sarama, Germeroth, 2016). They can see that a set of three toy bears is smaller than a set of five.

subitizing The ability to look at a small set of objects (four or fewer) and know how many there are without counting.

In other ways, young children's thinking is abstract. Consider 4-year-old Francine counting her stuffed animals. She touches each one as she says, "One, two, three, four, five." Her teacher asks, "How many animals do you have?" Francine answers, "Five," which seems like a very simple thing to do. However, this little girl had to know and say the counting words in the right order; connect each word to one and only one bear; and know that the last word said in the sequence not only stood for the last bear but also represented the total number of bears. That is, she had to remember that she had counted five bears in order to answer that she had five altogether—she had to hold two thoughts in her head at once. And she had to think about a very abstract concept—what *five* is. Five is still five whether it refers to five bears, five chairs, five children, or five fingers. She also sees, reads, and has to interpret an abstract symbol—the numeral 5—in different places. The numeral 5 is posted near the climbing loft because only five children are allowed at a time.

Conceptions and Misconceptions Children are actively thinking all the time as they try to make sense of their world. Some of these conceptions are accurate, such as Francine's computation of the five bears, while others are not. For example, a common "mistake" young children make is to assume that a "skinny," elongated triangle cannot be a triangle; they think that true triangles can only be equilateral triangles—ones with three equal sides (Clements, Sarama, and Gemeroth, 2016). Children also form their own hypotheses about events, some of which seem like magical thinking. They may assume that the sun goes to bed because they do, not the other way around. Even primary-grade children may think that a coat provides its own warmth rather than heat coming from inside their bodies.

Most misconceptions are actually partial hypotheses, or early theories, about how the world works. For example, 5- to 7-year-olds can readily state that the earth is round because they have been taught this fact. However, when asked to draw a picture of the earth and where the people live, their representations reveal their understanding (Hannust & Kikas, 2007). They may actually think the earth is a flattened sphere with the people living on top or that the earth is hollow and the people live inside. These partial hypotheses are gradually replaced by more accurate ones because, as children get older, their thinking becomes more abstract, and experience challenges their earlier ideas. Some misconceptions can be prevented by broadening children's experiences. For example, unless children are helped to understand the common properties that make a shape a triangle, they will persist in thinking that "skinny" versions are not really triangles.

It is normal for children to make "errors" as they learn math and science; errors provide clues for teachers to scaffold next steps (Nguyen et al, 2017). For example, Lacy skips a dot as she counts five dots on a card. Her teacher simply says, "Try touching each circle as you say the number." Teachers should be cautious about correcting "errors." It is more important to focus on children's thinking and problem solving than only on answers, which may be less revealing of their understanding (Goldenberg, Miller, Carter, & Reed, 2017). In addition, teachers should encourage children's enthusiasm instead of making them hesitant to voice their ideas (NRC, 2009).

Language and Cognition

Language plays a key role in cognitive development and, therefore, in learning mathematics and science. By age 2, children begin learning the language of counting. The first 10 or so number words are essentially meaningless—children memorize these words by rote (NRC, 2009). Even though this skill is learned before it has true meaning, knowing the number sequence is not the same thing as being drilled on it. Children memorize the sequence by playfully repeating it over and over, the same way they learn the alphabet sequence by singing the alphabet song long before the letters are fully meaningful. Knowing the alphabet sequence, however, is useful only

Young children are more capable of sophisticated reasoning and problem-solving than previously thought. Preschoolers are interested in and enjoy learning about mathematics and science.

for *alphabetizing*, a skill that preschoolers do not yet need; by contrast, learning the number sequence is absolutely essential.

The Language of Mathematics   Beyond the first 19 numbers, language reflects the underlying structure of the number system. For example, in English, after the child learns "twenty," all she has to do is repeat "twenty" and add on the numbers one to nine up to "twenty-nine." Thus, saying the number words goes beyond simple memory to reflect the organization of the **base-10 place value system**. The base-10 system is a highly efficient way of using just 10 symbols—0, 1, 2, 3, 4, 5, 6, 7, 8, 9—to write any counting number, no matter how large (NRC, 2009). To do so, we use place value in which the meaning of a numeral depends on where it is placed within the number—that is, the numeral 1 can stand for 1 or 1 trillion.

Children also learn other kinds of mathematical language, such as the names of shapes and words for quantity (*more*, *less*), position (*under*, *inside*), and relationship (*bigger*, *smaller*, *first*) (Ginsburg et al., 2008). These words are so commonly used that we don't even think of them as mathematical or scientific terms. Most important, language is necessary to express and explain mathematical thinking. Consider this example:

> Mr. Blaine's kindergarten class needs to divide into four groups. He explains that there will be four chaperones to accompany children to different sections of the zoo, and he asks for suggestions:
>
> *Naomi suggests:* Let's just pick the group we want.
>
> *Darius notes:* But what if we all pick the same one? It will be too crowded and we won't learn different things to tell the other kids about.
>
> *Flair:* There are twenty kids. How can we divide up? We could line up in four lines.
>
> *Mr. Blaine asks:* How would that help?
>
> *Flair:* We need four groups and four lines are four groups.
>
> *Doug jumps in:* That would work. But it would be easier if we just drew four lines on the chart paper and wrote our names where we want to go.
>
> *Darius is still skeptical:* But what if we all put our name in the same box?
>
> After each suggestion, Mr. Blaine asks each child to explain why her or his idea would work. The explanations reveal and extend their ideas about how to compose equal-size groups.

The Language of Science   Science, too, has its own vocabulary and exposes children to a vast array of words—both nouns and verbs—that they might not otherwise encounter. Children are eager to and capable of learning "big" words, such as *hypothesis, prediction, experiment, observe, reflect*, and *decide*. They learn the vocabulary attached to scientific and engineering information—words like *incline, magnifier, telescope, pulley*, or *lever*.

Science information books are rich sources of language along with hands-on experiences. Language is such an important part of children's cognitive development, as well as science and mathematics learning, that teachers should take every opportunity to introduce and reinforce this rich vocabulary (Gelman & Brenneman, 2004).

Mathematical Language and the Achievement Gap

Evidence suggests that the mathematics achievement gap exists because low-income children do not have sufficient opportunity to learn the language of mathematics (Ginsburg, 2006; Ginsburg & Pappas, 2004). How do we know this? Observations of lower- and middle-income preschoolers find little difference in the everyday mathematics they

---

base-10 place value system Highly efficient system of using just 10 numerals to write any counting number no matter how large, in which the meaning of a numeral depends on where it is placed within the number.

spontaneously demonstrate during free play (Ginsburg, 2006). Both groups exhibit a good deal of mathematical competence on which to build.

Informal, Everyday Mathematics

One of the first words babies utter is *more*—evidence of their intuitive understanding of quantity. As they grow, they pay considerable attention to who is bigger and when something is "All gone." Well before school entry, children of all socioeconomic groups demonstrate considerable informal math knowledge.

Informal knowledge about math, including basic ideas about quantity (more and less), size, shape, and pattern, is also called **everyday mathematics** (Ginsburg et al., 2008). Research demonstrates that beginning in infancy, everyday mathematical knowledge is a universal aspect of cognitive development (McClure et al., 2017). Even babies and toddlers demonstrate basic understandings about some math and science concepts. When they reach out to make a toy move or repeat a sound, they begin to understand the idea of cause and effect (Gelman & Brenneman, 2004). These intuitive ideas about mathematics and science are prior knowledge on which teachers can build.

Children's play is full of mathematical and scientific ideas. This informal knowledge provides a foundation for later mathematics learning when intentional teachers introduce the language of math—words that describe quantity and relationships. They order blocks by size, create and extend interesting patterns, and conduct their own experiments, such as seeing if a ball rolls faster down a steeper incline (Seefeldt, Galper, & Stevenson-Garcia, 2012). The main difference is that children living in poverty are generally provided less support and opportunity to learn the language that connects their informal, basic math knowledge to later, more abstract school mathematics. To do so, teachers must help children *mathematize* their everyday experiences, a critically important process described next.

Learning to Mathematize Experience

To **mathematize** means to understand and think about everyday problems and experiences in explicitly mathematical terms (NRC, 2009). When children mathematize, they focus on the mathematics aspect of a situation, they learn to represent and think about its quantitative or spatial aspects, and they create a mathematical model of the situation to solve problems (NRC, 2009).

Mathematical models can be created with objects (such as beads or paper), actions (such as counting), or through solving real-life problems mathematically. For example, children building a house create a model of mathematics learning when they figure out how many more blocks they need to make the house twice as tall.

To link the concrete world to the abstract world of math, teachers need to help children learn to mathematize, to connect the informal experiences they have to mathematical ideas and symbols (National Science Foundation, 2012). Consider the following situation. Children are often asked to share toys. Teachers tend to think of sharing as a social skill, but it can also be considered mathematically—as addition, subtraction, and division. When 4½-year-old Corky wants more toy cars than Eugene has, the situation is actually a math problem. If he takes two cars from Eugene, he is adding, while Eugene experiences subtraction (take away). If Corky gets two more cars from the shelf, Eugene's pile stays the same. Corky then has to figure out whether either solution gives him more than Eugene has. Unless he knows how many they both started with, he can't be sure whether either of his solutions worked. His teacher could step in and simply prevent a squabble by dividing the cars herself or telling Corky he has to share. Or she could engage them in a conversation about how to create two equal sets of cars or one set that is two cars larger.

everyday mathematics Informal, intuitive knowledge about math, including basic ideas about quantity (more and less), size, shape, and pattern.

mathematize To understand and think about everyday problems and experiences in explicitly mathematical terms.

 Check Your Understanding 13.2

Effective Mathematics Curriculum and Teaching

Teaching mathematics involves several key elements. First, teachers must know the math concepts and skills or operations themselves. This should go without saying, but many teachers do not fully understand the mathematics concepts they are expected to teach (Ginsburg et al., 2008). In fact, college-level math courses are often not helpful or relevant to early childhood mathematics. For this reason, the 2009 NRC report includes a chapter, "Foundational Mathematics Content," that explains the fundamentals of beginning mathematics for teachers.

The other elements of teaching mathematics are interrelated. Teachers need to know (1) the math content and processes that children need to learn and when they are most effectively taught, and (2) how to plan and implement effective curriculum and teaching strategies

Mathematics Curriculum Content

A broad consensus exists about the early childhood mathematics curriculum (NRC, 2009; National Council of Teachers of Mathematics (NCTM), 2000). The K–12 Common Core Mathematics standards identify the math content to focus on at each grade level to ensure that children gain deep understanding of the key concepts and skills needed for later learning. (Common Core State Standards [CCSS] Initiative, 2011).

Video Example 13.1:

Word Problems

In this video a kindergarten teacher works with two children to solve word problems their friends wrote during a previous class. What problem-solving strategies do the children use? How does solving word problems promote understanding and critical thinking?

The Common Core calls for three key changes in how mathematics should be taught (CCSS Initiative, 2015). First, there should be more focus on deep understanding of fewer topics. In the past, the math curriculum has been described as a "mile wide and an inch deep," with students exposed to many different skills but failing to understand and apply them. Another emphasis is on enhancing curriculum coherence by linking topics across grade levels. Finally, a key change is that the standards are more rigorous, requiring equal emphasis on understanding, skills, and real-world problem-solving. For example, compare these two activities: (1) children complete a worksheet with addition problems such as 6 + 3 and 4 + 5, or (2) teachers present an equation such as 6 + ? = 9 and ask the children to make up word problems that can be represented this way.

These standards identify the *big ideas of mathematics*—the overarching concepts and skills of the early childhood curriculum. From age 3 to grade 3, the content goals focus on number and operations, geometry, spatial relations, and measurement.

Mathematics Learning Trajectories   The NRC (2009) report on early childhood mathematics specifies the learning trajectories for children age 2 to first grade (which they called teaching–learning paths). These describe the goals or significant steps, with each new step building on the earlier step. Learning trajectories (Clements & Sarama, 2014) are also called *developmental* or *learning continua*, and they are a key part of curriculum planning.

Learning trajectories have two sources:

1. The content of the discipline—that is, the mathematics skills and knowledge that provide the foundation for later learning
2. What is achievable and understandable for children at a certain age.

Learning trajectories are linked to age/grade levels and are valuable because they can guide curriculum planning and help teachers use formative assessments to scaffold children's learning along the path (IOM & NRC, 2015). For an example, read the feature *Learning Trajectory: Mathematics*, which is based on the NRC report and the Common Core Standards for K–3 mathematics.

Learning Trajectory: Mathematics

Approximate Age Group	Widely Held Expectations
2-year-olds	• Use subitizing to recognize 1, 2, or 3 objects • Rote count, may skip some numbers ("1, 2, 3, 5") • Identify basic shapes • Count 1 to 3 objects
3-year olds	• Know number names and count 1 to 10 in sequence • Count objects with one-to-one correspondence • Know relationships such as more than, less than, equal • Do simple put-together/take-apart problems (2 apples and 2 more is 4)
4-year-olds	• Understand cardinality—the last number said represents the total number of objects • Write numbers 1 to 10 (not always legibly) • Count objects accurately to 10 and beyond (about 30) • Solve simple number word problems • Count backwards • Use mental subitizing of up to 5 objects to solve problems up to 10 (automatically know that adding 2 crackers to 4 is 6) • Recognize and describe attributes of 2- and 3-dimensional shapes
5-year-olds	• Compare numbers • Understand addition as putting together and adding to, and subtraction as taking apart and taking from • Work with numbers 11–19 to gain foundations for place value • Describe and compare measurable attributes (length, weight) • Classify objects and count the number of objects in categories • Analyze, compare, create, and compose shapes
6-year-olds	• Count to 100 from any number • Represent and solve problems involving addition and subtraction • Extend the counting sequence (count on from any number) • Begin to understand base-10 number system and place value concept (pattern of ones, tens, hundreds) • Tell and write time • Reason with shapes and attributes
7-year-olds	• Consistently conserve number (i.e., knows quantity remains the same despite rearrangement of objects) • Skip count forward and backward, with meaning • Represent and solve problems involving addition and subtraction (i.e., measuring length) • Understand and use place value to add and subtract • Work with equal groups of objects to gain foundations for multiplication • Work with time and money
8-year-olds	• Represent and solve problems involving multiplication and division • Understand the relationship between multiplication and division • Use place value understanding to perform multi-digit arithmetic • Multiply and divide within 100 • Develop understanding of fractions as numbers

Sources: Based on Common Core State Standards Initiative, 2011. *Common Core Standards for Mathematics*, Washington, DC: Council for Chief State School Officers and National Governor's Association; and D. H. Clements & J. Sarama, 2014. *Learning and teaching early math: The learning trajectories approach* (2nd ed.). New York, NY: Routledge

One important recommendation in planning math curriculum is that equal attention should not be given to all topics (CCSS Initiative, 2011b; NRC, 2009). There is always limited time in the school day, and decisions need to be made about priorities. In preschool, more focused time should be devoted to number competence (NRC, 2009). The K–2 curriculum should emphasize concepts, skills, and problem solving related to addition and subtraction (CCSS Initiative, 2011b). This does not mean that number is taught in isolation, nor does it mean that geometry and measurement are unimportant. In fact, learning in these areas can promote learning number concepts. Nevertheless, the goal is that children achieve the foundational number and operations goals necessary for their continued progress in later grades.

The seemingly simple act of finger counting involves understanding and applying several different mathematical principles. Physically using and seeing fingers helps children learn about the number system.

© ZouZou/Shutterstock

Number and Operations Understanding number, even the seemingly simple act of counting—called **enumeration**—involves several key concepts (Gelman & Gallistel, 1978). Children need to know that number words should be said in the same order every time—the **stable order principle**. They need to know **one-to-one correspondence**—that one and only one number word should be attached to each object. They also need to learn **cardinality**, the concept that the last number said stands for the total number in the set. Another key idea, called **abstraction**, is that anything can be counted, whether bears, toes, or people. Finally, counting involves the **order irrelevance principle**, the idea that counting can begin with any object in the set as long as each is counted only once.

The term **operations** refers to working with and solving problems about relationships, such as *more than* or *less than*, and addition and subtraction. Teaching operations should involve real objects and word problems. For example, in meeting with her kindergartners, Ms. Guiffre raises a real-world math problem:

> *Ms. Guiffre:* There are 4 people absent today, and we usually have 22 people in our class. We need to send our lunch count to the cafeteria staff. How can we figure out the number of lunches we need?

The children offer several suggestions and then try out some of them:

> *Melissa:* We can count out 22 little blocks and take away 4, and then count out how many we have left.

> *Tyrone:* I know. Let's count our coat hooks. But not the ones for the kids who aren't here.

Learning trajectories help teachers scaffold children's progress (Clements & Sarama, 2013; NRC, 2009). For example, teachers use strategies to help children learn to count accurately and efficiently, such as slowly touching each object as each number name is said. Teachers should also encourage children to use their fingers to count and explore part/whole relationships (a concept that underlies addition and subtraction). The teacher might say, "Brianna is showing us how old her brother is by holding up five [fingers] and two. What's another way to show seven with your fingers?"

Geometry, Spatial Relations, and Measurement In addition to number and operations, a second area of focus for the early childhood math curriculum is geometry, spatial relations, and measurement (NRC, 2009).

Geometry Children are naturally motivated to engage with **geometry**, the study of shapes and space, including flat, two-dimensional space and three-dimensional space (Clements & Sarama, 2014). Geometry involves size, position, direction, and movement, and describes

enumeration The act of counting.

stable order principle The concept that number words need to be said in the same order every time.

one-to-one correspondence Attaching one and only one number word to each object being counted.

cardinality The concept that the last number said stands for the total number in the set.

abstraction The concept that anything can be counted.

order irrelevance principle The concept that counting can begin with any object in the set as long as each is counted only once.

operations Working with and solving problems about relationships such as *more than* or *less than*.

geometry The study of shapes and space, including flat, two-dimensional space and three-dimensional space.

spatial relations Spatial sense and familiarity with shape, structure, and location.

measurement The process of determining size, length, area, or volume using a standard unit.

and organizes the physical world in which we live. Children can learn about angles, shapes, and solids by observing and manipulating objects in the physical world and in the virtual one via technology (NRC, 2009).

Research finds that most curricula severely underestimate children's ability to learn geometry (Clements & Sarama, 2013). Teachers continue to focus only on naming basic shapes (circle, triangle, square) long after children have mastered these concepts. Geometry is far more complex and involves the ability to put together and take apart shapes (composing and decomposing), as well as talk about the properties of shapes (number of angles, sides, orientation).

Video Example 13.2:

Geometry, Spatial Relations, and Mathematizing

The children in this video are engaged in the challenging task of instructing the teacher to re-create their shape pattern that is hidden from her view. What geometry and other math competencies does this task require? How does it teach the children to mathematize?

Spatial Relations   Learning about spatial relations gives children an awareness of themselves in relation to the people and objects around them. Spatial sense and familiarity with shape, structure, and location help children understand both their spatial world and also other mathematics topics (NRC, 2009). For instance, as Carmel examines a three-dimensional pyramid, her teacher encourages her to explore number concepts as well. For example, the teacher asks: "How many sides does a pyramid have? Why is it hard to figure out?"

Measurement   Measurement is the process of determining size, length, area, or volume using a standard unit (inch, gallon). Children look for and analyze relationships in the real world using measurement. Measurement is a learning goal in itself, but it also plays a useful role in building children's understanding of number and spatial relations. When children measure and compare the length, height, and weight of objects, they use *units* such as inches, feet, or pounds. When measuring, children focus on how big, little, long, or short things are and how to figure that out.

Children will sometimes explore measurement by using parts of their body or toys in the classroom—what are called *nonstandard units*. For example, Damien and Issata use their own feet to measure the length of the boat they've built and discover that they get two different answers. Because children naturally use and can learn from nonstandard measurement, many state math standards call for children to use nonstandard and standard units of measurement. Such a standard has sometimes been misinterpreted to mean that teachers should withhold standard measurement tools such as rulers. But this is not the case. Children enjoy and can learn about standard units using rulers and scales, and doing so can prevent the development of misconceptions about measurement (NRC, 2009).

For example, Mina puts out rulers for her kindergartners to explore during center time. At first, they play with the rulers, pretending that they are objects such as magic wands or pirate swords. But when the children become interested in earthworms on the playground, Mina brings out the rulers and the children begin to pay attention to the numbers on the rulers and what they mean. They get excited about measuring and comparing the length of the worms, and begin to use the rulers for other purposes as well.

A relatively simple, enjoyable activity such as measuring a table or comparing strips of paper helps children learn spatial relationships and basic geometry concepts.

Measuring Time: A Word of Caution

Many teachers spend time every morning "doing" the calendar because they think it is a good way to teach math. In fact, more than 90% of kindergarten teachers teach the calendar every day (NRC, 2009). Although the calendar can be used to plan and anticipate future events, it has limited value as a math teaching tool (Beneke, Ostrosky, & Katz, 2008; NRC, 2009).

The calendar's organization—seven-day weeks—bears no resemblance to the base ten number system that children need to master (NRC, 2009). Most of the time, children simply recite the numbers in order while someone points to blocks on the calendar. This task is repeated long after the children have mastered the number list and long before they can fully understand the concept of time (Beneke et al., 2008). In addition, pointing to the spaces on the calendar is not as effective for teaching number as counting real objects. The amount of time spent on the calendar each day could be better spent helping children make progress on the mathematics learning paths. More valuable experiences that help children begin to develop understanding of time concepts include the following:

- Children compare one activity with another in terms of which takes more time: "Who can stand on one foot longer?"
- Teachers point out the time schedule and the passing of time, with ideas like *after lunch* or *before story time*, or using more abstract notions like *yesterday, today*, and *tomorrow*, although they don't expect children to fully comprehend.
- Teachers use a calendar in much the same way people use one in their homes—to note, plan for, anticipate, and remember significant events such as birthdays, trips, and visitors. They place calendars in the house or office center, where it is used in the real world. They introduce names of days of the week and months of the year, but don't drill children on these ideas.

Mathematics Process Skills

Math experts consistently identify five general cognitive process goals that cut across content areas and that should be interwoven throughout the teaching and learning of mathematics for all age groups (NRC, 2009). These processes are problem solving, reasoning, communicating, making connections, and designing and analyzing representations. Any mathematics learning experience might involve all of these processes. These processes are also relevant for science and engineering. Perhaps most important, these learning processes build children's curiosity, creativity, and willingness to take risks, all of which may be the most long-lasting and important goals of mathematics education.

Problem Solving and Reasoning

Mathematics is about thinking. It is not simply manipulating objects, but constructing mathematical meaning from the experience (Whittaker, 2014). To become mathematical thinkers, children need to solve problems and reason about number and operations, geometry, spatial relations, and measurement. They need to understand that different ways exist to solve a problem and that more than one answer is often possible. Even in situations where one correct answer exists ("We need 15 chairs for 15 children"), there are usually a number of ways to arrive at that solution ("We can give each person his or her own chair" or "We can count 15 chairs").

Reasoning is thinking logically to come to a conclusion or find a result. As children tackle problems, teachers should encourage them to talk about—mathematize—their thinking. This brings their reasoning to a conscious level, where other children or the teacher can expand on it. Teachers need to create a learning environment in which children feel free to take risks and search for solutions.

reasoning Thinking logically to come to a conclusion or find a result.

Communicating

To promote children's mathematical thinking, one of the most important things teachers can do is to talk with them about problems, relationships, and mathematical connections. Listening to what they say is equally if not more important. When children discuss their thinking and describe what they are doing, their own thoughts become clearer.

In addition, when children and teachers describe and debate their reasoning, they use the language of math. Then teachers can introduce and reinforce math vocabulary. Open-ended questions such as "How do these blocks compare to each other?" and "How do you know that a square is a rectangle?" increase the amount of math talk. Gradually children internalize these questions (ask them of themselves) and are more likely to understand the world from a mathematical perspective.

Making Connections

connections Refers to understanding links between different areas of math and connecting math concepts to real-world problems.

In mathematical terms, making **connections** refers to understanding links between different areas of math as well as connecting math concepts to real-world problems. For example, measurement can be connected to number because it involves counting units of measurement (that is, inches), or it could be used to figure out if a shoe fits.

Designing and Analyzing Representations

representing Expressing mathematical ideas with words, diagrams, pictures, and/or symbols.

Exploring ways of expressing mathematical ideas with words, diagrams, pictures, and/or symbols, called **representing**, is an essential part of mathematizing. Imagine a group of four-year-olds singing the song "Five Little Monkeys Jumping on the Bed." The teacher first uses her fingers to represent the monkeys as the children sing "One fell off and bumped his head." Soon the children follow her lead with their own fingers. From these concrete representations, the children begin to picture the monkeys in their heads—they form a mental image. Other ways they can represent the monkeys include scribbling circles or drawing pictures of them. Their representations gradually become more abstract. They may make marks on the page to represent the monkeys as the number goes from 11111 to 1111 down to 1. Eventually, children will represent these subtraction problems in symbols: 5 − 1 = 4.

Composing and decomposing Mathematical processes of putting together and taking apart (for example, addition and subtraction).

There are many ways to involve children in designing and analyzing representations of math concepts and problems as well as talking about them. Figure 13.1 graphically depicts a first grader's collection and analysis of data about her classmates' breakfast choices. Note how her analysis of results represents her understanding of quantity as well as her creative invented spelling—*cerel* for cereal and *choies* for choices.

In addition to these general processes, some specific mathematical processes are used across content areas, such as identifying patterns, solving problems that involve putting together/taking apart, and unitizing, which we discuss next.

Identifying Patterns

In recent years, math standards have included learning about patterns. The ability to identify patterns, however, is a process skill that cuts across all math content areas (NRC, 2009). For instance, geometry and spatial relations involve composing and analyzing patterns. The number list is a pattern in which each new number is one more than the last; counting can be done in patterns (by twos, fives, or tens). Classifying objects by some attribute such as size or shape also involves seeing patterns. Following are strategies for building children's awareness of patterns:

- Help children find patterns (*ab, ab* or *abc, abc*) in designs and pictures, as well as in movement and in recurring events such as the daily schedule.
- Sing songs with patterns—"If You're Happy and You Know It"; march or move to a rhythm; and clap patterns.
- Play detective and spy patterns in the classroom, on the playground, or in children's clothes.
- Engage children in creating and noticing patterns as they string beads, place shapes or blocks into arrays, and arrange other materials. Over time children can reproduce and create more complex patterns.

Putting Together and Taking Apart

Mathematics at all levels involves putting groups together and taking them apart—the processes of **composing and decomposing** (NRC, 2009). These processes are the basic components of addition, subtraction, multiplication, and division. Measurements are composed of larger units (feet) that can be decomposed to smaller units (inches).

FIGURE 13.1 First Grader's Mathematical Representation and Analysis This first-grader is learning how to represent and compare quantity by creating a graph, and then interpreting what the graph means.

Understanding these concepts begins with early experiences. From age 2 through primary grades, children create collections of objects. Toddlers love stacking toys and filling and dumping containers. Preschoolers will repeatedly compose and decompose puzzles, challenging themselves to do it faster each time. Children can sing a song like "B-I-N-G-O" in which the word starts out composed (with all the letters), and then is decomposed as each letter of the word is no longer articulated. Primary-grade children learn about fractions by dividing a pizza.

Unitizing Finding or creating a mathematical unit, **unitizing**, is important in learning number, geometry, and spatial relations (Sophian, 2013). When children count, they have to use or create a unit of what they are going to count. For example, they can count people, or couples, or people's hands. When they measure length, they use a unit, whether it is their feet, their body, or a yardstick. When they count by 2's, 5's, or 10's, the units are 2, 5, and 10.

> **unitizing** Finding or creating a mathematical unit.

Mathematics is based on understanding and applying the concept of a unit. For example, to understand the base-10 place value system, children must be able to recognize that 10 ones can form a single unit of 10. For this reason, the concept of unit should be a core idea in the early childhood math curriculum (Sophian, 2013). Of course, children learn this abstract idea through many meaningful, concrete experiences such as making patterns or counting.

In the previous sections, we described the important mathematics content and processes that children are learning in progressively more complex and sophisticated form from infancy through the primary grades. Next we describe mathematics curriculum and teaching strategies.

Effective Mathematics Curriculum

Responding to children's natural interest in math and problem solving and taking advantage of the teachable moments during children's play and routines are valuable ways to promote math learning, but they are not enough (Stipek, 2017). An effective curriculum is more than a collection of activities; it must be coherent, focused on important mathematics, and well articulated across the grades (CCSS Initiative, 2015).

Despite the fact that the amount of focused time on math instruction strongly predicts children's outcomes, very little time is devoted to mathematics in early childhood classrooms (Farran, Lipsey, & Wilson, 2011). Most programs do not include experiences in which mathematics is the primary goal. Instead, they address math as part of an integrated curriculum in which mathematics is a secondary goal; as a result, math teaching occurs only occasionally and rarely in depth (Jenkins & Duncan, 2017). In one study, researchers observed only 58 seconds of math teaching during an entire preschool day (Farran, Lipsey, Watson, & Hurley, 2007). In general, studies have found that integrated math instruction is less effective than activities in which mathematics is the primary goal (Jenkins & Duncan, 2017).

A focused mathematics curriculum not only improves children's math skills but also increases their interest in math (Arnold, Fischer, Doctoroff, & Dobbs, 2002). Teachers, too, report that they increase their knowledge and enjoyment in implementing math activities. Studies on the effects of mathematics curricula indicate that more intentional teaching of math leads to better math outcomes for children, especially dual language learners and children from low-income families (Schoenfeld & Stipek, 2011).

Even very young children experiment with basic mathematics and science concepts—such as sorting and classifying.

© Jules Selmes/Pearson Education

An effective curriculum involves children actively in "doing mathematics." With a coherent curriculum, such as *Building Blocks—Foundations for Mathematical Thinking* (Clements & Sarama, 2007), children encounter math experiences in small and large groups, and in everyday experiences with blocks, art, puzzles, dramatic play, and music. They learn math by using specially designed software that makes the most of digital media's capacities for supporting learning. *Building Blocks* significantly improves not only children's math outcomes but also their oral language and general reasoning (Sarama, Lange, Clements, & Wolfe, 2012). Similarly *Big Math for Little Kids*, a play-based, developmentally appropriate math curriculum for 4- and 5-year-olds has been found to significantly increase children's math achievement as compared to children in classrooms that do not use such a curriculum (Presser, Clements, Ginsburg, & Ertle, 2015).

Technology is an essential component of *Building Blocks* (Clements & Sarama, 2007). For example, young children are limited in their ability to mentally manipulate shapes—to imagine the shapes turned or flipped. After children accumulate experiences in sliding, rotating, and flipping objects—whether with physical objects or a computer tool—they will be able to develop skills of mental imagery and understand the possibilities for manipulating shapes. Digital environments, in which children need to think abstractly and give concrete and precise commands, can be particularly helpful in getting a feel for such transformations and for other aspects of mathematical thinking.

Effective Mathematics Teaching

In this section, we present research-based ways of intentionally teaching mathematics. They include specific teacher behaviors that relate to positive outcomes, math talk, and grouping.

Teacher Behaviors   Research demonstrates the effectiveness of specific teaching behaviors that are related to positive learning outcomes for children (Clements & Sarama, 2008). Clements and Sarama (2007b) developed the *Classroom Observation of Early Mathematics—Environment and Teaching* (COEMET), a useful observation instrument to evaluate the quality of mathematics instruction. Some specific teacher behaviors on the COEMET are listed next that relate to children's improved math knowledge (Clements & Sarama, 2007, 2008; Sarama & Clements, 2007):

1. How much time the teacher is actively engaged in math activities
2. Whether the teacher builds on and elaborates children's mathematical ideas and strategies
3. How much the teacher facilitates children's responding to math questions and situations

The COEMET describes both high-quality and poor-quality teaching, some examples of which appear in Figure 13.2. Other teacher behaviors that strongly relate to children's math learning include (Clements & Sarama, 2007b, 2008; Sarama & Clements, 2007):

- Teachers' curiosity about and enthusiasm for mathematics
- Teachers' ability to set high but realistic expectations
- Teachers' observations of children, note taking to record their observations, and use of learning trajectories to individualize instruction

Math Talk   Tamara's kindergarten is well stocked with board games that the children enjoy playing. But Tamara observes that some children rarely use them. One day, she invites four of the reluctant players to join her. Tamara introduces the activity: "For this game, we need to roll the dice. Look carefully at this cube. What do you observe about the dots?" As the children examine the dice and count the dots on each side, Tamara extends the math talk: "What's the largest number you can get when you roll one die?" After turning the dice around, the children agree on "six." As the conversation continues, Tamara

EXAMPLE 1: The teacher showed curiosity about and enthusiasm for math ideas and connections to other ideas or real-world situations.

- commented on or discussed mathematical ideas in reading a story
- showed interest in the mathematics that emerged in children's play, construction, or discussions

Situation

The children are building with blocks. The teacher says, "What are you making?"
Children respond that it's a skyscraper.

Low-Quality Instruction	High-Quality Instruction
• The teacher says, "Nice. Be careful it doesn't fall on you."	• The teacher says, "It looks the same on this side [gesturing] as it does on this side [gesturing]. It's symmetrical! Are you going to keep building a symmetric building?" • The teacher asks, "I wonder how tall it is?" • The teacher says, "I see you put the long blocks at the bottom and the smaller ones on top. Could you tell me how that helped you make your building?" "What might happen if you put the long ones on the top?" • The teacher asks, "If you put these curved ones here, can you build more on top of them or not? What would happen if you did?"

EXAMPLE 2: The teacher facilitated children's responding.

- elicited many solution methods for one problem
- encouraged elaboration of children's responses
- waited for and listened attentively to individual children
- responded to errors as learning opportunities

Situation

The teacher asks one child to figure out how many 1 more than 3 is.

Low-Quality Instruction	High-Quality Instruction
• When a child has difficulty, the teacher says, "Someone else can answer." • When another child gives the correct answer, the teacher moves to the next task.	• When a child has difficulty, the teacher says, "Can you show me 3 to get started?" • The child says, "Four." The teacher asks, "Can you teach us how you did that?" • The teacher asks, "Did anybody do it a different way?"

FIGURE 13.2 Examples of High- and Low-Quality Mathematics Teaching This figure compares and contrasts examples of high-quality effective math teaching strategies with ineffective practices.
Source: From Clements, D. H., & Sarama, J. (2000/2017). COEMET: The Classroom Observation of Early Mathematics Environment and Teaching instrument Denver, CO: University of Denver. Re-printed with permission.

introduces math talk such as "What do you observe about the number of dots on each side of the cube? How are they different? Do you see a pattern? The dice is shaped like a cube. What do the dots tell you about cubes?" After the children have mastered the game using one die, Tamara brings out a second one and further extends the math learning, "You rolled a four and a five, so how many spaces can you move?"

math talk Using the language and vocabulary of mathematics.

This scene from Tamara's classroom demonstrates how even a simple board game provides a great opportunity for math talk. Given the critical role of language in learning math, it is not surprising that one of the most effective teaching strategies is what is simply called *math talk*. Teachers should also point out that in these situations children are "doing" math.

The amount of math-related talk children experience is positively related to their mathematical knowledge (Klibanoff, Levine, Huttenlocher, Vasilyeva, & Hedges, 2006). However, there is an enormous amount of variation in the amount of math talk that children experience. One study found that in a one-hour observation of 26 preschool classrooms, teachers' math talk ranged from 1 to 104 math-related words (Klibanoff et al., 2006). An even greater difference occurs in parent-child interactions. A longitudinal study that recorded math talk between parents and their children, between the ages of 14 and 30 months, found that over 7½ hours of observation, some parents spoke as few as 4 math words with their children whereas others produced 287 (Levine, Suriyakham, Roe, Huttenlocher, & Gunderson, 2010). The researchers interpreted this finding to mean that over the first 2½ years of life, some children heard 600 times as many number words as other children.

Given the importance of math talk to children's mathematical understanding, the question arises, what if the children don't speak the same language as their teachers? Teaching math to dual language learners requires adapting curriculum and individualizing instruction.

Grouping for Instruction

Alice's preschool children love it when she brings out the plastic attribute blocks, which vary by color, shape, size, and thickness. She introduces the activity by saying, "There are so many ways these blocks are the same, but they are also different. Yesterday, we sorted them into groups by two attributes: color and shape. Today, let's see if we can sort them another way. Does anybody have an idea?"

> Alfredo says, "Some are big and some are little."
> "That's boring," counters Bernadette.
> "Okay, you want a challenge," Alice responds. "We'll play a game. I'll give clues and you try to find the shape. Alfredo, can you find the big, fat, blue pentagon?"

Small-group activities for four to six children are especially useful for teaching mathematics, and the skills children acquire during small-group instruction can transfer to knowledge and abilities that have not been taught (Clements & Sarama, 2007).

Although whole-group time can also be used to teach mathematics, to be effective, it should be only one component of instruction, along with small groups, individual activity, and technology (Clements & Sarama, 2007, 2008). The most effective whole-group interactions include a combination of teacher-led brief discussions, problem solving with a partner (another child or an adult), and physical activities such as marching while counting or doing a shape hunt (Clements & Sarama, 2007, 2008).

In previous sections, we described the importance of building a firm foundation in mathematics understanding for all young children. Next, we turn to the topic of science and engineering, which is frequently integrated with mathematics curriculum in the early years.

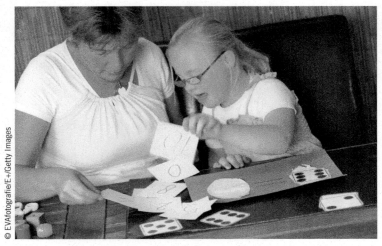

Effective teachers use various ways of grouping for instruction, including individual activity, whole group, small groups, and technology.

© EVAfotografie/E+/Getty Images

Check Your Understanding 13.3

Effective Science and Engineering Curriculum and Teaching

Young children tend to be curious and inquisitive. They constantly ask questions such as "What's that?" "Why?" "How come?" They also are inclined to actively explore and observe their environment. They want to know "What would happen if …?" To find answers, they readily dig in the mud, dump and splash water, or move their bodies in every way imaginable. At the same time, they try to make sense of these experiences, so they develop and test their own theories about how the world works. As a result, children are often called "natural scientists" (McClure, 2017).

In the following sections, we describe the early childhood science curriculum—the content and processes that children from infancy through third grade can and should be learning. Then, we describe effective teaching strategies to promote children's scientific knowledge and understanding. We begin with the role of science and engineering in an integrated curriculum.

Science and Engineering Curriculum

The purpose of **science** is to study and understand the physical and natural world, especially by observing and experimenting. Science plays two important roles in the early childhood curriculum. The primary role is to lay a foundation of conceptual understanding and knowledge that will deepen and broaden as children move through school. Second, science exploration is an excellent way of integrating learning across the curriculum, as the following example illustrates:

science Study of the physical and natural world, especially by observing and experimenting.

> Rose Grindel's first graders are studying life science and exploring concepts such as living and nonliving things and growth and change. As part of their study, they visit a nearby apple orchard. Before their visit, Rose brings in types of apples for tasting (Macintosh, Granny Smith) and the children graph their preferences. A lively debate ensues about why apples look and taste different. Theo comes to the wise conclusion that apples must be kind of like people: They are the same in most ways, but they look different.
>
> Rose continues, "I guess we need to find out the kind of apples that grow at the orchard. Are there other things you want to find out? Do you think apples are alive?" This last question draws laughs, but then some other queries. Grason says, "Well, trees are alive and apples grow on trees. So they could be alive, too." Grason's comment sparks a debate about what the word *living* means. This topic will be further explored throughout the month as children explore the characteristics of living and nonliving things.
>
> At the orchard, children write down the farmer's answers to their questions and take photos to document their visit. Hunter wants his picture taken next to a tree as a way to measure it. Later in the year, the class will return and compare their photos of the fruit-bearing trees to the flowering trees in spring. Their documentation will pique memories. Hunter thinks his photo will show how much the tree grows.
>
> At the farm, each child picks 10 apples (counting by ones), and back at school they group the apples by tens. The children come up with several ways to figure out that the total number they picked is 210! They also organize the apples by size, and choose the smallest to cook and the larger ones to eat. Because they picked so many apples, Ebony suggests that they donate some to the food bank. When the children cut the apples, they work with halves and quarters. They also bake apples and make applesauce, all the while predicting and observing the changes that take place.

In the previous example, life science is the main curriculum focus. Children learn science facts and concepts while *doing* science—asking questions, predicting, observing, and drawing conclusions. But other curriculum areas are well integrated. Children represent their learning in many ways—drawing pictures, taking photos, and writing about the apple orchard. Mathematics learning includes number and operations (counting, adding, using the base-10 system, and dividing); classifying; creating and analyzing data (graphing); and measurement. Language and literacy are also involved, with children reading information books and learning new vocabulary (Gelman, Brenneman, MacDonald, & Román, 2010).

Science Content

A coalition of scientists and science educators agree on the goals of the K–12 science curriculum, which are articulated in the *Next Generation Science Standards* (Achieve, Inc., 2013). The content of early childhood science is directly related to young children's natural interest and curiosity about how the world works, living things, their bodies, the earth, insects and animals, and other topics they find fascinating (Seefeldt, Galper, & Jones, 2012).

As in mathematics, both content and process are not only essential, but integrally connected. Children can't do a science experiment that isn't connected to science knowledge and concepts, nor can they make sense of discrete facts and concepts presented apart from meaningful context. In short, children can't learn science from a book alone; they have to *do* science.

physical science Basic ideas about the properties of liquids and solid materials, how things move and change position, and cause-and-effect relationships.

life science The study of the characteristics, life cycles, and environments of organisms.

Scientific Knowledge Goals
As important as it is to foster children's interest and active engagement in doing science, equally important is to expand their content knowledge. The *Next Generation Science Standards* (NGSS) call for the curriculum to include physical science, life science, earth and space science, and engineering. Following are definitions of these science topics and some related goals (Achieve, Inc., 2013).

Physical Science   In the area of physical science, children learn basic ideas about the properties of liquids and solid materials and objects (size and shape). They learn how things move and change position. They show increasing understanding of cause-and-effect relationships—for instance, how force affects the distance a ball rolls. They also explore characteristics of sound and light—how shadows are produced and change, or how sound results from vibrations.

From infancy, children gain knowledge of the physical world by acting on objects to see what happens; babies love to throw their bottle out of a high chair over and over to see what happens. At times they act to get a desired effect—rolling, pushing, and dropping objects. To extend learning, teachers can ask children what will happen if they squeeze an object or challenge them to blow on a spool to make it move. Often children explore and manipulate effects without knowing how they achieved the results; when teachers ask children how or why they think something happened, an everyday experience is turned into a scientific event (Seefeldt, Galper, & Jones, 2012).

Video Example 13.3:

Physical Science in Kindergarten

The kindergarten children in this video are having fun playing with balls but they are also learning one of the big ideas in physical science—forces and interactions: pushes and pulls. What does the teacher do to ensure that they focus on this important goal in the *Next Generation Science Standards*? How does she extend their learning?

Life Science   Life science is the study of the characteristics, life cycles, and environments of organisms. Children identify features of plants and animals, their habitats, and needs (food and water). They learn about living and nonliving things, and how living things grow and change. They also learn parts of the human body, how they function, what people need to stay healthy, and how human beings are alike and different.

Earth and Space Science   This topic involves studying properties of earth materials, changes on the earth, and patterns of movement and changes of the sun and moon. Once thought to be a topic beyond their understanding, many young children are fascinated and knowledgeable about space as demonstrated by the kindergartner's drawing shown in Figure 13.3. The learning goals of earth and space science include:

- Recognizing repeating patterns in nature (day and night; seasons)
- Observing weather changes
- Understanding the effect of people on the environment
- Learning about geographic features of the earth (mountains, oceans) and the movement of objects in the sky

Engineering Maynardo arrives at preschool breathless because a huge tree fell in his backyard over the weekend. His dad emailed photos to the teacher, which she projects on a screen. The children begin to wonder how the tree could ever be lifted and removed from Maynardo's yard. This question involves engineering—figuring out how to move very heavy objects; then designing, constructing, and experimenting with pulleys and levers.

FIGURE 13.3 Kindergarten Child's Representation of the Solar System This kindergartner's drawing of the solar system reveals both his scientific understanding and his representation skills. Used with permission of Annemarie.

earth and space science Studying properties of earth materials, changes on the earth, patterns of movement, and changes of the sun and moon.

Engineers create, design, and build structures and machines to help people solve problems and make things work better. Although engineering has only recently been an articulated learning goal in early childhood, young children are natural engineers as anyone who has observed block play can attest (Christenson & James, 2015). *Next Generation Science Standards*, which have been adopted by more than half the states, include engineering design beginning in kindergarten.

The engineering design process includes several steps: define a problem; design possible solutions using representations such as sketches, drawings, physical models; test the solutions; redesign to make it better; and share results. Consider children who want to solve the problem of building a road over a barrier or get objects to move farther at faster speeds—these are engineering challenges The children need to think about and research the problem; build a possible solution; test the creation; find out if it works and make it better; and discuss it with others (Heroman, 2017).

Young children love and excel at such "making and tinkering" as Heroman (2017) describes engineering design. But the learning environment must support tinkering. Teachers need to provide basic equipment and tools such as safety goggles, PVC pipe, pulleys, hammers, and screwdrivers. In addition, children need access to a wide variety of consumable materials that include things to build with (cardboard, wood scraps); connectors (tape, glue sticks); modeling materials and tools (clay, Play-Doh), and decorations such as fabrics, stickers, or feathers. Electronics, technology, and simple machines such as old phones that can be taken apart, batteries, and on/off switches also inspire engineering.

Big Ideas in Science Across the content areas of science are several key concepts or big ideas that help children make connections and create a strong foundation for later science learning. These concepts include *understanding change* and *cause-and-effect relationships*. Another concept that is revisited through school is the idea of a *system*—that a whole is composed of related parts that affect each other. For example, the human body is a system; there are weather systems; engineers design and build systems, and, of course, there is the vast solar system.

These complex concepts are vital to the work of all scientists. Preschoolers can grasp such concepts at a basic level when teachers draw attention to them in planned and spontaneous learning experiences. For example, when Jonah asks why insects and birds fly but fish that also have wings don't fly, his teacher poses the question to the class. A lively discussion ensues about the differences between wings and fins and how some birds, like ducks, both swim and fly.

Video Example 13.4:

Effective Science Teaching

In this video second graders are actively engaged in a science study. What science content are these children learning? In what ways are they "doing" science? What effective strategies is the teacher using?

Children's conceptual understanding deepens when they have a variety of experiences related to the same concept (French & Woodring, 2013). For example, children deepen their understanding of the concept of life cycles by planting and tending a garden, observing a class pet, and studying how humans grow.

Change can be continually observed in the natural world. Some changes occur too rapidly to be observed without special tools such as microscopes, whereas others occur too slowly for children to fully comprehend, such as the changing seasons. On the other hand, some changes can be readily observed and investigated by any age child. Teachers can encourage children to look for all sorts of changes:

- What happens to the plant when it is left in the dark?
- What happens to your shadow at different times of the day? Is your shadow there every day?
- What changes can be reversed? Can water be turned into ice and back into water?
- Why don't very tall buildings fall down?

Effective Science Teaching

The fact that most young children are naturally curious and inclined to explore and investigate does not mean that they "naturally" or automatically learn science concepts and processes. To understand concepts and acquire skills, children need intentional teachers who plan and implement a coherent science curriculum. Science learning is too important to be left to chance.

Intentional teachers promote science learning by carefully organizing the environment, providing focused learning experiences and information, and integrating science into children's play and everyday routines, but most of all, engaging children in the scientific process.

Organize the Environment   Science requires a planned environment, materials, and tools, such as cups, containers, trays, and jars, to help children observe, collect, organize, and display evidence. Children need tools for investigation, including a variety of magnifying glasses, binoculars, mirrors, flashlights, magnets, levers, pulleys, and scales. Information books and access to the Internet are also essential resources for studying science.

Children learn by doing science. They need to use the methods of scientists—questioning, predicting, investigating, experimenting, and drawing conclusions.

Recording and representing evidence and conclusions requires tools as simple as notebooks, writing implements, and chart and graph paper, and as technologically sophisticated as digital and video cameras, tablets, computers, and whiteboards. For example, an Eyeclops™ is a computerized magnifier that can project onto a wall or screen. Children can aim it at all kinds of objects—their skin, the inside of a seed, or a butterfly in a jar.

Provide Focused, Sequential Experiences   An effective science curriculum should reflect a coherent progression of science skills and content (French & Woodring, 2013). Learning goals and topics should build on one another so that children develop progressively more complex understandings. Content should align with state or national science standards.

Teachers can plan in-depth projects or topics of study related to science knowledge that build on and expand children's interests. Sufficient time should be devoted to topics for children to go into some depth. For instance, in a class study of animals, small groups of children or individuals might study one animal and report their findings to the others in the group.

Curriculum should focus on knowledge that is familiar and meaningful to children, such as concepts of temperature based on their experiences with weather. Although children are more capable of abstract learning than previously thought, it is usually easier to begin with more concrete, accessible experiences such as scientific phenomena that can be directly seen, touched, tasted, or heard (French & Woodring, 2013). In addition, teachers shouldn't impose scientifically accurate explanations for phenomena before children are able to grasp their meaning (Worth & Grollman, 2003).

Engage Children in the Scientific Process An overarching aspect of the curriculum is the process of doing science, or **scientific inquiry**. Scientific inquiry involves children in several processes such as questioning, predicting, observing, investigating, experimenting, recording, and documenting (National Center on Quality Teaching and Learning, 2013). In Table 13.1, we list these processes and illustrate them with a physical science example—children studying shadows to learn the properties and characteristics of light.

scientific inquiry Involving children in observing, predicting, and investigating.

Application Exercise 13.1
Scientific Investigation

Intentionally Teach Science Providing a scientifically engaging learning environment and opportunities to explore are essential, but children do not learn science from manipulating materials alone. Research shows that when teachers explicitly introduce children to science concepts, vocabulary, and processes during brief circle time lessons, children spend more time and are more engaged in science, and their scientific knowledge increases (Hong & Diamond, 2012; Nayfeld, Brenneman, & Gelman, 2011). For example, in one study, researchers introduced children to a balance scale during in whole group lesson; then the children tried weighing various objects and came to understand the function of the tool. During choice time, the children spontaneously experimented with the balance scale in the science center, which they had previously

---

TABLE 13.1 Scientific Inquiry Processes in Children

Children engaging in a shadow study, as described here, use the same inquiry processes as professional scientists.

Process of Scientific Inquiry	Example: Properties of Light
Noticing, wondering, exploring, and asking questions out of curiosity or to further existing knowledge	On a bright, sunny day outdoors, preschoolers notice and play with their shadows, exploring how to make the shadows longer or shorter and wondering whether they can "get away" from them. The teacher asks, "Where do you think a shadow comes from?"
Formulating preliminary predictions, explanations, or hypotheses to answer questions	Children offer their theories about shadows: People make shadows; shadows follow you; shadows are skinny; only the sun makes shadows. Some think shadows go away at night and some disagree.
Gathering evidence by actively observing, investigating, and/or experimenting	The children observe and gather evidence about shadows: They trace their shadows at different times of the day outdoors; they play with a shadow theater indoors (a sheet in front of a large window), guessing the objects creating the shadows.
Recording, reporting, explaining, discussing, and reflecting on evidence	The children refine their ideas about shadows: Other sources of light make shadows, not just the sun; people need light to make shadows; shadows change shape.
Refining questions, refocusing observations, and engaging in more focused explorations	The teacher sets up an overhead projector for children to focus on what more can be learned about shadows. The teacher sends home a letter to families encouraging them to help children observe shadows at night.
Sharing and discussing ideas, listening to other perspectives, and asking new questions	Children share their observations from home, such as street lights can make shadows, and they ask new questions: "Can the moon make shadows?" The study continues with new questions and interests.

Source: K. Worth & S. Grollman, 2003. *Worms, Shadows, and Whirlpools: Science in the Early Childhood Classroom*, Portsmouth, NH: Heinemann.

© Pearson Education

Video Example 13.5:

Intentionally Teaching Science

In this video, a first grade class is participating in a science lesson on camouflage. The day before, the teacher showed a video to engage the children's interest and activate their prior knowledge. What does she do in this lesson to involve the children in exploring, explaining, and elaborating about the concept of camouflage?

ignored (Nayfeld, Brenneman, & Gelman, 2011). Similarly, when teachers facilitate engineering design, children spend more time and are more likely to finish the engineering activity (Wang et al., 2013).

Children need intentional teachers to connect their experiences to scientific concepts and vocabulary, as described in the feature titled *Becoming an Intentional Teacher: Early Childhood Engineering*.

Table 13.2 lists key strategies that teachers can use to promote children's enthusiasm and understanding of science and engineering knowledge, concepts, and methods. These strategies are also effective for teaching mathematics.

Engaging All Children in STEM Learning

Science is interesting and fun for many children. But every child is different. Teachers need to pay particular attention to adapting learning experiences for children with special needs and for dual language learners. They also need to be mindful of providing girls with equal opportunities to learn science and mathematics.

Becoming an Intentional Teacher

Early Childhood Engineering

© Monkey Business Images/Shutterstock

Here's What Happened The block area was running smoothly, but my preschoolers seemed to become bored. Their constructions were repetitive and lacked imagination. Together we took the following actions:

1) *Identified the problem.* During whole group time, I shared my observation and asked the children to think about it. They brainstormed ideas and agreed that there wasn't enough floor space in the block area.

2) *Did research.* I invited Manuela's mother, who is an architect, to visit and describe how she does her work. She showed the children blueprints (2-D representations) and 3-D models of projects she has done. We read information books on architecture and storybooks such as *Iggy Peck, Architect*.

3) *Created and built solutions.* Lucy suggested designing elevated platforms to provide more building space. She drew pictures of her idea while other children came up with variations using LEGO and other table toys.

4) *Tested and made it better.* After much trial and error, using various building materials and connectors such as duct tape and wire, the elevated platforms stayed in place and supported small block structures. Most children agreed that Lucy's plan provided more building space. But Addison still wanted to make the area more interesting. He suggested adding materials for ramps and tunnels to move between the different levels (such as plastic tubing and open molding).

5) *Shared with others.* We invited the other preschool class in our school and listened to their opinions about our solution. We got ideas about adding decorative consumable materials that don't take up much space.

Here's What I Was Thinking Engineering and physical science are at the heart of block construction. But I felt that in my classroom we weren't using the full potential of blocks to explore these concepts and processes. I wanted the children to actively engage in engineering design to solve a problem that they identified, not one I created for them.

I brought in an expert because I wanted them to engage deeply in the *build and create* phase of the process. Seeing her design representations made the process meaningful and interesting. When the first few structures collapsed, I encouraged them to stick with it. In these situations, children will often try just one solution and give up if it doesn't work. Or if it does work, they won't try another, potentially better solution. I wanted to extend their thinking without interfering with their play.

I also found that using large- or small-group time worked well for introducing a new challenge or materials. I found that the children discussed them—with me and each other—yet the construction and play were under their control. By the end of the engineering project, the children were the experts.

Reflection What do you think about this teacher's approach to integrating engineering and science content in play? In what other ways could she intentionally support STEM learning?

Source: J. Lee, D.A. Collins, & L. Winkelman, 2015. "Connecting 2-d and 3-d: Drafting blueprints, building, and playing with blocks." *Young Children, 70*(1), 32–35; and R. DeVries and C. Sales, 2011. *Ramps and Pathways: A Constructivist Approach to Physics with Young Children,* Washington, DC: National Association for the Education of Young Children.

TABLE 13.2 Effective Science Teaching Strategies

The strategies listed and described here are not only effective in teaching scientific knowledge, concepts, and methods but also motivate children's interest in and enthusiasm for science.

Science Teaching Strategy	Explanation
Model and welcome curiosity, openness, and flexibility to questioning without needing to know all the answers. Teachers are sometimes intimidated by science because they don't have enough knowledge themselves.	Although teachers don't need vast knowledge before tackling a topic, they do need to prepare and learn as much as possible. When they don't know an answer to a child's question, the best response is, "I don't know. What do you imagine?" or "I'm curious about..."
Be open to and appreciate creativity and beauty in science. Sometimes science is erroneously thought to be only about cold, hard facts.	Examine NASA-produced photos of sunrise on Mars or the rings around Saturn. Watch a butterfly emerge from its cocoon. Such experiences can inspire children to produce their own creative representations of the natural and physical world.
Encourage children to reflect on their experiences and share their ideas with others. Direct experience with materials is important to their science learning, but it is not enough.	Engage children in thinking about, representing, and discussing their experiences and observations. Discussion among teachers and children, informally and in planned groups, gives children the chance to hear others' thinking and perspectives and to develop skills communicating about science.
Teach children observation skills.	Encourage children to go beyond just looking. Have children describe, draw, discuss, redraw, and describe again to refine observation skills and build vocabulary. Ask, "What did we learn about...?"
Provide a variety of ways for children to document and represent their work.	Give children journals, writing tools, and digital cameras to record their observations, gather data, and communicate their findings to others.
Listen to children and ask about what they are seeing and doing.	When children talk about what they see, hear, and think, they do more noticing, wondering, and reflecting. They make connections, think about causes, and learn new, often rare words.
Build on and extend children's interests in the natural world and living things.	Use information books, field trips, technology, and visitors, to open up the classroom.
Engage children in formulating their own questions (*What do you want to know?*), designing experiments (*How can we find out?*), and making predictions (*What do you think will happen if ...?*).	Children attend more closely to what they see, hear, smell, and feel when they have put forth their own prediction or question or have considered how to go about investigating something. They are more likely to think about what their observations mean.
Don't bombard children with talk as they explore and investigate. Instead, watch closely and use a well-timed question or comment.	Prompt children to: • Make a prediction (*What will it look like if...?*). • Think aloud (*What are you doing now? What next?*). • Reflect on their actions (*What did you do before that happened? How do you know? How did you figure that out?*).
Integrate science in play and routines	Science is everywhere. Children learn science when they play in the water table, ride down a slope on a tricycle, or observe ants on a sidewalk. Rich science opportunities occur in blocks, sand, clay, cooking, art, music, movement, stories, and outdoors.

Sources: Based on *Benchmarks for Science Literacy*, American Association for the Advancement of Science, 2009, Washington, DC: Author, retrieved May 16, 2018, from http://www.project2061.org/publications/bsl/default.htm; *Using the Scientific Method* by National Center on Quality Teaching and Learning, 2013, Washington, DC: U.S. Department of Health and Human Services, Office of Head Start.

Children with Special Needs Providing access to science experiences for children with disabilities is an especially important task for teachers. To widen your view of effective science teaching, read the *Including All Children: Science Exploration* feature.

Dual Language Learners STEM presents an opportunity as well as a challenge for children who are learning English. Because science involves real things and events, it can help children learn vocabulary words, especially names of objects, living things, and tools. On the other hand, specific scientific terms such as *inquiry* or *evidence* can be especially difficult for dual language learners (Albert Shanker Institute, 2009). These

© Pearson Education

Video Example 13.6:

Second Grade Scientific Inquiry

In this video, primary grade children are working at the Look and Learn science center in their classroom. How are the children engaged in the scientific inquiry process and what are they learning? What effective strategies does the teacher use to teach science?

children will need lots of cues, gestures, and repetition to learn these words in meaningful context. Read the *Language Lens: Teaching STEM to Dual Language Learners* to learn more.

Gender Differences During a visit to the nature center, first-grade teacher Trula Mann is startled when the naturalist brings out a snake for the children's inspection. She hates snakes and cringes at the thought of touching it. She sees that the boys eagerly gather around the snake while many of the girls look frightened and withdraw. Trula swallows her anxiety and reaches out to touch the snake. She is surprised to find that it is not at all slimy. The naturalist asks, "How can a snake find food or defend itself since it doesn't have arms or legs?" At the end of the discussion, the children conclude that they would bite, too, if they were a snake who was threatened.

In overcoming her trepidation, Trula served as a valuable model for the children, especially some of the girls. Such modeling behavior is important for girls because gender differences in science are apparent as early as preschool. For example, one study found that boys demonstrated more curiosity, spontaneity, and extensive knowledge about nature and vertebrate and invertebrate (snakes, worms) animals than did girls (Desouza & Czerniak, 2002). On the other hand, girls, although more fearful, were also more concerned about the welfare of animals. Boys

Including All Children

Science Exploration

Most children are naturally interested in science topics and motivated to engage in investigations using all of their senses. However, children with sensory disabilities may lose out on such learning unless teachers make appropriate accommodations.

Sheila Kohn loves science, and so do the children in her first-grade class. Currently, the curriculum topic is earth science. The children have formulated questions and are exploring a wooded area near the school. They want to know what lives under the ground and how it survives. They have brought little shovels, collection containers, and magnifying glasses for observation. Their questions include these: How does the earth smell? How does it feel? What lives in a small amount of earth? How do they breathe? What do they eat? What happens if it rains?

Most of the children are very excited and eagerly approach the investigation. Delores, however, has a vision impairment. The trek outside intimidates her, and all the talk of observing and using the magnifying glass makes her feel left out. Sheila discusses the situation with Delores and they agree on a plan. Together they will visit the outdoors in a small group, and Delores will use her other senses to investigate the earth. Delores will be in charge of the questions that she is most able to address: What does the earth feel like and how does it smell? Delores is an especially astute listener as well, so she will also report on what she hears outside. Because the other children focus on what they see, they usually miss a great

deal of information that can be obtained through their other senses.

Ira has a different special need—sensory integration disorder—which requires an altogether different accommodation. Children who have sensory integration disorders have difficulty processing and connecting sensory information. Each of the five senses obtains information from the environment in different ways. In the course of typical development, the senses work together to sort out and make sense of the input. Children with sensory integration disorders, however, may be overly sensitive to one or more of the senses—touch or sound, for example. Or they may fixate on one sense such as sight or smell.

In Ira's case, the busyness of the classroom overwhelms him at times. He is especially disturbed by confusing experiences like science study that seem to come at him from all directions. To ensure Ira's successful participation, Sheila includes him in the small group with Delores on the walk. Unlike Delores, however, who is encouraged to use as many senses as possible, Sheila helps Ira limit his sensory input. She gives him earplugs to lessen the noise and sunglasses to minimize the light. Under such conditions, Ira is an astute observer and spends a long time carefully watching a worm wiggling through his pile of earth.

As we see from Delores's and Ira's situations, successful inclusion of all children requires knowledge of each child's needs and strengths and individually planned accommodations and modifications.

Language Lens
Teaching STEM to Dual Language Learners

At times, there is an assumption that because mathematics is about numbers and quantity, language is less of a barrier. However, mathematics itself is a language, and as we have seen, math talk is what makes its abstract concepts comprehensible for children. Each area of STEM has its own vocabulary and involves academic language that children do not encounter in everyday conversations. In short, STEM learning presents unique challenges for dual language learners.

Many of the same strategies for teaching dual language learners in general are effective in teaching STEM. For example, gestures such as a circling motion help young children understand basic concepts such as the whole amount or putting together and taking apart. Children readily count or form shapes with their fingers. Teachers can set up indoor and outdoor games for children to use their whole bodies to learn position words such as *above*, *below*, *between*, and *through*. A strategy for older children is to create a math, science, or technology dictionary of relevant terms. Such a resource helps children use different ways of representing a concept—in this case, words that can be referred to later.

Another strategy is having children talk to one another in pairs or small groups. When children are learning a new language, it is important not to put them on the spot. They shouldn't be expected to respond in front of the whole class. In a small group, practicing concepts is easier and "errors" are more likely to be viewed as part of the learning process. In fact, cultivating a classroom culture in which children focus on how to solve a problem as opposed to seeking the one correct answer is a useful learning strategy for all the children.

Introducing a math or science concept to the whole class can be done effectively using an interactive whiteboard. Children can then be prompted to respond to questions chorally as a whole group. Not every child will answer correctly, and no one child's response will be singled out. Another proven strategy when introducing a math or science concept is to explicitly teach it by modeling, supplying the specific name, and having children repeat the word.

Problem solving is playing a larger role in curriculum due to the Common Core standards, but word problems complicate the challenge of math instruction for dual language learners. Teachers should avoid tricky word problems that create confusion, such as, "Jonas has 2 cars and 3 trucks; how many vehicles does he have?" Such a question is a language test rather than a math problem. A related challenge presented by word problems is the culturally implicit knowledge they often require. Solving a problem usually requires that a child understand the situation in which it occurs, whether it's purchasing groceries or driving a car at a certain speed.

Manipulatives are hailed as an excellent tool to teach STEM, and yet many children cannot relate to these toys. Few such toys reflect the racial, cultural, and gender diversity of our classrooms. LEGO® has introduced some plastic figures portraying people of color as doctors, scientists, architects, and other STEM occupations. However, most STEM toys still promote stereotypes of only white males in these roles.

What works most effectively are the practices that are developmentally appropriate for all children—hands-on, meaningful experiences coupled with teacher scaffolding, as opposed to worksheets that test what children should have already learned. Dual language learners need to actively "do" science, technology, and engineering tasks—as teachers and other children supply the words. And most important of all, teachers need to have high expectations that *all* children can learn challenging STEM content.

Sources: Based on B. Austin, 2014. Tips when discussing math with the English language learner. Chicago: Erikson Early Math Collaborative, retrieved May 8, 2018 from http://earlymath.erikson.edu/6-tips-discussing-math-english-language-learner; and M. Weinstock, 2015. It's Time for More Racial Diversity in STEM Toys. *Scientific American*, Voices: Exploring and Celebrating Diversity in Science, retrieved May 8, 2018 from https://blogs.scientificamerican.com/voices/it-s-time-for-more-racial-diversity-in-stem-toys/

and girls also differed in their play preferences, with boys more active and more likely than girls to bring into their play the science concepts that were introduced at group time the day before.

As for math, researchers find that girls and boys start kindergarten with about the same skills, but the gender gap widens over the first years of school (West, 2017). The gap is no doubt related to the fact that teachers rate girls' math skills lower than those of boys even when they score the same on direct assessments of math ability (Cimpian et al, 2016; Reardon & Portilla, 2016).

Research finds that first- and second-grade girls whose female teachers had math anxiety were likely to be anxious about math themselves (Beiland, Gunderson, Ramirez, & Levine, 2010). By the end of the school year, the girls came to believe that boys are good at math and girls are good at reading. Most important, young girls' anxiety negatively effects their beliefs about their own competence and in turn, their math achievement (Gunderson et al., 2018).

African American Boys In the previous section we presented research on gender differences in STEM achievement. However, these studies do not reflect the experience of African American boys. In reality, racial disparities in math achievement exist at kindergarten entry, especially for African American boys, and these gaps continue through school (Friedman-Krauss, Barnett, & Norris, 2016). An explanation for this phenomenon is that expectations are lower for African American boys even when they are high achieving (Zilanwala et al., 2017). As a result, they are often denied access to challenging curriculum. They come to believe that they are not good at math, which leads to negative attitudes about math that powerfully predict their achievement. Throughout school, African American children are less likely to experience challenging math curriculum and effective instruction (Farran et al., 2017). Providing the kind of high-quality and engaging STEM experiences described in this chapter is necessary but not sufficient to close the racial achievement gap (Davis & Farran, 2018). True progress depends on confronting racism and providing equity in educational opportunity for all children (Bowman, Comer, & Johns, 2018).

Because the science and engineering professions have been traditionally dominated by white males, particular efforts need to be made to address stereotypes and open the fields early on to children of color and girls. Given that gender, racial, and cultural disparities in STEM begin early and persist, it is never too early to introduce powerful role models such as female, African American, and Latino astronauts, inventors, or architects via real-life examples, toys, materials, and books. An excellent series of books by Andrea Beaty stars young girls as role models: *Rosie Revere, Engineer* (2013); *Ada Twist, Scientist* (2017), and *Iggy Peck, Architect* (2007). Especially relevant are true-story books. For pre-K to third-graders, *Starstruck: The cosmic journey of Neil deGrasse Tyson* (Krull & Brewer, 2018) is a picture book biography of the world famous director of the Hayden Planetarium in New York City. Tyson is an outstanding scientist role model for all children but particularly for African American boys. *Hidden figures: The true story of four black women and the space race* (Shetterly, 2018) is a picture book for 4- to 8-year-olds that tells the inspiring story of African-American female mathematicians and their ground-breaking work at NASA (made famous in the movie by the same name).

✓ Application Exercise 13.2
Science and Math in Kindergarten

✓ Check Your Understanding 13.4

🏠 Teaching about and with Technology

technology Tools used to change or modify the natural world to meet human needs.

Whereas science is the study of the natural world, the goal of **technology** is to change or modify the natural world to meet human needs (NRC, 2012). Technology, in its many forms, is a tool for all kinds of learning throughout life. It can be as simple as a handheld magnifying glass or as complex as the Hubble space telescope exploring the origins of the universe. Both of these tools make it possible for people to see things beyond the capability of the human eye.

Technology in itself is neither good nor bad; the same tool—such as a computer—can be used productively or destructively. A major curriculum goal is to improve STEM skills and understanding, with *T* standing for technology. In other words, children need to think critically about how technology is used to solve problems as well as learn how to use technological tools in intentional and creative ways.

A Developmentally and Technologically Appropriate Classroom

A preschool teacher creates a class website that is updated regularly. The children create a slide show about their class pet using Kid Pix software to share with families. For an integrated science study on the properties of water, kindergartners produce information books on the computer using digital photos of their water experiments.

First-graders work together using an interactive whiteboard, a large digital touchscreen with a computer, and the Internet. They explore pictures and information about birds in different parts of the world. They e-mail their questions to a first-grade class in Australia.

These are some examples of how creative teachers use technology to expand children's worlds beyond the classroom. In some cases, a relatively inexpensive form of media such as a digital camera is used, whereas an interactive whiteboard constitutes a much larger investment. Given the costs, educators must make informed decisions and be taught to use the tools effectively. For example, teachers may use digital tablets with individual children or pairs to differentiate reading instruction. A handheld device allows teachers to match apps, games, or other instructional tools to a child's learning level and needs. An interactive whiteboard, on the other hand, is most effective for larger groups or even whole-class instruction in which children actively participate (Linder, 2012). Teachers can introduce a new concept via the whiteboard and then children can solve problems in small groups or individually.

Use Interactive Media Effectively   Hundreds of children's media products flood the marketplace every year for both home and school use. Given limited budgets and the vital importance of choosing developmentally and culturally appropriate tools, early educators need help making decisions. Warren Buckleitner, an authority on interactive media for children, provides an online service for this purpose: *Children's Technology Review*, which is the world's largest online collection of educational reviews of children's interactive media. In addition, the NAEYC Technology and Young Children Interest Forum provides an interactive support group for teachers through its website.

Decisions about technology should be based on how well the particular tool serves the purposes of the classroom and the teaching and learning goals for children. "Technology does not drive purposeful learning; teachers' intentional instructional planning does" (NAEYC Technology and Young Children Interest Forum, 2008, p. 50).

Technology has many uses, from complex problem solving to practice on individual skills, managed at the children's level of thinking (Donohue, 2015). Working with appropriate software builds collaboration, creativity, and language. In fact, preschoolers actually talk almost twice as much at the computer than during any other activity, including blocks and art (Clements & Sarama, 2003).

Children need to learn with and about technology. How can teachers use interactive digital media to promote mathematics and science in learning?

© Monkey Business Images/Shutterstock

Digital media allow children to break free of the physical world and manipulate objects and space in ways that are otherwise impossible, using virtual manipulatives (Linder, 2012). For example, when children put together a wooden puzzle, there are strict limits on how pieces can be placed. Similarly, trying to correct or change marks formed on paper can be difficult and frustrating. By contrast, with Kid Pix drawing software and many other programs like it, a child can take actions that are impossible in the real world—change the shape of a design or instantly change colors—and easily alter their creations. In this way, digital media helps children become explicitly aware of and intentional about what they are doing (Clements & Sarama, 2007).

Ensure Access for All Children   Technology raises the issue of equity because some children have considerable access to technology at home whereas others do not. In addition, when digital media devices are available, boys tend to choose them more often than girls and to work on them longer.

For interactive media to be effective, teachers need to encourage experimentation with open-ended problems. They also need to use a wide range of teaching strategies to encourage, question, prompt, model, demonstrate, and give children choices without taking over or limiting children's opportunities to explore. Developmentally appropriate interactive media allows children to be in control, to function independently, and to create and invent their own activities; it also needs to be flexible and allow for more than one correct response (NAEYC and Fred Rogers Center for Early Learning and Children's Media, 2012).

Every developmentally appropriate math and science curriculum incorporates children's play. In the next section, we describe and give examples of how various types of play can be used effectively to promote STEM learning.

✔ Check Your Understanding 13.5

The Role of Play in Learning and Teaching STEM

Some early childhood educators inaccurately believe that teaching mathematics and science in preschool is not developmentally appropriate. The fact is that young children are capable STEM learners. To be developmentally appropriate, teachers need to provide playful, fun math and science experiences (Stipek, 2017). Opportunities for learning STEM content and processes abound in different types of play: block building, playing games, using table toys (manipulatives, pattern blocks, and so on), socio-dramatic play, exploration and practice during play, and book reading.

Block Building

Children enjoy building with blocks and they naturally engage in mathematical play with them (Seo & Ginsburg, 2004). Wooden unit blocks—called *unit blocks* because each block is a fraction or multiple of the standard unit—provide open-ended tools to promote children's creative play. But block play also provides valuable opportunities for children to explore and engage in math and engineering learning (Christenson & James, 2015; Lindeman & Anderson, 2015). As children build with blocks, they measure and classify them by size and shape;

Playing board or card games is very effective for teaching mathematics. What other kinds of games might be fun ways of learning mathematics?

© Corbis Super RF/Alamy Stock Photo

explore symmetry, balance, and stability; unitize; discover the mathematical relationships among the blocks (for example, two small blocks equal one longer block); and
work and solve problems together.

Young children's spontaneous activities with blocks do, in fact, include mathematical
play and exploration of spatial relationships (Seo & Ginsburg, 2004). Research suggests
that benefits from block play persist over the years (Wolfgang, Stannard, & Jones, 2009).
However, block building during free play alone doesn't automatically result in math learning. When teachers discuss mathematical ideas with children during block play, their learning is enhanced (Tepylo, Moss, & Stephenson, 2015). Teachers can introduce new words
such as *unit* or *equal*, and raise problems, such as "How can you make your bridge high
enough for the biggest boat to go under?" When teachers provide this kind of support, it
enhances children's learning at the time, but is also valuable because children incorporate
these new ideas when they play on their own. Block building contributes to children's
knowledge of geometry and spatial relations, especially three-dimensional shapes (Wang
et. al., 2013).

Games

Board games in which children count spaces along a number list (numbered squares) are
an effective way to develop children's numerical knowledge. The power of such games
is demonstrated in an experiment conducted in a Head Start program (Siegler & Ramani,
2008). Children who played a board game similar to Chutes and Ladders (that used a linear
rather than a circular pattern) became more skilled at counting, comparing, naming, and
estimating numbers. This study showed how something as basic as playing a board game
with numbered squares can significantly improve the number knowledge of children from
low-income families, many of whom don't have the opportunity to play such games at
home. Games such as cards and dominoes are also fun as long as they don't become too
competitive.

Further research on number board games finds that more effective games engage
children in "counting on" rather than counting from 1 every time. For example, if a child's
marker is on the square marked 18 and she rolls a 3, instead of counting 1, 2, 3, she counts
19, 20, 21 (Laski & Siegler, 2014). Children need prompting by adults to successfully play
the game but it can greatly expand their knowledge of the number system as described in
the feature *Promoting Play: Math Games*.

Manipulatives and Table Toys

One of the most effective ways for children to learn math is to use concrete materials such as
puzzles, matching games, and manipulatives. Manipulatives are small-sized blocks, cubes,
pattern blocks, beads, pegs, and the like that are designed for children's play and learning.

Puzzles and manipulatives can enhance math knowledge, especially geometric and
spatial thinking, in preschool as well as elementary-age children (Clements & Sarama,
2014). Up to about age 5½, children need concrete objects to learn counting and to solve
larger number problems using addition and subtraction (Levine, Jordan, & Huttenlocher,
1992). Manipulatives make abstract tasks meaningful.

However, simply providing manipulatives and concrete materials does not ensure
learning. Rather, teachers need to scaffold children's use of manipulatives if they get stuck
using the materials in the same way over and over. Six-year-old Martha loves to play with
Unifix cubes, and for several days she creates one row of 10 cubes. Her teacher says,
"Martha, you seem to like counting to 10. What if we make two rows of 10? How many
cubes do you think we'll need altogether?"

manipulatives Small-sized
blocks, cubes, pattern blocks,
beads, pegs, and the like that
are designed for children's play
and learning.

Application Exercise 13.3

Learning Math through Play

Promoting Play

Math Games

One of the most joyful and effective ways to teach math is using math games. Because math is a sequential discipline, children's ability to successfully play depends on their knowledge of math and the difficulty of the game. Teachers need to observe, model, and use math talk to ensure that the fun game helps them progress in understanding number and operations.

Teachers can make such games easily and inexpensively and relate them to a project study such as animal habitats. Typically, games with objects like table toys work best for younger children. For example, children may match plastic animals or wooden cubes to the number of dots on a card. Grid games are a little more challenging. They can be used to match objects to pictures on the squares and then count and compare them.

Grids are also effective for teaching big ideas such as sorting and classifying. Shoe sorting is a fun game in which children classify their own shoes into categories: tennis, sandals, slip-ons, and so on. Then they can count, graph, and compare which category has more or less, requiring addition, subtraction, and data analysis. Number path games help children learn one-to-one correspondence as they move their marker only one space along the path for each number. Shorter paths are best for younger children using one die, which supports development of subitizing. After children master the number sequence and one-to-one correspondence, they move on to more challenging longer path games using two dice; these teach addition, conceptual subitizing (numbers larger than six), and counting-on.

Shape puzzles using pattern blocks to match the design promote geometry and spatial relations. In one kindergarten class, children create and challenge each other to solve 3-D riddles: "I have one vortex, and one face. Party hats are shaped like me. What shape am I?" or "I have eight vertices and six faces. Dice are shaped like me." The children also make their own geoboards by hammering nails into blocks of wood and creating various shapes with rubber bands or string.

Some early educators still worry that focusing on math and standards is not developmentally appropriate and will take away from joyful preschool experiences. But too often adults underestimate children's capacities. Given the opportunity, as when playing games, children demonstrate that they love math and are amazingly competent.

Sources: A.I. Byers, E.A. Cottone, D. & Cameron, 2018. "From design copying to mathematics in the early childhood classroom." *Young Children*, *73*(1), 80–85; S. Moomaw, 2017. "Not all preschool math games are created equal." *Young Children*, *72*(3), 14–21; and D. Stipek, D., 2017. "Playful math instruction in the context of standards and accountability." *Young Children*, *72*(3), 8–13.

Socio-Dramatic Play

Sociodramatic play contributes to the development of self-regulation and executive function in children (Bodrova & Leong, 2007). Because these two basic cognitive abilities are essential for mathematics understanding, socio-dramatic play is an important opportunity to promote math and science learning.

Socio-dramatic play provides a context for children to use their developing math skills. For example, while playing restaurant, children write and read the prices on a menu, count their "money," and use one-to-one correspondence as they set the table. Pretend play also provides many opportunities for children to practice their developing math skills, as we describe next.

Exploration and Practice during Play

Many mathematics competencies such as counting require a lot of practice as well as demonstration, modeling, or scaffolding from adults (Fuson, 1988). Children need practice to master these skills, but such practice should be meaningful and motivating for children—and play is an excellent context for it.

During play, children will often initiate their own practice. For example, 2-year-olds will repeat a drumbeat until adults get tired. Three- and 4-year-old children will repeatedly string a set of beads in a pattern until they have mastered the skill to their personal satisfaction. While swinging, several girls take turns pushing each other and count the pushes as they go along. When they get to 20, they switch places. Seven-year-old Garrett repeatedly asks his mom to try to stump him with two-digit addition and subtraction problems as she puts him to bed each night.

Digital Play

Choosing appropriate apps is an important responsibility for teachers. The best apps have some of the same benefits as traditional play (Gray, 2015). When playing, children will often stay engaged for long periods of time, until they have mastered a task to their own satisfaction, repeating an activity such as putting together a puzzle or playing a matching game. These facts about play have important implications for choosing appropriate software for digital tools. Many apps emphasize extrinsic rewards like bells, gold stars, or flashing lights; but apps that engage children's intrinsic motivation to create, invent, think, and solve problems are more likely to promote imaginative play and its benefits.

Traditional play provides a context for children to develop social skills as they interact with other children. Some popular apps are designed to promote social interaction in several ways. Research shows that children often share a tablet, taking turns touching the screen, and talking. For example, Toca Boca provides a large selection of apps that promote play and creativity on a range of topics such as nature, construction, and transportation, and in settings such as a hair salon or pet doctor (Gray, 2015). *Toca Tea Party* enables a child to create an imaginary tea table and serve a meal to a favorite stuffed animal or toy figure. With *Toca Tea Party* or the other Toca apps, a child can also pretend with another child or an adult. Some shared apps enable children to interact with one another via the Internet.

Book Reading

Books have great potential for teaching mathematics and are often used to integrate math into other areas of the curriculum, especially literacy (Casey, Erkut, Ceder, & Young, 2008). Math concepts can be found in an enormous number of storybooks. In some stories, such as *The Three Bears*, math concepts are readily apparent (Ginsburg, 2016). In other stories, the math is more implicit, such as in *Rosie's Walk* (Hutchins, 1968), which uses spatial vocabulary to describe a fox following a hen on her winding way (Schickedanz, 2008). In such books, math learning is secondary to another goal, usually language and literacy. Numerous children's books are also published each year for the explicit purpose of teaching math, science, and engineering.

The use of books is powerful when the primary goal is teaching math. The work of Beth Casey and her colleagues (2008) provides strong evidence that presenting math content (such as spatial and number skills) as part of a meaningful story is more effective than teaching the content alone. They developed *Storytelling Sagas*, a series of specially written math storybooks for children in preschool through grade 2 that have proven to be very effective—especially with girls—in teaching math. Seeing and counting groups of things in books

© Pearson Education

Video Example 13.7:

Books and Math Learning

The children in this video are looking at a book that shows an octopus. The pictures that the children draw reflect what they've learned. What strategies does the teacher use to help the girls learn not just about an octopus, but about number and geometry concepts as well? What specific math content are the children learning?

helps children understand that three-dimensional objects can be represented as pictures on a two-dimensional space (Clements, Fuson, & Sarama, 2017b).

In this chapter, we explored the importance of providing developmentally appropriate, effective curriculum and intentional teaching in the related areas of science, technology, engineering, and mathematics (STEM). We described how teachers can help children become effective problem solvers and investigators, and how children learn STEM through play and intentional teaching. With this knowledge in mind, we return to Ms. Duncan's classroom.

Revisiting the Case Study

... Ms. Duncan's Classroom

At the outset of this chapter, we visited Celinda Duncan's kindergarten class on the 100th day of school, where the children were actively and enthusiastically engaged in learning math and other goals. Having now explored the current knowledge base about STEM learning, we can analyze what Ms. Duncan and her kindergartners were doing and why.

Several tasks clearly support development of executive function. Counting and stringing 100 beads places high demands on inhibitory control and working memory. Children must focus attention for an extended period of time to remember the counting sequence and not lose count as they carefully string the beads. They must exercise flexible thinking so as not to be distracted by all that is going on around them.

An entire day focused on the big number—100—supports many math learning goals. The project directly and indirectly teaches number and operations. The children aren't rotely counting; they must count on from any number in the sequence. They also use operations including addition and subtraction. Geometry and measurement are involved in doing puzzles and creating and measuring lengths of unifix cubes. Playing grid games promotes understanding of the base-10 number system.

In addition to math, the kindergartners are learning engineering design and using technology by constructing a skyscraper that doesn't fall down. The self-serve snack table also calls on executive function to count 100 pieces of food, and relates to physical science goals—how living things require food.

Other areas of the curriculum are integrated as well. Writing 100 words brings in language and literacy but also draws heavily on executive function: Children must concentrate to think of the words they know how to write and apply what they know about temporary spelling. Composing stories about reaching 100 years of age draws on creativity and narrative skills. Tinkering with various materials brings in the creative arts.

This visit to Celinda Duncan's classroom demonstrates that kindergartners are capable and competent STEM learners given developmentally appropriate teaching and learning experiences. Obviously the first 100 days have been productive; no doubt the rest of the year will be as well. ■

13 Chapter Summary

- A math achievement gap among lower-SES and higher-SES groups of children is present at the time of kindergarten entry and widens as children progress through school. This knowledge gap exists to a large extent because children living in poverty do not have sufficient opportunity to learn the language of mathematics that connects their informal, basic math knowledge to more abstract school mathematics. Lack of opportunity to learn is also related to disparities in math achievement between White European American children and children of color who are disproportionately low income.

- Children's cognitive development and abilities, such as their thinking, reasoning, and problem solving, develop over time as their experience increases and becomes more complex, and their brains mature. Executive function, which includes working memory, cognitive flexibility, and mental self-control, is strongly related to how children learn mathematics and science; conversely, math and science learning promotes the development of executive function.

- Young children are capable of learning sophisticated mathematics, and they are interested in learning it. Teachers can contribute to narrowing the achievement gap and improving the math learning of all children by helping children mathematize their play and everyday experiences as well as by planning specific, math-focused curriculum.

- Broad consensus exists among mathematics experts that from age 3 to grade 3, content goals should focus on these topics: number and operations and geometry, spatial relations, and measurement. Mathematics process goals include problem solving, reasoning, communicating, connecting, and designing and analyzing representations.

- Early childhood science curriculum includes knowledge and concepts of life science, physical science, earth and space science, and engineering. Learning the process of scientific inquiry—questioning, predicting, observing, investigating, and documenting—is an essential goal of the curriculum.

- Intentional teachers promote science learning by organizing the environment, providing focused experiences, intentional teaching, and integrating science in play and routines.

- Interactive digital media are effective tools for teaching young children curriculum content and for expanding their thinking and communication skills.

- Various types of child-initiated and teacher-guided play—blocks, games, table toys, pretend play, books, and digital play—are effective in helping children learn math, science, and engineering.

Key Terms

- abstraction
- base-10 place value system
- cardinality
- cognitive (mental) flexibility
- composing and decomposing
- connections
- earth and space science
- enumeration
- everyday mathematics
- geometry
- inhibitory control (also called cognitive self-control)
- learning trajectories
- life science
- manipulatives
- math talk
- mathematize
- measurement
- one-to-one correspondence
- operations
- order irrelevance principle
- physical science
- reasoning
- representing
- science
- scientific inquiry
- spatial relations
- stable order principle
- subitizing
- technology
- unitizing
- working memory

 Flash Cards 13.1

Readings and Websites

Clements, D. & Sarama, J. (2014). *Learning and teaching early math: The learning trajectories approach* (2nd ed.). New York, NY: Routledge.

Early Childhood Math Collaborative, Erikson Institute. (2014). *Big ideas of early mathematics: What teachers of young children need to know.* Upper Saddle River, NJ: Pearson.

Edson, M.E. (2013). *Starting with science: Strategies for introducing young children to inquiry.* Portland, ME: Stenhouse.

Heroman, C. (2017). *Making and tinkering with STEM: Solving design challenges with young children.* Washington, DC: National Association for the Education of Young Children.

Stone-MacDonald, A., Douglass, A., Wendell, K., & Love, M.L. (2015). *Engaging young engineers: Teaching problem-solving skills through STEM.* Washington, DC: National Association for the Education of Young Children.

DREME—Development and Research in Early Math Education

This website provides a wealth of resources to help teachers improve math learning opportunities for children from birth through age 8, with a focus on preschoolers. The site features videos of high-quality practice, examples of games and curriculum activities, webinars, research, and publications.

Erikson Early Math Collaborative

The Erikson Early Math Collaborative website provides a wide range of practical resources for pre-K to third-grade teachers to help children learn foundational mathematics through effective, developmentally appropriate approaches to teaching and learning.

Joan Ganz Cooney Center at Sesame Workshop

The Center conducts research and promotes high-quality, innovative educational technology practices. Their website includes resources and information for teachers, families, and media producers.

National Science Teachers Association

On this website, you will find an interactive version of the *Next Generation Science Standards* and many resources for planning science curriculum to help children in kindergarten through third grade meet the standards.

TEC (Technology in Early Childhood) Center

This website is the work of a cutting-edge technology center at Erikson Institute in Chicago. Here you'll find all the latest research and applications for using digital media with children in developmentally appropriate ways.

Shared Writing 13.1

Effective STEM Curriculum and Teaching

14

Teaching Children to Live in a Democratic Society: Social-Emotional Learning and Social Studies

Learning Outcomes

After studying this chapter, you should be able to

14.1 Discuss the social and emotional foundations of early learning.

14.2 Describe how teachers use the continuum of social and emotional development to foster children's learning.

14.3 Explain the role of play in children's social-emotional learning.

14.4 Apply effective curriculum and teaching strategies to promote children's social and emotional competence.

14.5 Formulate effective social studies curriculum and teaching strategies.

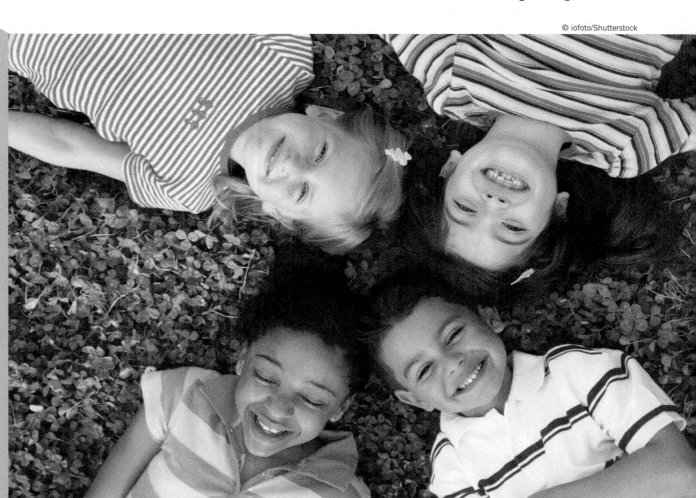

Related NAEYC Professional Preparation Standards

The NAEYC Professional Preparation Standards (NAEYC, 2011) that apply to this chapter:

1: Promoting Child Development and Learning

Key elements:

    1a. Knowing and understanding young children's characteristics and needs

    1b. Knowing and understanding the multiple influences on development and learning

    1c. Using developmental knowledge to create healthy, respectful, supportive, and challenging learning environments

2: Building Family and Community Relationships

Key elements:

    2b. Supporting and engaging families and communities through respectful, reciprocal relationships

    2c. Involving families and communities in their children's development and learning

4: Using Developmentally Effective Approaches to Connect with Children and Families

Key elements:

    4a. Understanding positive relationships and supportive interactions as the foundation of their work with children

    4b. Knowing and understanding effective strategies and tools for early education

    4c. Using a broad repertoire of developmentally appropriate teaching/learning approaches

    4d. Reflecting on their own practice to promote positive outcomes for each child

5: Using Content Knowledge to Build Meaningful Curriculum

Key elements:

    5a. Understanding content knowledge and resources in academic disciplines

    5b. Knowing and using the central concepts, inquiry tools, and structures of content areas or academic disciplines

    5c. Using their own knowledge, appropriate early learning standards, and other resources to design, implement, and evaluate meaningful, challenging curricula for each child

Case Study

It is Waylon's birthday and he gets to be the "Big Cheese" in his kindergarten class at Jefferson Elementary School. He bounds in the door with his "About Me, My Family, and My Community" poster, featuring a collage of photos including his grandparents' wedding, his first birthday, his first haircut, and his pets. His mom will visit at circle time to share the story of how they picked his name and what it means. Waylon gets to deliver the attendance sheet to the office and select a classmate to accompany him. Later, Waylon's teacher, Ms. Hans, asks the class to vote for which of Waylon's two favorite books to read. A few more votes are cast for *Leonardo the Terrible Monster*, and the children know that the majority rules. The children excitedly gather on the rug looking for spots with their names, sometimes stumbling over each other. Ms. Hans says in a soothing voice, "Close your eyes. Now pretend to smell a flower." Each child takes a deep breath and holds it. Then she says very calmly, "Now pretend to slowly blow out some candles." Ms. Hans begins reading, and the children visibly relax while listening to the story about friendship.

Down the hall, Mr. Bell is working with a small group of third-graders on their maps of the Gulf Coast, which has recently been hit by a damaging hurricane followed by a massive oil spill. Four children are working on a report about severe weather and its effects on geography, the economy, and people's lives. One group is working on a report about oil: what it is used for, how much we use in America, and how much we get from foreign sources. The group is huddled around a tablet, searching the internet for some of these answers. Another group is brainstorming ways to support the children whose homes or schools have been destroyed. They decide on a stuffed toy drive for the younger children, a "letter buddy" system, and a school supply collection. The group excitedly tells Mr. Bell about the buddy project.

Eight-year-old Tasha explains, "Well, you see, third-graders—like us—will work with kindergarten and first-graders to help write e-mails and letters to our neighbors and businesses around here to get them to donate."

Mr. Bell tells the children that he likes the idea and they need to figure out how much it will cost and what materials they will need. Mr. Bell's class has been working on this project for several weeks. He incorporates reading, writing, and mathematics into the social studies unit. ■

social-emotional learning Children's ability to recognize and regulate their emotions, establish and maintain positive relationships, make responsible decisions, and solve social problems constructively. Also called *social competence.*

social studies The integrated study of the history, geography, economics, political science, and other related aspects of societies of the past, present, and future.

engaged citizens Children as change agents in schools, communities, and eventually in the world.

In this chapter, we discuss how social-emotional learning and the social studies curriculum prepare children for life in a democracy and in a global society. **Social-emotional learning** (also called *social competence*) is children's ability to recognize and regulate their emotions, establish and maintain positive relationships, make responsible decisions, and solve social problems constructively (Institute of Medicine [IOM] & National Research Council [NRC], 2015). **Social studies**, the integrated study of history, geography, economics, political science, and other related subjects, contribute to the development of competent citizens (National Council for the Social Studies [NCSS], 2017). During early childhood, social studies and social-emotional learning are inextricably connected. Learning to live in a democratic society—the overarching goal of social studies—is predicated on social-emotional competence.

In this chapter, we focus on how the social studies prepare children to be **engaged citizens**—change agents in their schools, communities, and eventually the world. As we saw in Mr. Bell's class, he extends his class's learning beyond the local community and helps children learn economics and geography while working to make the world a better place. In Ms. Hans' kindergarten, she lays the foundation for engaged citizenry by focusing on social-emotional learning and beginning democracy through voting.

We begin with a discussion of how social-emotional development lays the foundation for all learning. Next, we present an overview of the continuum of social and emotional development from birth through age 8 and ways teachers can foster children's social-emotional learning. We describe research-based curriculum approaches to teaching social problem solving. Then we discuss social studies content and effective curriculum and teaching.

Social-Emotional Foundations of Early Learning

Research demonstrates the critical importance of social-emotional learning for success in school and life (Jones, Greenberg, & Crowley, 2015; Zhai, Raver, & Jones, 2015). Development in the social and emotional domains is inextricably linked; consequently, they are often referred to as one concept, *social-emotional development.* When children establish warm and responsive relationships with adults—the foundation of social development—they are more likely to develop important emotional skills such as identifying feelings and learning to regulate their emotions and express them appropriately. In turn, these emotional skills pave the way for the development of interpersonal problem solving, an essential social skill. The following example illustrates the interaction of social and emotional development.

> Louise was overjoyed the day her daughter Katie was born. Louise's friends tease her that she never puts Katie down for a moment. Indeed, Louise often holds and gazes at her baby. She imitates her expressions and, at first, picks her up whenever she cries. As a newborn baby, Katie is beginning to trust Louise to meet her needs. Katie generalizes this trust to other adults in her life. In the context of these relationships, Katie is also learning key emotion words that eventually will help her to regulate her emotions and, in turn, to solve interpersonal problems. Ever since Katie was a tiny baby, her parents have labeled her various states with feeling words, "You are feeling sad. ... Katie is feeling frustrated. ... Katie loves her mommy. ... Katie is feeling so happy to see her grandma. ..." When Katie begins to talk, her sentences are often peppered with feeling words that help her parents, teachers, and peers understand what she needs and how to help.

This snapshot of Katie's daily life reveals how early interactions contribute to the development of essential social-emotional foundations of learning. These include the ability to express feelings, establish positive relationships, and the overarching construct called self-regulation.

Emotional Development

Emotional development begins at birth, and continues through the lifespan. Over time, children's emotional development is shown in their ability to identify their own and others' emotions, and to express emotions in a healthy way (IOM & NRC, 2015). Emotional literacy refers to recognizing emotions in self and others, having words to express feelings, and knowing how emotional expression can affect others. Emotional literacy helps children express their emotions appropriately, in personal situations, such as when they become frustrated or discouraged, and in social contexts, such as when their feelings are hurt.

Teachers must understand that emotions play a significant role in early learning. For example, some children are especially sensitive to criticism. Working in a pre-K through third-grade project, Sharon Ritchie (2011) found that if teachers ignored or embarrassed children in any way, they were likely to disengage mentally or physically from the task at hand and not re-engage for up to an hour. Over the course of a school year, consider how much learning time these children will lose.

Teachers should never humiliate children. Creating a negative climate in classrooms is disruptive to children's social and emotional development and their academic learning. When teachers tease, use sarcasm or humiliation, children may start to avoid the classroom with excessive trips to the bathroom or nurse's office. Some may even claim to feel sick in order to stay home and avoid school altogether. Children need to be kept emotionally safe and provided with supports to help them learn key social emotional skills such as self-regulation.

Self-Regulation

When kindergarten teachers are asked to define school readiness, they rarely mention letters and numbers. Instead they inevitably say that children entering school need to be able to "follow directions, pay attention, delay gratification, and get along with others." These abilities are aspects of what developmental psychologists now call *self-regulation* (Diamond, 2012). Recent research suggests that parents feel the same way. The Trust for Learning (2017) conducted a survey of parents which found that academic readiness and achievement are not their primary goals for their children's early education. Instead, parents reported that academic achievement and knowledge building happen organically as their children develop the social and emotional skills they need to become capable, well-rounded adults.

Self-regulation in preschool has been found to be a strong predictor of academic achievement across ages, ranging from the early school years to college.

Experienced teachers understand that self-regulation is the underlying ability that makes learning possible in all areas from reading to science. When children are self-regulated, they control their impulses, transition smoothly from one activity to another, learn how to work with others in a group, and pay attention when the teacher gives directions. They are more likely to think before they speak or act, and not behave impulsively (Willis, 2015). Of course, these abilities do not emerge automatically even in the most self-regulated of children. They develop over time and with experience and support from parents and teachers. However, preschool plays a crucial role in the development of children's self-regulation because it is often the first structured place that children spend significant amounts of time outside of the home.

When children use self-regulation, they manage their thoughts and emotions in order to control their behavior and impulses and use constructive problem-solving to achieve their goals (Murray, Rosanbalm, Christopoulos, & Hamoudi, 2015). In fact, a study of 1,000 children born in the same city in the same year found that children with less self-control (that is, less persistent, more impulsive, and poorer attention regulation) had worse health, earned less, and committed more crimes as adults *30 years later* than did those with more self-control as young children, regardless of IQ, gender, social class, and family circumstances (Moffitt, Poulton & Caspi, 2013). Self-regulation in preschool predicts children's academic success in the early grades, in both literacy and math, over and above their intelligence or family backgrounds (Blair, 2016; Bohlmann & Downer, 2016; Nesbitt, Farran, & Fuhs, 2015).

Studies such as these provide important guidance for educators. Problems in self-regulation are strongly related to learning difficulties. Many efforts are underway to close the readiness and achievement gaps in schools, but most of them focus on directly teaching academic skills without attention to the underlying issue of self-regulation. Academic skills are important but should not be taught in ways that undermine children's self-regulation and social-emotional development.

Individual differences in self-regulation are apparent almost at birth (Montroy et al., 2016). Some babies quickly fall into regular patterns of sleep and wakefulness and almost entertain themselves; others struggle mightily to adjust as their parents may become more frustrated and feel more inadequate. Over time, these differences can be worsened by harsh or critical parenting or caregiving, environmental conditions such as community violence, or negative school experiences and peer relationships. But on a positive note, these problems can also be lessened by providing evidence-based parenting supports, and experiences in preschool and the early grades that promote the development of self-regulation (National Academies of Sciences, Engineering, and Medicine [NASEM], 2016).

✔ **Application Exercise 14.1**
Promoting Self-Regulation

Social Development

Social development refers to the process by which children learn to form and sustain positive relationships with adults and other children. Like other domains, social learning occurs along a developmental continuum, which we describe later in this chapter.

Skills become more complex as children are placed in more demanding social situations such as early childhood programs, schools, after-school programs, and special interest clubs and classes.

As children grow, their ability to establish friendships with peers becomes more important and influences how they view themselves and the world (Cigala, 2015; Slaughter, 2016). Within the context of these relationships, children learn and practice cooperation, the ability to form and sustain friendships, and the ability to solve problems in positive ways. Cooperation with peers requires that children understand another's perspective, empathize, and balance their own needs and desires with those of others. For example, when Kobe, James, and Larisha want to play restaurant, they can't all be the cooks; they have to figure out who will do what. Similarly, when Sasha tries to join the group, further cooperation is required to see how she will fit in.

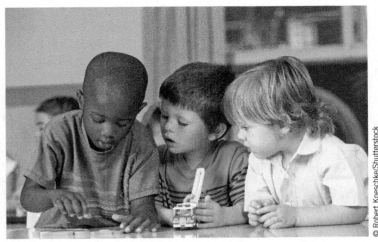

One of the greatest joys of childhood is making friends. Having friends contributes to social-emotional development and later success in school and life.

Stress in Children's Lives

As discussed previously, many children experience considerable stress in their lives, which can negatively impact their social-emotional development and success in school. About 10 percent of kindergarten children demonstrate some symptoms of emotional behavior problems, and among low-income children the number approaches 20 percent (Thompson, 2010). Head Start teachers report that increasing numbers of children show signs of depression, aggression, and other emotional difficulties. Importantly, early childhood teachers have also self–reported high rates of depression and stress (Soderberg & Joseph, 2016).

Some childhood stress is actually positive and necessary. Exposure to the typical moderate stresses of childhood such as starting school or visiting the dentist is a normal and essential part of healthy development and helps children learn coping skills (Thompson, 2010). At times, children are exposed to unique but relatively tolerable stressors such as an illness in the family or an injury to themselves. Although difficult, these situations can be weathered if they are short-lived and children have the support of loving relationships with parents and teachers.

However, increasing numbers of children are exposed to adverse childhood experiences (ACEs) leading to toxic stress (Center on the Developing Child at Harvard University, 2010). Toxic stress can result from single adverse events of trauma such as abuse, neglect, natural disaster, or injury. It can also result from ongoing patterns of trauma and stress such as parental mental illness, dangerous neighborhoods, or domestic violence (Zero to Six Collaborative Group, 2010). Childhood trauma is not so rare. In a now classic study, research suggests that two-thirds of all adults experienced at least one traumatic event during their childhood (Felitti et al., 1998). Early trauma has potential to cause the most harm, because young children often do not have the cognitive and emotional skills to process and express how the trauma has affected them.

Brain development in the early years is especially susceptible to toxic stress caused by adverse childhood experiences (ACEs). According to epigenetics research, toxic stress has the capacity to physically change a child's brain and be hardwired into the child's biology via genes in the DNA. Trauma or toxic stress cause a child to feel unsafe and includes physiological responses of racing heart, fast breathing, and the release of stress hormones, such as cortisol, into the body. This constant activation of the stress system can impair brain development, leading to lifelong problems in behavior, health, and learning

Video Example 14.1:

Social and Emotional Foundations

In this video, two preschool teachers describe how they support children's social and emotional development by creating a classroom of caring and respect. Which of their strategies do you think are most effective? Why do they spend so much time building a foundation of social and emotional learning for every child?

(Zero to Six Collaborative Group, 2010). Infants and toddlers who experience trauma may be developmentally delayed, display frequent tantrums, and become easily frustrated. They may have difficulty attaching to caregivers. School-age children who experience trauma may have difficulty with school skills and peer relationships, sleep problems, and trouble focusing and organizing their learning—and appear to have ADD/ADHD (American Academy of Pediatrics, n.d.).

Teachers' Roles

Early childhood educators are in a unique position to play a role in early identification of ACEs and to contribute to the development of resilience (Sciaraffa, Zeanah, & Zeanah, 2017). Teachers and related service staff, such as family support workers or counselors, can assist in increasing physical health and mental well-being for children who have encountered ACEs. Safe and healthy environments that allow the child to play and explore are examples of how individual protective factors can be enhanced. Teachers can support the child's protective system by building the child's personal attributes associated with resiliency, such as self-efficacy and self-regulation.

Teachers can provide a secure relationship, which is especially critical for children who have experienced trauma because it can provide extra support in times of stress. Additionally, by working collaboratively with families, teachers provide an additional layer of protection for children who experience adversity. Lastly, at the community level, teachers can bring awareness to the public and private sectors by informing others of ACE's effect on early brain development and the link to later outcomes on individuals and society. Society is positively impacted when ACEs are reduced and individuals are raised in thriving families and communities.

When teachers learn that children in their care have experienced trauma, they need to draw on all the tools in their strategy toolbox as well as consult with early intervention and mental health professionals. The National Child Traumatic Stress Network (NCTSN) Core Curriculum on Childhood Trauma Task Force (2012) provides resources for teachers and schools to help understand and support children and families who experience traumatic stress. Next, we turn to a description of the continuum of typical social-emotional development and how teachers can support children's social and emotional competence.

✔ Check Your Understanding 14.1

🏠 Continuum of Social and Emotional Development

In this section, we describe some of the typical social and emotional accomplishments that occur for children from birth through age 8. These descriptions are followed by examples of how teachers can support children's progress. Social-emotional learning is to a large extent the product of development—relatively predictable, age-related changes in children. At the same time, social and emotional skills are learned and, therefore, can be taught.

Infants and Toddlers

The major social-emotional task for babies is a healthy attachment to their primary caregivers (Shonkoff & Phillips, 2000). Between birth and 12 months, an indicator of emotional development is the ability to quiet when comforted. Babies also begin to show preferences for primary caregivers and work to maintain interactions with caregivers. For example, babies imitate caregivers' gestures and sounds and also initiate interaction by patting the caregiver or through eye gaze and smiles.

Toward the first birthday, babies show a preference for familiar people. This time period may also be marked by **separation anxiety**, in which a child cries when the caregiver is not in sight or clings to a caregiver in the presence of strangers; such anxiety diminishes over time. In the second year, toddlers continue to demonstrate a strong attachment to caregivers and initiate interactions with familiar adults.

Emotional Development in Infants and Toddlers

During their first year, infants experience a range of emotions, starting with expressions of comfort and discomfort, and emerging

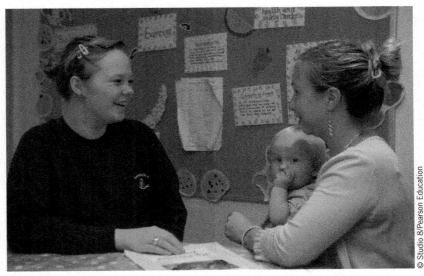

Separation anxiety is a natural part of social-emotional development at about 8 to 10 months of age, but it can make parents anxious as well. What can teachers do to help ease this experience for babies and families?

into a wide variety of emotions including fear, joy, and frustration. In the second and third year of life, toddlers begin to name their own and other's emotions, and they demonstrate empathy by noticing how adults or peers feel and trying to comfort them. For example, Marleco brings a stuffed animal to Raina, who is sad because her mommy just left. His teacher quickly reinforces Marleco's behavior: "What a caring friend you are, Marleco. You saw that Raina was feeling sad and you brought her a stuffy."

These first years are also marked by tremendous growth in self-awareness and awareness of others. Infants will observe themselves in mirrors and notice other's physical characteristics and also note when a member of the group is missing. For example, a toddler may pat a child's head to feel her curly hair. They explore their own body, observing their hands or reaching for their toes; they may explore the face and body parts of others.

Toddlers begin to identify gender, skin color, and other basic similarities and differences, although they may think that changing clothes changes their gender. They also begin to test limits and strive for independence. They notice when others are looking at them, and they often exaggerate movements or act silly when they are being watched.

Social Development in Infants and Toddlers

During the first year, babies show interest in other children, particularly siblings, by watching them and tracking their behavior. They smile spontaneously and show enjoyment in interactions with peers, as expressed in gestures, facial expressions, and vocalizations. They may reach out to touch other children or grab their toys. Babies begin to take turns with teachers during play, as in peek-a-boo, laying a foundation for turn taking with other children, which develops during the second and third years of life.

Toddlers and 2-year-olds often engage in **parallel play**, playing next to each other but not interacting. They observe and imitate another child's behavior or activity and, by age 3, they initiate social interactions with peers. They may approach another child and ask to play, but will also be quick to assert ownership of toys by saying "Mine." Between 2 and 3 years of age, children start to show preferences for familiar playmates.

The *Developmental Continuum: Social-Emotional Development in Infants and Toddlers* feature describes social-emotional development in infants and toddlers and ways that teachers can help promote these competencies.

separation anxiety Feeling a baby experiences when the caregiver is not in sight; the baby may cry or cling to a caregiver in the presence of strangers; usually occurs around 8 months of age.

parallel play Children play next to each other, but not with each other; they may speak, but don't really converse.

Developmental Continuum
Social-Emotional Development in Infants and Toddlers

Widely Held Expectations	How Teachers Can Help
Bonds and forms attachment with parents and other special people in life.	Encourage and support parent-child relationships (such as enabling mothers' breastfeeding).
Enjoys when familiar adult cuddles and talks with them.	Hold, cuddle, hug, smile, and laugh with the child.
Exhibits separation anxiety by crying when familiar caregiver leaves.	Provide environment with consistent, small number of trustworthy adults.
Establishes an attachment with a consistent adult other than the primary caregiver.	Respond to child's emotional and physical needs, verbal and nonverbal communications.
Explores the environment, but checks in with caregiver.	Encourage exploration, and reassure child that you are still present. Reassure child when you leave the setting, "I'll be back," and when you return, "See, I'm back."
Smiles spontaneously at other children and shows interest in other children by watching them and tracking their behavior.	Provide opportunities for children to play and interact with other children; carefully supervise so that children don't hurt each other.
Seeks adult assistance with challenges.	Respond positively to child's questions and calls for assistance.
Plays side by side with other children at times.	Provide enough toys of the same kind so children can play side by side but don't have to share.
With adult support, waits for turns during play (usually 2-year-olds).	Play turn-taking games like pat-a-cake with babies. Help children learning turn-taking skills: "It's Curtis's turn to sit on my lap. You're next, Cassie."
May frustrate easily when unable to achieve a desired goal (e.g., building tower of blocks).	Observe child for emerging frustration, and offer support when needed (but not too soon).
Toddlers follow social routines with reminders (e.g., put your coat in your cubby).	Encourage independence and reinforce learning of social routines ("Thank you for putting your coat away!").

Sources: Based on *North Carolina Foundations for Early Learning and Development*, by North Carolina Foundations Task Force, 2013, Raleigh, NC: Author; *Washington State Early Learning and Development Benchmarks*, by State of Washington, 2012, retrieved February 22, 2015, from http://www.del.wa.gov/publications/development/docs/guidelines.pdf.

Video Example 14.2:

Social and Emotional Development in Infants and Toddlers

This video illustrates the social and emotional development of infants and toddlers. Reflect on the competence they demonstrate. How is their behavior different from what you might expect from children of this young age?

Preschool and Kindergarten

During preschool and kindergarten, children develop the ability to regulate their emotions more competently, allowing them to become increasingly adept at building relationships. Preschoolers begin to try to please adults and use adults for assistance in solving problems, for getting their needs met, and for emotional support.

Emotional Development in 3- through 5-Year-Olds   During these years, most children become increasingly capable of regulating their own emotions. Most preschoolers can wait for a turn and sometimes, though not always, show patience during group activities, a skill that improves in kindergarten. With guidance from teachers, most preschoolers can calm themselves after feeling strong emotions, going to a quiet corner or requesting a favorite book to be read when upset. At this age, children can associate emotions with words and facial expressions and use pretend play to understand and respond to emotions, such as when pretending to be a fierce animal to express negative emotions.

Preschool and kindergarten children also demonstrate growth in self-concept and self-esteem. They describe themselves as a person with a mind, body, and feelings, and they often exert their will and have strong preferences for certain foods, toys, or activities. They also tend to overestimate their own competence, and experiment with their own abilities, try new activities, and test limits such as "skipping bars" on the monkey bars at the playground.

All the social-emotional skills described here require teachers to provide more or less assistance, depending on individual children's needs and abilities.

Social Development in 3- through 5-Year-Olds Enhanced emotional development and increased self-understanding allow children to develop stronger peer relationships. In fact the preschool and kindergarten years are marked by tremendous growth in interactions with peers. Children initiate interactions with other children and will make and maintain a friendship with at least one other child. These relationships contribute to cognitive and language development and to overall well-being (Buysse, Goldman, West, & Hollingsworth, 2007). With occasional assistance from teachers, children can share toys and materials during play and use simple strategies to solve social problems appropriately, as discussed later in this chapter.

Preschoolers can give reasons for a position, such as "I don't want to play right now because I'm tired." By the end of preschool, children can understand the effects of their actions on others, as in "I took the marker away from her and now she is crying." This accomplishment is essential to interpersonal problem-solving. Read the *Developmental Continuum: Social-Emotional Learning in 3-through 5-Year-Old* feature for a description of social-emotional learning in 3- through 5-year-old children and effective teaching strategies to promote it.

Developmental Continuum
Social-Emotional Learning in 3- through 5-Year-Olds

Widely Held Expectations	How Teachers Can Help
Demonstrates affection and comfort with significant adults.	Warmly welcome and return appropriate affection.
Begins to self-regulate attention, feelings, and behavior, and sometimes needs adult support.	Model calmness and patience. Teach children words to use to express emotions, and help them practice these skills in real-life situations.
Seeks adult support for emotional, physical and social support, including solving problems and approval.	Support and validate child's feelings and efforts at cooperation, and reinforce the child's positive problem-solving skills.
Enjoys learning and enthusiastically plays with other children.	Provide opportunities for child to engage in a variety of play activities with other children (e.g., dramatic play, art projects, free play outside, and dance and movement).
Makes and maintains a friendship with one or more children.	Provide opportunities for children to choose activities that interest them, the time to pursue these activities, and the freedom to interact with preferred playmates who share similar interests. Give ample time for children to be silly and enjoy each other's company. Read stories about friendship and discuss the behaviors that made the character in the story a good friend.
Demonstrates understanding of social rules in interactions with children; shares materials and toys during play, increasingly cooperative.	Acknowledge cooperation when child plays with other children and provide opportunities for children to share materials.
Demonstrates awareness that their behavior can affect others' feelings.	Provide opportunities for dramatic play so that child can practice taking another's role or perspective ("Pretend you're Gera and can't have a turn. How do you feel?").
Describes reasons for feelings, and uses strategies for managing strong emotions.	Name and discuss feelings throughout the day (e.g., "You're feeling disappointed because … ").
Uses social skills such as sharing, taking turns, and resolving conflicts in interactions with other children.	When there is a conflict between two children, demonstrate empathy for both children.
Demonstrates awareness of group membership ("I'm a boy") and acknowledges own abilities ("I'm good at soccer").	Provide opportunities for children to describe and see positive images of their own cultural and physical characteristics.

Sources: Based on *North Carolina Foundations for Early Learning and Development*, by North Carolina Foundations Task Force, 2013; *Washington State Early Learning and Development Benchmarks*, State of Washington, 2012, retrieved February 22, 2015, from http://www.del.wa.gov/publications/development/docs/guidelines.pdf.

Primary Grades

During the primary grades, close friends are vital to children's healthy development. Research suggests that children who lack friends can suffer emotionally later in life. Friendships are not just playmates; they help children learn social skills, such as how to communicate, cooperate and solve problems. Children practice controlling their emotions and responding appropriately to the emotions of others. They develop the ability to think through and negotiate different situations that arise in their relationships. Most primary-grade children show loyalty to friends. They sustain friendships by cooperating, helping, sharing, and suggesting new ideas for play. Having a good friend also affects a child's school performance. Children tend to have better attitudes about school and learning when they have their good friends there (Ferrer & Fugate, 2007).

Interpersonal problem solving becomes more complex during the primary grades. Children attempt to settle disputes or solve problems with another child through negotiation, addressing their own rights as well as the other child's needs, sometimes needing assistance from teachers. Children in primary grades can participate in cooperative groups and take different roles at times—sometimes leader, sometimes follower. Primary-grade children become excessively concerned about fairness and can recognize stereotypes and culturally or linguistically unfair or biased behavior.

In terms of self-esteem, a major development during the primary years is that children gain the ability to realistically judge and compare their own academic, physical, and social abilities to those of other children. Unlike preschoolers, who overestimate their competence, primary-grade children may judge themselves too harshly; for example, "I'm not smart like Natalie" or "I can't play baseball."

Read the *Developmental Continuum: Social-Emotional Learning in the Primary Grades* feature for a description of social-emotional development and learning during the primary grades and effective ways teachers can support this learning.

Developmental Continuum
Social-Emotional Learning in the Primary Grades

Widely Held Expectations	How Teachers Can Help
Describes their emotions and the situations that cause them and demonstrates constructive ways to deal with emotions.	Have children discuss situations that trigger strong emotions and role-play strategies to cope with them.
Identifies own likes and dislikes. Describes things they do well and not well.	Help children to make accurate, realistic assessments of their own competence ("It's true that this math lesson is hard, but I can see how hard you're working and how much you've learned since last week.").
Understands expectations and responsibility to promote a safe and productive environment. Demonstrates understanding of when to bring issues to adult attention.	Help children feel comfortable in coming to you with questions and assistance, but also encourage them to try to solve problems independently. Model cross-cultural communication and provide strategies for child to address bias. Actively address bullying or children's attempts to exclude others.
Shows loyalty to friends; prefers same-sex peers.	Provide opportunities for children to play and work with friends in self-selected groups. At times, organize mixed-gender or other diverse groups to ensure that children do not limit their interactions or consistently exclude others.

(continued)

Widely Held Expectations	How Teachers Can Help
Follows suggestions given by a friend about how to proceed in their play.	Provide opportunities for children to be part of group activities (e.g., games, cultural events).
Works with other children to overcome challenges.	Discuss and demonstrate how different things can be achieved when children work together (dramatizing a story or building a model). Children can read (or be read to) and write stories about actual people who have overcome challenges, such as Jackie Robinson. Model and promote respect for diversity in all its forms.
Uses multiple strategies to resolve social conflicts.	Guide children through conflict resolution. Support children's attempts to solve social problems.
Feels empathy for other people and describes how own actions make others feel and behave. Recognizes that others may have different perspectives or feelings than own. Recognize words and actions that hurt others.	Read or help children read chapter books, such as *Charlotte's Web*, about emotionally challenging events or social situations. Demonstrate and provide opportunities for children to take another's perspective before making decisions (e.g., "What would Ella think if you gave her your book?").
Participates cooperatively in large- and small-group activities, play, and games.	Provide opportunities for small-group projects (creating a map, carrying out an experiment). Encourage participation in group games, allowing children to make or modify rules.
Communicates about others' feelings.	Provide opportunities for children to share and discuss feelings. Discuss why a character reacts as he or she did in a story, taking cultural differences into consideration.

Source: Based on *O. McAfee & D..J. Leong, 2016. Assessing and Guiding Young Children's Development and Learning,* 6th ed. Upper Saddle River, NJ: Pearson.

Teachers need to understand the continua of social-emotional development to have realistic expectations for children's behavior and to provide effective amounts and kinds of assistance. For example, willful behavior on the part of 2-year-olds is typical, as is strong insistence on fairness among third- and fourth-graders. Knowledge of the social-emotional continua can also help teachers to assess where individual children are on the trajectory and to decide how to intervene when they are not making expected progress. Although we offer these descriptions of "typical" social and emotional learning, teachers need to remember that there is no such thing as a typical child, as we discuss next.

Diversity and Social-Emotional Development

Individual and cultural differences play significant roles in how children express their emotions and how they behave in groups. Individual differences are present even at birth, and children's experiences at home, in child care, and at school make a big difference in how and when they develop these abilities. Because children's social and emotional development are linked to the contexts, cultures, and relationships in which they grow and learn, adults play a critical role in shaping children's positive social and emotional development.

Cultural Values and Emotions The values and practices of each child's family and community shape the feelings, knowledge, and expectations that influence emotional development (Hanson & SooHoo, 2007). Children are socialized into understanding ideal affect and emotional expression. In some cultures, "collectivism" is valued over "individualism," and this influences what is considered to be the most valued emotions. In collectivist cultural groups, such as East Asian cultures, low-arousal positive states such as getting along with others and being responsive to others' needs are valued. Therefore, ideal emotions are low-arousal positive states such as feeling calm, content, and peaceful.

On the other hand, in individualistic cultures, such as the United States, where value is placed on influencing others, the ideal positive emotional states are more high-arousal such as excitement and enthusiasm.

A study of preschoolers from various cultural backgrounds (Tsai, Louie, J., Chen, & Uchida, 2007) found evidence of the many ways culture influences emotional development—from facial expressions to preferred activities. The researchers also found that children's story books from different cultures convey very different emotional expressions among the characters. In one study, preschoolers from European-American backgrounds considered bigger, deeper smiles as "happier" than smaller smiles. In reverse, children from Taiwanese cultural backgrounds perceived the smaller smiles to be happier. Differences were also detected in the types of preferred activities. Children from American backgrounds preferred activities intended to produce high-arousal emotional states versus the children from Taiwan who preferred activities that produced more low-arousal positive states. Think back to Waylon's demonstrative enthusiasm for being the "Big Cheese" in his classroom. How might cultural backgrounds affect how widely this enthusiasm might be shared? How could a teacher adjust this activity to better reflect the cultural differences in her classroom?

Cultural differences also influence social development of young children. Children need to develop respect for people with ideas and experiences that are both similar to and different from their own. Lulu's best friend in preschool is Bethel. When Lulu invites Bethel to her birthday party and Bethel doesn't come, Lulu's feelings are hurt. Quianna, the girls' teacher, notices that Lulu doesn't want to play with Bethel anymore. Quianna explains to Lulu that Bethel's family does not celebrate birthdays or holidays. Her not attending Lulu's party doesn't mean that Bethel doesn't like Lulu. Quianna draws a parallel to Lulu's family being vegetarian. When this is explained to Lulu, she understands and readily seeks out Bethel as a playmate again.

Healthy social-emotional development is influenced by the match between children's feelings and expressive behaviors and the expectations of the social situation in which they find themselves. Teachers need to provide a respectful atmosphere in which cultural, religious, racial, linguistic, age, gender, and ability differences are valued.

Children with Disabilities   Children who have disabilities, developmental delays, or who are at risk for developmental delays may require special attention and support to promote their social-emotional development. Many children with disabilities face particular challenges in developing successful peer relationships. Children with even mild delays tend to participate less in sustained play, spend more time alone when other children are playing, express more sadness when playing with other children, get angry more, and use less effective conflict resolution strategies (Strain & Joseph, 2006).

Successful inclusion requires that children with disabilities actively participate and that their needs are met. Among those important needs is the need for positive social relationships with other children. Indeed, early friendships are the most powerful single predictor of long-term adjustment for children with disabilities (Strain & Schwartz, 2001). To consider social-emotional development through the wider lens of special education, read the *Including All Children: Fostering Friendships in the Inclusive Classroom* feature.

Successful inclusion requires that children with disabilities fully participate in the classroom community. Making friends is especially important to their healthy development.

© Ktaylorg/E+/Getty Images

Including All Children
Fostering Friendships in the Inclusive Classroom

Children from ages 3 to 5, especially those with disabilities, may not naturally acquire the skills to function socially with their peers, which can be a barrier to developing friendships. They need teachers to help them. Young children's social relationships involve three main concepts, which occur along a continuum in inclusive settings: friendships, social acceptance, and social rejection. More passive than friendship, social acceptance occurs when a child is treated as a member of the group; other children play, smile, and sit beside the child throughout the day. By contrast, social rejection occurs when peers do not choose to play with a child or outwardly refuse the child's requests to join in their play.

Not only are friendships a critical component and predictor of positive mental health, but children develop and learn important social and communication skills in the context of social relationships. Therefore, it is critically important that teachers use proven strategies to promote friendships among children with disabilities and their typically developing classmates. Following are effective strategies teachers can use to facilitate social relationships in inclusive settings:

- Teachers and peers model specific behaviors for children with disabilities.
- Pair two children to complete classroom jobs or during transitions (go outside together, do errands).

- Compose small groups in order to provide peer models for children with disabilities.
- Read books and have class discussions about friendship, coping with difficult feelings, expressing anger and disappointment, problem solving, and conflict resolution.
- Use puppets to model problem solving and friendship skills during whole-group discussions.
- Set up a "pal" center during choice time where children use toys and games that require two children to play.
- Arrange "buddy" days where teachers pair children with disabilities and typically developing peers.
- Use toys and materials and teach games that require social interaction (for example, a teeter-totter or board game).
- Prompt children to play together (for example, suggest reversing roles—"You have been the patient, how about being the doctor now.").
- Support children to rehearse and practice in advance (for example, before choice time ask children what they are going to do, who they are going to play with).

Source: Based on "Social Skills Interventions for Young Children with Disabilities," by S. Vaughn et al., 2003. etc. *Remedial and Special Education, 24*(1), 2–15.

 Check Your Understanding 14.2

The Role of Play in Social-Emotional Learning

The importance of play is very apparent in the previous descriptions of the continuum of social-emotional learning. Because peer relationships are such a critical component of social-emotional development, play is an especially important context for children to acquire and practice self-regulation and social skills.

Emotional Development and Play

Play has long been linked with emotional development and helps children in several ways (Hyson, 2004; Veiga, Neto, & Rieffe, 2016). Play provides a context for children to address their fears, develop coping skills and resilience, and feel in control of their environment.

Play and Fears During the preschool years and as children's cognitive development progresses, they acquire a well-developed imagination. Along with this new flexibility in thinking comes an increase in their fears. Three-, 4-, and 5-year-olds may be afraid of animals, the dark, monsters, or whatever they can conjure up. Given the dangers in today's world—strangers, violence, and abuse—their fears may be real as well as imaginary. Consider this example:

> Four-year-old Taylor is afraid of dogs, especially the big boxer that just moved in next door. He cries every time he leaves home and doesn't want to go to school anymore. After talking to Taylor's mother, Ms. Jerome purchases a set of plastic dogs for the classroom and sets up a pretend dog training school. Taylor gradually begins to play with the plastic dogs and Ms. Jerome overhears him saying to the boxer, "Bad dog. Don't jump. Stay in your yard. No barking." After a few days, Taylor takes over the dog training school, and tells the stuffed dogs that they better be good or he will tell their mommies. Taylor's mother also talks to the neighbor about controlling the dog, but his play experiences at school help Taylor work through his fear.

In play, children like Taylor can pretend to be mighty and strong and conquer their fears. They fantasize that they are the giant animal or the monster, thus giving themselves power over the feared creature.

Building Coping Skills and Resilience As we described earlier, young children experience all kinds of stresses in their everyday lives: going to child care when they want to stay home, moving to a new house, going to the doctor, and so forth. At times, extraordinary stressors occur—serious illness or injury in the family, homelessness, observing or being a victim of violence. Play helps children develop the ability to cope with life's traumas and acquire resilience (Marcelo & Yates, 2014).

Play can serve as a cathartic activity for children to express the negative emotions that life events precipitate. When children are angry, they can take out their feelings by pounding Play-Doh or hammering nails. Or they can pretend to be a turtle and go into their "shell" until the strong feelings pass. When they are tense, they can pretend to be a rag doll or curl up like a kitten. Three-year-old Grace has a new baby brother, Miles. Her mother assures her teacher that Grace just loves the baby and isn't jealous at all. But during playtime, her teacher observes that Grace wants to be the baby and is acting like an infant asking her classmates and teacher to feed and cuddle her. The teacher perceives that Grace is a little jealous of the attention her baby brother is receiving at home and trying to get some of it through play at school. By playing out her jealousy at school, however, she can cope more effectively with this major change in her life.

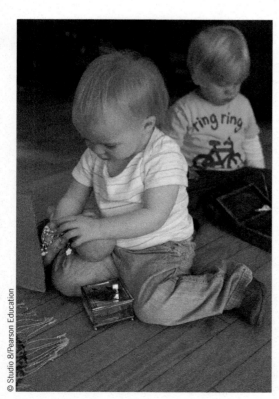

Social development begins in play. These toddlers are parallel playing, a first step in learning to play with other children.

Gaining Control through Play In general, young children's lives are not in their control. Grown-ups and older children make them do things that they don't want to do: eat what is served, pick up their toys, get dressed, go outside, or take a nap. Sometimes they resist even when they want to do something simply because it wasn't their idea.

Children love to play (and it is so emotionally supportive) because it is *child initiated* and controlled (Weisberg et al, 2015). They decide when to start and stop, what to do, and whom to do it with. If teachers intrude on children's play—try to take over or direct the play to their own ends—children will usually stop playing. It's no longer fun. Child-initiated play affords children power in a safe environment and also helps them learn to make choices and live with the consequences of their choices. If Chloe chooses to build with blocks, she may not have time to paint at the easel.

Social Development and Play

Children's play has been a topic of study for centuries. Early in the 20th century, researchers began to systematically observe and record how young children's social interactions during play changed over time. Now-classic studies conducted by Parten (1933) identified four developmental levels of social play and approximate ages when each type of play dominates, as presented in Table 14.1. Parten also identified unoccupied and onlooker behavior as two situations in which children do not engage in play.

Although most play researchers still agree that children engage in these different types of social play, they do not agree about the order or the ages at which children progress in their play (Lillard, 2015). For example, parallel play, where children play side by side but do not interact, is now considered the least mature form of play, rather than solitary play. Older children continue to engage in solitary play and, at times, switch back and forth between cooperative and solitary play. Solitary play can involve toys/objects or make-believe. For example, Toya enjoys the cooperative scenario of taking the trip, but afterward she sits by herself and pretends to drive the bus. Even after children develop more socially complex play abilities, they will use all types of play at times. Imelda may share her stethoscope with Lora, who also wants a turn—associative play—without cooperating in the shared goal of running a hospital.

In fact, solitary play may be evidence of a personality trait; some people are just more social than others. But if children never play with others, they miss the valuable learning opportunities that play affords. Additionally, if children do not move beyond solitary play, this may signal a difficulty in children's social development (Johnson et al., 2005). Children with disabilities, such as autism, can also benefit

© Pearson Education

Video Example 14.3:

Cooperative Play

In this video, kindergartners are building a ship in the block area. What type of play are they engaged in? How do you think this type of play contributes to their social development?

TABLE 14.1 Levels of Social Play

Based on systematic observation of children over time, this chart identifies and describes four developmental levels of social play.

Type of Social Play	Approximate Age	Example
Solitary play—children play alone, usually with toys or objects.	2 to 2-1/2 years old (according to Parten) All ages (as understood today)	Two-year-old Jeannette pounds her plastic hammer on her workbench or tucks her baby doll into bed. Five-year-old Imelda pretends to be a doctor, dresses up in a lab coat with a stethoscope, and starts treating the dolls and stuffed animals.
Parallel play—children play next to but not with each other. They may speak but don't really converse.	2-1/2 to 3-1/2 years old	Three-year-olds Nina and Dora sit next to each other with their dolls. Nina says, "My baby is sick." Dora says, "I'm going to grandma's house."
Associative play—children play and share with each other, usually one other child.	3-1/2 to 4-1/2 years old	Four-year-olds Chris and Cory are each building a tower with blocks. Cory says, "You need a pointy one on top. Here's one."
Cooperative play—children assume different roles and share a purpose for the play.	4-1/2 years and older	Four preschoolers build a bus with the hollow blocks. Sasha says, "I'm the driver, but I need a ticket taker. You take the tickets, Rinaldo." Toya states, "Me and Isaac will be passengers. Take us to the circus. Then I get to drive."

solitary play Children play alone, usually with toys or objects.

parallel play Children play next to each other, but not with each other; they may speak, but don't really converse.

associative play Children play and share with each other, usually one other child.

cooperative play Children assume different roles and share a purpose for the play.

Source: Based on "Social Participation among Preschool Children," by M. Parten, 1933, *Journal of Abnormal and Social Psychology, 27,* 243–269.

from teachers' support in developing play skills (Wong, 2013). Teachers need to be aware of children's play patterns and intervene if necessary; for example, if children watch others play and appear to want to join in but don't know how or are rejected by their peers, teachers need to model the words to say or suggest other strategies to use.

✔ Application Exercise 14.2
Play and Social-Emotional Learning

✔ Check Your Understanding 14.3

Effective Social-Emotional Curriculum and Teaching

Teachers and children interact constantly in early childhood programs, so social-emotional development is naturally and almost invisibly interwoven into the day. Because of this, some people don't think it necessary to include social and emotional development in a planned curriculum. However, the increase in challenging behaviors and emotional difficulties among very young children has led to the need for a more intentional approach to social-emotional curriculum.

Social and Emotional Curriculum Goals

As discussed earlier, the main goal of a social-emotional curriculum is to promote children's social competence and self-regulation. Widely used comprehensive curriculum models such as *HighScope* (Epstein & Hohmann, 2012) and *Tools of the Mind* (Bodrova & Leong, 2007) integrate these goals throughout. In recent years, more focused evidence-based curricula have been developed that include whole- and small-group teacher-guided lessons designed to be incorporated in a larger curriculum framework. Among these curricula are *The Incredible Years* (Webster-Stratton, 1999); *Second Step* (Committee for Children, 2011), *I Can Problem Solve* (Shure, 2000), *Al's Pals* (Lynch, Geller, & Schmidt, 2004), and *Preschool PATHS* (Domitrovich, Greenberg, Cortes, & Kusche, 2005). Research finds that these curricula are effective in improving children's knowledge and understanding about emotions, their social problem-solving skills, and their social behavior (Barton et al., 2014).

Social Problem Solving Children's problem-solving skills are a key feature in the development of social competence (Webster-Stratton, 1999). The power of problem solving lies in three areas. First, these skills travel well with children; they can be used in any social situation to resolve any number of social dilemmas. Second, these skills prevent challenging behavior. Finally, problem-solving skills enable children to quickly repair breaches in their relationships with peers, such as typical squabbles over toys, taking turns, or competition among friends.

Problem solving is a highly effective deterrent to aggression and antisocial behavior. Consequently, every validated curriculum designed to teach social competence includes instruction in these skills

© 2xSamara.com/Shutterstock

© Intentional teachers help children learn many alternative strategies to solve social problems among themselves.

(Joseph & Strain, 2004). Teachers can help children learn the following problem-solving steps that are common to most evidence-based curricula:

1. What is my problem?
2. What are some solutions?
3. What would happen next?
4. Give the solution a try!

Step 1: *What is my problem?* As a first step in problem solving, children should be taught to pay attention to their feelings. When they are experiencing an uncomfortable emotion such as loneliness, anger or frustration, it is their cue that they have a problem.

After children recognize they have a problem, they need to describe it. This is why teaching young children an emotional vocabulary is essential for effective problem solving (Joseph & Strain, 2003; Webster-Stratton, 1999). Adults and/or puppets can model the process of describing a problem for children. Initially, children will need guidance to reframe the situation from the other person's problem to their own. For example, instead of "Jordan has the red ball and won't give it to me," the problem becomes "I want to play with a ball, but they are all being used." This reframing, although subtle, helps children generate more appropriate solutions.

Step 2: *What are some solutions?* Young children need help generating several alternative solutions to interpersonal problems. Children who engage in aggression and anti-social behavior have fewer solutions than their typically developing peers (Joseph, 2002). These children may in fact have a positive solution in their repertoire, but tend to have only one, such as saying "please." Their other solution is aggression, which in the short run is often more effective and efficient at getting their needs met.

Children who have more solutions to choose from usually solve the problem before resorting to aggression. For these reasons, teachers need to teach children alternative solutions to common problems and have children generate their own solutions. Because no one solution is always effective, the key is to teach children to generate as many different solutions as possible, as illustrated in the following example:

Preschool teacher Ms. Trina brings hypothetical as well as real problems to the group and challenges the class to come up with multiple solutions to the problem. Yesterday, Ms. Trina asked the class what they would do if they were feeling lonely and wanted to join a group of children playing on the Big Toy structure.

Tobias: You could ask them.

Ms. Trina: Yes, you could ask them. That is a solution. What else could you try?

Savannah: If they said no, you could find another friend to play.

Ms. Trina: Yes, that is another solution. So far we have two solutions. Let's try to think of five more.

Step 3: *What would happen next?* After children generate many alternative solutions to problems, they can begin to evaluate consequences. Teachers ask, "What would happen next?" Three questions can guide a child's decision to determine if the consequences would be good or bad (Webster-Stratton, 1999):

- Will this solution keep our bodies, feelings, and things safe?
- Is the solution fair?
- How will everyone feel?

Once again, teachers can use role-play to help children learn these strategies. Feeling satisfied with the number of diverse solutions the children generated, Miss Trina helps them evaluate the consequences of solutions, using a puppet to introduce the three criteria for evaluating solutions. For example, the puppet demonstrates their solution of taking turns, and then asks the children, "Is it safe?" Aaron and Javier shout, "Yes!" The puppet congratulates them on good thinking and then demonstrates another solution, grabbing toys. The puppet asks, "Is it safe?" When the children respond, "No," the puppet asks, "Why not?"

Video Example 14.4:

Social Problem Solving

In this video two kindergarten teachers discuss how they encourage social-emotional development. What strategies do they use? Why are these successful ways to teach social problem solving?

mindfulness noticing one's sensations, thoughts, and feelings in the present moment, without judgment

Step 4: *Give the solution a try!* At this step, children are taught to act on the best solution that they generated and what to do if a solution does not work. When a prosocial solution does not work, children can draw on the other solutions they generated in Step 2 that might have positive consequences. When teachers focus on building problem-solving skills, children are likely to begin supporting and encouraging each other's efforts.

Solve Problems in the Moment Many unanticipated social-emotional problems occur throughout each day. Teachers need to assist children with problem solving on a moment-to-moment basis. At times, it's enough for teachers to anticipate a problem and be nearby to prompt a child through the problem-solving steps. For example, 6-year-old Oralie got off the bus this morning with a scowl on her face. Her teacher keeps an eye on her, and when Oralie squabbles with Clancy over the computer, her teacher is there to encourage them to think of and try various solutions.

Children need support from teachers to remember the problem-solving steps and to stay in the situation. Those who are not skilled problem solvers may be prone to flee. Others may lose control of their temper and have an emotional meltdown. Teachers need to be equipped with strategies to support children through these difficult moments. Recent research suggests that mindfulness-based and relaxation practices can be used effectively in classrooms (Flook, Goldberg, Pinger, & Davidson, 2015; Schonert-Reichl et al., 2015). Mindfulness refers to noticing one's sensations, thoughts, and feelings in the present moment, without judgment. When children are taught to notice their breathing and bodily sensations and emotions—in the present moment—they may develop better self-regulation (Zelazo & Lyons, 2012). They may even develop better cognitive and social skills. Another research-based strategy that helps children respond to stressful situations, the snow globe, is described in the *What Works* feature.

Relationships with Peers Mr. Wilson's kindergarten class meeting begins with a question: "Do you know how to make a new friend?" Hands shoot up immediately and children chant, "I do, I do." Almost whispering, Mr. Wilson says, "We don't need hands yet. Now stop and think for a second." The children know this routine by now. After a few seconds, Mr. Wilson calls on children in turn and most of them say some variation of "play with them." So Mr. Wilson asks, "How would you invite a friend to play?" and he writes down their ideas to post on the wall: What can we play? Want to go to the park? Do you like Clay Boy? Want to play frog? He continues writing as their ideas become more creative and detailed.

Mr. Wilson's planned lesson is to help the children practice self-regulation and friendship skills in advance. By asking the children to think before they answer, he encourages impulse control. By posting their ideas, he provides a scaffold to revisit when children need to work on friendship skills later.

Social-Emotional Competence in the Whole Group On the wall in Ms. Colello's inclusive preschool classroom is the list of rules depicted in Figure 14.1. Ms. Colello helped the preschoolers re-word the rules in positive phrases. For example, if the children offered, "Don't hit," Ms. Colello said, "Great—so use gentle touch—is that it?" When the children agreed, she wrote it on the board. By establishing the rules together, children gain a sense of ownership and are more likely to remember and abide by them. Thinking and articulating them in advance promotes self-regulation and commitment to caring about each other and their school.

A major goal of the Far Hills Elementary School is to create a school-wide community of learners. The principal and teachers have high expectations for academic achievement but they also know that learning is founded on social-emotional development. They have created a school culture of caring and compassion. At every grade level, children are expected to practice three acts of kindness every day—whether holding the door for someone, saying you're sorry for interrupting, or just smiling at a new student. The primary-grade children keep a running list of acts of kindness and are striving to reach 100.

What Works

Relaxation for Children: The Snow Globe

Tyler just turned 5 years old and has been in his pre-K program since September. Tyler is an active boy and loves to play ball on the playground. Like many children, Tyler has strong preferences for certain activities, people, toys, and materials. He also gets disappointed and upset very easily. This week alone, Tyler had several meltdowns—when he didn't get called on for a turn at circle time, when two classmates got too close to his block structure during free choice, when his teacher told him it was time to clean up, and when his dad told him they needed to go straight to the grocery store after school and not stop at the park. Tyler's teacher, Raychael, noticed that Tyler seemed anxious on most days.

Raychael shared her concerns about Tyler with her colleague Scott. He told Raychael that he had started using some relaxation activities and was already seeing reduced levels of stress and increased moments of calm in his classroom. Raychael was skeptical; she had heard of mindfulness for adults but didn't think it could work with young children. But Scott insisted that fostering relaxation through small tools such as pictures, objects, food, simple movements, and music for preschoolers can help them to stay calm and to develop an ability to focus attention at a higher level. Raychael arranged times to observe Scott teach these lessons. She saw several lessons and decided to start with teaching her class sailboat breathing and the "snow globe."

Sailboat breathing teaches young children to focus on and slow their breathing. Imagine a sailboat riding the waves going up (breathing in) and going down (breathing out) over and over again. A visual of the waves—starting small and then getting bigger (so breathing becomes deeper and the exhale becomes longer).

The snow globe validates how children can sometimes feel stressed and "shaken up" and it is hard to think or see clearly. When children feel "shaken up" like the snow globe, they can shake an actual snow globe or glitter jar and then practice mindful breathing as the snow or glitter falls to the bottom and the water becomes clear again.

Raychael embedded mindful breathing each day after the children came in from the playground. They found a place on the carpet and Raychael moved her fingers over the waves as the children breathed in and out. She could already see more moments of calm in the classroom.

After a few days, Raychael introduced the snow globe at circle time. She talked about a time she got really frustrated and shook the globe to demonstrate how upset her feelings were. She asked the children if they ever felt that way. She noticed Tyler's hand shoot up and his head nod. She asked the children if anyone would like to volunteer a time they felt shaken up. Tyler raised his hand again, and Raychael called on him to come up front and tell the class when he felt shaken up. He told everyone that he felt shaken up that morning when his dad told him he couldn't watch television. Raychael told him to shake the snow globe until the swirling snow was as upset as he was. Tyler shook the globe vigorously then handed it back to Raychael for the class to see. Raychael asked Tyler to take a few sailboat breaths until the "snow settled" and the rest of the class joined in with him. When the water was clear, after several deep breaths, she asked Tyler how he felt now. "I feel calm," he said, and then sat down. Raychael then told the children that they would each get to make their own snow globe to help them whenever they needed it. The children eagerly walked to small group and started filling babyfood jars with water, food coloring, and lots of glitter. Raychael loved seeing the children practice their mindful breathing.

Source: M. Thompson, & J. Gauntlett-Gilbert, 2008. Mindfulness with children and adolescents: Effective clinical application. *Child Psychology and Psychiatry, 13*(3), 395–407.

> **Class Rules**
> 1. Use gentle hands
> 2. Listen to the teacher
> 3. Take care of our things
> 4. Have fun

FIGURE 14.1 Classroom Rules Generated by Preschoolers When children themselves generate the classroom rules, as these preschoolers did, they are more likely to feel a sense of ownership and abide by them.

✔ Application Exercise 14.3:
Social-Emotional Competence in the Whole Group

The foundation of active citizenship is the ability to establish positive relationships with other people and solve social problems. In the *Promoting Play* feature, learn the true story of how a teacher and school counselor created a "game show" to support emotional learning for energetic second-graders.

We now turn to the related area of the curriculum in which children see these skills in action in themselves and other people—social studies.

Promoting Play

Learning Interpersonal Problem-Solving Skills through Games

Atty is in her third year of teaching second grade in an urban school that serves a diverse student body. She loves how diverse her class is and how engaged they are in learning. The school principal always remarks on the energetic buzz that emanates from her classroom, and the real sense of belonging the children have. Atty has worked hard to create a fun, caring community. One thing that her students really enjoy are the games Atty plans. Sometimes they are competitive, but positive and fun. For example, last month, she divided the students into equal, but diverse groups and has them work as teams to build the tallest tower using only ten sheets of paper and a role of tape. The students enjoyed the challenge and applied math, engineering, and social skills to create paper skyscrapers.

Recently, however, there has been an increase in children arguing on the playground which has sometimes ended in fights and definitely is brought into the classroom—disrupting the community spirit and interfering with learning. Atty shared this observation with Bryan, the school counselor. Together they decided to build on the children's love of game play and came up with, "Peace Maker or Peace Breaker."

Atty and Bryan divided the class into two teams. They let the teams name themselves. They ended up with the "Super Star Heroes" and the "Fierce Friends." Then Bryan and Atty told them the objective and rules of the game. It was set up a bit like a television game show. Bryan even came to class wearing a sparkly blazer and they had a pretend microphone. Bryan and Atty were the hosts, and they alternated giving the teams questions. The questions were common scenarios and ways that children might act and the team had to decide whether the children in the scenario were acting as "peace makers or peace breakers."

Atty read the first scenario to the Fierce Friends: "Tommy and Michael were playing wall ball at recess. Julio approached and asked if he could join the game. Tommy said, 'No! Find your own ball.' Then Atty asked the team if Julio was being a "peace maker or a peace breaker" and the children shouted, "Peace Maker." How about Tommy? The children shouted, "Peace Breaker." Then the children were given a three-minute lightning round to brainstorm as many "peace making" responses as they could for Tommy.

Then Atty read a different scenario to the "Super Star Heroes." Each team had four turns. Then each team had to come up with a cheer for the other team to celebrate. Atty and the children started using the peace maker language throughout the day. They created a box to nominate a classmate or teacher for a "Peace Maker" prize. The nominations were read on Friday afternoons. Atty and Bryan continued to make the scenarios more complex and were happy to see the second-graders meet the challenge. The children looked forward to the afternoons when they had some time to play a round of "Peace Maker or Peace Breaker."

The peace-making efforts spread throughout the building and soon several teachers were incorporating peace-making activities that included random acts of kindness in the school and community. It became a focus of the school's social studies curriculum on citizenship. The art teacher taught fifth graders how to make origami doves and they decided to make a "peace tree" in front of the school. Whenever a child nominated as peace maker, a dove with her or his name on it was hung on the tree. The peace tree became a visual reminder of what was valued in the school community.

Sources: The real life adventure of elementary school counselor, Bryan Manzano, at Sand Point Elementary in Seattle, WA; and R. Joshee, & M. Thomas, 2017. "Multicultural citizenship education in Canada: Slow peace as an alternative to social cohesion," in J. A. Banks (Ed.),*Citizenship education and global migration: Implications for theory, research, and teaching*, 91–106. Washington, DC: American Educational Research Association.

✓ Check Your Understanding 14.4

Effective Social Studies Curriculum and Teaching

Positive social-emotional development is integrally connected to other areas of development and to learning curriculum content, particularly in social studies. In Chapter 10, we described a model for curriculum planning that draws on content knowledge from the disciplines as well as knowledge of child development. Social studies content comes from the subject matter disciplines of history, geography, political science, and economics. These provide the key concepts—the "big ideas"—and processes that children need to learn. Understanding typical patterns and sequences of child development determines which of these concepts to include in the curriculum for different ages. In addition, knowing children's predictable interests and capabilities makes it possible to teach relatively complex concepts in ways that are meaningful and accessible for children.

For example, one big idea in social studies is that institutions such as the family, community, and government play key roles in individuals' lives. At the college level, these concepts are part of courses in sociology and political science. By contrast, in preschool, teachers tap into children's natural interest in their families as a theme for organizing curriculum and teaching how people depend on and help each other. This same topic can be explored in greater complexity as children get older. First-graders might study how their community supports families by investigating if the park is accessible for persons with disabilities and, if not, contacting town council members to call for change.

What Is Social Studies?

Social studies is not a single topic or field of study. According to the National Council for the Social Studies (NCSS), social studies is the "integrated study of the social sciences and humanities to promote civic competence. ... The primary purpose of social studies is to help young people make informed and reasoned decisions for the public good as citizens of a culturally diverse, democratic society in an interdependent world" (NCSS, 2010, p. 1).

Social studies includes the political, economic, cultural, and environmental aspects of societies of the past, present, and future. Children learn about their community and the world as well as developing skills in problem solving, decision making, collaboration, collecting and analyzing information, and making informed judgments. Above all, social studies helps children become responsible, participating citizens, whether in their play group, the school, the community, or the world. As we see, considerable overlap exists between the goals inherent in teaching social-emotional learning and in social studies.

Social Studies Content Goals

Although social studies includes a vast amount of content, a relatively small share of curriculum time is allotted to it, especially in primary grades (Mindes, 2016). So what can and should children learn about social studies in the early years? The NCSS (2010) suggests thematic strands that serve as the basis for social studies standards in many states. Each theme includes concepts that are most easily understood as well as relevant and engaging for children. Table 14.2 lists nine social studies themes and key concepts for young learners.

In the sections that follow, we briefly describe many of the themes and ways teachers can help children learn key social studies concepts.

Foster Children's Sense of Identity
A major goal of the social studies for young children is to help them develop a positive **identity**. Children need to understand that they are unique, but they also have commonalities with other children. General principles for helping young children develop a sense of identity include:

- Have children share information about their interests and families.
- Provide opportunities for children to make appropriate and varied decisions.
- Delight in children's accomplishments and explorations.
- Ensure that children can see themselves in books, pictures, and play materials.
- Help children distinguish people and relationships.

identity The collection of characteristics that individuals recognize as constituting their sense of self and belonging to a group.

TABLE 14.2 Social Studies Themes and Concepts

Social studies in early childhood integrates several traditional subject matter disciplines and translates them into developmentally appropriate, key concepts for children to learn.

Theme and Traditional Discipline(s)	Big Ideas from the Discipline	Key Concepts for Young Learners
Individual Development and Identity (Psychology)	Personal identity is shaped by one's culture, by groups, and by institutional influences.	Developing a positive self-concept and feelings of self-efficacy; making and keeping friends.
Individuals, Groups, and Institutions (Sociology, Political Science)	Institutions such as families, schools, government agencies, and the courts play a role in people's lives.	Different kinds of families, making group decisions, living in a democracy.
Culture (Anthropology)	Aspects of human cultures—art, language, history, and geography—exhibit both similarities and differences.	Concepts such as alike and different, appreciation and respect for diversity in all of its forms.
Time, Continuity, and Change (History)	Children come to understand themselves in terms of the passage of time and develop the skills of the historian.	Routines that teach time sequencing; projects that teach how things change over time.
People, Places, and Environment (Geography, Archeology, Ecology)	Children learn to locate themselves in space, become familiar with landforms in their environment, and develop an understanding of the human-environment interaction.	Mapping for young children, beginning with picture maps of their classroom and extending to their community; caring for and protecting the environment.
Production, Distribution, and Consumption (Economics)	Projects address questions such as "What is to be produced?" and "How is production to be organized?"	Understanding that everyone has wants and needs and how these can be fulfilled.
Science, Technology, and Society (Mathematics, Science, and Technology)	The modern world is greatly affected by technology and the sciences that support it.	Becoming familiar with, evaluating, and using various technologies.
Global Connections (Political Science, Ecology, Economics)	We have connections and tensions with the rest of the world.	Being stewards of the environment; human rights; economic competition.
Civic Ideals and Practices (Political Science, Civics)	Children need an understanding of civic ideals and the practices of citizenship.	Involving children in developing the rules and holding class meetings to resolve conflicts.
Power, Authority, and Governance (Political Science, History, Civics)	People work together to bring about change in democratic societies.	Helping children understand the basic ideas of fairness, rights, and responsibilities in various contexts.

Source: Based on *National Curriculum Standards for Social Studies: A Framework for Teaching, Learning, and Assessment,* by National Council for the Social Studies, 2010, Silver Spring, MD: Author.

Value Diversity and Equity An overarching goal of social studies is to create an engaged citizenry in which democratic values are an essential element of early education. James Banks (2008), founding director of the Center for Multicultural Education at the University of Washington, coined the term *equity pedagogy*, the idea that teaching about differences needs to include teaching about equity, justice, oppression, and the rights of diverse people, as this example illustrates:

> Gail and Jim co-teach in a preschool classroom and decide to read some classic fairy tales. Fully aware that fairy tales often convey racism, sexism, and ageism, the two decide to incorporate the goal of teaching about equity. After reading versions of *Sleeping Beauty* and *Cinderella*, Jim asks the children why they think the princesses always have blonde hair and light skin. The children decide that this was because the author chose to draw only white people. The class collectively decides to "rewrite" and illustrate the fairy tales, featuring characters of color. The children also reenact the stories with princesses saving princes. In this example, Jim and Gail are teaching children to value both diversity and equity. And the children learn to think critically about books, movies, television, and other media.

Equity is not the same thing as equality. However, achieving equality—the American ideal—requires recognition of unfair and unequal starting points for learners. The goal is to provide fair and equitable opportunities for all children to reach their full potential which requires adapting practices for cultural, linguistic, and individual variation as we have described throughout this book.

Video Example 14.5:

Learning Social Studies

In this video, preschoolers check on their school garden to see if anything is ripe for harvest. How does this experience help them learn about ecology and economics? What other social studies themes and concepts could the garden project promote?

equity pedagogy The idea that teaching about differences needs to include teaching about oppression and equity.

Implement Culturally Sustaining Practices Helping young children develop a sense of self and a positive identity begins with learning about the important people in their environment. A wide variety of activities help children think about who is in their family—immediate and extended—and community. These themes date back to the *widening horizons approach* to social studies curriculum developed by Lucy Sprague Mitchell and incorporated in the Bank Street approach (Mitchell & David, 1992). This approach to curriculum planning is designed to begin where "children are" and then expand outward. Although the basic concept of widening horizons is still relevant, social studies should not be limited to immediate, firsthand experiences. Children's horizons are and can be much wider today.

The widening horizons approach also provides the teacher with opportunities to use *culturally sustaining practices*. Culturally sustaining practices are teaching strategies that acknowledge and sustain the language, literature, and cultural practices of all children, and in particular children of color (Paris & Alim, 2017). Consider how this approach is used in the following example:

widening horizons approach Approach to social studies curriculum planning designed to begin "where children are" and then expand outward.

culturally sustaining practices teaching strategies that acknowledge and sustain the language, literature, and cultural practices of all children, and in particular children of color

> Lily Nguyen teaches in an inclusive preschool classroom. For a study about families, she plans a project that families can work on together. Lily sends home colorful construction paper, child-sized scissors, glue sticks, crayons, stickers, and directions to trace one foot from each person in the family, decorate it, and then glue it to the large piece of construction paper. When the foot pages come back, Lily is delighted. The families are very creative and many note that they had great fun. She had asked families to also note how to say feet and shoes in their home languages. After laminating the pages and compiling them into a book, Lily shares the completed project with the children, stopping after each page to count and discuss the members of each family. She noted that some families kept their shoes on and others did not. The children talk about if their families take their shoes off or keep them on inside their homes. The children then help graph the number of family members each child has.

In this project, Lily has many opportunities to talk about and demonstrate respect for diverse families. The children come from a variety of family structures, such as single parents, LGBTQ families, extended families, and foster families. An additional subject emerges as Lily's class discusses families. Some children talk about relatives who are no longer living. This topic leads into another social studies theme and related concepts—history and how people change over time.

Learning about diversity naturally focuses on differences; however, children need to understand that people are similar as well as different (Thompson & Gauntlett-Gilbert, 2008). Read the feature *Culture Lens: Learning about Cross-Cultural Similarities,* which describes resources to accomplish this important goal.

Learn about the Past and the Concept of Time   Social studies can equip young children with knowledge and understanding of the past and how things, people, and places change over time. Preschoolers begin learning concepts of time by experiencing a predictable schedule. As children get older, they are increasingly able to mark the passage of time and how things change over days, weeks, months, and seasons.

Children can also learn to use the methods used by historians, such as identifying problems and questions, collecting information and artifacts, and observing and reaching conclusions about the past. Elementary-age children learn about the past by engaging in "living history" projects in which they interview older members of their family or community. The *Becoming an Intentional Teacher* feature illustrates how one teacher engaged children in a living history project to integrate social studies and other curriculum areas.

Learn about Where We Live: Geography and Mapping   Geography is an important part of our daily lives and of the early childhood curriculum. Children learn geographic concepts through active experiences and engaging in geographic thinking. For example, preschoolers and kindergartners can take a walk around the school or neighborhood, collect objects or take pictures along the way, and then create a map of their surroundings. Primary-grade children's geography understanding can go well beyond their immediate experience as in the following example:

> Second-grade teacher Ms. Polan introduces a unit on maps and globes designed to meet the state geography standards. First, each child prepares their own K-W-L chart identifying their current knowledge and questions. Then with the whole group, the teacher uses the smartboard and the website, Brainpop Jr., to help children learn how to read a map, view videos of various land forms, and play related games. Other activities include using Google Earth to tour the world's continents and oceans. The children create a map of the United States, identify rivers and mountains, and locate

Culture Lens

Learning about Cross-Cultural Similarities

When teachers think about culture, the focus is almost always on differences. However, human beings from diverse cultural backgrounds are not only different, they also share many similarities. The OxFam Education Modules are designed to focus more attention on the ways people across cultural groups are alike.

Given divisive world events such as ethnic cleansing, religious hatred, and racism, teaching children about various cultural groups and building empathy has never been more important. This is the focus of the OxFam Education Modules, which are based on the premise that children love learning from other children. This resource helps children explore their own lives—and

the world around them—by looking at the lives of four children from around the world. The stories of children from Ethiopia, Brazil, Russia, and India allow discussion of themes such as "myself," "helping out," and "caring and sharing."

Developers believe that if more people could see how all humans are alike, people would be more accepting, understanding, and respectful of each other. The OxFam Education Modules are available free to download and include multiple lesson plans, photos, and videos that can be easily incorporated into lessons by any teacher.

Becoming an Intentional Teacher

Integrating Social Studies Content to Meet Standards

Here's What Happened   I teach second grade in a rural public school. Seven-year-old Amy's great-grandmother, whom she calls Gigi, recently came to live with the family. Prior to this move, Gigi lived in the same farmhouse where she grew up. Amy tells me that Gigi isn't happy. Amy tries to cheer Gigi up by asking her to tell stories, which sometimes works.

With Amy's agreement, I invite Gigi to visit our class to talk about what life was like in our community when she was a little girl. At first Gigi is hesitant, but with much encouragement, Gigi agrees to come. To prepare for her visit, the children generate a list of questions to ask her: "What was your school like?" "How did you get there?" "How did you talk to people far away?" "How did you get food?" The list goes on and on. Carl suggests that it would be neat if we could videotape Gigi's interview, and she grants permission.

On the day of Gigi's visit, Amy proudly introduces her great-grandmother, who says that she is 89 years old. The children do the math to figure out what year she was born and how much older she is than they are. The interview lasts 30 minutes. The children can hardly imagine what it must have been like not to have e-mail or cell phones, much less not to have phones at all! They also can't believe that Gigi's father was a blacksmith and that, in earlier days, people used horses to travel. A few people had cars, but they were very expensive and there weren't many paved roads. Gigi has brought some black-and-white photos that show her family and farm and the buildings in the small town back then.

Gigi's visit generates a great deal of interest among the children. She returns for several more interviews, and the children produce a documentary video as the culmination of their living history project. The children seek out other elders in the community to learn about their lives when they were young, their jobs, and how the area looked at the time.

Here's What I Was Thinking   Our school curriculum reflects the state learning standards. For second grade, the history, geography, and economics standards require

children to learn key concepts and processes for studying the discipline. One such history concept—continuity and change—is related to the standard "Children understand that basic human needs remain the same but how they are met changes with technology."

I find it difficult to teach abstract concepts such as this. And there isn't time in the day to address all of these standards, especially because in second grade we need to focus so much on reading and math. In my experience, however, children learn best when their interests are piqued and they actively inquire about a meaningful problem or question.

I saw an opportunity for integrating many key social studies concepts into the living history project. After the children generated their list of questions and decided how they would get answers, I went through the state standards and noted which ones related to this study. I also planned for children to use the actual processes and tools of historians. For example, they interviewed subjects, recorded data, examined old photos and documents, read books about the period, and came to conclusions based on the evidence. Thus, children practiced their reading and writing skills during the living history project as well.

A serendipitous outcome of the project was that Gigi became an honorary member of our second-grade class. Children frequently consult her when they have questions about past and even current events. And since Amy taught her to use e-mail and Skype, communication with her became even easier.

Reflection   People often think that history is developmentally inappropriate for young children because they cannot experience it concretely and they will not develop a fully accurate sense of time until they are older. But all children and their families share stories about the past. What are some other project ideas for teaching history to preschool and primary grades?

their own state and its geographic characteristics. During the two-week study, they explore interactive maps such as the Rand McNally website and also learn mapping terminology such as *birds-eye view* and *legend* by examining a school map.

The *Geography for Life* national standards (Heffron, 2012) identify big ideas to be used in geographic inquiry. One basic concept is location, where in the world something is and why things are located in certain places. A related concept is how the characteristics of any given place tell a lot about where people live, why they settle there, and how they use natural resources. By asking questions with this geography concept in mind, teachers can help children develop an understanding of places and their distinctive characteristics (Seefeldt, Castle, & Falconer, 2014). A related idea is movement, which focuses on how people, things, ideas, products, and information move from one place to another. The most common movement children see and think about is people traveling every day to school or work. Some children will have traveled much farther afield or have family members around the globe.

Children can also learn about relationships within places. This concept, which has been getting more attention because of issues such as climate change, explores how humans impact the environment as well as how the environment influences human behavior (Seefeldt et al., 2014). Another big idea is geographic regions—how they are united by similar physical conditions and common cultural traits. Related questions include how human actions modify the physical environment, how physical systems affect human systems, and the changes that occur in the meaning, use, distribution, and importance of resources.

The national geography standards, *Geography for Life* (Heffron, 2012), are designed for older children; however, they identify skills that children begin developing during their preschool and primary years. These are listed in Table 14.3 with suggestions for how teachers can help children learn these skills.

Learn about Wants and Needs: Early Economics

Economic concepts are basic to children's lives. Teachers sometimes avoid the topic of economics, however, because it raises sensitive issues around social class (Odhiambo, Nelson, & Chrisman, 2016). However, the economic conditions in the world raise this topic in everyone's consciousness. At one end of the economic spectrum, increasing numbers of children are falling into poverty and their basic needs are not being met. At the other end, many children get everything they ask for and more.

Teachers need to be sensitive to families' economic situations. They can help children take pride in how their family cares for them regardless of their work or home situation (Odhiambo, Nelson, & Chrisman, 2016). Children's attention can be drawn to economics and poverty across the globe through children's literature (Dunkerly-Bean, Bean, Sunday & Summers, 2017). Constantly drawing attention to children's possessions such as new clothes or toys can be painful for some children. More appropriate ideas to introduce early economics include helping children learn not to waste resources or to think critically about television advertisements.

All young children have wants and needs that act as powerful motivation to begin understanding economic systems. This topic can be an opportunity to raise awareness about commercialism in society. Table 14.4 presents six key early economics concepts young children can learn, along with examples of teaching strategies

TABLE 14.3 Geography Education Standards

Geography can be a topic of great interest to children if teachers use strategies such as those described here.

Geographic Skill	Teaching Strategies
Asking geographic questions	Acknowledge and encourage geographic questions. Join children in their sense of wonder about the natural world and how it formed (e.g., "Where does rain come from?" "How do mountains grow?"). Model asking geographic questions ("Which way do you come to school?").
Acquiring geographic information	Provide children with resources such as maps, globes, map puzzles, relief maps, and books depicting other lands and people.
Organizing geographic information	Provide children with materials and inspiration to draw maps, construct graphs, and tell and write stories about places they have been or want to go.
Analyzing geographic information	Show children how to locate themselves on maps and globes. Locate the places of origin of children's families, especially immigrant families.
Answering geographic questions	Have children present their maps, stories, buildings, drawings, and findings of other places to their peers. Teachers and peers can ask questions about the child's work.

Source: Based on S. Heffron (Ed.), 2012. *Geography for Life: National Geography Standards*. Washington, DC: National Council for Geographic Education; and E.A. Odhiambo, L.E. Nelson, & J.K. Chrisman, J.K., 2016. *Social studies and young children*. Upper Saddle River, NJ: Pearson.

TABLE 14.4 Teaching Early Economics

Economics may seem too advanced a topic for young children, but developmentally appropriate strategies such as these can make it highly accessible and engaging.

Economics Concept	Teaching Strategies
Scarcity means that there is always a conflict between never-ending wants and limited resources.	Comment on the scarcity of materials when children engage in conflict over them. Explain that there are limited numbers of toys, and more children want them than there are toys to go around.
Because resources are limited, people must choose some things and give up others.	Building on the preceding example, this is a time to talk about other solutions to problems involving scarce materials. Ideas include sharing, getting another toy to play with, or waiting for a turn.
People produce and consume. When they produce, they make goods. When they consume, they use goods and services.	Ask family members to share their work with the class, and (if possible) to share active experiences with the children (cooking, making art, writing). Create a "market day" where children produce and sell things. The class can vote on how the profits will be spent.
Money and trade or barter are used to obtain goods and services.	Create a store in the classroom. Include merchandise, a cash register, play money, pads for receipts, and props for workers and consumers.
People work in a variety of jobs.	Take field trips to local businesses and organizations or invite parents to visit the class and discuss what they do.
Helping others who do not have their basic needs met is socially desirable.	Host a class clothing drive. Children can make signs about the drive, collect and organize clothing, and count and graph the types and sizes of clothing collected.

Sources: Odhiambo, E.A., Nelson, L.E., & Chrisman, J.K., 2016. *Social studies and young children.* Upper Saddle River, NJ: Pearson; and C. Seefeldt, S. Castle, & R.C. Falconer, R. C., 2014. *Social studies for the preschool/primary child* (9th ed.). Upper Saddle River, NJ: Pearson.

Learn to Live in a Democracy: Making Choices and Voting
John Dewey strongly believed that an essential purpose of education is to empower an engaged citizenry. In a democracy, people have the power to make a variety of meaningful choices pertaining to their daily lives—to become agents of change. In early childhood programs, children are not just preparing to become members of a democratic society; they actually are citizens of a democracy (Dewey, 1916). Therefore, teachers need to engage them in group decision making and discussion of differing opinions during class meetings and help them understand the concepts of voting and majority. As children get older, their understanding of history and current events expands and they engage more with American democratic experiences. The following scenario shows how voting can be incorporated into preschool schedules.

Gayla teaches a Head Start classroom of 4-year-olds in an urban setting. One of the favorite times of the day is large group or circle time. It is short, but is a time to acknowledge everyone who is there, wish the absent children well, sing songs, make music and movement, and read a good book together. Gayla has a board with the title "Circle Time Democracy" on it. Each day she posts two books, or two songs on the board and the children vote for which one she will lead or read. The children count the votes, talk about not being able to vote twice and the importance of franchise. The children extend the concept of "Circle Time Democracy" to other areas of their preschool day. They sometimes call a vote for the snack offering or art projects.

Social-emotional learning and social studies during early childhood lay the foundation for children to become engaged citizens in their community and the world.

In previous sections, we presented some of the social studies curriculum themes recommended by the National Council for the Social Studies, the key concepts for children to learn, and examples of teaching strategies. Next we discuss effective approaches for planning and implementing social studies curriculum.

Effective Strategies for Teaching Social Studies

One of the biggest challenges in teaching social studies is deciding what content and topics are developmentally appropriate for young children; that is, which learning goals are achievable for children and when? These decisions are particularly difficult in social studies because subjects such as history and geography involve highly abstract ideas. For example, comprehending history requires understanding chronological time—an ability that is not fully developed until age 11 or later (Seefeldt et al., 2014). Similarly, geography requires an understanding of complex concepts such as location and direction, and that maps and globes are abstract representations of reality (Seefeldt et al., 2014).

Using the NCSS themes to plan early childhood social studies curriculum is a good way to make such abstract concepts more understandable for young children and, therefore, more developmentally appropriate. It is also important to use teaching strategies that build on what children already know, help them make sense of new experiences, and connect facts to larger concepts and ideas. Three commonly used, developmentally appropriate approaches to social studies curriculum meet those criteria: (1) engaging children in play and active learning, (2) using a project approach to integrate social studies, and (3) using technology to expand children's firsthand experiences and worldview.

Play and Active Learning Experiences
Children are born into social studies. From birth, they begin exploring their world (Mindes, 2016). In good schools for young children, social studies take place almost naturally (Seefeldt et al., 2014). Such schools allow children to experience the curriculum firsthand through child-guided exploration and play within a carefully planned environment. Children learn social studies when they interact to solve problems such as how to produce a guidebook for school visitors.

Teachers can extend this learning by inviting guest speakers for children to meet and interview. However, teachers should prepare guests in advance; people who have not had experience with young children may have inappropriate expectations for their behavior, such as expecting them to remain quiet for a lecture. A more successful approach is for guests to bring hands-on materials such as antique tools from the history museum for the children to see, touch, and talk about.

Field Work
Field work is another active way to extend social studies learning, whether in the form of an exploration of the school building, a visit to the florist, or a trip to the history museum. However, like all early childhood experiences, field trips must be planned and structured carefully to be safe and support active learning (Seefeldt et al., 2014). It is important to have a clear purpose for a field trip that identifies specific learning goals. In addition to following school procedures and policies related to field trips, teachers should visit the field trip site in advance, noting parking facilities and safe walking paths, and how children with disabilities might be accommodated. It is also important to prepare the adults at the field trip site with information about the children in your group and their learning goals for the trip.

Children should also be prepared for the field trip. In addition to discussing safety and expected behavior, providing background content is helpful. This does not mean that field trips should necessarily come at the end of a study, and in fact, having a field trip at the beginning of a project to ground the children's learning in real experiences is often more useful. Either way, children should learn about the field trip schedule and activities and have an opportunity to see photos or videos and ask questions. Teachers should plan for children to document their experiences. They can use a tablet, recorder, camera or other tool to record photos, videos, and interviews. They can also draw pictures or take notes.

Children should be helped to document their learning when they return to school. They can discuss and record their memories in writing, drawing, painting, or through other forms of creative expression. They can work their experiences into their play with appropriate props; for example, they might create a pretend flower shop after a visit to the florist. They can extend learning by reading books and through technology such as looking on the Smithsonian website following a museum visit.

Field trips have the potential to expand children's horizons in many ways. However, trips can also be missed opportunities for learning if the experience is just a whirlwind of unfocused activity. When asked what they remember from a trip to the nature center, children might say "Tasha got sick" or "I jumped in the puddle of water." While these reports are undoubtedly factual, they should not be all the children bring back from the experience.

An Integrated Approach to Teaching Social Studies There is a limited amount of time in the school day and year to address all the content that comprises the social studies. Fortunately, the various strands of social studies lend themselves to project work and integrated curriculum, as the following example illustrates:

Video Example 14.6:

Social Studies Field Trip

In this video, a preschool teacher reviews the class's long-term project designed to learn about the university where the center is located. The children plan the route for their upcoming field trip using the map and discuss prior knowledge. What social studies content goals does this study address? How does this whole group time adequately prepare children for their field work?

> One winter day, Gabriella Johnson notices that someone put several unkempt duffle bags and a sleeping bag on the back porch of the child care center. Gabriella sees a note that reads: "I am homeless right now. Please do not remove my things. If I need to move them, let me know."
>
> At circle time, Gabriella reads the note to the children and describes the possessions. The children have many questions. Lani asks why the person is homeless. Leo asks if it is a man or a woman. Jeremiah wants to know where the person is right now. Helen wonders if he is going to sleep there. A rich discussion ensues, and Gabriella explains that she doesn't have the answers to the questions.
>
> The children take a vote and decide the things can stay. Alexa wants to write the person a note. Gabriella helps the children write notes explaining that the stuff can stay and asking some of their questions. The next day, the notes are gone, but the person leaves one for the children that says "Thanks." The children are disappointed that the person didn't answer their questions and think of reasons why, but also are glad the belongings are still there. Leo worries that the person might not have enough to eat, so he asks if they could put the leftovers from lunch on the back porch.
>
> The discussions, note writing, and caretaking continue for several weeks, until the person removes the bags. The children make up stories about where he went. Jackson wonders aloud if the person moved into the shelter he and his mom stayed in at the beginning of the year. Gabriella decides to invite one of the soup kitchen volunteers to visit and talk about her work. This inspires the children, and Gabriella arranges for a service learning opportunity for them to organize a food drive. Tanya suggests that the food drive include pet food, too. The children make signs, set goals, write letters, and graph the amount and types of food they collect.

Gabriella takes an opportunity to build a powerful social studies project from this event. Throughout the project, the children learn concepts of wants and needs, power and privilege, fairness, culture, similarities and differences, and the importance and value of service learning—all while building language, literacy, and math skills.

Technology and Social Studies Children can also use global positioning system (GPS) devices during field trips to learn about geography. To learn more about the world at large, children can explore diverse cultures and places with Internet searches and electronic pen pals. Many schools, for example, Skype with or send e-mails and photos of their drawings to children in other schools, particularly ones in the hometowns or countries of children in the class.

Children can also produce and disseminate projects on the web. For example, young elementary-age children might put together a web page about the topics they are studying. Children could also prioritize a "wish list" that includes items to be used in the class; this allows the class to explore economics learning.

virtual field trip   Trip taken via the Internet in which children can go anywhere in the world.

Travel costs and supervision concerns often limit opportunities to take field trips. However, **virtual field trips** allow children to use the internet to go anywhere in the world. In this way, children can explore another community, state, or even country. They also can interview experts online via e-mail or participate in live chats with other children or workers in various jobs. The possibilities of using technology to teach social studies are limited only by the technology available to children.

✔ Check Your Understanding 14.5

Revisiting the Case Study

... Jefferson Elementary School

At the beginning of this chapter, we visited the kindergarten and third-grade classrooms at Jefferson Elementary School. Having discussed social-emotional development and learning as well as social studies curriculum and teaching, we can now revisit the school and see more clearly what and how children are learning about social studies.

It is evident from Waylon's experiences in kindergarten that his teacher focuses on both social-emotional development and social studies in her curriculum. Each child has an opportunity to develop a strong sense of identity, while all the children learn about each other, their family history, and the community in which they live. Ms. Hans, his teacher, operates her classroom as a mini-democracy in which children make choices, accept responsibility, and learn how voting functions to make group decisions.

The in-depth study of the Gulf Coast in Mr. Bell's third grade is an example of integrated social studies curriculum. Current events in the news motivate the children to learn more and get actively involved as citizens in helping others. They express empathy and concern for other people. They also learn about global connections between products developed and used in different places. The topic is rich with opportunities to learn geography, economics, and the environment while also developing skills in reading, writing, and researching. ■

14 Chapter Summary

- Social-emotional learning (also called social competence) is children's ability to recognize and regulate emotions, establish and maintain positive relationships, make responsible decisions, and solve social problems constructively.

- Teachers need to understand the developmental continuum of significant social-emotional accomplishments across the period from birth to third grade to have appropriate and realistic expectations for children's behavior, and to know how and when to effectively promote social-emotional learning.

- Play is a vital context for children to develop positive peer relationships and practice social skills. Play is

equally important for emotional development, providing a context for children to address their fears, develop coping skills and resilience, and feel in control of their environment.

- Effective social-emotional curricula include specific strategies for teaching social problem-solving skills, friendship skills, and self-regulation.

- Social studies—the integrated study of history, geography, economics, political science, and other related subjects—contribute to the development of competent citizens. During early childhood, social studies topics and social-emotional learning are inextricably connected. Learning to live in a democratic society—the overarching goal of social studies—is predicated on social-emotional learning.

- Developmentally appropriate, effective approaches to teaching the social studies in early childhood programs include engaging children in play and active learning experiences, using an integrated approach to link social studies learning and other curriculum areas, and using technology to expand children's worldviews.

Key Terms

- associative play
- cooperative play
- culturally sustaining practices
- engaged citizens
- equity pedagogy
- identity
- mindfulness
- parallel play
- separation anxiety
- social studies
- social-emotional learning
- solitary play
- virtual field trip
- widening horizons approach

 Flash Cards 14.1

Readings and Websites

Bohart, H., Charner, K., & Koralek, D. (Eds.). (2015). *Spotlight on young children: Exploring play.* Washington, DC: National Association for the Education of Young Children.

Mindes, G. (2016). *Social studies for young children: Preschool and primary curriculum anchor* (2nd ed.). Lanham, MD: Rowman & Littlefield Education.

Paris, D. & Alim, H.S. (2017). *Culturally sustaining pedagogies: Teaching and learning for justice in a changing world.* New York, NY: Teachers College Press.

Procopio, R. (Ed.). (2018) *Spotlight on young children: Social and emotional development.* Washington, DC: National Association for the Education of Young Children.

Cultivate Learning

This website, sponsored by the University of Washington, offers numerous free resources for supporting the social and emotional learning for young children, as well as for primary grade children and youth in before and after school programs.

National Center for Pyramid Model Innovations

This website provides a resource library for schools, centers, families, and states to implement the *Pyramid*

Model for Supporting Social Emotional Competence in Infants and Young Children, including activities to promote emotional literacy and self-regulation.

Center for Early Childhood Mental Health Consultation

Developed for Head Start programs, this website provides resources for supporting children's social and emotional development, and addressing challenging behavior.

National Childhood Traumatic Stress Network

This website offers resources for teachers, designed to support children and families who have experienced traumatic events and toxic stress.

Collaborative for Academic, Social, and Emotional Learning

This website offers resources to support primary-grade children's social and emotional learning, and documents the benefits of social-emotional competence for academic achievement.

National Council for the Social Studies

This website offers social studies resources for teachers, including textbooks, lesson plans, and assessment and curriculum ideas.

 Shared Writing 14.1
Social Studies in the Primary Grades

15 Teaching Children to Be Healthy and Fit: Physical Development and Health

Learning Outcomes

After studying this chapter, you should be able to:

15.1 Explain the importance of children's physical fitness and health.

15.2 Outline the continuum of gross motor, fine motor, and perceptual motor development.

15.3 Analyze the role of play in children's physical development and health.

15.4 Describe health and safety standards for early childhood programs.

15.5 Synthesize effective curriculum and teaching strategies to promote physical fitness and health.

© Sue Bredekamp

The NAEYC Professional Preparation Standards (NAEYC, 2011) that apply to this chapter:

1: Promoting Child Development and Learning

Key elements:

   1a. Knowing and understanding young children's characteristics and needs

   1b. Knowing and understanding the multiple influences on development and learning

   1c. Using developmental knowledge to create healthy, respectful, supportive, and challenging learning environments

4: Using Developmentally Effective Approaches to Connect with Children and Families

Key elements:

   4b. Knowing and understanding effective strategies and tools for early education

   4c. Using a broad repertoire of developmentally appropriate teaching/learning approaches

5: Using Content Knowledge to Build Meaningful Curriculum

Key elements:

   5a. Understanding content knowledge and resources in academic disciplines

   5b. Knowing and using the central concepts, inquiry tools, and structures of content areas or academic disciplines

   5c. Using their own knowledge, appropriate early learning standards, and other resources to design, implement, and evaluate meaningful, challenging curricula for each child

Case Study

Ms. Perez's class of 3- to 5-year-olds joyfully bounds out the door for their favorite part of the day—outdoor play. A well-planned environment greets the children on the playground. In addition to choosing from the permanent options of a climbing structure and tricycle path, today they can paint on a long piece of paper attached to the fence, water the class garden, or play with the ball collection in the large grassy area.

In less than a minute, all the children except 3-year-old Allison choose an activity and are busy playing. She is standing by the balls, but hasn't picked one up. Ms. Perez asks, "Allison, do you want to play catch?"

Allison replies, "No, I want to kick the ball but I can't do it."

Ms. Perez smiles and says, "I can help you learn." The teacher sets the balls up in a straight line, positions Allison in front of one ball, stands next to her, and demonstrates how to kick the ball. Allison tries and the ball rolls slowly away to the side without much motion. Ms. Perez says, "You kicked it! Let's see what happens to the next kick. I bet it goes farther." Allison is excited about this possibility. Ms. Perez demonstrates again, commenting on the positions of each foot in relation to the ball. Allison kicks the ball again—a longer way this time. Ms. Perez steps back and says, "That was a big kick."

Allison continues to kick the balls until they are all over the playground. Drew arrives and says, "I want a turn." Ms. Perez suggests that Drew ask Allison if he can play. He does, and Allison says, "Yes, but I go first." Drew agrees and together Allison and Drew collect the balls, line them up, and kick each one. They run off to collect the balls to repeat the game and play together until it is time to go inside.

After 45 minutes outside, Ms. Perez calls the children inside. They wind down by doing quieter activities. JaNaye and her two friends continue working on the collages they began this morning,

© AndrewLilley/E+/Getty Images

using objects such as buttons, foam cutouts, scraps of ribbon, and lace. Mitchell and Carletta write notes to friends. The assistant teacher, Ms. Aliote, assists four children as they string beads and use small pegboards to create patterns. Seth and Asia use a computer program to draw pictures, changing colors and line width by clicking the mouse. Amos, whose fine-motor development is less well-developed, works on a touchscreen tablet.

As lunch arrives, Regina and Alexei help set the table, and the children take turns at the sink next to a child-sized poster reminding them how to properly wash their hands.

Their meal is served family style, with children maneuvering serving spoons and passing dishes to each other. Brooks exclaims, "Look, Ms. Perez, I poured my milk and no spills." ∎

As in any high-quality early childhood program, movement is an essential part of living and learning in Ms. Perez's classroom. From tiny babies to active third graders, young children take on and embrace the world with their whole bodies. Healthy children of all ages love physical activity and play, but more than fun is involved. With the help of families and teachers, children master critically important physical skills and also establish habits related to fitness and health that can last a lifetime.

In this chapter, we address the critical health and fitness issues facing our nation's children today. We discuss the continuum of children's motor development from birth through age 8, and how intentional teachers promote optimal development through play and focused teaching of physical skills. We also discuss curriculum and teaching practices that promote children's fitness, health, and nutrition, and those that prevent illness and injury.

The Importance of Physical Fitness and Health

physical fitness Children's overall physical condition: growth, strength, stamina, and flexibility.

Physical fitness refers to children's overall physical condition: growth, strength, stamina, and flexibility. Children's physical fitness depends on a number of factors, including heredity, access to good nutrition and health care, and participation in fitness-enhancing activities. Most physically active children grow up to be physically active adults. On the other hand, few adults who were inactive as children become active later in life (Nekitsing, Hetherington, & Blundell-Birtill, 2018).

Benefits of Physical Fitness

When they feel strong and fit, children are more confident; they are likely to gain self-esteem, enjoy playing and learning with others, and eagerly take on new challenges (Sanders, 2015). Ample evidence (CDC, 2017) confirms that regular physical activity helps children by:

- Building and maintaining healthy bones, muscles, and joints
- Controlling weight
- Building lean muscle and reducing fat
- Preventing or delaying high blood pressure and cholesterol and type 2 diabetes

- Reducing feelings of depression, stress, and anxiety
- Improving physical fitness
- Increasing capacity for learning

Healthy physical development is closely and consistently linked to children's subsequent academic success throughout schooling (Active Living Research, 2015). For example, one study of preschoolers, half of whom were Head Start children, found that higher active play was associated with better self-regulation, which, in turn, was associated with higher reading and math achievement (Becker, McClelland, Loprinzi, & Trost, 2013).

Health-related fitness is the aspect of health that can be improved by exercise and activity. It consists of the following four components (Goodway, Ozmun, & Gallahue, 2013):

1. The **cardiorespiratory (aerobic) system** includes the heart, lungs, and blood. When working well, this system provides the stamina needed to actively participate for a long period of time.
2. **Muscular strength and endurance** allow for effective use of muscles. *Strength* allows children to use force to perform a task such as kicking a ball or hammering a nail. *Endurance* is the ability to keep moving without stopping because of fatigue.
3. **Flexibility** is the ability to bend and stretch easily, which helps prevent muscle and tendon injuries.
4. **Body composition** refers to weight and body fat. Excess fat puts stress on ligaments, tendons, bones, and tissues that support the body's weight.

All of these components are important parts of children's fitness and health. Each should be considered in planning effective early childhood programs. In recent years, however, children's health-related fitness has become an urgent concern as the rate of childhood obesity in America has increased significantly (Ogden, Carroll, Kit, & Flegal, 2014).

health-related fitness Any aspect of health that can be improved by physical exercise and activity.

cardiorespiratory (aerobic) system Body system made up of the heart, lungs, and blood; provides the stamina needed to be active for a long period of time.

muscular strength and endurance The ability to keep moving without stopping because of fatigue.

flexibility The ability to bend and stretch easily.

body composition Weight and body fat.

Childhood Obesity Crisis

Because children's physical development is so variable, their weight status is defined as their body-mass index (BMI) in relation to what is typical for their age and sex. Children are considered overweight when their BMI is above the 85th percentile for their age and sex, and obese when their BMI is above the 95th percentile (CDC, 2012b). The CDC reported dramatic increases in childhood obesity during the past 30 years. Although obesity rates among preschoolers have declined recently (Ogden et al., 2014), 23% of 2- to 5-year-olds are overweight or obese. These rates are higher for preschoolers who live in low-income families, and among African American, Latino, Native American, and Alaskan Native children (CDC, 2012b). Over a third of 6- to 11-year-olds are overweight or obese. These problems often continue into adulthood: 70% of severely overweight children become obese adults (CDC, 2014).

The causes of obesity are complex and involve genetics, lifestyle, and poor nutrition. But the consequences are profound. Overweight children are at greater risk of cardiovascular disease, diabetes, and other serious illnesses, miss four times as much school as normal-weight children, and can suffer from other health consequences such as depression and anxiety disorders (CDC, 2012b). Obese children are also more likely to be socially isolated from their peers and have low self-esteem, which negatively affects their academic performance (CDC, 2010). A higher percentage of children from low-income families have limited access to healthy food, poor nutrition, and are also more likely to be overweight or obese (CDC, 2012b), which becomes another risk factor associated with poverty. Children whose parents are obese are at greatest risk (McLoone & Morrison, 2014). So although predicting whether overweight/obese children will grow to be obese adults is difficult, making physical health a central aspect of the early childhood curriculum for all children makes sense.

Implications for Programs and Schools

Early childhood programs have a responsibility to counter the obesity crisis and improve physical fitness in all children by complying with the following recommendations for children's physical activity (CDC, 2015; SHAPE America, 2014):

- Children should engage in 60 minutes or more of moderate to vigorous physical activity every day. When children engage in moderate aerobic activity, their heart beats faster and they breathe faster than normal; during vigorous exercise, heart and respiration rates are much faster.
- Preschoolers need between 60 minutes and several hours of daily, unstructured free play every day. Unstructured free play is chosen and initiated by children, such as that which occurs on a playground.
- Physical activity for preschoolers should include at least 60 minutes of structured physical activity (in short, 15-minute segments), which is adult-guided play designed for a purpose such as increasing endurance or flexibility, such as when a teacher leads a game of Simon Says). Toddlers need 30 minutes of this type of play.
- Children should not sit for more than 60 minutes in any activity. Television viewing should be limited to less than two hours per day.
- Children's diets need to be improved with decreased intake of fast food and increased intake of fruits, vegetables, and whole grains.

unstructured free play Play that is chosen and initiated by children, such as that which occurs on a playground.

structured physical activitye Adult-guided play that is designed for a purpose such as increasing endurance or flexibility.

These recommendations have direct implications for early childhood programs and schools, especially considering a program's hours of operation. For example, in a full-day child care center where children might spend 8 to 10 hours a day, providing significant amounts of time for structured and unstructured physical activity is essential. The children may have limited time for active play after they leave the center. If children spend three or four hours in a program, teachers should plan at least 30, and preferably 45 minutes, of gross-motor play, in one or two time periods. Family child care may provide greater flexibility.

Video Example 15.1:

Physical Fitness and Health

Physical development is largely controlled by biological growth, but children do not acquire physical skills automatically. In this video, an intentional teacher and her pre-kindergartners transform the dramatic play area into a pretend exercise studio. How does using workout equipment and practicing yoga exercises help the children gain more control over their bodies, teach them motor skills and healthy habits? What else are they learning from this experience?

We know from research, however, that preschool children are not engaging in sufficient amounts of physical activity. For example, one study (Brown et al., 2009) of 24 preschools found that children spent less than 4% of the day engaged in moderate to vigorous physical activity, mostly outdoors. Indoor activity was essentially sedentary, except for rarely occurring teacher-initiated music and movement experiences A similar study of 10 child care centers observed for 50 days found that 88% of the time children did not have active play opportunities (Tandon, Saelens, & Christakis, 2017).

Given the benefits of physical activity for young children, as well as the risks of poor levels of fitness, teachers need to ensure that promoting physical development and health are core curriculum goals and not simply add-ons. Movement is fun, and most children love it, but the many benefits of physical activity for children's health and well-being are a serious justification for including it in the early childhood curriculum.

How Physical Development Occurs

Physical development during early childhood may seem a little magical; it begins at the moment of conception and continues throughout the life span. Yet physical development is anything but effortless. Individual children's physical growth and development vary considerably, depending on heredity, environmental factors, nutrition, gender, and access to health care. Over time, the interplay brings on dramatic, noticeable changes in children.

Changes in physical development are rapid, with later abilities, skills, and knowledge building on already acquired skills. Although children's development follows a relatively predictable sequence, variation exists—most notably in the pace of development. For example, although most children jump first with both feet and then learn to balance on one foot, Kinisha begins to balance at age 3; Jarrod acquires this skill at age 4.

Children's ways of perfecting physical skills are also different. Brent tries hopping, but falls when he loses his balance. Amalie hops while holding hands with a friend or while holding onto a railing. Li watches others hop, learning from their successes and failures before trying the skill. Another aspect of individuality is the sporadic and uneven nature of development. Physical growth in children sometimes occurs in spurts; at other times development is steady and incremental.

Types of Physical Development

There are three types of physical development:

1. **Gross-motor development** refers to physical skills related to moving the whole body or major parts of the body. For babies, one of these skills is gaining control of the head, neck, and torso to enable sitting and, later, standing. In preschoolers, gross-motor skills are walking, running, and jumping.

2. **Fine-motor development** involves changes in skills related to the small muscles found in individual body parts, especially those in the hands and feet. As children increasingly direct the movements of their fingers, hands, and wrists, they learn to perform more complex fine-motor tasks such as tying shoes and drawing or writing.

3. **Perceptual-motor development** involves children using their senses to take in information about objects in the environment and then using this information to coordinate their movements. Information collected by the senses helps determine how the muscles of the body respond.

gross-motor development
Physical skills related to moving the whole body or major parts of the body.

fine-motor development
Physical skills related to the small muscles found in individual body parts, especially those in the hands and feet.

perceptual-motor development
Occurs when children use their senses to take in information about objects in the environment and use this information to coordinate their movements.

Characteristics of Physical Development

Although individual differences exist, three general principles of muscle development apply:

1. In general, the *direction* of muscle development is from the top of the head to the tips of the toes. Babies learn to lift their heads before they can raise their torsos and use their arms before they can stand with, and then without, support.

2. The *sequence* of muscle development begins with those closest to the center of the body and progresses to those in the extremities—the hands and feet. Most children learn to crawl before they can pick up objects using the thumb and forefinger, called the **pincer grasp**. Thus, children refine their gross-motor movements, such as those used to walk or throw a ball, before they can control the fine-motor skills used to zip a jacket or turn the pages of a book.

3. The *process* of physical development is a result of experience—the opportunities children have to explore, practice, refine, and increasingly coordinate those motor movements that drive physical development.

pincer grasp Grasp used to pick up objects with the thumb and forefinger.

As children learn to roll over, sit, stand, walk, and run, the impact of free exploration and practice is clear in gross-motor skill acquisition. In addition, adult guidance and, sometimes, direct teaching stimulate physical development, as when children learn to swim, balance on a beam, or throw a basketball through the hoop. The direction, sequence, and process of physical development are not the same for all children, especially for those with disabilities. However, relatively predictable, though not rigid, sequences exist in each of these areas of motor development, as we see in the next section.

 Check Your Understanding 15.1

The Continuum of Physical Development

During the first three years of life, the pace of physical development is staggering: children go from newborn helplessness to competence in controlling their own bodies in space and coordinating their arm, hand, and finger movements. The pace slows down somewhat during the preschool years as children gain greater control over these skills. During the primary years, children develop increasing coordination of their arms and legs as well as better control and refinement of skills.

Phases of Motor Development

The four broad phases of motor development from infancy to age 8 (Gallahue, Ozmun, & Goodway, 2012) are presented in Table 15.1. Although the sequence of motor skill acquisition is similar in typically developing children, the age range varies considerably. For example, children learn to skip between 5 and 7 years of age (Gallahue et al., 2012). As children get older, individual differences increase because children have such widely varying opportunities to participate in physical activities—for instance, while one child constantly watches television, another child may ski and swim regularly.

These phases and related skills constitute the goals of the physical education curriculum. From ages 2 to 7, the goal is for children to develop and refine the following fundamental movement skills (Goodway, Ozmun, & Gallahue, 2013):

- **Locomotor movements**, through which the body proceeds in a horizontal or vertical direction from one place to another, such as walking, running, leaping, or jumping.
- **Gross-motor manipulative movements**, through which the body gives or receives force from objects such as throwing, catching, or kicking.
- **Stability movements**, in which the body remains in place but moves around its horizontal or vertical axis, such as balancing, dodging, starting, and stopping.

In the sections that follow, we present the typical expectations for gross-, fine-, and perceptual-motor development and explain how teachers can foster development in each area.

locomotor movements Movements that allow the body to proceed in a horizontal or vertical direction from one place to another, such as walking, running, leaping, or jumping.

gross-motor manipulative movements Large muscle movements involving giving or receiving force from objects, such as throwing, catching, or kicking.

stability movements Movements in which the body remains in place but moves around its horizontal or vertical axis, such as balancing, dodging, starting, and stopping.

Gross-Motor Development

Even though physical development is strongly influenced by biological growth, teachers need to be intentional in promoting children's physical development. The *Developmental Continuum: Gross-Motor Skills from Birth through Age 8* feature describes gross-motor skill acquisition for children from birth through age 8.

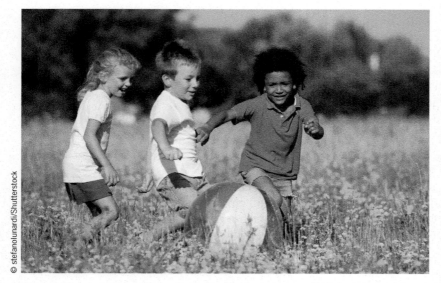

When children's motor skills develop optimally, they are more likely to enjoy and engage in physical activity. Fun outdoor play and physical activity can build children's health and fitness and fight today's childhood obesity crisis.

TABLE 15.1   Phases of Motor Development

Motor skill development follows a predictable sequence, as described in this table, but a wide range of variation exists in the ages when individual children acquire these skills.

Typical Age	Movement Phase	Movement Characteristics
Infants—birth to age 1	Reflexive movement phase	Babies gradually replace inborn reflexive movements such as sucking with more voluntary movements.
Toddlers—to age 2	Rudimentary movement phase	As infants become toddlers, they gain more control over their bodies as characterized by grasping, sitting, standing, and walking.
From ages 2 to 7	Fundamental movement phase	During this phase, children master most of the locomotor skills of walking, running, jumping, hopping, galloping, and skipping.
Begins about age 7 and continues to adolescence	Specialized movement phase	Children combine fundamental movements with other skills to develop coordinated, specialized skills such as running and kicking a soccer ball.

Source: Based on *J.D. Goodway, J.C. Ozmun, & D.L. Gallahue,* 2013. Motor development in young children, in O.N. Saracho & B. Spodek (Eds.), Handbook of research on the education of young children, 88-101. New York: Routledge.

Developmental Continuum
Gross-Motor Skills from Birth through Age 8

Approximate Age	Widely Held Expectations
Infants (Birth to 12 months)	• Gradually gain control over reflexes • Excitedly wave arms and legs • Lift head when on tummy • Sit with support • Roll over • Sit without support • Move around by crawling, scooting, or creeping • Stand with help • Cruise by holding furniture • By first birthday, stand without support and may start to walk
Toddlers (About 12 to 36 months)	• Walk on their own • Like to pull and carry toys while walking • Run awkwardly • Climb stairs one at a time by about 18 months • Eager to explore world • Delight in jumping, marching, walking backward, propelling a riding toy with their feet • Love to run but can't control stopping and turning • Throw a ball a short way • By age 3, run and jump with control • Pedal a tricycle
Preschoolers and Kindergartners (Age 3 to 6)	• Gradually increase control and refinement of fundamental motor skills • Walk up and down stairs alternating feet without support • Balance on one foot for several seconds, walk on a balance beam • Master fundamental motor skills including walking, running, hopping, galloping • Increasingly able to coordinate hands and arms to roll, throw, catch (traps object against body), and kick a ball
Primary Grades (Ages 6 to 9)	• By age 7, skip easily • Coordinate fundamental motor skills into skills needed to play organized games and sports • Jump and catch a ball, kick a ball while running • Jump rope • Perform motor skills in adult-like manner

Sources: Based on *J.D. Goodway, J.C. Ozmun, & D.L. Gallahue,* 2013. Motor development in young children, in O.N. Saracho & B. Spodek (Eds.), Handbook of research on the education of young children, 88-101. New York: Routledge.

Gross-Motor Development from Birth to Age 3 Remarkable physical change happens to babies during the first year or so of life. During infancy, babies learn to control and lift their heads and turn from side to side. Next, they roll from back to side, then front to side, and then completely over. This ability to change position is followed fairly rapidly by scooting, sitting, crawling, pulling to a stand, and walking with support.

Between 14 months and the second birthday, toddlers typically perfect walking without support and learn to squat down and stand back up, carry large objects, and sweep things off of tables and shelves. Twos are quite good at dumping out containers of toys and materials, propelling riding toys with their feet, walking tentatively up stairs one foot at a time, and carrying large objects from one place to another.

As toddlers continue to explore the world and begin to mimic the gross-motor behaviors of older children and adults, their actions become more purposeful. Two-year-old Chad is helped out of his car seat by his mother and stands by the car as she hands him his diaper bag. He puts it on his shoulder, bending his body sideways and raising his arm high in the air to keep it on his shoulder. This awkward position barely keeps the bag from dragging on the ground as he takes his mother's hand and walks toward his child care center. When his mother offers to carry it, he says emphatically, "No, my bag!" and toddles off.

Fostering gross-motor development during this stage is often about getting out of the way! During this period, most children have a built-in drive to master and move on. Creating safe and well-supervised opportunities to continue gross-motor practice is the primary task for teachers of babies and toddlers.

It is also important to remember that cultural groups differ in their views of appropriate child-rearing practices; therefore, infants' and toddlers' gross-motor experiences will vary among diverse cultural groups. For examples of diverse cultural practices that impact gross-motor development, read the *Culture Lens: Cultural Influences on Gross Motor Movement and Development* feature.

Gross-Motor Development in Preschoolers and Kindergartners Gross-motor play continues to be important during the preschool and kindergarten years. Children during this period need physical activity throughout the day to maintain their focus and on-task behavior during the more structured parts of the school day. By age 3, children learn to climb stairs, walking up and down, as well as how to alternate feet as they climb. Preschoolers get better at running, pedaling a tricycle, and jumping up and down on both feet. Endurance increases, although younger children still fatigue easily. Coordination and balance improve as kindergartners learn to jump rope, hop on one foot, and skip. An increasing awareness of their own skills and abilities leads to better understanding of unsafe behaviors; however, children can still lose control and become overexcited or unable to manage during large-group activities.

motor planning The ability of the brain to conceive, organize, and carry out a series of unfamiliar actions.

The ability of the brain to conceive, organize, and carry out a series of unfamiliar actions is called **motor planning** and takes center stage as children work to gain control over their growing bodies. For example, 2½-year-old Lena tries to catch a ball by extending her arms. She knows what should happen, yet ends up with the ball bouncing off. By contrast, 4-year-old Derek moves his body so he can enclose the ball in his arms. Finally, kindergartner Julianne moves her body around so she can catch the ball between her hands with no assistance from her forearms.

The primary goal of the curriculum for preschoolers and kindergartners is to help them make progress on fundamental motor skills. In acquiring physical skills, competence leads to confidence and further persistence, so success matters. Therefore, it is important for teachers to intentionally teach fundamental motor skills, just as Ms. Perez did with Allison at the beginning of this chapter. Intentional teachers provide encouragement, coaching, and modification of the toys and materials to increase the chances of

© Rawpixel.com/Shutterstock

Culture Lens

Cultural Influences on Gross-Motor Movement and Development

Children's physical development is strongly influenced by biology, and yet cultural experience plays a key role. Consider two very different approaches to infant caregiving and their effects on babies' motor development.

The Pikler Institute located in Budapest, Hungary (previously an orphanage), was founded after World War II to serve children left without families. Dr. Emmi Pikler created a program for children from birth through age 3 that focuses on freedom of movement, which means that babies are not put in positions that they cannot get into on their own. For example, they aren't placed in restrictive devices such as infant seats, high chairs, jumpers, or walkers. They lie on their backs, awake or asleep, until they are able to roll over by themselves and move into different positions. In general, adults do not to interfere with children's movement.

Allowing infants to move freely results in remarkable competence, balance, coordination, and calculated risk-taking. Visitors to the Pikler Institute are impressed with the ease and confidence with which very young children move their bodies. The children have impressive equilibrium and their body awareness is far above average. In addition, there is a very low accident rate at the Institute. Freedom of movement promotes gross-motor development as well as a strong sense of competence within babies who find out that they can move and learn on their own without the assistance of an adult.

Magda Gerber, a major leader in the field of infant-toddler development, introduced the Pikler philosophy to the United States by founding Resources for Infant Educarers (RIE) in the 1980s. The basis of the RIE approach is respect for babies and toddlers—treating them as human beings in an authentic way. Parents and caregivers demonstrate respect by trusting in children's competence to explore and initiate learning, providing just enough help as needed. Gerber stated that RIE is a cultural approach to child-rearing that would not fit all cultural contexts.

Contrast the Pikler and RIE approach to the child-rearing practice of the Au people of Papua, New Guinea. Anthropologist David Tracer has documented that during the first 12 months of life, Au babies are carried by their mothers or siblings 86% of the time. When they are put down, they are usually placed in a sitting position, not on their stomachs. Instead of crawling, Au babies go through a "scooting" phase—pushing themselves along with their hands and scooting on their backsides. Au parents discourage crawling to reduce the risk of their babies contracting disease. Their babies do not crawl; they learn to walk, although a few months later than children in the United States and Europe.

These examples and countless others demonstrate how cultural practices influence children's development—even their physical development—which is so dependent on biology and maturation. Consider how these approaches compare to the expectations for babies' freedom of movement in your own cultural group.

Sources: M. Gerber, 1998, "RIE Basic Principles," Retrieved from https://www.rie.org/educaring/ries-basic-principles; J. Gonzalez-Mena, E. Chahin, and L. Briley, 2005, "The Pikler Institute: A Unique Approach to Caring for Children," 2005, *Exchange, 166*, 49–51; National Science Foundation Discoveries, 2004, "Will Baby Crawl?" Retrieved from http://www.nsf.gov/discoveries/disc_summ.jsp?cntn_id=103153&org=NSF.

successful skill learning. They offer cues about how to perform specific skills, such as suggesting that children widen their stance to increase stability while bending forward. They also challenge children to extend, hold, or repeat skills as they practice, or they may add a challenge such as "Recite a poem while balancing on one foot." Table 15.2 describes effective strategies and examples of how teachers can promote gross-motor development in children from birth to kindergarten.

Inclusion of children with disabilities requires that they participate as fully as possible in all activities. Embedding interventions in the regular classroom day is an excellent way to meet the needs of all children during one activity. For example, Caden, a 2-year-old with severe disabilities, cannot roll over on his own. His physical therapist works with him on the floor, gently rolling his body from side to side. To the other

TABLE 15.2   Effective Strategies: Gross-Motor Skills from Birth through Age 5

Intentional teachers use effective strategies such as these to support children's gross-motor development, which is not an automatic process.

Teaching Strategy	Examples
Respond to babies and take delight in their motor skills.	Smile and laugh as babies kick their legs over and over. Provide constant supervision and a safe environment (e.g., no objects that might be swallowed).
Give babies opportunities to control their own bodies without restraint or external support.	Avoid the use of infant seats, swings, playpens, and other equipment that restricts movements or limits explorations and repetition.
Give babies places and spaces to explore in a safe environment.	Provide floor time ("tummy time" for non-crawlers) with a clean carpet or blanket on the floor.
For toddlers, provide sufficient space and low indoor climbing equipment for them to practice new skills.	Pay particular attention to children's safety as they explore and take risks.
Include periods of time for uninterrupted gross-motor play.	Organize the classroom to provide sufficient indoor space so that children can move without getting in each other's way.
Provide active outdoor play.	Provide space and time for children to freely engage in unstructured play and physical activity such as running, climbing, digging, and tricycle riding.
Plan structured opportunities to build and practice gross-motor skills indoors.	Act out the movements to songs, rhymes, chants, and finger plays.
Provide gross-motor opportunities that use a range of different skills and combine skills in novel and interesting ways.	Set up an obstacle course or play a game such as having children move to music and freeze their bodies in place when the music stops.
Use a variety of developmentally appropriate toys and materials.	Supply balance beams, ladders, large wooden and plastic blocks, jump ropes, balls, floor puzzles, push carts, tumbling mats, scooter boards, and so forth.
Provide structured play experiences that help children build and practice fundamental motor skills.	Engage children in activities such as rolling balls, bowling, tossing bean bags into baskets, climbing stairs, or tumbling on mats. Have children play games using hula hoops, streamers, parachutes, or beach balls. Have them participate in music activities such as marching to the beat of a musical selection.
Use motor movements during routines and transitions.	Have children waddle like a duck or jump like a frog to get from the classroom to the cafeteria.
Integrate movement with other curriculum topics such as literacy or music.	Select action-oriented books to read to children and then add movements to the stories (e.g., *Dinosaur Roar!*).
Consciously choose, adapt, and use materials to ensure maximum participation by all children, including children with disabilities.	Provide equal encouragement to boys and girls. If children have difficulty with materials, adapt them by adding handles, buttons, or knobs; prevent slipping with Velcro or mats. Simplify the task by limiting the range of difficulty; by adding sensory cues such as color, sound, textures, or scents; or by encouraging cooperation among children who can do the gross-motor activities and those who cannot.

Sources: Based on K. Albrecht & L.G. Miller, 2004. Innovations: The comprehensive preschool curriculum. Beltsville, MD: Gryphon House; H. B. Tomlinson & M. Hyson, 2009. Developmentally Appropriate Practice in the Preschool Years—Ages 3–5: An Overview, in C. Copple & S. Bredekamp (Eds.), Developmentally Appropriate Practice in Early Childhood Programs Serving Children from Birth through Age 8, revised edition, 111–148. Washington, DC: NAEYC.

children in the class, this looks like great fun, and soon five other children are rolling on the floor and laughing along with Caden.

Gross-Motor Development in the Primary Grades During the primary grades, children practice and perfect a wide range of gross-motor skills, often connected to their interests. They have high energy levels and rarely show physical fatigue. Interest in group games increases as children are able to coordinate more than one gross-motor activity at a time, such as hitting a pitched ball. They

TABLE 15.3 Effective Strategies: Gross-Motor Skills in the Primary Grades	
The structure of elementary schools may make it difficult to support children's gross-motor development so teachers must use multiple strategies such as those illustrated here.	
Teaching Strategy	**Examples**
Arrange the classroom to allow for movement activities.	Arrange desks or tables to provide room for calisthenics and movement accompanied by music.
Plan breaks throughout the day for physical exercise and stress relief.	Have children stand, stretch, do motor mirroring (pairs of children mirror each other's movements), or move from place to place.
Integrate motor skill learning and practice into other areas of the curriculum.	Have children act out rhymes and stories, dance, repeat rhythms, express emotions with the entire body, play charades, and pantomime stories.
Offer opportunities for children to create, modify, and play group games and child-initiated team sports.	Encourage children to choose and participate in noncompetitive games such as hopscotch, jump rope, parachute games, hula hooping, and playing tag and games such as Red Light/Green Light.
Plan activities in which everyone has a chance to participate as opposed to organized sports where only the best players make the team and get to play.	Because of primary-grade children's growing inclination to compare themselves with others, avoid competitive activities. Instead, help children compete with their own prior performances rather than those of other children ("Last time you hit the target only once. Today you hit it three times").
Collaborate with physical education, music, and fine arts specialists to make sure that children have opportunities for motor-skill learning every day.	At the elementary level, teachers are not likely to be in control of physical education activities, but they can work with other professionals to ensure that children have many rich opportunities to learn and practice motor skills throughout the school day.

Source: Based on H. B. Tomlinson, 2009b. Developmentally appropriate practice in the primary grades—ages 6–8: An overview, in C. Copple & S. Bredekamp (Eds.), Developmentally appropriate practice in early childhood programs serving children from birth through age 8, revised edition, 257–288. Washington, DC: NAEYC.

can coordinate the movements required for dancing, skating, bike riding, swimming, and playing games such as soccer, basketball, and volleyball. As they practice using motor, balancing, and manipulative skills, they become increasingly competent and coordinated, often perfecting the skills needed to participate successfully in a wide range of games and sports. Table 15.3 lists strategies and examples of how teachers can promote gross-motor development in the primary grades.

Because the primary-grade day is so full, one of the best strategies is to integrate physical education with other subject areas. For example, one elementary school has periodic field days during which children move from station to station using different muscles and skills such as rope climbing or bike riding that are fun but challenging. To link to the broader curriculum, the children take photos and write about the experience. As is evident in Figure 15.1, one second-grader had a great time.

Importance of Recess Because motor skill development is closely tied to opportunity, recess is not a luxury for children in the primary grades (American Academy of Pediatrics, 2013). As the pressure to improve scores on standardized tests has increased, as many as 40% of elementary schools have severely limited or eliminated recess (Robert Wood Johnson Foundation, 2010). This trend is troubling and potentially damaging to children's academic achievement—opposite of the desired effect (Goodway, Ozmun, Derringer, & Lee, 2013). Only 16% of states require that schools provide recess, leading parents in many states to lobby legislators on behalf of their children (Reilley, 2017). One mother explains that her children came home in tears because the day was so long and they had no time to play.

Video Example 15.2:

Gross-Motor Development in Preschoolers

The two children in this video are playing together outdoors. They have been friends for a long time. In what ways is their motor development typical for children of this age? What, if any, differences in gross motor development do you observe between them?

Yahoo, yahoo, Today is feild day. Their was 11 stashens. stashen was the My favorit inflatubles. The bikes where really fun too acshuly their all fun I got to be owt side all morning. I got nine pickers taken of me.

FIGURE 15.1 Second Grader's Field Day Story This second grader's documentation of her field day experience illustrates how gross-motor experiences can be incorporated into the school day and link to other areas of the curriculum such as literacy.
Source: Second Grader.

A large body of research demonstrates the educational, social, and physical benefits of recess (American Academy of Pediatrics, 2013). Playful breaks maximize children's ability to perform higher-level cognitive tasks and improve social competence, adjustment to school, and physical health. In a study of almost 11,000 third-graders, children who had at least 15 minutes of daily recess behaved more positively than those who didn't (Barros, Silver, & Stein, 2009). And children of color from low-income families in urban areas were less likely to have recess—the very children who may need it most. Ironically, eliminating recess is the strategy schools often use to try to close the achievement gap for this same group of children (Goodway, Ozmun, Derringer, & Lee, 2013).

Some think that recess interferes with children's attention spans, but the opposite is true; research finds that in kindergarten and primary grades, children are more inattentive before than after recess (American Academy of Pediatrics, 2013). Recess increases the amount of time children stay on task and reduces fidgeting (Jarrett et al., 1998). Furthermore, because children in the primary grades have more advanced gross-motor skills and can play games with rules, many enjoy learning how to play sports with their classmates.

Read the *Promoting Play* feature to learn how one teaching team introduced sports to their second-grade class.

fine-motor manipulative movements Control, precision, and accuracy of small muscle movement.

Fine-Motor Development

The term **fine-motor manipulative movement** refers to control, precision, and accuracy of small muscle movement, such as those inherent in picking up objects with the thumb and forefinger, tying shoes, cutting with scissors, or using a keyboard. Fine-motor skills allow children to explore how things work, get dressed, use writing tools, put puzzles together, prepare snacks and meals, and engage in many more activities that require hand, finger, and wrist movements. Strength, control, and coordination of hand, finger, and wrist movements are part of fine-motor development. Strength is needed to cut

© Jules Selmes/Pearson Education

Children need a lot of practice to master fine-motor skills and eye-hand coordination.

Promoting Play

Teaching Sports Skills in Primary Grades

While observing children on the playground in fall, second-grade teachers Alex and Mel noticed that children were beginning to put teams together and play "sports." They watched as children put together a soccer game, which rapidly devolved into arguments about rules and all abandoning the game. Alex and Mel recognized that primary-school children enjoy games with rules, and that the gross-motor play during recess would help their learning and development. But they also realized that the children needed support with playing more complex games. At class meeting the next Monday, they surveyed children about their interest in sports, asking which ones children liked most and would like to learn to play. The children voted for soccer, and agreed they would like to learn to play baseball (whiffle ball) in spring.

Using visuals and clips of soccer from YouTube, Alex and Mel introduced soccer during large-group time—especially for children who were not familiar with the game from family and friends. They were sure to explain that these professional soccer players were so skilled because of years of practice. Focusing on the skills used in soccer, Mel and Alex developed a series of games around kicking balls, kicking while running, and aiming at a target. They provided many balls and used cones to mark places on the playground to run around and kick through. For the last 10–15 minutes of every 45-minute lunch recess, they helped the children play a short game of soccer. They organized the children's teams daily, making sure to mix up the team membership. Mel and Alex emphasized teamwork with the children—assists in scoring were celebrated as much as the scoring.

The children's skills grew, and Mel and Alex began to teach the children more of the rules, and higher-level skills, such as passing the ball. In addition to their growing gross-motor skills, the teachers noticed that children began to develop more confidence in their interactions. They negotiated in their other areas of play, and got along better with children in general. Over the course of the fall, Mel and Alex were less needed during the soccer games and were available to support disputes and made certain that all children had equal opportunities to play. Not all children played soccer every day—some children preferred sports more than others. But children who did play benefited in important ways. Alex and Mel looked forward to the spring, when they would teach whiffle ball, which would help children learn different skills and rules.

---

with scissors; control allows for buttoning and zipping; coordination is used to put together puzzles and thread beads on laces.

Fine-motor skills are connected to healthy brain development. When the small muscles of the body move, brain circuitry is stimulated and strengthened, and the coordination between neurons and between the parts of the brain improves (Levitt, 2008). As children repeat fine-motor skills, such as stringing beads, working with clay, and putting pegs in pegboards, they not only refine these skills but also improve brain connections. In fact, a study of thousands of children from birth to kindergarten found that fine-motor skills in preschool are a strong predictor of later achievement (Grissmer, Grimm, Aiyer, Murrah, & Steele, 2010).

Fine-motor development progresses slowly as individual children experience different degrees of difficulty in performing fine-motor tasks. Children often encounter failure and become frustrated as they try to master these difficult skills; consequently, they need adequate time and adult support to keep them interested enough to practice. Read the *Developmental Continuum: Fone-Motor Skills from Birth through Age 8* feature for a description of fine-motor skill acquisition in children from birth through the primary grades.

Developmental Continuum
Fine-Motor Skills from Birth through Age 8

Approximate Age	Widely Held Expectations
Birth to about 9 months	Small muscles respond reflexively in newborns (automatically grasp object) Reach for and grab objects with hands, hold rattle Gradually gain control in grasping and explore objects (often mouths them)
About 9 to 18 months	May use pincer grasp (thumb and forefinger) to pick up objects Gain control in exploring and manipulating objects Use both hands, may show preference for one hand May undress self, untie shoes, begin to feed self Scribbles with crayons
About 18 to 36 months	Can hold utensils and feed self (with spills) Dress self with loose clothing, except for buttons and shoelaces Does three- to five-piece puzzle Scribble, paint, and draw making recognizable lines and shapes
3- and 4-year-olds	Gain more control over fine muscles Build complex patterns and structures using interlocking pieces such as LEGO blocks, pegboards, puzzles, beads Increasingly able to take care of own needs including hand washing, toileting, feeding, and dressing (may unbutton and unzip) Can use scissors, glue, collage materials
5- and 6-year-olds	Increasingly skilled in drawing and writing Hold pencil with fingertips Demonstrate handedness Eye-hand coordination increases Dress independently, tie shoes Use a fork and knife
7- and 8-year-olds	Independently use fine-motor skills to accomplish tasks and goals Control handwriting, begin cursive writing Use keyboard easily Use tools such as saw, hammer, and nails successfully

Sources: Based on C. Copple & S. Bredekamp, with J. Gonzalez-Mena, 2011. Basics of developmentally appropriate practice: An introduction for teachers of infants and toddlers. Washington, DC: NAEYC; C. Copple & S. Bredekamp (Eds.), 2006. Basics of developmentally appropriate practice: An introduction for teachers of children 3 to 6. Washington, DC: NAEYC.

Fine-Motor Development from Birth to Age 3 Babies spend the first year of life working on grasping objects and tracking movements with their eyes and heads. They perfect picking up objects with their whole hand, pointing, putting objects into containers, and drinking from a cup.

Toddlers begin to use a spoon to eat, turn pages, stack blocks, scribble with crayons or markers, hold drinking cups, and remove clothing. By age 2, they are able to remove shoes and some clothing, hold a cup or glass in one hand, unbutton large buttons, turn doorknobs, stack small blocks, fit large pegs in pegboards, pour and fill containers at a sensory table, unzip large zippers, and begin to show a preference for one hand. Toward the end of toddlerhood, children tackle toileting, which involves many motor skills such as pulling underwear down and up and controlling the small muscles that hold and release bodily functions. Table 15.4 provides examples of ways teachers can promote fine-motor skills in very young children.

Fine-Motor Development in Preschoolers and Kindergartners By age 3, children usually exhibit a preference for one hand (although they don't know left from right) and can complete puzzles, string beads, put pegs in pegboards, easily turn the pages of a book, grasp a pencil or marker (though not always with an adult-like grip), and draw and write with crayons and markers. Four- and five-year-olds complete board and floor puzzles; draw recognizable images; copy shapes, letters, and numbers; cut with scissors; button their clothes; and pour from a pitcher into a glass.

Many preschoolers and most kindergartners print letters recognizably, disassemble and reassemble manipulative constructions, use scissors to accomplish desired tasks, hit nails with a hammer head, and use a keyboard and mouse with age-appropriate computer programs. By age 5, children's drawings are more detailed and they may be able to tie their own shoes. When children's fine-motor skills are well developed and practiced, their creativity can take off. Five-year-old Sandi loves creating things using items from her family's recycling box and a non-hot glue gun. By contrast, her twin sister, Ella, has little interest in doing the same kind of projects.

Gender differences in motor skills are evident in this period. In general, girls tend to be more advanced than boys in fine-motor skills and in gross-motor skills that require precision, whereas boys tend to do better with skills that require force and power (Berk, 2012). Therefore, teachers need to provide opportunities and encouragement for every

TABLE 15.4 Effective Strategies: Fine-Motor Skills in Infants and Toddlers

Providing developmentally appropriate materials and lots of supervised play, as exemplified here, are excellent ways to promote fine-motor development in infants and toddlers.

Teaching Strategy	Examples
Give babies and toddlers many opportunities to explore objects, people, and things using the muscles necessary for reaching, grasping, pulling, picking up, chewing, holding, and letting go.	Play interactive games like peek-a-boo; look at picture books, particularly books with textures, sounds, and actions to imitate; display images that are interesting from a baby's or toddler's perspective, taking into account that very young infants are usually looking up from their backs at the world.
Provide developmentally appropriate toys such as action/reaction toys that help children connect cause and effect as well as stimulate fine-motor skills.	Provide appropriate toys that make noise and respond to the child's manipulation in interesting ways such as rattles, teethers, toys to stack and sort, pull toys, soft blocks, and toys that pop up or roll away. Children who aren't mobile like play mats with objects to kick or reach for; toddlers can do puzzles with a few separate pieces, stack blocks, and roll wheeled toys.
Provide developmentally appropriate equipment.	Provide eating utensils for children in graduated sizes and complexity to provide incremental motor practice using the small muscles of the fingers and the hand; e.g., spoons, then forks; bowls, then plates.
Provide age-appropriate materials. Ensure that most fine-motor toys and materials are easy to clean and sanitize and large enough that they do not present a choking hazard.	Babies put almost everything into their mouths—as they use the sense of touch, taste, and smell to gather information about the object with which they are playing. Toddlers like to tear paper, pull things off of shelves, dump toys out of containers, and play with miniatures such as interconnecting blocks. Banging and clapping are great fun, as is playing with sand, water, and playdough.
Provide art materials such as large crayons, watercolor markers, and a variety of sizes and types of paper.	Let children explore materials. Be realistic about the amount of mess.

Sources: Based on K. Albrecht & L.G. Miller, 2000a. Innovations: The comprehensive infant curriculum. Beltsville, MD: Gryphon House; K. Albrecht & L.G. Miller, 2000b. Innovations: The comprehensive toddler curriculum. Beltsville, MD: Gryphon House; K. Albrecht & L.G. Miller, 2000b. Innovations: Infant and toddler development. Beltsville, MD: Gryphon House.

TABLE 15.5 Effective Strategies: Fine-Motor Skills in Preschool and Kindergarten	
During preschool and kindergarten, children's fine-motor skills become more refined if teachers provide developmentally appropriate materials and experiences such as these.	
Teaching Strategy	**Examples**
Provide a range of materials and activities for children.	Use materials and activities in which children with different levels of fine-motor skills can participate with success, such as puzzles with different numbers of pieces and more or less complexity.
Provide appropriate toys and materials.	Supply objects to sort, count, and put into patterns; pegboards and beads to string; clothing and other items that zip and button for dress-up play; a variety of drawing and writing tools and paper; scissors, paint, and clay.
Offer opportunities to practice functional skills.	Allow children to pour milk, hammer nails, and use other tools. These activities may require accommodation or modification for all children to use them successfully or when materials cause frustration or fatigue.
Provide open-ended activities that enable children to practice fine-motor skills. Choose activities that fit their current level of competence as well as those that are more challenging yet within reach.	Arrange for open-ended experiences such as drawing and painting, working with playdough or clay, building with blocks, and constructing with DUPLO and LEGO blocks and other interconnecting blocks.

Sources: Based on K. Albrecht & L.G. Miller, 2004. Innovations: The comprehensive preschool curriculum. Beltsville, MD: Gryphon House; C. Copple & S. Bredekamp (Eds.), 2006. Basics of developmentally appropriate practice: An introduction for teachers of children 3 to 6. Washington, DC: NAEYC.

Video Example 15.3:

Fine Motor Skills

In this video, children are working in an ideally equipped art center. What fine motor skills are they developing? How do creative art materials support fine motor development?

child to acquire these skills. Table 15.5 presents ways to help preschoolers and kindergartners master fine-motor skills.

When fine-motor experiences lead to frustration and fatigue or when children prefer gross-motor activities, they need encouragement and support and sometimes instruction in skills or models of what to try next. Teachers need to carefully observe children to be sure they are ready to tackle the next challenge.

Fine-Motor Development in the Primary Grades Fine-motor development in primary-grade children is all about refinement. Writing, drawing, and keyboard skills are more precise. By second grade, wrist, hand, and finger muscles are more coordinated, writing becomes more uniform, and drawing skills include detail and display early attempts at perspective. Primary-age children master the ability to coordinate movements: They can cut with scissors while turning the paper to make arches, angles, borders, and other cutouts. They enjoy working on projects or crafts over time and, rather than finish an activity in one session, they will return repeatedly to it if it interests them.

In general, during this time, girls are ahead of boys in fine-motor development (Haywood & Gretchell, 2005). However, gender differences are at least partially the result of differences in practice opportunities, with boys and girls developing at a similar pace given similar opportunities (Craig & Baucum, 2002). This research highlights the importance of providing equal opportunities to all children to develop physical skills.

Children in the primary grades like to use real things such as hammers and nails and scrap lumber rather than toys. They need instruction about how to use the tools but will often resist the offer of support until they have tried their own ideas. Teachers can draw on their interests, arranging for them to create friendship bracelets, birdhouses, or race cars. Six- to 8-year-olds will work for extended periods of time on projects, particularly if they result in "real" products.

Perceptual-Motor Development from Birth through Age 8 Perceptual-motor development plays an important role in learning fundamental movement skills. Perceptual-motor skills include auditory, visual, and tactile-kinesthetic skills as well as body awareness. Children develop these skills while using their senses to collect, monitor, interpret, and respond to information from the environment. As their ability to collect and use information improves, motor skills grow and develop, as we see in the following example.

Fourteen-month-old Tara sits on her teacher's lap with her finger in the air. Her teacher, Miss Laura, begins the finger play she knows Tara is asking her to say. She points to Tara's facial features gently as she repeats the rhyme: "Eye winker (touches one eyelid), tom tinker (then the other eyelid), nose smeller (touches the tip of her nose), mouth eater (points to her mouth), chin chopper (touches her chin), gully, gully, gully (gently tickles her neck)." Tara is already showing her teacher how she perceives input from her senses (the words she hears, the touch she feels) and combines them with her memory of previous times when the teacher played this game to anticipate what will happen next. Tara closes her eyes before they are touched, sticks her nose in the air as Laura says "nose smeller," and lowers her chin and laughs heartily in anticipation of the gentle tickle on her neck.

Perceptual-motor development is maturational—as attention to and perception of sensory information improves, subsequent motor coordination improves. This growth is largely dependent on the development of the brain and central nervous system, although the timing of such maturity varies. Perceptions of where the body is (spatial awareness), speeding up or slowing down a movement (temporal awareness), anticipating which way to go (directional awareness), and listening to verbal input or distinguishing between different sounds (auditory awareness) are all part of perceptual-motor development.

> **spatial awareness** Perceptions of where the body is.
>
> **temporal awareness** Speeding up or slowing down a movement.
>
> **directional awareness** Anticipating which way to go.
>
> **auditory awareness** Listening to verbal input or distinguishing between different sounds.

Perceptual-Motor Development in Babies and Toddlers Babies and toddlers learn through movement. As they move their arms, legs, and bodies, they encounter the world by touching it and being touched by it. They explore using all the senses, particularly touch and taste. Babies begin processing sensory information and trying to make sense of it, anticipating, for example, that pushing a button on a toy will produce a sound. They manipulate tools, such as spoons or a cup, and demonstrate a basic understanding of quantities of more or less.

Toddlers continue the exploration, now from an upright vantage point. They increasingly manipulate objects with a purpose, such as stacking blocks or lining up cars. They gather sensory data from watching others and imitate other children and adults.

Perceptual-Motor Development in Preschoolers and Kindergartners During the preschool and kindergarten years, the senses of sight, smell, touch, taste, and hearing are all well developed. Young children delight in exploring the world and preschool teachers often use the senses as an engaging curriculum topic.

However, in spite of their physical capacities for excellent sensation and perception, this age group's processing of the incoming information is not complete; children have yet to develop some of the cognitive strategies and language needed to make sense of all the information coming in through their senses. Children's ability to perceive patterns and discriminate various forms improves during the preschool years. Visually, preschool children are farsighted; they have trouble switching focus between close and distant targets and are still developing binocular vision (the ability of the eyes to work together), which necessitates larger print. Their depth perception is still developing and they tend to run into things and each other (Pica, 2006).

Preschoolers and kindergartners may make letter reversals (confusing the letters *q* and *p* or *d* and *b*), but this is not a perceptual problem. It is a natural confusion based on experience with objects in the physical world that have the same function regardless of their directional orientation—a chair is still a chair whether it is facing left or right.

Hearing is also well developed; this age group loves listening to music, stories, and conversations. They recognize rhyming words and play with the sounds of language. They perceive when two words sound the same or begin with the same sound (Schickedanz & Collins, 2013). If children do not participate or respond during these activities, it may be a sign of hearing problems due to chronic middle ear infections or other causes that should be evaluated by a physician.

Perceptual-Motor Development in the Primary Grades

Children in the primary grades have learned to use all the senses to influence their motor movements. As their ability to simultaneously take in sensory input and make modifications to their motor movements improves, so does motor coordination, balance, and timing. Increasingly, children are able to integrate previously acquired skills into more complex actions, particularly if they have had considerable practice.

Environments filled with interesting things to touch, smell, see, listen to, and manipulate provide sensory input for children to perceive and interpret. From birth to age 8, similar types of experiences promote perceptual-motor development, as listed in Table 15.6.

TABLE 15.6 Effective Strategies: Perceptual-Motor Development from Birth to Age 8

Intentional teachers use effective strategies such as these to promote perceptual-motor development in children from birth to age 8.

Teaching Strategy	Examples
Provide a variety of interesting sounds and rhythms to hear.	Use songs, rhymes, finger plays, and chants to provide interesting sounds and rhythms. Finger plays (such as "The Itsy, Bitsy Spider"), which require the coordination of the spoken word with hand or body movements, are good perceptual motor experiences for children ages 5 and under. Primary-age children often add hand and body movements to familiar songs, rhymes, and chants. Build auditory awareness by adding novel input such as the sounds of orchestra instruments or nature.
Stimulate visual acuity for all ages by providing interesting pictures and displays at children's eye level in the environment.	Provide visual stimulation for young children. Babies spend long periods of time gazing at things that interest them; toddlers and 2's will explore photographs and pictures. Have preschoolers, kindergartners, and primary-grade children examine pictures from a variety of sources, including the Internet and magazines, and use digital and video cameras to enhance visual awareness.
Offer a variety of textures and objects to feel, see, smell, and manipulate to provide sensory input for children to perceive and interpret.	Provide experiences that require children to use the senses independently, such as having them identify hidden objects by touch or various odors by smell. Also have them use the senses together to figure things out: They might smell the results of a cooking project and see food change form as it is cooked.
Help children explore space to build awareness of their body to learn about the parts of their bodies, to become aware of how much space their bodies take up, and to learn how to control their body as they move from one place to another.	Support perceptual-motor skills by giving children freedom to explore under tables and chairs and inside of cozy spaces. Balance the familiar perspective of not being as tall as adults with the unfamiliar perspective of being taller by encouraging children to visit the loft or use the climber.
Give children a variety of points of view within and beyond the classroom.	Provide multiple levels with raised platforms or use foam structures or pits. Peek-a-boo hideouts and windows into the next classroom are sources of visual and auditory stimuli, as are low windows that provide a view of the world beyond the classroom.
Provide experiences that promote visual, body, and directional awareness.	Use obstacle courses to build understanding of directions in space such as *under, over, around,* and *through*. Ask children to imitate body movements: move like an animal, insect, or amphibian. Have children use their body to make letters or numbers.

Sources: Based on K. Albrecht & L.G. Miller, 2004. Innovations: The comprehensive preschool curriculum. Beltsville, MD: Gryphon House; H. B. Tomlinson, Developmentally appropriate practice in the kindergarten year—ages 5–6: An overview, 187–216, and H. B. Tomlinson & M.L. Hyson, Appropriate practice in the preschool years—ages 3–5: An overview, 111–148, both in C. Copple & S. Bredekamp (Eds.), 2009, Developmentally appropriate practice in early childhood programs serving children from birth through age 8, revised edition. Washington, DC: NAEYC.

As children gain perceptual-motor skills and their body awareness increases, teachers can increase the level of difficulty and challenge of the tasks to help them refine these skills further. However, the most effective strategy is to provide experiences that support all areas of physical development at once, as described in the feature *Becoming an Intentional Teacher: Supporting Physical Development in Toddlers*. In the next section, we turn to the all-important contribution of play to children's physical fitness and health.

Becoming an Intentional Teacher

Supporting Physical Development in Toddlers

Here's What Happened   I have worked in an infant-toddler program for several years. I am now the teacher in a group of eight children who range in age from approximately 18 months to 3-year-olds. I have a few children who are just pulling themselves up, cruising by holding onto furniture, and walking on their own. Other children are developing fundamental motor skills including climbing, sliding down ramps, and running though in an uncontrolled way. All are developing perceptual-motor skills and body awareness.

In my classroom, there is a large open carpeted area for safe free play and exploration. Toddler-size furniture enables children to sit independently and reach the table to feed themselves finger food or begin to use utensils. A wooden climbing apparatus has three steps and a slide. There are windows to the outside at child-height and peek-a-boo windows into the hallway so children can see what else is going on in the center. The children love crawling in and out of the tunnel and over and under the other large-muscle equipment. Soft rubber mats invite them to tumble. They carefully climb into the low loft, which gives them more of a bird's-eye view of the classroom. We play lots of games to develop perceptual motor skills—moving like animals or singing.

Some parents seem to think that physical development is a competition among their children, comparing their children to others and bragging about how early they rolled over, sat up, or walked. One mother has begun to question why her son isn't walking as well as the other children. She wants me to hold her child's hands and "teach" him to walk and help him practice walking by putting him in a walker. A father is concerned that his daughter isn't climbing up the stairs yet.

Here's What I Was Thinking   The children in my group are naturally at various levels of physical development because of their individual differences. My philosophy is that providing them with lots of time for supervised free play and exploration in a carefully planned, safe environment is the best way to promote their perceptual and gross motor development. I believe that "baby walkers" and similar equipment deprive children of the joy of achieving major developmental accomplishments on their own. I explained to the parents that it is better to let children of this age develop physically with support and scaffolding but without too much adult interference. They need to accomplish as much as possible on their own. I also assured the families that I will continually assess the children's development to ensure that it is within the typical range.

Reflection   Do you agree with this teacher's approach? Does it reflect her own cultural perspective? What other ways could this teacher promote perceptual- and gross motor development in very young children?

✔ Check Your Understanding 15.2

 The Role of Play in Physical Development and Health

From our previous discussion of types of motor skill learning, we have seen that play is an essential context in which children acquire and practice physical abilities. Different types of play have different benefits and are developmentally appropriate for children at different age levels (Milteer, Ginsburg, & Council on Communications and Media Committee on Psychosocial Aspects of Child and Family Health, 2012). Here, we focus on the

rough-and-tumble play or big body play The boisterous, large-motor, physical activity children seem to crave.

critical roles of outdoor play and, particularly, rough-and-tumble or "big body" play, the "boisterous, large motor, physical activity children seem to crave" (Carlson, 2015; Huber, 2016). The outdoors is one of the most stimulating, engaging contexts for children's development and learning and for this type of play. However, current changes in children's lives threaten their exposure to nature, as described next.

Childhood Experiences with the Natural Environment

Richard Louv, in his book *Last Child in the Woods* (2005), chronicles changes in children's exposure, contact, and experience with the natural world and concludes that something important has been lost as children's time in natural environments has diminished. This concern is shared by many early childhood educators (Honig, 2015; Rivkin, 2014). As the late Jim Greenman, author of *Caring Spaces, Learning Places*, stated: "Children are losing habitat—the real world of people and nature and machines and an opportunity to explore that world (directly, not just electronically) and be a part of it" (Greenman, 2005b, p. 2).

nature-deficit disorder Hypothetical disorder related to lack of exposure and experience outdoors and in the natural world.

Address Nature Deficit   Louv (2005) proposes that children, families, and communities are experiencing "nature-deficit disorder." The hypothetical disorder describes the human costs of alienation from nature that include "diminished use of the senses, attention difficulties, and higher rates of physical and emotional illnesses" (Louv, 2005, p. 34). These concerns led to an examination of how outdoor environments are designed and constructed and to a movement toward more natural outdoor playgrounds (Keeler, 2008; Rivkin, 2014).

A growing trend among playground planners rejects the idea of playgrounds full of commercially purchased plastic, metal, or wood structures surrounded by safety zones filled with wood chips (Natural Learning Initiative, 2012). Instead, these planners favor environments that make creative use of natural features and objects while still meeting the health and safety standards required for children's outdoor playgrounds (see American Academy of Pediatrics, American Public Health Association, & National Resource Center for Health and Safety in Child Care and Early Education, 2011). They believe that playgrounds should have areas with trees, grass, shrubs, planters, pots, and paths to show children what the world is made of—the real stuff, not a plastic or simulated version (Rivkin, 2014).

Benefits of Natural Environments   Contact with nature has restorative powers for children. Nature buffers the impact of life stresses and lowers the incidence of behavior disorders, anxiety, and depression; children who play outside are sick less often and have a higher measure of self-worth (Rivkin, 2014). Exposure to nature has a calming effect that helps children focus attention. For example, children who play in natural environments show fewer symptoms of attention deficit/hyperactivity disorder (ADHD) than do children who play mostly with manufactured playground equipment (Torquati, Gabrie l, Jones-Branch, & Miller, 2011). Even a walk in the park can reduce symptoms of ADHD and improve concentration (Faber Taylor & Kuo, 2009).

The quality of children's experience is different when they play in natural environments; it is more diverse, imaginative, and creative. Such play fosters language and collaborative skills and stimulates social interaction between children (American Academy of Pediatrics, 2013). Children who play regularly in natural environments show more advanced motor fitness, including coordination, balance, and agility, and are better able to concentrate after contact with nature (Goodway, Ozmun, Derringer, & Lee, 2013).

Natural environments also build an understanding of science concepts and engage them in scientific inquiry (Meier & Sisk-Hilton, 2013). For those children experiencing developmental, psychological, or relational disorders, research suggests that their symptoms are relieved after contact with nature (Kuo, 2010; Taylor, Kuo, & Sullivan, 2001) and that bullying behavior is reduced by frequent play in natural environments (Malone & Tranter, 2003).

Outdoor Play Environments

Good outdoor environments have similar characteristics (Rivkin, 2014). Space is typically divided into defined areas for different kinds of activities. Areas are dedicated to motor activities such as:

- Climbing, sliding, and crawling
- Riding wheeled toys and transporting things
- Building and construction
- Gross-motor activities such as running, jumping, throwing, kicking, bouncing, and balancing
- A messy play area for sand and water play
- Places to pretend and for creative expression
- A gardening or digging area
- A place for swings and other dynamic equipment
- An area for art activities
- Places to watch, get away from it all, or slow down

Children today are more likely to spend time watching television or playing video games than experiencing active physical play outdoors. Children need both child-initiated free play and teacher-guided physical activity.

On playgrounds, climbing structures for children need to be sturdy and well anchored. But children also need equipment and materials that they can arrange in a variety of ways—providing experience with controlling the environment. Children like to rearrange crates, planks, boxes, blocks, and toys. They like tents, fabric scraps, and beach umbrellas to create places to climb into, under, or around.

Spacious settings equipped with age-appropriate toys, materials, and apparatus are also important for primary-grade children. Outdoor settings with hills, obstacle courses, softball diamonds, mazes, basketball hoops, tunnels, four-square and hopscotch grids, and volleyball nets are likely to interest children. Walking and running tracks, tether-ball poles, and plenty of movable parts such as planks, large blocks, and tree trunks and branches help children sustain gross-motor play. Additional materials, such as balls of all types (large and small playground balls, softballs, basketballs, soccer balls, sensory balls), parachutes, jump ropes, hoops, cones, and beanbags add variety and give children opportunities to practice a variety of physical skills.

Schools should have outdoor equipment such as balance beams that are low to the ground to encourage children to practice skills at their own level. Such equipment limits spills to tumbles instead of serious falls. Digging in the sand or soil is another great outdoor motor activity for children. Water added to dry sand and soil or placed in a water table adds interest as children explore these components of the natural world.

✓ Application Exercise 15.1

Outdoor Play Environments

When children are given ample time to play outdoors, they can practice and perfect many physical skills; they feel powerful and successful. For this reason, most children love the outdoors—it is a "can do" place. Yet the fast-paced activity of the outdoors can also be overstimulating and overwhelming for some. Children need quiet places to cool off, calm down, or rest; they also need water available to quench their thirst. A blanket in the shade can provide a place for children to spend some time with a teacher or friend, refueling and recharging before heading back out to explore the world again. Time outdoors provides a change of pace, freedom from being close to other children, and a constant source of interesting stimuli.

Many people worry that technology interferes with children's outdoor experiences. However, teachers can integrate technology goals and activities outdoors (Blagojevic & Thomes, 2014). While exploring the natural environment, children can use tablets to photograph and document nature-based art, and can research their discoveries online. They can document aspects of nature they find exciting or beautiful and integrate these into their writing projects back in the classroom.

Outdoor Environments for Children with Disabilities

Creating outdoor play environments and supporting participation in natural environments for children with disabilities can be complicated. Depending on their particular developmental challenges, children with disabilities often have motor delays and may have difficulty with balance and visual-motor tasks. Furthermore, they may need extra support in following directions and understanding and following safety guidelines. Teachers should plan carefully for accommodating the outdoor play needs of all children, and programs must ensure inclusive outdoor play spaces.

Universal design—creating materials and environments that are accessible to all—is one way programs can accommodate all children. For example, many programs use play surfaces such as wood chips or tire pieces. However, these surfaces are very difficult for children who move with a walker or wheelchair to navigate. Teachers must observe how children with and without disabilities access their current outdoor play space, and introduce materials and structures that allow children to participate more fully, including interacting with peers while playing.

The Value of Rough-and-Tumble Play

With childhood obesity hitting epidemic proportions, and academic pressure and technology leading to more sedentary lifestyles, early childhood educators call for greater awareness of the importance of "big body" play, where children literally use their whole bodies to run, jump, roll, climb, fall, tumble, somersault, and generally engage in vigorous, playful activity (Carlson, 2011). When such activity involves contact with another child, such as chasing, wrestling, tickling, rolling on top of each other, or play-fighting, it is usually called rough-and-tumble play.

Perhaps because there is so much emphasis today on protecting children, rough-and-tumble play has gotten a bad name. Some people interpret it as aggression or misbehavior and actually forbid it. However, there are important differences between fighting and other intentionally harmful acts and roughhousing—the goal of which is to have fun. I clearly remember rolling on the ground with my best friend in the yard one day and my mother calling from the front porch, "Are you playing or fighting?" "Playing!" we both hollered back immediately. The distinction, which children are well aware of and is easily observable, is that they are smiling, and they not only want to participate but they want to extend the play (Carlson, 2011). By contrast, fighting is something that most children obviously do not enjoy, would prefer to avoid, and want to stop.

As we've seen from discussing the research on active play, there are developmental benefits to rough-and-tumble play. Children practice and learn to control their bodies in space. They also learn self-regulation, social, and cognitive skills; to sustain the play, they have to take another person's point of view (a difficult cognitive skill) and read their friend's nonverbal cues. As long as Susie is smiling and giggling with her eyes shut, it's fine to continue, but as soon as she starts to frown, stare, and pull away, it's time to stop (Carlson, 2011).

Individual and cultural differences also exist in rough-and-tumble play. On average, boys are rougher and more physical in their play than girls are, and boys are more often disciplined by teachers (Goodway, Ozmun, & Gallahue, 2013). But girls need active play, too, and teachers could help by modeling actions such as hopping, jumping, skipping, and twirling games like ring around the rosie. Individual children may hold back from rough-and-tumble for many reasons, such as fear, shyness, or aversion to being touched. Cultural groups also play with children differently—some more gently than others. Teachers need to consider all of these factors in planning for and supporting rough-and-tumble play.

Given the benefits of rough-and-tumble play, however, teachers need to facilitate it in several ways. The class can establish a few clear rules such as keep hands below the neck, no pinching, no hitting, and stop when the other person says, "Stop!" (Carlson, 2011). Because big body play can easily turn into real fighting, supervision is critical (Carlson, 2015). Teachers need to make sure the environment where children play is safe and stay close by to supervise at all times, key elements of health and safety standards in early childhood programs, which we discuss in the next section.

✓ Check Your Understanding 15.3

🔺 Health and Safety Standards: The Teacher' Role

Children's success in school and life is integrally connected to their health. To protect young children, early childhood programs must comply with legally mandated health and safety regulations. In addition, teachers have a responsibility to keep children safe and prevent disease. In the sections that follow, we discuss ways of supporting children's health and wellness, and teaching practices that prevent illness and injury.

Adults must be vigilant to protect young children's health and safety. The American Academy of Pediatrics, American Public Health Association, and the National Resource Center for Health and Safety in Child Care and Early Education (2011) has established national model standards for programs. Keeping children safe requires adequate and attentive supervision during all activities and experiences, and providing safe, appropriate furniture, toys, and materials and systematic monitoring to keep them that way (Aronson, 2012).

By nature, children are messy beings. In the early childhood setting, this translates into the need to keep everything clean and sanitized so as to prevent the spread of germs. Adults who model keeping the environment clean teach children how to clean up after themselves. Disease prevention starts with pre-enrollment requirements such as immunization and physical checkups, and continues with instilling habits that will lead children to eat well, get adequate rest, and participate in plenty of vigorous exercise.

Emergency preparedness is another dimension of health and wellness. In schools, sheltering-in-place strategies and evacuation procedures and drills need to be understood by all and practiced until they become routine for adults as well as children (Head Start, 2015b). Natural disasters such as hurricanes, tornadoes, or earthquakes are prevalent in certain geographic areas and require specific disaster preparedness plans. In addition to natural disasters, our world today is threatened by terrorism and criminal behavior, and emergency preparedness must address these possibilities as well (Greenman, 2001). One difficult challenge facing teachers today is conducting newly required "active shooter" drills while at the same time supporting children's sense of security and emotional health. In these situations, warm, positive relationships between teachers and children become even more essential.

Prevent Illness

Preventing the spread of germs is an essential disease-prevention strategy for young children to learn. Most experts agree that the single most effective practice that prevents the spread of germs is proper hand washing by adults and children. Teachers can stop the

- Always use warm, running water and a mild, preferably liquid, soap. Antibacterial soaps may be used, but are not required.

- Wet the hands and apply a small amount (dime to quarter size) of liquid soap.

- Rub hands together vigorously until a soapy lather appears and continue for at least 15 seconds. Be sure to scrub between fingers, under fingernails, and around the tops and palms of the hands.

- Rinse hands under warm running water. Leave the water running while drying hands.

- Dry hands with a clean, disposable (or single use) towel, being careful to avoid touching the faucet handles or towel holder with clean hands.

- Turn the faucet off using the towel as a barrier between your hands and the faucet handle.

- Discard the used towel in a trash can, lined with a fluid-resistant (plastic) bag. Trash cans with foot-pedal operated lids are preferable.

- Consider using hand lotion to prevent chapping of hands. If using lotions, use liquids or tubes that can be squirted so that the hands do not have direct contact with container spout to avoid contaminating the lotion inside the container.

- When assisting a child in handwashing, either hold the child (if an infant) or have the child stand on a safety step at a height at which the child's hands can hang freely under the running water. Assist the child in performing all of the above steps and then wash your own hands.

FIGURE 15.2 Proper Hand-Washing Procedures The Centers for Disease Control and Prevention recommends the following steps as the most effective way to prevent illness in both adults and children.
Source: Centers for Disease Control and Prevention. (2018). *Wash your hands.* Atlanta, GA: U.S. Department of Health and Human Services. Retrieved August 17, 2018 from www.cdc.gov/washyourhands.

Video Example 15.4:

Teaching Proper Handwashing

This video explains how to teach children proper hand washing and its role in preventing the spread of illness in group programs. What other strategies could teachers use to ensure correct handwashing procedures and prevent illness?

spread of germs by washing their hands and teaching children correct hand-washing practices. NAEYC accreditation standards as well as state licensing standards require regular, systematic hand washing at specific times for adults and children, such as before and after eating, using the toilet, or diapering. Despite the critical importance of these procedures, these standards are among the least frequently met in early childhood programs. Hand washing that actually prevents the transfer of germs is a process with specific steps, as described in Figure 15.2.

Prevent Injury

When children are involved in active play, the role of the teacher is to provide constant attention and supervision. Teachers need to observe zones of the outdoor area and pay close attention to what children are doing so that they can intervene quickly, remind children of safety considerations, and be close enough to step in and stop risky behavior when it occurs.

Teachers also need to teach children about accident prevention, tricycle and bicycle safety, walking in traffic, and preparedness for emergencies. The majority of injuries that occur at school happen on the playground (CDC, 2012a). Nonfatal playground injuries are most often caused by falls. Children under age 4 are likely to suffer head and face injuries, whereas children ages 5 to 14 are likely to suffer injuries to the arms and hands, but head injuries, including concussions, are becoming more common as children play youth sports (CDC, 2012a)

Balance Risk and Challenge

In striving to protect children's safety and health, however, early childhood educators need to understand the impact of the amount of risk and challenge in the environment, what is called the risk vs. challenge continuum (Greenman, 2017). The concept is that extremes of either risk or challenge—too much or too little—are not in the best interest of children (Greenman, 2017). Too little risk, and children may withdraw or try harder to make something happen by using inappropriate or dangerous behaviors. Too much risk will certainly result in accidents and injuries.

Concern for children's safety is absolutely necessary, and environments should be designed to minimize risks and eliminate hazards as much as possible. A hazard is a serious danger that must be avoided; a risk is a possibility of harm that can be minimized with planning and supervision (Greenman, 2017). An attempt to eliminate all risk can lead to eliminating all challenge. Children not only need to be safe, they also need to be challenged if they are to advance their skills and learn how to keep themselves safe.

From infancy on, children try out challenging activities that might put them at risk for injury, most of them as a part of normal exploration. Consider the concept of risk vs. challenge in deciding whether children should be allowed to climb trees. One teacher might consider the risk of injury is too high and, therefore, that tree limbs on playgrounds should be trimmed to prevent tree climbing. However, from the perspective of a veteran child care center director, tree climbing is a learnable skill that can be safely taught to children and practiced with careful supervision (Curtis, 2010).

risk vs. challenge continuum Concept that children not only need to be safe but they also need to be challenged if they are to advance their skills and learn how to keep themselves safe.

hazard A danger that must be avoided.

risk A possibility of harm that can be minimized with planning and supervision.

✓ Check Your Understanding 15.4

🔺 Effective Curriculum and Teaching to Promote Physical Fitness and Health

The purpose of developmentally appropriate physical education is to help children learn to move and learn through movement (Gallahue, 1995). In the sections that follow, we first describe curriculum and teaching strategies to promote physical development. We then address how to plan a health education curriculum.

Curriculum for Physical Development

You will recall from Chapter 10 that curriculum planning draws on both the content of the disciplines and knowledge of child development. In planning curriculum for physical development, the disciplines of physical education, nutrition, and health provide the learning goals for children. To make these goals meaningful and accessible to young children, teachers need to translate them into topics of interest. The teachers then plan the learning experiences keeping in mind what they know about the continuum of physical development so they can set achievable goals for children's gross-motor and fine-motor skills. Then, based on their observation and assessment, teachers set goals for individual children, as the following example illustrates:

The 4-year-olds in Betty Bartock and Jake Springer's child care class eagerly anticipate the arrival of the circus in their town. Betty and Jake decide to make the circus the big idea for planning curriculum to address their goals for children's physical development and health. The group has read books about the circus and learned circus songs and games. When they discuss the topic with the children in a group meeting, many ideas are generated. "I'll be the tightrope walker," says Durrell, who is proud of his skill on the high balance beam. "We can have a parade. We can be acrobats and do somersaults and cartwheels," suggests Deretha. "Let's dress up like clowns," says Maggie.

The circus project becomes one of the highlights of the year. Betty and Jake use it to motivate several of the reluctant children to try out new physical skills like balancing on one foot. They observe that Barton's eye-hand coordination is exceptional for his age. Although Barton is often disruptive in class, the circus tasks focus his attention, and he becomes the "juggler"—perfecting his ability to toss a small ball hand to hand.

After a few weeks of circus-inspired physical activity, Betty and Jake decide to share the fun with families. The children write invitations to their circus, plan costumes, and paint advertising signs. For the big day, they need refreshments. This generates a lengthy discussion of what kinds of "circus" foods are healthy. The children settle on unbuttered popcorn and fresh fruit cups, which they prepare. Many family members attend the circus, watching the parade and enjoying the children's performances of songs and skills. Then they visit the various "acts" arranged in sections of the room or stop to pay a penny for a treat at the food booth.

The circus project was a big hit with children, families, and teachers. But it also provided a framework for Betty and Jake to help children make progress in the areas of physical development, motor skill acquisition, and health. They were able to use children's interests to help them achieve goals such as building Barton's fine-motor skill or getting a less-skilled child to try out the balance beam.

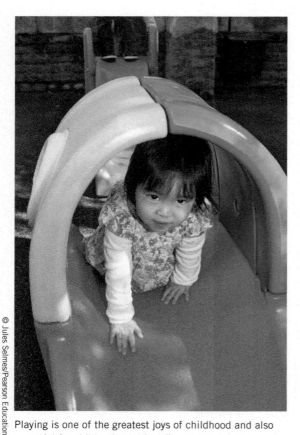

Playing is one of the greatest joys of childhood and also essential for children's physical fitness and health.

The context of a meaningful curriculum topic such as the circus provides numerous opportunities for children to learn and practice physical skills. Just growing up is not enough to ensure that all children develop the fundamental motor skills they need. They require more than an appropriate environment and supportive adults; children also need instruction (Goodway, Ozmun, & Gallahue, 2013). Effective teaching strategies to build physical skills include movement exploration, explicit teaching, and teacher-supported practice (Goodway, Ozmun, & Gallahue, 2013).

Movement Exploration   Movement exploration gives children a role in learning the skills being taught and allows for wider experimentation as the learning unfolds (Pica, 2014). Tina Sabuco, the founder of *Arts Alive!* in Houston, Texas, asks preschool and kindergarten children during her movement classes to find a way to connect with each other without touching. As children explore this idea, they discover ways to encircle each other's legs or arms, straddle another person's reclined body, crawl through spread legs, or mirror another child's hand or foot movements—all appropriate though different solutions to the challenge. As children discover their own motor solutions, they develop self-confidence and independence, and their fear of failure lessens. In the current educational milieu of high-stakes testing, where there is often only one right answer to any question, movement exploration is invaluable for solidifying children's view of themselves as able to make things happen and to figure out solutions.

Explicit Teaching   Some children benefit from a more direct approach. Teachers using a direct approach describe, model, and demonstrate the necessary components of the physical skill being taught. A benefit of the direct approach is that it is immediately clear if children can or cannot perform the skills.

An additional benefit of explicit teaching is that it is efficient. It takes less time to show children how to do movements than to let them figure them out on their own. Children also learn to do the skills correctly, which can prevent injuries. On the other hand, the direct approach leaves little room for creativity and individuality. During early childhood, the direct approach should be used in an individualized way rather than as a primary teaching strategy (Pica, 2014).

Some examples of explicit teaching include:

- Model and describe the sequence of a skill such as kicking a ball—"Put your right foot down, then your left foot, then swing your right foot to hit the ball."
- Break down motor tasks into smaller steps—if a child cannot throw a ball yet, have them bat a balloon to practice the motion.
- Give cues to help them learn a skill more quickly such as when learning to catch, "Keep your eye on the ball" or "Hold your hands up like this."
- Use games and playful experiences—for example, put out mats and challenge children to get to the other side in different ways (by hopping, jumping, running, somersaulting).
- Always individualize—children will be at different skill levels. Teaching should be adapted so as to challenge but not frustrate them.
- Use a variety of equipment of various shapes and sizes such as bean bags, rubber and plastic balls, basketball hoops, and cornhole games.

Teacher-Supported Practice Young children are usually highly motivated to master new skills. But even when teachers use appropriate teaching strategies, children still need plenty of practice to master physical skills. In one research-proven, child-centered strategy called "mastery motivational climate," teachers provide materials and plan lesson components, but children initiate and participate according to their preferences (Goodway, Ozmun, Derringer, & Lee, 2013).

Without opportunities to practice and perfect what they are learning to do, children may never achieve proficient levels of skill, particularly children living in poverty who are often found to be significantly delayed in motor skills development (Goodway, Robinson, & Crowe, 2010). When children are learning new skills, and even while they are practicing, children need verbal prompts and reminders, feedback on performance, and encouragement to keep trying (Goodway, Ozmun, Derringer, & Lee, 2013).

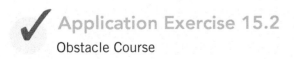

Application Exercise 15.2
Obstacle Course

Teachers' attitudes are extremely important. When adults are not enthusiastic about motor play and do not engage with children, children are unlikely to be enthusiastic and persist. The first step to effective teaching is for teachers themselves to be physically active and interested in meaningful physical activity.

Children do not master physical skills without adult support but that does not mean that unstructured free play should be sacrificed to organized teacher-directed experiences. This is another area where *both/and* approach is necessary especially because free play opportunities are in jeopardy. To learn more about the important benefits of free play, read the feature: *What Works*: *Unstructured Play Activities Support Children's Executive Functioning*.

What Works

Unstructured Play Activities Support Children's Executive Functioning

Many children today lead heavily scheduled lives. Much of their time is spent in adult-supervised and organized structured activities with formal rules or instructions designed to achieve specific goals, such as soccer practice or music lessons. Little time is available for unstructured leisure activities such as free play or choosing to read or draw whatever they want. During unstructured activities the child is in charge—deciding what to do and how to do it.

A new study raises concerns about the impact of heavily structured activities on children's development. Researchers asked parents of 6-year-olds to record their children's activities for a week and then measured the time spent in unstructured and structured experiences. Then they tested the children on measures of executive function. The researchers found that spending more time in structured activities negatively affected children's ability to work toward goals, make decisions, and regulate their own behavior. Researchers found that the children who spent more time in less structured activities had more highly developed, self-directed executive function.

As we have seen, executive function processes such as planning, decision making, and flexible thinking strongly predict later success in school and life. The researchers conclude

that opportunity for unstructured play and leisure helps children take responsibility for what they're going to do with their time. When children are in control and decide how they spend their time, they practice executive function skills. By contrast, too much adult-structured time may hinder the development of self-regulation and executive function. The researchers caution that more study is needed because it could be that children with better EF prefer less-structured activities while those with worse EF gravitate toward adult-directed experiences.

Nevertheless these results present a cautionary tale. Increasingly free playtime in preschool and kindergarten is being replaced in favor of more structured experiences, and the same is true in homes and communities. The study supports the importance of child-directed free play in classrooms and outdoors for the acquisition of all-important executive function abilities.

Source: J.E. Barker, A.D. Semenov, L. Michaelson, L.S. Provan, H. Snyder, H. & & Y. Muakata, Less-structured time in children's daily lives predicts self-directed executive functioning, 2014, *Frontiers in Psychology*, https://doi.org/10.3389/fpsyg.2014.00593

© Suzanne Clouzeau/Pearson Education

Family-style dining promotes children's self-rgulation and fine-motor skills as well as their interest in healthy eating.

Effective Health Curriculum and Teaching

Teaching children healthy and safe practices is the best way to support health and wellness. Nutrition education is also an essential part of the curriculum.

Learning Safety An important curriculum goal is educating children about accident prevention, particularly on the playground. Accidents are actually preventable. Teachers need to teach children safe ways to play and interact in indoor as well as outdoor environments to prevent injuries. Safety should be considered from the perspectives of adults as well as children.

Learning how to use wheeled toys safely is an important curriculum goal. Universal use of helmets by children ages 4 to 15 when riding tricycles or bicycles could prevent deaths, head injuries, and scalp and face injuries (CDC, 2013). Children need to understand how to operate wheeled toys without injuring themselves or others—in other words, they need to learn the rules of the road.

Learning Wellness The curriculum goal of disease prevention is a natural extension of children's interest in their own bodies. Children's shared experiences of visiting the doctor and dentist and getting regular immunizations are conceptual organizers for this topic. They can also learn about germs and how germs are spread from one person to another. Many children's books address the topic of visiting the physician and other health and wellness topics. Examples include *Corduroy Goes to the Doctor* (Freeman, 2001), *Wash Your Hands!* (Ross, 2000), and *Germs Are Not for Sharing* (Verdick, 2006).

Nutrition Education Good nutrition in early childhood is related to children's readiness for school and academic success (Pascoe, Shaikh, Forbis, & Etzel, 2007). Children who eat a nutritionally poor diet, such as fast food, score lower on tests of reading and math achievement (Tobin, 2013). Skipping breakfast is associated with poorer cognitive performance (Food Research and Action Center, 2016) and eating breakfast cereal improves mood and alertness (Smith, 2010). However, attention and memory are improved with breakfast cereal that is lower in sugar content (Ingwersen, Defeyter, Kennedy, Wesnes, & Scholey, 2007).

Video Example 15.5:

Nutrition Lesson

The teacher in this video is teaching a nutrition lesson. How does the teacher encourage healthy eating and incorporate playful experience and physical activity into the nutrition lesson?

The goals of nutrition education are teaching children about healthy eating, introducing children to different types of foods, and promoting exploration of and interest in a well-balanced diet (Kalich, Bauer, & McPartlin, 2014). The U.S. Department of Agriculture's Choose MyPlate symbol, depicted in Figure 15.3, is a good vehicle for helping children to learn about the kinds and amounts of food to eat each day and developing heathly eating habits. The message of Choose MyPlate is that half of children's daily diet should be fruits and vegetables. They also should eat more whole grains and, after age 2, they should drink 1% or nonfat milk.

Application Exercise 15.3

Figure 15.3: Choose MyPlate

One effective strategy to help children make better nutritional choices is to teach them about *anytime* foods and *sometime* foods. This idea is part of the Healthy Habits for Life curriculum developed by Sesame Workshop, Nemours Health and Prevention Services, and KidHealth.org (2007). One of children's favorite characters, Cookie Monster, makes it clear that cookies are a "sometime" food, like potato chips or ice cream; whereas bananas or carrots can be eaten anytime. Research shows that children's eating habits can be powerfully influenced by role models. For example, in one study, when children watched Elmo promote eating broccoli rather than chocolate, their interest in eating broccoli increased 127% (Cohen & Kotler, 2005).

Nutrition education has the potential to affect children's health behaviors for a lifetime, particularly when the family is included in the education process. Educating children begins by offering them a variety of foods as part of a balanced diet. Nutrition education continues by interesting children in where food comes from, how it is prepared, and the wide variety of food that is available for inclusion in a balanced diet to help children grow up healthy. Serving meals family style controls portion size because children tend to choose the amount they will eat and not more.

Eating involves more than taste; all the senses are engaged. How foods look, feel, and sound during eating effect children's food preferences. One strategy is to make healthy eating a multi-sensory learning experience using sight, sound, touch, and smell (rather than taste) to introduce children to

FIGURE 15.3 Choose MyPlate The U.S. Department of Agriculture uses the image MyPlate to teach children to make healthy food choices.

Source: Reprinted from Choose MyPlate, U.S. Department of Agriculture, no date, retrieved April 26, 2018, from http://www.choosemyplate.gov.

new foods. A study of children ages 12–36 months found that introducing unfamiliar vegetables by looking, listening, feeling, and smelling them during playtime increased the children's willingness to taste the foods at lunch time (Nekitsing, Hetherington, & Blundell-Birtill, 2018). Such an approach has the added benefit of promoting perceptual-motor development.

For babies and toddlers, teachers can start by offering food on demand and at regular intervals. Then, as toddlers begin to eat table food, teachers give them repeated opportunities to try new foods. Color, texture, and temperature of food may be as important as taste during initial offerings.

Preschool and kindergarten children often have a reputation as picky eaters. This suggests refraining from too much external pressure to try new things. However, children need repeated *opportunities* (5 to 10) to try new foods, especially vegetables (Nekitsing, Hetherington, & Blundell-Birtill, 2018). One strategy is to set up a self-serve snack center, similar to the other learning centers in the classroom (Bernath & Masi, 2006). Food is presented in small store-bought packages or preproportioned in cups with napkins, plates, and utensils for children to serve themselves.

While children should be exposed to new foods and encouraged to try them, they should not be coerced to try foods, using "one bite" rules. When adults control children's eating practices in this way, children can develop unhealthy relationships with food and mealtimes (McBride & Dev, 2014). Some children are reluctant eaters due to their developmental disabilities. It is particularly important in this situation to work with children's parents to support children's nutrition while also supporting healthy eating behaviors. In the feature, *Including All Children*, read how one teacher supported a child with autism in his nutrition and eating.

▶

Video Example 15.6:

Self-Serve Snack

The classroom in this video uses a self-serve snack center. How do you think a self-serve snack facilitates healthy eating habits, self-regulation, and social skills?

Including All Children

Nutrition and Children with Developmental Disabilities

Snack time is busy in Mara's preschool classroom. After washing their hands, 16 children gather for snack at two tables. They talk about the food, ask questions, and pass dishes family style. One child, Henry, passes the snack dishes, but does not take food. Mara puts out an additional dish of crackers, and Henry, a child with autism, takes some of these and passes to his classmates. Henry eats only crackers at school. When Henry first started in her class, he would not sit at the snack table. He would take a cracker and run around the room, and would scream and cry when encouraged to take tastes of the snack food. Mara was concerned that Henry was not able to join the class at snack time, and that he might not be getting sufficient nutrition.

Working with Henry's parents and a nutrition therapist, Mara learned about Henry's sensory sensitivity and his difficulty joining in meals. She learned that Henry was not just a "picky eater," but that he was very afraid of trying new foods and was anxious when around new

foods. She also learned that Henry drank a fortified drink several times a day to meet his nutritional needs while he was learning to eat a variety of foods.

Mara, Henry's parents, and the nutrition therapist developed a set of goals around mealtimes, including washing hands, sitting at the table for initially short and increasing periods of time, and using a spoon to serve a small amount of crackers that his parents provided. Mara asked if his parents would provide crackers for all the children, so that Henry could experience sharing the food with others. At first, Henry sat only a few seconds at the table, but after a while he was able to stay at the snack table for almost the entire time with his classmates. Last week, Henry even tried a piece of toast that was offered at snack time. Henry's parents were thrilled that he was making progress, and Mara was very happy that she had found a way for Henry to join the other children during this very special time of the preschool day.

Cooking with Children Cooking is an excellent way to introduce and encourage children to try new foods. Classroom cooking offers many learning opportunities including seeing foods change state as they cook (science), measuring and mixing ingredients (mathematics), introducing new vocabulary and reading recipes (language and literacy), and predicting outcomes (science) and preferences. Many resources such as children's books and simple recipes are available to help early childhood teachers cook with children in the classroom (Colker, 2005). Also, cooking can be a way to reinforce understandings about food allergies and why some foods such as peanuts may not be allowed in the classroom.

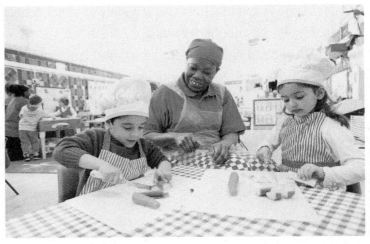
Young children can be picky eaters. Cooking is one of the most effective ways to get them to try new, more healthy foods.

Routines That Promote Health and Wellness Young children need adult support to remember and practice what they have learned about health and wellness. Without including healthy practices in the daily, weekly, and monthly routines, children aren't likely to integrate them into their lives and apply them at home and in other spheres.

Children's health is also affected by their growing independence in carrying out personal routines, their awareness of health and safety concerns, and their ability to follow rules and take steps to keep themselves safe and healthy. Teachers can use different strategies with different children to teach health and wellness practices, such as hand washing or sanitizing table tops before lunchtime, offering specific feedback (such as washing the front, back, and in between the fingers), creating or adding a challenge such as washing for as long as the child sings "Happy Birthday," twice or modeling appropriate hand washing for a child who skips steps.

We began this chapter with alarming statistics about the health and fitness of our nation's children and the disturbing childhood obesity crisis. Having explored the continuum of motor development and effective curriculum and teaching strategies for promoting health and fitness, we return to Ms. Perez and Ms. Aliote's classroom to see how they implement these practices.

Video Example 15.7:

Routines as Learning Opportunities

In this video, pre-kindergarten children clean up after lunch. What healthy behaviors are they learning during this daily routine? What are they learning from separating waste into compost, recycling, and trash?

 Check Your Understanding 15.5

Revisiting the Case Study

… Ms. Perez and Ms. Aliote's Classroom

At the beginning of this chapter, we visited the classroom of Ms. Perez and Ms. Aliote. These teachers plan indoor and outdoor environments that foster children's physical development and learning. They encourage gross-motor and fine-motor skills with a wide variety of materials and experiences in the classroom and on the playground. These activities promote children's body awareness and perceptual-motor development.

Outdoors, children engage in unstructured play, such as tricycle riding, climbing, and running, as well as structured physical activities—learning how to kick a ball at a higher level of proficiency and playing kickball with a friend. These teachers use a variety of effective teaching strategies and adapt for individual children's needs. Ms. Perez intentionally taught Allison the skills she needed for kicking the ball. At the same time, she helped Drew build his social-emotional and language skills as she encouraged him to ask Allison if he could play, and they began to play cooperatively.

The teachers incorporate health education in their day by offering healthy food choices and prompting children to wash their hands before eating. Children's physical fitness and health are priorities in this classroom. Their teachers integrate these topics in fun and meaningful ways throughout the day. The end result is that these children are more likely to remain active and healthy throughout their lives. ■

15 Chapter Summary

- Given the benefits of physical activity for young children as well as the risks of poor levels of fitness, teachers need to ensure that promoting physical development and health are core curriculum goals and not simply add-ons. Children's physical fitness and health have become urgent concerns as the rate of childhood obesity in America has increased significantly.

- Physical development—gross-motor, fine-motor, and perceptual-motor development—follows a relatively predictable sequence that is influenced by both maturation and experience.

- Teachers foster children's physical development by providing age-appropriate materials and learning environments, supporting play and movement exploration, and explicitly teaching motor skills.

- Children need opportunities for unstructured and structured play, including rough-and-tumble play, throughout the day to promote physical activity and develop skills. Outdoor play is a particularly valuable context for promoting physical development. Some children today do not get enough exposure to nature and its many benefits.

- Physical fitness and health and wellness habits are formed early in life. Children benefit from teachers who intentionally plan engaging curriculum to promote physical development and fitness.

- Health education curriculum goals include teaching children health and safety procedures such as emergency preparedness, practices for preventing illness and injury, and good nutrition.

Key Terms

- auditory awareness
- body composition
- cardiorespiratory (aerobic) system
- directional awareness
- fine-motor development
- fine-motor manipulative movements
- flexibility

- gross-motor development
- gross-motor manipulative movements
- hazard
- health-related fitness
- locomotor movements
- motor planning
- muscular strength and endurance

- nature-deficit disorder
- perceptual-motor development
- physical fitness
- pincer grasp
- risk
- risk vs. challenge continuum

- rough-and-tumble play or big body play
- spatial awareness
- stability movements
- structured physical activity
- temporal awareness
- unstructured free play

 Flash Cards 15.1

Readings and Websites

Administration for Children and Families, U.S. Department of Health and Human Services (2015). *Caring for our children basics: Health and safety foundations for early care and education.* Retrieved from http://www.acf.hhs.gov/sites/default/files/ecd/caring_for_our_children_basics.pdf.

Greenman, J. (2017). *Caring spaces, learning places: Children's environments that work!* Lincoln, NE: Exchange Press.

Honig, A. S. (2015). *Experiencing nature with young children: Awakening delight, curiosity, and a sense of stewardship.* Washington, DC: National Association for the Education of Young Children.

Huber, M. (2016). *Embracing rough-and-tumble play: Teaching with the body in mind.* St. Paul, MN: Redleaf Press.

Action for Healthy Kids

This organization provides programs and resources for professionals, families and communities to achieve the goal of every child becoming healthy, active, and ready to learn.

Nature Action Collaborative for Children (NACC)

Visit this website to find out about developmentally appropriate educational resources designed to enhance children's connection with nature.

Natural Learning Initiative

This website highlights how the environment can act as a third teacher, including "Preventing Obesity by Design," using landscape architecture, natural materials, and developmentally appropriate play settings to create natural playgrounds.

SHAPE America: Society of Health and Physical Educators

The membership organization for physical education and health instructors, SHAPE establishes National Standards for K-12 physical education. Its website provides resources on health and physical education, physical activity, dance, and sport.

Shared Writing 15.1
Risk vs. Challenge Continuum

16 Putting It All Together in Practice: Making a Difference for Children

Learning Outcomes

After studying this chapter, you should be able to:

16.1 Describe what life is like as a teacher of infants and toddlers, preschoolers, kindergartners, and primary-grade children.

16.2 Apply the NAEYC Code of Ethical Conduct and describe professional obligations of early childhood educators.

© Kathryn Tunstal

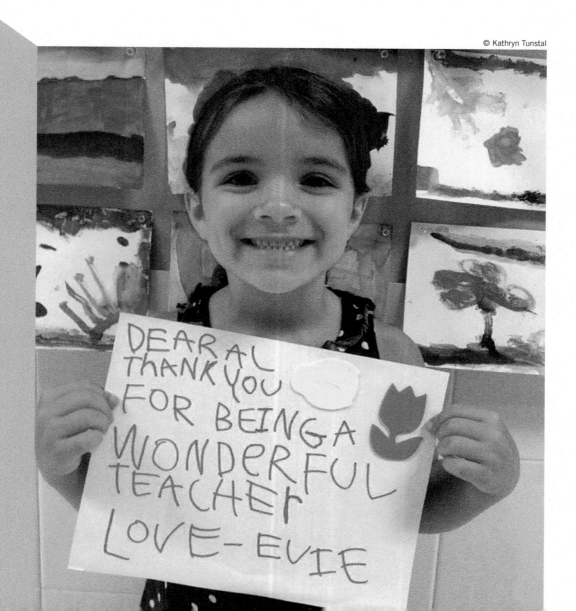

Case Study

Students are gathering on the first day of class in a college course titled *Foundations of Early Childhood Education*. Each individual contemplates the next semester from his or her own experience. Consider how their diverse paths have led them to this shared place. Aisha has always wanted to be a teacher. Her mother and grandmother were teachers before her, and education is strongly valued in her family. When she was a little girl, her favorite thing to do was to "play" school. She is excited that this class will begin her journey toward that lifelong dream. Laron is a little surprised to find himself here. He never thought of education as a career goal. But the last two summers, he worked as a lifeguard and discovered that giving swimming lessons to preschool-aged children was the most fun he'd ever had in a job. He felt so good every time a 4-year-old gave him a giant smile after overcoming that initial fear of the water. Now he's considering early childhood education as a major. Julienne is certain about why she is here. She has decided to get a dual major in early childhood education and early intervention in order to be certified as an early childhood special educator. Her twin brother has cerebral palsy, and she is committed to serving children with disabilities in inclusive settings.

Compared to Aisha, Laron, and Julienne, Rita is feeling nervous. She is a 32-year-old single mother of three who is starting college now that her children are all in school. She can't help feeling a little out of place with all these younger people. But raising her own children and taking care of nieces and nephews made her want to become a teacher herself. Oralie has a similar story. She volunteered in her children's Head Start program, obtained a CDA Credential, was employed as an assistant teacher, and now is pursuing her college degree with support from her supervisors.

The other students in the class have their own stories—all different. Some will learn that they have little interest or aptitude for becoming teachers. If so, it is wise for them to pursue another field. Others will be amazed at all there is to learn about young children. They assumed that teaching young children would be simple compared to older children, but they will come to understand the complexity as well as the challenge of this work. Eventually a number of them will be better parents for having taken this course of study. Most important, many of them will become the effective teachers that every child needs and deserves. ■

Every morning in communities across the country, young children arrive at child care centers and family child care homes, preschools, Head Start programs, and K–3 primary schools. Their teachers are there to greet them and to help them take another step on the lifelong journey of development and learning. At the same time, the teachers themselves are on a journey—to be and become the most caring, informed, and effective early childhood professionals possible. In this chapter, we visit some of those teachers to see what life is like for them in their chosen careers. Then we discuss some of the broader aspects of an early childhood professional's journey.

Throughout this book, we describe ways that effective teachers help build strong foundations of development and learning for young children. This work has three interconnected dimensions. Effective teachers must:

- Know children—*who* they teach.
- Understand *how* to teach—the complex roles of the teacher, which include building caring relationships with children, partnering with families, planning and implementing curriculum, assessing children, and adapting teaching strategies.
- Know *what* to teach—the goals and content for children's learning and development.

Experienced teachers know that these dimensions of their work cannot be separated. They teach the whole child. And they do not work in isolation; they are connected to colleagues, families, and communities. One of the biggest challenges for teachers is putting it all together.

 ## Life as an Early Childhood Educator

Among the major questions early childhood educators face is which age group they would most like to work with and why. Many teachers change jobs, settings, and/or age levels over the course of a career; however, most early childhood teachers gravitate toward one age group and stay there.

The following sections describe things to consider as you weigh your career options. After reading about a "day in the life" of teachers in diverse settings, you will see some ways in which teachers engage in effective practices. In reality, there is no such thing as a typical day in any program for children. There should be a predictable schedule and routine, a prepared age-appropriate environment, and a planned curriculum. But children themselves are unpredictable. They change from day to day, in wonderful and challenging ways, and they come up with great ideas that lead in new directions. In addition, conditions impinge that are beyond a teacher's control—for example, an emergency or a serendipitous event. Teachers need to be prepared to handle any and all situations.

In many ways, it is the unpredictable nature of teaching young children that makes it such fascinating work. A career in early education is filled with never-ending rewards and challenges. It is a field like no other, as we see from brief visits to classrooms in the following sections.

Caring for and Educating Infants and Young Toddlers

Some people do not consider those who work with babies and toddlers to be teachers. Because much physical care is required for this age group, the term *caregiver* is often used for this role. Nevertheless,

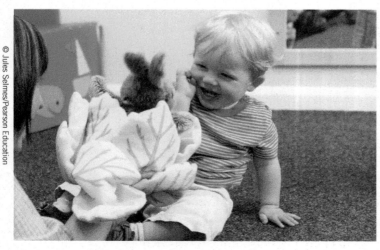

High-quality early childhood programs provide a joyous experience for both children and teachers.

babies are always learning in the context of loving care (Copple, Bredekamp, Koralek, & Charner, 2013a). We choose to call all professional caregivers *teachers*.

A Day in the Life of an Infant/Toddler Teacher Victoria Thomas and Luisa Franco co-teach a group of eight babies and young toddlers. Their children stay with them for about 2½ years to provide continuity of care and secure relationships for the children and their families. Each morning as the children arrive, Victoria and Luisa greet them warmly and casually chat with the family member who drops them off. They learn vital information about the baby's sleeping and eating patterns, as well as who is feeling fussy or especially happy. Luisa positions the three nonmobile babies where they can watch the action and hear her talking as she picks up little Lyla, who is clearly in need of a diaper change. Throughout the day, the teachers will engage in feeding, diapering, and hand-washing routines as the children eat and rest on their own schedules.

After meeting Lyla's immediate needs, Luisa puts Sam down for his midmorning nap and then positions Foster and Lydia on the rug, who soon demonstrates her newly acquired skill of rolling over. Luisa gets down and plays with them at their eye level with a ball that makes music as it rolls. The babies love swatting the ball to produce the sounds.

Meanwhile, across the room, Victoria calmly plays on the rug with the mobile toddlers, who are just beginning to talk. They are enchanted by a set of large, plastic, colored blocks that they can pick up and place together, forming a big pattern on the floor. Victoria describes what they are doing as it happens: "Alan has a red peg. He put it next to the green one." Alan starts to fuss when Wanda pushes against him. "Wanda, you are in Alan's space. Can you move just a little?" asks Victoria in a soft voice. Alan calms and Wanda smacks a kiss on his cheek. Victoria smiles, "You're a good friend, Wanda."

As the play time comes to an end, Victoria says, "Let's see who is big and strong and can help me pick up the pegs." As Victoria places the full bin onto the shelf, Gary holds on, too. Victoria says, "It's heavy. We have to lift it up high." Gary responds, "Up," and Victoria says, "Yes, let's put it *up* on the shelf. Now, let's go outside. It's warm and we can play on the ride-on toys or go for a walk in the stroller."

In this brief scene, we see effective practices in action. Victoria and Luisa create a calm and warm climate for these young children, focusing on building a relationship with each child. They model kindness and social skills, which even these very young children are starting to emulate. They weave into play ways to support all areas of development and learning. The teachers help the children develop physical skills (rolling the ball, placing the pegs) and knowledge about the world while building language skills. They model rich vocabulary such as spatial relation words like *next to* and *up* and explain the phrase "You're in his space." And they are keen to create new experiences to stimulate children's senses and interests, such as being outside in nature, the beginning of science learning.

Throughout the day, Victoria and Luisa keep careful records about each baby—what they eat and drink, bowel movements, their moods, and any special accomplishments—to share with parents at the end of the day. Observing and recording is an effective way of assessing children and communicating what families want and need to know. These exchanges help build close relationships with the families, who then feel more secure about leaving their precious babies in the care of others.

© Pearson Education

Video Example 16.1:

Teaching Infants and Toddlers

This video takes you inside a high-quality infant and toddler program. Pay attention to the interactions between the teachers and children. How do the teachers feel about their work? What do you think are the most gratifying aspects of working with this age group?

Considerations for Teaching Infants and Toddlers Some people would never consider working with babies and toddlers; others can think of nothing more rewarding. Teachers of infants and toddlers usually work in child care centers, Early Head Start programs, or family child care homes. Table 16.1 lists some considerations in deciding whether to work with these very young children.

TABLE 16.1 Considerations for Infant/Toddler Teachers	
Working with infants and toddlers can be difficult but also delightful as described in this table. IF YOU ARE THINKING OF TEACHING INFANTS AND TODDLERS, YOU MIGHT CONSIDER THAT:	
On the One Hand	**On the Other Hand**
A great deal of physical care is required—diapering, feeding, dressing, frequent hand washing, and constant supervision.	Caregiving routines provide time to connect and talk one-on-one with babies and to build loving relationships.
Babies' actions are repetitive and can be frustrating—they drop the cup off the high chair again and again to see what happens.	Babies' actions are obvious evidence of their development and opportunities to share in their joy of discovery.
Babies and toddlers grow and develop so rapidly that just when you think you know what to expect, they change.	From the earliest moments of life, young children demonstrate that they are unique, so life with them is always challenging and never boring.
Caring for babies requires close, constant communication with families. Relationships can be difficult due to competition, differences of opinion, or diverse cultural values.	Relationships with families can be close and rewarding, marked by shared power and responsibility as teachers and parents learn from each other and work toward common goals.
Babies and toddlers are so vulnerable and dependent on adults to protect their health, safety, and emotional security that the responsibility can feel overwhelming.	Protecting very young children from harm as they discover and rediscover the world every day is immensely rewarding.
Babies and toddlers can't tell you what they want and need. They cry and fuss and can make adults feel helpless or inadequate.	Babies and toddlers communicate their needs and wants through cries, expressions, and gestures. Nothing compares with a baby's or a toddler's smile and belly laugh.

Teaching the Whole Child in the Preschool

Three- to five-year-olds are some of the most interesting people in the world. They are miniature navigators, explorers, writers, artists, acrobats, linguists, and comedians (although much of their humor can be silly or of the bathroom variety). At this age, their potential seems boundless.

Teachers who are drawn to preschoolers have many choices of work site or employer. They may choose Head Start, a child care center, family child care, a public prekindergarten, or private preschool. The length of time the children spend in the program will make some difference in what a teacher's day is like. Although preschoolers are more capable of taking care of their own needs, they continue to need vigilant supervision and a lot of physical care and attention. They also need experiences that engage their minds and actively involve them in the world around them (Copple, Bredekamp, Koralek, & Charner, 2013b). Most of all, they need intentional teachers to help them achieve their full potential (Epstein, 2014).

A Day in the Life of a Preschool Teacher As a white van pulls up at Children's Learning Center, Masami and his assistant teacher, Ana, greet the preschoolers—some in English and some in Spanish. The children head off to wash their hands and settle in for breakfast. Ana helps them serve oatmeal and orange slices and pour their own milk, while Masami sits and begins a conversation about the bus ride.

The sixteen 3- and 4-year-olds live in an economically challenged community. Some have been exposed to violence and a few have serious emotional problems. Masami and Ana's program places a strong emphasis on building social skills and emotional self-regulation. They use a comprehensive curriculum that promotes language and thinking through interesting projects that build science, math, engineering, and literacy skills. It also includes lots of art and music. To achieve the curriculum goals and build secure, continuous relationships, Masami and Ana each work with a group of eight children at times during the school day, which lasts from 8:30 a.m. to 3:30 p.m. For instance, half the group will go outside with Ana while the rest stay in with Masami, and then they switch.

After breakfast, Masami leads the children in singing and then reads a book about a new baby. The group is involved in a long-term science project about how people grow

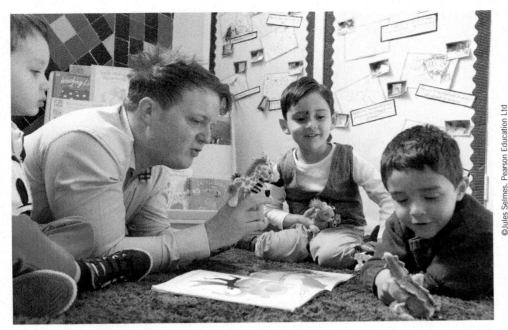

©Jules Selmes. Pearson Education Ltd

Intentional preschool teachers engage with small groups of children throughout the day to scaffold their learning.

and change. Then they discuss the choices for center time. Learning centers include dramatic play (set up as a hospital with props and dress-up materials), creative art, math/manipulatives, writing center, library area, and blocks. Masami talks with the children about where they plan to play and what they'd like to do, which helps them regulate their behavior and thinking. The children are becoming better listeners. As they describe their plans, Ana helps them leave the group and transition to the next activity. Sharde calls out, "I got room at my table for Keyona's wheelchair."

During center time, Masami works with a small group in the art center. They examine their own baby pictures, look in the mirror, and use different media including digital cameras to represent how they look. The discussion centers on how big they can make their drawings. They get excited at the idea of projecting their faces on the large interactive whiteboard. Some children write recognizable letters on their pictures, while others dictate their thoughts for Masami to write. In the dramatic play area, Assata dresses as the doctor while Ben and Rhonda bring their new baby for a checkup. Ayah goes to the writing center, makes marks on a piece of paper, and hands it to Assata, "Here's a letter."

Mia, who has just turned 3, heads toward the restroom. Ana congratulates her on listening to her body and getting to the toilet in time. Mia beams in response. Ana helps her get her pants buttoned (she pulls them up all by herself) and then they wash their hands. In the library area, Arturo studies an information book about baby animals. Ana talks with him about how some look like their mothers, and some do not. Their conversation continues as Arturo, who was adopted from Costa Rica, explains that he doesn't look like his mom, either.

After cleanup, the children join Masami on the carpet and tell him about what they did during activity time. Mia proudly says she went to the toilet (although that is not exactly what she said). Arturo says he read a book; others talk about how they observed each other's drawings of themselves—"Marco has brown eyes and he made them blue."

On the playground, Arturo and Kiesha ride on the wheeled toys. Mia starts climbing to the loft of the playhouse. Jorge calls to her to join him in the sandbox. Masami asks Mia if she heard Jorge's invitation. She nods. He coaches her to tell Jorge she wants to climb, so he will know what her answer is.

After lunch, the children settle in for naps. Ana and Masami play soft music, pat a few backs and soon the children sleep. After naptime, the children find several activity areas,

© Pearson Education

▶

Video Example 16.2:

Teaching Preschool

In this video a preschool teacher describes why she chose early childhood education as her career path. Which of these considerations weighed most heavily in her decision?

including a self-service snack area. Children write their names or make a mark by their photo when they wash their hands and serve themselves a snack.

At the end of the day, Masami and Ana meet to review the day and record their observations of the children's progress. Masami plans to inform Mia's mother about her toileting success, and Arturo's mother about his reflections on adoption. They also plan ways to build vocabulary through children's interests in babies and their growing bodies.

Considerations for Working with Preschoolers Ana and Masami's day is far busier than this general portrait can communicate. As we saw in the brief interactions with Mia, they must know each child and how to support her or his progress. They plan ahead but are constantly thinking on their feet as they interact with individuals and groups. Table 16.2 lists some things to consider in contemplating becoming a preschool teacher.

Teaching the Whole Child in the Kindergarten

Kindergarten holds a special place in children's lives. Even if a child has been in child care for the previous five years, entering kindergarten marks the major transition to formal school. Given this momentous event, kindergarten teachers are very important to children. They help

TABLE 16.2 Considerations for Preschool Teachers

Preschoolers are usually enchanting and enthusiastic explorers, which makes preschool teaching a fun and rewarding career.
IF YOU ARE THINKING OF TEACHING PRESCHOOL, YOU MIGHT CONSIDER THAT:

On the One Hand	On the Other Hand
Preschoolers become increasingly capable of taking care of their own physical needs, but still need help with skills like toileting, feeding, and dressing (zipping, tying). Messiness and spills are normal.	Routine caregiving and meals provide times to interact one-on-one or in small groups and enjoy children as individuals. They also provide learning opportunities.
Many preschoolers have difficulty regulating their emotions and behavior and can be aggressive. Teachers can feel like they spend all their time guiding behavior.	Effective teachers help children make great strides in social-emotional learning and development. Behavior is less of a problem when children have interesting things to do and learn.
Preschool children are active and curious and can be loud and boisterous. Teaching them requires patience and can be exhausting.	Preschoolers are competent, active learners both physically and mentally. They try to make sense of the world and take on new challenges. Preschool teachers are constantly learning with and about them, and taking on new challenges, too.
Preschool children are all different in so many ways, making it hard to teach a large group. Working with diverse cultural groups and languages can be daunting. Successful inclusion of children with special needs can be difficult.	Individual differences in children are what make preschoolers so interesting and enjoyable. Cultural backgrounds and languages are fascinating aspects of everyone's identity. Inclusion, with appropriate support, benefits all children.
Preschool programs must meet standards for operation that can seem onerous. Some preschools measure child outcomes and stress teachers' accountability for children's learning.	Standards are designed to protect children and support their healthy development. Meeting them also protects teachers. Professional educators care about children achieving developmentally appropriate goals and are willing to be accountable for children's progress and learning.
Preschools are usually staffed with a teacher and an assistant, requiring skills for working with and perhaps supervising another adult, as well as working with children.	Having two teachers provides better teacher-child ratios, creating more opportunity for individual attention and small-group interaction. Different teachers have different interests and abilities to bring to the class. Collaborating, they can be more creative and effective than alone.
Working with preschoolers requires frequent, almost daily communication with families. Some families are demanding, whereas others are uninvolved.	Partnering with families makes teachers more effective. Children sense when their parents are respected and feel more comfortable and connected to teachers.

children negotiate a significant life change and build the foundation for their future educational career.

A Day in the Life of a Kindergarten Teacher

The morning bell rings as Hope Millner greets her 21 kindergartners at the classroom door. Toting backpacks and displaying mostly grins, these 5- and 6-year-olds feel very grown up as they navigate the corridors and expectations of "real" school. After a brief settling-in period, the group gathers on the rug for a morning meeting.

"Let's review what happened yesterday, and think ahead to today's plans," Hope suggests. The children wave their hands in the air for a turn to talk about the visit to the aquarium. Although the sharks made the biggest impression, some children were enthralled by the stingrays. "I hear from your descriptions that you were observing very care-

Most public school kindergartens today set high expectations for children's reading progress. How can kindergarten teachers use developmentally appropriate practices to help children build early literacy skills?

fully," Hope says. "I know that most of you used your clipboards, made some drawings. During choice time this morning, I'd like you to refer to those and write in your journals about what you saw and learned. We also have digital photos that we'll put on the computer and project on the wall to help you remember details. Now, I'm going to read parts of an information book about sea life that you can look at later in the library area."

During the morning activity period, two children feed the fish in the classroom aquarium and write a brief note: "Fsh et." Hope assists the children in their journal writing, helping them with letters and words, but emphasizes communicating their ideas rather than correct spelling. She also works with a small group who are still struggling with recognizing letters. An inviting library area is stocked with a variety of diverse, high-quality books at varying reading levels, including multiple copies of kindergarten-level texts. Storybooks and information books reflect the cultural and linguistic diversity of the group. Some children listen to audio books and follow along in the printed book.

Following the midmorning snack, children independently browse or read self-selected familiar books, especially ones that Hope has previously read aloud, such as the fish book. The field trip, books, and ongoing science study of sea life broaden the children's background knowledge and vocabulary. To build reading comprehension, Hope guides discussions about what is being read or listened to. She asks the children to predict events, retell or act out stories, and notice when a text does not make sense.

The kindergartners also have physical education classes three times a week. Working with Hope, the PE teacher plans related movement activities—how would you move like you're swimming? What if you were a fish and there was no water? In the classroom, Hope has a creative art center where some children make representations of their favorite fish and underwater environments; others create simply from their imaginations. After lunch and outdoor play, the children have another 60-minute choice period before dismissal. This is a favorite time for many because they especially like dramatic play, block building, and board games. During this time, Hope works with small groups on the mathematics curriculum goals. Today, a group spontaneously decides to replicate the aquarium with unit blocks. This leads to lengthy debates about how to re-create the water because a flat piece of blue paper wouldn't really hold up the fish. At the end of the day, the group meets to reflect on their day and look forward to tomorrow.

Considerations for Teaching Kindergarten

Hope Millner has taught kindergarten in a suburban school district for 15 years. In that time, she has seen changes in the curriculum, especially recently with the Common Core standards on English language arts and mathematics, and less administrative support for play. She has also observed that a higher proportion of her students now attend preschool and enter school with more

FIGURE 16.1 Kindergarten Child's Image of Her Teacher As is clear from this kindergarten child's drawing, teachers play an enormously important role in children's lives. Used with permission from Kaylee Rojas

knowledge about how the written language system works. At the same time, Hope knows that, developmentally, 5- and 6-year-olds haven't fundamentally changed and that they benefit from both "learningful play and playful learning" (Weisberg et al., 2015). Her task is to make the curriculum meaningful and engaging and to use play and other effective teaching strategies to intentionally promote each child's continuing progress. Most of all Hope is committed to a building positive, warm relationship with every child. One of the children's drawings reminds Hope of how important her job is; she literally "looms large" in the lives of her kindergartners (see Figure 16.1).

One of the biggest challenges for kindergarten teachers is to provide developmentally appropriate practice, while also implementing an increasingly rigorous curriculum (Copple, Bredekamp, Koralek, & Charner, 2014b). Teaching kindergarten today involves balancing some potentially conflicting needs and goals, as demonstrated in Table 16.3.

TABLE 16.3 Considerations for Kindergarten Teachers

With the increased academic demands of kindergarten, committed teachers must strive to engage in developmentally appropriate, effective practices that meet the needs of the whole child.

IF YOU ARE THINKING OF TEACHING KINDERGARTEN, YOU MIGHT CONSIDER THAT:

On the One Hand	On the Other Hand
Kindergarten is part of the formal school system, more structured and with more challenging learning standards and curriculum expectations than in the past.	Teachers are still the most important influence on the quality and appropriateness of children's experiences in school. The school system tends to offer higher salaries, better benefits, and more job security than do child care or preschool programs.
Kindergartners vary widely in their prior learning opportunities both at home or in preschool. Teachers face the challenge of teaching a general curriculum to diverse learners.	Effective teachers don't expect all the children to achieve the same thing, at the same time, in the same way. By individualizing teaching and working with small groups, teachers experience the rewards of seeing children make great strides.
Kindergartners don't think and learn exactly like adults and older children—there are limits to their understanding of complex concepts.	Kindergartners are more competent learners and thinkers than many people assume. They strive to make sense of the world, solve problems, and are fascinated by learning about topics that interest them.
Kindergarten classes are larger than those in preschool and teachers do not usually have the benefit of an assistant, making it more difficult for teachers to individualize their teaching.	Most schools have multiple kindergarten classrooms, and teachers can collaborate with colleagues within grade level and across grades. Family members as well as specialists in music, art, physical education, and special education may be available to offer support.
Kindergartners can function independently in self-help skills and need less adult support than preschoolers.	Kindergartners are still young children who rely on teachers for emotional as well as physical support and usually want to please their teachers.
The kindergarten curriculum tends to focus on literacy and math, raising concerns that there is insufficient attention to social-emotional and other areas of development.	Good kindergarten teachers know that both children's cognition and social development are essential. Their teaching integrates academic skills and concepts with positive social-emotional development and warm, responsive relationships.
Kindergarten may be included in school district accountability requirements. Children are sometimes tested inappropriately.	Effective teachers use ongoing assessment of children's learning to adapt curriculum and teaching. They don't place undue emphasis on formal tests but do hold themselves accountable to children and families.

Teaching the Whole Child in the Primary Grades

A great deal of growth and change takes place from ages 6 through 8. Similarly, the curriculum and, therefore, teachers' experiences will vary if they are teaching in the first, second, or third grade (Copple, Bredekamp, Koralek, & Charner, 2014a). Here we visit a first-grade classroom, but the considerations for teaching in the primary grades generally apply across the age span.

Video Example 16.3:

Teaching Kindergarten

In this video, two kindergarten teachers describe their daily life. What motivates them to teach kindergarten? What brings them the greatest joy? What are their challenges?

A Day in the Life of a First-Grade Teacher Lina Truesdale's 22 first-graders have very different backgrounds and abilities. Early in the school year, Lina spent time getting to know the children and assessing their abilities. She found that five of them were reading at the second-grade level or above, and four did not know all the letter-sound combinations. The district curriculum is designed for children somewhere in the middle. But like every good first-grade teacher, Lina knows that she teaches children first and curriculum second.

The school district requires that there be a 90-minute language arts block each morning in first grade. Lina knows that the children are more likely to stay energetic and focused if she varies the activities during this time, and makes sure that the children are as active as possible, both mentally and physically. She begins the morning with whole-group instruction and discussion of new concepts, introducing and explaining new vocabulary words in everyday language. Then the class divides into smaller groups. Each day, Lina works with small groups on guided reading, during which she assesses their reading comprehension and ability to monitor themselves for understanding. She coaches them to ask questions such as "Does that make sense?" "What does that mean?" and "How you know?"

At the same time, others read independently or in pairs. Then, children continue with individual work, such as writing in journals, while Lina observes and offers individual help as needed. She ends the language arts period with a whole-group read-aloud, which the children love. At this point in their reading journey, the books the children can decode on their own have limited vocabulary and are not as interesting as the stories that Lina reads to them. Lina keeps careful records of children's reading progress. She takes great pride in their achievements while also focusing on ways to adapt her teaching for those who are behind.

Some days the class has physical education before lunch, and other days they have music. After lunch, they play outside for 20 minutes and then return for focused math time. Again, Lina varies the teaching context. She may introduce a new math concept, such as a put-together/take-apart problem, to the whole group. Then she gives them a problem to discuss with their neighbors: "Sixteen plus what number equals 21?" The children report their solutions and reasoning to the whole group. Seven-year-old Nancy explains, "We got 5. We started with 16 and counted 17, 18, 19, 20, 21, and that's five numbers." Lina says, "That's one way to solve the problem. Is there another way?"

Lina observes children's grasp of the problem. Then, she follows the whole-group time with small-group work, during which she focuses on those who haven't grasped the new concept, or gives more difficult problems to those who need challenge. Science or social studies projects follow that integrate literacy, language, and mathematics goals.

At the end of her day, Lina meets with the other first-grade teachers to talk about effective ways of helping struggling readers and children who are having trouble grasping basic math concepts. She also seeks their advice on ways to assist Irina and Carlos, who are learning English. She plans to communicate with their families as well.

A major portion of the day in primary grades is devoted to reading and writing instruction. What are some ways that intentional teachers can integrate other areas of the curriculum, such as science and social studies, with reading and writing?

© Pearson Education

Video Example 16.4:

Teaching Primary Grades

In this video, primary-grade teachers talk about the rewards of their work. Reflect on your own goals for a career in education. What challenges and rewards do you expect?

Considerations for Teaching in the Primary Grades Do you remember your first-grade teacher? What experiences come to mind? Of all your teachers between kindergarten and third grade, which ones do you remember best, and for what reasons?

The primary grades—first through third—are prime time for learning. They set the stage for much that comes after. Primary-grade teachers have a significant, measurable impact on children's educational careers and, hence, their lives. They have the opportunity to make lasting contributions to the world; their work is both demanding and stimulating, as described in Table 16.4.

In this section, we used broad strokes to paint images of life in classrooms for teachers of children from birth through age 8. However, teachers lead important professional lives beyond the classroom, as discussed in the next section.

TABLE 16.4 Considerations for Primary Grade Teachers

During the primary grades, children need to acquire the fundamentals of literacy and mathematics, which increases the emphasis on accountability but also the rewards of teaching.
IF YOU ARE THINKING OF TEACHING IN THE PRIMARY GRADES, YOU MIGHT CONSIDER THAT:

On the One Hand	On the Other Hand
Primary-grade children have longer attention spans and are increasingly capable of independent work.	Primary-grade children are still in their early childhood. They become more inattentive and exhausted from sitting and listening for long periods than from movement. Good teachers respect their need to be physically and mentally active.
By third grade, children's self-concepts, academic ability, and social skills are well established and become more difficult to change.	Teachers have the power to really make a difference to children's self-concept and academic and social success through positive relationships and intentional teaching.
The primary-grade curriculum tends to be so focused on reading that little time is left over for other subject areas.	Teaching a child to read, which for some children is a relatively easy task but for others is a seemingly overwhelming hurdle, is one of the most satisfying experiences of a teacher's life.
The primary-school curriculum is usually dictated by the district or state and can be overly prescriptive with little room for flexibility on the part of teachers.	Teachers know that children cannot be scripted. They take their cues from children and follow their lead more than they follow the prescribed lesson plan.
Primary-grade children tend to develop focused interests such as collecting, sports, music, or art.	Children's interests can be the vehicles for teaching them important skills and content. They can read and write about sports or practice number problems with a collection of their favorite objects.
Schoolwork gets harder during the primary grades, requiring greater attention and sustained effort. This discourages some learners.	Throughout the primary grades, if they have engaged and talented teachers, most children are motivated to learn and, therefore, like school.
Standardized achievement testing in third grade (and sometimes earlier) can place considerable stress on teachers and children who may be retained if they are not reading at grade level. Test scores may be used as the sole measure of accountability.	Teachers can work across grade levels and with families to focus on helping every child learn and succeed, resisting the pressure to narrow the curriculum to what is tested. Good teachers have high expectations for every child and do not assign blame when children are behind or need extra help.

 Application Exercise 16.1

Which Teacher to Hire

 Check Your Understanding 16.1

Beginning Your Journey as an Early Childhood Professional

Becoming a professional early childhood educator involves commitments in addition to working with children and families. In its *Standards for Early Childhood Professional Preparation*, NAEYC (2011b) describes the following aspects of becoming a professional:

- Identifying and involving oneself with the early childhood field
- Knowing about and upholding ethical standards and other professional guidelines
- Engaging in continuous, collaborative learning to inform practice
- Integrating knowledgeable, reflective, and critical perspectives on early education
- Engaging in informed advocacy for children and the profession.

Video Example 16.5:

Are Younger Children Easier to Teach?

Early childhood educators work with children from birth through age 8. In this video, Sue Bredekamp interviews the director of a high-quality NAEYC-accredited program serving 3-year-olds through kindergarten. Do you agree with the director's views about teaching different age childen? What age group would you prefer and why?

Become a Professional

A **profession** is an occupation that requires extensive education and/or specialized training, such as the legal or medical professions. Professionals draw on this specialized body of knowledge and expertise to guide their decisions and behavior, but not prescribe it (Feeney & Freeman, 2018). Professions also mandate requirements for entry and standards for practice by their members. They tend to be exclusive in that only those individuals who meet the requirements can call themselves members of the profession (Goffin, 2015).

Although some positions in the early childhood field abide by this strict definition of a professional, others do not. In general, teachers at the elementary level are considered professionals because they are required to have baccalaureate degrees and licenses and to participate in continuing professional development to stay current in the field. By contrast, there are no uniform educational requirements for teachers of children from birth to age 5. The fragmented nature of the field is a barrier to professionalization and ensuring quality for all children (Bornfreund, & Goffin, 2016). Nevertheless, early childhood education is evolving and can boast several key characteristics of a profession, such as a commitment to a greater good—the welfare of children, a body of knowledge to guide practice, professional associations, and a code of ethics (Feeney & Freeman, 2018; NAEYC, 2016).

profession An occupation that requires extensive education and/or specialized training.

Given the expanding scientific knowledge of child development, efforts are underway to further professionalize the field of early education (Institute of Medicine [IOM] & National Research Council [NRC], 2015). In addition, the National Academies of Sciences, Engineering, and Medicine [NASEM] (2018) calls for transforming the financing of early education to ensure a high-quality system for all children and compensation commensurate with teachers' qualifications and professional responsibilities. A related effort, *Power to the Profession*, is a national collaboration led by NAEYC (2018) to establish uniform career paths, standards, qualifications, and compensation for early educators across all sectors.

Become Involved in the Early Childhood Field One of the most valuable steps in becoming a professional is joining an organization that offers resources and services to its members, such as conferences and publications. These affiliations provide a sense of identity, the opportunity to establish relationships with like-minded people, and access to the most current research and information about the field. Professional associations, such as the American Medical Association, restrict membership to qualified individuals. Early childhood education, on the other hand, has several professional associations, but membership in them is open to all.

The National Association for the Education of Young Children (NAEYC) is the largest association of individuals who work with and for children from birth through age 8. Other organizations also strengthen individuals' ties to their chosen field and advocate on behalf of children, including the National Black Child Development Institute, Unidos US (formerly National Council of La Raza), National Head Start Association, and the National Association for Family Child Care. Most national associations also have state and/or local affiliate groups through which new and experienced teachers can find support from colleagues and mentors.

Elementary school teachers usually belong to one of the two teacher unions: the National Education Association or the American Federation of Teachers. Increasingly, child care professionals are also joining unions in order to band together for improved wages and working conditions. Many primary-grade teachers belong to content organizations such as the International Literacy Association, National Council of Teachers of Mathematics, or National Science Teachers Association.

Uphold Professional Standards

Because young children are at such a critical point in their development, and because they are vulnerable and cannot articulate their own rights and needs, early childhood professionals must know about and uphold professional and ethical standards (Feeney & Freeman, 2018).

Standards and guidelines vary depending on the type of program or school, but they may include those for program accreditation (NAEYC, 2016) and for developmentally appropriate practice (NAEYC, 2009). Other relevant professional standards may include:

- Child care licensing requirements
- National, state, or local standards for curriculum content and child outcomes
- Requirements for reporting and preventing child abuse, which we discuss in detail later in this chapter.

Uphold the NAEYC Code of Ethical Conduct

One of the hallmarks of a profession is the existence of a **code of ethics**, which defines the core values of the field and provides guidance for what professionals should do when they encounter difficult or conflicting obligations or responsibilities in their work. The *NAEYC Code of Ethical Conduct* (NAEYC, 2011a) guides early childhood educators in their relationships with children, families, colleagues, and the broader society. Supplements to the code also exist for program administrators, principals, teacher educators, and others involved in professional development.

Individual people have their own personal views about **morality**—what they think is right and wrong and how they should behave. **Ethics** involves critical thinking about morality and the ability to make choices about one's own values. In contrast to individual morality, **professional ethics** are "the kinds of actions that are right or wrong in the workplace and are a public matter" (Feeney & Freeman, 2018). They help individuals resolve moral dilemmas they encounter in their work.

Understanding Ethical Responsibilities

Ethical responsibilities refer to the obligations that every teacher agrees to uphold with honesty, integrity, and respect. In fulfilling these responsibilities, early childhood educators should adhere to principles articulated in NAEYC's Code of Ethical Conduct. For example, the first principle is the most important and takes precedence over all others:

> Above all, we shall not harm children. We shall not participate in practices that are emotionally damaging, physically harmful, disrespectful, degrading, dangerous, exploitative, or intimidating to children (NAEYC, 2011a, p. 3).

Other examples of teachers' ethical responsibilities include never sharing confidential information about a child or family with a person who has no legitimate need for knowing, obeying relevant laws (especially those regarding child abuse), and respecting the rights of children with disabilities. In difficult situations, teachers should consult the code for guidance about their ethical responsibilities, as illustrated in the following situation:

> Daniel is a child in Kiera Blaine's kindergarten class. His parents are divorcing and involved in a nasty custody battle. Kiera has had several conferences with Daniel's father because he is concerned about the effect of the divorce on his son. Daniel's

code of ethics Defines the core values of a profession and provides guidance for what professionals should do when they encounter difficult or conflicting obligations or responsibilities in their work.

morality Personal views about what is right and wrong and how to behave.

ethics Critical thinking about morality and people's ability to make choices about their own values.

professional ethics The kinds of actions that are right or wrong in the workplace and are a public matter.

ethical responsibilities The obligations that every teacher agrees to uphold with honesty, integrity, and respect.

mother hasn't said anything to Kiera. After several months, Daniel's father asks Kiera to testify on his behalf in the custody case. Kiera feels bad for Daniel's father and wants to help him, but isn't sure if she should.

Here is a case in which consulting the code can ease Kiera's mind and help her do the right thing. The code clearly states: "In cases where family members are in conflict with one another, we shall work openly, sharing our observations of the child, to help all parties involved make informed decisions. We shall refrain from becoming an advocate for one party" (NAEYC, 2011a, p. 4).

Over the course of your teaching career, you are likely to encounter difficult situations when you aren't sure about the right decision. In these cases, NAEYC's Code of Ethical Conduct will help you resolve ethical dilemmas.

Resolving Ethical Dilemmas Sometimes the right answer in a difficult situation is not clear. An **ethical dilemma** involves deciding the right thing to do when two or more values conflict, as in the following case:

> Little Achievers is a well-respected child care center in a relatively affluent community with a long waiting list for admission. Beverly Stanos is excited to get a job there as an infant/toddler teacher that pays more than any other position she has had. Soon she begins to feel bewildered and conflicted. The center moves the babies and toddlers to a new group every six months; the director explains that they do this so that the babies don't get attached to the teachers.
>
> Beverly is upset; this practice goes against everything she has learned in her teacher education program about the importance of early attachments for babies' development. She checks the licensing standards and finds nothing to prohibit the practice. Finally, she meets with the director to try to get her to change the policy based on research about child development. The director dismisses Beverly's ideas because she says the policy is a good selling point with parents who don't want their babies to become attached to anyone but them. On the one hand, Beverly thinks she should quit this job, but she knows that if she just quits nothing will change. On the other hand, she feels an obligation to tell the parents that the policy is wrong.

ethical dilemma Deciding the right thing to do when two or more values conflict.

Although many early childhood professionals choose their jobs based on the philosophy of the school or program, many find that at some point in their career, they may encounter an ethical dilemma, as Beverly does, in which values conflict. In Beverly's case, several principles in the code apply and she should weigh them as she attempts to resolve the dilemma:

- The code states that early childhood professionals should be familiar with the knowledge base of the profession and appreciate the vulnerability of children and their dependence on adults, which Beverly clearly does in this case.
- The code also guides her to acknowledge families' child-rearing values and their right to make decisions for their children.
- The code directs early childhood educators "to do nothing that diminishes the reputation of the program in which we work unless it is violating laws and regulations designed to protect children or is violating the provisions of this Code" (NAEYC, 2011a, p. 5).

Beverly's dilemma causes her to feel stress and discomfort and forces her to consider:

- Who she is most obligated to in this situation
- What she should do to address her dilemma
- Examining the code for additional guidance

As an early childhood professional, you will most likely encounter ethical dilemmas of your own. Knowing the resources and tools to refer to is a first step in resolving the conflict. It is also important to understand the philosophy of any place where you are considering

Promoting Play

Resolving an Ethical Dilemma about Play

You teach 3- and 4-year-olds in a large, diverse child care agency. Your personal teaching philosophy is that children learn a great deal through play, especially socio-dramatic play. Your classroom environment includes a large housekeeping area. You regularly provide specific props related to children's interests or the current topic of study to encourage and extend their pretend play. Many of the families, however, are members of cultural groups that object to the children taking on pretend roles that they do not consider culturally appropriate. For example, some of the Latino parents are upset to see boys playing in the housekeeping area. Some of the Arabic families do not want boys and girls playing together at all. You personally are opposed to gender stereotyping and try to counteract it in your classroom whenever possible.

You are faced with an ethical dilemma. To resolve it, you consult the NAEYC Code of Ethical Conduct, which leads you to first consider the knowledge base about child development and learning. You are already convinced that socio-dramatic play is valuable. Research informs you that preschool children often show preference for playmates of their own gender. At the same time, research indicates that young children become aware of and often react negatively to differences among people, which requires straightforward anti-bias teaching and learning experiences to counteract.

Next, you consult the code of ethics, which includes an important, applicable principle that early childhood environments must support each child's culture, language, ethnicity, and family structure. A similar principle requires that professionals respect the dignity and preferences of families to ensure a culturally consistent environment for children. And that families must be listened to and involved in program decisions.

No simple resolution to the situation exists. However, applying both the code of ethics and what you know about child development, here are some appropriate actions:

- Meet with families to listen to their specific concerns and desires for their children.
- Provide interesting socio-dramatic play themes that do not involve housekeeping.
- Encourage but don't force friendships between children or across genders.
- Foster positive relationships among all children and teach anti-bias approaches to diversity.
- Respect children's choice of playmates but prohibit expressions of bias toward other children for any reason.
- Provide toys and play experiences that appeal to both genders.
- Explain to families, through a translator if necessary, how you are working to accommodate their concerns, respect their cultural values and preferences, and also provide a developmentally appropriate program for their children.

taking a position. If Beverly had known from the start what the program's practice was for moving children from one group to the next, she very well might have continued her job search. Read the *Promoting Play: Resolving an Ethical Dilemma about Play* feature and consider how you would use the Code of Ethical Conduct to address this dilemma.

As we see in the Promoting Play feature, diverse cultural experiences and perspectives can often lead to ethical dilemmas for teachers. In our complex society, resolving such dilemmas can be difficult. Read the *Culture Lens: Professional Ethics in Challenging Times* for suggested guidance.

Engage in Continuous, Collaborative Learning to Inform Practice

Knowledge about child development and learning and about effective curriculum and

Culture Lens
Professional Ethics in Challenging Times

The United States is composed of millions of diverse people of every race, ethnicity, and religion. We speak English but also a variety of other languages. We share a broad cultural experience, but every one of us is also a member of families and cultural groups with differing experiences and world views. We live in challenging— often divisive—political times.

There are rightfully different perspectives and opinions on public policies, many of which directly affect the well-being of vulnerable children. Teachers and parents have their own opinions and may often disagree. But every day educators encounter children and families who are anxious and fearful due to economic insecurity, immigration status, racism, or Islamophobia. The U.S. Constitution protects the right of every child to an education regardless of immigration status; nevertheless, many families are afraid to send their children to school.

What should educators do in these challenging times? Use their professional Code of Ethics to guide their conduct. The first principle (1.1) takes precedence: "Above all, we shall not harm children." Other applicable principles are: We shall support each child's culture, language, ethnicity, and family structure (1.2); We shall not discriminate against children by denying benefits, giving special advantages, or excluding them from programs or activities based on their sex, race, national origin, religious belief, medical condition, disability, or the marital status/family structure, sexual orientation, or religious beliefs or other affiliations of their families (1.3). The Code also calls for relationships of mutual trust with all families, and respecting the dignity and preferences of each family about its structure, culture, language, customs, and beliefs.

Resolving ethical dilemmas in these times can be challenging given all our different perspectives and experiences. Louise Derman-Sparks and Julie Olsen Edwards (2017), well-known advocates for anti-bias education, articulated their commitment to implement these ethical principles in the following "Pledge to All Children and Families," which they encourage programs to adopt and post in their classrooms:

All Children Belong Here: This is Our Promise to You

We will build an open, safe, and mutually respectful school community in which each child and each family is an important and equal member.

We will never allow differences of any kind to be an excuse to make fun of, exclude, or hurt you.

We will listen carefully and lovingly to what worries you and give you thoughtful, age-appropriate information and support.

We will nurture you to feel strong and proud about yourself and your family.

We will facilitate your skills to be friends with classmates who are alike and different from you.

We will honor your family's importance to you by building respectful partnerships with them.

We will provide support to you and your family when they feel stress, anxiety, or fear because of current events or acts of prejudice or hate.

We will learn about and help your family use legal and community resources to keep you safe.

We will work to uproot our own personal biases as adults and will speak out against prejudice and bias wherever we encounter it.

We will mobilize our courage and become active with others to resist and change any policies and practices that threaten to hurt you or your family.

We are in this together—working for a world where every child is protected and honored, exactly as they are.

Sources: Derman-Sparks, L., & Edwards, J.O. (2017). *Living our commitments: A pledge to all children and families. Exchange.* Retrieved May 23, 2018 from https://www.childcareexchange.com/article/living-our-commitments-a-pledge-to-all-children-and-families/5023432/; Day, C., Derman-Sparks, L., & Hernandez, L. (2017). *Honoring our professional ethics, conduct, and commitment in challenging times.* Presentation at NAEYC Professional Learning Institute, San Francisco, CA; and National Association for the Education of Young Children (NAEYC), 2011a. *Code of ethical conduct and statement of commitment,* (reaffirmed and updated May 2011). Retrieved May 12, 2018 from http://www.naeyc.org/files/naeyc/file/positions/PSETH05.pdf

teaching is always changing and expanding. Early childhood educators have an obligation to keep up to date with the latest research developments in the field (IOM & NRC, 2015; Pre-kindergarten Task Force, 2017). Professional education doesn't end with completion of a degree or initial licensure. Rather, teachers commit themselves to lifelong professional learning. Technology greatly facilitates collaborative practice and continuous learning.

Becoming an Intentional Teacher

I Wish My Teacher Knew

Here's What Happened I've been teaching second grade for three years, but this year I have had more behavior problems than ever before. More children arrive late and absenteeism has increased. One child falls asleep in the afternoon. I've tried to talk with parents, but either I can't reach them or they aren't forthcoming.

A fellow teacher alerted me to a viral Twitter hashtag "#iwishmyteacherknew" which linked to an article in the *New York Times*. A third-grade teacher in Colorado, Kyle Schwartz, decided she wanted to get to know her students better so she asked them to complete the sentence: *I wish my teacher knew*. The responses she received were both heartbreaking (I wish my teacher knew I live in a shelter) and inspiring (I wish my teacher knew I love science).

I decided to try the strategy myself. I knew that my students' lives were more complicated than my own but I never imagined all that was happening. It was enlightening to read: I wish my teacher knew that my Mom is going to Afghanistan soon. I wish my teacher knew that I get a stomach ache during reading lesson. I wish my teacher knew that I'm hungry. I wish my teacher knew that I'm afraid someone will shoot us at school.

Here's What I Was Thinking I've always known that it is important to get to know each child, build positive relationships, and individualize teaching. But I felt something was missing. This relatively simple assignment opened windows into my students' lives that had been closed to me. Focusing on outward behaviors such as being late or absent masked what I really needed to know. After this experience, I'll work harder at understanding their lives and won't be so quick to make assumptions.

Reflection Think about your own years in school. What do you wish your teachers knew about you? How did that change over time?

Source: De La Cruz, D. (2016). What kids wish their teachers knew. *New York Times*, August 31. Retrieved May 22, 2018 from https://www.nytimes.com/2016/08/31/well/family/what-kids-wish-their-teachers-knew.html

Teachers can learn a great deal from other teachers. For this reason, NAEYC (Lutton, 2012) calls for teachers to collaborate with colleagues on their own classroom-based research, investigate ways to improve their own practices, participate in conferences, and stay current by reading and discussing publications and Internet sites. For example, a group of kindergarten teachers might figure out how to share a limited set of materials across classrooms to enhance the complexity of hands-on learning experiences. A team of preschool teachers might meet regularly to compare observations of children's interests and thinking. The staff of a child care center might read an article on biting and agree on ways to handle the problem with toddlers and families. Most important of all, teachers need to learn directly from children as described in the feature *Becoming an Intentional Teacher: I Wish My Teacher Knew*.

Integrate Knowledgeable, Reflective, and Critical Perspectives on Early Education Even relatively routine decisions about which book to read, how to help children settle a dispute, or how to organize a safe, educational field trip require teachers to draw on professional knowledge and values. Developmentally appropriate practice is a decision-making process that requires teachers to be knowledgeable about the latest research findings in the field.

However, none of the professional guidelines or standards, including the Code of Ethical Conduct, contains one simple, true answer to any of the myriad questions teachers confront. In fact, early childhood professionals who share the same core values do not agree on the answers to some of the most central questions such as the name of the field, the proper balance of teacher-guided and child-guided experience, or what *developmentally appropriate* really means (Bredekamp, 1997; Goffin, 2015). Therefore, professionals need to be reflective and critical, analyzing and evaluating the effectiveness of their own practices to improve their work with children of all ages. They also must be open to views that differ from their own.

Become an Informed Advocate for Children and the Profession Early childhood education is an imperfect field. The quality of services for children is uneven and, in many cases, inadequate. High-quality programs are expensive, and many families cannot afford them. Early childhood teachers, whose jobs require a high level of professional knowledge and responsibility, are grossly undercompensated (Thomason et al., 2018). This disparity is finally being widely publicized as occurred when the *New York Times* (Interlandi, 2018) published an in-depth expose entitled, "Why are our most important teachers paid the least?"

To make a real difference in children's lives, early childhood professionals have the additional obligation of becoming informed advocates for children and the profession (Lutton, 2012). **Advocacy** is aiding a cause that you believe in. It can be as personal as referring a family for counseling or as political as lobbying your representative for an increase in Head Start funding.

advocacy Aiding a cause that you believe in.

The key word is *informed*. Effective advocates present valid, accurate information and draw on their knowledge of research and real-world experience. Representatives are more likely to vote for increased funding if they are convinced that such programs work. Successful advocates present research on program effectiveness, but they also share the stories of children and families whose life experience is represented by the data.

Informed advocacy requires that early childhood professionals be familiar with the central policy issues affecting the field, including compensation for teachers, financing of

- Join a child advocacy organization such as NAEYC, NBCDI, or NHSA, and stay informed about policy via their listservs, websites, and meetings.
- Get to know and collaborate with other professionals who work across the age-span and in diverse sectors. Avoid pitting the needs of one sector against another.
- Organize opportunities for colleagues with a variety of political opinions to come together in an informal setting to listen and learn from each other about their views on early childhood education.
- Advocate for sufficient funding for high-quality early childhood programs for all children and to improve compensation and benefits for teachers.
- Listen to parents and engage them in advocating for their children and quality programs for all.
- Attend meetings of policy makers at all levels—city council, county commissioners, Congressional representatives—and follow them on social media to learn their views on issues impacting young children.
- Express your views on legislation and policy decisions via social media, op-ed pieces, email, phone, and letters.
- Attend school board meetings and speak up about issues affecting young children such as curriculum adoption, testing practices, grade retention, and suspension/expulsion policies.
- Build your knowledge of cultural and linguistic diversity through wide reading and joining diverse civic, community, volunteer, and faith-based organizations.
- Provide online critical reviews of violent videos, inappropriate apps, or other substandard products intended for children.
- Invite elected officials to visit high-quality programs and share the research on the long-term effects of high-quality early education.
- Vote in every election at the local, state, and national levels and encourage others, including families, to register and vote.

FIGURE 16.2 Become an Informed Advocate Effective teachers not only focus on the children in their classrooms, but also advocate for high-quality education for all children and families, and better work environments for professionals.

Source: National Association for the Education of Young Children. (no date). *Be a proactive early learning advocate.* Retrieved May 4, 2018 from https://www.naeyc.org/get-involved/advocate/be-proactive

the early education system, standards for curriculum, and appropriate methods of assessment (IOM & NRC, 2015; NASEM, 2018). They also need to understand how public policies are developed and demonstrate essential advocacy skills, such as clear verbal and written communication skills and the ability to work effectively with others toward a common goal (NAEYC, no date).

Change requires a broad base of advocates, particularly parents and grandparents who are consumers of the services. Truly informed advocacy requires listening to and involving parents. Read the feature, *What Works: Parents as Partners in Advocacy*, to learn how parents make choices for their children and the implications.

Figure 16.2 lists ways in which informed advocates act on behalf of children and the profession.

To learn more about the importance of critical, reflective practice and informed advocacy, read the feature *Including All Children: Advocating for Effective Inclusion of Children with Disabilities*.

Protect Children from Abuse and Neglect

Early childhood educators tend to focus on the positive and want only the best for young children. But our responsibility goes beyond providing excellent care and education for children to protecting them from harm to the extent possible. For this reason, reporting suspected cases of child abuse and neglect is not only one of our most difficult professional responsibilities but also the most sacred. To meet this responsibility, teachers need to know the signs and symptoms of child abuse and also the legal requirements surrounding it. The federal government's Child Welfare Information Gateway website provides up-to-date resources to help professionals fulfill these obligations.

What Works

Parents as Partners in Advocacy

© Karen H Ilagan/Shutterstock

To advocate for better quality, educators need to understand families' needs and goals for their children. NAEYC commissioned a bi-partisan polling organization to conduct a market survey of parents' opinions about quality and financing. Similarly, the Trust for Learning conducted a research program to discover how parents make choices about their children's care and education from birth through age 5. Overwhelmingly, parents agree that early education has a positive impact on their children's social and academic development. And 84 percent of parents believe that there should be more public funding for these programs.

Predictably, the research found that parents want their children to become capable, well-rounded contributors to society. In general, parents' views are congruent with the science of child development and research on effective practice. Both surveys found that parents place the most value on social-emotional competence followed by academic readiness.

Approximately two-thirds of parents agree that enrolling their child in a program prior to school is valuable, but a large percentage acknowledge that they cannot afford the best program.

Not surprisingly, more affluent parents place greater emphasis on quality while less affluent families stress affordability. However, across the income spectrum, parents agree that they have the primary financial responsibility and are not looking for a government handout. But they acknowledge that improving teacher qualifications and compensation will put costs out of reach, necessitating some public support.

Parents consider teacher quality and safety to be the most important factors in choosing a program. Regardless of race or income, parents value high-quality early childhood education. Parents' views must be respected and included if advocacy for improved quality and sufficient funding is to be effective.

Source: National Association for the Education of Young Children (NAEYC), 2017. *Growing the demand for quality: Parents and early childhood educators talk about the financing of early learning in market research from NAEYC*. Retrieved My 22, 2018 from https://www.naeyc.org/our-work/initiatives/profession/advancing-profession-market-research; and Trust for Learning, 2017. *Parents as consumers of early childhood education*. Retrieved May 23, 2018, 2018 from https://www.trustforlearning.org

Including All Children

Advocating for Effective Inclusion of Children with Disabilities

Inclusion of children with disabilities and special needs raises important questions for teachers and requires them to reflect on their own practices. Consider the following classroom example:

> Two children with disabilities and IEPs are in my first-grade class. April has Tourette's syndrome and Willis has autism. I learned about inclusion in my college classes, but until now I haven't encountered children with disabilities as severe as theirs. In searching the internet for help, I found the joint position statement on Early Childhood Inclusion by the Division for Early Childhood and NAEYC, which says that the defining features of inclusion are *access, participation,* and *systemic supports.* The next time that I attended each child's IEP team meeting, I spoke up. I confessed that in each case, the child was present in the classroom but not really participating. I asked for resources to read and the opportunity to attend some workshops to help me learn more effective strategies. My biggest concern is that neither the children nor I are getting the systemic supports we need to be successful. As a result, I spoke with the principal and

April's and Willis's parents. We arranged meetings with the school district special education coordinator to advocate for changes in how the children are served, such as having therapists work with them in the regular classroom rather than pulling them out.

This teacher demonstrates her commitment to professional standards. She collaborates with colleagues, continues to learn, and integrates knowledgeable, reflective, and critical perspectives into her work. After reading and reflecting on the position statement, she realized that April and Willis weren't really included in the class. Although they had access, they weren't fully participating and they needed more support to achieve their IEP goals and the goals of the regular curriculum. Reflecting on and thinking critically about her own behavior, she realized that she wasn't fully participating in team meetings and was unsure about how best to teach Willis and April. The teacher and the children were not getting the supports they needed from the school system. She exercised her professional responsibilities working with families and colleagues to advocate on their behalf.

Signs and Symptoms of Child Abuse and Neglect There are several types of child abuse, including physical abuse, neglect, sexual abuse, and emotional abuse. In most cases, however, children experience these abuses in combination—a sexually abused child is also harmed physically and mentally. Teachers need to be alert to general warning signs for abuse. If a teacher suspects a parent or other adult of abusing a child, it is important to observe both the child's and adult's behavior individually and also to observe the interaction between them. For example, a child might be always watching as though waiting for something bad to happen, a parent may show little concern for the child, and when together they may avoid looking at or touching each other (Child Welfare Information Gateway, 2007). Teachers also need to know the typical warning signs of specific types of abuse, which are listed in Table 16.5.

Reporting Requirements Almost every day the media report tragic incidents of child abuse that could have been alleviated if someone had reported their suspicions to the proper authorities. Too many people feel that it is none of their business or they are afraid of offending parents or colleagues. Although anyone can and should report suspected abuse, teachers, child care workers, and school officials are *mandatory* reporters. They are required by law to report maltreatment of children. Every state has child abuse reporting procedures, but the specific regulations regarding confidentiality and how to report vary from state to state. The Child Welfare Information Gateway provides links to each state's requirements.

Teachers are not only legally mandated to report suspected child abuse but also have an ethical responsibility to do so. The NAEYC Code of Ethical Conduct (NAEYC, 2011a) states that even when another person tells us of their suspicion, we should assist them in taking action, and if a child protective service agency fails in its responsibilities, we should advocate for improved services. Being the one person in a child's life who intervenes to

TABLE 16.5 Recognizing Potential Signs of Child Abuse

Knowing these potential warning signs is essential for teachers to fulfil their legal and moral responsibility to report suspected incidents of child abuse and neglect.

Type of Abuse	Consider the Possibility of Abuse When the Child:	Consider the Possibility of Abuse When the Parent or Adult Caregiver:
Physical Abuse	• Has unexplained burns, bites, bruises, broken bones, or black eyes • Has fading bruises or other marks noticeable after an absence from school • Seems frightened of the parents and protests or cries when it is time to go home • Shrinks at the approach of adults • Reports injury by a parent or another adult caregiver	• Offers conflicting, unconvincing, or no explanation for the child's injury • Describes the child as "evil," or in some other very negative way • Uses harsh physical discipline with the child • Has a history of abuse as a child
Neglect	• Is frequently absent from school • Begs or steals food or money • Lacks needed medical or dental care, immunizations, or glasses • Is consistently dirty and has severe body odor • Lacks sufficient clothing for the weather • States that there is no one at home to provide care	• Appears to be indifferent to the child • Seems apathetic or depressed • Behaves irrationally or in a bizarre manner • Is abusing alcohol or other drugs
Sexual Abuse	• Has difficulty walking or sitting • Suddenly refuses to change clothes or to participate in physical activities • Reports nightmares or bedwetting • Experiences a sudden change in appetite • Demonstrates bizarre, sophisticated, or unusual sexual knowledge or behavior	• Is unduly protective of the child or severely limits the child's contact with other children, especially of the opposite sex • Is secretive and isolated
Emotional Abuse	• Shows extremes in behavior, such as overly compliant or demanding behavior, extreme passivity or aggression • Is either inappropriately adult (parenting other children, for example) or inappropriately infantile (frequently rocking or head-banging, for example) • Is delayed in physical or emotional development	• Constantly blames, belittles, or berates the child • Is unconcerned about the child and refuses to consider offers of help for the child's problems • Overtly rejects the child

Source: Child Welfare Information Gateway, retrieved from https://www.childwelfare.gov/pubs/factsheets/ques.cfm.

stop the horror of abuse is probably the most difficult task of any teacher's career but would also make the biggest difference in an individual child's life.

Join a Profession That Makes a Difference

Throughout this book we cite research demonstrating incontrovertably that high-quality early education makes a significant contribution to children and families, and to the larger society. As we have seen, the most important determinant of quality is an effective teacher.

Effective Teachers Most people intuitively know that good teachers make a difference in how well children learn. In fact, some studies show that the most effective teachers can contribute as much as an extra year's growth in academic achievement for the fortunate children in their classes. But conducting such research is difficult because it is hard to know whether the differences were caused more by the children's inborn abilities or their environmental circumstances than by the teacher's practice.

A well-designed study addressed the question of cause and effect directly by measuring the reading achievement of identical and fraternal twins who had more- or less-effective teachers (Taylor, Roehrig, Hensler, Connor, & Schatschneider, 2010). Using twins enabled the researchers to control for genetics because identical twins share 100% of their genes, and fraternal twins share 50%. In the study of more than 800 first- and second-graders, teacher effectiveness was measured by how much the twins' classmates' reading ability improved over the course of the year. What the researchers found was that among identical twins with different teachers, the twin with the more effective teacher had better reading skills. Looking at fraternal and identical twins, the researchers concluded that if teachers are equally excellent, genetics plays a larger role in reading achievement, but that poor-quality, ineffective teaching inhibits children's ability to reach their full potential.

Advocates for effective teaching can cite rigorous research to support their positions. The RAND Corporation reviewed evaluations of 115 programs that serve children and families prenatally to school entry (Cannon et al., 2017). Most were group programs for children, but some were home visiting, parent education, or a combination approach—all of which are career options for early childhood educators. Eighty-nine percent (89%) of the programs showed positive effects on children's learning, development, or health. Similarly, an analysis of 22 well-designed studies conducted between 1960 and 2016 found that participation in early education significantly reduces special education placements and grade retention and increases high school graduation rates (McCoy et al., 2017)—all positive effects that have lifelong benefits.

Application Exercise 16.2
Making a Difference

Commitment to Children Although not an official part of NAEYC's Code of Ethical Conduct, the *Statement of Commitment* (NAEYC, 2011a) in Figure 16.3 is a personal acknowledgment of the individual's willingness to embrace the values and

---

As an individual who works with young children, I commit myself to furthering the values of early childhood education as they are reflected in the ideals and principles of the NAEYC Code of Ethical Conduct. To the best of my ability I will:

- Never harm children.
- Ensure that programs for young children are based on current knowledge and research of child development and early childhood education.
- Respect and support families in their task of nurturing children.
- Respect colleagues in early childhood care and education and support them in maintaining the NAEYC Code of Ethical Conduct.
- Serve as an advocate for children, their families, and their teachers in community and society.
- Stay informed of and maintain high standards of professional conduct.
- Engage in an ongoing process of self-reflection, realizing that personal characteristics, biases, and beliefs have an impact on children and families.
- Be open to new ideas and be willing to learn from the suggestions of others.
- Continue to learn, grow, and contribute as a professional.
- Honor the ideals and principles of the NAEYC Code of Ethical Conduct.

FIGURE 16.3 NAEYC Statement of Commitment The NAEYC Code of Ethical Conduct and all the organization's work is based on this foundational statement of commitment to children and families.

Source: From *Code of Ethical Conduct and Statement of Commitment*, revised edition, 2011a, Washington, DC: NAEYC. Reprinted with permission from the National Association for the Education of Young Children.

moral obligations that lead to becoming part of the early childhood profession. This statement undergirds the association's other positions including developmentally appropriate practice.

The Joy of Teaching Young Children   Teaching young children is a career that brings great personal fulfillment. Every hour, your small charges burst into laughter, need comforting, figure something out, and learn new words. Each day has its small rewards—a wilting dandelion, a shared joke, an "Ah-ha!" expression of understanding, or a whispered "I love you, Teacher." Looking back at the end of every year, teachers can't believe how far most of their children have come, and they regret that some have not come further. Over time, teachers learn more *about* children but mostly *from* children, and they are humbled by the job. They realize how much they don't know and that there are no simple answers to complex questions. They are awed by the trust that children and parents place in them and they use their power wisely. Most of all, they know that the lives they touch will be changed, as will their own. They are committed to making a positive difference in children's lives.

✓ Check Your Understanding 16.2

Revisiting The Case Study

... the College Classroom

At the outset of this chapter we saw into the thoughts and motivations of several college students as they embarked on an early childhood education class. Those brief descriptions reveal only some of the diverse paths that individuals take into the field. Undoubtedly, their paths will diverge again as they make decisions about which of the many career options, settings, and age groups they want to pursue. We've shined a light on what future days might be like, and some of what they need to consider in their choices.

We began this journey by looking back at the beginnings of early childhood education and the contributions of dauntless women and men who provided the foundations on which it stands today. While those foundations are firm, they are not limiting. The future of children and of early childhood education continues to be built as we learn more about effective practices and our country commits more resources to improving schools for young children. Early childhood education is indeed a field on the rise. If you join this profession, you will discover that you have the power to shape that future for the better. ■

16 Chapter Summary

- A career in early childhood education is filled with never-ending rewards and challenges. Among the major questions early childhood educators face is which age group(s) they would most like to work with and why. For each age group/position, there are interesting points to consider.

- The NAEYC Code of Ethical Conduct guides early childhood educators in making decisions about their professional responsibilities and resolving ethical dilemmas that arise in their relationships with children, families, colleagues, and society.

- Early childhood educators are also effective advocates for children and the profession. They know about the central policy issues in the field, including professional compensation, financing of the early education system, and standards for curriculum and assessment.

- Teachers must know the warning signs of child abuse and neglect, and are required by law to report suspected abuse to the proper authorities.

- Early childhood teachers have the opportunity to make lasting, positive contributions to the lives of children and to make a significant difference in the world.

Key Terms

- advocacy
- code of ethics
- ethical dilemma
- ethical responsibilities
- ethics
- morality
- profession
- professional ethics

✓ Flash Cards 16.1

Readings and Websites

Chenfeld, M. B. (2014). *Still teaching in the key of life: Joyful stories for early childhood settings*. Washington, DC: National Association for the Education of Young Children.

Feeney, S., & Freeman, N. K. (2018). *Ethics and the early childhood educator: Using the NAEYC code* (3rd ed.). Washington, DC: National Association for the Education of Young Children.

Sykes, M. (2014). *Doing the right thing for children: Eight qualities of leadership*. St. Paul, MN: Redleaf Press.

Washington, V. & Gadson, B. (2017). *Guiding principles for the new early childhood educator: Building on strength and competence*. New York: Teachers College Press.

Child Welfare Information Gateway

On this government website, you will find information on identifying signs of child abuse and neglect, reporting requirements, and effective ways to prevent child abuse.

MenTeach

MenTeach is a clearinghouse for both men and women seeking information and resources about men teaching.

This website provides information on careers and resources for recruiting men into early education.

National Black Child Development Institute

The National Black Child Development Institute works with policy makers, professionals, and parents on critical issues that directly impact African American children and their families. This website provides culturally relevant resources on early childhood education, health, child welfare, literacy, and family engagement, addressing the unique strengths and needs of Black children.

New America Early and Elementary Education Program

New America Early and Elementary Education Policy Program brings together diverse perspectives to address current issues and promotes a high-quality and continuous system of early care and education for all children, birth to age 8. Read and subscribe to their blog, EdCentral, to stay informed on the latest developments and research in the field.

✓ Shared Writing 16.1
Confronting an Ethical Dilemma

Glossary

5- to 7-year shift—Major transition in cognitive abilities that gradually occurs between 5 and 7 years of age, resulting in increased ability to think logically, self-regulate, and solve problems.

absorbent mind—Maria Montessori's image of the child as actively learning from sensory experiences.

abstraction—The concept that anything can be counted.

academic discourse—The language of school, which is important for school success.

accommodation—When new information or experience doesn't fit within an existing concept (scheme), the child must modify it or construct a new scheme.

accommodations—Changes in assessment procedures, materials, or setting to eliminate barriers related to the child's disability that might keep children from demonstrating their full capabilities.

accountability—The process of holding teachers, schools, or programs responsible for meeting a required level of performance.

accreditation system—NAEYC's voluntary system for identifying high-quality early childhood centers and schools serving children from birth through kindergarten.

acculturation—The process whereby children learn expected rules of behavior.

achievement tests—Tests designed to measure what children have learned in general or in a content area such as reading or mathematics.

acknowledging—Giving positive verbal or nonverbal attention that promotes the child's persistence and effort.

adaptation—The mental process of altering concepts (schemes) in response to experience, which occurs in two ways: through assimilation and accommodation.

advance organizers—Ways of introducing new information that serve as a bridge between what the student already knows and the new learning.

adverse childhood experiences (ACEs)—Parents' substance abuse, physical emotional or sexual abuse, or neglect that creates toxic stress.

advocacy—Aiding a cause that you believe in.

age appropriate—Age-related human characteristics that allow teachers to make general predictions within an age range about what materials, interactions, and experiences will be safe, interesting, challenging, and within reach for children, and thus likely to best promote their learning and development.

aggressive communication—Speaking the truth in a hurtful way.

Alignment or Continuity—Coordination of the curriculum and experiences from one level of education to the next in order to build on what children have already learned and to ease transitions for students between schools and school levels.

alliteration—Two words beginning with the same sound.

alphabetic principle—The understanding that there is a systematic relationship between letters and sounds, and that all spoken sounds and words can be represented by a limited set of agreed-on symbols called *letters*.

anecdotal records—Short descriptions written by teachers and based on observations of incidents or anecdotes involving one or more children.

anti-bias education—Learning experiences and teaching strategies that are specifically designed not only to prepare all children for life in a culturally rich society, but also to counter the stereotyping of diverse groups, and to guard against expressions of bias

apprenticeship—The process of children learning by observing adults and more accomplished peers performing tasks and by practicing the skills themselves with adult guidance and support.

approaches to learning—Behaviors or typical patterns that children use in learning situations that include both how they feel about learning—their level of enthusiasm, interest, and motivation—and how they engage with learning—their curiosity, initiative, and creativity.

aptitude tests—Tests designed to measure children's potential for learning in the future.

assertive communication—Telling the truth in a thoughtful and considerate way; considered the most effective form of communication.

assessment—The ongoing process of gathering evidence of children's learning and development, then organizing and interpreting the information to make informed decisions about instructional practice.

assimilation—When new information or experience is understood in connection with existing knowledge (schemes).

assistive technology—A piece of equipment or product that is used to increase, maintain, or improve the functional capabilities of individuals with disabilities.

associative play—Children play and share with each other, usually one other child.

attachment theory—The theory that children's ability to learn depends on their developing trusting relationships with caregivers.

auditory awareness—Listening to verbal input or distinguishing between different sounds.

authentic assessment—Determines what children know and can do from their demonstration of a skill or their creation of a product.

autism spectrum disorder (ASD)—Complex developmental disabilities that impact the normal development of the brain processes related to social interaction and communication skills.

babble—Produce consonant/vowel sounds such as "ba ba."

background knowledge—Concepts and basic information about how the world works that is essential for reading comprehension.

balanced approach—Effective reading instruction that helps children master the alphabetic principle *and* acquire meaning from text.

Bank Street approach—Originating with Lucy Sprague Mitchell at Bank Street College and later called the Developmental–Interaction approach, a curriculum framework based on individual children's development, emphasizing that learning begins in children's experiences in the immediate environment (here and now).

base-10 place value system—Highly efficient system of using just 10 numerals to write any counting number no matter how large, in which the meaning of a numeral depends on where it is placed within the number.

behavior intervention plan—Describes the strategies adults will use to prevent a child's negative behavior and to teach more acceptable behavior.

behaviorism or behavioral learning—Theory that learning is a change in behavior that is controlled by the consequences, either positive or negative, that follow the behavior.

bias—Negative feelings and expressions toward groups or individuals.

bicultural—Capable of operating successfully in both the home environment and the dominant culture of the larger world.

body composition—Weight and body fat.

bullying—Occurs when a person repeatedly commits aggressive acts that intend to harm, and an imbalance of power makes it hard for the victim to defend himself or herself.

cardinality—The concept that the last number said stands for the total number in the set.

cardiorespiratory (aerobic) system—Body system made up of the heart, lungs, and blood; provides the stamina needed to be active for a long period of time.

caring community of learners—A group or classroom in which children and adults engage in warm, positive relationships, treat each other with respect, and learn from and with each other.

challenging behavior—Any behavior that interferes with children's learning, development, and success at play; is harmful to the child, other children, or adults; or puts a child at high risk for later social problems or school failure.

charter schools—Independently operated, publicly funded schools that have greater flexibility than regular schools in meeting regulations and achieving goals.

checklists—Practical and versatile tools for gathering assessment information about children's behavior, skills, or attitudes.

Child Care and Development Block Grants (CCDBG)—Federal funds allocated to states for low-income working families to purchase child care.

Child care center—Group program that provides care and education for young children during the hours that their parents are employed.

Child care licensing standards—Minimum requirements legally established by each state for a child care program to operate.

Child Development Associate (CDA) credential—National competency-based credential for entry-level early childhood educators.

child study movement—Early 20th-century effort to scientifically observe and systematically document children's individual development under the leadership of G. Stanley Hall and Arnold Gesell.

child-centered curriculum—John Dewey's idea that curriculum should reflect the concepts and topics that the child is interested in and capable of learning.

child-initiated experiences—Experiences that allow children to gain knowledge and skills through their own exploration and interactions with objects and other children.

children with disabilities—Children who have been identified as having a specific category of disability, such as autism or cerebral palsy.

children with special needs—A broad term used to describe children who may have multiple risk factors, specialized health care needs, mental or emotional health concerns, severe allergies, or physical and/or cognitive disabilities.

chronosystem—System that refers to effects of circumstances over time.

classification systems—Systems teachers use to help children build concepts by identifying similarities and differences or by comparing and contrasting objects and ideas.

Classroom Assessment Scoring System (CLASS)—Preschool and elementary classroom observational instrument that assesses the quality of teachers' relationships and interactions with children and the instructional strategies used to support children's learning.

closed questions—Lower-level questions that have one right answer and usually require children to recall information or facts.

co-player—Teachers actually join in and take an active role in children's play.

code of ethics—Defines the core values of a profession and provides guidance for what professionals should do when they encounter difficult or conflicting obligations or responsibilities in their work.

code switch—The ability to understand and use both the mainstream version of English and the home dialect or language.

cognitive (mental) flexibility—The ability to find new solutions or revise plans in response to changing circumstances.

cognitive development—Thinking, intelligence, and language abilities.

Common Core State Standards—Rigorous national standards in English language arts and mathematics for kindergarten through grade 12 developed by the Council of Chief State School Officers (CCSSO) and the National Governor's Association (NGA).

competent child—The image of children as active players in their own development and learning.

completion prompt—A prompt that requires the child to verbally complete the end of a sentence.

Composing and decomposing—Mathematical processes of putting together and taking apart (for example, addition and subtraction).

comprehension—The ability to understand what is read and to interpret and analyze the author's meaning; the ability to make sense of what is read.

concepts of print—Beginning understandings about the forms and functions of written language, such as that words carry messages.

conceptual frameworks—Mental models that connect new learning to prior knowledge, enhance memory, and deepen understanding.

conceptual organizer—Ways of organizing curriculum, such as the project approach, that make content knowledge more meaningful, interesting, and understandable for children.

connections—Refers to understanding links between different areas of math and connecting math concepts to real-world problems.

consequences—Principle of operant conditioning that behavior changes as a result of what occurs immediately afterward.

conservation—The understanding that the quantity of objects stays the same regardless of changes in appearance.

constructivism—Learning theory derived from the work of Jean Piaget, which assumes that children actively build their knowledge from firsthand experiences in stimulating environments.

constructivism—Learning theory derived from the work of Jean Piaget, which assumes that children actively build their knowledge from firsthand experiences in stimulating environments.

content standards—Describe what students should know and/or be able to do within a particular discipline such as math or science.

conventional reading—Reading in which the reader gains meaning from unfamiliar text.

cooing—Vocalizing vowel sounds.

cooperative play—Children assume different roles and share a purpose for the play.

Council for Exceptional Children (CEC)—The national professional association for special educators.

criterion-referenced tests—Tests that compare a person's score to a predetermined level of performance.

cultural competence—The ability to work respectfully and effectively with people of all cultures, languages, socio-economic classes, races, ethnicities, religions, and other aspects of diversity.

culturally appropriate—Applying knowledge of the social and cultural contexts in which children live, which helps teachers build on children's prior knowledge and make experiences meaningful and responsive.

culturally sustaining practices—teaching strategies that acknowledge and sustain the language, literature, and cultural practices of all children, and in particular children of color

culture—The explicit and implicit values, beliefs, rules, and expectations for behavior of members of a group that are passed on from one generation to the next. These rules determine to a large extent what group members regard as important and what values shape their actions and judgments.

curriculum—a written plan that describes the goals for children's learning and development and the learning sequences, experiences, materials, and teaching strategies used to help children achieve those goals.

curriculum approach—Describes the main elements or direction of a program; is less detailed than a curriculum model.

curriculum framework—A guide for designing or choosing a curriculum.

curriculum model—A research-based, idealized version of what and how teaching and learning should occur.

curriculum-embedded assessment—Formative assessment that is integrated into the curriculum; this assessment does not occur as a separate procedure.

day nurseries—Programs designed to serve working families in the late 19th and early 20th centuries; the forerunner of present-day child care centers.

decode—The ability to figure out what written symbols—letters of the alphabet—represent.

decontextualized speech—Talk about events, experiences, or people that are beyond the here and now or that inhabit children's imaginations.

demonstrating—Showing the correct way to perform a skill or procedure while children observe the outcome.

development—Age-related change that results from an interaction between biological maturation and physical and/or social experience; development occurs as children grow, adapt, and change in response to various experiences.

developmental continuum—A predictable, but not rigid, sequence of typical accomplishments within age ranges that is used to plan curriculum; also an effective assessment tool used to focus teacher attention on what is important to assess—what children can do—and to identify goals for continued progress.

developmentally appropriate practice (D.A.P.)—Ways of teaching that engage children's interests and adapt for their age, experience, and ability to help them meet challenging and achievable learning goals.

diagnostic tests—Tests designed to identify the specific learning or developmental problems a child has and to plan interventions; must be administered by specially trained professionals.

dialogic reading—Interactive, shared picture book reading during which the adult and the child gradually switch roles so that the child learns to become the storyteller with the assistance of the adult, who plays the role of active listener and questioner.

differentiated instruction—The creation of multiple paths so that children of different abilities, interests, and learning needs experience equally appropriate ways to achieve important learning goals.

digital literacy—The ability to obtain, use, interpret, and evaluate information available through multimedia digital sources.

direct instruction—Explicitly giving directions for completing a task; providing facts, verbal labels, or other specific information; or providing instructions for a child's action or behavior.

directional awareness—Anticipating which way to go.

disequilibrium—An imbalance in thinking that occurs when new information or physical experience cannot be understood in terms of what is already known (cannot be assimilated).

disorganized/disoriented attachment—Seen in children who lack secure attachments with adults due to having experienced neglect, abuse, or violence in the home and who have not developed useful strategies for seeking comfort or attention or handling difficulties.

distancing questions—Questions that relate pictures and words in the book to children's own experiences beyond the book.

Division for Early Childhood (DEC)—Subdivision of the Council for Exceptional Children that is the national professional organization for early childhood special educators and early intervention specialists.

domain-general processes—Broad abilities that cut across traditionally defined developmental domains.

domains of development—Areas of human development and functioning that include cognitive, social, emotional, and physical.

dual language learners—Children who simultaneously learn two languages: the home or first language as well as English or another second language.

dual language learning—Simultaneously learning two languages: the home, or first, language and English or another second language.

dynamic assessment—Analyzes a child's performance not just in terms of what the child can do independently, but what the child can do with the assistance of a teacher or peer.

early childhood education—Education and child care services provided for children from birth through age 8.

Early Childhood Environment Rating Scale (ECERS-3)—Observational instrument used to rate program quality on a seven-point scale from inadequate to excellent.

early childhood special education—Services for children with disabilities or special needs who meet eligibility guidelines that are determined on a state-by-state basis according to the Individuals with Disabilities Education Act.

Early Head Start—Federally funded program serving low-income pregnant mothers, infants, and toddlers that promotes healthy family functioning.

early intervention—Services for infants and toddlers who are at risk of developmental delay and their families.

early learning standards—Guidelines that describe what children should know and be able to do before entering kindergarten.

early literacy—Skills and knowledge that come before and lead up to (forerunners) conventional reading and writing.

earth and space science—Studying properties of earth materials, changes on the earth, patterns of movement, and changes of the sun and moon.

ecological systems theory—Bronfenbrenner's theory that describes the diverse, interactive contexts that influence children's development over time.

effective teaching—The use of approaches that are proven to be successful based on scientific evidence and that have a high probability of enhancing children's learning and development.

efficacy—Children's belief in their own ability to accomplish what they set out to do.

effortful control—Children's ability to act purposefully including controlling thoughts, emotions, and behaviors.

egocentrism—The process whereby very young children tend to see everything from their own intellectual and emotional points of view.

Elementary and Secondary Education Act (ESEA)—Law governing how the federal government distributes education funds to states and holds public schools accountable for the use of funding.

eligibility guidelines—Guidelines established on a state-by-state basis according to IDEA that determine whether children may receive special education services.

emergent curriculum—Curriculum that develops in an educational environment in response to children's interests and needs rather than according to predeveloped plans.

emotional development—Acquisition of important emotional skills, such as identifying feelings and learning to regulate emotions and express them appropriately.

emotional literacy—Children's ability to identify their own and others' emotions, to express emotions in a healthy way, and to self-regulate their feelings.

encode—Translating speech sounds into symbols—the letters of the alphabet—to create writing.

encouragement—Verbal comments or nonverbal signs such as pats or high fives that promote the child's persistence and effort.

engaged citizens—Children as change agents in schools, communities, and eventually in the world.

enumeration—The act of counting.

equilibration—The process whereby humans try to make sense of new experiences by creating new concepts (schemes) or adapting existing ones.

equity pedagogy—The idea that teaching about differences needs to include teaching about oppression and equity.

ethical dilemma—Deciding the right thing to do when two or more values conflict.

ethical responsibilities—The obligations that every teacher agrees to uphold with honesty, integrity, and respect.

ethics—Critical thinking about morality and people's ability to make choices about their own values.

ethnicity—The shared characteristics and experiences of a group of people, such as nationality, race, history, religion, and language.

evaluation—The process of making a judgment about assessment results; frequently considered the last step in assessment.

Every Student Succeeds Act (ESSA)—Reauthorization and revision of the Elementary and Secondary Education Act (effective 2016), provides for more local and state control of schools, new accountability systems, and more support for early learning.

everyday mathematics—Informal, intuitive knowledge about math, including basic ideas about quantity (more and less), size, shape, and pattern.

evidence—An outward sign or indication of children's learning, such as their response to a question or their solution to a problem.

evidence-based curriculum—Derives from research evidence about what kinds of learning outcomes relate to later achievement, and what types of teaching and learning experiences help children acquire those outcomes.

exceptional children—An all-encompassing term used to communicate inclusion of gifted and talented children as well as children whose development is below the expected range.

executive function—Mental abilities including working memory, mental flexibility, and inhibitory control that enable children to remember, think flexibly, focus attention, control impulses, plan, and think ahead (sometimes called self-regulation).

exosystem—Systems that affect the child's microsystems but that the child doesn't directly participate in, including economic, media, education, health, legal, and political entities that directly affect a person or circumstance in the child's microsystem.

expressive language—The ability to communicate; use and knowledge of spoken language.

extended discourse—Talking with children in ways that build on and expand what they say.

extinction—The process whereby a conditioned behavior diminishes and eventually disappears when reinforcers are removed.

facilitating—Providing short-term, temporary assistance to help a child achieve the next level of functioning.

family child care home—Child care in which caregivers provide care in their own homes for a small group of children, often multi-age groups.

family systems theory—Views family members as interconnected parts, with each member influencing the others in predictable and recurring ways.

family-centered practice—Providing resources and supports to families that promote children's development and learning while at the same time strengthen the competency of families in their role.

feedback loop—Back-and-forth communication between a teacher and a child or small group of children in an effort to reach deeper understanding.

fidelity—Faithful implementation of a curriculum model.

fine-motor development—Physical skills related to the small muscles found in individual body parts, especially those in the hands and feet.

fine-motor manipulative movements—Control, precision, and accuracy of small muscle movement.

flexibility—The ability to bend and stretch easily.

fluency—Rapid, efficient, and accurate word recognition skills that permit the reader to comprehend the meaning of text.

formal assessment—Assessment that follows a specific procedure and uses a specially designed instrument or tool.

formative assessment—The process of gathering information about children and using it to plan effective and individualized instruction.

free appropriate public education (FAPE)—Education for children with disabilities that is required by IDEA, so that children with disabilities are not denied the same opportunities offered to everyone else.

frequency counts—Method used by teachers to keep track of how often a behavior occurs.

Froebel's occupations and gifts—Invented by Friedrich Froebel for kindergartners.

Occupations were planned experiences designed to train children's eye-hand coordination and mental activity; gifts were concrete materials, many of which influenced later toy development.

functional behavioral assessment—The process of determining why a child is behaving a certain way, based on the principle that all behavior serves a function or purpose.

functional skills—The essential abilities needed to fulfill goals parents have for their children, such as communicating, making friends, and learning self-help skills.

funds of knowledge—Experiences, traditions, goals, resources, and rich culture that families bring to their roles.

generative skills—Skills that can be used across settings, people, events, and objects.

geometry—The study of shapes and space, including flat, two-dimensional space and three-dimensional space.

graphic representation—The process of depicting thoughts and ideas through drawing, modeling, or other media.

gross-motor development—Physical skills related to moving the whole body or major parts of the body.

gross-motor manipulative movements—Large muscle movements involving giving or receiving force from objects, such as throwing, catching, or kicking.

guidance—The process of teaching children the life skills they need to function productively with other children.

hazard—A danger that must be avoided.

Head Start Program Performance Standards—National standards that establish the level of quality of services provided by every Head Start program.

Head Start—Federally funded national program that promotes school readiness by enhancing the social and cognitive development of children ages 3, 4, and 5 through providing educational, health, nutritional, social, and other services to the nation's poorest children and families.

health-related fitness—Any aspect of health that can be improved by physical exercise and activity.

high-context culture—Culture in which communication relies less on words and more on contextual cues, such as facial expressions, gestures, or other physical clues, to convey meaning.

high-stakes testing—Using standardized test scores to make decisions about individual children, teachers, or schools that have potential long-term consequences.

home visiting—Visits made by a teacher to the child's home on a regular basis to get to know children and their families.

home-based programs—Programs based on visits to families designed to support parents in the parenting role, involve them in their children's education, and help them achieve their own life goals.

hypothesis generating and testing—Applying previously acquired knowledge to a new situation by making a prediction and then observing and reflecting on the outcome.

hypothesis—An assumption about or tentative explanation of a phenomenon.

Idea webbing (also called webbing or concept webbing)—a planning tool that teachers and children create together to organize curriculum content.

identity—The collection of characteristics that individuals recognize as constituting their sense of self and belonging to a group.

implict bias—attitudes or stereotypes that unconsciously affect our thoughts, actions, and decisions.

inclusion—Participation and services for children with disabilities and special needs in programs and settings where their typically developing peers are served.

individualistic cultural groups—Cultural groups that focus on the needs of the individual, independence, self-expression, and personal property and choice.

individualized education program (IEP)—A written plan designed to meet the unique needs of a child with a disability or special need; it is developed, reviewed, and revised by an IEP team during meetings for each child who is eligible for special education services.

individualized family service plan (IFSP)—Documents and guides the early intervention process for children with disabilities from birth to age 3 and their families; contains information about the services necessary to facilitate a child's development and enhance the family's capacity to facilitate the child's development.

individualized intervention—A systematically planned and implemented set of actions designed to alter the course of a child's development or learning.

individually appropriate—Information about the strengths, interests, abilities, and needs of each individual child in a group that enables teachers to adapt to and be responsive to individual variation.

Individuals with Disabilities Education Act (IDEA)—Federal law governing provision of services for children with disabilities and special needs.

informal assessment—Gathering information for teacher's use to make everyday classroom decisions or adjustments to teaching.

inhibitory control (also called cognitive self-control)—The ability to think before we act and to focus attention on what is necessary.

insecure–ambivalent/resistant attachment—Children's inability to trust adults to keep them safe due to neglect, abuse, or other difficult circumstances that results in a lack of social competence.

insecure–avoidant attachment—Rejection and insensitivity from adult caregivers that causes children to turn away from or avoid adults and not seek their comfort.

integrated curriculum—Learning plan that addresses goals across multiple areas of the curriculum at the same time.

intentional teachers—Teachers who have a purpose for the decisions they make and can explain that purpose to others.

interdependent cultural groups—Cultural groups that focus on the needs of the group rather than those of the individual, also called collectivist.

interviews—Teacher-created, predetermined questions that are designed to reveal what children understand.

invented spelling—Developmental or phonetic spelling that represents children's initial attempts to associate sounds with letters.

kindergarten—Typically considered the first year of formal schooling; serves 5- and 6-year-olds.

K-W-L—An advance organizer strategy in which teachers ask children what they already know (K) about the topic of study, what they want (W) to know, and then what they learned (L).

laboratory school—School operated by colleges and universities that usually serves children of students and faculty and also acts as a model of excellent education for student teachers.

Lanham Act—Federal legislation to provide emergency child care and other services for families employed in the war effort during World War II.

learning centers—Defined areas of the classroom that have a particular purpose and contain relevant furnishings and materials.

learning continuum, learning trajectory, or learning path—Similar to a developmental continuum, but focuses on sequences of knowledge or skill in a content area.

learning standards—Expectations for student learning.

learning strategy—How children construct meaning in any context or situation.

learning—A change in knowledge or skill that results from experience or instruction.

life science—The study of the characteristics, life cycles, and environments of organisms.

listening—The process of taking in information through the sense of hearing and making meaning from what is heard.

locomotor movements—Movements that allow the body to proceed in a horizontal or vertical direction from one place to another, such as walking, running, leaping, or jumping.

logico-mathematical knowledge—The relationships that are constructed in our minds between objects or concepts.

low-context culture—Culture that focuses on direct, logical, precise verbal communication.

macrosystem—System that includes the overarching cultural context of the values, beliefs, laws, and policies of a society.

manipulatives—Small-sized blocks, cubes, pattern blocks, beads, pegs, and the like that are designed for children's play and learning.

math talk—Using the language and vocabulary of mathematics.

mathematize—To understand and think about everyday problems and experiences in explicitly mathematical terms.

maturationist—Theory of development that assumes that the sequence of changes in abilities and behavior is largely predetermined by children's biological growth processes rather than by their experiences or learning.

measurement—The process of determining size, length, area, or volume using a standard unit.

mesosystem—Interaction of different microsystems in a child's life.

metacognitive activities—Activities that engage children in thinking and reflecting about their own learning.

microsystem—System in which the child directly participates on a regular basis and includes the family, child care, school and faith-based settings.

mindfulness—noticing one's sensations, thoughts, and feelings in the present moment, without judgment

mistaken behavior—Alternative term for children's misbehavior, recognizing the fact that young children are still learning acceptable behavior and that they are bound to make mistakes.

modeling—Teacher showing children a skill or desirable way of behaving or speaking; also children imitating the behavior of others.

modifications—Changes in an assessment that alter what the assessment measures or what the results mean.

morality—Personal views about what is right and wrong and how to behave.

motor planning—The ability of the brain to conceive, organize, and carry out a series of unfamiliar actions.

multi-language learners—Children who are learning more than two languages.

muscular strength and endurance—The ability to keep moving without stopping because of fatigue.

narrative records—Teachers' attempts to record detailed descriptions of children in a situation or event that is the focus of the observation.

narrative—A story with a beginning, middle, and end; characters; dialogue; and a plot with a problem to solve or a dilemma to be resolved.

National Association for the Education of Young Children (NAEYC)—The world's largest organization of early childhood educators whose mission is to promote high-quality early learning for children ages birth through 8 by connecting practice, policy, and research; to advance a diverse, dynamic early childhood profession; and to support all who care for, educate, and work on behalf of young children.

natural learning environments—Settings that are natural or normal for the child's same-age peers without disabilities, such as child care centers, parks, a neighbor's house, or the zoo, as opposed to hospitals, clinics, and therapy offices.

naturally occurring reinforcers—Consequences that are likely to occur *whenever* the child performs the skill and are, therefore, highly effective.

nature-deficit disorder—Hypothetical disorder related to lack of exposure and experience outdoors and in the natural world.

nature—The hereditary or genetic contributions to human development.

negative reinforcement—An unpleasant consequence that is avoided if the person performs a desired behavior more frequently.

neurons—Nerve cells in the brain that receive information through the senses or from other neurons, and then communicate information back to other parts of the body.

norm-referenced tests—Tests that compare an individual's score to that of other test takers.

normal curve—A distribution of scores that looks like a bell shape, with most people scoring at the midrange and fewer scoring at the higher and lower ends.

nursery schools—Schools serving children younger than kindergarten age; out-of-date term for preschool or prekindergarten.

nurture—Environmental factors and experiences that influence human development and behavior.

object permanence—A concept that babies lack early in the period of sensorimotor development so that when an object is no longer in their sight, it ceases to exist for them.

one-to-one correspondence—Attaching one and only one number word to each object being counted.

onlooker—Teachers act as the audience for children's play.

open-ended questions—Questions that require children to analyze information in some way and that have many possible answers.

operant conditioning—The process of using pleasant or unpleasant consequences to control behavior.

operations—Working with and solving problems about relationships such as *more than* or *less than*.

order irrelevance principle—The concept that counting can begin with any object in the set as long as each is counted only once.

parallel play—Children play next to each other, but not with each other; they may speak, but don't really converse.

parent cooperative—Preschool program owned, operated, and partially staffed by parents.

parentese—The high-pitched tone of voice that adults and even children tend to use naturally with babies; also called *motherese*.

passive communication—Speaking in a way that is sensitive to the listener's feelings, but so vague that the message is easily misunderstood.

pedagogy—What a teacher says or does that engages children and contributes to their learning and development.

perceptual-motor development—Occurs when children use their senses to take in information about objects in the environment and use this information to coordinate their movements.

performance assessment or authentic assessment—Determines what children know and can do from their demonstration of a skill or their creation of a product.

performance standards—Describe the knowledge or skill that students should acquire by a particular point in their schooling, usually tied to grade or age level; also known as *benchmarks*.

person-first language—Language that recognizes that a child is a child first, whether or not he or she has a disability (e.g., saying "child with special needs" as opposed to "special needs child").

phonemes—The individual sounds of spoken language; changing one in a word changes the meaning of the word.

phonemic awareness—Recognizing that spoken words are made up of individual sounds that can be manipulated.

phonics—A system of teaching the correspondences between letters or groups of letters and the sounds they represent.

phonological awareness—Consciousness that the stream of spoken language is made up of smaller units or chunks of sound.

physical development—Biological growth and acquisition of fine-motor and gross-motor skills.

physical fitness—Children's overall physical condition: growth, strength, stamina, and flexibility.

physical knowledge—Understanding how objects move and function in space and how the physical world works.

physical science—Basic ideas about the properties of liquids and solid materials, how things move and change position, and cause-and-effect relationships.

pincer grasp—Grasp used to pick up objects with the thumb and forefinger.

planning—Requires children to make intentional choices and encourages them to identify their goals, consider the options for achieving them, make predictions, and anticipate consequences; helps build children's higher-level thinking and problem solving.

plasticity—The brain's ability to develop and change in response to experiences.

play leader—Teachers participate in children's play; includes making deliberate attempts to enrich and extend the play episode.

play-based assessment—Similar to curriculum-embedded assessment, but the context for observing and interacting with children is the children's play.

play-by-play language—Language that describes what is happening during routines and social interactions with babies and toddlers; also called *running commentary*.

portfolios—Systematic and organized collections of children's work and demonstrations of their progress relevant to the goals of the curriculum.

position statement—A document that articulates a stance, usually research-based, that an organization is taking in response to an issue or a problem.

positive behavior support (PBS)—A method of identifying the causes and functions of problem behaviors in order to develop support strategies that prevent challenging behaviors and teach new, more appropriate skills.

positive reinforcement—A reward or pleasant consequence that follows a behavior, causing that behavior to be repeated.

predictable books—Books with controlled vocabulary using parallel text structures that become familiar to children.

predictors—Set of early literacy skills and knowledge that increase the likelihood of later success in learning to read and write.

prekindergarten (pre-K)—Educational program serving 3- and 4-year-olds, usually in public schools.

preschool—Educational programs serving 3- and 4-year-olds delivered under various sponsorships.

primary grades—First, second, and third grade; sometimes includes kindergarten.

print awareness—Beginning knowledge about written language.

private speech—The process whereby interpersonal understanding or socially constructed knowledge is turned into intrapersonal knowledge (thinking aloud becomes thinking to oneself).

process quality—The quality of the relationships and interactions among teachers and children and the appropriateness of the materials, learning experiences, and teaching strategies occurring in an early childhood program.

profession—An occupation that requires extensive education and/or specialized training.

professional ethics—The kinds of actions that are right or wrong in the workplace and are a public matter.

professionals—Members of an occupational group that make decisions based on a specialized body of knowledge, continue to learn throughout their careers, and are committed to meeting the needs of others.

program evaluation—The process of gathering information about a program's quality and effectiveness.

progressive education movement—Major effort to reform schooling in the early 20th century to make it more democratic and responsive to children's needs. This movement was highly influential on early childhood education and later ideas about developmentally appropriate practice.

project approach—Strategy for conceptually organizing curriculum by engaging children in in-depth investigation of a topic, focused on finding answers to questions posed by the children, the teacher, or the teacher working with the children.

project—An in-depth investigation of a topic worth learning more about, usually involving a small group but occasionally the whole class.

prompts—Gestural, model, physical, pictorial, or verbal clues that elicit responses from children to assist them in using a specific skill.

protective factors—Mechanisms, both inherited and experiential, that may minimize the potentially negative effects for children living in identified high-risk situations.

proximal processes—Interactions in the context of daily living that have the most impact on a child's development due to their frequent, ongoing nature, often over extended periods of time.

pruning—The process whereby the brain eliminates unnecessary or unused synapses, which contributes to efficient brain operation, aids learning and memory, and increases the brain's flexibility.

punishment—An unpleasant consequence that stops or decreases the frequency of a behavior.

push-down curriculum—Content previously taught in a higher grade that's being expected to be learned in an earlier grade.

quality rating and improvement systems (QRIS)—State-operated tiered systems that evaluate and rate the quality of child care programs according to achievement of benchmarks beyond those required for minimal licensing, such as having more highly qualified teachers or better ratios.

questioning—Eliciting different types of responses and promoting different types of thinking.

rare words—Multisyllable words that are not typically part of a young child's vocabulary.

rating scales—Method of recording teacher's judgments about how a child's performance compares to that of peers or to a predetermined standard.

readiness tests—Achievement tests administered to children at entry to kindergarten.

reasoning—Thinking logically to come to a conclusion or find a result.

recall questions—Questions asked by the teacher about a book to see what children remember.

receptive language—The ability to understand what is being said.

reciprocal relationship—A two-way relationship in which information and power are shared evenly.

reciprocal teaching—A strategy that promotes children's reading comprehension and higher-order thinking by engaging them in summarizing, questioning, clarifying, and predicting.

redirection—Drawing a child's attention or behavior toward a more desirable alternative than the one on which the child is currently focusing.

reflection—Teaching strategy in which teachers help children go beyond remembering what they did to becoming aware of what they learned, what was interesting, how they felt about the experience, and what they can do to build on and extend the experience.

reinforcer—Consequence—either positive or negative—that increases or strengthens a behavior.

reliability—The extent to which the results obtained from a test are accurate and consistent over time.

replacement behaviors—Desirable prosocial behaviors that replace problem behaviors.

representing—Expressing mathematical ideas with words, diagrams, pictures, and/or symbols.

resilience—A child's ability to overcome, adapt to, or minimize the damaging effects of adversity.

Response to Intervention (RTI)—A three-tiered framework intended to prevent learning delays in primary grades from becoming learning disabilities.

rhymes—Two words ending with the same sound.

risk factors—Inherited or experiential conditions that potentially contribute to poor developmental outcomes for children, such as peer rejection, academic failure, juvenile delinquency, and school expulsion.

risk vs. challenge continuum—Concept that children not only need to be safe but they also need to be challenged if they are to advance their skills and learn how to keep themselves safe.

risk—A possibility of harm that can be minimized with planning and supervision.

rough-and-tumble play or big body play—The boisterous, large-motor, physical activity children seem to crave.

rubrics—Descriptive rating scales that detail the qualities related to each rank on the scale; includes clear descriptions of each point on the scale or guidelines for making judgments about a rating.

running record—A chronological record, like a diary, of an individual child's behavior that helps teachers better understand that behavior.

scaffolding—The assistance, guidance, and direction teachers provide children to help them accomplish a task or learn a skill (within their ZPD) that they could not achieve on their own.

scheme or schema—The organization of mental structures people use to think or guide behavior; the structures develop and change with experience.

school readiness—Children's competencies related to success in kindergarten, including physical development, health, and well-being; social-emotional development and learning; cognitive development and general knowledge such as mathematics and science; positive approaches to learning such as curiosity and motivation; and language development and early literacy skills.

science—Study of the physical and natural world, especially by observing and experimenting.

scientific inquiry—Involving children in observing, predicting, and investigating.

scientific method—Method of beginning with a hypothesis, testing it with an experiment, making observations and gathering data, and then confirming or disconfirming the initial hypothesis.

scope—The particular focus of the curriculum at a given point in time; that is, how much of a larger content area will be taught.

screening tests—Tests administered to all children, usually in preschool or kindergarten, as the first step in a process to determine which children are at risk of a possible disability or learning problem; also called *developmental screening*.

script language—The typical ways that people communicate in different contexts or settings.

secure attachment relationship—A responsive and sensitive relationship with caregivers that allows children to venture forth and comfortably explore and learn about the world.

secure base—An attachment figure (mother or caregiver) who serves as an anchor for children to rely on and from which children can safely venture out and explore.

self-actualization theory—Maslow's view that behavior and learning are motivated by a hierarchy of needs.

self-concept—Children's stable perceptions about themselves despite variations in their behavior.

self-esteem—Children's perception of their own worth.

self-regulated learning—Bandura's theory that people not only learn by modeling the behavior of others, but by observing and evaluating their own.

self-regulation—The ability to adapt or control behavior, emotions, and thinking according to the demands of the situation, control impulses, and delay gratification (sometimes called executive function).

separation anxiety—Feeling a baby experiences when the caregiver is not in sight; the baby may cry or cling to a caregiver in the presence of strangers; usually occurs around 8 months of age.

sequence—The order in which knowledge and skills will be taught.

sequential language learning—Learning a second language *after* the first language is relatively well established.

serve and return—the back-and-forth interaction between a caregiving adult and a child in which each response is contingent upon the response of the "partner."

shaping—Teaching a new skill or behavior by rewarding each step or successive approximation toward the goal.

simultaneous acquisition—Learning two languages at the same time during the earliest years of life.

slippery egg messages—Communications that are difficult to "toss" (send) and "catch" (receive), and must be expressed gently

to be sure that the "catcher" receives the communication as intended.

social cognitive theory—Bandura's theory that people can learn efficiently from observing the consequences of another person's behavior.

social development—The ability to establish positive relationships with adults and peers, make friends, cooperate, and resolve conflicts.

social studies—The integrated study of the history, geography, economics, political science, and other related aspects of societies of the past, present, and future.

social-conventional knowledge—The culturally agreed-on names and symbols that need to be transmitted to the learner directly.

social-emotional learning—Children's ability to recognize and regulate their emotions, establish and maintain positive relationships, make responsible decisions, and solve social problems constructively. Also called *social competence*.

sociocultural theory—Vygotsky's theory that children learn from social interaction within a cultural context.

socioeconomic status (SES)—Family income level.

solitary play—Children play alone, usually with toys or objects.

spatial awareness—Perceptions of where the body is.

spatial relations—Spatial sense and familiarity with shape, structure, and location.

specialized instruction—Involves teachers matching an individual child's goals and objectives with appropriate teaching methods and materials, deciding what amount of assistance each child with special needs requires, providing the assistance, and then determining whether the instruction was effective.

stability movements—Movements in which the body remains in place but moves around its horizontal or vertical axis, such as balancing, dodging, starting, and stopping.

stable order principle—The concept that number words need to be said in the same order every time.

stage manager—Teachers set the stage for children's play by providing the props and theme and being available to respond to children's requests.

standardized assessment—Assessment of all children using the same procedures and performing the same task under the same conditions.

standardized testing—Uses prescribed methods for administering and scoring.

structural quality—Features of an early childhood program, such as maximum group sizes, teacher/child ratios, and teacher qualifications, that are relatively easy to quantify and measure.

structured physical activity—Adult-guided play that is designed for a purpose such as increasing endurance or flexibility.

subitizing—The ability to look at a small set of objects (four or fewer) and know how many there are without counting.

successive approximations—Behaviors that are reinforced (shaped) that are not the actual desired behaviors, but each approximate behavior that is closer to the goal.

summative assessment—Assessing student learning at the end of an educational experience to evaluate the effectiveness of the experience.

supporting—Providing assistance that helps the child accomplish a difficult task by making it easier.

symbolic representation—the process of mentally using one thing to stand for something else

synapses—Connections in the brain that carry information between neurons.

syntax—Grammar and sentence structure.

teacher-initiated experiences—Learning experiences in which teachers take the lead by providing explicit information and modeling or demonstrating a skill, as determined by the teacher's goals and direction.

teaching strategy—A behavior or activity that a teacher deliberately selects and flexibly applies to help students construct meaning.

technology—Tools used to change or modify the natural world to meet human needs.

telegraphic speech—Combining words into two-word utterances.

temperament—The pattern of arousal and emotionality that is characteristic of an individual.

temporal awareness—Speeding up or slowing down a movement.

Temporary Assistance for Needy Families (TANF)—Federally funded program, more commonly known as Welfare to Work, that provides temporary financial aid but requires recipients to move into the labor force or schooling.

tennis ball messages—Communications that are easily "tossed" and received and that help form the foundation of a relationship; they constitute the everyday chitchat between teachers and parents.

testing—A systematic procedure for evaluating a child's behavior and knowledge that is then assigned a score.

thematic curriculum—Way of integrating curriculum in which a broad topic of interest or a "big idea" provides the basis for making connections across learning goals.

theory of multiple intelligences—Theory developed by Howard Gardner that identifies eight different intelligences as opposed to a single score on an intelligence test; this theory is useful for thinking about variation among children and teaching to their strengths.

theory—An explanation of how information and observations are organized and relate to one another.

time-out—Removing a child to a specified chair or area of the room for a period of time following an unacceptable behavior.

tourist curriculum—An approach in which a culture is visited as though it were an exotic destination where people dress, talk, dance, and eat differently before returning to the "normal" place where we all live.

toxic stress—Children's experience of intense, frequent, and/or prolonged anxiety such as abuse, neglect, violence, or economic deprivation without adult support to help them cope.

transactional theory of development—Theory that development is the result of both biology and experience and how they influence each other.

transitions—Changes from one activity or place to another.

unitizing—Finding or creating a mathematical unit.

universal design—The concept that materials and environments need to be usable by everyone, including those with disabilities, to the greatest extent possible.

universal voluntary prekindergarten—Publicly funded preschool, usually for 4-year-olds but sometimes 3-year-olds; available to any family that chooses to use it.

unstructured free play—Play that is chosen and initiated by children, such as that which occurs on a playground.

utility—Used to benefit children.

validated curriculum—Curriculum that has been evaluated and its effectiveness demonstrated.

validity—The degree to which an instrument measures what it purports to measure.

vicarious learning—Learning by observing the effects of other people's behavior, rather than experiencing rewards or punishments directly.

virtual field trip—Trip taken via the Internet in which children can go anywhere in the world.

visual arts—Creative processes and products that involve drawing, painting, sculpting with clay, or making models of objects using a variety of materials.

visual literacy—Ability to create visual messages and to interpret messages contained in visual communications.

vocabulary—A combination of receptive and expressive language; the number of words a person knows and uses when listening or speaking.

wait time—The length of time that a teacher waits for a response after asking a question or responding to a comment.

Wh-**questions**—Questions that begin with "why" or "what" to get children thinking about characters' motives or feelings.

widening horizons approach—Approach to social studies curriculum planning designed to begin "where children are" and then expand outward.

windows of opportunity—Periods of time during which human brains are particularly susceptible and responsive to certain types of experience.

word identification—The process of decoding unfamiliar words and recognizing high-frequency (both regularly and irregularly spelled) words by sight.

working memory—The ability to retain information for a short period of time, which enables transfer to long-term memory.

WPA nurseries—Federal emergency relief nursery schools funded by the Works Progress Administration (WPA) during the Great Depression. Designed to support the economy by providing jobs for those who worked on the site and child care services to families seeking work.

zone of proximal development (ZPD)—The distance between the actual developmental level an individual has achieved (her independent level of problem solving) and the level of potential development she could achieve with adult guidance or through collaboration with other children.

References

Chapter 1

Abbott, K. (2017). Keeping the "kinder" in kindergarten: Developmentally appropriate practice in New York. *Preschool Matters Today*. Retrieved November 9, 2017, from NIEER.org

American Academy of Pediatrics. (2013). The crucial role of recess: Policy statement. *Pediatrics, 131*(1), 183–188. doi:10.1542/peds.2012–2993

Annie E. Casey Foundation. (2017a). *Child population by race and age group*. Retrieved October 25, 2017, from http://datacenter.kidscount.org/data/tables/8446-child-population-by-race-and-age-group

Annie E. Casey Foundation. (2017b). *The 2017 Kids Count data book*. Retrieved November 9, 2017, from www.aecf.org/databook

Annie E. Casey Foundation. (2017c). *Child in foster care*. Retrieved November 8, 2017, from http://datacenter.kidscount.org/data/tables/6243-children-in-foster-care

Barnett, W. S., & Friedman-Krauss, A. H. (2016). *State(s) of Head Start*. New Brunswick, NJ: National Institute for Early Education Research.

Barnett, W. S., Friedman-Krauss, A. H, Weisenfeld, G. G., Horowitz, M., Kasmin, R., & Squires, J. H. (2017). *The state of preschool 2016: State preschool yearbook*. New Brunswick, NJ: National Institute for Early Education Research.

Bassok, D., Latham, S., & Rorem, A. (2016). Is kindergarten the new first grade? *AERA Open, 1*(4), 1–31.

Berrueta-Clement, J. R., Schweinhart, L. J., Barnett, W. S., Epstein, A. S., & Weikart, D. P. (1984). *Changed lives: The effects of the Perry preschool program on youths through age 19*. Ypsilanti, MI: High/Scope Press.

Bialystok, E., & Werker, J. F. (2016). The systematic effects of bilingualism on children's development. *Developmental Science, 20*(1).

Bipartisan Policy Center. (2017). *A bipartisan case for early childhood development*. Washington, DC: Author.

Bishop-Josef, S. (2017). *High-quality child care: A two-generation solution for a productive American workforce*. Council for a Strong America. Retrieved November 5, 2017, from www.strongnation.org/articles/489-how-child-care-contributes-to-a-productive-american-workforce

Brown, C. (2017). *All work and no play needs to change for kindergarteners. Here's why*. World Economic Forum blog. Retrieved November 8, 2017, from www.weforum.org/agenda/2017/04/its-all-work-and-almost-no-play-in-kindergarten-but-does-it-matter

BUILD Initiative. (2017). *Quality rating and improvement systems*. Retrieved November 9, 2017, from www.buildinitiative.org/TheIssues/EarlyLearning/-QualityQRIS.aspx

Calderon, V. J., & Jones, J. M. (2017, October 12). Superintendents say too little invested in early education. *Gallup News*. Retrieved November 5, 2017, from http://news.gallup.com/poll/220541/superintendents-say-little-invested-early-education.aspx

Carlson-Paige, N., McLaughlin, G. B., & Almon, J. W. (2015). *Reading instruction in kindergarten: Little to gain and much to lose*. Alliance for Childhood and Defending the Early Years. Retrieved November 4, 2017, from https://deyproject.files.wordpress.com/2015/01/readinginkindergarten_online-1.pdf

Center on the Developing Child at Harvard University, 2017. *Executive function and self-regulation*. Retrieved November 5, 2017, from https://developingchild.harvard.edu

Center on the Developing Child at Harvard University. (n.d.). *8 things to remember about child development*. Retrieved November 4, 2017, from developingchild.harvard.edu/resources/8-things-remember-child-development

Child Care Aware of America. (2017). *Child Care Aware state licensing database*. Online at http://licensingdatabase.usa.childcareaware.org

Children's Defense Fund. (2017). *Child poverty in America 2016: National analysis*. Washington, DC: Author.

Colasanti, M. (2007). *Kindergarten entrance age: A 30 year trend analysis*. Denver, CO: Education Commission of the States. Retrieved November 24, 2014, from http://inpathways.net/kindergarten_trend_analyses.pdf

Colker, L. (2008). Twelve characteristics of effective early childhood teachers. *Young Children, 63*(2), 68–73. Retrieved from https://www.naeyc.org/files/yc/file/200803/BTJ_Colker.pdf

Copeland, K. A, Sherman, S. N., Kendeigh, C. A., Kalkwarf, H. J., & Saelens, B. E. (2012). Societal values and policies may curtail preschool children's physical activity in child care centers. Retrieved November 5, 2017, from https://www.ncbi.nlm.nih.gov/pmc/articles/PMC3269117

Copeland, K. A, Sherman, S. N., Kendeigh, C. A., Kalkwarf, H. J., & Saelens, B. E. (2012). Societal values and policies may curtail preschool children's physical activity in child care centers. Retrieved from http://pediatrics.aappublications.org/content/early/2012/01/02/peds.2011-2102.full.pdf+html

Copple, C., & Bredekamp, S. (Eds.). (2009). *Developmentally appropriate practice in early childhood programs serving children from birth through age 8* (Rev. ed.). Washington, DC: National Association for the Education of Young Children.

Council for a Strong America. (2017). *Early education*. Retrieved November 3, 2017, from www.strongnation.org/topics/early-education

Covert, B. (2017). The U.S. already has a high-quality, universal child care program—in the military. *Think Progress*. Retrieved November 9, 2017, from https://thinkprogress.org/universal-military-childcare-9bb2b54bd154

De La Cruz, D. (2016, October). Opioids may interfere with parenting instincts, study finds. *The New York Times*.

Division for Early Childhood & National Association for the Education of Young Children. (2009). *Early childhood inclusion: A joint position statement of the Division for Early Childhood (DEC) and the National Association for the Education of Young Children (NAEYC)*. Chapel Hill: The University of North Carolina, FPG Child Development Institute. Retrieved from http://npdci.fpg.unc.edu/sites/npdci.fpg.unc.edu/files/resources/EarlyChildhoodInclusion_0.pdf

Dobbins, D. (2017). *Child Care Aware of America Announces Child Care Licensing Database Launch*. Retrieved November 24, 2017, from https://usa.childcareaware.org/2017/06/child-care-aware-of-america-announces-child-care-licensing-database-launch

Duncan, G. J., & Magnuson, K. (2012). Socioeconomic status and cognitive functioning: Moving from correlation to causation. *Journal of Child Psychology and Psychiatry, 3*(3), 377–386.

Fernald, A., Marchman, V. A., & Weislader, A. (2013). SES differences in language processing skill and vocabulary are evident at 18 months. *Developmental Science, 16*(2), 234–248.

Fight Crime: Invest in Kids. (2017). *Members agree: Early education is key to a safe and prosperous America*. Retrieved November 3, 2017, from www.strongnation.org/articles/490-members-agree-early-education-is-key-to-a-safe-and-prosperous-america

First Five Years Fund. (2017). America speaks: New poll shows investing in early childhood education is a national priority. Retrieved June 29, 2015, from http://ffyf.org/wp-content/uploads/2014/07/F_FFYF_ResearchSummaryHandout_071414.pdf

Flores, A. (2017). *How the U.S. Hispanic population is changing*. Washington, DC: Pew Research Center.

Foundation for Child Development. (2008). *America's vanishing potential: The case for preK–3rd education*. New York: Author.

Friedman-Krauss, A., Barnett, W. S., & Nores, M. (2016). *How much can high-quality universal pre-k reduce achievement gaps?* Center for American Progress & NIEER. Retrieved November 1, 2017, from http://nieer.org/wp-content/uploads/2017/01/NIEER-AchievementGaps-report.pdf

Garcia, J. L., Heckman, J. J., & Ziff, A. L. (2017). Gender differences in the benefits of an influential early childhood program. Retrieved November 6, 2017, from https://heckmanequation.org/assets/2017/05/abc_treatmenteffects_2017-05-11b_jbb.pdf

Garcia, J. L., Heckman, J. J., Leaf, D. E., & Prados, M. J. (2016). *The life-cycle benefits of an influential early childhood program*. Retrieved October 31, 2016, from https://heckmanequation.org/assets/2017/01/Garcia_Heckman_Leaf_etal_2016_life-cycle-benefits-ecp_r1-p.pdf.

Generations United. (2017). *In loving arms: The protective role of grandparents and other relatives in raising children exposed to trauma*. Retrieved November 8, 2017, from www.gu.org

Gormley, W. T. (2008). *The effects of Oklahoma's universal pre-kindergarten program on Hispanic children*, Washington, DC: Center for Research on Children in the U.S. (CROCUS), Georgetown University, retrieved July 28, 2009, from http://www.crocus.georgetown.edu

Hamre, B., La Paro, K., Pianta, R., & Locasale-Crouch, J. (2014). *Classroom Assessment Scoring System (CLASS) manual, infant*. Baltimore: Paul H. Brookes.

Harms, T., Clifford, R. M., & Cryer, D. (2014). *Early Childhood Environment Rating Scale (ECERS-3)* (3rd ed.). New York: Teachers College Press.

Head Start. (2016). *Head Start Program facts fiscal year 2016*. Retrieved November 1, 2017, from https://eclkc.ohs.acf.hhs.gov/about-us/article/head-start-program-facts-fiscal-year-2016

Head Start. (2017). *Head Start Early Learning Outcomes Framework*. Retrieved November 3, 2017, from https://eclkc.ohs.acf.hhs.gov/school-readiness/article/head-start-early-learning-outcomes-framework

Heckman, J. J. (2008). *Schools, skills, and synapses*. Retrieved October 21, 2017, from https://-heckmanequation.org/assets/2017/01/Schools_Skills_Synapsis.pdf

Hernandez, D. J. (2011). *Double jeopardy: How third grade reading scores and poverty influence high school graduation.* Baltimore: Annie E. Casey Foundation. Retrieved August 29, 2011, from http://gradelevelreading.net/wp-content/uploads/2012/01/Double-Jeopardy-Report-030812-for-web1.pdf

Institute of Medicine (IOM) & National Research Council (NRC). (2015). *Transforming the workforce for children birth through age 9: A unifying foundation.* Washington, DC: National Academies Press.

Jacobson Chernoff, J., Flanagan, K. D., McPhee, C., & Park, J. (2007). *Preschool: First findings from the preschool follow-up of the Early Childhood Longitudinal Study, Birth Cohort (ECLS-B)* (NCES 2008-025). Washington, DC: U.S. Department of Education, Institute of Education Sciences, National Center for Education Statistics.

Jiang, Y., Granja, M. R., & Koball, H. (2017). *Basic Facts about Low-Income Children: Children under 6 Years, 2015.* New York: National Center for Children in Poverty, Columbia University Mailman School of Public Health.

Kagan, S. L., Moore, E., & Bredekamp, S. (Eds.). (1995). *Reconsidering children's early development and learning: Toward common views and vocabulary.* Washington DC: National Education Goals Panel: Goal 1 Technical Planning Group.

La Paro, K., Hamre, B., & Pianta, R. (2012). *Classroom Assessment Scoring System (CLASS) manual, toddler.* Baltimore: Paul H. Brookes.

Minervino, J. (2013). Quality in center-based early learning: High-level findings and trends. In *Lessons from research and the classroom: Implementing high-quality pre-K that makes a difference for young children* (September 2014, pp. 3–7). Seattle, WA: Bill and Melinda Gates Foundation. Retrieved from https://docs.gatesfoundation.org/documents/Lessons%20from%20Research%20and%20the%20Classroom_September%202014.pdf

National Academies of Science, Engineering, and Medicine. (2017). *Promoting the educational success of children and youth learning English.* Washington, DC. The National Academies Press. Retrieved October 31, 2017 from https://doi.org/10.17226/24677

National Alliance for Public Charter Schools. (2017). *Estimated public charter school enrollment, 2016–2017.* Retrieved November 4, 2017, from www.publiccharters.org/wp-content/uploads/2017/01/EER_Report_V5.pdf

National Association for the Education of Young Children (NAEYC) & the Fred Rogers Center for Early Learning and Children's Media. (2012). *Technology in early childhood programs serving children from birth through age 8. Joint Position Statement.* Washington, DC: Authors.

National Association for the Education of Young Children (NAEYC). (2016). *Overview of the NAEYC Early Childhood Program Standards.* Washington, DC: Author. Retrieved October 28, 2017, from www.naeyc.org/academy/files/academy/OverviewStandards.pdf

National Association for the Education of Young Children (NAEYC). (2017). *Revised criteria and guidance for assessment: NAEYC early learning program standards and accreditation criteria.* Retrieved November 2, 2017, from www.naeyc.org/academy/files/academy/Revised%20Criteria%20and%20Guidance%20for%20Assessment%20April%202017.pdf

National Association for the Education of Young Children (NAEYC). (2009). *Developmentally appropriate practice in early childhood programs serving children from birth through age 8: Position statement.* Washington, DC: Author.

National Association for the Education of Young Children (NAEYC). (2011a). *Code of ethical conduct and statement of commitment* (Reaffirmed and updated May 2011). Retrieved September 9, 2011, from http://www.naeyc.org/files/naeyc/file/positions/PSETH05.pdf

National Association for the Education of Young Children (NAEYC). (2011b). *2010 NAEYC Standards for Initial & Advanced Early Childhood Professional Preparation Programs: For use by Associate, Baccalaureate and Graduate Degree Programs.* Washington, DC: Author.

National Center for Education Statistics (NCES). (2016). *Primary early care and education arrangements and achievement at kindergarten entry.* (NCES 2016–070).

National Center for Education Statistics (NCES). (2017). *Preschool and kindergarten enrollment.* The Condition of Education. Washington, DC: U.S. Department of Education. Retrieved November 9, 2017, from https://nces.ed.gov/programs/coe/indicator_cfa.asp

National Center on Early Childhood Quality Assurance. (2017). *Early learning and developmental guidelines.* Retrieved November 5, 2017, from https://childcareta.acf.hhs.gov/sites/default/files/public/075_1707_state_elgs_web_final.pdf

National Center on Family Homelessness at American Institutes for Research. (2015). *America's youngest outcasts: A report card on child homelessness.* Waltham, MA: Author.

Neuman, S. B. (Ed.). (2008). *Educating the other America: Top experts tackle poverty, literacy, and achievement in our schools.* Baltimore: Paul H. Brookes.

Parkinson, J., & Rowan, B. (2008). Poverty, early literacy achievement, and education reform. In S. Neuman, (Ed.), *Educating the other America: Top experts tackle poverty, literacy, and achievement in our schools* (pp. 73–90). Baltimore: Paul H. Brookes.

Pianta, R. C., La Paro, K. M., & Hamre, B. K. (2008). *Classroom assessment scoring system (CLASS).* Baltimore: Paul H. Brookes.

Pre-kindergarten Task Force. (2017). *The current state of scientific knowledge on pre-kindergarten effects.* Brookings & Duke Center for Child and Family Policy. Retrieved November 1, 2017, from www.brookings.edu/wp-content/uploads/2017/04/duke_prekstudy_final_4-4-17_hires.pdf

Reynolds, A. J., Temple, J. A., Robertson, D. L., White, B. A. B., & Ou, S. R. (2011). Age 26 cost–benefit analysis of the Child-Parent Center early education program. *Child Development, 82*(1).

Schweinhart, L. J., Barnes, H. V., & Weikart, D. P. (1993). *Significant benefits: The High/Scope Perry Preschool study through age 27.* Ypsilanti, MI: High/Scope Press.

Schweinhart, L. J., Montie, J., Xiang, Z., Barnett, W. S., Belfield, C. R., & Nores, M. (2005). *Lifetime effects: The High/Scope Perry Preschool study through age 40* (Monographs of the High/Scope Educational Research Foundation, 14). Ypsilanti, MI: High/Scope Press.

Schweinhart, L. J., Xiang, Z., Daniel-Echols, M., Browning, K., & Wakabayashi, T. (2012). *Michigan Great Start Readiness Program evaluation: High school graduation and grade retention findings.* Ypsilanti, MI: HighScope Educational Research Foundation.

Shonkoff, J. P. (2011). Protecting brains, not simply stimulating minds. *Science, 333*(6045), 982–983.

Shonkoff, J. P., Garner, A. S., & the Committee on Psychosocial Effects of Child and Family Health. (2012). *Pediatrics, 129*(1), e232–e246. Retrieved from http://pediatrics.aappublications.org/content/129/1/e232.full.pdf+html

Tandon, P. S., Saelens, B. E., & Christakis, D. A. (2015). *Active play opportunities at child care.* American Academy of Pediatrics. Retrieved November 5, 2017, from http://pediatrics.aappublications.org/content/pediatrics/early/2015/05/12/peds.2014-2750.full.pdf

Teachstone. (2017). *Effective teacher-child interactions and child outcomes: A summary of research on the Classroom Assessment Scoring System (CLASS) Pre-K–3rd Grade.* Charlottesville, VA: Author.

TEC Center at Erikson Institute & National Association for Media Literacy in Education (NAMLE). (2017). *Media literacy in early childhood education: A critical conversation.* Retrieved November 24, 2017, from http://teccenter.erikson.edu/publications/medialitecreport

Vaala, S., Ly, A., & Levine, M. H. (2015). *Getting a read on the app store: A market scan and analysis of children's literacy apps.* New York: The Joan Ganz Cooney Center at Sesame Workshop. Retrieved November 9, 2017, from http://-joanganzcooneycenter.org/wp-content/uploads/2015/12/jgcc_gettingaread_exec.pdf

Vandell, D. L., Belsky, J., Burchinal, M., et al. (2010). Do effects of early child care extend to age 15 years? Results from the NICHD Study of Early Child Care and Youth Development. *Child Development, 81*, 737–756.

Vogel, C. A., Yange, Y., Moiduddun, E. M., Kisker, E. E., & Carlson, B. W. (2010). *Early Head Start children in grade 5: Long-term follow-up of the Early Head Start Research and Evaluation Study sample.* OPRE Report #2011-8. Washington, DC: Office of Planning, Research, and Evaluation, Administration for Children and Families, U.S. Department of Health and Human Services.

Walters, C. (2014, October). *Inputs in the production of early childhood human capital: Evidence from Head Start.* Berkeley, CA: National Bureau of Economic Research. Retrieved November 25, 2014, from http://www.nber.org/papers/w20639

Whitebook, M., & McLean, C. (2017). *In pursuit of Pre-K pay parity: A framework for understanding and advancing for policy and practice.* Center for the Study of the Child Care Employment and National Institute for Early Education Research. Retrieved November 9, 2017, from http://nieer.org/wp-content/uploads/2017/04/Pre-K-Parity-Brief_Final-1.pdf

Whitebook, M., Phillips, D., & Howes, C. (2014). *Worthy work, STILL unliveable wages: The early childhood workforce 25 years after the National Child Care Staffing Study.* Berkeley, CA: Center for the Study of Child Care Employment, University of California, Berkeley.

Workman, E. (2014). *50 state comparison: State kindergarten policies.* Denver, CO: Education Commission of the States. Author. Retrieved November 4, 2017, from www.ecs.org/kindergarten-policies

Yazejian, N., Bryant, D. M., Hans, S., Horm, D., St Clair, L., File, N., & Burchinal, M. (2017). Child and parenting outcomes after 1 year of Educare. *Child Development, 88*, 1671–1688.

Yoshikawa, H., Weiland, C., Brooks-Gunn, J., Burchinal, M. R., Espinosa, L. M., Gormley, W. T., et al. (2013). *Investing in our future: The evidence base on preschool education.* New York: Foundation for Child Development. Retrieved from http://fcd-us.org/sites/default/files/Evidence%20Base%20on%20Preschool%20Education%20FINAL.pdf

Chapter 2

Anderson, C. J. (2013). Child champion, professionals' mentor, hothead: Substance of "A Giant in the Field." In B. F. Hinitz (Ed.), *The hidden history of early childhood education* (pp. 215–237). New York: Routledge.

Ansari, A., & Winsler, A. (2014). Montessori public school pre-K programs and the school readiness of low-income Black and Latino children. *Journal of Educational Psychology, 106*(4), 1066–1079.

Aries, P. (1962). *Centuries of childhood: A social history of family life.* New York: Vintage Books.

Barazzoni, R. (2000). *Brick by brick: The history of "SSV Aprile" People's Nursery School of Villa Cella*. Reggio Emilia, Italy: Reggio Children.

Barnett, W. S., Friedman-Krauss, A. H, Weisenfeld, G. G., Horowitz, M., Kasmin, R., & Squires, J. H. (2017). *The state of preschool 2016: State preschool yearbook*. New Brunswick, NJ: National Institute for Early Education Research.

Bassok, D., Latham, S., & Rorem, A. (2016). Is kindergarten the new first grade? *AERA Open*, *1*(4), 1–31.

Biber, B. (1977). A developmental-interaction approach: Bank Street College of Education. In M. C. Day & R. K. Parker (Eds.), *The preschool in action: Exploring early childhood programs* (2nd ed., pp. 421–460). Boston: Allyn and Bacon.

Bredekamp, S. (2001). Improving professional practice: A letter to Patty Smith Hill. In *NAEYC at 75: Reflections on the Past, Challenges for the Future* (pp. 89–124). Washington, DC: National Association for the Education of Young Children.

Bredekamp, S., & Copple, C. (Eds.). (1997). *Developmentally appropriate practice in early childhood programs* (Rev. ed.). Washington, DC: National Association for the Education of Young Children.

Bredekamp, S., & Glowacki, S. (1996). The first decade of NAEYC accreditation: Growth and impact on the field. In S. Bredekamp & B. A. Willer (Eds.), *NAEYC accreditation: A decade of learning and the years ahead* (pp. 1–10). Washington, DC: National Association for the Education of Young Children.

Bunseki Fu-Kiai, K. K., & Lukondo-Wamba, A. M. (1988). *Kindezi: The Kongo art of babysitting*. New York: Vantage Press.

Cagliari, P. M., Castagneti, M., Giudici, C., Rinadi, C., Vecchi, V., & Moss, P. (Eds.) (2016). *Loris Malaguzzi and the schools of Reggio Emilia: A selection of his writings and speeches, 1945–1993*. New York: Rouledge.

Cantor, P. (2013, May). Elizabeth Peabody: America's kindergarten pioneer. *Young Children*, *68*, 92–93. Retrieved September 10, 2014, from http://www.naeyc.org/yc/files/yc/file/201305/0513_OPH_Elizbeth_Peabody.pdf

Cerda, N., & Hernandez, C. M. (2006). *History of bilingual education*. Cervantes, A., & Callanan, M. (1998). Labels and explanations in mother-child emotion talk: Age and gender differentiation. *Developmental Psychology*, *34*(1), 88–98.

Cunningham, C. E., & Osborn, D. K. (1979). A historical examination of blacks in early childhood education. *Young Children*, *34*(3), 20–29.

Dewey, J. (1900). *The school and society*. Chicago: University of Chicago Press.

Dewey, J. (1916). *Democracy and education*. New York: Free Press.

Dewey, J. (1929). *My pedagogic creed*. Washington, DC: Progressive Education Association.

Elkind, D. (2007). *The hurried child: Growing up too fast, too soon* (25th Anniversary ed.). Cambridge, MA: Da Capo Press.

Elkind, D. (2015). *Giants in the nursery: A biographical history of developmentally appropriate practice*. St. Paul, MN: Redleaf Press.

Ervin, B., Wash, P. D., & Mecca, M. E. (2010). A 3-year study of self-regulation in Montessori and non-Montessori classrooms. *Montessori Life*, *2*, 22–31.

Field, S. L., & Baumi, M. (2014). Lucy Sprague Mitchell: Champion for experiential learning. *Young Children*, *69*(4), 94–99.

Gaylord, J. (2012). Maria Montessori and 10 famous graduates from her schools. *The Christian Science Monitor, August 31, 2012*. Retrieved March 29, 2018 from https://www.csmonitor.com/Technology/Tech-Culture/2012/0831/Maria-Montessori-and-10-famous-graduates-from-her-schools/Jeff-Bezos

Giardiello, P. (2014). *Pioneers in early childhood education*. New York: Routledge.

Greenberg, P. (1987). Lucy Sprague Mitchell: A major missing link between early childhood education

in the 1980s and progressive education in the 1890s–1930s. *Young Children*, *42*(5), 70–83.

Hall, E. L., & Rudkin, J. K. (2011). *Seen & heard: Children's rights in early childhood education*. New York: Teachers College Press.

Head Start. (2016). *Head Start program facts, fiscal year 2016*. Retrieved October 18, 2017, from https://eclkc.ohs.acf.hhs.gov/sites/default/files/pdf/hs-program-fact-sheet-2016.pdf.

Hewes, D. W. (1976). Patty Smith Hill: Pioneer for young children. *Young Children*, *31*(4), 297–306.

Hewes, D. W., & the NAEYC Organizational History and Archives Committee. (2001). NAEYC's first half-century: 1926–1976. In *National Association for the Education of Young Children (NAEYC), NAEYC at 75: 1926–2001* (pp. 35–52). Washington, DC: Author.

Hill, P. S. (1926/1987). The function of the kindergarten. *Young Children*, *42*(5), 12–19.

Hinitz, B. S. F. (2014, May). Head Start: A bridge from past to future. *Young Children,69*, 94–97. Retrieved September 10, 2014, from http://www.naeyc.org/yc/files/yc/file/201405/YC0514_OPH_Hinitz.pdf

Lascarides, V. C., & Hinitz, B. F. (2000). *History of early childhood education*. New York: Routledge.

Levin, D., & Kilbourne, J. (2008). *So sexy, so soon: The new sexualized childhood and what parents can do to protect kids*. New York: Ballantine Books.

Liebovich, B. (2016). Abigail Eliot and Margaret McMillan: Bringing the nursery school to the United States. *Young Children*, *72*(2), 93–95.

Lillard, A. S. (2005). *Montessori: The science behind the genius*. New York: Oxford University Press.

Lillard, A. S., & Else-Quest, N. M. (2006). An evaluation of Montessori education. *Science*, *313*, 1893–1894.

MacKenzie, B. (2011). Caring for Rosie the Riveter's children. *Young Children*, *66*(4), 68–70.

Mbiti, J. (1992). *African religions and philosophy* (2nd ed.). Portsmouth, NH: Heinemann.

Mitchell, A., & David, J. (1992). *Explorations with young children: A curriculum guide from the Bank Street College of Education*. Mt. Rainier, MD: Gryphon House.

Montessori, M. (1909/1964). *The Montessori method*. New York: Schocken.

Montessori, M. (1912/1964). *The Montessori method*. Translated by A. E. George. New York: Schocken.

Moore, M. R., & Campos, D., et al. (2010). Inspiration to Teach—Reflections on Friedrich Froebel and why he counts in early childhood education. *Young Children*, *65*(4), 74–76.

Neugebauer, B. (1995, January/February). Meet cover advocate Winona Elliott Sample, Santa Clara, California. *Child Care Information Exchange*, 57–58.

Nourot, P. M. (2005). Historical perspectives on early childhood education. In J. L. Roopnarine & J. E. Johnson (Eds.), *Approaches to early childhood education* (5th ed., pp. 3–43). Upper Saddle River, NJ: Pearson.

Osborn, D. K. (1991). *Early childhood education in historical perspective* (3rd ed.). Athens, GA: Daye Press.

Pestalozzi, J.H. (1894/2012). *How Gertrude teaches her children: An attempt to help mothers to teach their own children and an account of the method (Classic Reprint)*. Forgotten Books.

Pratt, C. (1948). *I learn from children*. New York: Simon & Schuster.

Reagan, T. (2005). *Non-Western educational traditions: Indigenous approaches to education thought and practice* (3rd ed.). Mahwah, NJ: Lawrence Erlbaum Associates.

Reggio Children. (1995). *A journey into the rights of children*. Reggio Emilia, Italy: Author.

Rumbaut, R. G. (2006). The making of a people. In M. Tienda & F. Mitchell (Eds.), *Hispanics and the future of America* (pp. 16–65). Washington, DC: National Academies Press.

Shapiro, E. K., & Nager, N. (1999). *The developmental-interaction approach to education: Retrospect and prospect*. New York: Bank Street College of Education. Retrieved from https://s3.amazonaws.com/bankstreet_web/media/filer_public/filer_public/2013/02/12/occasional-papers-1.pdf

Simpson, J. (2012, November). Oneida Cockrell: Pioneer in the field of early childhood education. *Young Children*, *67*, 58–60. Retrieved September 10, 2014, from http://www.naeyc.org/yc/files/yc/file/201211/Heritage1112.pdf

Simpson, J. W., & McConnell-Farmer, J. L. (2013). Selected African-American pioneers of early childhood education. In B. F. Hinitz (Ed.), *The hidden history of early childhood education*, 143–158. New York: Routledge.

Simpson, W. J. (n.d.). A biographical study of black educators in early childhood education. Unpublished dissertation, Fielding Institute.

Simpson, W. J., & McConnell-Farmer, J. L. (2013). Selected African-American pioneers of early childhood education. In B. Hinitz (Ed.), *The hidden history of early childhood education*, 143–158. New York, NY: Routledge.

Snyder, A. (1972). *Dauntless women in early childhood education, 1856–1931*. Washington, DC: Association for Childhood Education International.

Some, S. (1999). *Welcoming spirit home: Ancient African teachings to celebrate children and community*. Novato, CA: New World Library.

Stoltz, L. M. H. (1977). *An American child development pioneer: Lois Meek Stoltz* (Interview by R. Takanishi, typescript). Washington, DC: National Archives.

United Nations Convention on the Rights of the Child, 1989, retrieved from www.ohchr.org/en/professionalinterest/pages/crc.aspx

Wolfe, J. (2000). *Learning from the past: Historical voices in early childhood education*. Mayerthorpe, Alberta: Piney Branch Press.

Wortham, S. C. (2002). *Childhood: 1892–2002*. Wheaton, MD: Association for Childhood Education International.

Zellizer, V. (1981). The price and value of children: The case of children's insurance. *American Journal of Sociology*, *86*(5), 1036–1056.

Chapter 3

Barbarin, O. A., & Wasik, B. H. (Eds.). (2009). *Handbook of child development and early education: Research to practice*. New York: Guilford Press.

Barker, K. (2005, November 30). Paparazzi get an audience with the panda. *Washington Post*, p. B5.

Barnett, W. S., Jung, K., Youn, M.-J., & Frede, E. C. (2013). *APPLES, Abbott Preschool Program longitudinal effects study: Fifth grade follow-up*. New Brunswick, NJ: National Institute for Early Education Research, Rutgers University. Retrieved from http://nieer.org/sites/nieer/files/APPLES%205th%20Grade.pdf

Bassok, D., Latham, S., & Rorem, A. (2016). Is kindergarten the new first grade? *AERA Open*, *1*(4), 1–31.

Bierman, K. L., Domitrovich, C. E., Nix, R. L., Gest, S. D., Welsh, J. A., Greenberg, M. T., et al. (2008). Promoting academic and social–emotional school readiness: The Head Start REDI program. *Child Development*, *79*(6), 1802–1817.

Bowman, B. T., Donovan, M. S., & Burns, S. (Eds.). (2001). *Eager to learn: Educating our preschoolers* (National Research Council, Committee on Early Childhood Pedagogy Report). Washington, DC: National Academies Press.

Bredekamp, S. (1997a). Developmentally appropriate practice: The early childhood teacher as decision maker. In S. Bredekamp & C. Copple (Eds.), *Developmentally appropriate practice in early childhood programs* (Rev. ed., pp. 33–52). Washington, DC: National Association for the Education of Young Children.

Bredekamp, S. (1997b). NAEYC issues revised position statement on developmentally appropriate practice in early childhood programs. *Young Children*, 52(2), 34–40.

Bredekamp, S. (Ed.). (1987). *Developmentally appropriate practice in early childhood programs serving children from birth through age 8* (Expanded ed.). Washington, DC: National Association for the Education of Young Children.

Bredekamp, S., & Copple, C. (Eds.). (1997). *Developmentally appropriate practice in early childhood programs* (Rev. ed.). Washington, DC: National Association for the Education of Young Children.

Bronfenbrenner, U. (Ed.). (2004). *Making human beings human: Bioecological perspectives on human development*. Thousand Oaks, CA: Sage.

Bronson, M. B. (1995). *The Right Stuff for Children Birth through Age 8: Selecting Play Materials to Support Development*. Washington, DC: NAEYC.

Brown, C. P., Feger, B. S., & Mowry, B. (2015). Helping others understand academic rigor in teachers' developmentally appropriate practices. *Young Children*, 70(4), 62–69.

Campaign for Commercial-Free Childhood. (2017). *Children's Screen Time Action Network*. Online at www.commercialfreechildhood.org/blog/-announcing-childrens-screen-time-action-network

Cannon, J. S., Kilburn, M. R., Karoly, L. A., Mattox, T., Muchow, A. N., & Buenaventura, M. (2017). *Investing early: Taking stock of outcomes and economic returns from early childhood programs*. Santa Monica, CA: RAND Corporation. www.rand.org/pubs/research_reports/RR1993.html. Also available in print form.

Carle, E. (1969). *The very hungry caterpillar*. New York: Philomel, Penguin Group.

Carlson-Paige, N., McLaughlin, G. B., & Almon, J. W. (2015). *Reading instruction in kindergarten: Little to gain and much to lose*. Alliance for Childhood and Defending the Early Years. Retrieved November 4, 2017, from https://deyproject.files.wordpress.com/2015/01/readinginkindergarten_online-1.pdf

Common Core State Standards Initiative. (2011a). *Common core standards for English language arts*. Washington, DC: Council for Chief State School Officers and National Governor's Association. Retrieved February 17, 2012, from www.corestandards.org

Common Core State Standards Initiative. (2011b). *Common core standards for mathematics*. Washington, DC: Council for Chief State School Officers and National Governor's Association. Retrieved February 17, 2012, from http://www.corestandards.org

Copple, C., & Bredekamp, S. (2006). *Basics of developmentally appropriate practice: An introduction for teachers of children 3 to 6*. Washington, DC: National Association for the Education of Young Children.

Copple, C., & Bredekamp, S. (Eds.). (2009). *Developmentally appropriate practice in early childhood programs serving children from birth through age 8* (Rev. ed.). Washington, DC: National Association for the Education of Young Children.

Copple, C., Bredekamp, S., Koralek, D., & Charner, K. (Eds.). (2013a). *Developmentally appropriate practice: Focus on infants and toddlers*. Washington, DC: National Association for the Education of Young Children.

Copple, C., Bredekamp, S., Koralek, D., & Charner, K. (Eds.). (2013b). *Developmentally appropriate practice: Focus on preschoolers*. Washington, DC: National Association for the Education of Young Children.

Copple, C., Bredekamp, S., Koralek, D., & Charner, K. (Eds.). (2014a). *Developmentally appropriate practice: Focus on children in first, second, and third grades*. Washington, DC: National Association for the Education of Young Children.

Copple, C., Bredekamp, S., Koralek, D., & Charner, K. (Eds.). (2014b). *Developmentally appropriate practice: Focus on kindergartners*. Washington, DC: National Association for the Education of Young Children.

Costanza, V., Northey, K., Riley-Ayers, S. (2017). Academic rigor and DAP: Implementing high-quality teaching practices in K–3. Paper presented at annual conference of the National Association for the Education of Young Children, Atlanta, GA.

Dahlberg, G., Moss, P., & Pence, A. R. (2007). *Beyond quality in early childhood education: Languages of evaluation* (2nd ed.). New York: Routledge.

Diamond, K. E., Justice, L. M., Siegler, R. S., & Snyder, P. A. (2013). *Synthesis of IES research on early intervention and early childhood education*. (NCSER 2013-3001). Washington, DC: National Center for Special Education Research, Institute of Education Sciences, U.S. Department of Education. Retrieved from http://ies.ed.gov/

Donahue, C., & Schomburg, R. (2017). Technology and interactive media in early childhood programs: What we've learned from five years of research, policy, and practice. *Young Children*, 72(4), 72–78.

Donohue, C. (Ed.). (2015). *Technology and digital media in the early years*. New York: Routledge Taylor & Francis Group.

Epstein, A. S. (2014). *The intentional teacher: Choosing the best strategies for young children's learning* (Rev. ed.). Washington, DC: National Association for the Education of Young Children.

Fred Rogers Center & TEC Center at Erikson Institute. (2017). *Technology and interactive media for young children: A whole child approach connecting the vision of Fred Rogers with research and practice*. Chicago, IL: Author.

Garcia, J. L., Heckman, J. J., Leaf, D. E., & Prados, M. J. (2016). The life-cycle benefits of an influential early childhood program. Retrieved October 31, 2016, from https://heckmanequation.org/assets/2017/01/Garcia_Heckman_Leaf_etal_2016_life-cycle-benefits-ecp_r1-p.pdf

Gee, E., Takeuchi, L., & Wartella, E. (Eds.). (2017). *Children and families in the digital age: learning together in a media saturated culture*. New York, NY: Routledge.

Gilliam, W. (2016). *Issue Brief: Early childhood expulsions and suspensions undermine our nation's most promising agent of opportunity and social justice*. Robert Wood Johnson Foundation. Retrieved December 6, 2017, from http://bma.issuelab.org/resources/25852/25852.pdf

Graue, M. E., & Delaney, K. (2011, November 4). *Being developmentally and culturally responsive*. Paper presented at the annual meeting of the National Association for the Education of Young Children, Atlanta, GA.

Guernsey, L. (2014). *Envisioning a digital age architecture for early education*. Washington, DC: New America Foundation. Retrieved from http://www.newamerica.net/sites/newamerica.net/files/policy-docs/DigitalArchitecture-20140326.pdf

Hamre, B. K., & Pianta, R. C. (2005). Can instructional and emotional support in the first-grade classroom make a difference for children at risk of school failure? *Child Development*, 76(5), 949–967.

Hamre, B. K., & Pianta, R. C. (2007). Learning opportunities in preschool and early elementary classrooms. In R. C. Pianta, M. J. Cox, & K. Snow (Eds.), *School readiness, early learning, and the transition to kindergarten* (pp. 49–83). Baltimore: Paul H. Brookes.

Hamre, B. K., & Pianta, R. C. (2010). Classroom environments and developmental processes: Conceptualization and measurement. In J. L. Meece & J. S. Eccles (Eds.), *Handbook of research on schools, schooling, and human development* (pp. 25–41). New York: Routledge.

Hamre, B., Hatfield, B., Pianta, R., & Jamil, F. (2014). Evidence for general and domain-specific elements of teacher–child interactions: Associations with preschool children's development. *Child Development*, 85(3), 1257–1274.

Heroman, C., & Copple, C. (2006). Teaching in the kindergarten year. In D. F. Gullo (Ed.), *K Today: Teaching and Learning in the Kindergarten Year*. Washington, DC: NAEYC.

Hill, C. J., Gormley, W. T., Adelstein, S., & Willemin, C. (2012). *The effects of Oklahoma's pre-kindergarten program on 3rd grade test scores*. Washington, DC: The Center for Research on Children in the U.S. (CROCUS) at Georgetown University. Retrieved from http://fcd-us.org/sites/default/files/Long-term%20Policy%20Brief_05-22-2012%20(2).pdf

Honig, A. S. (2010). *Little kids, big worries: Stress-busting tips for early childhood classrooms*. Baltimore: Paul H. Brookes.

Institute of Medicine (IOM) & National Research Council (NRC). (2015). *Transforming the workforce for children birth through age 8: A unifying foundation*. Washington, DC: National Academies Press.

Jenkins, J. M., & Duncan, J. G. (2017). Do pre-kindergarten curricula matter? In Pre-kindergarten Task Force, *The current state of scientific knowledge on pre-kindergarten effects*, 37–43. Brookings & Duke Center for Child and Family Policy, Retrieved November 1, 2017 from https://www.brookings.edu/wp-content/uploads/2017/04/duke_prekstudy_final_4-4-17_hires.pdf

Kostelnik, M. J., Soderman, A. K., Whiren, A. P., & Rupiper, M. Q. (2014). *Developmentally appropriate curriculum: Best practices in early childhood education* (6th ed.). Upper Saddle River, NJ: Merrill/Pearson.

Martin, B. (1996). *Brown bear, brown bear, what do you see?* New York: Henry Holt.

Mashburn, A. J., Pianta, R., Hamre, B. K., Downer, J. T., Barbarin, O., Bryant, D., et al. (2008). Measures of classroom quality in pre-kindergarten and children's development of academic, language and social skills. *Child Development*, 79(3), 732–749.

Matychuk, P. (2005). The role of child-directed speech in language acquisition: A case study. *Language Sciences*, 27, 301–379.

McCoy, D. C., Yoshikawa, H., Ziol-Guest, K. M., Duncan, D. J., Schindler, H. S., Magnuson, K., . . . & Shonkoff, J. P. (2017). Impacts of early childhood education on medium- and long-term educational outcomes. *Educational Researcher (46)*8, 474–487.

National Association for the Education of Young Children (NAEYC) & the Fred Rogers Center for Early Learning and Children's Media. (2012). *Technology in early childhood programs serving children from birth through age 8. Joint Position Statement*. Washington, DC: Authors.

National Association for the Education of Young Children (NAEYC) & the Fred Rogers Center for Early Learning and Children's Media. (2012). *Technology in early childhood programs serving children from birth through age 8. Joint Position Statement*. Washington, DC: Authors.

National Association for the Education of Young Children (NAEYC). (2009). *Developmentally appropriate practice in early childhood programs serving children from birth through age 8: Position statement*. Washington, DC: Author.

Pianta, R. C., Barnett, W. S., Burchinal, M., & Thornburg, K. R. (2009). The effects of preschool education: What we know, how public policy is or is not aligned with the evidence base, and what we need to know. *Psychological Science in the Public Interest*, 10(2) 49–88.

Pianta, R. C., Barnett, W. S., Justice, L. M., & Sheridan, S. M. (Eds.). (2012). *Handbook of early childhood education*. New York: Guilford Press.

Pre-kindergarten Task Force. (2017). *The current state of scientific knowledge on pre-kindergarten effects*. Brookings & Duke Center for Child and Family Policy. Retrieved November 1, 2017, from www.brookings.edu/wp-content/uploads/2017/04/duke_prekstudy_final_4-4-17_hires.pdf

Ritchie, S., & Gutmann, L. (Eds.) (2014). *FirstSchool: Transforming preK–3rd grade for African American, Latino, and low-income children*. New York, NY: Teachers College Press.

Schweinhart, L. J., & Weikart D. P. (1997). The High/Scope preschool curriculum comparison study through age 23. *Childhood: A Global Journal of Child Research, 143*(1997), 117–143.

Schweinhart, L., Weikart, D., & Larner, M. (1986). Consequences of three preschool curriculum models through age 15. *Early Childhood Research Quarterly, 1*(1), 15–46.

Shanker, S. (2012). *Calm, alert, and learning: Classroom strategies for self-regulation*. Pearson Education Canada, Toronto, Ontario, Canada.

Shonkoff, J., & Phillips, D. A. (2000). *From neurons to neighborhoods: The science of early childhood development*. Washington, DC: National Academies Press.

Squires, J. (2014). "First you work, and then it's play." *Preschool Matters Today: A blog of the National Institute for Early Education Research*. Retrieved from http://preschoolmatters.org/2014/06/19/first-you-work-and-then-its-play/

Stipek, D. (2011). Classroom practices and children's motivation to learn. In E. Zigler, W. S. Gilliam, & W. S. Barnett (Eds.), *The pre-k debates: Current controversies and issues* (pp. 98–103). Baltimore: Brookes.

Teachstone. (2017). *Effective teacher-child interactions and child outcomes: A summary of research on the Classroom Assessment Scoring System (CLASS) pre-K–3rd grade*. Charlottesville, VA: Author.

Weiland, C., & Yoshikawa, H. (2013). Impacts of a pre-kindergarten program on children's mathematics, language, literacy, executive function, and emotional skills. *Child Development*, p. 11.

Weiland, C., Ulvestad, K., Sachs, J., & Yoshikawa, H. (2013). Associations between classroom quality and children's vocabulary and executive function skills in an urban public prekindergarten program. *Early Childhood Research Quarterly, 28*(2), 199–209. doi:10.1016/j.ecresq.2012.12.002.

Yoshikawa, H., Weiland, C., Brooks-Gunn, J., Burchinal, M. R., Espinosa, L. M., Gormley, W. T., et al. (2013). *Investing in our future: The evidence base on preschool education*. New York: Foundation for Child Development. Retrieved from http://fcd-us.org/sites/default/files/Evidence%20Base%20on%20Preschool%20Education%20FINAL.pdf

Chapter 4

Alliance for Childhood. (2010). *The loss of children's play: A public health issue*. College Park, MD: Author. Retrieved from http://www.allianceforchildhood.org

Ames, L. B., & Ilg, F. (1979). *The Gesell Institute's child from one to six*. New York: Harper & Row.

Bailey, B. A., & Brookes, C. (2012). Thinking out loud: Development of private speech and the implications for school success and self-control. In C. Copple (Ed.), *Growing minds: Building strong cognitive foundations in early childhood*, pp. 105–110. Washington, DC: National Association for the Education of Young Children.

Bandura, A. (1973). *Aggression: A social learning analysis*. Upper Saddle River, NJ: Prentice Hall.

Bandura, A. (1986). *Social foundations of thought and action: A social-cognitive theory*. Upper Saddle River, NJ: Prentice Hall.

Bandura, A. (1997). *Self-efficacy: The exercise of control*. New York: Freeman.

Baumrind, D. (1971). Current patterns of parental authority. *Developmental Psychology, 4*, 1–103.

Berk, L. E. (2006). Looking at the kindergarten child. In D. F. Gullo (Ed.), *K today: Teaching and learning in the kindergarten year* (pp. 11–25). Washington, DC: National Association for the Education of Young Children.

Bodrova, E., & Leong, D. J. (2007). *Tools of the mind: The Vygotskian approach to early childhood education*. Upper Saddle River, NJ: Pearson.

Bodrova, E., & Leong, D. J. (2012a). Developing self-regulation in kindergarten: Can we keep all the crickets in the basket? In C. Copple (Ed.), *Growing minds: Building strong cognitive foundations in early childhood* (pp. 119–122). Washington, DC: National Association for the Education of Young Children.

Bodrova, E., & Leong, D. J. (2012b). Scaffolding self-regulated learning in young children: Lessons from Tools of the Mind. In R. C. Pianta, W. S. Barnett, L. M. Justice, & S. M. Sheridan (Eds.), *Handbook of early childhood education* (pp. 352–369). New York: Guilford Press.

Boyd, J., Barnett, W. S., Bodrova, E., Leong, D. J., & Gomby, D. (2005, March). *Promoting children's social emotional development through preschool* (Preschool Policy Report). New Brunswick, NJ: National Institute for Early Education Research.

Bredekamp, S. (2004). Play and school readiness. In E. F. Zigler, D. G. Singer, & S. J. Bishop-Josef (Eds.), *Children's play: The roots of reading* (pp. 159–174). Washington, DC: ZERO to THREE Press.

Bronfenbrenner, U. (1979). *The ecology of human development: Experiments by nature and design*. Cambridge, MA: Harvard University Press.

Bronfenbrenner, U. (Ed.). (2004). *Making human beings human: Bioecological perspectives on human development*. Thousand Oaks, CA: Sage.

Bronfenbrenner, U., & Morris, P. A. (2006). The bio-ecological model of human development. In R. M. Lerner & W. Damon (Eds.), *Handbook of child psychology* (6th ed.), *Vol. 1, Theoretical models of human development* (pp. 793–828). Hoboken, NJ: John Wiley & Sons.

Bustamante, A. S., et al. (2017). Approaches to learning and school readiness in Head Start: Applications to preschool science. *Learning and Individual Differences, 56*, 112–118.

Case, R., & Okamoto, Y. (1996). *The role of central conceptual structures in the development of children's thought* (Monographs of the Society of Research in Child Development, Vol. 61, No. 2, Serial no. 246). Chicago: University of Chicago Press.

Center on the Developing Child at Harvard University (2016). *From best practices to breakthrough impacts: A science-based approach to building a more promising future for young children and families*. Retrieved October 21, 2017, from www.developingchild.harvard.edu

Center on the Developing Child at Harvard University. (2010). *Early experiences can alter gene expression and affect long-term development: Working paper #10*. Retrieved October 28, 2011 from http://www.developingchild.harvard.edu

Clements, D. H., & Sarama, J. (2009). *Learning and teaching early math: The learning trajectories approach*. New York: Routledge.

Copple, C., & Bredekamp, S. (Eds.). (2009). *Developmentally appropriate practice in early childhood programs serving children from birth through age 8* (Rev. ed.). Washington, DC: National Association for the Education of Young Children.

Diamond, A., & Lee, K. (2011, August 19). Interventions shown to aid executive function development in children 4 to 12 years old. *Science, 333*(6045), 959–964. doi:10.1126/science.1204529

Division for Early Childhood. (2014). *DEC recommended practices in early intervention/early childhood special education 2014*. Retrieved October 21, 2017, from www.dec-sped.org/recommended-practices

Eason, S. H., & Levine, S. C. (2017). Math learning begins at home. *ZERO TO THREE, 3*(5), 35–43.

Elkind, D. (2008). *The power of play: Learning what comes naturally*. Cambridge, MA: Da Capo Press.

Erikson, E. (1950/1963). *Childhood and society* (2nd ed.). New York: Norton.

Frost, J. L., Wortham, S. C., & Reifel, S. (2012). *Play and child development* (4th ed.). Upper Saddle River, NJ: Pearson.

Fusaro, M., & Nelson, C. A., III. (2009). Developmental cognitive neuroscience and education practice. In O. A. Barbarin & B. H. Wasik (Eds.), *Handbook of child development and early education: Research to practice* (pp. 57–77). New York: Guilford Press.

Galinsky, E. (2010). *Mind in the making: The seven essential life skills every child needs*. New York: Harper.

Gapin, J., & Etnier, J. L. (2010). The relationship between physical activity and executive function performance in children with Attention Deficit Hyperactivity Disorder. *Journal of Sport & Exercise Psychology, 32*(6), 753–763.

Gelman, R. (2000). Domain specificity and variability in cognitive development. *Child Development, 71*, 854–856.

Gesell, A. (1940). *The first five years of life*. New York: Harper & Row.

Gilpin, A., Boxmeyer, C., DeCaro, J., & Lochman, J. (2014), *Power PATH universal preschool intervention effects on executive function*. Paper presented, July 7, 2014, at Head Start's 12th National Research Conference on Early Childhood, Washington, DC.

Gopnik, A., Meltzoff, A. N., & Kuhl, P. K. (1999). *The scientist in the crib: Minds, brains, and how children learn*. New York: William Morrow.

Hassinger-Das, B., Hirsh-Pasek, K., & Golinkoff, R. M. (2017). The case of brain science and guided play: A developing story. *Young Children, 72*(2), 45–50.

Hirsh-Pasek, K., Golinkoff, R. M., Berk, L. E., & Singer, D. (Eds.). (2009). *A mandate for playful learning in preschool: Applying the scientific evidence*. New York: Oxford University Press.

Institute of Medicine (IOM) and National Research Council (NRC). (2015). *Transforming the workforce for children birth through age 8: A unifying foundation*. Washington, DC: The National Academies Press.

Johnson, J. E., Christie, J. F., & Wardle, F. (2005). *Play, development, and early education*. Upper Saddle River, NJ: Pearson.

Jones, S., & Bailey, R. (2014). *Mapping executive function: Technical and applied definitions and their implications for the classroom*. Paper presented July 7, 2014 at Head Start's 12th National Research Conference on Early Childhood, Washington, DC.

Kohn, A. (2014). *The myth of the spoiled child: Challenging the conventional wisdom about children and parenting*. Boston: Da Capo.

Kuhl, P. K., Ramirez, R. R., Bosseler, A., Lin, J. L., & Imada, T. (2014). Infants' brain responses to speech suggest Analysis by Synthesis. Retrieved April 18, 2018 from http://www.pnas.org/content/pnas/111/31/11238.full.pdf

Lally, J. R., & Mangione, P. (2017). Caring relationships: The heart of early brain development. *Young Children, 72*(2), 17–24.

Leong, D. J., & Bodrova, E. (2012). Assessing and scaffolding make believe play. *Young Children, 67*(1), 28–34.

Lieberman, D. A. (2006). What can we learn from playing interactive games? In P. Vorderer & J. Bryant (Eds.), *Playing video games: Motives, responses, and consequences*. Mahwah, NJ: Lawrence Erlbaum Associates.

Lifter, K., Foster-Sanda, S., Arzamarski, C., Briesch, J., & McClure, E. (2011). Overview of play: Its uses and importance in early intervention/early childhood special education. *Infants and Young Children, 24*(3), 225–245.

Maslow, A. H. (1954). *Towards a psychology of being*. New York: Van Nostrand.

A Maslow, © 2013. Motivation and personality. Reprinted and electronically reproduced by permission of Pearson Education, Inc., Upper Saddle River, NJ.

McWayne, C. M., Owsianik, M., Green, L. E., & Fantuzzo, J. W. (2008). Parenting behaviors and preschool children's social and emotional skills: A question of the consequential validity of traditional parenting constructs for low-income African Americans. *Early Childhood Research Quarterly, 23*, 173–192.

Moffat, T. E., Arseneault, L., Blsky, D. W., & Harrington, H. L. (2011). A gradient of childhood self-control predicts health, wealth, and public safety. *Proceedings of the National Academy of Sciences*. Retrieved April 18, 2018 from https://www.researchgate.net/publication/288449926

Murphy, S. (2014). Finding the right fit: Inclusive strategies for students with characteristics of ADHD. *Young Children, 60*(3), 66–71.

National Association for the Education of Young Children (NAEYC). (2009). *Developmentally appropriate practice in early childhood programs serving children from birth through age 8: Position statement*. Washington, DC: Author.

Palmer, K., Miller, M., & Robinson, L. (2013). Acute exercise enhances preschoolers' ability to sustain attention. *Journal of Sport & Exercise Psychology, 35*(4), 433–437.

Papert, S. (1999, March 29). Time 100: Piaget. *Time* magazine. Retrieved October 9, 2009, from http://www.time.com/time/time100/scientist/profile/piaget.html

Partnership for 21st Century Learning. (2017). *Skills for today research series*. Retrieved April 18, 2018 from http://www.p21.org/our-work/4cs-research-series.

Piaget, J. (1930). *The child's conception of physical causality*. Harcourt Brace & Co.

Piaget, J. (1952). *The origins of intelligence in children*. New York: International Universities Press.

Piaget, J. (1962). *Play, dreams, and imitation in childhood*. New York: Norton.

Rogoff, B. (2012). Learning without lessons: Opportunities to expand knowledge. *Infancia Y Aprendizaje /Journal for the Study of Education and Development, 35*(2), 233–252. doi:10.1174/021037012800217970.

Sameroff, A. J. (Ed.) (2009). *The transactional model of development: How children and contexts shape each other*. Washington, DC: American Psychological Association.

Sameroff, A., & McDonough, S. (1994). Educational implications of developmental transitions: Revisiting the 5- to 7-year shift. *Phi Delta Kappan, 76*(3), 188–193.

Shonkoff, J. P., Garner, A. S., & the Committee on Psychosocial Effects of Child and Family Health. (2012). The lifelong effects of early childhood adversity and toxic stress. *Pediatrics, 129*(1), e232–e246. Retrieved from http://pediatrics.aappublications.org/content/129/1/e232.full.pdf+html

Siegler, R. S., & Ramani, G. B. (2008). Playing board games promotes low-income children's numerical development. *Developmental Science, 11*(5), 655–661.

Slavin, R. (2015). *Educational psychology: Theory and practice* (11th ed.). Upper Saddle River, NJ: Pearson.

Smilansky, S. (1968). *The effects of sociodramatic play on disadvantaged preschool children*. New York: Wiley.

Smilansky, S., & Shefatya, L. (1990). *Facilitating play: A medium for promoting cognitive, socio-emotional, and academic development in young children*. Gaithersburg, MD: Psychological and Educational Publications.

Stetsenko, A., & Vianna, E. (2009). Bridging developmental theory and educational practice: Lessons from the Vygotskian project. In O. A. Barbarin (Ed.), *Handbook of child development and early education: Research to practice* (pp. 38–54). New York: Guilford Press.

Thompson, R. A. (2008). *Connecting neurons, concepts, and people: Brain development and its implications* (Preschool Policy Brief, Issue 17). New Brunswick, NJ: National Institute for Early Education Research.

Tierney, A. L., & Nelson, C. A., III. (2009). Brain development and the role of experience in the early years. *Zero to Three, 30*(2), 9–13.

Vygotsky, L. S. (1962). *Thought and language*. Cambridge, MA: MIT Press.

Vygotsky, L. S. (1977). Play and its role in the mental development of the child. In M. Cole (Ed.), *Soviet developmental psychology* (pp. 76–99). Armonk, NY: M. E. Sharpe.

Vygotsky, L. S. (1978). *Mind in society*. Cambridge, MA: Harvard University Press.

Wiltz, N. W., & Klein, E. L. (2001). "What do you do in child care?" Children's perceptions of high and low quality classrooms. *Early Childhood Research Quarterly, 16*(2), 209–236.

Wong, C., Odom, S. L., Hume, K. Cox, A. W., Fettig, A., Kucharczyk, S., et al. (2014). *Evidence-based practices for children, youth, and young adults with Autism Spectrum Disorder*. Chapel Hill, NC: The University of North Carolina, Frank Porter Graham Child Development Institute.

Chapter 5

Ali, S. S. (2013, November 30). A brief review of risk-factors for growth and developmental delay among preschool children in developing countries. *Advanced Biomedical Research, (2)*91. doi: 10.4103/2277-9175.122523.

Allington, R. L. (2009). *What really matters in response to intervention: Research-based designs*. Upper Saddle River, NJ: Pearson.

Barbu, S., Cabanes, G., & Le Maner-Idrissi, G. (2011). Boys and girls on the playground: Sex differences in social development are not stable across early childhood. *PLoS ONE, 6*(1), e16407. http://doi.org/10.1371/journal.pone.0016407.

Bates, J. E. (2012). Temperament as a tool in promoting early childhood development. In S. L. Odom, E. P. Pungello & N. Gardner-Neblett (Eds.), *Infants, toddlers, and families in poverty: Research implications for early child care* (pp. 153–177). New York: Guilford Press.

Bennett, T., Eatman, J., Garcia, G. E., Halle, J., McCollum, J. et al. (2001). *Cross-Cultural Considerations in Early Childhood Special Education* (Technical Report #14). Urbana-Champaign, IL: University of Illinois, Culturally and Linguistically Appropriate Services (CLAS). Retrieved April 20, 2018, from http://clas.uiuc.edu/techreport/tech14.html#4b

Brillante, P. (2017). *The essentials: Supporting young children with disabilities in the classroom*. Washington, DC: National Association for the Education of Young Children.

Burchinal, M., & Willoughby, M. (2013). The Family Life Project: An epidemiological and developmental study of young children living in poor rural communities: IV. Poverty and associated social risks: Toward a cumulative risk framework. *Monographs of the Society for Research in Child Development, 78*(5), 53–65.

Casey, M. B., Erkut, S., Ceder, I., & Young, J. M. (2008). Use of a storytelling context to improve girls' and boys' geometry skills in kindergarten. *Journal of Applied Developmental Psychology, 29*, 29–48.

Center on the Developing Child at Harvard University. (2010). *Early experiences can alter gene expression and affect long-term development: Working paper #10*. Retrieved October 28, 2011 from http://www.developingchild.harvard.edu

Center on the Developing Child at Harvard University. (n.d.) *8 things to remember about child development*. Retrieved November 4, 2017, from http://-developingchild.harvard.edu/resources/8-things-remember-child-development.

Center on the Developing Child at Harvard University. (n.d.) *Resilience*. Retrieved December 31, 2017, from https://developingchild.harvard.edu/science/key-concepts/resilience/

Christensen, D. L., Bilder, D. A., Zahorodny, W., Bilder, D., Charles, J., Constantino, J. N., Daniels, J., et al. (2016) Prevalence and characteristics of autism spectrum disorder among 4-year-old children in the Autism and Developmental Disabilities Monitoring Network. *Journal of Behavioral Pediatrics, 37*, 1–8.

Clements, D. H., & Sarama, J. (2011). Early childhood teacher education: The case of geometry. *Journal of Mathematics Teacher Education, 14*(2), 133–148. Retrieved from https://www.researchgate.net/-publication/226486133_Early_childhood_teacher_education_The_case_of_geometry.

Coleman, M. R., & Shah-Coltrane, S. (2015). Children of promise: Dr. James Gallagher's thoughts on underrepresentation within gifted education. *Journal for the Education of the Gifted, 38*, 70–76. doi: 10.1177/0162353214565556.

Coleman, M. R., Roth, F. P., & West, T. (2009). *Road-map to Pre-K RTI: Applying Response to Intervention in preschool settings*. New York: National Center for Learning Disabilities. Retrieved October 9, 2009, from http://www.rtinetwork.org/images/roadmaptoprekrti.pdf

Copple, C., & Bredekamp, S. (Eds.). (2009). *Developmentally appropriate practice in early childhood programs serving children from birth through age 8* (Rev. ed.). Washington, DC: National Association for the Education of Young Children.

Dinnebeil, L. A., Boat, M., & Bae, Y. (2013). Integrating principles of universal design into the early childhood curriculum. *Dimensions of Early Childhood, 41*(1), 3–14.

Division for Early Childhood & National Association for the Education of Young Children. (2009). *Early childhood inclusion: A joint position statement of the Division for Early Childhood (DEC) and the National Association for the Education of Young Children (NAEYC)*. Chapel Hill: The University of North Carolina, FPG Child Development Institute. Retrieved from http://npdci.fpg.unc.edu/sites/npdci.fpg.unc.edu/files/resources/EarlyChildhoodInclusion_0.pdf

Division for Early Childhood of the Council for Exceptional Children (DEC), National Association for the Education of Young Children (NAEYC), & National Head Start Association (NHSA). (2014). *Frameworks for response to intervention in early childhood: Description and implications*. Article first published online December 17, 2013; issue published February 1, 2014. https://doi.org/10.1177/1525740113514111.

Division for Early Childhood of the Council for Exceptional Children. (2014). *DEC recommended practices in early intervention/early childhood special education*. Los Angeles, CA: Author. Retrieved

February 1, 2015, from http://www.dec-sped.org/recommendedpractices

Dunst, C. J. (2011). *Family-centered practices, parent engagement, and parent and family functioning.* Paper presented at the June 7, 2011, meeting of the Head Start Advisory Committee on Research and Evaluation, Washington, DC. Retrieved from http://www.acf.hhs.gov/programs/opre/hs/advisory_com/index.html.

Dunst, C. J., Hamby, D., Trivette, C. M., Raab, M., & Bruder, M. B. (2000). Everyday family and community life and children's naturally occurring learning opportunities. *Journal of Early Intervention, 23,* 151–164.

Eliot, L. (2009). *Pink brain, blue brain: How small differences grow into troublesome gaps—and what we can do about it.* Boston: Houghton Mifflin Harcourt.

Gadzikowski, A. (2013). *Challenging exceptionally bright children in early childhood classrooms.* St. Paul, MN: Redleaf Press.

Gallagher, K. C. (2013). Guiding children's friendship development: An essential part of the early childhood curriculum. *Young Children, 68,* 5.

Gardner, H. (2004). *Frames of mind: The theory of multiple intelligences* (20th Anniversary ed.). New York: Basic Books.

Gardner, H. (2006). *Multiple intelligences: New horizons in theory and practice.* New York: Basic Books.

Gartstein, M. A., Putnam, S. P., & Rothbart, M. K. (2012). Etiology of preschool behavior problems: Contributions of temperament attributes in early childhood. *Infant Mental Health Journal, 33*(2), 197–211.

Guralnick, M. J., & Bruder, M. B. (2016). Early childhood inclusion in the United States: Goals, current status, and future directions. *Infants & Young Children, 29*(3), 166–177.

Hamre, B. K., & Pianta, R. C. (2010). Classroom environments and developmental processes: Conceptualization and measurement. In J. L. Meece & J. S. Eccles (Eds.), *Handbook of research on schools, schooling, and human development* (pp. 25–41). New York: Routledge.

Hart, B., & Risley, T. R. (1999). *The social world of learning to talk.* Baltimore: Paul H. Brookes.

Hemmeter, M. L., Fox, L., & Snydor, P. (2013). A tiered model for promoting social-emotional competence and addressing behavior. In V. Buysse & E. Peisner-Feinberg (Eds.), *Handbook of Response to Intervention in Early Intervention.* Baltimore, MD: Brookes.

Heward, W. L. (2014). *Exceptional children: An introduction to special education* (10th ed., Pearson new international edition). Upper Saddle River, NJ: Pearson.

Howes, C., & Ritchie, S. (2002). *A matter of trust: Connecting teachers and learners in the early childhood curriculum.* New York, NY: Teachers College Press.

Hume, K., Turner-Brown, L., & Boutot, E. A. (2016). Play focused interventions for young children with autism. In E. Boutot (Ed.), *Autism spectrum disorders: Foundations, characteristics, and effective strategies* (2nd ed.), 169–180. Boston, MA: Pearson.

Hyson, M. (2008). *Enthusiastic and engaged learners: Approaches to learning in the early childhood classroom.* New York, NY: Teachers College Press.

Institute of Medicine (IOM) & National Research Council (NRC). (2015). *Transforming the workforce for children birth through age 9: A unifying foundation.* Washington, DC: National Academies Press.

Jensen, A. R. (1980). *Bias in mental testing.* New York: Free Press.

Krinzinger, H., Wood, G., & Willmes, K. (2012). What accounts for individual and gender differences in the multi-digit number processing of primary school children? *Zeitschrift für Psychologie, 220*(2), 78–89. http://dx.doi.org/10.1027/2151-2604/a000099

Martin, C. L., Kornienko, O., Schaefer, D. R., Hanish, L. D., Fabes, R. A., and Goble, P. (2013). The role of sex of peers and gender-typed activities in young children's peer affiliative networks: A longitudinal analysis of selection and influence. *Child Development, 84,* 921–937. doi: 10.1111/cdev.12032.

Masten, A. S. (2014). *Ordinary magic: Resilience in development.* New York, NY: Guilford Press. Paperback edition 2015. German edition 2016. http://www.guilford.com/books/Ordinary-Magic/Ann-Masten/9781462523719.

Masten, A. S., & Cicchetti, D. (2016). Resilience in development: Progress and transformation. In D. Cicchetti (Ed.), *Developmental psychopathology, vol. 4: Risk, resilience, and intervention* (3rd ed.), 271–333. New York, NY: Wiley. doi: 10.1002/9781119125556.devpsy406.

McClelland, M. M., Acock, A. C., Piccinin, A., Rhea, S. A., & Stallings, M. C. (2013). Relations between preschool attention span-persistence and age 25 educational outcomes. *Early Childhood Research Quarterly, 28*(2), 314–324.

McWilliam, R. A. (2010). *Routines-based early intervention: Supporting young children and their families.* Baltimore: Brookes.

National Academies of Science, Engineering, and Medicine. (2017). *Promoting the educational success of children and youth learning English.* Washington, DC: The National Academies Press. Retrieved October 31, 2017, from https://doi.org/10.17226/24677.

National Association for Gifted Children. (2008). *Pre-K–Grade 12 gifted education programming standards.* Retrieved December 2, 2011, from http://www.nagc.org/index.aspx?id=960

National Association for Gifted Children. (2010). *Pre-K–Grade 12 gifted education programming standards.* Retrieved December 31, 2017, from http://www.nagc.org/sites/default/files/standards/K-12%20programming%20standards.pdf.

National Association for Gifted Children. (2010). *Redefining giftedness for a new century: Shifting the paradigm.* Retrieved August 1, 2014, from http://nagc.org

National Center on Response to Intervention. (2010). *Essential components of RTI—A closer look at Response to Intervention.* Retrieved January 16, 2011, from http://www.rti4success.org.

National Center on Universal Design for Learning. *About UDL: What is universal design for learning?* Retrieved December 27, 2017, from www.cast.org/udl.

National Professional Development Center on Inclusion (NPDCI). (2007). *Research synthesis points on early childhood inclusion.* Chapel Hill: The University of North Carolina, FPG Child Development Institute.

National Professional Development Center on Inclusion. (2012). *Response to intervention (RTI) in early childhood: Building consensus on the defining features.* Chapel Hill, NC: University of North Carolina, Frank Porter Graham Child Development Institute. Retrieved from http://npdci.fpg.unc.edu.

Neitzel, J., & Wolery, M. (2009). *Overview of prompting.* Chapel Hill, NC: The National Professional Development Center on Autism Spectrum Disorders, Frank Porter Graham Child Development Institute, The University of North Carolina. Retrieved September 10, 2014, from http://csesa.fpg.unc.edu/sites/csesa.fpg.unc.edu/files/ebpbriefs/Prompting_Overview.pdf

Özçalışkan, S., & Goldin-Meadow, S. (2010). Sex differences in language first appear in gesture. *Developmental Science, 13*(5), 752–760.

Parke, R., & Gauvain, M. (2008). *Child psychology: A contemporary viewpoint.* New York, NY: McGraw Hill.

Quinlan, C. (2016). The beginning of 'two cultures': By preschool, boys and girls are already segregated. Retrieved January 17, 2017, from https://thinkprogress.org/the-beginning-of-two-cultures-by-preschool-boys-and-girls-are-already-segregated-219b6b4e76d0/.

Rothbart, M. K. (2011). *Becoming who we are: Temperament and personality in development.* New York: Guilford Press.

Rudasill, K. M., Gallagher, K. C., & White, J. M. (2010). Temperamental attention and activity, classroom emotional support, and academic achievement in third grade. *Journal of School Psychology, 48,* 113–134.

Sabol, T. J., & Pianta, R. C. (2013). Relationships between teachers and children. In W. M. Reynolds, G. E. Miller & I. B. Weiner (Eds.), *Handbook of psychology, Vol. 7: Educational psychology* (2nd ed., pp. 199–211). Hoboken, NJ: John Wiley & Sons.

Sameroff, A. (2010). A unified theory of child development: A dialectic integration of nature and nurture. *Child Development, 81*(1), 6–22.

Sandall, S. R., & Schwartz, I. S. (2008). *Building blocks for teaching preschoolers with special needs* (2nd ed.). Baltimore: Paul H. Brookes.

Shahaeian, A., Razmjoee, M., Wang, C., Elliott, N., & Hughes, C. (2017). Understanding relational aggression during early childhood: An examination of the association with language and other social and cognitive skills. *Early Childhood Research Quarterly, 40,* 204–214.

Shonkoff, J., & Phillips, D. A. (2000). *From neurons to neighborhoods: The science of early childhood development.* Washington, DC: National Academies Press.

Skinner, B. F. (1953). *Science and human behavior.* New York: Macmillan.

Skinner, B. F. (1968). *The technology of teaching.* New York: Appleton-Century-Crofts.

Stright, A. D., Gallagher, K. C., & Kelley, K. (2008). Infant temperament moderates relationships between maternal parenting and children's adjustment in first grade. *Child Development, 79*(1), 186–200.

Sullivan, D. R. (2016). *Cultivating the genius of black children: Strategies to close the achievement gap in the early years.* St. Paul, MN: Redleaf Press.

Tarullo, L., Aikens, N., Moiduddin, E., & West, J. (2010). *A second year in Head Start: Characteristics and outcomes of children who entered the program at age three.* Washington, DC: U.S. Department of Health and Human Services, Administration for Children and Families, Office of Planning, Research and Evaluation.

Tomlinson, C. A. (2014). *The differentiated classroom: Responding to the needs of all learners* (2nd ed.). Alexandria, VA: Association for Supervision & Curriculum Development.

Wolery, M., & Wilbers, J. (1994). *Including children with special needs in early childhood programs.* Washington DC: National Association for the Education of Young Children.

Wong, C. S. (2013). A play and joint attention intervention for teachers of young children with autism: A randomized controlled pilot study. *Autism* (*17*), 340–357.

Wong, C., Odom, S. L., Hume, K. Cox, A. W., Fettig, A., Kucharczyk, S., et al. (2014). *Evidence-based practices for children, youth, and young adults with Autism Spectrum Disorder.* Chapel Hill, NC: The University of North Carolina, Frank Porter Graham Child Development Institute.

Woolfolk, A., & Perry, N. E. (2015). *Child and adolescent development* (2nd ed.). Upper Saddle River, NJ: Pearson.

Chapter 6

Allen, R. (2017, June 13). *Promoting kindness and resilience in turbulent times: Why social and emotional skills matter now more than ever*. Presentation at the annual Professional Learning Institute, NAEYC, San Francisco, CA.

Annie E. Casey Foundation. (2017). *Child population by race and age group*. Retrieved October 25, 2017, from http://datacenter.kidscount.org/data/tables/8446-child-population-by-race-and-age-group.

Banks, J. A. (2016). *Cultural diversity and education: Foundations, curriculum, and teaching* (6th ed.). New York, NY: Routledge.

Barbarin, O. (2011). *Imagining auspicious environments for the development of African American boys*. Paper presented at the ETS Addressing Achievement Gaps Symposium co-sponsored with Children's Defense Fund, June 14, 2011, Washington, DC: Educational Testing Service. Retrieved August 11, 2011, from http://www.ets.org/s/sponsored_events/achievement_gap/pdf/2011_conference/oscar_barbarin_presentation.pdf

Barbarin, O. A. (2015). Parental practices and developmental challenges of boys of color: Opportunities for early intervention. *ZERO TO THREE*, (35)3, 9–17.

Barbarin, O. A., Murry, V. M., Tolan, P., & Graham, S. (2016). Development of boys and young men of color: Implications of developmental science for My Brother's Keeper Initiative. *SRCD Social Policy Report*, 29(3).

Bates, D. (no date). *Digital story helps dual language learner connect with classmates*. Washington, DC: National Association for the Education of Young Children, retrieved August 27, 2014, from http://www.naeyc.org/technology/ digital-story-helps-dual-language-learner

Bialystok, E. (2015). Bilingualism and the development of executive function: The role of attention. *Child Development Perspectives*, Society for Research in Child Development, DOI: 10.1111/cdep.12116.

Bowman, B. T., Donovan, M. S., & Burns, S. (Eds.). (2001). *Eager to learn: Educating our preschoolers* (National Research Council, Committee on Early Childhood Pedagogy Report). Washington, DC: National Academies Press.

Bredekamp, S. (1997a). Developmentally appropriate practice: The early childhood teacher as decision maker. In S. Bredekamp & C. Copple (Eds.), *Developmentally appropriate practice in early childhood programs* (Rev. ed., pp. 33–52). Washington, DC: National Association for the Education of Young Children.

Bredekamp, S., & Copple, C. (Eds.). (1997). *Developmentally appropriate practice in early childhood programs* (Rev. ed.). Washington, DC: National Association for the Education of Young Children.

Bronfenbrenner, U. (1979). *The ecology of human development: Experiments by nature and design*. Cambridge, MA: Harvard University Press.

Bronfenbrenner, U. (Ed.). (2004). *Making human beings human: Bioecological perspectives on human development*. Thousand Oaks, CA: Sage.

Bromer, J., Modigliani, K., and Callahan, C., no date. *Perspectives in childrearing values*. The Family Child Care Accreditation Project, Boston, MA: Wheelock College

Church, V. (1997). *Colors around me*. Chicago: African American Images.

Dahlberg, G., Moss, P., & Pence, A. R. (2007). *Beyond quality in early childhood education: Languages of evaluation* (2nd ed.). New York: Routledge.

Day, C. B. (2006). Every child is a cultural being. In J. R. Lally, P. L. Mangione, & D. Greenwald (Eds.), *Concepts for care: Essays on infant/toddler development and learning* (pp. 97–99). San Francisco: WestEd.

Delpit, L. (2006). *Other people's children: Cultural conflict in the classroom* (Updated ed.). New York: New Press.

Derman-Sparks, L., & Edwards, J. O. (2010). *Anti-bias education for young children and ourselves*. Washington, DC: National Association for the Education of Young Children.

Derman-Sparks, L., & Ramsey, P. G., with Edwards, J. O. (2011). *What if all the kids are white? Anti-bias, multicultural education with young children and families* (2nd ed.). New York: Teachers College Press.

Gannon, M. (2016). Race is a social construct, scientists argue: Racial categories are weak proxies for genetic diversity and need to be phased out. *Scientific American*. Retrieved December 12, 2017, from www.scientificamerican.com/article/race-is-a-social-construct-scientists-argue/

Gilliam, W. (2016). *Early childhood expulsions and suspensions undermine our nation's most promising agent of opportunity and social justice*. Robert Wood Johnson Foundation.

Gilliam, W. S., Maupin, A. N., Reyes, C. R., Acavitti, M., & Shic, F. (2016). *Do early educators' implicit biases regarding sex and race relate to behavioral expectations and recommendations of preschool expulsion and suspensions? A Research Policy Brief*. New Haven, CT: Yale University Child Study Center.

Gonzalez-Mena, J. (2008). *Diversity in early care and education: Honoring differences* (5th ed.). New York: McGraw-Hill.

Graue, M. E., & Delaney, K. (2011, November 4). *Being developmentally and culturally responsive*. Paper presented at the annual meeting of the National Association for the Education of Young Children, Atlanta, GA.

Hale, J. E. (1994). *Unbank the fire: Visions for the education of African American children*. Baltimore: Johns Hopkins University Press.

Hamayan, E., Genesee, F., & Cloud, N. (2013). *Dual language instruction from A to Z: Practical guidance for teachers and administrators*. Portsmouth, NH: Heinemann.

Hanson, M. J. (2011). Diversity in service settings. In E. W. Lynch & M. J. Hanson (Eds.), *Developing cross-cultural competence: A guide for working with children and their families* (4th ed., pp. 2–19). Baltimore: Paul H. Brookes.

Hanson, M. J., & Lynch, E. W. (2004). *Understanding families: Approaches to diversity, disability, and risk*. Baltimore: Paul H. Brookes.

Harms, T., Clifford, R. M., & Cryer, D. (2014). *Early Childhood Environment Rating Scale (ECERS-3)* (3rd ed.). New York, NY: Teachers College Press.

Head Start. (2010b). *Revisiting and updating the multicultural principles for Head Start programs serving children ages birth to five: Addressing culture and home language in Head Start program systems and services*. Retrieved from http://eclkc.ohs.acf.hhs.gov/hslc/tta-system/cultural-linguistic

Head Start. (n.d.). *Multicultural principles for early childhood leaders*. Retrieved December 13, 2017, from https://eclkc.ohs.acf.hhs.gov/culture-language/article/multicultural-principles-early-childhood-leaders.

Heath, S. B. (1983). *Ways with words: Language, life, and work in communities and classrooms*. Cambridge: Cambridge University Press.

Heath, S. B. (1989). Oral and literate traditions among Black Americans living in poverty. *American Psychologist*, 44, 367–373.

Killen, M. (2012). *Kids on race: The hidden picture*. Report for CNN *AC360°*. Retrieved August 28, 2013, from http://www.cnn.com/2012/04/02/us/ac360-race-study/

Kuh, L. P., Keenan, D. L., Given, H., & Beneke, M. R. (2016). Moving beyond anti-bias activities: Supporting the development of anti-bias practices. *Young Children*, 71(1). Retrieved December 16, 2017, from www.naeyc.org/resources/pubs/yc/mar2016/moving-beyond-anti-bias-activities.

Li, K., Hu, B. Y., Pan, Y., Qin, J., & Fan, X. (2013). Chinese Early Childhood Environment Rating Scale (trial) (CECERS): A validity study. *Early Childhood Research Quarterly*, 29(3), 268–282.

Lopez, M., Hofer, K., Bumgarner, E., & Taylor, D. (2017). *Developing culturally responsive approaches to serving diverse populations: A resource guide for community-based organizations*. National Research Center on Hispanic Children and Families. Available online at www.hispanicresearchcenter.org/resources/publications.

Lynch, E. W. (2011). Developing cross-cultural competence. In E. W. Lynch & M. J. Hanson (Eds.), *Developing cross-cultural competence: A guide for working with children and their families* (4th ed., pp. 41–77). Baltimore: Paul H. Brookes.

Lynch, E. W., & Hanson, M. J. (Eds.). (2011). *Developing cross-cultural competence: A guide for working with children and their families* (4th ed.). Baltimore: Paul H. Brookes.

Mallory, B. L., & New, R. S. (Eds.). (1994). *Diversity and developmentally appropriate practices: Challenges for early childhood education*. New York: Teachers College Press.

National Academies of Science, Engineering, and Medicine. (2017). *Promoting the educational success of children and youth learning English*. Washington, DC: The National Academies Press. Retrieved October 31, 2017, from https://doi.org/10.17226/24677.

National Association for the Education of Young Children (NAEYC). (2017). *Revised criteria and guidance for assessment: NAEYC early learning program standards and accreditation criteria*. Retrieved November 2, 2017, from www.naeyc.org/academy/files/academy/Revised%20Criteria%20and%20Guidance%20for%20Assessment%20April%202017.pdf.

National Association for the Education of Young Children (NAEYC). (2009). *Developmentally appropriate practice in early childhood programs serving children from birth through age 8: Position statement*. Washington, DC: Author.

Nemeth, K. N. and Simon, F. S. 2013. Using technology as a teaching tool for dual language learners in preschool through grade 3, *Young Children*, 68(1), 48–52

Oertwig, S., Gillanders, C., & Ritchie, S. (2014). The promise of curricula. In S. Ritchie & L. Gumann (Eds.), *First school: Transforming pre-K–3rd grade for African American, Latino, and low-income children*. New York: Teachers College Press.

Office of Head Start. *Multicultural principles for early childhood leaders*. Retrieved December 13, 2017, from https://eclkc.ohs.acf.hhs.gov/culture-language/article/multicultural-principles-early-childhood-leaders

Olsen, L., Bhattacharya, J., & Scharf, A. (2007). *Cultural competency: What it is and why it matters*. Sacramento: California Tomorrow.

Paradis, J., Genesee, F., & Crago, M. G. (2011). *Dual language development and disorders: A handbook on bilingualism and second language learning* (2nd ed.). Baltimore: Paul H. Brookes.

Ramsey, P. G. (2015). *Teaching and learning in a diverse world: Multicultural education for young children* (4th ed.). New York, NY: Teachers College Press.

Ritchie, S., & Gutmann, L. (Eds.). (2014). *First school: Transforming pre-K–3rd grade for African American, Latino, and low-income children*. New York: Teachers College Press.

Rogoff, B. (2003). *The cultural nature of human development*. New York: Oxford University Press.

Rotner, S., & Kelly, S. M. (2010). *Shades of people*. New York: Holiday House.

Sandall, S. R., & Schwartz, I. S. (2008). *Building blocks for teaching preschoolers with special needs* (2nd ed.). Baltimore: Paul H. Brookes.

Sanders, K. E., Diehl, A., & Kyler, A. (2007). DAP in the 'hood: Perceptions of child care practices by African American child care directors caring for children of color. *Early Childhood Research Quarterly, 22*(3), 394–406.

Souto-Manning, M. (2013). *Multicultural teaching in the early childhood classroom: Approaches, strategies and tools preschool–2nd grade*. New York, NY: Teachers College Press.

Sparrow, J. (2011). *Culture, community, and complex systems: Touchpoints in intervention, adaptation, and co-construction*. Paper presented at the September 21, 2011, meeting of the Head Start Advisory Committee on Research and Evaluation, Washington, DC. Retrieved from http://www.acf.hhs.gov/programs/opre/hs/advisory_com/index.html

Sullivan, D. R. (2016). *Cultivating the genius of black children: Strategies to close the achievement gap in the early years*. St. Paul, MN: Redleaf Press.

Teaching Tolerance. (2012). *Teaching tolerance anti-bias framework*. Montgomery, AL: Teaching Tolerance, a Project of the Southern Poverty Law Center. Retrieved August 27, 2014, from http://www.tolerance.org/anti-bias-framework

Trawick-Smith, J. (2013). *Early childhood development: A multicultural perspective* (6th ed.). Upper Saddle River, NJ: Pearson.

U.S. Department of Education. (2014, March 21). *Expansive survey of America's public schools reveals troubling racial disparities: Lack of access to preschool, greater suspensions cited*. Retrieved August 26, 2014, from http://www.ed.gov/news/press-releases/expansive-survey-americas-public-schools-reveals-troubling-racial-disparities

Wardle, F. (2008a, February 10). *Multicultural and multilingual education in early childhood (infants to age 8) programs*. Denver, CO: Center for the Study of Biracial Children.

Wardle, F. (2014, August 14). *Do mixed-race (Black/White) people have an ethical obligation to identify as Black?* Center for the Study of Biracial Children. Retrieved August 27, 2014, from http://csbchome.org/?p=57

Woolfolk, A., & Perry, N. E. (2015). *Child and adolescent development* (2nd ed.). Upper Saddle River, NJ: Pearson.

York, S. (2016). *Roots and wings: Affirming culture and preventing bias in early childhood* (3rd ed.). St. Paul, MN: Redleaf Press.

Zepeda, M., Rothstein-Fisch, C., Gonzalez-Mena, J., & Trumbull, E. (2006). *Bridging cultures in early care and education: A training module*. Mahwah, NJ: Lawrence Erlbaum Associates.

Chapter 7

Allen, K. R., & Henderson, A. C. (2017). *Family theories: Foundations and applications*. West Sussex, UK: John Wiley & Sons.

Annie E. Casey Foundation. (2016). *Kids count data book: 2002 through 2016 American community survey*. Retrieved February 24, 2018, from www.aecf.org/resources/2016-kids-count-data-book/

Baum, A. C., & McMurray-Schwarz, P. (2004) *Early Childhood Education Journal, 32*(57). https://doi.org/10.1023/B:ECEJ.0000039645.97144.02.

Bredekamp, S. (1997a). Developmentally appropriate practice: The early childhood teacher as decision maker. In S. Bredekamp & C. Copple (Eds.), *Developmentally appropriate practice in early childhood programs* (Rev. ed., pp. 33–52). Washington, DC: National Association for the Education of Young Children.

Bredekamp, S. (1997b). NAEYC issues revised position statement on developmentally appropriate practice in early childhood programs. *Young Children, 52*(2), 34–40.

Bronfenbrenner, U., & Morris, P. A. (2006). The bio-ecological model of human development. In R. M. Lerner & W. Damon (Eds.), *Handbook of child psychology* (6th ed.), *Vol. 1, Theoretical models of human development* (pp. 793–828). Hoboken, NJ: John Wiley & Sons.

Cabrera, N. (2013). Minority children and their families: A positive look. In National Black Child Development Institute, *Being Black is not a risk factor: A strengths-based look at the state of the Black child*. Washington, DC: National Black Child Development Institute. Retrieved October 27, 2014, from http://www.nbcdi.org/resource

Center on the Developing Child at Harvard University. (n.d.). *8 things to remember about child development*. Retrieved February 4, 2018, from https://developingchild.harvard.edu/resources/8-things-remember-child-development/

Child Trends Databank. (2015). *Family structure*. Available at www.childtrends.org/?indicators=family-structure.

Child Welfare Information Gateway. (2014). *Philosophy and key elements of family-centered practice*. Washington, DC: Administration for Children and Families. Retrieved November 13, 2014, from https://www.childwelfare.gov/famcentered/philosophy.cfm

Children's Defense Fund (2017). *The state of America's children*. Washington, DC: Author.

Christian, L. G. (2006). Understanding families: Applying family systems theory to early childhood practice. *Young Children, 61*(1), 12–20.

Dearing, E., Kreider, H., Simpkins, S., & Weiss, H. (2007). *Family involvement in school and low-income children's literacy performance* (Family Involvement Research Digest). Cambridge, MA: Harvard Family Research Project. Retrieved February 27, 2018, from www.gse.harvard.edu/hfrp/publications_resources/publications_series/family_involvement_research_digests/family-involvement-in-school-and-low-income-children's-literacy_performance

Dearing, E., Kreider, H., Simpkins, S., & Weiss, H. (2007). *Family involvement in school and low-income children's literacy performance* (Family Involvement Research Digest). Cambridge, MA: Harvard Family Research Project. Retrieved January 18, 2012, from http://www.gse.harvard.edu/hfrp/publications_resources/publications_series/family_involvement research_digests/family-involvement-in-school-and-low-income-children's-literacy performance.

Dearing, E., Sibley, E., & Nguyen, H. N. (2015). Achievement mediators of family engagement in children's education: A family-school-community systems model. In S. M. Sheridan & E. Moorman Kim (Eds.), *Processes and pathways of family-school partnerships across development* (2), 17–39. Basel, Switzerland: Springer International.

Division for Early Childhood. (2014). *DEC recommended practices in early intervention/early childhood special education 2014*. Retrieved February 25, 2018, from www.dec-sped.org/recommended-practices.

Division for Early Childhood. (2016). *DEC recommended practices with examples*. Retrieved February 24, 2018, from www.dec-sped.org/-recommendedpractices.

Driscoll, K. C., Wang, L., Mashburn, A. J., & Pianta, R. C. (2011). Fostering supportive teacher-child relationships: Intervention implementation in a state-funded preschool program. *Early Education and Development, 22*(4), 593–619.

Ellis, R. R. & Simmons, T. (2014). *Co-resident grandparents and their grandchildren: 2012*. Retrieved November 10, 2014, from http://www.census.gov/content/dam/Census/library/publications/2014/demo/p20-576.pdf

Fagan, J., Day, R., Lamb, M. E., & Cabrera, N. J. (2014). Should researchers conceptualize differently the dimensions of parenting for fathers and mothers? *Journal of Family Theory & Review, 6*, 390–405.

Fisher, R., Ury, W., & Patton, B. (2011). *Getting to yes: Negotiating agreement without giving in* (Rev. ed.). Penguin.

Gonzalez, N., Moll, L. C., & Amanti, C. (Eds.). (2005). *Funds of knowledge: Theorizing practices in households and classrooms*. Hillsdale, NJ: Lawrence Erlbaum Associates.

Grove, A. (2016). Trends in community engagement: How K–12 schools are meeting the expectations of parents for digital communications. *Blackboard*. Retrieved December 12, 2017, from www.blackboard.com/k12.

Head Start. (2016). *Head Start Program facts fiscal year 2016*. Retrieved November 1, 2017, from https://eclkc.ohs.acf.hhs.gov/about-us/article/head-start-program-facts-fiscal-year-2016.

Hennon, C. B., Palm, G., & Olsen, G. (2012). *Home and school relations: Teachers and parents working together*. New York: Pearson.

Iruka, I. U. (2013). *The Black family: Re-Imagining family support and engagement for children*. In National Black Child Development Institute, *Being Black is not a risk factor: A strengths-based look at the state of the Black child*. Washington, DC: National Black Child Development Institute.

Iruka, I. U. (2013). *The Black family: Re-Imagining family support and engagement for children*. In National Black Child Development Institute, *Being Black is not a risk factor: A strengths-based look at the state of the Black child*. Washington, DC: National Black Child Development Institute. Retrieved from http://www.nbcdi.org/resource

Kaldor, T. (2015). Technology as a tool to strengthen the home-school connection. In C. Donohue (Ed.), *Technology and digital media in the early years: Tools for teaching and learning* (pp. 201–217). New York: Routledge.

Keyser, J. (2017). *From parents to partners: Building a family-centered early childhood program* (2nd ed.). St. Paul, MN: Redleaf Press.

Koball, H., & Jiang, Y. (2018). *Basic facts about low-income children: Children under 18 years, 2016*. New York: National Center for Children in Poverty, Columbia University Mailman School of Public Health.

Krogstad, J.M. (2014). *5 facts about the modern American family*. Pew Research Center. Retrieved February 28, 2018, from http://www.pewresearch.org/fact-tank/2014/04/30/5-facts-about-the-modern-american-family/

Lerner, C., & Barr, R. (2014). *Screen sense: Setting the record straight. Research-based guidelines for screen use for children under three years old*. Washington, DC: ZERO to THREE.

Levine, E., Kaufman, R., Hammar, C., & Fagan, J. (2015). *FRPN research brief: How involved are fathers with their children? A study of fatherhood programs*. Fatherhood Research and Practice Network. Available at www.frpn.org/asset/frpn-research-brief-how-involved-are-fathers-their-children-study-fatherhood-programs.

Lim, S. (2012). Family involvement in education. In G. Olsen & M. L. Fuller (Eds.), *Home and school relations: Teachers and parents working together* (4th ed., pp. 130–155). Upper Saddle River, NJ: Pearson.

Minnesota Fathers and Families Network. (2013). *Linking fathers: Father involvement in early childhood programs.* Plymouth, MN: Author. Retrieved from http://www.mnfathers.org/wp-content/uploads/2013/06/Early-Childhood-Sector-Analysis.pdf

Moore, K. A. (2006). *Defining the term "at risk"* (Research to Results Briefs). Washington, DC: Child Trends.

Moore, K. A., Chalk, R., Scarpa, J., & Vandivere, S. (2002). *Family strengths: Often overlooked, but real* (Research Brief). Washington, DC: Child Trends.

National Academies of Sciences, Engineering, and Medicine. (2016). *Parenting matters: Supporting parents of children 0–8.* Washington, DC: The National Academies Press.

National Association for the Education of Young Children (NAEYC). (2016). *Overview of the NAEYC Early Childhood Program Standards.* Washington, DC: Author. Retrieved February 27, 2018, from www.naeyc.org/academy/files/academy/Overview-Standards.pdf.

National Association for the Education of Young Children (NAEYC). (1998). *The leading edge workbook.* Washington, DC: Author.

National Research Council (NRC). (2014). *New directions in child abuse and neglect research.* Washington, DC: Author.

Nemeth, K. N. (2015). Technology to support dual language learners. In C. Donohue (Ed.), *Technology and digital media in the early years: Tools for teaching and learning* (pp. 115–128). New York: Routledge.

Novoa, C., & Taylor, J. (2017). *Home visiting programs are vital for maternal and infant health.* Center for American Progress. Retrieved February 24, 2018, from www.americanprogress.org/issues/early-childhood/reports/2017/09/12/438414/home-visiting-programs-vital-maternal-infant-health/

Office of Head Start. *Parent, family, and community engagement interactive framework.* Retrieved February 28, 2018, fromhttps://eclkc.ohs.acf.hhs.gov/school-readiness/article/pfce-interactive-framework

Pakulak, E., Gomsrud, M., Reynolds, M. M., Bell, T. A., Giuliano, R. J., Karns, C. M., . . . & Neville, H. (2017). Focusing on families: A two-generation model for reducing parents' stress and boosting preschoolers' self-regulation and attention. *Young Children, 72*(2), 25–37.

Partenan, A. (2011). What Americans keep ignoring about Finland's school success. *The Atlantic.* Retrieved February 26, 2018, from www.theatlantic.com/national/archive/2011/12/what-americans-keep-ignoring-about-finlands-school-success/250564/

Paula, A., & da Silva, P. (2014). Supporting gay and lesbian families in the early childhood classroom. *Young Children, 69*(4), 40–44.

Powell, D. R. (2013). Involving parents and community members: Coming together for children. In D. R. Reutzel (Ed.), *Handbook of research-based practice in early education* (pp. 46–61). New York: Guilford Press.

Scully, P., Barbour, C. H., & Roberts-King, H. (2015) *Families, schools, and communities: Building partnerships for educating children* (6th ed.). Upper Saddle River, NJ: Pearson.

Sheridan, S. M., Holmes, S. R., Smith, T. E., & Moen, A. L. (2016). Complexities in field-based partnership research: Exemplars, challenges and an agenda for the field. In M. S. Sheridan and E. Moorman Kim (Eds.), *Family-school partnerships in context*, 1–23. Cham Switzerland: Springer International.

Trivette, C. M., Dunst, C. J., & Hamby, D. W. (2010). Influences of family-systems intervention practices on parent-child interactions and child development. *Topics in Early Childhood Special Education, 30*(1), 3–19.

U. S. Bureau of Labor Statistics. (2017). *Employment characteristics of families 2016.* Retrieved from www.bls.gov/news.release/pdf/famee.pdf.

U.S. Department of Health and Human Services. (n.d.) *Home visiting evidence of effectiveness.* Available at https://homvee.acf.hhs.gov/Models.aspx.

U.S. Department of Health and Human Services. (n.d.) *Risk and protective factors for mental, emotional, and behavioral disorders across the life cycle.* Retrieved July 31, 2015, from http://www.crpcorp.com/Mandatory_Capacity_Building_Initiative_(Cohort_10)/Matrix_ReportBrief.pdf

Chapter 8

Ainsworth, M. D. S., Blehar, M. C., Waters, E., & Wall, S. (1978). *Patterns of attachment.* Hillsdale, NJ: Lawrence Erlbaum Associates.

Allen, R., & Steed, E.A. (2016). Culturally responsive pyramid model practices: Program-wide positive behavior support for young children. *Topics in Early Childhood Special Education, 36,* 165–175.

Barbarin, O. (2011). *Imagining auspicious environments for the development of African American boys.* Paper presented at the ETS Addressing Achievement Gaps Symposium co-sponsored with Children's Defense Fund, June 14, 2011, Washington, DC: Educational Testing Service. Retrieved August 11, 2011, from http://www.ets.org/s/sponsored_events/achievement_gap/pdf/2011_conference/oscar_barbarin_presentation.pdf

Barbarin, O. (2013). A longitudinal examination of socioemotional learning in African American and Latino boys across the transition from pre-K to kindergarten. *American Journal of Orthopsychiatry, 83,* 156–164. doi:10.1111/ajop.12024

Barbarin, O., Iruka, I. U., Harradine, C., Winn, D. C., McKinney, M. K., & Taylor, L. C. (2013). Development of social-emotional competence in boys of color: A cross-sectional cohort analysis from pre-k to second grade. *American Journal of Orthopsychiatry, 83,* 145–155. doi:10.1111/ajop.12023

Beckh, K., & Becker-Stoll, F. (2016). Formations of attachment relationships towards teachers lead to conclusions for public child care. *International Journal of Developmental Science, 10*(3–4), 103–110.

Bernier, A., Beauchamp, M. H., Carlson, S. M., & Lalonde, G. (2015). A secure base from which to regulate: Attachment security in toddlerhood as a predictor of executive functioning at school entry. *Developmental Psychology, 51*(9), 1177–1189.

Bettencourt, A., Gross, D., & Ho, G. (2016) *The costly consequences of not being socially and behaviorally ready by kindergarten: Associations with grade retention, receipt of academic support services, and suspensions/expulsions.* Baltimore, MD: John Hopkins University.

Blair, C., & Raver, C. C. (2015). School readiness and self-regulation: A developmental psychobiological approach. *Annual Review of Psychology, 3*(66), 711–31.

Bowlby, J. (1969/2000). *Attachment and loss: Volume I: Attachment.* New York: Basic.

Brock, L. L., & Curby, T. W. (2016). The role of children's adaptability in classrooms characterized by low or high teacher emotional support consistency. *School Psychology Review, 45*(2), 209–225.

Buyse, E., Verschueren, K., & Doumen, S. (2011). Preschoolers' attachment to mother and risk for adjustment problems in kindergarten: Can teachers make a difference? *Social Development, 20,* 33–50.

Caldarella, P., Williams, L., Hansen, B., & Wills, D. (2015). Managing student behavior with class-wide function-related intervention teams: An observational study in early elementary classrooms. *Early Childhood Education Journal, 43*(5), 357–365.

Center on the Social and Emotional Foundations for Early Learning. (n.d.). *Pyramid model for supporting social and emotional competence in infants and young children.* Retrieved February 2, 2012 from http://csefel.vanderbilt.edu.

Cole, P.M., Armstrong, L.M., & Pemberton, C.K. (2010). The role of language in the development of emotion regulation. In S.D. Calkins & M.A. Bell (Eds.), *Human brain development: Child development at the intersection of emotion and cognition,* 59–77. Washington, DC: American Pyschological Association.

Cook, C., Miller, F., Fiat, A., Renshaw, T., Frye, M., & Joseph, G. E. (2017). Promoting secondary teachers' wellbeing and intentions to implement evidence-based practices: Randomized evaluation of the achiever resilience curriculum. *Psychology in the Schools, 54*(1), 13–28.

Curby, T. W., Brown, C. A., Bassett, H. H., & Denham, S. A. (2015). Associations between preschoolers' social–emotional competence and preliteracy skills. *Infant and Child Development, 24*(5), 549–570.

DeMeulenaere, M. (2015). Promoting social and emotional learning in preschool. *Dimensions of Early Childhood, 43*(1), 8–10.

DeVries, R., & Zan, B. (2012). *Moral classrooms, moral children: Creating a constructivist atmosphere in early education* (2nd ed.). New York: Teachers College Press.

Division for Early Childhood. (2017). *DEC Position Statement on Challenging Behaviors.* Arlington, VA: Author.

Driscoll, K. C., & Pianta, R. C. (2010). Banking time in Head Start: Early efficacy of an intervention designed to promote teacher-child relationships. *Early Education and Development, 21,* 38–64.

Durlak, J. A., Weissberg, R. P., Dymnicki, A. B., Taylor, R. D., & Schellinger, K. B. (2011). The impact of enhancing students' social and emotional learning: A meta-analysis of school-based universal interventions. *Child Development, 82*(1), 405–432.

Early, D. M., Iruka, I., Ritchie, S., Barbarin, O., Winn, D., Crawford, G., et al. (2010). How do prekindergarteners spend their time? Gender, ethnicity, and income as predictors of experiences in prekindergarten classrooms. *Early Childhood Research Quarterly, 25*(2).

Fox, L., Dunlap, G., Hemmeter, M. L., Joseph, G. E., & Strain, P. S. (2003). The teaching pyramid: A model for supporting social competence and preventing challenging behavior in young children. *Young Children, 58*(4), 48–52.

Friedman-Krauss, A., Raver, C., Neuspiel, J., & Kinsel, J. (2014). Child behavior problems, teacher executive functions, and teacher stress in Head Start classrooms. *Early Education & Development, 25*(5), 1–22.

Fuhs, M. W., Farran, D. C., & Nesbitt, K. T. (2013). Preschool classroom processes as predictors of children's cognitive self-regulation skills development. *School Psychology Quarterly, 28*(4), 347–359.

Galinsky, E. (2010). *Mind in the making: The seven essential life skills every child needs.* New York: Harper.

Gallagher, K. C. (2013). Guiding children's friendship development: An essential part of the early childhood curriculum. *Young Children, 68,* 5.

Gallagher, K. C., & Sylvester, P. (2009). Supporting peer relationships in early education. In O. Barbarin & B. H. Wasik (Eds.), *Handbook of child development and early education: Research to practice* (pp. 223–246). New York: Guilford Press.

Gallagher, K. C., Kainz, K., White, K. M., & Vernon-Feagans, L. (2013). Development of student-teacher relationships in early education. *Early Childhood Research Quarterly, 28,* 520–528.

Gartrell, D. (2006, March). Guidance matters. In *Beyond the journal: Young children on the web*. Retrieved December 14, 2014, from https://www.naeyc.org/files/yc/file/200603/GuidanceBTJ.pdf

Gartrell, D. (2011). A guidance approach for the encouraging classroom. Clifton Park, NY: Wadsworth Cengage Learning.

Gilliam, W. (2016). *Early childhood expulsions and suspensions undermine our nation's most promising agent of opportunity and social justice*. Robert Wood Johnson Foundation.

Giménez-Dasí, M., Fernández-Sánchez, M., & Quintanilla, L. (2015). Improving social competence through emotion knowledge in 2-year-old children: A pilot study. *Early Education and Development*, 26(8), 1128–1144.

Graziano, P., Garb, L., Ros, R., Hart, K., & Garcia, A. (2015). Executive functioning and school readiness among preschoolers with externalizing problems: The moderating role of the student–teacher relationship. *Early Education and Development*, 27(5), 573–589.

Greenman, J. (2017). *Caring spaces, learning places: Children's environments that work!* Lincoln, NE: Exchange Press.

Greenman, J., Stonehouse, A., & Schweikert, G. (2007). *Prime times: A handbook for excellence in infant and toddler programs* (2nd ed.). St. Paul, MN: Redleaf Press.

Gregg, K. (2017). Communication disorders and challenging behaviors: Supporting children's functional communication goals in the classroom. *Early Childhood Education Journal*, 45(4), 445–452.

Hamre, B. K. (2014). Teachers' daily interactions with children: An essential ingredient in effective early childhood programs. *Child Development Perspectives*, 8(4), 223–230. doi:10.1111/cdep.12090

Hamre, B. K., & Pianta, R. C. (2005). Can instructional and emotional support in the first-grade classroom make a difference for children at risk of school failure? *Child Development*, 76(5), 949–967.

Hartigan, B. (2017). Mindfulness in teacher education: A constructivist approach to stress reduction for teacher candidates and their students. *Childhood Education*, 93(2), 153–158.

Hemmeter, M. L., Hardy, J. K., Schnitz, A. G., Adams, J. M., & Kinder, K. A. (2015). Effects of training and coaching with performance feedback on teachers' use of "Pyramid Model" practices. *Topics in Early Childhood Special Education*, 35(3), 144–156.

Hemmeter, M. L., Snyder, P. A., Fox, L., & Algina, J. (2016). Evaluating the implementation of the Pyramid Model for promoting social-emotional competence in early childhood classrooms. *Topics in Early Childhood Special Education*, 36(3), 133–146.

Hemmeter, M. L., Snyder, P., Fox, L., & Algina, J. (2011). *Professional development related to the Teaching Pyramid Model for addressing the social emotional development and challenging behavior of young children*. Presentation at the 2011 International Society on Early Intervention Conference, May 5, 2011, New York, NY.

Howes, C., & Ritchie, S. (2002). *A matter of trust: Connecting teachers and learners in the early childhood curriculum*. New York: Teachers College Press.

Janson, G. R., & King, M. A. (2010). Creating emotionally healthy learning environments: Eliminating emotional maltreatment from your school. *Focus on Elementary*, 23(1), 1–7. Silver Spring, MD: Association for Childhood Education International.

Johnson, S. R., Seidenfeld, A. M., Izard, C. E., & Kobak, R. (2013). Can classroom emotional support enhance prosocial development among children with depressed caregivers? *Early Childhood Research Quarterly*, 28, 282–290. doi:10.1016/j.ecresq.2012.07.003

Joseph, G. E. 2002. *Center for social and emotional foundations for early learning preschool training module 2*.

Joseph, G. E., & Strain, P. S. (2003a). Enhancing emotional vocabulary in young children. *Young Exceptional Children*, 6(4), 18–27.

Joseph, G. E., Webster-Stratton, C., & Reid, J. (2006). *Fostering social and emotional competence: Implementing Dina Dinosaur's social skills and problem solving curriculum in inclusive early childhood programs*. Retrieved from http://www.incredibleyears.com/Library/items/fostering-social-emotional-curriculum_06.pdf

Joseph, G., Strain, P. S., & Ostrosky, M. M. (2006). *Fostering emotional literacy in young children: Labeling emotions* (What Works Brief No. 21). Champaign, IL: Center on the Social and Emotional Foundations for Early Learning. Retrieved October 14, 2009, from http://www.vanderbilt.edu/csefel/briefs/wwb21.html

Kaiser, B., & Rasminsky, J. S. (2017). *Challenging behavior in young children: Understanding, preventing, and responding effectively* (4th ed.). Upper Saddle River, NJ: Pearson.

King, M., & Janson, G. R. (2010). The special needs of boys. In B. Erford (Ed.), *Professional school counseling: A handbook of theories, programs and practices* (2nd ed.). Austin, TX: Pro-Ed.

King, M., with Gartrell, D. (2004). Guidance with boys. In D. Gartrell (Ed.), *The power of guidance: Teaching social-emotional skills in early childhood classrooms*. Clifton Park, NY: Delmar Learning.

Kusché, C. A., & Greenberg, M. T. (2012). The PATHS Curriculum: Promoting emotional literacy, prosocial behavior, and caring classrooms. In S. R. Jimerson, A. B. Nickerson, M. J. Mayer, & M. J. Furlong (Eds.), *Handbook of school violence and school safety: International research and practice* (2nd ed., pp. 435–446). New York: Routledge/Taylor & Francis Group.

Lawner, E. K., & Terzian, M. A. (2013). *What works for bullying programs: Lessons from experimental evaluations of programs and interventions*. Bethesda, MD: Child Trends. Retrieved December 2, 2014, from http://www.childtrends.org/wp-content/uploads/2013/10/briefing_bullying5_anm1.pdf

Lengua, L. J. (2012). Poverty, the development of effortful control, and children's academic, social and emotional adjustment. In V. Maholmes & R. King (Eds.), *The Oxford handbook of poverty and child development*, 491–511. New York: Oxford University Press.

MacEvoy, J., Papadakis, A., Fedigan, S., & Ash, S. (2016). Friendship expectations and children's friendship-related behavior and adjustment. *Merrill–Palmer Quarterly*, 62(1), 74–104.

Main, M., & Solomon, J. (1990). Procedures for identifying infants as disorganized-disoriented during the Ainsworth strange situation. In M. Greenberg, D. Cicchetti, & E. M. Cummings (Eds.), *Attachment in the preschool years: Theory, research, and intervention* (pp. 161–184). Chicago: University of Chicago Press.

Malone, L., Hulsey, L., Aikens, N., West, J., & Tarullo, L. (2010). *ACF-OPRE Report: Data Tables for FACES 2006 Head Start Children Go to Kindergarten Report*. Washington, DC: U.S. Department of Health and Human Services, Administration for Children and Families, Office of Planning, Research and Evaluation.

McCoy, D., Yoshikaw, H., Ziol-Guest, K. M., Duncan, G., Schindler, H., Magnuson, K., Yang, R., Koepp, A., & Shonkoff, J. P. (2017) Impacts of early childhood education on medium- and long-term educational outcomes. *Educational Researcher*, 46(8), 474–487.

McIntosh, K., Barnes, A., Morris, K., & Eliason, B. M. (2014). *Using discipline data within SWPBIS to identify and address disproportionality: A guide for school teams*. Eugene, OR: OSEP Technical Assistance Center on Positive Behavioral Interventions and Supports.

Moffitt, T. E., Arseneault, L., Belsky, D., Dickson, N., Hancox, R. J., Harrington, H. L., et al. (2011). A gradient of childhood self-control predicts health, wealth, and public safety. *Proceedings of the National Academy of Sciences*, 108(7), 2693–2698.

Montroy, J. J., Bowles, R. P., Skibbe, L. E., McClelland, M. M., & Morrison, F. J. (2016). The development of self-regulation across early childhood, 52(11), 1744–1762.

Morhard, R. H. (2013). *Wired to move: Facts and strategies for nurturing boys in an early childhood setting*. Lewisville, NC: Gryphon House.

National Association for the Education of Young Children (NAEYC). (2011). *NAEYC code of ethical conduct and commitment position statement*. Retrieved from www.naeyc.org/sites/default/files/globally-shared/downloads/PDFs/resources/position-statements/Ethics%20Position%20Statement2011_09202013update.pdf

Neuenschwander, R., Friedman-Krauss, A., Raver, C., & Blair, C. (2017). Teacher stress predicts child executive function: Moderation by school poverty. *Early Education and Development*, 28(7), 880–900.

Perlman, M., Falenchuk, O., Fletcher, B., McMullen, E., Beyene, J., & Shah, P. S. (2016). A systematic review and meta-analysis of a measure of staff/child interaction quality (the Classroom Assessment Scoring System) in early childhood education and care settings and child outcomes. *PLoS ONE* (Vol. 11).

Pianta, R. C., La Paro, K. M., & Hamre, B. K. (2008). *Classroom assessment scoring system (CLASS)*. Baltimore: Paul H. Brookes.

Raikes, H. H., & Edwards, C. P. (2009). *Extending the dance in infant and toddler caregiving: Enhancing attachment and relationships*. Baltimore: Paul H. Brookes.

Ramming, P., Kyger, C. S., & Thompson, S. D. (2006). A new bit on toddler biting: The influence of food, oral motor development, and sensory activities. *Young Children*, 61(2), 17–23.

Raver, C. C., Garner, P. W., & Smith-Donald, R. (2007). The roles of emotion regulation and emotion knowledge for children's academic readiness. In R. C. Pianta, M. J. Cox, & K. L. Snow (Eds.), *School readiness and the transition to kindergarten in the era of accountability* (pp. 121–147). Baltimore: Paul H. Brookes.

Riley, D., San Juan, R. R., Klinkner, J., & Ramminger, A. (2008). *Social and emotional development: Connecting science and practice in early childhood settings*. St. Paul, MN: Redleaf Press.

Rueda, M. R. (*2015*). *Effortful control*. In M. Zentner & R. L. Shiner (Eds.), *Handbook of temperament*, 145–167. New York: Guilford Press.

Sagi-Schwartz, A. (2016). Important evidence highlights the meaning of teacher–child relationships for child development. *International Journal of Developmental Science*, 10(3–4), 115–116.

Saracho, O. (2017a). Bullying prevention strategies in early childhood education. *Early Childhood Education Journal*, 45(4), 453–460.

Saracho, O. N. (2017b). Bullying: Young children's roles, social status, and prevention programs. *Early Child Development and Care*, 187(1), 68–79.

Scroufe, L. A. (1996). *Emotional development: The organization of emotional life in the early years*. New York: Cambridge University Press.

Scroufe, L.A. (2005). Attachment and development: A prospective, longitudinal study from birth to adulthood. *Attachment and Human Development*, 7(4), 349–367.

Sprung, B., Froschl, M., & Gropper, N. (2010). *Supporting boys' learning: Strategies for teacher practice, pre-K–grade 3*. New York: Teachers College Press.

Stadnick, N., Chlebowski, C., & Brookman-Frazee, L. (2017). Caregiver-teacher concordance of challenging behaviors in children with autism spectrum disorder served in community mental health settings. *Journal of Autism and Developmental Disorders*, 47(6), 1780–1790.

Strain, P. S., & Hemmeter, M. L. (1999). Keys to being successful when confronted with challenging behaviors. In S. Sandall & M. Ostrosky (Eds.), *Practical ideas for addressing challenging behaviors* (pp. 17–25). Denver, CO: Division for Early Childhood of the Council for Exceptional Children.

Temkin, D. (2014). *Five things to know about bullying*. Bethesda, MD: Child Trends. Retrieved December 2, 2014, from http://www.childtrends.org/wp-content/uploads/2014/10/2014-51CT5Bullying.pdf

U.S. Department of Education Office of Civil Rights. (2014, March 21). *Civil rights data collection: Data snapshot: Early childhood education*. Retrieved December 14, 2014, from http://www2.ed.gov/about/offices/list/ocr/docs/crdc-early-learning-snapshot.pdf

Vance, E. (2013). *Class meetings: Young children solving problems together* (Rev. ed.). Washington, DC: NAEYC.

Vinh, M., Strain, P., Davidon, S., & Smith, B. J. (2016). One state's systems change efforts to reduce child care expulsion: Taking the Pyramid Model to scale. *Topics in Early Childhood Special Education*, 36(3), 159–164.

Waller, R., Dishion, T. J., Shaw, D. S., Gardner, F., Wilson, M. N., & Hyde, L. W. (2016). Does early childhood callous-unemotional behavior uniquely predict behavior problems or callous-unemotional behavior in late childhood? *Developmental Psychology*, 52(11), 1805–1819.

Wheeler, E. J. (2004). *Conflict resolution in early childhood: Helping children understand and resolve conflicts*. Upper Saddle River, NJ: Pearson.

Williford, A. P., Vick Whittaker, J. E., Vitiello, V. E., & Downer, J. T. (2013). Children's engagement within the preschool classroom and their development of self-regulation. *Early Education & Development*, 24, 162–187. doi:10.1080/10409289.2011.628270

Williford, A., LoCasale-Crouch, J., Whittaker, J., DeCoster, J., Hartz, K., Carter, L., . . . & Hatfield, B. (2017). Changing teacher–child dyadic interactions to improve preschool children's externalizing behaviors. *Child Development*, 88(5), 1544–1553.

Chapter 9

Ausubel, D. P. (1978). *Educational psychology: A cognitive view* (2nd ed.). Boston: Holt McDougal.

Bailey, M. (2017). *Inspiring and empowering young children: Exploring innovative uses of exciting new digital tools*. Presentation at the annual conference of the National Association for the Education of Young Children, Atlanta, GA.

Bates, C. C. (2013). Flexible grouping during literacy centers: A model for differentiating instruction. *Young Children*, 68(2), 30–33.

Beck, I. L., McKeown, M. G., & Kucan, L. (2013). *Bringing words to life: Robust vocabulary instruction* (2nd ed.). New York: Guilford Press.

Beneke, S. J., & Ostrosky, M. M. (2013). The potential of the project approach to support diverse young learners. *Young Children*, 68(2), 22–28.

Blair, C., & Raver, C. C. (2014). Closing the achievement gap through modification of neurocognitive and neuroendocrine function: Results from a cluster randomized controlled trial of an innovative approach to the education of children in kindergarten. *PLoS ONE*, 9(11), e112393. doi:10.1371/journal.pone.0112393

Bodrova, E., & Leong, D. J. (2007). *Tools of the mind: The Vygotskian approach to early childhood education*. Upper Saddle River, NJ: Pearson.

Bodrova, E., & Leong, D. J. (2015). Vygotskian and post-Vygotskian views on play. *American Journal of Play*, 7(3).

Bowman, B. T., Donovan, M. S., & Burns, S. (Eds.). (2001). *Eager to learn: Educating our preschoolers* (National Research Council, Committee on Early Childhood Pedagogy Report). Washington, DC: National Academies Press.

Boyd, B. A., Kucharczyk, S., & Wong, C. (2016). Implementing evidence-based practices in early childhood classroom settings. In B. Reichow, B. Boyd, E. Barton, & S. Odom (Eds.), *Handbook of early childhood special education*, 335–347. Cham, Switzerland: Springer.

Burchinal, M. (2017). Measuring early care and education quality. *Child Development Perspectives*. Society for Research in Child Development. DOI: 10.1111/cdep.12260.

Burchinal, M., Zaslow, M., & Tarullo, L. (Eds.). (2016). Quality thresholds, features, and dosage in early care and education: Secondary data analysis of child outcomes. *Monographs of the Society for Research in Child Development*, 81(2), 1–128.

Cabell, S. Q., DeCoster, J., LoCasale-Crouch, J., Hamre, B. K., & Pianta, R. C. (2013). Variation in the effectiveness of instructional interactions across preschool settings and learning activities. *Early Childhood Research Quarterly*, 28(4), 820–830.

Cabell, S. Q., Justice, L.M., McGinty, A.S., Decoster, J., & Forston, L.D. (2015). Conversations in preschool classrooms: Contributions to children's vocabulary development. *Early Childhood Research Quarterly*, 30(1), 80–02.

Cameron, C. E., & Morrison, F. J. (2011). Teacher activity orienting predicts preschoolers' academic and self-regulatory skills. *Early Education and Development*, 22(4), 620–648.

Clark, K. F., & Graves, M. F. (2005). Scaffolding students' comprehension of text. *The Reading Teacher*, 58(6), 570–580.

Cohen Group. (2011). *Young children, apps, and iPads*. U.S. Department of Education Ready to Learn Program. Retrieved February 7, 2011, from http://www.mcgrc.com

Cohrssen, C., Church, A., & Tayler, C. (2014). Purposeful pauses: Teacher talk during early childhood mathematics activities. *International Journal of Early Years Education*, 22(2), 169–183.

Common Core State Standards Initiative. (2011a). *Common core standards for English language arts*. Washington, DC: Council for Chief State School Officers and National Governor's Association. Retrieved February 17, 2012, from www.corestandards.org

Copple, C. and Bredekamp, S.2006. *Basics of developmentally appropriate practice: An introduction for teachers of children 3 to 6*. Washington, DC: NAEYC

Copple, C., & Bredekamp, S. (Eds.). (2009). *Developmentally appropriate practice in early childhood programs serving children from birth through age 8* (Rev. ed.). Washington, DC: National Association for the Education of Young Children.

Crawford, G. M., Cobb, C. T., Clifford, R. M., & Ritchie, S. (2014). The groundswell for transforming prekindergarten through 3rd grade. In S. Ritchie & L. Gutmann (Eds.), *First school: Transforming PreK–3rd grade for African American, Latino, and low-income children*, 9–28. New York: Teachers College Press.

Dean, C. B., Hubbell, E. R., Pitler, H., & Stone, B. J. (2012). *Classroom strategies that work: Research-based strategies for increasing student achievement* (2nd ed.). Alexandria, VA: ASCD; & Denver, CO: McREL.

Dickinson, D. (2001). Large-group and free-play times: Conversational settings supporting language and literacy development. In D. Dickinson & P. Tabors (Eds.), *Beginning literacy with language:*

Young children learning at home and school (pp. 223–256). Baltimore: Paul H. Brookes.

Dickinson, D. K. (2011, August 19). Teachers' language practices and academic outcomes of preschool children. *Science*, 333(6045), 964–967. doi:10.1126/science.1204526

Division for Early Childhood & National Association for the Education of Young Children. (2009). *Early childhood inclusion: A joint position statement of the Division for Early Childhood (DEC) and the National Association for the Education of Young Children (NAEYC)*. Chapel Hill: The University of North Carolina, FPG Child Development Institute. Retrieved from http://npdci.fpg.unc.edu/sites/npdci.fpg.unc.edu/files/resources/EarlyChildhoodInclusion_0.pdf

Donohue, C., & Schomburg, R. (2017). Technology and interactive media in early childhood programs: What we've learned from five years of research, policy, and practice. *Young Children*, 72(4), 72–78.

Early, D. M., Iruka, I., Ritchie, S., Barbarin, O., Winn, D., Crawford, G., et al. (2010). How do pre-kindergarteners spend their time? Gender, ethnicity, and income as predictors of experiences in pre-kindergarten classrooms. *Early Childhood Research Quarterly*, 25(2).

Edwards, C., Gandini, L., & Forman, G. (Eds.). (2012). *The hundred languages of children: The Reggio Emilia experience in transformation* (3rd ed.). Santa Barbara, CA: Praeger.

Elias, C. L., & Berk, L. E. (2002). Self-regulation in young children: Is there a role for sociodramatic play? *Early Childhood Research Quarterly*, 17(2), 216–238.

Epstein, A. S. (2012). How planning and reflection develop young children's thinking skills. In C. Copple (Ed.), *Growing minds: Building strong cognitive foundations in early childhood* (pp. 111–118). Washington, DC: National Association for the Education of Young Children.

Epstein, A. S. (2014). *The intentional teacher: Choosing the best strategies for young children's learning* (Rev. ed.). Washington, DC: National Association for the Education of Young Children.

Forman, G. (1994). Different media, different languages. In L. G. Katz & B. Cesarone (Eds.), *Reflections on the Reggio Emilia approach*. Urbana, IL: ERIC Clearinghouse on Elementary and Early Childhood Education.

Fuller, B., Bein, E., Bridges, M., Kim, Y., & Rabe-Hesketh, S. (2017). Do academic preschools yield stronger benefits? Cognitive emphasis, dosage, and early learning. *Journal of Applied Developmental Psychology*, 1–11.

Gadzikowski, A. (2013). Differentiation strategies for exceptionally bright children. *Young Children*, 68(2), 8–14.

Goble, P., & Pianta, R. C. (2017). Teacher–child interactions in free choice and teacher-directed activity settings: Prediction to school readiness. Early Education and Development, 28(8), 1035–1051.

Goble, P., Hanish, L. D., Martin, C. L., Eggum-Wilkens, N. D., Foster, S. A., & Fabes, R. A. (2016). Preschool contexts and teacher interactions: Relations with school readiness. *Early Education and Development*, 1–19. DOI: 10.1080/10409289.2016.1111674.

Gonzalez, J. E., Pollard-Durodola, S. Simmons, D. C., Taylor, A. B., David, M. J., Fogarty, M., & Simmons, L. (2014). Enhancing preschool children's vocabulary: Effects of teacher talk before, during and after shared reading. *Early Childhood Research Quarterly*, 29(2), 214–226.

Hamre, B. K., & Pianta, R. C. (2005). Can instructional and emotional support in the first-grade classroom make a difference for children at risk of school failure? *Child Development*, 76(5), 949–967.

Hamre, B., Hatfield, B., Pianta, R., & Jamil, F. (2014). Evidence for general and domain-specific elements of teacher-child interactions: Associations with preschool children's development. *Child Development*, 85, 1257–1274.

Hassinger-Das, B., Hirsh-Pasek, K., & Golinkoff, R. M. (2017). The case of brain science and guided play: A developing story. *Young Children*, 72(2), 45–50.

Head Start. (2016). *Report on Head Start CLASS data: Fiscal years 2012–2015*. Retrieved January 16, 2017, from https://eclkc.ohs.acf.hhs.gov/ publication/report-head-start-classroom-assessment-scoring-system-classr-data-fiscal-years-2012.

Heidemann, S., Menninga, B., & Chang, C. (2016). *The thinking teacher: A framework for intentional teaching in the early childhood classroom*. Redmond, WA: Exchange Press.

Hirsh-Pasek, K., & Golinkoff, R. M. (2011). The great balancing act: Optimizing core curricula through playful pedagogy. In E. Zigler, W. S. Gilliam, & W. S. Barnett (Eds.), *The Pre-K debates: Current controversies & issues*, 110–116. Baltimore, MD: Paul H. Brookes.

Hirsh-Pasek, K., Zosh, J. M., Gonlinkoff, R. M., Gray, J. H., Robb, M. B., & Kaufman, J. (2015). Putting education in "educational" apps: Lessons from the science of learning. *Psychological Science in the Public Interest*, 16(1), 3–34.

Holland, A. L., Crawford, G. M., Ritchie, S., & Early, D. M. (2014). A culture of collaborative inquiry. In S. Ritchie & L. Gutmann (Eds.), *First school: Transforming PreK–3rd grade for African American, Latino, and low-income children*, 57–80. New York: Teachers College Press.

Hong, S.-Y., & Diamond, K. E. (2012). Two approaches to teaching young children science concepts, vocabulary, and scientific problem-solving skills. *Early Childhood Research Quarterly*, 27(2), 295–305.

Howes, C., Burchinal, M., Pianta, R., Bryant, D., Early, D., Clifford, R., et al. (2008). Ready to learn? Children's pre-academic achievement in pre-kindergarten programs. *Early Childhood Research Quarterly*, 23(1), 27–50.

Institute of Medicine (IOM) and National Research Council (NRC). (2015). *Transforming the workforce for children birth through age 8: A unifying foundation*. Washington, DC: The National Academies Press.

Johnson, J. E., Christie, J. F., & Wardle, F. (2005). *Play, development, and early education*. Upper Saddle River, NJ: Pearson.

Johnson, J. E., Eberle, S. G., & Hendricks, T. S. (Eds.). (2015). *Handbook of the study of play*. New York: Rowman & Littefield.

Jones, E., & Reynolds, G. (2011). *The play's the thing: Teachers' roles in children's play* (2nd ed.). New York: Teachers College Press.

Justice, L. M., Mashburn, A. J., Hamre, B. K., & Pianta, R. C. (2008). Quality of language and literacy instruction in preschool classrooms serving at-risk pupils. *Early Childhood Research Quarterly*, 2, 51–68.

W. Kane, April 4, 2017. Meet Julia, Sesame Street's new character. www.commonsensemedia.org/blog/ meet-julia-sesame-streets-new-character

Keyser, J. (2017). *From parents to partners: Building a family-centered early childhood program* (2nd ed.). St. Paul, MN: Redleaf Press.

Landry, C. E., & Forman, G. (1999). Research on early science education. In C. Seefeldt (Ed.), *The early childhood curriculum: Current findings in theory and practice* (pp. 133–158). New York: Teachers College Press.

Linebarger, D. L., McMenamin, K., & Wainwright, D. K., (n.d.). *Summative evaluation of Super Why!: Outcomes, dose, and appeal*. Philadelphia: Annenberg School of Communications, Children's Media Lab.

Malaguzzi, L. (1998). History, ideas, and basic philosophy: An interview with Lella Gandini.

In C. Edwards, L. Gandini, & G. Forman (Eds.), *The hundred languages of children: The Reggio Emilia approach—Advanced reflections* (2nd ed., 49–97). Greenwich, CT: Ablex.

Mares, M. L., & Pan, Z. (2013). *The effect of Sesame Street around the world: A meta-analysis from 15 countries*. Retrieved January 26, 2017, from www.comminit.com/sesame_workshop/content/ effect-sesame-street-around-world-meta-analysis-15-countries.

Marzano, R. J. (2017). *The new art and science of teaching*. Alexandria, VA: ASCD & Solution Tree.

Marzano, R. J., Pickering, D. J., & Pollock, J. E. (2001). *Classroom instruction that works: Research-based strategies for increasing student achievement*. Alexandria, VA: Association for Supervision and Curriculum Development.

McDermott, M. J. (2012, June/July). Using graphic organizers in preschool. *Teaching Young Children*, 5(5). Washington, DC: National Association for the Education of Young Children. Retrieved October 13, 2014, from http://www.naeyc.org/tyc/article/ using_graphic_organizers_in_preschool

Meacham, S., Vukelich, C., Han, M., & Buell, M. (2014). Preschool teachers' questioning in sociodramatic play. *Early Childhood Research Quarterly*, 29(4), 562–573.

Mehigan, K. R. (2005). The strategy toolbox: A ladder to strategic teaching. *The Reading Teacher*, 58(6), 552–566.

National Academies of Science, Engineering, and Medicine. (2017). *Promoting the educational success of children and youth learning English*. Washington, DC: The National Academies Press. Retrieved October 31, 2017, from https://doi .org/10.17226/24677.

National Association for the Education of Young Children (NAEYC) & the Fred Rogers Center for Early Learning and Children's Media. (2012). *Technology in early childhood programs serving children from birth through age 8*. Joint Position Statement. Washington, DC: Authors.

National Early Literacy Panel (NELP). (2008). *Developing early literacy: Report of the National Early Literacy Panel. A scientific synthesis of early literacy development and implications for intervention*. Washington, DC: Author. Retrieved from http:// lincs.ed.gov/publications/pdf/NELPReport09.pdf

National Institute of Child Health and Human Development (NICHD). (2000). *Report of the National Reading Panel. Teaching children to read: An evidence-based assessment of the scientific research literature on reading and its implications for reading instruction*. Washington, DC: Author.

National Research Council (NRC). (2009). *Mathematics learning in early childhood: Paths toward excellence and equity*. Washington, DC: National Academies Press.

National Research Council. (2018). *How people learn II: Learners, contexts, and cultures*. Washington, DC: The National Academies Press.

Neuman, S. B., & Wright, T. S. (2013). *All about words: Increasing vocabulary in the common core classroom, PreK–2*. New York: Teachers College Press.

Oczkus, L. D. (2010). *Reciprocal teaching at work: Powerful strategies and lessons for improving reading comprehension* (2nd ed.). Newark, DE: International Reading Association.

Ogle, D. M. (1986). KWL: A teaching method that develops active reading of expository text. *The Reading Teacher*, 39(6), 564–570.

Ornstein, P. A., Coffman, J. L., & Grammer, J. K. (2009). Learning to remember. In O. A. Barbarin & B. H. Wasik (Eds.), *Handbook of child development and early education: Research to practice*, 103–122.

Paciga, K., Donahue, C., Myers, K. S., Fernandes, R, & Li, J. (2017). *Carrying Fred Rogers' message

forward in the digital age*. Fred Rogers Center for Early Learning and Children's Media at St. Vincent's College & Erikson Institute Technology in Early Childhood Center. Retrieved November 2, 2017, from www.fredrogerscenter.org/wp-content/ uploads/2015/07/Carrying-Fred-Rogers-Message-Forward-in-the-Digital-Age.pdf.

Palincsar, A. S., & Brown, A. L. (1984). Reciprocal teaching of comprehension: Fostering and comprehension-monitoring activities. *Cognition and Instruction*, 1(2), 117–175.

Pianta, R. C., La Paro, K. M., & Hamre, B. K. (2008). *Classroom assessment scoring system (CLASS)*. Baltimore: Paul H. Brookes.

Puerling, B. (2018). *Teaching in the digital age for preschool and kindergarten: Enhancing curriculum with technology*. St. Paul, MN: Redleaf Press.

Rideout, V. (2017). *The Common Sense census: Media use by kids age zero to eight*. San Francisco, CA: Common Sense Media.

Riley-Ayers, S., Ryan, S., Figueras-Daniel, A., & Costanza, V. J. (2017). *Giving young students a bigger piece of the pie*. New Brunswick, NJ: NIEER. Retrieved January 16, 2017, from http://nieer .org/2017/03/17/giving-young-students-bigger-slice-pie-chart.

Rogoff, B. (1990). *Apprenticeship in thinking*. New York: Oxford University Press.

Rogoff, B. (2003). *The cultural nature of human development*. New York: Oxford University Press.

Strasser, J. & Bresson, L.M. (2017). *Big questions for young minds: Extending children's thinking*. Washington, DC: National Association for the Education of Young Children.

Sullivan, D. R. (2016). *Cultivating the genius of black children: Strategies to close the achievement gap in the early years*. St. Paul, MN: Redleaf Press.

Teachstone. (2017). *Effective teacher–child interactions and child outcomes: A summary of research on the Classroom Assessment Scoring System (CLASS) Pre-K–3rd Grade*. Charlottesville, VA: Author.

Tharp, R., & Entz, S. (2012). From high chair to high school: Research-based principles for teaching complex thinking. In C. Copple (Ed.), *Growing minds: Building strong cognitive foundations in early childhood* (pp. 131–136). Washington, DC: National Association for the Education of Young Children.

Timmons, K., Pelletier, J., & Corter, C. (2016). Understanding children's self-regulation within different classroom contexts. *Early Child Development and Care*, 186(2), 249–267.

U.S. Department of Education. (2016, September 16). Using evidence to strengthen education investment. Retrieved January 30, 2017 from www2.ed.gov.

Vaala, S., Ly, A., & Levine M. H. (2015). *Getting a read on the app store: A market scan and analysis of children's literacy apps*. New York: The Joan Ganz Cooney Center at Sesame Workshop. Retrieved November 9, 2017, from http://joanganzcooneycenter.org/wp-content/uploads/2015/12/jgcc_ gettingaread_exec.pdf.

Vygotsky, L. S. (1978). *Mind in society*. Cambridge, MA: Harvard University Press.

Weisberg, D. S., Hirsh-Pasek, K., Golinkoff, R. M., Kittredge, A. K., & Klahr, D. (2016). Guided play: Principles and practices. *Current Directions in Psychological Science*, 25(3), 177–182.

Weisberg, D. S., Kittredge, A. K., Hirsh-Pasek, K., Golinkoff, R. M., & Klahr, D. (2015). Making play work for education. *Phi Delta Kappa International*, 26(8), 8–13.

Whitehurst, G. J., & Lonigan, C. J. (1998). Child development and emergent literacy. *Child Development*, 69(3), 848–872.

Wiltz, N. W., & Klein, E. L. (2001). "What do you do in child care?" Children's perceptions of high and low quality classrooms. *Early Childhood Research Quarterly*, 16(2), 209–236.

Wood, D., Bruner, J. S., & Ross, G. (1976). The role of tutoring in problem solving. *Journal of Child Psychology and Psychiatry, 17,* 89–100.

ZERO TO THREE. (2014). *Screen sense: Setting the record straight. Research-based guidelines for screen use for children under three years old.* Washington, DC: Author.

Chapter 10

Baldini, R., Cavallini, I., Moss, P., & Vecchi, V. (Eds.). (2012). *One city, many children: Reggio Emilia, a history of the present.* Reggio Emilia, Italy: Reggio Children.

Bierman, K. (2011, April 13). *Thinking across broad domains: Integrating curricula and instruction.* Paper presented at the meeting of the Advisory Committee on Head Start Research and Evaluation. Washington, DC.

Blair, C., & Raver, C. C. (2014). Closing the achievement gap through modification of neurocognitive and neuroendocrine function: Results from a cluster randomized controlled trial of an innovative approach to the education of children in kindergarten. *PLoS ONE, 9*(11), e112393. doi:10.1371/journal.pone.0112393

Bodrova, E., & Leong, D. J. (2007). *Tools of the mind: The Vygotskian approach to early childhood education.* Upper Saddle River, NJ: Pearson.

Bredekamp, S. (2008). Malaguzzi's metaphors: The power of imagery to transform educational practice and policy. In L. Gandini, S. Etheredge, & L. Hill (Eds.), *Insights and inspirations from Reggio Emilia: Stories of teachers and children from North America* (pp. 48–49). Worcester, MA: Davis Publications.

Bredekamp, S. (2009). Early learning standards and developmentally appropriate practice: Contradictory or compatible? In S. Feeney, A. Galper, & C. Seefeldt (Eds.), *Continuing issues in early childhood education* (pp. 258–271). Upper Saddle River, NJ: Pearson.

Bredekamp, S., & Rosegrant, T. (Eds.). (1992). *Reaching potentials: Appropriate curriculum and assessment for young children* (Vol. 1). Washington, DC: National Association for the Education of Young Children.

Bredekamp, S., & Rosegrant, T. (Eds.). (1995). Reaching potentials through transforming curriculum, assessment, and teaching. In S. Bredekamp & T. Rosegrant (Eds.), *Reaching potentials: Transforming early childhood curriculum and assessment* (pp. 15–22). Washington, DC: National Association for the Education of Young Children.

Bronfenbrenner, U., & Morris, P. A. (2006). The bioecological model of human development. In R. M. Lerner & W. Damon (Eds.), *Handbook of child psychology* (6th ed.), *Vol. 1, Theoretical models of human development* (pp. 793–828). Hoboken, NJ: John Wiley & Sons.

Burchinal, M. (2017). Measuring early care and education quality. *Child Development Perspectives.* Society for Research in Child Development. DOI: 10.1111/cdep.12260.

Cagliari, P., Castagnetti, M., Giudici, C., Rinaldi, C., Vecchi, V., & Moss, P. (Eds.). (2016). *Loris Malaguzzi and the Schools of Reggio Emilia: A selection of his writings and speeches.* New York: Routledge.

Carlson-Paige, N., McLaughlin, G. B., & Almon, J. W. (2015). *Reading instruction in kindergarten: Little to gain and much to lose.* Alliance for Childhood and Defending the Early Years. Retrieved November 4, 2017, from https://deyproject.files.wordpress.com/2015/01/readinginkindergarten_online-1.pdf.

Clements, D. H., & Sarama, J. (2007a). Early childhood mathematics learning. In F. K. Lester, Jr. (Ed.), *Second handbook of research on mathematics teaching and learning* (pp. 461–555). New York: Information Age Publishing.

Collaborative for Academic, Social and Emotional Learning (CASEL). (2013). Retrieved February 10, 2018, from https://casel.org/preschool-and-elementary-edition-casel-guide.

Commeyras, M. (2007). Scripted reading instruction? What's a teacher educator to do? *Phi Delta Kappan, 88*(5), 404–407.

Common Core State Standards Initiative, 2011. *Common Core standards for English Language Arts.* Washington, DC: Council for Chief State School Officers and National Governors Association. Retrieved February 2018 from www.corestandards .org/ELA-Literacy/ All rights reserved

Common Core State Standards Initiative. (2011a). *Common core standards for English language arts.* Washington, DC: Council for Chief State School Officers and National Governor's Association. Retrieved February 17, 2012, from www .corestandards.org

Common Core State Standards Initiative. (2011b). *Common core standards for mathematics.* Washington, DC: Council for Chief State School Officers and National Governor's Association. Retrieved February 17, 2012, from http://www.corestandards.org

Core Knowledge Foundation. (2013). Core knowledge sequence: Content and skill guidelines for preschool. Retrieved January 13, 2015, from http://www.coreknowledge.org/mimik/mimik_uploads/documents/494/CKFSequence_PreK_Rev.pdf

David, J. L. (2008). What research says about . . . project-based learning. *Educational Leadership, 65*(5), 80–82.

Diamond, A., & Lee, K. (2011, August 19). Interventions shown to aid executive function development in children 4 to 12 years old. *Science, 333*(6045), 959–964. doi:10.1126/science.1204529

Dodge, D. T., Colker, L. J., & Heroman, C. (2010). *The creative curriculum system for preschool* (5th ed.). Washington, DC: Teaching Strategies.

Edwards, C., Gandini, L., & Forman, G. (Eds.). (2012). *The hundred languages of children: The Reggio Emilia experience in transformation* (3rd ed.). Santa Barbara, CA: Praeger.

Espinosa, L. (2015). *Getting it right for children from diverse backgrounds: Applying research to improve practice with an emphasis on dual language learners* (2nd ed.). Upper Saddle River, NJ: Pearson.

Espinosa, L. M., & Calderon, M. (2015). *State early learning and development standards/guidelines, policies & related practices: How responsive are they to the needs of young dual language learners?* Build Initiative. Retrieved February 11, 2018 from www.buildinitiative.org.

Fantuzzo, J. W., Gadsden, V. L., & McDermott, P. A. (2010). An integrated curriculum to improve mathematics, language, and literacy for Head Start children. *American Educational Research Journal, 48,* 763–793.

Fleming, D. (2006). *Alphabet under construction.* New York: Square Fish.

Fountas, I. C., & Pinnell, G. S. (1996). *Guided reading: Good first teaching for all children.* Portsmouth, NH: Heinemann.

Gandini, L. (2008). Introduction to the schools of Reggio Emilia. In L. Gandini, S. Etheredge, & L. Hill (Eds.), *Insights and inspirations from Reggio Emilia: Stories of teachers and children from North America* (pp. 24–27). Worcester, MA: Davis Publications.

Garcia, J. L., Heckman, J. J., & Ziff, A.L. (2017). Gender differences in the benefits of an influential early childhood program. Retrieved November 6, 2017, from https://heckmanequation.org/assets/2017/05/abc_treatmenteffects_2017-05-11b_jbb.pdf.

Garcia, J. L., Heckman, J. J., Leaf, D. E., & Prados, M. J. (2016). The life-cycle benefits of an influential early childhood program. Retrieved October 31, 2016, from https://heckmanequation.org/assets/2017/01/Garcia_Heckman_Leaf_etal_2016_life-cycle-benefits-ecp_r1-p.pdf.

Grissmer, D. W., Grimm, K. J., Aiyer, S. M., Murrah, W. M., & Steele, J. S. (2010). Fine motor skills and early comprehension of the world: Two new school readiness indicators. *Developmental Psychology, 46*(5), 1008–1017.

Head Start. (2017). *Interactive Head Start Early Learning Outcomes Framework: Ages birth to five: A guide to what children should know and in five central developmental domains.* Retrieved February 10, 2018, from https://eclkc.ohs.acf.hhs.gov/interactive-head-start-early-learning-outcomes-framework-ages-birth-five.

Head Start. (2018). *Making it work! Connecting cultural learning experiences in American Indian and Alaska Native classrooms and communities with the Head Start Child Development and Early Learning Framework.* Online at https://eclkc.ohs.acf.hhs.gov.

Heckman, J., Pinto, R., & Savelyev, P. (2013). Understanding the mechanisms through which an influential early childhood program boosted adult outcomes. *American Economic Review, 103*(6), 2052–2086.

Helm, J., & Katz, L. (2016). *Young investigators: The Project Approach in the early years.* New York, NY: Teachers College Press.

Institute of Medicine (IOM) & National Research Council (NRC). (2015). *Transforming the workforce for children birth through age 9: A unifying foundation.* Washington, DC: National Academies Press.

Jacobs, G., & Crowley, K. (2014). *Supporting students, meeting standards: Best practices for engaged learning in first, second, and third grade.* Washington, DC: National Association for the Education of Young Children.

Jenkins, J. M., & Duncan, J. G. (2017). Do pre-kindergarten curricula matter? In Pre-kindergarten Task Force, *The current state of scientific knowledge on pre-kindergarten effects,* 37–43. Brookings & Duke Center for Child and Family Policy. Retrieved November 1, 2017, from www.brookings.edu/wp-content/uploads/2017/04/duke_prekstudy_final_4-4-17_hires.pdf.

Jones, E., & Nimmo, J. (1994). *Emergent curriculum.* Washington, DC: National Association for the Education of Young Children.

Kagan, S. L., Castillo, E., Gomez, R. E., & Gowani, S. (2013). Understanding and using early learning standards for young children globally. *International Journal of Child Care and Education Policy, 7*(2), 53–66.

Katz, L. G., & Chard, S. C. (2000). *Engaging children's minds: The project approach.* Norwood, NJ: Ablex.

Kauffman, D., Johnson, S. M., Kardos, S. M., Liu, E., & Peske, H. G. (2002). "Lost at sea": New teachers' experiences with curriculum and assessment. *Teachers College Record, 104*(2), 273–300.

Malaguzzi, L. (1993). For an education based on relationships. *Young Children, 49*(1), 9–12.

McAfee, O., Leong, D. J., & Bodrova, E. (2016). *Assessing and guiding young children's development and learning* (6th ed.). Upper Saddle River, NJ: Pearson.

Muccio, L. S., Kuwahara-Fujita, R., & Otsuji, J. J. Y. (2014). 'Ohana math: Family engagement to promote mathematical learning for Hawai'i's young children. *Young Children, 69*(4), 24–30.

National Academies of Science, Engineering, and Medicine. (2017). *Promoting the educational success of children and youth learning English.* Washington, DC: The National Academies Press. Retrieved October 31, 2017, from https://doi.org/10.17226/24677.

National Center for Families Learning. (2018). *CIRCLES: A culturally appropriate curriculum for American Indian preschool children.* Louisville, KY: Author.

National Center on Early Childhood Development, Teaching ,and Learning. (2017). *Framework for effective practice.* Retrieved February 9, 2018, from https://eclkc.ohs.acf.hhs.gov/teaching-practices/article/ framework-effective-practice

National Center on Early Childhood Development, Teaching and Learning (NCECDTL). (2017a). Curriculum scope and sequence. Retrieved February 10, 2018, from https://eclkc.ohs.acf.hhs.gov/sites/default/files/pdf/ncedtl-ecc-curriculum-scope-sequence.pdf.

National Center on Early Childhood Development, Teaching and Learning (NCECDTL). (2017b). *Framework for effective practice.* Retrieved February 9, 2018, from https://eclkc.ohs.acf.hhs.gov/teaching-practices/article/framework-effective-practice.

National Center on Early Childhood Development, Teaching and Learning (NCECDTL). (2017c). *Research-based curriculum.* Retrieved February 9, 2018, from https://eclkc.ohs.acf.hhs.gov/sites/default/files/pdf/ncedtl-ecc-research-based-curriculum.pdf.

National Center on Quality Teaching and Learning (NCQTL). (2015). *Guidance on comprehensive and domain-specific preschool curriculum consumer reports.* Retrieved February 10, 2018, from https://eclkc.ohs.acf.hhs.gov/sites/default/files/pdf/-curriculum-report-guidance.pdf

National Early Literacy Panel (NELP). (2008). *Developing early literacy: Report of the National Early Literacy Panel. A scientific synthesis of early literacy development and implications for intervention.* Washington, DC: Author. Retrieved from http://lincs.ed.gov/publications/pdf/NELPReport09.pdf

National Research Council (NRC). (2009). *Mathematics learning in early childhood: Paths toward excellence and equity.* Washington, DC: National Academies Press.

National Research Council. (2018). *How people learn II: Learners, contexts, and cultures.* Washington, DC: The National Academies Press.

Nayfeld, I., Brenneman, K., & Gelman, R. (2009). *Science in the classroom: Finding a balance between autonomous exploration and teacher-led instruction in preschool settings.* Paper presented at the bi-annual meeting of the Society for Research in Child Development.

New Zealand Ministry of Education. (2017). *Te Whariki (needs long accent over a): Early childhood curriculum.* Wellington, NZ: Author. Available online at www.thechair.miniedu.govt.nz.

NGSS Lead States. (2013). *Next generation science standards: For states, by states.* Washington, DC: The National Academies Press.

P21 Partnership for 21st Century Learning. (2011). *Framework for 21st century learning.* Retrieved February 13, 2018, from http://www.p21.org/our-work/p21-framework.

Reggio Children & Project Zero. (2001). *Making learning visible: Children as individual and group learners.* Reggio Emilia, Italy: Reggio Children.

Rinaldi, C. (2006). *In dialogue with Reggio Emilia: Listening, researching and learning.* New York: Routledge.

Roopnarine, J., & J. E. Johnson (Eds.). (2013). *Approaches to early childhood education* (6th ed.). Upper Saddle River, NJ: Pearson.

Rosegrant, T., & Bredekamp, S. (1992). Reaching individual potentials through transformational curriculum. In S. Bredekamp & T. Rosegrant (Eds.), *Reaching potentials: Appropriate curriculum and assessment for young children, Volume 1,* 66–73. Washington, DC: National Association for the Education of Young Children.

Sarama, J., Brenneman, K., Clements, D. H., Duke, N. K., & Hemmeter, M. L. (2016). *Connect4 Learning: The Pre-K curriculum.* Lewisville, NC: Gryphon House.

Schickedanz, J., & Dickinson, D. (2011). *Opening the world of learning: A comprehensive early literacy program* (2nd ed.). Parsippany, NJ: Pearson Early Learning.

Schweinhart, L. J., Montie, J., Xiang, Z., Barnett, W. S., Belfield, C. R., & Nores, M. (2005). *Lifetime effects: The High/Scope Perry Preschool study through age 40* (Monographs of the High/Scope Educational Research Foundation, 14). Ypsilanti, MI: High/Scope Press.

Scott-Little, C., Kagan, S. L., Reid, J. L., Sumrall, T. C., & Fox, E. A. (2015). *Common early learning and development standards analysis for the North Carolina EAG Consortium: Summary report.* Retrieved February 11, 2018, from www.buildinitiative.org.

Shanahan, T. (2006, August/September). Shanahan responds. *Reading Today, 24*(1), 16.

Vecchi, V. (2002). *Theater curtain: The ring of transformations.* Reggio Emilia, Italy: Reggio Children.

Vecchi, V. (2010). *Art and creativity in Reggio Emilia: Exploring the role and potential of ateliers in early childhood education.* New York: Routledge.

Weiland, C., & Yoshikawa, H. (2011, March). *The impact of an urban universal pre-kindergarten program on children's early numeracy, language, literacy, and executive function outcomes.* Paper presented at the Society for Educational Effectiveness Conference, Washington, DC. Retrieved from: http://www.eric.ed.gov.novacat.nova.edu/PDFS/ED519342.pdf

Weiland, C., & Yoshikawa, H. (2013). Impacts of a pre-kindergarten program on children's mathematics, language, literacy, executive function, and emotional skills. *Child Development 84*(6), 2112–2130,.

Wilson, S. J., Dickinson, D. K., & Rowe, D. W. (2013). Impact of an Early Reading First program on the language and literacy achievement of children from diverse language backgrounds. *Early Childhood Research Quarterly, 28*(3), 578–592.

Wittmer, D. S., & Petersen, S. (2017). *Infant and toddler development and responsive program planning: A relationship-based approach* (4th ed). Upper Saddle River, NJ: Pearson.

Yoshikawa, H., Weiland, C., Brooks-Gunn, J., Burchinal, M. R., Espinosa, L. M., Gormley, W. T., et al. (2013). *Investing in our future: The evidence base on preschool education.* New York: Foundation for Child Development. Retrieved from http://fcd-us.org/sites/default/files/Evidence%20Base%20on%20Preschool%20Education%20FINAL.pdf

Chapter 11

Ackerman, D. J., & Friedman-Krauss, A.H. (2017). Preschoolers' executive function: Importance, contributors, research needs and assessment options. *ETS Research Report Series,* 1–11, https://doi.org/10.1002/ets2.12148.

American Educational Research Association (AERA), American Psychology Association, & National Council on Measurement in Education. (2014). *Standards for educational and psychological testing.* Washington, DC: AERA.

Arnett, J. J., & Maynard, A. (2017). *Child development: A cultural approach* (2nd ed.). New York: Pearson.

Au, W. (2007). High-stakes testing and curricular control: A qualitative metasynthesis. *Educational Researcher, 36*(5), 258–267.

Au, W. (2014). Hiding behind high-stakes testing: Meritocracy, objectivity and inequality in US education. *International Education Journal: Comparative Perspectives, 12*(2), 7–20.

Batshaw, M., Roizen, N., & Lotrecchiano, G. (2013). *Children with disabilities* (7th ed.). Baltimore, MD: Paul H. Brookes.

Carlson, S. M., & Zelazo, P. D. (2014). *Minnesota Executive Function Scale: Test manual.* St. Paul, MN: Reflection Sciences.

Cohen, D. H., Stern, V., Balaban, N., & Gropper, N. (2016). *Observing and recording the behavior of young children.* New York: Teachers College Press.

Czik, A., & Lewis, K. (2016). Family involvement in the assessment and instruction of dual language learners. *Advances in Early Education & Day Care, 20,* 143–158. doi:10.1108/S0270-40212016000020005.

Division for Early Childhood of the Council for Exceptional Children. (2014). *DEC recommended practices in early intervention/early childhood special education.* Los Angeles, CA: Author. Retrieved February 1, 2015, from http://www.dec-sped.org/recommendedpractices

Epstein, A. S., Marshall, B., & Gainsley, S. (2014). *COR Advantage.* Ypsilanti, MI: HighScope Press.

Espinosa, L. (2015). *Getting it right for children from diverse backgrounds: Applying research to improve practice with an emphasis on dual language learners,* 2nd ed. Upper Saddle River, NJ: Pearson.

FairTest. (2012). What's wrong with standardized tests? Retrieved from www.fairtest.org/facts/whatwron.htm.

Fuhs, M.W., Farran, D. C., & Nesbitt, K. T. (2015). Prekindergarten children's executive functioning skills and achievement gains: The utility of direct assessment and teacher ratings. *Journal of Educational Psychology, 107,* 207–221.

Great Schools Partnership. (2015). Norm referenced test. *The Glossary of Education Reform.* Retrieved from www.edglossary.org/norm-referenced-test.

Hamre, B., La Paro, K., Painta, R., & LaCosale, J. (2014). *Classroom Assessment Scoring System manual, infant.* Baltimore, MD: Paul H. Brookes.

Harms, T., Clifford, R. M., & Cryer, D. (2014). *Early Childhood Environment Rating Scale (ECERS-3)* (3rd ed.). New York: Teachers College Press.

Helm, J. H., Beneke, S., & Steinheimer, K. (2007). *Windows on learning: Documenting young children's work* (2nd ed.). New York: Teachers College Press.

Hills, T. W. (1992). Reaching potentials through appropriate assessment. In S. Bredekamp & T. Rosegrant (Eds.), *Reaching potentials: Appropriate curriculum and assessment for young children* (Vol. 1, pp. 43–63). Washington, DC: National Association for the Education of Young Children.

Macy, M., & Bagnato, S. J. (2010). Keeping it "R-E-A-L" with authentic assessment. *NHSA Dialog, 13*(1), 1–20.

McAfee, O., Leong, D. J., & Bodrova, E. (2015). *Assessing and guiding young children's development and learning* (Enhanced e-text, 6th ed.). Upper Saddle River, NJ: Pearson.

McInerney, M., & Elledge, A. (2013). *Using a response to intervention framework to improve student performance: A pocket guide for state and district leaders.* Retrieved from https://rti4success.org/sites/default/files/Response_to_Intervention_Pocket_Guide_2.pdf.

McLoughlin, J.A., Lewis, R. B., & Kritikos, E.P. (2017). *Assessing students with special needs* (8th ed.). New York: Pearson.

Meisels, S. J., Marsden, D. B., Dombro, A. L., Weston, D. R., & Jewkes, A. M. (2003). *The Ounce Scale.* Upper Saddle River, NJ: Pearson Education.

Meisels, S. J., Marsden, D. B., Jablon, J. R., & Dichtelmiller, M. (2013). *The Work Sampling System* (5th ed.). New York: Pearson Education.

Michael-Luna, S. (2013). What linguistically diverse parents know and how it can help early childhood educators: A case study of a dual language preschool community. *Early Childhood Education Journal, 41*(6), 447–455. doi:10.1007/s10643-013-0574-9.

Mindes, G., & Jung, L. A. (2015). *Assessing young children* (5th ed.). New York: Pearson.

National Academies of Science, Engineering, and Medicine (NASEM). (2017). *Promoting the educational success of children and youth learning English.* Washington, DC: The National Academies Press. Retrieved October 31, 2017, from https://doi.org/10.17226/24677.

National Association for the Education of Young Children (NAEYC) & National Association of Early Childhood Specialists in State Departments of Education (NAECS/SDE). (2003). *Early childhood curriculum, assessment, and program evaluation: Building an effective, accountable system in programs for children birth through age 8. Joint position statement.* Washington, DC: National Association for the Education of Young Children.

National Association for the Education of Young Children (NAEYC). (2011). *NAEYC code of ethical conduct and commitment position statement.* Retrieved from www.naeyc.org/sites/default/files/globally-shared/downloads/PDFs/resources/position-statements/Ethics%20Position%20Statement2011_09202013update.pdf.

National Research Council (NRC). (2008). *Early childhood assessment: Why, what, and how.* Washington, DC: National Academies Press.

Parks, S., & Vort Corporation. (1994). *HELP charts (birth to 3 years): Hawaii Early Learning Profile.* Palo Alto, CA: VORT Corp.

Pianta, R. C., La Paro, K. M., & Hamre, B. K. (2008). *Classroom assessment scoring system (CLASS).* Baltimore: Paul H. Brookes.

Quinn, S. F., & Parker, L. (2016). Developing and articulating pedagogic principles: A case study of early childhood teacher trainees learning to use pedagogic documentation techniques. *Journal of Teacher Education, 37(1),* 96–113.

Ravitch, D. (2010). *The death and life of the great American school system: How testing and choice are undermining education.* New York: Basic Books.

Regenstein, E., Connors, M. C., Romero-Juradao, R., & Weinder, J. (2017). Uses and misuses of kindergarten readiness assessments. *The Ounce Policy Conversations, 6(1),* 1–48.

Regenstein, E., Connors, M. C., Romero-Jurado, R., & Weiner, J. (2018). Effective kindergarten readiness assessments. *Young Children, 73(1),* 36–43.

Reggio Children & Project Zero. (2001). *Making learning visible: Children as individual and group learners.* Reggio Emilia, Italy: Reggio Children.

Robins, D., Fein, D., & Barton, M. (2009). *Modified Checklist for Autism in Toddlers, Revised with Follow Up (M-CHAT R/F).* Retrieved from www.autismspeaks.org/sites/default/files/docs/sciencedocs/m-chat/m-chat-rf.pdf?v=1.

Santos, R. M. (2004). Ensuring culturally and linguistically appropriate assessment of young children. *Young Children, 59(1),* 48–50.

Snow, K. (2011). *Kindergarten readiness and other large-scale assessment systems: Necessary considerations in the assessment of young children.* Washington, DC: National Association for the Education of Young Children.

P. O. Tabors and L. M. López, 2005. How can teachers and parents help young children become (and stay) bilingual? 14–16; V. F. Gutiérrez-Clellen, 2005. Assessment of English language learners: Challenges and strategies, 47–51. Both in *Head Start Bulletin: English Language Learners, Vol. 78,* Washington, DC: Head Start Bureau, Administration on Children, Youth and Families, U.S. Department of Health and Human Services

Valencia, S. W., & Buly, M. R. (2004). Behind test scores: What struggling readers *really* need. *The Reading Teacher, 57(6),* 520–531.

Wortham, S. C. & Hardin, B. J. (2015). *Assessment in early childhood education* (7th ed.). Upper Saddle River, NJ: Pearson

Chapter 12

Bates, C. C. (2013). Flexible grouping during literacy centers: A model for differentiating instruction. *Young Children, 68(2),* 30–33.

Beck, I. L., McKeown, M. G., & Kucan, L. (2013). *Bringing words to life: Robust vocabulary—instruction* (2nd ed.). New York: Guilford Press.

Bialystok, E. (2015). Bilingualism and the development of executive function: The role of attention. *Child Development Perspectives,* Society for Research in Child Development, DOI: 10.1111/cdep.12116.

Bodrova, E., & Leong, D.J. (2015). Vygotskian and post-Vygotskian views on play. *American Journal of Play, 7(3).* 371–388

Boutte, G. S. (2015). Four things to remember about African American language: Examples from children's books, kindergarten through grade 3. *Young Children, 70(4),* 38–45.

Brown, E. D., Benedett, B., & Armistead, M. E. (2010). Arts enrichment and school readiness for children at risk. *Early Childhood Research Quarterly, 25(1),* 112–124.

M. B. Bronson, B. D. Goodson, J. L. Layzer, & J.M. Love, 1990. *Child Behavior Rating Scale.* Cambridge, MA: AbtAssociates

W. Buckleitner, 2017. *Inspiring and empowering young children: Exploring innovative uses of exciting new digital tools.* NAEYC Annual conference presentation, Atlanta, GA

Cabell, S. Q., Justice, L. M., McGinty, A. S., Decoster, J., & Forston, L. D. (2015). Conversations in preschool classrooms: Contributions to children's vocabulary development. *Early Childhood Research Quarterly, 30(1),* 80–02.

Carlson-Paige, N., McLaughlin, G. B., & Almon, J. W. (2014). *Reading instruction in kindergarten: Little to gain and much to lose.* Jamaica Plain, MA: Defending the Early Years and the Alliance for Childhood. Retrieved from https://deyproject.files.wordpress.com/2015/01/readinginkindergarten_online-1.pdf

Chaparo-Marino, L. J., Reali, F., & Maldonado-Carreno, C. (2017). Wordless picture books boost preschoolers' language production during shared reading. *Early Childhood Research Quarterly, 40,* 52–62.

Common Core State Standards Initiative. (2011). *Common Core standards for English language arts.* Washington, DC: Council for Chief State School Officers and National Governor's Association. Retrieved March 10, 2018, from www.corestandards.org.

Common Core State Standards Initiative. (2011a). *Common core standards for English language arts.* Washington, DC: Council for Chief State School Officers and National Governor's Association. Retrieved February 17, 2012, from www.corestandards.org

Common Core State Standards Initiative. (2015). *Key shifts in English language arts.* Washington, DC: Council for Chief State School Officers and National Governor's Association. Retrieved March 10, 2018, from www.corestandards.org/other-resources/key-shifts-in-english-language-arts.

Connect Module—*Embedded Interventions.* (2010). Retrieved March 10, 2018, from http://community.fpg.unc.edu/connect-modules/learners/module-1.

Dickinson, D. K. (2011, August 19). Teachers' language practices and academic outcomes of preschool children. *Science, 333(6045),* 964–967. doi:10.1126/science.1204526

Duke, N. K. (2014). *Inside information: Developing powerful readers and writers of informational text through project-based instruction.* New York: Scholastic.

Duke, N. K., Halvorson, A. L., & Knight, J. A. (2012). Building knowledge through information text. In A. M. Pinkham, T. Kaefer, & S. B. Neuman (Eds.), *Knowledge development in early childhood: Sources of learning and classroom implications,* 201–219. New York: The Guilford Press.

Eckhoff, A. (2017). Meaningful art and aesthetic experiences for young children. *Young Children, 72(5),* 14–20.

Eisner, E. W., & Day, M. D. (Eds.). (2008). *Handbook of research and policy in arts education.* New York: Routledge.

Espinosa, L. (2015). *Getting it right for children from diverse backgrounds: Applying research to improve practice with an emphasis on dual language learners* (2nd ed.). Upper Saddle River, NJ: Pearson.

Farran, D. C., Meador, D., Christopher, C., Nesbitt, K. T., & Bilbrey, L. E. (2017). Data-driven improvement in prekindergarten classrooms: Report from a partnership in an urban district. *Child Development, 88,* 1466–1479. doi:10.1111/cdev.12906.

Fernald, A., Marchman, V. A., & Weisleder, A. (2013). SES differences in language processing skills and vocabulary are evident at 18 months. *Developmental Science, 16(2),* 234–248.

Fernald, A., Marchman, V. A., & Weisleder, A. (2013). SES differences in language processing skill and vocabulary are evident at 18 months. *Developmental Science, 16(2),* 234–248.

Gardner-Neblett, N., & Iruka, I. (2017). Viewing African American children's oral language skills as a strength. In I. U. Iruka, S M. Curenton, & T. R. Durden (Eds.), *African American children in early childhood education (Advances in Race and Ethnicity in Education, Volume 5),* 123–141. Emerald Publishing Limited.

Golinkoff, R. M., Can, D. D., Soderstrom, M., & Hirsh-Pasek, K. (2015). (Baby)Talk to me: The social context of infant-directed speech and its effects on early language acquisition. *Current Directions in Psychological Science, 24(5),* 339–344.

Gonzalez, J. E., Pollard-Durodola, S. Simmons, D. C., Taylor, A. B., David, M. J., Fogarty, M., & Simmons, L. (2014). Enhancing preschool children's vocabulary: Effects of teacher talk before, during and after shred reading. *Early Childhood Research Quarterly, 29(2),* 214–226.

Graham, S., & Harris, K. R. (2013). How do you write? Writing for young children. In D. R. Reutzel (Ed.), *Handbook of research-based practice in early education* (pp. 380–394). New York: Guilford Press.

Greenberg, J., & Weitzman, E. (2014). *I'm ready! How to prepare your child for reading success.* Toronto: The Hanen Centre.

Grissmer, D. W., Grimm, K. J., Aiyer, S. M., Murrah, W. M., & Steele, J. S. (2010). Fine motor skills and early comprehension of the world: Two new school readiness indicators. *Developmental Psychology, 46(5),* 1008–1017.

Guernsey, L., & Levine, M. H. (2015). *Tap, click, read: Growing readers in a world of screens.* New York: Jossey-Bass.

Guernsey, L., & Levine, M. H. (2016). Getting smarter about e-books for children. *Young Children, 71(2).*

Hart, B., & Risley, T. R. (1995). *Meaningful differences in the everyday experience of young American children.* Baltimore: Paul H. Brookes.

Hart, B., & Risley, T. R. (1999). *The social world of learning to talk.* Baltimore: Paul H. Brookes.

Hart, B., & Risley, T. R. (2003, Spring). The early catastrophe: The 30 million word gap by age 3. *American Educator, 27(1),* 4–9. Retrieved January 25, 2015, from http://www.aft.org/pdfs/american-educator/spring2003/TheEarlyCatastrophe.pdf

Head Start. (2003). *The Head Start leaders guide to positive child outcomes: Strategies to support positive child outcomes.* Washington, DC: U.S. Department of Health and Human Services.

Hetland, L., & Winner, E. (2004). Cognitive transfer from arts education to nonarts outcomes: Research evidence and policy implications. In E. W. Eisner & M. D. Day (Eds.), *Handbook of research and policy in arts education,* 135–162. New York: Routledge.

Hirsch, E. D. (2007). *The knowledge deficit: Closing the shocking education gap for American children.* Boston: Mariner Books.

Hirsh-Pasek, K., Adamson, L. B., Bakeman, R., Owen, M. T., Golinkoff, R. M., Pace, A., Yust, P. K., & Suma, K. (2015). The contribution of early communication quality to low-income children's language success. *Psychological Science, 26*(7), 1071–83. doi: 10.1177/0956797615581493.

Huntsinger, C. S., Jose, P. E., Krieg, D. B., & Luo, Z. (2011). Cultural differences in Chinese American and European American children's drawing skills over time. *Early Childhood Research Quarterly, 26*(1), 134–145.

Institute of Education Sciences (2007). *Dialogic reading* (*What Works Clearinghouse intervention report*). Washington, DC: U.S. Department of Education. Retrieved March 10, 2018, from www.eric.ed.gov/ERICDocs/data/ericdocs2sql/content_storage_01/0000019b/80/29/e1/30.pdf.

Institute of Medicine (IOM) and National Research Council (NRC). (2015). *Transforming the workforce for children birth through age 8: A unifying foundation.* Washington, DC: The National Academies Press.

International Literacy Association. (2017a). *Early literacy learning for immigrant and refugee children: Parent's critical roles.* Newark, DE: Author.

International Literacy Association. (2017b). *Second-language learners' vocabulary and oral language development.* Newark, DE: Author.

International Literacy Association. (2018). *What effective pre-K literacy instruction looks like.* Newark, DE: Author.

International Reading Association (IRA) & National Association for the Education of Young Children (NAEYC). (1998). *Learning to read and write: Developmentally appropriate practices for young children: A joint position statement, adopted May, 1998.* Retrieved October 14, 2009, from http://208.118.177.216/about/positions/pdf/PSREAD98.PDF

Isbell, R., & Yoshizawa, S. A. (2017). *Nurturing creativity: An essential mindset for young children's learning.* Washington, DC: National Association for the Education of Young Children.

Isenberg, J. P., & Jalongo, M. R. (2018). *Creative thinking and arts-based learning: Preschool through fourth grade.* (7th ed.). New York: Pearson.

Jalongo, M. R. (2008). *Learning to listen, listening to learn: Building essential skills in young children.* Washington, DC: National Association for the Education of Young Children.

Johnson, M. H. (2008). Developing verbal and visual literacy through experiences in the visual arts: 25 tips for teachers. *Young Children, 63*(1), 74–79.

Jones, C. D., Clark, S. K., & Reutzel, D. R. (2012). Enhancing alphabet knowledge instruction: Research implications and practical strategies for early childhood educators. *TEaL Faculty Publications,* Paper 404. Retrieved from http://digitalcommons.usu.edu/teal_facpub/404

Kim, J. S. (2008). Research and the reading wars. *Phi Delta Kappan, 89*(5), 372–375.

McAfee, Oralie; Leong, Deborah J., Assessing and Guiding Young Children's Development and Learning, 5th ed., © 2011. Reprinted and electronically reproduced by permission of Pearson Education, Inc., Upper Saddle River, New Jersey

McAfee, O., Leong, D. J., & Bodrova, E. (2016). *Assessing and guiding young children's development and learning* (6th ed.). Upper Saddle River, NJ: Pearson.

McGee, L. M. (2013). Read me a story: Reaping the benefits of reading for children. In D. R. Reutzel (Ed.), *Handbook of research-based practice in early education* (pp. 364–379). New York: Guilford Press.

McKissack, P. (1986). *Flossie and the fox.* New York: Dial Books for Young Readers.

Morrow, L. M., Berkule, S. B., Mendelsohn, A. L., Healey, A. L., & Cates, C. B. (2013). Learning through play. In D. R. Reutzel (Ed.), *Handbook of research-based practice in early education.* New York: Guilford Press.

Morrow, L. M. (2015). *Literacy development in the early years: Helping children read and write* (8th ed.). Upper Saddle River, NJ: Pearson.

Munsen, S. (2013). No fine art left behind: Creative and expressive education. In D. R. Reutzel (Ed.), *Handbook of research-based practice in early education* (pp. 309–325). New York: Guilford Press.

National Academies of Science, Engineering, and Medicine (NASEM). (2017). *Promoting the educational success of children and youth learning English.* Washington, DC: The National Academies Press. Retrieved October 31, 2017, from https://doi.org/10.17226/24677.

National Center for Quality Teaching and Learning. (2015). *Language and literacy preschool curriculum consumer report.* Retrieved March 10, 2018, from https://eclkc.ohs.acf.hhs.gov/curriculum/article/choosing-preschool-curriculum.

National Center on Cultural and Linguistic Responsiveness, n.d. *Code switching: Why it matters and how to respond.* Washington, DC: U.S. Department of Health and Human Services, Office of Head Start. Retrieved February 21, 2018, from http://eclkc.ohs.acf.hhs.gov/hslc/tta-system/ cultural-linguistic/fcp/docs/code-switching.pdf

National Coalition for Core Arts Standards. (2014). *National core arts standards: Dance, media arts, music, theatre, and visual arts.* Retrieved January 24, 2015, from http://nationalartsstandards.org/

National Early Literacy Panel (NELP). (2008). *Developing early literacy: Report of the National Early Literacy Panel. A scientific synthesis of early literacy development and implications for intervention.* Washington, DC: Author. Retrieved from http://lincs.ed.gov/publications/pdf/NELPReport09.pdf

National Institute of Child Health and Human Development (NICHD). (2000). *Report of the National Reading Panel. Teaching children to read: An evidence-based assessment of the scientific research literature on reading and its implications for reading instruction.* Washington, DC: Author.

Neuman, S. B., & Wright, T. S. (2013). *All about words: Increasing vocabulary in the common core classroom, PreK–2.* New York: Teachers College Press.

Neuman. S., & Moland, N. (2016). The consequences of income segregation on children's access to print. *Urban Education.* doi.org/10.1177/0042085916654525.

Pelatti, C. Y., Piasta, S. B., Justice, L. M., & O'Connell, A. (2014). Language- and literacy-learning opportunities in early childhood classrooms: Children's typical experiences and within-classroom variability. *Early Childhood Research Quarterly, 29*(4), 445–456.

Pinkham, A. M., Kaefer, T., & Neuman, S. B. (Eds.). (2012). Knowledge development in early childhood: Sources and learning and classroom implications. New York: The Guilford Press.

Price, L. H., Bradley, B. A., & Smith, J. M. (2012). A comparison of preschool teachers' talk during storybook and information book read-alouds. *Early Childhood Research Quarterly, 27*(3), 426–440.

Puerling, B. (2018) *Teaching in the digital age for preschool and kindergarten: Enhancing curriculum with technology.* St. Paul, MN: Redleaf Press.

Puranik, C. S., & Lonigan, C. J. (2012). Name-writing proficiency, not length of name, is associated with preschool children's emergent literacy skills. *Early Childhood Research Quarterly, 27*(2), 284–294.

Ramirez-Esparza, N., Garcia-Sierra, A., & Kuhl, P. K. (2014). Look who's talking: Speech style and social context in language input to infants are linked to concurrent and future speech development. *Developmental Science, 17*(6), 880–891.

Rasinki, T. V. (2012). Why reading fluency should be "hot." *Reading Teacher, 65*(8), 516–522.

Rivera-Gaxiola, M., Silva-Pereyra, J., & Kuhl, P. K. (2008). Brain potentials to native and non-native speech contrasts in 7- and 11-month-old American infants. *Developmental Science, 8*(2), 162–172.

Rogow, F. (2015). Media literacy in early childhood education: Inquiry-based technology integration. In C. Donohue (Ed.), *Technology and digital media in the early years: Tools for teaching and learning,* 91–103. Washington, DC: National Association for the Education of Young Children.

Roskos, K. A., Tabors, P. O., & Lenhart, L. A. (2009). *Oral language and early literacy in preschool: Talking, reading, and writing* (2nd ed.). Newark, DE: International Reading Association.

Ruppert, S. S. (2006). *Critical evidence: How the arts benefit student achievement.* National Assembly of State Arts Agencies & Arts Education Partnership. Retrieved January 29, 2015, from http://www.nasaa-arts.org/Publications/critical-evidence.pdf

Schickedanz, J. A., & Collins, M. F. (2013). *So much more than the ABCs: The early phases of reading and writing.* Washington, DC: National Association for the Education of Young Children.

Shanahan, T., & Lonigan, C. J. (2013). *Early childhood literacy: The National Early Literacy Panel and beyond.* Baltimore: Brookes.

Snow, C. E., Burns, M. S., & Griffin, P. (Eds.). (1998). *Preventing reading difficulties in young children.* Washington, DC: National Academies Press.

Stahl, K. A. D. (2014). Research into practice: New insights about letter learning. *The Reading Teacher, 68*(4), 261–265.

Stanovich, K. E. (1986). Matthew effects in early reading: Some consequences of individual differences in the acquisition of literacy. *Reading Research Quarterly, 24,* 402–433.

Strasser, J., & Bresson, L. M. (2017). *Big questions for young minds: Extending children's thinking.* Washington, DC: National Association for the Education of Young Children.

Strickland, D. S. (2011). *Teaching phonics today: Word study strategies through the grades* (2nd ed.). Newark, DE: International Reading Association.

Strickland, D. S., & Schickedanz, J. A. (2009). *Learning about print in preschool: Working with letters, words, and beginning links with phonemic awareness* (2nd ed.). Newark, DE: International Reading Association.

Taylor, J., Davis, M., & Rastle, K. (2017). Comparing and validating methods of reading instruction using behavioural and neural findings in an artificial orthography. *Journal of Experimental Psychology: General, 20(4), 1–34.*

Thompson, C. M. (2013). Reposition the visual arts in early childhood education: Continuing reconsideration. In O. N. Saracho & B. Spdek (Eds.), *Handbook of research on the education of young children* (3rd ed., pp. 219–240). New York: Routledge.

Towson, J. A., Gallagher, P. A., & Bingham, G. A. (2016). Dialogic reading: Language and preliteracy outcomes for young children with disabilities. *Journal of Early Intervention, 38*(4), 230–246.

Vecchi, V. (2010). *Art and creativity in Reggio Emilia: Exploring the role and potential of ateliers in early childhood education.* New York: Routledge.

E. Weitzman & J. Greenberg, 2002. *Learning language and loving it: A guide to promoting children's social, language, and literacy development in early childhood settings* (2nd ed.). Toronto: The Hanen Centre

Wigfield, A., Gladstone, J. R., and Turci, L. (2016). Beyond cognition: Reading motivation and reading comprehension. *Child Development Perspectives, 10*(3), 190–195.

Williams, L. (1988). *The little old lady who was not afraid of anything.* New York: HarperCollins.

Winner, E., Goldstein, T., & Vincent-Lancrin, S., (2013). *Arts for arts' sake?: The impact of arts education.* Educational Research and Innovation, OECD Publishing. https://dxdoi.org/10.1787/9789264180789-en.

Zero to Three (2016a). *Your child's development: Age-based tips from birth to 36 months.* www.zerotothree.org/early-development.

Zero to Three. (2016b). *Learning to write and draw.* Retrieved February 21, 2018, from www.zerotothree.org/resoures/305-learning-to-write-and-draw.

Zucker, T. A, Cabell, S. Q., Justice, L. M., Pentimonti, J. M., & Kaderavek, J. N. (2013). The role of frequent, interactive prekindergarten shared reading in the longitudinal development of language and literacy skills. *Developmental Psychology, 49*(8), 1425–1439.

Chapter 13

Achieve, Inc. (2013). *Next Generation Science Standards, for states, by states.* Retrieved from http://www.nextgenscience.org/search-standards-dci

Albert Shanker Institute. (2009). *Preschool curriculum: What's in it for children and teachers.* Washington, DC: Author.

American Association for the Advancement of Science. (2009). *Benchmarks for science literacy.* Washington, DC: Author. Retrieved September 15, 2009, from http://www.project2061.org/publications/bsl/default.htm

Arnold, D. H., Fischer, P. H., Doctoroff, G. L., & Dobbs, J. (2002). Accelerating math development in Head Start classrooms. *Journal of Educational Psychology, 94*(4), 762–770.

Austin, B. (2014). Tips when discussing math with the English language learner. Chicago: Erikson Early Math Collaborative. Retrieved May 8, 2018 from http://earlymath.erikson.edu/6-tips-discussing-math-english-language-learner.

Beaty, A. (2007). *Iggy Peck, Architect.* Harry N. Abrams.

Beaty, A. (2013). *Rosie Revere, Engineer.* Harry N. Abrams.

Beaty, A. (2016). *Ada Twist, Scientist.* Harry N. Abrams.

Beiland, S. L., Gunderson, E. A., Ramirez, G., & Levine, S. C. (2010). Female teachers' math anxiety affects girls' math achievement. *Proceedings of the National Academy of Sciences, 107*(5), 1860–1863.

Beneke, S. J., Ostrosky, M. M., & Katz, L. G. (2008). Calendar time for young children: Good intentions gone awry. *Young Children, 63*(3), 12–16.

Bodrova, E., & Leong, D. J. (2007). *Tools of the mind: The Vygotskian approach to early childhood education.* Upper Saddle River, NJ: Pearson.

Bowman, B.T., Comer, J.P., & Johns, D.J. (2018). Addressing the African American achievement gap: Three leading educators issue a call to action. *Young Children, 73*(2), 14–23.

Byers, A.I., Cottone, E.A., & Cameron, .D. (2018). From design copying to mathematics in the early childhood classroom. *Young Children, 73*(1), 80–85.

Casey, M. B., Erkut, S., Ceder, I., & Young, J. M. (2008). Use of a storytelling context to improve girls' and boys' geometry skills in kindergarten. *Journal of Applied Developmental Psychology, 29,* 29–48.

Center on the Developing Child at Harvard University. (2011). *Building the brain's "air traffic control" system: How early experiences shape the development of executive function: Working Paper #11.* Retrieved from http://www.developingchild.harvard.edu

Christenson L.A. & James, J. (2015). Building bridges to understanding in a preschool classroom: A morning in the block center. *Young Children, 70*(1), 26–31.

Cimpian, J., Lubienski, S., Timmer, J., Makowski, M., & Miller, E. (2016). Have gender gaps in math closed? Achievement, teacher perceptions, and learning behaviors across two ECLS-K cohorts. *AERA Open, 2*(4), 1–19.

Clements, D. H., & Sarama, J. (2003). Young children and technology: What does the research say? *Young Children, 58*(6), 34–40.

Clements, D. H., & Sarama, J. (2007). Effects of a preschool mathematics curriculum: Summative research on the Building Blocks project. *Journal for Research in Mathematics Education, 38*(2), 136–163.

Clements, D. H., & Sarama, J. (2007b). Effects of a preschool mathematics curriculum: Summative research on the Building Blocks project. *Journal for Research in Mathematics Education, 38*(2), 136–163.

Clements, D. H., & Sarama, J. (2008). Experimental evaluation of the effects of a research-based preschool mathematics curriculum. *American Educational Research Journal, 45,* 443–494.

Clements, D. H., & Sarama, J. (2013). Solving problems: Mathematics for young children. In D. R. Reutzel (Ed.), *Handbook of research-based practice in early education* (pp. 348–363). New York: Guilford Press.

Clements, D. H., Fuson, K. C., & Sarama, J. (2017b). What is developmentally appropriate teaching? *Teaching Children Mathematics, 24*(3), 179–188.

Clements, D.H. & Sarama, J. (2014). *Learning and teaching early math: The learning trajectories approach* (2nd ed.). New York, NY: Routledge.

Clements, D.H., Sarama, J., & Germeroth, C. (2016). Learning executive function and early math: Directions of causal relations. *Early Childhood Research Quarterly, 36*(3), 79–90.

Common Core State Standards Initiative. (2011). *Common core standards for mathematics.* Washington, DC: Council for Chief State School Officers and National Governor's Association. Retrieved May 7, 2018, from http://www.corestandards.org

Common Core State Standards Initiative. (2011b). *Common core standards for mathematics.* Washington, DC: Council for Chief State School Officers and National Governor's Association. Retrieved February 17, 2012, from http://www.corestandards.org

Common Core State Standards Initiative. (2015). *Key shifts in mathematics.* Washington, DC: Council for Chief State School Officers and National Governor's Association. Retrieved May 7, 2018, from http://www.corestandards.org/other-resources/key-shifts-in-mathematics/

Davis, D.B., & Farran, D.C. (2018). Positive early math experiences for African American boys: Nurturing the next generation of STEM majors. *Young Children, 73*(2), 44–51.

Desouza, J. M. S., & Czerniak, C. M. (2002, Summer/Spring). Social behaviors and gender differences among preschoolers: Implications for science activities. *Journal of Research in Childhood Education, 16*(2), 175–188.

DeVries, R. and Sales, C., 2011. *Ramps and Pathways: A Constructivist Approach to Physics with Young Children,* Washington, DC: National Association for the Education of Young Children

Diamond, A. (2012, January 20). *What nurtures the human spirit may also be best for executive functions and school success.* Presentation at the Maryland State Department of Education Early Care and Education Research Forum, Towson, MD.

Donohue, C. (Ed.). (2015). *Technology and digital media in the early years.* New York: Routledge Taylor & Francis Group.

Duncan, G. J., Dowsett, C. J., Claessens, A., Magnuson, K., Huston, A. C., Klebanov, P., et al. (2007). School readiness and later achievement. *Developmental Psychology, 43,* 1428–1446.

Engel, M., Classens, A., Watts, T., & Farkas, G. (2016). Mathematics content coverage and student learning in kindergarten. *Educational Researcher, 45*(5), 293–300.

Farran, D. C., Lipsey, M. W., Watson, B., & Hurley, S. (2007). *Balance of content emphasis and child content engagement in an Early Reading First program.* Paper presented at the American Educational Research Association, Chicago, IL.

Farran, D., Lipsey, M., & Wilson, S. (2011). *Experimental evaluation of the Tools of the Mind Pre-K Curriculum* [Working paper]. Retrieved from https://my.vanderbilt.edu/toolsofthemindevaluation/files/2011/12/Tools-Report-8-10-11-Appendices-Removed1.pdf

Farran, D.C., Meador, D., Christopher, C., Nesbitt, K.T., & Bilbrey, L.E. (2017). Data-driven improvement in prekindergarten classrooms: Report from a partnership in an urban district. *Child Development, 88,* 1466–1479. doi:10.1111/cdev.12906.

French, L. A., & Woodring, S. D. (2013). Science education in the early years. In O. N. Saracho & B. Spodek (Eds.), *Handbook of research on the education of young children* (3rd ed., pp. 179–196). New York: Routledge.

Friedman-Krauss, A., Barnett, W.S., & Nores, M. (2016). How much can high-quality universal pre-k reduce achievement gaps? Center for American Progress & NIEER. Retrieved November 1, 2017 from http://nieer.org/wp-content/uploads/2017/01/NIEER-AchievementGaps-report.pdf.

Fuson, K. C. (1988). *Children's counting and concept of number.* New York: Springer-Verlag.

Gelman, R., & Brenneman, K. (2004). Science learning pathways for young children. *Early Childhood Research Quarterly, 19*(1), 150–158.

Gelman, R., & Gallistel, C. R. (1978). *The child's understanding of number.* Cambridge, MA: Harvard University Press.

Gelman, R., Brenneman, K., MacDonald, G., & Román, M. (2010). *Preschool pathways to science: Facilitating scientific ways of thinking, talking, doing, and understanding.* Baltimore: Paul H. Brookes.

Ginsburg, H. (2016). Finding the math in storybooks for young children. KQED MindShift. Retrieved May 10, 2018 from https://ww2.kqed.org/-mindshift/2016/02/02/finding-the-math-in-storybooks-for-young-children/.

Ginsburg, H. P. (2006). Mathematical play and playful mathematics: A guide for early education. In D. G. Singer, R. M. Golinkoff, & K. Hirsh-Pasek (Eds.), *Play = learning: How play motivates and enhances children's cognitive and social-emotional growth* (pp. 145–165). New York: Oxford University Press.

Ginsburg, H. P., & Pappas, S. (2004). SES, ethnic, and gender differences in young children's informal addition and subtraction: A clinical interview investigation. *Journal of Applied Developmental Psychology, 25,* 171–192.

Ginsburg, H. P., Lee, J. S., & Boyd, J. S. (2008). Mathematics education for young children: What it is and how to promote it. *Social Policy Report, 22*(1), 3–23.

Goldenberg, E.P., Miller, S.J., Carter, C.J., & Reed, K.E. (2017). Mathematical structure and error in kindergarten. *Young Children, 72*(3), 38–44.

Gray, J. (2015). Digital play and traditional play have more in common than you may think. Sparking Kids' imagination with digital toys. Retrieved from http://tocaboca.com/magazine/sparking-imagination/.

Gunderson, E. A., Park, D., Maloney, E. A., Beilock, S. L. & Levine, S. C. (2018) Reciprocal relations among motivational frameworks, math anxiety, and math achievement in early elementary school. *Journal of Cognition and Development, 19*(1), 21–46.

Hannust, T. & Kikas, E. (2007). Children's knowledge of astronomy and its change in the course of learning. *Early Childhood Research Quarterly, 22*(1), 89–104.

Heroman,C. (2017). Making and tinkering: Bringing design challenges to the classroom. *Young Children, 72*(2), 72–79.

Hong, S.-Y. , & Diamond, K. E. (2012). Two approaches to teaching young children science concepts, vocabulary, and scientific problem-solving skills. *Early Childhood Research Quarterly, 27*(2), 295–305.

Hutchins, P. (1968). *Rosie's walk*. New York: Simon & Schuster.

Institute of Medicine (IOM) & National Research Council (NRC). (2015). *Transforming the workforce for children birth through age 9: A unifying foundation*. Washington, DC: National Academies Press.

Jenkins, J.M. & Duncan, G.H. (2017). Do pre-kindergarten curricula matter? In Pre-kindergarten Task Force, The current state of scientific knowledge on pre-kindergarten effects, 37–43. Brookings & Duke Center for Child and Family Policy. Retrieved May 8, 2018 from https://www.brookings.edu/wp-content/uploads/2017/04/duke_prek-study_final_4-4-17_hires.pdf

Klahr, D., Zimmerman, C., & Jirout, J. (2011). Educational interventions to advance children's scientific thinking. *Science, 333*(6045), 971–975.

Klibanoff, R. S., Levine, S. C., Huttenlocher, J., Vasilyeva, M., & Hedges, L. V. (2006). Preschool children's mathematical knowledge: The effect of teacher "math talk." *Developmental Psychology, 42*(1), 59–69.

Krull, K. & Brewer, P. (2018). *Starstruck: The cosmic journey of Neil deGrasse Tyson*. Crown Books for Young Learners.

Lee, J., Collins, D.A., & Winkelman, L. (2015). Connecting 2-D and 3-D: Drafting blueprints, building, and playing with blocks. *Young Children, 70*(1), 32–35.

Levine, S. C., Jordan, N. C., & Huttenlocher, J. (1992). Development of calculation abilities in young children. *Journal of Experimental Child Psychology, 53*, 72–103.

Levine, S. C., Suriyakham, L. W., Roe, M. L., Huttenlocher, J., & Gunderson, E. A. (2010). What counts in the development of young children's number knowledge? *Developmental Psychology, 46*(5), 1309–1319.

Linder, S. M. (2012). Interactive whiteboards in early childhood mathematics: Strategies for effective implementation in pre-K–grade 3. *Young Children, 67*(3), 26–35.

Martin, M. O., Mullis, I. V. S., Foy, P., & Hooper, M. (2016). TIMSS 2015 International Results in Science. Retrieved from Boston College, TIMSS & PIRLS International Study Center website: http://timssandpirls.bc.edu/timss2015/international-results/

McClure, E. (2017). More than a foundation: Young children are capable STEM learners. *Young Children, 72*(5), 83–89.

McClure, E.R., Guernsey, L., Clements, D.H., Bales, S.N., Nichols, J., Kendall-Taylor, N., & Levine, M.H. (2017). *STEM starts early: Grounding science, technology, engineering, and math education in early childhood*. New York: Joan Ganz Cooney Center at Sesame Workshop.

Mongeau, L., (2017, October 2). New research finds 'Magic 8' preschool classroom practices. Hechinger Report.

Moomaw, S. (2017) Not all preschool math games are created equal. *Young Children, 72*(3), 14–21.

Mullis, I. V. S., Martin, M. O., Foy, P., & Hooper, M. (2016). TIMSS 2015 International Results in Mathematics. Retrieved from Boston College, TIMSS & PIRLS International Study Center website: http://timssandpirls.bc.edu/timss2015/international-results/

National Association for the Education of Young Children (NAEYC) & the Fred Rogers Center for Early

Learning and Children's Media. (2012). *Technology in early childhood programs serving children from birth through age 8*. Joint Position Statement. Washington, DC: Authors.

National Association for the Education of Young Children (NAEYC) Technology and Young Children Interest Forum. (2008). Meaningful technology integration in early learning environments. *Young Children, 63*(5), 48–50.

National Association for the Education of Young Children (NAEYC) & the Fred Rogers Center for Early Learning and Children's Media. (2012). *Technology in early childhood programs serving children from birth through age 8*. Joint Position Statement. Washington, DC: Authors.

National Center on Quality Teaching and Learning. (2013). *Using the scientific method*. Washington, DC: U.S. Department of Health and Human Services, Office of Head Start. Retrieved March 8, 2015, from http://eclkc.ohs.acf.hhs.gov/hslc/tta-system/teaching/eecd/Domains%20of%20Child%20Development/Science/using-scientific-method-poster-1.pdf

National Council of Teachers of Mathematics. (2000). *Principles and standards for school mathematics*. Reston, VA: Author. Retrieved from http://standards.nctm.org

National Research Council (NRC). (2009). *Mathematics learning in early childhood: Paths toward excellence and equity*. Washington, DC: National Academies Press.

National Research Council (NRC). (2012). *A framework for K–12 science: Practices, crosscutting concepts, and core ideas*. Washington, DC: National Academies Press.

Nayfeld, I., Brenneman, K., & Gelman, R. (2011). Science in the classroom: Finding a balance between autonomous exploration and teacher-led instruction in preschool settings. *Early Education & Development, 22*(6), 970–988.

Nayfeld, I., Fuccillo, J., & Greenfield, D.B. (2013). Executive functions in early learning: Extending the relationships between executive functions in school readiness to science. *Learning and Individual Differences, 26*, 81–88.

Nguyen, H.N. Laski, E.V., Thomson, D.L. Bronson, M.B., & Casey, B.M. (2017). More than counting: Learning to label quantities in preschool. *Young Children, 72*(3), 22–29.

Nguyen, H.N., Watts, T.W., Duncan, G.J., Clements, D.H., Sarama, J., Wolfe, C., & Spitler, M.E. (2016). Which preschool math competencies are most predictive of 5th grade achievement? *Early Childhood Research Quarterly, 36*(3), 550–560.

Presser, A.L., Clements, M., Ginsburg, H., & Ertle, B. (2015). Big Math for Little Kids: The effectiveness of a preschool and kindergarten mathematics curriculum. *Early Education and Development, 26*(3), 399–426.

Reardon, S., Portilla, X. (2016). Recent trends in income, racial, and ethnic school readiness gaps at kindergarten entry. *AERA Open, 2*(3), 1–18.

Sarama, J., & Clements, D. H. (2007, March 12). *Manual for classroom observation of early mathematics—Environment and teaching (COEMET), Version 3*. Retrieved from http://www.UBTRIAD.org

Sarama, J., Lange, A. A., Clements, D. H., & Wolfe, C. B. (2012). The impacts of an early mathematics curriculum on oral language and literacy. *Early Childhood Research Quarterly, 27*(3), 489–502.

Schickedanz, J. A. (2008). *Increasing the power of instruction: Integration of language, literacy, and math across the preschool day*. Washington, DC: National Association for the Education of Young Children.

Schoenfeld, A. H., & Stipek, D. (2011). *Math matters: Children's mathematical journeys start

early*. Berkeley, CA: Heising-Simons Foundation. Retrieved February 28, 2015, from http://earlymath.org/earlymath/wp-content/uploads/2014/09/Math-Matters-Report_2ndEd1.pdf

Seefeldt, C., Galper, A., & Jones, I. (2012). *Active experiences for active children: Science* (3rd Ed.). Upper Saddle River, NJ: Pearson.

Seo, K.-H., & Ginsburg, H. P. (2004). What is developmentally appropriate in early childhood mathematics education? Lessons from new research. In D. H. Clements, J. Sarama, & A.-M. DiBiase (Eds.), *Engaging young children in mathematics: Standards for early childhood mathematics education* (pp. 91–104). Hillsdale, NJ: Lawrence Erlbaum Associates.

Shetterly, M.L. (2018). *Hidden figures: The true story of four black women and the space race*. New York, NY: Harper Collins.

Siegler, R. S., & Ramani, G. B. (2008). Playing board games promotes low-income children's numerical development. *Developmental Science, 11*(5), 655–661.

Sophian, C. (2013). Mathematics for early childhood education. In O. N. Saracho & B. Spdek (Eds.), *Handbook of research on the education of young children* (3rd ed., pp. 169–178). New York: Routledge.

Starkey, P. (2007, December 1). Presentation to the National Research Council Committee on Early Childhood Mathematics, Washington, DC.

Starkey, P., & Klein, A. (2008). Sociocultural influences on young children's mathematical knowledge. In O. N. Saracho & B. Spodek (Eds.), *Contemporary perspectives on mathematics in early childhood education* (pp. 253–276). Charlotte, NC: Information Age Publishing.

Stipek, D. (2017). Playful math instruction in the context of standards and accountability. *Young Children, 72*(3), 8–13.

Szekely, A. (2014). *Unlocking young children's potential: Governors' role in strengthening early mathematics learning*. Washington, DC: National Governors Association center for Best Practices. Retrieved from http://www.nga.org/files/live/sites/NGA/files/pdf/2014/1410UnlockingYoungChildrensPotential.pdf

Tepylo, D. H., Moss, J., & Stephenson, C. (2015). A developmental look at a rigorous block play program. *Young Children, 70*(1), 18–25.

Wang, J., Werner-Avidon, M., Newton, L., Randol, S., Smith, B., & Walker, G. (2013). Ingenuity in action: Connecting tinkering to engineering design processes. *Journal of Pre-College Engineering Education Research, 3*(1), Article 2. Retrieved May 10, 2018 from https://docs.lib.purdue.edu/jpeer/vol3/iss1/2/

Weinstock, M. (2015). It's time for more racial diversity in STEM toys. Scientific American, *Voices: Exploring and Celebrating Diversity in Science*. Retrieved May 8, 2018 from https://blogs.scientificamerican.com/voices/it-s-time-for-more-racial-diversity-in-stem-toys/

West, J. (2017). National longitudinal studies of kindergarten children: Historical context and ongoing contributions. *AERA Open*, Published online http://journals.sagepub.com/doi/10.1177/2332858417701684.

Whittaker, J.V. (2014). Good thinking! Fostering children's reasoning and problem solving. *Young Children, 69*(3), 80–89.

Wolfgang, C.H., Stannard, L.L., & Jones, I. (2009). Block play performance among preschoolers as a predictor of later school achievement in mathematics. *Journal of Research in Childhood Education, 15*(2), 173–180.

Worth, K., & Grollman, S. (2003). *Worms, shadows, and whirlpools: Science in the early childhood classroom*. Portsmouth, NH: Heinemann.

Zilanawala, A., Marin, M., Noguera, P.A., & Miney, RB (2017). Math achievement trajectories among black male students in the elementary and middle school years. *Educational Studies*, 54(2), 143–164.

Chapter 14

American Academy of Pediatrics. (n.d.). *Trauma guide*. Retrieved March 1, 2015, from https://www.aap.org/traumaguide

Barton, E. E., Steed, E. A., Strain, P., Dunlap, G., Powell, D. & Payne, C. J. (2014). An analysis of classroom-based and parent-focused social-emotional programs for young children. *Infants and Young Children*, 27(1), 3–29.

Blair, C. (2016). Moderating effects of executive functions and the teacher and child relationship on the development of mathematics ability in kindergarten. *Learning and Instruction: The Journal of the European Association for Research on Learning and Instruction*, 41(February), 85–93. Published online 10.1016/j.learninstruc.2015.10.001

Bodrova, E., & Leong, D. J. (2007). *Tools of the mind: The Vygotskian approach to early childhood education*. Upper Saddle River, NJ: Pearson.

Bohlmann, N. L., & Downer, J. T. (2016). Self-Regulation and task engagement as predictors of emergent language and literacy skills. *Early Education and Development*, 27(1), 18–37.

Buysse, V., Goldman, B. D., West, T., & Hollingsworth, H. (2007). Friendships in early childhood: Implications for early education and intervention. In W. H. Brown, S. L. Odom, & S. R. McConnell (Eds.), *Social competence of young children: Risk, disability, and evidence-based practices* (2nd ed.). Baltimore: Paul H. Brookes.

Center on the Developing Child at Harvard University. (2010). *Early experiences can alter gene expression and affect long-term development: Working paper #10*. Retrieved October 28, 2011 from http://www.developingchild.harvard.edu

Cigala, Ada. (2015). Learning others' point of view: Perspective taking and prosocial behaviour in preschoolers. *Early Child Development and Care*, 185(8), 1199–1215.

Committee for Children. (2011). *Second step: Social emotional skills for early learning*. Seattle: Author.

Dewey, J. (1916). *Democracy and education*. New York: Free Press.

Diamond, A. (2012, January 20). *What nurtures the human spirit may also be best for executive functions and school success*. Presentation at the Maryland State Department of Education Early Care and Education Research Forum, Towson, MD.

Domitrovich, C. E., Greenberg, M. T., Cortes, R., & Kusché, C. A. (2005). *The Preschool PATHS Curriculum*. Deerfield, MA: Channing-Bete Publishers.

Dunkerly-Bean, J., Bean, T. W., Sunday, K., & Summers, R. (2017). *Poverty is two coins: Young children explore social justice through reading and art. Reading Teacher*, 70(6), 679–688.

Durden, T. R., Escalante, E., & Blitch, K. (2015). Start with us! Culturally relevant pedagogy in the preschool classroom. *Early Childhood Education Journal*, 43(3), 223–232.

Epstein, A. S., & Hohmann, M. (2012). *The HighScope preschool curriculum* (4th ed.). Ypsilanti, MI: High/Scope Press.

Felitti, V. J., Anda, R. F., Nordenberg, D., Williamson, D. F., Spitz, A. M., Edwards, V., & Koss, M. P. (1998). The relationship of adult health status to childhood abuse and household dysfunction. *American Journal of Preventive Medicine*, 14, 245–258.

Ferrer, M. & Fugate, A. (2007). *The importance of friendship for school-age children*. Gainesville, FL: Department of Family, Youth and Community Sciences, Florida Cooperative Extension Service, University of Florida.

Flook, L., Goldberg, S. B., Pinger, L., & Davidson, R. J. (2015). Promoting prosocial behavior and self-regulatory skills in preschool children through a mindfulness-based kindness curriculum. *Developmental Psychology*, 51(1), 44–51.

Hanson, M. J., & SooHoo, T. (2007). Cultural influences on young children's social competence. In W. Brown, S. Odom, & S. McConnell (Eds.), *Social competence of young children: Risk, disability, and intervention*. Baltimore: Paul H. Brookes.

Heffron, S. (Ed.). (2012). *Geography for life: National geography standards* (2nd ed.). Washington, DC: National Council for Geographic Education.

Hyson, M. (2004). *The emotional development of young children: Building an emotion-centered curriculum*. New York: Teachers College Press.

Institute of Medicine (IOM) & National Research Council (NRC). (2015). *Transforming the workforce for children birth through age 8: A unifying foundation*. Washington, DC: National Academies Press.

Johnson, J. E., Christie, J. F., & Wardle, F. (2005). *Play, development, and early education*. Upper Saddle River, NJ: Pearson.

Jones, D. E., Greenberg, M., & Crowley, M. (2015). Early social-emotional functioning and public health: The relationship between kindergarten social competence and future wellness. *American Journal of Public Health*, 105(11), 2283–2290.

Joseph, G. E. (2002). *If you're happy and you know it: The emotional literacy and social information processing scripts of young, high-risk children*. Paper presented at Conference on Research Innovations in Early Intervention, San Diego, CA.

Joseph, G. E., & Strain, P. S. (2004). Building positive relationships with young children. *Young Exceptional Children*, 7(4), 21–29.

Joshee, R. & Thomas, M. (2017). Multicultural citizenship education in Canada: Slow peace as an alternative to social cohesion. In J. A. Banks, (Ed.), *Citizenship education and global migration: Implications for theory, research, and teaching*, 91–106. Washington, DC: American Educational Research Association.

Lillard, A.S. (2015). The development of play. In L. Liben and U. Mueller (Eds.), *Handbook of Child Psychology and Developmental Science, Vol. 3: Cognitive Development*, 425–468. New York, NY: Wiley-Blackwell.

Lynch, K.B., Geller, S.R., & Schmidt, M.G. (2004). A multi-year evaluation of the effectiveness of a resilience-based prevention program for young children. *Journal of Primary Prevention*, 24(3), 335–353.

Marcelo, A. K., & Yates, T. M. (2014). Prospective relations among preschoolers' play, coping, and adjustment as moderated by stressful events. *Journal of Applied Developmental Psychology*, 35(3), 223–233.

McAfee, O., & Leong, D. J. (2016). *Assessing and Guiding Young Children's Development and Learning*, 6th ed. Upper Saddle River, NJ: Pearson

Mindes, G. (2016). Social studies from early childhood to the world. In Bohart, H., Collick, H. B. & Charner, K. (Eds.), *Spotlight on young children: Teaching and learning in the primary grades*. Washington, DC: National Association for the Education of Young Children.

Mitchell, A., & David, J. (1992). *Explorations with young children: A curriculum guide from the Bank Street College of Education*. Mt. Rainier, MD: Gryphon House.

Moffitt, T. E., Arseneault, L., Belsky, D., Dickson, N., Hancox, R. J., Harrington, H. L., et al. (2011). A gradient of childhood self-control predicts health, wealth, and public safety. *Proceedings of the National Academy of Sciences*, 108(7), 2693–2698.

Montroy, J. J., Bowles, R., Skibbe, L. E., McClelland, M. M., & Morrison, F. J. (2016). The development of self-regulation across early childhood. *Developmental Psychology*, 52(11), 1744–1762.

Murray, D. W., Rosanbalm, K., Christopoulos, C., & Hamoudi, A. (2014). *Self-regulation and toxic stress: Foundations for understanding self-regulation from an applied developmental perspective*. OPRE Report #2015–21, Washington, DC: Office of Planning, Research and Evaluation, Administration for Children and Families, U.S. Department of Health and Human Services.

National Academies of Sciences, Engineering, and Medicine (NASEM). (2016). *Parenting matters: Supporting parents of children 0–8*. Washington, DC: The National Academies Press.

National Child Traumatic Stress Network (NCTSN) Core Curriculum on Childhood Trauma Task Force (2012). *The 12 core concepts: Concepts for understanding traumatic stress responses in children and families*. Core Curriculum on Childhood Trauma. Los Angeles, CA, and Durham, NC: UCLA-Duke

National Council for the Social Studies. (2010). *National curriculum standards for social studies: A framework for teaching, learning, and assessment*. Silver Spring, MD: Author. Retrieved from http://www.socialstudies.org/standards/execsummary

National Council for the Social Studies. (2017). *About National Council for the Social Studies (NCSS)*. (2017, October 26). Retrieved April 04, 2018, from https://www.socialstudies.org/about.

Nesbitt, K.T., Farran, D.C., Fuhs, M. W. (2015). Executive function skills and academic achievement gains in prekindergarten. *Developmental Psychology*, 51(7), 865–878.

North Carolina Foundations for Early Learning and Development, by North Carolina Foundations Task Force, 2013, Raleigh, NC: Author; *Washington State Early Learning and Development Benchmarks*, by State of Washington, 2012, retrieved February 22, 2015, from http://www.del.wa.gov/publications/development/docs/guidelines.pdf

Odhiambo, E.A., Nelson, L.E., & Chrisman, J.K. (2016). *Social studies and young children*. Upper Saddle River, NJ: Pearson.

Paris, D. & Alim, H.S. (2017). *Culturally sustaining pedagogies: Teaching and learning for justice in a changing world*. New York, NY: Teachers College Press.

Parten, M. (1933). Social participation among preschool children. *Journal of Abnormal and Social Psychology*, 27, 243–269.

Ritchie, S. (2011, November). *FirstSchool: Improving the preK–3rd grade experience of African-American, Latino, and low income children*. Paper presented at the annual meeting of the National Association for the Education of Young Children, Orlando, FL.

Schonert-Reichl, K. A., Oberle, E., Lawlor, M. S., Abbott, D., Thomson, K., Oberlander, T. F., & Diamond, A. (2015). Enhancing cognitive and social–emotional development through a simple-to-administer mindfulness-based school program for elementary school children: A randomized controlled trial. *Developmental Psychology*, 51(1), 52–66.

Sciaraffa, M. A., Zeanah, P. D., & Zeanah, C. H. (2017). Understanding and promoting resilience in the context of adverse childhood experiences. *Early Childhood Education Journal*, 46(3), 343–353.

Seefeldt, C., Castle, S., & Falconer, R. C. (2014). *Social studies for the preschool/primary child* (9th ed.). Upper Saddle River, NJ: Pearson.

Shonkoff, J., & Phillips, D. A. (2000). *From neurons to neighborhoods: The science of early childhood development*. Washington, DC: National Academies Press.

Shure, M. B. (n.d.). *ICPS: I can problem solve*. Retrieved from https://www.researchpress.com/sites/default/files/books/addContent/ICPS-research.pdf

Slaughter, V. (2016). Theory of mind and prosocial behavior in childhood: A meta-analytic review. *Developmental Psychology*, 52(8), 1192–1205.

Soderberg, J. & Joseph, G.E. (2016). *Internal Validity of Early Achiever Standards.* Report submitted to Washington State Department of Early Learning. https://del.wa.gov/sites/default/files/public/QRIS/EarlyAchievers_Validationstudy.pdf.

Strain, P. S., & Joseph, G. E. (2006). *You've got to have friends* (Young Exceptional Children Monograph Series 8: Social Emotional Development). Longmont, CO: Sopris West.

Strain, P. S., & Schwartz, I. S. (2001). Applied behavior analysis and the development of meaningful social relations for young children with autism. *Focus on Autism and Developmental Disabilities, 16,* 120–128.

Thompson, M., & Gauntlett-Gilbert, J., 2008. Mindfulness with children and adolescents: Effective clinical application. *Child Psychology and Psychiatry, 13*(3), 395–407.

Thompson, R. A. (2010). *Social and emotional development: Foundations for learning in preschool.* Presentation to California Community College Early Childhood Educators, April 9, Long Beach, CA.

Trust for Learning (2017). *Parents as consumers of early education: Research findings 2017.* Trust for Learning. Retrieved May 1, 2018 from https://trustforlearning.org/assets/F_TFL_ParentasConsumers_FullResearchBooklet_2017_PRINT.pdf

Tsai, J.L., Louie, J., Chen, E. E & Uchida,Y. (2007). Learning what feelings to desire: Socialization of ideal affect through children's storybooks. *Personality and Social Pyschology Bulletin, 33*(1), 17–30.

Veiga, G., Neto, C., & Rieffe, C. (2016). Preschoolers' free play: Connections with emotional and social functioning. *International Journal of Emotional Education, 8*(1), 48–62.

Webster-Stratton, C. (1999). *How to promote children's social and emotional competence.* London: Paul Chapman Publishing.

Weisberg, D.S., Kittredge, A.K., Hirsh-Pasek, K., Golinkoff, R.M., & Klahr, D. (2015). Making play work for education. *Phi Delta Kappa International, 26*(8), 8–13.

Willis, E. (2015). An empathetic beginning in education: Exploring the prospects of self-regulation skills on pro-social behaviour in the early childhood environment. *Early Child Development and Care,* 1–9.

Wong, C. S. (2013). A play and joint attention intervention for teachers of young children with autism: A randomized controlled pilot study. *Autism, 3,* 340–357.

Zelazo, P. D., & Lyons, K. E. (2012). *The potential benefits of mindfulness training in early childhood: A developmental social cognitive neuroscience perspective.* University of Minnesota. Retrieved March 3, 2015, from http://research.familylife.com.au/wp-content/uploads/2012/05/the-potential-benefits-of-mindfulness-training-in-early-childhood.pdf

Zero to Six Collaborative Group, National Child Traumatic Stress Network. (2010). *Early childhood trauma.* Los Angeles, CA, & Durham, NC: National Center for Child Traumatic Stress.

Zhai, F., Raver, C. C., & Jones, S. M. (2015). Social and emotional learning services and child outcomes in third grade: Evidence from a cohort of Head Start participants. *Children and Youth Services Review, 56*(September), 42–51. doi:10.1016/j.childyouth.2015.06.016

Chapter 15

Active Living Research. (2015). *Active education: Growing evidence on physical activity and academic performance—Research brief.* Retrieved April 26, 2018 from https://activelivingresearch.org/sites/default/files/ALR_Brief_ActiveEducation_Jan2015.pdf

Albrecht, K., & Miller, L.G., 2000a. Innovations: The comprehensive infant curriculum. Beltsville, MD: Gryphon House.

Albrecht, K., & Miller, L.G., 2000b. Innovations: The comprehensive toddler curriculum. Beltsville, MD: Gryphon House

Albrecht, K., & Miller, L.G., 2004. Innovations: The comprehensive preschool curriculum. Beltsville, MD: Gryphon House.

American Academy of Pediatrics, American Public Health Association, & National Resource Center for Health and Safety in Child Care and Early Education. (2011). *Caring for our children: National health and safety performance standards: Guidelines for early care and education programs* (3rd ed.). Elk Grove Village, IL: American Academy of Pediatrics; Washington, DC: American Public Health Association.

American Academy of Pediatrics. (2013). The crucial role of recess: Policy statement. *Pediatrics, 131*(1), 183–188. doi:10.1542/peds.2012-2993

Aronson, S. S. (2012). *Healthy young children: A manual for programs* (5th ed.). Washington, DC: National Association for the Education of Young Children.

Barker, J.E., Semenov, A.D., Michaelson, L., Provan, L.S., Snyder, H. & Muakata, Y. (2014). Less-structured time in children's daily lives predicts self-directed executive functioning. *Frontiers in Psychology.* 17 June 2014. https://doi.org/10.3389/fpsyg.2014.00593

Barros, R. M., Silver, E. J., & Stein, R. E. K. (2009). School recess and classroom behavior. *Pediatrics, 123*(2), 431–436.

Becker, D.R., McClelland, M, M., Loprinzi, P. & Trost, S.G. (2013). Physical activity, self-regulation, and early academic achievement in preschool children. *Early Education and Development, 25*(1), 56–70, DOI: 10.1080/10409289.2013.780505

Berk, L.E. (2012). *Child Development* (9th ed.). PHI Learning.

Bernath, P., & Masi, W. (2006). Smart school snacks: A comprehensive preschool nutrition education program. *Young Children, 61*(3), 20–24.

Blagojevic, B., & Thomes, K. (2014). Preschoolers take tech outdoors. *Teaching Young Children, 7*(2), 30–31.

Brown, W. H., Pheiffer, K. A., McKiver, K. L., Dowda, M., Addy, C. L., & Pate, R. R. (2009). Social and environmental factors associated with preschoolers' nonsedentary physical activity. *Child Development, 80*(1), 45–58.

Carlson, F. M. (2011). *Big body play: Why boisterous, vigorous, and very physical play is essential to children's development and learning.* Washington, DC: National Association for the Education of Young Children.

Carlson, F. M. (2015). Infants through third grade—big body play: Understanding and supporting it. In H. B. Bohart, K. Charner, & D. Koralek (Eds.), *Spotlight on young children: Exploring play* (pp. 107–117). Washington, DC: National Association for the Education of Young Children.

Centers for Disease Control and Prevention (CDC). (2012a). *Playground injuries: Fact sheet.* Retrieved April 5, 2015, from http://www.cdc.gov/-HomeandRecreationalSafety/Playground-Injuries/playgroundinjuries-factsheet.htm

Centers for Disease Control and Prevention (CDC). (2012b). Trends in the prevalence of extreme obesity among U.S. preschool-aged children living in low-income families, 1998–2010. *Journal of the American Medical Association, 308* (24), 2563–2565.

Centers for Disease Control and Prevention (CDC). (2013). *Bicycle-related injuries.* Retrieved April 5, 2015, from http://www.cdc.gov/-HomeandRecreationalSafety/Bicycle/

Centers for Disease Control and Prevention (CDC). (2014). *Childhood obesity facts.* Retrieved April 5, 2015, from http://www.cdc.gov/healthyyouth/obesity/facts.htm

Centers for Disease Control and Prevention (CDC). (2015). *How much physical activity do children need?* Retrieved March 15, 2015, from http://www.cdc.gov/physicalactivity/everyone/guidelines/children.html

Centers for Disease Control and Prevention (CDC). (2015). *How much physical activity do children need?* Retrieved March 15, 2015, from http://www.cdc.gov/physicalactivity/everyone/guidelines/children.html

Centers for Disease Control and Prevention (CDC). (2017). *Physical activity facts.* Retrieved March 22, 2018 from https://www.cdc.gov/healthyschools/physicalactivity/facts.htm

Centers for Disease Control and Prevention [CDC]. (2010). *The association between school-based physical activity, including physical education, and academic performance.* Atlanta, GA: U. S. Department of Health and Human Services.

Centers for Disease Control and Prevention. (2018). *Wash your hands.* Atlanta, GA: U.S. Department of Health and Human Services. Retrieved August 17, 2018 from www.cdc.gov/washyourhands.

Cohen, D., & Kotler, J. (2005). *Preschoolers' perception of healthy food.* Paper presented at the Biennial Meeting of the Society for Research in Child Development, Atlanta, GA.

Colker, L. (2005). *The cooking book: Fostering young children's learning and delight.* Washington, DC: National Association for the Education of Young Children.

C. Copple & S. Bredekamp, with J. Gonzalez-Mena, 2011. Basics of developmentally appropriate practice: An introduction for teachers of infants and toddlers. Washington, DC: NAEYC; C. Copple & S. Bredekamp (Eds.), 2006. Basics of developmentally appropriate practice: An introduction for teachers of children 3 to 6. Washington, DC: NAEYC.

Craig, G. J., & Baucum, D. (2002). *Human development* (9th ed.). Upper Saddle River, NJ: Prentice Hall.

Curtis, D. (2010). What's the risk of no risk? *Exchange, 32*(1), 52–60.

Faber Taylor, A., & Kuo, F. E. (2009). Children with attention deficits concentrate better after walk in the park. *Journal of Attention Disorders, 12*(5), 402–409.

Food Research and Action Center. (2016). *Research brief: Breakfast for learning.* Retrieved March 22, 2018 from www.FRAC.org

Freeman, D. (2001). *Corduroy goes to the doctor.* New York: Penguin Putnam.

Gallahue, D. L. (1995). Transforming physical education curriculum. In S. Bredekamp & T. Rosegrant (Eds.), *Reaching potentials: Transforming early childhood curriculum* (Vol. 2, pp. 125–144). Washington, DC: National Association for the Education of Young Children.

Gallahue, D. L., Ozmun, J. C., & Goodway, J. D. (2012). *Understanding motor development: Infants, children, adolescent, adults* (7th ed.). Boston: McGraw-Hill.

Gerber, M. (1998). *RIE Basic Principles,* Retrieved May 4, 2018 from https://www.rie.org/educaring/ries-basic-principles

Gonzalez-Mena, J. Chahin, E., & Briley, L. (2005). The Pikler Institute: A unique approach to caring for children, *Exchange, 166,* 49–5.

Goodway, J. D., Ozmun, J. C., & Gallahue, D. L. (2013). Motor development in young children. In O. N. Saracho & B. Spodek (Eds.), *Handbook of research on the education of young children* (3rd ed., pp. 80–101). New York: Routledge.

Goodway, J. D., Ozmun, J. C., Derringer, S. T., & Lee. J. (2013). Promoting physical literacy and activity in young children. In D. R. Reutzel (Ed.), *Handbook of research-based practice in early education* (pp. 293–308). New York: Guilford Press.

Goodway, J. D., Robinson, M. A., & Crowe, H. (2010). Developmental delays in fundamental motor skill development of ethnically diverse and disadvantaged preschoolers. *Research Quarterly for Exercise & Sport, 81,* 17–25.

Greenman, J. (2001). *What happened to my world? Helping children cope in turbulent times.* Cambridge, MA: Bright Horizons Family Solutions. Retrieved October 14, 2009, from http://www.brighthorizons.com/resources/pdf/talktochildren/docs/what_happened_to_my_world.pdf

Greenman, J. (2005b). Places for childhood in the 21st century. *Beyond the Journal, Young Children on the Web.* Retrieved July 26, 2008, from http://journal.naeyc.org/btj/200505/01Greenman.pdf

Greenman, J. (2017). *Caring spaces, learning places: Children's environments that work!* Lincoln, NE: Exchange Press.

Grissmer, D. W., Grimm, K. J., Aiyer, S. M., Murrah, W. M., & Steele, J. S. (2010). Fine motor skills and early comprehension of the world: Two new school readiness indicators. *Developmental Psychology, 46*(5), 1008–1017.

Haywood, K. M., & Gretchell, N. (2005). *Life span motor development* (4th ed.). Champaign, IL: Human Kinetics.

Head Start. (2015b). *Head Start emergency preparedness manual: 2015 edition.* Retrieved July 8, 2015, from http://eclkc.ohs.acf.hhs.gov/hslc/tta-system/health/docs/head-start-emergency-prep-manual-2015.pdf

Honig, A. S. (2015). *Experiencing nature with young children: Awakening delight, curiosity, and a sense of stewardship.* Washington, DC: National Association for the Education of Young Children.

Huber, M. (2016). *Embracing rough-and-tumble play: Teaching with the body in mind.* St. Paul, MN: Redleaf Press.

Ingwersen, J., Defeyter, M. A., Kennedy, D. O., Wesnes, K. A., & Scholey, A. B. (2007). A low glycaemic index breakfast cereal preferentially prevents children's cognitive performance from declining throughout the morning. *Appetite, 49*(1), 240–244. doi:10.1016/j.appet.2006.06.009

Jarrett, O. S., Maxwell, D. M., Dickerson, C., Hoge, P., Davies, G., & Yetley, A. (1998). The impact of recess on classroom behavior: Group effects and individual differences. *Journal of Educational Research, 92*(2), 121–126.

Kalich, K., Bauer, D., & McPartlin, D. (2014). Creating the nutritionally purposeful classroom. *Young Children, 69*(5), 8–13.

Keeler, R. (2008). *Natural playscapes: Creating outdoor play environments for the soul.* Redmond, WA: Exchange Press.

Kuo, F. E. (Ming). (2010). *Parks and other green environments: Essential components of a healthy human habitat.* Ashburn, VA: National Recreation and Park Association. Retrieved April 5, 2015, from http://www.nrpa.org/uploadedFiles/nrpa.org/Publications_and_Research/Research/Papers/MingKuo-Research-Paper.pdf

Levitt, P. (2008). Building brain architecture and chemistry: A primer for policymakers. In A. Tarlov & M. P. Debbink (Eds.), *Investing in early childhood development: Evidence to support a movement for educational change.* New York: Palgrave Macmillan.

Louv, R. (2005). *Last child in the woods.* Chapel Hill, NC: Algonquin.

Malone, K., & Tranter, P. (2003). School grounds as sites for learning: Making the most of environmental opportunities. *Environmental Education Research, 9,* 282–303.

McBride, B. A., & Dev, D. A. (2014). Preventing childhood obesity: Strategies to help preschoolers develop healthy eating habits. *Young Children, 69*(5), 36–42.

McLoone, P., & Morrison, D.S., (2014). Risk of child obesity from parental obesity: Analysis of repeat national cross-sectional surveys. *European Journal of Public Health, 24*(2), 186–190.

Meier, D. R., & Sisk-Hilton, S. (Eds.). (2013). *Nature education with young children: Integrating inquiry and practice.* New York: Routledge.

Milteer, R. M., Ginsburg, K. R., & Council on Communications and Media Committee on Psychological Aspects of Child and Family Health. (2012). The importance of play in promoting healthy child development and maintaining strong parent–child bonds: Focus on children in poverty. *Pediatrics, 129*(1), e204–e213. Retrieved from http://www.pediatrics.aappublications.org

National Association for the Education of Young Children (NAEYC). (2011). *2010 NAEYC Standards for Initial & Advanced Early Childhood Professional Preparation Programs: For use by Associate, Baccalaureate and Graduate Degree Programs.* Washington, DC: Author.

National Science Foundation Discoveries (2004). *Will Baby Crawl?,* Retrieved May 4, 2018 from http://www.nsf.gov/discoveries/disc_summ.jsp?cntn_id=103153&org=NSF

Natural Learning Initiative. (2012). *Benefits of connecting children with nature: Why naturalize outdoor learning environments.* NC State University College of Design. Retrieved March 22, 2018 from www.naturallearning.org

Nekitsing, C., Hetherington, M.M., & Blundell-Birtill, P. (2018) Developing healthy food preferences in preschool children through taste exposure, sensory learning, and nutrition education. *Current Obesity Reports, 7,* 60–67. https://doi.org/10.1007/s13679-018-0297-8

Ogden, C. L., Carroll, M. D., Kit, B. K., & Flegal, K. M. (2014). Prevalence of childhood and adult obesity in the United States, 2011–2012. *Journal of the American Medical Association, 311*(8), 806–814. doi:10.1001/jama.2014.732

Pascoe, J. M., Shaikh, U., Forbis, S. G., & Etzel, R. A. (2007). Health and nutrition as a foundation for success in school. In R. C. Pianta, M. J. Cox, & K. L. Snow (Eds.), *School readiness and the transition to kindergarten in the era of accountability* (pp. 99–120). Baltimore: Brookes.

Pica, R. (2006). Physical fitness and the early childhood curriculum. *Young Children, 61*(3), 12–19.

Pica, R. (2014). *Preschoolers and kindergartners moving and learning: A physical education curriculum.* St. Paul, MN: Redleaf Press.

Reilley, K. (2017, October 23). Is recess important for kids or a waste of time? Here's what he research says. *Time.com.* Retrieved May 4, 2018 from http://time.com/4982061/recess-benefits-research-debate/.

Rivkin, M. S. (2014). *The great outdoors: Advocating for natural spaces for young children* (Rev. ed.). Washington, DC: National Association for the Education of Young Children.

Robert Wood Johnson Foundation. (2010). *State of play: Gallup survey of principals on school recess.* Princeton, NJ: Author. Retrieved March 20, 2012, from http://www.playworks.org/sites/default/files/d6/StateOfPlayFeb2010.pdf

Ross, T. (2000). *Wash your hands.* San Diego, CA: Kane/Miller Book Publishers.

Sanders, S. (2015). *Encouraging physical activity in preschoolers: Moving matters.* (2015). Lewisville, NC: Gryphon House.

Schickedanz, J. A., & Collins, M. F. (2013). *So much more than the ABCs: The early phases of reading and writing.* Washington, DC: National Association for the Education of Young Children.

Sesame Workshop, Nemours Health and Prevention Services, & KidHealth.org. (2007). *Healthy habits for life child care resource kit.* New York: Sesame Workshop. Retrieved March 20, 2012 from http://sesamestreet.org

SHAPE America. (2014). *National standards and grade-level outcomes for K–12 physical education.* Reston, VA: Author.

Smith, A. P. (2010). An investigation of the effects of breakfast cereals on alertness, cognitive function and other aspects of the reported well-being of children. *Nutritional Neuroscience, 13*(5), 230–236. doi:10.1179/147683010X12611460764642

Tandon, P. S., Saelens, B. E., & Christakis, D. A. (2017). Active play opportunities at child care. *PEDIATRICS, 135,* DOI: 10.1542/peds.2014–2750

Taylor, A. F., Kuo, F. E., & Sullivan, W. C. (2001). Coping with ADD: The surprising connection to green play settings. *Environments and Behavior, 33*(1), 54–77.

Tobin, K. J. (2013). Fast-food consumption and educational test scores in the USA. *Child: Care, Health & Development, 39*(1), 118–124. doi:10.1111/j.1365-2214.2011.01349.x

Tomlinson, H. B., 2009b. Developmentally appropriate practice in the primary grades—ages 6–8: An overview, in C. Copple & S. Bredekamp (Eds.), Developmentally appropriate practice in early childhood programs serving children from birth through age 8, revised edition, 257–288. Washington, DC: NAEYC.

Torquati, J., with Gabriel, M. M., Jones-Branch, J., & Miller, J. L. (2011). Environmental education: A natural way to nurture children's development and learning. In A. Shillady (Ed.), *Spotlight on young children and nature* (pp. 8–14). Washington, DC: National Association for the Education of Young Children.

Verdick, E. (2006). *Germs are not for sharing.* Minneapolis, MN: Free Spirit Publishing.

Chapter 16

Bornfreund, L., & Goffin, S. (2016). *You can't have professionals without a profession.* New America Foundation. Retrieved May 12, 2018 from https://www.newamerica.org/weekly/edition-134/you-cant-have-professionals-without-profession/

Bredekamp, S. (1997). Developmentally appropriate practice: The early childhood teacher as decision maker. In S. Bredekamp & C. Copple (Eds.), *Developmentally appropriate practice in early childhood programs* (Rev. ed.), 33–52. Washington, DC: National Association for the Education of Young Children.

Cannon, J.S., Kilburn, R., Karolyn, L.A., Mattox, T., Muchow, A.N., & Buenaventura, M. (2017). *Investing early: Taking stock of outcomes and economic returns for early childhood programs.* Santa Monica, CA: RAND Corporation.

Child Welfare Information Gateway. (2007). *Recognizing child abuse and neglect: Signs and symptoms.* Retrieved March 20, 2012, from http://www.childwelfare.gov/can

Copple, C., Bredekamp, S., Koralek, D., & Charner, K. (Eds.). (2013a). *Developmentally appropriate practice: Focus on infants and toddlers.* Washington, DC: National Association for the Education of Young Children.

Copple, C., Bredekamp, S., Koralek, D., & Charner, K. (Eds.). (2013b). *Developmentally appropriate practice: Focus on preschoolers.* Washington, DC: National Association for the Education of Young Children.

Copple, C., Bredekamp, S., Koralek, D., & Charner, K. (Eds.). (2014a). *Developmentally appropriate practice: Focus on children in first, second, and third grades.* Washington, DC: National Association for the Education of Young Children.

Copple, C., Bredekamp, S., Koralek, D., & Charner, K. (Eds.). (2014b). *Developmentally appropriate practice: Focus on kindergartners.* Washington, DC: National Association for the Education of Young Children.

Day, C., Derman-Sparks, L., & Hernandez, L. (2017). *Honoring our professional ethics, conduct, and commitment in challenging times.* Presentation at NAEYC Professional Learning Institute, San Francisco, CA

De La Cruz, D. (2016). What kids wish their teachers knew. *New York Times,* August 31. Retrieved May 22, 2018 from https://www.nytimes.com/2016/08/31/well/family/what-kids-wish-their-teachers-knew.html

Derman-Sparks, L., & Edwards, J.O. (2017). Living our commitments: A pledge to all children and families. *Exchange.* Retrieved May 23, 2018 from https://www.childcareexchange.com/article/living-our-commitments-a-pledge-to-all-children-and-families/5023432/

Epstein, A. S. (2014). *The intentional teacher: Choosing the best strategies for young children's learning* (Rev. ed.). Washington, DC: National Association for the Education of Young Children.

Feeney, S., & Freeman, N. K. (2018). *Ethics and the early childhood educator: Using the NAEYC code* (3rd ed.). Washington, DC: National Association for the Education of Young Children.

Goffin, S. (2015). *Professionalizing early childhood education as a field of practice: A guide to the next era.* St. Paul, MN: Redleaf Press.

Institute of Medicine (IOM) & National Research Council (NRC). (2015). *Transforming the workforce for children birth through age 8: A unifying foundation.* Washington, DC: National Academies Press.

Interlandi, J. (2018). Why are our most important teachers paid the least? *New York Times,* January 9. Retrieved May 22, 2018 from https://www.nytimes.com/2018/01/09/magazine/why-are-our-most-important-teachers-paid-the-least.html

Lutton, A. (Ed.). (2012). *Advancing the early childhood profession: NAEYC standards and guidelines for professional development.* Washington, DC: National Association for the Education of Young Children.

McCoy, D.C., Yoshikawa, H., Ziol-Guest, K.M., Duncan, G.J., Schindler, H.S., Magnuson, K., Yang, R., Koepp, A., & Shonkoff, J.P. (2017). Impacts of early childhood education on medium- and long-term educational outcomes. *Educational Researcher, 46*(8), 474–487.

National Academies of Sciences, Engineering, and Medicine (NASEM). (2018). *Transforming the financing of early care and education.* Washington, DC: The National Academies Press.

National Association for the Education of Young Children (NAEYC). (2011a). *Code of ethical conduct and statement of commitment* (Reaffirmed and updated May 2011). Retrieved May 12, 2018 from http://www.naeyc.org/files/naeyc/file/positions/PSETH05.pdf

National Association for the Education of Young Children (NAEYC). (2011b). *2010 NAEYC Standards for Initial & Advanced Early Childhood Professional Preparation Programs: For use by Associate, Baccalaureate and Graduate Degree Programs.* Washington, DC: Author.

National Association for the Education of Young Children (NAEYC). (2016). *NAEYC Early Childhood Program Standards.* Washington, DC: Author. Retrieved March 1, 2018, from http://www.naeyc.org/academy/files/academy/OverviewStandards.pdf

National Association for the Education of Young Children (NAEYC). (2017). *Growing the demand for quality: Parents and early childhood educators talk about the financing of early learning in market research from NAEYC.* Retrieved My 22, 2018 from https://www.naeyc.org/our-work/initiatives/-profession/advancing-profession-market-research

National Association for the Education of Young Children (NAEYC). (2018). *Power to the Profession.* Retrieved May 12, 2018 from https://www.naeyc.org/our-work/initiatives/profession/overview

National Association for the Education of Young Children (NAEYC). (no date). *Be a proactive early learning advocate.* Retrieved May 4, 2018 from https://www.naeyc.org/get-involved/advocate/be-proactive

National Association for the Education of Young Children (NAEYC). (2009). *Developmentally appropriate practice in early childhood programs serving children from birth through age 8: Position statement.* Washington, DC: Author.

Pre-kindergarten Task Force. (2017). *The current state of scientific knowledge on pre-kindergarten effects.* Brookings & Duke Center for Child and Family Policy. Retrieved November 1, 2017 from https://www.brookings.edu/wp-content/uploads/2017/04/duke_prekstudy_final_4-4-17_hires.pdf

Taylor, J., Roehrig, A. D., Hensler, B. S., Connor, C. M. & Schatschneider, C. (2010). Teacher quality moderates the genetic effects on early reading. *Science, 328*(5977), 512–514.

Thomason, S., Austin, L.J.E., Bernhardt, A., Dresser, L., Jacobs, K., & Whitebook, M. (2018). *At the wage floor.* Berkeley CA: Center for the Study of the Child Care Workforce. Retrieved May 22, 2018 from http://cscce.berkeley.edu/at-the-wage-floor/

Trust for Learning. (2017). *Parents as consumers of early childhood education.* Retrieved February 24, 2018 from https://www.trustforlearning.org.

Weisberg, D.S., Kittredge, A.K., Hirsh-Pasek, K., Golinkoff, R.M., & Klahr, D. (2015). Making play work for education. *Phi Delta Kappa International, 26*(8), 8–13.

Name Index

Subject Index